PROLETARIAN CHINA

PROLETARIAN CHINA
A Century of Chinese Labour

Edited by
Ivan Franceschini and Christian Sorace

First published by Verso 2022
Collection © Verso 2022
Contributions © Contributors 2022

Editorial assistance from Nicholas Loubere with support from the Libraries at Lund University
All rights reserved
The moral rights of the editor and authors have been asserted

1 3 5 7 9 10 8 6 4 2

Verso
UK: 6 Meard Street, London W1F 0EG
US: 20 Jay Street, Suite 1010, Brooklyn, NY 11201

versobooks.com

Verso is the imprint of New Left Books

ISBN-13: 978-1-83976-633-6
ISBN-13: 978-1-83976-634-3 (UK EBK)
ISBN-13: 978-1-83976-635-0 (US EBK)

British Library Cataloguing in Publication Data
A catalogue record for this book is available from the British Library

Library of Congress Cataloging-in-Publication Data
Names: Franceschini, Ivan, 1983– editor. | Sorace, Christian P., 1981– editor.
Title: Proletarian China : a century of Chinese labour / edited by Ivan Franceschini and Christian Sorace.
Description: New York : Verso Books, 2022. | Includes bibliographical references.
Identifiers: LCCN 2021027212 (print) | LCCN 2021027213 (ebook) | ISBN 9781839766336 (paperback) | ISBN 9781839766350 (ebk)
Subjects: LCSH: Labor – China – History. | Working class – China – History. | Communism – China – History. | Zhongguo gong chan dang. | China – Politics and government – 1949-
Classification: LCC HD8736.5 .P76 2022 (print) | LCC HD8736.5 (ebook) | DDC 331.0951 – dc23
LC record available at https://lccn.loc.gov/2021027212
LC ebook record available at https://lccn.loc.gov/2021027213

Design and typesetting by Tommaso Facchin; cover design and illustration by Roberto La Forgia.
Proofreading by Jan Borrie and Emily Bickerton.
Printed and bound by CPI Group (UK) Ltd, Croydon CR0 4YY

Table of Contents

Introduction   15
The Proletariat Is Dead, Long Live the Proletariat!
Ivan FRANCESCHINI and Christian SORACE

1898   26
'A Cheaper Machine for the Work'
Corey BYRNES

1902   35
Techno-Utopias and Robots in China's Past Futures
Craig A. SMITH

1915   43
An Extraordinary Journey: Chinese Labourers on the
Western Front during the Great War
XU Guoqi

1920   51
A Day Trip to Changxindian
DENG Zhongxia

1921   56
Setting Sail: The Foundation of the Chinese Communist Party
LIN Chun

1922   66
The Anyuan Strike of 1922: Lessons in Leadership
Elizabeth J. PERRY

1923   74
The 7 February Massacre
LUO Zhanglong

1925   87
From the May Thirtieth Movement to the
Canton–Hong Kong Strike
Apo LEONG

1925 96
Everyday Politics in Tianjin Factories
Gail HERSHATTER

1925 104
The Founding of the All-China Federation of Trade Unions
WANG Kan

1927 111
The Third Armed Uprising and the Shanghai Massacre
S.A. SMITH

1927 120
Organising Rural Society: Disintegrating Rural Governance,
Peasant Associations, and the Hailufeng Soviet
Alexander F. DAY

1928 129
Feminist Agitation inside Chinese Factories
Yige DONG

1929 138
Striking for Rice: The Struggle for the 'Rice Allowance'
in Republican China
Seung-Joon LEE

1938 145
Resurgence of Labour Activism in Prewar Hong Kong
LU Yan

1941 155
The *New China Daily* and the Moral Language of Class in
Wartime Chongqing
Joshua H. HOWARD

1942 167
The Rise and Fall of Wu Manyou, China's First Labour Hero
Bo Ærenlund SØRENSEN

1946   176
Production in Revolution: Agricultural and Political Labour during Land Reform
Brian DEMARE

1948   184
Women Workers and the Shanghai Cotton Mill Strike of 1948
Emily HONIG

1949   192
On the People's Democratic Dictatorship (Excerpt)
MAO Zedong

1949   194
Continuity and Change: Women Workers in the Early People's Republic of China
Robert CLIVER

1949   203
A Spark Extinguished: Worker Militancy in Taiwan after World War II (1945–1950)
Po-chien CHEN and Yi-hung LIU

1951   212
Li Lisan on the Relationship between Management and Unions
LI Lisan

1951   221
Revolutionising the Factory through the Mass Political Campaign
Jake WERNER

1952   230
Housing the New Socialist Worker: The 'Workers' New Village' in Shanghai
Mark W. FRAZIER

1952 240
The First Patriotic Locust Extermination Campaign: Rural Labour
Mobilisation and Pest Control in the Early People's Republic of China
John WILLIAMS

1955 250
The Short-Lived Eternity of Friendship: Chinese Workers
in Socialist Mongolia (1955–1964)
Christian SORACE and Ruiyi ZHU

1957 265
How Do Unions Handle Contradictions among the People?
LAI Ruoyu

Confronting the State: The Strike Wave of 1957
CHEN Feng 274

1958 282
Beyond the Wage: Zhang Chunqiao, Bourgeois Right,
and Maoism as Theory
Benjamin KINDLER

1958 291
Reorganising Chinese Labour: The Establishment of
the Household Registration System
Jane HAYWARD

1960 301
Workers' Peril in the Workers' State: The Laobaidong
Colliery Disaster
Tim WRIGHT

1960 310
The Angang Constitution: Labour, Industry and
Bureaucracy during the Great Leap Forward
Koji HIRATA

1960 319
Production First, Life Second: The 1960 Ban on Hand
Spinning and Hand Weaving
Jacob EYFERTH

1961 327
Anatomy of a Woman Worker: Collectivisation and
Labour during the Great Leap Forward
Aminda SMITH and Fabio LANZA

1962 337
Working Together in Agricultural Production Teams:
The Work Lives of the Majority of Chinese Under Mao
Jonathan UNGER

1963 346
Gods, Ghosts, and Workers: 'Feudal Superstition' and
the Socialist Education Movement, 1963–1966
S.A. SMITH

1964 356
Learning from the Daqing Oilfields
Maggie CLINTON

1964 365
The Third Front Campaign
Covell F. MEYSKENS

1967 375
The January Storm of 1967: From Representation to
Action and Back Again
Patricia M. THORNTON

1967 387
The Hong Kong Riots of 1967
Ray YEP

1968 395
The Establishment of the First Workers' University
Andrea PIAZZAROLI LONGOBARDI

1969 405
'Oppose Restoring the Old!': The Culmination of
the Rebel Workers' Movement in Wuhan during
the Cultural Revolution
Joel ANDREAS

1970   415
Building *Uhuru*: Chinese Workers and Labour Diplomacy
on the Tan–Zam Railway
Matthew GALWAY

1972   426
Transforming Urban Youth into Peasants: The Maoist
Rustication Movement of the 1960s–1970s
Michel BONNIN

1976   436
The Blank Exam: Crises of Student Labour and Activism
in the Late Cultural Revolution Film *Juelie*
A.C. BAECKER

1980   448
Echoes of the Rise of Solidarity in Poland
Jeanne L. WILSON

1981   457
Abandoning Collective Farming and the Effects on Labour
Jonathan UNGER

1983   466
Dagongmei: Gendered Troubles in the City of Dreams
Mary Ann O'DONNELL

1986   477
Sex Workers in China: From Criminalisation and
Abuse to Activism
Tiantian ZHENG

1988   486
The Lifting of Martial Law and the Rise of Taiwan's
Independent Labour Movement
Ming-sho HO

1989   495
Workers on Tiananmen Square
Yueran ZHANG

1993   505
Voices from the Zhili Fire: The Tragedy of a Toy Factory
and the Conditions It Exposed
Anita CHAN

1994   513
One Law to Rule Them All: The First Labour Law of
the People's Republic of China
Sarah BIDDULPH

1995   525
From Green Shoots to Crushed Petals: Labour NGOs in China
Jude HOWELL

1995   534
The Blocked Path: Political Labour Organising in the
Aftermath of the Tiananmen Crackdown
Kevin LIN

1997   544
Xiagang: The Fifteenth Party Congress and Mass Layoffs in
State-Owned Enterprises
William HURST

2001   552
China Joins the World Trade Organization: Implications
for Workers
Dorothy J. SOLINGER

2002   559
The Liaoyang Strike and the Unmaking of Mao's Working
Class in China's Rustbelt
Ching Kwan LEE

2003   567
The Sun Zhigang Case
Chloé FROISSART

2007 577
Slaving Away: The 'Black Brick Kilns Incident' of 2007
Ivan FRANCESCHINI

2008 586
The Labour Contract Law and Its Discontents
Mary E. GALLAGHER

2008 598
'Make Contributions and Offer Your Youth for Tomorrow's Dream': The Establishment of the Shenzhen Migrant Worker Museum
Eric FLORENCE and Junxi QIAN

2009 607
Zhang Haichao's 'Open-Chest Case'
Ralph LITZINGER and Yanping NI

2010 616
The Nanhai Honda Strike
Chris King-Chi CHAN and Elaine Sio-leng HUI

2010 625
The Foxconn Suicide Express
Jenny CHAN

2011 635
Rupture at the Centre: Evicting Migrant Schools in Beijing
Eli FRIEDMAN

2013 644
Chinese Workers on the Belt and Road
Aaron HALEGUA

2014 655
Bearing Witness to History: *Dagong* Poets from the 1980s to the Present
Wanning SUN

2014 664
The Yue Yuen Strike
Marc BLECHER

2015 674
Replacing Humans with Machines
HUANG Yu

2015 684
Labour NGOs under Assault
Chloé FROISSART and Ivan FRANCESCHINI

2018 692
The Jasic Struggle
Manfred ELFSTROM

2018 701
Factories of Turkic Muslim Internment
Darren BYLER

2019 712
The Birth of a New Trade Union Movement in Hong Kong
Anita CHAN

The Future 722
Folding Time: Futuristic Reflections on Class Divisions
in Contemporary China
Carlos ROJAS

The Affective Fallacy
CHEN Qiufan 730

Acknowledgments 743

References 744

Contributors 862

The Proletariat Is Dead, Long Live the Proletariat!

Ivan FRANCESCHINI and Christian SORACE

> 'The workers at Changxindian saw us arriving and were very welcoming and cordial to us. We saw them as friendly brothers, too, and there was fraternity among the workers themselves. I was rather fond of the solidarity and unity. I often resent how heartless people nowadays in society can be, cheating and battling each other, so the harmony and solidarity among the Changxindian workers gave me infinite hope.'
>
> — Deng Zhongxia, 1920[1]

Deng Zhongxia was twenty-six when he wrote these words. Forged in the fire of the May Fourth Movement, he was one of the earliest student activists to discover Marxism and glimpse the potential of the Chinese working class to bring forth revolutionary change in a country marred by profound social and political divisions.[2] With other young students, he would visit the workers of Changxindian in their workshops of the northern section of the Beijing–Hankou railway. He and his comrades established a night school where they provided literacy classes and more advanced political training for workers. As the workers learned how to read and write and acquired a basic understanding of Marxist politics, the student activists gained first-hand knowledge of the plight of the Chinese working class, its potential and limitations. The exchange was so successful that in the summer of 1921, when Marxist groups from all over the country gathered to establish the Chinese Communist Party, the founding resolution stressed the indispensable role of education in order to raise the class consciousness of workers.

Fast forward to one century later. On the afternoon of 6 August 2018, outside a police station in Shenzhen, a crowd of onlookers watched as workers, university students, retired state employees, and even old Communist cadres, made speeches to protest against the recent arrests of several workers who were involved in a unionisation campaign at Jasic, a welding equipment manufacturer with around one thousand employees.[3] As portraits of Mao Zedong appeared among the crowd and participants wore T-shirts with black-and-white sketches of their detained comrades accompanied by the words 'Solidarity Is Power' in red, several speeches exalted the importance of the unity between workers and intellectuals. As one of the orators said: 'Today's students are tomorrow's workers.' Unbeknownst to the onlookers, the Jasic unionisation campaign and the ensuing mobilisation was the result of a deliberate strategy by Marxist students who had entered the factory as early as 2016 to operate as underground labour organisers in order to plan confrontational collective action.[4] The response of the Chinese Communist Party was swift and brutal, with students belonging to Marxist groups in several universities throughout the country who had joined the Jasic campaign, or simply expressed support for it, subjected to surveillance, discipline, and intimidation.[5]

As we write from Canberra and Colorado Springs during a global pandemic in 2021, we are brought to reflect on these two anecdotes that mark the origin and present of the Chinese Communist Party in its first one hundred years of existence. This century has seen what is now one of the largest and most powerful political parties on earth transform from a revolutionary organisation whose foundations were built on the promise of the emancipation of the working class and pursuit of an alternative to capitalist modernity, into a capitalist machine decorated with socialist ornamentation that violently crushes any expression of labour organisation and working-class solidarity. How to explain this *volte-face*, and what it has meant, at different moments in history, for the lives of Chinese workers?

Any account, or collection of accounts, of history faces what Rebecca Karl describes as 'the problem of narration': 'Which facts do we use to tell our story? How is the story organized? In whose voice is it told?'[6] In the case of labour history in the People's Republic of China, the politics of representation turn on the question of the relationship between the Communist Party and the working class. Is the Party a conduit of worker voices, which might otherwise be inaudible without its amplification? Or is it a ventriloquist whose script dominates what can be said and who must remain silent? Prior to 1949, what kinds of dreams, longings, and demands animated workers? How were these realised, or disappointed, after workers' supposed liberation in 1949? How does China's role in global capitalism transform, and mediate, the relationship between the Party and Chinese workers?

This book does not attempt to harmonise the polyphonic voices, dialects, and silences of Chinese workers and their interlocutors by providing yet another master narrative. We are not seeking to replace the stentorian 'official' voice of the Communist Party with 'authentic' voices from the grassroots, let alone offer our own non-diegetic voice-over narration. Rather, in editing this volume, our hope is to bring into conversation different perspectives from China's past and present about the central role of the working class and its future in China and the world. But the fraught question of representation and narration raises a much thornier, profound, and fundamental conceptual problem: *who is the Proletariat*?

The Birth Pangs of the Chinese Proletariat

What do workers belonging to different geographies and moments in history share in common? What do weavers in textile mills in the 1940s in Shanghai have in common with today's migrant construction workers building China's gleaming cosmopolitan cities? What does a Communist militant being persecuted by the Nationalist Party in the early twentieth century have in common with a labour organiser being repressed by the Communist Party in the twenty-first century? The common denominator between these very different situations can be found under the signifier of the 'Proletariat'.

The very title of this book—*Proletarian China*—represents a conscious effort to retrieve the concept of 'Proletariat' from the dustbin of history. Although there have always been and will always be workers, the Proletariat is a relatively recent political and conceptual invention, naming an organised working class in revolutionary struggle against the bourgeois, whose historic mission is to bring about a transition to Communism. In Mandarin, Proletariat is translated as 无产阶级—the 'propertyless class'—faithful to Marx and Engels' definition in the *Communist Manifesto* as the class with 'nothing to lose but their chains'.[7] The Proletariat, then, is the name for a subject awaiting its birth. As Jacques Rancière argues in *The Philosopher and His Poor*, 'the Proletariat exists only by virtue of its inscription in the Book of Science'—Marx's *Capital*.[8] In the formation of the Proletariat, empirical workers with varying interests and backgrounds become a class acting for-itself as a political subject. Unable to give birth to itself, the Proletariat requires a midwife, an organised political party to compose, as Hobbes described of the Leviathan, an artificial body from 'the motley crowd of laborers'—an inorganic body constantly threatened with 'decomposition into simple individuals,' doubles, vagrants, and swindlers.[9] Since its birth whose gestation required decades and date remains imprecise, the Proletariat has resembled a powerful agentic body, a cumbrous prosthetic body, a moribund body, and perhaps, one day a phoenix-like body.[10]

The founding of the Chinese Communist Party in 1921, one hundred years ago from the date of publication of this volume, on a boat in Jiaxing's South Lake, brought forth the emergence of the Proletariat as a political entity in China.[11] Although labour unions, movements, factory struggles, and competing political visions pre-existed the Communist Party, the concept and arrival of the Proletariat in China as a historical and political agent was a programme of the Party.[12] At that time, China's working class was a coastline in a vast sea of agriculture, one rife with divisions related to gender, native place, clientelist networks, and even secret-society affiliation, merely an 'empirical dispersion' of workers.[13] For the first half of the twentieth century in China, the Proletariat remained a conceptual notion, a political aspiration, and birth announcement.

The 1949 Watershed

This identification of the Proletariat with the Communist Party was—and is—rife with contradictions, which became a permanent field of tension when the Party achieved a monopoly over political legitimacy in 1949, and which were further intensified after the nationalisation of industry in 1956. What did the establishment of the People's Republic of China mean for the Chinese working class? According to the official narrative, 1949 liberated workers from their exploitation under previous regimes of nascent capitalism, and semi-feudalism/semi-colonialism. Sounding a less enthusiastic note, some academics have suggested that the sustained worker activism of the Republican era dissipated when the Communist Party came to power, bringing workers to heel under the symbolic promise of their emancipation.[14] Others have argued that the Party's victory subjected workers to a new regime of dependency in and on their workplace that substantially undermined their organised power.[15] Although the idea of worker quiescence in the Mao era has long been exposed for what it was—a myth—and new sociological studies have pointed out the continuity in labour conditions before and after the Communist takeover, 1949 marked a symbolic and discursive watershed for Chinese workers.[16] If workers were now in power through the Communist Party, what possible reason could they have to raise their voices to complain and protest? And yet complain and protest they did, as many essays in this volume demonstrate.

Indeed, one of the vexing questions about twentieth-century communism in China and beyond its borders has been: why would workers be unhappy and accumulate grievances in a workers' state led by a Communist Party? As we will see throughout this volume, despite a relationship of intimate embodiment, in China the Communist Party and workers did not always see eye-to-eye, which is why Mao, among other leaders, entertained and tolerated at various points the seemingly unorthodox right for workers, in a workers' state, to strike.[17] For a long time, the myths of the 'socialist heroism' and 'dedication' of Chinese workers—or their 'passivity' and 'quiescence', depending on one's political perspective—drew attention away from these political debates and the extent of workplace activism in Maoist China. Although the Communist Party claimed to represent the working class, the working class and the Party have never fully coincided without remainder—these 'remainders' being the ongoing targets of the state's disciplinary apparatus and the Party's thought reform.

The Leninist paradox that China inherited from the Soviet Union is that the logic of worker emancipation depends on the Communist Party to give it political form in the dictatorship of the proletariat (无产阶级专政). Under these conditions, the working class can only achieve self-identity and sovereignty by way of its mediation through the Communist Party, which installs a permanent gap at the heart of representation. The amorphous category of the Proletariat acts like the Holy Spirit which fuses together the Party (the Father) and the working class (the Son) in a Holy Trinity. This trinitarian structure explains both how workers could experiment with insurgent democratic forms during the Cultural Revolution and how the Communist Party could later shed the skin of the Proletariat in its metamorphosis to capitalism.

Since it is not an empirical given, the Proletariat is bestowed flesh in aesthetic representations of glowing workers, tools in hand, immersed in the strenuous activity of building the future. Cultural production and aesthetic education are required for workers to see themselves as belonging to the Proletariat. Thus, the worker is doubled, yet again, in the aesthetic luminescence of the Proletariat, which both magnifies and diminishes her power. Although such proletarian dreamworlds are by now faded slogans on abandoned factory walls, sold as capitalist trinkets, or studied by the dispassionate gaze of academics, their spectral presence continues to haunt the imagination of the present.

These underlying paradoxes and doubles constitutive of twentieth-century communism would occasionally irrupt in the political debates that took place at times of crisis (for instance in 1951, 1956, and 1966).[18] For these reasons, the Chinese Communist Party under Mao maintained strict control over who was admitted to the Proletariat and who was its enemy. The revolutionary goal to emancipate the working class reinscribed and reified their identities in the dossier (档案), or personnel file.[19] Although dossiers and the household registration system (户口) functioned as the tiered basis of social organisation and work in Maoist China, one of the defining features of Maoist thought was an unease and suspiciousness of the reduction of the political to the sociological, which is why one's political standpoint (立场) or attitude (态度) could atone for one's class background, under certain conditions.[20]

As Joel Andreas has pointed out, the Chinese experiment stands out from all variations of the twentieth-century communist project in several respects.[21] First, under the work unit system (单位), the Chinese Communist Party managed to make employment relatively permanent (for some), going as far as to promise workers an 'iron rice bowl' (铁饭碗) of lifelong employment.[22] Second, due to the centrality of the work unit system, workplaces were turned into sites of worker participation, fostering strong norms of industrial citizenship and participation in spite of the workers' lack of autonomy. Finally, the Party in China adopted a radical programme of social levelling, which Mao Zedong episodically extended to include the political power and privileges of Party cadres.[23]

To its credit, at various moments in the early history of the PRC, Maoism—as a political project—also sought to break down the rigid sociological hierarchies and barriers, which consigned workers to their functions in the factory. Workers were encouraged to read, speak, philosophise, engage in politics, write poetry, paint, and expand their capacities as human beings, which is among the reasons which made Maoism so inspiring globally.[24] Although many of these experiments were episodic and short-lived, they ought to be recognised as meaningful attempts in China to create a 'rupture in the order of things … in the traditional division assigning the privilege of thought to some and the tasks of production to others.'[25]

One of the central paradoxes of labour in Maoist China, torn between developmental and political imperatives, is that the Communist Party both sought to tie workers to their place and set them free.

The Death of the Chinese Proletariat

Although the workplace in the Maoist years was definitely no paradise, the reform era saw a growing gap between the rhetoric of the Communist Party and the lived reality of the workers. While millions of workers in the state and collective sectors were laid off as the 'iron rice bowl' of lifetime employment shattered, wave after wave of migrants from the countryside with no other choice than to work in awful conditions in sweatshops arrived in the cities. Even as the Party attempted to rein in the worst labour rights abuses through the promulgation of detailed labour legislation, new forms of precarious labour entailing different dynamics of exploitation mushroomed.

Discursively, after the exhaustion of Maoism as a political project of 'class struggle' (阶级斗争), the sociological (and a-political) understanding of class defined as 'strata' (阶层) has become the hegemonic framework of analysis within and outside China. Since reform and opening, new sociological categories have proliferated, such as 'vulnerable groups' (弱势群体), 'floating population' (流动人口), 'second generation of migrant workers' (新生代农民工), 'ant tribe' (蚁族), among numerous other classifications—the 'class antagonism' that structures society through division, according to classical Marxism, has become an anamorphic blur in a 'moderately prosperous society'.[26] Similarly, the discourse of the working class as the 'master' (主人翁) of the country and the enterprise has been displaced by an anodyne language of detailed individual rights rooted in a set of labour laws that systematically undermine collective rights.[27] This new emphasis on the law has been interpreted by scholars as a means through which the Communist Party has re-created its hegemony over labour politics, while re-defining the meaning of work.[28] As demonstrated by the anecdote about the Jasic campaign at the beginning and by numerous chapters in this volume, attempts by Chinese workers and intellectuals to resurrect the body of the Proletariat as a political subject have been met unflinchingly with repression sanctioned by the Communist Party.[29]

At the same time, however, the Chinese Communist Party still holds on to its legitimating claim to represent 'the vanguard of the working class', which to this day features prominently in the opening line of the Party Constitution. As Alessandro Russo has argued, this is 'an assertion with a precise organisational thrust—an injunction that the CCP remains the only legitimate political organisation in China, and that no independent political organisation of wage-earning slaves can be tolerated. The category "working class" is an essential component of the government's discourse, albeit shorn of its political value.[30] This hegemony, however, is increasingly contested, as workers defy the risk of state repression to stage strikes and protests, and a contentious civil society dares to help workers advance demands that go beyond the narrow boundaries permitted by Party-State legalism in the reform era—or at least this was what was happening until Xi Jinping's crackdowns on labour nongovernmental organisations in the mid-2010s.[31]

In these circumstances, does it still make sense to talk about the Proletariat in China today, when the Party who supposedly gave it life has abandoned its creature? We believe it does, at least as a political aspiration. The common sense of post-socialism has been to dismiss the Proletariat as a political Frankenstein—a monstrous, distorted body—whose shadow eclipses the lives of actual workers. In our post-ideological and de-politicised age of positivist fundamentalism, people have eagerly sloughed off 'the fatal weight of words without bodies, of these phantoms, called the people, the proletariat, equality, or class struggle'[32] in the utopian search for *reality as it is*, for the ordinary worker shorn of revolutionary illusions. The problem with this account is that the ordinary worker, like the Proletariat, does not exist apart from the political and epistemological frameworks which inscribe its concept and representation. Again, Rancière is a helpful guide through the perils and paradoxes of representation. He does not critique the socialist celebration of labour in the name of an 'authentic' working class reality beyond the distorted mirror of propaganda but in order to deconstruct the pernicious binary between representation and reality altogether: 'We are not going to scratch images to bring truth to the surface, we are going to shove them aside so that other figures may come together and decompose there.'[33] Following Rancière, a goal of this volume is to allow a multiplicity of figures of labour to appear, the configuration remains open-ended, contestable, and ongoing. We still need to talk about the Proletariat today, because we still live under capitalism.

In China, as else and everywhere under late capitalism, we are witnessing an unrelenting process of *proletarianisation*—masses of people whose survival is dependent on aridifying trickles of capital— without the coming of the Proletarian as the political subject who was promised would dig capitalism's grave.[34] Even without the Proletariat, the world is indeed proletarian. We decided to title this book *Proletarian China* first as a commitment to the core Marxist insight into one of the main contradictions of capitalism: workers are dispossessed from the world that they make and depend on for survival. We also chose *Proletarian* in particular due to its ambiguous occupation of the space between adjective, noun, and subject, in which the composition and decomposition of political worlds takes place.

At the same time, while accepting the fact that Proletariat as a political aspiration still has value today, it is important to admit that the Proletariat, in China as elsewhere, is dead. Separated from the Party, the Proletariat once again has become disembodied and returned to its spectral status. Whether there will be incarnations of it in China or globally is a question of political composition. The Chinese Communist Party's new body is adorned with the costumery of 5,000 years of civilisational progress and gilded through the last several decades of capitalist accumulation. Today, what remains of the Communist Party's embodiment of The Proletariat is Mao's sallowish, embalmed corpse on Tiananmen Square, which may in the end, be only a wax figurine from Madame Tussauds.[35] As Alessandro Russo puts it: 'If the main barrier against the political existence of workers is the reference to a mummified working class enshrined in official discourse, nothing that is politically novel will be able to come into being unless there is an explicit, conscious effort to keep this fiction at bay.'[36] Even after its political de-throning and mummification, the phantom of the Proletariat continues to haunt the working class.

Nurturing Utopian Dreams

After so many disappointments, it is difficult to avoid the nihilistic gaze under which all attempts to build a better world appear doomed to failure. As Peter Sloterdijk wrote: 'The historical world was nothing but a graveyard of enthusiasms.'[37] Glancing at the remnants of past utopias from the perspective of today conjures an eerie feeling, as if we were looking at, and being looked at by, the ruins of a dreamworld. As the late Mark Fisher pointed out, gazing at ruins opens a series of questions about agency: who built and inhabited what are now ruins? What happened to produce these remains?[38]

In the case of the People's Republic of China, what is eerie is the sense of incommensurate worlds superimposed on each other. In the Great Leap Forward, people laboured and sacrificed themselves for a 'utopia of material plenitude' which turned out to be a deadly mirage;[39] during the Cultural Revolution, people's labour was given meaning by the 'utopia of proletarian power';[40] after the abandonment of Maoist utopias, labour chased after the pragmatic utopia of wealth and modernity; in the Xi era, while pursuing 'private paradise', Chinese people's labour is enlisted in the utopia of national rejuvenation and glory on the world stage—personal interests being enmeshed in, while not entirely reducible to, the ideologies of their time.[41] And this does not even touch upon all the utopias that workers attach to their work, and their lives beyond it, in private reveries. From the mass utopias of the past, utopia in China has been de-collectivised, individuated, and then re-incorporated into the glory of the national body politic. As the writer China Miéville so beautifully puts it: 'We live in a utopia: it just isn't ours.'[42]

About This Book

In its attempt to retrieve the shards of broken utopian promises, this volume builds on our previous editorial endeavour, the book *Afterlives of Chinese Communism*, published by Verso and ANU Press back in 2019. While *Afterlives* revisited the complicated and contested legacies of Chinese Communism through a series of essays focusing on keywords and concepts in the political vocabulary of the Chinese Communist Party, this volume adopts a different approach. Here, each chapter is linked to a specific event, so that on the whole the volume is structured as a timeline of the development of Chinese society from the early twentieth century to this day, which is not meant to construct but rather disrupt notions of teleological historical development.

Some of the episodes chosen for inclusion in this timeline can be considered landmark events in contemporary Chinese history—for instance, the Anyuan strike of 1922, the Shanghai uprising and massacre of 1927, the January Storm of 1967, the worker protests of 1989, among others—but most episodes are drawn from occurrences and situations that rarely feature in history books. These range from a boat trip up the Yangzi river in 1898 to a long-forgotten strike for rice in the early 1930s; from the temporary closure of a communist propaganda newspaper in wartime Chongqing in 1941 to the establishment of the first workers' universities during the Cultural Revolution; from the passing of laws that criminalised sex work in the late 1970s to a tragic fire that killed dozens of workers in 1993; from kiln slaves in the 2000s to the prospect of workerless automation of the future. Geographical diversity adds another layer of complexity to the book, as the essays engage with different places in Greater China, including Hong Kong and Taiwan, and globally to the trenches of Europe in the First World War, as well as Mongolia and Tanzania.[43] Finally, while the Chinese Communist Party plays an important role in the volume, especially in the years that make up the Maoist era, it is far from the only actor on a crowded stage.

Although this style leads to a certain, unavoidable episodic nature—which we tried to address by adding to each chapter a short introduction to provide some context—this was a deliberate choice. As mentioned earlier, this volume does not attempt to construct yet another grand narrative about Chinese labour history, to track the supposed rise and fall of China's working class, and predict its future. Without claiming to provide a comprehensive overview of Chinese labour history, the book is composed of different voices, perspectives, and interpretations of what constituted the experience of working in China in the past century. Each chapter of this book is a record of proletarian existence.

Like *Afterlives of Chinese Communism*, the volume that preceded this one, published by Verso and ANU Press back in 2019, this volume is also rooted in the work that we are doing with the open-access publication *Made in China Journal*. The ethos of the *Made in China* project is rooted in accessibility. We believe in the need to go beyond the insular confines of academia and reach a general audience. This entails a commitment to open access and the democratisation of knowledge. This book is written with a general audience in mind and made available simultaneously for sale with Verso Books and for free download on our website. As we pointed out in the introduction to *Afterlives*, this is also our way to think outside the confines of traditional academic publishing as we want our readers to imagine new political possibilities beyond capitalist models.

In the end, one might wonder what utopias do we, the editors of this volume, strive for? Our aspiration here is to rekindle passion for the project of finally overcoming the alienation of labour and gaining democratic control over the economic decisions that condition our lives. By looking at what animated workers at various moments throughout Chinese history to transform the cramped space of their conditions of possibility through political agency, unlikely solidarities, refusal of the given, and rebellion for the unrealised, we hope to revive some of the ideals that pushed them forward.

Canberra and Colorado Springs
13 February 2021

1898

Our journey begins on the banks of the Yangzi River, where, in the latter half of the nineteenth century, the Western colonial imaginary encountered its Other in the figure of the river tracker, whose supposed ability to endure pain without complaint was interpreted as a sign of both China's stagnant present and its magnificent future. Drawing on racialised typologies, Western observers described river trackers as less than human—both animal and mechanical. Even the boatmen's songs were heard only as 'tremendous noise', calling to mind Aristotle's differentiation of the human from the animal on the grounds 'that this speech is understood as discourse and another as noise', which Rancière argues is the logic of the police, subtending colonial, racialised and class-based conceptions of humanity.[1] Lost to foreign eyes and ears was the fact that Chinese trackers, just like other 'coolies', were all too conscious of the physical and economic vulnerabilities that made them into 'beasts of burden'. Complaints of being treated like 'oxen and horses' and other pleas to respect the human dignity of workers would resonate in Chinese protests for years to come.[2] This language would eventually become a mainstay of the early Communist discourse on labour. As Communist organiser Li Lisan's rousing call for miners and railway workers in Anyuan in the early 1920s went: 'Once beasts of burden, now we will be human' (see Perry's essay in this volume).

'A Cheaper Machine for the Work'
Corey BYRNES[3]

> All work such as tracking boats against the swift current of the Chinese rivers ... is done by overtaxed hand labour, and thus the mass of the people are little better than the beasts of burden, docile to a degree, but with few more wants than the animals, with the additional quality of being a cheaper machine for the work.
>
> — Archibald Little (1910)[4]

On the morning of 9 March 1898, Archibald Little's fifty-foot long, teak-hulled, twin-screwed, Shanghai-built steamship, *Leechuen* (利川), 'made a triumphal entry' into the port of Chongqing, the first steamship to traverse the treacherous Yangzi River gorges that separated the watery plains of Hubei from the riches of Sichuan—the 'Land of Heaven's Storehouse' (天府之国).[5] In 'demonstrating the possibility of navigating the Upper-Yang-tse, and drawing attention to its necessity', Little and his *Leechuen* (meaning roughly, 'Benefit Sichuan') helped loosen the ties binding travel and trade to the wide seasonal fluctuations and the forms of labour and technology that had defined life on the river for millennia.[6] For Little, a Shanghai-based British merchant who had actively lobbied to make an experimental steamer journey up the Yangzi as early as the 1880s, regular steam navigation promised not only riches for businessmen such as himself, but also the liberation of 'the present army of wretched trackers [who] will gradually be set free for more remunerative work'.[7]

To the Western writers who first began to reinscribe the Yangzi's Three Gorges as empirically and scientifically knowable landscapes starting in the 1860s, the men who pulled boats up the river's treacherous rapids were figures of fascination.[8] The work of tracking was harrowing, and trackers appeared to foreign eyes as simultaneously subhuman and superhuman. While Chinese sailors had mastered methods of ascending portions of the Yangzi River by sail, boats had to be pulled through many parts of the gorges, where massive rapids, whirlpools, hidden reefs and boulders created formidable obstacles. Individual boats generally had their own crews of trackers, though they frequently supplemented these with seasonal labourers, including large numbers of men and women who established temporary villages during the winter season at especially difficult spots, such as the Xintan Rapids.[9] Cargo was often transshipped there and at other rapids, though large boats still sometimes required upwards of 300 trackers (or 'rapid coolies', as one traveller called them) to pull them across serious obstacles.[10] At best, trackers inched their way along the towpaths constructed alongside sections of the river, some of them little more than narrow, low indentations hacked into the sides of sheer cliffs. More often, they clambered over enormous boulders and precipitous, rocky shores, wading through frigid waters (the upriver journey was easiest during winter, when the water level was at its lowest) or diving into the river to free the thick bamboo hawsers that yoked them to their boat. Men who fell while tracking were often dragged along until they could extricate themselves. To fall overboard in midstream meant almost certain death. Trackers worked naked or wearing only a thin jacket, with no protection from the elements or the dangers of their work; the harshness of their labours was etched on to their bodies.

'Immemorial Methods'

By the end of the nineteenth century, the tracker, with his naked body and 'immemorial methods', had long been a potent symbol of both the supposed Chinese ability to endure pain and the 'lack of imagination' that had locked the nation in its eternal past.[11] The failure to rationalise the work of tracking by introducing mechanical devices rendered it a tragicomic ritual of endless, crazed repetition. For Lawrence John Lumley Dundas, second Marquis of Zetland, tracking was little more than a farcical allegory of geopolitics:

> The thought that not unnaturally occurred to me was, what a marvellous thing it is that in the whole course of the two or three odd millenniums during which the Chinese have been struggling with the navigation of the Yang-tse, they have failed to evolve so simple a mechanical contrivance as a windlass! With the most primitive hand-winch a couple of men could have effected all and more than the dozen delirious maniacs in a quarter of the time, and at an expenditure of an infinitesimal fraction of the human

> force. It would be difficult to find a more striking example of that complete lack of imagination which has doomed China to a perpetual back seat among the competing Powers in the present advanced stage of the progress of humanity.[12]

Without the spark of imagination necessary to transcend the physiological limits of the human body or the willingness to adopt innovations from abroad, China was doomed to a struggle of repetition without progress. Dundas's equating of progress with labour-saving devices and stagnation with the 'delirious' movements of Chinese bodies shows how the interaction of labour, technology and race in the navigation of the gorges was filtered through the lens of popular conceptions of national difference. The idea of hard labour with minimal gain that figures in many Western descriptions of trackers evokes not only the 'not unnatural' idea of Chinese history as stagnant, but also a more complex conception of labour in a specifically 'Chinese' mode.

In the late nineteenth century, the figure of the 'coolie' was seen to possess a 'biological' capacity to work hard and long on a meagre diet of rice (and opium) while enduring 'low levels of constant pain'.[13] This trait made him a 'machine' far better suited (economically and physiologically) to the depredations of industrialised work or hard labour than the meat-eating white man, whom he threatened to supplant.[14] Beneath the surface of this 'yellow peril' rhetoric lurked even greater perceived threats—that familiar forms of labour would be (or had already been) supplanted by transnational and industrialised modes of production and that the appearance of such modes and the men who brought them into being destabilised what Eric Hayot describes as 'the measure of "humanity" itself'.[15]

For the 'measure of "humanity"' to have been thrown into doubt at the end of the nineteenth century must have seemed especially dire. Just as the world was measured, mapped and scientifically reinscribed during this period, so, too, was the human body subjected to an unprecedented degree of measurement and classification. With the articulation in the middle of the nineteenth century of the first law of thermodynamics (which holds that the energy of a closed system remains constant), French and German scientists came to see 'nature as a vast machine capable of producing mechanical work or ... "labor power"'.[16] The physiologists who followed in their footsteps treated the body as a 'human motor' that worked according to the same principles found in nature. If the energy contained within nature was inexhaustibly productive, the same might hold for the human body, assuming it could be managed properly. Freed from earlier religious and moral frameworks, the human body entered a realm of scientific measurement, rationalisation and systematisation that promised to unlock its natural capacity for work and, with it, the door to social progress (that is, increased production).[17]

As a paragon of Chinese endurance—and 'a cheaper machine' than even a beast of burden, as Little describes him in the epigraph to this chapter—the tracker would seem to pose two related problems for European productivist theories. First, his 'labour power' is disconnected from the models of socioeconomic development in which the idea was first developed. The foreign visitor was confronted by a system in which the transfer of natural forces through the human failed to fuel the progress of society. The human machine and the natural machine found along the Yangzi was in many ways superior to those in the West, but their social manifestation was profoundly out of order. As a result, energy was wasted in the maintenance of an ancient way of life, absorbed by the vacuum of Chinese history. Second, while his capacity to perform backbreaking work on a meagre diet seemed to fulfil the dream of labour without fatigue, he achieved this ideal without scientific rationalisation, through a specifically racial, and thus threatening, capacity. It is his Chineseness that allowed him to work in a manner that was not just unlike the work of Euro-Americans, but subhuman, animal and thus potentially superhuman.

'Absence of Nerves'

The idea that one could clearly define racial and national qualities was developed over the course of the nineteenth century through both mainstream scientific thought and the closely related pseudo-sciences of phrenology, physiognomy, eugenics and social Darwinism. As part of far-reaching expansionist ideologies, the bodies of non-Europeans were subjected to methods of physiological and ethnographic measurement that naturalised racial difference, usually defining the other as deficient, degraded or primitive.[18] Popular racial theories were even used to distinguish between different 'types' of Chinese. Archibald Little refers to his boat's lead sailor and his brother—among the 'first specimens of the "Four Streams" (Szechuan meaning Four Streams) province [he] had yet met'—as 'tall, fair-skinned [and] dolicocephalic', which was a term used in craniometry, phrenology and eugenics to describe a long, thin head type associated with northern Europeans.[19] In European accounts of China, this sort of racial typology was based mostly on anecdotal information (from travellers and missionaries, exported images and journalistic and scholarly works) rather than direct 'scientific' measurement. By the turn of the twentieth century, it had developed into part of an extensive discourse of racialised bodies and national 'types' distinct from universalist scientific theories of human productivity.[20] The ideal body might still be a 'human motor', but there were as many makes and models of motor as there were nations and races.

The most influential account of Chinese difference was Arthur Smith's *Chinese Characteristics*, published in 1890 and reprinted numerous times since, which presents a taxonomy of Chinese national character in twenty-seven chapters. Smith's style—what Lydia Liu calls his 'grammar of truth'—relies on a 'discursive power that reduces the object of its description to a less than human animal through rhetorical and figurative uses of language'.[21] In his chapter on the 'Absence of Nerves', Smith begins with a description of nervous agitation as an inescapable effect of 'modern civilisation'—a condition that 'include[s] all our readers'.[22] It is against the ubiquity of nervous afflictions in 'modern' nations that the Chinese 'absence of nerves' signifies. As he points out, however, this difference is unlikely to be physiological:

> It is not very common to dissect dead Chinese, though it has doubtless been done, but we do not hear of any reason for supposing that the nervous anatomy of the 'dark-haired race' differs in any essential respect from that of the Caucasian. But though the nerves of a Chinese as compared with those of the Occidental may be, as the geometricians say, 'similar and similarly situated', nothing is plainer than that they are nerves of a very different sort from those with which we are familiar.[23]

Through an imaginary, but still gruesome, dissection of 'dead Chinese', Smith repeats the dialectic that structures his entire work: though part of a single humanity, defined here by the geometrical arts of modern medical science, the Chinese remain unmistakably different. Having failed to find this difference under the skin, Smith locates it in a catalogue of Chinese characteristics: the ability to 'remain in one position' for a long time, to go without exercise, to 'sleep anywhere', to breathe without ventilation, to bear overcrowding and to endure 'physical pain'. In each case, 'freedom from the tyranny of nerves' is empirical evidence of a Chineseness that leaves neither outward nor inward trace, as well as a reminder that the Chinese may one day pose a threat to 'the Caucasian'.[24] Throughout, Smith's catalogue of difference poses the Chinese as not just other, but also threatening, especially in an imagined future in which China has modernised: 'We have come to believe, at least in general, in the survival of the most fit. Which is best adapted to survive in the struggles of the twentieth century, the "nervous" European, or the tireless, all-pervading, and phlegmatic Chinese?'[25]

Smith makes only one reference to 'boat-trackers', in a chapter titled 'Content and Cheerfulness', on the 'chronic state of good spirits ... [called] "cheerfulness"' and the form of 'conservatism' that makes the Chinese perfectly content with 'the system under which they live'.[26] He describes trackers as 'some of those whose labour is most exhausting ... [and yet] not only are [they] not heard to murmur at the unequal distribution of this world's goods, but when they have opportunities of resting do so in excellent spirits'.[27] As the most extreme, and thus most typical, of labourers, they prove the general rule of Chinese industry and endurance that Smith and others are at pains to establish, and of which cheer and contentment are merely subsidiary characteristics. But even this easy accommodation to harsh conditions poses a potential threat, as he reminds his readers: 'We repeat that if the teaching of history as to what happens to the "fittest" is to be trusted, there is a magnificent future for the Chinese race.'[28] The tracker is thus poised to enter the future with pain as pleasure and biology as destiny.

'Same as Oxen and Horses'

In reality, trackers and other boatmen were all too conscious of their physical and economic vulnerabilities. What appeared to the Western writer as contentment and cheer belied a tragic sense of self. Linguistically inaccessible to most Western travellers, this sense of self was expressed orally through the boatmen's work songs, or *haozi* 号子. As numerous travellers noted, these songs and chants were an integral part of the Yangzi soundscape, though usually they registered as little more than 'tremendous noise', loud enough to drown 'the roar of the rapid' or damage one's hearing.[29] The most common *haozi* consisted of a call-and-response structure that provided a clear and flexible system for pacing the work of tracking, while others constituted 'mind maps' of the region or expressed romantic longing.³⁰ Songs complaining about meagre pay, cruel bosses and middlemen and the dehumanising labour of tracking were also common. Not unlike the Westerners who were so shocked by their labour, boatmen frequently compared themselves to animals:

> 日子不如牛和马
> Our lives cannot compare to those of oxen and horses

> 船工终年如马牛
> The boatmen through the year are as horses and oxen

> 我们船工的生活真悲惨
> The lives of us boatmen are tragic indeed

> 风里来雨里去牛马一般
> In wind we come, in rain depart, same as oxen and horses³¹

Unlike Western writers, whose animal metaphors were grounded in racist conceptions of Chinese atavism, however, boatmen described themselves in this manner to draw attention not only to the harshness of tracking but also to how their poverty impinged on their ability to establish and maintain proper social ties, especially marriage.³² As in the leftist literature that made rickshaw-pullers iconic urban workers, the *haozi* of Yangzi boatmen drew attention to the bestial nature of tracking to reassert the humanity of the tracker.³³

A 'Decrescent Order'

The 'all-pervading … Chinese', of which the tracker was an extreme example, were both excluded from modernity and deemed to possess a super/subhuman capacity to weather the shocks of modernity because they offered a site for the schizoid marriage of the West's superiority complex and its anxiety over modernity's enervating effects. If the first law of thermodynamics makes possible a productivist ideology of labour power, the second law of thermodynamics, which holds that entropy in a closed system increases over time, forces a reckoning with the 'inevitability of decline, dissolution, and exhaustion'.³⁴ According to Anson Rabinbach:

> [T]he paradoxical relationship between energy and entropy is at the core of the nineteenth-century revolution in modernity: on the one side is a stable and productivist universe of original and indestructible force, on the other an irreversible system of decline and deterioration ... The powerful and protean world of work, production, and performance is set against the decrescent order of fatigue, exhaustion, and decline.[35]

Whereas the fatigue, nervous ailments and physical illnesses of modernity in industrialised Europe and America threatened to blunt the competitive edge that had raised the Caucasian races so far so quickly above the Chinese, the Chinese 'absence of nerves' conjured the (enduring) spectre of a role reversal. As both proof of Western progress and promise of Western decline, the tracker of Smith's *Chinese Characteristics* was an essential partner within the 'paradoxical relationship' of modernity.

In Smith's account, the tracker as coolie functions as both harbinger of a Chinese future and symbol of the Chinese past because he embodies a timeless racial essence—the telos of progress could be just as easily fuelled as foiled by the stagnant East. There is no irony here. After decades of scholarship dedicated to dissecting orientalist discourse, it is easy to recognise such antinomy as the engine of difference propelling colonial power structures and maintaining their latter-day manifestations. Just as the 'Chinese landscape' might refer to a timeless land of wonder or a region scientifically mapped and measured, the tracker came to embody contradictory conceptions of Chineseness. Shaped by the rhetorical template of Smith's book, the tracker and the coolie were simultaneously primitive and primed for future dominance. What is missing from Smith's secondhand account, however, but present in most firsthand accounts of trackers, is a sense of horror at the brutality of their labour and sympathy for their suffering. If evolving ideas of 'labour power' allowed observers to pit the tracker and coolie against labourers of other nationalities and races, an older and more powerful discourse of sympathy encouraged them to consider the tracker as part of a shared humanity, even as they described him as a 'less than human animal'.

1902

At the twilight of the Qing Empire, China's nascent working class was concentrated in a handful of urban centres—first and foremost, Shanghai. Up to the end of the nineteenth century, Shanghai's waged labourers consisted mostly of two categories: handicraft workers and workers in transportation, with the latter generally seen as belonging to a 'floating population' that was frequently associated with vagabonds and rogues.[1] Things began to change quickly at the turn of the century with the opening of cotton mills, silk filatures, tobacco factories, and other manufacturing plants, and by 1911, the city's modern sector employed close to 100,000 workers.[2] Women and children—in most cases recruited into factory jobs by foremen from their own regions—constituted the majority of this burgeoning factory workforce and were subjected to horrible exploitation. The most extreme working conditions occurred under the baoshenzhi (包身制) system, under which parents signed contracts agreeing that their daughter's wages would go to the contractor for the duration of the contract—usually three years—in return for a small sum of money, and the contractor in return would provide housing, food, and clothing to the worker, thus gaining total control over her.[3] Three types of proto-labour organisations dominated the social landscape: guilds (行会), mutual help societies (帮口), and secret societies (秘密结社).[4] The guilds were hierarchically organised corporations of those who practised a particular craft or trade. These bodies, which often were internally divided between workers and employers, sought to regulate the market by fixing prices, but also undertook the collection of taxes, organisation of public works, and maintenance of public order. Mutual help societies, meanwhile, were groups of workers, often from the same region, who monopolised a particular sector. This led to a notable fragmentation of the working class—a situation of which employers did not hesitate to take advantage. In those dire circumstances, some began dreaming about a future when machines would replace human labour and lead to the emancipation of workers.

Techno-Utopias and Robots in China's Past Futures
Craig A. SMITH

Long before Liu Cixin's novels became science fiction bestsellers in China and abroad, Chinese intellectuals dreamed of a utopia in which a robotic workforce could relieve humans of the need to labour. At the *fin de siècle*, utopian hopes for robots to emancipate human labourers were adapted to particular situations in different locales around the world. In China, the elite literati had always been able to adjust Confucianism to new epistemic issues, and even robots found a place in redesigned Confucian utopias. This essay examines discourses on robotisation in the late Qing Dynasty (1644–1912), showing that China's early techno-utopias included important discussions about the emancipation of labour that remain relevant today in light of both their dystopian fears and their utopian visions. The writing and limited dissemination of Kang Youwei's seminal *Book of Great Unity* (大同书)—which was first compiled into a complete draft in 1902—serve as a temporal marker for this chapter.

Labour Technology at the *Fin de Siècle*

The turn of the century crested on one of the many waves of industrialisation in modern China. In 1895, the Qing government officially opened the country's doors to foreign industry, allowing capital investment and industrialisation to flood the treaty ports. Even before this, industrialisation in Japan rippled throughout China's economy, as the mass production of textiles in Japanese factories increased the price of Chinese cotton and prompted a decline in profitability for spun yarn during the final decades of the Qing Dynasty.[5] As both traditional labour markets and regional handicraft industries were forced to adapt, these changes reverberated through the population. The large-scale importation of machinery and widespread curiosity about the implications of these new tools were particularly evident in the burgeoning print industry—an area that was already being revolutionised by new printing technologies that allowed the spread of information beyond the confines of the traditional elite.

In the waning years of the nineteenth century, Chinese newspapers were flooded with writings about machines. News reports announced the latest inventions, from tractors to typewriters. Foreigners, especially missionaries, played significant roles in encouraging this interest in industrialisation. For example, in 1894 the famous missionary Joseph Edkins published in the Chinese-language press an article titled 'On the Benefits of Machines' (论机器之益), in which he explained British economic success in light of the enhancement of economic and productive capabilities.[6] This discourse, and the clear material superiority of invading merchant and military forces, forced Chinese intellectuals to connect political change with industrialisation and technological enhancement.

In 1897 and 1898, at the height of China's dramatic political reforms known as the 'Hundred Days' Reform', a surprising number of articles on machines were published in reformist journals, including *Jicheng Bao* (集成报), *Xiangbao* (湘报), and *Nongxuebao* (农学报). Although many of these writings were translations from foreign newspapers, a considerable number of articles were written by local authors and focused on machinery relevant to Chinese labour and markets, particularly the production of rice and tea.

This was a time of optimism about China's future. China's loss to Japan in the First Sino-Japanese War, of 1894–95, had prompted a burst of political and literary activity from reformist intellectuals. However, just as their political idealism was accompanied by anxieties over China's future, their interest in industrialisation came with fears about the potential ills that machines would introduce. In an 1897 article in Shanghai's *Sin Wan Pao* (新闻报) titled 'Rise of the Machines' (机器盛行)—published more than a century before the *Terminator* film of the same title—an excited writer discussed the new machinery to be used at Hangzhou's Wulinmen Wharf.[7] The author explained that this trend was following existing practices in the West but acknowledged that the reduction in labour costs would result in a reduction in incomes, and 'there is a fear that this will anger all the workers'.

Although articles like this one indicated wariness towards machines and expressed serious concerns about labour issues, including reports of workers and children injured by machines, the elite recognised that technological advancements were necessary to save the country. A technologically ascendant China—which nationalists imagined as their redemption—was immediately reflected in the popular fiction that had recently become a motivating force for the increasingly literate population.

Decades before the word 'robot' was coined, mechanical humanoids began playing a role in these imagined techno-utopias in a new genre that would later be known as 'science fiction'.

The China Dream of the Electric Sheep

The idea of animated or mechanical humanoid servants and labourers appeared in classical Chinese texts. Mozi, a utilitarian philosopher active in the fifth century BCE, even created mechanical birds and beasts, and is now the namesake of a technology company. However, the concept of a 'machine-man' (机器人) only made its way from elite texts into the popular imagination towards the end of the Qing Dynasty.

Around the turn of the century, the entire world became fascinated with the idea of humanoid automatons and their potential for labour. The most memorable example of this in the West is the Tin Woodman from *The Wonderful Wizard of Oz* (1900), a depressed cyborg lumberjack yearning for a heart. Chinese fiction was in step and introduced labour automatons but with decidedly Chinese characteristics. In 1905 and 1906, the newspaper *Southern News* (南方报) serialised a lengthy novel by Wu Jianren entitled *The New Story of the Stone* (新石头记). Although other Chinese science fiction writers penned stories with automatons at the time, Wu's novel was a wonderland, its plot following Jia Baoyu, the protagonist of the eighteenth-century *Dream of the Red Chamber* (红楼梦), China's most famous novel, into a twentieth-century technological utopia.

Passing through a technological device called a 'civilisation mirror' (文明镜), Jia enters this utopia and is immediately served tea by a talking automaton 'boy' servant. The journey then proceeds through a melange of advanced technologies, including flying machines and submarines.[8] Wu's novel is a fascinating exploration of the desire for the preservation of Chinese tradition and the nation through technology, although it has also been criticised for its 'techno-ethnocentrism', as the author presents technology as instrumental to ensuring China's superior place in the modern world.[9] Wu placed his utopia in service of a revived imperial politics. This was not a modern technocracy but a Confucian empire led by an emperor named 'Eastern Civilisation' (东方文明). The symbolism of this techno-utopian ruler may be overly perspicuous in its positing of China's future in its past, but a better-known intellectual went much further into China's past to find no ruler at all for his own utopia: Kang Youwei.

Techno-*datong* and Confucian Robots

It might have been around this time that Kang Youwei wrote the *Book of Great Unity*, the most influential utopian imaginary published at the intersection of the imperial and Republican eras, and a crucial text for understanding modern China's political thought on labour. The utopia of *datong* that Kang described was first outlined in the Confucian classic *Book of Rites* (礼记), but due to Kang's bridging of this concept with modern understandings of labour and capital, *datong* became a keyword in Chinese revolutionary and Communist Party discourse.[10] The *Book of Great Unity* would become a seminal text after the 1911 revolution, but before this it remained unpublished and knowledge of it was limited to a tight circle of highly influential intellectuals.

Although Kang states in the introduction that he wrote the book in 1884—and although many from his army of disciples and influential associates long had access to the book—the first chapters were not published until 1913. As Kang would not allow it to be published while he was alive, the complete volume did not appear in regular print until 1935, eight years after his death, leading to controversy and numerous studies on the dating of the text.[11] Tang Zhijun's extensive research has shown that Kang most likely finished his manuscript in 1902, a finding corroborated by Wang Hui, who further argued that, although Kang was distributing early drafts in the 1880s, he completed a draft very similar to the published text by 1902.[12] This would indicate that Kang and Wu did not influence each other but were writing in a shared discourse.

Those years were a transitional period, in which new concepts flooding into China by way of Japan were assimilated into existing concepts and terminologies, producing a syncretic worldview. In this vein, the intellectuals of that time produced syncretic techno-utopias as well. Like his contemporaries, Kang did not use the term *laodong* (劳动), a modern word for labour that entered the Chinese lexicon around the turn of the century from the Japanese *rōdō*. Instead, he followed the long-held tradition of breaking society into four categories based on occupation: the scholars or officials (士, *shi*); the farmers (农, *nong*); the craftspeople, artisans, and workers (工, *gong*); and merchants and traders (商, *shang*). Although the *shang* had traditionally been seen as the least important of the four, since the Song Dynasty (960–1279), they had been significantly elevated in position.[13] While none of these divisions would find a place in Kang's utopia, in a remarkable fusion of Confucian and Marxist horizons, he maintained their use in steps leading up to the 'Great Unity' of *datong*, when all such hierarchies and categories will dissolve. In making this argument, he resorted to the traditional category of *gong* as a close equivalent of labour.

To explain the benefits of *datong* for labourers, Kang turned to foundational texts of early Chinese thought and constructed a comprehensive vision of the future and the pathway needed to arrive there. Building on a few short chapters from the *Book of Rites* and contextualising these ideas within the modern reality of nation-states and new political economies, Kang envisioned a future world with no suffering. He saw robots playing an important role in his Confucian utopia, yet his position as a member of the literati class shaped his understanding of how robots would bring an end to the traditional hierarchies: 'There will be no slaves or servants [奴仆], but their functions will be performed by machines, shaped like birds and beasts.'[14]

Just like H.G. Wells in his 1905 *A Modern Utopia*, Kang was also a fierce protector of animals, and insisted that future generations would all be strict vegetarians. However, unlike Wells, he did see animals such as monkeys and parrots as servants in our future world, with the caveat that the use of animals and birds would be limited to ensure that these creatures were also free from suffering.[15] In his view, the qualities of *ren* (仁), which is often translated as 'humaneness', extended to all birds and beasts.[16] Mechanical creatures, or automatons, had no *ren* and therefore could not suffer.

Kang saw industrialisation as the bane of the workers in the contemporary Age of Chaos (乱世)—as he defined our current age according to the classical Confucian cyclical history—but through industrialisation he also saw a liberating mechanism for workers in the time of the Great Peace (太平之世) that will follow once humanity achieves the Great Unity of *datong*. He argued that the struggles between labour and capital (工业之争) had increased in recent years 'because of machines being used to make things', and the only way to ensure that the rise of machines would not result in increased suffering was to remove ownership of capital from private hands.[17]

Kang imagined that 'in the time of the Great Peace, there will be no suffering. Labourers [为工者] will only find enjoyment.'[18] This will be possible because they will only put their skills to use in creating works of art, as the heavy lifting will all be done by robots. Again, like Wells, Kang saw technological advancements bringing an end to toil and opening the door to universal leisure: 'One will order by telephone, and food will be conveyed by mechanical devices—possibly a table will rise up from the kitchen below, through a hole in the floor. On the four walls will be lifelike, "protruding paintings".[19]

This great trust in the emancipatory potential of science continued throughout the twentieth century, and revolutionaries, including Mao Zedong in his youth, found Kang's work inspirational.[20] However, largely due to his promotion of constitutional monarchy, Kang is now remembered as a conservative opponent of revolution.

From Techno-Utopianism to Scientific Utopianism and Back Again

Despite Kang's fascination with science, and his detailed explanations of the ways in which scientific invention and robotics could relieve labourers of their suffering, his socialism is generally referred to as utopian socialism (or, in Chinese, 空想社会主义)—an approach that, as Frederick Engels indicated in his popular 1880 pamphlet *Socialism: Utopian and Scientific*, is inadequate when compared with scientific utopianism.[21] Scientific utopianism refers to a methodically argued model based on the dialectics of history, rather than—as the Chinese translation indicates—'fantastical socialism'. Engels' categorisation, along with the dismissiveness inherent in the Chinese term, has limited the genre of utopian socialism in post-1949 writings. However, China's current robotisation of labour—the replacement of human workers with industrial robots (以机器换人, to use the language of the Chinese authorities)—returns us to these texts today.

As China has become the biggest market for Tesla and other self-driving cars in the twenty-first century, and as Chinese investment in artificial intelligence research now leads the world, discussions of a robotic *datong* have resurfaced with urgency. In Guangdong, projects at both the provincial and the municipal levels have resulted in significant financial support for the robotisation of the labour force, with the provincial government claiming to have deployed 80,000 robotic units in 2017.[22] Research by Huang Yu has shown that, although the Chinese media has emphasised that robotisation will ultimately create jobs, many labourers, particularly those from rural areas, have already lost employment due to this push.[23] At the same time, in 2016, China's Thirteenth Five-Year Plan called for most farming practices to be largely mechanised before 2021.[24] This indicates the possibility of a massive reduction in demand for traditional labour markets, especially for rural peasants. These tremendous changes have great potential for the future, but without a corresponding reimagining of social organisation, they may result in the exploitation and suffering of Chinese workers.

Contemporary proposals to address the crisis in labour markets—such as the idea of an unconditional universal basic income—seem at home in the techno-utopian socialism of Kang Youwei's *datong*, but these concepts have yet to attract the attention of the Chinese leadership in the twenty-first century. In the *Book of Great Unity*, Kang argued that only by ending private ownership of labour, agriculture, industry, and commerce, and only by destroying boundaries of class, race, sex, family, and nation, could we end the suffering of labourers. In light of all this, the conservative monarchist is perhaps at the vanguard of the future being pursued by the Chinese Communist Party.

1915

The new Chinese republic was still trying to figure out its place in the global order—including how to deal with encroaching Japanese imperialism—when World War I erupted. Even as the prospects for China's formal entry into the war remained uncertain, in 1915, in a bid to ensure that China's voice would be heard once the conflict was over, senior politicians in Yuan Shikai's government came up with the idea of sending Chinese workers to Europe to support the Allied war effort. Eventually, 140,000 Chinese, most of whom were illiterate peasants, journeyed to the Western Front to aid the war efforts of the British, French, and US governments. Although labourers from many other countries travelled to France during the Great War, China sent by far the largest number of men and suffered the highest number of casualties—a sacrifice that has often been overlooked in historical accounts. The dispatch of workers also represented the first attempt by a Chinese government to engage in labour diplomacy—a practice that would become more prevalent in the Maoist era and of which we can still find traces in China's global engagements today.

An Extraordinary Journey: Chinese Labourers on the Western Front during the Great War

XU Guoqi

There have been many different types of Chinese labourers in Chinese and world history. There are many different kinds of Chinese emigration as well. But the 140,000 Chinese labourers who managed to go to the Western Front during World War I were unique and extraordinary. With their sacrifice and contribution, they not only helped the Allies' war efforts, thus doing their share to tilt the fate of Western civilisation, but also served as messengers between China and the West, contributing to China's renewal and great transformation. South Africans, Indians, Vietnamese, and many other labourers went to France during the Great War to support the British and French. Many went because they were citizens of colonial countries and had to answer the call from their imperial masters, but China—which was not a colony of any country—sent by far the largest number of men, and its labourers worked in Europe the longest.

Labourers in Place of Soldiers

The Great War coincided with a period of tremendous change in China, including the collapse of the Confucian civilisation, the rise of the New Culture Movement, and the undoing of a strong central government. During such a tumultuous period globally and domestically, the Chinese people were determined to transform their country and join the world on an equal footing. The outbreak of the Great War provided just such an opportunity. Hopes of recovering Qingdao, a Chinese territory in Shandong Province that had been under German control since 1898, first compelled the Chinese to try to join the war in 1914 but their effort was blocked by the United Kingdom. However, China's resolve was strengthened the following year, when Japan advanced its Twenty-One Demands aimed at turning China into a dependant state.

The challenge was how to win a place at the eventual peace conference to make sure China's voice would be heard and the country's national interests respected. In 1915, Liang Shiyi, a trusted advisor to President Yuan Shikai and a powerful politician in his own right, developed the 'labourers in place of soldiers' (以工代兵) scheme, which was designed to join hands with the Allied cause even as the official entry of the country into the war remained uncertain.[1] In 1915 and 1916, respectively, France and the United Kingdom reluctantly concluded that Chinese support was essential to win the conflict. Given the huge number of casualties they had suffered and the near bankruptcy of their national coffers, more human resources were crucial.

Through the collaboration between four parties—the Chinese volunteer labourers and the governments of China, the UK, and France—140,000 Chinese, most of whom were illiterate peasants, went to Europe during World War I. Initially, these workers were recruited by the British and French governments to aid their war efforts against the Germans; when the United States joined the war in 1917, the Americans utilised Chinese labour as well. All these governments considered Chinese labourers as critical for the fate of their war effort. While for the British and French authorities the Chinese labourers meant vital help in winning the war, the Chinese authorities saw these labourers as a means to allow China to join the Allied cause and promote the country's entry into the world community as an equal member.

The Chinese decision to send labourers to Europe was unprecedented. Both the Ming (1368–1644) and Qing (1644–1912) dynasties discouraged Chinese from going abroad and even persecuted those who had. In 1712, with considerable numbers of Chinese already residing abroad, an edict from the Qing court decreed: 'Those who stay overseas permanently are liable to capital punishment and will be extradited from foreign countries by the provincial governors for prompt beheading.'[2] The Qianlong Emperor of the Qing (in power from 1735 to 1795) once called overseas Chinese 'deserters of the Celestial Empire', who would therefore receive no protection from China if they encountered trouble in other countries.[3] In spite of this, many Chinese still went abroad, including those who travelled to the United States and built America's Trans-Pacific railway. Yet the prohibition against emigration remained official policy until 1893, when the Qing government finally abolished it by accepting its diplomat

Xue Fucheng's argument that adopting a friendly policy on emigration would 'have the benefit of bridging the gap between China and the West'.[4]

When China became a republic in 1912, official policy on emigration changed dramatically. The West was no longer dismissed as a society of demons but was painted as an example for China to follow; going abroad became a glorious privilege. As a result, the status of overseas Chinese was enhanced a great deal and, in 1912, Republican China passed a series of laws, including the *Provisional Constitution and Organisation Act* of congress, which legalised representation of overseas Chinese in domestic politics. In 1916, as Chinese labourers started to leave for France, the Ministry of Agriculture and Commerce and the Ministry of Foreign Affairs deliberated over new legislation to protect overseas workers.[5] The new law soon passed and, in 1917, with a huge number of Chinese labourers already in Europe, the government in Beijing established an office called the Bureau of Overseas Chinese Workers (侨工事务局).[6] The 1915 'labourers in place of soldiers' program should be understood in this context of the transformation in Chinese thought and society, in addition to being an expression of China's eagerness to join the war.

Extraordinary Experiences

Although the Chinese workers who travelled to the Western Front of the Great War were part of a grand strategy devised by the country's elite, most of those who undertook the voyage simply wanted to make a living. Most were poor, uneducated peasants from Shandong Province who volunteered to go to Europe to earn money they were promised they would make. However, the Chinese labourers' journey from China to France was extremely challenging. Some groups went to France via the Suez Canal or Cape of Good Hope, but most travelled by way of the Pacific, Canada, and across the Atlantic.[7] About 3,000 Chinese lost their lives either on their way to Europe or in Europe, including several hundred who died *en route* due to German submarine attacks. After landing in Europe, they were often shocked by the appalling living conditions. Many Chinese considered France the centre of so-called Western civilisation, but at that time the civilised West was mired in a terrifying war and it was not in a position to show off its cultural, intellectual, or political triumphs, revealing only its ugliest, most barbarous capacities. Nobody had prepared the Chinese labourers for this kind of culture shock, nor taught them how to adjust to this new life. The food, the language, the customs, and the management—all of these came as a shock, and there was no time or opportunity for them to ponder, digest, and ask questions, since their labour was urgently needed.

While on the Western Front, the Chinese worked in trenches, factories, and ports. They repaired tanks and roads, dug foundations, worked in arsenals, loaded and unloaded trains and boats, and manned paper factories. Although the French assigned Chinese labourers a variety of tasks, trench-digging occupied most of the time and labour of those working under the British. Trench warfare was of course a key feature of the Great War and, although no records indicate how much the Chinese were involved in trench-digging, it is safe to say they played a critical role in trench warfare. Before they were recruited to France, these workers had rarely ventured far beyond their village borders. Now their daily life was filled with racism, suffering, confusion, misunderstandings, mistreatment, and many other hardships. In addition, the Chinese who worked under the British had to deal with more stress and greater challenges, since at the end of each day they were confined in barbed-wire enclosures, facing boredom after hours of backbreaking work.

The Chinese came to Europe to help Britain and France win the war and, after the war, many would remain to help France with reconstruction. Many Chinese under British supervision stayed in France until 1920, and most of the Chinese under the French stayed until 1922. In fact, the Chinese were the last of the British labour forces to leave France. The Great War lasted about 1,500 days, but the war experience of many Chinese labourers was longer and more horrifying as they stayed behind to clear the battlefields and bury the dead. Anyone would count this work as gruesome, but it was especially hard on the Chinese, who believed that touching the dead was inauspicious. The men suffered nightmares and feared they would be cursed by the dead. The most dangerous task was clearing away unexploded ordnance. Nobody bothered to train the Chinese in how to handle these materials, and we still do not know with certainty how many died as a result. Although it is impossible to arrive at a concrete figure due to a lack of authoritative evidence, it is estimated that around 3,000 Chinese lost their lives in Europe or on their way there due to enemy fire, disease, or injury. To this day, their graves can be found in France and Belgium, among other places.

Chinese sacrifices were not meaningfully recognised after the war. At the Paris Peace Conference, British Secretary for Foreign Affairs Arthur Balfour claimed that China's contribution during the war had involved neither 'the expenditure of a single shilling nor the loss of a single life', completely disregarding the deaths of Chinese labourers.[8] The contributions of these Chinese workers were soon forgotten not only in Europe, but also by their own country, to the point that Chinese scholar Chen Sanjing described their experience as 'a great tragedy'.[9] Over the years, several historians have questioned the importance of the Chinese experience in the Great War in Europe. Marilyn A. Levine has claimed that Chinese labourers 'did not fulfil the expected foreign policy objective',[10] and Judith Blick has suggested that the whole idea of labourers as soldiers was merely a commercial one and the Chinese had nothing to do with the actual war effort.[11] However, this misses the crucial role the Chinese played in the Allied war effort. As the London *Times* wrote at that time:

> The coming of the Chinese Labour Corps to France relieved our own men from an enormous amount of heavy and miscellaneous work behind the lines, and so helped to release a much larger proportion than otherwise would have been possible for combatant duties.[12]

In other words, 140,000 Chinese labourers freed up at least 140,000 Allied soldiers. More importantly, the Chinese not only contributed to the infrastructure of the war, but also acted as messengers between East and West, thereby taking part in China's renewal and transformation.

Bridging the Gap between East and West

Most of the Chinese workers in France were common villagers who knew little of China or the world affairs when they were selected to go to Europe. Still, these men directly contributed to helping China transform its image at home and globally. Their new transnational roles reshaped China's national identity and internationalisation, which in turn contributed to shaping the emerging global system. From their experience of Europe in a time of war and their work with the American, British, and French militaries, as well as fellow labourers from other countries, they developed a unique perception of China and of world affairs.

In the words of historian James Joll, the Great War marked 'the end of an age and beginning of the new' world order.[13] This observation applies to China as well. With the Great War, China embarked on a journey of internationalisation and national renewal. As Chinese writer Yi Feng noted in an article published in late 1918: 'The Great War was soon to end, it would end with the collapse of nineteenth-century civilisation. And twentieth-century civilisation started immediately. In other words, the world has entered a new era.'[14] He encouraged his readers to understand the importance of these transformations and take advantage of the changes they brought. 'China will be discarded' in the new era if the Chinese failed to develop a 'great awareness' (大觉悟) and prepare themselves well, he warned.[15] At a Young Men's Christian Association (YMCA) conference in the spring of 1919, Wang Zhengting, a member of the Chinese delegation to the Paris Peace Conference, said in his address to the YMCA secretaries, including the Chinese secretaries who worked with the Chinese labourers in Europe, that present conditions in China demanded above all things a 'fighting spirit'. That included a 'spirit of justice and righteousness, a spirit of principle that will make one fearless of death or the loss of selfish interest and ambition'.[16]

The Chinese labourers in Europe, to a great extent, represented such fighting spirit. If we approach the 'labourers in place of soldiers' idea from the perspective of China's search for a new national identity and national renewal, the journey of these workers has historic importance. Or, to put it differently, it is possible to argue that Chinese labourers not only made important contributions to the Allied war effort, but also contributed to the postwar peace conference and China's subsequent development. After all, thanks to its presence on the Western Front, China was able to participate in the peace conference and voice demands for respect and equality. The workers' labour, sacrifices, and lives provided these diplomats with a critical tool in their battle for recognition and inclusion on the world stage.

Therefore, instead of being a 'tragedy', the journey of these workers succeeded in helping China actively participate in national and world affairs. Although nobody has given them this credit, they were an important part of China's own 'greatest generation'—that is, the generation of those who came of age in the 1910s and 1920s and fundamentally changed China's direction. From the very beginning of the modern era, Chinese elites have linked emigration with China's internationalisation, and nowhere is this point illuminated more clearly than in the case of Chinese labourers during the Great War.

These largely untold stories resonate with historical and contemporary issues related to migration within China and without. Today, Chinese people live all across the world as labourers, immigrants, or students.

As the late Philip A. Kuhn, a prominent China historian, recently wrote: 'Emigration has been inseparable from China's modern history ... At least for the period since the 1500s, I suggest that neither Chinese history lacking emigration nor emigration lacking the history of China is a self-sufficient field of study.'[17] By studying the Chinese labourers in Europe and their stories, we can not only recover a neglected chapter in Chinese history but also improve our understanding of how this seemingly obscure episode affected both Chinese and Western societies on which the modern world order is built.

1920

Before the First Congress of the Chinese Communist Party in July 1921 declared the chief aim of the Party to be the organisation of labour, student activists baptised in the fire of the May Fourth Movement of 1919 were already attempting to build bridges with the working class. Among them was Deng Zhongxia. Three months after the May Fourth demonstrations, then twenty-five-year-old Deng organised a cooperative residence that housed about thirty students from Peking University, many of whom would soon join the Communist cause.[1] They shared a common interest in the labour movement and mutual aid, believing that intellectuals should be judged not only on the grounds of scholarship, but also in terms of their participation in labour. As would later become a tenet of Maoism in China and globally, they called for investigations of the living and working conditions of the working class. To raise the workers' class awareness, the students established a 'Labour School for Continuing Education' in Changxindian—the centre for the workshops of the northern section of the Beijing–Hankou railway, quite close to Beijing and employing around one thousand workers. However, they quickly stumbled on the perennial obstacles to organising. Differences in social and cultural backgrounds made it very difficult for the students to connect with the workers.[2] Zhang Guotao, another student leader who had spearheaded the endeavour, reminisced about his first visit to Changxindian. The workers had warmly welcomed him and his fellow activists, offering the utmost hospitality despite their meagre means, but he was the only one who eagerly ate everything, unfazed by the flies flying around the food. As he recounted half a century later: 'I was the only one who gulped the food down noisily, like the workers, while talking patriotism with them. Perhaps because of my conduct the workers did not create a mental division between me as a student and themselves as workers. I was able to establish an intimate relationship with some of them as a result.'[3] The following recollection of a trip to Changxindian was written by Deng Zhongxia on 19 December 1920 and published two days later in Chenbao (晨报) under a pen-name.

A Day Trip to Changxindian
DENG Zhongxia

(Translated by ZHOU Ruixue)[4]

The workers in Changxindian invited us to help with a planning meeting to organise a labour school for continuing education. I woke up early today and, with my three comrades Tailei, Renji, and Guotao, rushed to the West Qianmen railway station, where we took the train to Changxindian. Changxindian is twenty-one kilometres from Beijing, and the train was supposed to arrive around 1 o'clock. It is a large village, with three big factories and 2,500 workers. These factories are managed by the Jinghan Railroad Administration. According to the Railroad Administration, there are three departments: train services, machinery, and railroad maintenance. The four of us were chatting and laughing on the train, so cheerful that the harsh cold weather seemed to have withdrawn. When the train passed the Yongding River, I gazed in the dawn at Lugou bridge, set against a shabby old town. Two or three curtains were swaying in the wind. It was quite beautiful, like a magnificent natural painting. That moment aroused my artistic impulse, and my hands were itching to paint, but sadly I had not brought my painting supplies with me. Also, the train did not stop at the bridge, so I wouldn't have been able to paint anyway. As the train went further, my heart was still attached to the memory of that place. The train arrived at Changxindian, but the scenery of Lugou bridge remained in my heart.

When we got off the train at Changxindian, I saw many famine survivors—men and women, elders and youth—crowded by the station. Their gaunt appearance and shabby clothes stirred the inside of my eyes, and my heart then felt hurt, in painful compassion. I did not know where the good mood that I had chatting on the train and my interest in painting had suddenly gone. My heart was just in great discomfort, as if I were also suffering from starvation and poverty. I pondered how they, the famine survivors, did not have clothes to wear, food to eat, or shelter to live in the freezing snow of the harsh winter. And yet the bureaucrats and politicians were enjoying large buildings, fancy clothes, and luxury food. They also were merrily cuddling their concubines around the fireplace, whereas the famine victims were outside sleeping on the ground, freezing or starving to death. Their pain and pleasure are as distinct as heaven and earth. Alas, this is truly the most unjust thing in society. Why did they come to be this poor? Who has stolen their property? How could we possibly save them just by donating a little money? I have a word of caution to every gentleman keen to relieve the famine: please broaden your horizons and be concerned about their permanent state of famine and poverty. This requires that we fundamentally dismantle the things that produce social injustice. Everyone should try to resolve this.

The workers at Changxindian saw us arriving and were very welcoming and cordial to us. We saw them as friendly brothers, too, and there was fraternity among the workers themselves. I was rather fond of the solidarity and unity. I often resent how heartless people nowadays in society can be, cheating and battling each other, so the harmony and solidarity among the Changxindian workers gave me infinite hope. Because the warm-hearted worker leader Mr Deng Shouting had opened a citizen school for women, which has made great achievements in recent years, the residents of Changxindian gave him a plaque, on which is written the motto 'Joyfully Educating Students' (乐育英才). Today, he was hosting a feast. There were many men, women, elders, and youth, most of whom were workers. We happened to be there at its height and got a taste of the village social feast, which was much fun. We envied their ways of life as ordinary people and their intimate, bustling habits.

After we ate, the planning meeting began. First, worker leader Mr Mingke announced the procedures to organise this labour school, its current methods, and the meeting agenda for the day. Perhaps because this labour school is organised by the Changxindian workers themselves, the funding is by donation. Next, Mr Guotao explained why it is necessary to start a labour school. Basically, he said, why do we workers have to work diligently every day, and yet still struggle to feed ourselves, whereas those idle bureaucrats, politicians, and capitalists enjoy lavish buildings, clothing, and food? Where does their money come from? What about their clothing and food? It is all from us workers, from our blood and sweat. This is why we have no enjoyment and have become so poor. Now we want to achieve happiness, but that is not possible if we don't have the intellect and knowledge first. Therefore, we are starting this school. Furthermore, education is equal, and everyone has a right to it. Are we workers alone not supposed to receive it? As Adam Smith eloquently put it: 'All men are created equal.' Therefore, we have to know that workers have the same status as the capitalists and should enjoy the same level of education and happiness. While he was speaking, all the workers present were nodding as if to show emotional approval and awareness of his words. The labour school will probably host its commencement meeting on 1 January 1921 and will start classes on the fifth. That day will most likely be bustling with excitement.

After the meeting, a few worker leaders gave us a tour of each factory. Because today is the weekend, most of the workers were not working. Due to special circumstances such as their poverty or not understanding the point of resting, a small number of workers were still working. They work around ten hours in winter and eleven or twelve hours in summer. The wages vary, depending on the project and the individual, from 0.3 yuan to 1 yuan. Overtime in the evening used to be paid at 25 percent more than ordinary time, but now it is paid at the same rate. (I heard that the workers in Tangshan southern factory have already gone on strike since the sixteenth because of this situation.) Living costs per month for workers range from 3 or 4 yuan to 15 or 16 yuan (for those who have family). We visited a place where many bricks were on the ground, and I asked whether they were supposed to be used to build something. One worker smiled and replied: 'We have had these bricks for six years already. They said they will be used to build a hospital for us workers. You see that newly built small house over there? But they have not started on the rest of the buildings in six years.' I said jokingly: 'Wouldn't it be convenient for you all to get sick [if the hospital is built]?' He responded: 'Don't you know the dark side of this? Thank heavens we have not been sick. If we do get sick, they will not treat us; they will say either that we don't have the disease or that they don't have the medication. Only if you have status can you get a bit of medicine!' I was outraged hearing this. I warned the Railroad Administration: you absolutely have to take care of the workers' happiness. Do not spend a large amount of tax revenue and hardly any of it for workers living in poverty.

The workers in Changxindian are intelligent and united. They are already organised into strong collectives and publish a journal called *Voice of Labour* (劳动音), each issue of which sells more than 2,000 copies.

Unfortunately, I do not have training in machinery, so I cannot write about any lessons that I learned after touring the factories. I only remember that one factory was for maintaining steamers, one for fixing machines, and the other for making iron bars; inside the general engine, we saw countless belts and wires. Each worker gave me explanations and I truly appreciate the knowledge that I acquired from them. At 5.50pm, we took the train back to Beijing. When passing Lugou bridge, the scene of natural beauty had already been covered by the dark haze of night. I could not see it again and was disappointed.

1921

The summer of 1921 witnessed the founding congress of the Chinese Communist Party (CCP) in Shanghai, a development that had momentous implications for the Chinese labour movement. In the early years of the republic, labour organising had been the realm of anarchists and socialist organisations.[1] Sun Yat-sen and his Nationalist Party, formed in August 1912, had championed the need for workers to organise, although this was as much to improve working conditions as to build a strong national economy.[2] With the creation of the CCP, a new actor entered and transformed history. The founding resolution of the CCP defined the basic mission of the Party to be the establishment of industrial unions. Learning from the recent experiences of some members in running worker schools, the document stressed the indispensable role of education: 'Because workers' schools are a stage in the process of organising industrial unions, these sorts of schools must be established in every industrial sector ... The main task of the workers' schools is to raise workers' consciousness, so that they recognise the need to establish a union.' As Elizabeth Perry has noted, this emphasis on proletarian education not only drew on the Russian precedent and contemporary experiments within China, but also was a result of the central place that education occupies in Chinese political culture.[3] This essay traces the relationship between the CCP and the labour movement in those momentous early years, arguing that the Party and its designated class nature were born in China's domestic structural conditions and global position as an exploited and oppressed nation in the epoch of capitalist 'uneven and compressed development'.

Setting Sail: The Foundation of the Chinese Communist Party

LIN Chun

On a hot summer day in July 1921, thirteen people representing the earliest Communist groups in China gathered in Shanghai to hold their first national congress. From 23 July, they started using the residence of Li Shucheng, the brother of co-organiser of the congress Li Hanjun, at 106 Wangzhi Road (now 76 Xingye Road) in the French concession. During an evening session on the thirtieth of the month, a stranger came into the house and then rushed out. Suspecting he was a spy, the group dispersed and reconvened the next day on a boat in Jiaxing's South Lake, about 100 kilometres away, in the hometown of Wang Huiwu, the wife of co-organiser Li Da. Minutes later that evening, the police surrounded and searched the house for four hours to no avail. As a result of these providential origins, 1 July was designated the anniversary of the monumental event of the founding of the Chinese Communist Party (CCP).

Of the fifty-three formal members that made up the total membership of the Party at that time, each major Communist group elected two people to attend the congress. Participants included Li Da and Li Hanjun from Shanghai, Zhang Guotao and Liu Renjing from Beijing, Mao Zedong and He Shuheng from Hunan, Dong Biwu and Chen Tanqiu from Hubei, Deng Enming and Wang Jinmei from Shandong, and Chen Gongbo and Zhou Fohai from Guangdong. Chen Duxiu and Li Dazhao, the two intellectuals who had led China's first formal Communist organisations, respectively in Shanghai and Beijing, were unable to attend the congress, but Chen was represented by Bao Huiseng. Absent also was any deputy of the Chinese Communists in Europe, who had set up a branch in Paris in late 1920. Others present included Maring (Henk Sneevliet), an experienced Dutch Communist representing the Communist International (Comintern), and Nikolski (Wladimir Abramowitsch Neumann), a young Russian representing the Comintern's Far East Secretariat and the Red International of Labour Unions (Profintern). Maring gave a long speech at one of the first meetings, translated by the delegate Liu, a nineteen-year-old Peking University student.

The delegates elected a provisional Central Bureau. Chen Duxiu became general secretary, with Zhang Guotao and Li Da directors of organisation and propaganda, respectively. The congress adopted a Party platform that set the goals of 'overthrowing the state power of the capitalist class' and 'accepting a dictatorship of the proletariat until class struggle is over and all class distinctions are eradicated' (as was similarly stated in the 'Declaration of the Communist Party of China' adopted by the Shanghai group in November 1920).[4] More specifically, it demanded the 'abolishment of capitalist private property and the expropriation of machines, land, factories, and intermediate products, so as to turn the means of production over to public ownership'.[5] The congress also passed a resolution on 'present works' that emphasised the importance of politically mobilising industrial workers. 'The fundamental task of this Party is to organise trade unions ... in which the Party should imbue the spirit of class struggle'.[6] Chen's written intervention was mainly concerned with organisation, stressing democratic centralism, membership rules, and discipline as critical to building a strong party capable of bringing with it the masses. Concluding that unionised workers should form a 'natural' unity with the peasants striving towards 'a social revolution', the Party centre subsequently assigned key members to develop local branches, unions, and educational classes among urban and rural workers.

Without tracing the diverse personal trajectories of the congress attendees, a minimal sketch is necessary. After the Nationalis Party's (Guomindang, or GMD) betrayal and slaughter of tens of thousands of Communists and sympathisers in 1927 (see S.A. Smith's essay in the present volume), Chen Duxiu and Liu Renjing took separate 'left opposition' positions, for which they were expelled from the Party in 1929. Chen remained a believer, whose two sons, both leading Communists, were killed by the GMD. Despite his commitment, the official historical verdict on his 'erroneous line of rightwing opportunism' remains unchanged. In 1929, Liu visited Trotsky in Turkey on his way back to China from Moscow, but he later distanced himself from the Chinese Trotskyites. Along with Mao Zedong, Dong Biwu, and Li Da, he lived to work in the new China after 1949. Wang Jinmei, Li Hanjun, Deng Enming, He Shuheng, and Chen Tanqiu died as martyrs during valiant revolutionary struggles between 1925 and 1943. After 1923, Chen Gongbo, Zhou Fohai, and Bao Huiseng variously slipped into reactionary camps. Zhang Guotao became a top commander of the Red Army but joined the GMD after the Long March. Of the two foremost Party founders, Li Dazhao was hanged by an anti-Communist warlord in 1927, and Chen Duxiu died from illness in 1942.

Catalysts of the Voyage

For decades since the Opium Wars and before 'the salvo of October' 1917 that shook the world and brought Leninism to China, the country had been devastated by both domestic unrest and foreign invasions. As rival imperialist powers violently 'dismembered' the country with the help of local warlords, landlords, and compradors, the late-Qing reformers' illusions of imitating the West were shattered. The Xinhai revolution of 1911 failed to either repel foreign domination or reorder society. Riddled by ever-increasing obstacles, Sun Yat-sen's government was unable to materialise his 'three people's principles' of nationalism, democracy, and popular welfare. Despite China's shortcomings, Lenin congratulated Asia's first republic with a series of commentaries on the 'awakening of Asia', in recognition of the significance of national liberation. He regarded events in China as a breakthrough for proletarian revolutionaries wanting to unite with the world's 'toiling masses'.[7] In 1919, the Comintern was established to promote revolutions globally to provide support, solidarity, and security for the still young and embattled Soviet regime. Communism and internationalism were twinned at birth.

Modern revolutionary nationalism arose in China in what was later theorised as its 'semicolonial, semifeudal' conditions inherited from the mid-nineteenth century.[8] In the capitalist epoch of uneven and combined development, the CCP emerged from an agrarian society as an innovative working-class organisation. Although only about two million strong, China's proletariat in the early twentieth century was politically vital and militant, in response to the substantial foreign presence in the Chinese economy. Li Dazhao articulated this relationship between class nationalism and social transformation by arguing that the 'victory of Bolshevism for the subalterns' was 'of world significance' and that China's 'self-determination' and liberation as a nation from exploitation and oppression would also be indispensable for reconstructing the globe.[9] The condition of being under siege in a 'class war' (阶级战争) between 'the world's proletarian subalterns and capitalists' was ripe for a worker-centred 'national people's revolution' (国民革命), in which democracy meant the 'populism of labour'.[10] Li's critiques of Japan's military expansionist 'pan-Asianism' underlined a 'new Chinese nationalism' (新中华民族主义) and 'new regionalism' (新亚细亚主义) of equality and peace free of imperialism. For him, anti-imperialist and class struggles were mutually indispensable.

In the runup to the formation of the CCP, competing ideas and thoughts—from social Darwinism, vitalism, and pragmatism to guild socialism, anarchism, and Marxist communism—were introduced to China by students returning from Japan and Europe. Liberalism did not find a receptive audience, largely due to its initial arrival in the guise of liberal imperialism. Chinese Communist theory powerfully argued that, since the liberal capitalist path was foreclosed by imperialist intrusion, revolution in China could only pave the way for socialism. In 1915, Chen Duxiu launched *Youth* magazine (青年杂志) and soon renamed it *New Youth* (新青年) during the New Culture Movement that sought to recast millennia of repressive Confucian hierarchy and despotism. On the eve of the May Fourth Movement of 1919, he condemned the 'darkness' of Chinese society and greeted 'Mr Science and Mr Democracy', advocating a cultural and moral sweep 'to clean up the old mucks with blood'.[11] The movement was triggered by the Treaty of Versailles, which transferred the former German concessions in Shandong Province to Japan. Demanding the government reject this imperialist deal, student demonstrations and labour strikes in Beijing diffused throughout other cities, making an age of radical mass politics in China part of the global postwar anticolonial and modernising realignments. It indicated a historical moment for the Chinese working class as an independent political subject making history.

The landmark May Fourth Movement moulded the first cohort of CCP cadres. Recognising their position within class politics, the Communist intellectuals were an organic component of the growing proletariat. In May 1919, *New Youth* became a firmly Marxist publication with a special issue on Marxism edited by Li Dazhao. He continued to elaborate his views in 'My Conception of Marxism' (我的马克思主义观) and several other articles, delineating how economics, socialism, and historical materialism were 'fundamentally connected by a golden line of class struggle'.[12] Li Hanjun wrote extensively as well. He translated and edited an introductory text to Marx's *Capital*, explaining capitalist commodities and surplus value, and the 'Russian road' as an alternative.[13] In debating with the anarchists and reformists, Chen Duxiu elucidated a materialist conception of history, labour value, and the proletarian state. With Chen's 'On Politics' (谈政治) as a Marxist declaration in September 1920, *New Youth* was reissued, with Chen remaining the chief editor.[14]

At this time, the Chinese translation of Marx and Engel's *Communist Manifesto* by Chen Wangdao was published. Ample publications associated with Communist networks were in circulation, such as *Weekly Review* (每周评论) edited by Li Dazhao, *Consciousness* (觉悟) by Zhou Enlai, *New Society Quarterly* (新社会) by Qu Qiubai, *Voice of Labour* (劳动音) by Deng Zhongxia, and the underground *Communist Party* monthly (共产党) by Li Da. The last two were launched simultaneously on 7 November 1920 as a tribute to the Russian revolution. *The Pioneer* (先驱), edited by Deng and Liu Renjing, was briefly the official newsletter of the Socialist Youth League, instituted in August 1920 with Yu Xiusong as its secretary.

By the time the Bolsheviks came to China, local agitation was well under way. In the spring of 1920, Grigori Voitinsky, the deputy head of the Russian Communist Party's East Asian Bureau, went to Beijing and Shanghai, where he assumed the position of acting president of the Comintern's Far East Secretariat, established in May 1920. On his trips, he was accompanied by his translator and assistant Yang Mingzhai, a Chinese worker and Bolshevik Party member in Russia. Zhang Tailei was the first Chinese Communist to head the Comintern's China division. He travelled to the Vladivostok office, attended the second Comintern World Congress in July 1920 concerning national and colonial questions, and accompanied Maring and Nikolsky to Shanghai in June 1921. Voitinsky's team joined meetings and activities, helped prepare for a May Day rally (which fell through after the police raided Chen Duxiu's headquarters), oversaw a conference of socialists and anarchists in July 1921, and jointly ran the *Shanghai Chronicle* (上海生活报, in Russian), *Society Daily* (社会日报), and *New China* (新中国) among their propaganda organs. Moscow and its dispatches played an important advisory role in the creation of the CCP as a branch of the Comintern, despite resistance from Chen Duxiu and Li Hanjun. Scores of Chinese were sent to the 'red Mecca' to attend the Communist University for Labourers of the East in the 1920s. Despite these affinities, from the outset, the CCP was distinctly independent politically, organisationally, and financially; the funds from internationalist donations were negligible. Neither Voitinsky nor Maring could have accomplished anything in China without what had already solidly developed locally. The CCP's roots in Chinese soil allowed it to cultivate its own distinctive revolutionary ideology and strategy.

Sacred Labour

Seeing the emancipation and empowerment of labour as its mission, the CCP possessed a proletarian (self-)identity, which informed the way its leaders engaged with China's labour movement. In April 1920, Chen Duxiu spoke about 'labour's consciousness' (劳动者底觉悟) to an assembly of Shanghai dockers.[15] Li Dazhao's 1920 speech at the Beijing University May Day rally popularised the notion of the dignity of labour—dubbed 'sacred labour' (劳工神圣) by the May Fourth intellectuals.[16] In a contribution to the May Day commemoration issue of *New Youth*, he narrated the international eight-hour workday movement, and quoted Karl Liebknecht on why the world's labour should unite against imperialism.[17] Lamenting that May Day was not yet established among workers in China but was only 'a movement of pen and ink on paper', he concluded with a call: 'Rise! Rise!! Rise!!! Hard working workers, today is the day of your awakening!' In August, Chen Duxiu and Li Hanjun initiated *Labour* (劳动界) as a popular weekly digest written by workers themselves. In its short run of twenty-four issues, workers described their experiences and views in their own words in the form of commentaries, poems, stories, and letters. For instance, in 'A Worker's Manifesto' (一个工人的宣言), the author, Li Zhong, a shipbuilder, imagined a 'future society as a workers' society, and the future China as a workers' China'.[18] More publications were launched later, including *Jinan Labour Weekly* (济南劳动周刊), established in May 1921 with the aim of 'raising the consciousness of common labourers', which was soon joined by the *Labour Weekly* (劳动周刊) in Shanghai and the *Workers' Weekly* (劳工周刊) in Hunan, among others.

Although it was not until the Second National Congress of 1922 that the Party delineated its program outlining a phased revolution from a 'new bourgeois democratic' to a socialist one, the Communist revolution's dual nature was defined from the beginning as national and social liberation under the leadership of the working class. The Party and the labour movement literally grew together, as exemplified in a strike by 8,000 workers over humiliating treatment from 20 July to mid-August 1921 in the British American Tobacco factories in Pudong, near the Party's founding congress. Li Qihan, who had worked with tobacco, machinery, textile, and print workers, was dispatched to lead the victorious strike. Prior to the congress, a number of major worker clubs and unions had been established. For instance, the Beijing Communist group created the Changxindian Railway Workers' Club (see Deng Zhongxia's translation in the present volume), while the Shandong group launched the Jinan Dahuaishu Machinery Workers' Club, and Wang Jinmei organised rail, coalmine, and iron factory workers in the Shanhaiguan and Qinhuangdao regions. In Hong Kong, the Seamen's General Union, which acquired its formal name from Sun Yat-sen, was led by Su Zhaozheng, who would go on to become a leading member of the CCP before his premature death.

On 11 August 1921, right after the meeting on the South Lake, the Party moved to found the Chinese Trade Union Secretariat (中国劳动组合书记部). Zhang Guotao was its general secretary and *Labour Weekly* its official organ. The founding statement, published in the magazine *Communist Party*, proclaimed the imminent advent of a new world belonging to the workers.[19] Five subdivisions of the secretariat were opened, in Beijing, Wuhan, Changsha, Jinan, and Guangzhou. In Hunan's *Workers' Weekly*, Mao Zedong, director of the Hunan chapter, wrote a short article in November 1921 to celebrate the anniversary of the provincial trade union: 'The purpose of labour unions is not only to gain workers better wages and shorter time through such tools as strikes, but also and especially for workers to acquire self-awareness and cohesion of the whole class for its fundamental interest.' He called for the 'right to strike' and the acknowledgement of the 'sacredness' of labour, and concluded with the resounding Marxist slogans 'from each according to his ability, to each according to his worth' (各尽所能，各取所值) and 'workers of the world, unite!'[20]

The central secretariat tasked itself with promoting Marxism, organising unions, and liaising with the international proletariat. Under its leadership, a triple struggle against foreign imperialism, warlordism, and capitalist conditions brought about the first tide of China's labour movement in the early 1920s. Most legendary were strikes by the seamen in Hong Kong, miners in Anyuan (Hunan) and Kailuan (Hebei), railroad workers along such arteries of communications as the Lanzhou–Lianyungang, Beijing–Fengtian, and Beijing–Hankou railways, and textile and service workers in Shangdong and the Yangzi River Delta. Luo Zhanglong, a leader of several of these strikes who also edited the Party's northern regional newspaper, *Workers' Weekly*, specified the basic distinctions between proletarian unionisation and 'yellow' or fake company unions for grassroots labour, against the backdrop of 'red unions' being sabotaged by foreign capital and reactionary strike-breakers.[21] Deng Zhongxia, who led the secretariat's northern China division before taking its general leadership, argued for conjoined economic and political struggles, and the importance of both strategies and tactics. To 'eventually achieve the complete emancipation of labour' while facing powerful enemies, he argued, it was necessary that workers seek allies as widely as possible and embrace both reformist demands and 'the fiercest forms of class struggle'.[22] Against localist cleavages, Wang Jinmei advocated for democratically structured institutionalisation by trade across regions. He made the Shanhaiguan Workers' Club into a model of direct elections to layered steering committees backed by standing workers' pickets, of which the Communist core had to be underground. In May 1922, as workers' demands became increasingly political, the CCP held its first National Labour Convention, in Guangzhou, with more than 100 unions in attendance. It was followed in the summer by a high-profile campaign for labour legislation based on the Communist proposal sketched in 'An Outline of the Labour Law' (劳动法大纲).[23] The Second Party Congress's 'Resolution on the Union Movement and the CCP' reaffirmed 'the final goal of the labour movement' as 'completely overthrowing the capitalist system of wage slaves and transforming society by Communist principles'.[24]

In parallel, the CCP focused on mass education and labour training. In the autumn of 1920, Li Qihan and Liu Shaoqi began a part-time workers' school in west Shanghai that offered literature and maths classes as well as political discussions and sports. On New Year's Day in 1921, the Beijing Communists opened the 'Labour School for Continuing Education' (劳动补习学校), soon followed by a workers' club and Party cell, in Changxindian—an important node on the railway that connected Beijing to Hankou. In the summer of 1921, Mao Zedong and He Shuheng started the Hunan Self-Study University for workers in Changsha. Encouraged by Li Dazhao, an evening workers' school also operated in Tianjin. Similar schools and training facilities appeared widely, often using books and pamphlets published by the central Trade Union Secretariat and local labour journals as textbooks. Typically, the Anyuan workers' evening school, set up by Li Lisan in January 1922, played a big part in preparation for the great strike that took place in September that year (see Perry's essay in the present volume). Moreover, the Party also pioneered a Women's School (平民女校) in Shanghai to train its female cadres. Not only did these schools enrich workers and foster their collective identity, they also became vehicles of class consciousness and sources of disciplined Party recruitment.

A Century Later

The sailors of the Communist revolution in China embarked young—the average age of the thirteen representatives at the 1921 congress was twenty-eight. Most of the millions who sacrificed their lives for the cause also died young, including the first generation of Communist labour leaders: Gu Zhenghong, Xiao Chunü, Xia Minghan, Peng Pai, Yun Daiying, and Ruan Xiaoxian, to name only a few who have not been mentioned earlier in this short account.

This revolution was extraordinarily idealistic, daring, and costly. Time and again, the Party narrowly escaped extinction and did not shun difficulty and danger. The tiny groupings represented on that small boat a century ago have firmly coalesced and developed into one of the largest and most consequential political parties in history. 'Party-building' (党的建设) is paramount among Mao's 'three magic weapons' (三大法宝) of the Chinese Communist revolution, along with armed struggle and the United Front after 1927. China's vulnerabilities and challenges today can be understood and traced in the same vein of the Party line and its class foundation. The ultimate question is whether the CCP can recover its founding commitment to labour, or whether the break from its 'original heart' (初心) is beyond repair.

1922

Nowhere were Communist efforts at labour organising as successful as in Anyuan, Jiangxi Province, a coal-mining centre and railway terminus that in the 1910s employed more than 10,000 miners and 1,000 railway workers. In the autumn of 1921, at a time when the mine was experiencing severe economic difficulties and battling warlords were forcibly conscripting miners, Mao Zedong—then in charge of labour organising in neighbouring Hunan Province—personally travelled to Anyuan to understand the situation of workers in the area. In December, he returned for a second, brief visit and, soon thereafter, sent fellow Hunanese Communist Li Lisan to set up a school for workers. Li was only twenty-two and had just returned from France. Taking advantage of his family networks and proving extraordinarily adept at dealing with the secret societies that dominated the area, he managed to obtain the support of the local authorities for the endeavour. With the permission of the local government, on 1 May 1922, the Communists publicly inaugurated the Anyuan Railway and Mining Workers' Club with a gala parade in which hundreds of workers carrying red flags marched, shouting revolutionary slogans—a display that Mao criticised with the conviction that mobilisation had to proceed gradually. In the following months, the club would establish a consumer cooperative that challenged the mining company's monopoly over workers' lives and organise its own militia. After Mao again visited Anyuan, in the summer of 1922, he decided that the time was ripe for a major strike and dispatched another up-and-coming Hunanese Communist, Liu Shaoqi, to assist in the negotiations. The strike began at 2am on 14 September 1922 and quickly spread to the whole workforce. Demands included payment of back wages, improvements in working conditions, reform of the labour contract system, and a guarantee of recognition and financial support for their newly established workers' club. It was a resounding success. Not only would Anyuan serve as the paramount centre of the Communist labour movement in China in the following years, but also the town would become a revolutionary mecca for decades to come.

The Anyuan Strike of 1922: Lessons in Leadership

Elizabeth J. PERRY

On 14 September 1922, the first major industrial strike mobilised and led by operatives of the newly founded Chinese Communist Party (CCP) erupted at the Anyuan (安源) coalmine in Jiangxi Province.[1] Launched in the name of the CCP-sponsored Anyuan Railway and Mining Workers' Club (安源路矿工人俱乐部), the dramatic five-day walkout by more than 13,000 miners and railroad workers succeeded in winning major concessions for the strikers: payment of back wages, improved working conditions, reform of the labour contract system, and a guarantee of recognition and financial support for their workers' club.[2]

The Anyuan 'great strike' of 1922 has attained iconic status in the history of the Chinese Communist revolution as an early expression of proletarian prowess. The Marxist intellectual and labour organiser Deng Zhongxia highlighted its signal importance in his canonical chronology of the labour movement: 'The strike demonstrated the great enthusiasm and courage of the masses … It was a complete victory.'[3] Even an anti-Communist historian acknowledged its significance, characterising Anyuan as 'the most notorious strike in the annals of the Chinese labour movement'.[4]

The impressive size and success of the strike, coming so soon after the establishment of the CCP and directly attributable to its organisational efforts, were certainly sufficient to justify a prominent place in the history books. But more important than the event itself were the lessons in mass mobilisation that Anyuan bequeathed to future Communist efforts. Here in embryonic form was a pattern—derivative of and yet distinctive from Russian precedents—that would inform the CCP labour movement for years to come.

The Role of Secret Societies

Labour unrest at Anyuan pre-dated the advent of the Communists. For decades before the 1922 strike, the coalmine had been the site of frequent protests. This is not surprising when one considers the industrial setting. The mining company at Anyuan also owned the adjoining railway that transported coal across provincial lines for use in enterprises throughout the Yangzi River Delta. Sociologists Clark Kerr and Abraham Siegel, in their influential cross-national study of labour strife, identify coal mining and railroads as the two most consistently strike-prone industrial sectors due to the concentrated and interconnected working conditions.[5] Anyuan was a combustible combination of the two.

Structural conditions alone do not automatically produce insurgency, however. To move beyond wildcat strikes requires premeditation and organisation. Social movement theorists point to the critical role of mobilising networks in marshalling popular protest.[6] In the case of Anyuan, a secret society known as the Red Gang (红帮) had performed this intermediary function since the opening of the mine in 1892. The Red Gang's chieftain, known as a 'dragon head' (龙头), not only controlled the local opium and gambling dens, pawnshops and brothels; his lieutenants also acted as labour contractors for the mining and railway company, introducing fellow villagers to jobs in return for a hefty share of their wages. Quasi-religious initiation rites, magical charms and amulets, martial arts routines, loyalty oaths, clandestine codes, and the like heightened members' deference to Red Gang patrons and strengthened fraternal bonds of association and mutual aid among the rank and file. The gangsters-cum-contractors, while closely connected to company management, nevertheless stood to gain financially from increases in workers' wages. For that reason, they were motivated to leverage the secret society's symbolic and coercive power over the workers to organise strikes for higher wages.

When Mao Zedong and his fellow CCP cadres in the Hunan Labour Secretariat targeted Anyuan as a promising site for the nascent Communist labour movement, they realised that the Red Gang's hold over the workers would pose the biggest challenge to their ambitions. Following Lenin's revolutionary playbook, which was standard operating procedure for the new CCP, they initiated night-time classes for workers in hopes of instilling a radical ideology to replace the 'feudal superstition' of the secret society. Important as this pedagogical effort was, it soon became clear that CCP activities at Anyuan were not carbon copies of Soviet practices. Rather, these efforts showed an ingenuity and originality that would come to distinguish Chinese communism from its Russian roots.

Enter CCP Organisers Li Lisan and Liu Shaoqi

Credit for the tactical innovations that allowed CCP operatives to supplant Red Gang chieftains as leaders of the Anyuan workers belongs above all to Li Lisan, a young activist from the neighbouring county in Hunan Province who had just returned from a work-study program in France. Introduced to Anyuan by fellow Hunanese Mao Zedong, Li leveraged both his insider knowledge of local customs and his cosmopolitan credentials to cultivate a charismatic persona that proved immensely appealing to the workers. His lively teaching style, eye-catching apparel, and reliance on familiar folkways—from lantern festivals and lion dances to religious processions—all contributed to Li's ability to recruit a large and loyal following among railroad workers and miners alike. Uninhibited in both personality and work style, Li Lisan's flamboyant manner was as alluring to ordinary workers as it was alarming to his Party superiors. Li sashayed ostentatiously around the grimy coal-mining town, dressed either in a long Mandarin gown or in a Western coat and tie, in a fashion designed to attract attention. When the shiny metal badge (acquired in France) that he sported on his chest generated rumours of his invulnerability to bullets, Li did nothing to dispel them. On the contrary, taking a cue from the Red Gang's 'dragon head', whose authority resided in his reputation for supernatural powers, Li actively encouraged the belief that he enjoyed the magical protection of foreign countries.

Li's personal magnetism and imaginative approach to labour organising enabled swift progress in moving from a workers' night school to a labour union (known euphemistically as a 'workers' club') to an all-employee walkout. On the eve of the planned work stoppage, Mao sent to Anyuan another young Hunanese labour organiser, Liu Shaoqi, to provide overall direction to the impending strike. Having just returned from training in the Soviet Union, Liu was known for his dour demeanour and a disciplined Leninist work style that Mao evidently believed would be useful in tempering the instincts of the exuberant and impetuous Li Lisan. Together, Li and Liu fashioned a winning formula that combined enthusiasm and energy with calculated restraint. The result was an ability to secure the support of secret-society notables and other key members of the local elite in addition to ordinary workers, garnering widespread public sympathy for the demands of the strikers. This was an approach that would serve the CCP well not only in the Anyuan strike of 1922, but again three years later in Shanghai's momentous May Thirtieth Movement.

Li Lisan came up with a stirring strike slogan: 'Once beasts of burden, now we will be men' (从前是牛马，现在要做人). Significantly, the plea was framed not in terms of class struggle, but as a cry for human dignity.

This *cri de coeur* was elaborated in a strike manifesto, also composed by Li Lisan, that emphasised the desperate and defensive motivation behind the work stoppage:

> Our work is so hard and our pay is so low. We are often beaten and cursed, robbing us of our humanity ... We want to live! We want to eat! We are hungry! ... Forced to the breaking point, we have no choice but to go on strike as a last resort ... We are willing to give our lives to reach our goal. Everyone, strictly maintain order![7]

As the manifesto implied, and as Liu Shaoqi insisted, public support would hinge on the ability of the strikers to prevent disorder. With thousands of unemployed workers milling about the town of Anyuan at the time, the possibility of violent conflict between strikers and strike-breakers was of particular concern. Aware that the key to keeping order was the cooperation of the Red Gang, Liu Shaoqi instructed Li Lisan to pay a visit to the 'dragon head' to seek his assistance. Bearing a bottle of liquor and a rooster—the elements of a Triad sworn-brotherhood ritual—Li and several members of the workers' club who were also Red Gang members proceeded together to the secret society lodge. Li strode into the main hall, placed his gifts on the altar, and, using Red Gang codewords that his followers had taught him, indicated his desire to be inducted as a member of the secret society. Seeing that the dragon head was pleased to welcome him into the fraternity, Li shared news of the impending strike and requested that the secret society shutter its opium and gambling dens and suspend all looting operations for the duration of the walkout. When the Red Gang leader pounded on his chest to indicate assent, the strike was called.

The strike began at 2am in the railway yard. Within two hours it had spread, by careful prearrangement, to the entire workforce. At each of the more than forty work stations, yellow flags bearing the characters for 'strike' (罢工) were unfurled and patrols were stationed to ensure that no-one entered the premises. Workers were instructed to return to their homes or dormitories to reduce the likelihood of violence. The impressive public order that prevailed during the strike reassured local officials and the business elite, who played an important part in negotiating a generous settlement. After five days off the job, with no injuries or major property damage, the strikers won agreement to their demands, resulting in a substantial wage increase along with the company's pledge of recognition and financial support for the CCP-sponsored workers' club.

From Anyuan to Shanghai

Historians and activists alike have attributed the stunning strike victory at Anyuan to the power of a unified, militant workforce, but leadership was also decisive. Li Lisan's unbridled ebullience and Liu Shaoqi's steely discipline made for a powerful combination that was at once appealing and effective. While studies of contentious politics have paid considerable attention to the importance of structural conditions and network mobilisation in generating and sustaining popular protest, they have had far less to say about the catalytic contributions of protest leaders.[8] Yet an examination of the history of the Chinese labour movement makes clear that skilful leadership was a key factor in distinguishing CCP-sponsored actions from wildcat strikes or strikes sparked by secret societies.

From its inception, the CCP was attentive to the importance of leadership. Systematic instruction in leadership techniques figured prominently in the training of cadres, beginning with the Peasant Movement Training Institute (农民讲习所) established in Guangzhou in 1923—and continuing with the nearly 3,000 Party schools (党校) that operate across China today.[9] The earliest teachings were based on Soviet methods of agitprop, but over time the revolutionary experiences of the CCP itself provided rich material for emulation. The Anyuan 'great strike' is among these paradigmatic exemplars.

That the CCP regarded the Anyuan strike of 1922 as a model of labour movement leadership was already clear three years later, when the Party tasked Li Lisan and Liu Shaoqi with joint responsibility for directing another critical labour protest.[10] In the spring of 1925, a strike wave broke out in Japanese-owned cotton mills in Shanghai. On 15 May, a Japanese foreman killed a cotton worker active in the strike during a factory confrontation. CCP propagandists took the initiative in publicising the worker's death, generating widespread sympathy for the mobilisation. On 30 May, throngs of supporters—mostly workers and university students—marched through the streets of Shanghai's International Settlement to express solidarity with the strikers. When British police unexpectedly fired on the demonstrators, leaving ten dead and another fifty seriously wounded, the historic May Thirtieth Movement (五卅运动) was born.[11]

The tragedy of May Thirtieth presented the Chinese Communists with an extraordinary political opening, which they were quick to seize. The very next day, the CCP-sponsored Shanghai General Labour Union (总工会) (GLU) was inaugurated under the chairmanship of Li Lisan and general management of Liu Shaoqi. As had been the situation at Anyuan, domination of the labour force by secret societies—in the case of Shanghai, the infamous Green Gang (青帮)[12]—posed a major obstacle to Communist inroads. As had also been the pattern at Anyuan, Liu laboured quietly behind the scenes to curb the threat of violence and cultivate support among the local business elite while Li cut a more flamboyant figure. At the invitation of a Green Gang bathhouse proprietor, and with Party approval, Li was duly initiated into the secret society. As a British police report observed with alarm at the time, 'Red and Green Gangs have joined forces with labour agitators ... and given allegiance to Li Lisan'.[13] In part because of these gangster connections, the GLU was able to turn the May Thirtieth Movement into a strike wave of unprecedented scale. In Shanghai alone, more than 200 enterprises with more than 200,000 workers participated. Factory foremen and labour contractors, many of whom had gang connections, were crucial in sustaining the walkout. They assisted the GLU in distributing strike pay to the idled workers from a fund donated by the city's Chinese Chamber of Commerce.

Maintaining order in the industrial metropolis of Shanghai proved a good deal more complicated than had been the case in the company town of Anyuan, however. Rival labour unions controlled by competing gangster networks presented an ongoing challenge to the GLU. So, too, did unruly workers who insisted on grabbing more than their fair share of strike pay. The resulting disruption of public order generated concern among the business elite, who—three months into the strike—were growing tired of the GLU's incessant demands for strike fund contributions. By late August, the GLU felt compelled to declare an end to the work stoppage. Although the negotiated settlement offered only modest gains for the strikers, it served the important political purpose of establishing the GLU as the recognised representative of organised labour in the city. For the next year and a half, until Chiang Kai-shek turned on the Communists in the bloody massacre of 12 April 1927 (see S. A. Smith's essay in the present volume), the CCP wielded considerable influence as the voice of labour in China's industrial capital.

Mandarins and Rebels

The Anyuan strike of 1922 and the Shanghai May Thirtieth Movement of 1925 marked milestones in the early development of the CCP labour movement. In both cases, many of the workers who participated in the events were seasoned veterans of labour protests that pre-dated the founding of the CCP. But the appearance of Communist cadres introduced a newfound dynamism and discipline to these ongoing struggles. Although CCP organisers followed a Soviet script that called for establishing night schools and trade unions as a prelude to strike actions, they also improvised to adapt to local conditions. In Republican China, where workers laboured under the thumb of gangster-contractors, access to the working class by would-be revolutionaries required first infiltrating and then inhibiting secret-society activities. Success in conducting this dangerous mission demanded not only deep familiarity with native conventions, but also daring, bravado, and steely discipline. Individual cadres evidenced such traits in unequal measure, however, and leadership training, useful as it was, could not always override innate temperament. A noteworthy feature of CCP operations—first adopted at Anyuan and later elaborated in Shanghai—was a judicious and self-conscious balancing of mobilisation styles that checked charisma with caution by deploying leaders known for contrary yet complementary personalities and proclivities.

Political scientist Lucian Pye pointed to a dichotomy in Chinese political culture between 'mandarins' who enforced centralised control and orthodox thought, and 'rebels' who embraced a free-wheeling relaxation of central controls and freedom from orthodoxy.[14] According to Pye, this dualism runs through the history of both Confucian and Communist China, helping to account for radical policy swings when one type of leader is replaced with its opposite. But contrasting leadership styles may appear concurrently as well as consecutively, with the two types acting in concert to fulfil a common objective. The history of the Chinese labour movement illustrates the powerful role that such complementarity can play in facilitating strikes. It thus supports an argument that has been put forward with respect to social movements more generally: 'When leaders with opposing styles are able to work out an effective modus vivendi that affords due play to their competing approaches, the likelihood of success is greatly enhanced.'[15]

1923

Although 1922 was a high-water mark for the Chinese labour movement, most strikes advanced simple economic demands. Concerned by the lack of political motivation among the workers, the Communist leadership focused its efforts on shifting the terrain of labour struggle to more political grounds, mobilising workers against imperialism and warlordism, while calling for freedom of association. The most high-profile attempt at politically organising workers occurred on the Beijing–Hankou Railway, where the influence of the Chinese Communist Party (CCP) was particularly strong. In addition to the workers' club at Changxindian, by the end of 1922, sixteen similar groups had been set up at other stations along the line. After a series of preliminary meetings, in January 1923, a preparatory committee comprising representatives from most of these clubs announced its decision to formally inaugurate the Beijing–Hankou Railway Federation of Trade Unions in Zhengzhou on 1 February. Even in the face of the manifest displeasure of the warlords who then dominated northern China—first and foremost, Wu Peifu and Cao Kun—the meeting went ahead as scheduled but, as the representatives began to disperse, several delegates were arrested. In response, some 30,000 workers went on strike on 4 February—a mobilisation that was eventually drowned in blood. According to Tony Saich, it was the 7 February massacre that caused the CCP leadership to realise that the Party could not rely on the strength of the workers alone in its struggle against foreign imperialists and domestic warlords.[1] The following account, written just weeks after the strike by Luo Zhanglong, a Communist labour organiser who played an important role in those events, offers a detailed description of the strike and the ensuing slaughter.

The 7 February Massacre
LUO Zhanglong
(Translated by Tony SAICH)[2]

In line with the decision to call a general strike, on the morning of 4 February, each branch put up leaflets informing passengers of the justness for workers to organise trade unions to improve their living standards and to fight against oppression. The railway authorities and warlords should not interfere so harshly and unreasonably as to prohibit the development of trade unions. The trade union is the workers' second life and therefore cannot, under any circumstances, be allowed to suffer harm. It must be supported even to the extent of sacrifice. We warmly hope that you will forgive us for our attempt to attain freedom.

They took an official letter to the factory director and handed over their work tools, left the factory in an orderly fashion and in a quiet manner declared the start of the Zhengzhou strike. At Changxindian, within a few hours of nine o'clock, all workers had stopped. By twelve o'clock, all passenger, freight, and military trains had stopped running. All workers acted in accordance with the Federation of Trade Union's orders that did not allow individual negotiations, compromise, or mediation. During the period of the strike, no worker was permitted to act alone. If something important arose, and it was necessary to leave, the worker had to request a permit from the trade union. With this, the pickets could let the worker pass; without it, the worker would be detained. In addition to the picket groups, investigation teams were organised. The picket groups were responsible for maintaining public order during the strike, while the investigation teams were in charge of secret inquiries and sometimes carried out sentry duties or night patrols. Each ten trade union members formed one group, electing one as the group head, who would be responsible for them. Thus, it only took a few minutes to convene a meeting of several thousand.

Deployment was decided upon and the confrontation with the railway authorities lasted three days. Before the 7 February massacre broke out, order was extremely strict. For the sake of convenience, let me note below the events at Changxindian, Zhengzhou, Jiang'an, and the other large stations.

Changxindian

After the delegates to Zhengzhou returned, they convened a committee meeting to report on the crushing of the federation and its decision. They began to prepare strike procedures. The day after next [4 February], at Niangnianggong, they convened a general meeting of all trade union members. Three thousand workers attended. After the committee delivered a report on the situation, the masses were incensed and their shouts shook heaven and earth. All were willing to fight for freedom ...

At noon on the day of the strike, a train arrived from Baoding. As soon as it arrived at Changxindian, the trade union ordered it to stop. In the night, a train travelling northwards from Hankou was also ordered to stop. The workers treated the passengers quite politely: they hired horse-drawn carriages for the male passengers and invited female passengers to stay in the workers' houses, sending them on to Beijing the next day. As a result, the ordinary people formed a good impression of the workers.

On the morning of 5 February, the railway authorities received a secret order from Wu [Peifu] and Cao [Kun] calling on them to treat the strike severely. At the same time, waiters at the railway's Beijing General Bureau held a sympathy strike, causing it to become extremely quiet. On the same day, [Director of the Beijing–Hankou Railway Bureau] Zhao Jixian issued a bulletin full of threatening words and ordering workers to return to work. Seeing that the workers paid no attention to it, he sent three propagandists to lure the trade union to negotiate. His general idea was that first they should return to work and that then conditions could be discussed. The workers refused. They left without any result. At that moment, Wu Peifu sent a telegram saying that he had 500 engineers who could shoulder the task of restoring communications and giving Zhao a free hand. From one o'clock onwards that afternoon, several batches of fully armed troops brought by railway officials had reached Changxindian. They were: the battalion of patrol commanded by Zhang Guoqing, the second battalion of the brigade commanded by Shi Quansheng, and the sixth company of Liulihe. On arrival, they were stationed at strategic points. The workers went to them to demonstrate and distributed leaflets to them. This moved the soldiers very much ...

Six battalions of troops encircled Changxindian. They prohibited workers from walking up and down, talking, and holding meetings, and they set up a sentry post every ten paces. They also sent many secret agents to the trade union to find out the addresses of the union's leading personnel. However, crafty Zhao Jixian moderated his attitude and sent emissaries to make contact with the trade union delegates. It was clear that he was investigating the circumstances of the trade union leaders to arrange his vicious intrigue.

On the morning of 6 February, a trade union investigation team reported that army actions were uncertain and it was said that a large number of troops would arrive from Zhuzhou. For a short while, the atmosphere in the city became more tense. The workers could see that the serious situation in Changxindian would lead to tragedy, but they would not regret dying for freedom and thus did not change their attitude. To put an end to the rumours, the trade union issued its second manifesto on 6 February …

On the same day, Zhao Jixian issued an order to arrest about fifty trade union committee and other staff members. At 12.50pm, 120 new workers were brought here from the Tanggu shipyard. They were sent to Changxindian, Baoding, Zhengzhou, and other stations under the protection of troops commanded by Han Zhengqing, an adjutant of the fourteenth brigade, and Meng Bingxiang, a representative of the Beijing–Hankou Railway Bureau and director of a printing house. Scabs, who had been expelled from the trade union, were chosen as foremen and 500 soldiers were sent to train with them. It was declared that if the striking workers did not return to work quickly, they would be dismissed and sent home by force. In addition, wages already paid would be recovered and their families would also be arrested. The workers paid no heed to these threatening words. Later, Mr Tang, a representative of the Beijing Mayor and concurrently magistrate of Wanping County, and others arrived at the trade union. They claimed to be willing to act as mediators, but their words were full of threat and deceit. The workers said that conditions had to be decided on by the federation and that the branch had no right to negotiate. Negotiations should be conducted between the railway authorities and the federation. If the federation issues an order to return to work, naturally our branch will obey the order. Having failed in his objective, Tang went away. Indeed, Tang came with other intentions: to spy on the true circumstances of the trade union so as to catch the whole lot in a trap.

In the afternoon, two battalions of troops that had arrived from Zhuzhou and the heads of small stations took over as engine drivers and workers. Shi Quansheng's troops arrived at Changxindian in full battle array and stood in combat readiness. At 11pm that night, troops were ordered to arrest trade union leaders. The trade union staff and leaders were living in the workers' homes. Thus, when the troops reached the trade union, they arrested no-one but robbed the trade union of money and furniture and intended to set the house on fire. Luckily, this was avoided through the persuasion of a certain man. Later, they searched the workers' families one by one and arrested, among others, Shi Wenbin, Chen Limao, Wu Ba, Hong Yinfu, and Wu Ruming, a teacher at the trade union school—eleven people in all. It was late on a severe winter night. While carrying out the search, the soldiers engaged in looting and beating. This disturbance caused great misery throughout the city. The workers' wives and children cried out loudly. The eleven arrested were stripped of their clothes and sent naked to the brigade headquarters. The brigade commander shouted out an order for them to be savagely beaten, not allowing them to speak. They were manacled and left on the ground until daybreak when they were to be sent to Baoding for a reward to be claimed. This angered the workers, and their pitiful cries filled the air.

At daybreak, 3,000 or 4,000 people gathered in front of the brigade headquarters. They carried a big banner with the words 'Release the arrested workers' and several small flags. Together, they shouted, 'Send back our fellow workers!' and 'Return our freedom!' Finding that the masses possessed great strength and were highly motivated, the brigade commander ordered his troops to charge. A large body of fully armed soldiers dashed out from inside and fiercely attacked the workers. For a short while, bullets fell like rain, knives and swords flew through the air. This was followed by a cavalry charge. Sadly, those among the many thousands hit by the bullets fell to the ground. In the end, four were killed, over thirty were seriously wounded (some died the next day), over thirty were arrested, and countless numbers were slightly wounded or were forced to flee. Soldiers seized the opportunity to loot and kill people wantonly. Inhabitants closed their doors and order in the city disintegrated. The Changxindian Trade Union was compelled to move elsewhere. The eleven arrested were sent under guard to Baoding …

Seeing the dead and wounded workers, Zhao thought he had succeeded with his scheme. On the one hand, he urged Baoding to kill the eleven staff members and, on the other hand, he fabricated a telegram saying the workers had died because they had fought the soldiers with pistols. His trick was the same as those of Xiao Yaonan and Feng Yun. At that time, Changxindian workers were forcibly dragged into the factory to work.

If they refused, they were shot on the spot. Countless numbers died in this way. Zhao did not even allow the wounded workers to go out or go to a doctor, with the result that the majority of them also died.

After the workers had been compelled to go to the factory, they were not allowed to talk to each other or ask for leave. This would risk severe punishment. In addition, he [Zhao] took the opportunity to put his trusted followers in key positions and to expel all the workers who had ever worked for the trade union and to compel their families to return wages that had already been paid. The crowd was extremely harassed. They organised a group of guards, each carrying a pistol, to look for enemies and daily they took their revenge. By this time, the warlords had forcibly occupied the railway as if it was their private property and Zhao claimed himself their domestic servant and running dog. Yet his various methods could not subdue the minds of the workers. Over several days, the workers fled. He could not restore communications. Order in the factory was extremely chaotic. It was the inhabitants of Changxindian who suffered from the daily encirclement. Troops and horses walked back and forth and the people suffered unbearable disturbances such as arrest.

Zhengzhou

At twelve o'clock in the morning of 4 February, Zhengzhou began a general strike in accordance with the orders of the federation. It issued a manifesto to explain it clearly to the outside world. At the same time, every worker carried a leaflet saying: 'Fellow workers! Because we suffer from numerous oppressions, we are obliged to call a general strike on the whole railway. It is distressing for us to do so. With heart and mind, we must carry it through to the end. We must adhere strictly to orders and await the federation's settlement.'

This leaflet tells us that the strike is being held in a consistent spirit of unity. That afternoon [4 February], Jin Yun'e, division commander of the fourteenth division, called in Gao Bin, Jiang Haishi, and Liu Wensong, presidents of the Zhengzhou Trade Union, to the division's headquarters. As soon as he saw them, he began to use foul, abusive language. Gao, paying no attention to this abuse, handed him the Strike Bulletin issued by the federation. After seeing it, he said, 'You obey the orders of the federation. You have no powers so there is no need to talk with you.' They went out.

On 5 February, all was peaceful. That night, a police officer went to Gao Bin's and Jiang Haishi's homes saying that the division commander had invited them to the fourteenth division's club for a talk. When Gao and Jiang arrived, Huang Diancheng was also there. Huang ordered their arrest and had them manacled like robbers. Liu Wensong thought that three were responsible for the trade union. Hearing the news that two of them had been put in prison, he felt that he should not escape and try to live ignobly. Immediately, he rushed to the club and asked to be treated the same as the other two. On hearing this, the people were indignant at the abuse of power by the troops and the police and they were moved by Liu's spirit. This intensified even more their hatred of the warlords.

On the morning of 6 February, another two people were arrested: Wang Zongpei and Qian Nenggui. Wang was arrested by plainclothes police while cleaning up at home. His comings and goings made it appear that he was not a good man. Qian had a problem with the police because of his son and the police, harbouring a hatred for him, used this chance to take revenge. They were also manacled. Qian's hands were bound so tightly that his wrists became swollen.

The same morning, the five were driven to the station where they were to be put on public show to intimidate the workers. But the workers were not afraid; on the contrary, they were aroused and indignant. In the afternoon, the police hired men to beat gongs, calling on the workers to return to work. However, the workers paid no attention to them. On 7 February, Jiang and Wang were released. Jiang was forced to go from door to door with a white flag to persuade the workers to return to work. The workers paid no attention to him. Later, Wang was sent under escort to the northern section to try the same form of persuasion. It was said later that Wang fled from Shundai Station to go to Beijing to present a petition to the assembly.

The same morning, Gao, Liu, and Qian were sent under escort to the trade union. The fourteenth division spent twenty-five yuan on light refreshments for their consumption. In addition, they ordered the adjutant Lin Baobi (once a worker, his father and son were workers, a fact that enabled him to come into contact with the workers) to persuade the three to issue an order to return to work. They were unmoved.

On 8 February, Huang Dianchen coerced the president of the county chamber of commerce to collect together thirty or forty rascals to hold a People's Assembly at the Puluo Theatre. A large number of troops were stationed inside and outside of the meeting place. Huang was in sole charge of the whole show. He printed 1,000 leaflets and made 400 flags. After the meeting, he hired a bunch of rural beggars to parade waving the flags and to distribute leaflets. The main points of the leaflets are as follows:

First the strike on the Beijing–Hankou Railway is knowingly intended to stir up trouble. Second, the workers should consider six factors:

(1) Within twelve hours, the workers should be compelled to return to work. If not, all supplies will be cut off. If anyone dares to supply workers and their families, he or she will be treated as a disruptive partisan.

(2) If a worker does not go to work, the landlord will cancel their lease. If anyone secretly puts up workers and their families, the house will be confiscated.

(3) All workers willing to return to work may go to the station to collect a pass.

(4) Troops and police will help drive the undesired workers out of the district.

(5) If workers are robbed by bandits, troops and police should not protect them.

(6) Since the workers on the Long–Hai Railway have not taken part in the strike, troops and police should give them special protection.

The twelve-hour limit passed but neither did the merchants cut off supplies to the workers nor did the landlords cancel the workers' lease. Thus, was the farce of the fake People's Assembly exposed. The workers laughed at it. On 9 February, Tang Tingxi made use of his connections to get his job back. He was an engine driver who had been brought in to organise a training class to destroy the trade union. Because of this, he came under attack and the trade union demoted him. When he regained his position, his son was promoted from fireman to engine driver. He collected together his followers to surrender to the warlords in order to destroy the strike. Through threats and tricks, he got together a bunch of ignorant workers. Thus, about 100 workers got passes for work. The other workers, on hearing of the 7 February Hankou massacre and seeing that the fight was as good as lost, swallowed the insults and were obliged to return to work on the condition that Gao, Liu, and Qian be set free.

That day, two incidents worthy of note occurred: 1) Vice director Wan Yulin, on seeing the workers return to work, asked, 'Did you not say that you should go to work according to federation orders? Why are you going to work now?' Those in the training class on hearing of this reported it to the fourteenth division. Wan was arrested at once. 2) Engine driver Peng Zhanyuan, unwilling to return, asked for leave but was caught and beaten 200 times by the military batons of the fourteenth division. Craftsman Ma Dingqing, unwilling to return to work, on asking for leave, was slapped in the face by the Director of the Beijing–Hankou Police, Hu Bo. After he had been beaten black and blue, he was arrested. Fortunately, later on, Gao, Liu, and Qian were released. However, to date, we do not know how Wan, Peng, and Ma have been dealt with.

During the strike at Zhengzhou, no worker died but about 300 workers lost their jobs. The warlord has sent more and more soldiers to work, to date some 800. None of the trade union staff could remain in Zhengzhou. Most fled to various places and tried to find work there.

Jiang'an

The second day of the general strike (5 February), Xiao Yaonan sent his chief-of-staff, Zhang Housheng, to Jiang'an. First, Zhang ordered a local police officer to threaten the trade union and to hand over Yang Defu, Zhu Lantian, Zhang Lianguang, Luo Haichen, and Lin Xiangqian. The trade union replied, 'If Cao, Wu, and the Ministry of Communications send a responsible delegate here, the federation will, of course, send a plenipotentiary to establish contacts. If not, we regret that we cannot receive you.'

By noon, it was reported that the factory had been occupied by a large number of troops and that the Dazhimen Station had begun to sell tickets. Zhang Housheng had found two engine drivers and, under threat from the troops and police, had ordered them to drive at once. On hearing of this, the branch committee sent pickets to make inquiries. Within a moment, about 2,000 workers met in front of the factory gate and they tried to break through the defence line of the troops and police to rescue their two fellow workers. The trade union sent four special delegates—Zhang Lianguang, Xiang Feilong, Luo Haichen, etc.—to ask the troops and police to free the three workers who had been arrested without any reason. Despite the many threats of the troops and police, even threats to kill, the delegates stood firm. When the troops and police had run out of ideas, they decided to set the three workers free. The failure of the enemy's threat was followed by defeat.

After Wuhan Trade Union delegates returned from Zhengzhou, they told the public of the oppression and repression of freedoms they had encountered. Some wept bitterly, others burned with anger. Their rousing attitude and militancy moved heaven and earth and made the ghosts and gods weep. As a result, despite all the sacrifices, the trade union delegates decided to show solidarity with the other workers on the Beijing–Hankou Railway.

On the third day of the strike, the trade unions sent over 100 flag-waving delegates to Jiang'an to bring greetings. A meeting was held in Jiang'an to express sympathy and about 10,000 participated. First, comrade Yang Defu, the President of the Executive Committee of the Beijing–Hankou Federation of Trade Unions, reported on the significance of receiving and greeting the delegates and stated the importance of and prospect for the general strike. Following Yang's speech, dozens of trade union delegates and *Zhenbao* journalists spoke passionately. Finally, comrade Li Zhenying, General Secretary of the Federation, delivered a speech for the federation, saying: 'This general strike of ours is the key to the fate of the working class in our country. Our aim is not for wage increases and a decrease in working hours but to fight for freedom and human rights. We are the defenders of freedom and of the interests of the Chinese people. Fellow workers! We must understand what a great responsibility we the Beijing–Hankou Railway workers are shouldering. The apathetic society needs to be immersed in our blood. Fellow workers! We should be the vanguard in the overthrow of the warlords. Only advance! Don't retreat!'

All at once someone in the crowd shouted again and again: 'Long live the Federation of the Beijing–Hankou Railway!'; 'Long live the Federation of the Hubei Trade Unions!'; 'Proletarians of the world unite!' The masses joined in, shouting thunderously. The masses, full of indignation, held a large-scale demonstration. It lasted for two hours, starting from Jiang'an and passing through the foreign concessions. Some 3,000 people joined in along the way. Many merchants on the route shouted, 'Welcome!' The police on point duty did not dare intervene.

This is a situation that is rarely seen. Who could have known that the delegates of the Military Governor, Xiao Yaonan, and the foreign capitalists were holding a meeting in the concession to prepare a slaughter?

On 7 February, four days and nights had passed since the beginning of the strike. Several times, Xiao Yaonan sent his chief-of-staff, Zhang Housheng, to entice the support of key people. These visits were rejected by the trade union. The trade union raised eleven preconditions for mediation and negotiation. The meeting between the two sides was to be conducted on the basis of equal responsibility. At the same time, it was said that Feng Yun had crossed the river to entreat Xiao to suppress the strike by military force. Each day, Xiao and Wu exchanged several telegrams. At two o'clock on the afternoon of 7 February, a police officer came and said: 'On Military Governor Xiao's order, I have come to ask the federation to send plenipotentiaries for negotiations. If you agree, chief-of-staff Zhang will come immediately to meet and talk. To show his sincerity, he will put on civilian clothes. The six conditions you raised can be recognised. First, please send the list of your plenipotentiaries.' Then the federation's plenipotentiaries, Li Zhenying and Zhang Lianguang, received him and the police officer's politeness amid the troop and police encirclement aroused suspicions of insincerity. As a result, they did not use their real names during the talk.

Later, the opposition changed its tricks and invited the federation's plenipotentiaries to meet at 5.20pm at the trade union, saying that the chief-of-staff would come himself. After delivering the message, the police officer hurried away. At 5.20pm as the delegates were on their way to the meeting, they suddenly heard many shots. Thus, the bloody tragedy began. Having lured all the leaders of the trade union to meet together, they felt that their chance had come. The chief-of-staff sped at the head of two battalions of fully armed troops to encircle the trade union and they fired over five volleys. Several hundred workers were waiting for news in front of the gates at the time. They had no time to escape. Barehanded, they had no means of resistance. Zeng Yuliang and thirty-two other workers were killed in the confused gunfire and the rattle of sabres. Over 200 workers were wounded. After this massacre in front of the trade union, the soldiers began to hunt people down and carried out various robberies. The younger brother of the branch president was murdered and the nephew of the federation's president had his legs chopped from under him. They killed at will and looted without restraint. According to statistics, there were three successive robberies a night on Fujian Street.

They even made a clean sweep of the smallest belongings of the workers' families. The situation was unbearable, so much so that the tears shed would empty the Yangzi and Han rivers.

During the robbery at the Jiang'an Branch, about sixty workers were arrested including Lin Xiangqian, president of the Jiang'an Branch Committee. Lin was bound to the station pole and forced to give an order to return to work. Comrade Lin resolutely refused, saying: 'The strike is a matter of life and death for 30,000 workers on the whole railway. Our branch will not return to work without the federation's order. You may cut off my head, but I won't give an order to return to work.' The same question and reply were repeated three times. Zhang Housheng shouted an order to 'cut off his head and hang it up as a warning to all'. His head was indeed hung up in the station. Observing strict discipline, he did not give in before his death. How could a man do otherwise if he was fighting for the benefit of the working class? Xiao Yaonan issued an open telegram saying that Lin Xiangqian had been killed in a fight with a pistol. This was a rumour fabricated entirely by the warlords to cheat the people. If the workers had had weapons how could such a massacre have occurred? Why had none of the soldiers been killed or wounded? Anyone with common sense could understand the reality of the situation ...

After the Jiang'an massacre happened, all the Wuhan working people were filled with righteous indignation. To support the Beijing–Hankou workers, they called a general strike in the name of the Hubei Federation of Trade Unions ...

At this time, Xiao Yaonan was alarmed, unable to sit down or sleep easily. A terrible atmosphere reigned in Wuhan. Xiao convened a special meeting to proclaim martial law ...

After the orders were issued, the Wuhan market was desolated and the situation became increasingly serious. Each concession recruited a team of volunteers to protect itself. For a time, a state of anxiety existed as if a great disaster would come. But it was only a trick. Xiao Yaonan's intention was to use this special martial law to murder those whom he perceived to be enemies. Later, he ordered the arrest of seventeen trade union leaders and related personnel such as Yang Defu and Chen Tian.

Xiao Yaonan bitterly hated the lawyer Shi Yang because he had become the legal adviser to the federation. Thus, he had him arrested on 7 February and sent under escort to the Military Governor's office. Being a leader of the Wuhan working class, Shi Yang devoted himself to the labour movement. He did not regret that this destroyed his family nor that it created extra work. On 15 February, Xiao had him shot in Wuchang on the charge of inciting the strike. After he killed Shi, he drove his wife and younger son out of Hubei. Being so cruel and unreasonable, he was inferior to the wild beasts.

Other Stations

Needless to say, since Changxindian and Jiang'an had suffered the same disaster, every other branch on the small stations was also trampled on. He Liquan and Bai Yueyao, the presidents of the Baoding Branch Committee were arrested by Cao Kun and killed and 500 trade union members were either killed or fled. Trade union property was confiscated. Two staff members of the Gaobeidian Trade Union and Comrade Kang Jing, the President of the Zhending Branch, were arrested and were almost shot. Now, they are imprisoned by the Baoding army section for law enforcement. Staff members of the Zhangde trade union were put in prison while others fled, unable to go home. Hu Chuandao, an executive member of the Xinyang Branch, was forced to drive the engine but, because he refused, one of his arms was chopped off. He still did not give in. We do not know yet whether he died. In addition, Zhao Mi, a telegram student in Xinxiang, was arrested together with five Zhengzhou workers and sent to Baoding to be tortured cruelly. The stations to the south and north of Yancheng suffered the same disasters. It is a pity that there has been no detailed investigation and thus we are unable to provide a complete picture.

1925

After the 7 February Massacre of 1923, the Chinese Communist Party (CCP) had to reevaluate its strategy of relying on the strength of the working class alone to gain power. In light of their defeat, the Communist leadership not only began considering a broader alliance to wage the struggle, but also, prompted by their Soviet advisors, started taking Sun Yat-sen's Nationalist Party (Guomindang, or GMD) more seriously as a possible partner during the stage of national revolution. In January 1924, this rapprochement resulted in the First United Front between the two parties, which allowed leading members of the CCP to take up important positions in the ranks of the GMD as individuals, while retaining their separate CCP membership. As a result, Communists were able to recover from previous setbacks and build their strength not only among workers but also among peasants. The alliance was always uneasy and largely held together by the personal prestige of Sun Yat-sen and the pressure of the Soviet Union, which saw the GMD as the local actor most likely to succeed in launching a national revolution in China. However, the First United Front also took important steps forward for the Chinese labour movement under the aegis of the struggle against imperialism—the first and foremost example being the general strike that took place in Guangzhou and Hong Kong in 1925, which is the focus of this essay.

From the May Thirtieth Movement to the Canton–Hong Kong Strike
Apo LEONG

> These strikes, at first skirmishes, sometimes result in weighty struggles; they decide nothing, it is true, but they are the strongest proof that the decisive battle between bourgeoisie and proletariat is approaching. They are the military school of the working men in which they prepare themselves for the great struggle which cannot be avoided.
>
> — Friedrich Engels, *The Conditions of the Working Class in England* (1845)[1]

> We are resolved to lay down our lives in the struggle against imperialists and capitalists: never will the workers of Hong Kong allow the imperialists within our territory freely to crush us.
>
> — Canton–Hong Kong Strike Committee (1925)[2]

For the past century, the May Thirtieth Movement in China and the subsequent Canton–Hong Kong Strike (省港大罷工) of 1925-26 have been glorified in both the pro–Chinese Communist Party (CCP) and the pro–Nationalist Party (Guomindang, or GMD) history books.[3] The strike, in particular, was a turning point in contemporary Chinese history as union power swelled in Guangzhou at a time when the city was administered by the joint partnership between Nationalists and Communists commonly known as the 'United Front'.[4] Unfortunately, this brief honeymoon would come to an end in 1927 when the GMD launched a brutal purge, imprisoning and killing thousands of worker activists throughout China, particularly in Shanghai, Wuhan and Guangzhou, leading to the demise of China's burgeoning militant labour movement (see S.A. Smith's essay on 1927 in the present volume). One century later, this essay reflects on the contributions and tribulations of the revolutionary working class in China in those early years.

The May Thirtieth Movement

In the early 1920s, Shanghai was China's manufacturing hub and a favourite destination for foreign investment. Its many foreign concessions under British, French and Japanese control formed the city's International Settlement, which was governed by its own municipal council. Strategically, the newly born Communist Party set up its Chinese Trade Union Secretariat there in August 1921 to coordinate labour-organising activities, including evening schools, publications and confrontational collective actions.

On 15 May 1925, in response to labour unrest, the managers at the Japanese-owned No. 7 Cotton Mill (Nagai Wata Kaisha) locked out the workers and stopped paying their wages.[5] When Japanese supervisors beat Chinese workers in the ensuing confrontation, a twenty-year-old Communist named Gu Zhenghong challenged them but was shot four times and subsequently died. This incident enraged the general public in Shanghai. The CCP instantly launched a campaign calling for solidarity with the textile workers, a boycott of Japanese products and a public funeral for Gu. In response, the Shanghai International Settlement authorities arrested many more workers and students. To counteract the repression, a public procession was announced for 30 May 1925. Nearly 10,000 protestors marched along Nanjing Road and demonstrated outside the police station in which more than 100 demonstrators were being detained. By 2pm, a British inspector ordered the police to open fire at point-blank range, killing thirteen and seriously wounding several dozen protestors.[6] This violence triggered the mass mobilisation that went down in history as the May Thirtieth Movement.

The CCP quickly called on all the local trade unions for an emergency meeting and established the Shanghai General Labour Union (上海总工会). Together with the student and traders' associations, the Party formed a citywide alliance that launched a 'triple strike' (三罢)—a joint mobilisation by workers, students and businesses to protest against the reckless brutality of the foreign powers. The alliance put forward seventeen demands, including the removal of the emergency measures that had been put in place to manage the popular unrest, the punishment of those responsible for the violence, compensation for the victims, respect for Chinese workers' rights to publish, assemble and speak freely, and equal rights for Chinese citizens in the International Settlement. In response, the imperialists reinforced their armed units to stifle the general strike with more violence. Within one month, the business circle unilaterally decided to sabotage the general strike by resuming business as usual and the Shanghai General Labour Union had to negotiate settlements with the foreign employers one by one.

In spite of its short life, the Shanghai general strike spread like wildfire, with 135 solidarity strikes occurring in various provinces in its wake, the most notable being the Canton–Hong Kong Strike.[7]

The Canton–Hong Kong Strike

A British colony since 1840, Hong Kong was not immune to industrial strife and class conflict. Time and again, workers rose up to demand their economic, social and political rights against all odds, such as the mechanics' strike of 1920 and seamen's strike of 1922.[8] Hong Kong unions in those early days were mainly craft unions, clanship or dialect groups, or triad societies. They had close ties with their Chinese counterparts, particularly those from Guangzhou.[9] During his days in exile, GMD leader Sun Yat-sen used Hong Kong as a revolutionary base to plan the overthrow of the Qing Dynasty and was well connected with waterfront workers, seafarers and mechanics, who helped him smuggle weapons and occasionally mobilised as combatants for uprisings inside the mainland. He encouraged the formation of modern trade unions along industrial lines—his most significant successes being the seamen's and the mechanics' unions.[10]

The 1911 revolution opened up political space for trade unions in southern China, whereas the northern and central parts of the country were ruled by different warlords who were natural enemies of the labour movement. Under these conditions, the Chinese labour movement in the south was becoming increasingly militant and anti-imperialistic. On 1 May 1925, the Second Labour Congress, representing 166 trade unions, was convened in Guangzhou and declared the foundation of the All-China Federation of Trade Unions (ACFTU), which immediately decided to affiliate with the Red International of Labour Unions (see also Wang Kan's essay in the present volume).

When the shocking news of the Shanghai massacre of 30 May 1925 arrived in the south, the ACFTU and other groups called for a demonstration on 2 June in Guangzhou and started to plan a solidarity strike. A working team comprising key union figures from Hong Kong and the mainland was formed to prepare a general strike similar to the one taking place in Shanghai but also drawing from the experiences of the previous mechanics' and seamen's strikes in Hong Kong. Deng Zhongxia, representing the ACFTU, Su Zhaozheng, the leader of the seamen's union, and others were dispatched to Hong Kong to gain support from local unions from different factions.[11] The call easily won support from the local patriotic Chinese community, including the triads, and the final mass turnout surprised even the organisers.

On 19 June, the first salvo of the strike was fired by seamen, tramway workers and printers. Simultaneously, Hong Kong students began their mobilisation. Soon, employees in Western-style businesses, waterfront workers, coal workers, postal workers, cleaners, construction workers, laundry workers, food workers, gas workers and electrical workers joined the swirling ranks of the 250,000 strikers—nearly one-third of the total population of Hong Kong and half of its labour force. The whole city was paralysed as outbound and inbound transportation came to a stop.

The strike committee adopted a statement in two parts originally released by the All-Hong Kong Federation of Trade Unions.[12] The first part stated the strikers' support for the struggle that was taking place in Shanghai and its demands. The second part advanced a series of requests, including: freedom of speech, publication, association and to live in any district; the right to strike and collective bargaining; equality under the law and the suspension of deportation and flogging for local Chinese; universal suffrage; and labour legislation covering things such as an eight-hour workday, social insurance and a minimum wage.

Lured by the promise of food and lodging, and with full support from the Guangdong revolutionary government, the strikers began to drift back to Guangzhou or to nearby villages. The left wing of the GMD faction pledged a subsidy of 10,000 Chinese dollars per month to the strike committee.[13] Abandoned houses, casinos, brothels and boats were requisitioned and turned into dormitories, dining halls and offices for strikers. By 21 June, as a full embargo against the foreign powers was imposed, 3,000 Chinese workers collectively left Shamian, a joint British and French settlement on an islet in central Guangzhou, to join the general strike. With foreign warships moored nearby, the Hong Kong and Shamian administrations declared an emergency curfew.

Two days later, on 23 June, a public procession in solidarity with the May Thirtieth Movement, comprising 100,000 soldiers, workers, farmers, students and traders, was organised in Guangzhou. When the students were marching along the opposite bank of Shamian, the joint foreign security force suddenly opened fire, killing fifty-two people and wounding more than one hundred.

To consolidate worker power during the general strike, the organisers established the Canton–Hong Kong Strike Committee (省港罢工委员会; hereinafter, 'Strike Committee') under the ACFTU. This new body was labelled by foreign observers a 'second Guangdong government' because it was entrusted with judicial, legal and police powers and had its own armed pickets, schools, hospitals, court, detention centres and publications.[14] The 2,000-strong armed picketers received training from the officers of the Whampoa Military Academy. They even controlled a 'navy' of twelve patrol boats to deter smugglers along sea and land routes of Guangdong Province. In several operations, though poorly armed, these fighting units exchanged gunfire with the British forces in Hong Kong and with pirates, and 120 picketers died while carrying out their duties.

The highest governing body of the strike was the Delegates' Congress, which counted about 800 members, each of whom was democratically elected.[15] They met publicly every second day and the meetings were open to all striking workers. By the end of 1926, the conference had met 178 times. The congress chose a thirteen-member Strike Committee represented by the ACFTU (two members), Hong Kong unions (seven members) and the Shamian/Guangzhou unions (four members). Supported by an advisory committee, the Strike Committee headed six special organisations: the Picketing Department, Financial Department, Stores and Auction Department, Joint Hearing Department, Workers' Hospital and the Workers' Propaganda Training School. Under its executive council, there were five departments: transportation and communication, public relations, reception, propaganda, and recreation.

Throughout the strike period, the organisers emphasised training and propaganda work. They put out a weekly newspaper named *Workers' Path* (工人之路), which reached a circulation of 10,000 copies at its peak. The Strike Committee also ran eight primary schools for the children of the strikers, eight extramural schools for the workers and a labour institute to train militant labour activists, similar to the famous Peasant Movement Training Institute run by Mao Zedong in Guangzhou. Special schools were also organised for women and youth.[16]

Sustaining the Strike

Economically, Hong Kong was devastated by the strike, with a wave of bankruptcies, bank runs, property market and entrepot trade collapses and ships stranded in the harbour. Hong Kong, which literally means 'fragrant harbour', in those days was mocked as a 'stinky harbour' due to the public health emergency caused by sanitary workers, rubbish collectors and cleaners joining the strike. The strike caused the city to lose seven million Hong Kong dollars every day, turning the government account from a surplus into a deficit.[17] Although the colonial ruling class tried to lobby the British Parliament to send an army to defeat the Guangdong 'Bolshevik' Government, as in the good old days of the Opium War, the British Government was preoccupied with mounting domestic labour problems.[18] The home authorities limited themselves to loaning £3 million to the Hong Kong Government to cover its deficit. By adopting a 'wait and see' approach, they were hoping the Chinese warlords would defeat the revolutionary government. The Hong Kong Government also tried to subsidise and arm the reactionary forces in China to overthrow the revolutionary government, but these forces were quickly quelled by the new revolutionary army.

To sustain the strike, the Strike Committee decided to limit the embargo to only British interests. Ships that did not display a British flag, did not carry British goods and did not call at Hong Kong were allowed to trade with Guangzhou. This measure boosted Guangdong trade, as merchandise was no longer routed through Hong Kong.

In May 1926, the Third Labour Congress was convened in Guangzhou, with the participation of 699 labour organisations claiming to represent 1.24 million members. The congress summed up the labour struggle of the previous year and made an open appeal for the launch of a Northern Expedition to defeat the warlord forces that still controlled most of China and to reunify the country under the banner of the GMD.

As the Northern Expedition kicked off in July 1926, all human, financial, political and diplomatic resources were drawn together to support this new endeavour. As well as those who enrolled as soldiers in the army, 3,000 strikers joined as porters, medical aids and auxiliary personnel. Many prominent labour leaders took up new official positions or helped to build new unions in the recently captured cities. By October, the revolutionary army seized Wuhan and set up a national government there, with Su Zhaozheng as the Minister of Labour.[19] In January 1927, armed picketers broke the British barricade and occupied the Jiujiang and Hankou foreign settlements. After negotiation, the British surrendered. This daring but assertive move paved the way for the armed uprising in Shanghai in the spring of 1927.

The Strike Committee and the revolutionary government reached a consensus that unification of China was the paramount task and, as a result, they declared the suspension of the strike. While many strikers returned to Hong Kong to look for employment, around 30,000 were left behind in Guangzhou; a special import levy of 2.5 percent was collected to alleviate their difficulties. The Strike Committee continued to operate for a few more months, even as it was forced to go underground after military rule was imposed in the wake of the GMD coup of April 1927. The fateful Guangzhou uprising led by the CCP in December 1927 caused many more strikers to lose their lives (see Day's essay in the present volume). Only in November 1927 was the sign board of the Strike Committee forcefully removed by the GMD government—an act that drew the final curtain on the Canton–Hong Kong Strike.

The Post-Strike Scene

The Hong Kong Government was not slow in suppressing the humiliated labour movement. By 1927, it had hastily enacted the notorious Illegal Strikes and Lockouts Ordinance, which joined the existing Boycott Prevention Ordinance and Emergency Regulations and Societies Ordinance. At least fifteen trade unions and labour organisations were outlawed during that period. Based on the UK model that had been enacted after the 1926 General Strike in Britain, the new law aimed to 'suppress the illegal activities of unions rather than to encourage their legal ones'.[20] A strike would become illegal if it had any objective other than the resolution of a trade dispute and if it was designed to coerce the government, either directly or by inflicting hardship on the community or any substantial portion of the community. The law further banned civil servants and workers in essential public services from participating in any industrial action. To sever the umbilical cord of the China–Hong Kong union relationship, the law outlawed the control of any Hong Kong union by any trade union or organisation from outside the territory, as well as the use of union funds for any political purposes.[21] Instead, the colonial government attempted to domesticate the local unions into 'bread and butter' or 'responsible' unions, with a focus on purely economic and livelihood interests that did not touch on political issues, particularly those related to China. In the 1930s, the government established the consultative Labour Advisory Board comprising union and management representatives to discuss labour legislation and related labour issues but with an agenda dominated by officials. The colonial government also utilised culture to defuse radical sentiments and the influence of the CCP by promoting traditional Chinese culture and literature, subsidising anti-Communist newspapers and elevating members of the Chinese elite to state offices.[22]

Many returned strikers and Communist members continued to support the national liberation movement from Hong Kong, under the watchful eyes of the Hong Kong police in close cooperation with their GMD counterparts. As the white terror was unleashed in China, Hong Kong became a haven and a coordination centre for the Communists. Time and again, small pockets of Communist militants were mobilised in the colony in flash gatherings to distribute leaflets or to shout slogans in public areas, only to be dispersed or arrested by the police. The police's Anti-Communist Squad rounded up Communist activists in ongoing raids, deporting the unlucky ones to mainland China, where they faced further persecution, including the death penalty.[23]

1925

While the Chinese Communist Party (CCP) continued its labour organising work at the national level through the foundation of the All-China Federation of Trade Unions, labour militancy continued unabated at the grassroots level. Jean Chesneaux's pioneering The Chinese Labor Movement (1919–1927), *first published in French in 1962, had a huge influence in promoting the view of the period between the May Fourth Movement of 1919 and the split between the CCP and the Nationalist Party in 1927 as being a golden age for labour activism in China, an era in which the proletariat achieved maturity as a class, pursuing ever broader and better organised strikes. However, our understanding of the labour movement during that period might be biased by excessive attention to these instances of worker mobilisation. From the 1970s onward, a new generation of scholars began challenging this narrative. By focusing on shop-floor relations and manifestations of worker culture, they put into sharp relief how Chinese workers in that era were still split by profound divisions related to gender, native place, sector, clientelistic networks, and even secret-society affiliation. In this vein, the following essay takes us to the shop floors of Tianjin in the mid-1920s.*

Everyday Politics in Tianjin Factories
Gail HERSHATTER

On 11 August 1925, newly unionised workers at the Japanese-owned Yu Da Cotton Mill in Tianjin presented a list of demands to the mill's management, including a wage increase, a shortened workday, and an office for the union. Details about the management's response are murky, but when millhands finished their shift and headed out for an organising meeting in a nearby saltyard, they found their way blocked by a hundred military police deployed by the local warlord Li Jinglin. Workers immediately called a strike and sent for reinforcements from nearby mills. Chasing some of the police and factory security forces into the mill courtyard, they fought the police with pickaxes, cut the factory phone lines, destroyed the factory office, and smashed all the windows. On the factory floor, as the *North-China Herald* reported, 'the cotton milling machinery crumpled up before them like wooden houses in a tornado ... a tangled mass of broken machinery, spindles, and debris'.[1] Damage to the mill was estimated to exceed half a million taels of silver. The next day, armed police ambushed mill workers at their saltyard meeting, killed at least ten and wounded a dozen more, drove some into the Hai River, and arrested more than four hundred. Li Jinglin shut down unions across the Chinese-controlled sections of Tianjin, sent police to surveil unions in the foreign concessions, and closed several factory schools that the fledgling Chinese Communist Party (CCP) had established to recruit and organise workers. That was the end of the episode known as 'Smashing Yu Da' (砸裕大事件).[2]

To the labour historian, the Yu Da factory-smashing incident is a seductive one. Newly militant workers join forces and take action against a repressive foreign management that is backed by a corrupt warlord state apparatus. The workers' outrage is audible, visible, and leaves a paper trail. Young Communist organisers are involved both inside and outside the mills, drawing the uprising into a larger narrative of protest, party-building, and budding working-class consciousness.[3]

And yet, in spite of its attractions, tracing militant labour uprisings is not the best way to understand worker history in Tianjin, for at least two reasons: they were infrequent and they involved only a small segment of the city's fragmented workforce.

Instability and Industry

In northern China's most important industrial city during the Republican period, strikes and associated disturbances were rare and brief. The Tianjin economy grew in fits and starts because of constant political instability; workplaces were run by a continuously shifting cast of would-be industrialists and were often in financial trouble. From 1918 to 1926—a fervid period of upheaval and union organising in major coastal cities—Shanghai recorded 638 strikes; Tianjin had only fourteen. Until 1928, successive warlord regimes routinely called in troops to prevent or suppress worker protests, and worker leaders were routinely assaulted, detained, and sometimes tortured.

At the beginning of the Nanjing Decade (1928–37), the Nationalist government moved aggressively to ensure labour peace and limit Communist influence by establishing official workplace unions that emphasised political training. The municipal government, through its Bureau of Social Affairs, attempted to mediate labour disputes to prevent strikes, with some success: in 1928 the city had one strike; in 1929 and 1930, only three each year. In 1922, as the world economic crisis deepened and cotton mills began to close, cotton millhands at every Chinese-owned mill in the city engaged in work stoppages aimed at preventing pay cuts and layoffs, sometimes locking themselves inside the buildings to avoid being ejected. By 1935, forced into an increasingly defensive stance as mills abruptly closed, they appealed unsuccessfully to the municipal government for the restoration of their jobs.[4] Most mills subsequently were sold to Japanese owners.

During the Japanese occupation of Tianjin (1937–45), the mill workforce initially expanded, but labour organisations were banned, and many factories were garrisoned. The Japanese authorities regarded strikes as politically treasonous acts. The Pacific War drained Japanese military resources in the early 1940s, and worker efforts focused on survival as machinery was melted down to make war materiel and mills closed once again.

The return of the nationalists to Tianjin in 1945 brought a resumption of official unions controlled by foremen and skilled workers, an ideology of cooperation between workers and owners, labour disputes mediated by the government, and government limits on the ability to strike. Government-sponsored unions were not expected to concern themselves with pay and working conditions, but the late 1940s was nonetheless Tianjin's brief high tide of labour disputes. Compared with previous decades, the workforce was older and less inclined to move back and forth from factories to their villages of origin. The state apparatus was weaker and less able to constrain labour activism. Communist organisers, particularly in the cotton and wool mills, established a consistent presence, and for the first time included women cadres who made headway in mobilising the increasing number of women millhands. Workers agitated, with only limited success, for improved wages, an end to layoffs, and severance pay, in an environment increasingly constrained by high inflation, intermittent martial law, political repression, and the exigencies of civil war with the Communists. Ultimately, working-class protest was of very limited importance to the entry of the CCP-led People's Liberation Army into Tianjin in January 1949.

Working-Class Fragmentation

The second reason labour militancy is an incomplete guide to Tianjin's working-class history is that the Tianjin workforce was fragmented, and many workers never encountered any form of open unrest. In 1929, more than 40 percent of Tianjin workers laboured at ironworking, carpet weaving, and other jobs in the artisanal sector. Many were unpaid apprentices in their mid-teens, connected to the shopowners by kinship or native place. In warehouses and working-class homes, casual labourers and outworkers glued matchboxes, cracked walnuts, spun wool, and wove mats, changing jobs frequently. Most of those who laboured in Tianjin came from rural villages, returning there annually or whenever economically troubled workplaces laid them off. Throughout the Republican period, they remained temporary sojourners in the city, participating little in workplace organising movements. Freight haulers and rickshaw pullers were more likely than other workers to be Tianjin natives, but their rootedness in the city did not lead to class-based action. Their world was divided into territories controlled by individual guilds and bolstered by vertical alliances between workers and transport bosses.

Even in the cotton mills—Tianjin's most organised and militant sector— the workforce was unstable and variegated in ways that constrained labour militancy. Children, for instance, made up more than one-quarter of cotton millhands in the early 1920s and, although the percentage of child workers dropped in the 1930s, it rose again during the Japanese occupation to somewhere between one-third and two-thirds of the mill workforce.[5] Unlike Shanghai, where women became the majority of the cotton mill workforce by the mid-1920s, in Tianjin, women accounted for less than 10 percent of the workforce in 1929, rising to 39 percent with the Japanese occupation and barely half in the late 1940s.[6] Children and women were not necessarily quiescent, of course, but they were hired as part of a search for cheap and tractable labour, and, at the very least, mobilising them inside the cotton mills had to entail different networks and strategies from those centred on adult men.

In this formation of inconstant industrialists and a fragmented working-class operating in an often-violent political environment, organising and strikes were sporadic, dangerous, and frequently unsuccessful. Concentrating on moments of labour militancy or CCP leadership is necessarily going to miss most of what workers experienced in Tianjin's industry and how they coped with circumstances well beyond their control. A more comprehensive approach to labour history must resist the seductive organising device of a labour action timeline and focus instead on the everyday politics of surviving, and attempting to thrive, under conditions of extreme instability. As Ben Kerkvliet writes: 'Everyday politics involves people embracing, complying with, adjusting, and contesting norms and rules regarding authority over, production of, or allocation of resources and doing so in quiet, mundane, and subtle expressions and acts that are rarely organised or direct.'[7]

Patterns of Everyday Politics

In the realm of everyday politics—unlike that of militant labour activism—significant commonalities appear among workers in small-scale workshops and mechanised factories. In the ironworks and machine-building shops of Santiaoshi, boys and young men were hired through family or native-place ties, often working for a relative. In the cotton mills, too, workers entered as members of kinship or geographical networks. Such networks, encompassing foremen as well as workers, might channel them into a particular workshop and offer them protection. Once inside the mills, some workers formed additional associations for mutual aid. Associations were usually single-gender and secret: sworn brotherhood or Green Gang membership for men, sisterhood and religious groups for women.[8] Sworn brothers watched out for one another in the workplace, but also drank together, watched plays, and attended weddings and funerals outside the strictures of the working day. Gang alliances sometimes led to conflicts with gang factions within or beyond one's own factory, drawing male workers into violent confrontations with other workers. Sisterhood groups were less formalised and less visible in the historical record, as was membership of religious sects.

Everyday politics included deploying these networks in survival strategies of withholding and concealment, in contrast to the open confrontation and historical visibility of conventionally recognised worker militancy. Regardless of the size of the workplace, exhausted workers engaged in a strategy known in local slang as 'soaking mushrooms' (泡蘑菇), or slowdowns, which were common before and during the Japanese occupation. When supervisors were not around, ironworkers in Santiaoshi and labourers in cotton mills would nap by the side of the machines or turn them off altogether. Sometimes soaking mushrooms was overtly political as when, for example, ironworkers in 1947 engaged in slowdowns in response to managers blocking their union organising efforts. Although it often emerged as a spontaneous shop-floor strategy, soaking mushrooms required a high degree of coordination among workers. Common techniques included smearing oil on machine belts to slow cotton mill machinery, cutting machine belts to be able to rest while the machines were repaired, sneaking off to the lavatories for extended cigarette breaks, and posting lookouts who would wave a cloth or throw a yarn tube into the workshop to warn that a foreman was returning.

The everyday politics of Tianjin workplaces also entailed removing some of what one produced from the factory—stealing, from the management's point of view. During the latter years of the Japanese occupation, cotton mill workers routinely stuffed yarn into their clothing and lunchboxes to sell outside the factory to supplement their increasingly inadequate wages. Individual pilfering was common, and mill owners responded with increasingly elaborate inspections and even body searches as workers exited the mills. As with soaking mushrooms, however, the most effective stealing required organisation: lookouts, coordinated efforts to remove thread from spindles, men bringing goods to women to conceal under their jackets, guards who were induced to slough off on their searches with the promise of a payoff. When managers erected partitions so that guards could not see the faces of the workers they were searching, workers put signals on their socks and shoes. Outside the factory, buyers acquired the stolen yarn for resale in the countryside. Everyone involved took a cut, and millhands did not get rich from stealing, but they did manage to bring their incomes up beyond the margin of subsistence, risking beatings, firing, imprisonment, and even sexual assault to do so.

Political Agendas

All of these social networks and activities, even if they had no initial connection to labour organising, could be deployed to advance political agendas. During the Japanese occupation, for instance, the Communist base areas across northern China were desperate to acquire goods blockaded by the Japanese, including paper, ink, salt, sugar, metals, medical supplies, cigarettes and matches, kerosene, machines and machine parts, and tubes, capacitors, and resistors needed for telecommunications. When the Jinchaji base area, which encompassed parts of Shanxi, Chahar, and Hebei, sent people to Tianjin to purchase these goods, they worked with mechanics, staff members, and workers of various factories to forge papers and procure the goods, which were then smuggled out to the base areas, concealed in double-bottomed boats, under cartloads of manure, or in piles of coal.[9] When the Japanese built northern China's largest power plant near Tianjin, the underpaid workers stole everything, from batches of red copper to bottles of turbine oil. Two boiler workers stripped the lead coating from the plant's electrical cables and removed it from the factory. A shipment of several tonnes of iron disappeared overnight. Workers gathered in the plant repair shop at noon, when Japanese supervisors went home to eat, and broke up iron rods, copper plates, and anything else that could be taken out of the factory and sold. The line between everyday politics in the service of survival and deliberate political sabotage blurred in the course of these activities.[10]

The everyday politics of workplace networks also made labour organising possible. Yu Da, the cotton mill that was 'smashed' in the summer of 1925, was the last Tianjin cotton mill to unionise after a spring and summer of intensive Communist organising activity, and the breakthrough was based on family and native-place networks. The mill was Japanese-owned and tightly controlled by the chief foreman, who was a member of the Green Gang. Workers at other mills suggested that one of the chief Communist organisers could make use of a family network at Yu Da: a millhand named Xiang Ruizhi and his three brothers, along with his father, who cooked in a nearby canteen. Known as the Five Tigers of the Xiang Family, they had close connections with many fellow natives from Baodi County who were also employed at Yu Da. The Communist organiser challenged Xiang Ruizhi by suggesting that perhaps Yu Da workers could not organise because they were afraid of the foreman. Xiang flushed, vowed that he could organise the mill, and within a few weeks had mobilised his brothers to sign up workers for the union as they ate in the kitchen run by his father. This activation of a family network, augmented by a native-place network, was the prequel to the union demands that resulted in the smashing of Yu Da.

Two decades later, when women CCP organisers found employment in Tianjin's cotton and wool mills to conduct underground organising, they integrated themselves into the lunchtime leisure activities of girls and women—teaching them to read, telling stories, and performing Beijing opera. Slowly, by means of activities that had no obvious connection to labour conditions, they built networks that could be activated to express the dissatisfaction of workers with their wages and government-sponsored unions. Although women were excluded from some of the networks that could be used to mobilise men, they were perhaps less constrained by the patronage of powerful foremen than some of their male coworkers, and thus easier to organise.

When workers developed a range of 'quiet, mundane, and subtle expressions and acts' centred on the workplace, it was not necessarily because they were attracted to communism or even unionisation, nor because they had a stable sense of themselves as part of an emergent working class. Activities such as soaking mushrooms, pilfering, or organised smuggling, along with the demonstrations, riots, and strikes that we recognise as the signal events of labour history, were not neatly arranged on a linear continuum. Tianjin workers sometimes began, as E.P. Thompson described it, to 'feel and articulate the identity of their interests as between themselves, and as against other men [and women] whose interests are different from (and usually opposed to) theirs'.[11] But the networks they created could be used to secure cross-class protection as well as to forge alliances for change. Labour activities developed in contingent and unpredictable formations, as workers created an everyday politics of the workplace that offered the possibility of ameliorating the difficult immediate conditions of working lives in Tianjin.

1925

In the 1920s, the efforts of the Chinese Communist Party (CCP) at labour organising reached their apex with the organisation of a series of national labour conferences (全国劳动大会) aimed at bringing together trade unions of all political stripes to seek common ground for their struggles. The first conference took place on 1 May 1922 in Guangzhou and saw the participation of 160 delegates from 200 trade unions in twelve cities, claiming to represent around 300,000 workers.[1] On that occasion, the participants appointed the CCP-affiliated Chinese Trade Union Secretariat to be the coordinating body for the labour movement in China until a proper national trade union federation could be established—a decision that some see as a watershed moment for the CCP's assertion of leadership over the Chinese labour movement.[2] It took three more years for the Second National Labour Conference—which took place in May 1925, with the presence of 230 delegates representing more than half a million workers—to establish a national umbrella organisation for Chinese labour organisations in the form of the All-China Federation of Trade Unions (ACFTU, 中华全国总工会).[3] This was the first truly national trade union in China—an organisation that, despite a long and tortuous history, remains in existence to this day. This essay reflects on the significance of the ACFTU's foundation in the context of the CCP's strategy in those years.

The Founding of the All-China Federation of Trade Unions

WANG Kan

On 1 May 1925, the All-China Federation of Trade Unions (中华全国总工会, ACFTU) was founded in Guangzhou to organise Chinese workers to struggle against the political and economic systems of the time, bringing together 166 affiliated trade unions, comprising more than 540,000 members.[4] Considered the first formally established umbrella organisation for all 'true' worker unions in China, the ACFTU was first and foremost a sign of cooperation between the Chinese Communist Party (CCP) and the Nationalist Party (Guomindang, or GMD).[5]

The formation of this organisation reflected the interest and growing influence of the Communist International (Comintern) in China. Acting as an international arm of the Soviet Union to promote global communism, the Comintern was heavily involved in the Chinese Revolution, providing military advisors, weapons and money to both the CCP and the GMD. This policy was motivated by the belief of the Soviet leadership that only a united workers' movement of the CCP and GMD could hasten the Chinese Revolution and would better serve Soviet interests in the Far East.

As a result of this alliance under the Comintern, the ACFTU was not a CCP department. Instead, it functioned as a platform to coordinate different forces among workers, including non-party actors.[6] A party faction system (党团制度) was introduced in what could be considered a 'nondenominational' organisation. Under this system, the CCP in the ACFTU functioned as a corporatist organ to democratically represent its own interests amid other factions and was therefore unable to dominate the decision-making process through its own model of democratic centralisation.[7] However, there was precedent for such a powersharing arrangement, as the Bolsheviks in the Soviet Union implemented a party faction system in their trade union and other mass organisations. In this case, the CCP sacrificed its dominant position among the Chinese working class in return for the opportunity to build a broader labour movement.

Changing Worker Mobilisation Strategy

Localism, clan cultures and regional economic disparities negatively affected any effort to organise Chinese workers in those early years. In addition, most workers laboured in small and medium-sized workshops, as there were few large factories. They lacked class consciousness and, in most cases, cared only about their immediate material interests, rather than labour rights or unionisation.[8] To overcome such fragmentation, the CCP had to build a durable and extensive organisational structure and develop sophisticated mobilisation techniques. To pursue this goal, in 1921, the Communist leadership established the Chinese Trade Union Secretariat (中国劳动组合书记部) in Shanghai—an organisation that operated as the *de facto* worker organising department of the CCP (see Lin Chun's essay in the present volume).

When the CCP decided to unionise workers in a certain region or firm, it would name a special commissioner. Under the principle of democratic centralism, the special commissioner exercised the final say in every decision in her or his domain. Although this organisational arrangement was designed for secret worker mobilisation in a repressive environment, its success relied heavily on the individual talents of the special commissioners.[9] A series of failed organising attempts, including the thwarted 7 February Strike (二七大罢工) launched by Beijing and Hankou railway workers in 1923 and the setbacks that followed the initial successes of the worker movement in Anyuan (see Luo Zhanglong's and Perry's essays in the present volume), alerted the Comintern and the CCP to the shortcomings of this mobilisation strategy.[10] Institutional adaptations and improvements were necessary.

First, at the Fourth National Congress of the CCP in January 1925, the Party's leadership acknowledged that since the Chinese working class was weak, they needed to form a coalition between workers, peasants and women's and youth movements to build a revolutionary force.[11] The ACFTU reflected this new strategy. Contrary to the claim by mainstream researchers in China that the founding of the ACFTU announced total leadership of the CCP over the Chinese workers' movement, by establishing this organisation, the Communist Party recognised factional politics in the Chinese workers' movement and opened a channel for all actors to raise demands and concerns related to labour struggles.[12] In other words, the introduction of the ACFTU represented a strategic move by the CCP to show its willingness to cooperate with all factions in the Chinese labour movement, rather than declaring its supremacy. This included the GMD and progressive gang leaders, who now could democratically participate in the decision-making by transforming the conventional Communist Party chain-of-command framework into a party faction system, under which the CCP was only one component. This was a direct outcome of the cooperation between the CCP and the GMD, which also saw CCP members of the ACFTU Executive Committee joining the GMD and playing active roles in its labour department.

A second innovation can be found in the ways Communist labour organisers began to engage gang leaders. Already in Anyuan, CCP organisers had begun to recognise the unavoidable importance of gang leaders in worker organising. Gangs were a societal response of the Chinese underclass to poverty and deprivation. In the early twentieth century, a deepening wealth gap haunted China. In Shanghai, the lowest wage of a worker was three to seven times higher than that of a peasant, but 80 percent of Shanghai's residents lived in poverty and could barely feed themselves or their families.[13] Gangs provided a collective network of protection and welfare for member workers. For these reasons, more than 80 percent of Chinese miners at that time belonged to gangs.[14] In addition, gangs were embedded in the workplace as a human resource management structure.[15] It was common practice for firms to contract out labour, with gangmasters serving as both recruiters and foremen.

To unionise, the CCP needed to understand how gangs operated and recruited their members.[16] With this aim in mind, senior Communist leaders, such as Deng Zhongxia and Li Lisan, interacted with and even joined gangs like the Green Gang (青帮) and the Hong Men (洪门). The CCP used this approach to hijack the gang structure and to plant Party cells in Chinese workplaces, so as to remake the gangs into modern trade unions.[17] At the same time, the GMD was using a similar mobilisation approach to manipulate gang influence.[18]

Organisational Structure

The Comintern exerted a decisive influence over the organisational design of the ACFTU. The highest authority was the Executive Committee (执行委员会), led by a chairman and three vice-chairmen. The National Congress (全国代表大会) of the federation met once a year. The number of representatives was determined by the Executive Committee, which comprised twenty-five members elected by the National Congress.

The first Executive Committee was elected at the Second National Labour Conference (第二次全国劳动大会), in May 1925—the event, organised by the CCP-affiliated Chinese Trade Union Secretariat and attended by both Communist and Nationalist participants, which inaugurated the ACFTU. The chairman and vice-chairmen of the organisation's first Executive Committee were men. Lin Weimin, a noted CCP labour leader, was elected chairman but fell ill after less than a year and had to quit the post (he died in September 1927). The three vice-chairmen were Liu Shaoqi, Deng Pei and Zheng Yimin, alias Zheng Zesheng. As Lin relinquished his position due to illness, Liu—who had made a name for himself as a labour organiser during the Anyuan strike of 1922 (see Perry's essay in the present volume)—became the ACFTU's acting chairman. In the following decades, Liu would remain active in the Chinese workers' movement while also climbing the ranks of the CCP bureaucracy, eventually becoming Vice-Chairman of the Party and President of the People's Republic of China after 1949, before being dragged into a power struggle with Mao Zedong and suffering a violent death in 1969 during the Cultural Revolution.

Liu's two colleagues on the first Executive Committee of the ACFTU followed different trajectories. After being elected vice-chairman, Deng Pei became a strong supporter of workers' armed struggle. He also took the position as chairman of the Guangdong Federation of Trade Unions. As a CCP member, Deng followed the orders of the Comintern and joined the GMD to strengthen the coalition between the two parties. After the 1927 split, the GMD army raided the ACFTU's facilities in Guangzhou; Deng was arrested and executed that year. Zheng Yimin maintained his position as ACFTU Vice-Chairman for only one year, when his name simply disappeared from the Executive Committee and little is known about what became of him.

Despite fluctuation in its leadership, the ACFTU had a clear organisational structure. There was an Executive Bureau (干事局) under the direct supervision of the Executive Committee, with personnel appointed by the latter. The Executive Bureau had four departments: the Organisation Department (组织部) was responsible for unionising workers; the Secretariat (秘书部) looked after administrative affairs; the Propaganda Department (宣传部) was responsible for public relations and worker education; and the Economy Department (经济部) was in charge of accounting and finance. In addition, according to the ACFTU Constitution passed in 1925, the Executive Committee could establish special field offices and special commissions/organisations for its 'convenience'.[19]

These special units were designed to cope with the secrecy required for labour organising. In practice, they opened a space for the Executive Committee to bypass the formal channels of the ACFTU and to conduct covert actions.

The CCP's control over the Executive Committee gave it an advantage in the democratic process in the ACFTU. All twenty-five elected members of the ACFTU's first Executive Committee were CCP members. Despite the fact that most ACFTU Executive Committee members also held GMD membership, the CCP membership was more disciplined when compared with the GMD and therefore better equipped to exert their influence within both the federation and the GMD itself. In fact, the Comintern secretly insisted that the CCP monitor GMD activities and stand against any attempt by the Nationalists to 'hook up' with anti-Soviet forces.[20]

Heightening Distrust and Conflict

Founding the ACFTU was part of the Comintern and Soviet Union's China strategy. They planned for the CCP and GMD to join forces and confront the warlord government, which it was hoped would expand Soviet interests in China.[21] By introducing a party faction system within the ACFTU, the CCP and the Comintern signalled their willingness to share power among different facets of the labour movement. However, other dynamics were also in play. While openly adopting such a system, Communist leaders covertly hoped to reduce the suspicion of the GMD and gangs towards their ranks, which would enable the CCP to establish Party cells in all major trade unions and worker organisations.

Senior worker leaders within the CCP were keen to use the ACFTU as a platform to increase CCP power in the labour movement. They saw the cooperation with the GMD as a tactical move to transform Nationalist-led trade unions into CCP affiliates. In the words of Deng Zhongxia, an Executive Committee member and first general secretary of the ACFTU in 1925, the party faction system was a method to extend Communist reach in trade unions. As a result, the ACFTU always prioritised mobilising workers against the political and economic status quo.[22]

Soon gang leaders became dissatisfied with escalating worker militancy led by the ACFTU. As the ACFTU hastened workers' struggle, GMD leaders viewed the Comintern and the CCP as rival forces and began to resent what increasingly felt like imposed cooperation with the CCP. A forceful collision was on the horizon, and eventually things came to a head in 1927, when the alliance between the two parties broke down and GMD forces, assisted by gangs, slaughtered workers and Communist labour organisers in Shanghai (see S.A. Smith's essay on 1927 in the present volume). Among the four chairmen of ACFTU's First Executive Committee in 1925, only Liu Shaoqi lived to witness the founding of the People's Republic of China in 1949.

1927

After the death of Sun Yat-sen in March 1925, the Nationalist Party (Guomindang, or GMD) was marred by increasing tensions between a 'left' and a 'right' wing. The Nationalist leadership was also concerned that the Chinese Communist Party (CCP) was taking advantage of the collaboration with it to grow its own following, on top of a mounting uneasiness among GMD rank and file about the violence unleashed by the land reform policies in rural areas under CCP control. In spite of these tensions, in July 1926, the GMD, supported by its junior partner, launched the Northern Expedition, a military campaign aimed at defeating the warlords who controlled large swathes of the country. Boosted by a remarkable mobilisation of both urban and rural masses, the endeavour was so successful that, by late November, the GMD had already set up a national government in Wuhan dominated by its left wing. Knowing that Shanghai was the next target and with the local working class suffering from a rapid rise in prices, the first months of 1927 saw a spectacular resurgence of unions in the coastal city. The Communist-led Shanghai General Labour Union (上海总工会) (GLU), which had been shut down in 1925 but continued to exist informally, experienced a surge in membership and, taking advantage of the favourable political conjuncture, launched two insurrections in the city, on 22–23 February and 21–22 March. With the Nationalist army getting close, on 21 March, the GLU launched a third armed uprising to rid the city of the warlord forces that controlled it. Although victory was swift and the GLU immediately set up a provisional municipal government that declared support for the Nationalist government in Wuhan, tensions within the GMD and between the GMD and the CCP quickly came to a head. A massacre ensued, and with it the First United Front collapsed.

The Third Armed Uprising and the Shanghai Massacre
S.A. SMITH

On 22 March 1927, workers in Shanghai—China's industrial and commercial heartland and the material and symbolic centre of foreign power—briefly took power through a triple strike (三罢), with merchants and students, in an uprising that defeated the warlord forces that controlled the city. The success of what became known as the 'third armed uprising' (第三次武装起义) marks a heroic chapter in the history of the Chinese working class—unparalleled in ambition before or since. The role of workers, however, cannot be divorced from a complex set of relationships that involved the Executive Committee of the Communist International (Comintern) (ECCI) in Moscow; the Central Executive Committee (CEC) of the Chinese Communist Party (CCP); the Shanghai regional organisation of the CCP; rival power centres within the Nationalist Party (Guomindang, or GMD); the British and French authorities who controlled large swathes of the city; uneasy interactions between workers, students, capitalists, and shopkeepers; and, finally, between Communist-dominated labour unions and the secret societies whose influence within the world of labour capitalised on ties of clientelism and native place that cut through class-based solidarity.[1] Fundamentally, however, the history of the uprising and its brutal suppression by Chiang Kai-shek, commander-in-chief of the National Revolutionary Army (NRA), is inexplicable except in the context of fast-changing shifts in military and political power.

Shanghai in Turmoil

The third armed uprising took place against the backdrop of the Northern Expedition by the NRA that aimed to reunify China by defeating regional warlords and the Beiyang government, which was controlled by rival northern warlords; it also hoped to roll back the influence of the foreign powers. Beginning in Guangdong in July 1926, this military expedition swept north and, by December 1926, had allowed the formation of a GMD government in Wuhan led by the left wing of the Party. The defeat or cooption of warlords allowed Communists and left GMD members to mobilise peasants, workers, and women around a program of socioeconomic reforms. This mobilisation increased the influence of Communists within the GMD and, together with the dominance exercised by Mikhail Borodin, Soviet adviser to the GMD, heightened opposition to the United Front within the GMD. Chiang Kai-shek refused to recognise the GMD government in Wuhan, and a real possibility of a split in the Party loomed—something the ECCI hoped to avoid.

As the NRA edged towards Shanghai, the Communists began to prepare an uprising aimed at defeating the forces of Sun Chuanfang, the warlord who controlled the Chinese areas of the city. The hope was to do this prior to the arrival of the NRA to strengthen the left within the GMD and NRA and ensure that an incoming Nationalist administration in the city would carry out a far-reaching program of democratic and socioeconomic reforms. This was the aim of both the first armed uprising in November 1926, which hardly merits that name, and the second armed uprising, from 19 to 22 February 1927, which massively increased the influence of organised labour and the popularity of the GMD and the CCP in the city. In line with the United Front policy imposed by the ECCI, the CCP sought to involve the left wing of the GMD in the uprisings. However, Niu Yongjian, the GMD veteran sent to liaise with the CCP, showed more interest in persuading Sun Chuanfang to come over to the NRA than in the niceties of insurrection.

In the wake of the May Thirtieth Movement in 1925 (see Leong's essay in the present volume), the Shanghai General Labour Union (上海总工会) (GLU) had been shut down. However, the prospect of the arrival of Chiang Kai-shek—seen by many workers as the embodiment of the national revolution—together with vigorous efforts by leftist activists, engendered a surge of labour militancy during the second uprising. During the four-day strike, 420,970 industrial and commercial employees in nearly 6,000 enterprises (including many small businesses) halted work—a larger number than in the May Thirtieth Movement.[2] Many of the strikers worked in Chinese-owned enterprises, which meant that financial support for the strike from Chinese capitalists was much lower than in 1925.[3] The GLU failed to achieve legal status but did manage to create the embryo of an ill-disciplined and scantily armed workers' militia, somewhat distinct from the pickets that maintained order during strikes and demonstrations.

Planning the Third Armed Uprising

In the light of the surge in labour organisation and the rapid rise in CCP and GMD membership, the CEC determined that it must launch a third armed uprising. The NRA was in Jiaxing, about 100 kilometres south of Shanghai, but the expectation was that it would soon resume its advance. Moreover, during the first days of March, Sun Chuanfang's garrison was replaced with northern warlord troops who were heartily detested by the citizens of Shanghai, not least by local business owners who knew that the Shandong warlord who controlled them, Zhang Zongchang, had flooded the areas he controlled with unsecured currency. This created some potential for a renewed alliance between workers, students, and merchants, focused on the ideal of an autonomous government for Shanghai.

On 23 February, the CEC formed a special committee to accelerate the uprising, chaired by CCP general secretary Chen Duxiu, who attended thirty of its thirty-one sessions.[4] Attention was given to building an effective workers' militia. Zhou Enlai, who had arrived in Shanghai in late December, led a new military commission and Soviet military adviser A.P. Appen oversaw the training of the militia. According to Zhou, by the second week of March, there were 1,200 volunteers in what he called the 'workers' shock brigade' (工人突击队), although he reported that they had a mere 250 pistols and 200 hand grenades, and only half had undergone any weapons training.[5] The special committee also stressed the need to explain the aims of the insurrection, resulting in the creation of 154 propaganda teams made up of 1,270 students and 205 teams directly answerable to the Greater Shanghai Bureau of the GMD.[6]

Lines of authority within the CCP were blurred. The CEC, which had its headquarters in the French Concession, had been ordered to move to Wuhan but key members, including Chen Duxiu, preferred to stay in Shanghai. The ECCI was represented in Shanghai by the Far Eastern Bureau, most of whose members were young, inexperienced, and had little knowledge of China. Like the CEC itself, as events unfolded rapidly, these agents of Moscow became disoriented, united only by mistrust of their boss, Grigorii Voitinskii, who was the chair of the bureau. Voitinskii himself was a critic of Borodin, whom he accused of imposing too centralist and authoritarian a structure on the GMD. Things were further complicated by tensions between the CEC and the Shanghai regional Party and between the latter and the GLU.

As far as the United Front was concerned, relations between the CCP and the GMD in Shanghai were worsening. The left wing of the GMD was rather strong in the Greater Shanghai Bureau and Jiangsu Provincial Bureau, but a new power centre emerged on 27 February in the form of the Shanghai branch of the GMD Political Council, which was dominated by right-wing opponents of the United Front. The Communists were under orders from Moscow to avoid a split within the GMD and thus refrained from any public criticism of Chiang Kai-shek. A key issue that galvanised conflict between the two parties was the nature of the government to be formed in Shanghai following the overthrow of the northern warlords. The CCP wished to see a citizens' assembly to which an elected municipal government would be accountable. The Shanghai regional committee argued that such a government should be as much like a soviet as possible, though not all Communists agreed. Niu Yongjian, the GMD veteran sent to liaise with the CCP, dismissed as 'almost comic' the proposal to give workers a plurality of votes in the citizens' assembly and to make the municipal government accountable to it. Instead, the GMD insisted that a new municipal government accept its 'leadership and supervision'.[7]

The Uprising

On 18 March, the forces of NRA general Bai Chongxi arrived in Songjiang, about thirty kilometres south of Shanghai. Thereupon the CEC special committee resolved that the work stoppage–insurrection begin on Monday, 21 March. On 16 March, the GLU resurrected the demands raised during the second uprising. These included calls to develop the anti-imperialist movement, destroy the warlords, support the Wuhan government and implement a popular democratic government in Shanghai, protect civil rights and the right to strike, institute workers' armed defence, implement safety legislation, and improve wages and working conditions.[8] On the evening of Sunday, 20 March, the GLU held an emergency meeting, attended by 300 delegates, half of whom were said to be Communists.[9] It approved the plan of action of the special committee and agreed to strike on the following day.[10]

The triple stoppage began promptly at midday on Monday, 21 March. Within hours, Shanghai was at a standstill. The labour unions sent teams to all parts of the city to announce the impending arrival of the NRA—

something Shanghai newspapers were prohibited from reporting. GMD flags and slogans appeared everywhere. Shops closed. Students in some twenty colleges walked out of classes, and student speaker teams busily urged traders and workers to support the stoppage.[11] The GLU reckoned that 200,000 workers walked out.[12] The British authorities in the International Settlement responded by declaring a state of emergency, and troops disembarked from the thirty to forty foreign warships that were anchored in the river. *Shenbao* claimed that 800,000 people stopped work, closed their businesses, or left school to demonstrate their support for the NRA.[13] A later source calculated that around 300,000 workers went on strike, and around 4,000 enterprises shut.[14] Following the defeat of the northern warlords, the GLU on 23 March called for a return to work, but insisted that the militias should not disband.

At 1pm on 21 March, the workers' militias took up their agreed positions. Many acted under the authority of their trade unions rather than under the CCP military commission. Hongkou was the first district to fall to the rebels, since there were no northern troops there. In Yangshupu, the militia—poorly organised and heavily reliant on the secret societies— also met minimal resistance, with the 1,500 US marines stationed in the district refusing to intervene.[15] The battle in Nanshi threatened to be fierce since the district was home to the Jiangnan arsenal and shipyard, the headquarters of the Wusong-Shanghai constabulary, and about one-third of the city's 2,000-strong police force. The principal militia at the Compagnie Française de Tramways et d'Éclairage Électrique de Shanghai (French Company of Tramways and Electricity) had 139 members but only five pistols and 40 axes. As soon as the arsenal was liberated, weapons became plentiful and both police and warlord forces gave up without much of a struggle. By far the fiercest challenge came in Zhabei, where the bulk of Zhang Zongchang's troops—numbering around 3,000—were concentrated. These were well-armed men, with machines guns, heavy artillery, and armoured cars, concentrated around the North Station. The insurgents comprised mainly printers, postal workers, electricians, and railway workers.

Everywhere workers bore the brunt of the fighting but students from Fudan, Shanghai, and Jinan universities also took part, as did members of the merchant militia.[16] Noteworthy—since it was pregnant with significance for the immediate future—was the part played by members of the Green Gang and Red Gang, who pledged allegiance to Bai Chongxi and the GMD right wing. Among them, the most significant was a unit led by Xu Langxi, master of the Yuyun Mountain Lodge in the Red Gang and bearer of the highest (大) generational status in the Green Gang, who had been active in the 1911 revolution.[17] Three times in the course of battle the insurgents sent emissaries to Bai Chongxi to beg him to proceed at once to the city.[18] Each time Bai prevaricated. After the third delegation arrived, however, Xue Yue, the Cantonese commander of the first division of the 26th corps, refused any longer to stand by and, at 3pm, Bai finally gave orders for the NRA troops to enter the city.[19] Xue's division arrived in Zhabei in the late afternoon, having come up the railway loop via Jessfield Station, which was occupied by British soldiers. Around 5pm they and some 800 members of the militia, many still without arms, finally captured the North Station. At least 200 insurgents were killed and 1,000 wounded in the course of liberating the city, not counting casualties among the northern forces.[20]

On the morning of 22 March, an exultant citizens' assembly hailed the victory of the NRA and endorsed a list of nineteen members, drawn up by the GMD, who would form the provisional municipal government. In the afternoon half a million people poured into the Public Recreation Ground in Nanshi to welcome the 20,000 NRA troops who were passing through the city. On 26 March, another big meeting was held to welcome the arrival of Chiang Kai-shek himself. Although the municipal government was inaugurated on 29 March, political pressure from the GMD right meant that business and professional representatives refused to take up their seats in view of the large number of Communists and GMD leftists in its ranks. However, on 27 March, the GLU was legalised and announced that the number of unions affiliated with it had risen from 187 at the beginning of 1927 to 502, and that affiliated membership had risen from 76,245 to 821,280 in the same period.[21] The critical issue, however, over which the left and right clashed bitterly was whether the workers' militias should continue to exist. Bai Chongxi was determined to suppress this unruly force, and there was outrage in GMD ranks when news percolated through that the CCP and GLU were toying with the idea of taking the strike–insurrection into the foreign settlements.

The Massacre

The first person Chiang Kai-shek met on arrival in Shanghai was Huang Jinrong, chief of the French Concession detectives and one of three leaders of the Green Gang. They agreed that the Green Gang should raise a force from secret-society members, which took the name of the Common Progress Society (公进会), to liquidate the workers' militias. The CCP had always tried to cultivate good relations with the Green Gang, since it carried such clout at all levels of Shanghai society. No less a person than Wang Shouhua, president of the GLU, was a disciple of Du Yuesheng, the principal leader of the Green Gang. However, the CCP and GLU leaders were under no illusions about the threat posed by the machinations of Chiang and Du. The arrival in Shanghai on 1 April of Wang Jingwei, leader of the GMD left wing, muddied the political waters since Wang prevailed on Chen Duxiu to publish a declaration affirming the inviolability of the United Front. More revealing of sentiment within the CCP, however, was the decision by Luo Yinong, secretary of the Shanghai regional committee, to ignore an order from the ECCI to hide all weapons. It seems to be this insubordination that led to his removal on 10 April by the CEC in Wuhan.

On the night of Monday, 11 April, Wang Shouhua was invited to dine with Du Yuesheng, whereupon he was leapt on, trussed in a sack, and buried alive. It was the first act of the drama that would unfold during the night. With the cooperation of the police in the foreign settlements, 500 members of the Common Progress Society, wearing white armbands bearing the character for 'labour', passed into the Chinese areas and began to pick fights with the militias. This served as the pretext for soldiers of Bai Chongxi to intervene to 'suppress internal strife among the workers'. After desperate fighting, by the morning of 12 April, the militias had been crushed.

Mass protests erupted in the course of the day, and the GLU issued an order for a general strike. The following day as many as 240,000 workers walked out.[22] At 1pm a parade set off from Zhabei, led by a military band and union banners. As the protestors filed in the pouring rain along Baoshan Road, machine gunners opened fire and attackers swarmed out of the alleyways, stabbing, shooting, and clubbing the panic-stricken crowd. More than 100 people were killed, 200 wounded, and around fifty simply disappeared. Amazingly, the strike stayed solid the next day even though the decision of the GLU to condemn Chiang Kai-shek publicly as a 'new warlord' who was in cahoots with foreign imperialism apparently disconcerted many workers. Wholesale arrests of Communists were now under way. On 15 April the GLU estimated that more than 300 trade-union activists had been killed, more than 500 arrested, and more than 5,000 were missing or had fled the city.[23] The terror gradually abated but was still occurring at the end of the year. It is estimated that, between 12 April and 31 December, up to 2,000 Communists and worker militants lost their lives and thousands more were arrested or fired from their jobs.[24]

Shifting Strategy

The slaughter unleashed by Chiang Kai-shek exacerbated the conflict that was in full spate within the Soviet Communist Party between Joseph Stalin and the left opposition. Despite their profoundly different diagnoses, both sides ascribed the disaster to poor leadership and political errors. No doubt errors were inevitable, given the fast-changing circumstances. Nevertheless, the idea that the armed insurrection could have been successful with better leadership massively underplays the significance of the objective balance of military and political forces. As Mao Zedong recognised in August 1927, in a context where there was no centralised state power and society was severely fragmented, 'power comes from the barrel of a gun' (枪杆子里面出政权).[25] Only when the CCP finally had built its own armed force was it able to chart a way out of this deadlock. More positively, the uprisings firmed up a version of nationalism that defined the nation in terms of the common people and construed national liberation in terms not only of emancipation from warlordism and foreign control, but also of emancipation of the popular masses from poverty, exploitation, and ignorance.[26] This was to shape Chinese national identity in lasting ways.

1927

As the Chinese Communist Party suffered a major defeat at the hands of Chiang Kai-shek in the wake of the massacre and purge of leftists in April 1927, Party leaders once again found themselves questioning the feasibility of a strategy that relied on raising the political consciousness of and organising the urban proletariat. Instead, their attention shifted to the countryside as a site of potential revolutionary change. This essay centres on the formation of the Hailufeng Soviet in 1927 and the emergence of the peasantry as a political category. The particular socioeconomic context of the early twentieth century created a situation in which Communist activists like Peng Pai could see peasant activism and unrest as forming a historically significant 'peasant movement'. For Peng, peasants were becoming landless in Haifeng because of the depredations of global capitalism, and thus were becoming proletarians. The movement to create peasant unions in Haifeng reached its peak in 1927 with the formation of the soviet. The Nationalists repressed the radical government in 1928, and Peng was killed a year later.

Organising Rural Society: Disintegrating Rural Governance, Peasant Associations, and the Hailufeng Soviet

Alexander F. DAY

It is not easy to date the beginning of the Hailufeng Soviet (海陆丰苏维埃). Localised uprisings, the formation of peasant associations, landlord killings, and shifting territorial control were ongoing in the years leading up to 1927. Although Communist control over rural areas was far from complete, it was increasingly hard for anti-Communist forces to enter areas of the countryside in the two counties of Haifeng and Lufeng in Guangdong Province.[1] On 1 May 1927, Communist-led peasant forces briefly took over the Haifeng County seat, only to lose it and return to the countryside nine days later. That autumn, Communist and peasant activists pushed for rent resistance under the slogan 'Land to the Tillers' (耕者有其田). In September, in a town in the northern part of the county, a small mutiny resulted in a Communist takeover, which the Central Committee of the Chinese Communist Party (CCP) designated as a 'soviet' (苏维埃). Despite soon losing control of the town, they successfully formed soviets in the countryside in fourteen districts across the two counties. Peasant militias and local Communists entered Haifeng again, forming the Provisional Revolutionary Government, on 1 November—a date often associated with the founding of the Hailufeng Soviet, although the formal name came a few weeks later.[2]

This chaotic period in the spring of 1927 began when the Nationalists split from and suppressed the CCP (see S.A. Smith's 1927 essay in the present volume). Following the advice of the Communist International (Comintern), the Communists shifted to an insurrectionary strategy. The 'Nanchang Uprising' in August and the 'Autumn Harvest Uprising' in September were rapidly crushed by ascendant Nationalists, scattering CCP forces in different directions. Mao Zedong famously established a base in the Jinggang Mountains on the border of Jiangxi and Hunan provinces, while other Communist forces from the Nanchang Uprising ended up briefly in eastern Guangdong before dispersing under attack by a much larger Nationalist army. Among the Communist forces was Peng Pai, a local activist and the son of a landlord from Haifeng. Peng fled to Hong Kong, returning to the newly formed soviet in Haifeng in the middle of November. If the CCP was to survive under these changing political and military conditions, a new social form of political organisation and of relating to the local population was clearly necessary. As a consequence, as it was pushed out of the cities, the Party refocused on the peasants. The Hailufeng Soviet was the first soviet formed in the Chinese Revolution, providing a model for the spread of insurrectionary action and for the transformation of peasant activism into revolutionary power. Soon led by Peng Pai, the soviet would become 'the most radical attack on the rural order until that time'.[3]

The 'Peasant' as a Political Category

The formation of the Hailufeng Soviet was not the beginning of the peasant movement nor even of militant action in the area, as the zone was already considered a model for rural revolution before the soviet was established. The soviet was, in fact, the result of a long series of events and shifting conditions in which Communist politics and forces joined together with peasant activism, with the 'peasant' (农民) becoming a political category in the process. This political category emerged in the context of China's entry into global capitalism, rapid agrarian change, and sharpening political tensions, at a time when rural networks of labour disintegrated or were restructured. The particular socioeconomic conditions of the late-Qing and early Republican periods created a situation in which people like Peng Pai, who had been actively organising peasants in the area since the early 1920s, could see and frame the activity of peasants as a historically significant 'peasant movement' (农民运动). At the same time, peasants in Haifeng came to view the new peasant political organisation as a powerful intervention in the degraded rural power structure that had emerged since the late Qing.

According to historian Robert Marks, peasants were particularly receptive to Peng's radical talk about injustice and oppression because of recent dislocations triggered by China's incorporation into global capitalism and the tensions this caused among the peasantry. 'It took Peng Pai,' Marks states, 'to articulate issues in such a way as to create a new type of social organisation among peasants, clearing the way for collective action along class lines.'[4] Yet Marks argues that we should not use the term 'peasant movement' to describe this struggle even though Peng used the term himself. In Marks's view, peasants had been shaping Haifeng's rural society since the late Ming, and this history is erased by seeing Peng as the creator of a recent 'peasant movement'. In his words: 'Peasants had their own history, forms of organization, goals, and experiences in collective action long before what has been called the "peasant movement" began.'[5]

My purpose in this essay is different. That Peng could see the activity of peasants as a 'peasant movement' was a significant moment in the Chinese historical-political imagination of the peasantry and for the development of the revolution[6]—one shaped both by the political and economic contexts of the time and by the transnational circulation of radical ideas of historical and social change. None of this, of course, should be taken to mean that Peng simply created the peasant actions by naming them a 'movement' or that peasants were not active agents in historical transformation. Rather, this essay stresses that the revolutionary event of the Hailufeng Soviet was the result of the interaction of radical practices both local and external to the Haifeng area, which took place in the economic context produced by China's colonial encounter with capitalism as well as the disintegration of rural governance from the late Qing.

Global Capitalism, Control over the Labour Process, and the Transformation of Rural Governance

The complexity of the economic effects resulting from the incorporation of Chinese peasant labour within global capitalist markets in the late-Qing and early Republican periods is well described by Marks, who argues that, in the late nineteenth century, there was a period of benefit for the peasants of Haifeng County, as they accessed wider markets for their goods.[7] Rural handicraft industries in the area—specifically, sugar refining and cotton spinning and weaving—initially expanded with growing markets. Yet, as the market grew, foreign and domestic merchants increasingly took control over the labour process, bringing about the industrialisation of handicrafts and the emergence of putting-out systems and wage labour. In other words, rural households were losing control of their own labour and becoming more dependent on global capitalist markets. Those markets were transformed over time to the detriment of the Chinese peasantry in the area. In particular, late-Qing peasants who were engaged in raw sugar production for foreign-owned processing factories were especially damaged when, in 1907, the sugar market collapsed because of financial dealings in New York as well as new competition from the Japanese in

Taiwan, the Dutch in Java, and the United States in Cuba and the Philippines. The fact that much of this sugar production was enabled by loans to poor peasants magnified the effects of the market crash, bringing about a concentration of land in the hands of landlords—as noted by Peng—and the predominance of less secure forms of tenancy.[8] In addition, women's sideline work in spinning and weaving was also impaired by the introduction of machine-made yarns at the end of the nineteenth century, dividing labour processes originally integrated within the household, and increasing the dependency of households on expanding markets. By the end of World War I, weaving, too, was concentrated among and done by wage labour. Thus, the restructuring and industrialisation of spinning and weaving resulted in the end of this important handicraft industry among the peasantry of Haifeng.[9] Add to these changes the high inflation of the cost of daily necessities, and increasing rural tensions come into greater focus as rural social relationships and the economy were permanently altered. As Marks concludes: 'Imperialism created the conditions under which collective action along the vertical lines of lineage and Flag would be replaced by collective action along the horizontal lines of social class.'[10]

Other scholars detail a similar trajectory in different regions of China. Kathy Walker describes the transformation of the spinning and weaving industry in the northern Yangzi Delta as a 'semicolonial process' that benefited urban capital at the expense of most peasants.[11] Kamal Sheel argues that the incorporation of rural Jiangxi into global capitalism brought about an increasing vulnerability of the peasantry to 'obscure market forces', an 'agrarian crisis', and the collapse of the moral economy of the peasantry, leading to rural revolution.[12] Like Walker, Sheel views this colonial process as leading to the loss of security in landholding and other rights that peasants had gained from the late Ming on. Sheel finds a trajectory for the spinning and weaving industries in the Xinjiang region of Jiangxi similar to that which Marks finds in Haifeng: local weavers first shifted to machine-made yarn, but then were put out of business by cheaper cloth from the textile industry, bringing about the 'total collapse' of home weaving and 'a massive loss of jobs in rural households'.[13]

Less clearly delineated in the abovementioned texts was the concomitant degradation of rural governance. While late-Qing attempts at modernising rural governance as part of the post-Boxer New Policies had varied effects, in many areas, they led to a breakdown of traditional rural governance as the state put more pressure on peasants to fund modernising projects.[14] This often led to the emergence of 'predatory state brokers', who used their official or semi-official positions to exploit rural residents for personal gain.[15] As Roxann Prazniak argues, the New Policy reforms ended up augmenting the power of the rural elite, compounding the already tense situation in the countryside, and helping to lead to a series of peasant revolts in the last few years of the Qing.[16] Looking at Haifeng, Yuan Gao sees a similar process, arguing that the 'semiformal governance' that grew in rural China from the late Qing and extracted greater resources from the rural population brought about escalating local violence and the rise of revolutionary politics.[17]

Bringing Revolutionary Practices to the Countryside

In the last decade of the Qing, philologist and revolutionary activist Liu Shipei interpreted these local revolts against rural modernisation and China's colonial incorporation into global capitalism as the emergence of a revolutionary peasantry capable of transforming China.[18] During a period of study in Japan from 1917 to 1921, Peng Pai joined a populist socialist group, the Builders' League, and took these insights further as he involved himself in the Japanese peasant movement.[19] The Builders believed the peasantry were the bearers of a natural human cooperative spirit that needed to be mobilised against an invasive capitalist and competitive culture—a position similar to Liu Shipei's radical agrarian humanism.

Carrying the political practices and ideas of the Japanese peasant movement back to Haifeng in 1921, Peng soon threw himself into local politics and education reform.[20] Increasingly believing in the revolutionary overthrow of private property, Peng argued that peasants in Haifeng were getting poorer as land was being concentrated in the hands of landlords.[21] The force of this revolution would be the proletariat—a group that, for Peng, included anyone who did not own property, including most peasants who were not landlords. But that force for revolution—the people—had to be 'awakened' by radical intellectuals.[22] In 1922, a year after his return from Japan and increasing proximity to Marxism, Peng began organising peasant associations to push for rent reduction in Chishan township, Haifeng.

Though Peng was consciously attempting to organise a 'real movement' (实际运动), the idea for a peasant organisation came from peasants themselves.[23] Though initially very small, the peasant association was able to block a local elite from intervening in a minor dispute over the death of a child bride and settle it themselves, thus marginalising the authority of the predatory semiformal power structure. This newly emerging dispute-mediation mechanism, as Gao Yuan argues,

> embodied both the continuity of the Chinese tradition of rural mediation that sought to settle disputes within the community rather than to resort to county courts, as well as modern notions and innovations introduced through revolutionary rural politics, namely that peasant organizations and a class standpoint were to play a pivotal role in rural life.[24]

These early successes in a practical struggle, together with rising local tensions, facilitated the expansion of the peasant association, and, by the end of 1922, Peng estimated that 20,000 households in the county had joined, forming the Haifeng General Peasant Association (海丰县总农民协会) on New Year's Day, 1923. This successful organising effort led Peng to believe he had divided 'the county into two classes: the peasant and the landlord'.[25]

This initial organising effort ended in repression, but Peng returned to this work again in 1924, when the Nationalist–CCP alliance and the focus on the Northern Expedition helped create a climate more open to such work. Peng, who was now a CCP member, joined the Nationalists and began to work as secretary of the peasant department and principal of the Peasant Movement Training Institute (later taken over by Mao), graduating hundreds of peasant organisers. As the Nationalists moved towards expanding their control in southern and eastern China from 1925, Peng led peasant resistance in Haifeng and reorganised peasant associations there, gaining nearly 200,000 members by 1926.[26] With conflicts between peasant associations and the local elite growing in number and intensity, the associations formed 'peasant self-defence corps' (农民自卫军) and carried out rent-reduction campaigns.[27] As elites fled, landownership by landlords decreased dramatically. The peasant associations had effectively taken over rural governance, sidelining the local predatory brokers and elite power structure that had sedimented since the late Qing.

As peasant demands radicalised, they outpaced the tamer proposals of the CCP.[28] As the Nationalists moved further to the right, more clearly condemning class struggle, the CCP vacillated over whether it should represent peasant interests and take a more formal leadership role in peasant organisations. With the Nationalists controlling Guangdong in

1926, the peasant movement there came under increased repression and was no longer seen as necessary to the national revolution. As a result of its increasing marginalisation, Peng lost his argument within the CCP for a heightened role for the Party in peasant work in Guangdong; conversely, the peasant movement in Hunan received support as it was on the Northern Expedition's planned route, and Mao was made the head of the Central Committee's new peasant department, penning his famous 1927 report on the peasant movement in Hunan soon after. Peng would publicly refute the CCP, coming to the conclusion, as Marks argues, 'that the large cities had become centres of reaction, while the countryside was the only place keeping the revolution alive'.[29] In effect, Peng's connections with an organised peasant force collided with the Party's historical teleology, which suggested that the national and anti-feudal revolution was the current political task and that the land revolution should be put off to the future.[30]

The Soviet and Its Defeat

While the Nationalists had made instrumental use of mass organisations, especially the peasant movement, during its Northern Expedition, once in Shanghai in April 1927, Chiang Kai-shek turned on the mass movements and, from then, relied primarily on military means for reunifying China. Out of the chaos into which CCP strategy was thrown, the peasant movement and the attempt to transform rural social relations reemerged. With peasant and Communist control of Haifeng from 1 November 1927, the newly formed Haifeng Provisional Revolutionary Government went about transforming the county by wiping out landlord power. Many landlords fled; others were caught and executed. Rents and debts were quickly abolished, elections were held for an assembly, and the Hailufeng Soviet was officially proclaimed at a massive meeting led by Peng Pai. At the time, the Party saw the soviet as a transitional political form through which the democratic revolution could be turned into a socialist one.[31]

Once formed, the revolutionary government, unofficially led by Peng, shifted to carrying out a land revolution—a task far more difficult than Party leaders initially assumed. Deciding how to define landlords, how to establish who should get land, and how to reallocate land was not easy, and, in the end, the county leadership only promulgated general guidelines, leaving most details up to individual village peasant associations. By the end of January 1928, the process was considered complete, if uneven.³² This unevenness was a symptom of how pivotal village power structures were to the land revolution, as peasant activists attempted to transform the local balance of class forces, leading to different outcomes in different areas. Nonetheless, Hailufeng provided the Party with a model for intervening in the degraded structure of rural governance and the weakening economic environment—a model that grew out of particular local circumstances, though the forces impinging on the area were global. Top-down approaches to understanding this revolution fail to account for the power of local peasant activists, yet, in the end, this power could only be sustained as long as the military power of the Nationalists was focused elsewhere, as it largely had been until early 1928.

This revolutionary process was dramatically cut short. After the Communists attempted to spread soviet control to neighbouring counties, and with Peng outside Haifeng, the Nationalists invaded at the end of February. As conscription efforts failed and the county town was initially abandoned, the Communists attempted to maintain control in the villages. But this time, they failed in the countryside as well, and the Nationalists and their local supporters regained control. New land deeds were written for returning landlords, and the soviet and peasant associations were defeated. After fighting in the area for a few months, Peng was moved to work underground as a Communist organiser in Shanghai, but he was betrayed and killed at the end of August 1929.³³

1928

By the early 1920s, China had more than 200,000 women workers, mostly concentrated in the textile mills and tobacco factories in the Yangzi River Delta. Far from being passive, these women workers repeatedly staged strikes and protests to demand higher wages, shorter working hours and better labour conditions. This posed a conundrum for the newly established Chinese Communist Party (CCP): were female workers supposed to have their own dedicated organisations? Or were they to be subsumed in class-based trade unions that paid no attention to gender distinctions? After initial hesitations, in 1923, the Party passed a motion that made it explicit that women workers' movements should not be separated from the labour movement at large. To build their base, prominent female Party members such as Xiang Jingyu and Yang Zhihua went to work on the shop floor, building workers' schools and leading strikes themselves. Despite the tragic interruption of their work in the wake of the breakdown of the First United Front between Communists and Nationalists in 1927, these early efforts laid the foundation for women-work in factories when the CCP returned to the cities after taking power in the 1940s. Starting from Xiang Jingyu's tragic execution on 1 May 1928, this essay looks back at the CCP's engagements with women workers in those momentous years.

Feminist Agitation inside Chinese Factories
Yige DONG

At dawn on 1 May 1928, thirty-three-year-old Xiang Jingyu was publicly executed by the police of the Nationalist Government in Hankou. According to witnesses' recollections, on her way to the execution ground, Xiang shouted revolutionary slogans at the huge crowd that had gathered. As one of the earliest members of the Chinese Communist Party (CCP) and the inaugural head of the Party's Women's Department, Xiang's martyrdom marked the end of the earliest feminist initiatives within the CCP.

In recent assessments of the CCP's gender politics during revolutionary times, the consensus is that, in general, the Chinese Communists subsumed gender issues under the imperative of a masculine class politics.[1] Evidence of this includes the CCP's overall hostility towards 'bourgeois feminism' and autonomous women's organisations, as well as the marginalisation of women leaders within the Party. Despite the persistent struggles and calculated manoeuvres of Communist feminists, the Party to this day has remained male-centred and has displayed, overall, a strong masculinist, misogynist culture. However, by revisiting the literature on the earliest interaction between labour activism and the CCP's 'women-work' (妇女工作), this essay brings to light a more ambiguous and contested relationship between gender and class politics during the communist revolution. Following Delia Davin, I use 'women-work' instead of 'women's work' in translating 妇女工作, which covers all sorts of activities the CCP sponsored to empower women, including revolutionary struggle, production, legal reform, literacy and hygiene campaigns, and so on.[2] This essay seeks to elucidate how political processes, especially those involving women revolutionaries, were deeply intertwined with individual agency and contingency—hardly fitting into teleological narratives featured either in the Party's official accounts or in some recent popular discussions.

An Inclusive Feminist Agenda within the Party

On its establishment in 1919—mainly thanks to German Marxist feminist Clara Zetkin's efforts—the Communist International (Comintern) requested its branches in each country set up a women's bureau and recruit proletarian women to join the Communist-led unions. While the first congress of the CCP in 1921, an all-male event, could only briefly comment on the general principles of women-work, at this incipient stage, the Party maintained a much more inclusive attitude towards independent feminist movements than it would in later periods.[3] In Beijing, Miao Boying had been active in Marxist study groups since 1919 and became the first woman to join the Party, in July 1921. Later, in 1922, Miao and her colleagues formed the Women's Rights League (女权运动同盟会), an organisation that sought to compete with the liberal-leaning Women's Suffrage Association (女子参政协进会) to broaden the latter's suffragist agenda by transforming gender relations in all sectors such as legal equality in marriage, equal pay, paid maternity leave and women's access to all educational institutions.[4]

In Shanghai, although she was not counted as a formal member in the first Party congress, Wang Huiwu, the wife of founding Party member Li Da, took care of the logistics of the meeting and was entrusted with developing the CCP's women's program together with Gao Junman, the wife of Chen Duxiu, the General Secretary of the CCP from 1921 to 1927. At the same time, in the autumn of 1922, along with a fellow feminist named Wang Yizhi, Wang Huiwu also worked on cultivating informal ties with prominent women activists outside the Party, including women in the Nationalist Party (Guomindang, or GMD) and Young Women's Christian Association (YWCA) activists who specialised in labour conditions and taught at the CCP-sponsored Shanghai Pingmin Girls' School.

It is worth noting that this strategy of reaching out to women's rights groups with different political backgrounds was far from a universally endorsed strategy within the Party in this period. While these women's vocal claims and Wang Huiwu's anarchist tendencies encountered strong resistance and attacks from male feminist Party members such as Mao Dun and Chen Wangdao, others were more supportive. Chief among them was Li Dazhao, then head of the CCP's Beijing branch, who maintained that 'as long as China is under warlord control, all civil rights groups of this type essentially promote the interests of the public and should be supported'.[5] He advocated for women's rights organisations, whether under the rubric of the Women's Rights League or the Women's Suffrage Association, to be established in every province in China.

Non-Communist Mobilisations of Women inside Factories

The early 1920s also saw the culmination of the first wave of industrial labour activism in Chinese history, in which women workers played a crucial role. As the CCP had just been established in Shanghai, local Communists considered linking up with women workers to be a great opportunity to build up their base and strengthen their forces.

To be sure, women workers had protested and joined strikes as industrialisation began in China in the late nineteenth century. Concentrated in the silk, cotton and tobacco industries, women became the bulk of the labour force and frequently participated in episodes of labour unrest. For example, in Shanghai, the first recorded women's strike took place in 1894 as textile workers in Yangshupu District protested against a pay cut—a mobilisation that ended with eight of them being arrested.[6] In August 1911, 2,000 women from four silk filatures went on strike, asking for a raise—and were successful. In May 1912, the Shanghai Women Silk Workers' Association (上海缫丝女工同仁会), the first proto-union for Shanghai filature workers, was founded, with a strong focus on upgrading women workers' low skills as a means to protect their jobs. In the summer of 1917, more than 1,000 women workers in the British American Tobacco Company (BAT) went on a strike that lasted several weeks to push back against pay cuts, which was followed by another, three-day strike by 1,000 women workers in the Japanese-owned Nikka Spinning Company. Both strikes ended with the factory owners partially compromising.[7] Overall, from 1895 to 4 May 1919, it was estimated that there were no fewer than fifty-seven strikes in which women were the main participants.[8]

Workers' activism in this period was mostly defensive rather than an offensive strategy born of class consciousness. In most cases, their mobilisations were facilitated by native-place associations and gangs, and their demands revolved around higher wages, shorter hours, better working conditions and more employment opportunities. This is why, when both the Nationalists and the Communists tried to mobilise them to unionise— which inevitably disrupted production, not necessarily resulting in gains and oftentimes causing a backlash—many women workers initially saw 'unionisation' as the cause of rather than the solution to their problems.⁹

Women workers' struggle peaked in 1922. According to available data, that year more than 30,000 women workers went on strike eighteen times in about sixty factories in Shanghai, Hubei and Guangdong.¹⁰ The most notable strike was in August, when more than 10,000 women workers from the Shanghai Zhabei Silk Factory went on strike for ten days, demanding higher wages, shorter hours and the right to establish an independent, women-only union, the so-called Shanghai Women's Industrial Progress Union (SWIPU, 上海女子工业进德会).¹¹ However, this union was not a spontaneous creation of the silk workers but was organised by Mu Zhiying, a female gangster from the Subei region who had the support of a gang and was backed by assemblymen who were also from Subei and were filature owners themselves.

Having just passed the 'Resolution on the Women's Movement' (关于妇女运动的决议) at the Second Congress of the CCP a month earlier, Communist leaders regarded the strike in August 1922 as a milestone in Shanghai's labour history, and male feminists such as Shao Lizi started to write extensively about the event.¹² However, interestingly, no-one within the CCP at the time of the strike was able to make real connections with the women workers on the ground. This was mainly because at the time, the CCP's women's program was undergoing a major leadership transition, from Wang Huiwu to Xiang Jingyu, and they did not have spare capacity to build ties inside the factories.

Xiang Jingyu's United-Front Approach

A member of the New Citizen's Study Society (新民学会) that was co-founded by Mao Zedong in Hunan Province in 1918, Xiang had sailed to France in December 1919 with her fellow Hunanese Cai Hesen, Cai Chang and their mother, Ge Jianhao. In France, Xiang and Cai Hesen formed the 'Xiang–Cai Alliance' (向蔡同盟), a new form of marriage based on revolutionary romance. The couple and their fellow students— including Li Lisan, who in the following years would become one of the most prominent Chinese labour leaders (see Perry's essay in the present volume)—studied French and Marxist theories while actively taking part in the struggle for the rights of Chinese student-workers being waged at that time. Their political activism so upset French authorities that it led to their deportation in September 1921. On returning to China in December that year, the couple settled in Shanghai, joining the CCP's bourgeoning Shanghai branch.

At that time, Wang Huiwu had just started publishing the Marxist feminist journal *Women's Voices* (妇女声). Originally, Xiang did not show interest in dedicating herself to the Party's women-work and in fact kept her distance from Wang's projects. Xiang's writing during this period was mainly focused on China's national liberation. However, at the Second Party Congress in 1922, Wang's husband, Li Da, failed to be reelected and his position was taken over by Cai Hesen. It was believed that Xiang's appointment as the inaugural head of the Women's Department was partly due to the fact that she was Cai Hesen's spouse. However, even after taking over the leadership of the Women's Department, Xiang remained ambivalent about involving herself in women-work.[13]

Having assumed this leadership role quite abruptly and facing a host of preexisting organisations that were already organising women in the factories, including native-place associations, gangs and the YMCA, Xiang found it difficult to penetrate the shop floor. The most noticeable connection between Xiang and female labour activism at this stage was a few articles Xiang wrote in the autumn of 1923, praising the Zhabei strike of the previous year, supporting a detained silk worker in the SWIPU and calling for feminist associations in Shanghai to support women workers.

The turning point in her engagement with women-work came at the Third Party congress in the summer of 1923. The bloody 7 February Incident earlier that year had dampened prospects for the Communists' ambition to launch a workers' revolution (see Luo's essay in the present volume). In despair, the CCP accepted the Comintern's proposal to form an alliance with the GMD, which came to be known as the first GMD–CCP Cooperation (国共合作) or the First United Front (统一战线). It was in this context that Xiang Jingyu shifted her attitude about taking charge of the Women's Department. Maintaining strong nationalist sentiments that she had acquired while growing up in Hunan and then studying in France, Xiang was pleased to see that the Party had finally committed itself to promoting a national revolution. Now, she could begin women-work in earnest, focusing especially on strengthening ties with independent feminist groups.[14]

It was through the United Front that Xiang showed her political vision and talent in advancing women's rights. From the Third Congress of the CCP until mid-1925, utilising the resources of the GMD to consolidate her own program, she channelled an extraordinary amount of energy into establishing the foundation for a broad-based women's movement. Although Xiang had a record of criticising women's suffrage movements, she still acknowledged the importance and legitimacy of these struggles. To her, the only way to develop a mass movement truly for women was to integrate the struggles of feminist groups with those of workers.

Communists Making Inroads Among Women Workers

During this period of cooperation between the CCP and the GMD (1924–27), Communist organisers were able to make significant inroads among women workers and cultivate a number of Communist women labour leaders. Much of the credit goes to Yang Zhihua, then a sociology student enrolled at the CCP-sponsored Shanghai University, who, after 1949, would become the architect of women-work within the All-China Federation of Trade Unions (ACFTU, 中华全国总工会).[15] Since being recruited by Xiang in 1924, Yang had put great effort into establishing links with the women workers at the BAT factories by fully immersing herself in the workers' daily lives, taking time to befriend them and 'even adopting their style of dress'.[16] Yang and her colleagues also taught literacy classes in working-class neighbourhoods during this period.

Having gained the trust and respect of these female tobacco workers, Yang mobilised a large number of them to join the general strike in the wake of the May Thirtieth Incident of 1925 (see Leong's essay in the present volume) and serve as propagandists for the cause. By September 1925, the number of women recruits into the Party had risen sharply to about 1,000—ten times the number before the May Thirtieth Incident. The following year, this organising effort eventually facilitated the demise of the power base of gangster Mu Zhiying among women silk workers, signalling that the CCP was finally making inroads into social space previously dominated by gang societies.[17]

Xiang's Final Years and Legacy

In October 1925, three years after the first leadership transition, the CCP's Women's Department was shaken up again, as Xiang Jingyu and Cai Hesen were sent to Moscow for a study trip and Yang Zhihua became deputy head. Xiang's abrupt departure was due to personal reasons that were inevitably entangled with political power plays. In late 1925, she started a relationship with Peng Shuzhi, then an important theorist in the Party and later an exile and leader of the Fourth International. The Party stepped in to save the endangered relationship by sending Xiang and Cai away from Shanghai. Despite the Party's efforts, they divorced in Moscow in 1926.

When Xiang returned from Moscow in early 1927, Yang Zhihua had already become the *de facto* head of the Women's Department, and Xiang was instead assigned to work in the Party committee in Hubei Province, based in Wuhan. In Shanghai, Yang continued mobilising women workers until the 12 April Incident, when the GMD started to brutally purge Communists nationwide (see S.A. Smith's essay in the present volume).[18] In July the same year, when attacks on the Communists reached their peak in Wuhan and the local Party branch was forced to relocate, Xiang insisted on staying. Xiang and another Communist, Xia Minghan, were arrested by the police in March 1928, and her public execution on 1 May served as a final testimony that the heyday of mass women's movements in Chinese urban areas had ended.

It was not until the late 1940s that the Communist Party returned to the cities and resumed its women-work by establishing the All-China Democratic Women's Federation (ACDWF, 中华全国民主妇联), in 1949. This new mass organisation was originally designed as a united-front organisation, serving to liaise between women across all social sectors—an approach that resembled Xiang Jingyu's vision of woman-work. Also in 1949, after two decades of tumultuous trajectories in her personal and political life, Yang Zhihua became the inaugural head of the Women's Department of the ACFTU. Thanks to her earlier experience in the Shanghai factories, Yang maintained a close relationship with workers on the ground and designed policies that were based on firsthand observations and were highly beneficial to the workers, such as the 'Regulations on Protections for Women Workers' (女工保护条例) of 1953, which included fifty-six days of paid maternity leave, employer-sponsored childcare services and other benefits.

Some Lessons

By restoring agency to these feminist members in the CCP and revealing both the structural limitations to and the historical contingency conditioning their fates, this essay makes two interventions in our current discussion about gender and labour politics in this period. First, I suggest that the CCP in its earliest days took the issue of women workers seriously not only because it was ingrained in Marxist dogma, but also because women made up a substantial portion of the industrial working class and, therefore, were crucial to the CCP's base-building efforts. Despite the disappointing and tragic results, these earlier mobilisations and the organisational infrastructure that was built for this purpose shaped the nature of the CCP's later women-work. It was only after 1957 that the feminist mass-line umbrella organisation of the ACDWF was completely subjugated to the Party's absolute authority.[19]

Second, while it has been well recognised that the CCP subsumed gender issues under the imperative of a masculine class politics, I highlight that, in its incipient stage of development, feminist causes did not always toe the class line. Women-work led by Xiang and her colleagues in fact recognised the importance of building a coalition with women in all social sectors and dedicated much effort to networking with them—a strategy that was largely made possible by the cooperation between the CCP and the GMD but unfortunately ended with the collapse of that fragile alliance.

1929

After the breakdown of the First United Front in April 1927, the regime of the Nationalist Party (Guomindang, or GMD) unleashed a wave of terror that eliminated almost all labour activism in the cities under its control. As the Communists fled to the countryside and guerrilla bases and were no longer viable opponents in labour politics, gangster-controlled unions took over. At the same time, the Nationalist administration proposed a raft of progressive labour and industrial legislation, including the eight-hour working day, the prohibition on employing children under fourteen, and guidelines for safety in the workplace and welfare facilities. The expectation was that workers, placated by these concessions, would swear absolute political allegiance to the GMD. Despite this wager, Chinese industrial workers did not lose their penchant for activism. Although not politically militant as before, labour protests kept occurring in Chinese factories—in particular, around issues related to food prices and subsidies, as Shanghai would discover in 1929, in the wake of an intolerable increase in rice prices.

Striking for Rice: The Struggle for the 'Rice Allowance' in Republican China
Seung-Joon LEE

Chiang Kai-shek's military coup in April 1927 was a turning point in Chinese labour history (see S.A. Smith's 1927 essay in the present volume). In the following decade, the regime of the Nationalist Party (Guomindang, or GMD) secured control over most of China's industrial heartland through the middle and lower Yangzi areas and, in the process, eliminated almost all of the labour activism in the cities. In Shanghai, the Communists were no longer meaningful political opponents of the regime, at least in the arena of labour politics, as they fled to the countryside and guerrilla bases. Gangster-controlled yellow unionism dominated labour politics in the city.[1] However, this is not to suggest that Chinese industrial workers lost their political presence and became subservient to regime-sponsored thugs. Labour unrest, if not militant, never ceased as the fluctuation of food prices constantly haunted the Chinese economy, situating food at the centre of labour politics in industrial China in the 1930s. Inflation and the subsequent rise in the cost of living were what united workers at the point of consumption, rather than production. While Chinese workers in the workplace were divided by skill, gender, and native place belonging, as consumers, they all suffered from highly volatile rice prices in the marketplace.

Food-related labour disputes were seemingly apolitical as they appeared to be limited to the domain of 'economic struggle', without developing into class consciousness and political militancy. For that very reason, however, the issue of food prices provided historical actors with more latitude to play a new game. For GMD authorities and 'yellow union' (黄色工会) leaders, offering food-related benefits was a comparatively straightforward measure to ameliorate worker discontent. However, the volatility of global food prices and its effect on domestic markets prevented GMD-style labour management from providing minimum benefits to the workers in the name of Sun Yat-sen's 'Principle of People's Livelihood' while eradicating Communist influences. Instead, the workers' growing distress provided an opportunity for the Communists to realise—if belatedly—the political potential of food issues.[2] Industrial workers ushered in a new phase of industrial food politics.

The Genesis of the 'Rice Allowance'

The labour policies advanced by the Nationalist Party entailed much more than violent suppression of labour activism. By initiating a series of labour and industry legislation that incorporated many progressive elements, the Nationalists demonstrated their eagerness to expedite state-led labour reform. The Factory Law that took effect in 1929, for example, stipulated working days of no more than eight hours, prohibited the employment of children under fourteen, and provided guidelines for safety in the workplace and welfare facilities, including dormitories, factory canteens, and clinics.[3] In return for these material benefits, the GMD demanded from workers absolute political allegiance. The GMD also took particular pride in the self-proclaimed success of labour-favoured arbitrations, at the centre of which was the unique presence of the 'rice allowance' or 'rice voucher' (米贴)—a compensation voucher that many industrial plants offered to their workers who could not afford to buy a minimum amount of staple food.

The GMD authorities preferred the rice allowance to wage increases for several reasons. They placed the rice allowance issue in the category of 'treatment' (待遇), separated from the category of wage, which was the most common cause of labour disputes at that time. The rice allowance was a temporary additional payment when rice prices rose over a certain amount and was supposed to cease when prices returned to normal levels. In keeping with the Party's paternalistic attitude promoted by its 'founding father', Sun Yat-sen, the rice allowance solved workers' immediate food security issues without constituting a large and permanent financial burden on employers. Having witnessed various 'rice strikes' in the 1920s, GMD leaders concluded that the granting of a rice allowance was an effective tool for ending labour disputes caused by the inflation of rice prices. However, if a deal was not reached, a broader mobilisation by the workers usually ensued.[4]

The authorities' dispensation of the rice allowance generally had a successful outcome for the workers. In 1930, for example, of eighty-seven labour disputes in which the Shanghai Municipal Bureau of Social Affairs intervened, approximately 10 percent fell under the category of 'treatment', including those related to the rice allowance. Unlike other controversies, all nine disputes in this category ended with complete or partial approval of workers' demands.[5] According to historian Peng Guizhen, who researched sixteen labour disputes over the rice allowance in the Shanghai cotton textile industry during the Nanjing Decade (1927–37), only two cases were rejected by management, while in ten cases, management accepted the workers' rice allowance demands either entirely or partially.[6] Employers also preferred the rice allowance to wage increases. Paying the rice allowance for a designated period was much cheaper than installing new canteen facilities, which, given the perennial problem of lack of space caused by population density and the high price of land in Shanghai, would entail enormous costs. Furthermore, offering a rice allowance only when it was necessary effectively dampened the workers' outrage as much as spikes in food prices easily stoked it.

This is not to say that the rice allowance—a tiny benefit—was given to workers as a purely benevolent act. It was a concession born of a series of fierce contentions between the rapidly politicising workers and management. In other words, the rice allowance was the most notable consequence of the militant labour strikes that took place in the 1920s. This concession took numerous forms. Some companies offered it in cash—usually no more than a few coppers. In most cases, however, payment was through a type of voucher. Workers were given a small piece of paper on which was written 'rice allowance' when they left the factory at the end of the workday that they could redeem in small neighbouring shops. Although both the amount and the quality of rice hinged on workers' political leverage, many companies tried to define the standard grade and maximum amount of rice, granting an average of 'five *sheng* [升] of rice'.[7]

The British American Tobacco Company was the first business to introduce a set of rice allowances for its workers, in 1920.[8] Far from being moved by purely altruistic reasons, management carefully used the allowance to improve labour discipline in the workplace—for instance, by granting it to workers on the condition that the recipient would not be absent from work for more than two days in a month.[9] If the management of British American Tobacco first introduced the rice allowance as a managerial technique, the labour union at the Commercial Press (商务印书馆) elaborated it as a labour entitlement through a series of struggles. Organised largely by skilled male workers, such as typesetters, printers, and mechanics, this union played a pioneering role in framing the issue of rice subsidies on the grounds that constantly rising rice prices caused suffering for hardworking families.[10] Though it has been marginalised in the Chinese Communist Party's official narrative of the May Thirtieth

Movement for its purely 'economic' character, the Commercial Press union's first 'rice allowance' strike in 1925 had significant repercussions for labour politics in subsequent years.

In the summer of 1925, the employees of the Commercial Press complained about the mismanagement of rice subsidies, which amounted to two dollars a month for workers whose wages were no more than fifteen dollars. However, payment was not guaranteed: managers arbitrarily deducted the amount, for example, when workers were too sick to show up at work; factory supervisors often embezzled the allocated budget for workers' rice subsidies; and management, workers claimed, also discriminated against female workers by paying lower amounts for their subsidy.[11] When the Commercial Press workers went on strike in August 1925, the management's first response was intransigence. The riot police were called and arrested sixteen union leaders, three of whom were prosecuted. In response, 300 workers went on strike to demand the release of the union leaders. This time, the management took a more conciliatory stance and, once the negotiation began, settlements were achieved quickly, including an improved rice subsidy scheme, together with a wage increase and work-hour reduction.[12] Afterwards, the rice allowance deal the Commercial Press union made became something of a normative precedent in Shanghai's industrial scene.

The Fate of a Conciliatory Benefit

Having successfully dampened labour militancy by 1927, the Shanghai industrialists found plenty of ways to dilute their commitment to paying the rice allowances. Their strategies included manipulating the price and lowering the grade of standard rice, and limiting who was eligible for the allowance. Underneath the self-laudatory facade of the GMD labour arbitration system, some workers complained that the GMD-controlled labour unions took on only 'light issues, while eschewing heavy ones' (避重就轻), such as 'demands to improve life and treatment' (改善生活待遇的要求).[13] Whether the GMD-style yellow unionism would succeed hinged on the fluctuation of rice prices in the marketplace. The regime's early successes soon gave way to a backlash.

Shanghai saw an unusual increase in rice prices in 1929. Shanghai rice consumers—both the haves and the have-nots—knew they needed to provision themselves for the period of rice scarcity that usually spanned from rice planting time in early May to harvesting in September.[14]

As the market price showed no sign of descending even after autumn came, however, a panic occurred. Average prices continued to grow until the end of the year, when they reached a level nearly 75 percent higher than usual.[15] This pressure opened a crack in the GMD's dominance of labour politics. Even labour unions under GMD control petitioned the local authorities to devise mechanisms for price control, as many members complained they could not make end meets with the conventional level of the rice allowance granted through arbitration by the GMD authorities.[16] In October, the press workers' union publicly requested an increase in the rice allowance, and many other unions followed suit.[17] Demands for the rice allowance across industries turned into a tremendous financial and political burden for company management and the GMD authorities. This was the beginning of what the Communists retrospectively dubbed the 'struggle for the rice allowance' (米贴斗争).[18]

Yellow Unionism in Crisis

To make matters worse for the GMD, yellow unions turned into hotbeds of Communist subversion. Many yellow union leaders were not necessarily GMD loyalists but, as historian Brian Martin has argued, they preferred reformist tactics to secure a 'legitimate place for organized labour in the GMD polity'.[19] Underground Communist cadres seized the opportunity presented by popular discontent over rice allowances to infiltrate the Nationalist-led union movement. An underground cadre named Ren Bishi argued that the revolutionary cause should not abandon yellow unions, as 'many yellow unions were organised by workers themselves to protect their economic interests'.[20] A series of strikes over the rice allowance that culminated in 1930 constituted a profound crisis for the yellow unionism of the GMD.

It all started with a strike related to the rice allowance at the French Tramways Union in the summer of 1930—an event that lasted 54 days and became the focal point for labour politics in Shanghai's French Concession and beyond.[21] This mobilisation also shook the dominance in the French Concession of the Green Gang—the secret society that had played a fundamental role in supporting Chiang Kai-shek's crackdown on red unions in Shanghai in 1927. Contemporaries dubbed Du Yuesheng, the Green Gang boss, the 'Al Capone of the French Concession', describing his ability to manipulate labour as 'a combination of Al Capone and Rockefeller'.[22] The leader of this strike, Xu Amei, was one of the few

Communist labour activists who insisted on the need to promote the workers' economic interests to broaden support for the Communist cause among the Chinese working class, regardless of whether the workers were Communist sympathisers or scabs. Xu opted for a slowdown rather than an immediate strike—a tactic that enticed a broader number of workers into the mobilisation while not giving the management an excuse to call the riot police.[23] To end the prolonged stalemate, Du had no choice but to yield his private money to pay off significant portions of the $300,000 settlement, although nobody knows how his money was utilised.[24]

The French Tramways Union struggle ignited a series of strikes over the rice allowance across industries, genders, and skill levels. A few weeks afterwards, workers at the Wing On Textile No. 2 Factory—mostly female and unskilled—demanded payment of the allowance. Although the management refused on the grounds that there was no precedent in a textile business owned by Chinese, before tensions could escalate to an explosive point, the Municipal Bureau of Social Affairs intervened in arbitration. After arbitration, the management agreed to purchase rice at thirteen dollars per dan—five dollars less than the market price at that time—to provide a 'rice allowance' to the workers.[25] The rule was that those who worked at least four days at the factory could claim a rice voucher equivalent to one dollar; those who worked more than nine days could claim two vouchers; and those who worked more than a month could claim four vouchers. There was no stipulated agreement on the grade of rice, and workers had no choice but to purchase rice as arranged by the management. Furthermore, this was in-kind aid, and was therefore not very helpful for those who did not cook their own meals.[26]

This partial victory for management is not the end of the story. Like a chain reaction, shortly afterwards, workers in Japanese-owned textile companies in Pudong, an industrial district notorious for being a Green Gang stronghold, began a series of disputes over the rice allowance.[27] Although such strikes might seem trivial, they nonetheless cast a portentous shadow over the fragile labour regime imposed by the GMD, reliant as it was on yellow unionism and the informal alliance with gangsters.

1938

After the high tide of the mid-1920s, the labour movement in Hong Kong entered a low ebb. In the wake of the Great Strike and Boycott of 1925 and 1926, the British colonial authorities increased their repression of labour activism and other expressions of social discontent. With trade unions effectively outlawed, the Illegal Strikes and Lockouts Ordinance of 1927 succeeded in eradicating collective labour action. The 1930s witnessed the rise of two interwoven movements: a citywide mobilisation for national salvation and a concurrent resurgence of labour activism. This essay looks into how the convergence of these two movements eventually rekindled Hong Kong's labour movement.

Resurgence of Labour Activism in Prewar Hong Kong

LU Yan

One day in early October 1938, a quiet meeting of three young men took place in a small apartment at Hung Hom, across Victoria Harbour from Hong Kong Island. Liao Chengzhi (1908–83), the oldest of the three, had been in Hong Kong for only ten months since his appointment to lead the semi-open Eighth Route Army Liaison Office in January. The other two, Zeng Sheng (1910–95) and Wu Youheng (1913–94), were still in their twenties but had spent years in Hong Kong, during which they had become secret members of the Chinese Communist Party (CCP). A Party directive had come through Liao's radio transmitter, urging them to develop guerrilla resistance against the Japanese occupation of South China. During that meeting, they reached the conclusion that Wu's responsibility for more than 600 Party members in the colony should keep him in Hong Kong, while Zeng, a native of the East River basin, was better suited for leading armed resistance there.[1]

Later that month, more than 120 young workers and students left a Hong Kong that was still safe and peaceful. They travelled alone or in small groups to Pingshan, Zeng Sheng's hometown, some thirty miles (forty-eight kilometres) north of the British colony. Most would be working among villagers as 'people's motivators' (民运员), operating as a civilian front for the new guerrilla force.[2] About thirty took up arms and fought on the battlefield. Coming from Hong Kong's factories and schools, these initial participants would form the core of the East River Column (东江纵队), as this new guerrilla force came to be known after 1943.

This meeting occurred at a pivotal moment for the colony's resurgent labour activism. Through the 1930s, Hong Kong witnessed two interwoven movements—a citywide mobilisation for national salvation and the resurgence of labour activism—in which Zeng and Wu emerged as leaders. As the two movements converged, they rekindled a once-vibrant tradition from the previous decade, which had made Hong Kong the leader of China's labour movement. If the rendezvous of the trio was to bring labour activism in Hong Kong to a new frontier, their planning for future battles was only the logical outcome of political developments that had taken place throughout the decade.

From Trading Post to Industrial Centre

In 1931, Hong Kong entered its tenth decade under British rule. Built on the nearly absolute power of the London-appointed governor and sustained by evolving legal institutions, the colonial system appeared to be more secure than ever. Repression of labour activism and social discontent attained a new level of comprehensiveness in the wake of the Great Strike and Boycott of 1925–26 (see Leong's essay in the present volume). Labour unions were outlawed. The Illegal Strikes and Lockouts Ordinance of 1927 effectively put an end to all collective labour action. The Chinese business elite, who had traditionally collaborated with the British administration, drummed up a 'red scare' in local newspapers and generated a political climate that stigmatised social and political protest.[3] Although Communists found in Hong Kong a temporary safe haven after 1927, when the White Terror swept the mainland, they were quickly caught by the police and deported over the border to Guangdong, where they were tried and executed. By the early 1930s, the Communist organisation in Hong Kong was crushed.[4]

Beneath its seeming quiescence, Hong Kong was on the brink of profound transformations. The sixth decennial census, conducted in 1931, noted for the first time that the number of people employed in manufacturing surpassed those engaged in trade, commerce, insurance, and banking.[5] A new industrial area emerged in Shaukiwan, the northeastern part of Hong Kong Island. Across Victoria Harbour to the north, far more factories and workshops were being erected on the Kowloon Peninsula. Leading this industrial expansion were mostly Chinese-owned light industries producing for distant markets. As war ravaged the mainland through the decade, more and more factories, especially those in Shanghai, chose to move south to Hong Kong in the hope of gaining protection under the British flag. Quantitatively, Chinese-owned factories were more numerous, yet often smaller in size than the European firms that continued to dominate the economy.

As Hong Kong transitioned from trading post to industrial centre, it attracted more people from neighbouring Guangdong Province, as well as from Fujian, Guangxi, and other provinces further north. More Shanghai workers relocated to Hong Kong when their factories opened branches there. Wages varied and could be as high as HK$150 per month for a skilled artisan or as low as HK$13 for a male labourer. The average wage for skilled workers was between HK$30 and HK$45, but female workers—predominant in light industry—were paid by piece rate and received only between HK$6 and HK$15 a month. Since a large proportion of their income had to be spent on food, nearly all workers had no choice but to live in subdivided apartments. Usually, those with family rented 'cubicles' whereas single workers squeezed themselves into 'bedspaces' or even shared a bedspace with their mother or sworn sister.[6]

Regardless of the distance from their point of origin or the length they lived there, workers in Hong Kong never thought they belonged to the colony. They were the so-called internal migrants who were merely following a time-honoured survival strategy in China.[7] They never considered themselves as Hong Kongers, only mere sojourners. A telling indication of this mentality can be found in the way these Chinese named their native-place associations and other mutual help organisations, which often carried the phrase 'sojourning in Hong Kong' (侨港).[8] The hearts and minds of Chinese workers in Hong Kong were always, in life and death, homebound.[9]

A Patriotic Resurgence

Towards the end of the 1920s, Chinese in Hong Kong reacted with alarm and anger to Japan's first major military move against China. In 1928, the massacre of 2,000 Chinese civilians by Japanese marines in Jinan, Shandong Province, made headlines in Hong Kong. Newspapers controlled by the merchant elite, particularly the *Wah Kiu Yat Po* (华侨日报, *Overseas Chinese Daily*) and *Kung Sheung Yat Po* (工商日报, *Industrial and Commercial Daily*), gave the event extensive coverage for weeks. In defiance of colonial law, some unusually brave Chinese gave public speeches on the streets calling for mass protests against the Japanese invasion. They were quickly arrested, fined, and sentenced to hard labour. These flashes of protest became preludes to a sustained movement. In September 1931, just a few days after the outbreak of the Manchurian Incident, tens of thousands of Chinese in Hong Kong responded with huge rallies in assembly halls and on the streets. These peaceful protests turned violent during a mass rally in downtown Wanchai, when a few Japanese sneered at the crowd. Protesting Chinese clashed with the police who had been called in to stop the disorder. As protests spread throughout the colony, the government found the police inadequate to quell the disturbance and mobilised regular troops to maintain order.[10] In the end, the governor's official report cited fourteen deaths—six Japanese and eight Chinese—but information circulated within the colonial administration indicated that British troops had killed at least 400 Chinese demonstrators. Another 200 were arrested and thrown into jail. As the Second Police Magistrate noted, anti-Japanese feeling among the Chinese was 'very bitter indeed'.[11]

Bitterness against the Japanese invaders alone was not enough to cause widespread and sustained protest. Authorities identified the Ko Shing Theatre, a popular stage for Cantonese opera, as a venue that facilitated anti-Japanese activities, and suspended its performances for three days in early October. The Barbers' Guild, accused of 'actively fomenting disaffection in connection with the anti-Japanese movement', was outlawed.[12] Actual organisational nodes, however, were far too numerous for an alien regime to identify. In fact, each neighbourhood had its own informal network, with links that stretched well beyond its boundaries, to mobilise fellow Chinese. The indignation and sorrow had been so widely shared that a boycott at one store would always draw a large crowd of passers-by, whose cheers and shouts merged with the sound of the smashing and burning of Japanese goods. Under severe censorship, newspapers often were published with 'empty windows' where articles with anti-Japanese content had been deleted. But the Chinese had their ways of circumventing the censorship. For instance, in place of the usual greetings of 'wishing you a great fortune', that year's New Year's cards featured mainland heroes who had fought the invading Japanese Army. Through these unmistakable images, the Chinese in Hong Kong made a loud statement that they supported their homeland in its resistance.[13]

A New Generation of Labour Leaders

Amid spontaneous civic activism for national salvation emerged a new generation of young leaders. They were either individual Communists without Party connections or local activists who rallied around the cause of national salvation. The Hong Kong Anti-Japanese National Salvation Association (香港抗日救国会, HKNSA) was probably the earliest national salvation organisation with a working-class base led by individual Communists. One major leader, Zhou Nan (1907–80), came from a poor peasant family in Guangdong and had to cut short his education on finishing primary school. He joined the CCP in 1927 while working in a battery factory in Hong Kong, but he lost organisational connection three years later when his contact was captured.[14] Surviving on odd jobs, Zhou became an avid reader of works by Marx, Lenin, and Chinese

Marxist writer Ai Siqi (1910–66). He also contributed articles to the *Public Herald* (大众日报), the newspaper sponsored by the Chinese National Revolutionary Alliance (中华民族革命同盟), a dissident organisation of political and military leaders who set up their base in Hong Kong after a failed rebellion against Nanjing in 1933. Zhou's writings for the *Public Herald* attracted other like-minded youth. Their secret study group, formed in the autumn of 1935, soon transformed into the HKNSA. Without contact or instruction from any political party, members of the HKNSA—estimated 400 to 500—were mostly workers, plus a smaller number of students, teachers, and shop clerks. In September 1936, the HKNSA suffered a fatal blow, when police raided a meeting as members held a commemoration of the Manchurian Incident. Zhou Nan happened to be in Shanghai attending the All-China Conference of National Salvation Associations and escaped arrest.[15]

Although the HKNSA was gone, young activists quickly rallied around another organisation, the South China Branch of the National Salvation Association (华南救国会), jointly formed by individual Communists and members of the Chinese National Revolutionary Alliance.[16] Wu Youheng, whom we met at the beginning of this essay, had just arrived from Guangzhou in the spring of 1936 in hopes of boarding a ship for Manchuria to join the armed resistance in the northeast. Instead, he connected with the South China Branch and remained in Hong Kong. In September, the twenty-three-year-old Wu became a member of the Communist Party and was appointed almost immediately to lead its recently formed city branch when local Party members reconnected with the CCP centre in the north. As a representative of the South China Branch, Wu made contact with the remaining members of the disbanded HKNSA.[17] Before he left for Yan'an in 1940 as Hong Kong's representative to the CCP's Seventh National Congress, Wu also became a keen observer of mass movements in Hong Kong.[18]

In the less repressive political climate in Hong Kong of the late 1930s, workers rapidly regrouped amid colony-wide national salvation activism. Among the newly revived labour organisations, the Hong Kong Seamen's Union (香港海员工会), which had led the first general strike in Hong Kong but was banned after the General Strike and Boycott, once more became the most prominent and active. Former union activists who had survived anti-Communist repression quietly played a key role in organising fellow Chinese seamen into recreational clubs tolerated by the colonial state. The Music Society for Leisurely Entertainment (余闲乐社)

was just this kind of labour union in the guise of a recreational society. First formed in 1929 on the ocean liner *Empress of Japan*, the society organised Chinese seamen to perform Cantonese opera while at sea and aided them in times of sickness and unemployment on shore. Zeng Sheng, mentioned at the beginning of this essay, had fled arrest in Guangzhou for national salvation activism, worked as a bell boy on the *Empress of Japan*, and rose to the union's leadership. In 1937, the seamen made two attempts to register their organisation with the colonial government as a union. Their first application was flatly rejected, but the second, which included the signatures of more than 1,000 seamen, succeeded and the society was registered as the Hong Kong Seamen's Union.[19]

Strikes, Boycotts, and Fundraising

Regrouped Chinese labour in Hong Kong was again at the forefront of the effort to aid China's struggle against foreign invasion. Soon after total war broke out in July 1937, the 3,500 Chinese seamen working on Japanese ships left their jobs. Among those working on the four 'Empress' ocean liners owned by the Canadian Pacific Line—*Empress of Japan*, *Empress of Canada*, *Empress of Russia*, and *Empress of Asia*—845 left the ships to boycott the shipment of war material to Japan. Labour activism spread further on shore. In the second half of 1937, seventeen boycotts by seamen and dockhands marshalled support from 8,399 participants.[20] Between November 1937 and February 1938, four strikes with 3,000 participants broke out at Hong Kong's dockyards. A nine-day strike occurred at the Hong Kong and Kowloon Wharf and Godown Company when 2,000 dockhands refused to unload Japanese goods and prevented them coming ashore. At Standard Oil, 500 workers refused to load a shipment for Japan, forcing the company to cancel the contract. Communists played an active role in some of these mobilisations, but the workers themselves also initiated anti-Japanese boycotts. At Hongji, Hong Kong's largest Chinese grain firm, 400 dockhands refused to load grain for shipment to Japan. On their own initiative, other dockhands dumped strategically important tungsten ore into the sea rather than load it on a ship bound for Japan. Five thousand workers at the Taikoo Dockyard refused to repair Japanese ships and convinced replacement workers hired by the company to boycott as well.[21] Under censorship and the attentive watch of the Japanese Consul-General in Hong Kong, news of Chinese workers' anti-Japanese strikes and boycotts could not appear in local newspapers.

Nevertheless, their activism appeared in internal reports by Communists who participated in or closely observed these collective actions. In hundreds of pages, their detailed descriptions recorded a rapid surge of anti-Japanese boycotts by Chinese workers in Hong Kong between 1936 and 1939.

Beyond subversive actions against Japan, Chinese workers in Hong Kong also assisted China's resistance through fundraising. The year 1938 saw their most enthusiastic participation, epitomised by an impressive campaign started by hawkers. It began accidentally at Shamshuipo, an emerging industrial area on the Kowloon Peninsula. In the wake of a colony-wide commemoration of the Marco Polo Bridge Incident that marked the outbreak of total war, three vegetable hawkers decided to hold a three-day charity sale. Among the poorest of the poor, making only slim profits from the daily sale of perishable produce, the hawkers' heroic decision to put the nation's wellbeing before their own was contagious. Word went out to textile workers in the neighbourhood, who immediately followed with an ingenious scheme: they challenged the factory owners to match their donations. Under public pressure, employers complied, and others quickly emulated this strategy across the colony. As a result, 'every market held charity sales'.[22] Factory workers devised a surprising way to move the public. They gathered in groups of several hundred to march through Hong Kong's streets, shouting in unison with a 'mountain-shaking' voice: 'Help our country [救国呀]!'[23] In just three weeks, they raised HK$700,000. On 13 August 1938, the first anniversary of the 'Shanghai Incident' in which the National Army of China stood up to the Japanese invaders, hawkers alone raised HK$1,180.[24] Their charity sale continued through the following year and raised a total of HK$300,000.[25]

While Chinese workers spearheaded the participatory civic movement in Hong Kong, merchant elites in the colony also joined in. Eurasian millionaire Robert Ho Tung was the principal donor when the Chinese Government announced a 'donation for airplanes campaign' in 1935. Others in the business community contributed as well, though they observed the legal boundary delineated by the colonial state and discreetly collected donations for the campaign. When the war broke out in 1937, the Chinese Chamber of Commerce became the official intermediary that transmitted donated funds to the Chinese Government. By then, national salvation had become a Hong Kong–wide movement, involving rich and poor, famous and humble alike. Actors in the film industry, singsong girls, factory workers, street hawkers, shop clerks, teachers, and students of all ages formed their own associations for national salvation.[26] One observer counted 150 such organisations that suddenly appeared in the colony in the second half of 1937.[27]

The Colonial State Steps into Labour Affairs

The upsurge of national salvation activism and labour activism in the late 1930s reflected Hong Kong's political environment, in which colonial repression moderated out of necessity. In 1936, British Asia began to feel a direct threat when Japan signed the Anti-Comintern Pact with Germany. With war imminent in Europe, Britain wished to avoid a fight on two fronts. It adopted a calculated attitude of 'benevolent neutrality', gave China 'moral support and limited material aid, but at the same time avoided confrontation with Japan'.[28] The British authorities allowed more than thirty official and semi-official Chinese establishments to operate in Hong Kong, channelling funds and purchasing strategic materiel from abroad.[29] Hong Kong's colonial state also slightly relaxed its anti-Communist stance when the Nationalist Party formed a United Front with the Communists to fight their common enemy. In 1938 the Communist-led Eighth Route Army was allowed to set up a liaison office in Hong Kong, with Liao Chengzhi as the director.

Urged by the imperial centre to reform colonial affairs and in recognition of Hong Kong's new reality of industrial development, the colonial state appointed its first labour officer in 1938. Yet its record of dealing with a major industrial dispute left much doubt as to the extent to which the colonial state would go to change its pro-business tradition. From 1937 to 1939, three waves of labour protest erupted at the Hong Kong branch of the Chung Hwa Book Company (中华书局), which was officially designated as China's currency printer. Workers took collective actions against the company's decisions to lengthen work hours in 1937, levy an unusually large fine for three banknotes ruined during printing in 1938, and enact a large-scale dismissal of workers in late 1939. Labour officer Henry Butters, a fair-minded progressive, recognised the workers' economic grievances and successfully mediated the first dispute to their satisfaction, but he was then excluded from the following disputes. On those occasions, the colonial state resorted to the police to assist the company in expelling workers from the factory. Although the protest by

1,200 dismissed workers continued for months thanks to donations from people in Hong Kong and elsewhere, eventually the workers were forced to accept the severance package and leave Hong Kong on an order by the Secretary for Chinese Affairs.

By the time the labour protest at Chung Hwa subsided, colonial Hong Kong was no longer the same as it was a decade before. It was on the rise to becoming yet another industrial centre on China's coast with a growing number of industrial workers. By establishing a labour office, the colonial state had departed from the tradition of indirect rule over the majority of local Chinese. Labour activism, once largely influenced by the Nationalist Party, witnessed the ascendance of a new leadership of activists forged in the national salvation movement, who soon chose to become Communists. This resurgent labour activism would move to a new frontier soon after Liao Chengzhi, Wu Youheng, and Zeng Sheng made their deliberation at Hung Hom. As many more activists were to recognise soon, the battlefields of guerrilla warfare against the Japanese invasion would serve as a training ground for a new wave of labour activism when peace returned to Hong Kong.

1941

Faced with the common threat of the Japanese invasion of China, from 1937 the Chinese Communist Party (CCP)—which since the conclusion of the Long March in 1935 had been entrenched in Yan'an, Shaanxi Province— and the Nationalist Party entered into an uneasy alliance commonly known as the Second United Front. This already fragile relationship was thrown into crisis in January 1941, in the wake of the so-called New Fourth Army Incident, when Nationalist troops ambushed and killed several thousand Communist soldiers. One of the casualties—at least temporarily, as it was soon allowed to resume publication—of the breakdown in the relations between the two parties was the New China Daily, *a newspaper that was the sole legal entity of the Communists in the Nationalist wartime capital of Chongqing. Besides disseminating the CCP line and covering international and domestic news, the paper provided literate workers with a forum in which to express their grievances. Through analysis of the workers' letters published in its pages, this essay explores the role of participatory journalism in the process of working-class formation in China.*

The *New China Daily* and the Moral Language of Class in Wartime Chongqing

Joshua H. HOWARD[1]

Prohibiting the more than 50,000 arsenal workers in Chongqing from reading *New China Daily* (新华日报), Ordnance Director Yu Dawei condemned the Communist paper's subversive message:

> The thought of *New China Daily* is biased, the writing extreme. It presents a grave threat to the future prospects of the War of Resistance and Reconstruction. We remain vigilant to prevent it from running rampant, but there are many national defence industrial workers. If they come under its sway, the momentum will be difficult to stop.[2]

One month later, in April 1941, *New China Daily*'s director, Pan Zinian, documented the crackdown:

> Police, spies, and Three People's Principles Youth League members go everywhere prohibiting the reading of the paper, destroying copies, arresting vendors, and even blocking the transmission of dispatches from the Central News Agency and drafts from the Censorship Inspectorate. Factory security guards have arbitrarily arrested newspaper delivery workers; readers have been arrested; cities and counties throughout the provinces have prohibited sales.[3]

The wave of anti-Communism that targeted the sole legal entity of the Communists in the Nationalist's wartime capital was due in part to the fallout from the New Fourth Army Incident. To retaliate against the Communist New Fourth Army's refusal to obey Chiang Kai-shek's orders to withdraw from Anhui and Jiangsu, Nationalist troops ambushed and killed several thousand New Fourth Army soldiers in January 1941. The conflict damaged the political alliance between the Chinese Communist Party (CCP) and the Nationalists that was known as the United Front and threatened to rekindle the civil war. Formed under the auspices of the United Front, *New China Daily* now fell victim to this broader political conflict.[4]

Within weeks, sales collapsed and the paper was forced to cut down to two pages for a year. Acknowledging that some semblance of the United Front had to remain in place, Chiang Kai-shek allowed the paper to continue publishing until February 1947—a decision he would come to regret as his 'biggest mistake vis-à-vis the Communists'.[5] By 1943, the paper had rebounded and achieved widespread popularity among the working people of Chongqing. As one militant worker put it: 'Xinhua [*New China Daily*] stands on the side of workers and speaks for us.'[6] Workers appreciated the Communist newspaper for the same reasons it inspired periodic crackdowns. It reported on the suffering brought about by Japanese bombing raids. It described the boom and bust of the wartime economy. It told of the massive influx of migrants and refugees, which doubled the city's population to over the million mark. It recounted the rapid and forced industrialisation that transformed the city from a commercial entrepot into Nationalist China's industrial base.

New China Daily reflected and facilitated working-class formation. As well as disseminating the Communist Party line and reporting on both international and domestic news, the paper provided literate workers with a forum in which to assess class relations and express their grievances. Engaging with sociologist Charles Tilly's observation that storytelling that helps shape people's identities can sustain social movements,[7] in this essay, I explore the role of participatory journalism in the process of working-class formation.

Promoting Mass Work

In *New China Daily*'s inaugural issue, editor Wu Min introduced the column 'Our Mailbox' (我们的信箱), stating that any reader could also be a writer for the paper. Wu argued that dissolving the aura and hierarchy associated with professional expertise was necessary for journalism to represent the voice of working people: 'A worker, for example, can write about specific living conditions and work experiences inside the factory, national salvation activities, and all the vexations and hopes accumulated over the years that a professional writer cannot achieve.'[8] Wu thus made the notion of popularisation appealing: 'Only when all the people—workers, farmers, sales clerks, soldiers, and students—write about their production, their work, their thoughts and difficult problems, will our paper accurately reflect developments of the entire country during the War of Resistance.'[9]

On a practical level, by soliciting testimonials and letters from the public, the paper could offset reliance on the Nationalist government's Central News Agency for dispatches, and could promote 'mass work' (群众工作). Even though most CCP members had gone underground by 1939, the fact that *New China Daily* circulated in Nationalist territory reinforced its function as an opposition paper. In contrast to *Liberation Daily* (解放日报), which used propaganda in the Communist base areas to 'explain policy or to teach cadres how to do things',[10] *New China Daily* fostered an 'active sphere' of news.[11] Party leaders recognised that popular participation in the pages of the Communist daily would attract a readership in Nationalist territory.

Undertaken in the name of combating dogmatism, bureaucratism, and sectarianism, the Rectification Campaign (整风运动) of 1942–43 prompted *New China Daily* to deepen its commitment to mass work. While the Rectification Campaign served to muzzle intellectual dissent in the Communist base areas, where mass criticism sessions exerted psychological pressure to enforce Party discipline, in Nationalist China, it had the opposite effect. In Nationalist territory, there were no public campaigns against intellectual dissenters. The need to maintain the discipline of a clandestine underground party, which by 1942 had been reduced from 60,000 to a core of 5,000 members throughout Nationalist China, meant that the campaign perforce could not be prosecuted in public.[12] In the wake of rectification, the paper redoubled its efforts to promote popularisation, use colloquial Chinese, and encourage the printing of letters written by people from all walks of life. In print for more than nine years (from 11 January 1938 to 28 February 1947), *New China Daily* published more than 500 letters (of a total of 700) from self-identified workers. Some 86 percent of these letters were published between 1943 and 1946, after the Rectification Campaign.

The following table highlights the dramatic increase in labour-related coverage during these years:

Number of *New China Daily* Articles Reporting Labour Issues, 1938–1946

Articles	1938	1939	1940	1941	1942	1943	1944	1945	1946
Labour Conditions	17	46	70	27	4	99	153	51	21
Labour movt (domestic)	78	24	32	14	28	19	21	338	414
Labour movt (international)	71	40	47	31	34	120	56	150	232
May First commemoration	28	36	32	20	21	19	14	7	18
Chinese Association of Labour	na	2	3	1	13	14	8	7	126
Unemployment	29	0	0	0	0	17	30	17	11
Total	223	148	184	93	100	288	282	570	822
Worker letters	10	19	37	0	5	47	147	171	69

Source: 新华日报索引编辑组编 [*New China Daily* Index Compilation Group, ed. 1987. 新华日报索引 [Indices to *New China Daily*], 9 vols. Shanghai: Shanghai Shudian.

Along with numerous reports about wartime social life, the letters also related stories of injustice, suffering, and aspirations for a better life—all of which helped workers create an 'imagined community' of class that fuelled the postwar labour movement that emerged in 1945–46.[13]

A New Community of Class

Although labour historians have often eschewed narratives of class formation and emphasised regionalism[14] or the aim of status recognition,[15] my analysis of worker testimonials highlights how they used 'rightful resistance',[16] employing the rhetoric of the powerful to curb the exercise of power, and a language of rights and class. By the mid-1940s, many letters constituted appeals in which workers related their suffering and requested help in their struggle to maintain a livelihood and secure basic worker rights. These concerns with economic and social justice are typical of exclusive notions of class. Demands for human dignity and various freedoms—of mobility, the press, and assembly—are class-inclusive by being grounded in universal human rights.[17] If some letters were openly critical of capitalists and the exploitation of workers, many did not talk about class in such straightforward terms. But, by identifying themselves as 'we the workers', the writers assumed a collective political identity that masked differences of personality, region, craft, and education. Moreover, the letters created a community of class by using a highly moralistic language that juxtaposed workers against corrupt authority figures. Indeed, moral and ethical norms informed letter writers' understanding of class relations. Workers' moral concerns and the recognition that their precarious existence was based on unjust social relationships were an integral part of working-class formation.

By giving voice to workers' concerns, *New China Daily* attracted literate workers, who could have made up to 70 percent of its readership, according to the publication's own internal survey.[18] Workers became an important constituency of the paper, because it paid attention to their needs. Even the Nationalist propaganda English-language journal *China at War* had to admit: '[T]he life of students and workers is more fully reported in the newspaper [*New China Daily*] than in any other.'[19] The CCP recognised that it could attract an existing mass audience among labouring people in Chongqing. The implementation of factory literacy campaigns, coupled with workers' quests for education, which reflected their demands for dignity and status in an effort to combat the stigma associated with manual labour, contributed to higher-than-expected literacy rates. One reason Yu Dawei was so concerned that the paper would hold sway over arsenal workers was their relatively high literacy rate. Surveys conducted of some 6,760 arsenal workers found 82 percent were literate.[20] Owing to limited schooling opportunities, women workers had lower literacy rates, but factory relief teams operating in Chongqing's textile mills organised literacy classes that were attended by 30,000 participants. Instructors indicated that, on arriving in 1939, illiteracy rates were as high as 90 percent, but had dropped to 42 percent by the spring of 1943.[21]

The Communist press found a ready audience among numerous reading societies, which proliferated in Chongqing factories. Police reported that, by the late 1930s, reading societies and other cultural associations had gravitated towards the CCP: 'Their method of action is to organise National Salvation groups—reading societies, wall newspaper societies, theatrical groups, choruses—and in this way gradually attract leftist-inclined workers to read their outline and become acquainted with Communist ideology.'[22]

Just as reading societies assumed a political bent, the act of writing letters to *New China Daily* became political. These letters served as a status marker for workers wanting to be treated with respect and swayed public opinion and the government to recognise worker demands. It remains difficult to authenticate the letters since the originals were destroyed on publication to avoid retribution. But, despite some editing by the Communist daily, certain redundancies, simple direct language, the use of Sichuanese dialect in quoted dialogues, and grammatical mistakes do suggest that the letters were written by less formally educated writers. A few letters even served as pedagogical texts by the editors keeping an incorrect character in place and putting the correct character in brackets.[23] The specificity of the content, even when exaggerated, and the parallels one can draw between the issues raised in workers' letters and petitions and strike demands indicate the letters were not fabricated by Communist propagandists.

Rhetoric of Gendered Sacrifice

Given the wartime context and the CCP's strategy of rendering all interests, including class interests, subservient to national interests,[24] workers often employed a rhetoric of sacrifice for the nation:

> We are a group of young women workers. For our livelihood, for our national liberation and in keeping with the mission 'everyone has a responsibility for the rise and fall of the nation', we have left our beloved families and small children to participate in production work. We resolved not to stop working on account of

family affairs. Although we receive low wages, as long as we can maintain ourselves we haven't complained, but now with the daily rise of prices how can we survive on just 60 cents a day? Because of inflation male workers received an hourly wage increase of 2 cents but we women workers have not received any raise. We feel aggrieved, because we work hard and put in just as many hours as male workers. During this war of national liberation the factory divides men and women, but is the War of Resistance only for men? We selected a few representatives to present our demands to the factory director but he responded: 'Women workers are temporary. If they want to work they should work, if they don't, they can get lost.'[25]

The letter is a combination of bold, assertive demands for gender equality and calculated appeals to nationalism. As a form of rightful resistance, the letter references the government's slogan of collective responsibility for the fate of the nation. It highlights how this group of young women has placed the public good over personal interests, by leaving their families and loved ones to work in a factory. The authors indict the factory director for his callousness, but the factory goes unnamed—a form of self-censorship that would have avoided any confrontation with factory authorities while remaining in line with the Communists' United Front tactic of forging cross-class alliances. Ultimately, the women workers sought recognition for their contribution to the war effort and demanded gender equality.

Although both male and female workers couched their demands in terms of national salvation, gender-specific experiences led women to highlight their oppression as women, and to condemn the factory's control over their bodies. Textile mills, the main employers of young women, were notorious for conducting body searches and banning pregnant women—in some cases, causing the abandonment of babies or infanticide. Hui Ying recounts how, after losing her husband in an air raid, she sought employment at a cotton mill because she had to 'feed the little treasure in my stomach'. She then narrates the cruel irony of sacrificing for a job that likely would take her life:

> Soon after joining the factory, the baby in my stomach began to get bigger by the day. Up until I went into labour I kept working hard and didn't tell the foremen for fear that if they found out they would have me fired. I then asked for a five-day

sick leave and gave birth. It was a plump baby boy! As soon as I saw him, I thought of his father and I couldn't stop from crying.

Five days of leave went by very quickly. On the fourth day after my delivery, I was carrying around the baby while thinking about my job. The factory had already fired many women workers for bearing children. Could I hide my child? Could I raise my child without working? A thousand thoughts ran through my head. I don't know where my cold heartedness came from but I decided to abandon my child. That evening as I was sobbing I placed the child in a latrine pit. In a crazed like state I fled without looking back.

Over the past five years, I have worked every day inside the factory. The cotton that flies around the workshop settles on my hair and eyebrows. On hot days the cotton mixed in with my sweat drips into my eyes, nose and mouth. As I breathe, the cotton filaments penetrate my nostrils and lungs. Five years of work has cost me my life and the only thing I have gained is tuberculosis.[26]

In narrating the decline of her health, Hui Ying's account is typical of the textile industry, in which a large percentage of workers contracted tuberculosis. In 'A Woman Worker's Personal Account' (一个女工的自述), author Bing Bing tells of her initial excitement at seeing an advertisement recruiting young women from the countryside to join a cotton mill. The ad promised an eight-hour workday, eight hours of education, and eight hours of sleep. She became disillusioned on realising that the already long twelve-hour work shifts were lengthened up to an hour by manipulating the clocks in the workshops. She recounted the abuses on the night shift and lack of dignity accorded to workers. In referring to her 'life in hell' (地狱的生活), Bing Bing creates a morally charged mood that juxtaposes good against evil. Her letter, published in 1940, when Communist United Front policy still stressed the multi-class alliance, is noteworthy for being directly critical of capitalists:

> [A]s the night deepens I get a headache and blurred vision. When I can't stand it any longer, I'm tempted to go to the workshop director and ask for leave, but he'll say that I'm 'faking illness'. Some workers who are denied leave the first time often ask again and then get kicked or slapped in the face. Because of this, even if I get sick and don't have the strength to breathe, I still don't dare ask for leave and prefer to have my illness drag out. I shed my bitter tears at this inten-

sity and heartless life that is even worse than for a beast of burden.

> When I have my period, there is no chance for a brief rest ... I do need to rest a minute when I get cramps and panic stricken, but it's impossible. It's as dark as hell here without a trace of human sympathy ...
>
> I have endured life in hell for so long. Society can't imagine that among us there is this pitiable group of animals. We have been hoodwinked by the capitalists' slogan of the 'eight-hour system' and thus I accurately describe our lives in the hope of gaining assistance from public figures of society and from women's circles. I hope that the factory owners can make at least some minimal improvements to our lives.[27]

Inequality, Divisions, and Corruption

Bing Bing's letter uses the metaphor of beasts of burden, evoking workers' demands for human dignity—the most frequent subject of their letters. The quest for dignity coincided with descriptions of inequality and deep divisions between production workers and technical and administrative staff, resonating with longstanding cultural biases against manual labour. During the war, this antagonism increased because the ratio between staff and workers rose rapidly as industries sought to rationalise production systems and oversee factory communities numbering in the thousands. In addition, worker–staff tensions were overlaid with ethnic tensions as 'downriver people' (下江人) from central China and coastal areas monopolised administrative and managerial posts. These divisions are evident in the following condemnation of corrupt factory officials and staff for betraying the nation's trust and for their indifference to workers' plight:

> Mr Editor,
> I am a labourer working in the defence industry. Upon joining this factory, I discovered that the officials and the staff gentlemen often compete against each other. Both sides seek personal fame and gain without any regard for the work of the nation and going so far as to arbitrarily oppress workers. The high-ranking officials and staff spent several tens of thousands of yuan to build a new Western style villa for themselves while we workers live in thatched sheds that they built without concern for our safety. The state provides them with over 100 yuan in salary in addition to subsidies for coal, water and electricity, while they turn a blind

eye to the suffering we workers [endure]. If this continues for long, it will have grave effects on the War of Resistance. We have failed to persuade them to change course. Please listen to our appeal![28]

By the mid-1940s, letters addressed factory-based disparities and state policies that affected the entire city. Workers expressed their grievances in terms of the unjust treatment they received relative to supervisory personnel—for example, with regard to food rationing, which they said favoured staff personnel.

Whereas management used the term 'treatment' (待遇) to refer to benefits other than wages, workers associated the word with their quest for higher social standing and respect. For example, a machinist demanded a more egalitarian workplace after being criticised by the manager's wife for inviting a friend to the factory canteen. The privilege of having a guest at the canteen was reserved for staff officers: 'Why is the status of workers lower than [that of] staff? We reject this kind of thinking! What could you do without workers? We demand equal treatment and oppose this injustice!'[29] Workers intermingled status recognition with a language of class and rights. Here, the anonymous writer questions the monthly rationing of food after being informed that only staff members could purchase a catty (500 grams) of sugar:

> I'm also human and also Chinese. Why does even the appreciation of food have to be divided by class? Is it possible that workers are constitutionally different from staff officers? Staff are people just as workers are people. Why does one have to make such distinct class divisions? That workers have no rights to purchase sugar is just one of numerous forms of unequal treatment between 'staff' and 'workers'.[30]

Advancing the Labour Movement

New China Daily's participatory journalism had consequences in both the short and the long terms. Besides shaping class consciousness through the reading, writing, and sharing of the paper, the Communist press facilitated the advance of the labour movement. Reports on the labour movement in Nationalist China and abroad served to foster a sense of common cause among workers. By 1945, under the guidance of the CCP's Southern Bureau, the paper pivoted from its wartime policy of 'justification, advantage, and restraint' (有理, 有利, 有节) to a strategy of mobilising students and workers in social movements. Contributing to workers' politicisation, *New China Daily* publicised worker demands with sympathetic reporting, and enlisted public support for labour.

Demands for dignity, economic justice, and human rights that had been expressed in letters resurfaced in the labour movement. In one of the first episodes of labour protest, the Hu Shihe Incident (胡世合事件), named for the electrician gunned down by Nationalist military intelligence in February 1945, 80,000 residents viewed his body lying in state in a Buddhist temple.[31] Workers adopted the same moral language of rights and class in their elegiac couplets as they had in their *New China Daily* letters. Spies were described as 'demons and monsters' (九妖十八怪) who helped prop up the power of the privileged. Workers cried out for justice and the rule of law: 'Theft of electricity and murder, where is the law of the land? Sacrifice for the public, honour despite death.'[32]

Many of the issues that workers raised in their letters had an impact on the social policies and political campaigns of the Communist regime during the early 1950s. Maoist policies and factory campaigns were not merely a 'revolution from above' that 'would at all times be guided by, and serve the interest of, the Chinese Communist Party'.[33] Rather, the campaigns and social policies that sought to bridge the divide between mental and manual labour and to impart workers with human dignity were responses to the grievances and aspirations workers had expressed in the previous decade.

Finally, one should consider the legacy of *New China Daily* on the press of the People's Republic of China (PRC). Participatory journalism flourished during the initial phase after 1949. Indeed, the political language promoted by the PRC through its propaganda and press in the 1950s built directly on the language of class the workers had so richly pioneered in *New China Daily*.

1942

For a long time in China, the dissemination of stories about heroes had been a mainstay of Confucian education. While in the past it was mostly emperors, military officers, officials, poets and virtuous widows who were upheld as models worthy of emulation, towards the end of the 1930s, the Chinese Communist Party started its own cult of revolutionary martyrs and heroes in Yan'an. Now model workers were the ones worthy of emulation. Taking a page from the Stakhanovite Movement that had recently emerged in the Soviet Union, in 1939, the Communist leaders began to designate labour heroes and model workers. In the following years, especially after 1942, the Party media would publish articles about peasants, workers, cadres and soldiers who had been conferred these titles, often assigning them significant prizes. This essay tracks the spectacular rise and fall of Wu Manyou, one of the earliest labour heroes, who was singled out by Mao Zedong himself for his achievements.

The Rise and Fall of Wu Manyou, China's First Labour Hero
Bo Ærenlund SØRENSEN

In May 1944, for the first time in five years, foreign reporters were able to visit Yan'an, Shaanxi Province, where the Chinese Communist Party (CCP) was then headquartered.[1] Harrison Forman and Günther Stein, two of the journalists, both noted the enormous prestige that was accorded to China's first 'labour hero' (劳动英雄), Wu Manyou. According to Forman:

> His [Wu Manyou's] portrait is hung prominently in the galleries, homes and public places alongside those of Mao Tse-tung, Chu Teh and other high political and military figures … As a Labour Hero, Wu [Manyou], and others like him, are not only held in high esteem by the people but are invited to attend all public and state functions, at which they occupy seats of honour along with the highest government military officials.[2]

What Forman witnessed was the unfolding of a campaign to improve governance through the dissemination of stories about the actions and attitudes of particularly industrious individuals who were awarded the titles of 'labour hero' and 'model worker' (劳动模范).[3] This was the beginning of a tradition that has continued until the present and over the decades has come to be known by everyone in China through news stories, documentary films, action movies, songs, dances, badges, postage stamps, museums and primary school textbooks. By telling the story of how Wu Manyou was catapulted to fame only to be excised from public memory shortly thereafter, this essay will draw some general lessons about labour governance in the People's Republic of China.

Creating the Model

The dissemination of stories about heroes worthy of emulation was not an invention of the CCP, but had long been a 'mainstay of Confucian education in the form of stories about great emperors, generals, poets, magistrates and filial children'.[4] Historian Donald Munro has pointed out that the Party-State's dissemination of model-worker narratives draws on a long pedagogical tradition: 'Much of the historical scholarship for which the Chinese are famous was concerned with unearthing models from the past for the education of the people.'[5] The CCP, however, would bring a new level of purposeful control and intentional design to this process.

The immediate inspiration for selecting model workers for popular emulation seems to have come from the Soviet Union of the mid-1930s, where a young miner from the Donbass region named Aleksei Stakhanov was celebrated in a nationwide campaign in 1935 for surpassing his quota by a prodigious margin. The Stakhanovite Movement was first noted in a CCP publication in 1936 as a useful way of stimulating productivity.[6] From 1939, the Communist Party in Yan'an began to designate labour heroes and model workers and, from April 1942, the *Liberation Daily* (解放日报) began to publish a steady stream of articles about peasants, workers, cadres and soldiers who had been conferred these titles along with significant prizes.

If we are to understand why labour heroes in general—and Wu Manyou in particular—came to feature so prominently in CCP propaganda, it is important to note that Mao Zedong favoured the use of such models as a means of popular education. In an interview with reporter Günther Stein, Wu explained: 'In 1941 Comrade Mao Tse-tung asked the people to find out who among the peasants were model farmers and could be regarded as candidates for the first Labour Hero elections.'[7] Shortly thereafter, in a report presented to the Senior Cadres Conference of the Shaanxi–Gansu–Ningxia Border Region in Yan'an in December 1942, Mao recommended the propagation of knowledge about those who had stood out for their efforts in the CCP-dominated areas, so that others might emulate their achievements.[8] In particular, Mao singled out the achievements of the farmer Wu Manyou, quoting at length extracts about Wu published in the *Liberation Daily*.

Mao's recommendation was turned into reality within weeks. In addition to news reporters, the CCP's cultural apparatus became involved in the celebrations. In early February 1943, the *Liberation Daily* began to publish reproductions of woodcuts featuring the icon of Wu Manyou. Figure 1, one of several woodcuts produced by the young and promising artist Gu Yuan—who would eventually be appointed President of the Central Academy of Fine Arts in Beijing—shows Wu's likeness surrounded by domestic animals and crops below the injunction to 'Emulate Wu Manyou' (向吴满有看齐).

Figure 1. Gu Yuan, 'Emulate Wu Manyou', in *Liberation Daily*, 10 February 1943, 4.

Around the same time, having been requested to write a long poem celebrating the achievements of Wu, well-known poet—and future father of celebrated artist Ai Weiwei—Ai Qing visited the Wu household for several days to gather knowledge and inspiration.[9] Just as Gu Yuan and his visual art colleagues had done, Ai heeded Mao's call to place the masses at the centre of the arts, and his poem about Wu Manyou marks a point of departure in his work: where the poet had previously represented peasants as objects of pity, Wu was depicted as capable and resourceful.[10] According to Wu, he convinced Ai to change a line about him enjoying good luck in his old age to a new line emphasising his hard work.[11] The finished poem was published in *Liberation Daily* on 9 March 1943 and took up almost the entire fourth page. Roughly at the same time, Wu's life story was also transformed into a *yangge* dance, several short stories and songs.[12]

The cultural artefacts produced to celebrate Wu Manyou show that the artists who became involved with the model-worker campaign of those years were among the first prominent artists to produce art that responded to Mao's call to make art *for* the masses *about* the masses.[13] These works of art also reveal that, in attempting to create a 'new China' through propaganda, the CCP constantly had to make use of older idioms, as reflected in the adoption of China's traditional *nianhua* motifs by the urban-educated artists who came to Yan'an.[14] Making use of established forms, however, threatened to undermine the ability of the CCP to control the message received by the audience. As Xiaofei Tian has argued, even the story of the most widely publicised model worker of all time, the young soldier Lei Feng, is shot through with Buddhist and Daoist motives that quite probably accounted for its popular resonance.[15]

Political and Economic Uses of the Wu Manyou Campaign

Wu Manyou's story seems to have served two functions. First, by focusing on the active role of labour heroes such as Wu, whose name came to figure as a synonym for the production drive itself—for instance, in the phrase 'the Wu Manyou direction' (吴满有方向), which was frequently employed in the *Liberation Daily*—the CCP sent the message that local peasants and workers were at the forefront of policy development. Second—and related to the first point—the CCP sought to make use of the distribution of labour hero titles to gain a foothold in local society. This can be seen in the fact that very few of the individuals selected as labour heroes and model workers in this period were cadres or Party members; rather, the CCP selected its models from residents who enjoyed local prestige and whose life stories fit in with the narrative of socialism overturning the feudal order. Mao himself made clear that this was one of the prime purposes of model workers in a speech at a conference in honour of labour heroes in the Shaanxi–Gansu–Ningxia Border Region in 1945, when he said: 'You are the bridge between the leaders above and the broad masses below. Through you, the opinions of the masses are transmitted to the leadership; the opinions from above are transmitted below.'[16] As such, the model-worker tradition is part and parcel of the CCP's very successful efforts to coopt a broad swathe of social actors into its governance apparatus.

In terms of economic policy, the Communist authorities used Wu to send a very clear message. Again and again, Wu is praised in the *Liberation Daily* for his diligence and for paying his taxes—even exceeding his obligations. What the articles about Wu highlight are the intensely practical and pressing needs of both the general populace and the CCP elite at that time. Under the harsh circumstances facing the CCP with the tightening of the Nationalist blockade of the area in 1941, the government of the border region sought to make peasants and workers devote more hours to their work and increase their willingness to contribute, through taxation and voluntary schemes, to the building up of the local economy.

The CCP's devotional reliance on model workers is also revealed by the considerable value, in terms of both material handouts and social prestige, of the prizes. In late 1943, the CCP held its first model-worker conference and awarded no less than 185 model workers with certificates of merit autographed by Party leaders.[17] The models also received material rewards, such as money, draught animals and farm equipment.[18] After the conference, woodcut portraits of twenty-five individuals singled out as 'special model workers' (特等劳动英雄) were prominently displayed on the front page of the *Liberation Daily*.[19] At this point, the CCP displayed no qualms about relying on material incentives to motivate the populace to increase production.

There was, however, a vocal minority who felt that this reliance on material incentives did not fit well with socialist ideology. This contradiction became especially glaring as many of those chosen as models were already among those doing best for themselves in their local communities. By Wu's explicit admission, he was by far the richest man in his village, and even hired others to work for him.[20] The fact that Wu made his living by extracting surplus value from the labour of others led some readers of *Liberation Daily* to take exception to giving him the title of labour hero. In response, the newspaper editors repeatedly explained that, although these practices shared certain exploitative aspects with capitalism, they were certainly better than the previous system of feudal oppression.[21] In an internal publication, the editors argued that the development of some economic aspects of capitalism among the peasantry was both 'natural and desirable', resting their defence on the arguments that Mao had advanced in his 1940 essay 'On New Democracy'.[22]

The fact the government-sponsored adulation of labour heroes could be controversial is probably also part of the reason Mao, in his speech at the 1945 conference mentioned above, warned model workers:

> [Y]ou must always remember not to become conceited ... if you are not modest and cease to exert yourselves, and if you do not respect others, do not respect the cadres and the masses, then you will cease to be heroes and models. There have been such people in the past, and I hope you will not follow their example.[23]

This and many similar injunctions to maintain good relations between model workers and their surrounding community point to the fact that, while models might serve to boost social governance and control for the CCP, they could also provoke animosity in local society.[24]

And Then It All Went Wrong

Judging from the continued dissemination of news stories about Wu Manyou in the *Liberation Daily*, the CCP leadership must have found the campaign useful. In July 1946, the newspaper announced that a movie about Wu was being produced and, in August, a new film studio was established in part to realise this project.[25] Well-known filmmaker Chen Bo'er—who had herself been named 'labour hero on the cultural and educational battlefront' (文教战线上的劳动英雄)—was charged with writing the script for *Working Hero in the Communist Base: Wu Manyou* (边区劳动英雄: 吴满有).[26]

The movie would trace the events of Wu's adult life and, in so doing, describe the land reforms in northern Shaanxi in 1935, the reorganisation of the Communist army, the fight against the Japanese invasion, the great production drive and other major historical events and movements.[27] In other words, the film would link the personal history of Wu with the teleological march of socialism in China—a link between personal and political history that the CCP has often made to legitimate its policies.[28]

With the resumption of armed hostilities between the CCP and the Nationalist Party, Chen left the area to take up other responsibilities. A committee of writers—which included Jiang Qing, the former Shanghai actor who married Mao—took up the task of revising the script ahead of production, which began in September 1946. Before the movie was released, however, catastrophe hit: Wu was taken prisoner by the Nationalists and appeared in a radio broadcast to publicly denounce the CCP. A telegram from the Northwest Party Bureau put an effective end to the film's production by noting that 'Wu Manyou has been taken prisoner. Appears to have lost all integrity ... Do not recommence shooting on the film concerning him.'[29]

Following this public relations disaster, the CCP had to decide what to do with the public memory of Wu. Interestingly, they responded not by casting aspersions on Wu, but rather by erasing him from history. To this end, woodcuts of Wu were left out of published selections, Ai Qing's poem was not included in his collected works and the movie about Wu does not figure in the published catalogues of early CCP movies.[30] In the 1950 edition of Ding Ling's award-winning *The Sun Shines Over the Sanggan River*, a novel originally published in 1948, the two references to Wu were replaced with references to Liu Yuhou, another well-known labour hero.[31]

Memory can, however, be recalcitrant, and Wu did eventually re-emerge from captivity, claiming it was a voice-actor, not he, who had disparaged the CCP. Unable to provide any proof of this claim, Wu, however, was never able to clear his name. To this day, his descendants are still fighting to clear their family name by publishing rebuttals and appealing to politicians and historians. At times, they have been successful, such as when the influential CCP member Li Rui—a former secretary of Mao's who had personally known Wu Manyou—published an article in the influential historical journal *Yanhuang Chunqiu* (炎黄春秋) in 1995 in which he claimed Wu was innocent of the charges against him.[32]

Model Workers Today

The CCP has continued to select model workers and propagate their stories ever since, with thousands of individuals selected annually at local, provincial and national levels. The most celebrated model worker of recent years is Guo Mingyi, a worker at a well-known steel factory in Anshan, whose exploits have been publicised widely by China's national media in the form of books, a play, a biopic and hundreds of articles and news reports since 2010. In the somewhat more open first decade of the 2000s, influential voices criticised the practice of selecting model workers. Most notably, perhaps, Qinghua sociology professor Sun Liping recommended retiring the institution of the model worker, comparing it to old holiday stickers peeling off government office doors because no-one could be bothered to take them down.[33] In recent years, the Party-State has been more forceful in its attempts to quell such criticism, as civil rights lawyer Pu Zhiqiang found out in 2015 when he was charged with, among other things, ridiculing model worker Shen Jilan.[34]

There are probably many reasons the CCP continues to propagate stories about model workers. In recent decades, celebrating model workers has become a way of sprinkling celebrity stardust on the CCP, such as in 2005 when the famous athletes Liu Xiang and Yao Ming were thus honoured at the Thirteenth National Conference of Model Workers in Beijing. Selecting model workers is a low-cost way of rewarding industrious and compliant individuals and a means of creating inspirational stories for use in Party-State media and school textbooks. Perhaps most importantly, continuing the tradition has enabled the CCP to signal that it remains the guardian of China's working class through a period when many workers have had reason to doubt this.

1946

Ownership of land has always been an existential issue for Chinese farmers. Although both the Nationalist and Communist parties recognised the need to reorganise agricultural landholdings, during the Republican era, there was considerable reluctance to act. Under Sun Yat-sen, the Nationalists issued a call to give 'land to the tiller', which proved very popular among the people, but after the rise of Chiang Kai-shek, the Nationalist Party increasingly relied on village landlords and rural power-holders who had little interest in agrarian reform. As for the Communists, following the Soviet model, they initially sought to carry out a proper Marxist revolution by organising the urban proletariat. Only after the Communists were purged from the cities in the late 1920s did some Party members—Mao Zedong, in particular—begin to consider rural revolution as the key to Communist survival and victory. Starting with the Jiangxi Soviet of the early 1930s, the Communists experimented with how far they could push land reform. Experiments in this sense started again more cautiously in 1945 as the war against Japan ground to a close and accelerated once the Communists obtained state power, lasting until 1952. This essay explores how these campaigns created dramatic but short-lived changes in the relationships between farmers, land, and labour.

Production in Revolution: Agricultural and Political Labour during Land Reform

Brian DEMARE

In the late summer of 1946, only a few months after the official launch of land reform (土地改革), the Chinese Communist Party's promotion of the successes of the Bureau Work Team (分局工作组) began in earnest. Organised by the Central China Bureau, the Bureau Work Team boasted leaders with impeccable revolutionary credentials. Team leaders, instructed to experiment with redistributing land from wealthy villagers to their poor neighbours, possessed decades of experience in carrying out rural revolution. One of them, a poor peasant woman hailing from Guangdong Province, had joined Peng Pai's peasant movement in the 1920s (see Day's essay in the present volume) before surviving the Party's famed Long March (1934–35). After carrying out land reform in E'qian village, Jiangsu Province, the team's approach to rural revolution was heralded as a model for future campaigns. In a glowing account of the Bureau Work Team's time in E'qian, a top Party leader praised the team for mobilising the village masses to attack not just landlords, who typically did not personally take part in agricultural production, but also well-off farmers.[1]

These farmers, classified as 'rich peasants' (富农) by the Work Team, regularly engaged in agricultural production; they were, by definition, hardworking labourers. But their relative wealth allowed them to rent out their excess lands or hire agricultural workers. So while these rich peasants were among the most productive farmers in E'qian, the Bureau Work Team treated them as little more than parasites, full of tricks (投机取巧), and ready to hog (独吞) any and all property. By organising the village poor, who were said to have nothing to lose and everything to gain (不怕损失), to attack E'qian's rich peasants and confiscate their property, the Central China Bureau declared that the Work Team had discovered the key to rural revolution.[2] E'qian was only a single village, but the message from this model work team reverberated throughout the Chinese countryside for a half-dozen years: revolutionary activism, often violent and always divisive, came before the practical concerns of agricultural production.

Redefining Rural Labour

The period of land reform, the most formative years of the Maoist rural revolution, created dramatic but largely short-lived changes in the relationship between farmers, land, and labour. These transformations began in 1945 as the war against Japan ground to a close, kicking into high gear with the release of the May Fourth Directive in 1946.[3] This document launched the Party's first land reform campaigns—massive events designed to fundamentally alter all aspects of rural life, including the ownership of land. These campaigns, which did not come to a close until 1952, were carried out in an endlessly diverse countryside against an always changing political backdrop. At the start of land reform, the Communists were locked in a life-and-death battle against their Nationalist rivals. By the end of the campaigns, Communist Party leaders were in the final stages of cementing their hold over the newly established People's Republic of China (PRC). Most of the changes to rural labour that land reform wrought were short-lived due to the subsequent implementation of collectivised farming. But the land reform classification scheme—theoretically predicated on a family's relationship with land and labour—endured even after collectivisation. The Maoist class system became a defining characteristic of China until the reform era.

Maoist theories of rural classes, based on the exploitation of labour in the countryside, were unheard of when they arrived in Chinese villages; previously rural labour was understood in practical rather than in abstract or theoretical terms. While not discounting the possibilities of serious complications from weather and human factors, there existed in rural China an obvious relationship between labour and the household economy. Through agricultural production, farming families had the opportunity to earn profits, which could be reinvested, most often in the purchase of more and better land. It was thus not unreasonable for villagers to dream of gaining wealth through labour, often with the goal of not having to work the land themselves but renting their fields to tenants or hiring labourers.

Party reports framed the rural rental and hiring systems in terms of inequality and exploitation, emphasising how a small number of landlords permanently controlled large tracts of land.[4] In the vast Chinese countryside, there were indeed many instances of fabulously wealthy landlords living extravagant lives. The Party used such examples to promote the idea that landlords, parasitically living off the labour of their tenants and workers, were immoral and worthy of denunciation if not direct verbal and physical abuse. Intellectuals visiting the countryside on behalf of the Party, meanwhile, went to great lengths to provide theoretical justification for the argument that it was impossible for poor peasants to prosper under the old regime. The feudal nature of the countryside, they reasoned, ensured the eternal prosperity of the landlord class at the expense of the rural poor. Villagers, however, had good reason to doubt such theoretical assertions. As Xiaojia Hou has argued, there was no clear relationship between landholding and wealth: renters might even be more prosperous than landholders.[5] The long-accepted tradition of partible inheritance among sons, moreover, made maintaining a large estate for multiple generations inherently difficult. The result was a fluid rural social order in which labour was essential for survival and offered the possibility of prosperity.

A Tectonic Shift

The arrival of land reform work teams, dispatched by the Communist Party to remake the countryside, turned this rural order and its assumptions about labour upside down. Changes to landholding patterns were, by definition, among the most fundamental of the campaign's many aims. The accumulation of wealth, including the ownership of excess land—long a bedrock of economic security—was now labelled as nothing more than a form of exploitation. Not having adequate access to land—once an existential crisis for Chinese farmers—now offered a path to prosperity through revolutionary activism. Labour, particularly one's relationship to land and agricultural production, stood at the centre of this tectonic shift.

Under the careful guidance of visiting land reform work teams, villagers were taught to rethink their labour, as well as the labour of their neighbours, through the lens of exploitation. The Party released a host of guidelines and policy documents to help work teams and local cadres determine class status, emphasising the centrality of calculating the ways in which some villagers exploited the labour of others. Those who rented out land or hired farmworkers were given the loathsome labels of landlord or rich peasant; those who were not involved in any serious exploitation of labour were cast as middle peasants; farmers who were tenants or hired out their labour, finally, were declared poor peasants or hired hands. During the process of class division, better-off families took great pains to emphasise their own labour in hopes of receiving a more favourable class label.[6] All members of rural society, from landlords to the landless, were best served by calling attention to their poverty in hopes of keeping their property, and perhaps gaining greater distributions from their wealthier neighbours.[7] In the process of class determination, two critical stress points emerged, both involving labour. First, how much labour could a middle peasant exploit without being classed as a rich peasant? Second, what to do with rich peasants who farmed their own land while also exploiting others by renting out extra fields or hiring workers? In both cases, the theoretical assumptions underlying these questions were pushed aside in the search for greater wealth to distribute to the rural poor.

In theory, work teams dispatched by the Party teamed with local cadres to determine class status by calculating the amount of income families earned by exploiting the labour of their neighbours. In practice, however, other concerns crept into the process of class determination. Most notably, poor activists pushed for greater gains from fields that wealthier peasants were farming themselves. Early land reform directives were highly contradictory—on one hand, instructing cadres that the lands personally farmed by rich peasants, including land they farmed with the help of hired labour, should not be touched.[8] Yet as early as 1946 the Central China Bureau, while noting that no more than 10 percent of households should lose land, also allowed cadres to take the lands rich peasants personally farmed if these fields were needed to satisfy the needs of poor peasants.[9]

This directive foreshadowed a troubling trend of encroaching on the wealth generated by the non-exploitative labour of Chinese farmers. By 1947, for example, the East China Bureau began warning against the continued existence of a 'rich peasant line' (富农路线). According to this report, compiled one year after the start of land reform, landlords still had excess and good land.[10] And because cadres had not confiscated any rich peasant land, many poor peasants and hired hands did not have enough land. For Party leaders in the East China Bureau, past land reform policy had erred in taking care of landlords and especially rich peasants before considering the needs of their poorer neighbours. As a result, work teams and local cadres were instructed to settle accounts with landlords, giving them a share of property only after taking care of poor peasants and hired hands. In a major blow to hardworking farmers, the Party now approved the confiscation of the lands rich peasants farmed themselves to make up for past exploitation.¹¹ A push to equalise landholdings, meanwhile, made the property of middle peasants another attractive target for activists.

Political Labour in the Countryside

The radical turn towards egalitarianism in land reform in 1947 firmly established a new form of work in the countryside: political labour. Now, instead of the endless drudgery of agricultural production, villagers could receive material rewards through revolutionary activism—most importantly, struggling against their neighbours for property and hidden wealth. The choice between agricultural production and political activism represented a major contradiction in the Maoist rural revolution. As historian Fangchun Li has demonstrated in his study of land reform in northern China, although the Party presented production (生产) and liberation (翻身) as compatible, if not perfectly harmonious, in reality, attempts to stress rural liberation invariably damaged agricultural production.¹²

During the first land reform campaigns in 1946, the Party had pushed back against the tendency of poor activists to attack wealthier neighbours to the detriment of agricultural production. Early land reform directives, for example, stressed limiting struggle to keep production going. For most landlords, 'struggle' (斗争) was to be confined to open discussion to facilitate the transfer of land; only the most obstinate of landlords were to be subject to confrontational attacks.¹³ But as early as the autumn of 1946, poor peasant activists were moving against not only rich peasants, but also middle peasants. As the Central China Bureau warned, this threatened the agricultural production of middle peasants, which was essential to the rural economy.¹⁴ As one report from the Taihang base area made clear, while rich peasants exploited the labour of hired hands, the result of this exploitation was a high level of agricultural production.¹⁵ Targeting these rich peasants could only damage the local economy.

Yet land reform directives continued to suggest that agricultural and political labour could coexist without friction. In the summer of 1947, for example, a report from the Northeast instructed work teams and local cadres to combine struggle with production. But the nature of the struggle proposed by the report—a campaign of 'digging out treasures' (挖财宝) to end peasant poverty—was exactly the sort of political labour that wreaked havoc on agricultural production.¹⁶ During this and similar land reform campaigns, which went by a variety of colourful names, peasant activists tortured and killed class enemies in search of hidden wealth. Because these class enemies invariably included rich and middle peasants, agricultural production suffered mightily. Later campaigns, especially those launched following the establishment of the PRC in 1949, attempted to limit violent struggle for economic gain, in no small part to promote agricultural production. But throughout the many years of land reform, villagers tended to approach rural revolution with economic gains in mind.[17]

Legacies

The impact of the Party's successive land reform campaigns on agricultural production was incredibly diverse, but one common trend was an initial reluctance to commit to farm work due to fears of future redistributions. Xi Zhongxun, one of the Party's most important leaders in the Northwest Bureau, raised this issue in early campaigns in a letter to Mao Zedong. Xi, now better known as the father of Xi Jinping, noted the plight of hardworking peasants after land reform: now hailed as labour heroes due to their hard work, they might find themselves attacked by neighbours jealous of their excess grain.[18] Many of those who remained poor in the aftermath of land reform, meanwhile, were lazy or gamblers, not to be trusted with leadership positions. According to Xi, the prospect of future redistributions brought fear of prosperity to the countryside. However, once villagers felt land reform was truly complete, the traditional belief in the value of labour returned. Thus, many Party reports emphasised how land reform fuelled agricultural production. One such report, penned by future Minister of Agriculture and eventual Cultural Revolution victim Liao Luyan, stressed how peasants, now owners of land and agricultural tools, were eager to produce.[19] The flipside of this belief also returned: a strong disdain for those who were considered lazy or simply bad at farming, including many new to the harsh realities of rural labour.[20]

In the aftermath of land reform, new labour practices offered the possibility of redefining China's rural classes. Taking part in labour after the close of the campaigns, for example, offered a path for class enemies to join with the peasant masses. This started with punishing criminal landlords with forced labour (劳役); minor offences such as selling or hiding property might receive a one-year sentence, while major crimes such as spreading rumours or handing out bribes could fetch up to five years of forced labour. Such punishments, however, were designed to be rare. The final rounds of land reform featured better treatment for rich peasants and even landlords, who were guaranteed a share of land to farm. In this way, land reform seemed to create a path towards the creation of villages full of owner-cultivators, entirely free from exploitation and class conflict. Landlords, now taking part in agricultural production, were to have their class status reevaluated after five years of labour.

This oft-promised milestone, however, was never reached. First, the landholding system created in the wake of the campaigns was short-lived. At the start of land reform, Deng Zihui, a Party specialist on agricultural affairs, had written to Liu Shaoqi arguing in favour of a 'middle peasant economy' (中农经济) made up of owner-cultivators, as opposed to Soviet-style collectivisation.[21] But only a few short years after land reform, the Party forcibly moved to collectivise rural farms—a policy shift that would have profound impacts on rural labour practices. As for landlords and other class enemies, taking part in agricultural production was never enough to remove their class labels. They and their descendants would remain class enemies, pariahs for the remainder of the revolutionary era. Despite engaging in labour for decades, rich peasants and especially landlords remained useful to the Party as symbols of exploitation. For this reason, the class statuses that work teams gave to villagers, based on a snapshot of labour practices viewed through the lens of exploitation, remained the true legacy of land reform.

1948

As the civil war between the Chinese Communist Party (CCP) and the Nationalist Party was drawing to a close, labour unrest was again on the rise. However, in those years, the CCP's relationship with worker activism was ambiguous. Although some radical voices in the Party still held that final victory for their cause would come through a series of worker uprisings, the Party leadership did not want to risk alienating capitalists and entrepreneurs whose cooperation would be necessary for postwar reconstruction. Already in April 1945, the Seventh Congress of the CCP pledged to improve labour conditions while protecting the interests of entrepreneurs in the spirit of Mao Zedong's 'New Democracy'. In the same vein, in August 1948, the Sixth All-China Labour Congress revived the old Nationalist slogan of cooperation between labour and capital (劳资合作), reframing it as 'mutual benefits for labour and capital' (劳资两利). The primary message was that workers should be discouraged from confrontations with employers and instead focus on forming 'factory protection teams' to prevent destruction of machinery and raw materials as the CCP took over cities like Shanghai. This essay looks at the role of women in the labour unrest of that period.

Women Workers and the Shanghai Cotton Mill Strike of 1948
Emily HONIG

In early 1948, at the Shen Xin Number Nine Cotton Mill in Shanghai, 6,000 women went on strike. Their demands included distribution of rice and coal rations and enforcement of provisions for paid maternity leave. The women occupied the mill for four days. They selected representatives from each workshop to demand a meeting with the mill's management. Meanwhile, in the spinning room, women sat on top of bobbin bins; in the weaving workshop, they made themselves comfortable on bolts of cloth; and in the roving room, they collected bundles of roving and fashioned them into pillows. Initially, groups of women in each workshop sat, eating dried melon seeds, and chatted.

As both mill managers and the police pressured them to end the strike, workers began to collect bricks, machine parts, metal food bowls and oil drums filled with rocks to use as ammunition, moving them to the factory roof on bobbin and yarn-transporting carts. Ultimately, it took several hundred policemen equipped with three army tanks, deploying tear and vomit gas, to force them out of the mill, killing three women workers and injuring five hundred. So violent was this strike that it came to be known as the 'February Second Bloodbath' at Shen Xin Nine.

In the context of the Shanghai labour movement in the first half of the twentieth century, this episode stands out as an almost unparalleled instance of women workers boldly and decisively unifying to demand improved conditions. Yet understanding the significance of this strike requires consideration of industrial development in Shanghai, the composition of the labour force and organisations that shaped labour activism, including the Green Gang, the Chinese Communist Party (CCP) and the Young Women's Christian Association (YWCA).

Social and Economic Divisions

The Shen Xin cotton mill was one of a number of mills established in Shanghai by the Rong family in the early twentieth century. With mills owned by British, Japanese and other Chinese capitalists, the cotton textile industry accounted for roughly half of the industrial workforce in Shanghai from the 1920s through to the 1940s, with women representing 75 percent of the workforce.[1] Most mills employed male workers for machine repair and transport of cotton and yarn, while women were the overwhelming majority of workers in the spinning, roving and weaving workshops.

In almost all sectors of the Shanghai workforce, labour activism was conditioned by divisions among workers. As with workers in other enterprises, women in cotton mills were neither a unified nor a homogeneous group; rather, they were divided both socially and economically by native place. The majority of skilled workers came from the relatively wealthy Jiangnan and the parts of Jiangsu and Zhejiang south of the Yangzi River, such as Wuxi, Changzhou and Ningbo; most of the unskilled workers migrated from poverty-stricken Subei, the area of Jiangsu north of the Yangzi, including Yangzhou, Taizhou and Yancheng.[2] Depending on which area they came from, women spoke different and mutually unintelligible dialects, dressed differently and had distinctive eating habits.

Within the cotton mills, women from Jiangnan and Subei worked in different workshops. In general, women from the north, who were considered by mill managers to be strong, robust and accustomed to dirt, were concentrated in workshops where the work was most arduous and dirty—for instance, reeling and roving—while those from Jiangnan dominated jobs in the higher-paying weaving shops. Thus, although they technically worked in a single enterprise, workers from different native places did not necessarily have much contact with one another.

Segregation was only one aspect of the relationship between women from Jiangnan and Subei, who often treated each other with contempt and hostility. Membership of their own mutual aid and social organisations, the 'sisterhoods', invariably consisted of women from the same native place. In some cases, the sisterhoods included supervisors and even gang members from their home counties. Native place, then, took precedence over status in the workforce. And, in pledging sisterhood, women workers confirmed bonds among those from the same native place, while emphasising the separateness of those from different native places.

Women on Strike

In spite of these divisions among workers of different origins, the historical record abounds with strikes involving thousands of women. From the opening of the first cotton mills in Shanghai through to the 1940s, there were occasions when women workers shut off their machines and left the factories. One of the most dramatic moments in the labour movement centred on the May Thirtieth Movement of 1925 (see Leong's essay in the present volume), which triggered numerous strikes in the cotton mills, with statistical records indicating that often the majority of the strikers were women. However, the simple fact that women struck does not necessarily represent a radical or revolutionary agenda. For example, one of the strikes in 1925 was instigated by male workers in the roving department who had been dismissed from their jobs and replaced with women. During the protest, activists physically barred women from going into the mill. So, although women did not go to work and therefore appeared to be 'on strike', they were not acting voluntarily to assert their own demands. In another strike, when many hundreds of male workers smashed machinery as they rushed through the cotton mill to begin a strike, women workers fled outside. Again, in the statistical record, it appears that women workers who had exited the mill were on strike.

There were, to be sure, strikes in the 1920s that were initiated and organised by women workers themselves. While some issued demands for pay increases and protested beatings by foremen and supervisors, many strikes organised by women sought to defend traditional loyalties. In one case, police were summoned to control a strike involving 3,000 women workers protesting management's refusal to hire the woman introduced for a job by their supervisor. As Elizabeth Perry points out, male cotton mill workers, too, sometimes participated in strikes for less-than-radical reasons. For instance, she quotes one worker who recalled student members of the CCP instructing workers to strike, which they did because of the promise the Party would provide their pay during the time they did not work.[3]

During this period, it appears that the most radical participants in the Shanghai labour movement were not the unskilled cotton mill workers, but rather the educated artisans—printers, postal workers and mechanics—most of whom came from Jiangnan and were most sympathetic to the cause of the CCP. In cotton mills, CCP membership in the mid-1920s consisted primarily of the skilled male workers: copper fitters, woodworkers and mechanics.[4] It is possible that the inability of the CCP to effectively organise women mill workers may be partly due to the fact that it had only a few female organisers, all of whom came from Hunan and therefore did not speak a dialect intelligible to women in the cotton mills. In addition, viewing the sisterhoods as 'feudal' organisations, the CCP did not use them as a basis for organising. It may also be because, as S.A. Smith points out in his study of Shanghai labour, CCP leaders in the 1920s did not approve of separate organisations for women workers, aspiring as they were to the expression of an undivided class solidarity among factory workers.[5]

Between the YWCA and the Communist Party

Understanding the militant activism of women workers during the 1948 Shen Xin strike requires consideration of several transformations that took place during the 1930s and 1940s. One of the most important changes concerned the role of the YWCA, the first external organisation that women workers joined. Although the number of women who participated in YWCA programs was never more than a small fraction of the female workforce, an overwhelming majority of the women workers who became activists in the labour movement and in the CCP attributed their initial 'political awakening' to the night schools for women workers run by the YWCA.

Offering programs in several Chinese cities since the late nineteenth century, the YWCA began with a primarily foreign staff who focused on providing general social welfare for women. Ironically, its project of educating women workers to become leaders in the labour movement emerged in the wake of the White Terror of 1927 that resulted in most CCP activists fleeing cities such as Shanghai (see S.A. Smith's essay on 1927 in the present volume). From then until the outbreak of war with Japan in 1937, the Nationalist government enacted a series of laws prohibiting labour organising and strike activity. This left the YWCA as one of the only organisations in Shanghai that quietly and modestly tried to instil in women a radical understanding of their position as both women and workers. In addition to classes on writing, geography and history, the night schools offered ones on imperialism, capitalism and labour laws, as well as training the students in public speaking. Meanwhile, by the late 1920s, most of the YWCA staff, including the heads of most of its bureaus, were Chinese rather than European or American women.

A second transformation concerned the CCP, particularly its role and organising strategy during the war with Japan. During the war, tactics the CCP had used during the 1920s—such as making speeches and distributing leaflets—were not viable, as the Japanese arrested blatantly political activists. Under these circumstances, the CCP began to adapt organisational forms that already existed among women workers, such as the sisterhoods and YWCA schools, adhering to directions issued by CCP labour leaders such as Ma Chunji. Rather than viewing sisterhoods as 'backwards', CCP activists began encouraging women workers to pledge sisterhood with other workers; they accompanied them to Buddhist temples, burned incense with them and pledged loyalty to each other. Like the traditional sisterhoods, those encouraged by the CCP sometimes included supervisors and women married to gang members. In fact, some CCP activists pledged to become the goddaughters of supervisors. During the war, the CCP did not try to mobilise its recruits to engage in a revolutionary movement, but instead tried to organise women workers to subvert production in as many inconspicuous ways as possible in the mills now owned primarily by the Japanese, whether by stealing yarn and cloth from the workshops or slowing the speed of the machines to decrease production and therefore Japanese profits.

Many of these practices continued into the postwar period. For instance, the CCP continued to use the tradition of pledging sisterhood as a way of organising women who worked together in the mills. The sisterhoods initiated by the CCP moved further and further away from the relative spontaneity of the traditional sisterhoods, becoming much more calculated and deliberate. In some instances, the CCP conducted sisterhood-pledging ceremonies in each workshop of particular factories, establishing aggressive political groups rather than the defensive mutual aid organisations of the past. Furthermore, they often held meetings under the guise of innocuous sisterhood get-togethers.

The YWCA of the late 1940s was also far different from the foreign-run missionary organisation it had been in the 1920s. It may not have espoused revolution, but it provided women the education, social analysis skills and organisational ability they needed to become both active participants in and leaders of a revolutionary worker's movement. In addition, the CCP recognised the crucial role the YWCA played and strategised to have Party members get jobs as teachers in the schools—some decades later claiming that the Party actually ran the YWCA night schools. All of this meant that, from the vantage point of the women mill workers, the CCP was no longer an alien organisation, composed of outsiders and intellectuals who spoke unintelligible dialects. Most of the Party activists responsible for organising women in the mills now were coworkers, neighbours, friends, classmates at the night schools or pledged sisters of the women they sought to organise.

United for Tomorrow

This, then, is the context in which the 1948 strike at the Shen Xin Number Nine Cotton Mill took place. The role of women workers in that strike, subsequent research suggests, is somewhat more complicated than the image of several thousand unskilled women workers uniting in a quasi-revolutionary movement. Elizabeth Perry points out that the CCP leader of the strike was a male metalworker and the strike headquarters were in the machine shops, dominated by skilled male workers.[6] Male and female strikers were not always unified, as indicated by Perry's account of male CCP members in the mill physically assaulting a leader of women workers, accusing her of being sympathetic to the Nationalist Party.

This does not mean that the role of women workers should be underestimated. Even if the CCP continued to focus on recruiting skilled artisans in the postwar period, women workers nonetheless played an active role in the labour movement. In the Shen Xin mill, they reportedly stood on tables in the workshops to deliver speeches; some, who had taken classes at the YWCA night schools, went from workshop to workshop performing skits to dramatise strike issues and teaching workers inspirational songs. Learning about the strike at the YWCA night schools, women workers from other factories established support committees and organised to bring supplies of bread and vegetables for the striking workers. Among those who came to express support for the strike were representatives of the Shanghai dance hostesses' organisation, who were themselves engaged in a protest movement. By the strike's end, three women activists were dead, 500 injured and more than 100 arrested.

Although a number of the strikers' demands were eventually granted by mill managers, the aftermath of the strike was overshadowed by much larger political events. By mid-1949, victory for the CCP was imminent. Although the success of the strike was cheered at the All-China Labour Congress held by the CCP in Harbin in August 1948, the primary message of the meeting was that workers should be discouraged from conflicts and confrontations with mill managers and owners and instead should form 'factory protection teams' to prevent destruction of the machinery and raw materials before and during the CCP takeover of cities like Shanghai.

The Shen Xin strike was not forgotten, however. The women who participated were celebrated as revolutionary heroines in one of the first feature films made by the Shanghai Film Studio after liberation, *United for Tomorrow*. The film's message was that the strike was no less than a dramatic display of 'sisterly solidarity'. Unrecognised by the film, however, was that even if the strike highlighted a dramatic shift in women's role in the Shanghai labour movement from the 1920s to the 1940s, the display of solidarity was almost invariably informed by native-place loyalties and divisions. As David Strand, in his study of Beijing labourers, points out, a strike—like any other mass movement—was 'not a solvent capable of breaking down barriers based on status, native place or division of labor so much as it was an opportunity to display these divisions in public'.[7]

1949

In 1949, the Chinese Communist Party (CCP) achieved victory over the Nationalist Party in the Civil War. As he addressed the first plenary session of the Chinese People's Political Consultative Conference on 21 September 1949, a triumphant Mao Zedong famously proclaimed that 'the Chinese people have stood up' and China would 'no longer be a nation subject to insult and humiliation'. In little more than twenty-eight years, the CCP had gone from an underground network of like-minded revolutionaries, surviving near extinction, to the formidable party solely in charge of China's future. In the following excerpt from a speech Mao gave in June that year to celebrate the anniversary of the founding of the CCP, it is possible to see the horizon of revolutionary promise and workers' liberation imagined during that period—a horizon that over time would fade into obscurity.

On the People's Democratic Dictatorship (Excerpt)

MAO Zedong[1]

The first of July 1949 marks the fact that the Communist Party of China has already lived through twenty-eight years. Like a man, a political party has its childhood, youth, manhood and old age. The Communist Party of China is no longer a child or a lad in his teens but has become an adult. When a man reaches old age, he will die; the same is true of a party. When classes disappear, all instruments of class struggle—parties and the state machinery—will lose their function, cease to be necessary, therefore gradually wither away and end their historical mission; and human society will move to a higher stage. We are the opposite of the political parties of the bourgeoisie. They are afraid to speak of the extinction of classes, state power, and parties. We, on the contrary, declare openly that we are striving hard to create the very conditions which will bring about their extinction. The leadership of the Communist Party and the state power of the people's dictatorship are such conditions. Anyone who does not recognise this truth is no communist. Young comrades who have not studied Marxism-Leninism and have only recently joined the Party may not yet understand this truth. They must understand it—only then can they have a correct world outlook. They must understand that the road to the abolition of classes, to the abolition of state power and to the abolition of parties is the road all mankind must take; it is only a question of time and conditions. Communists the world over are wiser than the bourgeoisie, they understand the laws governing the existence and development of things, they understand dialectics and they can see farther. The bourgeoisie does not welcome this truth because it does not want to be overthrown. To be overthrown is painful and is unbearable to contemplate for those overthrown, for example, for the Guomindang reactionaries whom we are now overthrowing and for Japanese imperialism which we together with other peoples overthrew some time ago. But for the working class, the labouring people, and the Communist Party the question is not one of being overthrown, but of working hard to create the conditions in which classes, state power, and political parties will die out very naturally and mankind will enter the realm of Great Harmony.

1949

After the Communist victory, the promises of liberation did not always translate into immediate changes on the ground for China's workers. While the establishment of the People's Republic in 1949 undoubtedly represented a revolutionary break for Chinese labour politics on a symbolic-discursive level, many workplaces initially simply carried on as before. Elements of continuity and change in workers' experiences in those early years of Communist rule varied across regions, industries and social groups. Taking the example of women workers in Wuxi's silk filatures, this essay argues that women were much less likely to benefit from the new opportunities opened up by the emerging order in China.

Continuity and Change: Women Workers in the Early People's Republic of China

Robert CLIVER

Shen Gendi was a young woman who worked in the Number Five Filature in Wuxi, Jiangsu Province, a silk thread mill operated by the state silk company, the China Sericulture Company (中国丝绸公司). The factory was unusual among filatures (silk mills) as it was one of the few taken over by the Government of the People's Republic of China (PRC) in 1949; most remained in private hands. Different groups of workers in different cities and industries experienced the Chinese Revolution in different ways and, for many, like the young women employed in Wuxi's filatures, little changed in their workplaces and daily lives in the first years after the Communist takeover. Even the 'feudal' management system (封建管理制度) in silk filatures, which included the beating of young women by older male supervisors, continued under Communist management. In August 1951, Miss Shen's supervisor beat her so severely she died in hospital.[1]

In the past, this might have elicited a strike wave of women workers engaging in work stoppages, protests and even violence (see Honig's essay in the present volume). But by 1951 the Chinese Communist Party (CCP) was firmly in control in cities like Wuxi, and the unions that all Chinese workers were made to join after 1949 frequently failed to protect their interests. Recognising the need for action, in September 1951, Party leaders launched the Democratic Reform Campaign (民主改革运动) in Wuxi's silk filatures, specifically targeting the feudal management system, along with counterrevolutionaries and agents of the defeated Nationalist Party (Guomindang, or GMD) among the filatures' supervisors. The campaign elicited a flood of complaints and accusations about the brutal mistreatment of women workers at the hands of male supervisors, as well as many other inequities that had remained unchanged in the factory regime since 1949.[2]

The Communist victory and establishment of the PRC in 1949—known as 'Liberation' (解放) in Communist Party parlance—is often treated as the break of dawn, a decisive moment when everything changed and the old society gave way to the 'New China'. A key question for labour histories of the PRC is, what difference did the revolution make for China's workers? What difference did it make that the new rulers' goals included liberating and empowering the working class, especially women? The answer is complicated and depends a great deal on which group of workers one studies. In general, workers in high-priority industries like steel and machine-building won substantial benefits and even some degree of control over their working conditions, while changes came more slowly for workers in construction and textiles, especially in smaller cities and in the private and collective sectors of the economy. Although things were not neatly divided along gender lines, male workers were usually better able to take advantage of new opportunities after 1949 than their female counterparts. The revolutionary changes Chinese workers experienced during the two years from Liberation in 1949 to the Democratic Reform Campaign in 1951 developed unevenly across regions, industries and social groups.

Chinese Workers under New Democracy

Efforts at liberating workers in the first years of the People's Republic developed in the context of Chairman Mao Zedong's theory of New Democracy (新民主主义)—a set of policies intended to foster and develop capitalist industry while protecting workers' interests and employment in pursuit of rapid economic recovery and, ultimately, state-led socialist industrialisation.[3] The promise was that compromise and cooperation with capitalists in the early years of the revolution would result in economic growth that would benefit the entire population, especially industrial workers, who could then enjoy the fruits of their labour in the form of health care, housing, education and consumer goods. Subsequent events show how difficult these goals were to achieve in practice, especially the promise of making workers the 'masters of the factory and the nation' (工厂与国家的主人翁).

In contrast with the 'dictatorship of the proletariat', theoretically inaugurated in the Russian Revolution of 1917, New Democracy did not include the expropriation of most private firms (excluding businesses in the 'commanding heights' of the economy such as steel, shipping, coal and power generation, most of which had already been nationalised under the GMD).[4] On the contrary, private industry and commerce expanded in the early years of the PRC, before the entire economy was rapidly 'socialised' in the winter of 1955–56.

In the context of the devastation of war, rampant inflation and the collapse of trade in 1949, protections for private businesses were entirely necessary and the Communist Party encouraged workers to compromise with employers on issues like wages, working conditions and dismissals. As Communist Party leader Ye Jianying put it to workers in Guangzhou in 1950:

> We must be good at uniting our own class, raising our political consciousness, and distinguishing between immediate and long-term interests and between partial and overall interests, and must subordinate immediate and partial interests to long-term and overall interests ... and so, under certain circumstances, it will sometimes be necessary to make some concessions to other classes.[5]

At the same time, the new regime also established protections for workers to prevent mass unemployment and social unrest. The CCP was, after all, the 'vanguard of the working class' (工人阶级的先锋队) and could not risk alienating its urban base. Two of the most important symbols of workers' newfound power under New Democracy were democratic management (民主管理) of the enterprise and the enrolment of industrial workers into union organisations established in every factory, city and industry. It was hoped that establishing a degree of worker control over production through organs for democratic management would obviate the need for workers to engage in more radical actions like strikes, walkouts and 'methods of struggle which harm production'.[6]

'Liberating' Women

Women workers were one group that stood to benefit from the Communist revolution, which promised not only the liberation of China's working class, but also gender equality and the transformation of traditional gender roles. As Delia Davin put it:

> More importance was attached to the mobilization of women factory workers than of any other group, in part because they

were members of what the Party taught was now to be the leading class in China, and also because they had an immediate role to play in the restoration of the economy.[7]

Unions played an important role in the mobilisation of women workers. In the early 1950s, the CCP rapidly established or reorganised industrial unions in cities throughout China and, by 1952, about ninety percent of industrial workers were enrolled in union organisations. These unions were not always under CCP leadership, however, nor did they always protect or represent workers' interests effectively. Many unions were controlled by criminal gangs or holdovers from the old regime and remnants of organisations created under the GMD. Many unions were controlled by employers and management, while others were loyal to and appreciative of CCP policies but wanted to preserve their autonomy.[8]

Many women workers had no existing union organisations—less because these had been prohibited than because they had proved too easy to coopt or suppress—so many female proletarians, such as silk filature workers, preferred to protect their interests through informal networks and direct action rather than establishing union organisations.[9] When the CCP insisted that all workers join the new unions, this frequently resulted in labour organisations that did not represent their constituents effectively, or even unions dominated by management, as was the case for Wuxi filature workers in the early 1950s.[10]

Even in unions that were both loyal to the CCP and effectively represented their members' interests, women faced an uphill struggle to achieve effective representation and advance their interests as workers and women. The fact is that, despite the Party leadership's emphasis on women's liberation, many CCP cadres in villages and factories harboured sexist attitudes towards women and ignored or downplayed the specific needs and problems of women workers. Even high-ranking women labour leaders disparaged women workers' roles in the labour movement and in production, ignoring the important role women had played in strike actions and protests throughout the first half of the twentieth century.

For instance, Cai Chang, a national leader in 'woman-work' (妇女工作) in the unions, stated in a 1950 report that it was especially difficult to mobilise Chinese women for union work because they had to defer to their parents or husbands and could not be 'their own masters'.[11] She stated that it was necessary to carry out education work among women in industry to 'raise their consciousness' and eliminate the mentality of 'relying on men to carry out union work'. Such passivity was thought to be a product of women's double oppression under the old society. Older workers, although praised as 'veterans on the production front', were considered 'ideologically confused' because they had been raised in a 'feudal' society. Younger workers, on the other hand, were characterised as more active and enthusiastic about politics and union activities, but union reports criticised younger women as vain, liking to 'make themselves pretty' and lacking in 'character' (个性), such that they feared hardship, did not value labour and had certain '*petite bourgeois* characteristics'. This is but one example of the Communists' penchant for defining anything corrupt, decadent or feminine as 'bourgeois'—a prejudice with obvious negative consequences for 'woman-work' in Chinese unions.

One means put forward for addressing the specific needs of women workers—so important symbolically and practically to the new regime in 1949—was the establishment of women workers' departments (妇女部) in union organisations. The first Trade Union Law of the PRC, implemented in 1950, required that unions in enterprises employing more than fifty women create a women's committee and those employing more than 300 women employ a full-time union official in charge of 'woman-work'.[12] Although often underfunded, sidelined and ignored by male union leaders, women workers' departments were essential in addressing some of the specific difficulties women faced in Chinese factories in the early 1950s. Health care and maternity leave were just two important issues the women workers' departments addressed. Marriage reform, domestic violence, unequal pay, childcare and working conditions were other problems the departments struggled to address, often facing opposition from Party and union cadres more concerned with the economic demands of New Democracy than with the liberation of working-class women.[13]

As with the unions, the organs for democratic management in Chinese factories were also less accessible for women workers than for their male counterparts. This was the case in both state-run and privately owned factories. In privately owned factories employing mostly women, like the silk filatures of Wuxi, the organs for democratic management (called 'labour–capital consultative conferences'; 劳资协商会议) were not established at all or were simply an empty façade, despite being legally required in all large enterprises.[14] Even in government-administered factories in which the majority of workers were women, such as the Tianjin Third Cotton Mill, it proved almost impossible for women to participate in the organs for democratic management given the prevailing prejudices.[15]

If anything, private employers seem to have been more responsive to women workers' demands for implementation of legislated improvements like health insurance and medical care, especially after the reform campaigns from the autumn of 1951 to the summer of 1952. In Wuxi's silk thread mills, for example, the kinds of changes that workers in other industries enjoyed from 1950 only began in the summer of 1952. These included literacy education, provision of medical care and childcare, protections for women workers and improvements in working conditions in the city's filatures, especially improved ventilation and temperature and humidity control.[16]

The Impact of Patriotic Production Campaigns

One of the more ubiquitous changes to appear in Chinese industry in the early 1950s were the patriotic production campaigns (爱国增产运动) of the Korean War (1950–53). Production competitions of various kinds had appeared sporadically in both private and state-run factories in the 1930s, but in the 1950s the practice spread throughout Chinese industry (see Sørensen's essay in the present volume). Modelled largely on Soviet practices such as 'shock work' and Stakhanovism, Chinese production campaigns were initially limited to state-run factories, but by the end of the war in Korea had become a common feature throughout Chinese industry. Production campaigns were one of the few CCP initiatives in private industry that capitalist employers were enthusiastic about implementing. Even if factory owners resented the high taxes and compulsory 'donations' to the war effort, having the strength of Communist Party propaganda behind a movement to get workers to improve productivity and quality was a potential benefit.

In the context of Wuxi's silk filatures, the wartime production campaigns were one of the few revolutionary initiatives implemented by unions dominated by managerial personnel hostile to women workers' liberation. The filature unions were mostly controlled by management and many factories managed to avoid their legal obligations to establish health insurance provision or organs for democratic management, but they nonetheless launched patriotic production campaigns. The women employed in Wuxi's silk mills were reminded how important their product was for the war effort, as the PRC exchanged silk thread and cloth with the Soviet Union in return for steel and petrol. Workers were told to 'sweat a bit more to help the Volunteer Army bleed a bit less'.[17] Of all the CCP's initiatives affecting women workers in the early 1950s, the production campaigns were the most widespread and successful, as output and product quality saw impressive, if short-lived, improvements in 1951.

By the autumn of 1951, however, the shortcomings of the unions described above—ineffective representation, sometimes due to control of the unions by management or even criminal elements hostile to the revolution—had produced problems serious enough for the Party-State to launch a nationwide campaign to reform the unions. The Democratic Reform Campaign, as it was known, entailed investigation of union leaders and, if necessary, their replacement with more reliable activists.[18]

Controlled Class Struggle through Mass Campaigns

Despite the dramatic changes in Chinese factories resulting from the Communist takeover, the fact that Shen Gendi was beaten to death by a supervisor in a state-run silk filature in August 1951 reveals how little had really changed for this group of women workers more than two years after Liberation. The Wuxi labour authorities' response was to focus the Democratic Reform Campaign on removing 'counterrevolutionary elements' from union leadership and reforming the 'feudal' management system in place in the city's silk thread mills. Party cadres carefully controlled the process, first meeting with workers in small groups to identify the worst offenders, then organising mass struggle meetings at which women were encouraged to voice their accusations, and ultimately punishing the perpetrators. The last part of the process was disappointing and frustrating as very few of these men were, in fact, punished, and some even kept their jobs at the factory. But this was less important to Wuxi's Communist leaders than the opportunity to 'cleanse the class ranks' of the union organisation and elect new leaders who were more representative of the filatures' workers, but also more loyal to the Party-State.

This form of controlled class struggle, which under the Democratic Reform forbade criticisms of capitalist factory owners or government policy, was only somewhat successful in achieving the Party's goals, and in fact failed to eliminate or replace the 'feudal' management system in factories, with complaints about the treatment of workers continuing to surface at least until 1953.[19] Nonetheless, it was not until after the Democratic Reform and the Three Antis and Five Antis campaigns (三反五反运动) in 1952 (aimed, respectively, at corrupt officials and law-breaking capitalists) that the city of Wuxi began to implement the improvements in welfare provision and working conditions described above. The Party-State might be blind to the difficulties many workers faced, but it was not impervious to influence and could achieve many positive benefits for workers once moved to action.

As the country's transition to socialism accelerated from the publication of the *General Line for the Transition to Socialism* (社会主义改造总路线) in October 1953 to the proclamation of the Socialist High Tide (社会主义改造高潮) in January 1956, China's women workers continued to see rapid changes in politics, society and the economy, even as many things—including unequal pay and representation, male chauvinism and the sidelining of women workers' interests—remained unchanged. China's New Democratic experiment was revolutionary in its scope and ambition, but the contradictions between liberation and democracy, on the one hand, and the state's overarching goal of economic development and industrialisation, on the other, posed immense challenges for women workers' efforts to advance their interests. As the Chinese economy plunged into the frenzy of production and destruction known as the Great Leap Forward (大跃进) (1958–62), women found themselves working harder than ever before and losing many of the protections they had won in the interim, while watching their hopes for liberation and empowerment recede over the horizon.[20]

1949

As the Civil War was nearing its end, the Nationalist Party (Guomindang, or GMD) retreated to the island of Taiwan. At a time when the United States was forging its anticommunist networks in East Asia against both the Soviet Union and the People's Republic of China, the GMD-led Republic of China with its strategic location and its claim to represent the only legitimate government of 'free' China constituted an important ally for the US Government, an alliance that was sealed as the Korean War broke out. The two Chinas then began an intense diplomatic competition that lasts to this day. Internally, the GMD ruled with an iron fist. To impose order on the island in the face of increasing popular unrest, in May 1949, the Nationalist authorities declared martial law. They would not lift it for thirty-eight years until July 1987. This essay looks at the tumultuous period for labour in Taiwan in the aftermath of World War II, before the GMD managed to annihilate any social force that went against its authoritarian rule.

A Spark Extinguished: Worker Militancy in Taiwan after World War II (1945–1950)

Po-chien CHEN and Yi-hung LIU

> On the day of the strike, around three to four hundred workers took a boat to the shipyard but didn't go into the workplace. Instead, with our own toolboxes in hand, we assembled and blockaded the offices. Then, workers with military training background subdued the armed factory police and put them into the shipyard's privately built iron cages. The shipyard was surrounded by the sea. To prevent the managers and supervisors from running away and sending out information, the trained workers patrolled the seashore and hence the island [on which the shipyard was located] was sealed off. The strike went on from morning to night for around twelve hours. The employers eventually gave in and accepted the workers' demand for a pay raise. That night, the strike was over and we won!
>
> — Ruan Hung-Ying, Keelung shipyard worker and leader of Keelung Metal Workers' Union in the late 1940s[1]

Towards the end of 1949, the regime of the Chinese Nationalist Party (Guomindang, or GMD) retreated to the Province of Taiwan as a result of the Chinese Civil War. Albeit defeated, the GMD was once again supported by the United States due to the outbreak of the Korean War and the US strategy of containing communism—a Cold War arrangement that led to the establishment of the Republic of China (ROC) in Taiwan and the ensuing diplomatic competition with the People's Republic of China for the representation of China that lasts to this day. Although the GMD would impose military rule on Taiwan for the next thirty-eight years, the ROC regime—in opposition to 'communist China'—was referred to as 'free China' by both the GMD and its allies, most notably the United States.

A Strike-Less 'Free China'

On 4 July 1976, the bicentenary of the US Declaration of Independence, the ROC Government in Taiwan paid for an advertisement in *The New York Times*. It read:

> [The labour force in Taiwan] is the best bargain in Asia, if not the world, when efficiency as well as cost is taken into account. And the island's workers are well disciplined; there is practically none of the costly labor strife that characterizes industries in many parts of the world. There are no strikes.[2]

From the late 1960s, a so-called economic miracle occurred in 'free China'. Current studies have attributed this successful economic growth to Taiwan's low labour costs and meek workers, with some researchers even suggesting that prior to the 1980s a worker movement did not exist on the island.[3] This led to the widespread belief that Taiwanese workers have always been docile and easily tamed.

Yet, in the post–World War II years, workers in Taiwan were militant, often instigating radical strikes and industrial action, courageously fighting for improved labour conditions. Taiwan was not innately 'an island without strikes'. The 'strike-less island' was an outcome of the imposition of martial law and the GMD's brutal suppression of the left. Under martial law, the ROC Government systematically annihilated thousands upon thousands of workers, peasants, indigenous people and members of the underground Chinese Communist Party (CCP) to eliminate any social force that went against the grain of its authoritarian rule.

Legacies

In 1895, the defeated Qing Dynasty and the victorious Japanese Empire signed the Treaty of Shimonoseki, in which China ceded the island of Taiwan to Japan. Taiwan had been under the jurisdiction of the Qing imperial government since 1684 and, in 1885, it had even been established as a Chinese province under Qing rule. For centuries, Han Chinese immigrants from the coastal region of mainland China had constituted the majority of the local residents. Due to the Treaty of Shimonoseki, the Japanese Empire took hold of Taiwan and began a process of colonisation that would last five decades.

In the early years of Japanese colonisation, Taiwan was mainly an agrarian society. For the purposes of governance and exploitation, the Japanese Empire developed Taiwan into a colonial economy and modernised the island to some extent. For instance, to enlarge sugar exports from Taiwan to Japan, the Japanese Government introduced semi-automated and fully automated production techniques. Mechanical operations gradually replaced manual labour and the scale of mechanisation and factories expanded. To facilitate the export of the colony's resources, the Japanese Government also devoted itself to the construction of port facilities. As a result, cement factories were built and the demand for port workers increased. Because of this process of industrialisation, the population of waged workers in Taiwan began to increase.

The mid-1920s witnessed the thriving of peasant and labour movements for the first time in the history of Taiwan.[4] For instance, an unprecedented island-wide strike broke out in 1927 as mechanics in southern Taiwan initiated a labour dispute. These movements were organised and led by anticolonial, nationalist cadres.[5] In particular, towards the end of the 1920s, a nationwide peasant union with a membership of more than 20,000 came under the directorship of the Taiwanese Communist Party (台灣共產黨, TCP), a newly established party aspiring to overthrow the Japanese regime. Meanwhile, a left-wing reformist party, the Taiwan People's Party (台灣民眾黨, TPP), led a general labour union of more than 10,000 members, as well as some related worker organisations.

Yet, in the early 1930s, the Japanese colonial government severely suppressed these thriving movements. The TCP was branded an illegal organisation and almost fifty of its cadre members were arrested and prosecuted. Higher-ranking leaders were sentenced to more than ten years in prison, although some of them managed to escape to mainland China. The TPP was disbanded by the colonial government in 1931, in the year the Japanese invaded northeastern China. As the Imperial Japanese Army gained power, the Japanese Empire embarked on a series of expansionist wars. Japan picked Taiwan as a base for its invasion of Southeast Asia and the Pacific Islands, and hence accelerated the industrialisation of the island to meet the empire's military demands. This meant the peasant and labour movements had to be subdued.

Fast forward to the end of World War II. On 15 August 1945, Emperor Hirohito announced the surrender of Japan to the Allies. As per the 1943 Cairo Declaration, Taiwan was restored to the ROC and, in October 1945, the ROC Government sent a number of GMD officials to the island to accept the surrender of Japan and simultaneously take over the administration of the now former colony.

During the last two years of the war, those who had once been imprisoned or under surveillance by the Japanese colonial government, as well as members of the TCP and TPP, had restarted their organising work. Witnessing the impending downfall of Imperial Japan, organisers and leaders of peasant and labour movements began to rebuild connections and networks, marshalling in secrecy members of the past movements, ready to rise again when the moment arrived.

The restoration of Taiwan to the ROC ended five decades of Japanese colonisation. Having been discriminated against under Japanese rule, most Taiwanese people fervently welcomed the return to China. Nevertheless, because of the language barrier—learning Chinese was banned in the late Japanese colonial period—and the condescending attitude of GMD officials, the very people who had been so welcoming of the new rulers soon began again to feel discriminated against. Moreover, the GMD regime in Taiwan was incompetent and continued to engage in corruption and abuse of power, exactly as it had done in mainland China.

Less than eighteen months after the return to China, towards the end of February 1947, uprisings broke out all over Taiwan, culminating in an extensive anti-government movement that came to be known as the 'February 28 incident' (二二八事件). The movement was violently suppressed as the GMD called for troops from the mainland to launch a brutal crackdown. More than 10,000 civilians died.[6]

Organisational Work from the Left

Between 1946 and 1949, before and after the February 28 incident, Taiwanese workers instigated at least twenty-five major industrial actions, which included wildcat strikes, work-to-rule protests, assemblies, appeals and petitions. As evidenced by news reports from that time, those who organised and instigated radical industrial action came from all walks of life. These Taiwanese labourers and activists, from both urban and rural areas, were railway workers, dock workers, shipyard workers, printing workers, bus drivers, sugar mill workers, low-level employees at government agencies, teachers and physicians.

Before the February 28 incident, the cadres and members of the TCP who had been arrested and imprisoned during Japanese colonisation played an important role in organising and assisting these persistent industrial actions. Yet, after the restoration of Taiwan to the ROC, the GMD intelligence service had obtained a great amount of information about these political activists and placed them under surveillance. After the February 28 incident, the already stringent discipline tightened even further. Most experienced cadres and members were compelled to flee to Hong Kong or mainland China. The deteriorating political situation prevented them from continuing their organisational work in Taiwan, not to mention assisting worker and peasant movements on the island.

Nevertheless, when the GMD took over the administration of Taiwan, some Taiwanese who had been based in mainland China for several years were sent back to the island to conduct underground activities on behalf of the CCP. These Taiwanese communists had escaped to the mainland to avoid being captured by the Japanese colonial government and, once there, joined the CCP. In collaboration with a few Taiwanese communists still unknown to the GMD intelligence, they established the Taiwan Province Mission Committee of the CCP (台灣省工作委員會) to organise social movements and recruit new underground party members.

Although the ROC authorities managed to suppress the uprisings and popular resistance by deploying military forces, the February 28 incident further intensified resentment of the GMD regime among the local population. Under such circumstances, more and more intellectuals and students joined the underground party, which in turn was able to establish strongholds in critical factories and workplaces in Taiwan. In some shops and industries that offered better conditions, the underground party successfully organised the cadres and gained leadership posts in some unions. Prior to 1949, when the GMD regime eventually imposed martial law, the underground party even prompted extensive demonstrations and well-planned work-to-rule actions throughout the island.

Collective Resistance

In 1946, one year before the February 28 incident, two similar strikes broke out in the two most important port cities in Taiwan, Keelung in the north and Kaohsiung in the south. In the face of extreme inflation, shipyard workers in both ports went on strike in June and September, respectively, to fight for a reasonable pay raise.

In June, workers at the Keelung shipyard—a factory built during Japanese colonisation and then taken over by the GMD regime—launched their strike. They not only blockaded the factory, but also subdued the armed police deployed to stop them. They even detained the factory director and some senior managers (who had been appointed by the GMD), demanding face-to-face negotiations. Within a day, the employers agreed to the workers' request for a pay rise. The strike gave rise to the Keelung Metal Workers' Union (基隆鐵器職業工會), a union co-organised by the shipyard workers and the mechanics of two other nearby factories.

A few months later, workers at the Kaohsiung shipyard in southern Taiwan started a strike that bore a significant resemblance to the action in Keelung. Both shipyards, in fact, belonged to the same company and, after World War II, were taken over by the GMD. In September 1946 at the Kaohsiung shipyard, more than 1,000 workers blockaded the factory, subdued the armed police and detained the director and other senior managers. Workers also demanded immediate, face-to-face negotiations. Similar to what happened in June at the Keelung shipyard, the striking Kaohsiung workers won a reasonable pay rise with their one-day action.

The Kaohsiung strike benefited from the assistance of left-wing organisers who had been active in the late 1920s during the Japanese colonial era. It is likely that the strike at the Keelung shipyard in June, sharing a number of characteristics with the one in Kaohsiung, might also have received the same support. Supported by organisers from the TCP and TPP, these two strikes can be considered the most coherent, militant industrial actions in the postwar years in Taiwan. Precisely because of this, during the White Terror of the 1950s, when the GMD regime launched a bloody anticommunist campaign, many cadres and members, as well as low-level workers of the two shipyards, were arrested and received severe sentences.

After the February 28 incident, most organised labour movements were developed by the underground groups and members of the Taiwan Province Mission Committee of the CCP. In 1949, their efforts bore fruit. By May of that year, as the GMD regime lost ground in the mainland and prepared for a total retreat to Taiwan, the Taiwan Province Mission Committee had already obtained full or partial leadership in the two main unions in Taipei: the Employed Drivers' Union (台北司機工會) and the Postal-Telecommunications Workers' Union (台灣省郵務工會). After three years of organising efforts, the committee was now ready to instigate collective actions for workers' rights.

In March 1949, to negotiate a pay rise, the Employed Drivers' Union had launched a work-to-rule action, in which all city bus drivers drove at a speed of twenty kilometres per hour. Although the action caused inconvenience for passengers, residents of Taipei City considered the union's request reasonable and thus supported the workers. As a result, after a day of work-to-rule, the city government agreed to a pay rise as demanded by the union.

Mobilising the workers in the postal-telecommunications department was tougher. Even though the sector employed around 6,000 people, dispersed all over Taiwan, the underground party organised the workers in Taipei and established a branch there. It also made every effort to contact and bring together workers at different locations. Many postal-telecom employees joined the underground party and broke through the GMD's control of the union. Some underground party members were elected to leadership positions in the union.

The GMD officials never hid their condescending attitude towards Taiwanese postal-telecom workers. After the return of the island to the ROC, the GMD regime regarded the 6,000 postal-telecom workers who were hired by the Japanese colonial government as temporary rather than permanent employees. For this reason, Taiwanese postal-telecom workers received a wage that was only one-fourth to one-fifth of that of the permanent postal-telecom workers from mainland China. This unfair treatment caused a strong sense of discontent and resentment.

In 1947, a former Nationalist intelligence agent from mainland China was appointed by the GMD as president of the Postal-Telecommunications Workers' Union. Under the new leadership, the workers' requests to be recognised as permanent employees remained unanswered. Meanwhile, by the end of 1946, the Taiwan Province Mission Committee of the CCP had effectively mobilised the low-level employees of the postal-telecom department in Taipei. Through activities such as labour education and journal publications, the committee established underground working teams to contact and connect postal-telecom workers. The workers' demands to be granted permanent employment became more and more intense.

At the end of March 1949, more than 400 postal-telecom workers gathered in Taipei. After the GMD-appointed department director disregarded their request, the workers promptly launched a street demonstration, marching from the department headquarters to the Taiwan Provincial Government building—where the GMD troops had fired the first shot two years earlier, in February 1947. Throughout the march, people supportive of the workers' demands joined the demonstration one after another and, by the time they arrived at their destination, the crowd had grown to around 2,000 people—enough to surround the Provincial Government building. The demonstration shocked the GMD regime, which was then preparing for a complete retreat to Taiwan.

The demonstration led to the recognition of the 6,000 Taiwanese postal-telecom workers as permanent employees. In fact, this mobilisation in Taipei was the largest of all those in the postwar years. And yet, it also marked the last action by Taiwanese workers' movements for decades to come.

Annihilation

On 19 May 1949, not long after the work-to-rule action by the Drivers' Union and the postal-telecom workers' demonstration, the GMD regime declared martial law in Taiwan, under which all industrial action and strikes were banned. According to the martial law order, those who encouraged or instigated workers' movements could be sentenced to death.

In December 1949, the GMD regime—defeated in the Chinese Civil War—retreated to Taiwan. From 1950, the underground organisations and groups, including the postal-telecom workers' branch and the Drivers' Union, were repeatedly raided and destroyed. A great number of cadres were arrested and sentenced to severe punishment. Some were even convicted of treason and executed. During the White Terror of the 1950s, about 1,000 people[7]—including farmers and workers, left-wing intellectuals and students, union cadres and apolitical civilians—were executed.

From 1950, the GMD regime began to regulate and control all union organisations and factories in Taiwan. It pressed for the restructuring of the unions, assigning directors to each union and sent out intelligence agents to factories to conduct onsite surveillance. Workers were also encouraged to watch over and report on 'suspicious characters'.

Under martial law, any collective action by Taiwanese workers could be considered 'treason' and hence lead to arrest or even execution. Union organisations, at the same time, were reduced to GMD-manipulated 'yellow unions'. As the ROC Government strived to thoroughly eliminate every trace of resistance, the Taiwanese workers' militancy inherited from the anticolonial tradition of the Japanese colonial era was exterminated.

1951

We encountered Li Lisan in 1922 at Anyuan, where he was establishing a workers' school and organising miners and railway workers into one of the most consequential strikes of that era. In the following years, he experienced several political setbacks and ended up spending fifteen years in disgrace in the Soviet Union. We now meet him again in Beijing in 1951, holding the concurrent positions of Minister of Labour and head of the revived All-China Federation of Trade Unions (ACFTU). Founded in 1925 as a coordinating body for leftist unions nationwide, the ACFTU had fallen into disuse in the 1930s and was reestablished only in 1948 as the Chinese Communist Party (CCP) was gearing up to take power. In those early years, when the institutions of the new Party-State were still in flux, it was unclear what role a trade union was supposed to play in a new order in which power was held by a political party that claimed to represent the 'vanguard of the working class' and pledged to work for improvements in workers' conditions while at the same time vouching to protect the interests of entrepreneurs and maintain appropriate levels of profit.

The first months after liberation were chaotic. According to Mark Frazier:

> [T]housands of private-sector employees left unemployed by the collapse of industrial activity during the civil war returned to their factories to demand their jobs back. They wanted higher wages, improvements in benefits and working conditions, and guarantees of full-time employment. In the State-owned factories, Communist military cadres who had been placed in certain critical factories to 'supervise' factory directors often seized power from them, with predictable upheavals in basic operations.[1]

This led to a situation in which 'workers struck at will and frightened capitalists closed their factories'.[2] Speaking at an international union conference in November 1949, even Li Lisan had to concede that the situation in the previous months had been untenable:

In private enterprises, after the liberation of each city, waves of workers' struggles immediately ensued. As the capitalists lost the support of the reactionary regime, they could not but make concessions to the demands of the masses ... However, the demands of the workers were sometimes too high. Their actions and forms of struggle were in some cases inordinate. This had effects on the close down of some enterprises, stoppage of production, and the passive running away of the capitalists; these are detrimental to the paramount interests of the resumption and development of production.[3]

The necessity to restore production and regain control over the economy led the Party to strengthen the political role of the ACFTU—a move that caused widespread mistrust and even hostility among the workers, who perceived the union as a tool in the hands of management. In response, in August 1950, the authorities launched a campaign against 'bureaucratism' (官僚主义) within the ACFTU, encouraging it to be more open and responsive—and less formal and rigid—to the needs of workers.[4]

Against this uncertain background, in August 1950, the People's Daily and Workers' Daily published a speech by a Party cadre named Deng Zihui on the work of the ACFTU in southern and central China.[5] According to Deng, the union had become detached from the masses. Going even further, he argued that, although in the public sector the union and the Party were both working for the wellbeing of the workers and the country, some differences between the functions of the union and those of the Party could not be avoided. For this reason, he reckoned it was necessary to admit that, in certain circumstances, it was possible for the union to adopt a 'standpoint' (立场) different from the Party's.

Li Lisan intervened in support of Deng's thesis. In a speech given in March 1951, he affirmed that, although under the new government the administration and the working class converged, it was inevitable for 'some minor contradictions' (些小的矛盾) between workers and management to survive. For instance, even in the state sector there could be disagreements regarding wages.[6] Still, Li was careful to express his disagreement with Deng regarding the existence of different standpoints between the union and the administration. Such a distinction was substantively wrong because

under the 'New Democracy', public and private interests overlap and therefore the standpoint of the union and the administration

> also overlap. Wherever there is a difference, it can just be said that it is a matter between 'essential standpoint' [基本立场] and 'particular standpoint' [具体立场].

In other words, the Party determines the essential standpoint, while details may require modification to suit particular situations.

In a draft official document written on behalf of the ACFTU in September 1951, Li further distinguished between two sets of potential contradictions that could affect the work of the union: the contradiction between 'general interests' (整体利益) and 'individual interests' (个人利益), and that between 'long-term interests' (长远利益) and 'ordinary interests' (日常利益).[7] In his view, while

> in the state enterprises the workers are the owners and there are no class conflicts nor exploitation, therefore the effects of the development of production are always beneficial for both the individual and general interests of the working class, as well as for its long-term and ordinary interests, [it was impossible to deny that] there remain some contradictions in the practical problems of workers' lives, on issues regarding labour conditions.

On this basis, he argued that it was of the utmost importance that even state enterprises be equipped with a union strong enough to represent the workers and protect their interests. A few months later, in October 1951, Li Lisan repeated his views in a report directly addressed to Mao Zedong, urging him to take a position in the debate, but received no response.[8]

The clash quickly came to a head at the end of 1951. On 20 December, during an enlarged meeting of the Party group of the ACFTU, Li was subjected to ferocious criticism.[9] In strict Party jargon, he was accused of having committed three fundamental mistakes: first, he had 'completely misunderstood the nature of state enterprises', confusing the relations between workers and enterprises under the new socialist government with the previous situation under the rule of the Nationalist Party; second, he had 'denied the role of the Party as a guide of the union, considering the latter as the highest representative of the working class'; and third, he was guilty of 'subjectivism' (主观主义), 'formalism' (形式主义), 'routinism' (事务主义), and 'paternalism' (家长制的作风). The Party group relieved

Li Lisan of his position in the organisation on the grounds that he had encouraged worker autonomy to the detriment of Party control; three years later, he was dismissed from the Ministry of Labour as well.

In this speech given in March 1951 at the Second National Congress of the Electric Industry, we hear in Li's own voice what he thought about the contradictions between management and unions at that critical juncture in Chinese history.[10]

Li Lisan on the Relationship between Management and Unions

LI Lisan

(Translated by Malcolm THOMPSON)

Yesterday, I had a conversation with a few representatives who do union work. During this discussion, I learned that the relations between management and unions in many of our factories are not good enough, so I would like to take this opportunity to talk about this relationship with everybody concerned. If the relationship between management and unions is not good enough, in the first place, it is the responsibility of our comrades who do union work, or at least it shows that these comrades are not good at actively persuading management. As Chairman Mao says: 'Unions must actively persuade management to rely on the masses and must actively persuade the capitalists to unite with the masses.' We should earnestly study and realise this instruction.

There are people who say that the bad relations between management and unions are due to their different standpoints: unions represent the interests of workers while management represents the interests of the state, and the state is a dictatorship of four classes, so the standpoint of management is that of the four classes. This formulation is of course incorrect, because in our new democratic country, public and private interests are essentially the same, and the essential standpoint of both management and unions is thus naturally also the same. If there are still differences, we can only say that it is a question of differences between the essential standpoint and particular standpoints.

China is currently in the stage of New Democracy, so only by working together can the labouring masses be paid according to their work, and the principle of 'to each according to their needs' remains out of the question.[11] As a result, in the wage system that is in effect today, some minor contradictions between the public and the private inevitably remain. For instance, the management side, in order to implement economic accounting to reduce costs, will inevitably wish to reduce wages a bit; conversely, the union side, in order to attend to the lives of the workers, will, equally, wish to raise wages a bit. This is because management represents public interests more, and unions represent private interests more.

It is not at all the case that management represents *only* public interests and unions *only* private interests. The contradiction that arises in this way between public and private is by no means an antagonistic contradiction, but rather a contradiction between the essential standpoint and particular standpoints. It can be resolved using the method Chairman Mao has indicated of 'balancing public and private interests'. If we wish to resolve this contradiction, we must first of all improve relations between unions and management.

There are people who say: 'If this is the case, let management implement the balancing of public and private interests. Why bother with unions?' We say that not involving unions is impossible. This is because the responsibility of the factory manager is to increase production and reduce costs, and anyone who is good at these things makes a good factory manager. In circumstances like this, if there is no union, it is very easy for management to focus only on this aspect and discard the other aspect. The union has the function of crying out. The union uses the method of crying out and always making sure management is paying attention, so that the measures taken by it will not lean too far towards one extreme or another and give rise to deviations. Actually, this is the principal assistance that the union gives to management. Without it, management can easily forget about the balance of public and private interests, and it can place public interests first and private interests last or give everything over to public interests and leave nothing to private ones. There is still some sense in the principle of placing public interests first and private ones last, but wishing to give everything over to public interests and nothing to private ones simply will not work. However, in their work of persuading management, our comrades who work in the unions must never forget that public and private interests are essentially the same, and that basically means improving production. If this is forgotten, they will commit the error of one-sided unionism. Our comrades who do union work must realise: the standpoint of the essential is higher than that of the particular, and the particular standpoint should be subordinated to the essential standpoint. In this way, contradictions can be integrated.

The form of union work often adds to the troubles of management, but in its essence, it is management's only support. This is because if management wishes to improve production, it must rely on the masses. The organisational form of management's reliance on the masses is its reliance on the union. Without the union, management would have no support and it would be impossible to improve production. Since management must necessarily rely on the union, the union must also maintain this support and not let its side of things break down. Because of this, management has a responsibility to help the union to be strong and must foster the masses' trust in the union. How can this be done? First, under current conditions of possibility, management must try its best to resolve the demands made by the union on behalf of workers. For instance, if workers raise a demand for drinking water in the workshop, if management does its best under current conditions of possibility to provide a satisfactory solution, then the workers will feel that the union can get things done for them, and then they will believe in the union. If management then wishes at some point to rely on the support of the union to launch a production competition, the workers will have the power to speak, they will be easily appealed to, and it will be easy to improve production. Having resolved the minor problem of drinking water for workers in the workshop, trust in the union has been fostered; when the union has this trust, it is possible to solve major problems in production. If this is not the case, the working masses will say that the union has become the tail of management, which will be harmful not only to the workers' trust in it but especially to the improvement of production. Second, also under current conditions of possibility, it is necessary that the union does more of the things that incur gratitude and management does more of the things that incur blame. In reality, though, the opposite is often the case. I remember that a certain factory was unable to distribute a tonne of coal to each worker as scheduled due to transportation problems. Management asked the union to explain this to the workers, and it took a lot of effort for workers just to understand the situation. When the transportation problem was resolved and the coal arrived, management did not tell the union, and issued a notice on its own allowing workers to come and get the coal. After seeing the notice, the workers sought out the president of the union and said that they could now get the coal, and because the president did not know this in advance, he carried on as before, to the point that the workers had to drag him over to look at the notice himself. This way, it was management that got the gratitude and the union that got the blame, which greatly undermined workers' trust in the union. Henceforth such incidents must be given attention and corrected.

However, the labour union cannot simply function as a loudspeaker for every demand the workers make. Workers' demands can basically be divided into three types. The first type are demands that are both reasonable and achievable. With this type of demand, the union must persuade management, and management must do everything it can, and if it cannot be resolved, it must be reported to higher authorities. The second type are demands that are reasonable but impossible to achieve. With this type of demand, the union must first explain the situation to the workers and explain the obstacles to its achievement, and then confer with management about whether or not the demand can be at least partially met. If management considers the results of this consultation and a portion of the demand still cannot be met, this must be patiently explained to the workers. This way, after repeated explanations and consultations, the problem will be solved in the end. The third type are demands that are both unreasonable and impossible to achieve. With this type of problem, the union can only actively persuade the workers according to the real situation, and if it is unable to, it must convene the masses for a discussion and use the power of the masses to sanction individual workers. These are the three approaches that the union should take in representing the interests of the masses.

The Trade Union Law was promulgated by the Central People's Government. It is not only the law of union members, but also the law of relevant management personnel. As a result, the relevant management personnel also have a responsibility to observe or actively implement it. If the Trade Union Law is to be put into effect well, it must be observed and implemented by both the union and management together. Over the past year, every factory has implemented the Trade Union Law and, although some have certainly done very well, the great majority have not. Take, for instance, the problem of union cadres. According to the regulations of the Trade Union Law, they can be transferred by management, but management must first seek the consent of the union. But in reality, there are many factories that transfer union cadres without having sought the approval of the union in advance, and this gives rise to problems. The union side complains about the instability of its cadres, and the management side has the sense that it is being diverted from its tasks and bothered by the union. In fact, the union has a responsibility to develop cadres for management, and management can of course transfer cadres from the union, but it must take the work of the union fully into consideration before the transfer is done. If the transfer is done without full consideration and without seeking unity, this will affect the work of the union. So, there are a number of union cadres that have been transferred out this year who need to be transferred back to the union.

We must be aware that management and unions are an integrated whole and recognise that unions help management to accomplish its tasks. Therefore, management must also come up with a way to help unions solve their cadre problems, and properly consider which cadres are suitable for union work. If technical personnel are used for union work, obviously this is harmful to production. If cadres who are unnecessary for production are transferred from the trade union, this is similarly harmful to union work. The interests of management and unions are basically the same, and there is no contradiction. If contradictions arise, it is the result of feelings of resentment. Only if management and unions are united can production be improved. Generally speaking, union cadres are worse than management cadres, so management is responsible for giving assistance to union work and providing stability to union cadres. Without the help of the factory director, it is difficult to improve the work of the union. If the work of the union is not improved, neither can production work be improved. This year we have examined the relations between management and unions in every factory. We have done better in factories in Shijingshan, Nanjing, and Xi'an. We should extend their model achievements to other factories.

1951

After taking power in 1949, the Chinese Communist Party pursued a staggeringly ambitious transformation of every facet of the productive economy. The pivot from which factories and other workplaces were revolutionised was the mobilised working class, organised by the Party through a series of mass political campaigns—starting with the Democratic Reform Campaign launched in 1951—targeting corrupt or abusive managers and labour bosses. At first glance, this seems to fit cleanly within orthodox Marxist-Leninist tenets: a vanguard party seizing state power, shepherding the workers to class consciousness and overcoming capitalism. Yet the structure that emerged from this process was a far cry from the Party's promise to make the workers masters of their factories and of society. Instead, campaign mobilisation established top Party cadres as the centres of authority in the factories and imposed on them and those they oversaw the compulsions of the state plan. The new system repudiated the free market and violent exploitation of the prior period by integrating the working class into a form of exploitation that was in many respects deeper because it was more egalitarian.

Revolutionising the Factory through the Mass Political Campaign

Jake WERNER[1]

The mass political campaign of the Chinese Communist Party (CCP) was a social form at once political, cultural and technical that simultaneously democratised the factory and intensified labour discipline. It was a technique that drove a rapid restructuring of the labour process and a significant increase in productivity and output even in the old industrial centre of Shanghai, which, unlike previously underinvested areas, did not benefit from substantial new capital commitments.

For most of the country, the initial months following the takeover left economic relations largely untouched as the Party built its administrative apparatus, addressed potential political threats and revived economic growth. Though confrontation with labour bosses and factory managers was put off, new institutions were quickly established that would allow workers a voice in the workplace. Labour–capital consultative conferences (劳资协商会议) were set up in private factories; factory management committees (工厂管理委员会) in state-owned enterprises; and staff and worker representative conferences (职工代表会议) and trade unions in companies of all ownership types. The Party also began to organise the workforce into 'small groups' (小组) of around ten employees each. These were to become the organisational foundation for the Party's remoulding of workplace relations and workers' consciousness, the basic unit in which everyday political study would be carried out and through which mass campaigns would be brought to the lowest levels of the organisation.[2]

The crucial factory campaigns began with the Democratic Reform Campaign (民主改革运动 or 民改, *mingai*) in 1951. The aim of *mingai* was not to destroy enemies but to redeem those members of the working class who had made 'mistakes' under the influence of the old society. Both the victims and the victimisers were organised and guided towards reconciliation. To those with grievances, it was explained that their abusers were also exploited labourers who had been under the influence of the old ruling class. The targets of the campaign—who included both labour bosses and regular workers 'estranged' from their fellow workers due to their work style, regional identity or gang membership—were coached on performing self-criticism and seeking forgiveness in front of other workers. They were told that their past mistakes were primarily due to the reactionary system under which they had lived but they also had to accept some responsibility, which gave them a chance to earn the respect of the other workers.[3] The second principal aim of the campaign was to animate the new structures of authority that were often little more than words on the factory organisational chart. The factory Party committee was to be consolidated as the locus for unified leadership in the factory, and the labour boss system was to be replaced with elected production group heads.

Following *mingai* came two additional campaigns—the Three Antis Campaign (三反运动 or 三反, *sanfan*) in state-owned factories and the Five Antis Campaign (五反运动 or 五反, *wufan*) in private factories—which targeted graft and corruption. These campaigns aimed to extirpate the 'bourgeois hedonist thinking' (资产阶级享乐思想) that had arisen among complacent factory cadres since the takeover and to stop the private capitalists' volleys of 'sugar-coated bullets' (糖衣炮弹; bribery and dissolution) that were corrupting cadres.[4] They focused on leaders such as the factory director and secretary of the factory Party committee, as well as administrative staff like accountants, but their ambit extended as well to petty theft among the workers.

The Party's ultimate targets in all of these early campaigns were not its 'competitors' but the conditions that produced these social groups. The instrumentality with which the Party treated the masses was more than mere cynical manipulation. It was an attempt to make the masses fit their concept as understood in Party theory, which would in turn allow the masses to realise their historical mission. As one pamphlet explained: 'The working class is rich in organisational capacity and discipline, but under the oppressive rule of the old society and the old enterprise, it suffered all kinds of injury and restriction.'[5] Party leaders believed they were not coercing compliance but actively remaking subjectivities—from those deformed by the 'old society' into those required by a truly democratic society. They thought there was a potential among the workers that had been suppressed and could be unleashed through participation in the mass campaign.

The Campaign Process

The first stage of the campaigns took place behind closed doors within the Party committees at individual factories, with an intensive series of meetings convened to 'unify thought' (统一思想) among Party members. Members of the Party committee conducted self-criticism—some of them more than once, if they were judged inadequate. A variety of infractions might be uncovered, ranging from visiting prostitutes to using factory property for personal reasons and, at one factory, to arranging separate banquets to celebrate production of the plant's first boring machine for the owner and for the workers—but serving inferior food to the latter.[6] Party leaders were told to use their own self-criticism as a model for the other Party members, making a deep and thorough confession of their mistakes along the lines laid out in campaign directives. Hearing these confessions often inspired panic among factory leaders who did not belong to the Party, and they rushed to harshen their own self-criticism.

In the next stage, the now unified Party organs brought the campaign to the non-Party 'masses' at the factory. The first step was to collect complaints and accusations and to educate workers on the campaign. Demonstrating the central importance of the campaign's performative elements, a key aim of gathering this information was to ensure that the wider factory assembly would be 'lively' in expressing their discontent. A number of 'active elements' (积极分子)—non-Party individuals willing to take an active part in the campaign—were recruited to provide information and assume roles in the larger assemblies.[7]

With preparations complete, the staff and workers' representative conference was then convened. The main event was a presentation of top leaders' self-criticism—again, meant to set the tone and provide a model for all those observing. As in the intraparty meetings, small groups were convened after the self-criticism session to critique the performances of the leaders. At the same time, these meetings provided a chance for the workers' representatives and small-group leaders to formulate their own confessions of graft, waste and bureaucratism, which would then be presented to the workers on the shop floor. A representative at one factory noted that he had initially thought the campaign would only target leaders, but he now understood that the failure to draw a clear line between proletarian and bourgeois thinking was a much wider problem.[8]

The meeting of the representative conference concluded with an announcement of the names of those suspected of corruption who had been singled out in the preparatory stages. With this, the campaign shifted directly to the grassroots. Rumours were already circulating among the workers; anxieties were growing among those who, having witnessed earlier campaigns, feared they might be targeted, and many began clamouring for a chance to come clean and seek forgiveness.[9]

During *sanfan* in Shanghai, the city-level managers of the campaign judged this phase to have gone well overall, but they believed the leadership at a few plants was 'suppressing democracy': Party members were few in number or cowed into silence. At this point, the higher-level district or sectoral committee could step into the process and rally the workers of the factory against their domineering administrators. The East Shanghai District Committee (沪东区委), for example, organised the workers at two different plants to confront the factory directors with allegations of corruption raised by Party members at the factory. The confrontation was exhilarating for some employees and improved the standing of the Party committee within their factory. One worker embraced a Party member afterward and admitted he had made a mistake in blaming him for the failure to implement his rationalisation suggestion.[10]

With the arrival of *sanfan* at the factory grassroots, the 'masses' were now called on to make their own accounting (交代). Pilfering of materials was found to be very common, both before and after 1949. At Shanghai Iron and Steel (上海钢铁 or 上钢, Shanggang) Factory No. 1, 476 of 509 workers admitted to petty theft. Stealing funds, while less widespread, was not uncommon. At Shanggang No. 1, sixty-nine workers were implicated in graft. After the representative conference meetings, workers came forward fairly quickly to confess. Only a small number refused to cooperate at all, primarily those implicated in larger corruption cases involving connections with professional staff. As these minor cases moved forward, the masses were exhorted to make a clean break with the past and to participate in locating the criminal ringleaders within their factory.[11] In this way, it was made clear to the workers that they had been absolved and could, with relief, join the Party in its battle against the real targets of the campaign. As attention shifted from the workers to the staff, the campaign moved towards its climax.

In this final stage, the primary targets of the campaign were isolated and tremendous social pressure was exerted on them to confess wrongdoing. This pressure was leveraged through factory-organised 'tiger-beating teams' (打虎队), which were enjoined to carefully prepare the ground for interrogations, gathering accusations from others in the factory and marshalling incriminating documents to confront any uncooperative targets with damning evidence. To allay the fears of their targets, they were to constantly reiterate the policies of the campaign—that those who confessed and cooperated would be treated with leniency or even let off without punishment. Confessions were important not only for their own sake, but also because they allowed the tiger-beaters to isolate others who refused to confess by turning their accomplices against them.

The interrogation teams fell prey to a variety of abuses and mistakes. The Party centre always insisted that any kind of physical pressure had to be forsworn, but inevitably there were tiger-beating teams that resorted to literal beatings.[12] Even without physical violence, the intense pressures exerted by the campaign could produce false or unsound confessions; if those running the campaign did not immediately verify the information they elicited, the case against their target might eventually fall apart.[13] Targets were sometimes pushed to breaking point. By late February 1952, eleven people in the Shanghai campaign had committed suicide and an additional nineteen had attempted it.[14]

There were also tiger-beaters who failed to prepare adequately when interrogating their targets. One team faced a suspect who rambled on and on in response to their questioning, never coming to anything on which they could pin him down. Finally they took a severe attitude and forbid him from being so 'long-winded' (啰嗦). He closed his mouth and stopped talking altogether. The team, because it had failed to prepare independent evidence, was stymied. Ultimately, they gave in: 'Ok, why don't you be a little more long-winded?'[15]

In Shanghai, the campaign culminated with five mass meetings held around the city in which a select number of major cases were aired before the workers. At each meeting, around a dozen of the accused were placed before an audience of more than 1,000 and encouraged to confess and turn in their accomplices. A key aim of these meetings was to 'clearly embody the Party's policies by dealing with specific individuals'.[16] To this end, individuals considered to be representative were chosen—'living emblematic types' (活的典型事例), as they were called. Those who readily confessed were released without punishment while those who resisted were arrested.[17] Making a vivid example of these individuals was meant to terrify the holdouts who had been placed in the audience. Immediately after the meeting, these individuals would be taken back to their factories and interrogated—deep into the night if necessary. One said: 'This is the first time in my life I've ever been to a meeting like this, I was so afraid that I cried. I swear that I'll come clean on all the problems.' After attending one of the meetings, the factory director at Shanghai State Textile (上海国营棉纺织 or 国棉, Guomian) Factory No. 15 was called on to write out his confession, but his hands were shaking so violently he could not form the characters.[18]

The other key aim of the mass meeting was to 'overcome bureaucratism and reluctance among [factory] leaders'.[19] Some factories were criticised for conducting the campaign with inadequate vigour, due to fears that targeting management would leave the company rudderless and holding so many meetings for the campaign would reduce production.[20] Such ideas were branded 'rightist', causing leaders to lag behind the masses in their prosecution. At Guomian No. 5, the lack of Party leadership left the non-Party masses to act on their own initiative. At the representative conference, they raised complaints against the factory director and set their own deadline for him to do a self-criticism. They posted their own, undirected accusations against individuals among the staff. A group of 'active elements' even broke into the home of one suspect, looking for his ill-gotten gains. Returning to the factory, they exhibited at the door of the union an overcoat and other items as evidence.[21]

Transformational Effects of the Campaign Form

As these examples illustrate, the campaign form was not simply a performance for passive onlookers. On the contrary, it opened up powerful new possibilities of participation for those at the bottom of the factory power structure—opportunities that ranged from serving as workers' representatives or volunteering as 'active elements' to joining the crowd in the clamour for a more exacting self-criticism from the factory director. The campaigns of the early 1950s exposed widespread accumulated frustrations and grievances against factory leaders, technical personnel, managers and labour bosses. By unleashing these energies, the Party presented factory leaders with a straightforward choice: they could either work in concert with the masses in an attempt to channel grassroots participation in a constructive direction or risk bearing the brunt of undirected wrath. The campaign form thus squeezed staff and management—including Party, union and youth league leaders—between the mobilised workers below and municipal and central Party authorities above. By institutionalising and legitimising worker participation, the Party centre established a powerful means of disciplining lower-level cadres who might be less than enthusiastic in following the centre's guidance.

At the same time, the campaigns of the early 1950s cemented the factory Party committee as the ultimate locus of power in the factory. They targeted the Party committees' main rivals in the factories—labour bosses, gang networks, professional staff and factory management—battering if not destroying them. They also pioneered new modes of gathering operational intelligence. Through the systematic investigations carried out in preparation for the campaigns, which involved combing through factory records and speaking with numerous workers and staff, the Party committees compiled detailed information on both work conduct and personal relationships at their factories. As a third party antagonistic to management (in the context of the campaign), the Party committee could take advantage of bottom-up resentment against overseers to establish its credibility among workers, thereby gaining unprecedented access to their knowledge. This gave the Party a mastery of functional details that had always proved elusive to management in the past.

By establishing the Party committee as the only force to which the besieged targets of the campaigns could appeal, it was ultimately the campaign dynamic itself that breathed life into the new structures of authority in the factory. The process of producing this authority was often very direct and personal. As one report on *sanfan* put it:

> Most high-level skilled personnel start out arrogant and condescending and they look down on the Party committee. So in certain situations it's entirely proper to shake them up a bit and wipe that smug expression off their faces ... leading them to bow their heads and meekly seek the help of the Party committee with their self-criticism. Thereafter they will earnestly do their work.[22]

The Party did not manufacture the tension between management and workers. Such hostilities had been a persistent feature of Shanghai's factories before 1949, but they had been crosscut by numerous other divisions and deflected by ideology, fear and repression. The campaigns of 1951–52 crystallised the worker–management divide as the privileged axis of conflict, suppressed competing expressions of animus and encouraged the workers to articulate their grievances through the newly authorised language of proletarian identity and the collective good. The process was intended to be transformational—to purify the workers into genuine members of the proletariat adequate to their historical mission, and to steel the recently established factory Party committees through leadership of the masses in struggle. The form of this struggle was, in turn, meant to enact an organic unity between the Party and the masses. Factory Party leaders stood before the masses, confessing their shortcomings and promising reform. Those workers who had erred were forgiven and welcomed into the fold. Then both the Party and the masses joined as one to confront the labour bosses and corrupt managers.

Yet the unity of the Party and the masses was ambiguous in nature. The Party committees' antagonistic stance against managers and technical staff was not structural but situational. Its solidarity with the workers against their superiors was likewise transitory. Even during the campaigns, this imperfect alignment was evident in the way the Party committee dominated the staff and workers' representative conference—the nominal organ of worker sovereignty. With the beginning of the first five-year plan, the tension would grow.

Yet the early campaigns also established a durable structure of identity and authority that would channel resentments away from Party rule, leaving individual managers and obstreperous workers to bear the brunt of popular anger. The Party committee was an independent third figure within the newly congealed power structure of the factory. It stood outside the immediate tensions between workers and management, sometimes aligning with one side and sometimes with the other. It represented an external authority—not a despotic Communist Party but something more fundamental. Its role was to enforce the impersonal compulsions expressed in the five-year plan. With the completion of the campaign cycle of 1951–52, the process of Taylorist rationalisation that would permit the plan's quotas to be met assumed a new course, and the campaign form was increasingly employed to tighten labour discipline and ratchet up labour intensity.

1952

As the Chinese Communist Party attempted to rein in labour unrest and navigate its already fraught relationship with the trade unions, it also had to live up to the expectations it had aroused in the working class. Given the chronic lack of affordable dwellings in the largest urban centres where China's industrial base was concentrated, construction of public housing became a priority. As this essay will show, Shanghai was particularly innovative in providing new solutions to the housing crisis. It is no mystery that twentieth-century state socialism in both the Soviet Union and China embraced the idea that ideology was embedded in material infrastructure. However, the origins of Shanghai's showcase for socialist living, the Caoyang New Village, came from the unlikely sources of the utopian socialist New Village movement in Japan and US neighbourhood unit planning. Although it did not solve Shanghai's housing shortage, this was nevertheless an important experiment in form, and now has become a historical landmark where migrant workers (the twenty-first century proletariat) lease the cramped dwellings amid the glittering towers of the city.

Housing the New Socialist Worker: The 'Workers' New Village' in Shanghai
Mark W. FRAZIER

When the Chinese Communist Party (CCP) took control of Shanghai in May 1949, an acute housing shortage loomed large as an obstacle to bringing socialism to China's most capitalist city. Some one million working-class households (four to five million residents) lived in 'dilapidated housing' found in the older *lilong* (旧式里弄), the lane-alley neighbourhoods that were home to the majority of Shanghai's population, and in shack settlements (棚户区) of rural migrants. The promise of the new socialist government was to replace these and other legacies of capitalist Shanghai with a new form of housing that in function and design represented the new era. A new socialist housing model was central to fulfilling this promise: the Workers' New Village (工人新村).

Construction of the first of what would become nine Workers' New Villages located around the outskirts of Shanghai started in September 1951 under the orders of Vice-Mayor Pan Hannian, who headed the municipal government's Worker Housing Construction Committee. The first Workers' New Village was completed quickly, in May 1952, and named Caoyang New Village (曹杨新村), Village Number One (after the nearby Caoyang Road). It was located near the main industrial zone in western Shanghai, in Putuo District, on land appropriated from Dongmiao village in Zhenru township (真如镇东庙前村).[1] The two-storey masonry and wood-beam buildings—48 units aligned in staggered rows—provided new housing for model workers and 'progressive producers' (先进生产者) from nearby factories. As additional units were completed, by 1953, there were 1,002 households in the Caoyang New Village complex, which was thus renamed the '1,002 Households Project' by the urban planning bureaucracy. Soon the Shanghai Municipal Government would receive permission from Beijing to embark on the '20,000 Households Project' (两万户) to build Workers' New Villages in Yangpu, Zhabei, and elsewhere in Putuo District.

Workers' New Villages would, in the end, house only a fraction of Shanghai's one million working-class households—and Shanghai's well-known housing scarcity under state socialism remained no better than it had been under the capitalism of the pre-1949 era.[2] But the significance of the projects lay less in housing policy than in the symbolic and political realms. This essay will analyse the Caoyang New Village as a material representation of Chinese socialism in 'post-capitalist' Shanghai. Labour history, in China and elsewhere, has paid close attention to the material culture and lived experience of workers. Housing is central to both. Although in most accounts of labour in Maoist China the lived experience of the 'work unit'—including factory housing—has been the central focus, the significance of Workers' New Villages (which were built not only in Shanghai, but also in Beijing and other first-tier cities) has received less attention.

The 'Village' in Workers' New Village

Scholars have traced the ideological origins of the 'new village' (新村) and its implications for the design and layout of Caoyang New Village to two sources: utopian socialist thought of the early twentieth century and the urban planning concept of the 'neighbourhood unit' (in Chinese, 邻里单位) informed by British and American designers in the 1920s.

According to Chinese urbanists' recent scholarship on Caoyang New Village, the 'new village' concept stems from the new village ideology (新村主义) of the iconoclastic 'White Birch School' (*Shirakaba-ha*) in early twentieth-century Japan, an artistic movement that rejected old tenets of Japanese philosophical thought in favour of individualism and humanism, as espoused by Leo Tolstoy.[3] The ideal society, in the view of literary figures such as Saneatsu Mushanokōji, would be one in which mutual aid and labour existed alongside the pursuit of artistic endeavours. Mushanokōji established the 'New Village' (Atarashiki Mura) as a social experiment, where peasants and artists engaged in mutual labour and shared in the output of the collective. The new village concept migrated from Japan to China by way of Zhou Zuoren, a literary figure and Japanophile more famous today as the younger brother of Lu Xun. In October 1919, Zhou published an essay in the New Culture Movement journal *New Tide* (新潮) reporting on his visit to Atarashiki Mura, heaping praise on the deeper meanings and social connectedness of arduous physical labour and mutual support. In enthusiastic tones similar to those in which foreign visitors would later speak of Caoyang New Village, Zhou proclaimed: 'Only those who have experienced it, are able to understand this spiritual joy. How happy the people of Atarashiki Mura are! I wish all the people in the world could share this joy!'[4]

Zhou never attempted to establish a 'new village' in China, but the practices of mutual aid, work–study collectives, and communal living were popular throughout the 1910s and 1920s among Chinese students and intellectuals. What was later labelled as 'utopian socialism' (乌托邦社会主义) drew the attention of the youthful Mao Zedong and others at the time of the May Fourth Movement.[5] The new village ethos resonated with the idea, later propagated in Maoism, of the integration of manual and mental labour, and the assimilation of the village and the city—not in terms of the urbanisation of the village, but in terms of the 'village-isation' of the (industrial) city. As Yang Chen has written: 'The creation of the Workers' New Village became the most important spatial realization of the socialist era in Shanghai.'[6]

Capitalist Origins of a Socialist Village

If the Workers' New Village was the spatial manifestation of early Marxist and Maoist thought in China and represented the essence of socialism in Shanghai, it was also derived from a significantly different line of socialist practice of Western origin. The lead designer of Caoyang New Village was the Chief Engineer and Deputy Director of the Shanghai Municipal Urban Planning and Management Bureau, Wang Dingzeng, who received an MA in Architecture in the 1930s from the University of Illinois at Urbana-Champaign. Wang explicitly drew on the urban planning concept of the 'neighbourhood unit'—a popular ideal in architecture and planning attributed to the New York City urban planner Clarence Perry.[7] Perry, who heavily influenced regional planning in that city in the late 1920s and 1930s, believed that clusters of housing should be arranged around a core of public institutions, including schools, churches, libraries, and post offices, with green spaces and small shops situated throughout the surrounding half-mile radius of the residential cluster. The neighbourhood unit, which could be designed adjacent to arterial roads but not disrupted by their traffic, would promote community at a time when the automobile and urban highways were destroying traditional neighbourhoods in New

York City. Perry's ideas held sway among urban planning programs of the sort that Wang Dingzeng attended at the University of Illinois, and in an interview late in his long life, Wang recounted the fact that many planners and architects returning to China from training in Europe and the United States had been influenced by the neighbourhood unit design concept:

> Of course, at the time [the 1950s], I didn't dare to say that it was European and American style. We had to learn from the big brother Soviet Union. In subsequent construction [at Caoyang New Village], we also added the former Soviet Union's residential architectural pattern and created a series of long blocks in the style of farmhouses [农庄式].[8]

The curious intellectual origins attributed to Caoyang New Village—in some ways both contradictory and complementary as alternatives to the mode of housing provision found in the capitalist West—would become a source of controversy only a few years after the completion of Village Number One in 1952. After urban planning, and economic planning more broadly, came under the sway of Soviet influences in the early 1950s, the spatial plans and generous open spaces in Caoyang New Village would stand out as flagrant violations of the Stalinist principle of high housing density.[9]

On a visit to Shanghai in 1953, a Soviet specialist was quoted as saying of Caoyang New Village:

> In recent years, many left-leaning architects have built some boring barracks-style square-box houses, and have created a so-called theory that streets are only for traffic, merely vessels of transportation, so there is no need to pay attention to street construction as an art form. As can often be seen, the housing units whose sides front the road cause the street to be rigid and boring.[10]

This criticism was quoted in a 1956 article in *Architecture Journal* (建筑学报), authored by none other than the chief designer of Caoyang New Village, Wang Dingzeng. In print at least, Wang acknowledged that his team had moved too hastily, with no consideration for the aesthetics of the street when placing the windowless sides of the housing units facing the road. Far more serious, as Wang wrote in the same article, was the paradoxical effect of creating in Caoyang New Village overly high densities within the two and three-storey housing units (about the same citywide four square metres per person), while the neighbourhood itself consumed valuable land with its winding streets, rows of willow trees, and meandering stream (which had once been a polluted, mosquito-infested brook). Wang also confessed to another major oversight in putting the buildings too close together, blocking sunlight for most rooms on the ground floor.[11]

These and other shortcomings, Wang concluded, were the result of failing to study the Soviet experience, but also showed the errors made when a major housing construction project is undertaken without first developing a comprehensive urban plan.[12] Caoyang New Village was built before urban planners had completed their work, and the results showed. If Shanghai were ever to grow out to its western reaches, Wang (accurately) surmised, the squat structures of Caoyang New Village would be pinched in amid a very different-looking city.[13] Subsequent housing units—village numbers two through nine—built in Caoyang New Village over the 1950s and 1960s would have six-storey rather than two-storey construction, and would provide more space between buildings. And, of course, the skyscrapers and towering apartment buildings of Shanghai would come to engulf Caoyang New Village by the late twentieth century.

Caoyang New Village as a Socialist Space

Despite its non-socialist origins and the criticism its designers came under in the 1950s, Caoyang New Village was soon celebrated as the shining symbol of Shanghai under state socialism, a material expression of the leading status of the working class. As most media descriptions note, Caoyang New Village was visited by some 7,200 foreign delegations from 155 countries over six decades, with former US president Jimmy Carter a commonly cited guest (he visited Caoyang New Village in the spring of 1981, soon after stepping down as US president, and then again in 1987).

Despite its origins with a New York regional planner and its adoption in the early 1950s by way of Wang and other US-trained architects, the neighbourhood unit connected well with the socialist collective ethos and urban management aspirations of the CCP. As several studies have noted, the neighbourhood unit concept, as a kind of cellular form of community services and governance, is not a radical departure from the Street Committees (街道委员会) and subordinate Residents' Committees (居委会) that the CCP overlaid on the existing neighbourhoods in Shanghai and all other cities in China during the 1950s.[14] Perry and the propagators of this idea never intended neighbourhood units to be aggregated into large administrative units like a Street Committee, nor to mobilise residents for political purposes and ideological work, but this type of cellular spatial formation clearly facilitated the CCP's aspirations.

Unfortunately, there is a scarcity of contemporaneous research material on what life was like inside Caoyang New Village Number One and in its subsequent extensions during the 1950s. Recollections of workers several decades later, found in media reports and journal articles, generally convey a sense of emancipatory personal experiences (翻身) from the impoverished living conditions in the 1940s to the simple but satisfactory dwellings in Caoyang New Village. Reports also note that the model workers and progressive producers who first moved into Caoyang New Village were allocated housing units so that workers from the same factory would be living on the same floor, or at least in the same building.[15] Shanghai's first twenty-four-hour bus service operated to take workers between Caoyang New Village and their factories, covering both the day and the night shifts.[16] By these retrospective accounts, the most significant effect of the Caoyang New Village was in the moulding of a collective consciousness through a shared material and lived experience. As Luo Gang, a scholar of twentieth-century Chinese literature and culture, notes: 'The significance of the New Workers' Villages thus lay not only in the functional value of actual living space. Even more important was that it signalled the arrival of a new working-class spatial regime, a production of a new space in the social imaginary.'[17]

Luo and others have analysed Caoyang New Village from the perspective of Henri Lefebvre's work on space, ideology, and power. As Lefebvre famously said: 'Space is political and ideological. It is a product literally filled with ideologies.'[18] If Caoyang New Village, by its layout, arrangement of public space, and provision of public services, was the material representation of the New China, and signalled the status of workers as the leading class in socialist China, it is with deep irony that the place had the look of an American suburban tract of housing units (though multi-family rather than single-family), with winding streets, sidewalks, surrounded by green space, and even a gentle stream flowing nearby. Chinese socialism was being produced spatially from an oddly mid-twentieth–century American ideal, thanks to the lineage of Clarence Perry and Wang Dingzeng. The novelist Zhou Erfu in his classic *Morning in Shanghai* (上海早晨) depicted Caoyang New Village Number One as follows:

The setting sun had turned half the sky red, giving the row of willows behind the houses a purple glow. Parallel to their house were rows of new two-story houses, a broad alley between them, and opposite the glass windows were, as with their house, a row of willows ... As everyone walked out of the school, the dusk gathered from all directions, and the houses, the willows, and the lawns seemed to melt, faintly and indistinctly, into the dusk. Only the stream next to the road flashed and glittered faintly. People's flickering shadows flitted by. In the New Village, only at the Cooperative were the lights bright and the voices loud.[19]

Morning in Shanghai (published in four volumes between 1958 and 1960) celebrated the agency of the new working class and their efforts to protect socialist China from the ruses of Shanghai's old capitalist classes. However, Caoyang New Village Number One and its extensions would end up becoming the exception, as other housing built in the city was done in Soviet-style concrete-exterior apartment blocks—a representation, in Lefebvre's framework, of a very different form of socialism, reflecting the power of five-year plans and the productivist imperative.

The Decline of Caoyang New Village

Caoyang New Village's distinctive traits lay in part with Western influences, and in part with a collectivist ethos reflecting the self-sufficiency of the early twentieth-century's New Village movement in Asia. Within the community were public spaces and public goods provision: schools, libraries, public baths, hotwater stoves, vegetable gardens, consumer cooperatives, medical clinics, auditoriums, and administrative departments for housing management and public security. During the 1950s, land was laid aside for future construction of banks, post offices, childcare centres, parks, what would become the famous Cultural Palace (established in 1953), and a movie theatre (established in 1960).[20] In keeping with Clarence Perry's intention in his neighbourhood unit designs, all these amenities at Caoyang New Village were placed within walking distance of the residents.

By the late 1950s, as Caoyang New Village grew from forty-eight two-storey buildings to 718 buildings of two to six storeys, overcrowding became a serious issue. A 1958 report from the Shanghai Municipal Party Committee noted that the low-density principles with which the community had been designed were now anything but. While the public space and amenities were plentiful, within the housing units, the workers lived in ever-closer quarters.[21] The specific numbers provided by the authors stated that, from a base of 929 households (4,247 residents) in 1952, the community had expanded to 8,584 households (47,563 residents) in 1958. Given that there were 680 buildings at that point, they should have accommodated the expansion, but the typical two-storey construction held only ten rooms. There were fifty cases in which two households shared the same room—the largest space for which was only 32.9 square metres. Crowding led to inevitable arguments and disputes among the residents. The original arrangement was for ground-floor shared kitchens to be used by five households, and toilets to be shared by the ten households in the building.[22] Subsequent construction at other Workers' New Villages in Shanghai after 1954 used improved standards in construction and had three or more storeys. They also had south-facing rooms, with kitchens and toilets placed on the north side of the buildings.

Still, as another Party committee report noted in 1959, workers' families were on waiting lists for housing stretching out from eight to ten years.[23] Not unlike conditions in the late 1940s, about one-fifth of the city's population, or about 1.1 million people in 200,000 households, lived in crude dwellings (简室) or shacks (棚户). Housing would remain chronically scarce until market reforms produced a new, if largely unaffordable, stock of private or 'commodity housing' in Shanghai. But the Workers' New Village project was never envisioned as solving Shanghai's housing shortage; as discussed in this essay, the power of the Workers' New Village was in the realm of the symbolic, not the practical.

Legacies

In 2005, the Shanghai Municipal Government made Caoyang New Village the first post-1949 structure to be designated as Heritage Architecture, thus legally protecting it from demolition. Just as Caoyang New Village was a kind of 'reverse template' of the drab concrete apartment blocks that were built for workers elsewhere in the city under state socialism, the housing styles in the era of 'state capitalism' in Shanghai have made the place an oddity again. Aerial photos show the village wedged amid towering luxury apartment buildings, as a low-lying array of tiled-roof dwellings among dense foliage; a common if dubious refrain is that the layout resembles the five-pointed red star and symbol of the CCP. But few of today's Shanghai residents choose to live in what looks to be a quaint leafy neighbourhood when viewed from above. The dwellings that were once celebrated as spaces of emancipation are now deemed to be so small by Shanghai standards that the only residents who take advantage of the location and the low rents are migrant workers, whose landlords are the remaining original residents, the model workers of the past.[24] Shanghai's twenty-first–century proletariat lives in housing that once celebrated workers as the 'masters of socialism'.

1952

Locust swarms had posed an existential threat to Chinese farmers for centuries, and the imperial state's efforts to control them relied on the mobilisation of rural labour. Though post-imperial states were aided by the development of pesticides and a better understanding of locust bionomics, locust control remained labour-intensive late into the twentieth century. In the early 1950s, the newly established People's Republic of China drew on both old and new methods to fight infestations, transforming in the process the way labour was mobilised and organised in significant and far-reaching ways. This essay looks at the role of labour in the 'First Patriotic Locust Extermination Campaign' of 1952 and beyond.

The First Patriotic Locust Extermination Campaign: Rural Labour Mobilisation and Pest Control in the Early People's Republic of China

John WILLIAMS

Catastrophic locust damage was a feature of Chinese agricultural history until the late twentieth century.[1] Between 1950 and 1952, the state mobilised an estimated 120 million labourers to fight insect pests over thirty-six million hectares.[2] In Hebei Province, nine locust extermination campaigns (灭蝗大战役) employed forty aircraft and millions of farmers as the People's Republic of China (PRC) built on late-imperial and Republican era practices to physically and discursively mobilise rural labour for pest control in new ways.[3] Although these efforts demonstrated features of ideology and organisation central to the mass campaigns of the Maoist era, those features were far less important for the eventual suppression of the locust threat than were pesticides and land reclamation. In fact, reduction of labour was from the outset a central goal of locust-control planning for both ideological and economic reasons.[4] To state entomologists, mass mobilisation was not an optimal choice, but rather one dictated by necessity.

The local cadres organising villagers into locust-fighting battalions inherited a long tradition of state practices conscripting peasants into war against orthopteran invaders. Shang oracle bones (ca. 1250–1045 BCE) and Western Zhou (1045–771 BCE) texts reference locusts, and detailed accounts of catastrophic infestations appear in official Han histories.[5] To fight them, imperial states relied on methods requiring intensive mobilisation of rural labour. After twentieth-century entomologists uncovered the mechanism by which devastating swarms appeared, modern states began to permanently dismantle it through environmental transformation of breeding grounds. In China, the threat of truly catastrophic swarms was largely eliminated by the 1970s.[6] The campaigns considered here transpired towards the beginning of that closing chapter, at the dawn of the People's Republic. Though they showed great operational continuity with locust-control methods in both the Republican and the late-imperial eras, they also applied new methods to the age-old struggle. Chemical pesticides superseded trenches and nets as frontline defences, while the development of spraying techniques reduced the labour required to apply them. Organisationally, the campaigns demonstrated the state's capacity to mobilise labour with an efficacy far surpassing its predecessor and drew heavily on the wartime experience of the Communist-base areas. In terms of scale and technique, these mobilisations foreshadowed the mass campaigns of the 1950s and 1960s.

Locust Disasters in Imperial Times

By 1949, locust disasters (蝗灾) had been recorded in China for thousands of years. Customarily ranked third after flood and drought in local histories' taxonomy of catastrophe (灾), they held a particular significance in political discourse. By the time of the Han Dynasty (206 BCE – 220 CE), political elites construed them as Heaven's response to immoral governance, and, despite the scepticism of a few notable critics, this remained a prominent interpretative frame through the late-imperial period.[7] Rural society also associated locust plagues with divine will. The earliest rites relating to agricultural spirits included prayers for their prevention, while popular belief in much of the imperial period attributed them to the Insect King (虫王) or similar deities.[8] In the Ming (1368–1644) and Qing (1644–1912) eras, temples to locust-quelling deities proliferated based on the belief that, if gods caused outbreaks, they could also control them.[9] These popular beliefs often prohibited human interference with the swarms and came to be regarded by local officials, modern entomologists, and twentieth-century revolutionaries alike as the epitome of self-defeating peasant superstition.[10] Though many cultures associated locust plagues with divine punishment, in China, such events had distinct political implications that persisted long after modern revolutionaries vanquished their supernatural aura.[11] This was because a basic measure of an imperial state's legitimacy had always been its capacity to perform disaster relief. Shorn of divine connotations, this premise remained a core principle of the modern state, which therefore assumed responsibility for locust control.

Locusta migratoria manilensis, the species common to northern China, goes through five developmental phases, or instars, between hatching and taking flight, and a population's stage in this process greatly influenced control measures. Depending on the growth rates of eggs, nymphs, and adults, a year might see four generations depending on several climatic and ecological variables. Northern China typically experienced two generations in an outbreak year, known as 'summer' and 'autumn' locusts. A single summer locust could lay more than 1,000 eggs, and an autumn locust almost 600; eggs laid in autumn survived the winter to hatch the following year.[12] Different developmental stages necessitated different control methods. Eggs laid in the ground could be destroyed by ploughing or harrowing, which either buried them more deeply or exposed them to the elements. But oviposition often transpired unwitnessed on reedy, uncultivated land where labour was in short supply. Newly hatched nymphs were the easiest to destroy, since they were smaller and less mobile than later instars. Nymphs aggregated in ever-larger bands as they sought food supplies, and the traditional control method was to dig trenches in which the bands could be buried or drowned.[13] But trenches had to be strategically placed, and wide and deep enough to prevent bands crossing or escaping. Fully fledged adult locusts in fast-moving swarms were the hardest to battle since, to save crops, they had to be scraped off vegetation before they consumed it.[14] Fire could be employed but was a last-ditch possibility usually reserved for uncultivated land. All of these techniques required an immense application of labour that had to be mobilised by the state.

Usually, the state placed this burden on local officials.[15] According to the history of the Song Dynasty, the court recruited commoners to dig up thousands of dan of eggs in Zizhou in 1034.[16] In 1075, it made county magistrates and subprefectural officials responsible for locust suppression, empowering them to exchange bounties of grain or cash for destroyed insects.[17] Qing Dynasty regulations elaborated these principles in ever-greater detail over the eighteenth and nineteenth centuries.[18] The Republic continued them. In 1934, the Nationalist government issued the 'Outline of Locust Control Methods', providing county officials with a detailed schedule of locust-control responsibilities, including appointing locust-control inspectors and disseminating propaganda to educate farmers about the insect threat.[19]

Though official and unofficial sources provide ample examples of such regulations, the degree to which they were enforced is difficult to discern. Locust-control work removed farmers from other agricultural tasks and, unless their own fields were directly threatened, they had little incentive to engage in the backbreaking labour required for control efforts, especially if they believed it might invite divine retribution. Hence the necessity of bounties, which essentially functioned as piece-rate wages. But here the state faced another quandary, since incentive programs provided ample opportunities for corruption. Though local officials paid the bounties from state granaries established for famine relief, they bore all the other costs of control efforts. This requisition of funds and labour, in turn, provided opportunities for exploitation. Thus, on the one hand, local officials who overlooked basic locust-control work endangered farmers' livelihoods through neglect; on the other, the lictors and yamen runners sent to muster them could be as rapacious as the locust swarms themselves. Qing laws and edicts meant to address these problems make clear their significance.[20]

Learning from the Republican Era

Although the Republican era (1912–49) saw the rise of scientific entomology and a modernist ruling elite that rejected the supernatural connotations of locust plagues, the state's ability to manage outbreaks remained an indicator of political legitimacy. In spite of the creation of entomological bureaus charged with controlling insect pests, Republican regimes lacked the capacity to effectively mobilise the rural populace to either prevent or manage outbreaks. Republican locust-control efforts often faced rural resistance stemming from multiple causes: popular beliefs about divine intervention, banditry in provincial border regions, and a distrust of predatory local officials.[21] The Japanese occupation of northern and eastern China effectively ended Nationalist locust-control programs and prevented any coordinated response from the various forces vying to control the countryside. (Locusts, of course, ignored territorial boundaries.)

In 1943, human and environmental factors converged in an unprecedented locust disaster that ravaged provinces across the Yellow River floodplain.[22] Witnesses reported seething runnels of nymphs flowing unimpeded through villages and over compound walls, while the sky turned yellow with multiple crisscrossing swarms.[23] During the crisis, Communist cadres in Henan's Taihang Revolutionary Base Area pioneered the organisational techniques that informed later campaigns in the PRC. Forced to rely on the labour-intensive catch-and-kill methods described above, they developed an administrative structure of locust-control organs extending to the village level. They also conducted extensive propaganda efforts to counter religious beliefs discouraging human intervention and develop an ideological consciousness that elevated communal over individual interests. Finally, they consciously employed military metaphors and modes of organisation that explicitly linked anti-locust campaigns to wartime struggle.[24] These efforts provided the fundamental blueprint for the later campaigns and vital experience in conducting them. In the process, the Party gained political legitimacy among the rural populace as it honed its capacity to mobilise them.

Hebei's Locust-Control Army

As the events in Ji County, Hebei, showed, that experience would prove valuable in the early 1950s, when a series of major outbreaks confronted the nascent People's Republic. Each year of that decade brought damaging swarms to the province, but those in 1951 and 1952 were especially intense.[25] Ji County was on the northern edge of the Yellow River floodplain's breeding zone and contained the Qingdian and Taihe basins, two low-lying depressions (洼) larger than 10,000 acres (4,000 hectares) apiece, where floodwaters routinely left vast expanses of standing water that evaporated slowly. The soft soil left behind was optimal for oviposition and rapid vegetation growth provided plenty of sustenance for newly hatched nymphs. A local saying held that Qingdian basin flooded nine years out of ten—and the dry year brought locusts.[26] Under the Yuan, Ming, and Qing dynasties, multiple catastrophic outbreaks occurred. The worst infestation of the Republican era was in the autumn of 1929, when villagers went into the fields before dawn for days on end to pluck sluggish insects from corn and sorghum—and still lost 40 percent of the crop.[27]

During the rainless spring and summer of 1951, evaporation exposed 13,000 acres (5,300 hectares) of basin land. As another local proverb said: 'Flood first, drought after, grasshoppers cover the area' (先涝后旱蚂蚱成片).[28] Towards the end of June, a sheet of insects more than 1.5 miles (2.4 kilometres) long and one-third of a mile (half a kilometre) wide draped approximately thirty locusts per square foot (929 square centimetres) across the Qingdian basin, spurring local cadres to form a Locust Suppression Joint Defence Committee. An emergency bulletin released on 25 June directed affected villages to provide no less than 30 percent of their available manpower for an extermination campaign commencing immediately.[29] By the end of the month, eight of the county's nine districts reported locusts covering 100,000 mu (about 6,600 hectares) of land. As Qingdian village's Party branch secretary Wu Cunchong recalled, 'buildings and courtyards were coated in bugs, everyone's windows were devoured, and they flowed across the ground like water—you could step on twenty or thirty with one foot'.[30]

On 1 August, local leaders ordered the mobilisation of 17,000 to 20,000 villagers. They suspended primary school classes in seven districts to free up teachers and older students, and required the participation of all able-bodied citizens, declaring the undertaking a 'political duty' (政治任务) required to prevent losses affecting thousands of livelihoods. Within two days, more than 14,000 people assembled to form a Locust-Control Army (治蝗大军) that, as the name implied, took the form of a military organisation. Each district created 500-person locust-control battalions organised into brigades and squads. The district chief or Party secretary commanded the battalions from a central command post, and assigned them communications, hygiene, and propaganda officers.[31]

Through August, this army faced the orthopteran onslaught using a combination of traditional tactics and new methods. Trenching units dug ditches sixty centimetres wide every 100 metres, then buried the insects herded into them by capture squads. In other cases, brigades surrounded the insects, driving them to interment in massive pits. Teams in uncultivated areas hacked weeds and brush to encircle the insects and then ignited it. Some teams led donkeys pulling rollers to crush the locusts. On 7 August, the Locust-Control Army was reinforced with 750 kilograms of '666' pesticide and sixty sprayers, which increased extermination rates so dramatically that Beijing sent an additional 5,000 kilograms by the end of the month.[32] But, along with the insecticide came orders for continued mobilisation, so local cadres also resorted to more traditional tactics to keep the campaign going, offering a bounty of one jin of corn for every three jin of locust carcasses. They mobilised more than 20,000 people in the first week of August; thousands more joined the effort before it concluded at the end of the month.[33] The local history stresses the zeal of the masses and the energetic leadership of local cadres. It is less forthcoming regarding the total number of insects killed or crops saved, but clearly the swarms were not prevented from reproducing, since they returned in force the next year.

The First Patriotic Locust Extermination Campaign

Indeed, 1952 saw an even greater mobilisation of human and discursive resources across the country to fight the greatest insect crisis the PRC had faced. The Bureau of Agriculture issued an emergency bulletin on 3 June. Observing that early appearing nymphs already threatened hundreds of thousands of mu in Hebei, Shandong, and northern Anhui, it warned that, if they were not destroyed within weeks, the damage to summer harvests would be compounded by the subsequent generation of autumn locusts: 'At this critical juncture each locale must earnestly grasp the situation, organise the strength of the farmers, and exhaust every method to thoroughly exterminate them.'[34]

The Qingdian basin was an early hotspot. County leaders scrambled to mobilise nearby farmers on 15 May. A week later, they summoned more distant villagers to form 'expeditionary teams' (远征队), declaring that locust-control efforts superseded all other activities. They also organised more than 1,000 able-bodied adults into mechanised dusting teams for the dispersal of the 666 insecticide.[35] At the end of the month, Beijing sent more manpower and supplies to help conduct what was termed the 'First Patriotic Locust Extermination Campaign' (第一次爱国灭蝗战役). It seems likely that pesticide was being improperly prepared and applied by inexperienced cadres and farmers, since the reinforcements were led by locust expert Chen Jiaxiang and included an additional nearly 35,000 kilograms of spray and 437 sprayers.[36]

As the first campaign commenced, locusts infested more than 128,000 mu (8,500 hectares) at a density of up to 120 insects per square foot, with three-fifths of them in the fourth or fifth instar. On 3 June, the 10,000 men and women of the Locust Extermination Expeditionary Army (灭蝗远征大军) began trenching and encirclement operations, while trucks pulled rollers to crush insects. After three days of arduous effort under the slogan 'To patriotically increase production, we must resolutely exterminate the locusts to keep them from becoming a disaster' (为了爱国增产,坚决要把蝗虫消灭,不使成灾), the campaign concluded and most participants returned home. Unfortunately, the overall acreage of infestation had actually *increased*. Locust-control headquarters thus ordered a second campaign, mobilising 43,000 people from five districts.

As in its depiction of the first campaign, the local history emphasises the fervour of the masses: a fifty-six-year-old woman demanded to join the pesticide teams, while residents of one hamlet slept on desks in the village school so that recruits from distant areas could use their lodgings. By 13 June, the infested area had dropped slightly to 124,530 mu (8,200 hectares), and cadres decided a third campaign was necessary. More than half of the 10,000 people mobilised were women or students. To emphasise that the success of the campaigns was due to the coordination of provincial, prefectural, and district resources, as well as the education and encouragement of the masses, the history quotes one villager's emotional exclamation: 'It's the People's Government that found a way. Before, everyone said they were "spirit insects" and that the more you fought, the more they came—but it's really that the more you fight the less there are. What past dynasty ever did such good things for us?'[37]

Though these early anti-locust struggles essentially ended in stalemate, they nevertheless prevented extensive damage. And yet, while pitched battles might keep a disaster from turning catastrophic, the caloric and economic value of crops always had to be measured against the energy and resources expended to save them. But what is significant about these early efforts is the degree to which the state was able to effectively mobilise the populace—and this is the point emphasised in nearly all accounts. As the doyen of twentieth-century locust control, Boris Uvarov, wrote: 'The success of an anti-locust campaign can always be guaranteed on the sole condition that the campaign is properly organized ... and in some cases even second-rate technical methods may give better results owing to good organization.'[38] These campaigns, moreover, informed the organisation of early detection regimens that greatly improved the state's ability to prevent or control outbreaks by the end of 1952.[39]

Between Maoist Radicalism and Technocratic Expertise

Sigrid Schmalzer has argued that early PRC agricultural policy not so much careened between poles of Maoist radicalism and technocratic expertise as integrated them in the pursuit of socialist ideals through scientific farming. PRC locust-control policies in the 1950s and 1960s support this claim. Though Maoist ideology privileged the conventional wisdom of the rural masses over the ostensibly colonialist outlook of foreign-trained scientific elites, in the most radical periods, the intent was to dialectically integrate these approaches into a unified sensibility embodying the ideals of the new society rather than establish a hegemony of the former through obliteration of the latter.[40] Nor, at least in the case of locust control, was this dualistic approach unprecedented. After all, Ming literatus Xu Guangqi (1562–1633) credited his pathbreaking 1630 description of *Locusta migratoria*'s lifecycle to accounts gathered from elderly farmers.[41] The exterminationist rhetoric, on the other hand, was a feature of modern applied entomological discourse.[42] And, while cultures across the centuries have commonly likened the struggle against locusts to warfare, the Communist Party's intentional construction of locust control as military campaign grew directly from wartime experience and reflected the organisational and discursive militarisation of mass campaigns in general.

From the vantage point of rural labour history, the early PRC's locust-control campaigns exhibited significant continuities with both a deeper and a more recent past. Many of the operational and organisational techniques deployed in the campaigns had deep antecedents in China's 'feudal' history, including the notion that the mobilisation of labour for prevention, control, and disaster relief was a fundamental state responsibility. It is significant that early in the era of the voluntarist mass campaigns that were such a hallmark of Maoist policies, the state also relied on traditional material incentives to get farmers to fill bags with locust carcasses. The efforts of Ji County Party officials to mobilise farmers to dig up locust eggs in the spring and autumn hearkened back to agricultural manuals and dynastic regulations from the imperial era that mandated such activities, as did their policy of providing cash rewards or grain at egg-purchasing stations.

Other aspects of the early 1950s campaigns stemmed from precedents established in the recent past: both the mode and the discourse of wartime organisation derived from the experience of control campaigns conducted in the Henan base areas during the anti-Japanese resistance. These, of course, came to be emblematic of the Maoist-era mass campaign and also signified the new reach and prerogative of the modern nation-state. What was once a tax obligation was now a patriotic duty inculcated through ideological education analogising orthopteran and foreign invaders.[43] Where county magistrates once dispatched yamen runners and cajoled village heads, the Party now deployed village cadres to muster farmers with an organisational efficiency that reflected the unprecedented penetration of local society by the Party-State. Given the crucial importance of the locust-control campaigns in the development of the state's capacity to mobilise rural labour, it is somewhat ironic that the reduction and elimination of large-scale labour mobilisation were from the outset central goals of locust-control planning, and the main impetus for the intensification of pesticide use in the 1950s.[44]

1955

Starting in the mid-1950s, Beijing experimented with 'proletarian diplomacy' as a new form of international relations with other socialist countries. By sending Chinese workers abroad, the Chinese authorities were not only pursuing pragmatic goals, but also responding to broader ideological imperatives rooted in the communist belief in internationalism, with all the paradoxes this entailed. This essay tracks how Chinese labour diplomacy panned out in Mongolia, in a short-lived experiment launched in 1955 and prematurely cut short by the Sino-Soviet rift of the early 1960s.

The Short-Lived Eternity of Friendship: Chinese Workers in Socialist Mongolia (1955–1964)

Christian SORACE and Ruiyi ZHU

Opening ceremony of the China–Mongolia–Russia railway in January 1956. The locomotive carries the portraits of Nikolai Bulganin, Yumjaagiin Tsedenbal, and Mao Zedong. Source: Ch. Dashdavaa and Ch. Bold. 2015. *Jou En'lai ba Mongol oron* [*Zhou Enlai and Mongolia*]. Ulaanbaatar: Selenge Press, 52.

> Long Live the Eternal Friendship between the Mongolian and Chinese People!
>
> 蒙中人民的永久友谊万岁!

In early May 1955, Chinese workers departed on a three-year extendable contract to 'assist' (支援) in the socialist construction of their fraternal neighbour, the Mongolian People's Republic (MPR, 1924–92). A few months later, on 24 September 1956, Mao Zedong explained to a visiting Mongolian delegation: 'Our ancestors exploited you for three hundred years, oppressed you, they ran up quite a debt; therefore, today we want to repay these debts.'[1] In the same speech, however, Mao also referred to China's aid to Mongolia as a model for the attitude of his own government towards China's national minorities, sowing doubt about how he conceptualised Mongolia's status and relationship with China.[2] Despite these misgivings, which permanently haunted Sino-Mongolian relations, labour assistance was celebrated as an expression of 'internationalist spirit' (国际主义精神)[3] and 'eternal friendship' (永久友谊).[4]

This eternity was short-lived, however, as Mongolia stood on the Soviet side of the Sino-Soviet rift that engulfed the international communist movement in 1962.[5] Although the Sino-Soviet split is an undeniable cause of the breakdown of Sino-Mongolian relations at the state level, in this essay, we look beneath the surface of international diplomacy to the lived experiences and realities of workers. Chinese workers were expected to do more than labour; they were to become models of socialist friendship that transcended national identities and overcame attitudes of 'big-power chauvinism' (大国主义). Chinese workers were expected to feel at home in Mongolia while remaining *Chinese* workers—a configuration that would later prove untenable. Instead, friendship between Chinese and Mongolian workers ran into mundane obstacles, such as language barriers, cultural misunderstandings, and less than desirable living and working conditions. Diplomatic disputes inflamed and instrumentalised these underlying tensions but were not the origins of them.

In this essay, we first establish the framework of big-power chauvinism, which the friendship intended to overcome. Next, we examine the lived realities of Chinese workers that hindered the realisation of international proletarian solidarity, and eventually culminated in a series of strikes, between 1961 and 1963. By 1964, when the agreement was suspended and most Chinese workers were repatriated,[6] the project of socialist friendship was already a failed experiment.

Between Internationalism and Chauvinism

Communist internationalism requires the abolition of borders. As Karl Marx and Friedrich Engels argued in *The Communist Manifesto*, under capitalism, the proletariat is 'stripped of every trace of national character'; therefore, under communist leadership, in their own countries, the working class would struggle for 'the common interests of the entire proletariat, independent of all nationality'.[7] The problem with this rosy view has been that workers tend to identify as national subjects and not international proletarians. Because of the geographic confinement of the October Revolution, the principle of internationalism had to work with a complicated diplomatic patchwork of national identities. In his final years, Lenin realised that proletarian internationalism was also being undermined by Stalin's policies, which risked reinforcing deeply ingrained attitudes of Russian big-power chauvinism and the alienation of different nationalities historically oppressed by Tsarist Russia and were antithetical to the promise of anti-imperialism. As a result, Lenin declared 'war to the death on dominant-nation chauvinism'[8] and espoused a policy of national autonomy according to which, as historian Moshe Lewin puts it, 'in order to make amends for the wrongs committed against the small nations, the big nation must accept an inequality unfavourable to itself'.[9] According to dialectical logic, the path to internationalism could only be achieved by resisting big-power chauvinism and respecting the autonomy and independence of smaller nations.

The dialectical tension between proletarian emancipation and national liberation was rendered in the paradoxical status of borders. As the border between China and Mongolia was being demarcated in 1963, the General Secretary of the MPR, Yumjaagiin Tsedenbal, and Chinese Ambassador to Mongolia, Zhang Canming, had the following exchange:

> Tsedenbal: Now they are putting up these border markers. In the future, during the communist period, borders will not be needed anywhere. They will remain as historic reminiscences for young people to study.
>
> Zhang: This is the law of dialectics. For example, now we have a proletarian dictatorship. Its aim is to annihilate classes. Now we are erecting border markers. Their aim is to annihilate borders in the future.
>
> Tsedenbal: Yes. It has to be like this. Borders are a product of class society. During that period, nation-states separated from each other. Now such borders are also needed. In the future, in the communist period, they will not be needed. In the future there will be no nation-states that close themselves up in a box.[10]

Within a few years, both sides would be militarising their borders in preparation for possible conflict.

In the Sino-Mongolian case, the contradiction between international solidarity and big-power chauvinism was particularly acute for historical reasons. Since Mongolia declared its independence from the Qing Empire in 1911, and obtained Lenin's blessing for national independence in 1921,[11] Mongolian leaders have been wary of China's irredentist ambitions—directly asserted by the Republican government and ambiguously insinuated by the Communist one.[12] As the Sino-Soviet relationship deteriorated, Mao's uncharacteristically aggressive remark to a delegation of Japanese communists in 1964 that the Soviet Union had annexed territories, including Mongolia, which historically belonged to China did the opposite of assuaging their fear.[13] According to historian Xiaoyuan Liu, Chinese Communist leaders had difficulty accepting Mongolia's socialist credentials and letting go of the belief that it would return to China by its own volition. As a result, the Sino-Mongolian friendship was internally fractured by a 'contradiction between their nationalist practices and internationalist pronouncements'.[14] As Cold War historian Sergey Radchenko puts it: 'Chinese claims on Mongolia did nothing to strengthen proletarian solidarity between the two parties.'[15]

Viewed from the perspective of proletarian internationalism, the sending of Chinese workers to Mongolia was intended as a gesture of good faith and friendship (although historian Gu Jikun points out that the origins of the arrangement were actually part of a failed negotiation to repatriate Chinese who were stranded in Mongolia after World War II).[16] When seen from the perspective of big-power chauvinism, however, it could appear as a Trojan horse for China's revanchist ambitions, as indicated in Soviet first deputy premier Asastas Mikoyan's confidential warning to Tsedenbal in March 1956: 'In order for you not to end up with a mainly Chinese working class, you should develop your own working class.'[17] It is no wonder that Mongolia initially requested China send ethnically Mongolian workers—a request the Chinese side rejected.

There is reason though to trust that the Chinese side ideologically believed in the project of proletarian friendship. In the 1956 speech in which Mao raised the issue of historical debt, he addressed the need to overcome chauvinist attitudes among Chinese workers:

> Some Chinese workers have gone to Mongolia. You should carry out propaganda work with them so that they do not commit the error of Great Han nationalist thinking, so that they do not

ride roughshod over you [*chengwang chengba*]. If the Chinese workers or laborers there commit mistakes, you should make this known to us.[18]

For the Chinese side, big-power chauvinism was an ideological problem that needed to be remedied through political education. In one of its April 1957 issues, the Chinese-language newspaper based in Mongolia, *Workers' Way* (工人之路), directly raised the question: 'What is big-power chauvinism and why must we oppose it?' (什么是大国主义，为什么必须反对它?).[19] The article defined chauvinism as a form of international relations in which larger countries 'look down' (卑视) on countries with a smaller population and surface area, and less-developed levels of cultural experience and economic development, resulting in a 'blind sense of superiority' (盲目优越感), which 'lacks the spirit of equality' (缺乏平等的精神) and 'does not respect the independence of other countries'.[20] Chinese workers were expected to receive 'equal pay for equal work' (同工同酬),[21] cultivate 'mutual solidarity, mutual respect, and mutual love' (互助团结，互敬互爱), and 'criticise big-power chauvinism in thinking and emotions' (批评某些员工大国主义的思想情绪),[22] while adhering to Mongolian law, factory norms, work discipline, and local customs. Conceptualised in this way, proletarian diplomacy was carried out at the level of workers' lives, thoughts, emotions, habits, and interactions.

Construction and Deterioration

For nine years (1955–64), China sent an estimated 26,000 Chinese workers and their families to Mongolia to engage in construction, industrial production, mining, agriculture, and numerous other professions. At that time, Mongolia relied on the Chinese workers to supplement its acute labour shortage and help it transition from a pastoral mode of production to build the industrial base of production necessary for 'socialist construction'.[23] For Mongolia, the main reason for the labour exchange was its desperate need for workers.

Chinese workers' contribution to the construction of Mongolia is still evident today. In the capital city, Ulaanbaatar, Chinese workers built the Peace Bridge, the Ulaanbaatar Hotel, the State Department Store, numerous downtown apartment complexes, several factories, and an electric generator. That the urban core of Ulaanbaatar was built by the Chinese is an uncomfortable and seldom discussed reality in Mongolia's current atmosphere of Sinophobia.[24] In the countryside, Chinese workers were engaged in the construction of cultural facilities, schools, and hospitals, in addition to working on farms and at factories of various kinds.[25]

When the diplomatic relationship started to fray, unsurprisingly, the status of Chinese workers became the subject of diplomatic disagreement. At the end of December 1962, Zhou Enlai and Tsedenbal engaged in a heated—to the extent of nearly coming to blows—exchange over China's relationship with the Soviet Union, the Sino-Indian border dispute, and the Albanian question. Aware of Mongolia's dependence on Chinese labour, Zhou attempted to leverage the issue of Chinese workers to extract diplomatic concessions. Tsedenbal refused this pressure by stating: 'We will not retreat in ideological terms and will not change the correct policy line of our party because of 8,000 workers.'[26] As a result of the breakdown in negotiations, Chinese workers were sent home ahead of the termination of their contracts. Their absence did in fact set back Mongolia's development, especially in the construction industry, resulting in campaigns to recruit and train Mongolians to engage in construction work as a civic duty, and utilisation of the labour of Soviet soldiers.[27]

The Mongolian side blamed the collapse of the friendship on the revival of Chinese big-power chauvinism and its willingness to 'destroy the internationalist Communist movement'[28] with the Sino-Soviet split looming in the foreground. But as Sergey Radchenko points out, on many issues, the Mongolian side took a *harder line* than the Soviets,[29] which suggests the possibility of deeper historical and political tensions—namely, the Mongolian fear of Chinese encroachment. For instance, on the fortieth anniversary of the MPR, Mongolia's state newspaper, *Ünen Sonin*, accused 'Chinese leaders [of] denying [Mongolia's] non-capitalist path of development, which in essence disregards the Mongolian people's historical experience of struggle'.[30] This dismissive attitude was due to the fact that 'Chinese leaders fell into the trap of big-power chauvinism' (中国领导人陷入大国主义).[31]

The ambiguous status of Chinese workers in Mongolia is perhaps best illustrated by the disagreement over how to handle the corpses of 89 Chinese workers who died on Mongolian soil due to labour-related accidents or natural causes. The 'Mongolian representative did not accept the Chinese suggestion to ship the remains of dead Chinese workers to Beijing but instead made accommodations to build a public graveyard for Chinese workers on Mongolian soil'.[32] Questions about soil, burial, and national identity undermine the putative international identity of the proletariat.[33] As Benedict Anderson famously argued, a 'Tomb of the Unknown Marxist' is absurd to imagine in contrast with the passionate linkages between nationalism, death, memory, and identity.[34] Thus, the deaths of Chinese workers in Mongolia were ambiguously framed as a *national sacrifice* on behalf of *proletarian internationalism*. At the Seventh Conference of Chinese Cadres held in 1962, Liu Runshen, an official within the Chinese Embassy in Mongolia, commemorated the 'many comrades [who] shed their blood, lost their health, and even gave their lives for the sake of the socialist construction on behalf of the Mongolian people' and consecrated them as 'labour warriors' (*khödölmöriin baildagch*).[35] In 1963, a Chinese newspaper suggested that Mongolia should construct a memorial for the dead workers, comparing their sacrifice to that of martyrs in the Korean War.[36] This did not sit well with the Mongolian comrades, who felt it overshadowed and minimised their own participation.[37] Only in recent years have representatives from the Chinese Embassy in Mongolia begun paying annual official visits to the graves of Chinese workers buried in Ulaanbaatar, as a patriotic ritual of tending to one's own dead.

Rough Conditions

Although Chinese workers were expected to treat Mongolia as their home, they had difficulty adapting to the strenuous living and working conditions. On arrival in May 1955, one month after the signing of the intergovernmental agreement, the first group of Chinese workers were confronted with an acute shortage of material facilities. Zhou Changchun, son of a carpenter from Changchun who arrived in Mongolia with his parents, recalled their first night.[38] Dispatched directly from Ulaanbaatar to Nalaikh, around 40 kilometres east of the capital, they discovered neither houses nor yurts prepared for them. Instead, they slept under the moon, in the duvets brought from home, surrounded by their luggage as a makeshift fence, and listened to the gunshots fired by Mongolian guards to ward off wolves.

The second day, they were welcomed by a Mongolian cadre, who outlined the blueprint of a new city they were invited to build on the very ground on which they were standing. Following the convention in their hometown, Changchun, the Chinese workers named the place 'New City Construction Site' (新街工地)—a name that was in use until 1964. Zhou's father, a skilled carpenter, joined his colleagues in building wooden houses for temporary use, with the hope of building brick houses before winter. However, they were soon disappointed to learn about the shortage of building materials such as cement and steel in Mongolia, making their plan virtually impossible. Faced with the coming winter, they decided to dig partially subterranean dwellings on a slope. Zhou recalled:

> A cave for a family measured three metres in width and four metres in length. The bachelors' dormitories were much more spacious. There was a *kang* [bed-stove] and a cooktop inside. The front of the cave was covered with a wooden door and window frames. The top was secured by logs and felt to be waterproof. They looked like buns from a distance.

The workers and their families lived in the caves for three years before moving into brick homes, with some of them developing rheumatism due to underground water seeping into the caves in spring. Soon, a Mongolian commercial cooperative opened on the construction site, providing a steady supply of flour, oil, salt, beef, mutton, and dairy products. Combined with regular official deliveries of staple and non-staple foods from China, the sustenance of Chinese workers and families was assured.

With the improvement in their material living conditions, social life on the construction site also expanded: an elementary school for the workers' children was started, along with a night school for the workers, many of whom were illiterate. In the Chinese literacy class, the workers were taught to read; if they did not learn, their salaries would be docked for poor performance. Zhou jovially remembered:

> My mother enthusiastically volunteered to take the class and earned an elementary school diploma after a few years. But my father, a model worker during the day, often dozed off during class at night and lost a considerable amount of salary as a result.

In addition, workers organised a Peking opera club and a dance group in their spare time. Despite the varied geographic origins of the Chinese workers, they cultivated a strong sense of solidarity and camaraderie through collective work and life in Mongolia.

The material conditions of Chinese workers living in apartments were also spartan and rough. According to an official Mongolian report dated 1 February 1962, Chinese Ambassador to Mongolia Xie Fusheng conducted an inspection of apartments in Zuun Ail district of Ulaanbaatar, where more than 800 Chinese workers and their families lived. The report found that the 'building's wall was cracked' to such an extent that 'when the ground thaws in the spring, it might collapse'.[39] Additionally, 'the steam heating system had deteriorated. In some buildings, there wasn't any heat at all and frost started to appear inside', which was exacerbated by the fact that 'water leaked from the ceilings' in several apartments. The report concluded that 'even Mongolians would not want to endure living in such a building, let alone Chinese' (*ene bairand khyatad baitugai mongol khün ch tesej suumaargüi baina*), who were not used to living in an environment where the temperatures in winter could easily drop to minus forty degrees. To make matters worse, the Mongolian Deputy Minister of Construction, who was supposed to accompany the inspection team, was several hours late—a 'disrespectful situation' noted by the Chinese side. The lateness was not out of character for Mongolian diplomats, who, according to Balázs Szalontai, frequently engaged in 'subtle insubordination' towards their more powerful neighbours; in 1960, for instance, Soviet diplomats lodged a 'formal complaint against their ill-treatment at the hands of various Mongolian cadres', while North Vietnamese diplomats complained about 'recurrent shortages of electricity and water'.[40]

Three Chinese workers on the Sukhbaatar Square, circa 1960. Courtesy of Wang Guangsheng.

The rough living conditions and diplomatic tensions, however, did not eliminate the possibilities for interpersonal amity. Li Zhi'an, who lived in Zuun Ail with his family from Changchun during his childhood, fondly remembered their friendly Mongolian neighbours.[41] As there was no tapwater in Zuun Ail when they first arrived in 1955, they relied on Soviet *gaz* cars to transport water specifically for Chinese workers. A few Mongolian neighbours would ask the Li's family to fetch water on their behalf, to which they gladly agreed. After transferring the water to other containers at home, their Mongolian neighbours would always return the basin full of food and snacks to thank the Chinese family.

Remittances

According to the labour agreement, Chinese workers were permitted to remit only 30 percent of their monthly salary and take with them no more than one month's salary when they permanently returned home. In addition to salary remittances, Chinese workers also disputed customs regulations over what they could take with them back to China. Given the conditions of scarcity in Mongolia, the Mongolian side expected Chinese workers to spend the majority of their salary in the country and to either consume or leave behind what they purchased.[42] Since their salaries in Mongolia were much higher than they would have been at home, even though the allowed remittance was a fraction of what they made, it was sufficient for supporting their families in China. Although most workers complied without complaint, disputes did occur, especially as the economic situation worsened in China.

In the context of the early 1960s and China's Great Leap Forward, in which millions perished, the question of remittances and customs took on necropolitical ramifications. According to historian Sang Ye, during the Great Leap Forward, 'Chinese people were sending meat back to China, which worried Mongolian officials about food security'.[43] At the border,

> people would cram their suitcases full with things they couldn't get in China at the time. This was a nightmare for the customs officials who eventually made them get down from their rail car, and open up their luggage right there in front of them. The luggage bulged so much, it was difficult to close.[44]

From archival materials in the Mongolian Ministry of Foreign Affairs, it is clear that Chinese workers were aware of the horror unfolding at home. One file contains dozens of requests to return to China due to a 'death in the family' or 'severe illness'; Mongolian officials observed, to their consternation, 'a dramatic increase' (*ers nemegdsen*) in the number of such requests. One report notes that, while it was acceptable for Chinese workers to leave before their contracts expired due to emergency situations, the frequency of this kind of occurrence peaked between late 1961 and early 1962.[45] Those workers who used their forty-five-day holiday once every three years to visit home were shocked by the abysmal state of famine, despite the information they had already been given by their family members via correspondence. 'If I had known people were suffering so much, I would have brought more food from Mongolia,' an interviewee who worked as an electrician in Mongolia recalled.[46] While famine caused starvation and deaths at home, in Mongolia, the food supply was reliable and offered items that would have been considered luxuries in China. He felt too ashamed to describe to his family the availability of cosmopolitan products he saw in Ulaanbaatar: Mongolian sausages, Soviet flour, North Korean rice, Vietnamese peanuts, and so forth. Tormented by the stark contrast in food supplies at home and in his host country, he was glad his hard-earned remittance—albeit a fraction of his income—could help his family survive the difficult period.

Tension Afoot

Despite initially rough conditions of material scarcity, most Chinese workers and their families interviewed for this chapter fondly recalled their lives in Mongolia. Worker diplomacy was beginning to bear fruit. However, the workers on both sides were not immune to the enveloping political context. Mongolian leaders accused the Chinese of politicising ordinary tensions into diplomatic disputes, insinuating that the Chinese Communist Party was behind Chinese worker unrest in Mongolia. A Mongolian report from the end of December 1963 concludes:

> But in the last few years, the Chinese side has magnified even small issues using various manners and artificially turned them into political conclusions. They have attempted to prove that the Mongolian government was intentionally organising these debatable problems against Chinese workers. Moreover, it is extremely

regrettable that some Chinese officials and organisations have supported Chinese workers who on their own or in a group are disrespectful, engage in illegal activities, infringe, and slander the internal affairs of border inspection, police, customs, and the factories and economy of the People's Republic of Mongolia.[47]

From the end of 1961 to the first quarter of 1963, there were twenty-six strikes involving Chinese workers, ranging from seven to 180 participants, the shortest strike lasting a few hours and the longest fourteen days. The 1964 summary report by Mongolian officials expressed regret over the decision to compensate Chinese workers for the days they missed during their first strike, mistakenly believing it was a one-time event.

Although Chinese officials attempted to leverage the strikes during diplomatic negotiations, the reasons for the mobilisations varied and most were work-related disputes about issues such as insufficient wages, workplace accidents due to the inadequate operational safety of equipment, lack of transportation to the worksite, and complaints over basic necessities, such as the absence of cotton or 'wood to heat steamed buns', and shoes that did not fit.[48] Chinese workers were also upset over what they perceived as mistreatment and bullying by Mongolian bosses and other workers; on one occasion, forty-three Chinese workers went on strike and demanded to return home after a fellow worker was beaten by a Mongolian. At the Tolgoit Brick Factory, nine workers went on strike for a day because of fears that the Mongolian guard might 'shoot them'.[49]

Chinese workers also went on strike to protect their own interests and protest restrictions on remittances and customs regulations, the importance of which we discussed in the previous section. One strike, which included the occupation of a government office, from 16 to 18 April 1962, successfully petitioned the Mongolian authorities to allow the workers to send 'cotton, milk, and meat through customs without restrictions'.[50] From these cases, it is possible to see that not all mobilisations were politically motivated, despite the Mongolian side's accusation that Chinese workers 'seized the slightest pretext' (*neg ül yalikh shaltgaanyug dalimduuldag*) to organise strikes.[51]

On the other end of the spectrum, several strikes were directly related to thorny issues of political and national identity. In Khövsgöl Province, Chinese workers went on strike demanding that Mao's picture be placed at the same height as that of Mongolia's leader, Tsedenbal. In Arhkhangai Province, on 6 December 1961, wind blew an official Chinese banner to the ground, causing a brigade of twenty-four Chinese workers to go on strike for two days. The workers complained to the provincial governor that: 'This was a deliberate action by the Mongolian people to undermine the Chinese government. As a result, Chinese workers have lost interest in working anymore.'[52] The Mongolian side considered these actions to be of a 'non-friendly nature' (*nairamdalt bish*).[53]

In the acrimonious dialogue between Zhou Enlai and Tsedenbal as the Sino-Mongolian friendship collapsed, neither side could agree on the nature of the strikes carried out by Chinese workers. Zhou explained that Chinese political culture permitted workers to strike even under socialism. Evidence for this can be found in Mao's 1956 proposal that: 'The workers should be allowed to go on strike and the masses to hold demonstrations.'[54] Although the right to strike would not be included in the Chinese Constitution until 1975—only to be removed in the 1982 version—under certain conditions, the Chinese Communist Party promoted a 'tolerant attitude towards strikes' on the basis of a 1957 policy document, 'Instructions for Dealing with Strikes of Workers and Students', issued by the Central Committee.[55] Anxious about the possible contagion of unrest, Tsedenbal's response was to insist that 'Mongolia has its own laws. We cannot agree that some workers can break and ignore the established order. Such a situation could, in the end, negatively influence the Mongolian workers.'[56]

Whereas Tsedenbal suspected political influence, Zhou attributed the strikes to hurt patriotic feelings over criticisms of China in the Mongolian press:

> As they were in touch with the Mongolian population, they are familiar with the Mongolian press, and this caused certain difficulties. 8,000 Chinese workers were in the midst of the Mongolian population. Zhou Enlai stressed that a man was not an inanimate commodity [Russian: *mertvy tovar*], but a living, politically thinking individual. We brought our people up in such a way that if they did not like something, then they could give up work. Therefore, we allow such order [of things]. Now, let's look at the situation of the Chinese workers in Mongolia. What you publish in Mongolia disposed the Chinese workers critically towards the [People's Republic of China]. This caused difficulties. What are we to do with these workers? Leave them in the MPR? But I already said these are people and not commodities.[57]

Neither side acknowledged that Chinese workers may have had their own reasons to strike.

Lost Alternatives

In today's global capitalist economy, in which transnational migrant labour is precarious, degraded, and hidden from view, the exchange of workers as a gesture of socialist friendship appears like a hieroglyph from another planet. In our current age of simmering ethnonationalist passions, the spirit of internationalism is even more remote, like an incandescent blur from outer space. For these reasons, it is imperative that we study these experimental formations of labour for clues to what might have been, what went wrong, and what could be.

Although the official archives and diplomatic history record a bleak story of failure, this is an incomplete picture. Several Chinese workers and their descendants described in interviews with one of the authors their fond relationships with their Mongolian neighbours, coworkers, and labour apprentices, despite the rough working and living conditions, and the political earthquakes shaking the communist world. If it were not for the ideological split, they would have remained in Mongolia not only as workers but also as cultural ambassadors. The underlying desire to live, work, and learn from one another is the key to any future proletarian internationalism.

That being said, socialist friendship was ambiguous and unstable because its aspiration for internationalism was articulated and felt as a patriotic duty. The utopian goal of moving beyond the framework of national identity was never achieved or earnestly pursued. One of the casualties was that the friendship could not withstand the geopolitical rifts between both countries. Even at the height of state socialism in China and Mongolia, workers were *national subjects* before they were *international proletarians*. A revolutionary politics of the future will require the inversion of these terms.

1957

In 1956, the Party-State completed the nationalisation of industry. Although official propaganda hailed this as a historic step towards the end of class struggle and capitalist exploitation, many workers saw their conditions deteriorate. In the past, they felt morally entitled to fight their employers and could even hope to receive some support from the union and the Party, but after the state assumed control over enterprises, they lost any moral and political ground on which to stake their claims.

In this period, management's despotic power over the working class, alongside a maladroit reform of the wage system carried out in the second semester of 1956, heavily hit the material interests of the workers, leading to a wave of strikes.[1] Politically, one of the consequences of labour unrest was a debate on the right to strike, which was missing from both the Common Program of 1949 and the Chinese Constitution of 1954. Mao Zedong first raised the issue during a meeting of the Central Committee in March 1956 when he stated that 'it is necessary to allow the workers to go on strike, allow the masses to protest. The demonstrations have their basis in the Constitution. If in the future the Constitution is to be amended, I suggest adding a freedom of strike, it is necessary to let the workers go on strike. This can benefit the resolution of the contradictions between the workers, the directors of the factories and the masses.'[2]

Mao took up the issue again in February 1957, in his famous speech 'On the Correct Handling of the Contradictions among the People'.[3] In it, he argued that contradictions among workers, and between workers and the national bourgeoisie, were to be considered 'contradictions among the people' (人民内部矛盾) and therefore had to be solved through the method of 'unity–criticism–unity' (团结-批评-团结). In his speech, Mao specifically quoted episodes of worker unrest that had taken place the previous year, labelling them 'disorders created by a small number of individuals', and explained that they had three different roots: the failure of the Party to satisfy the economic requests of the workers, a bureaucratic approach by the leadership and the inadequate political and ideological education of the workers. He blamed the masses for not understanding the long-term, *national and collective interests, but at the same time recognised that such events could occur again in the future and suggested using them as examples to improve the work of the Party.*

After less than a month, the Central Committee of the Chinese Communist Party (CCP) formally adopted Mao's ideas in an official document titled 'Directive of the Central Committee of the CCP on the Handling of Strikes by Workers and Students'.[4] This document—which to this day remains the only official public statement by the Communist leadership on how to deal with strikes—espoused Mao's point of view on the reasons for labour unrest in China. It claimed that, in the event the masses were deprived of their democratic rights and had no choice other than adopting extreme measures such as strikes or protests, these actions 'were not only unavoidable, but also necessary', and therefore had to be allowed. The directive stated that these actions absolutely did not go against the Constitution—and therefore there was no reason to forbid them—but at the same time suggested the Party committees penetrate the lines of the people on strike, to take the lead and prevent the masses from being 'stranded on the wrong way by some bad elements'. In the whole directive, the union was mentioned only three times—twice in passing and once just to emphasise that the Party committees had to 'lead the union and the youth league to actively reflect the opinions and the requests of the masses'.

Mao's February speech marked the launch of the Hundred Flowers Campaign. Under the slogan 'Let one hundred flowers bloom and one hundred schools of thought contend' (百花齐放, 百家争鸣), the Party leadership invited the people to freely voice their opinions and criticisms. It took a while for the campaign to gain momentum, but eventually more and more citizens, especially intellectuals and members of the democratic parties, started voicing their criticisms. In early May, the national leadership of the All-China Federation of Trade Unions (ACFTU) weighed in on the debate through the pages of the union mouthpiece, the Workers' Daily (工人日报). On 8 May 1957, Chen Yongwen, then chief editor of the newspaper, ran a long interview with Lai Ruoyu, the union official who had replaced Li Lisan as chairman of the ACFTU after his downfall in 1951.[5] In this exchange, republished the following day in the People's Daily (人民日报), Lai tackled the fundamental issue of the position of the union in relation to the Party—dangerous territory, the misnavigation of which had led to the political disgrace of his predecessor.

The following day, the Workers' Daily *published another critical piece—a report on a long investigative journey undertaken in the previous months by Li Xiuren, Deputy Director of the ACFTU General Office.*[6] *This '8,000 li' trip had taken Li and an unnamed member of the CCP Central Committee through a dozen cities along the Beijing-Hankou and Hankou-Guangzhou railway lines. In every city in which they stopped, Li and his companion found clear hints of the 'crisis of the union', with frustrated workers blaming the ACFTU for being nothing more than the 'tail of the administration' (行政的尾巴), a 'department for the management of the workers' (工人管理科) and a 'tongue of bureaucratism' (官僚主义的舌头). They found that workers were striving to establish their own autonomous organisations. Many union cadres complained about the difficulty of their position: even if they wanted to support the rightful requests of the masses, they could not, because they were pressed between their obligation to represent the masses and the imperative of respecting Party discipline. They were particularly concerned with being accused of 'syndicalism' (工团主义), 'tailism' (尾巴主义), 'independence from the Party' (对党闹独立) and even losing their Party membership. Some union cadres in Guangdong complained of being 'fourth-level cadres' (四等干部), subordinated to Party cadres, management and even technicians.*

The publication of these two articles opened a heated debate about the role and functions of the union in socialist China. In May and June 1957, the Chinese press published a great number of articles that dealt with the issue of the perceived impotence of the union in representing workers' rights.[7] *Some of these essays even put forward radical proposals, as in the case of Gao Yuan, then Director of the Archival Department of the ACFTU Central Office, who argued that, if necessary, the union should take up arms against the Party.*[8] *Unsurprisingly, on the receiving end of such criticisms, the Party once again stepped in. On 19 June 1957, the* People's Daily *published Mao's February speech, but the printed version was slightly different from the original one, for it emphasised ex post the boundaries that should not have been crossed in the debate—namely, the political legitimacy of the Party.*

The national leadership of the ACFTU was caught in the ensuing wave of repression. Exactly as had happened in 1951 with the fall of Li Lisan, in September 1957, an enlarged meeting of the ACFTU Party Group was called to deliberate on two fundamental issues: the validity of the resolu-

tion adopted in November 1951 on the struggle against economism and syndicalism and the functions and role of the union under the dictatorship of the proletariat.[9] On 5 September, Lai Ruoyu gave a long speech in which he substantially confirmed the validity of the 1951 report, attacking the line of Li Lisan and giving up any vestige of independence for the union.[10] Then, at the end of 1957, the Eighth Congress of the ACFTU laid the basis for the decentralisation of the union in anticipation of the Great Leap Forward. In the following months, at least twenty-two high-level cadres of the ACFTU were purged, among them the chief editor of the Workers' Daily, Chen Yongwen. In May 1958, Lai Ruoyu died of illness. This second crisis left the union weaker than ever, depriving it of its most outspoken personalities.[11] From that moment, the ACFTU stopped playing any meaningful role in the Chinese workplace, until its eventual dissolution during the Cultural Revolution (see Thornton's essay in the present volume).

In the following two chapters, we offer a translation of Lai Ruoyu's 1957 interview and an analysis of worker unrest in that momentous year.

How Do Unions Handle Contradictions among the People?

LAI Ruoyu

(Translated by Malcolm THOMPSON)[1,2]

When union organisations at all levels recently discussed the problem of how to handle contradictions among the people correctly, they raised some questions about how to understand them. On 7 May of this year, a reporter from Workers' Daily *interviewed Lai Ruoyu, Chairman of the All-China Federation of Trade Unions, and he provided his views on the reporter's question as follows.*

Do Contradictions Exist between Unions and the Working Masses?

Reporter: In discussing the correct handling of contradictions among the people, there are people who think that because the principal contradictions among the people are contradictions between the masses and the leadership, and unions are mass organisations, as a result, contradictions exist between the workers and enterprise management, but contradictions between union organisations and the working masses do not. Do you think this view is correct?

Lai Ruoyu: It is true that a union is an organisation of the masses themselves. But a union is in such a position that, on one side, it is a mass organisation and should represent the views of the masses and, on another side, it is not a single individual. It has a national unified organisation, and as a part of this kind of organisation it should understand the overall situation and the present state of the country. It should also represent the long-term interests of the masses and persuade the masses in a patient manner of the incorrectness of some of their views.

Being in this position results in a certain number of disadvantages for the union. Being in this position, the union should understand the situation of both the [enterprise] leadership and the masses, and bring the union organisation into play to perform a regulatory role in the correct handling of contradictions among the people. But this position that the union organisation occupies can give rise to contradictions with respect to both the leadership and the masses. When the union, reflecting the views of the masses, encounters bureaucratism among the enterprise leadership, this can give rise to contradictions. When it encounters certain incorrect ideas among the masses, the union engages in work to explain things, and here, too, contradictions may arise.

The question certainly is not whether contradictions will arise between the union organisation and the working masses. More importantly, it is how to handle the contradictions that may emerge. The union should, in the first place, stand on the side of the masses and back their correct views. And when the masses have incorrect views, they should likewise stand among them and persuade them. Only in this way will the masses be willing to listen to the union's views.

How Do Unions Handle Mass Disturbances?

Reporter: In industrial and mining enterprises, contradictions between the masses and the leadership sometimes develop into mass disturbances, and in some cases even strikes. When it encounters this situation, how should the union handle it? Some people think that because the union represents the masses, it should speak on their behalf; even if the views of the masses are incorrect, the union should represent their interests. Others hold the opposite opinion: they feel that the union should not participate in mass disturbances, and that it should only undertake to persuade the masses out of their incorrect opinions. Which of these views is correct?

Lai Ruoyu: Obviously the ideas of the masses are not always correct, or not entirely correct. With regard to the incorrect ideas of the masses, the union should persuade them of their errors. But the essence of the question is that the union cannot be separated from the masses. If the union loses contact with the masses, when it encounters the masses' incorrect ideas and needs to persuade them of their errors, the masses won't listen. Only if the union remains close to the masses will they be willing to listen to it and will its persuasive work be effective. We can see in this kind of situation that if the union is separated from the masses when there is a mass disturbance, the masses will abandon the union and establish their own autonomous organisations, with the result that the union cannot function. Thus, the principal task of the union lies in supporting the reasonable ideas of the masses; only after this aspect of the union's responsibilities has been fulfilled will it be possible to persuade the masses out of their incorrect ideas.

When we say that there may be incorrect ideas among the masses, we certainly cannot assume that all of the masses' opinions are incorrect, or that they are often incorrect. On the contrary, we must recognise that many of the masses' ideas are correct and reasonable. According to past statistics from many factories and mines, frequently over 60 percent of the ideas of the masses were related to various aspects of work, such as ideas about the organisation of labour, the use of raw materials, supply, production equipment, as well as systems of organisation and other matters. These views should be received with respect and supported. In political matters, the masses also usually have ideas and demands. These ideas and demands often involve the masses' democratic rights. If mass criticism of bureaucratism is met with retaliation, for instance, this is a violation of the masses' democratic rights, and the union should support the masses' demand that retaliation not occur. In matters of wages, benefits, recreation, and sports, the demands of the masses are often not excessive, and many of their ideas in these matters do not even involve the question of increases in wages and benefits, like their ideas about unhygienic canteens, poorly run nurseries and medical clinics, unreasonable wages, and so on. This also requires the support of the union. Demands concerning culture and technical training are the same. Most of these ideas are reasonable and correct, and the union should support them. This is the main point. Only by supporting the correct ideas of the masses will the union be considered to represent their interests. And it is only if you have the trust of the working masses that they will listen to you when situations develop.

As for the incorrect ideas of the masses, should the union also speak for the masses unconditionally? Obviously not. In a situation like this, the union should persuade. The question is not to persuade or not; the important question is how to persuade. The union should stand among the masses in order to persuade them. It should be recognised that even if there are incorrect opinions and excessive demands, there are reasons for this. That is, there is a reasonable aspect to them. Even if this reasonable aspect only comprises a small part, the union should in the first place recognise it, and moreover express sympathy. In that case, the union's persuasive efforts regarding the incorrect part can be accepted by the masses.

How should people be persuaded of the incorrectness of their ideas? It requires patient persuasion, not compulsion, and the method should be to stimulate the masses' own discussions and their own solutions. But what should be done if there is still no solution even after these discussions and the masses still persist in their original ideas? In a situation like this, the union must not be separated from the masses. The union has a responsibility, on one hand, to put the masses' ideas forward to the relevant parties and, on the other hand, if the union still considers the masses' ideas to be incorrect, to continue to make its own attitude clear, to continue to attempt to persuade the masses. From the perspective of the union organisation, certainly the ideas of the majority of the masses may not always be correct, but democracy is one of the principles of the union, and the minority should submit to the majority. Here, union cadres can only continue to have their ideas and engage in the gradual work of persuasion. Only in this way can the union adhere to correct ideas while remaining close to the masses. Clearly, getting this point right is not easy, but it is also not impossible. We don't have a great deal of experience in this, but we do have some.

Can Union Work Be a Form of 'Contending'?

Reporter: Can 'letting a hundred schools of thought contend' be a part of union work?

Lai Ruoyu: Regardless of the organisation, there are two types of work that are different in nature. One is work of an executive nature, and the other is work of an investigative nature. With executive work, once the way of doing something is decided, then that is how it is done. Work of an investigative nature promotes free thought and free discussion. In this sense it, too, can also be called a form of 'contending'. But this is not the same as 'letting a hundred schools of thought contend' in the academic sphere, because it cannot form itself into a tendency of thought.

Contradictions Also Exist within Union Organisations

Reporter: Are there contradictions within union organisations? How should these contradictions be understood?

Lai Ruoyu: At present, the main question of union organisation is to clarify the position of the union in the correct handling of contradictions among the people. As for the internal organisation of the union, clearly there are contradictions, like there are in any other organisation. Within the union there are questions concerning upper and lower levels, questions of the relations between the leadership and the rank and file, between various departments and levels, and so on. But these are questions internal to the union organisation, and these problems of daily work can be investigated without getting tangled up in the correct handling of contradictions among the people.

If the union is to play its proper role in the correct handling of contradictions among the people, the most important thing is the question of union democracy.

At Present, the Fundamental Question is the Promotion of Democracy

Lai Ruoyu: For unions, one of the fundamental questions at present is democracy. Only with democracy is it possible to show that the union is an organisation of the masses themselves. In order to be well adapted to the present situation, unions should resolve two major questions: the question of relations with management, and that of relations with the Party.

In terms of relations with management, in the past, unanimity was emphasised and the differences were not visible. Because of this, unions always stood with the leadership when situations arose, and they were unable to represent the ideas of the masses. This oversimplified approach to problems among the people often made unions hard and rigid in their methods of work, and they were unable to perform a regulatory role between the masses and the leadership. This is something that should be improved.

In terms of the relations with the Party, in the past, it was decided that unions must accept the leadership of the Party. This was correct, but insufficient attention was paid to the fact that, as a mass organisation, unions must also develop their own independent activities under the leadership of the Party's policies and ideology. Only by developing their own independent activities can they express their proper role.

In the past, we did not resolve these two problems well, and the role of union organisations was not fully brought into play. Because of this, the question of 'are unions even necessary' arose. The Central Committee and Chairman Mao have raised the question of the correct handling of contradictions among the people; union organisations should play their proper role better.

Confronting the State: The Strike Wave of 1957

CHEN Feng[1]

In January 1957, workers from the No. 296 Factory (an arms plant) in Chongqing surrounded the offices of the Chinese Communist Party (CCP) secretary and manager, demanding an immediate pay raise.[2] As more and more people gathered and the tension increased, soldiers equipped with machine guns were called in to disperse the crowd. With martial law enforced in the factory, hundreds of workers then marched to the Chongqing Municipal Party Committee building to file complaints. This was but one of many worker protests that broke out in Chinese factories in 1957. Although sporadic labour protests had occurred regularly in the early years of the People's Republic of China (PRC), that year witnessed worker unrest on an unprecedented scale. Why did workers protest then and what were their claims?

After coming to power in 1949, the CCP faced dire economic conditions. Skyrocketing inflation forced the government to adopt policies that caused bankruptcy and unemployment. In the meantime, the new regime's policies, aimed at restructuring the political economy of the country, such as the socialist transformation of industry and commerce of 1953–56, led to a decrease in real income for workers.[3] While scattered protests had already taken place in the country, pent-up discontent among workers erupted when the Hungarian uprising of 1956 and Mao's Hundred Flower Campaign of 1957 emboldened them to speak out and take to the streets (see Gipouloux's essay in the present volume).[4] Starting from this basic premise, this essay argues that the labour unrest of the 1950s was rooted in inherent tensions in the state's efforts to reconstruct its relations with labour. With the state's increasing control over industry and the emergence of paternalistic institutions, workers came to see the state, as it presented itself, as the patron of their interests and therefore expected economic protection from it. As a result, the disjuncture between the state's socialist promises and some of its policies and practices often disappointed workers and became a major source of grievance.

Dilemmas

It was crucial for the CCP, as a party that claimed to be the 'vanguard of the working class' (工人阶级的先锋队), to ensure the support of urban workers because it was a political and ideological prerequisite for its legitimacy. As early as March 1949, before the CCP declared the founding of the PRC, Mao Zedong stated that the Party 'must rely wholeheartedly on the working class'.[5] Yet, in its efforts to build relations with the working class, the new regime had to confront a profound quandary rooted in the tension between the state's heightened image as a workers' state and its actual practices, which were mostly concerned with policymaking and the daily performance of state actors and agencies down to the grassroots level. In particular, this essay identifies three dilemmas that reflect the inherent tension between the state's image and its practices.

First, the CCP's policies to reconstruct an economy in dire condition in the initial years of the PRC constrained the regime's capacity to deliver and satisfy workers' economic expectations. To fight hyperinflation in the early years after the takeover, the CCP enforced a series of austerity policies that resulted in extreme deflation, which, in turn, caused widespread bankruptcies and unemployment. In the same period, the CCP launched the Three-Anti Campaign (三反运动), which targeted Party bureaucrats (the three 'antis' being anti-corruption, anti-waste, and anti-bureaucracy), and Five-Anti Campaign (五反运动), which targeted private employers (the five 'antis' being anti-bribery, anti-theft of state property, anti-tax evasion, anti-cheating on government contracts, and anti-stealing state economic intelligence). This further depressed numerous factories and shops and caused massive layoffs. The Socialist Transformation (社会主义改造) campaign that followed in 1953, with the aim of nationalising private businesses, created even more difficulties. The new government's inability to prevent wage cuts or stagnation exacerbated workers' resentment.

Second, when it began to run modern industry, the new regime faced conflicting goals. In the pursuit of industrialisation, it had to adapt to certain new managerial practices that were incompatible with the Party's ideological goals. As the government pressed for the fulfilment of production targets and increased industrial efficiency, some workers felt they were still oppressed. To explain labour unrest, as well as other social protests in the 1950s, Mao and the CCP attributed it to the 'bureaucratism' (官僚主义) of state officials—a term that denoted the managerial style and practices that were considered to be opposed to socialist tenets such as equality and workers' participation in factory management.

Third, after taking over urban industry, the state began to establish a socialist factory system organised around 'work units' (单位). A substantial proportion of industrial workers benefited from the new system, which provided them with access to housing, education, and health care as well as lifetime employment.[6] However, the new model did not provide a universal pact for all working people. It was applied only to permanent employees within state-owned enterprises. In the process of the regularisation and institutionalisation of the workforce, a large proportion of workers who were once hired on an informal and temporary basis were dismissed, their demands for formal employment denied. Most were forced to return to the villages from which they came; many more found themselves in limbo. Many protests in the 1950s were triggered by workers' resentment about being excluded.

These three dilemmas created a discrepancy between the new regime's socialist rhetoric and the harsh reality with which workers had to live, causing disappointment and disillusion. Thus, their complaints were framed in terms of unfulfilled promises explicitly directed at the Party and the State.

Wages

Wages and welfare benefits were inflammatory issues that ignited much labour unrest in this period. For instance, in February 1953, as a result of the enforcement of very strict criteria imposed by the Industrial Department of East China, wage reform in the Second Plant of the Shanghai Steel Company shattered workers' expectations of a wage increase.[7] Angry workers surrounded the factory office, demanding an explanation from the Party secretary and director. The Party secretary showed them the document that proved that the criteria were actually set by the central government. However, the workers refused to believe this and claimed that they would write to Chairman Mao to clarify the matter. The protest turned nasty as workers discovered that their complaints could not be redressed. Similarly, in late 1956, workers' demands for a pay raise led to a series of strikes, work stoppages, and petitions in Tianjin. In one case, stevedores in the port city not only surrounded the port office, confronting administrative and union cadres, but also twice sent representatives to the Labour Ministry and the All-China Federation of Trade Unions to complain about their low wages and economic hardship.[8]

The year 1957 saw a dramatic rise in the number of labour riots, particularly in Shanghai. In May and June, protests involving 27,000 workers broke out in 548 enterprises in the city; 94 percent of these protests (that is, 518 of 548) occurred in joint-ownership enterprises and 42 percent (230 of 548) were triggered by wage disputes, while an almost equal number (41 percent, or 229 of 548) were over welfare benefits.[9] The *Internal Reference Report* described some cases. In one instance, on 19 May 1957, more than 600 workers from Xinfeng Textile Factory held a rally to demand the restoration of their wage rate, which had previously been reduced when the economy was in difficulty.[10] On the same day, more than 100 workers from Tianxiang Woollen Mill also gathered to demand the restoration of their wages to previous levels.[11] These incidents show how the protests were motivated by workers' demands for their wages to be restored to the levels experienced before the socialist transformation. They were angry about wage reductions and questioned why their wages in the new society should be lower than they were before liberation.

Working Conditions and Management

Slack regulations and labour protection were another cause of workers' disappointment with the new regime, and were exacerbated by poor management. According to the *Internal Reference Report*, industrial accidents were common in many enterprises due to negligent and lax management (see also Wright's essay in the present volume). For instance, compared with the preceding year, the death rate in Hunan Province in 1954 increased by 225 percent, with most deaths caused by mine accidents.[12] The data also show that, in the first seven months of 1953, Shanghai saw an increase in the number of industrial accidents that resulted in death or injury—double that of the same period in the preceding year.[13] In one factory, Shanghai First Steel Plant, there were 858 industrial injuries in 1952–53 alone. In total, the *Internal Reference Report* documented 722 industrial accidents in 1955–56, with more than 100 deaths.[14]

The reports mentioned above indicate that enterprise management was responsible for these industrial accidents. Although enterprises under the new socialist regime were not driven by profit and did not face market competition, they were under pressure to fulfil output targets set by the bureaucracy. Particularly towards the end of the First Five-Year Plan (1953–57), enterprises were pushed hard to complete production tasks. Forced overtime and excessive and intensified workloads were widespread. Management paid scant attention to safety and labour protection, and this was a major cause of industrial accidents and injuries. For instance, a factory in Shandong Province with an annual profit of 1.2 million yuan spent only 3,000 yuan on labour protection equipment.[15] In that province, 42 percent of industrial accidents were caused by a lack of labour protection measures.[16] Many enterprises and mines in Yunnan Province also failed to improve labour conditions or provide labour protection, and this caused many industrial injuries and occupational disease.[17] Workers were forced to work extra shifts, and fatigue led to accidents. In Shenyang, it was also common for workers to be forced to work extra hours; even pregnant women and young mothers less than four months after giving birth were not exempted. Jiangsu Province witnessed a high death rate from industrial accidents and overwork.[18] In Beijing, workers were asked to undertake additional hours, even on Sundays, as 'voluntary labour' (义务劳动).[19] One manager from Anshan Steel Company in Liaoning Province forced fifty-three workers to work twenty-four hours nonstop, telling them: 'You can't go home before the job is done; otherwise, you'll be fired or your salary will be reduced.'[20] Workers from Shanghai Guanghua Machinery Factory complained that 'the enterprise and trade union only want us to produce, produce, and produce more; they do not care about anything else.'[21] Management commonly practised 'commandism' (命令主义) and 'punishism' (惩罚主义) to deal with workers.[22]

Exclusion

An employment system that divided workers into regular and temporary employees came to be implemented during the rebuilding of China's industry in the 1950s. Not only did the two categories of workers have different pay scales and benefits (such as medical insurance, pensions, and so on), but also, more importantly, one group was entitled to lifetime employment while the other was not. During the economic recovery, unskilled labourers—including peasants and demobilised soldiers—were hired in large numbers for numerous construction projects that required heavy manual work and in enterprises that needed extra hands to catch up with output targets. However, they were treated very differently in terms of wages and benefits compared with regular workers. Thus, they demanded to be classified as regular workers.

For instance, in March 1957, the Wuhan Yangzi River Bridge Bureau decided to dismiss more than 100 temporary workers after the completion of several designated projects and send them back to their rural hometowns.[23] The meeting at which the decision was announced was instantly disrupted and thrown into chaos as angry workers shouted slogans and marched out of the venue. The workers expected to become regular workers as they were promised that they would be granted such status if they worked hard. They quickly held their own meeting and raised their demand to become regular employees and to 'stay with the bridge for good'. They organised a picket in the sheds where they were living to prevent cadres from entering and dividing the workers with private contracts. A deputy head from the provincial industrial bureau was sent to the site to handle the crisis. Although no promise was made to promote them to regular employees, these workers avoided immediate dismissal by being transferred to another construction site.

In the same year, 190 dockworkers in Wuxi started a hunger strike to demand their status be upgraded from temporary to regular workers.[24] They were afraid they might be laid off in the Increasing Production and Practising Frugality (增产节约) campaign, in which many temporary workers in the city had already been dismissed. Their action was quickly imitated by workers in several other districts, and eventually the whole city was affected. The workers made it clear that, if they did 'not kick [the cadres'] ass, the problem would not be solved'.

Workers in Action

The founding of the PRC brought 'liberation', which promised, among other things, a better life for the working class. The regime's socialist promises became a benchmark against which workers expressed their grievances. In Chongqing, protesting workers openly complained that the new government was 'no better than the old one' and 'the General Line [总路线] comes, we are unemployed'.[25] In Suzhou, it was reported that workers grumbled that 'the Communist Party has come, but we still have to work like an ox and a horse, from morning to night, from the beginning of the year to its end' and asked: 'Does this mean that we are the masters of the country?'[26] In Feng Feng Coal Mine in Hebei Province, as the management arbitrarily docked workers' wages, one older worker complained: 'I have been working here for over thirty years; I worked at the time of imperialism. Our current system is worse than that under imperialism.'[27] When the socialist transformation reduced the private sector, which led to layoffs, workers in Tianjin responded sarcastically that the policy was designed not to reform capitalists, but to reform workers.[28] In July 1956, the *Internal Reference Report* carried a speech by a construction worker—a Party member and model worker—at a Party conference in Qingdao.[29] He described the dreadful lives of his fellow workers and complained that they were forced to work almost to their physical limits. In his speech, he expressed the hope that Chairman Mao and the higher-level Party organisation would send people to take a look at their situation.

Clearly, disgruntled workers attributed their grievances to the new regime and blamed it for its failure to fulfil its socialist promises. The official rhetoric was not only a source of disillusionment among the working class; they also used it to criticise the regime. Workers' protests were often framed in terms of 'anti-bureaucratism' (反官僚主义) and even 'democracy' (民主). In March 1957, a protest broke out in No. 116 Factory in Henan as a result of the mishandling of the job assignments of more than 300 newly recruited apprentices.[30] When municipal officials stood by the factory cadres, the workers criticised this as 'bureaucrats shielding one another' (官官相护). In some other factories, in Shanghai, protesting workers distributed flyers that called for 'democracy and equality' (民主和平等). When they were detained by police, they claimed the police's actions were against the Constitution.

The scale and methods of action varied. In one case, 4,000 workers from the Northwest Construction Company rioted in May 1953; in another, 3,000 workers were engaged in making collective petitions in Chongqing in June 1956.[31] Most of the cases reported by the *Internal Reference Report* involved a few hundred people. In Shanghai, the scale of worker action was registered by the fact that about 27,000 workers participated in protests in May and June 1957.[32] Workers also used collective petitioning to articulate their grievances. Of sixty-one incidents in Shanghai reported in the *Internal Reference Report* of 28 September 1957, twenty-three involved collective petitioning. Moreover, the report also noted that, by the end of 1955, nineteen 'illegal organisations' (非法组织) had been formed by unemployed and itinerant construction workers in the city, with a membership ranging from twenty to two hundred.[33] These organisations were behind a number of actions. For instance, shop workers in Shanghai's Huangpu district formed an 'anti-bureaucratism group' (反官僚主义小组) with the stated aim of 'protecting workers' interests' (保卫工人利益).[34] As mentioned above, in several reported incidents, worker groups were founded to establish pickets and headquarters and send representatives to negotiate wages with management. Protesting workers also intentionally pursued a strategy of 'making a big noise' or 'making the thing bigger', as they believed that otherwise their grievances would not be taken seriously and redressed.

A Recurring Pattern

At the inception of the PRC, state–labour relations posed a challenge to the new regime. Despite its marginal role in the revolution, the working class was critical to the CCP in both ideological and political terms, as it had been consecrated as the most advanced social class, the one from which the regime derived its legitimacy. The Party ruled in the name of the working class, promising an industrial system that would ensure the social and economic status of workers. Nevertheless, the 'image' of the Party-State as the 'patron' as well as the incarnation of the working class was sometimes contradicted by many of the practices the workers experienced in the workplace, often on a daily basis.

The first labour protests in the history of the PRC arguably set a pattern of state–labour conflict that recurred in the years to come, especially during the period of industrial restructuring in the mid-1990s (see Ching Kwan Lee's and William Hurst's essays in the present volume).[35] As this essay has shown, the industrial system that was being built in the early 1950s already evinced characteristics of a 'moral economy' in which the state traded economic benefits in exchange for the workers' recognition of its legitimacy, and the workers derived their conception of justice and equity from the extent to which their interests were maintained by the state.[36] Such relations began to shape the workers' perception of the state as the patron that had a moral responsibility to ensure their interests. The installation of the paternalist enterprise system during the ensuing thirty years only served to entrench the workers' view of the state's responsibility for their wellbeing. This way the state's failure to maintain certain norms and standards that the workers expected from it came to be a major source of discontent, leading to extensive labour protests that reverberated well beyond the 1950s.

1958

In September 1958, Zhang Chunqiao, who was only an aspiring critic at the time, published an article titled 'Smash the Ideology of Bourgeois Right' in a Communist Party theoretical journal in Shanghai. In it, he argued that the wage marked a social relationship that reproduced a capitalist logic of labour and proposed prioritising the development of new ideological or moral incentives that would supersede the wage as the basis for stimulating production. With Mao Zedong's personal endorsement, this article opened a series of theoretical encounters that would have dramatic implications for the trajectory of the Chinese Revolution for years to come.

Beyond the Wage: Zhang Chunqiao, Bourgeois Right, and Maoism as Theory

Benjamin KINDLER

On 15 September 1958, the Shanghai-based theoretical journal *Liberation* (解放) published an article titled 'Smash the Ideology of Bourgeois Right' (破除资产阶级的法权思想) by aspiring critic Zhang Chunqiao. The article drew on the conceptual vocabulary of 'bourgeois right', derived from Marx's late writings on transition, as an attempt to theorise the reproduction of social inequalities under socialism in ways that would challenge the hegemony of the Soviet model as it had been previously applied. A copy of each published edition of *Liberation*, formed in 1958 as a local parallel to the national-level journal *Red Flag* (红旗), was delivered to Mao Zedong himself for his perusal. This opened a series of theoretical encounters that were to have dramatic implications for the trajectory of the Chinese Revolution.

Having read Zhang's article, Mao ordered that it be reprinted in the *People's Daily* (人民日报), where it promptly appeared on 13 October, complete with an editorial comment in which Mao asserted that 'this question'—referring to the question of bourgeois right—'needs to be discussed because it is a pressing question at the current moment. We believe that Zhang's article is fundamentally correct, but that it is somewhat too partial, which is to say, that its explanation of the historical process is incomplete.'[1] Mao's excitement and approval established Zhang's leading role as a theorist, whose interventions from this point on posed a series of crucial questions about the problem of socialist transition. For Zhang, the continued deployment of the wage-form under socialism could not, as Soviet theorists had assumed, be radically demarcated from the capitalist wage. If a socialist society relied on material incentives for stimulating productivity, and neglected the formation of new modes of consciousness, Zhang believed that, not only would there be no guarantee of an automatic transition to communism, but also the wage would create the material and ideological conditions for a capitalist reversal and the defeat of the revolutionary process. In the theoretical production of Chinese socialism, Zhang's article has the status of an *event*. We need to not only engage

Zhang's thought, but also recognise that the most original contributions of Maoism lie in the post-1949 period, consisting of a series of reflections on the social organisation of labour under socialism, and the extent to which transitional social forms—specifically, the wage—could be historically and theoretically demarcated from capitalist relations of production.

By arguing that the wage marked a social relationship that reproduced a capitalist logic of labour, and prioritising the development of new ideological or moral incentives that would supersede the wage as the basis for stimulating production, Zhang, together with Mao, sought to inaugurate a theoretical understanding of socialism that differed from the Soviet model in its most basic features. For Zhang, socialism itself encompassed certain social relations and forms that were drawn into socialism from capitalism, such as the wage, and which needed to be superseded through the constant transformation of social relations and consciousness. Zhang's intervention was therefore a theoretical rupture that offered radical insight into the heart of the Chinese Revolution and engendered a new series of debates until the exhaustion of Maoism in the late Cultural Revolution.

Marx at Beidaihe

The problem of 'bourgeois right' arose in China amid the tumult of the Great Leap Forward as part of an extended process of reflection on the inadequacies of the Soviet model of socialism. Over the course of key meetings held from early 1958, Mao began to rethink socialism in terms of the persistence of contradictions and modes of unevenness between different sets of social relations. This was, at the same time, a project of locating new theoretical categories that would not be dependent on the edifice of Soviet political economy as encountered in China, especially in the form of Stalin's 1952 *Economic Problems of Socialism in the USSR* and the Soviet textbook on political economy.[2] In the second half of August, at the Beidaihe Conference, Mao introduced the vocabulary of bourgeois right by asserting: 'We must smash the ideology of bourgeois right, for example, the competing for position, the competing over ranks, seeking bonuses, the fact that mental labourers earn higher wages, and manual labourers lower wages, all of these are manifestations of bourgeois right.'[3] He went on: 'Having resolved the problem of the status of ownership, the system of bourgeois right persists, for example in the system of ranks, and in the problem of relations between the leaders and the masses.'[4] Mao emphasised that changes in the formal status of ownership do not exhaust the problems of socialist transformation because socialism continues to be marked by social forms, relations, and modes of consciousness that originate from capitalism, and which therefore render socialism itself a site of contradiction rather than a stable or homogeneous mode of production. This was also the opportunity for a return to Marx as the basis for a new beginning that would be beholden neither to the Soviet experience nor to the strict letter of Marx's own categories. The Marx to which Chinese theorists returned was not the early Marx of humanism but rather the late Marx of 'bourgeois right'.

The formula of bourgeois right (in German, *bürgerliche Recht* is only ever used in the specific singular, not to be translated as 'bourgeois legal rights') is discussed mainly in Marx's 1875 *Critique of the Gotha Program*, which contains one of his only extended discussions of the problem of socialist transition.[5] Marx posits a society in which commodity production and the law of value have been abolished through the reorganisation of production on an immediately social basis. Yet, he also postulates that the early development of such a society will fall short of the communist society regulated according to the principle of 'from each according to his abilities, to each according to his needs', because, having emerged from the cultural and ideological conditions of capitalism, it is 'still stamped with the birthmarks of the old society from whose womb it emerges'.[6] For this reason, the adequate mode of distribution in this society is one of 'equal right' or, more precisely, 'bourgeois right', meaning a mode of distribution that remains premised on the exchange of equivalents, where 'the individual producer receives back from society—after the deductions have been made—exactly what he gives to it. What he has given to it is his individual quantum of labour.' As Marx acknowledges, in a statement that caused endless consternation for subsequent theorists, with the exchange of equivalents in the sphere of labour, 'the same principle prevails as that which regulates the exchange of commodities' in capitalist society—namely, the abstract norm of universal exchangeability, or remuneration according to labour done that does not account for the particularity of different individuals. Insofar as remuneration according to a universal norm of labour contribution fails to take account of differing needs and abilities, it 'is, therefore, a right of inequality, in its content, like every right'. The transcendence of this narrow horizon of right as an abstract norm that reproduces inequality is precisely the movement of transition towards communism. This 'higher phase of communist society', Marx anticipates, is one where

> after the enslaving subordination of the individual to the division of labour, and therewith also the antithesis between mental and physical labour, has vanished; after labour has become not only a means of life but life's prime want; after the productive forces have also increased with the all-around development of the individual, and all the springs of co-operative wealth flow more abundantly—only then can the narrow horizon of bourgeois right be crossed in its entirety and society inscribe on its banners: From each according to his ability, to each according to his needs![7]

Mao's deployment of the vocabulary of bourgeois right involved a stretching of Marx's categories. In the first place, there could be no suggestion that China had already abolished commodity production and the law of value as Marx described. Yet, for precisely this reason, in China, bourgeois right came to stand for a great deal more than its specific content in Marx's thought, encompassing the reproduction of social inequalities under socialism. The Maoist deployment of bourgeois right at this juncture was therefore intimately related to the transformation of everyday life that also figured as central to the Great Leap, insofar as it designated not only the central problem of the wage, which hewed closely to its 'original' Marxist connotation, but also acts of superiority on the part of officials, anticipating the radical anti-bureaucratic movements of the 1960s.[8] Most importantly, by speaking of the ideology of bourgeois right, Mao gestured at the dialectical relationship and dynamic tension between social forms and modes of consciousness and how a transformation of consciousness could bring about the transformation of social relations.

These early interventions created the space for a more systematic exploration of the problem of bourgeois right. When, having returned from Beidaihe, the Shanghai mayor Ke Qingshi (1902–65) informed Zhang Chunqiao of the discussions that had taken place, Zhang set to work writing his article.

Lenin in Shanghai

Zhang's article rests on and revisits the legacies of the return to Marx embodied by Mao's early deployments of 'bourgeois right'. Zhang's argument was distinguished less by its reading of Marx than by its recovery of the supply system during the revolutionary war that could be re-theorised and developed as part of a sustained transition to communism. The supply system consisted of the open, nonmonetary provision of goods to cadres and soldiers in wartime. For Zhang, the egalitarian relations of the Red Army in the 1930s encompassed 'communist mutual relations' not only within the army but also between the army and the masses, and offered an alternative to material incentives, such as the wage. In Zhang's terms, 'when comrades used to live under the supply system they did not envy wage labour, and so they enjoyed a life that expressed relations of mutual equality between comrades'. By contrast, Zhang posits, 'the core of the ideology of bourgeois right is the wage system' through which material incentives reproduce and naturalise bourgeois expectations that labour is compensated by wages and, as such, prevent the consciousness of communist forms of distribution. This intervention momentously called into question the absolute difference—central to the Soviet discourse on political economy—between the capitalist wage as the purchase and sale of labour power and the socialist wage-form, which, under the formula of 'remuneration according to labour' (按劳分配), was said to reward labourers in strict proportion to work done.

Zhang's text suggests that the socialist wage-form is not fundamentally different from the wage in capitalist relations of production, insofar as both participate in a shared logic of atomised labour that is incompatible with the formation of new communist social relations. To a greater extent than for Mao, for Zhang, 'bourgeois right' offered a way of establishing the continuity between capitalism and socialism, so that, for him, socialism became legible as a contradictory ensemble of social forms, with the wage relation itself a site of radical contradiction.[9] Throughout the text, Zhang refers to those who privilege the continued use of material incentives as 'the economists' (经济学家), which allows his own intervention to be posed as a question of politics. Zhang's article therefore embodies a strategic separation of politics from economics that is summed up in his explicit privileging of 'politics in command', whereby politics is understood in terms of the transformative capacities of consciousness to rupture with transitional social forms such as the wage.

One month after the publication of Zhang's essay, in October and November 1958, six meetings were held in Shanghai to discuss the problem of bourgeois right. Participants were overwhelmingly drawn from the circles of propaganda work rather than being the 'economists' whom Zhang disparaged. They followed Zhang in attending to a complex relation between politics and economics, and between the structure of the wage-form and the transformative capacities of consciousness. *Liberation* summarised these debates over bourgeois right by stating: 'It cannot be denied that definite economic relations always give rise to corresponding forms of consciousness, and that with distribution also being a kind of economic relationship, the remnants of inequality in distribution will also generate bourgeois consciousness.'[10]

The communist consciousness of labour, by contrast, was characterised as labour 'without remuneration'. These divergent modes of consciousness were characterised in terms of the distribution of desire and consciousness between the 'self' (私) and 'society' (公). In sketching the contours of such a consciousness, the radicals who agreed with Zhang made recourse to the early utopian days of the Soviet Union. They noted that 'Lenin had already taken great efforts to support "communist subbotniks" in the early days of the Soviet Union, because from this he could see "communist things", he could see the sprouts of communism'.[11] In his 1920 essay 'From the Destruction of the Old Social System, To the Creation of the New', Lenin described the *subbotniks* as labour performed on a voluntary basis 'for the benefit of society'. The supersession of bourgeois right would require the wholesale reconstruction of consciousness and social relations so that all labour would be 'for the benefit of society', no longer mediated by the wage and its attendant mode of consciousness. The layered references to Marx, Lenin, and the early phases of the Chinese Revolution allowed the language of bourgeois right to function as a critique of Stalinism from a specifically Maoist perspective.

The utopian phase of the Great Leap Forward soon ran into disaster, which forced a reckoning with the heady expectations that had accumulated during 1958, including the idea of an imminent abolition of bourgeois right through a supersession of the wage-form. At the Wuchang Conference in November, therefore, Mao urged that

> it is only possible to eliminate one part of bourgeois right, such as bureaucratic airs, excessive privileges, masterly attitudes, old relations, these must definitely be destroyed the more thoroughly the better. But the other part, such as the wage system, relations between upper and lower levels, and the definite compulsion of the state, cannot be done away with.[12]

He went on in even more striking terms, that 'there is a part of bourgeois right that is still of use under socialism, and which must be preserved and made to serve socialism'.[13] The question of how bourgeois right could be made to serve socialism deepened the complexity of the problem of the wage-form, consisting of how a social relation that marked the persistence of capitalist organisation of labour under socialism could be made to work in a way that would produce the material and ideological conditions for its eventual supersession in favour of the communist society described by Marx.

Towards Communist Labour

The cultivation of the new subject of communist labour that would enable the supersession of bourgeois right became the consistent problem of Chinese socialism from 1958, and yet was also the point of struggle that ultimately contributed to the ossification of the Chinese Revolution and the theoretical vocabulary of bourgeois right. The strategic bifurcation between politics and economics that had informed Zhang's 1958 article entered a new configuration during the Cultural Revolution when Zhang himself was charged with writing a new textbook of socialist political economy. In it, he and his fellow authors sought to develop an account of socialist political economy that replaced the Soviet understanding of socialism as a stable mode of production by revealing its contradictory character. The failure to restrict bourgeois right provided the basis for a retrospective critique of the Soviet Union as well as an explicit affirmation of the continuity between the wage relation of capital and remuneration according to labour under socialism:

> Under the socialist system, the production relations reflected by the wage are different from those production relations reflected by the wage under capitalism. Yet, the category of the wage and its specific form, whether it be piece or time rates, is ultimately an inheritance of capitalist society.[14]

The significance of this passage from the final version of the textbook drafted in 1976 lies not only in the restatement that the socialist wage remained basically consistent with its capitalist pre-revolutionary counterpart, but also that the wage relation would provide the foundation for a prospective reintroduction of capitalism, whereby the wage would be on hand to assist the reinsertion of labour power into a process of capitalist accumulation. Zhang presciently understood that socialism provided the 'ready-to-hand' possibilities for the process of capitalist restoration that emerged in the 1980s. The final version of this textbook was published in September 1976, preceding the coup following Mao's death.[15]

Zhang and his interlocutors, however, could only conceive of the supersession of the wage in the form of heroic acts of will that could not be sustained outside particular periods of exhausting mobilisation. Although they were unable to invent new communist forms of labour, the problems they highlighted—the continuity between the capitalist and the socialist wages, and the need for a systematic reconfiguration of desire to render communism possible—were, and remain, real problems. It falls to us to take up these challenges in our own time, amid the ruins of twentieth-century socialist experiments.

1958

In 1958, the Chinese Communist Party announced the Great Leap Forward, a campaign that was supposed to run for the whole of the Second Five-Year Plan (1958–63). The stated goal was to overtake the United Kingdom's industrial output within fifteen years and catapult China into the pantheon of great nations. As people's communes were established in the countryside, rapidly accelerating the collectivisation process, the Chinese state made major investments in heavy industry. Although efforts were made to involve workers in enterprise management, the trade unions had emerged considerably weakened from the crackdown that followed the Hundred Flowers Movement, and many of the concessions won by the workers in previous years were rescinded. Most importantly, the campaign set ambitious and unrealistic targets for production, which put industrial workers under pressure. Although it would be strictly implemented only at the beginning of the following decade, the household registration (hukou) system was established at this time, and it remains in place to this day. This essay looks into the historical roots of the system, its rationale and its legacies.

Reorganising Chinese Labour: The Establishment of the Household Registration System

Jane HAYWARD

Formally established under Mao Zedong in 1958, the household registration system (户口, *hukou*) was the central mechanism for the organisation of labour and production underpinning China's development model. It harnessed China's large rural labour force to support urban livelihoods and industrial development at a time when comprehensive engagement with the international capitalist economy was not possible. As the reform era dawned in the late 1970s, the *hukou* system stayed in place as Chinese social relations transformed around it. While continuing to promote urban industrial development through the exploitation of rural labour, paradoxically, it evolved from an institution designed to shield China's economy from global capital to one whose very *modus operandi* was the making available of low-cost labour to international corporations.

The International Environment

Throughout the past few centuries, the nation-states of Western Europe developed and industrialised through colonial expansion, utilising cheap labour and resources from overseas territories. China after 1949 did not have this option. Colonialism and imperialism were anathema to everything the Chinese Communist Party (CCP) stood for (in theory at least)—and with good reason. A century earlier, following its defeat by British troops in the Opium Wars, the weak Qing Government had been strong-armed into opening Chinese markets on very poor terms for China. Postwar concessions to the victorious British included not just disadvantageous trading conditions, but also the ceding of portions of Chinese territory. Other capitalist powers soon got in on the game and, before long, Britain, France, Germany, Russia, the United States and, eventually, Japan were all happily ensconced in treaty ports around China's coasts—special concession areas and trading hubs where foreign occupiers were immune from Chinese law. Any material benefits to the

Chinese economy from these foreign commercial activities had little impact beyond the treaty ports.[1] Instead, large swathes of China's inland and rural population, already mired in poverty, suffered all the more under a government whose prior failings were exacerbated by its subjugation to foreign powers.[2] During World War II, after the other powers had left, China was under partial occupation by a militarist Japan intent on establishing hegemony throughout Asia.[3] Little wonder the communists' eventual victory in 1949 hinged on a platform of virulent anti-imperialism. The incongruity of this stance should certainly be recognised, however. As Chris Bramall pointed out, 'it is one of the many ironies of the CCP "project" that a party committed to eliminating any imperial presence within China was nevertheless determined to preserve its own internal cohesion in Tibet, Qinghai, Xinjiang and Inner Mongolia'.[4] Even so, the experience of 'semicolonialism' at the hands of foreign capitalist powers was pivotal in shaping the communists' development strategy going forward.

Moreover, engagement in foreign markets was largely off the table. In today's world, in which the ideological tenets of economic liberalism have resoundingly triumphed over alternatives, economic pundits routinely take for granted the connection between foreign trade and national economic growth. From the perspective of China's communists, however, given both recent experience and their analysis of China's situation rooted in Marxist principles, imperialist relations were inherent to global capitalism. Therefore, opening up a weak China to foreign markets would only have meant more of the same: the economic and political subordination of the country to predatory foreign capitalists on disadvantageous terms, the extraction and depletion of national resources and the inability of the country to develop in a way that benefited the majority of the Chinese people.[5] In any case, in practical terms, the hostile Cold War environment of the early 1950s allowed few options in this respect. The United States, the newly crowned hegemon of the capitalist world order, which was then in the throes of anticommunist McCarthyism, pursued an aggressive containment policy towards China, including a trade embargo, military bases in Japan and South Korea and the deployment of the Seventh Fleet in the Taiwan Strait.[6] Given all of the above, any prospects for the new People's Republic of China (PRC) to develop its economy through engagement with global capitalism were severely restricted[7]. Instead, China's leaders had to look internally, to the resources of their own domestic population. The *hukou* system became the strategy by which this was to be achieved.

The Communist Understanding of Class

For any communist, the exploitative class relations at the heart of capitalism are the root of all social injustice. The problem lies with the concentration of private ownership of the means of production in the hands of a few, which compels those without property to sell their labour to the private owner, the capitalist, for a wage. Under this system, labour itself is a commodity. Thus, the goods produced by this labour belong not to those who produced them, but to the private capitalist, who pays the labourers only a fraction of what the product is worth and sells it for a profit, accumulating private wealth in the process. In this exchange, the labourers always lose out, making back less than the value of what they produced. The commodification of labour under private ownership is thus a form of exploitation, tending towards ever greater inequality as the private capitalist seeks to make greater profits by keeping wages as low as possible. It was literally unthinkable, therefore, for the CCP to organise the national economy according to the principles of private property or commodified labour.

Yet, as far as the communists were concerned, class inequality in China was not just an ideological matter or a moral issue of social justice; it was an existential question of national security. Global capitalism was, after all, always expansionist—always on the lookout for new territories and markets. Those within China able to benefit from commercial activities, particularly those who had done well under the previous imperialist occupiers, or those whose private wealth or property might somehow blossom as the new communist polity sought to establish itself, would always be susceptible to the lure of foreign trade, so it was presumed. Moreover, the Communists' recently vanquished rivals, the US-backed, pro-capitalist Nationalists, with whom they had fought a gruelling civil war throughout the 1930s and 1940s, were a continuing source of concern. Having fled to Taiwan after 1949 and now under American military protection, they harboured plans to reinvade and join forces with their capitalist allies on the mainland. Anyone accumulating individual wealth or property was therefore viewed with suspicion as a potential collaborator with the imperialist enemy, threatening to drag China back to its underdeveloped, semicolonial past.

China's *Hukou* System

All of this formed the backdrop of the fledgling communist state's Herculean task to rebuild a strong nation-state and a flourishing economy while, at the same time, both keeping social inequalities in check and keeping out the foreign powers which encircled them. Facing this dilemma, the *hukou* system became the solution. Under this system, agricultural labour was organised on the basis of large collective farms, or communes, and urban workers were organised into collective work units. Every member of the population was registered to their respective commune or work unit and, along with this registration, classified as either a peasant (*agricultural*, 农业) or an urbanite (*non-agricultural*, 非农业).

The public goods, facilities and infrastructure to which Chinese people had access were determined by these classifications. For urban dwellers, the state provided housing, food, health care, social security, schooling and other facilities, all of which were allocated on the basis of work unit registration. For those registered with agricultural *hukou*, however, the state did not provide such amenities; these were instead provided by the rural collectives themselves or by the production teams into which the rural workers were organised.[8] Moreover, mobility around the country was restricted under this system. The rationale behind this was to prevent China's rural population from converging on the cities, placing a strain on urban infrastructure and supplies. The goal was to preserve the bulk of state resources for the urban workforce to promote industrial development. Under the large-scale collective farms in the countryside, meanwhile, the abundance of agricultural labour could be managed and organised and grain could easily be extracted at cheap cost and transferred to cities.

Under the *hukou* system, labour was not commodified and class exploitation was impossible, supposedly, since peasants and urbanites were, nominally at least, the collective owners of the means of production. The produce extracted from the countryside was utilised for the collective project of nation-building, rather than marketised for private gain. This 'non-exploitative' social structure—hailed in state discourse as the worker–peasant alliance—underpinned the Chinese socialist state ideologically and was the overarching form of social organisation. Ironically, however, given the Communist Party's ideological foundations, the *hukou* system in fact rested on the structural subordination of the countryside to the cities. It was a mechanism of mass exploitation on a national scale, designed to uphold urban living standards on the backs of the peasant masses. According to the well-known agricultural economist Wen Tiejun, the *hukou* system under Mao constituted a form of national self-exploitation tantamount to internal colonisation.[9] According to Vivienne Shue, insofar as it segmented the population into different peoples of unequal status administered under different regulations, the *hukou* system is best understood not as a form of nation-state governance, but as a manifestation of imperial rule.[10]

The *Hukou* System in Historical Context

This *hukou* system, which took shape during the 1950s, in fact had a lengthy institutional history. Household registration of some kind had long been a practice of Chinese imperial dynasties for the administration of tax collection and for purposes of military conscription and social control.[11] One aspect of the last, the *baojia* (保甲) system developed during the Warring States period (third–fifth centuries BCE), involved the organisation of households into collectively administered groups with mutual responsibilities towards the state—effectively a surveillance mechanism whereby neighbours were expected to report on one another's suspicious activities to avoid collective punishment. Such a system re-emerged in various forms under the Song, Yuan, Ming and Qing dynasties. In the twentieth century, the Nationalist government of 1927–49 deployed a similar system to root out its enemies—particularly members of the CCP. From the late 1930s, the Communist Party also adopted the system in rural areas under its control to guard against anti-revolutionary activities and infiltration by Nationalists or the Japanese.[12] After the victorious communists entered the cities in 1949, they took over the urban *hukou* records kept by the Nationalists, drawing on these to flush out any remaining enemies or 'questionable persons' lurking in the cities.[13] Restrictions on population movement were not a priority at this stage. On the contrary, the PRC's first *de facto* constitution, the Common Program issued in September 1949, guaranteed freedom of residence and migration. In fact, the free flow of people between city and countryside during the formative years of the PRC facilitated economic recovery after decades of war.[14]

As the 1950s progressed, the focus of household registration shifted from the identification of enemies to national control of people and resources. With the Soviet influence on the PRC increasingly apparent, Chinese economic policy came to reflect the Stalinist prioritisation of heavy industry as well as the ideological pre-eminence of the urban workforce over the 'backward' peasantry. The Soviet *propiska*, an urban residency permit used to regulate the size of cities and restrict access for those from the countryside, served as an early model for restricting rural–urban migration.[15] Through a series of regulations, the Chinese state gradually asserted control over housing and migration, and grain purchasing, marketing and allocation through rationing, guaranteeing low-priced food for urban residents. A nationwide registration system regulating population movement across both cities and countryside appeared in 1955.[16] This early *hukou* system continued to be porous, however. As the state prioritised industrialisation, urban job opportunities burgeoned, attracting an influx of workers from the countryside, who often brought their families with them, despite misgivings from planning officials. Various regulations, such as guarantees for home leave, were promulgated in an attempt to keep such movements in check.[17]

In 1958, the *hukou* was established in its fullest form with the passing of the Regulations on Household Registration in the PRC. This extended registration to include members of the People's Liberation Army, so covering every Chinese citizen.[18] Yet, these regulations coincided with the fervent industrialisation push of the Great Leap Forward, a nationwide project which, of course, led to a further explosion of job opportunities in cities. While this was accompanied by the decentralisation of economic management intended to energise the grassroots, the central government lost its grip on the movement of labour just as it was attempting to tighten its fist.[19] Thus, paradoxically, at the moment the *hukou* took on its fullest form, '[t]he rush of millions of people into the cities in the years 1958–60 … constituted the most rapid burst of urbanization in the first three decades of the People's Republic, perhaps in any comparable period in human history'.[20] It was not until 1960 that China's leaders acknowledged the disaster and famine the Great Leap Forward had wrought on the countryside—in no small part as a result of the redirecting of massive amounts of labour out of agriculture and into industrial construction projects during the harvest seasons. From this point, the *hukou* system came to be strictly enforced, with large-scale state-led 'downsizing' programs put in place to shift migrant labourers out of the cities and back into the villages.[21]

The *Hukou* System of the Reform Era

The market reforms introduced after 1978 transformed the nature of the Chinese economy and urban–rural relations. The rural communes were dismantled and agricultural production was reorganised on a household basis. Special economic zones (SEZs) were set up on the southern and eastern coasts to attract investment from foreign companies, connecting China with the global capitalist economy. In rural areas, local cadres established town-and-village enterprises producing goods for export. With rural families now managing their own household plots, any extra hands were encouraged to seek off-farm work, as long as they remained within their own localities. A rural labour market began to emerge in the countryside, and a trickle of rural–urban migration began as some moved further afield to seek employment in the SEZs.[22]

In the latter half of the 1980s, work units in the cities began to move workers on to temporary contracts. Many were laid off—a traumatic social and cultural disruption after decades of having their employment and lifetime security guaranteed by the state (see the essays by Ching Kwan Lee, Hurst and Solinger in the present volume). Labour was becoming commodified on a national scale. In 1992, Deng Xiaoping undertook his historic Southern Tour—a promotional stunt to galvanise activities in the SEZs. As more investment poured in, rural–urban migration accelerated and, before long, millions of rural migrants were flooding from the countryside into the cities to join with the newly 'freed-up' urban workforce. According to Lin Chun, '[f]rom 1991 to 2013 there was a huge increase of 269 million in the urban workforce, 85 percent of which was accounted for by rural immigration.'[23]

Through all of this, the *hukou* system stayed in place. Local officials turned a blind eye to rural migrants' illegitimate status in the cities, as the massive influx of cheap labour fuelled China's new export-led growth model. But the state still had no obligation to provide for them—not housing, social security, health care, schooling for their children or pensions. What amenities they had remained back in the countryside, attached to their local *hukou* registration. Thus, the social reproduction of a large portion of the urban labour force took place in the countryside, at villagers' expense. The countryside served as a vast social safety net, with the expectation that migrant labourers would eventually return there when no longer required. Since neither city governments nor incoming corporations had to stump up the costs for work-related benefits, wages could be driven lower. Thus, the *hukou* system now constituted a new form of mass exploitation—the exploitation of rural migrant labour in the interests of both Chinese cities and global capital.[24] The *hukou* system now operated both to facilitate the production of the largest proletariat in world history and to make it readily available to global capital. The irony.

The *Hukou* System Today

The incapacity of major cities to incorporate rural migrants has been manifest, over the past two decades, in the appearance of urban villages. These are former farming villages that have been engulfed by urban expansion. Instead of being steamrollered and built over, they have been protected on account of their status as rural *hukou* localities, so they remain standing, incongruously, inside the city. Having lost their farmland, the villagers in these locations have sought to replace their agricultural income through building extra rooms to rent out. The city's failure to provide suitable accommodation for the millions of incoming rural migrants has ensured a steady supply of willing tenants for these new village landlords. Serious overcrowding has resulted, with local residents often outnumbered ten to one or more. With their limited infrastructure and often shoddily constructed buildings, urban villages increasingly came to resemble the slums of Latin America—havens for the urban underclass.

Despite the *hukou* system's longevity, Chinese policymakers have long been experimenting with reforming it, sometimes leading commentators to assume it is on the brink of being abolished. From the early 2000s, for example, some cities launched measures to unify the divided urban and rural categories into a single 'resident hukou' (居民户口), while, since 2010, certain cities in Guangdong began to experiment with a points-based system, awarding *hukou* to migrants who met certain criteria.[25] A turning point came in March 2014 when the central government published the *National New-Type Urbanisation Plan 2016–20*. This was closely followed by a circular from the State Council, one of China's highest legislative bodies, proclaiming the elimination of the urban–rural distinction for residence permits and the relaxation of restrictions permitting movement to small and medium-sized cities, with the goal of allowing 100 million rural migrants to permanently settle in cities.[26] On the surface, such measures appeared, finally, to award recognition to the rural workforce for their pivotal role in China's state-building and rapid economic growth, rewarding them with full inclusion in the modernity they helped create—the civilisation of urban life. A closer look, however, suggests otherwise. Despite the formal elimination of the urban–rural distinction for most Chinese urban centres, the *hukou* continues to determine the hierarchical status of a large swathe of Chinese people, based on local versus non-local distinctions.[27]

Behind the *hukou* reforms lie plans to limit the size of the largest cities—those with a population of more than five million—the epicentres of Chinese capital and modernity. In many such cities, low-paid rural migrants are the least welcome. Thus, the Chinese state is implementing all manner of measures to keep out the poorest and least-educated migrant workers, via the *hukou* reforms, and by other means, including restricting access to schooling for migrant children (see Friedman's essay in the present volume), moving manufacturing industries out of the cities, as well as the aforementioned points-based scheme.[28] Urban villages have also become targets, with a recent 'clean-up' campaign by state officials in Beijing evicting thousands of migrants from their homes with no warning.[29] Systemic bias against China's low-cost workforce is not going away. And nor is the *hukou*. Once again, it is simply changing shape.

1960

Both workers and peasants in China suffered from the ambitious and unrealistic targets for agricultural and industrial production set during the Great Leap Forward. While much has been written about how farmers ended up neglecting agricultural production for the sake of smelting steel in backyard furnaces—contributing to the famine that killed tens of millions of people—the impact the Great Leap had on workers in other sectors is less well known. This essay explores the toll this campaign took on the safety and wellbeing of workers in the coal mining industry.

Workers' Peril in the Workers' State: The Laobaidong Colliery Disaster
Tim WRIGHT

In 1960, well over 650 miners lost their lives following a massive explosion at the Laobaidong (老白洞) colliery in Datong, northern Shanxi Province.[1] This was China's second-worst mine disaster, and the fourth-worst in world history.[2] Both the leadup to and the aftermath of the disaster reflected the limited importance of workers' welfare in China's political economy.

Anatomy of a Disaster

At 1.45 pm on 9 May 1960, an electric spark in the underground area where coal wagons were parked ignited a large amount of accumulated coal dust, causing a huge explosion. The first sign for those aboveground came when a wall of smoke and fire exited Shaft Fifteen with the power of a force-twelve typhoon, destroying the facilities at, and anywhere within 2,000 metres of, the mine entrance. Workers queuing to start their shift down Shaft Sixteen were killed or injured when they were blown away by a wall of air. Underground, many workers were killed by the blast or when the roof fell in. The explosion also closed down the ventilation systems, allowing poisonous fumes to circulate, which, as in most similar mine disasters, suffocated many miners.

The authorities moved promptly to organise a rescue effort. Although the most experienced local rescue teams were out of town helping at another mining disaster, in Baotou, the remaining two teams quickly arrived, going down the mine within half an hour of the explosion but finding it difficult to make progress because of rock falls, fires, and smoke. At 5.15 pm a well-intentioned but disastrous decision to turn the ventilation system back on in fact fanned the fire underground and distributed poisonous smoke throughout the mine. Although rescue teams had established bases at the bottom of Shafts Fourteen and Fifteen, by 11.15 pm they had all been forced to leave the mine. At 11.50 pm a plume of smoke and 15-metre-high flames spurted out of Shaft Sixteen and cut off an escape route for miners who were still trapped. At 12.30 am the next day, the ventilation equipment was turned off and early that morning a new rescue attempt was made.

In total, 912 workers were underground at the time of the explosion. A group of thirteen was rescued late on 9 May and a further 104 around midnight. The last thirty-six survivors were brought out on 13 May. By 16 May it was decided that no-one could still be alive underground and, late the following day, the mine entrances were sealed. In all, 228 workers were rescued, five of whom later died. A total of 669 workers were killed underground. The official death toll was 684, though the Deputy Minister of Coal later suggested that more than 800 people may have died.[3]

Within an hour of the explosion, the leaders of the Datong Coal Bureau, which ran Laobaidong, arrived at the mine, followed within a day by senior officials from the central and provincial governments. The leaders in Beijing were notified and Premier Zhou Enlai kept Mao Zedong informed. The Ministers of Coal and Labour were summoned from a meeting in Hainan to provide oversight. Deputy Premier Luo Ruiqing assured the mine authorities that the Centre would provide whatever they needed, and more than 1,000 troops, including some equipped for chemical warfare (and therefore able to work through the poisonous gasses in the mine), were sent to Datong, as were rescue teams from leading mines across northern China.

At the first sound of the explosion, miners' families had begun to congregate at the mine. Despite appalling scenes of distress, the authorities assigned guards to keep the crowd away, lest they impede the rescue effort. As bodies began to be brought out, heartbroken relatives had to identify their loved ones, sometimes just by the clothes they were wearing. Because the weather was warming up, rural families, who took longer to reach the mine, sometimes arrived only after their relatives had to be buried. The authorities found a site suitable for a mass grave, burying many bodies there; others were taken back to their ancestral homes for burial. Yet others, including the mine manager, were not found until more than a decade later, leaving their families with no focus for their mourning and no grave to visit at the Qingming festival.

No Random Accident

This disaster was no random accident. Rather, as Ben Harvey writes: 'Mining disasters provide snapshots of society exposed and forced into action.'[4] Its causes lay deep within China's political economy, reflecting the

Party-State's adoption of an extensive development model that increased production by expanding the quantity of inputs, and in particular the extreme version of that model practised at the height of the Great Leap Forward (1958–60).

After 1949, the newly established Party-State took measures to promote the welfare of its workers, in the process 'remaking' China's working class as a—somewhat privileged—status group dependent on the state.[5] As part of worker welfare, there was at least a rhetorical commitment to work safety. As the Chief Engineer of China's state mines wrote in a 1990 retrospective of the industry: 'After 1949, the working class became the masters of the country, and coal safety was given a high priority.'[6] From 1953, the government established work-safety institutions on the Soviet model at national, regional, and local levels; by 1955, ten major coal regions and twenty-seven mine areas had established safety inspection organs.[7] Indeed, the official statistics from the early 1950s show a sharp fall in coalmine death rates from the very high figures for 1949–50, when the country had still not recovered from the chaos and disruption of the Civil War and the new safety measures had not yet been put in place.[8]

When concrete decisions had to be made at the basic level, however, the extensive development model limited the privileges that could be granted to workers and, even for union officials, safety often had a lower priority than other pressing needs.[9] In general, poorer countries aiming for rapid development and industrialisation have to make difficult choices when allocating resources, and often in practice give a low priority to work safety.[10] Even in the Britain, in what W. G. Carson described as the 'political economy of speed', the imperative to develop the North Sea oilfields in the 1970s led to the sidelining of safety and a high price paid in workers' lives.[11] So, at Laobaidong, when the mine was reopened in 1954 after having been closed during the Civil War, financial constraints and the state's urgent need to develop coal production meant the mine failed to implement key safety requirements, with, for example, Shaft Fifteen doubling as both a winding and a ventilation shaft.[12]

Problems accelerated during the Great Leap Forward, when the extensive mode of development was carried to extremes and widespread political fervour and repression prevented any questioning of policy. Central to the movement were ambitious and unrealistic targets for production and, under the slogan 'steel as the key link and coal supporting steel' (以钢为纲以煤保钢), coal mining played a crucial role. The 1959 target for coal production was 380 million tons—close to three times the output of 1957.[13] However, this mode of development ran into internal contradictions as any slack within the economy became exhausted and, by May 1960, when the Laobaidong disaster occurred, the extensive methods used to develop production in the industry had reached their limit, and coal output started to decline.[14]

Nationally, the Great Leap Forward led to a work-safety crisis in the coal-mining sector and beyond.[15] Mines were forced to cut corners to meet ever-higher targets. Despite rhetorical commitments, in practice, work safety was downgraded in a drive for production at all costs, with the slogan 'safety first' (安全第一) denounced as a manifestation of dogmatism.[16] Using the military terminology common during the Great Leap, foreign minister Marshall Chen Yi compared the movement to a battlefield and said fatalities were inevitable: 'Casualties have indeed appeared among workers but it is not enough to stop us in our tracks. This is a price we have to pay, it's nothing to be afraid of.'[17] The official statistics unambiguously show the cost in miners' lives. The number of workers killed in Chinese coalmines increased from around 600 in the mid-1950s to more than 6,000 in 1960, while the death rate in large state-owned mines (of which Laobaidong was one) increased from around four per million tons to almost fourteen in 1960, and was still eleven in 1961.[18] In other sectors, almost four times as many workers died annually in state and collective enterprises in the years 1958 to 1961 than during the First Five-Year Plan (1953–57), while in the construction industry the death rate in 1958 was more than three times that in 1957, with 117 of the 435 fatalities occurring through the collapse of buildings brought about by shortcomings in construction. The railways similarly experienced an increase in deaths during the Great Leap Forward and a sharp spike in 1960.[19]

At Laobaidong, the prioritisation of production was reflected in a blind push to increase output. The mine's installed capacity was 90,000 tons but already by 1958 it was producing way over that amount and the 1959 and 1960 targets raised the planned output to almost 150,000 tons. Overcapacity production is a major source of risk in coal mining, and this augured badly for safety at the mine. High and unrealistic targets for production by each shift meant that workers were often forced to work multiple shifts to try to reach their quotas. Just as in many areas of rural China, the cadres used the supply of ration tickets to browbeat workers into undertaking excessive shifts.[20] The day of the disaster, 9 May, had itself been scheduled as a 'high production day'.[21]

Under these circumstances, safety very explicitly came second. The Datong Mine Party Committee proclaimed to a workers' meeting: 'Production is the aim, safety the means. Where there is a contradiction between production and safety, we have first to obey the needs of production.'[22] At the same time, the department in charge of mine safety was downgraded.[23] Numerous unsafe practices rooted in the need to increase production were seen at Laobaidong. Large amounts of coal dust, sometimes up to 30 cm deep, were allowed to accumulate in the passageways. Even if it had been operating, the sprinkler system was unable to deal with so much dust. Moreover, the prohibition on welding underground was lifted and the frenzied atmosphere even allowed welding contests to be conducted within the mine.[24]

The imperative to increase production also led to the dilution of the workforce with large numbers of new, untrained workers who were often not properly registered with the mine management. These workers were less aware than experienced miners of the safety requirements. While in 1955 the mine's workforce was 1,978, by 1960, it had increased to 6,994, some 1,126 of whom were hired without going through the regular procedures. Management almost totally lost the ability to regulate labour, to the extent that workers who did not have suitable arrangements at home would take their children down the mine, where they could look after them, or bring their parents or other relatives sightseeing underground.[25]

The treatment of the survivors and the bereaved families also signalled the limits to worker welfare. The state did not attempt to abjure all responsibility, as did coal owners in nineteenth-century Britain or the United States.[26] Surviving workers were allocated to suitable jobs that they could manage despite their injuries, and widows were given preference in the recruitment process for appropriate positions. But, as in the Britain, the amount of monetary compensation paid was pitifully inadequate. The families of the dead were granted an allowance of 12.50 yuan per month (8.50 for rural residents).[27] Although later reports said these amounts were reasonable in light of the country's economic difficulties, they are unlikely to have been remotely enough to support livelihoods given the average miner's wage was about 60 yuan per month.[28]

Attributing Responsibility

The politics of the Great Leap Forward and of the Party-State in general contributed to the disaster and also prevented serious analysis from which future generations could learn. Before the disaster, those questioning unsafe work practices were denounced as rightists. One old worker was aware of the risks, having experienced an explosion while working in mines in Manchuria, but he nevertheless did not dare to refuse to go underground.[29] When he did go down the mine, he carefully noted escape paths and, after the explosion, guided fellow workers to a safe place where they could await rescue.

After the disaster, an investigation by a small group set up by the central authorities and led by the Ministers of Public Security, Labour and Coal, and the head of the All-China Federation of Trade Unions turned into a search for saboteurs and counterrevolutionary elements accused of triggering the explosion. The failure by the mine leadership to take this possibility into account was denounced as a lack of the spirit of 'politics in command'.[30] Workers who had been due to go on shift but for various reasons had not, or who had fled back to their home villages in fear after the disaster, were under suspicion, as were the technicians in charge of safety, electricity, and transport. Although the official report one year later found no link between counterrevolutionaries and the explosion, large numbers of workers and cadres suffered demotion or worse. In all, 709 people were struggled against, 398 cadres were replaced, and 462 'impure elements' (不纯分子) were transferred away.[31]

As with other aspects of the Great Leap Forward, the Party's response was to lay blame on local officials. At a meeting shortly after the disaster, the Minister of Coal pounded the table and shouted at mine officials: 'You should apologise to the people. So many dead, how can you justify yourselves? Have you no Party spirit, no conscience!'[32] The eventual official report also focused just on the immediate causes of the disaster, such as lapses in safety measures and in management, which was described as 'chaotic' (混乱), and identified mine managers as responsible.[33] A further report in 1963 likewise merely discussed the immediate causes and laid responsibility on officials at the Coal Bureau; the 'correct leadership of the upper levels of the Party' had led to the rapid development of the mine, but mine leaders had made key mistakes.[34] Even the local officials themselves blamed their own excessive enthusiasm, rather than the external pressures they were under: 'Our brains burned with enthusiasm for increasing production, management and safety provisions just could not keep up.'[35] No doubt those in the know could read between the lines and understand what had happened, but it was hardly an open and objective analysis of the causes of the disaster.

In fact, the chaos was not just local. As Xu Daben, then Vice-Minister of Coal, found when he visited other key mines in northern and northeastern China, it was general, even universal.[36] Crucially, however, no-one dared mention the policy settings or the ideological environment that created the chaos. At Laobaidong, one widow in the heat of the moment said: 'God damn it. Great Leap Forward, Great Leap Forward, a minute late down the mine won't do, they will only be happy when they have Great Leaped us to death.'[37] During the late 1950s, Minister of Labour Ma Wenrui recalled saying to a workers' meeting, 'This isn't a Great Leap Forward, it's a Great Leap Backward', though some scepticism about this recollection is probably warranted.[38] In general, however, criticism of the broader policies was virtually impossible and, as with the even more serious famine in rural areas, local officials—rather than Mao and the central leadership—were held responsible.[39]

Finally, except for one possible mention in a provincial government document published in late 1960,[40] information about the disaster was designated 'top secret' (绝密) by the leadership and there was no media coverage. In contrast, in China in the 1990s and 2000s, investigative journalists played a prominent role in raising consciousness of work safety and of the needs of those whose lives were destroyed by disasters.[41] Likewise, in Europe, press coverage and parliamentary inquiries in nineteenth-century Britain created pressure to improve safety and to better compensate the families of killed or injured workers, while in France a series of reports on the 1906 Courrières disaster allowed miners to voice demands for a safer work environment.[42] But, while in the Britain and France such press reports and the documents produced by public inquiries stimulated public discussion by providing rich detail on mining disasters (even though coroners' hearings and inquiries sometimes failed to uncover the real picture), in China, state control over the press has deprived the public of that detail for Laobaidong and, to a lesser extent, for more recent mining disasters.[43]

Unearthing Laobaidong

After the beginning of the reform period, restrictions on reporting were gradually relaxed and, from 1982, there were occasional brief references to the Laobaidong disaster in articles on work safety, in the *Labour Yearbook*, in the official gazetteer of the provincial coal industry, and in a speech by the Minister of Labour.[44] From 1992, the writer He Yuqing started to research the disaster, completing that research in 1998. Four decades after the explosion, excerpts of this first detailed account were published in several journals, including *China Coal News* (中国煤炭报), a daily newspaper published by the Ministry of Coal and its successors, at last bringing it to public attention.[45]

For a long time, this lack of transparency inevitably constrained any attempts to learn from, and to some extent even to understand, what had happened; in the short term, the managers at Datong just maintained their focus on increasing production.[46] Nevertheless, the disaster was an important factor behind the resuscitation of safety institutions in the early 1960s, under the slogan 'safety first'.[47] But politics intruded again during the Cultural Revolution, when those institutions were again dismantled. As a result, there was a steady increase in the death rate in large state-owned mines, from around four per million tons in the mid-1960s to over seven in 1970, though the increase was less marked than during the Great Leap Forward, and there was greater variation between provinces.[48] In fact, work in China's coalmines continued to be extremely perilous into the early twenty-first century, though from around 2003, China started to dramatically improve its record, by 2019 reducing the recorded death rate to 2 percent of what it had been in the early 2000s.[49]

1960

As the Great Leap Forward (GLF) ended in catastrophe, leaders of the Chinese Communist Party took a step back from the policies that caused the tragic famine that killed tens of millions and brought the country's economy to the brink of collapse. From late 1961, industrial relations in China began to be regulated by a new document entitled 'Regulation of Tasks in State-Owned Industrial Enterprises (Draft)' (most commonly known as the 'Seventy Articles', adopted on 15 September 1961). The new policy spelled the abandonment of the 'mass line' and the return to a management model based on the authority of the factory director, assisted by administrative and technical staff, which had been heatedly contested during the strike wave of 1956 and 1957. Concurrently, the material incentives that had been disdainfully discarded under the GLF were reinstated, albeit for a limited number of groups of unionised workers in state-owned enterprises. However, while these policies were consistently implemented until the eruption of the Cultural Revolution in 1966, not everyone in the Party's top leadership was ready to abandon the 'mass line' that had driven the GLF. Mao Zedong himself never hid his opposition to this reorganisation of labour relations—a position he made abundantly clear in 1960 when he publicly endorsed the so-called Angang Constitution. This document laid out the principles of putting politics in command of enterprises, assigning a stronger role to the Party in management, resorting to mass mobilisation within companies, blurring the boundaries between workers, technicians and managers, and pushing for technological revolution. The Seventy Articles and the Angang Constitution became the core documents in a 'struggle between two lines' in industry that would last into the reform era. This essay examines the local and national political dynamics at play behind the scenes in Mao's adoption of the Angang Constitution.

The Angang Constitution: Labour, Industry and Bureaucracy during the Great Leap Forward

Koji HIRATA

On 22 March 1960, at the height of the Great Leap Forward (GLF), Mao Zedong read a report about the Anshan Iron and Steel Works (鞍山钢铁公司), also known as Angang (鞍钢), written by the Anshan City Committee of the Chinese Communist Party (CCP). In the spirit of the GLF, the report argued that revolutionary spirit and mass campaigns could help industrialise China. It confirmed Mao's extremist policy line in opposition to a more moderate line: 'It is necessary to continue an ideological revolution [思想革命] without a break, maintain political leadership, totally eliminate superstitions, and liberate ideology.'[1] The report from Anshan pleased Chairman Mao, who commented: 'This … report is very good. The more I read it, the happier I become. I don't think it is too long.'[2] The importance of this document lay in the fact that Angang was the single largest enterprise in what at that time was the most important industrial sector in the People's Republic of China (PRC): steel-making. Reading it, Mao was excited to see his vision—industrialisation through unleashing the power of the masses—confirmed by the nation's most important state-owned enterprise (SOE).

Importantly, the report from Anshan also symbolised the end of an era in Chinese socialism—the period of building socialism by imitating Stalinism, which was best represented by the construction of new plants at Angang with the help of Soviet engineers during the First Five-Year Plan (1953–57). Aware of this change, Mao commented on the report:

> In the past, they thought that this enterprise [Angang] was already modernised and did not need the so-called technological revolution. They opposed implementing mass campaigns … They regarded the 'Magnitogorsk Constitution [马钢宪法]' [an authoritative method for managing a large steel enterprise in the Soviet Union] as sacred and absolute … This report [of March 1960] is

> more advanced. It is not the Magnitogorsk Constitution. It created the Angang Constitution [鞍钢宪法]. The Angang Constitution was born in the Far East, in China.³

Mao gave the report a charming new title, the 'Angang Constitution', the name under which the document would be circulated in the thousands during the Cultural Revolution.

Mao's approval of the technological innovation outlined in the Angang Constitution excited Angang's workers. Although in all likelihood the constitution was not published in newspapers or other media at that time, according to Anshan's official local history, its content was orally communicated in meetings. By the end of March 1960, about 90 percent of the staff and workers at Angang had heard about Mao's comments.⁴ According to a CCP internal report, the workers of Angang favourably compared the present situation as described in the Angang Constitution with the past, when their workplace was controlled by the managers. A number of workers proclaimed that, before the revolution, everything had been done 'just as the factory director says', but now 'our thought had been liberated greatly, and the rightists had been wiped away'.⁵

Reflecting the official Party line, conventional Chinese scholarship regarded the Angang Constitution as evidence of genuine grassroots efforts to create new forms of socialist factory management, and at least some of these efforts were successful.⁶ Criticising this interpretation, some revisionist historians have claimed instead that the Angang Constitution was mere propaganda created by the CCP's top-down policies.⁷ While I agree with the latter view—that the Angang Constitution was a work of propaganda—in this essay, I also show that its creation involved complex local political dynamics. The Angang Constitution was shaped not only by a diktat from the central state authority, but also by the political ambitions of local officials who tried to make use of the state's campaigns and discourse for their own interests.

Local Politics

Though it was called the Angang Constitution, the report actually was not produced by Angang itself; the document was drafted by the Anshan City Party Committee, Angang's local political rival. The leader of the City Committee at the time was First Secretary Yang Shijie, an experienced Party cadre with little experience in industry. In the first years of the PRC,

Yang played an active role in land reform, the 'Resist America Aid Korea Campaign' (抗美援朝运动) and the 'Suppress Counterrevolutionaries Campaign' (镇压反革命运动).[8]

The making of the Angang Constitution reflected the enhanced power of local governments vis-a-vis SOEs like Angang. During the First Five-Year Plan, the economic policymaking of the PRC was largely centralised in the hands of industrial ministries and bureaus in Beijing. In 1958, however, Mao took the planning power from the hands of bureaucrats in the capital and turned it over to provincial Party secretaries.[9] Mao's localism was also associated with anti-technocratic, egalitarian ideals. While criticising Soviet texts on economics in 1959 and 1960, Mao stressed the importance of reforming the management system of SOEs by levelling the relationship between cadres, technological experts and workers:

> It is necessary for leaders [of SOEs] to treat people equally ... When it comes to the management of enterprises, it is necessary ... to make worker-masses, leading cadres, and technical staff unite with each other such that cadres will participate in [political] campaigns, workers will participate in management, and inappropriate rules and systems will be reformed constantly.[10]

Newly empowered local cadres mobilised workers and encouraged them to take command of factories. Workers' initiatives in technological innovation were highly praised and SOE managers and engineers were required to learn from workers. Local cadres even attempted to give equal status to workers and better-educated managers and engineers.

Local city officials like Yang Shijie made use of the GLF to politically attack SOE managers and engineers and thus assert stronger control over enterprises like Angang. In Anshan, the GLF was implemented by combining the production forces of the large modern enterprises and small, mass-based facilities. At a Party conference in March 1959, First Secretary Yang stressed the importance of concurrently developing small furnaces and Angang, which he called, respectively, 'small, local-origin facilities' (小土群) and 'huge, foreign-origin facilities' (大洋群). According to him, the achievement of the GLF in steel production in Anshan in 1958 was made possible not only by Angang, but also from the 270,000 tonnes of 'local steel' (土钢) produced by small furnaces and by the new facilities at Angang built by local enterprises.[11]

During the GLF, the Anshan City Party Committee pressured Angang into taking a more ambitious attitude. On 27 April 1958, the committee produced the 'Five-Year Leap Plan' (五年跃进计划), which outlined ambitious goals for the development of Angang.[12] That day, the City Committee also decided that the goal of the GLF in Anshan was to 'complete the General Line, make efforts for five years, dramatically liberate thoughts, make cadres both red and expert, save half of investment, let all the people work for industry, and build "small Angang[s]"'.[13] In a meeting of the Anshan City Party Committee on 18 October 1960, the Secretary of the Liaoning Provincial Party Committee stated: 'Right now, the entire country is looking at the Northeast. The Northeast is looking at Angang. Simply speaking, the entire country is looking at Angang.'[14]

Just as Mao's anti-technocratic, decentralised vision during the GLF strengthened local CCP organisations' influence over SOEs, reports from local CCP organisations in industrial bases like Anshan also helped Mao consolidate his position within the top leadership. On 25 July 1959, the Liaoning Provincial Party Committee forwarded to the Party centre a report by the Anshan City Committee on production and mass mobilisation in Anshan. The report from Anshan pleased Chairman Mao, who then circulated it with his comments among CCP leaders.[15]

Mao's reference to Angang legitimated and empowered the Anshan City Committee to complete its ambitious goals for steel production. In a speech in August 1959, First Secretary Yang Shijie used Mao's statement to buttress the City Committee's authority: 'We think the instruction of the central leadership and Chairman Mao perfectly match the current reality of our city … [I]t has given us great forces and sharp weapons with which we will oppose rightist deviations and go all out.'[16] With Mao's imprimatur, Yang framed the GLF as 'the process of struggling with rightist, conservative thought'. In his view, problems in Angang's operations were 'inseparable from the rightist thought of some cadres' who cast doubt on the GLF by pointing out its shortcomings and arguing for lower goals. Instead, Angang's industrial production would increase only when 'advanced thought takes command, and the fighting spirit of the masses becomes high'. He stressed how Chairman Mao thought highly of the City Committee's leadership over Angang:

> [T]he Chairman commented on the report by us, the Anshan City Committee, because we are the nation's largest steel enterprise …
> We definitely must reply to the Chairman's words by completing

the production plan in an impressive way, prove the correctness of the Party's General Line, and protect the General Line through the real action in the Great Leap Forward of steel production.

In this way, Angang became a part of the 'we' (我们) of the collective directed by the City Committee.

Mass Mobilisation

Besides Mao's endorsement, another important source of power for the City Committee was its role as a local-level organiser of the mass mobilisation campaigns initiated by the chairman. On 23 August 1958, the Anshan City Party Committee and the City Government convened a meeting with 25,000 people to launch the 'leap' in steel production in the city. On 1 September 1958, the City Party Committee circulated instructions from the CCP's national leadership at a meeting of all the city's Party cadres to begin a campaign to save electricity and dig up abandoned steel.[17]

Local CCP committee cadres also mobilised workers against SOE managers and engineers. The City Committee, together with the Angang Party Committee, blasted Angang's managers and engineers as 'the major obstacle' (主要障碍).[18] In October 1958, the City Committee launched a 'Pull Out White Flags' campaign (拔白旗运动) at Angang. In a meeting at the Iron-Making Factory, the factory director and an engineer were criticised for their 'rightist conservative thought' (右倾保守思想). The campaign then spread to other parts of Angang.[19] By the end of 1958, thirty-nine factory directors and chiefs and 109 lower-level managers had been punished, some of them fired. In February 1960, Deputy Director of Angang, Ma Bin, was also criticised for his 'rightist thought'.[20]

Local CCP cadres also condemned the previous management system that had given managers a dominant status within SOEs—the so-called one-chief system (一长制) that had originated in the Soviet Union. Under this system, SOE managers such as factory directors had almost total control over all employees within their workplaces, while local cadres such as the secretaries of the Party committees played only a supporting role. Even though the CCP had abandoned the one-chief system in 1956, local cadres attacked the existing power of the SOE cadres as the 'remnant influence' (残余影响) of this Soviet-style management system. In March 1959, Yang Shijie stated that the 'unified leadership by the Party' (党的一元化领导) of industrial enterprises was the foundation of the success of the GLF. The unified leadership of the Party within enterprises had been strengthened since 1956 along with the introduction of a 'director responsibility system under the leadership of the Party committee' (党委领导下的厂长负责制), in place of the one-chief system. Yet, the attack on the one-chief system had not been thorough enough, and it was claimed that the 'remnant influence of the one-chief system still exists in many factories and mines'.[21] By criticising the workplace mentality that reinforced the status of SOE managers and engineers, local governments tried to educate SOEs in an effort to justify a new workplace order in which CCP local organisations took command.

According to the Party Committee of Angang's Steel Mill No. 2: '[S]ome cadres stubbornly hold up the one-chief system and oppose the Party's leadership and the escalation of mass campaigns.'[22] They further criticised these SOE cadres for thinking that 'the Party committee does not understand technology' and that 'the Party cannot guide enterprise'. Therefore, the Factory Party Committee decided to target factory directors in an anti-rightist rectification campaign. On 9 November 1959, Secretary Jin of the Factory Party Committee explained the purpose of the campaign. They split the participants into several discussion groups. The assembly first thoroughly criticised a team leader named Jin (not the Party Committee secretary). During the criticism, a leader of another team with the surname Liu challenged the rectification campaign by defending Jin, which resulted in a 'concentrated criticism and struggle' (重点批判和斗争) against Liu as well. Criticism and struggle against Jin and Liu lasted about one month. Overall, these campaigns constituted a serious and dynamic 'education in the General Line and education in Party-ness' (总路线教育和党性教育) targeting a wide range of managers and engineers.[23]

Mobilisation of workers during the GLF was also aimed at strengthening solidarity among workers within the same workplace. In the early and mid-1950s, under the one-chief system, work was atomised into small parts and workers were held individually responsible only for the piece of work allocated to them. During the GLF, however, at least some factories at Angang promoted the idea that workers were collectively responsible for the work of the entire workplace. For instance, steelworker Han of the first open-hearth furnace of Angang's No. 1 Steelworks made a proposal to abolish the division of workers into groups for the purpose of overcoming 'sectionalism' (本位主义). In its place, he argued that they should set up a 'small commune' (小公社) for the entire open-hearth furnace, in which all the tools were shared and the salary was equally distributed to all the workers. By this system, the furnaces would purportedly be better protected.[24]

The Angang Constitution was born from the mutually reinforcing relationship between Chairman Mao and the Anshan City Party Committee. Mao's policy was supported by certain segments of the local bureaucracy, including Anshan city officials like Yang Shijie. Unsurprisingly, Mao's support for the Angang Constitution further enhanced the City Committee's power in Anshan. After Mao's praise of the committee's report, it held three standing committee meetings and decided to implement a mass campaign to read Mao's writings and to further intensify the campaign for technological innovation and technological revolution. Between 11 April and 15 April 1960, the City Committee held a representative meeting, in which Yang Shijie stressed that it was necessary to criticise the one-chief system, eliminate the Magnitogorsk Constitution, establish the Angang Constitution and realise the goal of producing 6.55 million tonnes of steel.[25]

A Rebuttal

Despite its name, the Angang Constitution was actually a rebuttal of what Angang had originally represented: a Soviet-style technocratic management system tethered to the vertical line of control from the industrial ministry in Beijing. In a dramatic rupture from the centralised policymaking of the previous period, Mao empowered local Party organisations and cadres. The GLF strengthened the horizontal leadership of the city over Angang through the network of local cadres based in Party committees within individual factories. Making use of the chairman's new agenda, Party committees in provinces, cities and towns wrested control of SOEs in their jurisdictions away from industrial ministries in Beijing. Local cadres also strengthened their leadership by mobilising workers within factories and promoting the cult of the people's role in technological issues.

China's growth out of the Soviet model is clearly distilled in the 'Angang Constitution'. During the First Five-Year Plan, Angang served as a symbol of China's friendship with the 'Soviet Big Brother' (苏联老大哥), with its new plants built according to Soviet designs, its use of Soviet machines and the help given by Soviet engineers. Yet, in 1960, Chairman Mao provided Angang with a new, opposing role as a symbol of China's departure from

Soviet socialism. While the Angang Constitution was sidelined for a few years after the GLF, it was soon resurrected during the Cultural Revolution, when it was distributed in thousands of copies as a symbol of China's own independent vision for socialism.

Even after the GLF as an economic policy was retracted, its political consequences, which empowered local cadres and workers vis-a-vis SOE cadres and engineers, persisted to some extent. Mass mobilisation became more frequent and regular. The control of SOEs was decentralised and local CCP committees asserted more power over these enterprises than in the period prior to the GLF. Anti-technocratic ideology still possessed legitimacy. The tension between local cadres and SOE managers also continued. Some cadres looked at technicians with suspicion, thinking they might have political problems, which worsened the morale of the technicians. As one Angang engineer reportedly said in 1964: '[W]hile in primary school, I was a flower of the motherland. While in high school, I was the future of the motherland. After graduating from college, I became a target of remoulding.'[26]

1960

In 1960, the Central Committee of the Chinese Communist Party issued the 'Directive to Immediately End the Hand Spinning and Hand Weaving of Cotton'. This was neither the first nor the last time the government tried to ban rural textile production; indeed, the frequency of these bans indicates they had little effect. The survival of manual textile work speaks to the failure of the socialist state to transform or replace domestic reproduction. Rural women were mobilised for full-time work in the public sector, but also worked a second shift at home, feeding and clothing families, raising children, and comforting husbands. Rural women thus contributed twice to socialist accumulation: as underpaid collective labourers, and as producers of the labour force at home.

Production First, Life Second: The 1960 Ban on Hand Spinning and Hand Weaving
Jacob EYFERTH

On 7 February 1960, the Central Committee of the Chinese Communist Party (CCP) issued the 'Directive to Immediately End the Hand Spinning and Hand Weaving of Cotton'. This was neither the first nor the last time the government banned manual textile production. Between 1951 and 1965, the central authorities issued seven separate directives that aimed to abolish 'wasteful' (浪费) and 'backward' (落后) household-based cloth production. The frequency of these bans speaks to their limited effect: millions of rural people continued to wear handloom cloth until the very end of the collective period, and millions of rural women spent a large part of their working hours making cloth and clothes.

Rural handloom weavers were not, in any obvious sense, part of the working class. In fact, the Chinese state saw home-based textile production not as productive work but as a threat to production since it diverted scarce cotton away from state-owned factories. Rural women I interviewed concurred: in their view, hand spinning and hand weaving could not be considered labour (劳动), production (生产), or work (工作, in the sense of a steady job); rather, they were reproductive chores, similar to cleaning, cooking, and childcare. Yet spinning and weaving were undoubtedly important economic activities—as were gathering fuel wood, hauling water, threshing and milling grain, processing and preserving food, raising farm animals, composting excrement to make farmyard manure, and the myriad other tasks rural women performed on a daily basis. Textile work alone could take up half a woman's working time; a 1954 article in the *People's Daily* estimated that a woman who was the sole textile provider for a family of four spent six months every year spinning yarn, weaving cloth, and making clothes and bedding.[1]

A history of the Chinese working class—of any working class, in fact—needs to ask how its object is constructed. Not all work is created equal: all societies value some work over other types and exclude some activities from the category that others may include. The Chinese Revolution redistributed and reevaluated work along three axes: urban–rural, male–female, and productive–reproductive. Urban factory workers stood at the top of the hierarchy: they formed the working class (工人阶级), and they alone had full access to the benefits of industrial citizenship.[2] While the working class comprised women and men, its archetype was the male factory worker. Contract and temporary workers, apprentices, members of handicraft cooperatives, and so on made up the 'labouring people' (劳动人民)—a less prestigious category with access only to watered-down benefits. The rural population, too, were labouring people, but their livelihoods were not backed up by the state; instead, their 'rice bowl' depended on their own work in the fields and on the vagaries of the weather.

Social reproduction—the work of giving birth to children, nurturing them, and turning them into socially competent adults; of feeding, clothing, and emotionally comforting current and future workers; of caring for the elderly, sick, and dying—was not considered work at all. The socialist state understood work as paid employment in fields or factories; unremunerated work at home was nothing but a private chore. Urban housewives were initially described as 'parasites' (寄生虫) whose only path to liberation led through formal employment; it was only in times of economic downturns and male unemployment that the Party praised housewives as useful members of society and encouraged women to stay at home.[3] The 1952 Constitution stipulated that work was an honour and a duty for all able-bodied citizens and, after 1962, almost all urban women worked for wages, albeit in less well-paid and less prestigious sectors than men.

Production and Reproduction

The Party never considered rural women housewives. Like men, they were members of agricultural collectives (社员) and were expected to participate in farm work. The Women's Federation and other branches of the state recognised that domestic labour conflicted with work in the fields, yet even mothers with significant childcare and household duties were expected to perform at least fifteen days of collective work each month and, in the busy seasons, all able-bodied women were expected to work full-time.[4] The Great Leap Forward (1958–62) saw an expansion of collective childcare and other socialised services, but these were mostly seasonal and provided for less than half of rural children even at their peak. After the Great Leap, rural collective childcare was largely abandoned.[5]

Equally importantly, low rural cash incomes and a deficient supply network combined to deprive the countryside of modern consumer goods. Hand spinning and hand weaving survived because rural textile rations were set below replacement needs: the long-term rationing average of 5.5 metres of cloth fell far short of basic textile needs. Similarly, a shortage of coal in the countryside meant rural women spent much time collecting firewood or chopping up grain stalks for fuel; food shortages meant women had to collect wild plants to enrich a monotonous grain diet. Because synthetic fertiliser was in short supply, households composted manure—a laborious task mostly shouldered by women. An absence of modern building materials such as glass, cement, and kiln-fired bricks and rooftiles made it difficult to keep houses dry and clean. Material life in the countryside remained largely unchanged and uncommodified; almost everything people ate, much of what they wore, and most of what they used at home was grown on their own land and produced by the labour of their hands, or that of their neighbours.

What is at issue here is the boundary between production and reproduction. On the one hand, socialism cannot be built on the basis of self-sufficient peasant households that consume most of what they produce. Socialist states generally seek to enlarge the scope of public production and shrink that of domestic reproduction. They do so by providing public childcare and other social services that liberate women from mind-numbing chores and by supplying consumer goods that ease women's domestic burdens. In so doing, they shrink the domain controlled by domestic patriarchs and expand the realm in which socialist values hold sway. Commodity exchange between state industry and households is also one of the ways in which socialist states accumulate capital and finance their social and political ambitions. Soviet leaders from Lenin to Stalin thought of the *smychka* (the alliance between workers and peasants) as rooted in rural–urban exchange and, above all, the exchange of factory cotton cloth for grain.[6]

CCP leaders generally followed the Soviet model of accumulation by means of scissor pricing—that is, by buying agricultural materials at low state-set prices and selling industrial goods back to the countryside at prices that ensured a hefty profit. Yet China differed from the Soviet Union and other socialist states in that it relied heavily on forms of rural self-provisioning that it officially condemned. In theory, socialist China was committed to a circular exchange between state industry and urban population—an exchange that, ideally, would fill state coffers and make both urban workers and rural peasants better off. Sources from the early 1950s complained about peasants' penchant for 'self-sufficiency' (自给自足思想) and the 'abnormal' (不正常) growth of rural crafts and sidelines that blocked the path towards industrial development.[7] Already in 1949, the new government declared that domestic textile production competed with state industry for raw materials and markets and was to be phased out within the next three years.[8]

Yet, while the state managed to extract more and more raw materials from the countryside, little flowed back. The reason was scarcity. China at the outset of its First Five-Year Plan was a much poorer country than the Soviet Union at a comparable stage of development; its per capita output of grain, coal, and cotton cloth was less than half that of the Soviet Union, while its steel output was less than one-tenth.[9] Faced with conflicting demands on limited resources, the government prioritised urban markets and the crucial export sector. Rural retail outlets were typically the last to be supplied with consumer goods, state capital investment was by and large reserved for urban industry, and inputs for agriculture such as fertiliser and pesticides were expensive and in short supply.

The Case of Cotton

Let us briefly review this mechanism in the case of cotton, which was second only to grain in its importance for the state's development strategy. The modern mills built in the early 1950s were crucial motors of accumulation, generating high profits for the state. Hand weaving interfered with accumulation since it reduced the amount of cotton available for mechanised processing. Initial attempts to control rural sideline weaving had little effect, but, by 1954, cotton, cotton yarn, and cotton cloth were subject to 'unified purchase and marketing' (统购统销). From then, farmers had to sell their entire cotton harvest to the state, apart from a small amount of 'self-retained cotton' to be used for padding quilts and winter clothes.

At the same time, the state rationed cotton cloth and clothes. Rural rations fluctuated between six and seven metres per capita in the 1950s and 2.3 metres in the crisis years of 1960–62, with a long-term average of 5.5 metres. Actual consumption needs were at least nine metres a year for the average person, taking into account the reduced needs of children. This amount covered a lined and padded winter suit, an unlined summer suit, two pairs of cloth shoes, and some minimal bedding—all of which were patched and mended until they fell apart. Rations thus fell dramatically short of the most minimal consumption needs: a person with access only to ration cloth would soon have run out of clothes and would have been obliged to stay at home during inclement weather. People coped with scarcity by drawing down existing stocks of clothing—in particular, dowries that young brides had brought to the family when they married. When these stocks were depleted, people stole cotton from the fields and spun it into yarn. Collective leaders, concerned about the wellbeing of their members, routinely hid part of the cotton harvest from the state, and often closed their eyes when pickers pocketed some cottonwool.

Rural self-provisioning was both a problem for the socialist economy and a necessary condition for its functioning. It was a problem because it diverted scarce materials away from state industry. At its peak in 1965, peasant households and underground workshops produced an estimated 566 million metres of cotton cloth—12 percent of China's total cotton textile output in that year.[10] By setting the price for cotton low and that for cloth high, the state all but ensured that people would hang on to their cotton and transform it into cloth at home. Because of shortages, profits for black market weavers were extraordinarily high: a woman who was willing to risk fines and public censure could earn as much as eleven yuan for each kilogram of cotton she spun into yarn and wove into cloth, rising to twenty-four yuan in 1961–62. At seven to ten labour days for each kilogram of cotton, this translates into a daily income of 1.1 to 3.4 yuan—much more than one could hope to earn by working in the fields.[11]

Sources from the 1960s described a freewheeling black market economy, with millions of people in all cotton-growing provinces engaged in commercial weaving, often with the explicit encouragement of local governments. Handloom weavers drew on several sources: farmers stole from the collective fields, collectives embezzled cotton and distributed it to their members, and famine and disaster-stricken brigades petitioned for supplies of below-grade cotton or textile rags, which they unravelled and refashioned into yarn.[12] All this played into the tendency of state and collective units to hoard and misappropriate scarce raw materials and contributed to a dramatic 'cotton famine' in state mills.

At the same time, handloom weaving relieved the state of the obligation to clothe the rural population and freed it to direct scarce textiles to urban consumers and the export trade. If we assume, conservatively, that rural per capita rations fell one metre short of requirements, we arrive at an overall rural shortage of 600 to 700 million metres. Part of the gap was filled by black market workshops, but the lion's share came from rural women who spun and wove to provide for their families, using whatever cotton they could scrape together. They did so at little cost to the state: their labour was unpaid, and the cotton they used was often mildewed, short-stapled, and unsuitable for machine processing. Had the bans succeeded, the state would have had to provide the missing textiles—or risk a collapse of agriculture because people could not work outdoors without clothing. We can thus think of these 600 to 700 million metres as a subsidy or tribute paid by rural women to the planned economy. Incidentally, this subsidy corresponds to China's textile exports, which ranged from 500 to 700 million metres in the collective years. In short, women's unpaid textile work freed the state to sell fabric and garments abroad, where they earned the foreign currency that paid for technology imports from the Soviet Union and for emergency imports of grain during the 1960 famine.

Unrecognised Contributions

Official rhetoric did not acknowledge these contributions. Instead, it urged rural people to produce more and consume less—every pound of grain not eaten and every inch of cloth not used contributed to the construction of socialism.[13] Rural consumption needs were typically discussed under the rubric of 'life' (生活), which was contrasted with production. Official rhetoric left no doubt about priorities: 'Production first, life second' (先生产, 后生活) was a common slogan.

Already in 1949, the new government declared that domestic textile production competed with state industry for raw materials and markets and was to be phased out within the next three years.[14] The introduction in 1954 of the 'unified purchase and marketing' of cotton and cotton cloth should have put an end to household weaving, but it left several loopholes. Farmers who grew cotton on their private plots or on newly opened land were allowed to process it, as long as they sold the cloth to the rural supply and marketing cooperatives at state-set prices. Specialised weavers in traditional weaving districts were supplied with machine yarn and produced cloth under plan, but much of their output found its way on to rural black markets. Areas hit by flood, drought, or other natural disasters were often allowed to engage in 'emergency weaving'—that is, to sustain themselves by selling cloth until conditions had improved enough to resume farming.

These loopholes were gradually closed in the 1960s. A total ban on hand spinning and hand weaving was first proposed in 1956 by the Ministry of Textile Industry; Chairman Mao Zedong reportedly agreed, praising the ministry for generating income for the country and encouraging it to accumulate more.[15] In 1957, the government banned the long-distance trade of handloom cloth and the trade in ration coupons, which were collected by peddlers in rural areas and sold to urban consumers. The Great Leap Forward saw an explosive growth of weaving workshops, as communes and brigades used the Great Leap rhetoric of 'walking on two legs' (两条腿走路) as a pretext to revive handloom weaving. The 1960 ban, written in response to this development, called for an end to all manual textile production without exception. A revised and expanded ban was issued in 1963, followed by more detailed local regulations in 1964. None of these bans had any appreciable effect: handloom weaving began to decline only in the late 1970s and early 1980s, when hardwearing synthetics became widely available in rural areas.

1961

Launched in 1958 as a counterpart to rural collectivisation during the Great Leap Forward, the Urban Commune Movement mobilised city residents—mostly women—for production in small workshops and factories. The domestic work left behind by the newly employed 'housewives' was then socialised through the development of canteens, kindergartens, and service centres. While collectivisation in the countryside was slowed because of the great famine, urban communes were revamped in 1960–61 and, although social welfare services deteriorated, many of the factories survived through the decade. This essay takes us to one of these small female-staffed workshops in Beijing.

Anatomy of a Woman Worker: Collectivisation and Labour during the Great Leap Forward

Aminda SMITH and Fabio LANZA

In March 1961, there were 184 women working in a powder metallurgy factory at Beijing's Tianqiao Urban Commune. Established in 1958 as a neighbourhood enterprise, this factory in Xuanwu District employed almost exclusively women, all of whom were 'unskilled' labourers, supervised by thirty-one male managers and technicians. This was not unusual for urban commune factories, where a stated objective was to harness the 'reserve army' of labour—which referred mainly to women without paid employment, who were usually called 'housewives' (家庭妇女). Chinese Communist Party (CCP) policymakers claimed that this deployment of female labour would allow for a massive expansion in production while furthering the goal to 'complete women's liberation' (妇女彻底的解放).[1] Commune leaders thus aimed to transform 'housewives' into 'workers' (工人) and to free them from burdensome but 'non-productive' domestic chores.

But on 15 March 1961, when the Neighbourhood Office of the Beijing Party Committee reported on the situation at Tianqiao, they made no mention of women's liberation or industrial productivity and wrote instead about the workers' bodies. The committee claimed that fifty-eight of the 113 women surveyed were suffering from gynaecological problems. Twenty-four had vulvitis, vaginal infections, or chronic pelvic infections; nineteen had irregular periods (two among those had amenorrhea); six suffered from a prolapsed uterus; and nine suffered from cervical erosion (子宫颈糜烂).[2]

Unfortunately, we found only one other short and uninformative document about this particular factory, though there are a few sources on the Tianqiao Commune more generally.[3] Despite having little information about the site or the survey, this single report still offers significant insights into how CCP observers envisioned and constructed productive and non-productive female bodies during the Great Leap Forward (1958–62)—a time when an unprecedented number of women joined the industrial workforce as part of a radical effort to change social and gender relationships.⁴ What the surveyors saw in these women workers and how they interpreted material and bodily phenomena hint at the gendered assumptions that framed the CCP's understanding and utilisation of labour, and shaped the nature of women's experiences and their potential liberation during the Great Leap and beyond.

The Factory and the Report

It is difficult to ascertain the specific industrial processes that occurred in the Tianqiao factory. The term 'powder metallurgy' (粉末冶金) is vague and covers a wide range of techniques, from the relatively crude to the highly sophisticated. The document offers almost no information about the factory's products, other than references to workshops for 'iron oxide' (氧化铁) and 'bearings' (轴承). Earlier sources on the Tianqiao Commune note ferric oxide as one of the unit's major products, together with electric switches, mica condensers, and tungsten wire recycled from discarded light bulbs.⁵ The details in the report suggest this enterprise was like most commune factories, which were generally low-tech, sometimes makeshift, and reliant on residents' activism and initiative. It was often the workers themselves who provided the initial capital by toiling without pay for a few months. Larger state-owned factories might offer tools, equipment, and basic technical instruction, but mechanisation was minimal at best, and communes gathered their production materials from industrial scraps. These enterprises also employed mostly women labourers, who performed lower-skilled and repetitive tasks to produce everyday goods (clothing, shoes, etc.) or semi-finished objects for larger state-owned (and more heavily male-staffed) factories.⁶ The report's comments about workplace safety suggest that, like many such operations, the Tianqiao site lacked both the capacity and, to a certain extent, the will to properly care for its workers.

When the writers of the report described the women at the Tianqiao factory, they spoke of weak bodies, assailed by illness, at levels they found alarming. In their effort to ascertain the causes of what they saw as a health crisis, the surveyors pointed to three factors: poor hygiene; labour that 'was not suitable for women to perform'; and particular negative effects that cold and damp environments had on female bodies. The first problem apparently developed because the factory had only one small shower room with four showerheads. Women had to wait in long lines at the end of the working day and, as a result, 'many of the manufacturing personnel went long periods without bathing; some had even gone several months since their last shower'. Dirt mixed with metal powder from the factory thus 'soaked into their skin and penetrated into their bodies, giving rise to vulvitis and in some cases further developing into vaginitis and pelvic infection'.[7]

The surveyors also thought the women were working too hard, even by Great Leap standards. The report argued that women ought not engage in tasks that required heavy lifting, but apparently 'the heavy labour was all done by women' at Tianqiao. 'Their labour enthusiasm runs very high,' it continued, 'especially among many of the activists, who want to set a good example by performing hard labour.' Unfortunately, such strenuous activities were thought to 'lead to irregular periods or a prolapsed uterus'.[8] The head of the iron dioxide workshop—a twenty-four-year-old 'city-wide 8 March Red Banner pace-setter and district-wide model worker'— reportedly twisted her back while loading a truck. In the three months since the accident, she had not had a menstrual period, had developed 'weak legs', and periodically 'spit up blood'.[9] Finally, the committee noted that cold, damp conditions were notoriously bad for menstruating women. Part of the manufacturing process apparently required personnel to stand for long stretches in frigid rooms wearing high rubber boots and immersing their hands in cold water. Probably drawing on Chinese medical knowledge, which posits that such conditions allow poisonous *qi* (气) to enter the body, the committee explained that women who worked with cold water while menstruating could 'quite easily' develop gynaecological problems.[10]

The report concluded by suggesting these problems stemmed in part from the fact that 'the leadership in this factory did not take work safety issues as seriously as they should', but also from the inexperience of leaders and cadres who might not know, 'for example, that women are not suited to perform hard labour'.[11] The committee then made some basic recommendations: install extra showers, establish a women's committee, ensure that workers avoid cold water while menstruating, and stop heavy lifting altogether. 'All hard labour that is unsuitable for women should be performed by male workers,' the writers insisted, adding that men could be brought in from elsewhere if needed.[12]

Gendered Silences

Given the nature of the worksite and the historical context, it is surprising that the Tianqiao report made no mention of, or did not fully discuss, other aetiologies for gynaecological problems that ought to have occurred to the surveyors: diet, sex, and metal poisoning. The first two possibilities do not appear at all in the brief; metal poisoning does, but without reference to other, non-gynaecological symptoms, even as the committee describes metal powders that settled all over the women's skin, not solely on their genitals.[13] As all of these factors entered into other health-related discussions in the People's Republic, their omission here prompts several questions.

As the Tianqiao survey notes, the kinds of metal powders in use at the factory were very volatile substances, easily absorbed through the skin. Cadmium and other elements used in metallurgy are highly toxic and can cause gynaecological problems, but exposure can also have non-gynaecological effects. The committee makes no mention of coughs from inhaled powder or skin rashes where powder had lingered. Even if the report meant to address gynaecology alone, why would other symptoms caused by the same elements not be relevant? Was the CCP so focused on gendered illness that it glossed over visible—but not female-exclusive—issues?

Like so many sources from the Urban Commune Movement, this report is also silent about the potential effects of malnutrition. In 1961, Beijing was still feeling the devastation of the Great Leap famine. Capital-city residents enjoyed much better provisions than their rural compatriots, but one still wonders how much and what kinds of food were available to poor women workers in an urban commune factory that was reported to be in disrepair and possessing very few resources. Both Nicholas Lardy and Kenneth Walker have pointed to stagnation in overall average food consumption (and caloric intake) from the late 1950s into the 1960s.[14] This was connected, in urban areas, to rigid implementation of rationing by 1957 and to the collapse of agricultural output in the wake of the Great Leap. Grain procurement—to feed the cities and for export—had increased during the famine years, which made the food shortages even more disastrous in rural areas. But after procurement policy was relaxed in 1961, feeding the cities became a challenge, especially as urban populations had increased by 30 percent during the Great Leap.[15]

There is also anecdotal evidence of a decline in the quality of the food provided in cities, with coarse grains and potatoes making up for shortages of more nutritious foods. Food served in Beijing's communal canteens was reported to be of even lower quality than what other city residents ate—no meat and very little oil—as famine shortages were compounded by the need to keep commune expenses to a minimum. A 1961 report on citywide commune services admitted that cereal provisions were too low, canteen food was of poor quality, and most residents preferred home-cooked meals.[16] Thus, it seems likely that the Tianqiao workers had experienced a rapid decline in the quality of their diet. Missed periods and amenorrhea were common symptoms of malnutrition during the Great Leap (and otherwise). Moreover, risk of illness (including metal toxicity) also increased dramatically during the famine, as underfed or poorly fed bodies were less able to protect themselves against disease. The silence surrounding the famine might have led the writers of the report to hide diet as an important cause of the health problems at Tianqiao. Or gynaecological ailments may have served as code words—bodily conditions that were politically 'speakable', but that could still signal to others in the know the presence of the hunger that was not to be mentioned.[17]

Finally, there was another silence: sex. Although the CCP achieved remarkable success in its efforts to eradicate sexually transmitted infections (STIs), sexual activity often caused non-STI–related vaginitis, vulvitis, and pelvic infection.[18] It is difficult to know anything about these women's sex lives, but many of them were likely married and/or sexually active, as suggested by their status as housewives and the fact that commune enterprises were overwhelmingly staffed by young but adult women. The report admitted that the male supervisors in the factory had very little knowledge about women and their bodies. It may be that male observers saw a number of gynaecological problems that would have been common among sexually active women (compounded by the inaccessibility of hygienic facilities), and thus misinterpreted both their cause and their significance, which potentially deprived the women of needed care. In any case, the many silences in this report are most revealing not of issues related to women's health, but of specific male and Party-centred anxieties about women in general and the female labouring body in particular.

The Gender of Labouring Bodies

Political taboos would have made hunger off-limits in the Tianqiao discussion. But the silences around sex and metal poisoning seem more closely connected to the very notion of these women as a 'reserve' of otherwise unproductive housewives. To the state, these were women, not workers (not even women workers). They were 'potential' labourers, but until they laboured under the gaze of the Party, outside the home, they were cast as 'idle and unused' (闲散), and as-yet unproductive or 'not engaged in production' (不参加生产). CCP discussions of this 'reserve army' (后备军) further suggested that these women could be mobilised to enter factories and produce but they would never quite reach the productivity levels, or the political status, of other workers, whom CCP rhetoric tended to gender masculine. The Tianqiao report was rhetorically consistent with that vision. Surveyors focused on industrial aetiologies—metal poisoning and overwork—and ignored sex, which could be and was discussed elsewhere in conjunction with gynaecological issues, but which was also a part of the domestic and reproductive realm.[19] The observers also associated metal poisoning with gynaecological illness alone, and thus limited it to an issue for women workers and not a broader failure to care for worker safety in general. In this way, the reproductive associations with womanhood were both confined to the domestic space and deployed to excuse the failure of the state to serve the labouring people, by blaming harm to labourers on the relative inadequacy of female bodies—an inadequacy that was itself directly connected to the presumed fragility of women's reproductive organs.

When the report described 'mindsets' (思想), it further reinforced this vision of the labourers as women whose womanhood hampered their productive capacities—and, by extension, the capacity of the entire factory. While the report made mention of less obviously gendered attitudes, such as lack of concern for workplace safety, it paid more attention to the perceived femininity of the workers: 'Some of the personnel have feudal mindsets. When their period comes, they are too embarrassed to say so and just keep working on cold water tasks as usual.'[20] The report added that problems were exacerbated by the fact that the mostly male managers and cadres lacked experience dealing with female bodies.[21] Even as they worked, sometimes injuring their bodies in the process, the Tianqiao women were defined by their femininity more than their labour. Industrial production was supposed to transform 'unproductive housewives' into 'workers', but the Tianqiao report suggests that it could not, at least not in the eyes of the state. From the perspective of the state, these women were, first and foremost, female, reproductive bodies—bodies that were sickened by the demands of production, rendering them again 'unproductive' and potentially 'non-reproductive' as well.

The socialist category of the 'worker' was envisioned, in its archetypal form, as male, and thus women were always, at least implicitly, 'women workers'. The addition of the modifier put distance between the actors and the act of labour, and between women and the political category of 'labourers'. This gap provided a way to evade and displace larger questions about how well socioeconomic experiments were furthering the interests of the people. This distance might also be what led the Tianqiao surveyors to focus on the physical and mental manifestations of femininity and gendered relationships, which resulted in descriptions of weak and docile bodies, accustomed to domestic chores and 'ill-suited' to hard labour, as well as 'feudal' mindsets that hindered the operations of production. Even when summoned by the developmental call of the Great Leap, these housewives were still 'untrained' (培养教育不够) and 'unskilled' (根本没有技术), and suited, therefore, only to specific forms of work: tedious, repetitive, simple.

This gendered discourse extended well beyond a single factory. Wang Zheng has described the Great Leap Forward as a crucial, if brief, event in the history of Chinese feminism, a parenthetical moment in which the agenda of 'female liberation', through the socialisation of housework, temporarily replaced that of the more regressive 'double diligences'.[22] Yet, Wang also shows that, even during the high tide of this experiment, female labour was rarely viewed as equal to male labour. Most sources from the urban collectivisation campaign bear this out, describing labour in commune enterprises as cheap, low-quality, done mainly by women, and thus marked by the perceived weaknesses of female minds and bodies. This discourse had very concrete effects, such as helping to justify lower pay for women. CCP bureaucrats repeatedly stressed the importance of maintaining low-salary systems (低工资制) for 'reserve-army' commune workers. Paying these housewives only half of what many male workers would earn for similar tasks was key to the profitability of commune enterprises, a benchmark that was central to the state's evaluation of those enterprises even during the socialist period.[23] Simultaneously, a never fully severed connection to the realm of social reproduction made most female labour ultimately and easily disposable. In the words of commune authorities and policymakers with regard to women workers: 'If there is work to do, they can do it; if not, they can always go back [home] to cook and clean.'[24]

A Failed Liberation?

The sense that an army of housewives could be deployed as needed and move seamlessly between industrial and domestic production (and reproduction) may have partly caused, and certainly reinforced, the decline and eventual collapse of commune social-welfare systems. By 1960, communal services no longer seemed poised to liberate women from unremunerated domestic labour. Canteens and childcare centres were often poorly run, and they were also expensive. It had come to be expected that such services operate without economic support from the state or the commune, leading to rapidly rising fees, declining attendance, and closures.[25] While few women were truly relieved of domestic tasks, even in the most successful moments of Great Leap experimentation, the complete dissolution of communal services further increased the double burden of industrial labour and housework for housewives, who were now expected to report for factory duty whenever they were needed. The injustice was not lost on commune leaders, who expressed concerns about women being overworked, but there was little to be done as pressure to produce increased and resources declined. Reports quoted female labourers who mocked a 'liberation' they said consisted of nothing more than adding poorly remunerated, tedious industrial chores to women's already substantial workloads.[26] Some women reportedly argued that working in a commune factory and being a housewife were essentially the same, as 'both are a sheer waste of our talents'.[27] A subversive slogan alleged that women workers now suffered from the 'three lows' (三低) (that is, low salary, low services, and low rations) and 'two misfortunes' (两倒霉) (that is, not being able to find a partner or raise a family).[28]

Collectivisation during the Great Leap Forward aimed to generate a series of radical transformations and sometimes effected powerful changes, if only briefly. But the project of women's liberation through mass participation in industrial labour was contravened by a failure to rethink and reconfigure social reproduction. The assumption that housewives were unproductive and thus constituted an untapped reservoir of workers was born of and exacerbated a lack of critical analysis about the nature of socially reproductive labour. The notion that domestic work could simply be moved to non-domestic sites, without having to be reconstituted in a new form, reflected a lack of attention to how social reproduction would be transformed (and needed to be consciously refashioned) in the socialist transition.

A glimpse inside a small commune factory in the Tianqiao neighbourhood of downtown Beijing highlights the always unresolved tension between women's liberation articulated as participation in (often injurious) labour and the unchanging view of women's bodies as the crucial locus of, and best suited to, social reproduction. Never again did the CCP make such a radical attempt to promote gender equality. By the late 1970s, 90 percent of urban, working-age women were employed outside the home, making up nearly half of the industrial workforce, but that change did not come with improvements in divisions of labour, either at home or in non-domestic workplaces. Women remained largely responsible for housework and were usually assigned jobs that were 'suitable'. Notions of 'suitability' remained somewhat similar to their Great Leap versions, as women continued to be employed in lower-skilled and subordinate positions, and even those opportunities were often reduced if a woman became actively reproductive.[29]

1962

In 1962, the Party-State in Beijing decreed that China's farmers should participate in a new form of agricultural organisation that would persist for the next two decades. It not only entailed an entirely new collective system of property ownership within village neighbourhoods and hamlets, but also gave rise to new types of work relations, and dramatically reshaped social relationships in hundreds of thousands of villages. It constituted the final step in the tumultuous series of reorganisations of agriculture during the 1940s and 1950s.

Working Together in Agricultural Production Teams: The Work Lives of the Majority of Chinese Under Mao
Jonathan UNGER

The farmers of China experienced, first, land reform and then a succession of progressively higher forms of collectivisation, leading to the utopian and ultimately tragic Great Leap Forward of 1958–60. During the Great Leap period, a rural market town and all of the villages that surrounded it were declared a 'commune' (公社), and Chinese Communist Party officials in the market-town command posts of the new communes directed the labour of thousands of farmers. It was imagined that communes would provide the organisational foundation of material plenty. Stories circulated in China's mass media about miraculous achievements in far-flung parts of the country. In a competition to achieve similar miracles, large squads of farmers were instructed to plant seeds so tightly packed together that the seedlings crowded each other out; during the agricultural busy seasons, they were sent to work at hastily planned dam sites; they were told to eat free meals in public mess halls and to melt their own metal cooking utensils in primitive backyard steel furnaces that produced useless junk. Huge quantities of grain were shipped off to the cities and onward abroad as exports while rural officials competed to exaggerate the size of local harvest yields. The consequence of all this was a collapse in rural production during 1959 and 1960 and a plunge into starvation in many parts of the countryside.[1]

The specific system of collectives that will be the focus of this essay was created out of the ashes of that tragedy. The information about how it actually operated at the grassroots level derives from more than 100 interviews that Anita Chan and I conducted in Hong Kong during the 1970s and early 1980s with emigrants from about four dozen Chinese villages. At the time, it was not possible to conduct research inside China, and the constant flow of people into Hong Kong from the mainland provided a feasible alternative.[2]

Production Teams as the Basis for Landownership and Work

When the collectives were totally reorganised in 1962 in the aftermath of the Great Leap Forward, agricultural production within each village was placed in the hands of 'production teams' (生产队). Each production team contained some fifteen to forty neighbouring households who collectively owned a block of agricultural land, and its member households worked the land together and shared in the proceeds. In the wake of the Great Leap Forward's failure, the idea was to create a collective unit small enough for members to perceive the relationships between their own contributions of labour, their team's productivity, and their family's benefits.

To encourage the farmers to accept their team head's leadership, the head was normally either elected by team members or informally chosen by consensus, though in a minority of cases the team heads were selected by a higher-level Party organisation. In some other cases, even if elected, the production team head was chosen by one large kinship group or clique to the detriment of other such groups, and cases were reported of nepotism, favouritism, and abuses of power. But, despite such occurrences, on the whole the teams were relatively democratic in the way leaders were chosen—which had no parallel in any other parts of the Chinese political system.[3]

The new system contained a number of attractive features. By providing farmers with a share in a larger stretch of land than any family could farm on its own, it gave each household protection against natural disasters or unexpected illness. It also provided for a relatively equitable distribution of incomes among households, and it organised and paid for a range of public services. In many villages, by the late 1960s or 1970s, almost-free health care and elementary schooling were being provided through production-team revenues—reaching much of rural China for the first time in history. Production teams also paid for the sustenance of orphans, widows, and the childless elderly. In much of rural China, mortality rates declined dramatically and the length of villagers' lives began to approach that in developed nations.

The countryside was able to achieve these gains in part because the state under Mao was strong and penetrated communities effectively. The state's drive to transform villages had a downside, however, in both the political and the economic spheres. Although Mao Zedong and other Party leaders were now willing to tolerate a system of ownership and production by relatively small production teams, and allowed farmers to select their own production-team heads, at the same time the national leaders were unwilling to give the production-team members enough leeway in figuring out what crops to grow or enough say on how their own teams and villages were run. The system ultimately was top-down. The belief at the helm of the Party was that China's villagers, left to their own devices, would not continue to move China forward into ever higher forms of socialist society; the villagers needed to be controlled and prodded for their own good.

There was a second important factor. The national leadership was convinced that, to develop the national economy, agricultural surpluses needed to be squeezed from the countryside. However, without strong institutional mechanisms in place, the villagers would not so willingly sacrifice their own material interests for the greater good of China by providing the state with cheap agricultural provisions to help build up Chinese industry. The consequence was that, in the new system of governance that was put in place after the collapse of the Great Leap Forward, the production teams sat at the very bottom of a political hierarchy dominated by a top-down chain of Party rule that reached from Beijing into each and every village. The village was now called a 'brigade' (大队) and was headed by a Party secretary who was appointed by the Party leadership of the commune, who in turn were appointed by the Party leadership of the county, who were appointed by the next higher level of the Party.

Daily Work and the Complex Issue of Pay

The Party-State officialdom above the village was nowhere to be seen in daily life, though. Farmers soon became accustomed to a new work routine that some preferred. Before, they had worked on their own, on their own plots. Now, they normally worked together with neighbours in small squads. The men often engaged in different types of work than the women and so, depending on the time of year and the task, the women enjoyed a chance to work in a squad of fellow women; young people had opportunities to work and socialise in their own squads; and older men sometimes in their own groupings. The younger women, in particular, who in China always married into a village from outside, no longer felt socially isolated and continuously under the thumb of their parents-in-law and husband. Instead, they spent the day with their own network of acquaintances; they earned their own income from the team in 'work-points' (工分) and so could independently contribute to their household's income; and, through this and through their new social network, they saw their standing rise in both the household and the community. So, too, did the young men, who, with the strength of youth, often earned more than their fathers.

The men's tasks normally paid more than the women's. For instance, during the dry season in Chen Village, a community in Guangdong Province that I have studied,[4] when dredging the nearby river, the men were the ones who dug out the mud from the river bottom while the women hauled it up the riverbank and packed it into the dykes. The men were paid for each bucket they filled and the women for each bucket they toted. It was the women's work that required the greater skill and effort, since the dykes were tricky to ascend under the swaying loads of dredged mud. But over the course of an hour, the men's digging paid almost twice as much as the women's carrying. The village women did not publicly complain, however; they tacitly accepted that their lower status meant lower pay.

In a few agricultural seasons, ways were found to dispense with the complexities of recording and awarding payments by piece rate. For instance, the Chen Village farmers at harvest time worked in tightly knit squads of a dozen or so members of both genders, much as they had done even in traditional times in the rice regions of southern China. Without having to break their work rhythm, half of the squad members cut the crop; others would rush the sheaves to a small thresher at the side of the field; two men worked the hand threshing machine; and the two strongest men hustled the loads of grain into the village. Since the pace of the squad members' work was so closely interlinked, work-points were awarded to the squad as a whole based on the tonnage harvested. In this 'group task work', the squad members would hold a post-harvest session to appraise one another's labour contributions and determine among themselves how to divide up the totality of squad work-points.

During the height of radical national policies in the late 1960s and early 1970s, this method of payment was extended to all the work in what was titled the Dazhai system.[5] In this, all of a production team's members sat in judgement of one another at periodic team meetings. But, in a twist, they were to award work-points based not on what a team member had physically accomplished but rather on his or her attitude and effort.

Initially, this worked well. But, over time, the appraisal meetings descended into acrimony, as members began to vociferously defend their own work and took umbrage if awarded lower points. To avoid this, by the early 1970s the best men were being appraised as worth ten work-points a day, the average man was getting 9.5, and the worst nine points—a very narrow spread. Eventually, the best and most energetic workers resented this and stopped working as well, and the teams' production sputtered.[6] Ultimately, the Dazhai appraisal system had to be abandoned here and elsewhere across China.

Private Endeavours

The rights of farmers to engage in private sideline production had been guaranteed by the state (with temporary exceptions during radical campaigns) since 1962.[7] China's leaders had learned through the disastrous experiences of the Great Leap Forward that some private spare-time endeavours, particularly maintaining a family vegetable plot, were a 'necessary adjunct to the socialist economy'.[8] The regulations of 1962 let the production teams set aside 5 to 7 percent of their arable land for these family plots. Because most Chinese villages have little land per capita, the plots were relatively tiny. A family held only temporary use rights to them, and the size of its plot was readjusted from time to time as additional children were born and older children married out. Families were also permitted to privately raise animals such as pigs, chickens, and ducks, to plant limited numbers of fruit trees in courtyards and on hilltop wasteland, and to fish or produce cottage handicrafts after hours.

These private activities were essential to the farmers' livelihoods in two ways. Whereas the collective fields provided almost all of China's grain, the private sector provided the bulk of the farmers' vegetables and meat. This was reflected in the saying, 'For the bottom of the rice bowl, rely on the collective. For the top of the bowl, rely on ourselves.' Their private endeavours were also the farmers' most important source of cash income. At the end of each collective harvest, each household's cumulative work-points were computed and the family was paid in both kind and cash. Payment in kind came first, and the team was supposed to guarantee to each family the staple food grains that it needed even if it had earned insufficient work-points and had to go into debt to the team. Such families received no cash from the collective and depended entirely on their private sidelines for money to spend. In poor villages, many families found themselves in this circumstance. But even the best-off households in prosperous villages did not have much ready money to meet the costs of a family funeral or a son's wedding. On such occasions, farmers sold what they jokingly referred to as their 'piggy banks'—one or more of their hogs. For all farmers, prosperous or impoverished alike, a second rural saying applied: 'For eating rice, rely on the collective. For money, rely on your private sidelines.'

Under the government's own pricing mechanisms, much of the collective grain was sold cheaply to the state to fulfil a sales quota while vegetables and pork fetched far better prices. As a consequence, farmers could earn considerably more per hour from their private endeavours than from collective labour. All told, from among all the villages for which I have such information through interviewing, approximately one-quarter to one-third of the peasants' gross annual income (including both in kind and cash) derived from the private sector.[9] In two of the poorest villages for which I have interview data, where the earnings from the collective fields were very low, up to half of the family income was derived from such private activities.

This became a source of conflict between team leaders and farmers: the farmers' desire to focus on this valuable private production inevitably impinged on the productivity of the collective sector. Squad leaders were constantly on the lookout to stop team members sneaking off early from work, preventing them from clearing too much barren land to expand their private production, and haranguing members to rest during rest breaks rather than scramble off to their private endeavours.

From above, the Party-State periodically reacted to keep the private endeavours quite limited in extent and under tight control. One means, used especially during the 1970s, was to close the periodic farmers' markets in rural towns at which farmers sold their private produce. During radical periods, officialdom not only clamped down on this, but also sometimes launched campaigns to directly tighten the reins on families' vegetable plots. These campaigns were usually backed vociferously by the ideologues among Party leaders, who warned shrilly that private undertakings encouraged a selfish 'small-producer mentality'. The last major campaign of this type, the Line Education Campaign (路线教育运动) of 1974–75, was pushed by the group around Mao later dubbed the Gang of Four, and was so draconian that it needed to be removed from local cadres' hands to avoid retaliation against them by villagers. Squads of officials sent from above took over many of China's villages to push the campaign through; in Guangdong Province alone, 120,000 officials were dispatched to villages.[10] They forcibly reduced the size of the family vegetable plots, implemented very strict limits on the numbers of ducks, chickens, and pigs that farmers could raise, and imposed harsh fines equivalent to several days' wages on any team member who took leave during the day to attend to private matters.

The radical leadership also periodically launched directives during the 1970s that adversely interfered with the production teams' collective activities. Chen Village in subtropical Guangdong provides an illustration: one year the Maoist leaders in Beijing decided that each region should be 'self-reliant', so Chen Village's production teams were ordered to grow crops such as wheat and cotton that were woefully unsuited to the climate. Another time, the teams were ordered from above to forgo collectively planting profitable vegetable plots and to fill in money-making fishponds to plant more grain, and, when national slogans and policies flip-flopped, to reexcavate the fishponds and again 'diversify' the teams' crops.[11]

The End of Collective Farm Work

The farmers' support for collective agriculture could not endlessly be tested year after exhausting year by dysfunctional Party policies like these and by heavy grain exactions. Rural living standards were stagnating and by the late 1970s farmers' patience was running thin. Disillusionment and stalled production eventually led to the abandonment of agrarian socialism a few years after Mao's death. Coming almost full circle, Party officials in the early 1980s reintroduced household farming—with a twist: families could cultivate fields independently as though these were their own, but landownership remained in the hands of the production teams (on this, see my essay on 1981 in this volume).

The litany of failed radical programs during the 1970s should not lead us to believe that most of what occurred during the two decades of production-team work went against the interests of the farmers. There was much that was good in the collective system: the labour-intensive building of agricultural infrastructure and the provision of economic security, basic health care, and welfare for the needy. During the 1970s, émigrés from the countryside made it clear during interviews that the production teams, if left to their own devices, could have operated reasonably efficiently and productively. Had the state been less interventionist, had it allowed the production teams a much wider degree of independence in their economic operations, it is conceivable the system of teams could have persisted successfully over the long term. But for too much of the two decades in which Chinese agriculture operated through production teams, the Party-State was unwilling to keep its hands off.

1963

From the early 1950s, the Chinese Communist Party employed activist cadres and mass campaigns to limit or eradicate local religious practices. Whatever progress had been made on this terrain was seriously challenged by a massive revival of popular religion that occurred in the wake of the famine resulting from the Great Leap Forward (GLF), during which an estimated thirty million people died. Spurred by Mao Zedong's concerns about the political effects of the liberalising reforms introduced to repair the economic damage caused by the GLF, in February 1963, the Party leadership launched the Four Clean-Ups Campaign, also known as the Socialist Education Movement, which targeted corruption and embezzlement by rural cadres. In the cities, this was paralleled by the Five Antis Campaign, which targeted corruption and theft on the part of officials, along with speculation, extravagance and waste, poor coordination, and bureaucratism. The two campaigns soon broadened into movements to root out the 'three evils' of capitalism, feudalism, and extravagance. Work teams dispatched by the Party between 1963 and 1966 as part of these movements discovered ample evidence of a resurgence of popular religion among both workers in the cities and peasants in the countryside.

Gods, Ghosts, and Workers: 'Feudal Superstition' and the Socialist Education Movement, 1963–1966

S.A. SMITH

In August 1963, He Tingfu, a worker in Wuchang, went with his brother to see his sick mother, who lived in a remote mountain village. He was outraged to learn that an elderly neighbour had brought a spirit medium to his mother's house to exorcise the evil spirit that was supposedly causing her illness. Tingfu refused to allow the ritual, but his brother, also a worker, scolded him, saying: 'Why bother? It's enough that we don't believe in spirit mediums.' Tingfu thereupon wrote to the *Beijing Workers' Daily* (北京工人日报) to ask why 'feudal superstition' had returned to such a high level, fourteen years after liberation.[1] The editor curtly denied there was any such resurgence and went on to criticise the attitude of Tingfu's brother:

> To not believe in superstition is insufficient. We must also take the lead in doing away with it ... We workers have our destiny in our hands. We employ different kinds of machinery and harness water, fire, electricity—elements with which people in the past were not familiar ... It would hardly be a joke if we once again asked spirit mediums to ward off evil spirits and cure diseases or consulted fortune-tellers about our future weal and woe.[2]

Workers, in other words, had a special responsibility to combat feudal superstition, given their higher level of scientific knowledge.

The denial of the claim that feudal superstition was on the increase would have surprised Party leaders, even though public admissions to that effect were rare. Unusually, the Guangzhou United Front Bureau noted in late 1962 that 'religious thinking has grown owing to the economic difficulties of recent years'.[3] In fact, the Great Leap Famine, in which up to thirty million people died, had led to a massive revival of popular religion, the scale of which would gradually become apparent as work teams (工作队) were sent into the countryside between 1963 and 1966 as part of the Socialist Education Movement (SEM). The SEM originated in September 1962 when Mao Zedong warned the Central Committee to 'never forget class struggle' (千万不要忘记阶级斗争). Mao had become concerned that the liberalising reforms introduced in the wake of the famine were leading to 'revisionism' (修正主义).[4] In February 1963, this concern was cemented in the form of the 'Four Clean-Ups' (四清) campaign, which targeted corruption and embezzlement by rural cadres, who were, in effect, being made to carry the can for the famine. It was paralleled in the cities by the 'Five Antis' (五反) campaign, which targeted corruption and theft on the part of officials, along with speculation, extravagance and waste, poor coordination, and bureaucratism.[5]

The two campaigns remained distinct, but both broadened into movements to root out the 'three evils' of capitalism, feudalism, and extravagance. The work teams were initially under the tight control of provincial and county-level Party organisations and comprised a majority of Party and government officials, along with graduates, students, and white-collar workers from the towns. Local cadres were the targets of the SEM, and the work teams increasingly mobilised the 'poor and lower-middle peasants' to criticise them and advance their 'class education' (阶级教育).[6] From September 1964, the SEM entered its most intensive phase, as a purge of more than one million grassroots cadres began, and, from January 1965, the Five Antis merged into the Four Clean-Ups.[7] The reports of the SEM work teams provide rich evidence of feudal superstition as practised by cadres, in particular, and the masses in general.[8] The reports express alarm at the extent to which temple reconstruction, extravagant temple festivals, and lavish marriage and funeral rituals had revived in the wake of the famine. In the Handan mining region of Hebei Province, for example, the temples where miners prayed to the mine god for protection before 1949 had all been restored. At the Xiaobojian coalmine, 1,370 yuan had been spent repairing the temple, and the Party secretary was criticised for organising three feasts to celebrate the completion of this work.[9]

Anatomy of Feudal Superstition

Feudal superstition encompassed the entire field of popular religion, though it could extend to include certain nonreligious activities such as extravagant feasting or gambling.[10] Constitutionally, the Government of the People's Republic of China (PRC) recognised freedom of religion, but applied it only to five 'world' religions—Buddhism, Daoism, Islam, Catholicism, and Protestantism—which met the criteria of 'modern' religion by having institutionalised structures, canonical scriptures, a liturgy, trained clergy, and national representative associations.[11] The religion of the majority of the Chinese people failed to meet these criteria, since it was essentially local in character and family-centred, rooted in ancestor worship, networks of temple cults and festivals, veneration of a rich array of gods, and belief in spirit possession, divination, and loosely defined notions of karmic retribution, fate, reincarnation, and demonic threat.[12]

The official condemnation of feudal superstition comprised the following elements. First, it was a backward mode of thought that reflected a lack of understanding of science and rationality and that encouraged recourse to invisible entities to explain the world and to offer protection against its vagaries. Second, feudal superstition was seen as a social arena in which the masses were hoodwinked and exploited by unscrupulous practitioners such as spirit mediums, fortune-tellers, geomancers, and religious professionals such as lay Daoist priests (道士) and Buddhist monks. Such people, it was said, traded on the ignorance, credulity, and fatalism of the populace. Third, the central role played by spirit mediums in diagnosing and curing illness was extremely dangerous to the health of the population. Fourth, the tradition of extravagant weddings and funerals, along with the money spent on worship of gods, ghosts and ancestors, brought financial hardship to families. Fifth, feudal superstition had an adverse effect on the wider economy, since events such as temple fairs, pilgrimages, or searches for miraculous cures took people away from the collective and undermined production. It also led to corruption, since officials sought to cover up illicit expenditure. Finally, superstition gave rise to rumours that were often politically destabilising, and it was in this regard that the connection with class enemies was made. Many of these elements of critique could be traced back to Confucian elites in the imperial era and to the vigorous attack on feudal superstition that had been launched by the Nationalist government from 1928 to 1931.[13]

The Chinese Communist Party (CCP) saw the eradication of religion and superstition as a long-term task, the key to which lay in carrying out 'ideological education among the masses so as to raise their consciousness and help them do away with them self-consciously'.[14] In the early years, Party ideologists condemned the use of administrative methods to extirpate the two and, although they seldom referred to Soviet antireligious policy publicly, they consciously distanced themselves from it.[15] Nevertheless, in the aftermath of the famine, policy towards the officially recognised religions became more repressive. A key event was the Seventh National Conference on Religious Work, which met from December to January

1963, hot on the heels of the Tenth Plenum of the Central Committee, which had endorsed Mao's injunction to never forget class struggle. The Seventh Conference issued a report, the leitmotiv of which was that reactionaries were now using religion as a cover to sabotage progress towards socialism. In the preface to the document, the Religious Affairs Bureau declared: 'Reactionaries brazenly wrap themselves in the garb of religion in order to attack the Party; landlords, rich peasants and others use the revival of religion that is taking place to bring about restoration of the old regime.'[16] The conference put forward a host of policies designed to combat this danger, including a proposal for 'regular education in scientific knowledge and atheism among the people'.[17]

The reference to atheism (无神论) was something of an innovation in official ideology. Through the 1950s, the CCP had made little effort to promote Soviet-style 'scientific' atheism (still less the militant atheism of the 1920s and 1930s), although atheism was a requirement of Party membership. The content of atheist propaganda as it had developed within the European Marxist movement was hardly suited to China, since it related primarily to Christianity and concentrated on debunking the idea of a transcendent creator God and discrediting the Bible, as well as on lambasting the historical links between the churches and the ruling classes. China had its own tradition of materialist and rationalist philosophy, exemplified by the Han Dynasty scientist and philosopher Wang Chong (27 – ca. 100 CE), but the content of 'atheist' propaganda directed at workers and peasants during the SEM bore no relation to this tradition, barely rising above ritual denunciation of religion and superstition as tools of the class enemy. Significantly, the distinction between 'religion' (宗教, *zongjiao*) and 'superstition' (迷信, *mixin*), which had hitherto been sustained, came under increasing challenge, with references to *zongjiao mixin* proliferating. Typical of the new hardline discourse was the warning by the Shanghai Association for the Dissemination of Science and Technology in 1965 that 'in recent years under conditions of complicated class struggle, superstitious thinking in Shanghai has undergone a resurgence, with the five black categories using it to carry out wrecking [破坏运动]'.[18]

Chinless Ghosts, Fortune-Tellers, and Demon Hunters

By the time the SEM found its stride, the agricultural and industrial economies were recovering briskly from the famine, yet the public mood remained anxious—an anxiety that, in 1962, was compounded by the expectation that Chiang Kai-shek would launch a full-scale attack on the mainland and by the sharp deterioration in relations with the Soviet Union. Grassroots anxieties were projected into a spate of rumours of the supernatural that circulated in Shanghai in 1963. Women textile workers were too scared to leave the mills at night because they believed chinless ghosts—so-called stiff-corpse ghosts (僵屍鬼)—were waiting to catch them as they trudged home. This kind of zombie, whose soul had not been properly separated from its body through the correct performance of funeral rites, seemed to mirror the fate of the famine victims. Memories of the famine were still vivid, and the ghost stories attest to a sense that social control of the dead was failing, and that the boundary between the human and the supernatural world had become more permeable.[19] And since, as James Watson puts it, 'the world and the social structure of the living have meaning only through manipulation and preservation of the dead', the failure to properly deal with the famine dead appeared to be reflected in the ascendancy of chaotic spirits.[20]

It was in this context that some factory administrators decided to step up work to combat superstition. At the No. 9 Textile Mill in Shanghai, a group of nine women was asked why they thought the famine had occurred. Thirty-nine-year-old Wang Jinxiu said: 'During the past years there have been an awful lot of natural disasters—first we hear of floods, then of droughts, then of hailstorms, then of whirlwinds. This is all because people no longer believe enough in Buddha.'[21] Three different opinions emerged. The first, shared by six of the women, was that the disasters were sent by Buddha. The second, expressed by the youngest worker, Chen Huicong, was that bodhisattvas (菩萨) did not exist and the famine was a natural disaster. The third opinion, expressed by two women, was that both sides were partly right. As a worker named Ding Alin put it: 'We cannot not believe in the bodhisattvas, but nor can we believe in them fully. If we say there are no bodhisattvas, how do we explain thunder, rain, hail, and the whirlwind that comes from heaven?' In response to the discussion, the cadres arranged lectures to explain these phenomena.

A specific target of the SEM work teams was fortune-telling. In times of uncertainty, people seek guidance and spiritual comfort from those believed to be skilled at reading signs that reveal what fate has in store for them. At a rubber factory in Handan, Hebei Province, the work team discovered that Party member Wang Xinsong had returned to his native village to become the apprentice to a master in divination.[22] He copied out 12 *gua* (divinatory symbols), procured some bamboo slips (used in temples for divination), read a book on physiognomy, and then returned to the factory to set up shop as a fortune-teller. No less a figure than the deputy director consulted him and was told by Wang: 'Your nose is crooked, which means you have suffered since childhood and will never be able to count on another person.' The director replied: 'You are completely right.' Thereafter, more than 70 percent of the 127 employees, including ten of the twenty-eight members of the CCP, had their fortunes told by Wang. At the No. 12 Wireless Factory in Shanghai, a discussion on fortune-telling was organised among a work group of thirteen women and one man.[23] All said they consulted fortune-tellers regularly on such matters as marriage and divorce, whether they would give birth to sons, and whether they should change jobs. Told by the work team that they were being cheated by fortune-tellers, some became irate: 'If the CCP does not believe in superstition, why was the Prime Minister of Ceylon taken to the Jade Buddha Temple when he visited Shanghai?' 'The CCP advocates freedom of religion, so why is it against fortune-telling?'

The state healthcare system had developed slowly during the 1950s, but, with the financial retrenchment that came after the famine, services were cut back. Ordinary folk, who had used the biomedicine and herbal remedies on offer in local clinics, had not stopped using the services of spirit mediums, who were capable of drawing down spirits to defeat the demons that caused illness. Following the reduction in state healthcare provision, their services were in ever-greater demand. In the community around the Nantong coalmine, near Chongqing, there were ten notorious *guanhuapo* (观花婆) (a local type of female spirit medium), who were said to have 'run wild' since 1962. One woman, who had practised before 1949 and who had been put under administrative control (管制) during the 1950s, resumed performing exorcisms as a 'sideline occupation' when the economy liberalised in the early 1960s. Her fame spread far and wide, and soon 120 people were seeking her services each day, some coming by bus and sedan chair from as far as Guizhou across the provincial border.[24] In Taishan County, Guangdong Province, the SEM work teams launched an anti-superstition campaign in a brigade that lived by fishing, where 70 percent of the population was reputed to believe in gods and ghosts.[25] Attention focused on an influential male spirit medium, who was subjected to a denunciation meeting in the course of which some locals called for his execution. A variety of opinions was expressed about spirit mediums. Some said spirit mediums might be illiterate, but they nevertheless had the power to summon spirits and expel demons. Others said gods existed but demons no longer existed because the spirit medium had caught them all. Yet others opined that the presence of the CCP meant there were no longer demons but, without the Party, demons would return.

As the SEM radicalised from the autumn of 1964, the work teams' emphasis on class enemies and on the need to have faith in Chairman Mao intensified. In June 1965, in Dingzhuan Village in Ji County, Hebei Province, the work team urged villagers to 'abolish' (取消) their gods by burning or throwing images of them into a pit and to replace them with pictures of Chairman Mao.[26] Among twenty-nine women workers, twenty were said to have a good attitude towards the campaign, five were neutral, and four were hostile. During New Year in 1965, a campaign was launched in Chongqing to change customs and habits (移风易俗 的春节). Zhang Xiuying, a woman worker at the city's cement factory, was interviewed: 'My mother used to believe in gods (信神), but we lived in beggary. Now we have abandoned our belief and are living a better life thanks to the Party and Chairman Mao.'[27] She went on to say that making sacrifices to the gods was a tool used by class enemies to fool the people. Another member of her family added that in the old society he had been 'fooled by a landlord' into believing that 'poverty is my fate', and he used to pray to the gods for better wages and for his children not to be sick. Now, however, he had learned from the CCP that the 'bodhisattvas are nonsense conjured up by capitalists and landlords'. This emphasis on deceit and trickery was perhaps the most powerful weapon of persuasion in the armoury of the work teams.

Overcoming Superstition?

It would not be unreasonable to infer that the work teams were engaged in mass indoctrination. Even if we assume that Zhang Xiuying was saying what she was expected to say, it is unlikely she could think outside the framework of official ideology and establish conceptual ground from which to critique the statements she was making. In general, however, the above reports do not suggest that indoctrination is the term that best characterises the relationship between the work teams and working people. First, the format chosen by the work teams was that of the discussion group, and the reports of the debates show that individuals disagreed with one another and that some did not hesitate to oppose the line promoted by the team. The general impression is one of individuals facing a sharp intellectual challenge to what had hitherto been taken-for-granted knowledge and genuinely wrestling with the critique of supernatural belief with which they were confronted. Second, the participants had some control over the agenda of these discussions, even if it was only to turn rather abstract propaganda about the nonexistence of supernatural entities into debate about identifiable individuals and professions, and about practical problems of health, marriage, jobs, and poverty. Incidentally, although the work teams assumed that women workers were more captive to feudal superstition than their male counterparts, they operated on the assumption that women were capable of liberating themselves from backward thinking.

Does the evidence of workers' ongoing belief in higher supernatural entities make nonsense of the claim of the editor of *Beijing Workers' Daily* that workers, by dint of their exposure to modern technology and scientific knowledge, were destined to rise above feudal superstition? To some extent, certainly. There was, after all, a huge revival of religious belief throughout Chinese society during the reform era. Nevertheless, we should not underestimate the impact of the state-backed project of ideological and coercive secularisation. Regardless of the baroque excesses of Mao worship, belief in supernatural entities came under intense and sustained assault. No worker could be unaware that to be a religious devotee was, in some degree, to deviate from the officially approved model of a class-conscious proletarian. Nevertheless, in the long term, more corrosive of religious belief than the *Sturm und Drang* political campaigns of the Mao era were processes of economic, social, and cultural modernisation that served to dis-embed religious beliefs and practices from a body of shared local knowledge. Modernity certainly does not leave an ineluctable decline in religious belief in its wake, but it does change the nature of that belief, making it more a matter of contention and choice. And, for workers in the Mao era, especially those who were physically cut off from the rural cultures into which they had been born, assumptions about the power of invisible entities ceased to be what the philosopher Charles Taylor calls 'facts of life about the world'.[28] It would probably be too strong to claim that at this stage of historical development the acceptance or rejection of invisible entities had become a matter of personal choice for workers; but values and orientations that had once gone unexamined and unchallenged were now exposed to sharp contestation not only from the ideological apparatuses of the Party-State, but also from scepticism on the part of fellow workers. And, as He Tingfu's thoughtful letter attests, for a growing number of workers, it was a badge of pride to cast off feudal superstition and embrace the model of a rational individual and class-conscious worker.

1964

In September 1959, workers struck oil in China's northeast, near a stop along the Harbin–Qiqihar railway. As these new deposits were discovered at a time when China was facing international crises on multiple fronts that had severed its access to petroleum, this was cause for celebration, and, in 1960, the area was rechristened 'Daqing' (大庆, or 'Great Celebration'). As Daqing began pouring out millions of tonnes a year, allowing China to become self-sufficient in oil, in 1964, the Chinese Communist Party (CCP) began promoting the experience of the workers who had toiled in arduous circumstances to develop the deposits as an example for the whole nation to emulate.

Learning from the Daqing Oilfields
Maggie CLINTON[1]

'Into the ground drill bits tread / Reaching desired footage / Crude gurgles to the surface bed / Supporting the Vietnamese people and drowning the Yankees dead,' wrote model worker Wang Jinxi in a poem dated June 1966.[2] By luck or design, Wang went to Albania with an official petroleum delegation that month, just as the Cultural Revolution reached the Daqing oilfields and insurgent workers accused him, along with the state's increasingly powerful Petroleum Group (石油派 or 石油帮), of a litany of transgressions including denying them adequate time for rest.[3] Wang, a poor peasant turned lifelong oil worker, had been elevated to the status of 'National Model Worker' (全国劳动模范) in 1959 for his tireless devotion to oilfield development.[4] His poetry exalted the superhuman work ethic he and his fellow workers modelled and forged links between their own backbreaking manual labour and the nation's capacity to secure petroleum self-sufficiency to counter imperialist threats.

In April 1964, when the first national campaign to 'Learn from Daqing' (学习大庆) was announced in the *People's Daily*, Daqing appeared ready-made to mythologise.[5] Following a prospecting campaign scattered across Manchuria's central plains, in September 1959, workers struck oil near a stop along the Harbin–Qiqihar railway.[6] The first shipments of crude left the area—rechristened 'Daqing' (大庆, or 'Great Celebration')—in June 1960.[7] Daqing's deposits, located in proximity to China's heavy-industry heartland, promised enough oil to ensure the country's self-sufficiency according to its Mao-era demand.[8] These deposits were discovered amid China's split with the Soviet Union, which had severed its main foreign source of petroleum, and as the United States was increasing aid to South Vietnam. That Manchuria's Japanese occupiers through 1945 had not uncovered this oil—even as they forcefully developed the region's mining infrastructure and provoked a war with the United States in part to secure oil from the Dutch East Indies—rendered the discovery all the more poignant.[9] This context invigorated Daqing's workers and suffused the spotlight that 'Learn from Daqing' initiatives shone on them after 1964.

In certain respects, the particularities of Daqing's history, along with the specific technological and labour requirements of oil production, inhibited its utility as a model. Behind celebrated 'ironmen' (铁人) oil workers like

Wang Jinxi and female 'family dependants' (家属) like agricultural worker Xue Guifang (薛桂芳) stood some 30,000 People's Liberation Army (PLA) veterans redeployed to bring the Daqing fields into production.[10] Nevertheless, at conferences by late 1963 and on a national and mass scale by April 1964, Daqing was promoted as holding key lessons for the rest of the country.[11] These included its successful integration of industry and agriculture, of mental and manual labour, and the practical application of Mao Zedong's wartime treatises 'On Practice' and 'On Contradiction'.[12] Above all, Daqing was celebrated for the self-sacrificial spirit of its workers, who demonstrated how collective effort could tangibly contribute to national energy self-sufficiency and thereby advance the revolution at home and abroad.

Locating Daqing

In 1973, Radio Peking highlighted how Daqing departed from the 'predatory imperialistic ways of oil extraction'.[13] The broadcaster indicated that Daqing's development differed from the capitalist practice of wildcatting, in which lone entrepreneurs drilled recklessly for the sake of private profit and without regard for a site's long-term sustainability. While all evidence suggests that efforts to locate oil in Manchuria—spearheaded in 1956 during China's First Five-Year Plan by the Ministry of the Petroleum Industry (MPI)—took the form of state-organised wildcatting, it is certainly the case that once oil had been struck in 1959 plans were made to ensure Daqing's longevity and socialist tenor.[14] It is important to bear in mind that ecological sustainability 'was not a political value at the time', and thus the focus of Daqing's planners and workers during the Mao era remained on petroleum's role in socialist modernisation.[15]

MPI leaders, including Long March veteran Yu Qiuli and geologist turned Eighth Route Army fighter Kang Shi'en, were able to tap their PLA connections to secure the labour and resources necessary to turn Daqing into a functioning site of oil production, transport, and, soon, refining.[16] In February 1960, the MPI secured 30,000 PLA veterans, plus 3,000 officers recently demobilised from the Korean War, to build up the requisite infrastructure around the newly discovered wells.[17] This was conducted and described like a wartime mobilisation: a 'Great Battle for Oil' (石油大会战).[18] Seasoned PLA troops were joined by thousands of civilian engineers, geologists, planners, and workers from across the country.[19] Even when morale was high conditions were punishing. As historian Tai Wei Lim has written: 'Personnel had to work in a harsh natural environment during bitter[ly] cold months ... [with] scant material comfort. Modern equipment was inadequate with few motorized vehicles and accessible roads. The workers overcame technological deficiencies with sheer self-reliant brute labor.'[20] They had to build nearly everything from scratch, including their own shelter and food supply. Resolving food scarcities also took the form of organised campaigns. Responsibility for waging the battle for food soon fell to female family dependants, who, often fleeing Great Leap Famine conditions elsewhere, came to Daqing to join male relatives who had taken up oilfield posts.[21]

In the first half of the 1960s, Daqing's development was guided by specialised knowledge, technological leadership, and shared hardship. Amid a hierarchical management structure that respected worker contributions while deferring to scientifically trained experts, oilfield leaders like Yu Qiuli and Kang Shi'en encouraged universal asceticism.[22] Daqing's early days involved a 'leadership style in which leaders and led lived together with minimum status differences'.[23] With Mao's encouragement, Daqing's organisational structure drew on the 1960 Charter of the Anshan Iron and Steel Company (see Hirata's essay in the present volume).[24] The charter called on people to 'keep politics firmly in command and strengthen Party leadership; launch vigorous mass movements, have cadre participation in productive labor and worker participation in management ... close cooperation among cadres, workers, and technicians; and go all out with technological innovation and technological revolution'.[25] As the oilfields became a major generator of state revenue and as the power of MPI officials within central government ranks grew—giving rise to the 'Petroleum Group' moniker based on its affiliates' energy industry ties—Daqing's leaders still expected spartan living conditions. A perhaps apocryphal oilfield story has Yu Qiuli chastising 'ironman' Wang Jinxi for indulging in the luxury of purchasing an East German–made motorcycle. Only after Wang persuaded Yu that the motorcycle was not a luxury but rather a necessity for speeding between well sites and thereby enhancing work productivity did Yu agree to let him keep it.[26] Some accounts suggest that Daqing's leaders lived considerably better than its general workforce during this period, mostly in terms of food quality and quantity.[27] However, even with such stratifications, conditions were harsh for all. No-one lived or accumulated private profits in the manner of oil barons in the capitalist West.

Despite or because of the oilfields' technocratic leadership, Daqing's manual labourers received the bulk of media attention once the fields began to be publicised in 1964.[28] As scholars Li Hou and Yiyu Tian have explained, spotlighted workers included three broad categories that revealed the oilfields' starkly gendered divisions of labour: 'Ironmen', 'Iron Girls' (铁姑娘), and family dependants'.[29] Ironmen included figures like Wang Jinxi and other male workers with long-time oilfield experience.[30] Iron Girls—themselves modelled after female agricultural workers of the Dazhai Production Brigade in Shaanxi Province—were officially registered as workers and, like their male counterparts, 'challenged the limits of human bodies in their intense physical labor'.[31] Family Dependants were 'housewives in industrial and urban areas who were mobilized into productive labor by the state as "workers," but did not have officially-budgeted positions'.[32] In Daqing, dependants like Xue Guifang set to work cultivating fields surrounding the well sites. They thereby not only sustained the entire endeavour but also facilitated Daqing's emergence as a model of industrial and agricultural integration and self-sufficiency.[33] As Daqing developed, dependants took on other crucial tasks including caring for children, making clothes, and staffing public offices. To be sure, all of Daqing's residents performed many different roles and contributed in one way or another to its becoming a new kind of urban–rural oil town. But how a person was officially classified meant significant differences in job security and remuneration.[34] Chairman Liu Shaoqi—soon singled out for attack during the Cultural Revolution alongside Deng Xiaoping—reportedly discouraged oilfield workers from engaging in agricultural tasks because it was 'not worth the 50 yuan per month that we pay' for their labour.[35] Family dependants, as Tian has explained, felt their precarious employment status acutely even as they took great pride in contributing their varied skills to Daqing's success.[36]

When the Cultural Revolution erupted in May 1966, who performed what kind of work and how this work was socially valued and materially compensated became intensified sites of political struggle. While at the outset of the Cultural Revolution the oilfields continued to be nationally praised, Daqing and the Petroleum Group were soon recast as bastions of technocracy closely allied with Liu and Deng.[37] Red Guards and the Gang of Four accused Daqing and Petroleum Group leaders, including Yu and Kang, of capitalist tendencies. They also attacked Wang Jinxi for supplying Daqing with the veneer of worker leadership.[38] Significantly, and with Mao and Premier Zhou Enlai's apparent blessing, these upheavals were only briefly tolerated at Daqing. The PLA, long involved in Daqing's development, restored production at the oilfields as early as the autumn of 1967, 'making Daqing one of the earliest places during the Cultural Revolution to be placed under military control'.[39] Deposed senior cadres were soon restored to their posts and, by May 1968, Wang was appointed vice-director of the new Daqing Revolutionary Committee. 'The conservative workers, the so-called "royalists",' Hou explained, 'joined together under the leadership of the PLA to maintain order and to increase production ... The oil field remained one of the leading growth engines in the Chinese economy during the Cultural Revolution.'[40]

While Daqing's rank-and-file workers struggled against entrenched leadership, regional anti-Communist developments appeared to justify the PLA's effort to keep the oil flowing. The war between North Vietnam and the United States invoked in Wang's June 1966 poem was then in full swing; the 1965–66 coup against Sukarno in Indonesia had turned the region's foremost oil producer staunchly anti-communist.[41] Daqing, meanwhile, had proved so bountiful that China was exporting nominal amounts of oil to North Vietnam and North Korea and, by 1972, it also sent symbolic amounts to the Philippines and Thailand.[42] Since 1964, China had been importing refining equipment from Western Europe (Italy in particular) and Japan to process the volume of crude the oilfields were generating.[43] More consequentially, once the US–China normalisation in 1972 paved the way for the normalisation of relations between China and Japan, the latter two countries inked an 'oil for steel' deal that supplied Japan with Chinese oil just as Japan was hit by the 1973 Organisation of the Petroleum Exporting Countries (OPEC) oil embargo.[44] Although principles set forth by Zhou Enlai, who brokered the deal, stipulated that Chinese oil should not benefit US subsidiaries, Taiwan, or South Korea, this was difficult to enforce in practice.[45] Gang of Four members criticised these trade deals throughout the 1970s while scoring intermittent victories—particularly in the realm of cultural production, for instance, by delaying the release of a film about Daqing's early pioneers—against Daqing's restored technocratic and production-first ethos.[46] Jiang Qing, for her part, pointedly charged that, by 'exporting petroleum, China is shifting the international energy crisis on to the Chinese people and has saved the first and second worlds, i.e., the U.S., Japan, and Western Europe'.[47] After Mao's death and the arrest of the Gang of Four in 1976, suppressing oilfield struggles for the sake of increasing production and integrating China into global petroleum markets continued unabated.

Daqing's Mao-Era Lessons

On 20 April 1964, 'Daqing Spirit, Daqing People' (大庆精神, 大庆人) was the headline of the front-page story in the *People's Daily*.[48] In keeping with the secrecy that had shrouded the entire project since its inception, the article did not identify Daqing's actual location. The oilfields' headquarters had hitherto been publicly identified only as the 'Saertu General Land Reclamation Farm' (萨尔图农垦总场), rendering it indistinguishable from other worksites and prison camps elsewhere in China's far northeast.[49] Even after Daqing's achievements were publicised, further details about the oilfields were kept as quiet as possible until 1973, when Party leaders decided that the benefits of broadcasting China's reserves outweighed the potential security risks (prices in US dollars for Chinese crude tripled between late 1973 and early 1974 amid the OPEC embargo).[50] In this vein, when the campaign to 'Learn from Daqing' officially launched in 1964, Daqing's experiences were, on the one hand, generalised and distilled into exhortations about self-sacrifice and extreme endurance. On the other hand, Daqing's story supplied lessons about ways to integrate industry and agriculture and deploy Maoist philosophy to resolve practical problems.[51]

Readers of the *People's Daily* on 20 April 1964 learned that Daqing manifested the self-sacrificial and self-sufficient ethos of the Communist wartime base at Yan'an. They learned about Daqing's punishing weather, what the oilfields looked like, and how staff and workers offered mutual support and studied 'On Practice' and 'On Contradiction' together. Readers also learned anecdotes about Wang Jinxi and other male workers who risked life and limb for oil, and about the geologists and engineers who supplied the necessary expertise. 'Without a high degree of revolutionary consciousness, without dauntless revolutionary stamina, without esteem for a real scientific spirit, would any of this be possible?' the reporters asked. A piece in the newspaper's late edition profiled Daqing's 'lofty models' (崇高的榜样) and further clarified that the 'Daqing spirit' (大庆精神) was the 'revolutionary spirit of the working class' (无产阶级的革命精神).[52] Daqing's people were 'made of something special' (特种材料制成的人). Its workers were 'both red and expert' (又红又专). They had achieved such astounding results because they 'persisted in holding aloft the red flag of Mao Zedong thought' and had 'conjoined heightened revolutionary fortitude with a rigorous scientific stance'. In April 1964, 'Learning from Daqing' meant replicating this ethic and attitude.[53]

Daqing offered other lessons as well. Many of these focused on how Daqing's workers incorporated Maoist philosophy to resolve problems confronted at the oilfields. A striking example appears in a documentary by Belgian filmmakers Joris Ivens and Marceline Loridan, who visited Daqing in the mid 1970s. For their film *The Oilfields*, Ivens and Loridan interviewed many Daqing workers, including Xue Guifang, who in the film is identified by her honorific, 'Mama Xue' (Wang Jinxi had passed away from stomach cancer in 1970). In one scene, the filmmakers interview seamstresses in a workshop tasked with making and mending clothing for workers to help them endure Manchuria's bitter cold. As the camera pans over seamstresses pressing fluffs of cotton between sheets of fabric to make warm padded clothing, they discuss how they resolved the dire cotton shortage. One explained:

> According to metaphysics, material objects are unchangeable. But Chairman Mao's philosophy has taught us that things can be transformed into their opposites. That's how rags are turned into cotton. You discover truth by putting ideas into practice. We started out with the idea that cloth is made of cotton. Then we asked, if cotton can be transformed into cloth, why can't cloth be turned into cotton again? Practical experience proved that it was possible. When we tried to find a way to do this, we sometimes got discouraged. But finally, we succeeded in making cotton from cloth. We were really excited.

Another seamstress continued:

> At first our experiments didn't work. But we thought that since these rags were made of cotton fibre, there must be a way to make cotton again from the rags. It's a dialectical process. We tried seven times before we finally got it. Since 1970, we've made 300,000 pairs of gloves, with only 90,000 pounds of recycled cotton. Our interest in philosophy keeps growing. Because we can apply it to concrete situations, it's fascinating, and it encourages us to study philosophy.[54]

The proud work performed by these women—making clothes to keep oilfield workers warm enough to survive in the Manchurian cold—was integral to Daqing's emergence as a model. As the seamstresses in Ivens and Loridan's film attest, much of this grassroots work was fuelled by Maoist philosophy integrated into everyday practice.[55]

While the precise reasons Daqing was so successful as an oilfield remain a subject of debate, there is no question that its development facilitated China's capacity to continue its industrialisation and weather the split with the Soviet Union. Daqing supplied China with sufficient oil until consumption needs were recalibrated amid the market reforms of the 1980s and substantially contributed to China's emergence as one of the world's major oil producers.[56] Oil exploration hardly stopped at Daqing in the 1960s. However, as new fields were opened, officials demonstrated greater interest in extracting oil itself than in building up diversified, egalitarian communities around extraction sites. The geological formations that contained Manchuria's oilfields were understood to lead towards the Bohai Gulf and to the Yellow and East China seas. Chinese geologists noted the potential of these offshore regions as early as 1960.[57] Preliminary explorations of the shallow waters of the Bohai Gulf began by 1965; results from a United Nations–sponsored 1966 survey and another conducted by the US Navy in 1968 indicated that 'the continental shelf between Taiwan and Japan may be one of the most prolific oil reservoirs in the world', and China began offshore drilling in 1973.[58] While Wang Jinxi in 1966 sang the praises of drilling for Vietnam, petroleum industry officials were already thinking much more expansively about the meanings of national demand and how new demands could be met.

1964

In the early 1960s, the geopolitical environment was worsening. On one side, the United States had established a string of military bases around China, from South Korea to the Philippines, and was increasing its aid to the South Vietnamese regime; on the other side, the Soviet Union had transformed into an existential threat for China, amassing hundreds of thousands of troops along its northern border. To make matters worse, China still had not managed to develop an atomic arsenal of its own. As Chinese leaders were discussing the terms of the Third Five-Year Plan, Mao Zedong argued that, in preparation for war, the country should be divided into three fronts. The First Front would be along the coast, the Second behind coastal provinces, and the Third in central and western China. This entailed the secret construction of a large military-industrial complex in China's interior—often in hidden mountain locations. This essay looks at the circumstances of the workers involved in the construction of the Third Front.

The Third Front Campaign
Covell F. MEYSKENS

On 27 May 1964, Mao Zedong summoned Deng Xiaoping and a few other Chinese Communist Party (CCP) leaders to discuss China's Third Five-Year Plan.[1] Over the previous few months, Deng and other leading officials had drafted initial plans that concentrated on developing coastal areas and lifting the output of agricultural and consumer goods.[2] Mao disapproved of this economic strategy because it did not address China's worsening geopolitical environment. The United States had a string of military bases around China, from South Korea to the Philippines, and Washington was expanding its forward-deployed forces in Southeast Asia. The Soviet Union, meanwhile, had transformed in the wake of the Sino-Soviet Split from a close ally into an existential threat, with 200,000 troops on China's northern border. What made matters worse was that both the United States and the Soviet Union had thousands of nuclear weapons while China did not have a single atomic bomb, as Moscow had withdrawn its promised support to build one.[3]

Given China's imperilled security position, Mao argued that, 'in the age of the atom bomb, not having a military rear was no good'.[4] In preparation for war, the Party had to divide the country into three military fronts: the First Front along the coast, the Second Front behind coastal provinces, and the Third Front (or, hereinafter, the Front) in central and western China. In this final region, the Party had to secretly build a large military-industrial complex to serve as a backup economic motor for national defence in case the United States or Soviet Union invaded, and had to abandon established industrial areas and retreat into the interior like Chiang Kai-shek had done during World War II.[5] Provinces in the First and Second fronts also had to build small military-industrial bases. Like the CCP's revolutionary base areas, all Third Front projects had to be dispersed in hidden mountain locations. With this new industrial war machine, Beijing would be in a better position to fight off an assault by its Cold War enemies.[6]

Figure 1. Map of the First, Second, and Third fronts. The author owns the rights to this map.

Deng and other top Party leaders did not immediately back Mao's call to undertake such a big developmental drive to bolster national security. They instead recommended conducting preparatory surveys and drawing up plans for a few select projects. This policy stance was based on their concern about launching an industrialisation campaign like the Great Leap Forward (1958–62), during which the central government had decentralised authority to localities and commanded them to mobilise local resources to quickly expand China's industrial base. In the end, the Great Leap led to economic and administrative disorder and a famine that killed tens of millions of people.[7]

Party elites only endorsed building the Third Front in August 1964, when the United States bombarded North Vietnam in the wake of the Tonkin Gulf Incident. With the prospect of a great-power war on the immediate horizon, Party leaders greenlit the construction of a military-industrial complex in China's inland regions.[8] To ensure the Front did not experience the Great Leap's managerial problems, Party leaders granted central planners sole authority over its administration and did not allow local leaders to independently initiate projects.[9] Between 1964 and 1980, China dedicated to the Front about 40 percent of the national construction budget. Most investment occurred in two big waves. The first wave was concentrated in the southwest. Major projects included three railroads to connect the provincial capitals of Sichuan, Guizhou, and Yunnan, the large steel town of Panzhihua in Sichuan, the coke town of Liupanshui in Guizhou, and a conventional weapons complex in the mountains around Chongqing. In late 1966, the Cultural Revolution derailed these early efforts to build the Third Front.[10]

The Party leadership ordered a second wave of construction in 1969 in response to Sino-Soviet border clashes. While construction continued on projects in the southwest, hundreds of new initiatives were begun in central and northwestern China. The CCP's big push to industrialise the interior subsided in 1972 when Sino-American rapprochement significantly lessened Beijing's concerns about the threat of a great-power war on Chinese territory. About one-third of the national construction budget, however, was still allocated to completing existing projects until the late 1970s, when Party leaders decisively reoriented national development back towards the coast.[11]

Integral to the Third Front's construction was a huge labour force. In total, roughly fifteen million people took part in the campaign, with about one million labourers coming from urban areas and the rest mobilised from the countryside.[12] The remainder of this essay examines the experiences of Third Fronters and the products of their labour. The first section charts how people were recruited. The next section looks at what life was like at construction sites, while the last section discusses the Front's economic legacies.

Going to the Front

Since the Third Front was top secret, its creation was never officially announced, so people typically only learned about it when their workplace informed them that Mao had ordered the construction of a military-industrial complex in inland regions to protect China from rising American and Soviet military pressures. Before someone was transferred to the Third Front, a political background check was conducted to ensure they were not classified as a landlord, rich peasant, counterrevolutionary, or rightist and that they did not have any foreign contacts or personal reason to oppose the Party. The government instituted these recruitment criteria because it sought to enlist only people who could be trusted to remain dedicated to building the Front amid any hardships and who would not disclose its existence to domestic or foreign enemies.[13]

With this framing, the Party presented Front participation as a political privilege. Some participants were excited to have the opportunity to go where the Party thought they were most needed. Their enthusiasm was heightened by Mao's declaration that until the Front was built, he would 'not sleep well'.[14] Favourable views of this sort were most common among Party members, whose personal biographies were already deeply enmeshed with the CCP's project of building socialism in China, and youth who had grown up after the establishment of the People's Republic in 1949 and were eager to realise Mao's decrees on how to construct socialist China. Many other recruits were traumatised to learn they had been chosen to answer Mao's order to firm up national security by industrialising remote mountainous areas.[15]

Urban residents were particularly distressed because going to the Front amounted to a socioeconomic demotion. Instead of living in a city in China's northeastern or coastal industrial heartland, they would have to reside not just in the underdeveloped interior, but in its mountainous hinterlands. In many cases, when workers were mobilised, plans for their new workplace were still on the drawing broad, and construction had yet to begin. Workers were anxious about the sort of life that awaited them in this industrial world that they would have to build themselves. What sort of housing, medical facilities, and cultural activities would there be? Would there be schools for their children, and would they be any good? What would local weather and food be like, and would they be able to adapt? Would they be able to understand the local dialect? And, perhaps most importantly, when could they come back and live again with their family and friends?[16]

Figure 2. Third Front mobilisation poster. From the author's personal collection.

The administrators charged with overseeing the relocation of urban workers had their own concerns, too. Some provincial officials shared the worries of those in the Party centre who thought the Front might negatively impact the countryside like the Great Leap had, so they stressed that the campaign must be centrally directed and agriculture must receive adequate attention. Some northeastern and coastal officials also cautioned against ignoring the development of their regions and devoting too much consideration to the interior. While some inland provincial officials voiced similar words of warning, others sought to acquire more resources from developed parts of the country to advance local industrialisation.[17]

Officials in rural areas tended to view the Front more positively because it was a way for them to gain more resources by temporarily hiring labour out to projects in their vicinity. Employed in this way, a worker could earn about thirty-two yuan per month. A labourer's wage, however, did not go directly into their pocket. Their rural work unit first took a portion to cover the costs of food and lodging. Workers received the remainder, which was often about six yuan. This sum was a significant material benefit for rural folk who were typically compensated in work-points and earned, on average, eleven to fifteen yuan per year. The amount rural officials skimmed off the top was also more than they usually spent on local labour's livelihood, meaning they, too, obtained extra funding.[18]

The small number of rural residents hired as permanent employees accrued the even greater privilege of having access to the broad welfare guarantees of an urban state-owned enterprise. Despite these material advantages, some rural parents were still reluctant to let their children partake in the Front because they preferred to have more familial labour for their household, could not bear to part with their loved ones, or feared they might be maimed or killed in an accident. As this overview of people's responses to Third Front recruitment demonstrates, how people felt about being integrated into China's covert Cold War industrial defence apparatus was shaped by their specific social, economic, and geographical situations.[19]

Everyday Life

For urbanites, their departure for the Front was often filled with tears. Leading cadres tried to stimulate enthusiasm by playing revolutionary songs and coming to the train station to wish them farewell. These efforts were usually of little avail, as family members and workers welled up at not knowing when, if ever, they would see one another again. The hundreds or thousands of kilometres they had to travel before arriving at their destination reinforced the feeling of how far they were going from home. Their sense of heading into the middle of nowhere was further enhanced by the fact that, for most, their future workplace could only be reached by a truck-ride, snaking for hours, if not days, up dusty mountain roads. Although rural folk generally had to travel shorter distances to their new workplace, they rarely had the luxury of motorised transport and had to instead walk for tens or hundreds of kilometres along rugged mountain routes.[20]

Figure 3. Building a road for a Third Front factory. Source: '"三线文化" 三线建设部分老照片选登 ["Third Front Culture": Select Published Old Photos of Third Front Construction].' 每日头条 [Meiri Toutiao], 20 August 2017, available online at: kknews.cc/zh-cn/news/a8jbqa6.html.

On reaching their new workplace, many recruits were shocked to find not an established factory but a construction site in various stages of completion. Due to a shortage of motor vehicles, recruits regularly had to install heavy machinery by hand and lug in tonnes of supplies on shoulder poles and pushcarts. Whatever sort of work people were engaged in, it was militarised: people were organised into military units; administrators described project goals as battles in China's Cold War struggle against the United States and Soviet Union; and militaristic language and routines pervaded everyday life, from calling colleagues 'comrades-in-arms' (战友) to a regimented schedule of morning calisthenics, long work hours, and regular readings of Mao's works about the need to have a military mindset.[21]

At the end of a workday, the earliest recruits were lucky if they slept in tents on thin mats; many closed their eyes under the stars with no bedding at all. Even once labourers erected housing, it typically was a rammed-earth hut with a thatched roof. Provisions were similarly spartan, with water sourced from local streams and rice porridge and pickled vegetables the main sustenance, with fresh vegetables occasionally added as an accompaniment, and small morsels of meat served only once a month or so.[22] This regime of austerity was by design, resulting from the Party's policy of restraining consumption so that more resources were available for expanding China's economic infrastructure and increasing heavy-industry output.[23]

The Party's drive to quickly build up its military-industrial base in inland China came crashing to a halt in late 1966 when it collided with Mao's campaign to root out 'hidden enemies and traitors within Chinese intellectual circles and within the Party', who, in Andrew Walder's words, were putatively trying to 'overthrow Communist political power and restore capitalism'.[24] Third Fronters made the Cultural Revolution's political logic their own, claiming that barebones living conditions and their assignment to the Front were due to the actions of capitalist roaders in their midst. Party leaders, on the other hand, asserted that criticisms of this sort were the work of domestic elements collaborating with China's enemies in the United States and Soviet Union. The Party's efforts to clamp down on worker dissent intensified in 1969 when Sino-Soviet border skirmishes made it seem that Moscow might soon launch an invasion or carry out multiple nuclear strikes.[25]

In response to Sino-Soviet military tensions, the Party centre endorsed another big push to accelerate the expansion of China's military-industrial base. As in the first phase of Third Front construction, workers frequently replaced machine power with their muscles as they rushed to boost China's industrial defences before the outbreak of war. While many urban recruits were supportive of the Front's objective of bolstering national security through rapid industrialisation, many were also dissatisfied with their austere housing, diet, and cultural life. Even when projects were completed and standards of living began to improve in the late 1970s, many workers still longed for the day they could decamp from China's hinterlands and rejoin family and friends in more developed urban centres. While rural recruits also missed their families, they tended to better recognise the material benefits they had as urban state-owned enterprise employees compared with rural residents living just outside Third Front factory walls.[26]

Life After the Front

To assess the lives of the Third Fronters after the campaign, it is necessary to examine this issue from several different angles. If this topic is approached from the perspective of the workers themselves, the picture is decidedly ambivalent. While many Third Fronters recognise in their memoirs and oral interviews that their years of hard work endowed inland China with a larger industrial base than it would otherwise have had, they also often complain about the material privation of their everyday lives and the psychological adversity of being separated from family and friends. Those recruits who brought their children with them worried that their work unit's subpar schools would adversely impact their children's life chances and perhaps even lead them to suffer the same fate—having to reside forever in China's mountainous backwoods.[27]

If a different perspective is adopted and the Front is evaluated through the lens of its economic results, they, too, are unmistakeably mixed. From one perspective, the Front made significant contributions to the development of inland China. By building up regional industrial infrastructure, the Front integrated inland regions more into the Chinese economy, sped up the circulation of regional resources, and augmented manufacturing, mining, and hydropower facilities that made a society powered by hydrocarbons and electricity into more of an economic norm in inland China. Taken altogether, these economic changes helped to decrease the economic gap between the coast and the interior. On the other hand, they also established an industrial base whose continued growth would require ever more resources and whose development would place ever more stress on China's ecology.[28]

From another standpoint, the Third Front was massively wasteful.[29] According to a 1984 State Council report, only 48 percent of all projects were worthy of further development; the other 52 percent were abandoned.[30] This statistic is a stunning testament of how much of the Third Front passed into the dustbin of China's economic history. However, when considering the inefficiency of the Front, it is important to take into account the security logic embedded in its construction. According to Party policy, Front projects had to be in secluded mountain areas to keep them out of sight of enemy bombers. About one-quarter of Front funding was invested in factories that manufactured war materiel, and projects were rushed because of concerns that the Soviet Union or United States might soon attack. The policy of speeding up the building process ironically slowed project completion, as it resulted in shoddy construction and the need for years of repairs, which in turn raised construction costs.[31]

Given the many economic problems with the Third Front, it might seem most appropriate to conclude that, despite what it left in terms of industrial infrastructure, it must overall be viewed as an economic failure. This viewpoint, however, overlooks the fact that the Front was a development initiative that had ensuring national defence as its top priority. Critics might still object that, although certain inefficiencies are to be expected for an industrial defence project, the CCP leadership nonetheless still overreacted to Soviet and American military pressures by investing so much in the Third Front, and that the Communist Party could have guaranteed China's security with a more moderate industrial campaign.[32]

Perhaps the Third Front was too much, but stopping our analysis there neglects one particularly important point. The Front was not an isolated phenomenon. It was part of a slew of defence initiatives undertaken by Washington and Moscow during the Cold War, from the thousands of atomic bombs produced that if used would have annihilated the Earth many times over to the very long, bloody, and costly wars fought in Vietnam and Afghanistan. From this standpoint, the excesses of the Third Front appear not as a Chinese anomaly but rather as part and parcel of the irrationality of great-power competition during the Cold War, when massive reactions to perceived security threats became a defining feature of international statecraft.

1967

The mass mobilisation phase of the Cultural Revolution began as a student movement on the campuses of Beijing's universities and middle schools in the summer of 1966. However, under the direction of cadre work teams, the movement quickly degenerated into a crisis over political representation. After a fight to a stalemate, the withdrawal of the work teams triggered a new stage of direct but also violent political action that paralysed Chinese Communist Party and state administrations by the end of the year. Worker mobilisation in Shanghai led to the usurpation of the municipal government in early 1967, signalling a new phase in the movement. The so-called January Storm (一月风波), a dramatic wave of rebel power seizures in which workers figured prominently, swept the country. Its apogee was the declaration of the Shanghai People's Commune in early February; yet its denouement came only a few weeks later, when the rebel workers agreed to reorganise as a 'revolutionary committee', uniting forces with some of the cadres they had dispossessed as well as local military leaders. The January Storm thus marks an unresolved dilemma in the Party's history: the Cultural Revolution originated in a crisis over the Party's role in political representation, which the Maoist leadership sought to overcome through the direct political action of students and workers with the nominal aim of self-rule. But the Party's monopolisation of power deprived rebel workers of the resources necessary to build and sustain a lasting alliance. When the coalition quickly collapsed, Party leaders gradually reverted to the flawed mechanism of representation through delegation that triggered the initial crisis. This essay focuses on labour's role in the rise and fall of the Shanghai People's Commune through the question of labour's representation in the People's Republic of China.

The January Storm of 1967: From Representation to Action and Back Again

Patricia M. THORNTON

In January 1967, as China's Cultural Revolution transitioned from a largely student-based upsurge into a worker movement, a wave of rebel power seizures of Party and government agencies swept the country. For many, the so-called January Storm (一月风波) marked the culmination of the Cultural Revolution: what had begun as a sustained rebellion of high school and university students in Beijing not only widened to include the working class, but also quickly spread beyond the capital, to major cities up and down the east coast and into the hinterland. The grassroots efforts of rebel workers in Shanghai to overturn the municipal government, and the subsequent declaration of the founding of the Shanghai People's Commune (上海人民公社), were an instance not only of direct political action by the working classes, but also of the proletariat in China acting *for* itself as a political subject, rather than *in* itself as an object. Alessandro Russo hails the commune's founding as the culmination of a process of 'experimenting with a new political existence for workers who were no longer under the sway of the Stakhannovite model, and, hence, were able to organize their collective existence regardless of whether the party-state could endorse such an action'.[1] On the other hand, as Alain Badiou observed, this triumphant achievement was 'immediately paradoxical': the Shanghai People's Commune may have been originally intended as 'a complete countermodel of the party-state', but because the existing political landscape of the Cultural Revolution was already oversaturated, the newborn commune could 'obtain only a fragile unity'.[2] Thus, he argued, 'the entrance onto the scene of the workers' marked 'a spectacular broadening of the revolutionary mass base' and 'the short-lived outline of a new articulation between the popular political initiative and the power of the state' that ultimately could not challenge, but only reproduce, the existing structures of power.[3]

Others are considerably more sceptical about the grassroots nature of the Shanghai takeover and the upheavals of the January Storm, casting doubt on official portrayals of the event as worker-led. Independent historian He Shu argued that Central Cultural Revolution Small Group (CCRSG) members Zhang Chunqiao and Yao Wenyuan not only failed to support, but also actively suppressed, repeated attempts by rebel workers to topple the Shanghai Municipal Party Committee. He argues that although Zhang and Yao were in principle not opposed to power seizure per se, they actively thwarted any effort that they did not directly control.[4] More recently, Andrew Walder described the 1967 national power seizure as 'a top-down process of diffusion [that was] essentially a form of collective behavior by party-state cadres' responding to signals from the central leadership in Beijing.[5] In his analysis, the rapid diffusion of the power seizures to areas without large student and worker insurgencies, alongside the participation of cadres in these events, suggests that the mobilisation was driven by Party-State officials, calling into question basic assumptions about who, precisely, was seizing power from whom.

However, debates about the spontaneity of the January Storm elide a more profound dilemma in the Party-State's history: the unresolved problem of mass political representation, and its relationship to direct political action. This essay focuses on the January Storm, and what the brief life of the Shanghai People's Commune tells us about the unresolved question of labour's representation in the history of the People's Republic of China (PRC).

'Real' and 'Fake' Party Members

The mass mobilisation phase of the Cultural Revolution began in May 1966 with the hanging of a wall poster at Beijing University denouncing the university's president and Chinese Communist Party (CCP) secretary and two other municipal officials as 'revisionist elements' linked to a recently purged 'anti-Party clique'. The accusation created an uproar on campus, exacerbated by tensions within the faculty and student body that had been simmering for at least several months, if not years, and resulted in the widely publicised removal of those accused.[6] This, however, did not prevent instructors and students at other campuses from posting similar accusations, particularly following the publication of the original poster on the front page of the *People's Daily* a week later.[7] As the month wore on, Party and state officials attempted to defuse escalating unrest on school campuses by dispatching cadre work teams to investigate, instruct and contain rebellious young activists who had already begun forming the loose autonomous associations that came to be known as the Red Guards.

At the forefront of the escalating tensions between the student activists and work team members were questions of political representation: who had the right to speak on behalf of student interests, who represented various Party and state departments and, finally, who represented the Party centre and the revolutionary agenda itself? The front-page commentary of the *People's Daily* had described the members of the 'anti-party clique' as the representatives of a 'fake' and 'revisionist' Communist Party (假共产党, 是修正主义的党), and warned readers that anyone who opposed the instructions of Mao Zedong or the Party Central Committee—'no matter what banner they carry or how high their position or qualifications are'—were in reality 'representing' (代表) the interests of the overturned bourgeoisie, thereby placing the question of who was representing the 'real' Communist Party up for public debate and speculation as tensions soared.[8]

At Qinghua University, third-year chemical engineering student Kuai Dafu was singled out by the work team as a troublemaker and sequestered in his dorm room in early July. During his confinement, he produced his own wall poster arguing that the political power previously monopolised by the school's discredited Party committee—overthrown by student rebels—had been in effect transferred to the work team. Kuai called on all 'revolutionary leftists' on campus to ask themselves: 'Does this power *represent* [代表] us? If it represents us, then we'll support it, if it doesn't represent us, then we'll seize power again!'[9]

This broader battle ended in stalemate with the withdrawal of the work teams from Beijing's schools in August and inaugurated the start of a new phase marked by direct, and sometimes violent, political action: self-authorised student rebels and activists fanned out across the city and the country, seeking to mobilise support for various agendas, many of which targeted Party and state officials and agencies. The dislocation and disruption caused by student activists roaming the country in such large numbers succeeded in completely 'paralysing' (瘫痪) nearly one-third of provincial capital administrations by the end of 1966.[10]

From Students to Workers

The first major delegation of Red Guard representatives from Beijing arrived in Shanghai during the so-called blood-red August of 1966. Disembarking from the main train station, the members of the visiting Red Guard contingent announced they were the representatives of a genuine revolutionary movement seeking to 'light a fire' (点火) by spreading the Cultural Revolution to the Paris of the East.[11] They were not pleased with what they saw. Despite the fact that an official welcome had been staged for them at the city's Cultural Square, the delegation inveighed that their reception had been insincere and subpar. Within days, the Red Guard delegation followed up with additional complaints. First, they had been turned away from several Shanghai schools because they lacked proper letters of introduction; they were also dismayed to find that they had to purchase tickets when boarding public transportation, when they had become accustomed to free passage elsewhere; and, finally, the delegation members were frustrated that it had been difficult to arrange meetings with local CCP leaders. On receiving the complaints, the Municipal Party Committee offered its apologies, but the Red Guard delegates were not appeased. On the morning of 31 August, more than a dozen Beijing Red Guards marched to Yan'an Road, demanding a meeting with the municipal Party leadership. A crowd of more than 1,000 onlookers quickly gathered as the visiting Red Guards angrily rushed the building. They found mayor Cao Diqiu inside, meeting with two other self-described Beijing Red Guard representatives who had likewise demanded an official audience. In the fracas that ensued, Deputy Mayor Song Liwen was struck on the head by one of the Beijing Red Guard representatives, and the glass front door of the building was shattered.[12]

A few days later, on 10 September, a second wave, of tens of thousands of Beijing Red Guards organised into divisions and battalions, arrived in the city, calling themselves the 'Southern Touring Regiment of Capital Universities and Institutes' (首都大专院校红卫兵司令部南下兵团). Defying the Central Committee's September 1966 ban on allowing the Cultural Revolution to disrupt industrial production, the Beijing Red Guard representatives entered factories and workplaces around Shanghai in the name of establishing the 'Worker Student United Movement' (工人学生联合运动).[13] A third group, dispatched by CCRSG members

Jiang Qing and Zhang Chunqiao, arrived in early October and quickly established links with rebel workers in nearby factories with the goal of overturning the Shanghai Municipal Party Committee.[14]

Labour Ascendant

One month later, on 6 November, the Capital Red Guards Liaison Station in Shanghai organised a meeting that attracted at least thirty workers from seventeen different factories; on that occasion, the Shanghai Workers' Revolutionary Rebels General Headquarters (上海工人革命造反总司令部, hereinafter WGH) was founded, with Number 17 Cotton Mill security officer Wang Hongwen as its chair. At its inaugural meeting, held on the city's Cultural Square, the organisation demanded that the Shanghai Municipal Party Committee recognise it as a legitimate revolutionary mass organisation. The mayor and municipal Party secretary refused, with support from the Party centre, arguing that the WGH was riddled with internal contradictions and detrimental to maintaining industrial production.[15] When the mayor further declined to attend the 9 November inaugural ceremony, and moreover refused to 'participate, recognise or support' the new organisation, more than 1,000 angry workers surrounded the municipal Party committee building and staged a sit-in, before deciding to take their protest to Beijing.

Well over 1,000 self-declared representatives of the rebel workers headed to Shanghai North Station the next morning to join three trains bound for the capital, seeking recognition from the central leadership. A State Council directive from Premier Zhou Enlai halted the trains, snarling national rail lines for hours. The train that happened to be carrying WGH leader Wang Hongwen and 2,000 members was stopped outside Anting Station, approximately forty-five kilometres from Shanghai's city centre, leading to a standoff between the workers and local authorities. The WGH put forward five demands: 1) that the WGH be officially recognised as a legitimate revolutionary mass organisation; 2) that the WGH's founding meeting and the Anting incident be classified as revolutionary actions; 3) that the East China Bureau and the Shanghai Party Committee be held responsible for their part in the matter; 4) that the mayor offer a public self-criticism; and 5) that the WGH receive assistance from the Party and local government.[16]

The CCRSG dispatched Zhang Chunqiao to mediate the conflict. Within a few hours, he conferred official recognition on the new rebel workers' organisation—in violation of the instructions of the enlarged Politburo Standing Committee meeting held just prior to his dispatch—claiming to be representing the CCP Central Committee in so doing. At the Politburo meeting the following day, Mao supported Zhang's decision to recognise the workers' right to organise, based on their constitutional right to do so.[17]

The official recognition of the rebel WGH as a legitimate mass organisation triggered a flurry of grassroots organisation-building as other interests likewise sought official recognition conferring the associated right of representation in the new and still-emerging political hierarchy. For example, within days, Shanghai's 'conservative' workers—that is, those workers who supported the existing municipal Party committee and enjoyed a close relationship with local Party authorities—sprang into action, demanding a voice and a seat at the table as well. Li Jianyu, the soon-to-be local leader of the conservative Scarlet Guards (赤卫队) at the Number 31 Cotton Mill, approached his work team leader, requesting permission to assist in destroying 'black materials' following a call that 'representatives of all factions' participate.[18] Because the work team at the mill made up one of the factions there, and the rebel workers another, the team leader retorted: 'We represent organisations; what do you represent?' Li replied: 'Then I'll establish an organisation, too!' The mill's Scarlet Guard unit was founded a mere two hours later, and quickly joined forces with like-minded conservative workers across the city. Although short-lived, the organisation faced off against the rebel forces in two high-profile incidents in December before their popular support dwindled amid the widespread strikes, work stoppages and slowdowns that paralysed the city.

Word of the founding of the WGH in Shanghai set off a flurry of rebel activity across the country. Within days of the WGH's official recognition, more than 1,000 rebel workers from Chengdu in Sichuan headed to Beijing to petition central authorities, who hastily assembled forces to turn them back at Wuhan.[19] Hundreds of temporary workers in Beijing banded together to establish the All-China Red Labourer Rebels' Headquarters, colloquially known as the Quanhongzong (全红总), and quickly established branches in more than a dozen provinces. Throughout December and into early January, the organisation staged rallies and sit-ins targeting the official All-China Federation of Trade Unions (ACFTU) and the

Ministry of Labour in Beijing, demanding official recognition and labour policy reforms, while mobilising their branches elsewhere to engage in similar protests.[20]

Labour unrest had become sufficiently protracted in Nanjing by the end of 1966 that the municipal Party committee was dispatching ranked officials into factories to read aloud their self-criticisms to contingents of rebel workers in hopes of placating them. In Guangzhou, rebel workers succeeded in invading and closing the two major Party news offices in mid-December. In the smaller city of Shijiazhuang, a clash at a textile mill that wounded 300 rebel workers in early December escalated into calls to 'bombard' (跑打) municipal authorities, leading to an invasion of a municipal government office on 25 December. The net effect of these events—ranging from rebel invasions of Party and government offices to the seizure of local officials and the formation of sweeping coalitions of rebel workers—succeeded in paralysing Chinese cities, from provincial-level Shanghai down to prefectural-level small centres across the country.[21]

The January Storm

The power seizure that occurred in Shanghai on 6 January 1967—the first such seizure at the provincial level[22]—was chiefly motivated by rebel coalitions' desire to restore public order and resume public services to municipalities in which Party and government offices had effectively collapsed. Although the WGH and a coalition of allied rebel organisations staged a mass meeting to 'drag out' the municipal Party secretary, the mayor and other high-level cadres and subject them to public criticism, criticising local authorities was not the WGH's initial objective. Instead, at the organisation's core was a skeletal 'Frontline Command Post to Grasp Revolution and Promote Production' (上海市抓革命、促生产火线指挥部), with the relatively modest ambition of restarting Shanghai's transportation networks. One WGH leader at the time recalled how, on the evening of 7 January, the new Frontline Command Post's key concern was merely to reopen the rail links and Shanghai's main port, because the paralysis to which the city had succumbed was clearly 'a ploy by capitalist roaders to destroy production and suppress revolution'.[23] The grander ambition of self-rule seems to have been suggested by CCRSG members Zhang Chunqiao and Yao Wenyuan, who, in an early meeting with the Frontline Command Post, declared: 'This is a newly born thing, a new form of political power. We really must sum up this experience.'[24]

Meanwhile, on 8 January, Mao extolled Shanghai and its rebel coalition; the following day, the *People's Daily* published an 'Urgent Letter to the People of Shanghai', adding an editorial comment commending them for responding to Mao's call for workers to 'grasp revolution and promote production', underscoring that the lessons learned were relevant not just for Shanghai but also for the entire country.[25] The national media lavished praise on the WGH's takeover of the city beginning less than a week later in a series of articles and radio broadcasts urging rebels across the country to follow Shanghai's example.[26] The *People's Daily* on 16 January claimed that, in the 'experience of seizing power from a handful of capitalists within the Party', Shanghai's rebel coalition had 'provided correct principles, policies, forms of organisation and methods of struggle'.[27] Less than a week later, the newspaper called for a national bottom-up seizure of power through a great alliance to 'shake China' to its very core.[28]

By the end of January, more than half of China's 2,215 cities and counties had experienced seizures of power and, by the end of March, the authorities in more than 75 percent had been overturned.[29] Only days after the publication of the 'Urgent Letter', rebel organisations of workers in Shanxi established a 'grand alliance' (大联合) with 'revolutionary cadres' (革命干部) and members of the military and announced that they had 'seized power' (夺权) at the provincial level.[30] Permutations of the Shanxi experience involving alliances of cadres and army units alongside 'rebel revolutionary' workers soon followed in Shandong and Guizhou. Finally, on 31 January 1967, Heilongjiang became the first provincial power seizure carried out by a self-declared 'revolutionary committee' (革命会)—so named for the governing organ of the Paris Commune that had figured prominently in official newspaper commentaries during the earliest throes of the Cultural Revolution. Within the week, a coalition of thirty-two different rebel workers' groups declared the establishment of a 'People's Commune' in the place of their municipal government.

However, across the country, the January Storm had already taken events in a new direction. It was the model developed primarily in Heilongjiang— of a 'revolutionary committee' (革命委员会) formed as a 'triple combination' (三结合) uniting local military commanders, representatives of rebel mass organisations and local revolutionary cadres—that Mao favoured, and which was formally adopted in Shanghai before the month's end.

The autonomously formed WGH thus inaugurated and completed the five-week political sequence of the power seizure movement by serving as both midwife and gravedigger for the newborn Shanghai People's Commune, closing the circle from political representation to direct action and back again.

After the Storm

On the final day of January, in an article reprinted on the front page of the *People's Daily*, *Red Flag* referred to the power seizures collectively as the 'January Revolution', claiming 'the great storm of revolution started in Shanghai'.[31] Shanghai's model status notwithstanding, less than three weeks later, the Shanghai People's Commune was renamed a 'revolutionary committee' in accordance with Mao's 23 February instruction, conforming to the 'triple combination' arrangement that Shanxi, Shandong and Heilongjiang had inaugurated weeks before.[32] Zhang assumed chairmanship and Yao was appointed first deputy chairman. Locally, rebel worker Wang Hongwen, soon to be elevated to a seat on the CCRSG, served as principal deputy.[33]

More importantly, perhaps, the name change marked the beginning of the end of a political sequence: if the first battles of the Cultural Revolution were waged by students as struggles over political representation, and the second by workers as contests over direct political action, the renaming of the Shanghai People's Commune signalled the closure of the rebel workers' brief experiment in nominal self-rule by forcing them into a powersharing arrangement with some of the authorities they had overthrown. In 1972, the WGH likewise renamed itself the 'Shanghai Workers' Representative Congress' (上海市工代会); subordinate rebel units followed suit. By the following year, the former leadership of the WGH was absorbed into the Shanghai Municipal Federation of Trade Unions (上海市总工会), the local branch of the ACFTU, which had ceased operations when the Cultural Revolution began, but resumed functioning in 1970 under rebel worker control. Following the reopening of the municipal ACFTU, subordinate rebel units thereafter became known as 'union' branches and have largely remained as such to the present day.[34]

Writing in 2006, Li Xun remarked that, prior to the Cultural Revolution, whatever representation workers enjoyed in the political system had been merely 'symbolic' (象征性的). Those designated worker representatives who did exist were actually the heads of the Shanghai municipal

ACFTU, cadres who had led the CCP's underground labour organisations before 1949; none hailed from a working-class background, and all had only limited contact with those whose interests they were appointed to represent. Of the thirty-three key post-holders in the Shanghai Municipal Government in 1950—including the municipal Party secretary and Party standing committee members—only four were local ACFTU members. This number had dropped to a single representative by December 1965, on the eve of the Cultural Revolution.[35]

Although the events of January and February 1967 dramatically changed the structure of political representation for Shanghai's workers, it did so only temporarily and only at the local level; the worker representatives who made it to positions on the revolutionary committee had to compete against the more experienced cadre members for political influence under the 'triple combination' powersharing system, and were frequently accused of putting the interests of the union above those of the Party. A series of political campaigns targeting rebels in 1969 and 1970 further reduced their numbers. Of the 'worker rebels' who served in ten district government agencies under the Shanghai Revolutionary Committee, 135, or 43.5 percent, had been purged by 1971.[36]

On a deeper level, the new revolutionary committees also failed to resolve the crisis over political representation. Questions over who had the right to speak on behalf of particular collective interests, and who was authorised to represent the Party and the revolutionary agenda, were effectively taken off the table; the new revolutionary committees were not poised to 'represent' the masses so much as to *be* representative of them. On 19 February 1967, the CCP Central Committee issued a notice that the new organs of political power would ensure that, under the 'triple combination' system, the representatives who were leaders of revolutionary mass organisations would 'truly represent the broader revolutionary masses' (真正代表广大群众的革命群众).[37] A March 1967 *Red Flag* editorial republished in the *People's Daily* stipulated that, as provisional organs of revolutionary political power, all revolutionary committees must both display 'representativeness' (有代表性) and exercise 'proletarian authority' (有无产阶级权威的).[38] Mass representatives were enjoined to bring the masses 'into full play' (充分发挥) and value their opinions and warned to never 'use them as a foil' (当做陪衬); but beyond such blandishments, the central leadership declined to put in place formalised practices of accountability at the national level.

This failure undermined the ostensible aim of the revolutionary committee: to increase and institutionalise the political representation of revolutionary and rebel workers within the system. Political power in the PRC flows from the centre down by design; it is invested in local organs of government and grassroots actors through mechanisms of authorisation and delegation. The power seizure movement in 1967 thus triggered a desperate scramble at the grassroots, in Shanghai as elsewhere across the country, among local actors and groups seeking central authorisation to legitimise various political agendas. The Central Committee's order regarding the 'triple combination' arrangement of revolutionary committees attempted to guarantee 'genuine' mass representation in the new organ of governance. Yet by failing to designate methods of selection and recall, the actual mechanism of representation under the 'triple combination' system was left largely to local cadres to determine, virtually extinguishing the possibility of a radically new political existence for workers that the Cultural Revolution had promised to deliver.

1967

The crisis sparked by the anticolonial riots in 1967 is arguably the most important episode of the colonial history of Hong Kong in the postwar era. Triggered by an industrial dispute in May 1967, incessant waves of violence, demonstrations and strikes hit the colony, leading to fifty-one deaths and about 4,500 arrests. The territory was also haunted by extreme forms of confrontation, such as bombings and military clashes between British and Chinese forces at the border. Many commentators regard the events as the turning point in colonial governance, as post-riot Hong Kong underwent fundamental changes in socioeconomic policies. However, despite their origin as an industrial dispute against a backdrop of destitution and frustration among the working class in the colony, the events were primarily a spillover of the political radicalism in mainland China. The confrontation lasted more than six months and had a long-lasting impact on the trajectory of labour reforms in colonial Hong Kong.

The Hong Kong Riots of 1967
Ray YEP[1]

Factories in postwar Hong Kong were seen by many as poster-cases of 'blood and sweat workshops' of capitalism. Workers were paid low wages with few legal protections and limited benefits, and state regulations on industrial safety and working hours were yet to be introduced. The rapid population expansion in the postwar years further intensified the vulnerability of the underprivileged. Central to the desperation were the miserable living conditions endured by the majority. A study conducted in 1965 provides a vivid portrait of the abysmal lives of the locals, which were very much a mirror image of the desperation suffered by the English working class depicted by Charles Dickens:

> These buildings are mainly three storeys high. A very steep wooden staircase serves two adjacent buildings. The treads are so worn that hollows are formed in the central parts, and sometimes one or two treads are missing altogether. As the cleaning and maintenance of the stairs are nobody's responsibility (caretakers are unheard of) dirt and dust have accumulated over the years. The stairways are dark even in broad daylight and artificial lighting is never installed so that drug addicts who take advantage of the protective darkness are encountered on the landings.[2]

Colonial administrators attributed their reluctance to increase social investment and welfare provision to the 'China factor'. They argued that improvement in living standards in the colony would simply encourage more population inflows from the mainland—a discourse that had considerable mileage given the accelerated influx of illegal immigrants from China since the late 1950s as a result of the famines caused by the Great Leap Forward.

The apparent increase in social tension in the early 1960s is reflected in crime statistics. In 1965–66, 8,166 cases of serious crime were recorded—the highest level of serious crime since the late 1950s and a 40 percent increase over the level of 1961–62.[3] Even more worrying was the rising involvement of young people. The number of defendants under the age of sixteen witnessed an average annual growth rate of 17 percent between

1960 and 1966, and the number of young offenders between the ages of sixteen and twenty increased at an average of 13 percent during the same period.[4] With education and employment opportunities for young people few and far between, juvenile delinquency was a genuine concern. Signs of uneasiness were also evident in the workplace. Right before the 1967 riots, industrial disputes related to pay and working conditions occurred at Greenland Cement, the Central Taxi Company and Nanfung Textiles, threatening to escalate into major disturbances.[5] It was, however, the Kowloon disturbance of 1966 that finally forced the government to acknowledge the prevailing social tension. Triggered by a fare increase for the round-trip ferry service between Central District and Tsimshatsui, these disturbances lasted from 4 April to 10 April and ended with curfews, mass arrests and direct confrontations between the police and rioters. Although these were brief disturbances confined to districts in eastern Kowloon, they were a testament to the general restlessness among Hong Kong's young people.

The Riots as a Spinoff of China's Cultural Revolution

The 1967 riots started in an artificial-flower factory in Kowloon on 6 May, when an industrial dispute over the reduction of bonuses and allowances spiralled out of control. The employer refused to give in and eventually fired ninety-two workers. The police were soon called in and their violent handling of the situation left many workers injured. Eighteen workers were arrested. The local communists seized on this bickering to launch their anti-imperialist campaign in the colony. The communist-dominated Hong Kong Federation of Trade Unions (HKFTU) immediately intervened on behalf of the workers, putting forward four demands: the immediate release of the workers arrested, the punishment of the evildoers and compensation for the victims, guarantees of the workers' personal safety and no interference henceforth by the police in labour disputes.

The event was quickly politicised. The turning point was the intervention of the Chinese Ministry of Foreign Affairs on 15 May 1967. Chinese diplomats passed a protest statement to the British chargé d'affaires in Beijing, which was then followed by anti-British demonstrations in Beijing and Guangzhou and sympathetic editorials in the *People's Daily* (人民日報).[6] For many local radicals in Hong Kong, these events were a clear call to arms. The formation of the All Circles Anti-Persecution Struggle Committee (香港各界同胞反英抗暴鬥爭委員會) in Hong

Kong heralded the full-scale mobilisation of local communists for an anticolonial campaign across the whole colonial territory. The labour dispute was quickly subsumed by demonstrations, strikes, marches and bombings, and the original concern for industrial relations was replaced with the highly politicised slogans of anti-imperialism. For at least six months, the normal life of the colony was paralysed by thousands of protestors performing the rhetoric and postures of the mainland's Cultural Revolution, such as holding Mao Zedong's *Little Red Book*, although attempts at full-scale and sustained strikes remained unsuccessful.

In fact, the Chinese Communist Party (CCP) had been present in Hong Kong since the 1920s (see Leong's and Lu's essays in the present volume). In the early days of the CCP, the colony had been a safe haven from the Nationalist regime and Japanese aggression and, in the postwar years, it served as a centre for coordination during the Civil War and remained strategically significant during the Cold War period. After 1949, the CCP's policy towards Hong Kong remained pragmatic, following the guiding principle of 'long-term planning, full utilisation' (长期打算, 充份利用). That is, despite denying the legality of the colonial status of Hong Kong, the mainland authorities regarded acceptance of the status quo as in their best interest. As a result, their efforts to consolidate the Party's presence in the colony continued under the radar.

In such a context, the rising influence of the communists was partly a self-inflicted wound on the side of the British administration in Hong Kong. With their minimalist approach to governing and noncommittal stance in service provision, the colonial authorities had unintentionally created a wide constituency for the communists, who were prepared to provide a moderate but highly cherished support network for the locals. The colonial government's foot-dragging when it came to welfare provision and reticence to address the destitution faced by the working class contributed to the expansion of the communist presence in the local labour movement.

The development of trade unions had always been the primary concern of the local communists since the 1920s. Labour's vulnerability to economic cycles and the lack of safety nets simply drove more and more hapless workers to unions that would provide them with some support for their misfortunes. Founded in 1948, the HKFTU was the local communist-controlled umbrella labour organisation. In this role, it had been particularly successful in establishing its hold among workers in public utilities companies, playing a key role in organising the strikes and struggles of tram workers in 1949, 1950 and 1954.⁷ And it was also the force behind the success of the strikes at Dairy Farm in 1949 and the Hong Kong Naval Dockyard in 1957. The HKFTU was, however, not simply a labour organisation; it had also attempted to fill the void in welfare provision left by the colonial government, serving as a support network for its members and sympathisers. While the government was still pondering its involvement in education, the union had its own network of schools for workers' children. It also provided affordable health services, cheap meals, cultural entertainment and even relief support during crisis at a time when the notion of the welfare state remained very much a taboo for the colonial administrators.

The communist cause was further strengthened by the communist involvement in the media, education and cultural sectors. By the beginning of 1967, there were a number of broadsheets directly controlled by the communists in Hong Kong—*Wen Wei Po* (文匯報), *Tai Kung Po* (大公報), *New Evening News* (新晚報), *Ching Po Daily* (晶報), *Hong Kong Commercial Daily* (香港商報), *Ching Wu Po* (正午報) *and Tin Fung Daily* (田豐日報). These papers commanded a respectable audience: by early 1967, in total, they published 240,000 copies per day—about 16 percent of the daily newspaper circulation in the colony.⁸ By the early 1950s, the communists had also established their own filmmaking machinery in the territory. The three companies—Great Wall, Phoenix and New United—were highly successful in producing commercial films for local entertainment and occupied a key role in the colony's film industry, producing 262 films between 1950 and 1966.⁹

The communist camp was equally successful in consolidating its foothold in education. Hong Kong society had a demographic structure strongly tilted towards the young. According to the 1961 census, 41 percent of the 3.1 million people living in the territory were aged fifteen or under, with one-third of this group aged below five years.¹⁰ Although this distinctive pattern created a huge demand for education, the colonial administration was slow to react. By the early 1960s, government intervention in this area remained circumscribed and the private sector continued to play a leading role in providing schooling opportunities for the local population. The shortage of government-funded places was particularly acute in secondary education, as 70 percent of students were enrolled in private schools. Yet many of these private schools operated in unsafe premises, with limited resources and unqualified teachers. The infamous 'rooftop' schools—that is schooling offered by 'teachers' with no formal qualifications in makeshift facilities on the tops of buildings—for example, contributed about 20 percent of total places at the primary level.[10] Communist sympathisers ran a substantial portion of these informal education establishments.

In short, on the eve of 1967, there already existed an extended web of communist supporters across different sectors of the colony. This network could serve as an effective platform for leadership, mobilisation and coordination, and it was also a steady source of foot soldiers for violence, strikes, demonstrations and propaganda. The colonial government was not unaware of the danger but its policy of minimal intervention in welfare and development tied its hands. It was not until the summer of 1967 that the real impact of this potentially subversive machinery was felt.

The Riots as a 'Spontaneous Act' by Local Communists

The presence of networks, however, does not explain why the local communists mobilised them in 1967. Sir David Trench, the colonial governor at the time, was convinced of the 'spontaneous' character of the original industrial dispute in Kowloon and that it was not a premeditated act by Beijing. 'There is every indication that this was a spontaneous incident', he argued in a telegram, and that the latest wave of militant unionism was no more than 'a reflection of the increased freedom allowed to the "masses" as a result of local propaganda based on the Cultural Revolution in China'.[12] Trench's theory was that the later escalation of events was largely a result of the Hong Kong communist leaders' survival instinct.[13] In his opinion, they needed to win a victory for Mao Zedong Thought in Hong Kong, 'mainly to save their own neck'.[14] In other words, the confrontation was primarily a plot by local communist agents to prove their loyalty to the radical leadership in China. They were under pressure to deliver some 'success', especially after their counterparts in Macau had managed to bring the Portuguese administration to its knees after a confrontation in December 1966.

The colonial government responded to the challenge with firm measures.[15] For Trench, this was imperative as there was a danger that the extreme actions of radicals in Hong Kong might end up 'pushing' Beijing to support the Hong Kong communists. Under this logic, if Hong Kong managed to contain the disturbances before they spiralled out of control, Beijing could be spared this challenge. Through mass arrests of ringleaders and protestors, suspension of leftist newspapers, closure of communist schools, activation of emergency powers and deportation, social order was gradually restored by early 1968. However, these measures would probably not have amounted to much if not for Mao's anxiety to keep radicalism in the mainland in check by mobilising military control of local administration in China.

The Riots as a Catalyst for Social Reform

Labour conditions improved in the aftermath of the riots. State regulations on working hours and women's and child labour were introduced and debates on social insurance and other labour benefits resumed with a greater sense of urgency. As the potential repercussions of the neglect of working-class conditions were used as a justification for accelerating policy changes, the riots catalysed the discourse on the imperative of labour reform. However, the events of 1967 barely changed the mentalities of the social and political elites.

As Clayton has observed:

> During 1967, radicals wanted conflict between labour and capital, and sought the overthrow of a colonial state which, they argued, sided with capitalist interests. For the benevolent, 1967 was a sign, a warning that the state had to deal with market failures, and to try, once again, to foster strong, politically non-aligned, organisations of workers, able to use democratic institutions and lawful means. For pragmatists, however, the fear of social revolution soon waned. 1967 had, they must have realised, failed to change how the ordinary person in Hong Kong thought; the masses had backed the colonial state and backed away from radicalism.[16]

The riots, however, exerted a long-term impact on how the British establishment in London thought of the importance of social reforms. The British Government's rising concern with Hong Kong's development now attained a strategic dimension. For London, one of the major lessons of the 1967 riots was that British rule in Hong Kong beyond 1997 was simply untenable: the CCP would neither forget nor forgive the humiliation inherent to the alien rule of Hong Kong and Chinese nationalism would not disappear anytime soon. According to a Cabinet study on Hong Kong in the aftermath of the riots, 'it is inconceivable that any communist Chinese government would "negotiate" an extension of the Hong Kong lease', and 'the Chinese intention is to take over Hong Kong by 1997 at the latest'.[17] A stable and prosperous Hong Kong could at least put Britain in a good bargaining position and social reforms could contribute to this cause, the report contended.

The confrontations, however, also had a negative impact on the trajectory of labour reforms in the colony in that they tarnished the image of leftist trade unions. Left-wing unionists who had been fully engaged in the riots were now seen by many as troublemakers or communist agents. They were marginalised from both the mainstream of society and the policy process. As the most organised labour groups were forced to withdraw from the policy debate, the inferior bargaining position of the working class vis-a-vis capital in the colony was further exacerbated. It was not until the early 1980s, when the issue of the future of Hong Kong finally came to the forefront of global attention, that they resumed their role in local politics.

1968

In September 1968, the 'Workers' University' was established at a factory in Shanghai. Although it started as a nebulous project with only forty-five students in a unit of 6,000 workers, soon after its inauguration the experiment was publicly endorsed by Mao Zedong, leading to a proliferation of similar initiatives all over the country. This essay examines how workers' universities gained political prominence during the Cultural Revolution and how workers studying at these institutions engaged in theoretical debate over whether China was on the path to communism or simply reproducing aspects of a capitalist political economy.

The Establishment of the First Workers' University

Andrea PIAZZAROLI LONGOBARDI

In July 1968, two years after the beginning of the Cultural Revolution, the Chinese Communist Party (CCP) decided to disband Red Guard student associations. This decision was possible only because, in the early months of 1967, workers' mobilisation became the main vector of revolutionary significance. Considering their importance for the national economy, workers exerted substantial influence on local politics, which eclipsed the importance of squabbling students.

Student factionalism raised many questions about how to actualise the goals of the Cultural Revolution in the field of education. Since it was a revolution in the cultural sphere, education should have been a central part of it. However, it was never clear how to transform education according to communist principles. The first steps of economic transition to communism had already been roughly theorised, entailing measures to collectivise the means of production and to submit production and distribution to state planning, but what changes would be necessary in the educational field? This was one of the main questions at the centre of the Educational Revolution (教育革命) campaign, which started during the Great Leap Forward in the late 1950s and was escalated and radicalised during the Cultural Revolution, with the increasing participation of workers. As Zhang Chunqiao, one of the members of the Central Cultural Revolution Small Group (中央文革小组), remarked on the occasion of a visit to the Shanghai Machine Tools Factory (上海机床厂, SMTF) on 22 July 1968:

> Educational Revolution is not only a matter of schools. To lean only on schools to carry it—I will say an impolite phrase—is to do it wrong. It is better to rely on the Party, the workers, on poor and middle peasants, on the People's Liberation Army … So, the Educational Revolution really is not a matter of schools; after its rise in schools, it has to come to the factory and the commune.[1]

The SMTF exerted a substantial influence on Maoist educational experiments in the Great Leap Forward and Cultural Revolution. Mao himself visited the factory as early as 1957, making it a national example. Machine tools were a fundamental product for Chinese industrial development at the time, as they stood for national independence from Soviet technology and assistance. Promoting political and technical education to workers in this kind of factory meant supporting national technological development at the level of local initiatives. Some workers in the SMTF had actively participated since 1956 in political study groups, which later gained strength during the Cultural Revolution, particularly during 1967, when the focus of political mobilisation shifted from students to workers.

As workers were called on to 'take the leadership in everything' (工人阶级必须领导一切) in a famous article written in August 1968 by Yao Wenyuan, another member of the Central Cultural Revolution Small Group, a team of workers in the SMTF set up the first Workers' University (工人大学). Throughout the university's history, both its form and its content were debated, and different types of organisation were tried, some of which failed. Most importantly, the example of the Workers' University was replicated in different forms all over the country, to such an extent that, in 1974, the CCP calculated that around 330 formal schools had been established inside factories in all provinces.[2] One year later, the number grew to approximately 500.[3]

In this essay, I outline the events leading to the creation of the SMTF Workers' University, show how this initiative resulted in political experiments in production units and, finally, discuss some examples of the theoretical output produced in these universities.

Political Crisis and Invention

The events of the January Storm of 1967 (一月风暴; see also Thornton's essay in the present volume) and the aftermath of the Shanghai Commune unveiled the saturation and subsequent loss of meaning of some political categories then in use, such as 'class' (阶级), 'power seizure' (夺权) and even 'revolution' (革命). This does not suggest that this conceptual network was perceived as outdated or detached from reality, but rather that the complexity and practical contradictions of these concepts were on full display, particularly in a society engaged in what was believed to be a transition to fully fledged communism. Both Party leadership and grassroots militants questioned how to engage in a revolution that required taking over state power from the hands of the Communist Party. In December 1966, Zhang Chunqiao described the situation in these terms: 'Some people say: "This is revolution ... that is revolution." It is too much. These currents of thought are at all times reflected within the Party. This problem needs to be solved from practice.'[4] Zhang was referring to the different understandings of what 'revolution' actually was and how it would be actualised after the Communist takeover of the state. Probably alluding to Mao's 1937 essay 'On Practice', Zhang declared these conflicts could only be solved 'from the empirical experience' (从实践中解决), which meant that only practice, political mobilisation and experience could clearly answer how to carry the revolutionary process towards communism.

In 1966 and 1967, Red Guards disseminated political debates and examined the historical records of many cadres. This resulted not only in the dismissal of some officials, but also in violent acts during public criticism sessions. Another consequence with profound political meaning was the instilment in the population of the habit of scrutinising the Party leadership—both their words and their actions.[5] What Mao in 1967 called 'the Red Guard broom' (红卫兵扫帚) breached the separation between 'inside' and 'outside' the Party, paving the way for unprecedented grassroots supervision of and participation in the Party-State's agenda.[6]

These developments notwithstanding, the workers were the ones who started to actualise political inventions from within their units, while at the same time attempting to maintain production output.[7] In declaration after declaration, Mao, Zhou Enlai and the members of the Central Cultural Revolution Small Group emphasised the importance of consolidating a positive political direction to the uprisings—in this case, the criticism of the 'Seventy Articles', a particular document that regulated industrial management (see Hirata's essay in the present volume)—so that the revolutionary current would not be undermined by factionalism. Fundamental to the Cultural Revolution was the question of the construction of the 'new'—what Zhou called 'inventions' (创造) and Mao referred to as 'newborn things' (新生事物).[8]

Seven days before the meeting that officially dismissed the Red Guards on 28 July 1968, the *People's Daily* published a report about some experiments developed at the SMTF with a personal comment from Mao promoting the example to the whole country.[9] The article explained that, in that factory, there was a project to train technicians from among the workers, focusing in particular on four aspects: 1) engineers agreed to share technical information with workers; 2) engineers were working a few hours per week in the production line; 3) workers had joined the technical commission and were taking part in meetings regarding production management; and 4) there were committees comprising workers, cadres and technicians set up to manage sectors of the factory. The report stated that an engineer who had no direct experience on the production line was more susceptible to make mistakes; conversely, a worker who did not understand how to read a project, or the theory behind it, would be more likely to do something wrong in their practice. Moreover, efforts to keep manual labourers from participating in planning activities were to be considered a waste of resources and limitation on technological innovation. The report also declared that workers trained as technicians tended to have a degree of political consciousness and sense of collectivity that made it possible for them to consider productive labour as a contribution to society, while engineers may cultivate an 'individualistic' character, tending to work for profit or power.

On the occasion of his visit to the SMTF in July 1968, Zhang Chunqiao gave a speech in which he traced a 'historical line' connecting that moment in 1968 to an earlier visit Mao had paid to the factory, in 1957: 'At that time, we were in the middle of the Anti-rightist Campaign, and based on that debate, it became clear that workers should be trained and form a new class of intellectuals, otherwise the Dictatorship of the Proletariat could not be consolidated.'[10]

By relating the experience of 1968 with Mao's visit, Zhang attempted to combine popular initiative with the leadership of the Party—in other words, to present the experience of the SMTF as a democratic experiment with the imprimatur of authority. Zhang continued to argue that the experiments in the factory could be a prototype for a national revolution in education because they combined manual and intellectual activities, alternating workers, students and professors in positions of productive labour, study and teaching.

By including the experiments in the SMTF in the Educational Revolution, this and other speeches by prominent Party leaders promoted the rise of a new project: the Workers' University, which would be formally announced in September 1968 by a group of workers in the SMTF. The decision to use the word 'university' was particularly consequential, as would become clear in the following years.

Experiments and New Questions

In its first report, published in July 1969, the SMTF Workers' University declared it had started its activities with fifty-two students chosen from among the 6,000 workers in the unit.[11] Of this group, 'the majority had completed only primary education, the minority had finished high school, and eight have not finished primary education'. The word 'university' did not imply the existence of a building or even a specific room for the classes; in SMTF, as in most other work units, classes were simply held inside the factory, promoting political studies and literacy as much as technical knowledge.[12] Most professors in the workers' universities were experienced workers and intellectuals from conventional educational institutions.[13]

The experience of setting up a university in a production unit raised many questions. Should it have the same type of pedagogy as other universities? What defined its 'proletarian' or 'revolutionary' character, its students, its methods and its results? These and other topics were debated at least until the death of Mao and the imprisonment of the remaining members of the Central Cultural Revolution Small Group in 1976, and continued even until workers' universities were changed into common technical schools in 1978.[14]

When the first cohort of students graduated from the three-year course in engineering in 1971, part of the leadership of the SMTF Workers' University advocated that, after graduation, worker-students should go back to the production line instead of occupying positions as engineers or managers in the factory. Their aim was political: to discontinue a system in which the privilege of studying led to leadership positions and to prove that mental and manual labourers could work together in all spheres of production. Moreover, the clear implication was that anyone, proletarian or not, could make mistakes and act as capitalists if their political role reproduced old social structures. As one SMTF worker declared: 'The political environment of the Workers' University is good, but it is not a "red security box". I have the deepest consideration for Mao Zedong's policies and towards the Party, but a simple "class feeling" does not substitute the consciousness of the line struggle.'[15]

Nonetheless, the request that worker-students come back to the production line after graduation was not welcomed by all participants. Some questioned: 'This new type of graduate, is new in what way, exactly?'[16] Others asked: 'Some people ask what kind of "position" do I have [当一

个什么"员"]?'[17] The answers to these questions were idealistic: 'I believe it is not to forget I am a worker ... Every day, after class, I go back to the factory shed and work with all comrades ... when there is a problem, we solve it together.'[18] The objective was personal and political: to be able to take part in production and political mobilisation, to 'go up and go down' (能上能下)—that is, occupy positions in the leadership and in manual labour—and to 'be able to write and fight' (能文能武).[19]

Wang Defa, one of the leaders of the SMTF Workers' University, mentioned that some had criticised the institution as being a 'primary school with secondary school books and a "university" sign on the front door'.[20] Critiques like this were common even among workers and, in response, university members started to write reports with examples of graduated workers who devised technological innovations, highlighting their contribution to enhancing production output.[21] In fact, these reports were marred by deep contradictions. They attempted to prove the economic advantages of forming new technicians from among workers, however, output numbers could not reveal the political and social advantages of the program of study. The real breakthrough of the workers' universities was in their reconfiguration of the relations of production, which did not map easily into technical and economic language.

Analyses from the Factory Floor

As part of the adult education initiative that took off thanks to the newly established workers' universities, many writing manuals aimed at adults were published, starting in 1968. The increased literacy also resulted in innumerable collections of workers' articles, some of which were published in local and national journals.

A good example of this new editorial phenomenon can be found in an article published in 1975 about the production quota mechanism—one element of the socialist planned economy, by which production output and quality were predetermined by the government and assigned to each work unit.[22] This text attempts to distinguish between 'true and false' Marxism—that is, political practices that actually lead to communism and capitalist policies 'disguised' by Marxist-Leninist terminology.[23] It starts with a quotation from a factory worker named Wang Gongxiao, who in a letter to a colleague allegedly asked whether the production quota was, in fact, a capitalist or a communist policy.[24] On the one hand, he avers that production quotas help to advance backward technology and production output, which can be useful to the socialist construction. On the other hand, he continues, the system homogenises the labour capacities of different individuals, subsuming labour into abstract capital, thus acting as a capitalist dynamic.

The article continues in the form of a letter written by another worker, named Ye Baile, in reply to Wang. It starts with a common argument of the period, declaring that if capitalists have been defeated in the revolution, there are no exploiters who could 'take away' added value and perpetrate class exploitation, and therefore 'the quota system has gone through a fundamental change of its character and role' within socialism. This notwithstanding, Ye further elaborates the contradiction proposed by his interlocutor, declaring that the quota system also sets a specific time for production output, virtually equating the capacity of each worker, calculating it as time, not as labour, and thus reinforcing the division of labour. In his words: '[The quota system] uses a unified unit to measure each labourer, and does not consider the level of technical knowledge or physical force of each individual. Thus, in this aspect, it acts as capitalist legal power.'[25]

The text continues by situating this contradiction within the communist aim of bringing forth a society in which each person receives according to their needs and gives according to their abilities, proposing that if 'each gives according to their abilities', thus reinforcing the communist character of the contradiction, workers themselves might be able to restrain the capitalist aspect of the production quota system. Ye affirms that if the quota system is set without direct political control from the workers, it could reinforce capitalist policies such as the use of material incentives: 'Some people … use the quota system as an excuse to promote material incentives and awards—this is a way to reinforce the capitalist character of the quota system.'

To prevent this capitalistic resurgence, Ye proposes that production be directly managed by the workers: 'Production development and advances need to go through public debates, formulating new quotas, setting new strenuous targets.' This proposition is coherent with a coeval debate on the internal contradictions of socialism. These questions did not crop up overnight but developed throughout discussions that took place over the previous two decades. By 1975, there was a clear directive from the CCP to all study groups to analyse empirical situations and distinguish, in local and national policies, the contradictions between 'capitalist and communist vectors'—that is, policies that could lead the political economy back to capitalism or forwards to actual communism.[26] Accordingly, the way to limit capitalist structures remaining in socialism would be to reinforce communist policies and inventions—in particular, by strengthening the direct participation of workers in the spheres of administration and education.

Filling a Gap

The mobilisation campaigns carried out during the Cultural Revolution brought up important theoretical questions about the coherence and effectiveness of socialist policies. At times, the crises and even failure of some political campaigns triggered new theoretical debates, as was the case with Red Guard factionalism.

The brief history of the workers' universities and the debates to define their form and aims are important topics through which to comprehend the events of the Cultural Revolution from a grassroots perspective. This essay lingered in particular on two aspects of these institutions: the difficulty of defining their programs and role in the political economy, and the significance their members assigned to political experimentation, which was considered as important as theoretical and technical study. Studying in a workers' university actually entailed theoretical analysis of practical experiences.

Workers' universities, together with other study groups set in rural and urban production units, filled a social gap for individuals who previously were not considered apt to engage in political debates or set forth new theoretical hypotheses. However, there was never any consensus in Chinese society about the social and political economy value of these institutions, as shown in the persistent reports attempting to 'prove' their effective contribution to the national economy. Yet, those engaged in the project persisted and produced interesting and complex political analyses.

In the example of the article criticising the production quota system examined in this essay, we can see that workers who engaged in these universities were far from convinced about any ideas of a predetermined 'triumph' of socialism. This is in line with the belief—widely disseminated during the Cultural Revolution—in the persistence of the line struggle within socialism, based on the conviction that socialism was not a 'secure' society that would automatically lead to communism. Accordingly, the only chance to actually accomplish the transition to communism was to maintain an open space for political experimentation and for the direct participation of workers in the management of production and also in the educational field. This would be the only way to establish policies that would blur and eventually overcome class inequality. Yet, these articles were ripe with doubts, as befitted their experimental character and political ideals.

1969

In April 1969, Mao Zedong convened the Ninth Congress of the Chinese Communist Party, which was intended to put an end to the mass upheavals of the Cultural Revolution. At that moment, hundreds of thousands of workers joined a series of rallies in the central city of Wuhan under the banner 'Oppose restoring the old!'. The rallies were organised by the city's rebel factions, which—with Mao's support—had overthrown the local Party authorities, prevailed over the conservative workers' faction organised to support these authorities and taken control of the city's factories and newly organised municipal Workers' Congress. They had also engaged in violent factional conflicts among themselves, but they now united to challenge the direction of the Ninth Party Congress and oppose the marginalisation of their representatives in the new revolutionary committees created to govern Wuhan's factories and city administration. This essay examines this movement, which revealed in sharp relief the aspirations and tensions that animated the Cultural Revolution. The main analytical concern is the extent to which rebel workers' organisations during the Cultural Revolution acted autonomously.

'Oppose Restoring the Old!': The Culmination of the Rebel Workers' Movement in Wuhan during the Cultural Revolution

Joel ANDREAS

Modern Chinese history is replete with highly contentious workers' movements, but none as massive or widespread as that during the Cultural Revolution. Between autumn 1966 and the spring of 1969, workers organised huge rallies, marches, factory occupations, sieges and street battles involving tens of millions of people. Never before—or since—have Chinese workers mobilised in such large numbers or for such an extended period. The movement spanned cities and towns throughout the country, encompassed every sector of industry (and beyond) and the participants were highly politicised and class conscious. Workers across the country divided into rebel and conservative factions: the rebels were inspired by Mao Zedong's call to challenge local Chinese Communist Party (CCP) authorities, while the conservatives defended these authorities.

Some observers write off this historical chapter, reasoning that workers were not acting on their own, but rather were mobilised as part of a conflict between Mao and other CCP leaders. It is true, of course, that Mao initiated the Cultural Revolution and the mass factional conflicts of this period were shaped by contention among CCP leaders and local officials.[1] The questions I will address in this essay involve the extent of their autonomy: Were the rebel workers' organisations that emerged during the Cultural Revolution pursuing their own interests, as they perceived them? Were they acting on their own or were they simply following directives issued from above?

The answers to these questions, I will argue, must be nuanced. On the one hand, the rebel movement was inspired by Mao, it could not have existed without his support and rebel workers generally did their best to follow his lead. On the other hand, the rebels were self-organised, they effectively challenged factory and municipal Party authorities and they forcefully raised demands for popular participation (see also Thornton's essay in the present volume). The rebel camp was made up of small, loosely affiliated 'fighting groups', there was no hierarchy of authority that connected them to Beijing and, although they generally followed Mao's lead, there were critical moments in which they did not.

A few scholars have looked closely at these exceptional moments. There have been a number of accounts, for instance, of workers' efforts to raise economic demands, which took place mainly in the early weeks of the workers' movement, before Mao denounced 'economism' (经济主义). Many workers attempted to win improved conditions and welfare in their own work units and temporary workers organised a remarkable national movement to demand permanent status.[2] In addition, there has been scholarship about 'ultra-left' ideas and organisations, especially theorists of the *Shengwulian* (省无联) tendency in Hunan, who advanced a critique of the 'Red capitalist class' (红色资本家阶级).[3]

This essay examines what was in some ways rebel workers' most defiant coordinated action: the Oppose Restoring the Old (反复旧, *Fan Fujiu*) movement that took place in the spring of 1969. By that time, Mao and the leadership of the CCP had been trying to rein in the mass factional contention of the Cultural Revolution for well over a year. The *Fan Fujiu* movement, which mobilised massive rallies in major cities around the country, directly challenged the CCP leadership, especially because the most audacious actions coincided with the CCP's Ninth Congress, with which Mao intended to definitively signal an end to the mass upheavals of the Cultural Revolution. The *Fan Fujiu* movement exposed in sharp relief the aspirations and tensions that animated the Cultural Revolution, and it revealed both the extent and the limits of rebel autonomy.

While the *Fan Fujiu* movement encompassed many cities, in this essay, I will examine the movement in Wuhan, a large industrial city in Hubei Province that straddles the Yangzi River. Although the first skirmishes of the Cultural Revolution were in schools, by the end of 1966, workers had come to dominate the contending factions and, by the end of 1968, students had gone to the countryside, leaving workers to stage the *Fan Fujiu* movement. I was able to interview seventeen individuals who were involved in the upheavals of the Cultural Revolution in Wuhan, including several key leaders of the *Fan Fujiu* movement, as well as other rebel and conservative activists in a number of large factories. I have also made use of valuable information provided in accounts of the *Fan Fujiu* movement in Wuhan published by Shaoguang Wang and Lao Tian, as well as reports on how the movement developed in other cities.[4] Before examining the events of the spring of 1969, I will provide necessary context by briefly tracing the rise of the rebel workers' movement in China, and its specific trajectory in Wuhan.[5]

Rebels Loyal to Mao

The Cultural Revolution was a highly unusual social movement in which Mao called on students, workers and villagers to attack the local officials of his own ruling party. There are many theories about why Mao chose to do this. I have argued that the Cultural Revolution can best be understood as the culmination of a series of experiments intended to find effective means of 'mass supervision' (群众监督)—the CCP's term for mobilising the population to help the Party control its own cadres.[6] Although the CCP was a highly disciplined party with effective top-down controls, it was concerned that these had to be reinforced by bottom-up supervision. Mao and other Party leaders worried that, without supervision from below as well as from above, it would be impossible to effectively enforce Party policies and curb corruption, the abuse of power and especially 'bureaucratism' (官僚主义)—that is, isolation of cadres from the masses. The trick in managing mass supervision campaigns had long been finding a way to give workers and villagers enough autonomy to effectively criticise wrongdoing by local Party leaders without endangering central control over the movements.

In previous mass supervision campaigns, such as the Three Antis and Five Antis movements in the early 1950s and the Four Cleans campaign in the early 1960s, the CCP typically dispatched outside work teams of Party cadres to mobilise workers to criticise factory leaders. While these movements were effective in curbing corruption and other vices, by the mid-1960s, Mao was convinced they reinforced bureaucratic behaviour by only allowing the masses to raise their voices under work team tutelage. When he launched the Cultural Revolution in the summer of 1966, therefore, although he initially permitted Party officials to again send work teams to schools and factories, he then condemned the work teams for suppressing the masses and encouraged students and eventually workers to throw them out and form their own 'rebel groups'. Moreover, he gave these groups licence to attack factory Party leaders, all of whom were open to the charge that they were 'following the capitalist road'.

By the autumn of 1966, workers in Chinese factories had split into two camps: rebels, who attacked the enterprises' Party leadership, and conservatives, who defended it. The rebel camp was made up of many small, self-organised groups led largely by workers; some were disaffected rank-and-file Party members, but most had never joined the Party. The conservative camp—usually larger and better organised—was typically led by base-level cadres. Nevertheless, by the end of the year, the rebels—with Mao's support—had effectively paralysed factory Party organisations, leaving the conservative camp discouraged and in retreat. Then, in January 1967, Mao astonishingly called on the rebels to 'seize power' (夺权).

Mao, however, never intended the rebels to unilaterally take control of China's factories. Rather, he called on the military to dispatch small teams of officers to factories to oversee the formation of 'revolutionary committees' (革命委员会) comprising these officers, veteran Party cadres and 'mass representatives' (群众代表)—that is, leaders of the rebel groups. As might be expected, the formation of these committees was a highly contentious process and the military officers, contrary to Mao's instructions, were generally not inclined to support the rebels.

In Wuhan, as elsewhere, disparate rebel groups quickly coalesced into moderate and radical camps. The moderate alliance, which called itself the New Faction (新派), was more inclined to cooperate with the military, while the radical alliance, known as the Steel Faction (钢派), insisted that rebels take full control of factories. In February and March, the military detained leaders of the Steel Faction and drove the organisation underground. After Mao denounced the suppression of the rebels in April, however, the moderate and radical rebel factions joined forces and went back on the offensive. In response, conservative workers and cadres, with military support, also regrouped, forming a powerful confederation called the Million Heroes (百万雄师). Violent confrontations ensued as rebels and conservatives battled for control of factories, with rebels suffering the most casualties. In July, conservative militants kidnapped and beat up high-level envoys dispatched by Mao to mediate the conflict. Mao harshly condemned the 'Wuhan Incident' and removed the military units that had supported the Million Heroes from the city. The conservative confederation collapsed and rebels triumphantly took control of Wuhan's factories, violently settling scores with their adversaries.

Seeking to consolidate their newfound authority, rebel factions restored industrial production, while continuing to promote their own political agendas—efforts that were often at odds. 'The rebels took power in the work units and used work unit money to publish newspapers,' a rebel leader told me. 'If different rebel groups in a work unit had different thinking then they would publish different newspapers.'[7]

That autumn, workers in every work unit were instructed to elect delegates to municipal and provincial workers' congresses, who in turn—together with delegates elected to new peasants' and students' congresses—were to elect the members of the provincial revolutionary committee. A new cohort of military officers was dispatched to preside over the process. With the conservative faction sidelined, the Steel and New factions each vied to promote their own leaders and 'pull' old cadres to join their lists. After the two rebel coalitions failed to agree on a single list, the military leaders finally decided the composition of the provincial revolutionary committee in February 1968. Nearly one-quarter of the committee members, including the chair and vice-chair, were military officers, with the remaining seats divided evenly between the rebel leaders and old cadres nominated by each of the two rebel factions.[8]

The election of the provincial committee was followed by elections of municipal and enterprise committees, as well as workshop committees within factories. A rebel leader described the process to me this way: 'Each organisation held their own meeting to choose their own representatives. Then it was decided in a big meeting how many representatives each organisation would get. Everyone had to agree. They negotiated and compromised. It was relatively democratic.'[9] Nevertheless, competition for control over revolutionary committees led to a new round of violent confrontations, this time among the rebel groups. Finally, in the autumn of 1968, Mao insisted that rebel factions around the country disband, cease publishing their own newspapers and turn in their weapons.

Until that time, workers recalled, revolutionary committees had met regularly and rebels held sway in many of Wuhan's factories. Now military officers began to assert their authority more aggressively. They began reorganising Party committees, which excluded rebel leaders who were not Party members, and made decisions without consulting the broader revolutionary committees. They not only marginalised rebel leaders, but also began punishing the most recalcitrant as part of the Cleansing of the Class Ranks campaign.[10] 'That was the big question', a rebel leader told me, explaining why the rebels took to the streets again in early 1969. 'The mass representatives on the revolutionary committees could not play the role they were supposed to play. That's why they called it "restoring the old".'[11]

Opposing the Restoration of the Old

The *Fan Fujiu* movement was launched in Shandong Province in November 1968 and soon spread to Anhui, Fujian, Guangxi, Guizhou, Gansu, Henan, Hubei, Jiangsu, Jiangxi, Shanxi, Sichuan and other provinces.[12] The geographic extent of the movement was all the more remarkable because rebels had been barred from organising across provincial boundaries.

In January 1969, rebels in Wuhan joined the movement and began to openly defy the city's military leaders. As rebel organisations had been folded into workers' congresses, these organisations became key organising vehicles. 'Although our organisations have been disbanded, there is still the Workers' Congress,' a rebel publication declared. 'The Workers' Congress is the core of leadership for us. We do not acknowledge the authority of the military representatives. We do not acknowledge the authority of the puppet revolutionary committee.'[13]

The Steel Faction and the New Faction were still in a competitive mode, with the latter continuing to enjoy relatively favourable treatment by the military, but by mid-March leaders of the two factions decided to band together to resist efforts to sideline and suppress them. They understood it was a risky move. A radio factory worker who had become a leader of the New Faction and was instrumental in initiating the *Fan Fujiu* movement, told me: 'We decided we're all rebels. We'll go forward together, we'll live together or we'll die together.'[14]

On 16 March, leaders of the two factions penned a big character poster, titled—in dramatic Cultural Revolution style—'I shed my blood for the people and the liberation of mankind', calling on workers to once again take to the streets. Overnight, rebels plastered copies of the poster across the city, launching a movement sharply at odds with the message of 'unity' that was the watchword of the upcoming Ninth Party Congress.

Although the rebel organisations had been compelled to close their own newspapers, they controlled the official Workers' Congress newspaper, *Wuhan Workers* (武汉工人). Until then it had largely echoed the line emanating from Beijing; now they converted it into a vehicle to denounce the local military authorities. They began publishing the newspaper more frequently and used it to condemn increasing military control over the revolutionary committees, the sidelining of worker representatives, the suspension of revolutionary committees in factories in which the rebels held sway and the persecution of rebel activists.

The rebels hoped to consolidate their power in workers' congresses at the factory level and turn them into more autonomous organisations. Accordingly, they demanded that factory workers' congresses not be subordinated unilaterally to factory revolutionary committees, but instead also be accountable to the citywide workers' congress. In factories, they worked to enhance the power of workers' congresses they controlled, take over others they did not, and revive congresses that had become inactive. A wave of wildcat strikes swept Wuhan, encouraged by the municipal workers' congress.[15] While the central demands were about shifting the relative power of workers' congresses, revolutionary committees, Party committees and the military representatives, the movement was also inspired by debates and disputes about factory rules and practices, which had become grist for rebel accusations about the restoration of old power structures and old ways of management.

Starting in mid-March, rebel leaders employed the municipal and factory-level workers' congresses to mobilise a series of massive rallies, which grew in size as the Ninth Party Congress met in Beijing from 1 April to 24 April. On 27 April, they convened a mass rally reportedly attended by 500,000 people.[16] During the first weeks of May, they continued to hold huge rallies and rebel leaders became bolder in their denunciations of Hubei's military leaders, demanding they make self-criticisms before the masses. Rebel groups reorganised in hundreds of factories across the city and reportedly took power from the existing revolutionary committee leadership in 180 work units. On 11 May, 100 trucks carrying rebel activists surrounded the headquarters of the provincial and municipal revolutionary committees.[17]

In early May, more than twenty rebel leaders and military representatives were summoned from Wuhan to Beijing. The rebels travelled to the capital hoping to make their case to top Party leaders, as they had been able to do in previous meetings in Beijing. Over the course of nearly two weeks, they met numerous times with Zhou Enlai, Chen Boda, Kang Sheng and other top leaders. In the meetings, they were admonished for pursuing factionalism, but they defended their actions. 'We didn't give up,' the New Faction leader told me, recalling that they argued that their protests were justified because they were being marginalised and suppressed.[18] Ultimately, however, Mao approved a document, known as the '27 May Directive', that criticised the rebels for attacking the military and 'placing the workers' congress above the revolutionary committee'.[19]

The directive opened the way for military leaders in Wuhan to carry out a wave of repression against the rebels, who were no longer in a position to resist. 'Because the centre and Mao had criticised us,' the New Faction leader explained, 'what could we say?'[20] In November, more than 1,000 rebel leaders were sent to Beijing for 'study'—a euphemism for intensive interrogation and political pressure sessions, which lasted for six months. Thousands more endured such sessions in their own factories. This repression was folded into the nationwide 'One Strike and Three Antis' campaign and the drive to ferret out '16 May elements', during which thousands of rebels in Wuhan were locked up, some for several years.[21]

The rebels were able to regroup after Mao and the CCP leadership criticised the military representatives and removed them from factory and government administration in 1972. Over the next four years, with Mao's renewed support, rebels mounted a series of new offensives. During the Criticise Lin Biao and Confucius campaign in 1973–74, they revived factory workers' congresses and once again used them as vehicles for mass mobilisation. They abducted military officers, compelling them to face the wrath of workers in the factories they had managed, and thousands of workers surrounded the Party headquarters in Wuhan demanding—and winning—freedom for rebel leaders who remained in prison. Then, in 1975 and 1976, along with former rebel leaders around the country, they mobilised workers to support a new campaign that promoted radical policies and toppled Deng Xiaoping. Their movement, however, was decisively crushed after Mao's death in September 1976.

Discussion

Can we call a workers' movement that was completely dependent on Mao autonomous? Clearly, the rebels' autonomy was profoundly limited, as they had little choice but to follow Mao's agenda. That meant that, while they were free to attack cadres' privileges, corruption and authoritarian behaviour, they could not raise economic demands and, while they could overthrow local Party officials, they could not fundamentally challenge the Party's authority. Moreover, their complete dependence on Mao was revealed when he withdrew his support. Without it, they were unable to defend themselves against repression and retribution by the Party establishment. After Mao used the rebels to attack local Party officials, he abandoned them to their fate.

Rebels followed Mao's agenda, however, not simply because of practical power constraints; their worldview was fundamentally shaped—and limited—by the Maoist vision. All social movements, of course, wear ideological lenses and blinders fashioned within the societies they inhabit. The lenses and blinders worn by rebel workers during the Cultural Revolution gave them a particularly righteous and fervent class consciousness, which included the idea that workers should run the factories in which they work. The CCP, of course, had long promoted the slogan that workers were the 'masters of the factory'. During the Cultural Revolution, Mao gave this idea a subversive twist, telling workers they were being denied their rightful role by bureaucratic Party officials.

Regardless of the limits of their autonomy in terms of practical power and vision, the rebels were self-organised and not subordinate to any organisational hierarchy. Not only were they autonomous from the local Party organisation, but their overriding purpose was to challenge its authority and, although they sought to follow Mao, they had to interpret his unpredictable and sometimes ambiguous messages themselves. They, therefore, had no choice but to think for themselves and, at critical moments, their thinking—and actions—deviated from Mao's agenda. This essay has recounted one such moment, when rebels in Wuhan and other cities disagreed with the direction in which Mao was leading them and went their own way, hoping he would follow.

1970

In the wake of the Sino-Soviet split of the early 1960s, the Chinese Communist Party recast its foreign policy into a 'Third World' struggle against the twin imperialisms of the United States and the Soviet Union. In concrete terms, this translated into increased Chinese foreign aid to fellow non-aligned, autonomous socialist countries, with work teams from China having a hand in constructing dozens of turnkey aid projects all over the world. By committing their own labour power and expertise to develop infrastructure in these countries, Chinese leaders sought to position China as the beaming sun from which Third World socialism emanated. The African continent occupied a privileged position in this diplomatic effort. In particular, the Tanzania–Zambia (Tan–Zam) Railway, built in the first half of the 1970s, is to this day held up fondly by the Chinese authorities as a symbol of Sino-African friendship. This essay looks into the lived experiences of the Chinese workers and technical experts who helped build the railway.

Building *Uhuru*: Chinese Workers and Labour Diplomacy on the Tan–Zam Railway

Matthew GALWAY

'Serve the Revolutionary People of the World', 1971. Image courtesy of the IISH Stefan R. Landsberger Collection, chineseposters.net/posters/e39-614.php.

On returning from his visit to Tanzania in 1968–69, civil rights leader and author Robert F. Williams reflected on his ten-day, 1,470-mile (2,366-kilometre) round-trip motorcycle adventure from Dar es Salaam to Kapiri Mposhi in the journal *The Call*. During the trip, which he undertook to emulate 'the long marches of the young Red Guards' and 'the cross-country treks of China's youth', he was struck by the initial construction of the Tanzania–Zambia (Tan–Zam) Railway. As he rode along it, witnessing Chinese technicians working alongside Tanzanian and Zambian labourers, he concluded that 'Africa's potential will be unlimited'.[1] Similarly, at a banquet during his second visit to the People's Republic of China (PRC) in 1968, Tanzanian President Julius Nyerere reminisced about observing 'the revolutionary spirit' of the

Chinese people on the occasion of an earlier visit in 1965. He expressed the wish that 'all the people of Tanzania could visit China and witness for themselves what a determined people can accomplish.'[2] He continued:

> If we really want to move from national independence to the real independence of the people, and if we really want to make sure that the African revolution will ever move forward, and not degenerate into neocolonialism, then I say that we should learn from you [China]. Indeed, from what I have seen of China in 1965, I must say that if you found it necessary to begin a cultural revolution [to] make sure that the new generation would carry forward the banner of your revolution, then certainly we need one.[3]

Nyerere wondered how he might transmit the Chinese work ethic, discipline, and revolutionary spark to his homeland. After his return home, on inspecting Chinese-financed Tan–Zam construction sites and the Urafiki (Friendship) Textile Mill—another landmark Chinese-funded project—Nyerere was taken aback by Chinese technical workers' work ethic, vigour, zeal, and competence. 'Disciplined work is essential,' he noted, 'and here once again our Chinese technicians have set us a great example.'[4]

Although many Tanzanians made the journey to China to study and train, the Chinese Communist Party (CCP) also sent its nationals to Tanzania. In exchange for 'unfettered access' to Tanzanian ports, and only after Euro-American firms refused to pledge aid to the country, the PRC 'flooded Tanzania with teachers, doctors, technological support, monetary aid, cultural productions, and a range of other collaborative and unilateral assistance'.[5] Unilateral assistance, in particular, stood out as Maoist China's greatest contribution to the developing world. In 1964 alone, China dedicated more than US$45 million in aid to Tanzania— about half of Beijing's yearly aid commitment on the continent.[6] The sum also covered the transport of a Chinese Railway Expert Team (中国铁路专家组) of 40–50,000 technical personnel, their living accommodation, and the employment of 50–60,000 local labourers. In the midst of the Cultural Revolution, the Chinese authorities committed to loan to Tanzania and Zambia 988 million yuan, 868 million of which (approximately US$400 million) was interest-free, which both countries would use for infrastructure projects and repay over three decades after a five-year deferral.[7] Beijing's goal was twofold: 1) to spur economic development in both Tanzania and Zambia by linking the latter's Copper Belt (Zambia exported 700,000 tonnes of copper annually) to the former's ports; and 2) to decouple both countries from dependency on apartheid South Africa and white-dominated Rhodesia by securing cargo transport in East and southern Africa, thus facilitating Zambian support for anticolonial struggles in Angola, Southern Rhodesia, and South Africa.[8] As one Chinese Railway Expert Team member recalled, the Tan–Zam Railway 'accomplished its mission in both senses'.[9] A third goal, however, underpinned this substantial commitment: the export of model labour as the quintessence of Third World socialist solidarity.

A Leap Forward in African Development

Chinese labour on the Tan–Zam Railway was a material manifestation of the greater China–Tanzania friendship, which was solidified in a 1965 treaty that spanned the next decade. Du Jian, an interpreter who joined the Chinese labour team in Tanzania in 1969, witnessed the railway's construction firsthand and continued to track its growth across four decades. For him, the Tan–Zam Railway stood as a lasting embodiment of the friendship between China and Africa: 'It is no exaggeration to say that China exerted all its strength—in terms of manpower, materials, and funds—to build this railway.'[10] China was, of course, undergoing the radical iconoclasm and political tumult of the Cultural Revolution, yet the CCP insisted on fronting the whole cost of the railway's construction. 'China shipped out more than 1.5 million tonnes of materials, including steel rail, cement, and dynamite, and daily necessities, even though it suffered itself a dire shortage of all commodities,' Du recounted. Mao Zedong and Zhou Enlai, in fact, 'personally oversaw a nationwide mobilisation' to vouchsafe that China was sending only its highest-grade supplies to Tanzania, and that Chinese factories, including the Wuhan Iron and Steel Plant, 'operated day and night' to meet material production quotas for the railway.

Why did the CCP commit to such a selfless, yet costly, endeavour? Between 1949 and 1965, socialism in China shifted from emphasising class revolution to a widescale anticolonial project aimed at casting out Euro-American imperialism from the Global South (see also Sorace and Zhu's essay in the present volume).[11] In the wake of the Sino-Soviet split of 1962, Chinese leaders made rhetorical commitments to waging Third World struggle against both US capitalist and Soviet socialist imperialisms, with Zhou declaring on his 1964 African tour that the continent was 'ripe for revolution'.[12] But words only went so far. Sino-African relations in the 1960s were reflective of China's foreign policy, as Beijing fostered economic and diplomatic ties with newly independent countries and anticolonial movements in an 'international united front' (国际统一战线).[13] By 1972, Chinese work teams had a hand in constructing nearly 100 different turnkey aid projects globally, and in 1973 the CCP had pledged aid to nearly thirty African nations.[14] Through these accomplishments, China burnished its credentials as an epicentre of anti-imperialism during the global 1960s and well into the long 1970s.[15]

The CCP sent teams of railway workers, engineers, and technicians—all of whom had to possess 'strong bodies, strong minds, and strong skills' in conjunction with a high ideological loyalty—to Tanzania to assist in developing socialism autonomously.[16] As a living, labouring embodiment of the CCP's global vision and a show of Beijing's dedication to socialist development in Tanzania, these Chinese work teams laboured shoulder-to-shoulder with Tanzanians to build the Tan–Zam Railway from 1970 to 1975. As Jamie Monson wrote, Chinese workers' model labour 'conveyed the values of modernity and progress through the practice of self-discipline and hard work' and exhibited 'socialist principles ... [of] international solidarity and brotherhood [to] foster worker discipline'.[17] In this new type of 'labour diplomacy', Chinese leaders positioned the PRC as the beaming sun from which Third World socialism emanated, and Chinese experts and labourers stood as embodiments of that ideology.[18] Through infrastructural development, Chinese technicians were to plant the seeds of socialism so the sun's rays could nourish them. Chinese technical workers' work ethic and vigour—both shaped by the Cultural Revolution's radical ethos—were also to be transmitted to their East African comrades. As Deborah Brautigam recounted:

> A local farmer told me how he was inspired to follow the example of the Chinese, who worked in the paddy fields by lantern into the night. 'You see the Chinese man there [in the fields] and you come.' Once a visiting member of parliament came to consult a doctor and was surprised to find him scrubbing the floor of the office. While the World Bank recruited chiefs for its integrated agricultural development projects, the Chinese asked to work only with 'peasant' farmers ... [T]he mobilization spirit of the Cultural Revolution reached its zenith in China's most audacious achievement in Africa: the Tanzania–Zambia railway.[19]

If the Chinese sowed the seeds, Tanzanians and Zambians were to tend the saplings and cultivate the flowers of autonomous socialist development. As one Chinese instructor, Ya Peiji, explained:

> After we complete this railway, if they [Tanzanians and Zambians] themselves do not know how to manage it, they will not know how to operate the railway ... the management has to be localized, which means that we will help Tanzania and Zambia to cultivate their own talent to manage this railway ... we will not only build this railway for them but we will make them feel that they are managing the railway themselves.[20]

Decades after its 1975 opening to the public—two years ahead of schedule, no less—the Tan–Zam Railway's lasting legacy as a monument to both the friendship between China and Tanzania and the international aspirations of the CCP has been recoded in the discourses that the Chinese authorities put forward to justify their Belt and Road Initiative (see also Halegua's essay in the present volume). Despite the enduring materiality of the railway, China's post-Mao marketisation has abandoned the Maoist imperative of world socialism via interest-free development, in pursuit of profit-driven resource acquisition for China's benefit.

Building the Railway

According to an agreement signed on 5 September 1967, the CCP pledged nearly one billion yuan (US$406 million, or US$2.62 billion inflation-adjusted) to build the nearly 2,000-kilometre-long railway. Originally conceived as a north–south Africa rail link by late-nineteenth-century British imperialist Cecil Rhodes, the Tan–Zam Railway eventually became China's 'largest international development project and the third-largest infrastructure development project in Africa'.[21] After an initial 1968–70 survey and design period, for which the CCP dispatched its surveyors to conduct a comprehensive appraisal of the terrain, construction began in 1970. Conditions were unfavourable, and access to first aid was limited to the extent that when one Chinese surveyor suffered a poisonous bee sting, he died.[22]

Problems were compounded with the arrival of Chinese technicians and management personnel. Alongside local workers, the Chinese Railway Expert Team endured food shortages, sweltering heat, isolation, an omnipresent risk of disease, and limited availability of medical care for illness or injury. Work was highly regimented and the hours were long. As Jamie Monson wrote:

> Work on the project was organized through twelve base camps, with centers of operations at Dar es Salaam and Mang'ula in Tanzania. Teams of workers were sent out from the base camps in smaller sub-teams, directed by African foremen and Chinese field assistants. The work gangs varied in size; at one base camp in 1972 there were 64 labor gangs involving some 5,500 workers. Work took place in isolated conditions, as the gangs could be spread out two to three miles apart during the workday. In some critical sections work continued around the clock in 8-hour shifts, with diesel generators providing electric light.[23]

Food was shipped from China, but the half-month voyage meant that staff on the ground were confined to eating dehydrated vegetables. Even soy sauce was a luxury. Sometimes, when supplies arrived, the wheat flour was already mouldy. Living in tents in the wilderness was dangerous, too. The men always had to check their shoes for snakes before putting them on in the morning. At night they could hear lions roaring outside.[24]

Veteran workers also encountered hardships while working on the project. An interview that was part of a *China Central Television* (*CCTV*) program included one account by an anonymous veteran of the Tan–Zam Railway that told of water scarcity, overwork, and extreme pressure to meet construction deadlines. 'Sometimes we had to drink the water that we found in the elephants' footprints,' the interviewee noted.[25] In all, more than 160 workers, sixty-four of whom were Chinese, died during the railway's construction.[26] Yet, in spite of all this, what truly mattered to many of those workers were the bonds of friendship and solidarity that they forged through shared struggle in the face of the world superpowers, and the conviction that they were building world socialism.

On the Tanzanian side, local communities also experienced significant duress during the Tan–Zam Railway's construction, as Nyerere ordered state seizures of farmland to make way for the railway. The state offered limited compensation for these lands and holding the authorities to account was often extremely difficult. For years after workers drove the final spike into the Tan–Zam Railway, many farmers complained of long-ignored compensation payments due for their lost crops and revenues. These losses were compounded by Nyerere's massive '*Ujamaa*' villagisation program, as state authorities forcefully relocated more than 1,300 households to establishments closer to the railway to safeguard the structure from damage and contribute to the state's massive agricultural production initiatives.[27]

At the national level, there were growing fears that Chinese investment would signal a forfeiture of Tanzanian economic and political sovereignty. However, government officials in Dodoma held that the construction of the Tan–Zam Railway and the stipulation of economic treaties with the PRC did not imperil either. Nyerere fervently asserted that the Tan–Zam Railway, like any other project of that kind, 'was a railway whether it was built by Chinese or Italians and it was not necessarily Red'.[28] He reiterated that Chinese assistance did not mean that Tanzania had deviated from its resolute commitment to self-reliance, autonomous socialist development, and nonalignment. Tanzanian Minister for Communications, Labour, and Works, J.M. Lusinde, echoed Nyerere's statement: 'The Tanzanian people are determined to see to it that the whole of Africa is liberated. And the construction of the railway is a contribution to the total liberation of Africa.'[29] Nyerere often dismissed charges that China was manipulating Tanzanian affairs through the Tan–Zam partnership and stressed Tanzania's agency in international exchanges.[30] He even remarked in response to Euro-American media's interpretation of his wearing the widely imitated 'Tanzania suit'—itself somewhat resembling a Mao suit—as indicative of his desire to imitate Maoist China: 'I gather that even the suits I wear have been adduced as evidence of pernicious Chinese influence.'[31]

Remembering the Railway Labourers Today

Decades after its completion, the Tan–Zam Railway holds contemporary relevance as a lasting monument to Maoist China's commitment to global anti-imperialism. For many in contemporary China, it remains a 'pinnacle of the kind of struggle, hardship, and "glorious achievement" pushed by Mao'.[32] The PRC's emphasis on collective sacrifice, especially in memorialising veterans and Chinese Railway Expert Team members who perished, not to mention Tanzanian and Zambian workers who also paid a price, 'parallels the tales of Daqing's Iron Man Wang Jingxi' and the 'agricultural brigade at Dazhai' (see also Clinton's essay in the present volume).[33] State officials from both China and Tanzania continue to make widely publicised visits to commemorate the heroic sacrifices of Chinese workers on the Tan–Zam Railway. Most notably, on 23 June 2006, Tanzanian Prime Minister Edward Lowasa joined PRC Premier Wen Jiabao in Dar es Salaam, where both leaders paid their respects at the Chinese Railway Expert cemetery on the city's outskirts at Gongo la Mboto, where sixty-four Chinese technicians who died while working on the project are buried. Wen laid flowers and a wreath on the monument to the 'Glorious Sacrifices of the Comrade Chinese Aid Experts in Tanzania' (中国援坦专家光荣牺牲同志), after which the officials observed a moment of silence.[34]

That same year—which in China was celebrated as the 'Year of Africa'—Chinese state media ensured that the Tan–Zam Railway story was broadcast throughout the country.[35] 'It is hard to find a speech or newspaper account about contemporary Africa–China relations that does not contain a glowing reference to the Tan–Zam Railway project and the heroism of the men who built it,' one journalist recounted.[36] At a press conference on Chinese aid to Africa, Vice-Minister of Commerce Fu Ziying noted how moved he was when he visited the railway personally:

> A few days ago, when I was paying respect to the Chinese workers who sacrificed their lives for the construction of [the] Tanzania–Zambia Railway at a public cemetery in Tanzania, I could not help bursting into tears for the tens of thousands of Chinese workers who laboured side-by-side with the Tanzanian and Zambian people to build the railway successfully.[37]

Despite the Tan–Zam Railway's domestic significance when it was built, the railway project was not without its critics in its time. The criticisms levelled against it curiously resonate with discussions today about Chinese engagements abroad. As mentioned above, some in Tanzania pointed to deals with China as signals of an impending loss of sovereignty. In spite of Chinese pledges to 'resolutely implement' Mao's teachings, Zhou's eight principles of foreign aid, and later Chairman Hua Guofeng's instructions to help develop the national economies of Tanzania and Zambia, there were still grave concerns about the scale, cost, and labour involved in a foreign-funded project. Even more worrying was the fact that Tanzania and Zambia, although contributing most of the workforce for the railway's construction, committed to trade agreements favourable to Beijing.[38]

Activists pointed to these unequal trade agreements—most notably, one that gave the PRC unfettered freedom to pump its surplus goods into East Africa, effectively eliminating local competition. As one commentator noted, this rapid influx of Chinese products endangered local industries:

> African recipient countries are often in the difficult position of virtually having to take whatever is available [so] shops in Dar es Salaam are full of unsold 'make-weight' Chinese goods ... The influx of simple industrial goods tends to inhibit the recipient country from establishing that sort of industry within its borders.[39]

Several Tanzania-based African-Americans also highlighted unfair treatment of local workers by the Chinese Railway Expert Team, including degrees of discrimination in hiring practices and lack of protection of worker safety.[40]

After Mao's death in 1976, the gradual transition to Reform and Opening Up completely reoriented the relationship between China and Tanzania. Gone were the days of China's rhetorical, ideological, and material commitments to Third World anti-imperialism and autonomous socialist development. PRC-funded factory and rail-building aid initiatives for Tanzanian economic autonomy from apartheid South Africa gave way to a unilateral relationship in which Chinese profit was prioritised. PRC firms hired largely for 'capitalist exploitation' and depended primarily on easily exploitable 'casualized Tanzanian labor in enclaves of industrial production, resource extraction, and infrastructure construction'.[41] The situation in Tanzania also played a part. In pursuit of international debt cancellations for the country, Nyerere's successor, Benjamin Mkapa (who took power in 1995), discarded the socialist policies of his predecessor, privatised state-owned companies, and instituted liberal market policies to promote economic growth. The International Monetary Fund and World Bank enthusiastically supported these neoliberal measures.[42]

Such significant changes to the nature of the Sino-Tanzanian relationship in recent years notwithstanding, for many Chinese and Tanzanians alike, the Tan–Zam Railway stands for something much greater than the hazards brought about by the neoliberal world order. Tan–Zam Railway veteran Li Yongzen from Tianjin, who worked in Tanzania as an engineer in 1970, reflected on the symbolic importance of the railway as a monument of the China–Tanzania friendship: 'To have aided in the construction of the Tan–Zam Railway remains an unforgettable memory for me.'[43] His grandson, Li Shangyi, who followed in his grandfather's footsteps by working in Tanzania and, later, Malawi, as a technician for a project that connected thousands of rural households to satellite television, recognised the importance of carrying on the mantle of the China–Africa friendship. He said that in this new era, 'we from the younger generation ought to contribute as well to the traditional friendship between China and Africa'.[44]

1972

As an experiment in educating the new socialist subject, the Cultural Revolution saw the intensification of the practice of sending educated urban youths to the countryside to learn from the peasantry. In the mid-1950s, Chinese authorities began sending young people from the cities to rural areas so they could gain valuable life experience by toiling side-by-side with peasants. However, the policy really took off only after the disaster of the Great Leap Forward, when the Chinese Government began to relocate urban youths of bad class origins to alleviate pressure on employment, food provision and services in the cities. Although the flow of students had stopped with the breakdown of state institutions at the onset of the Cultural Revolution, in 1967, some Red Guards volunteered to go to the countryside to merge with the peasant masses and continue their revolution there. What initially was only a trickle became a torrent one year later, after Mao Zedong himself endorsed the practice. Taking as a starting point a letter a disgruntled parent wrote to Mao in 1972, this essay looks into the experience of the Chinese 'rusticated youth'.

Transforming Urban Youth into Peasants: The Maoist Rustication Movement of the 1960s–1970s

Michel BONNIN[1]

In 1972, Li Qinglin was a primary schoolteacher in Putian, Fujian Province.[2] He was annoyed because his elder son had been sent down to a rural village eighty kilometres away—a fate no ordinary urban family had been able to escape since the end of 1968. To add to Li's annoyance was the fact that, since his move to the countryside, the son had been unable to earn enough work points to feed himself properly. Just like the local peasants, the rusticated 'educated youth' (知识青年, abbreviated to 知青, zhiqing) had to earn work points every day to get a share at the time of the harvest, of grain and money, but most were given fewer points than the local peasants, in part because they were considered less skilled and robust and in part because the local cadres were unhappy about this burden imposed on them by the higher authorities, which reduced their meagre earnings. Rural labour was already plentiful, but they had been told that accommodating the zhiqing was a political task given to them by Chairman Mao. As a result, most zhiqing had to ask for help from their parents to sustain themselves. Li, for instance, had to provide food (bought on the black market) for his son, who had finished his yearly share after only six months, not to mention all the other necessary items, since the boy did not earn any money. In addition, even after four years of hard work, his son had no proper housing in the village.

As his younger son was almost sixteen and on the verge of also being rusticated, Li Qinglin became particularly worried. His own salary would not be enough to help sustain two hungry bellies. Li also resented the injustice of children of local cadres and leaders who were returning to urban areas 'through the backdoor' whereas the children of ordinary people had no idea how long their rural sojourn would last; theoretically, it could be forever. When Mao Zedong launched this movement with his famous directive of 22 December 1968, it was said that urban youth had to be re-educated by the 'poor and lower-middle peasants' (接受贫下中农的再教育) and transformed into 'new-type socialist peasants' (社会主义新式农民).[3] At the time, many young people were ready to enthusiastically answer any demand made by Chairman Mao; as for the others, they were not given a choice. However, after a few months in the countryside, even those who had been full of enthusiasm lost their zeal. Having lost their precious urban *hukou* (residence permit), they were not allowed to return to the cities, where they would be illegal residents without the ration cards necessary to buy food or anything else, and no possibility of obtaining a job or shelter. Only at the beginning of the 1970s were some *zhiqing* hired in their home city or recruited by the People's Liberation Army (PLA)—a phenomenon that became more frequent in 1972, when, after the failed escape and death of Marshall Lin Biao, most former leaders and cadres who had fallen victim to the Cultural Revolution were called back to the cities and given new positions. The first thing they did after being reinstated was to arrange the return of their children—by admission to the PLA or the universities that had just reopened. This was of course resented by those who had no special privilege or, worse, had 'bad class status' and thus no hope of ever leaving the countryside.

Stimulated by his desire to denounce injustice and, at the same time, get some help with his specific case, Li decided to do something that had traditionally been the last resort for people in China with a grievance: write a petition to the Emperor (告御状)—that is, Chairman Mao. Two letters were sent with no reply, but he did not lose heart. Having noticed that Wang Hairong, Mao's grandniece, who had by then become a leader at the Ministry of Foreign Affairs, received foreign dignitaries alongside the chairman himself, Li decided to send a third letter, through her. Then a miracle happened: on 25 April 1973, he received at home a letter containing three 100-yuan bills (almost seven months of salary for him) with a short letter in Mao's own hand, saying: 'Please find attached 300 yuan to help you a little with your problem. Such cases are widespread in the country, and will be dealt with in the standard manner.'

This was the first time Mao had directly sent a letter of reply to an individual, although he had already sent one to a group of Red Guards at the beginning of the Cultural Revolution.[4] As in the first case, the letter became a national political event and the name of Li Qinglin and the content of Mao's letter were soon known throughout the country. Mao was happy to appear as a benevolent ruler providing justice to the people and rectifying the ways of the bureaucrats who did not implement correctly his grand plans for the bright communist future of the country. His 'specialty' among the communist leaders of the world was precisely his regular use of the 'masses' to put pressure on other leaders and bureaucrats who did not follow his line—the Red Guards being a good example of a social group he had used and then discarded. Mao insisted that Li Qinglin should be given official positions at the local and even national level. Li, then, took this opportunity to denounce some local leaders and even became embroiled in the political infighting between the top leaders who had managed to survive the Cultural Revolution and the radical leaders who had been promoted through it.

Unfortunately for Li, after Mao's death on 9 September 1976, the top radical leaders were labelled the 'Gang of Four' (四人帮) and arrested, while the local bureaucrats whom he had denounced took their revenge. Considered the number-two representative of the Gang of Four in Fujian, Li was condemned to life imprisonment, which was later reduced to fifteen years. He was freed in 1994 and died ten years later in the humble house where he had written his letter to Mao. To this day, Li's image remains good among the former rusticated youth, not because of his later political activity, but simply because in 1972 he had dared to tell the truth to the Emperor. Mao had seized this opportunity to give a new start to the rustication movement, which was an essential part of his revolutionary strategy aimed at educating and training 'revolutionary successors'—a process he deemed essential to preserve the socialist system in China. After a slowdown due in part to the fierce political struggle that monopolised the attention of the highest leaders in 1970–71 and in part to the realisation that, after the worst of the political chaos, the cities needed fresh labour, the Chinese leadership recognised that if they wanted to relaunch the movement, it was necessary to improve somewhat the material conditions of the *zhiqing*, which in many cases were simply unbearable both for them and for their families.

Relaunching the Movement

Feeling that Mao's letter to Li was a covert indictment of the leaders in charge of the country's daily management, Zhou Enlai lost no time organising the National Working Conference on the Rustication of Educated Youth, which took place in Beijing from 22 June to 7 August 1973. Drawing on the information collected by seventy cadres who had been sent to different regions to discover the main problems affecting the *zhiqing* and their parents, the conference adopted a series of remedial measures. As the inquiries had revealed that at some military farms officers had raped dozens of female *zhiqing*, some of these rapists were arrested and condemned to death in a bid to reduce the anxieties of parents. But, with no systemic improvements concerning the rule of law in sight, the root of the problem remained, which explains why 10,000 cases of ill treatment of *zhiqing* (mostly rapes) were reported in 1976.[5]

Another decision taken at the conference was to insist on the responsibility of the leadership in the management of the system. At each level, 'small leadership groups in charge of rusticating the educated youths' (知识青年上山下乡领导小组) were established. The objectives of the measures taken during and after the conference were to improve the material situation of the *zhiqing* and to better control them. The subsidy paid to rural authorities for the installation of each *zhiqing* increased from 230 yuan to 480 yuan in the south and from 250 yuan to 500 yuan in the north. At the same time, the principle of equal pay for equal work was stressed in the hope of improving the number of work points given to the *zhiqing*. An important improvement for the wellbeing of the *zhiqing* was the insistence on regrouping them together for housing and for work wherever possible. More building materials were allocated. Having the *zhiqing* live in collective households (集体户) meant not only was it easier to rationally divide domestic tasks, but also the *zhiqing* felt less isolated and girls were less vulnerable to sexual harassment and rape. Where land and finance were available, the authorities encouraged the creation of *zhiqing* farms or plantations, where these youths worked together, sometimes with the help of an experienced peasant.

Working and living apart from the peasants reduced the occasions of conflicts between peasants and *zhiqing*, but it was at the expense of the original rationale of the movement: the integration of the *zhiqing* with the labouring masses and the re-education of young intellectuals by poor and lower-middle peasants. Regrouping *zhiqing* did, however, facilitate their monitoring, especially when the Chinese authorities established a new practice of sending 'accompanying cadres' to live in villages on a rotating basis to try to control the activities of the *zhiqing*, preventing them from evading work and organising political study in the evening. The presence of these cadres also gave some protection to the *zhiqing*, especially girls, against abuses. But they were not dispatched everywhere—the national ratio was about one for every 100 *zhiqing*—and the protection was far from sufficient, as we have seen.

Beginning in 1974, the city of Zhuzhou, Hunan Province, became the model for a new system, in which schools continued to designate those students who would have to leave for the countryside, but the parents' work units took over the task of mobilising them and organising transfers to the village to which the units were 'hooked'. It was even more difficult than before to resist the transfer, given the enormous power of the work unit over the life of every family and especially considering the fact that the best chance for *zhiqing* to return home was to be hired by their parents' work unit. The Zhuzhou model was thus an important element in the development of what became, at the end of the movement, a pervasive practice of hereditary hiring in Chinese urban areas.

The changes resulting from the 1973 conference were not implemented evenly in all areas, but they brought a real improvement for most *zhiqing*. The basic problem at that time, however, was that an improvement of the material conditions of the *zhiqing*'s rural sojourn could not really satisfy them or their parents. At that point, the only question in their minds was: when will I be able to go home?

States of Mind

This state of mind was already deeply entrenched among the *zhiqing* before the 1973 conference and it did not change with the new wave of youths who arrived in the countryside in the following years. The policy of rusticating urban youth first began in 1955 in imitation of the Soviet Union, but on a small scale. Before the Great Leap Forward (1958–62), less than 100,000 Chinese youths were rusticated and the policy stopped during the Leap. When this period of utopian frenzy ended in famine and economic breakdown, the pressure on employment, food provision and education in urban areas was so great it was decided to send large numbers of urban youths to the countryside. From 1962 to mid-1966, on the eve of the Cultural Revolution, 1,290,000 *zhiqing* were rusticated.[6] At that time, this policy focused mainly on youth of 'bad class origin', who were discriminated against in access to high schools and universities as well as jobs. These people were given the opportunity to 'redeem' themselves by going to 'places where the country needed them most'. After they discovered that those rural places were not as idyllic as they had been told and that their prospects of returning home were dim, their mood was quite low and a number used the Cultural Revolution as an opportunity to go home and 'make revolution' there, asking the authorities to stop the 'revisionist' rustication policy. However, the Maoist nature of the policy was eventually reiterated and they were all forcibly sent back to the countryside before the end of 1967.

After the beginning of the Cultural Revolution, there were no new departures to the countryside, as the chaotic situation did not permit this type of organised bureaucratic activity. But in 1967, some Red Guards, disappointed by the orientation taken by their movement and stimulated by some of Mao's speeches, asked to go to the countryside to merge with the peasant masses and continue the revolution there.[7] Only about 2,000 Red Guards left this way in 1967 but, by mid-1968, as Mao was already thinking of putting an end to the Red Guard movement and restoring order, some provinces encouraged secondary school students to go to the countryside in an organised way. This movement accelerated after Mao himself published an editorial and then a directive on the front page of the *People's Daily* on 5 September and 13 September, respectively, but there was still resistance from those Red Guards who refused to abandon their fight and from parents who were worried about sending their children away, often to faraway border regions, with no guarantees about their fate in the countryside or their future return. Mao, then, decided to strike hard. On 21 December 1968, a directive from him was read on the evening radio news and published on the front page of the *People's Daily* the following day. It said:

> It is absolutely necessary for educated young people to go to the countryside to be re-educated by the poor and lower-middle peasants. Cadres and other city people should be persuaded to send their sons and daughters to the countryside when they have finished junior or senior high school, college, or university. Let's mobilise. Comrades throughout the countryside should welcome them.

A huge mobilisation was immediately launched and, in the following months, most urban secondary school students were declared to have graduated and were sent to the countryside in an atmosphere of frenzied excitement. From the end of 1968 to the spring of 1970, about five million *zhiqing* went either to villages in their own province or, in the case of the biggest cities, to faraway border regions where they were often integrated into military farms that were later transformed into state farms. Such farms at least had the advantage of providing a monthly salary and enough food on which to survive, while in the villages there was no such guarantee, as we have seen. However, according to official statistics, only 15 percent of *zhiqing* were enrolled in farms (about 2.5 million of a total of 16.5 million sent to the countryside during the period 1967–79).[8] From 1974 to 1979, two million youths were sent to separate *zhiqing* farms or plantations, but these were only collective units without a guaranteed salary.[9]

The overhaul of the system prompted by Mao's letter to Li Qinglin was by then incapable of gaining the acceptance of the *zhiqing*, who tried all methods to end their rural sojourn—by bribing officials or by extreme actions like harming themselves physically, returning illegally to the cities or escaping to foreign places such as Hong Kong or Burma. Even those who had a good attitude in the countryside, openly praised the policy and went as far as becoming cadres at the lowest levels were hoping to be eventually rewarded with an urban posting. The few who found jobs in which their talents were not wasted, such as primary schoolteachers or 'barefoot doctors', were looking for opportunities to leave as well.

The Wind of Return

The rustication policy also became a bone of contention between the two main political factions at the top of the Party: the Maoist radicals insisted on the necessity for the *zhiqing* to 'take root'—that is, to become peasants for life—whereas the moderates favoured a rotation system. Although the former made more noise, the latter had more influence over the daily management of the country, so a steady flow of returns continued. However, the number of returns was always lower than that of departures, which explains why the peak in the number of *zhiqing* actually present in the countryside (almost nine million) came in 1977.[10] In addition, after Mao's death and the arrest of the Gang of Four, Mao's successor, Hua Guofeng (who had organised the 1973 conference), decided to continue to pursue rustication—another factor behind the 1977 peak. But the questioning of all Maoist policies in 1978 brought hesitation among the leaders. This was supposed to be solved by a new work conference, which took place from 31 October to 10 December 1978. The conference decided to reduce the numbers sent to the countryside, with the objective of stopping the transfers after a few years. At the same time, the gradual return of the *zhiqing* sent to villages was also scheduled. However, new problems arose as the Chinese authorities announced that *zhiqing* sent to state farms were no longer considered *zhiqing* but employees of the farms. This decision caused an uproar among the *zhiqing* concerned, which translated into a desperate, spontaneous movement that included petitions, strikes, hunger strikes and the dispatch of delegations. This resulted in a general 'wind of return' (回城风), which the authorities eventually decided to accept—although without saying so publicly. From 1978 until the end of 1980, there was a wave of returns that brought some six million *zhiqing* back to the cities.

Taking advantage of the political openness of late 1978, the *zhiqing* were then the first social group in the People's Republic of China to succeed in altering significantly the plans of the authorities in their favour. Of course, the new Party leadership's decision to prioritise economic development made the rustication policy untenable in the long run. The policy was indeed totally irrational from an economic as well as a sociological or psychological point of view. The active resistance of the *zhiqing* came after a decade of passive resistance, which had expressed itself in many ways and played an important role in fostering corruption in China and led to a general decline in idealism and basic ethics. Most of the opportunities to leave the countryside were arbitrary: entrance to university did not require passing an exam but only currying political support; being hired by the army or an urban work unit also depended on pulling strings; and return for medical reasons depended on a medical certificate, which could be bought.

Towards the end of the movement, the authorities acknowledged in internal discussions that by spending seven billion yuan, the state had just bought four discontents: that of the *zhiqing*, of their parents, of the peasants and of the state itself.[11] Considering the enormous cost of this movement, not only for the *zhiqing* and their parents, but also for the state and for the peasants who shared the financial burden of the installation and maintenance of a labour force that was not needed, the question is: why did this policy endure so long?

This movement served multiple purposes and, in the course of its long history from 1955 to 1980, the motivations of the leadership evolved with the situation. In border regions, the main objectives included land clearing and boosting the strategic presence of Han people in minority and/or scarcely populated areas. But in certain periods, the main motive was certainly economic—that is, to alleviate the problem of urban unemployment. Many people, including scholars, consider this the real rationale behind the whole movement, but this view is simplistic. It is true rustication was used in some periods for this purpose, especially after the catastrophic Great Leap Forward and at the end of the Red Guards movement, when it would have been difficult for the Chinese authorities to provide jobs for youth after years of turmoil. But in both these periods, the employment problem was mainly the result of a political movement that had turned bad. In 1968, the most pressing problem was how to put an end to the political threat represented by those Red Guards who were unwilling to end their revolution. But this was a contingent problem. Statistics show that during the period 1968–77, the number of people from the countryside hired in urban areas was roughly equivalent to the number of *zhiqing* who were permanently rusticated. The *hukou* system could have avoided this exchange of population, if it were not for another reason: the fact that Mao had said rustication was 'absolutely necessary'.

Mao insisted during his final years on the need to preserve and develop this 'new-born thing from the Cultural Revolution' (文化大革命的新生事物). And, for him, this was certainly not a question of economic rationality but of political necessity, to train 'revolutionary successors' and prevent China from 'changing its colour'. Even when his health was already very frail, in February 1976, he wrote a comment on a letter that had been sent to him, asking the Politburo to organise a new conference on the rustication movement.[12] This reaction—reminiscent of his earlier reply to Li Qinglin—shows his interest in the rustication of educated youth had not abated even at the very end.

This is why this movement endured so long—not because of a supposed economic rationale. When economic development did become a priority, after 1978, a large number of new jobs were created in the cities to accommodate both the wave of returning *zhiqing* and the new cohort of youths who had been born during the baby boom that followed the period of food shortages and economic slowdown in the cities. This was made possible simply by abandoning the constraints Mao had imposed for purely ideological and political reasons on individual and small collective enterprises as well as on the service and light-industry sectors. After their return home, many *zhiqing* expressed the idea that this movement had been equivalent to turning the wheel of history backwards. And indeed, only when, a decade later, the Chinese Government accepted a reverse labour migration of much larger numbers of young peasants going to work in urban areas was China able to develop its industrial and service sectors on a large scale, while relieving the countryside of its surplus labour.

1976

Although 'workers' universities' gained prominence during the Cultural Revolution, they were not the only experiment in moving beyond the elitist and 'bourgeois' values of the conventional university through the integration of mental and manual labour. Nor were they the earliest. First established in 1958, the Jiangxi Communist Labour University (江西共产主义劳动大学, or 'Gongda'), was one of the most notable attempts in this sense. Its students were taught through a curriculum of 'part-work, part-study' and, unlike other universities, Gongda was registered as both a university and a production unit, supporting its staff and students through the sale of products from its farms and factories. This essay looks at the Cultural Revolution's larger intellectual project of integrating the labour of education with the labour of production through the lens of the 1976 movie Juelie, a feature film depicting a fictional account of the university's founding. Through narrative references to the historic role students played in the Cultural Revolution, the film responded to the crises raised by student activism during the Cultural Revolution by reinscribing student subjectivity within the patriarchal and developmentalist structures of the state.

The Blank Exam: Crises of Student Labour and Activism in the Late Cultural Revolution Film *Juelie*

A.C. BAECKER

The dramatic conflict at the centre of the 1976 film *Juelie* (决裂, *Breaking With Old Ideas*, directed by Li Wenhua) involves a group of students' last-minute decision to skip an exam. When the local production brigade's ricefields are imperilled by a surprise infestation of a pest called the 'night bandit', which is capable of destroying the entire crop overnight, the students abandon their textbooks and rush off to save the harvest. They stay up late killing the bugs with insecticide, rescuing the brigade's rice but missing their exam the next morning.[1]

However, instead of recognising their heroism, conservative administrators at the students' university threaten them with expulsion. The school's vice-principal, a career educator named Cao Zhonghe (portrayed by character actor Chen Ying), had warned the students before they abandoned their books to mind their own business and focus on scoring well. But an impassioned plea from an idealistic student convinces the group otherwise. 'Classmates, what are we studying for?' she asks. 'How can we not use our scientific knowledge to serve the peasants?' The school's bureaucratic administrators disagree, and say that skipping the test constitutes submitting a 'blank exam' (白卷儿). The controversy surrounding the group's expulsion indicates there is clearly more at stake than just the academic futures of fifteen college students. Indeed, the success of the entire university model hangs in the balance.

Juelie depicts the establishment of a fictional branch of the real-life Jiangxi Communist Labour University (江西共产主义劳动大学, or 'Gongda'), an institution that sought to reject the elitist and 'bourgeois' values of the conventional university by integrating mental and manual labour. Its students were taught through a curriculum of 'part-work, part-study' (半工半学) and, unlike other universities, Gongda was registered as both a university and a production unit, supporting its staff and students through the sale of products from its farms and factories.[2] *Juelie*'s portrayal of students engaged in both classwork and productive labour contributed to the period's larger intellectual project of integrating the labour of education with the labour of production, understanding the experience of production itself as a legitimate site of education.

Thus, grading the students' 'blank exam' becomes a contested exercise pitting the university's progressive leadership against its traditionalists. In a heated faculty meeting, vice-principal Cao produces the blank exam papers, throwing them on the table as proof of the students' failure to perform to standard. 'We're not a farm, we're a college!' he shouts. 'We need to have universal standards!' But the university's popular principal, Long Guozheng (portrayed with hale gravitas by Guo Zhenqing), sees things differently: 'Actually, these blank exams demonstrate a great deal: they show a high political consciousness, and a deep feeling for the proletariat. They carry sweat from the students' brows, and represent the many tonnes of grains rescued for the lower-middle peasants [贫下中农].' Long concludes that 'the students did right', making the blank exam a Rorschach test revealing Cao's and Long's oppositional understandings of education's ultimate purpose.

Much like the blank exam at its centre, the film *Juelie* was itself a contested text, controversial during its time for its radical reconceptualisation of the position of the university and the student within society. In this essay, I argue that labour was the key site through which the student in the late socialist cultural imaginary transformed from the bespectacled urban intellectual of the May Fourth era into a diffuse, pluralistic subject embedded within the socialist project and its productive social relations. As the most extensive mainstream narrative from the period to depict higher education and its subjects, *Juelie*'s adaptation of real-life experiments in proletarian education and student rebellion should also be understood as both a response to and a mediation of the crises around student subjectivity raised by the student activism of the Cultural Revolution.

The Revolutionary Rural Undergraduate on Film

When *Juelie* was filmed in 1975, the release of a major motion picture enacted a very different set of cultural precepts than those operative in the release of a major movie today. A film made during the mid-1970s was neither a work of art made by a visionary auteur nor a work of consumer corporate entertainment. Rather, films were made to shape and reflect national mass culture, to defend national policies, and to showcase socialist culture and entertainment.[3] In those terms, *Juelie* was intended to celebrate the success of a new national education culture exemplified by Gongda. This culture was practical, cultivating useful skills such as animal husbandry and agricultural production, and rejected the class politics of theoretical knowledge divorced from real-world application, such as taking tests only for the sake of achieving high scores. It was also egalitarian, striving to offer rural students as much access to higher education as their wealthier urban peers.

Juelie's showcase of China's new national education culture was underwritten by a widespread reconsideration of the role of students in the labour of social reproduction. When the people's communes (人民公社) were formally established in 1958, their architects recognised that greater economic productivity could only be achieved by establishing wideranging social services that facilitated the full participation of all available potential agricultural workers. 'Farm cooperatives must be not only organisers of production, but also organisers of the way of life,' wrote the editors of *Red Flag* magazine in a 1958 article promoting the implementation of the commune.[4] This would be materialised through ambitious programs that collectivised the onerous burdens of domestic labour in the countryside—which fell nearly exclusively on women— including establishing commune-run public canteens, sewing circles, maternity wards, and nurseries.[5]

Education also fell under the purview of the communes, as organisers of 'the way of life', and their supporters believed that commune management of rural education would result in the Marxist realisation of the 'gradual elimination of the difference between mental and manual labour'.[6] Communes were therefore responsible for establishing not just nurseries and daycare centres, but also primary, secondary, and technical schools, the last of which were expected to conduct scientific research.[7] Thus, outside urban regions that were already equipped with education infrastructure, the adoption of the commune effectively integrated education within the purview of productive labour.

For many rural communities, commune responsibility for education meant establishing new schools and educating children who had not previously attended formal schools. Accordingly, the Great Leap Forward (1958–62) period saw a widespread expansion of the rural education system, particularly at the primary and secondary levels.[8] Where education had previously been seen as the prerogative of the moneyed urban classes, the rapid expansion of China's education infrastructure, particularly in the countryside, corresponded with a wider reconceptualisation of education as a social right, not a privilege—a shift that was also taking place elsewhere in the world during the middle of the century.⁹

Naturally, depictions of students in the cultural imaginary began shifting as well, transforming from the romantic, bespectacled, white-gowned May Fourth intellectuals portrayed in Yang Mo's 1958 novel *Song of Youth* (青春之歌) into *Juelie*'s ideal of the well-rounded peasant-intellectual. No character showcases the new student ideal better than Li Jinfeng, the Gongda student who spearheaded the overnight action to save the nearby brigade's imperilled rice crops, played with fiery resolve by Wang Suya. A farmer recruited from a poor mountain community to attend Gongda, Li is admitted to the university under new affirmative action higher education policies implemented during the Cultural Revolution. These policies allowed universities to enrol deserving members of the worker-peasant-soldier masses (工农兵群众) through political reccomendation, even if they did not possess the typical qualifications, such as a high school diploma.[10]

Like several other farmer-student characters in the film, Li Jinfeng is not a traditional undergraduate. Through the commune representative's testimony, the audience learns that, before Liberation, Li Jinfeng had starved as a child labourer, suffering daily abuse at the hands of her landlord, and was eventually sold as a child bride. Even after Liberation, her region remained too poor to set up local schools, so she only learned to read and write in night classes for poor farmers. When Gongda's progressive new principal comes to recruit students from her village, Li Jinfeng impresses him by writing the sentence 'Chairman Mao is our great liberator' in tidy calligraphy. Even though she did not sit for the entrance exam and does not hold a high school—or indeed, any—diploma, Long Guozheng considers her literacy and record of labour to be exemplary qualifications and admits her on the spot.[11]

Li Jinfeng and her fellow worker-peasant-soldier classmates at Gongda represent the reconceptualisation of 'the student' along multiple subject positions. This transformation is illustrated most clearly through the contrast drawn between Li, her cohort at Gongda, and a third-year male undergraduate whom Long encounters on a study tour of China's most prestigious universities. Like Li, the unnamed male undergraduate comes from humble origins in the countryside, but he treats the chance to attend university as an opportunity not to enrich his community, but to attain individual social mobility. When the student's mother comes to visit, Long watches as the student rejects one by one every handmade gift she has brought. He tells his mother that things are different now that he has been educated ('我现在是有知识的人!'), and the camera pans down as the mother takes stock of her son's inward and outward changes: the cross, exasperated expression he wears behind black-rimmed glasses, the button-down shirt with a pen tucked into its pocket, the slacks held up with a leather belt, and the black leather Oxfords on his feet. Distinctly unaffordable to the lower-middle peasant, each item signifies the privileged intellectual.

The smart clothes of the rural farmer's son serve not just as physical evidence of his elitist values, but also as a material manifestation of corrupted social relations. Although the village boy achieves social mobility, he no longer wishes to return to his home village, thus removing himself from the social relations of his birth. The knowledge he has attained while attending college has transformed him into the product of a system that equates learning with class standing. The village boy turned undergraduate illustrates the perils of education for education's sake: a fundamentally destructive path that prevents not only the reproduction of the labourer, but also the production of new socialist subjectivities—namely, that of the educated labourer.

Li Jinfeng, by contrast, demonstrates the virtues of being an educated worker. In addition to her rural background, Li is mother to a young daughter, who appears during her recruitment scene, playfully tugging on her mother's shirt. To the university's conservative administrators, Li's motherhood makes her unsuited to attend college, and one teacher who cannot bite his tongue after Li is admitted disdainfully asks whether she expects to take her daughter to campus with her.[12] Although her daughter appears on screen only twice, Li's motherhood is no coincidence or minor detail of her backstory. Unlike the male undergrad at the traditional university, Li actively expands and redefines the social identity of the student, allowing for students who are red, not experts; women, not men; labourers, not intellectuals; and of the country, not the city. Li is explicitly reproduced in the form of her daughter, who physically manifests Li's embeddedness within the generative social relations of her community, as well as her capacity for social reproduction.

By depicting university students who break the traditional mould, *Juelie* depicts a radically new university. Rather than serving as a stronghold of bourgeois class interests, the Gongda depicted in *Juelie* is a university where students do not need to be wealthy, male, traditionally educated, or come from the city. Instead, *Juelie* presents the university as a site for the socialisation of worker-students, integrating education with production to ensure that the university fulfils its potential as an incubator of productive forces and reproductive social relations. Li Jinfeng and her cohort demonstrate that the student is less a marker of class or identity than it is a diverse and pluralistic subject position within society.

Heroes of the Blank Exam

But Li Jinfeng rewrites the role of the student as much through her labour and activism as she does by simply attending university. During the Cultural Revolution, the production and reception of major feature films were embedded within a dialectic negotiating the boundary between narrative fiction and recent history—similar to films produced today depicting historical events. In particular, using the term 'blank exam' to frame Li and her cohort's decision to work in the fields rather than sit for an exam was a deliberate choice meant to connect the fictional students of Gongda with a real-life 'hero of the blank exam' (白卷英雄), Zhang Tiesheng.

Zhang Tiesheng was a sent-down youth working at Baita commune in Liaoning Province who first rose to fame in the summer of 1973 after submitting an empty answer sheet during county college entrance exams.[13] Rather than accept a failed test result, Zhang submitted his answer sheet with an explanation written on the back: 'I do eighteen hours of heavy labour every day, there's no time to study.' Moreover, Zhang believed the test was a poor indicator of who most deserved a college education. Although Zhang's time working at the Baita commune had not prepared him for the test, it was honest work, and he felt disdain for 'those bookworms who have never worked, and live leisurely, unprincipled lives. They truly disgust me, and this test is unwittingly complicit in giving them a monopoly over college.'[14] Zhang's action caught the attention of provincial officials, including Mao Yuanxin, Mao Zedong's nephew who was then Party secretary of Liaoning Province. Zhang's words were published first on the front page of the *Liaoning Daily* and then in the national press, turning him into a celebrity overnight.

Zhang's blank exam reflected a moment of deep inequity in the distribution of education resources, as well as deep suspicion of the traditional admission criteria to high school and college. With his failed exam elevated to a critique of the education system, Zhang's dissent crystallised the inherent contradictions of such a system: that the nation's youth could devote themselves to building socialism in the countryside and be denied an education because of it. To be certain, Li Jinfeng's cinematic 'blank exam' improves on Zhang Tiesheng's real-life one: where Zhang had not studied and was not capable of passing the test, Li makes the active choice not to sit for hers—a narrative gloss that neatly sidesteps the question of whether or not the rural student is capable of performing well on tests, a point of considerable anxiety.

Zhang was not alone in 'going against the tide' (反潮流),[15] nor was his dissent the only act of student rebellion written into *Juelie*'s script. Students were among the first to heed Mao's call to arms in the opening months of the Cultural Revolution, and, as the period writ large endured, accounts of righteous student rebellion were frequent highlights of media discourse. Notably, in 1974, a Nanjing University student's request for an assignment in the countryside was also published on the front page of the *People's Daily*. The student, Zhong Zhimin, was the son of a Long March veteran. He had been admitted to Nanjing University through family connections, but now he repudiated the nepotism that had got him there. He asked to withdraw from the university rather than attend through the 'back door' (走后门).

Zhong's story is evoked in the character Cao Xiaomei, the young daughter of the villainous career educator Cao Zhonghe. When she is first introduced, Cao Xiaomei is a bubbly and blithe young girl skipping by the riverside, but as the film unfolds, Cao's happy-go-lucky innocence gives way to consternation over her father's handling of university affairs. When her father makes 'backdoor' arrangements for her to be sent away to a prestigious university, she publicly disavows his actions and declares that she will remain at Gongda, where she will follow Mao's exhortation to make revolution in the countryside. Cao Xiaomei's fictional narrative mirrors the real-life Zhong Zhimin's, completing her transformation from the innocent, privileged, and politically uninitiated daughter of a disloyal intellectual into an active, mature, and enlightened political subject fully socialised within the rural mountain community. Cao Xiaomei and Li Jinfeng thus go against the tide from opposite directions and, in spite of their diametrically opposed backgrounds, they arrive on the same red path.

Student Activism and the Cultural Revolution on Screen

At its boldest, *Juelie* aimed to represent the Cultural Revolution on screen, adapting stories of real-life experiments in proletarian education and student rebellion for narrative cinema. But *Juelie* can also be understood as a response to the crises that had been raised by student activism during the period. On the eve of the Cultural Revolution, the student indexed a host of thorny contradictions and unresolved legacies, from issues of class, family background, and political engagement, to the enduring urban/rural disparity. Jonathan Unger argues that, by 1966, four distinct groups of students, with the corresponding opportunities strictly delimited between them, were apparent: cadres' children, worker-peasant children, middle-class children, and bad-class children.[16] Seventeen years after the founding of the People's Republic of China, it was clear that educational qualifications remained a key mechanism of class differentiation in socialist society. The Cultural Revolution was thus less a conflict *between* classes than it was a conflict *about* class, as Joel Andreas has argued.[17]

Students were famously among the first to respond to Mao's call for Cultural Revolution, and their activism enacted a politics that transgressed the boundaries of state-organised institutions. By forming alliances with factory workers, demobilised soldiers, and personnel in administrative organs, students created networks that traversed the given social and organisational boundaries such as the school and the work unit.[18] Student characters in narrative depictions of schools were simultaneously a reference to the inequality that the school produced and a depiction of a politics that exceeded the established order of the socialist state.[19]

Produced during the final years of the period that would retroactively be defined as the Cultural Revolution (1966–76), *Juelie* is set in 1959, during the Great Leap Forward—a temporality that is reinforced through character references to the vim of the period and its policies, as well as set pieces, such as banners celebrating the arrival of the Great Leap.[20] Yet I believe the film is better understood as a cinematic staging of the Cultural Revolution—a fact made clear not only through its presentation of historical acts of student dissent from that era, but also in the film bureau's internal review of the script. In their review, the committee noted that, by setting the film during the Great Leap Forward, when education policy was controlled by a few 'revisionists' like Liu Shaoqi, the screenwriters created continuity issues around the authority and narrative agency of the script's principal characters. After experiencing the Cultural Revolution, the committee explained, it was no longer plausible for one person to determine the course of sweeping social change, such as the establishment of Gongda. Rather, because the occurrence of the Cultural Revolution had enabled systemic grassroots change such as that showcased in *Juelie*, it was therefore imperative for the film to depict the Cultural Revolution.

'If you don't write about the Cultural Revolution, then don't make your film,' the committee concluded bluntly.[21] But because Gongda had been established in 1958, neither could the film be set wholly during the Cultural Revolution. The result was a finished product that straddled discrete historical periods, with explicit reference to the campaigns of the late 1950s made through the updated political language of the mid-1970s.[22]

In the film's final act, Li Jinfeng is called in for public criticism. The central debate during the session is the question of whether or not Li is a good student, with Cao Zhonghe and the deputy commissioner arguing in the negative and principal Long in the affirmative. Yet ultimately the act that brings Li in for judgement before the masses is not her 'blank exam', but rather her later opposition to new policies seeking to privatise the commune that the corrupt local Party secretary and his henchman try to ram through. For refusing to follow the new policies, Li Jinfeng is accused of inciting people to oppose the work team, in another echo of the historical opposition to work teams occurring at the start of the Cultural Revolution. Seeking to protect the public interest, Li acts not in her capacity as a university student, but as a member of the commune. Thus, by the film's final act, Li has been educated, skilled, and socialised by the university, all without sacrificing her embeddedness within productive social relations.

But where the Red Guard student activists of the historical Cultural Revolution challenged and disrupted the conditions that defined them, *Juelie*'s narrative delivers the student back into a socialist moral universe delimited by institutions of the state. Although Li Jinfeng's criticism session ends with mass support for Li and the university, the corrupt Party secretary and his allies remain in their leadership positions, and eventually take the opportunity to force a shutdown of the university. The film reaches its resolution only when the good Party secretary, Tang Ning, arrives in a sedan with a letter from Mao. Mao's letter is addressed to the university's leftist activists, and Mao's support both exonerates Li and reverses the closure of the school. 'Comrades, I am in full agreement with what you have done,' Tang reads from the letter—his dialogue an excerpt from the letter Mao wrote to the leadership of the real Gongda campus on 30 July 1961.[23]

While *Juelie* creates a narrative depiction of the Cultural Revolution that interacts with its historical one, the two differ in important ways: where the state's response to the historical Cultural Revolution was to foreclose the possibility of a student-articulated politics outside the state, Mao's letter at the film's conclusion arrives like a *deus ex machina* reinscribing Li's dissent within the auspices of the Party. Notably, the good Party leaders who rescue Li and the university are men, making a patriarchy of the structures that contain Li's gendered dissent. Through its depiction of an education fully integrated with production, *Juelie* reinscribes socialist subjectivity through student labour, delivering the student back into a historically and politically determined subject position devoted to the developmentalist projects of the state.

[1] Party secretary Tang Ning arrives at the film's conclusion to read Mao Zedong's vindicating letter to Gongda. [2] Gongda students stay up late to exterminate pests

[3] Wang Suya as Li Jinfeng and Xiang Hong as Cao Xiaomei. [4] Principal Long encounters a college student who has forgotten his village roots on a tour of bourgeois universities. [5] Xiang Hong as Cao Xiaomei.

1980

After losing any residual relevance in the wake of the confrontation with the Chinese Communist Party during the Hundred Flower Movement, the All-China Federation of Trade Unions (ACFTU) was dismantled at the beginning of the Cultural Revolution, as workers began setting up their own organisations. After a few years of gradual reconstruction of its regional and industrial branches, in October 1978, the Ninth National Congress of the ACFTU was finally convened in Beijing, signalling the organisation's comeback at a time when the Party-State was getting ready to start its ambitious program of economic reforms. On that occasion, Deng Xiaoping gave a speech in which he defined the trajectory of the union for years to come. Starting from the assumption that China was still underdeveloped, Deng emphasised that 'the union has to protect the wellbeing of the workers, which can only increase gradually following the increase in production, especially in labour productivity'. As the ACFTU struggled to keep up with the times, Chinese workers were increasingly restive, their discontent fuelled by the echoes of what was happening in far-away Poland.

Echoes of the Rise of Solidarity in Poland

Jeanne L. WILSON

In the summer of 1980, in the midst of worker protests, the independent trade union movement Solidarity was established in Poland. These events largely coincided with an outbreak of worker unrest in China. According to diplomatic sources in Beijing, twenty to thirty demonstrations and strikes occurred in the autumn of 1980.[1] In particular, both foreign and domestic regional press reported significant cases of labour unrest in the industrial cities of Wuhan and Taiyuan, in which workers' grievances culminated in demands for the establishment of free trade unions.[2] Instances of labour unrest were apparently largely due to economic causes, reflecting workers' discontent with the material circumstances of their lives. In at least one case, however, the call for an independent union was paired with the articulation of explicitly political, rather than economic, demands. As reported in the *Taiyuan Daily*, a 'minority of workers' at the Taiyuan steel mill, labelling themselves 'the poorest workers in the world', called for 'breaking down the rusted door of socialism', the right to decide their own fate, the end to dictatorship, and the overthrow of the system of political bureaucracy.[3]

Ever since the founding of the People's Republic of China (PRC), the leaders of the Chinese Communist Party (CCP) have displayed a keen appreciation of the potential for the diffusion of ideas and movements throughout the communist—and now post-communist—bloc. Just as Mao Zedong was influenced by political unrest in Hungary and Poland in 1956 to launch the short-lived 'blooming and contending' of the Hundred Flowers Movement (see Gipouloux's essay in the present volume), so, too, his successors, under the direction of paramount leader Deng Xiaoping, sought to apply a preventive response at home to the evolution of events in Poland.[4] The CCP was deeply alarmed by the unravelling of Communist Party rule in Poland and anxious to devise an appropriate strategy that would inoculate China against the reverberating effects of the 'Polish virus'. This essay examines the reaction of the Chinese leadership to events in Poland from 1980 to 1990, with a focus on the extent of their influence on

Chinese labour policy. From the perspective of the Chinese leadership, the Polish situation presented itself as a case that reflected in an exacerbated form problems and tensions also to be found in China itself.

The Chinese Reaction to Solidarity: 1980–1981

When labour unrest erupted in Poland in 1980, the Chinese press responded to the initial crisis with detailed coverage that was circumspect, factual, and, to a considerable extent, non-judgemental. Chinese reporting tended to treat the emergence of Solidarity with some sympathy, describing it as an understandable reaction by desperate workers to grim political and economic realities. Nonetheless, that the Chinese leadership considered the Polish situation to be serious business was indicated by an internal circular of 25 November 1980. Issued by the Propaganda Department of the Provincial Party Committee of an unnamed province, its title, 'Background Reference Material No. 17: Once Again on the Polish Affair', indicated that it was not the first directive on the topic.[5] Three main causes of the Polish situation were identified: errors in economic policy; popular dissatisfaction with the corruption of Party leadership; and a Polish crisis of self-respect resulting from the subordination of the Polish state to the Soviet Union.

Although the circular indicated that 'the significance and influence of the Polish affair were enormous and reached well beyond the boundaries of the Polish nation', the author(s) refrained from drawing explicit parallels with the Chinese conditions. Nonetheless, the circular's discussion of Polish popular dissatisfaction with the low standard of living and endemic shortages in the purchase of consumer goods invited a direct comparison with the Chinese situation, in which industrial wages in state industry in 1980 still lagged behind 1956 levels.[6] Moreover, the circular's identification of Poland's political problems—for example, corruption and special privileges within the Party, a lack of democratic mechanisms for popular consultation, and the low level of party prestige among the working class—reproduced a litany of abuses familiar in China in the aftermath of the Cultural Revolution and openly recognised by reformers in the Party's leadership. By implication, reform was the key to the resolution of Poland's troubles as well as the means to guard against the transmission of the 'Polish disease' to China. A number of statements by high-ranking Chinese officials explicitly identified reform as an antidote to the evolution of a Polish-style scenario in China. For example, Li Xiannian, the Vice-Chairman of the CCP, reportedly compared the conditions of China with those of Poland in a July 1981 conversation, noting that if China could not carry out its current economic readjustment, it would risk encountering the same difficulties.[7]

Nowhere did the challenge of Solidarity loom as large on the Chinese political scene as in the elaboration of trade union policy. By 1980, reformers had developed an array of proposals that were meant to rescue the trade unions from their dismal heritage of slavish submission to the Party. These measures in their most liberal incarnation sought to restructure authority relations to give the unions operational independence and the ability to represent the interests of the workers without falling prey to charges of 'economism' (经济主义) or 'syndicalism' (工团主义). As Liao Gailong, a close (although more liberal) associate of paramount leader Deng Xiaoping, pointed out in a work report delivered to high-ranking cadres in October 1980: 'We all know what happened in Poland. If we do not change our course, the same things will happen to us. Will the working class not rise in rebellion? Therefore our trade unions and mass organisations must be thoroughly reformed.'[8]

However, not everybody in the Party leadership shared this perspective. The aforementioned outbreak of strikes in the autumn of 1980 provoked unease, as did the scattered efforts by workers to establish independent trade unions. Possibly even more alarming were reports that dissatisfaction with the operation of trade unions extended beyond rank and file workers into the trade union leadership. Members of an Italian labour delegation visiting China in August 1980 reported, for example, that Chinese labour leaders were following the Polish workers' strikes with 'sympathy and great attention'.[9] Fearing that increased participation and democracy in the unions could be a precursor to societal destabilisation, more conservative voices curbed the reformist proposals at a Central Committee Work Conference held in December 1980, which issued a set of instructions on trade union work.[10]

The Spectre of Poland: 1982–1988

With the imposition of martial law in Poland on 13 December 1981 and the appointment of General Wojciech Jaruzelski as the head of the Polish United Workers' Party (PUWP), Polish labour unrest and the

Solidarity movement appeared to have been decisively crushed. Still, the CCP leadership continued to display a keen sensitivity to the potential reverberations of the Polish events on Chinese soil.

A Japanese press report in January 1982 claimed that the CCP had issued an internal document for cadre study in late December 1981 that called on key members of the Party to learn the 'valuable lesson' of the Polish situation and to analyse its causes.[11] The Polish crisis was also apparently a decisive factor in the leadership's decision to remove the clause guaranteeing the 'freedom to strike' (罢工自由) from the new Constitution of 1982. As a practical measure, the action had little significance, but China's leaders apparently feared—with reason—that discontented workers could seize on the phrase as a constitutional mandate for their actions. Significantly, the 'freedom to strike' clause had been ignored in the midst of a movement that culminated in the eradication of the 'four big freedoms' (四大自由)—namely, to 'speak freely', to 'air views freely', to write 'big character posters', and to engage in 'big debates'—from the Constitution in 1980 and did not come under attack until after the founding of Solidarity. Leadership sensitivity over autonomous trade unions and support for Solidarity on the part of workers and union cadres alike was also indicated in late 1983, when Li Xiannian chose the occasion of the Tenth All-China Federation of Trade Unions (ACFTU) Congress to reprimand Solidarity as an example of sham trade unionism (假工会主义) and to castigate those in the PRC who sympathised with Lech Walesa.[12] In particular, the Chinese leadership sought to maintain centralised vertical control over the trade unions, discouraging the formation of horizontal linkages that would facilitate communication between workers outside their own workplace. To this end, regulations issued in 1984 by the ACFTU specified that 'national, trans-regional, and trans-industrial mass activities should by all means be discouraged'.[13]

By the mid-1980s, it was becoming evident in China that the industrial reform movement launched with high hopes in 1984 was not achieving success comparable with what had been attained in the countryside. Price inflation began to erode and, in a significant number of cases, outstrip wages. The student demonstrations of December 1986 and January 1987 raised an explicit challenge to reform policy in calling for the acceleration of reform and societal liberalisation. Reportedly, Deng evoked the Polish situation in December 1986, when he issued instructions to CCP General Secretary Hu Yaobang on how to handle the demonstrators, noting: 'If worst comes to worst, we will impose military control just as the Polish are doing.'[14] Hu's handling of the students, however, proved insufficiently militant to placate Deng, who jettisoned his erstwhile protégé. The consequent reshuffling of leadership positions, with Li Peng replacing Zhao Ziyang as Premier and Zhao assuming the post of General Secretary within the CCP, proved to be only a temporary solution to the problem of increasing rifts between reformers and conservatives within the leadership.

This dissension within the top leadership was further reflected in labour policy. Although the workers had largely been passive observers during the earlier student demonstrations, by 1987 strikes and industrial go-slows were on the rise in China. Moreover, the development of strains in the Chinese economic reform movement coincided in 1988 with the outbreak of strikes in Poland and the resurgence of Solidarity as a force to be reckoned with on the Polish political scene. Despite the increased strength of the conservatives, policy decisions at the Eleventh Congress of the ACFTU, held in October 1988, indicated a victory for the reformist camp. The congress called for 'drastic changes' for the unions, greater independence, and more authority, with an eye to moulding them into a sort of interest group along the lines of the East European reform experience.[15] Reformist forces were also bolstered by the sudden appointment of Zhu Houze, a close associate of Hu Yaobang, to the number-two position in the trade union hierarchy as Vice-President and First Secretary of the ACFTU. With the Solidarity example lurking in the background, Chinese decision-makers apparently decided that increased democratisation within the ACFTU was preferable to attempts to build alternative structures outside it.

The Tiananmen Protests: 1989

The indecision with which the Chinese leadership reacted to the student movement that evolved after the death of Hu Yaobang on 13 April 1989 reflected a paralytic division between factions within the CCP as to an appropriate response. Fate seemed to will that Hu would die the week following the legalisation of Solidarity in Poland—an event with implications that were lost neither on China's leaders nor on its citizens. That China's leaders were highly sensitive to the possibility that the students and intellectuals would seek a Polish-style coalition with workers was indicated by a letter written by Party octogenarian Chen Yun to Deng in late April 1989, in which he noted: 'We must take strong action to suppress the student movement. Otherwise, it will only grow bigger and if the workers join in the consequences will be unimaginable.'[16]

In fact, as May passed, workers joined the demonstrations in increasing numbers (see Zhang's essay in the present volume). Speakers seeking to rally demonstrators made pointed references to Solidarity, which subsequently served as a model for students and workers in setting up associations independent of Party control.[17] The best-known worker organisation was the Beijing Workers' Autonomous Federation (北京工自联), set up in Beijing on 19 May 1989, which claimed to have a membership of 3,000 workers.[18] Subsequently, the movement spread to other Chinese cities. In just several weeks between late May and early June, autonomous unions were established in Beijing, Shanghai, Changsha, Hangzhou, Hefei, Hohhot, Guiyang, Jinan, Nanchang, Lanzhou, Nanjing, Xi'an, and Zhengzhou. In some cities, moreover, multiple autonomous unions sprang up.[19] Small in scale and lacking organisational coherence, these groups, with a membership that was apparently predominantly male and young, nonetheless posed a clear challenge to the positions of both the Party and the ACFTU. In its Provisional Charter, the Beijing Workers' Autonomous Federation stressed its intent to operate as an 'entirely independent autonomous organisation', defining one of its key functions as 'monitoring the performance of the Chinese Communist Party'.[20]

The establishment of independent trade unions, however, was only one indication of dissatisfaction in the ranks of labour. With the continual breakdown of traditional controls, cadres within the ACFTU itself became increasingly emboldened to present their case against the leadership. Journalists from the *Workers' Daily* were among those who expressed their support for the students' demand for freedom of the press. The publication of an article in the *Workers' Daily* in praise of Hu Yaobang in April 1989 reportedly so enraged President Yang Shangkun that he pressed for the removal of its author or the closure of the paper.[21] Even after publication of a 26 April editorial in the *People's Daily* that condemned the students' movement as illegitimate, the national committee of the ACFTU, as well as local-level trade union committees in Hunan and Shanghai, issued a statement praising the student movement and calling on the CCP and the State Council to engage in dialogue with student representatives.[22] The ACFTU even donated 100,000 yuan to the Beijing Committee of the Red Cross to be used for medical treatment for students on hunger strike.[23]

Although the evidence is inconclusive, the leadership's decision to impose martial law on 20 May was possibly spurred on by the growing militancy of China's workers and open signs of defiance by the ACFTU. Even before the Tiananmen incident of 4 June, workers came in for harsher treatment than students at the hands of the regime. As a journalist noticed at the arrest of four workers in Shanghai: 'These people said the same thing that the students were saying. Their crime was to be workers rather than intellectuals.'[24] In the crackdown that followed, the conditions of incarceration for workers were more severe than for students or intellectuals. In large part, these differences appear to be a function of the higher status and superior connections, both domestic and international, of students and intellectuals in Chinese society. It would appear, nonetheless, that a residual fear among the Chinese leadership of the potential for organised industrial unrest also accounts for some of the ferocity displayed in its treatment of workers. In the aftermath of the Tiananmen events, the CCP reoriented the ACFTU in a more conservative direction as well as purging those members of the trade union leadership (most notably, Zhu Houze) who were deemed too radical. The prominent message at the Third Meeting of the Eleventh Presidium of the ACFTU in July 1989 was the paramount importance of maintaining CCP leadership over the organisation.

The Polish Lesson

When worker strikes erupted in Poland in 1980, the Chinese leadership immediately recognised their significance for the Chinese domestic scene. As in Poland, workers in China were highly dissatisfied with their standard of living and regarded the ACFTU as an ineffectual structure that was unable to defend their interests. Chinese leaders were rightfully concerned about the potential for the 'Polish virus' to spread to China, inasmuch as Chinese labour issues tended to mirror those in Poland, albeit in a less inflamed context. China's leaders were in agreement that the Polish crisis was a cautionary lesson for China. The problem was that they disagreed about the policy implications of that lesson. The reformers sought a greater role for the voice of workers, largely through reforms within the ACFTU; conservatives, meanwhile, feared that greater liberalisation would undermine the leading role of the CCP. In fact, the evolution of events in Poland—as well as elsewhere in the communist bloc—indicates the immense difficulties in striking a balance between liberalisation and the maintenance of Communist Party control.

During the 1980s, the tensions engendered by the Chinese reform movement intensified, and were further aggravated by the unravelling of communist party-states in Eastern Europe and the Soviet Union. Over time, the conservatives overpowered the reformist wing of the CCP. The political protests of 1989 were deeply disturbing to the CCP leaders who had lived through the traumas of the Cultural Revolution and feared above all political instability. During the Tiananmen events, Deng set forth his own assessment of the events in Poland and the errors of the Polish Communist Party leadership. For Deng, the PUWP had been 'too soft'.[25] Moreover, as he noted: 'Concessions in Poland led to further concessions. The more they conceded, the greater the chaos.'[26] The preeminent lesson that Deng and many of his like-minded comrades drew from the Polish events was the imperative to never relinquish Party control. At the same time, however, this lesson—which remains relevant—not only eliminates the possibility of autonomous worker associations, but also dooms the ACFTU to a subservient existence.

1981

After three decades of collective agriculture (see Unger's essay on 1962 in the present volume), the return to family farming in the early 1980s was a seismic shift in the lives and labour of the majority of Chinese people. It did not, however, occur everywhere at the same time. The year 1981 witnessed the largest number of villages making this shift, but some villages did so earlier and some later. In fact, the conversion from collective agriculture to household farming was rolled out across China, one county and province after another, over four years, from 1980 to 1983.

Abandoning Collective Farming and the Effects on Labour
Jonathan UNGER

By the late 1970s, many of China's farmers were frustrated. Due to a wave of failed radical policies pushed in the 1970s by Mao Zedong's closest followers in Beijing (today pejoratively called the Gang of Four), earlier gains in rural livelihoods had begun to stagnate. Before the mid-1970s, many farmers had perceived benefits in owning and working the land together with some fifteen to forty neighbouring households in what were titled 'production teams' (生产对). Interviews I conducted in Hong Kong during the 1970s with émigrés from China's countryside revealed that previously there had been acceptance and a large degree of support for the team-based effort. Most villagers appreciated the economic security of being a member of a team in case they suffered personal illness or injury. Grassroots collective ownership and work had also provided the means to organise farmers' labour during slack seasons to level fields or improve irrigation systems and thereby raise yields. And it had provided a means to invest in agriculture on a scale beyond what individual households could ever afford. But things were turning sour in the 1970s. Political commands from above, pushed by the new radical leadership around Mao, forced production teams to convert fields devoted to cash crops to concentrate on low-priced grain crops. The teams were being told to 'volunteer' some of their grain free of charge to support the revolution. Farmers were prohibited from raising extra pigs and chickens privately in their spare time, denying them an important source of cash income. As one imposition after another descended from above, the farmers' willingness to work hard for the mutual benefit of the households in their production team was waning.[1]

However, the farmers did not abandon collective agriculture and revert to household-based farming on their own. Orders to do so came from above in the early 1980s. Chinese newspapers and journals of the time, however, painted a different picture. Much as they had erroneously reported about collectivisation in the 1950s, the official Chinese media made it seem that the abandonment of collective farming was a spontaneous grassroots movement. A flurry of English-language academic articles in the 1980s reiterated what the official Chinese writings averred.

But interviewees from Chinese villages repeatedly have reported otherwise, saying they were instructed to dismantle collective production and adopt household farming. By this point, many of them were disillusioned and happy to do so, but they were not the initiators.

The very first moves towards household farming had indeed originated with farmers during 1978–79 in two poor and remote counties of Anhui and Guizhou provinces, in hamlets where farmers had barely enough to eat. Their secret acts were quietly permitted by local officials and then, more publicly, by Anhui's Party secretary Wan Li. In 1980 Li was promoted to Beijing as the minister in charge of agriculture. China's new leaders were aware of the rural discontent and slowing work pace and, starting that year, Chinese Communist Party secretary Hu Yaobang, Premier Zhao Ziyang, and Wan Li, in separate and uncoordinated ways, pushed for relaxations in agricultural policy. But they did not specifically call for household farming and in fact were ambiguous about their intentions. One result was that provincial leaders had to figure out how to proceed. Coming after the repeated purges of officials during the 1960s and 1970s for being out of step with the Party line, they looked sideways to see what other officials were doing. As relaxations in rural policies gathered pace, they climbed aboard and ordered the parcelling out of collective fields to families to cultivate independently.[2]

As household farming was adopted in one province after another, there were significant increases in agricultural production in 1982–83, and this validated and embedded the new farming practices. As a consequence, by the end of 1983, 97.8 percent of all production teams in China had handed out their land to households.[3] In sum, a complex and unplanned interplay between the top leadership, which was hesitantly open (but not committed) to household farming, and provincial and subprovincial leaders, who felt strong tacit pressures to show their political loyalty by embracing new 'reform' policies, culminated in an entirely new agrarian order.

This national scenario was confirmed by interviews I conducted in Hong Kong in mid-1983 with twenty-eight emigrants from eleven Chinese provinces who had recently returned from extended visits to their home village, ranging from a week to several months.[4] Twenty-six of the twenty-eight villages in my sample had converted to family smallholdings by the end of 1982, and twenty-four of the interviewees related that in their own villages the decision was made exclusively by officials at levels far above that of the village. In only two villages had the production teams' cadres and peasants themselves taken the initiative, and in one of these they had jumped the gun and swung over to family smallholdings in a belief that instructions to do so would soon come down from above.[5] The other village was in Fengyang, the impoverished county in Anhui that became famous as the first place in China where farmers, in 1979, secretly began cultivating their fields as households.[6] All of the other twenty-six villages passively waited for upper levels to tell them what to do and, when the upper levels did move, in only two of these villages were the peasantry informed that they could choose for themselves which system they preferred. The remaining twenty-four villages were shifted, without choice, into exactly the same system of family smallholdings, called 包干到户, in which each family gained use rights to fields without rental charge, with the amount of land based strictly on how many people were in the family. The land remained the property of the production team as a whole, but individual households could use most of the land that was allotted to them to diversify into any crops they liked and they could sell those crops on their own. To all intents and purposes, team members had been transformed into independent smallholders—albeit without a right to sell the land or convert it to non-agricultural purposes. That same system prevails today in the majority of China's villages.

The Immediate Consequences to Livelihoods and Labour

According to my twenty-eight interviewees, families with a large number of dependants were worried about the return to family farming, as were the elderly without close relatives, and families headed by women or by weak or chronically ill men. According to an interviewee who was sympathetic to collective agriculture, 'before, if they weren't physically able-bodied, they were given lighter work and still got their work-point income, but now they'd have to take care of the entire agricultural process, including all the really heavy work'. However, the majority of able-bodied families simply looked after their own interests—and, going by the interviewees' accounts, in the surveyed villages something like three-quarters of the households were in favour of disbanding collective agriculture and the remainder were opposed.

Some of the opposing households soon found that they, too, were better off. In good part this was due to policies the government had initiated even before the disbandment of collective agriculture. In particular, the government in 1979–80 began offering better prices for most types of agricultural produce. Largely as a result of this, official statistics for China showed a rise of 67 percent in real per capita villager incomes between 1978 and the end of 1982.[7]

Prices for agricultural produce continued to rise for a few more years after 1982. Taking advantage of this, many households further raised their living standards by working more efficiently. Whereas in the last years of collective agriculture the pace of work had slowed, now, with their own families the sole beneficiaries, farmers pushed themselves. Households with adequate labour power could now strive to quickly plant and harvest sufficient grain on a portion of their fields and then use the remaining land to grow labour-intensive high-priced commercial crops. Many also found time to begin raising large numbers of hogs and poultry for the market, or rented village ponds to raise fish for urban consumption. Per capita peasant incomes leapt by 14.7 percent in real terms in 1983—a point at which all households were engaged in family farming—and climbed yet again in 1984 by exactly the same percentage: that is, by about 30 percent in two years.[8]

A downside, though, was that many women lost their status as independent income-earners. Before, they had worked together all day with other team members, often in squads of fellow women, and had developed their own social standing in the team. They had earned their own workpoints and their own share of the harvest yield, demonstrably contributing much-needed income to the family. This had especially enhanced the situation of the as-yet-unmarried daughters. Now, when family farming was introduced, they worked under the direction of the *paterfamilias*, they were no longer working alongside other women, and did not bring home their own income. In these respects, rural women's circumstances and personal status declined.

However, the return to household farming soon was accompanied by a release of spare family labour from the fields, including young unmarried women. During the 1980s and 1990s, the fastest-growing sector of China's economy was rural industry—still publicly owned by rural townships and villages—which thrived because it was based on considerably cheaper labour than China's urban state-owned factories. The young rural factory workers rode or walked to work from their village homes each day, brought home much-needed cash from their personal wages, and worked in their spare time in their family's fields. Some of the young adults soon began spreading out across China in search of job opportunities. When the teams had practised collective agriculture, they did not have permission to move, but now they were able to leave unimpeded. The number of migrant workers from the countryside has now swelled to more than 200 million—with major implications for farming that will be observed later in this essay.

An Egalitarian Legacy

The experiences of the previous period of collective agriculture had accustomed farmers to a commonly held moral premise that every household had a right to receive enough from the land to subsist. For instance, a plot of land had been distributed by the team to each household near its home to grow vegetables for its own consumption. The size of these plots (自留地) had expanded and contracted as families added and lost members, and each readjustment restored within the production team an equal per capita vegetable plot size. In addition, families who could not earn enough to feed all their children had obtained an annual grain ration 'on loan' from the production team for each of their young children; the cost of the loaned grain would be finally deducted from the family's earnings after the grown children entered the team's labour force. Villagers who had become accustomed to their production teams making these adjustments to balance out the family cycle were favourable to continuing such adjustments in the post-collective period in a different form, as being in their family's long-term interests.

They were glad that in the early 1980s, when all fields were handed over to households to farm independently, the same principle of equal per capita land size was used that had previously been applied to small household vegetable plots. Across China, farmers decided to retain this egalitarian principle into the future. Since the fields were still owned collectively by all of the team's households, they were able to recalibrate use rights over time. Starting in the 1980s and into the 2000s, every half decade or so they met as a group to readjust the team's fields. Each time, families that had grown in size through births or weddings and faced a shortage of land gained larger landholdings, and families that had decreased in size through deaths or the departure of daughters into marriage lost land, to recreate an equal per capita possession of land. The national government opposed these land readjustments, and passed regulations in 1993 and more strictly in 1998 to prohibit the practice. But the farmers ignored these official directives and reallocated land at least once and often periodically, meeting quietly to discuss and vote on whether the time had come to readjust landholdings yet again.

In mid-2008, a survey questionnaire I helped devise collected a wealth of information in fifty-seven of Anhui Province's rural counties from 476 production teams (now retitled by the government as 'villager small groups', 村民小组). The survey was implemented by students at Anhui Agricultural University who came from villages. They obtained answers to the questionnaire from their own and sometimes also one or two nearby 'villager small groups' when they went home for the summer of 2008. The findings were startling. Some 452 of the 476 villager small groups in the survey—that is, 95 percent—had reallocated their fields at least once since 1984 to recreate equal per capita landholdings, and most had done so more than once. A second survey using the same questionnaire was implemented that same year by seventy schoolteachers in one rural Anhui county. It found that all but one of the ninety-one surveyed villager groups (98.7 percent) had reallocated land and had conducted an average of 3.8 land redistributions since 1984.[9]

China's Migrant Workers and Their Ties to the Land

Practically all of the young villagers who sought work elsewhere in China after the disbandment of collective agriculture moved without their families, because China's system of household registration (户口, hukou) erected legal barriers to migration (see Hayward's essay in the present volume). The Chinese authorities tightly implemented the registration system in much the same way as the South African Government used the pass system in the days of apartheid—and, similarly, families could not accompany workers.[10] China's registration system is a legacy of the period of Mao's rule, when the government used it to segregate peasants and urban people by barring migration from rural to urban areas. In its original form, hukou required rural residents to remain in agricultural production in their own village to feed the urban populace, and urban population growth was strictly kept in check. In the post-Mao era in the 1980s and 1990s, the same system instead served as a way of making use of the huge cheap surplus labour power of rural areas in new labour-intensive export industries, while forcing the migrant workers' families to remain behind in the countryside. This policy saved city governments a lot of money, since they did not have to provide migrant families with access to urban health care and schools.

Most of the factories preferred to hire young unmarried women in the belief they were more 'obedient' (听话) (see Anita Chan's essay on 1993 in the present volume). The women were usually dismissed by the time they were twenty-four, on the grounds they were becoming too old to endure the fast-paced production-line work. Thus, the majority of the young women who left villages to find urban jobs had to then leave factory work and return home. The men often found jobs in construction and could continue working into middle-age. Agriculture became 'women's work', with young wives and their mothers-in-law and older men doing most of the work.

By the latter part of the 1990s, increasing numbers of the young wives began leaving their villages, even after giving birth, to take up low-end sweatshop or service-industry work, often in the same city as their husbands. It was too difficult to make ends meet otherwise, as crop prices were declining. They normally left their children behind in the care of grandparents. This trend accelerated after 2003 as China's export industry continued to expand rapidly and needed more labour than could be supplied just by young unmarried rural women. Factories therefore began opening their doors to migrant workers older than their mid-twenties, including men. It became increasingly common in poorer parts of the agricultural heartlands for villages to be occupied largely by grandparents and young children, with the younger generation of adults returning for a week each Chinese New Year. But many parents did not want to endure separation from their children and, within another half-decade, some of them began taking their young children to the city where they worked, sometimes bringing along a grandmother to care for them.

Most of the factory and construction jobs were temporary, though, and migrant workers regularly found themselves between jobs or became burned out and had to quit urban work for a while, returning to their village and farm work in the interim. A majority of migrant-worker families have experienced this type of circular migration between village and urban job, exacerbated by the fact that often their children, once of school age, cannot enter urban schools.[11]

Other families, though, departed the countryside for such a long period that it seemed permanent. It therefore became an issue as to whether those households should receive land in the next redistribution given they had left the village, had not personally cultivated land for an extended period, and instead had leased out their allotted fields. But, according to the Anhui survey, 76.5 percent of villager small groups continued to make land available to families who had moved away. They realised that access to land back home provided a much-wanted safety net for these migrant families, whose urban status remains precarious due to China's ongoing household registration policy. Almost all villagers have close relatives who have become migrant workers, and having land as a backup is an option many village householders obviously wish to keep open.

Notably, though, there was a drop-off in the frequency of land reallocations after 1995 that persisted through to the 2008 survey. My Anhui survey statistics show that, between 1996 and 2008, only 33 percent of the villager small groups reallocated land for demographic reasons. A major reason is that after increased numbers of young villagers started leaving the countryside to take up work in urban areas, they remitted part of their income to their relatives in the village, so there is now a lower dependency on agriculture; and also, with more labour working elsewhere, there is less population pressure on the land. These two factors work against a felt need for land readjustments.

In the past decade and a half, the national and regional governments have turned away from supporting household farming and, in many districts, have endorsed agribusiness as 'modernisation'. Pressures have been exerted on villager small groups to lease all their land to a large-scale farmer or corporation—sometimes on contracts lasting several decades.[12] While most of China's villages retain family smallholdings under villager small groups, in the villages where agribusiness has taken over, many of the households and migrant workers have lost their access to farming. Their precarity has worsened.

1983

As part of Reform and Opening Up, the Chinese authorities decided to allow some foreign investment in the country and permit private entrepreneurs to start businesses. With this goal in mind, in 1980 the Chinese Government approved the establishment of China's earliest Special Economic Zones (SEZs) in Shenzhen, Xiamen, Zhuhai, and Shantou. Although labour mobility remained limited until the mid-1980s, the companies that set up shop in the zones relied on a workforce coming from the Chinese countryside. Excluded from the perks of the 'iron rice bowl', these migrants took on temporary wage labour without many legal guarantees in the hope of earning higher wages that eventually would allow them to save enough money to return home and set up their own family or, possibly, stay in the city. Many of them were young rural women—a whole generation of 'working little sisters' (打工妹). Based on the experience of the Sanyo mei—female workers recruited from 1983 by one of the first Japanese firms to set up shop in the Shenzhen SEZ—this essay is a heartfelt tribute to that generation of Chinese women.

Dagongmei: Gendered Troubles in the City of Dreams

Mary Ann O'DONNELL

When Shenzhen was the world's factory during the 1980s and especially during the 1990s, migrants came to the city with the goal of finding jobs that would enable them to earn enough money to improve their lives and status. Men were referred to as *dagongzai* (打工仔) or 'working boys', while women workers were classified as *dagongmei* (打工妹) or 'working little sisters'. At the time of the establishment of Special Economic Zones (SEZs) in 1980, both men and women understood temporary wage labour (one possible translation of *dagong*) to be a transitional role that filled the years between leaving home to find work and setting up an independent family, usually back home, but possibly, through luck and hard work, in the SEZ itself. However, by the late 2010s in Shenzhen the term *dagongzhe* (打工者) had come to refer to temporary workers from rural areas who lived and worked in the city's outer districts or in second-tier cities such as Huizhou and Dongguan and had few life options other than leaving home to take up low-paying jobs that offered little hope for advancement and respectability. In this essay, I draw on fieldwork since 1995, sociocultural research on Shenzhen, the city's gazetteers, newspapers, and statistical reports, as well as *dagong* writing (打工文学), to discuss the emergence and degradation of Shenzhen's *dagongmei* within and against the city's gendered moral geography, tracking how roles such as wife and mother, sister and whore, girlfriend and female boss have shaped migration and belonging to Shenzhen through the real and imagined bodies of 'little sisters' (*mei* in Mandarin and *mui* in Cantonese).

Sanyo Mei: Normative Migration

> I remember once I was in an elevator, when a former colleague said to me: 'Are you still a Sanyo *mei*?!' At the time, I felt embarrassed because I was still working at Sanyo. But actually, I'm proud of what I did there. In fact, Sanyo *mei* could get jobs anywhere in the Special Zone. We had the best training and were the most conscientious workers. — A Wen, former Sanyo line girl[1]

Shenzhen is famously a city of migrants and more famously a city of opportunity. From the city's official establishment in 1979 to its fortieth anniversary in 2019, the population grew from roughly 300,000 to an unofficial estimate of twenty million people. Yet residents are quick to point out that population figures obscure more than they reveal because tens of millions have come and left China's oldest and largest SEZ. Maybe thirty, maybe forty million people have lived and worked in Shenzhen over the years—or so residents speculate over *dim sum* and pu'er tea, casually reckoning population, gross domestic product (GDP), and projected growth in billions and trillions because it seems impossible to exaggerate the scale and intensity of Shenzhen's boom times.

Before President Xi Jinping launched the China Dream campaign in 2012, before Shenzhen became the first Chinese city without villages in 2004, before the Handover accelerated the ongoing social and economic integration of Shenzhen and Hong Kong in 1997, before Deng Xiaoping came to Shenzhen to announce that Socialism with Chinese Characteristics would not be derailed in 1992, and before Yuan Geng went to Shanghai to participate in debates on extending Reform and Opening Up policies to China's coastal cities in 1984—before all this, the elevation of Bao'an County to Shenzhen City in 1979 and the subsequent establishment of the SEZ in 1980 symbolised a turn away from the austerities of Maoism towards more: more appliances, houses, cars, and democracy; more enlightened thinking, industry, j-pop idols, and Taiwanese crooning. Deng said: 'Let some people get rich first.' And they did.

Consider the first generation of Sanyo *mei*, who are still held up as exemplars of the success of Reform and Opening Up in transforming the destinies of ordinary people. From 1983 until roughly the end of that decade, Sanyo recruited female workers from cities and towns throughout Guangdong. The first Japanese firm to invest in Shekou—a former customs station of Bao'an County that in 1979 was made into a pioneering industrial zone—Sanyo produced electronic components, as well as radios, boomboxes, and televisions. At that time, urban unemployment was high throughout Guangdong, and provincial leaders hoped to manage it by limiting access to formal jobs in Shenzhen to workers with provincial urban *hukou* (household registration). In such circumstances, the first generation of Sanyo *mei* were not only thrilled to receive an offer to work in an international factory, but some also left existing jobs to take their chances in Shekou.

Getting an offer from Sanyo was a complicated process. The company's human resources department requested workers via the Shekou Industrial Zone Human Resources Department, which in turn arranged for urban labour departments to hold onsite tests in maths, science, and Chinese as well as interviews for female high school graduates, who had to be at least 1.6 metres tall. The tests aimed to identify the smartest applicants, while the interviews focused on Mandarin communication skills, manners, and self-presentation. After all, Sanyo recruiters reasoned, these young women would represent China in one of the country's first fully foreign-owned factories of the reform era.

Getting into the recruitment process was the first step, and many women—especially shorter applicants—relied on relatives to 'open a backdoor' (开后门) to secure a chance to sit the job exam and be interviewed by recruiters. Tests were graded after the exam and results posted the next day, along with the interview list. As many as 2,000 might sit an exam, but ultimately only one in ten or sometimes even one in twenty made the cut. A week after selection, hometown labour bureaus arranged buses to bring cohorts of seventy to 100 workers to Shekou. While recruits were excited to set off for the industrial park, most were disappointed to find themselves travelling on dirt roads through rice paddies and lychee orchards. They had departed relatively prosperous cities and towns only to discover that Shekou was a rural backwater. Consequently, most recruits did not stay. One former Sanyo worker remembered that her hometown cohort had seventy people, and only four or five stayed, while another recalled that of her 105-person cohort only five remained.

Recruits who stayed were employed as contract workers. The Shekou Industrial Zone Human Resources Department arranged for their files (档案) to be transferred from their hometowns to Shekou. As contract workers, Sanyo *mei* were entitled to subsidised housing and medical benefits. In contrast, workers who had not transferred their file to a company in Shekou were employed as temporary workers. The distinction between contract and temporary workers made a difference because only contract workers were eligible to transfer their *hukou* (户口) to Shekou, which in turn made them eligible to send their children to a local school and receive a retirement pension. The window of opportunity for Sanyo *dagongmei* to secure a Shekou *hukou* as a single woman was brief. By the late 1980s, Sanyo—like many manufacturers in Shenzhen—hired temporary line workers, rather than offering migrant workers a contract that included transferring one's *hukou* to the industrial zone. By the end of the decade, unlike the first generation of Sanyo *mei*, the majority of migrant workers came from villages and held rural *hukou*, complicating their ability to secure legal residence in Shenzhen because the SEZ only recognised city-to-city *hukou* transfers. This meant that rural migrants had to first transfer their village *hukou* to their hometown county seat, and from there make an urban-to-urban *hukou* transfer to Shenzhen; for many, this was not a viable option.[2] In addition, after 1990, when Shekou was incorporated into the SEZ, *hukou* allotments were assigned by the city government. In the majority of cases, men had priority in receiving *hukou*, not only because it was assumed that men were the heads of households, but also because most managerial jobs and work unit transfers that offered *hukou* transfers were given to men. In practice, this meant that women and children usually received Shenzhen *hukou* as dependants of husbands and fathers, blurring the distinction between a woman's status as a worker and her status as a household member.

Lisa Rofel's work on female silk workers in Hangzhou offers insight into why Sanyo *mei* have continued to derive pride from their time as wage labourers.[3] In particular, she describes how family roles shaped women workers' experience of revolution, arguing that a key factor in the respectability of female work was not the work itself, but rather its location. Before the nationalisation of the silk industry in 1956, wives, mothers, and daughters who worked inside the family home retained their respectability. In contrast, women who performed the same jobs outside the family home were seen as sexually available 'broken shoes' (破鞋). For these women, being brought into nationalised production repositioned them from outside to inside, affirming their moral status and respectability. Similarly, the sponsored bus ride that Sanyo *mei* took from their hometowns to Shekou protected and affirmed their moral status within the state apparatus, even as having a Shekou *hukou* enabled them to legally reside 'inside' the SEZ. In addition, like the first generation of female factory workers in Hangzhou, Sanyo *mei* experienced the work they did in Shekou factories as an improvement over previous work. The Sanyo factories were modern and clean, the uniforms were more international in style than uniforms in traditional work units, and wages were significantly higher, allowing young women to contribute to their natal households, purchase cosmetics and clothes, save for school tuition, or open a kiosk. Sanyo also provided workers with relatively spacious dormitories, a bicycle for local transportation, and training in production and management, giving these young women access to physical and professional mobility and independence.

Quintessential Outsiders: Situating Dagongmei

> For those Shenzheners who already have a 'green card', we wage workers are simultaneously respected and pitied. Without a long-term *hukou*, a house, investment capital, a stable work unit and speaking with northern and southern accents, we are scattered in construction sites and on factory lines, behind counters and between offices, drifting from job to job; we make lives out of precarity. — An Zi, Shenzhen author[4]

Sanyo *mei* and young female migrants to Shenzhen during the 1980s imagined factory labour as a pathway to changing their destinies. However, even as Sanyo recruits forged the normative path for *dagongmei* in Shekou, a second, more precarious, path emerged.

An Zi was seventeen when she migrated from Meixian, a rural district of Meizhou City, Guangdong Province, to downtown Shenzhen in 1984. Her home village was in the mountains and she writes that 'the vitality of the city filled the heart of a Hakka girl with hope'.[5] She joined a cousin at a privately owned factory in the Caiwuwei area. The company's five-storey dormitory had ten forty-square-metre rooms per floor, with beds for twenty-four women per room. That first night, An Zi's cousin brought her a bucket of water for washing because the line at the shower room was too long. The next day, the girl was assigned to the assembly line managed by a young man who was also from Meixian. The workday was twelve hours and entailed assembling small metal components. An Zi does not say what the components would be used for, but she does mention that within several days her hands were bruised. By calling attention to how manufacturing injured *dagongmei* bodies, specifically hands, her writing refutes a common stereotype that young women are best suited for assembly work because they have nimble fingers. In fact, these contradictions between the hype and the lived conditions were an important feature of Shenzhen's *dagong* literature in the 1980s and 1990s.[6]

A temporary worker, An Zi has written about the difficulties *dagongmei* experienced on the road from factory work to respectability. In the essay 'Luohu *Mei*' (罗湖妹), for example, she introduces Luo Ling, who is described as someone no longer young enough to be amused by romance and who instead just wants to get married.[7] While working in a factory, Luo hooks up with Ren Honghui, a Chaoshan migrant who 'has a head for business'. The two move in together. Luo gives her savings and free time to helping Ren start up a restaurant near the factory, anticipating that they will formalise their relationship once he has made enough money to support a family. When the restaurant succeeds, however, Luo realises that Ren is not a faithful lover. Failing to convince him to respect their relationship, Luo cuts her losses and moves from Luohu to Shekou, where she eventually sets up her own shop. Luo's takeaway from her failed romance–business venture is that she is better off as an independent businesswoman, and she starts donating money to support a *dagong* literary club.

When An Zi published this essay in 1991, the idea that hard work would facilitate self-transformation was already an established trope in Shenzhen.[8] However, the implication that Shenzhen *dagongmei* shacked up with boyfriends scandalised many outside Shenzhen, even if living together seemed a quasi-respectable option for young women who were 'temporarily' in the city and vulnerable to economic and sexual predators. Shenzhen was infamous as a place where Hong Kong businessmen set up second wives, where nightclubs included private rooms where men purchased time with 'three accompany mistresses' (三陪小姐), who ate, drank, and played with them, and where barbershops operated as low-end brothels. From the late 1980s and well into the 2000s, Shenzhen common sense held that, 'when men have money, they become bad. When women become bad, they get money' (男人有钱就变坏，女人变坏就有钱). The definition of 'bad' for both genders referred to having illicit sexual relations. Indeed, the three-line pun 'Bureau-level cadres play the hole [golf/vagina], division-level cadres play the ball [bowling/breast], and department-level cadres play with themselves [mahjong/masturbate]' (局级干部打洞、处级干部打波、科级干部自摸) reflected the institutionalisation of illicit sexuality in the SEZ.

The moral status of *dagongmei* was further degraded outside the SEZ. Built between 1982 and 1986, the Second Line (二线关) separated the SEZ from Bao'an County, which was reconstituted in about 1981. In practice, the Second Line operated as an internal border. Visitors were required to have travel passes (通行证) to enter the SEZ, while employers secured passes for contract workers. Anyone without a travel pass was inside the SEZ illegally and could be deported, making these workers vulnerable to policy shifts and economic swings. However, no Chinese citizen needed a travel pass to enter Bao'an. Consequently, Shenzhen City comprised the SEZ and Bao'an County, which functioned as interrelated ecosystems—one officially urban and the other rural, allowing for political, economic, and social exceptions to the already exceptional space that was the SEZ.[9] Inside the Second Line, the municipal apparatus and designated enterprises annexed collective land to build the city proper, while outside the Second Line, township and village enterprises thrived. In fact, Shenzhen's first urban plans (in 1982 and 1986) considered only the SEZ, and it was not until 1996 that the city promulgated a comprehensive urban plan for the entire city. This institutional geography not only echoed the themes of 'inside' and 'outside' that Rofel identified in Hangzhou and that Sanyo *mei* experienced as critical to their transition from unmarried migrant worker to respectable matron, but also appropriated the concomitant gendered morality of being inside and outside a 'proper' household to post-Mao society.

Shenzhen author Wu Jun has paid particular attention to how a *dagongmei*'s location inside or outside the Second Line was mobilised to mark, distinguish, and classify female bodies. In her first short story, 'From the Second to the Sixth Ward' (二区到六区), the narrator—a college graduate with urban *hukou* back home—happily migrates from northern China to Bao'an to work at a cultural station, the lowest level of cultural administration and production in Shenzhen City. On her arrival, the narrator discovers that she cannot enter the SEZ proper without a travel pass because her work permit is for Bao'an.[10] Lonely and isolated, she convinces her boss to offer a job to her hometown friend Guo Xiaogai. When the women first reunite, they cry and repeatedly exclaim how much they have missed each other. After their emotional reunion, the narrator notices that Guo's boyfriend, Xu Senlin, has also come. The relationship between the two women breaks down because both the narrator's boss and her friend believe she is having an affair with Xu. By the time the narrator breaks off her relationship with her friend, her reputation has been irreparably damaged. Eventually the narrator stops trying to make people see that she is a proper young lady and hooks up with 'Little Foreman', a married Cantonese-speaker (it is unclear whether he is local or from Hong Kong) who visits her dormitory and buys her clothing and small gifts. One night, a drunk and loquacious Xu stops by the dorm room, where he encounters Little Foreman. It is a strange and desperate cock block. Xu exhorts Little Foreman to treat the narrator better because she's a good girl, a college graduate. But on the wrong side of the Second Line, in her work place, she's treated like a whore. No one will marry her. No one will give her a decent job. She's doing random jobs just because she's from the Northeast and speaks Mandarin.[11]

Gendered Troubles in the World's Factory

Maybe it would be better if I teach my daughter to be selfish.
— Xiao Xu, migrant and young mother[12]

Pun Ngai has observed that *dagongmei* were aware that hard work would not secure them a place in the city, noting that 'the socialist machine had not smashed the patriarchal machine in the Maoist period, nor did the capitalist machine do so in contemporary China; in fact, these systems worked happily with each other, hand in hand; gear meshing with gear'.[13] In retrospect, it is clear that the life sequencing that Pun observed—from home to factory to home—was itself a normative path to respectability, if not in Shenzhen, then at least back home. Many of the *dagongmei* who came to Shenzhen not only enabled their parents to build new homes, but also helped finance their brothers' marriages. In rural areas, especially in the Hakka and Chaoshan areas of Guangdong, young men must own a house and provide a bride price to get married. Since the 1980s, sisters have earned much of the money that has transformed brothers into husbands and fathers. In turn, having paid back their natal family's investment in them, these daughters have 'married out' (嫁出去), becoming wives and mothers in houses partially paid for by their *dagongmei* sisters-in-law.

In 2018, the former employees of Shekou Sanyo celebrated the thirty-fifth anniversary of the opening of the factory and the fortieth anniversary of Reform and Opening Up. China Merchants, the state-owned corporation that first developed Shekou as an industrial zone, provided an exhibition space and former Sanyo employees donated more than 61,000 yuan, as well as exhibit items to the project, including their uniforms, ID cards, photographs, and copies of the *Shekou Sanyo Report*.[14] The exhibition documented how working at Sanyo facilitated the transformation of contract workers into Shenzheners who had not only contributed to the construction of the city, but also become members of the city's emergent middle class. Importantly, for many Shekou residents, Sanyo *mei* were not really *dagongmei*, even if, as the quotation that opened this essay suggests, they were viewed through the prism of Shenzhen's gendered labour regime. Sanyo *mei*, one of Shekou's early managers explained to me, were high school graduates, could speak Mandarin with northern leaders, and had an urban sensibility. That is why, he insisted, it was so easy for them to find husbands in Shekou. The implication was that 'authentic' *dagongmei* were uneducated, spoke Mandarin poorly, and remained lamentably rural, which not only made it difficult for them to find suitable husbands, but also put into question their reasons for being in Shenzhen. The subtext of his comments might have been implied, but it was nevertheless clear: how sexually promiscuous—he insinuated—were *dagongmei* (as opposed to legitimate employees)?

The normative path of Sanyo *mei* makes salient how pre-revolutionary moral geographies of inside and outside the home, as well as socialist geographies of being inside and outside the state apparatus, not only shaped how young women became *dagongmei*, but also how they were perceived within and against Shenzhen's gendered moral geography. This moral geography operated along two dimensions of interiority and exteriority. The first dimension of interiority referred to being 'inside' the state apparatus as an employee of an official enterprise; the second dimension referred to being 'inside' the SEZ proper. An SEZ *hukou* signified that a young woman had successfully achieved these two forms of interiority. Within and against this larger background, marriage and respectability were either a cause or a result of one's *hukou* status. For example, Sanyo *mei*, who enjoyed double inclusion—inside the state apparatus and inside the SEZ—often married for sentimental reasons because they already had an SEZ *hukou*. In contrast, as described by An Zi, rural *dagongmei*, who were physically located inside the SEZ but did not have Shenzhen *hukou*, faced institutional barriers when trying to transform their economic mobility into a respectable household. Many resolved this conundrum by prioritising one form of inclusion over the other. Some remained unmarried and focused on their career, while others contributed to their brothers' marriage costs and then married someone from back home. In contrast, outside the SEZ in Bao'an, even an urban *hukou* and a job at a government cultural station did not ensure an unmarried woman's respectability, let alone access to the SEZ. Under these circumstances, becoming a 'second wife' (二奶) was often preferable to—and/or an inevitable result of—navigating the suspicions about one's promiscuity that arose because both one's *hukou* and one's workplace were located 'outside' the SEZ.

Today, the first generation of Sanyo *mei* are respectable matrons and grandmothers. Many of the first generation of temporary *dagongmei* who made their way into the SEZ have small businesses and families, while others have households back in their hometowns. In 1990, Bao'an County was redistricted as Bao'an and Longgang Districts, the city's original 'outer districts'. Unmarried women workers who held Bao'an or Longgang *hukou* were eventually able to secure their status inside the SEZ when border-crossing protocols were relaxed in 2003 and then disbanded in 2010. Some first-generation *dagongmei* remained in Bao'an and Longgang despite the fact they did not secure a local *hukou*, continuing to find temporary work in factories and eventually setting up quasi-legal households in urban villages. When Shenzhen opened its public schools to children with 'outside' (非本地) *hukou* in 2009, even more women stayed to raise their families inside the city.

Today, these grandmothers embody the gendered contradictions of the 1980s and 1990s: their *hukou* status remains located 'outside' Shenzhen, but they are unable or unwilling to return to their hometowns. Their children are in but not of Shenzhen, inheriting their parents' *hukou* status. The conundrum, of course, is that migrating for work has become an inevitable journey for young people, especially those with rural *hukou*. Consequently, many unmarried rural women workers who have migrated to Shenzhen since the 2000s do not refer to themselves as *dagongmei*, the preferred term being the gender-neutral *gongyou* (工友).[15] *Gongyou* translates as 'work friend' and emphasises an individual's public roles as worker and friend, implying an alternative moral geography to that of *dagongmei*—the unmarried younger sister. The moral geography of *dagongmei* implicitly thrusts young women back into the pre-revolutionary moral landscape of working inside or outside a father's or husband's household, where one is sexually suspect merely for leaving home to find a job. In contrast, the moral geography of coworkers and friends, *gongyou*, offers young unmarried women places where they can make lives for themselves that are both independent and respectable.

1986

Not all women coming from rural areas found jobs in the new factories that were being established in China's Special Economic Zones. As China gradually introduced a market economy and pro-consumption policies, sex work, which had nearly been eradicated in the Maoist era, made its comeback in the country's major urban centres. As establishments such as nightclubs, saunas, hotels, hair salons, and karaoke bars began offering sexual services to their patrons, the Chinese authorities reacted with draconian measures that stipulated severe punishment for people who introduced others into sex work, offered venues for sex work, or organised or forced others into sex work, including the Criminal Law of 1979, the 1986 Regulations on Strictly Prohibiting Sale and Purchase of Sex, the 1987 Regulations on Eradicating Prostitution and Detaining Sex Workers for Labour Reeducation, the Criminal Law of 1984, and the Decision on Strictly Forbidding the Selling and Buying of Sex of 1991. This essay delves into the plight of sex workers in China in the reform era, highlighting how the repressive policies adopted by the Chinese Government not only have fuelled violence, exploitation, abuse, and health risks, but also have had terrible consequences for public health more generally.

Sex Workers in China: From Criminalisation and Abuse to Activism

Tiantian ZHENG[1]

In 1979, one year after the Third Plenary Session of the Eleventh Central Communist Party Committee ushered China into the new post-Mao era, the National People's Congress passed the first Criminal Law of the People's Republic of China. The law stipulated severe punishment, from imprisonment to the death penalty, for people who introduced others into sex work, offered venues for sex work, or organised or forced others into sex work. Since the law was enacted in 1980, the country's Public Security Bureaus have been tasked with periodic and nationwide crackdowns on sex work and police raids on the entertainment industry.

Maoist China boasted of its eradication of sex work through state policies such as the stringent household registration system, the isolation of peasants in the countryside, and the near prohibition of rural-to-urban migration. However, in the post-Mao era, the market economy and pro-consumption policies relaxed these restrictions, producing an explosion in the entertainment industry in major cities. In the 1980s and 1990s, the dire poverty and desperation of people in rural areas, accompanied by increasing social inequality, saw peasants stream into the cities, resulting in an influx of an estimated six million sex workers. The resurgence of sex work took place in establishments such as nightclubs, saunas, hotels, hair salons, discos and other dance halls, parks, video rooms, and karaoke bars.[2] On average, in the early 2000s, sex workers could earn more than 6,000 yuan a month—three times the average monthly income of a person with no special labour expertise, education, or skills.[3]

Adopting a feminist standpoint opposed to prostitution, the communist state perceives sex work as a violation of the human rights of women, as exploitation of their bodies, and degradation of their status. In the official view, sex work reduces women to the status of sexual objects, humiliated playthings, and exchangeable commodities, rather than respectable human beings. From such a perspective, women's social and political positions cannot be advanced unless sex work is outlawed. Since the ideology contends that no woman would voluntarily or willingly choose sex work in violation of her own legal rights, it is considered a forced occupation. Therefore, it is believed that sex workers need to be rescued, reeducated, and rehabilitated.

Rooted in this set of ideas, in the reform era, the Chinese Government continued the Maoist abolitionist policy of prohibiting all aspects of sex work, including solicitation, sale, purchase, and the third party's involvement in sex work. To do so, it adopted a wide array of laws and regulations, including the first Criminal Law of 1979, the 1986 Regulations on Strictly Prohibiting Sale and Purchase of Sex, the 1987 Regulations on Eradicating Prostitution and Detaining Sex Workers for Labour Reeducation, the Criminal Law of 1984, the Decision on Strictly Forbidding the Selling and Buying of Sex of 1991, the Decision on the Severe Punishment of Criminals Who Abduct and Traffic in or Kidnap Women and Children of 1991, the Law on Protecting the Rights and Interests of Women (Women's Law) of 1992, the Revised Criminal Law of 1997, and the Entertainment Regulations of 1999. These legal documents stipulate that it is forbidden to sell or purchase sex and that it is illegal to introduce people to sex work, offer venues for sex work, and organise or force people into sex work. People who transgress risk five to ten years of imprisonment, or the death penalty in severe situations.

Since 1989, local public security bureaus have been enforcing these laws and regulations through comprehensive, periodic 'strike hard' (严打) campaigns. These police raids target sex work as a 'social evil' (社会邪恶的东西) or 'ugly social phenomenon' (丑恶的社会现象) at odds with a 'socialist spiritual civilisation' (社会主义精神文明). Police crackdowns usually last about three months at a time and often occur more than once a year. Using techniques perfected during the communist revolution, the raids are often unexpected, sudden, and unannounced. As well as these attacks, plain-clothed police masquerade as customers to secure evidence to arrest sex workers.[4]

Elaine Jeffreys has argued that such crackdowns have successfully redressed the 'deteriorating' social order and that fines and the detention of sex workers in the wake of these raids are 'soft' and 'lenient', resulting in an 'amicable' relationship between local police and veteran sex workers.[5] As I will explain in this essay, my previous ethnographic fieldwork and recent research on this topic indicate that the opposite is the case. Police raids not only have fuelled violence, exploitation, abuse, and health risks among sex workers, but also have exacerbated public health problems and facilitated the transmission of HIV/AIDS.

Violence, Exploitation, and Abuse

Due to police raids and the criminalisation of sex work, sex workers live in constant fear of arrest and are unable to pursue police protection in case of violence. These women are at the mercy of both the police and male customers who feel they can inflict violence on and abuse them with impunity. Since it is the public security apparatus that wields the ultimate power to fine, arrest, and detain sex workers without due process, the police frequently abuse their arbitrary power, resulting in sex workers' mistrust of, and antagonistic relationships with, authority figures.

Legally and socially vulnerable, sex workers use fake names, fake identification, and fake family backgrounds in the cities where they work, making them easy victims of rape, violence, robbery, blackmail, as well as murder. In one shocking case in 2005, two male customers in Shenzhen not only beat and raped two sex workers, but also burned their breasts and vaginas with cigarette lighters. They dipped needles into ink and tattooed the words 'No 1. Sex Worker' and 'Slut' on the women's foreheads, breasts, and backs.[6] From 2004 to 2006, the bodies of more than sixty sex workers were discovered in Beijing alone, their identities unknown until their families reported them missing.[7] Since 2007, every week there have been at least one to two incidents of rape or murder of sex workers.[8] In the past decade, 40 percent of the unresolved murder cases in Beijing involved sex workers as victims.[9]

Police raids and criminalisation subject sex workers not only to violence from male customers, but also to police abuse. In 2010, during a police raid in Dongyuan, Guangzhou, several sex workers were paraded barefoot on the street and photographed, to subject them to public humiliation.[10] Elsewhere, sex workers reported being cruelly beaten by the police and forced to take nude pictures with male customers.[11] In a city in southern China, a journalist witnessed police charging at sex workers on a street with iron batons, beating and swearing at them.[12] Over the ensuing nights of this crackdown, the streets were periodically filled with the piercing screams of sex workers being mistreated by the police. Some police sprayed black ink or paint on the hair and faces of the women, before driving off while whistling songs. One sex worker told the reporter that her roommate, fleeing to avoid being beaten by a policeman, was hit by a car and died on the spot. The police were not held responsible for this incident.[13]

Because the police have the arbitrary power to arrest, fine, and detain them, sex workers are also compelled to comply with sexual exploitation at the hands of policemen. Seeking immunity from arrest and fines, some sex workers are kept by police officials as their personal harem to spy on others. My previous research showed that sex workers were petrified when plain-clothed customers revealed themselves to be policemen. To avoid arrest and fines, they were compliant with their sexual demands and exploitation.

In the absence of police protection and legal recourse, to ward off customer violence, sex workers are forced to look for protection from gangsters or establish long-term relationships with regular clients. In exchange for the protection provided by gangsters, sex workers have to provide free sexual services. Some sex workers are able to cultivate intimate relationships with regular customers, thus entering into contractual relationships with them. Living with a regular customer as part of a couple in a rented apartment, a sex worker is protected against police raids, arrest, and customer violence. However, since not using condoms is a prerequisite for such a relationship, sex workers are not protected against the risk of sexually transmitted infections (STIs), including HIV/AIDS.[14]

Fines and Abuses in the Rehabilitation Centres

Police raids often end in severe fines, arrests, and the detention of sex workers. Indeed, the 'strike hard' campaigns have become one of the ways in which police officials extort sex workers as well as owners of entertainment establishments.[15] The police arrested many sex workers during my own ethnographic fieldwork in karaoke bars.[16] If sex workers wanted to avoid being detained at a rehabilitation centre for up to two years, hefty fines immediately ensued. Over the years, fines have been arbitrarily imposed, from as low as 5,000 yuan (around US$800) to as high as 70,000 yuan (around US$10,000) in some special extortion cases.[17] The owners of some entertainment establishments also find it necessary to regularly bribe the police to avoid—or be notified in advance of—police raids.

Every year, more than 28,000 sex workers are arrested by the police or detained in about 200 rehabilitation centres.[18] Established in 1991 and managed by the local public security authorities, these centres house sex workers for a period ranging from six months to two years, providing 'reeducation' (再教育). Sex workers detained in these centres are often forced to engage in hard labour for many hours a day, seven days a week, without payment.[19] Such labour includes producing commodities such as toys and disposable chopsticks, some of which are for export. Women are not allowed to use the bathroom at night, are required to request permission for bathroom breaks during work hours, and are forbidden from using their local dialect when talking to their families. Often, they have to endure physical abuse such as severe beatings.[20] They are also required to pay for all the costs incurred by the centre on their behalf, including food, regular STI tests, bed linen and pillows, bathroom necessities such as soap and towels, and toilet paper. Family members must pay 200 yuan each for every visit. On average, sex workers end up spending 2,400 yuan during a six-month detention at a centre.[21] Having 'learned nothing', these women usually continue to engage in sex work after the completion of their 'rehabilitation education'.[22]

Mistreatment by Public Health Officials

Criminalisation of sex work engenders discriminatory public health policies. Sex workers are subjected to coerced HIV testing, their privacy is violated through the public release or withholding of the results of their medical tests, and they are mistreated by public health officials.[23] With the permission of the Ministry of Health, the Centres for Disease Control (CDC) test sex workers' HIV/AIDS status without their consent and, at times, without their knowledge. The CDCs also conduct HIV testing on all sex workers at a particular entertainment establishment after the health officials have established a relationship with the owners. Under such circumstances, sex workers feel compelled to comply with the business owners' orders to continue working there. Test results, however, are either released to the public or withheld from the sex workers themselves.[24]

Sex workers have reported prejudice, discrimination, and mistreatment by health officials in the CDCs.[25] They fear going to CDC clinics due to the poor treatment they receive from health officials and the possible cooperation between health officials and the police. As a result of this glaring rift between the official public health system and sex work, the health needs of sex workers are not met, while they are also humiliated and deprived privacy.

Health Risks

Police raids harm the health of sex workers. In addition to the violence and abuse mentioned above, police officials routinely confiscate condoms to use as evidence. During my research, sex workers, on arrest, were searched for condoms, the presence of which was deemed sufficient evidence to impose charges. This continued practice directly violates two Chinese laws: the 2006 Law on AIDS Prevention that instructs that condoms should not be used as evidence for arrest and a 2012 State Council document that mandates that condoms should be made available in public places.[26] This police practice discourages sex workers from carrying or using condoms, making them vulnerable to health risks related to unprotected sex, such as unwanted pregnancy and the transmission of disease.

Police raids also drive sex workers to clandestine or isolated locations to conduct their activities. Being in an unfamiliar area can render them helpless, thus augmenting the likelihood of customer violence and refusal to use a condom. Some sex workers are also forced into hiding, waiting for several months for police crackdowns to end. When they return to work after several months of forced inactivity and financial constraint, sex workers sometimes feel compelled to agree to unprotected sex with customers for immediate financial relief.

Sex workers in my previous research employed a variety of methods to mitigate the risks associated with unprotected sex, including emergency contraceptive pills, ineffective liquid condoms, cleansing liquids, and pre-sex antibiotic shots.[27] The overuse of these mediums, however, resulted in long-term physical suffering such as abdominal pain, vomiting, frequent pregnancies and abortions, infections, and infertility.

As mentioned above, sex workers avoid seeking help from health officials who are regularly judgemental and have connections with the police.[28] They also tend to stay away from major hospitals unless they are in need of serious surgery or urgent treatment for fear of high financial costs and potential arrest. As a result, they often seek temporary relief of symptoms from low-quality, unlicensed, and low-cost clinics, managed by unqualified practitioners with no professional training. As a result of police raids, sex workers are thus excluded from accessing essential healthcare services and face a wide array of health risks.

Activism

Calls for the legalisation of sex work and the abolition of the rehabilitation education system have proliferated in recent years in China. At every session of the National People's Congress and the Chinese Political Consultative Conference from 2003 to 2011, National People's Congress Representative Chi Susheng proposed legalising sex work. In her proposal, Chi enumerated the problems arising from the criminalisation of sex work, including police corruption, murder, abuse, heavy fines, an alarming HIV/AIDS transmission rate, and social discrimination. She advocated for the establishment of red-light districts, registration of sex workers, and regulation to ameliorate public health problems and increase national tax revenue. However, all her proposals were rejected.

In 2012, a group of nongovernmental organisations (NGOs) came together under the name Coalition of Chinese Sex Worker Organisations and published an online petition titled 'Sign On to End Violence against Sex Workers in China'.[29] The twelve organisations listed on the petition included the Beijing Zuoyou Centre, Shenzhen Xiyan, Shanghai Xinsheng, and Tianjin Xinai Culture and Media Centre. Some of these organisations are AIDS and LGBTQ activist groups. The letter cites 218 violent incidents against female, male, and transgender sex workers, including eight murders. Deploring the lack of protection for sex workers, the letter calls for an end to violence, stigma, discrimination against, and abuse of people in this line of work. These organisations have a marginal status in China, with only a few able to register as companies. These kinds of grassroots organisations and the state operate in a regime of 'contingent symbiosis', whereby the survival of the organisations hinges on their ability to benefit the state—a situation that constrains their activities.[30]

In 2006, activist Ye Haiyan created Hong Chen Wang (红尘网), the first website to provide sex workers with a platform to share their experiences and exchange information.[31] The website was blocked in 2010. One year earlier, Ye had organised the Chinese Folk Women's Rights Working Group (中国民间女权工作室)—an NGO intended to galvanise support from civil society to extend assistance to all kinds of marginalised women, including sex workers—and proposed 3 August as 'Sex Workers' Day'. In 2010, her NGO members and volunteers staged events on the main streets of Wuhan to appeal for the legalisation of sex work. A few days later, Ye was taken away by police for a 'trip' that lasted a few days.[32] Her organisation was also forced out of Wuhan and is currently located in a remote town in Guangxi Province. Over the following years, Ye was arrested and detained on several occasions.

Although the Chinese Government abolished the 'labour reeducation system' (劳动教养体制) in 2013, this reform has not impacted sex workers. In 2014, more than 100 lawyers, scholars, and retired Communist Party members signed a petition, appealing for the abolition of the reeducation system for sex workers.[33] The letter, which declared the system violated the Constitution and rule of law, was sent to the National People's Congress. Four years later, on 24 December 2018, the Legislative Affairs Commission of the Standing Committee of the National People's Congress also proposed the abolition of the reeducation system for sex workers.[34] These developments suggest that the system might be abolished within the next few years.[35] With this system gone, the goal of decriminalising sex work will probably be within reach. Although the system currently remains very active in major cities such as Beijing, certain areas such as Anhui Province have already closed their reeducation centres.[36] In these areas, sex workers are either detained at police stations or fined, but they are no longer sent to rehabilitation centres.[37]

The criminalisation of sex work not only spawns violence, abuse, stigmatisation, and the exploitation of sex workers by the police and customers, but also ignores the economic and social factors that lead women to engage in this work. Decriminalisation would mean respecting sex work as a legitimate profession, protecting workers from violence, ensuring workers' access to basic health services and justice, and promoting public health. Research around the world has shown that areas where sex work has been decriminalised experience lower HIV transmission rates thanks to sex workers' insistence on condom use, in collaboration with public health officials.[38] Embodying the spirit of the international movement for the rights of sex workers, the rising activism in Chinese civil society has lit a beacon of hope that decriminalisation of sex work is on the horizon.

1988

In 1987, Taiwan emerged from thirty-eight years of martial law and initiated a democratic transition. At the same time, workers began to agitate for their rights and better protection. This essay reviews the trajectory of Taiwan's labour movement since this political watershed. Taiwan's working class was formed under authoritarian industrialisation, and workers adopted a wide array of hidden resistance strategies under the façade of docile conformism. The termination of martial law lifted the prohibition on strikes and demonstrations, setting forth a wave of grassroots militancy, which was aligned with the political opposition. In the 1990s, the labour movement adopted a more institutional approach by making use of the national legislature and the local administrations controlled by the opposition party, thus significantly improving the legal framework for labour protection. The essay ends with a discussion of the multiple challenges in the new century.

The Lifting of Martial Law and the Rise of Taiwan's Independent Labour Movement
Ming-sho HO

In July 1987, Taiwan terminated thirty-eight years of martial law. In February the following year, the first Lunar New Year holidays after the thaw witnessed a spontaneous strike wave among Taiwanese workers demanding a higher year-end bonus (年終獎金). This unexpected insurgency marked the beginning of Taiwan's labour movement—a long-overdue development considering that by then the island had experienced high-speed growth for nearly three decades with a concomitant process of proletarianisation that saw the children of farmers leave their home villages to become urban wage labourers.

Taiwan under martial law was an inhospitable environment for labour activism. Besides curtailing freedom of speech and the press, the government outlawed strikes, political parties and unauthorised gatherings of more than ten people. The generals were in charge of managing protests and military rather than civilian police were deployed when needed. While these features of 'political exclusion of the working class' were also common among other newly industrialised countries in East Asia,[1] Taiwan's case was particular in that its ruling Nationalist Party (hereinafter, Guomindang or GMD) was able to implement a series of preemptive measures to control labour prior to the economic transformation that began in the 1960s, when Taiwan became an export-oriented economy by exploiting its cheap labour. Reflecting on its defeat in mainland China, the GMD installed party-state structures—that is party branches and loyal unions—in state-owned and large enterprises.[2] In addition, by adopting a state corporatist arrangement, the GMD fostered a cohort of pro-regime labour union leaders to make sure that workers were represented in decision-making processes in a politically safe manner.[3] In light of all this, martial law–era Taiwan did not see the emergence of labour protests until the mid-1980s. Yet, the lack of ostensible conflict should not be seen as an outcome of the inherent docility or conformism of the Taiwanese working class. Deprived of political freedom, workers dealt with their grievances through private and individualised strategies, such as moonlighting, frequent turnover, operating their own small businesses, and so on.

This essay will examine the nascent labour movement's explosive rise and precipitous decline in the interval between political liberalisation and democratisation. Let me begin with an episode of the 1988 spring strike for a fuller understanding of workers' situation after the lifting of martial law.

The Taoyuan Bus Strike

Since 1947, the Taoyuan Bus Company (桃園汽車客運公司) had been granted exclusive rights to operate some routes in Taoyuan County (now Taoyuan City). Like many regional monopolies, the company belonged to a powerful local family of GMD politicians, the Wus. The Wu family also owned businesses in the financial and health sectors at the local level, for which government permits were required. While the bus company was lucrative, its 700 bus drivers were mistreated. Their hourly overtime rate was barely NT$20 (roughly US$0.70) and they received a daily allowance of NT$100 (US$3.30) for working during the holidays. In spite of personal threats from gangsters, in 1987, bus drivers organised a labour union. As the Lunar New Year approached, drivers advanced three demands: four days of rest per month; a daily allowance of NT$1,000 (US$33) for working during the holidays; and a fairer distribution of the year-end bonus, as they knew the company was making record profits. After several rounds of negotiation, the management only agreed to increase the extra holiday payment to NT$300 (US$10). Humiliated by such a meagre offer, the drivers launched an unprecedented five-day strike starting on 14 February 1988.

Technically, this was a wildcat strike, as it did not fulfil the legal procedures for an official stoppage. Many bus drivers punched in for duty but did not drive their route or called in sick. Although the right to strike had been recently restored after the lifting of martial law, the requirements were nearly impossible to meet since the law demanded that unions hold a meeting of their members at which at least half of the participants had to vote in favour of going on strike. A platoon of armed military police deliberately marched around one bus station to intimidate workers. On the second day, the local government issued an emergency order citing the National Mobilisation Law to demand the bus drivers return to work. It was no light threat: the wartime legislation could put violators in prison for up to seven years.

Why did an industrial dispute invite such high-handed intervention by the military and the government? At that time, Wu Po-hsiung, the scion of the local political clan, was the Minister of the Interior and Zheng Shuizhi, who had served as the general manager of Taoyuan Bus Company for more than a decade, was the Commissioner of the Labour Affairs Council—the top labour administrative organ, created in 1987. In other words, activists in the nascent labour movement were facing a formidably interconnected web of power and wealth—a situation that was not uncommon in Taiwan's large enterprises. Nevertheless, largely thanks to the courageous leadership of a driver named Ceng Maoxing, the management conceded to pay extra year-end bonuses to drivers and promised not to punish the strike participants. This successful strike led to a wave of bus driver activism throughout the country.

In many ways, Ceng's biography exemplifies the profile of Taiwan's first generation of labour leaders. Born into an impoverished Hakka peasant family in 1941, Ceng had to give up his study after finishing junior high school. Before becoming a professional driver, he worked in a state-owned construction company and volunteered in a harbour project in Saudi Arabia for extra money, gaining experience and skill in operating construction machinery. He first encountered political trouble when he refused to wear the mourning symbol after Chiang Kai-shek's death in 1975, eventually leading to his departure from the company. Partly because of this incident, Ceng was a staunch supporter of the political opposition, highly critical of the GMD and vocally supportive of Taiwanese independence, long before his involvement in the labour movement.

Other political changes in the mid-1980s laid the foundations for organised labour activism, including the campaign launched by Ceng and his fellow workers. In 1984, the *Labour Standards Act* (勞動基準法) was enacted, largely due to pressure from the United States, which had grown increasingly uneasy with the way Taiwan exploited cheap labour to grow its trade surplus. Although this was the first comprehensive legislation on working hours, overtime, minimum wages and other labour protection measures, the Act did not immediately improve the conditions of rank-and-file workers as neither the government nor businesses were eager to implement the new rules. However, the gap between what was legally promised and what workers actually received provided activists with a powerful discursive tool to persuade workers to join their movement. After bringing the strike to a successful end, Ceng launched another campaign to demand from the company compensation for all underpaid overtime since 1984.

The bus drivers were also supported by several of the newly established civil society organisations. On May Day 1984, when the legislative review of the *Labour Standards Act* was about to be completed, a group of human rights activists and lawyers formed the Taiwan Labour Legal Support Association (台灣勞工法律支援協會). This intellectual-led organisation was part of the political opposition, and many of its early participants later became politicians in the Democratic Progressive Party (民進黨, DPP). During the strike, Ceng Maoxing constantly availed himself of their legal advice and members of the organisation also recorded the mobilisation on film as it developed. In addition to opposition intellectuals, Ceng was also supported by a local Catholic labour centre directed by Father Neil Magill. Hailing from an Irish family with a background in the republican movement, Magill had originally worked in South Korea until he was expelled by the government. In 1984, Magill established an outreach centre in Taoyuan to assist distressed workers, which provided the meeting space for Ceng and his union associates.

Finally, the Taoyuan bus drivers' strike was also symptomatic of how workers' grievances accumulated in Taiwan. Even though the ban on political parties was still enforced, in 1986, the DPP was established and obtained the tacit recognition of the government. Before the 1992 legislative election, a portion of seats were reserved for workers, farmers, schoolteachers and other occupational groups. The legislature's functional representative design was a part of the GMD's state corporatist ideal, and, as expected, these seats were easily won by the ruling party. In the legislative election at the end of 1986, one GMD labour union incumbent was unexpectedly defeated and his seat went to a rather obscure DPP candidate. Since the legislators for the worker group were elected by workers, the incident revealed the existence of widespread labour discontent and its potential political reverberations.

The Rise of an Independent Labour Movement

In the late 1980s, the end of authoritarian rule brought about a flourishing of labour activism in the context of what was generally referred to as an 'independent labour movement' (自主勞工運動). The name did not indicate nonpartisanship or political neutrality—in fact, as Ceng Maoxing's case indicates, many of the earliest participants embraced an anti-GMD outlook. The emphasis on independence highlighted the necessity of challenging the system of labour control built by the GMD over the previous several decades.

One of the first battles was for control of the labour unions at the company level. Typically, in state-owned and large private enterprises, there were preexisting labour unions, often managed by GMD cadres or management. To gain control of these entities, dissident workers coalesced to participate in union elections, in which they often competed against the GMD-sponsored candidates. For instance, in March 1988, barely one month after the conclusion of the Taoyuan bus drivers' strike, workers at the state-owned China Petroleum Corporation elected their first non-GMD union president. It is highly suggestive that the new president was the younger brother of veteran DPP politician Kang Ning-hsiang. In other words, the GMD's grip on the existing labour unions was swiftly collapsing. In addition to these developments, an organising drive was set in motion in workplaces where workers were not represented by a labour union.

The salient feature of Taiwan's young labour movement was grassroots initiatives pertaining to company-level issues, such as overtime, working hours, union representation, and so on. In many cases, rank-and-file workers initiated their protests with little or no assistance from outside. Wildcat strikes and work stoppages were weapons typically adopted by discontented workers in this period. On May Day 1988, more than 1,000 railroad workers collectively took leave, resulting in a nationwide shutdown of railroad transportation. Soon, newly forged militant unions began to build broader alliances across regions and industries. At the end of 1988, the Alliance of Independent Labour Unions (自主工聯) was formed, with Ceng Maoxing elected as its first president. Since these groups did not seek legal recognition as union federations, they were largely free to operate drawing from their own resources.

As Taiwan's political transition opened up more legislative seats for competition, elections emerged as another arena for participation for Taiwan's independent labour movement. Opposition intellectuals already involved with labour issues became the conduits through which labour activists joined the DPP. But there were also some labour activists who rejected the DPP's middle-class liberalism and chose to set up new parties, including the Workers' Party (工黨) in 1987 and Labour Party (勞動黨) in 1989. The 1989 legislative election saw intensified competition among these new contenders, particularly for the five worker-group seats. In the end, the GMD obtained three seats and the DPP two. After this defeat, the two parties that claimed to represent the working class became less active.

The focus on elections was also related to the ruling party's attempt to revise existing laws. In 1988, the government proposed amendments to the *Labour Union Act* (工會法) and the *Act for the Settlement of Labour-Management Disputes* (勞資爭議處理法) in the hope of containing the labour offensive—a particularly urgent task considering threats from the business community to cease investing in Taiwan. Later, officials claimed that the 1984 *Labour Standards Act* was excessively generous and thus drafted a proposed amendment. In light of these initiatives, the legislative arena became another battleground for the independent labour movement.

In short, Taiwan's first postwar wave of labour activism shared many features with the so-called social movement unionism of other democratising countries, such as Brazil, South Korea and South Africa.[4] As in other countries, in Taiwan, labour grievances were an integral part of social problems that had emerged under prolonged authoritarian rule. It was immediately clear that labour exploitation was a result of political domination and not vice versa. Union leaders were willing to take militant action to improve the working conditions of their members, but also saw themselves as an integral part of a broader campaign for justice, including democratisation. In such a context, the fact that Taiwan's early flourishing of labour protests became politicised and partisan was to be expected.

The Decline of Grassroots Militancy

By the time Taiwan's first full legislative election was held in 1992, the militant ethos of the Taiwanese working class appeared to be a spent force. The labour movement continued, but its focus shifted away from workplace organising and strikes to policy lobbying, which required less rank-and-file participation. There are several reasons for this shift.

First, the GMD government took an increasingly hostile attitude to grassroots militancy. In May 1988, workers of the Far Eastern Chemical Fibre Company launched a strike to protest the dismissal of a union leader. Riot police were sent in to break the picket line and many participants later faced criminal prosecution. Three months later, workers at the Maoli Bus Company went on strike to demand better pay. In response, the government coordinated a boycott by mobilising buses and drivers from neighbouring regions, until Maoli bus drivers were forced to end their three-week strike empty-handed.

Second, employers grew less tolerant of labour activists, summarily discharging many of them. Since company unions were the building blocks of Taiwan's independent labour movement, the edifice collapsed when their leaders were removed. Some union leaders decided to resort to the legal system, but by the time they won their lengthy lawsuits, they faced an entirely new workforce that no longer welcomed them or their activism.

This phase of Ceng Maoxing's trajectory serves as an illuminating case of the repressive collusion between government and business. After leading the successful strike at the Taoyuan Bus Company in early 1988, Ceng was fired. In 1991, after receiving a two-month prison sentence for his involvement in the Far Eastern Chemical Fibre Company strike, he decided not to appeal and thus became the first labour movement leader to be jailed in the post–martial law era. Until his death in 2007, Ceng remained active in the labour movement through his leadership of the Alliance of Independent Labour Unions, but he was never able to obtain another full-time job and hence return to being a grassroots union leader.

Lastly, Taiwan's political transition away from martial law and authoritarianism took place in the context of a rapid process of post-industrialisation. From the late 1980s, semi-skilled manufacturing jobs were offshored to mainland China and Southeast Asia, and the subsequent shrinkage of the manufacturing workforce made it difficult for the Taiwanese labour movement to expand. The service industry workers who became numerically dominant in the early 1990s were notoriously difficult to unionise. As the predominantly male leadership failed to pay enough attention to gender discrimination and sexual harassment in the workplace, women service workers did not find unionism a solution to their grievances. High-tech industry workers grew in numbers in tandem with Taiwan's transition to a knowledge-based economy, but they were reluctant to unionise because of profit-sharing schemes that tied them closely to management.[5]

As a result of these converging dynamics, the organising drive stimulated by the end of martial law quickly came to an end. According to official statistics, Taiwan's enterprise unions—then misleadingly called 'industrial unions' (產業工會)—started to grow in the mid-1980s and peaked in 1989 with 1,354 unions and 700,000 members. Thereafter, there was a persistent decline for two decades. By the time the Taiwanese people finally elected a non-GMD government, in 2000, workers who enjoyed the protection of active labour unions had become a shrinking minority, typically concentrated in state-owned enterprises, recently privatised enterprises or large private enterprises.

A Brief Awakening

The rise of Taiwan's independent labour movement represented a moment of awakening for the Taiwanese working class after a prolonged silence. The wave of strikes caught the government and businesses off guard and helped secure better pay and protection for workers. As workers became more conscious of their rights and entitlements, employers could no longer violate labour laws without consequence. In addition, as authoritarianism was so entrenched, workplace struggles were not only a manifestation of class politics, but also a critical battleground for democratisation. However, grassroots militancy was short-lived and, after the first few years after the end of martial law, labour activists found themselves unable to expand their organisational base.

To be sure, the labour movement did not vanish in Taiwan. In the 1990s and beyond, Taiwan's progressive democratisation opened more arenas of engagement for labour advocates, including the legislature, the courts, local labour administrations and tripartite decision-making channels. Nevertheless, the narrow focus of the post-1980s labour movement remained apparent even in the following decades, as unions relied on mostly male full-time workers in the manufacturing and transportation sectors. Until now, gender equality, discrimination against migrant workers, the plight of dispatch workers and youth poverty have seldom emerged on the agenda of Taiwan's mainstream labour unions, relegated to a wide variety of contentious politics engaged in by actors other than unions.

1989

Although at the end of the first decade of reforms Chinese workers' quality of life had improved, there was a growing sense of uneasiness caused by the incipient dismantling of the welfare system, widespread managerial corruption, and inflation. The death of beloved Chinese Communist Party leader Hu Yaobang in April 1989 catalysed the widespread discontent hanging in the air; to express their grief and grievances, students marched from their universities to occupy Tiananmen Square in Beijing. Workers were also eager to join the protest and, between April and May 1989, independent unions sprang up in several cities in China, the most famous being the Beijing Workers' Autonomous Federation (工自联). Over the previous decade, the official All-China Federation of Trade Unions (ACFTU) had attempted top-down reform—first, within the framework of the 'democratic management of the enterprise' (企业民主管理), and then through reform plans that would have laid the foundations for a truly democratic union had they been implemented. Now the time for this top-down approach was up. Sections of the ACFTU supported the students, organising marches, petitions, and donations. After martial law was declared, worker activists bore the brunt of state repression, while the conservative side of the ACFTU launched an internal purge that stripped the union of many of its reformist cadres. To make sense of the momentous events of 1989, this essay looks into the workers' role in the protests and how they shaped China's political landscape thereafter.

Workers on Tiananmen Square
Yueran ZHANG

The 1989 Tiananmen Democracy Movement is mostly remembered as a student-led one. In this telling, intellectuals and college students deeply influenced by Western liberalism hoped to push the Chinese Communist Party (CCP) to accelerate political liberalisation, which had been rolled out only intermittently during the 1980s. To the extent that this account mentions workers at all, it depicts them as playing a supplementary role: workers and working-class residents in Beijing and other major cities mobilised to demonstrate support for the liberal-minded students.

This dominant account obscures the agency of workers in the movement, for workers not only mobilised on a massive scale but also developed an independent political agenda and strategic outlook that was somewhat at odds with what the students had in mind. Understanding the role of the workers in the movement is thus crucial for understanding both the movement's trajectory and internal contradictions and how it shaped China's political landscape thereafter. Drawing on published scholarly research—particularly an important paper by Andrew Walder and Gong Xiaoxia from the early 1990s[1]—publicly available documents, and interviews I conducted with those who participated in the movement, this essay examines what transpired in 1989 from the perspective of the workers.

A Workers' Movement

After Hu Yaobang, a much-revered pro-reform CCP leader, passed away on 15 April 1989, students in Beijing's universities set up memorials on their campuses. At the same time, pockets of workers gathered in Tiananmen Square to exchange views about current affairs. On 20 April, after police suppressed a student sit-in in front of Zhongnanhai, the CCP leaders' residential compound, a few angry workers decided to form an organisation that would later evolve into the Beijing Workers' Autonomous Federation (北京工人自治联合会), henceforth referred to as *gongzilian* (工自联). According to Walder and Gong, this embryonic worker organisation was established even earlier than the Beijing Students' Autonomous Federation.

However, the *gongzilian* at that time was just an informal, loose network of dozens of workers without established organisational structures and did not operate publicly. Members barely knew each other. In April, students remained front and centre in the movement. But after 4 May, the student movement stagnated and declined. Students did not know what to do next and were hesitant to escalate further. Most of them returned to the classroom. Facing such a deadlock, a group of radical students planned a hunger strike to reenergise the movement. In this sense, the hunger strikers accomplished their goal. On 13 May, the first day of the hunger strike, a recordbreaking 300,000 people protested in and occupied Tiananmen Square.

The beginning of the hunger strike marked a turning point; despite a temporary revival of enthusiasm among the students, the movement unavoidably declined again, and after 13 May, the number of students participating in the occupation of Tiananmen Square dwindled. However, the students' hunger strike marked the beginning of workers' participation *en masse*. The enthusiasm of the workers was seen not only in their numbers, but also in the fact that they started to organise their own rallies and marches and display their own banners and slogans. From that point on, workers became a major force in the movement.

Many workers decided to participate due to both sympathy for the hunger-striking students and a sense of moral outrage against the CCP's indifference. A worker I interviewed told me that he decided to get involved 'simply because the state was treating students too badly'.[2] As the number of workers participating in the movement exploded, the *gongzilian* started to make itself publicly known and recruit members on a large scale.

What boosted workers' participation even further was the declaration of martial law on 20 May. As military regiments—most of which had been garrisoned nearby—marched towards Beijing from all sides, a huge number of workers and working-class residents spontaneously took to the streets in Beijing's outskirts, trying to obstruct the military. Workers erected barricades and assembled human walls. They brought water and food to soldiers to fraternise with them and convince them to abandon their arms and stop their march. According to one witness account, during the night right after martial law was declared, hundreds of ordinary working-class residents walked down an alley to stop about thirty military trucks.[3] The action was largely spontaneous, and the participants did not know each other. They were nervous to the point of not daring to use flashlights. People walked in darkness, with bricks in their hands to defend themselves, unsure of how they would be treated by the soldiers. Fortunately, they found out that the soldiers were not armed, and they engaged in a long and emotionally charged conversation.

In other words, it was workers, not students, who directly confronted the most powerful, repressive apparatus of the state. And workers won temporarily: the military was prevented from entering Beijing's inner core for two weeks.

As Rosa Luxemburg famously argued, the radical consciousness of the workers grows out of the process of struggle itself.[4] The events of 1989 in China proved this. During the struggle to obstruct the military, workers started to realise the power of their spontaneous organisation and action. A huge wave of self-organising ensued. The *gongzilian*'s membership grew exponentially and other worker organisations, both within and across workplaces, mushroomed (see also Wilson's essay in the present volume).

The development of worker organisations led to a radicalisation of action. Workers started organising self-armed quasi-militias, such as 'picket corps' (纠察队) and 'dare-to-die brigades' (敢死队), to monitor and broadcast the whereabouts of the military. These quasi-militias were also responsible for maintaining public order, so as not to provide any pretext for military intervention. A witness I interviewed recalled that, a week after the military was obstructed, there were a dozen workers' picket corps active in the Yuetan and Ganjiakou neighbourhoods, just north of the Muxidi area, where the bloodiest battles between civilians and the military took place on the night of 3 June.[5] Another witness said Beijing almost became a city self-managed by workers.[6] One could argue that the situation described here was somewhat reminiscent of Petrograd's self-armed workers organised in soviets in the months between Russia's February and October revolutions.

At the same time, Beijing workers built many more barricades and fortifications on the streets. In many factories, they organised strikes and slowdowns. Li Peng, then China's Prime Minister, later wrote in his diary that, at the end of May, it was rumoured that about 100,000 workers at the Capital Steel Factory were planning to go on strike, which unnerved the CCP's top leadership.[7] Capital Steel was one of the most important industrial plants in Beijing at that time. Had its workers gone on strike, a much larger strike wave would have been likely to follow. A possible general strike was put on the table as well, as several interviewees recalled and Walder and Gong also mentioned.[8] Another rumour widely circulated among the workers was that the All-China Federation of Trade

Unions (ACFTU), China's official labour union, was itself on the verge of proclaiming a general strike, which certainly further emboldened some.[9] To prepare for this possibility, many workers started to build connections between factories. These links remained mostly informal, with workers communicating with each other about the mood of coworkers in their respective workplaces, especially those where strikes and slowdowns had already occurred. It was unclear, however, whether any concerted action was taken to explicitly devise a plan for a general strike.

Self-arming, self-organising, and striking had altogether different meanings to marching, rallying, and occupying. The last three were self-expressive acts, whereas the first three entailed solidly building power over the production process and the management of society as a whole. The radicalism was not in the words workers proclaimed, but in their acts. This was where the movement stood towards the end of May and early June: the students were struggling with declining enthusiasm, dwindling participation, and constant infighting, but the workers were growing stronger and more radical by the hour through self-organisation and self-mobilisation.

There is no way to ascertain why the CCP leaders finally decided to order the military to enter Beijing 'no matter what' and crush the movement. But a plausible speculation is that what terrified the Party leaders was the rapidly growing and radicalising workers' movement. This is consistent with the fact that workers faced much more severe repression than students both during and after the massacre.[10] Indeed, during the final crackdown on the night of 3 June, workers fought an extremely heroic battle against the military. Historian Wu Renhua provided the following account:

> That night, a picket team comprising three dozen workers was on duty with [students] on the Square. When the gunshots of the bloody crackdown were fired, the workers rushed towards West Chang'an Street [from where the military was coming]. At around 1am, a young worker covered in blood returned to the Square, saying in tears that he was the only survivor. The other workers had all given their lives ... At that moment, the only two female members of the workers' picket team who were still on the Square threw away their coats and rushed towards West Chang'an Street with great impulse. The students and I cried and advised them

not to go. They fell on their knees, saying in tears: 'Our brothers are all dead, we can't be cowardly' … In the end, they left with the young man, and never came back.[11]

What Kind of Democracy?

What grievances drove workers' participation in the events of 1989? Some leftist accounts point to the widespread discontent with the liberalisation of prices and rampant inflation of the late 1980s.[12] These accounts are not wrong, but they do not tell the whole story. In fact, by focusing on economic grievances and material hardship alone, they buy into the somewhat condescending assumption that workers could not be bothered about democracy and other political demands.

In fact, over the course of the movement, the workers did articulate a vision of democracy to which they aspired. This vision, it should be emphasised, originated from workers' firsthand experiences of the lack of democracy on the shopfloor. What probably affected the lives of urban workers the most during the 1980s was not the liberalisation of prices, but the substantial expansion of managerial power over the operation of state-owned factories—something that had begun as an experiment in some localities in 1978 and then developed into a fully fledged nationwide reform in the name of 'strengthening the autonomy of enterprises' (增强企业自主权) in 1984. Managers gained almost unopposed power to allocate the means of production as they pleased, resulting in strengthened one-person rule in urban workplaces and de facto private ownership.

As staff and workers' congresses (职工大会 and 职工代表大会)—the bodies the Chinese authorities had charged with ensuring workplace democracy in those early years of reform—were systematically disempowered and deactivated, workers lost their limited power over decision-making in factories and directly experienced managerial despotism at the point of production.[13] Managerial despotism manifested in things as trivial as regulation over bathroom breaks and sick leave, and as significant as decisions about job assignment and promotion. Several workers I interviewed recounted that what they found most irritating in the late 1980s was the sense that their superiors in the workplace did not treat them with dignity.[14]

With workers feeling oppressed, mistreated, stripped of their dignity, and facing increasing power inequalities, they aspired to democracy first and foremost in the workplace. According to Walder and Gong's analysis of pamphlets published by the *gongzilian*, the organisation's democratic ideal was intertwined with sharp criticisms of China's official trade union system, which did not really represent workers, and with a vision of workers having the right to organise independent unions, supervise managers, and bargain collectively.

Therefore, it was no surprise that many workers developed an explicitly political understanding of their economic grievances. Again, as Luxemburg showed in *The Mass Strike*, economic and political demands were intricately intertwined in workers' movements. The *gongzilian*'s analysis of inflation, for example, attributed rising prices to the lack of democracy: the 'Stalinist dictatorial bureaucracy' (斯大林主义的专制官僚) had given rise to a layer of bureaucrats who controlled the pricing of domestic and imported goods and deliberately set the prices high to make room for their own hoarding and profiteering.[15] Therefore, the only way to eradicate inflation and inequality was to overthrow the bureaucracy as a whole and restore to the workers the power to control the production and circulation of goods. In articulating this democratic ideal, some workers drew on the Cultural Revolution rhetoric celebrating the self-emancipatory potential of the ordinary masses. This partly explains the prominence of certain Cultural Revolution symbols and slogans in the movement.[16]

Democracy as defined by the workers entailed the replacement of bureaucracy with workers' self-management, and the first step towards this goal was to establish democratic and independent workplace organisations. This vision of democracy clearly had a class character, premised as it was on the agency of the working class. In sharp contrast, the democratic ideal articulated by intellectuals and students comprised a set of supposedly universal liberal values. Even though students were also deeply dissatisfied with corruption and official hoarding, their discontent pointed towards an abstract notion of democratic rights and liberty, unlike the belief—widespread among the workers—that democracy should first be established in the workplace realm of the production process.

The Disconnect between Students and Workers

Given their different trajectories of participation and conceptions of democracy, it is not surprising that a notable disconnect existed between students and workers throughout the movement. Students constantly tried to exclude workers, seeing the movement as 'their own' and seeking to maintain its 'purity'. Walder and Gong pointed out that, until the end of May, students were adamant that workers' organisations not be allowed to enter Tiananmen Square proper. Students had little interest in communicating or coordinating with the workers, especially the organisation formed by construction workers, most of whom were villagers from Beijing's rural outskirts. Historian Maurice Meisner even argued that 'in the early weeks of the movement, student demonstrators often marched with arms linked to exclude workers and other citizens'.[17] A student who participated in the movement also recounted that students took great care to ensure that the logistical supplies donated by supporters in Hong Kong went to themselves, not to workers.

Excluded by students, many workers started to lose faith in them. They thought the students felt too good about themselves, did not respect workers, and were much better at talking than doing things practically. What alarmed workers most was that traces of bureaucratic elitism, which they deeply resented, started to appear within student organisations. My interviewees recounted how disgusted they felt towards the obsession of student leaders with official titles like 'General Commander' (总指挥) and 'Chairman' (主席) and their internal jockeying for power, position, and privilege.[18] In contrast, as Walder and Gong noted, the *gongzilian* and other worker organisations were much more horizontal in structure, with individual leadership playing a much smaller role.

At the same time, workers and students also disagreed about strategy. From the very beginning, students assumed a posture of petitioning the Party, seeking to convince Party leaders to make concessions. To win the Party's trust, students even held banners with slogans like 'We Support the CCP' (拥护共产党) during marches. In contrast, a significant portion of the vocal and organised workers were much more hostile to the Party and argued for an insurrectionary strategy. The *gongzilian*'s leaflets always called on people to rise up and overthrow the oppressors.

When disagreements about how to deal with the movement emerged among the CCP's top leadership in May, some students were inclined to cooperate with the 'moderate' leadership faction headed by Zhao Ziyang, then CCP General Secretary, against the 'hardliner' faction headed by Li Peng and Deng Xiaoping, the de facto supreme leader. For students, factional infighting among the CCP leadership provided leverage for the movement, which is why they firmly opposed the workers' call for a general strike, seeing such initiatives as 'instigating chaos', as one worker I interviewed recounted.[19]

However, the students' strategy did not make any sense to the workers, who saw Zhao Ziyang as a perfect example of a dictatorial bureaucrat who had used his power to make millions for his family during the reforms of the 1980s. They saw no difference between the moderate and the hardliner factions. The *gongzilian* argued that, if the movement sought cooperation with Party bureaucrats, only one thing would result: the movement would end up being appropriated by Party bureaucrats to advance their own interests, in a way similar to how Deng Xiaoping used the 1976 'April Fifth' Movement to strengthen his power.[20] The *gongzilian* believed that the only way for the movement to attain success was to build power through self-organising and self-arming until the Party bureaucracy could be overthrown. This is why its leaflets referenced the 1789 French Revolution in calling on the masses to 'storm the twentieth-century Bastille' (攻克二十世纪的巴士底狱).[21]

In this sense, one could argue that what transpired in 1989 was not one movement, but two. The student movement and the worker movement, though overlapping in time and place and somewhat related to each other, did not become one. Between students and workers there was little trust, insufficient communication, almost no strategic coordination, and only a very weak sense of mutual solidarity.

After 1989

The disconnect between students and workers during the movement foreshadowed their exceedingly divergent fates thereafter. The difference in the approaches the Party took towards students and workers was evident in the immediate aftermath of 1989: except for a few leaders, students were let go, whereas workers were violently prosecuted on a much wider scale.[22] This divergence remained pronounced during the 1990s.

The dramatic acceleration of market reforms in the 1990s provided ample economic opportunities for students who graduated from top universities in the late 1980s and early 1990s. Some Chinese observers have noted that, through the high tide of marketisation, many student participants in the 1989 movement transformed into the new urban middle class that developed a vested interest in supporting the CCP regime.[23] In a sense, the economic reforms of the 1990s were a way for the CCP to absorb and coopt the generation of students who participated in 1989. I have talked to dozens of people who studied at Beijing's top universities in the late 1980s, almost all of whom participated in the movement. Today, as middle-class residents of Beijing, they believe that 'political stability trumps everything'. They look back on their participation in 1989 as naive and manipulated.

Whereas the economic reforms of the 1990s greatly benefited intellectuals and students, they almost completely destroyed the urban working class. As the majority of state-owned enterprises were restructured, downsized, and privatised, workers lost jobs or faced much worse working conditions and meagre benefits and protections (see Hurst's and Lee's essays in the present volume). Scholars have generally attributed this wave of industrial restructuring to economic factors, but if we take 1989 into account, political considerations seem to have played a role as well. The power and radicalism of urban workers, as displayed in 1989, alarmed the Party leaders and made them determined to break down the urban working class.

The contrasting fates of the intellectuals who morphed into China's new middle class on the one hand, and the urban working class on the other, have remained a feature of Chinese society since 1989. To this day, this class-based strategy of 'divide and rule'—one of the most important legacies of 1989—remains crucial to sustaining the CCP regime.

1993

In 1993, a fire broke out in a small Hong Kong–owned toy factory in Shenzhen, claiming the lives of eighty-seven migrant workers, mostly young women. In those early days of China's opening up to foreign investors, little was known of the terrible working and living conditions of the migrant workers who had flocked to Shenzhen in search of a living. Dozens of the victims' private letters found in the rubble provided evidence of their plight; their authors complained, for instance, of constant hunger. Labour nongovernmental organisations (NGOs) in Hong Kong publicised the tragic incident and an effective international campaign was launched that linked the big-brand toy companies in the developed world to the exploitation that went on inside their supplier factories in Asia. This not only resulted in the international toy industry recognising a code of conduct drawn up by the Hong Kong labour NGOs, but also led to increased international scrutiny of labour conditions in Chinese factories at both the local and the international levels. In the decades since, Hong Kong NGOs and their counterparts in mainland China have taken on an important role in shaming global companies into putting pressure on their suppliers to improve working conditions.

Voices from the Zhili Fire: The Tragedy of a Toy Factory and the Conditions It Exposed

Anita CHAN

> 'I am now working in another factory. It's better than the Japanese umbrella factory. It's twelve hours work a day. If my factory needs people, I'll let you know.'
>
> Quote from a letter found in the rubble of the burnt-out Zhili Toy Factory

On 19 November 1993, eighty-seven workers lost their lives when the Zhili Toy Factory in Shenzhen caught fire. Their deaths aroused widespread public outrage in China, and the Zhili fire has since been equated to the notorious Triangle Shirtwaist Factory fire in New York City in March 1911—a tragedy that robbed the lives of 146 young immigrant workers. That fire marked a watershed in US labour law reform and is still commemorated annually.[1] Although the policy impact was not as significant, what happened at Zhili exposed how Chinese migrant workers lived in the early 1990s and the mechanisms that entrapped them in slave-like working conditions.

The Economic and Social Contexts

In 1980 China established its first special economic zone (SEZ), in Shenzhen, which was then a very small city sharing a border with Hong Kong (see O'Donnell's essay in the present volume). As China was still poor and inexperienced in global trade, a new manufacturing model was introduced in the SEZ known as the 'three-plus one' (三来一补) model. Foreign investors, mostly Asian suppliers to Western companies in the global production chain, were invited to build or rent factories to manufacture products for export. The investors then shipped in raw materials and machinery, employed their own foreign technology and product design, and China provided cheap labour. China desperately needed foreign exchange for its industrialisation project to take off and, as a result, the power relationship between foreign capital and the local Shenzhen Government was lopsided. In such an environment, the investor was allowed to depress wages to a level below subsistence.

As Hong Kong at that time was one of the world's major centres for the production of garments and toys, businesses in what was then still a British colony were the first to rush into the Shenzhen SEZ to take advantage of wages that were ten times lower than in Hong Kong.[2] Chinese villages in the Shenzhen area quickly threw together substandard factory buildings to accommodate the wave of new investment. As more and more factories from Hong Kong and, later, Taiwan, Japan, and South Korea relocated to the SEZ, the local supply of labour became inadequate. By the end of the 1980s, local Shenzhen people who had been working in these labour-intensive factories were earning enough from renting out buildings and providing services to investors that they no longer wanted to toil under the dreadful conditions that were prevalent at that time. Hence a massive number of young people from poor villages in inland provinces, desperate to escape rural poverty, were allowed to come to Shenzhen to fill the labour shortage.[3] In the belief that young women were more docile, most of the factories, including Zhili, preferred to hire women under the age of twenty-three or twenty-four rather than young men.

The Workers' Private Letters

Zhili was housed in a 'three-in-one factory building' (三合一厂房) that included workshops, storage areas, and a dormitory. Although this kind of arrangement had already been banned as a fire hazard, the company had a record of violating safety regulations and defying restrictions through bribing local officials. Raw materials were piled up on staircases, iron rods were installed on windows, and safety exits were blocked and locked to prevent theft. When the fire broke out on 19 November 1993, the workers were trapped in the inferno. Eighty-seven perished. Many of those who were lucky enough to survive were severely burned, scarred for life, and sent back to their home villages.

Living conditions in such a factory were extremely basic. During a tour of similar factories in the toy industry that I undertook in the mid-1990s, I recall being ushered through a converted warehouse filled with rows and rows of bunkbeds for more than 100 workers, with the floor strewn with garbage.

Soon after the Zhili fire, a Chinese industrial relations researcher visited the site and retrieved a few hundred personal letters from the remains of the dormitory. Most of the letters had been written by the friends and relatives of the Zhili victims, many of whom were themselves migrant workers in Shenzhen or other parts of China. Almost all the letters were penned by female workers. The researcher kindly passed on to me seventy-seven letters, which form the basis of this essay. Through these letters, the workers exchanged information on factory conditions and revealed their inner fears and aspirations. The descriptions of their work situations, living conditions, health, and feelings towards the factories were candid and intimate.[4]

Physical Survival and Hunger

What issues were the most important and urgent to the workers? Questions and comments about wages and money appeared most frequently in the letters (107 times), with some writers complaining that wages were too low to allow them to send any money home or even to eat properly.

Fifteen entries in the letters alluded to whether there was enough food. For instance, one worker asked her correspondent: 'In your factory do you have two meals or three meals? I hope you're not too frugal. If you're hungry, go buy something to eat.' Similarly, another worker wrote: 'Little sister, you should go to see the doctor. Don't take money too seriously. To have a body in good health is to have everything. Don't be stingy. Make sure you eat both breakfast and dinner.' The concern was quantity, not whether the food was nutritious or tasted good, which did not warrant even one entry in the letters. The letters allude to the fact that some workers skipped meals to save money, that some factories did not provide enough food in their messrooms, and also that, back home in the countryside, they sometimes experienced hunger. A decade later, when I visited factories during lunch breaks in the early 2000s, the situation was quite different. Generally, workers could help themselves to as many bowls of rice as they wanted, and the biggest complaints were about quality and taste, a lack of meat, and repetitive dishes.

A letter-writer advised her friend that 'to have good health is to have everything'. It was not just the food that took a toll on workers' physical and mental health. The writers mentioned extremely long working hours, repetitive tasks, a poor environment, abusive treatment, toxic air, and industrial injuries. Seventeen entries in the letters discussed work-related ailments; one entry complained of enervating weight loss, and eight others noted exhaustion, lack of sleep, and a death from poisoning related to paint, with the body of the deceased quietly sent back to her home village. The most frequent ailments were headaches, fevers, and leg pain. That was a time when occupational health and safety standards and knowledge about them were extremely low. In 1994, some 5,000 factories in Shenzhen were classed as hazardous according to occupational health and safety standards; 4,000 of these were foreign-owned factories employing approximately 250,000 workers. Despite the complaints of feeling unwell, only in one letter did a worker mention that she had taken a few days off. The others appear to have remained at work even when they were suffering—either too poor to afford any time off or, as I discovered in my fieldwork, afraid of the fines that some factories imposed on anyone taking sick leave.

Low Wages and Very Long Working Hours

To gain a full grasp of the anxiety felt by these workers, it is necessary to compare their wages with the legal minimum wage in Shenzhen, which at that time was 280 yuan a month for a forty-four-hour week. Back then, the legal minimum wage was set at the level of subsistence. Twenty-three letters provided the specific amount the writer earned. Of these, only four met the level of Shenzhen's legal minimum wage, and the rest earned less than that. Three wrote that their factory withheld a portion of their monthly wage and eleven wrote that they faced serious problems getting paid. The pay was so sporadic that workers were apt to ask each other in their correspondence whether they had yet been paid. With the usual response being 'not yet', it seems the norm was not getting paid on time.

In addition, twenty-seven workers wrote that they received irregular payments, had wages withheld, were paid as low as sixty yuan for the month, or were not paid at all. Of all the workers who mentioned wages without providing the exact amount in their letters, forty-six had serious problems in this regard. Many who had come to Shenzhen had spent all their families could afford to make the long journey and were desperate to find a job on arrival. Pressed by these hard circumstances, they had started work without knowing when and how much they would be paid.

In reality, the wage rates were even lower than they might seem at first sight. The minimum legal wage per month was set for an eight-hour workday. But the normal workday for these workers was eleven to twelve hours. Fresh from the impoverished countryside, where wage labour was uncommon and the daily work rhythm was flexible, and not knowing that there were legal maximum working hours or minimum pay, the workers had little idea that they were being cheated. They did not complain of the long working hours in their letters, only of being tired. Their fear was not so much that they would be required to work until they were dead tired, but rather that there would not be enough working hours to allow them to feed themselves and send some money home to their families. This would defeat their main purpose for leaving home. Several wrote about very long working hours at their factory being a positive inducement to work there. As the young woman quoted in the epigraph of this essay wrote: 'I am now working in another factory. It's better than the Japanese umbrella factory. It's twelve hours work a day. If my factory needs people, I'll let you know.'

Physical Entrapment

The second-largest number of letter entries related to workers asking each other about the conditions and wages in other factories in the hope they could escape their present situation and join their relatives or friends there. The letters contained a lot of comments comparing jobs, strategies to change jobs, and the difficulty of quitting one's current factory.

They had difficulty quitting because of the constraints imposed on them by China's household registration system (户口; hukou). Workers from the countryside were not only denied urban registration in the city where they worked; if they were without a job, they were also considered an illegal 'migrant' in much the same vein as an international illegal migrant is regarded today. At the time of the Zhili fire, a migrant worker picked up by police without a temporary work permit was usually placed in a jail-like detention centre. Unless a friend or relative came to pay bail of several hundred yuan, the worker would be sent back to the countryside. As the police found that they could make easy money by arresting illegal migrants, the number of arrests increased with time. This stringent control of migrant workers was relaxed only in 2003 after the Sun Zhigang incident, in which a migrant university graduate died in police detention (see Froissart's essay in the present volume). After a massive public outcry, the authority of the police to detain migrant workers was transferred to the Civic Affairs Bureau, which could no longer incarcerate migrants.

Making matters worse for migrant workers, it was a common practice for employers to hold on to the identification cards of employees; without these, the worker would not dare even to go out the factory gate. On top of that, employers normally demanded that workers pay a bond at the time of recruitment or withheld their wages for the first two months, so that if the worker ran away, she would lose a substantial sum. In reality, this first generation of migrant workers were bonded labourers—a situation that continued for the next decade and more. At some of the factories where I conducted interviews in the early 2000s, the workers' most serious grievance was that they could not afford to forfeit the bond and wages if they resigned.

Isolation

Thirty entries expressed loneliness and feelings of isolation or misery, of sorely missing friends and relatives, of crying and yearning for letters and photos from loved ones. This period pre-dated mobile phones and internet cafes, and it was not easy to access a public phone at the workplace. Since they worked such long hours, the window to lock in a time to talk on the phone was limited, and at the other end there often was only one phone in an entire village, usually at the production team or the production brigade office. In such circumstances, the only practical means of communication was by letter, but the mail service was slow and unreliable. The anxiety of waiting for a letter was sometimes palpable, as in the case of a worker who wrote: 'I sent you a letter a few days ago. Have you got it? I look forward to your letter every day but it never comes. I think of you very much.' Similar feelings can be found in another letter that a worker wrote after a sister or friend had just arrived in Shenzhen:

> Though we are so near, we can only see each other in our letters. Little sister, can you please send me a photo. I sent my photo to your home. Did you get it? I'll close off here. See you in a letter next time.

The Zhili Fire's Influence on the Labour Movement

Even though the Zhili tragedy was reported in Beijing, the families of the victims had difficulty claiming compensation for their loss. The local government took a hands-off attitude. Nor did the Zhili fire have an impact on China's labour laws, unlike the New York Triangle Shirtwaist Factory fire. The main impact of the tragedy with regard to legislation was stronger enforcement of the ban on three-in-one factory buildings; from then on, shopfloors, storage warehouses, and workers' dormitories had to be self-contained in separate buildings.

At the international level, the fire attracted the attention of newspapers and foreign trade unions, which began to pay closer attention to working conditions in China's growing export sector. In particular, the fire led Hong Kong labour NGOs to become more involved with the plight of Chinese migrant workers in the neighbouring Shenzhen region. Hong Kong labour NGOs continued to publicise the case in Hong Kong and internationally, and launched a campaign calling on the Zhili factory's Hong Kong owner to be held responsible for compensating the Zhili victims. They connected the Zhili fire with the Kaida Toy Factory fire in Thailand, which on 10 May 1993 claimed the lives of 188 workers, and used these cases as graphic illustrations of the serious violations of labour rights in the global production chain. The Hong Kong Toy Coalition was created to put pressure on the multinational toy corporations to accept their responsibility for the welfare of the workers who produced their merchandise.[5] Starting with the Zhili fire, Hong Kong labour NGOs became deeply involved in the international corporate social responsibility movement and in monitoring the violation of labour rights in China. Ever since, these organisations have played an important role as a bridge between Chinese labourers in Guangdong Province and the international labour movement.[6]

1994

In the Maoist era, the concept of rights occupied a very marginal position in the discourse on labour of the Chinese Party-State. While state workers acquired considerable social and economic entitlements under Communist rule, these were framed not in terms of rights but rather as being due to the revolutionary social transformation steered by a regime that ruled in the name of the working class.[1] As a result, China in the pre-reform era never adopted any substantial body of laws and regulations to regulate labour relations. As for the Chinese constitutions of 1954, 1975, 1978, and 1982, they granted people the right and duty to work, the right to labour protection and adequate working conditions, a right to be paid and to social security, a right to gender equality, and a right to rest. However, as Biddulph et al. have pointed out, constitutional labour rights in China do not confer on individuals a judicially enforceable entitlement against the state; they just impose a notional obligation on the state to create conditions under which individuals will enjoy those rights.[2]

The creation of a body of labour laws in China began in the 1980s with a series of regulations aimed at managing labour relations in the newly established special economic zones. Then, as the decade unfolded, further regulations were adopted to handle labour relations in specific industries, locations, and companies of different types of ownership. Due to unclear and often contradictory provisions, in the early 1990s, China's labour laws had become so convoluted the authorities felt they were starting to become a hindrance to foreign investment. At the same time, worker unrest underlined the need for the Party to find new ways to boost its legitimacy among the working class. In such a context, the Chinese authorities drafted a series of national laws that for the first time covered all the companies on Chinese territory regardless of ownership type or industry, the most important of which was the Labour Law of 1994, at the centre of this essay.

One Law to Rule Them All: The First Labour Law of the People's Republic of China

Sarah BIDDULPH[3]

After thirty drafts and more than a decade of debate, in 1994, the Standing Committee of the National People's Congress finally passed the first Labour Law of the People's Republic of China (PRC), to take effect on 1 January 1995.[4] This law is more than just an ordinary piece of legislation. Not only was it an important element in the ongoing process of dismantling the planned economy, establishing a labour market, and unifying the increasingly fragmented and inconsistent regulatory treatment of work across different sectors—state-owned, foreign-owned, township and village enterprises, and the emerging private sector—it was also part of the regulatory framework designed to smash the 'iron rice bowl' (铁饭碗) of guaranteed lifetime employment and benefits enjoyed by core workers in state-run firms in urban areas.[5] By 1994, economic reform had progressed to the point that legislation was needed to bridge the increasingly untenable and undesirable divisions between regulation of foreign and domestic work and economic activities more generally. But the final impetus to pass the law—as has often been the case with work-related laws—came from increasing labour unrest and a series of workplace disasters that occurred in 1993.[6]

The Labour Law sets out a framework that has provided the scaffolding for employment relations and subsequent work legislation. Although the law was amended in 2009, 2012, and again in 2018 to strengthen labour protections and address gaps in the existing regulatory regime, its fundamental elements remain unvaried to this day. This essay sets out the debates surrounding the process of drafting and the passage of the law and then discusses the basic framework established by the legislation.

History and Policy Context

The Labour Law attempted to consolidate an array of fragmented and inconsistent work laws that had been passed throughout the 1980s. It was not, however, cut from entirely new cloth but selectively incorporated regulatory choices made in Republican China in the 1929 Factory Law, which set basic labour standards for large industrial enterprises, and in the Maoist era before 1978.[7] The influence of the latter is particularly evident in the structurally weak position of unions to represent and protect workers and in the privileges accorded to urban industrial workers.[8] The Labour Law was not an organic development but the product of policy visions, heated debates, and decisions, which in the end privileged enterprise autonomy and established individual contracts as cornerstones of economic reform. On the losing side were advocates of strengthening the role of workers, industrial democracy, and collective decision-making through staff and workers' representative congresses (职工代表大会). Instead of collective participation in enterprise management, the Labour Law entrenched enterprise autonomy by empowering the firm manager under the enterprise responsibility system to manage labour relations through individual labour contracts.[9] Institutionally cemented in this law was the definition of economic reform, developed at the Fourteenth Congress of the Chinese Communist Party (CCP) in October 1992, as the construction of a 'socialist market economy' (社会主义市场经济).

By 1994, work-related laws had become complex, fragmented, and inconsistent. One of the ambitions of the Open Door Policy was to encourage foreign investment, and it was recognised that capitalist-friendly laws were needed to entice foreign enterprises into China. A bifurcated legal system emerged throughout the 1980s that regulated domestic and foreign-related economic activity differently. The distinction between the Economic Contract Law, which governed administrative contracts appropriate for use in the domestic planned economy, and the Foreign Economic Contract Law, aimed at regulating foreign-related contracts, was one example. Another was the division between economic law and civil law, with economic law covering the domain of economic activity in the vertically oriented planned economy and civil law carving out a narrower sphere of horizontal autonomous legal relations among and between citizens and entities, represented by the comparatively narrow scope of the 1986 General Principles of the Civil Law.

Legal regulation of work was divided between foreign-related and domestic sectors as well. Authorisation to pass the earliest foreign-related economic and labour regulations in advance of the rest of the country was given to the special economic zones (SEZs) established in Guangdong Province. Local regulations were passed in Shenzhen beginning in 1980 authorising the establishment of foreign-invested enterprises and allowing management in those companies greater autonomy to employ workers on a contract basis, which would make workers easier to manage and dismiss.[10]

Starting with some pilot sites in 1983, in 1986, the labour contract system was extended nationwide with the passage by the State Council of four regulations.[11] The Provisional Regulations on the Implementation of the Employment Contract System in State-Run Enterprises (Article 2) made the contract system applicable to all new hires in the state sector. Before then, most urban workers in the state sector were subject to administrative management, being allocated to a workplace they were not free to leave, but which was also responsible for the provision of social benefits such as education, housing, medical care, and a retirement pension. These 1986 regulations marked a decisive shift away from administrative allocation and management of work to a labour market and system of contracting. Between 1987 and 1989, further labour regulations covering domestic private enterprises were passed, with rules for township and village enterprises following in 1990.[12] The Labour Law constituted the first major step to unifying the existing fragmented and divergent set of regulations.[13]

In addition to the distinction between foreign-related and domestic enterprises discussed above, at the beginning of the economic reform period, a second important divide existed between urban and rural sectors and workers. Adoption of Soviet-style, industrial-led models of development in the pre-reform period privileged an elite urban industrial workforce. Under this development model, substantial economic transfers were made from rural to urban production, and the provision of state benefits was confined to small numbers of urban workers. Rural people were excluded from seeking work in urban areas by the household registration system (户口; hukou) and the coercive detention and repatriation measures that underpinned its effectiveness (see Hayward's and Froissart's essays in the present volume). While the hukou system has subsequently been reformed to an extent to permit some rural-to-urban movement, to this day, these rural migrants continue to suffer unequal protection at law, which has in turn contributed to enduring problems of inequality. The passage of the Labour Law did nothing to alleviate the discriminatory treatment of rural migrant workers or to alter the privileging of a small urban elite in terms of work law and conditions.

The Labour Law was intended to provide an overarching structure to regulate employment relations, but at the same time it did not represent a radical break from pre-reform labour regulation. It continued to reflect the existing distinctions, inequalities of opportunity, and differential protections that had previously been afforded to different categories of workers.

What the Labour Law Provided

The Labour Law sets out the basic legal framework for employment relations in the PRC. Its objectives were officially 'to protect [the] rights and interests of working people in the socialist market economy', and to use contracts as a way of improving flexibility in enterprise management and productivity.[14] It also unified labour standards across different forms of enterprise and industry and, as Cooney and others have noted, 'sought to give effect to those ILO [International Labour Organisation] Conventions that were compatible with [the] Chinese political system'.[15]

In this basic scheme, the individual labour contract is placed at the centre of regulation, supplemented by collective contracts. The law regulates labour rights in the realms of wages, working conditions, work health and safety, vocational training, and social insurance. Finally, it specifies how dispute-resolution mechanisms and enforcement by the labour bureaus and trade unions are supposed to work. However, since the Labour Law regulates basic labour standards in broad terms, the detailed interpretation required to implement it has relied heavily on subordinate rules and regulations issued by central agencies such as the Ministry of Labour—now the Ministry of Human Resources and Social Security—and local authorities. This form of regulation allows the law to set clear standards—for example, in terms of working hours and overtime—but also to create flexibility to enable these provisions to be both supplemented as needed and circumvented.[16]

Individual Labour Contracts

Even though there are precedents from the pre-1949 Republican era for the use of contracts as the primary legal form to regulate labour relations, in the early reform era, there were strong ideological and practical objections to this practice. The centrality of the individual labour contract in the law effectively individualised labour relations at the expense of any form of collective organised worker voice.[17] This policy decision was by no means uncontroversial and was debated extensively in the drafting process.

These objections reflected some of the key debates at that time about how economic reforms were to be carried out and their relationship to socialist ideology. The first objection to using the individual contract form was that contracts were by nature exploitative, as they commodified labour and alienated workers from the value of their labour. The virtue of socialism was precisely that it created secure lifetime employment. Those arguing for universal adoption of an individual contract system of employment had to spend considerable energy to rebut these objections, grounded as they were in the socialist discourse that Chinese workers were 'masters of the enterprise'.[18]

This ideological problem also fed into practical problems. As a framework law, the Labour Law failed to regulate some key aspects of contracting, such as formation, effect, and variation of contracts.[19] One consequence was that labour contracts were characterised as being distinct from ordinary civil contracting processes. Even the unified Contract Law of 1999 excluded labour contracts from its scope, to the detriment of workers who were unable to take advantage of that law's protective provisions, such as those prohibiting undue influence, misrepresentation, and oppressive conduct.

Another problem was the false presumption of formal equality between contracting parties, insisting that labour contracts were based on the principles of 'equality, voluntariness, and agreement through consultation' enshrined at Article 17 of the Labour Law. There was strong evidence, even by 1986, to show that, apart from skilled male workers, who had strong bargaining power, many workers employed under contract were much worse off, facing inferior working conditions, wage arrears, and work insecurity. In the early 2000s, the duration of the labour contract decreased from the average of between three and five years in the mid-1990s to predominately one-year fixed-term contracts.[20] Contract workers were often treated as badly as temporary workers had been: disdained, discriminated against, and subjected to arbitrary dismissal and punitive disciplinary regimes.[21] The Labour Law embraced the individual labour contract as the cornerstone of the labour relationship in spite of widespread awareness of the fact that the individual contract form, without effective protective mechanisms, would entrench injustices and insecurities produced by power imbalances in the emerging labour market.

Rights and Interests

To mitigate the consequences of the presumption of formal equality in stipulating individual labour contracts, the Labour Law specifies a number of labour rights that contracts may not derogate. These rights give specific legal form to general—and otherwise unenforceable—constitutional protections for labour. They include: the right to be paid the minimum wage; wage protections, such as the right to be paid periodically without unauthorised deductions, equal pay for equal work, and paid holidays; default rules on working hours, providing for an eight-hour day and forty-four-hour week; the right to rest and be paid overtime; leave, including annual holidays and parental leave; and gender-specific protections for women.[22]

In addition to individual labour contracts, collective contracts were designed to supplement labour contracts and specify baseline conditions. However, collective contracts are only subject to sketchy regulation in three articles of the Labour Law.[23] They provided that collective contracts should be concluded by the trade union acting on behalf of the staff and workers of the enterprise and the enterprise management and then reported to the local labour department. A collective contract can cover remuneration, working hours, rest, health and safety insurance, and welfare and, once stipulated, is binding for all staff and workers. While collective contracts were designed to provide a baseline of conditions below which individual contracts could not go, they were unequal to this task. First, collective contracts were initially conceived as operating only at the enterprise level as they were never intended to be a device to strengthen collective labour power. Second, the enterprise union that entered into these contracts, ostensibly on behalf of workers, lacked autonomy from the enterprise (often with management representation in the union) and was obliged to implement Party policies, including those that undermined workers' interests and emphasised increased productivity.[24]

In practice, the collective contract is the only mechanism in the Labour Law for the negotiation of interest claims about wages and working conditions. The rights set out in the concluded collective contract are enforceable through the same channels as the individual labour contract. Since the early 2000s, trade unions have sought to expand the use of collective contracts as a way to 'coordinate' and 'stabilise' the relationship between labour and capital.[25] However, for many years, collective contracts were effectively a dead letter. Before renewed policy attention to expand collective contracting at the turn of the millennium, the proportion of enterprises covered by these agreements was small. Even where an enterprise had entered into a collective contract, the benefit to workers was limited. Collective contracts were notoriously concluded in a top-down manner without substantial input from workers—a formalistic exercise in fulfilling quotas set by higher-level unions that did not go beyond restating minimum legal standards.[26] To this day, despite intense policy pressure to expand the proportion of enterprises concluding collective contracts, these documents remain marred by formalism. To overcome the problem, in the 2000s, some local administrations tentatively introduced industry-level agreements, but these experiments have not expanded into a more efficient and widespread form of collective bargaining. In fact, until the problem of the structural weakness of trade unions is addressed, the prospects for the transformation of collective contracts into a tool of industrial democracy remain poor.[27]

Hierarchies of Protection

The hierarchy of protection directs our attention to two related questions: *who* is included in the scope of the Labour Law and who is excluded; and *how* are different categories of workers that fall within the scope of the law regulated?[28]

The first question relates to the scope of the Labour Law, which is defined in Article 2. For the law to apply, the following conditions must be met: there must be a 'labour relationship' (劳动关系) between a person who 'engages in labour' (劳动者) and an 'employing unit' (用人单位) (comprising enterprises and individually owned economic enterprises). Article 16 further requires that, where there is a labour relationship, there must be a (written) labour contract.

As Cooney et al. have pointed out, this is as important for its definition of who is excluded as it is for whom it includes within the Labour Law regime.[29] Enactment of the legal concept of 'labour relationship' has effectively excluded large swathes of the Chinese workforce, leaving aside migrant workers, rural labourers, members of the armed forces, government officials, domestic workers, students on training programs, independent contractors, and retirees. Those work relationships that are excluded from the scope of the Labour Law are treated as a civil law commercial relationship and so fall outside the protective scheme established under the law. People employed by an individual or an illegally registered firm—a category that includes a significant number of people employed, for instance, in the construction industry—also fall outside the scope of the law as the employer must be an enterprise.

A labour relationship is created by way of a labour contract—as opposed to a labour contract documenting an existing labour relationship—and, while the law does not explicitly negate a labour relationship without a labour contract, a worker without a written labour contract faces difficulties in proving that a labour relationship has been established.[30] In the 1990s and 2000s in sectors such as labour-intensive manufacturing, construction, and services, a large proportion of people were employed without written labour contracts, which created sometimes insurmountable barriers to their ability to access systems provided in the Labour Law for wage protection, working conditions, specialised labour dispute resolution, social security, and safety net provisions in cases where wages were not paid or workplace injury had occurred.[31]

Another weakness of the law was that it very quickly became outdated due to the proliferation of dispatch labour and other types of informal and non-standard or precarious working arrangements. For example, the law did not contemplate the need to distinguish between real and false independent contractors, and so left workers vulnerable to employer avoidance devices like false contracting.

Regarding the regulation of different categories of workers that fall within the scope of the law, the regulatory regime of the Labour Law imagines a standard or typical worker employed full-time in a fixed workplace such as a state-owned enterprise or a foreign-invested enterprise. In light of this, the Labour Law thus pays little attention to, and protects poorly, the rights of people in short-term, part-time, casual, or project-based work, or who are employed under arrangements such as labour dispatch, where labour is supplied to an end user by a third-party organisation. For these reasons, labour dispatch arrangements became a very common way for the end user of labour to avoid application of the Labour Law. The system was not subject to detailed regulation until 2007, with the passage of the Labour Contract Law.[32]

Enforcement and Dispute Resolution

Like many laws, the Labour Law enacts state-led enforcement supplemented by private dispute resolution, primarily for disputes related to legal rights. Law enforcement comprises three components: private enforcement through dispute-resolution processes, enforcement by state administrative agencies, and enforcement by the unions.[33] Enforcement of the law has generally been weak, both because of structural power imbalances between workers and employers and because these enforcement mechanisms have not been effective. Poor law enforcement has gone hand in hand with poor compliance.

The Labour Law adopts the three-stage dispute-resolution system comprising mediation, labour arbitration, and litigation that was first established in the 1980s in foreign-invested and state-owned enterprises. Under this system, disputes are first to be mediated within the enterprise by a committee comprising representatives of the workers' congress, the enterprise union, and enterprise management. This form of mediation makes sense only where the enterprise has a union and a workers' congress, which were, at the time, primarily located in state enterprises. Labour arbitration is conducted by labour dispute arbitration committees—a tripartite committee comprising representatives of the local labour administration bureau, the district trade union, and enterprise management. As the process has in fact been dominated by local labour departments, this form of dispute resolution has been affected by conflicting policy incentives, corruption, and questions about competence.[34] Finally, an appeal can be made to a court if one is dissatisfied with the arbitration decision.[35]

Ultimately, this form of dispute resolution proved to be a time-consuming and costly process, which workers—especially if they had been dismissed from their employment—were less able to sustain than enterprises. Apart from time and cost, another limitation is that the labour dispute system is directed exclusively to breaches of labour rights, but not interest-based claims over wages and conditions. However, despite the cost and difficulty of pursuing claims, the number of claims heard by labour arbitration committees and courts continued to increase as labour dispute resolution was diverted away from mediation within the enterprise.[36] After some of the barriers and costs to accessing arbitration and litigation were reduced with the passage of the Labour Disputes Mediation and Arbitration Law in 2007, there was a further surge in the number of disputes filed, revealing large pent-up demand.[37]

But, in an economy now dominated by precarious work, the gig economy, and labour dispatch practices, an assertion of rights by a worker will commonly be preceded by an argument about the boundary issue of whether a 'labour relationship' exists. For workers, this threshold standard is often difficult to establish because of a lack of credible evidence in acceptable form and lack of resources to prosecute the argument. Those in precarious work are also the least able to sustain the cost and time required to pursue their rights through official channels.[38]

Article 88 of the Labour Law provides that the trade union is also responsible for 'safeguarding the legitimate rights and interests of labourers, and supervising the implementation of laws, rules and regulations on labour by the employing units'. However, enterprise unions are in a structurally weak position to perform their responsibilities either in dispute resolution or in law enforcement, because of their upward responsibility and obligation to implement Party policy—which may be counter to workers' rights and interests—and because enterprise unions often include or are led by representatives of management.[39]

The weaknesses of private dispute-resolution mechanisms to resolve disputes in a timely and fair manner, coupled with the lack of effective penalties for enterprises breaching mandated labour standards, have exacerbated labour unrest. From the mid-1990s to the late 2000s, failure to pay wages on time and without unlawful deductions, punitive labour discipline, and poor working conditions became widespread and acute, particularly in small privately owned businesses and labour-intensive export sectors. Private enforcement was unequal to the task of addressing these problems, with collective disputes ending up being individualised by courts and the unions mostly absent from any role in protecting worker rights and interests. Both by design and as a result of limitations in private dispute resolution, the burden of enforcement has fallen on the labour administration department and its labour inspectorate. However, the capacity of the department and inspectorate to enforce the law has been limited by a range of institutional and legal factors, such as chronic understaffing, budgetary limitations, lack of clear policy support by local governments, and high law enforcement costs and risks.[40] Increasing labour unrest has placed greater pressure on the labour administration to enforce the law, but more importantly to defuse and minimise conflict as part of broader stability maintenance responsibilities.[41] It is therefore unsurprising that local labour departments are often the first agencies to which workers turn to express grievances.[42]

What Came After

When it was passed, the Labour Law was intended to be the first of a suite of labour-related regulations. However, because of the disruption to the labour market and massive layoffs resulting from the reform of the state sector in the late 1990s (see Ching Kwan Lee's and William Hurst's essays in the present volume), this accompanying legislation was delayed.[43] Regulatory gaps and ambiguities in the law were addressed by implementing national or local regulations, often on an ad hoc basis and often ex post facto, in response to abusive practices. In some cases, local regulation was outside the scope of the Labour Law itself.

Widespread worker unrest galvanised the political will to address some of these deficiencies. The impetus for drafting new labour-related laws came alongside a three-year campaign to redress systemic problems of non-payment of migrant workers' wages between 2004 and 2007. In the wake of that campaign, more worker-friendly legislation—that is, the Labour Contract Law, the Labour Disputes Mediation and Arbitration Law (2007), and the Employment Promotion Law (2008)—was drafted and passed despite organised opposition from some employer groups (see Gallagher's essay in the present volume).[44]

But, as mentioned at the beginning of this essay, these reforms did not change the basic structure of or categories set out in the Labour Law. Despite the dramatic shifts in the nature of work and workplaces, the legislation passed in 2007 and 2008 did not adopt more creative ways of regulating work to address the challenges of precarious work, or even fundamentally reimagine the standard worker or the hierarchy of protection previously enshrined in the Labour Law.[45]

1995

In the early reform period, Chinese civil society began to take root and bloom. Taking advantage of a more relaxed political and legal framework, commercial, financial, cultural, and professional organisations sprouted throughout the 1980s. After 1989 and the ongoing repression in its wake, the political spaces available to these organisations shrank and state–society relations froze. It would not be until the United Nations Fourth World Conference on Women, held in Beijing in 1995, that the Chinese authorities would again allow some space for civil society. Nongovernmental organisations (NGOs) working on gender issues, some of which focused on migrant women, were the first to appear. The next wave, starting from the late 1990s, were labour NGOs that provided assistance to migrant workers in several urban centres, mostly in the capital and in Guangdong Province. This essay tracks the development of these organisations from their heyday in the mid-1990s to the crackdowns of the mid-2010s.

From Green Shoots to Crushed Petals: Labour NGOs in China
Jude HOWELL

When China hosted the 1995 United Nations Fourth World Summit on Women, who would have thought it would be a catalytic event in the growth of nongovernmental organisations (NGOs) in China? This meeting of UN representatives from all over the world and activists attending the shadow NGO conference held in Huairou County, Beijing, unleashed a raft of relatively independent women's organisations. With space prised open for Chinese citizens to organise, it also created opportunities for those concerned with the lamentable situation of workers to set up independent groups to provide services and counsel on rights. In the decades since this monumental event, China's labour NGOs have been subject to not only harassment and repression, but also governmental overtures towards them to cooperate in the provision of welfare services.

This essay charts the twists and turns of China's labour NGOs from 1995 onwards. It identifies three key stages in their growth: first, the period from 1995 to 2002, when the first seeds of labour NGOs were sown; second, the decade from 2002 to 2012, which was marked by China's entry into the World Trade Organisation (WTO) and its strategic move to 'go global'; and finally, the current period under President Xi Jinping during which labour NGOs have faced acute repression.

Green Shoots (1995–2002)

Though NGOs, often semi-governmental, began to develop from the mid-1980s onwards, China's hosting of the UN's Fourth World Summit on Women in 1995 catalysed the rapid growth of more independent women's organisations. Until that point, the strict 1989 Regulations on the Management of Social Organisations had stymied the growth of NGOs, and those that existed were in any case mainly commercial, industrial, and professional associations. Given international sanctions after the tragic events in Tiananmen Square on 4 June 1989, the government was keen to restore international relations. This grand UN meeting provided a pivotal moment for China to shed its pariah status internationally.

Not only did it open up opportunities for women to organise independently of the All-China Women's Federation (ACWF), but also it created an opening to organise for those with other concerns such as labour issues. Some of the first labour NGOs, as they came to be known, grew out of the ripples flowing from the UN summit. Astute activists capitalised on the implicit licence to establish NGOs and set up organisations relevant to female migrant workers. Journalists, lawyers, and academics leveraged their positions and contacts to create new organisations addressing migrant workers' rights and issues. Hong Kong academics and activists also used these openings to start organisations offering services for female migrant workers. International organisations such as aid agencies and foundations played a vital role in promoting concepts such as gender equality, facilitating international links, exchanges, and visits, offering advice on organisational development, building networks, and providing small funds for activities. Through these experiences, female activists and academics, as well as international organisations, accumulated contacts, knowledge, networks, and connections with sympathetic government officials.[1] New ideas, approaches, contacts, and international awareness began to extend beyond gender inequality concerns to other issues.

In the late 1990s, there was but a handful of labour NGOs, mainly concerned with female migrant workers. Perhaps the most well-known of these were the China Working Women's Network in Shenzhen, established by a group of concerned activists and academics in Hong Kong, and the Female Migrant Workers' Club in Beijing, which was initiated by a prominent female journalist. With good connections to the Party-State, these women were able to sustain these groups despite periods of government harassment and suspicion. However, a further tidying up of the regulations governing social organisations in 1998 curtailed any substantial growth or development of NGOs. Indeed, many of the existing NGOs were in a state of limbo, neither banned nor registered due to the strict criteria for registration and the reluctance of government departments to sponsor them, as required. It was with China's entry into the WTO in 2001, and the subsequent rapid globalisation of China's economy and society, that labour NGOs began to proliferate and blossom.

Blossoming (2002–2012)

Several interlinked factors underpin the proliferation and blossoming of labour NGOs from 2002 to 2012. These include China's entry into the

WTO in 2001, a change in leadership, the growing presence of international organisations, and the lameness of the All-China Federation of Trade Unions (ACFTU). At the end of the 1990s, there was just a smattering of labour NGOs in China, mainly located in Beijing, Shenzhen, and Guangzhou. By 2012, estimates of labour NGOs across China varied from forty to 100—precise statistics were not available because most were not registered. A key factor enabling the growth of labour NGOs was China's entry into the WTO in 2001. This not only opened China to more foreign investment and trade, but also spurred Chinese firms to 'go global' and seek investment abroad. Through these expanded economic relations, travel opportunities for government officials and ordinary citizens increased. There was more exposure to international ways of doing things, whether economically, culturally, or politically. Personal connections developed between businesspeople, academics and students, NGOs, labour activists, and trade unions, seeding partnerships, exchanges, and joint initiatives.

WTO entry coincided with a shift in the types of NGOs that were emerging. By now the social consequences of economic reforms were becoming more evident. This was soon mirrored in the growth of NGOs concerned with social issues and marginalised groups such as autistic children, migrant workers, or people living with HIV/AIDS. The Wenchuan earthquake of 2008 marked a turning point in state–NGO relations as the Party-State began to recognise the contributions that NGOs could make in disaster relief and in addressing social issues. Nevertheless, difficulties remained in gaining legal status through registration, and many groups affiliated with other organisations, such as research institutes or the ACWF, registered as companies or not at all. By 2012, unregistered groups were reported to far outweigh those that had registered.

The year 2002 also heralded a change in leadership, with Hu Jintao as Party General Secretary and Wen Jiabao as Premier, replacing, respectively, Jiang Zemin and Zhu Rongji. Like all leaders, they sought to put their own mark on their period in office. Central here were notions such as 'harmonious society' (和谐社会) and 'people-centred development' (以人为本), which subtly acknowledged the growing inequalities in China and 'the three rural issues' (三农问题), which signalled a move to address rural grievances. This rhetoric pointed to a leadership that strove not only for continued growth but also to improve the lot of those not benefiting as much from the reforms. It was a time of greater openness and experimentation, enabling new forms of government–NGO relations to develop, including those with labour NGOs. The outward thrust of the economy and society created more space for international institutions that provided aid, support, and opportunities not only for government officials but also for Chinese scholars and NGOs. The International Labour Organisation, for example, regularly discussed labour issues with businesses, the ACFTU, and the government, and also engaged with the emerging labour NGOs. The support of international NGOs, bilateral development agencies, and foundations was pivotal to the growth of some NGOs in China, especially those with a rights orientation.

Given Hong Kong's proximity to Guangdong Province, Hong Kong NGOs also began to enter China to establish new labour NGOs or partner with emerging ones.[2] Guangdong Province was home to the greatest concentration of foreign investment and attracted swathes of migrant workers to labour in the export-oriented factories (see O'Donnell's essay in the present volume). Working conditions in China were already under the spotlight in the mid-1990s, leading to a raft of new labour laws to protect workers (see Biddulph's essay in the present volume). But with this surge in export production, there was growing concern within China and abroad about the sweatshop conditions of labour. While in the early years of the millennium there was a greater concentration of labour NGOs in Guangdong Province, over time, these organisations began to sprout across the Yangzi River Delta and in other Chinese cities such as Hangzhou, Chengdu, Shanghai, Beijing, and Chongqing. The types of issues that labour NGOs took up varied according to the nature and degree of labour activism, the orientations of their founders (such as their interests in gender, law, journalism, occupational health, and so on), the type of enterprise (such as state, private, or joint venture), and the industrial sectors specific to certain geographic locations. The field of labour studies in China expanded as researchers analysed labour relations, while trade unions and labour NGOs abroad observed the rising number of protests and strikes and sought connections with activists and researchers. Furthermore, as labour NGOs raised awareness about labour laws, workers increasingly sought redress through mediation committees and courts.[3] Though most workers tended to vote with their feet, a growing minority was ready to voice their concerns, lobbying the Labour Bureau and local government officials, and leading workers to action and organisation.

As the official trade union, the ACFTU, proved ineffective in coming to the defence of workers, labour NGOs found fertile soil on which to grow. Though the ACFTU had a monopoly on the representation of labour, this was largely confined to state-owned enterprises (SOEs), whose workers enjoyed better working conditions, at least until SOE reforms in the mid-1990s (see Ching Kwan Lee's and Hurst's essays in the present volume). The ACFTU functioned as a transmission organisation, mediating between workers and government.[4] In practice, it was an appendage to the state, limiting itself to benign tasks such as arranging entertainment and rarely taking the side of labour against capital and local governments. In any case, it lacked the skills, desire, and capacity to bring migrant workers into its fold. In the new foreign-invested factories, the head of the trade union was often the owner of the factory or a relative of the owner. Under these conditions, workers had little incentive to seek ACFTU support. As most surveys revealed, workers viewed the ACFTU as ineffectual.

Having outlined some of the factors driving the development of labour NGOs at the beginning of the millennium, it is important to understand some of their basic features. There was considerable variation across NGOs in terms of size, activities, goals, origins, and relations with government. Most were small in scale, with few paid staff, relying on volunteers who were students or migrant workers.[5] Some were founded by academics, others by former workers, and some by lawyers. Their activities included providing services, such as legal counselling, secondhand clothes shops, libraries, hotlines, awareness-raising about law and labour rights, proffering advice in disputes, assisting workers injured in the workplace, and organising workers through choirs and cultural activities.[6] Some also engaged in advocacy work, seeking to influence government and trade union policies. Whether offering services or conducting advocacy, labour NGOs couched their activities in a language of rights that echoed the official discourse of the law. By appropriating the official legal language of rights and interests, they could protect themselves from potential accusations of seeking to undermine the regime.

Labour NGOs were different from independent trade unions in that they did not seek to become membership organisations that took up workers' grievances with management in the workplace. Compared with the ACFTU, labour NGOs were more innovative and experimental, introducing new ways of approaching and mobilising workers, such as contacting workers in dormitories or organising a mobile bus to provide advice and information on labour issues in industrial sites. Some engaged in corporate social responsibility activities for foreign brands such as monitoring codes of conduct. However, NGOs with transformative agendas insisted on doing this only if they could also undertake training in the factories, which would allow them to raise issues of legal rights and engage in consciousness-raising.[7] Some labour NGOs also became involved in supporting workers in collective bargaining processes, especially during and after the Honda strikes in 2010 (see Chris Chan's essay in the present volume).[8]

Nevertheless, labour NGOs were also controversial among some academics. In particular, Lee and Shen criticised labour NGOs for being 'anti-solidarity machines'.[9] They argued that many labour NGOs were predominantly concerned with individual workers seeking redress through the law rather than organising alternative trade unions or collective action. Though the criticism was harsh, it also generated debate and perhaps a more measured understanding of the contribution that labour NGOs made in redressing workers' grievances and in shaping a labour movement.[10]

During the Hu–Wen period, relations between government and labour NGOs were a mix of ongoing repression, toleration, and occasional collaboration. Repression involved a spectrum of actions, such as detention, physical brutality, harassment, surveillance, and spot-checks.[11] Labour NGOs were often forced out of their premises, only to relocate elsewhere and face further eviction a few months later.[12] However, they were also tolerated by some trade union and government officials who saw the NGOs' activities as providing services for which they lacked the capacity and skills. In some cases, local governments and trade unions even provided some funding to NGOs to deliver services such as legal counselling or support to migrant workers' children. However, there was always a constant drone of repression that rendered the existence of labour NGOs precarious. Indeed, the situation for most labour NGOs would worsen under the new administration of Xi Jinping from 2012.

Crushed Petals

The Chinese Government had long looked on NGOs with considerable suspicion. Yet government officials in the Ministry of Civil Affairs—which was responsible for welfare provision and NGO registration—were increasingly aware of the benefits of NGOs in addressing new welfare needs and filling service gaps. However, the regulatory environment was overly restrictive, preventing the government from capitalising on civil society initiatives. In the Hu–Wen period, pilot programs were launched from 2003 in contracting government service provision to NGOs.[13] The risk for government officials was how to achieve this without enabling the expansion of rights-based NGOs and sensitive groups.

It was under Xi Jinping that the strategy of welfarist incorporation was generalised across the country.[14] In this way, civil society was bifurcated into two distinct strands: service-delivery organisations and rights-based groups. While the government introduced a swathe of regulations enabling NGOs to register more easily and apply for government contracts, it also set about draining rights-based groups of external funding and clamping down on activists in general. In this way, the government could advance its goals of streamlining the public sector and reforming welfare, while mitigating risks.

To address the risk that purposively fostering the development of a services-oriented NGO sector might also encourage growth of rights-based and sensitive groups, the government used its coercive agencies to clamp down on perceived troublemakers. As Franceschini and Froissart relate in their essay in this volume, 2015 was a landmark year, when security agencies made a sweep of rights-based organisations and activists, including rights lawyers, feminists, dissidents, critical academics, and labour activists. This was followed in late 2016 by the passing of the Foreign NGOs Management Law, which severely constrained the room for manoeuvre of foreign foundations, NGOs, and other external funders, leaving rights-based groups starved of resources.

This strategy of welfarist incorporation took its toll on labour NGOs and activists. While labour NGOs had faced the constant threat of repression, the wave of arrests in 2015 also swept up several prominent labour NGO leaders, lawyers, and labour activists, who were detained and in some cases sentenced to prison. Over the next few years, the leaders of several labour NGOs were detained across the country, leading to the organisations becoming moribund or closing completely. In light of this, other activists and NGO leaders halted their activities, kept a low profile, distanced themselves from foreign actors, and sought alternative sources of income on which to survive.

However, repression was not the only story. Local government and trade union officials continued to court some labour NGOs to apply for government service contracts such as hosting activities for migrant children. Those that did so trod carefully, limiting their activities to the least controversial issues such as afterschool work with the children of migrants, and eschewing rights and advocacy work. Not all labour NGOs chose to take this path, fearing, like NGOs in other fields, that accepting government contracts could compromise their autonomy and goals, while inviting greater control over their organisations. As the trade-offs and uncertainties of contract renewal became evident, the option of government service contracting became less appealing. For most labour NGOs, it was a question of lying low until the repression lifted or adapting activities towards services funded through other means, and perhaps discreetly fitting in some rights work. Hong Kong labour NGOs also halted activities on the mainland, though maintaining contact and providing advice where possible.

The End of Labour NGOs?

Does this signal the end of labour NGOs in China? In smothering the rights-based work of labour NGOs, the Xi period also brought to a halt any innovation in approaches to resolving workers' grievances, such as collective bargaining with labour representation. Despite this, workers have continued to strike and protest, suggesting that the legacy of past activism has not been wholly lost. The experiences of worker organising and labour NGOs during the Hu–Wen era have left a significant residue of memories, connections, and tactics that can be leveraged for the future. The violation of labour laws and poor conditions of work continue to vex workers, who carry on striking, protesting, or voting with their feet. There is still a place for labour NGOs, which, though different to trade unions, have a role to play in improving worker conditions and building a labour movement. However, this may not be in the immediate future. The restrictions on foreign institutions funding NGOs in China, coupled with the imposition of the National Security Law in Hong Kong, severely constrain the possibilities for international support. Moreover, many labour NGO activists and rights lawyers remain in detention or under surveillance. If political conditions loosen, there may be space for labour support groups to reemerge, but whether they will take similar forms or harbour similar goals to those that operated in the past decades remains to be seen. Nevertheless, the genie is already out of the bottle and cannot easily be put back in. Crushed petals can still become new green shoots.

1995

Worker activists suffered disproportionately in the crackdown that followed the end of the democracy movement of 1989. While the ensuing years are generally considered a low point for the Chinese labour movement—at least until 1995, when the United Nations Fourth World Conference on Women, held in Beijing, signalled a thaw for China's civil society (see Howell's essay in the present volume)—some activists kept up their attempts at organising workers even during such a challenging time. With ideals forged in the democracy movements of the 1970s and 1980s, these individuals engaged in a form of labour activism that was openly political, often in collaboration with various opposition forces that managed to reemerge from the ashes of 1989. Although most of the leaders of these groups came from an intellectual background, the possibility of them linking up with state-sector and migrant workers to form proto-trade unions was threatening enough for the Party-State to engage in harsh repression. This essay looks into some of these organisations, what they stood for, and what their ultimate demise meant for Chinese labour activism.

The Blocked Path: Political Labour Organising in the Aftermath of the Tiananmen Crackdown

Kevin LIN

On 21 May 1995, Liu Nianchun found himself suddenly arrested without a warrant and disappeared from his family and friends after he presented a set of petitions to the National People's Congress (NPC). The police raided his home, confiscating letters, newspapers, magazines and photographs.[1] Liu's petitioning was part of a campaign by China's political dissidents to call for democratic reforms and rectification of human rights abuses. More than 100 other dissidents were also arrested in relation to the campaign, demonstrating a fierce determination by the authorities to stamp out any organised dissent.

Liu was neither naive about nor new to repression at the hands of the Party-State. A veteran democracy activist, he had been deeply rooted in the dissident milieu since the late 1970s, when he had taken part in the Democracy Wall Movement as a college student at the Beijing Normal Institute—a prestigious teaching college, from which he was later expelled due to his political activities.[2] In 1978, he became one of the editors of the prodemocracy literary journal *Today* (今天), along with the preeminent poets Bei Dao and Mang Ke. In 1981, his persistent activism landed him in jail for three years for 'counterrevolutionary propaganda and incitement' for his role in organising international support for his brother, Liu Qing, another veteran democracy activist, who would eventually spend fifteen years in jail. After being released, Liu went on undeterred and took part in the 1989 protests. Despite the harsher environment, he continued his political activism into the early 1990s, including joining the Peace Charter (和平宪章) movement with other political dissidents to demand the rehabilitation of the 1989 democracy movement and the release of political prisoners.

In all these activities, Liu was no different from many of his fellow political dissidents across China who had participated in earlier movements and remained engaged in political organising. However, Liu diverged in one aspect: his political vision included Chinese workers.

In 1994, amid his other activist projects, Liu and another activist named Wang Zhongqiu began preparation for the formation of the League for the Protection of the Rights of Working People (劳动者权利保障同盟, LPRWP), a civic organisation with a mission to protect workers' rights. Hoping to operate above ground and within the law, Liu applied for registration with the Ministry of Civil Affairs. Not taking kindly to this attempt, the authorities put him under 'home surveillance', only to release him without charge five months later.

Instead of staying put, Liu was soon back in prison—this time, for the 1995 petition campaign. On this occasion, his main 'crimes', according to the Beijing Municipal Government criminal case document, were petitioning the NPC and Communist Party leadership and the attempt to create an illegal organisation—that is, the LPRWP. After more than a year in detention, in June 1996, he was sentenced to three years of 'reeducation through labour' and was sent to a facility in Heilongjiang Province, where he was allegedly tortured and his health deteriorated significantly.

Liu's name, and his short-lived organisation, the LPRWP, were not widely known at the time nor are they remembered today even among labour activists. But his activism—a mix of democratic opposition and an orientation towards labour organising—was indicative of a nascent political project that recognised the power of workers in social change and democratisation.

Emerging Political Labour Organising

The suppression of the 1989 democracy movement did not extinguish the hope for political reforms. The fact that hundreds of students, workers and intellectuals supportive of the movement were imprisoned, executed or exiled failed to deter some from opposition movements in the 1990s. Among them, a diverse group of people—many college graduates, educated professionals and some workers, who, like Liu, usually had a background in the democracy movements of the 1970s and 1980s but also developed an orientation towards workers in the 1990s—emerged as leaders of new labour-oriented groups.

This development can be understood as a form of political labour organising. The leaders recognised the plight of workers under China's market transitions, but also the importance of workers' political power in challenging state power. Their activities represented a conscious and strategic project of organising workers around not only economic interests but also explicitly political demands. In many ways, this was a continuation of the short-lived Beijing Workers' Autonomous Federation (北京工人自治联合会) that grew out of the 1989 Democracy Movement (see Zhang's essay in the present volume).[3]

These were not just isolated attempts but part of a proliferation of dissident groups and networks. In December 1991, the Hong Kong–based *South China Morning Post* reported that Deng Xiaoping considered the birth of the Polish trade union Solidarity 'the single most important factor that led to the wholesale disintegration of communist regimes' in Eastern Europe (see also Wilson's essay in the present volume).[4] This was in the context of the Ministry of State Security targeting fourteen underground labour organisations in Beijing, which had memberships ranging from twenty to 300 people, at least two of which had modelled themselves after Solidarity.[5]

A Comparison of Three Groups

The many similarities aside, the labour-oriented groups sat on a spectrum of political positions and approaches. An examination of three of the most prominent groups is instructive.

One of the more radical groups, identified as being closest to the political opposition movement, was the Free Labour Union of China (中国自由工会, FLUC). Formed in 1991, the FLUC focused on the deteriorating conditions of state-sector workers as market reforms undermined their welfare. Envisioning itself as 'a mass organisation formed out of the conscious efforts of Chinese workers', its stated goal was to fight for the economic rights and political freedom of workers.[6]

One of the leading founding members was Liu Jingsheng, a former worker at a state chemical plant on the outskirts of Beijing, who, despite his working-class background, had also been a democracy activist for more than a decade. He, too, was involved in the democracy movement of the late 1970s and was an editor of a movement journal called *Tansuo* (探索) along with Wei Jingsheng, the famed democracy activist of the Democracy Wall Movement. Liu was already on the authorities' radar, having been briefly arrested in 1979 and released after a few months. Besides the FLUC, he was also involved in forming a Beijing-based underground opposition group in early 1991. Another founder, Hu Shigen, an academic at the Beijing Foreign Languages Institute, co-founded the China Liberal Democratic Party (中国自由民主党, CLDP) in 1992. The FLUC thus identified closely with the political opposition movement from which it emerged and with which its leadership overlapped.

After forming the FLUC, for three months between December 1991 and February 1992, Liu and other activists did make efforts to propagate their ideas, distributing pamphlets that advocated for autonomous trade unions among workers in Beijing. In a 1992 FLUC pamphlet that critiqued China's economic reforms, they contended that while the economic reforms raised the living standard of some people, the majority of the working class had not seen improvement but instead had their existing rights, such as social security, taken away from them.[7] The authors pointed to examples where state workers now had to pay considerable sums out of their own pocket for medical expenses that before the reforms would have been covered by their work units. The focus of their critique was on the breaking of the 'iron rice bowl' (铁饭碗)—namely, the erosion of rights and declining living standards of state-sector workers. The pamphlet then went further to say that the Communist Party was no longer the party of the working class and had itself become the 'real master of society' while workers now were simply 'its servants'.

In June the same year, FLUC activists were detained for distributing leaflets about the 1989 democracy movement. In these documents, they expressed their belief that to fight for a fair and just society, it was necessary to have 'a democratic and sound legislative structure so that workers' rights and welfare can be improved'. To them, workers were 'a main force for the promotion of democracy in China'. Although these activists were detained, their reports were shared at the International Labour Conference held in Geneva in June 1992 with the help of the International Confederation of Free Trade Unions (ICFTU).

Moving along the spectrum, Liu Nianchun's LPRWP was among the more moderate groups. Its stated intention in its charter was to serve only as an interest group that protected the interests of workers, peasants, intellectuals and entrepreneurs; it was not a political party nor an independent trade union, and it did not aim to challenge the rule of the Communist Party (a fact that was explicitly stated in the charter). Due to its positioning, Liu decided to register with the Ministry of Civil Affairs in Beijing as an independent labour rights group. Before the arrests of its leading activists, including Liu Nianchun, by the Beijing Public Security Bureau in March 1993, it had a self-reported national membership of about 120 people.[8]

Some of the proposals the LPRWP submitted to the National People's Congress in March 1993 provide a useful understanding of the group's analysis and agenda.[9] The document started by emphasising the organisation's twin goals: protecting the rights and interests of working people, and rooting out corruption. The first proposal argued for the restoration of the right to strike, which was removed from the Chinese Constitution of 1982. As China was undergoing 'a difficult process of evolving from a planned economy to a market economy,' the authors wrote, 'confronted with capitalist owners and their managers, workers and employees can only protect their own interests by invoking the specific rights of citizens bestowed on them by the law.' They went on to say that 'absolute power corrupts absolutely' and 'unrestrained wealth will also deteriorate into a source of social injustice'. For these reasons, they believed the right to strike was crucial for preventing 'the unjust use of wealth'.

The document included several other proposals. It demanded that government officials and Communist Party leaders report on their personal property and advocated for the establishment of unions for agricultural workers. It then tackled the rights of 'peasant workers' (农民工), who at the time were often overlooked, as attention was largely focused on state workers. Recognising peasants' contributions to China's economic development and their arduous working conditions, the LPRWP called for the NPC to investigate labour conditions and legislate to protect their rights. Finally, the authors contended that with more foreign-owned enterprises, private enterprises and joint ventures setting up shop in China, unions were either absent or not playing their role. Therefore, they suggested the congress come up with laws so that workers could unionise in these new enterprises. While the proposals fell short of calling for independent trade unionism as FLUC did, the LPRWP offered a more grounded analysis and practical direction for workers' struggles.

The group that was least grandiose in name but arguably came the closest to serious labour organising was the Federation of Hired-Hand Workers (打工者联合会). While references to the organisation at the time translated its name as 'hired-hand workers', the original Chinese refers to what we would simply call 'migrant workers'. The choice of the phrase was not accidental and reflected their deliberate focus on rural migrant workers in southern China.

One of the leaders was Li Wenming. After graduating from a technical school in Hunan Province, Li moved to Shenzhen in 1991, when he was in his late twenties. Following a few odd temporary jobs, Li secured a position as a reporter at the newspaper *Shenzhen Youth* (深圳青年). Li and his colleagues, some of whom participated in the 1989 democracy movement, were appalled by the conditions of rural migrant workers and believed the only solution was political education and independent trade unionism. For these purposes, Li and his colleagues set up an evening school for rural migrant workers and established the Federation of Hired-Hand Workers. They also published a bulletin called *Workers Forum* (打工广场) for distribution to workers. Supported initially by the local municipal Party leadership and the city trade union, Li was in charge of a Shenzhen Government program to disseminate knowledge about the Labour Law among rural migrant workers.[10]

The bulletin had a specific focus on rural migrant workers in Shenzhen. It discussed basic issues that we now take for granted, such as working conditions, wages, overtime and safety, but also more sensitive matters like trade unionism and workers' struggles. This was a distinct step towards understanding migrant labour and the potential for its empowerment. The first issue of the bulletin criticised the government for permitting the Zhili factory to continue operating despite it not meeting the safety standards before its deadly fire (see Anita Chan's essay on 1993 in the present volume).[11] It argued that only through struggle and solidarity could workers best protect their rights and safety.

A particularly striking article in *Workers Forum* posed the poignant question: Why must we unite?[12] It painted Shenzhen as a city of two worlds: the world of 'tall skyscrapers, highly developed commercial compounds and merchants busy making money' and the world of 'the real masters of Shenzhen, the millions of workers' with their 'oppressive working conditions, overtime work, and meagre wages'. Adopting a militant tone, the article argued that 'rights can never be bestowed on us, they depend on our own struggle' and 'if they are given to us, they can be easily taken away'. It concluded that 'only those [rights] obtained through our struggle can rest securely in our hands'. But previous struggles had been isolated efforts, and what was needed was unity. To those who feared repression, the authors argued that unity would bring strength, and they would not lose their jobs but feel safer and have more job opportunities. Finally, to avoid tragedies like the horrific Zhili fire of 1993, they believed it was critical to have 'our own strong trade union'.

While their messages tended to focus more on working conditions than on political opposition as such, their language of workers' struggles and working-class unity could be equally, if not more, threatening from the point of view of the Party-State. Furthermore, the leaders' networks and entanglement with the broad political opposition movement put them out of favour with the authorities. In 1994, the Shenzhen Public Security Bureau detained Li Wenming and Guo Baosheng for attempting to form an independent trade union. It would take the authorities until 1997 to sentence them to three and a half years for 'counterrevolutionary propaganda and incitement'.

The Blocked Path

All of the groups discussed above can be seen as a continuation of the democratic political movements in which the groups' leaders were embedded in the previous decades. Their analyses and demands reflected their preoccupation with democratic aspirations. Some maintained even more direct connections with attempts to form independent political groups and parties to challenge the government taking place in the same period. It should come as no surprise that many of these organisations were founded and operated in Beijing—an indication of the political nature of their organising and of the fact they were aimed at other dissidents as their constituencies and took the state as their target. Whatever the intention of the individual groups, most maintained an underground or semi-underground presence, with no prospect of operating openly and legally.

These groups were primarily led by intellectual dissidents and did not have a solid working-class base—a situation that went against their ambitions to build strong national organisations and movements. In their brief existence, no labour action was organised or concretely supported by the three groups discussed, and there was no evidence of these groups having rooted themselves in labour organising at the workplace level. This, however, was already a step further along from the democracy movement of 1989, when workers were excluded from the centre and leadership of the movement despite their wide participation. But without working-class membership, these groups were speaking in the name of workers rather than constituting mass working-class organisations or trade unions. It is hard not to see the risk of instrumentalising the working class and subordinating them to their political projects.

However, a minority of these groups did try to address directly the conditions of workers and raise grievances the workers would have endorsed. The erosion of workers' living standards and welfare entitlements that deepened and accelerated from the early 1990s, as well as the massive rural labour migration in the same period, were fertile ground for these groups' messages of rights protection. Although the 1980s and early 1990s did not see many large-scale worker mobilisations, this was the dawn of a new period of worker organising, including a series of industrial actions in 1993 and 1994.[13] Unfortunately, all of these attempts ended prematurely before they could develop further. The leaders and key participants in these groups were rounded up within a year or two, and many were handed harsh sentences. The possibility of intellectual dissidents and groups set up as proto–trade unions linking up with state-sector or migrant workers posed enough of a threat to the authorities to trigger harsh suppression.

By remembering this now largely forgotten episode, we see a glimpse of attempts at labour organising different from those that came after. By the mid to late 1990s, as the hope of any explicit political project was extinguished, the demands of rural migrant workers for social protection gave rise to largely non-political projects of mutual aid, legal protection and bargaining over economic benefits without a link to any political vision. Independent trade unionism remained an absolute taboo, but a new door was opened for legal rights–based civil society organisations that sprang up to support migrant workers (see Howell's essay in the present volume). Because of the near total suppression, there was an all but complete rupture between these early attempts at political labour organising and the later emergence of labour nongovernmental organisations in the 2000s and 2010s.

Had they been given the time to develop, would these labour-oriented groups have helped bring about mass labour and trade union organisations? They might have found a receptive constituency. The following two decades first witnessed state workers' resistance to state-owned enterprise privatisation and layoffs, and then the larger-scale mobilisation of rural migrant workers for better pay and conditions. The labour-oriented groups of the early 1990s could have acted as an organisational base and a political program for these movements to develop into more organised, national movements. Yet, it is just as likely that workers would find the intellectual dissidents untrustworthy and too risky to be associated with. What is certain is that just the prospect of such a path—namely, the political organising of Chinese workers in independent trade unions as part of, or in alliance with, a democracy movement—was so threatening for the Party-State that it could not be allowed to exist. Consequently, in the next two decades, it became ever more difficult—even against a trend of increasing workers' struggles—for an organised labour movement to emerge and take political or mass organised forms in China.

1997

In the second half of the 1990s, the Chinese Party-State decided to accelerate the reform of state-owned industry. The Fifteenth Congress of the Chinese Communist Party in 1997 is frequently considered a watershed moment in this process. On that occasion, then Party General Secretary Jiang Zemin gave an important speech in which he emphasised two key slogans that set the tone for what was to come: 'cutting workers to increase efficiency' (减员增效) and 'grasping the large [companies] while releasing the small' (抓大放小). The following years would see a massive wave of layoffs in state-owned and collective enterprises throughout the country, sparking misery and dislocation among workers who had long been considered China's proletarian aristocracy. This essay examines the 1997 congress, arguing that while it was indeed a significant inflection point, the dynamics it threw into sharp relief had been set in motion well before then.

Xiagang: The Fifteenth Party Congress and Mass Layoffs in State-Owned Enterprises

William HURST

For seven days in September 1997, the Chinese Communist Party (CCP) convened its Fifteenth Party Congress in Beijing. Emerging from the congress was a series of statements and documents that put reform of state-owned enterprises (SOEs), and particularly of labour relations within them, front and centre. Many observers have jumped to the facile yet erroneous conclusion that this marked the sharp injection of hard budget constraints into the logic of firms now expected to behave as market-rational actors and reduce their excess costs—the greatest of which, by far, were to be found in payrolls massively bloated by bureaucratic labour allocation under the planned economy. It is essential we remember, however, that, rather than a monocausal tale of hardening budgets, the reform of state-owned industry in China has been a meandering—and unfinished—journey of negotiation, experimentation and occasional desperation unfolding over four decades.[1] This essay recounts that journey, analyses the specific impacts of the moves made at the Fifteenth Party Congress and offers some updates in light of events up to early 2021.

The Two Decades before the Congress

The reform-era story begins with the contested process of decollectivisation of agriculture (see Unger's essay about 1981 in the present volume). Heralded by many scholars abroad (and by the Chinese Government at home after the fact) as an unqualified success, decollectivisation brought sharply differential results to different parts of China. In the northeast, in particular, it failed to deliver promised benefits and led to significantly decreasing rural incomes relative to the rest of China. Combined with early moves towards what became known as the 'dual-track system' (双轨制), under which SOEs were allowed to sell on the market products they manufactured outside or beyond plan quotas, reform left many heavy industrial firms in the northeast adrift, especially as they were unable to modify production to turn out goods demanded in the mainly light industrial and consumer-oriented market.

In a shifting political economic landscape, in which 'pigs were suddenly more valuable than pig iron had ever been', the northeast's heavy industrial behemoths faced especially sharp challenges if they were even to try to reap benefits from the market or make up for reduced assistance from the state plan.[2] Stagnant or declining local revenues conspired with worsening business environments and fraying ties with Beijing to drive many SOEs across the northeast into severe deficits and arrears, forcing them to lay off significant numbers of workers. Still, most such layoffs were concealed in official data and reports, and nearly all took place through various informal arrangements. By the end of the 1980s, a number of northeastern cities were filled with SOEs that had gone bankrupt in all but name, and perhaps millions of workers had already lost their jobs and incomes, even if they could not be reported formally as 'laid-off' (下岗) or 'unemployed' (失业); at that time, the former category did not yet exist under Chinese law or policy, while the latter was so politically sensitive and ideologically charged that most officials and enterprise leaders sought to avoid at all costs designating anyone as 'unemployed'.[3]

Starting in the early 1990s, however, the woes of the northeast began to spill over the Great Wall and into other regions of China's industrial heartland. Areas with high concentrations of extractive industries—like the coal-mining-dependent North-Central provinces of Shanxi, Henan and parts of Inner Mongolia—were an aberration. Here, SOEs *added* substantially to their workforces between 1990 and 1997. Elsewhere, however, as in the region I have called the Upper Changjiang (comprising Hunan, Hubei, Sichuan and Chongqing), many SOEs began shedding workers, as competition with foreign firms, private firms, and other SOEs became increasingly intense. Several SOEs had difficulty competing, in part due to structural disadvantages, such as antiquated equipment, restrictions on specific sectors or activities and locations selected based on national security rather than business principles during the Third Front (see Meyskens's essay in the present volume). Military enterprises were hit especially hard. The only region where firms came under intense pressure but were still largely able to stave off layoffs was the central coast (Tianjin, peninsular Shandong, Jiangsu and Shanghai), where the rich coffers of local governments played a vital supportive role.⁴ Meanwhile, the carnage across the northeastern provinces of Liaoning, Jilin and Heilongjiang continued apace, accelerated by new trends such as foreign competition in sectors like automobiles and structural changes like the exhaustion of important oil and coal deposits.⁵ Thus, by the time the Party congress delegates convened in 1997, mass unemployment was already a reality across much of the Upper Changjiang and had become a severe social problem in the northeast.

A Watershed?

At the famous Fifteenth Party Congress, General Secretary Jiang Zemin gave perhaps the single most notable and influential speech on SOE labour reform of the period, emphasising two key slogans: 'cutting workers to increase efficiency' (减员增效) and 'grasping the large while releasing the small' (抓大放小). Specifically, he proclaimed:

> We must look to do well by the whole state-owned economy, grasping well the large and letting go of the small, to achieve a strategic restructuring of the SOEs. Taking capital as the bindings we must, through the market, amass great enterprise groups that are of relatively strong competitive ability, multi-regional, multi-sectoral, multi-ownership system, and multi-national ... [We must also] implement and encourage annexations, standard bankruptcies, lay-offs and departures, cutting workers to increase efficiency and the re-employment project, give shape to a competitive mechanism of survival of the fittest for enterprises. With the deepening of enterprise reform, technological progress, and structural economic challenges, the movement of personnel and the laying off of workers are difficult to avoid.⁶

This bold declaration of the Party's intention to reform labour relations in the state sector, and of its willingness (even eagerness) to do so through the specific mechanisms of closing or selling off smaller and unprofitable firms and deliberately cutting workers from the labour force, marked an important departure. No longer did layoffs need to be kept hidden. Rather, firms were explicitly encouraged to use them as a primary, valid means for achieving profitability. This message was reiterated countless times in subsequent years, following the opening of the gates at the congress.

Indeed, within a few months, in December 1997, then Premier Zhu Rongji delivered an even starker directive in a high-profile speech entitled 'Resolutely and Unswervingly Follow the Road of Encouraging Annexations, Standard Bankruptcies, Layoffs and Departures, Cutting Workers and Raising Efficiency, and the Realisation of the Reemployment Project'.[7] By May 1998, the State Council and CCP Central Committee jointly convened the 'Work Conference on Basic Livelihood Protection and Reemployment of Laid-Off Workers in SOEs', at which both the demand to reduce staff to increase efficiency and a number of policy measures aimed at easing workers' dislocation were trumpeted. By the end of 1998, the number of laid-off workers had duly increased to at least thirty million.[8] It is important to note, however, that China's official formal 'unemployment' rate (城镇登记失业率) never rose to anything like a correspondingly high level. That category remained restricted and politically policed, with only workers whose firms had failed or who had other kinds of special status permitted to register formally as 'unemployed'. This left a conceptual and regulatory morass in which pinning down precise numbers and rates of joblessness was notoriously difficult.[9]

But how much had really changed? Did the Party congress and work conference actually reorient the political economy of China's SOEs? Or did they simply formalise and give official endorsement to measures already undertaken on an ad hoc basis for many years? Did thirty million workers lose their jobs in two years, in other words, or were they simply acknowledged and counted as laid-off, having been concealed in that de facto status before? The answers depend heavily on at which regions and sectors one chooses to look. While the official narrative was one of sharp redirection, we have seen that unemployment on a massive scale had already existed in places like the northeast for at least a decade. Many older Third Front and other heavy industries in inland regions, like the Upper Changjiang, had also been struggling, while international and domestic competition were hurting light industrial firms across those and other areas. Genuinely new unemployment was concentrated in resource-extractive sectors in regions like northern-central China and in the otherwise relatively economically healthy cities along China's central coast.[10]

In these regions, job losses occurred largely in direct response to *political* rather than *economic* pressures. Far from a natural hardening of SOE budget constraints, the orders disseminated from the state leadership and Party centre were programmatic commands. Firms received quotas for what percentage of staff should be laid-off and sometimes had to scramble to meet them, shedding workers they actually needed to maximise efficient production.[11] Such job losses by fiat constituted a critical subset of SOE layoffs that too often has gone unnoticed. Many observers have assumed that layoffs were a 'northeastern problem' and failed to recognise that a plurality of layoffs—and a majority of those that were verifiably novel in the late 1990s and early 2000s—occurred in places like Shanghai or Nanjing, rather than Shenyang or Anshan.

Another mechanism that became important was the policy of 'grasping the large while releasing the small'. This emerged from debates around the Ninth Five Year Plan (1996-2000) and was, in fact, already being implemented before the Fifteenth Party Congress, despite the erroneous insistence of some scholars that it emerged only after the congress.[12] But, after 1997, its implementation was expanded to facilitate state economic and political divestment from thousands of small and medium-sized SOEs, affording local governments and enterprise cadres wide latitude to restructure or close those firms as they saw fit.

While the Fifteenth Party Congress was certainly not the cause of all—or even most—layoffs across the Chinese state sector, it was indeed a significant inflection point, exacerbating existing trends in some regions and sectors and adding new pressures across others. The festering problems of the northeast and certain other places were formalised and brought into the open. Economically healthy regions and sectors were ordered to cut staff in response to political fiat. And the existing mechanism of encouraging divestment from smaller firms was broadened and bolstered to speed up the privatisations and closures leading to the loss of millions of jobs.

Grasping the Large and Releasing the Small

While many have remarked that the policy of grasping the large while releasing the small was a major contributor to layoffs, fewer have analysed its implications in detail, especially at the microlevel.[13] Across a great many small SOEs and urban collective enterprises, the policy was used to justify *de jure*, as well as *de facto*, privatisation and the mass layoff of nearly all employees. After being let go, workers could then apply for their old jobs, often at lower salaries and sans any other benefits or security. Many were never allowed to return at all. Others were asked to pay fees or bribes for the privilege of going back to work.[14]

In my own previous work, I examined the detailed case of a machine tool plant in a part of Hubei Province I called 'County J'.[15] Based on streams of enterprise and county government internal documents, I was able to piece together the tale of that firm's restructuring as it unfolded over about a year between the summer of 1996 and mid-1997, amid a broader process of policy involution that bent the implementation of general central directives to the particularistic advantage of enterprise cadres and local officials. Unsurprisingly, it rendered the plant's workers much worse off. In the end, the plant was transformed into a private corporation, with shares distributed among workers and managers, but in a manner requiring workers to pay to keep their shares (even as their jobs were in jeopardy). Those who could not pay saw their shares go up for auction to enterprise cadres or other workers with deeper pockets. By 2011, the reconstituted firm had achieved a high level of commercial success, but with a workforce only 40 percent the size of what it had been in 1996. A firm that had long been a critical employer in this county town had become profitable, but no longer offered many jobs. Similar stories were repeated all over the country, especially in county towns and smaller prefecture-level cities, where local SOEs and even smaller collective-sector enterprises predominated (and where other employment opportunities tended to be scarce).

2008 and Beyond: Cresting of the Wave?

Over the decade after the Fifteenth Party Congress, a new policy consensus came into focus around a more universalistic welfare relief program known as the 'minimum livelihood guarantee' (最低生活保障, or *dibao* for short).[16] This, combined with comprehensive healthcare and pension reform, constituted a new state welfare regime for Chinese workers (see also Solinger's essay in the present volume).[17] Social protection, though less generous and encompassing, was no longer tied nearly so closely to the work unit as it had been previously. Moreover, the political and economic logics of layoffs were evolving rapidly and changed markedly with the advent of the Global Financial Crisis in late 2008.

With job losses already slowing in the state sector from about 2005, China's response to the 2008 crisis halted them almost entirely and reversed many trends. Indeed, the massive fiscal stimulus the central government injected into the economy had a principal effect of showering credit and investment on SOEs, rendering workers still employed in them a new kind of 'blue-collar aristocracy'.[18] Wages and working conditions improved markedly, where they had been declining precipitously for most of the previous twenty-five years. Though layoffs returned to some industries by the 2010s (especially in coal mining and some other heavy industrial sectors), they never again approached the pace or severity of the precrisis years; for one thing, there were not many workers left to shed, with more than 60 percent of state-sector jobs already gone.

Reverberations

Much has been made of China's characteristic labour market fragmentation, dating back to before 1949.[19] In particular, many (myself included) have drawn sharp lines between the politics of state-sector workers and their counterparts among rural–urban migrants. The long-run effects of the changes that unfolded since the late 1980s have included a weakening of this division and a blurring of old lines. Gone are the days of 'iron rice bowl' security for the urban labour elite in the state sector. Meanwhile, the most invidious and discriminatory rules excluding rural migrants from urban China's economy and society have eroded to a much greater degree than many thought possible even a decade ago. But the division of China's working class into a privileged state-sector elite and a disadvantaged mass of migrants has also been strengthened in other ways. With lower-skilled and older workers now mostly gone from SOEs, those remaining occupy higher echelons of the social hierarchy than either migrants or many of their own predecessors. The earthquake that shook China's state-sector labour market for more than two decades will continue to reverberate in these and myriad other ways for many years to come.

2001

In 2001, after fifteen years of negotiations, the People's Republic of China joined the World Trade Organization (WTO). Although many hailed this event as a milestone for China's economic transition and a cause for rejoicing, others expressed concern over how China's joining would impact workers both domestically and globally. Within China, fears arose that the country's further integration into the global economy would result in massive unemployment; abroad, the concern was that China's comparative political economic advantages might undercut workers elsewhere, especially in the Global South. This essay tracks the process of China's accession to the WTO and looks into its impact on Chinese workers.

China Joins the World Trade Organization: Implications for Workers

Dorothy J. SOLINGER[1]

'To poor people, us ordinary folk, the World Trade Organization [WTO] doesn't have any benefits,' lamented a laid-off worker whom I encountered on the streets of Wuhan in October 2001, on the eve of China's accession to the organisation. This man, recently let go without notice from a temporary work unit, having earlier been sacked from his once-secure state enterprise posting, was pedalling a three-wheeled cart to sustain his livelihood when I spoke with him. The pedicab he drove—an innovative but short-lived solution in Wuhan, where 40,000 of these were said to operate at that time—garnered an income of about 30 or 40 US cents per mile for millions like him. But, he continued: 'Any other profession is no good [其他的职业不行].' What concerned him most was the possibility that the government might eliminate bicycle taxis like his, which indeed it did just a couple of years later. 'The WTO is good for the rich. But the poor, those doing bitter labour, will just increase; there'll be more criminals, a lot of people like me agree,' he pronounced with some authority. 'They say goods will be getting cheaper, but that's about high-class things, like cars. We can't afford those things anyway. What it's all about, we don't understand much, [but we do know] it will have a negative impact.'

On 11 December 2001, after fifteen years of tortuous negotiations, China formally entered the WTO. The government and media in both the United States and China hailed the event as a cause for rejoicing. But the rosy picture they painted turned bleak when analysts began to contemplate the possibility that a substantial section of the Chinese urban workforce might lose their jobs as a result. For instance, the investment bank Salomon Smith Barney predicted a year beforehand that as many as forty million people in China could lose their employment in the first five years after entry.[2]

In fact, with the benefit of hindsight, we can affirm that joining—and thus becoming more deeply enmeshed in the global economy—would not be directly responsible for job losses. Instead, membership intensified trends already under way: heightening competition would accelerate state firms' insolvency, and requiring China to train and employ higher-quality labour would make most of the extant Chinese urban workforce unsuitable for the employment on offer. It would also precipitate those workers' replacement with upgraded machinery, even as better educated, younger employees moved into newly created jobs. At the same time, an increased inflow of agricultural imports was apt to hurt Chinese farmers, and so spur migration of more rural labourers into the urban job market. Besides, from the latter half of the 1990s, rural industry's ability to absorb labour had begun declining.[3] Farm employment dropped by 17 million in 1998 alone and by almost 33 million throughout the late 1990s.[4] One Chinese commentator characterised the coming employment situation as 'frost appearing on top of snow' (雪上加霜)—a four-character metaphor meaning 'one disaster after another'.[5]

Yet one more factor was China's growing integration into the global economy. In late 2001, one of my newly unemployed informants in the medium-sized city of Zigong, Sichuan, bemoaned: 'A lot of factories have gone bankrupt because people prefer foreign-made electronics.' All of these tendencies spelt the discharge of dozens of millions of urban workers long assured that they could count on a steady job and paid retirement, with secure health care and other benefits, for their lifetimes. How did this come to pass?

First Steps

From the early 1970s, China had started, if gingerly, to open its economy to the world. In 1980, it resumed its pre-1949 seat on the United Nations Interim Commission for International Trade Organization, which appointed the Secretariat for the General Agreement on Tariffs and Trade (GATT, the predecessor of the WTO). This move indicated the Chinese Government's intention to take part in GATT affairs. The next year, China was authorised to act as an observer at GATT meetings and, in 1983, it applied to join GATT's Multifibre Agreement. The subsequent step took place in mid-1986, when the Chinese authorities formally notified GATT that they had decided to seek resumption of the country's status as a contracting party; in the following year, formal negotiations began. A critical point here is that one of the chief goals of politicians who favoured reform of the national economy was to push ahead with marketisation—and to ensure it was irrevocably set into place.[6]

Throughout the late 1980s and 1990s, China's leaders initiated structural changes in the economy, such as the phasing out of direct subsidies for exports, cutting tariffs and/or quotas on thousands of categories of merchandise and eliminating licensing requirements. These measures were taken, first, from a desire to enter the GATT, then in preparation for acceptance into the WTO (which succeeded the GATT in 1995).[7] From 1994 to 1997, the country's average tariff rate dropped from 43 to 17 percent; when China entered the WTO in late 2001, the overall average was just 15 percent.[8] In early 1999, Premier Zhu Rongji agreed to open many protected sectors to gain acceptance into the WTO, again—as had reformers of the 1980s—in a bid to use internationalisation to prod state-owned enterprises to press on with reforms.[9]

This lengthy background—marked first by China's leaders' aims, then by WTO members' conditions and, at last, by compromises—led to the final fulfilment of the requirements and expectations of the parties involved. It is true that pressure of a sort did come from the outside: after 1986 the then-GATT member parties did urge China to undertake multiple adjustments to its economic structure and practices before they would admit the country into their ranks. But the fundamental motive behind all the modifications the Chinese officials made to the nation's economy over more than a decade was clearly their own drive for China's inclusion in the WTO. So, in that sense, it was a choice the Chinese authorities took themselves and not the influence of the member states that mattered most.

Domestic Effects for Workers

As expected, as trade barriers fell away and obstacles to investment broke down, foreign firms found it more convenient to trade with and invest in China. This took place just as many state firms suffered crippling losses and collapsed, partly due to competition from non-state firms, but also to a growing degree as a result of competition from imports.[10]

Another issue was that foreign companies were prone to hire young, well-educated workers for their skills, good health, knowhow and energy, and to employ rural migrants for their willingness to serve as drudges for very low wages.[11] Chinese employers reasoned that their older workers would be more costly to employ, as their stamina declined and their medical bills rose; at the same time, their work experience and skills were outmoded and irrelevant.[12] Bosses also considered they could save money by engaging outside (that is, young, educated or migrant) labour rather than retraining their own workers.[13] As a Chinese WTO negotiator noted: 'There's a popular ceiling of 35 years of age for new jobs.'[14]

Except in a few major industrial bases along the east coast, most of the textile technology in China was by then obsolete, the equipment decades old, the varieties of fabric too plain and unmarketable and the mill workers too undereducated to suit the demands of modern industry.[15] Accordingly, in the textile sector—supposedly a winning industrial sector in foreign trade[16]—millions of mill hands were let go, with the intentional destruction of more than nine million out-of-date spindles by the end of 1999.[17] In the major inland industrial city of Wuhan, where more than 100 state-owned textile mills had existed in the 1980s, not one remained by 2001. In their place were joint ventures, whose new owners demanded the booting out of large numbers of employees. Other firms were merged with more successful plants or simply collapsed, unable to survive under competitive pressures from the burgeoning private sector and foreign firms.[18] In addition, the lowering of tariff and other barriers meant an increase in chemical fibre imports, which put new pressure on the domestic market.[19]

Numerous workers were sacked from plants in a range of other sectors, such as pharmaceuticals, instruments, automobiles, chemicals, petrochemicals, steel, paper and machinery manufacturing.[20] As Thomas Rawski statistically demonstrated, 'large inflows of foreign direct investment, most of it directed toward manufacturing, have not prevented a sharp decline in employment growth among China's secondary industries, a category dominated by manufacturing.'[21] In all, those finding new jobs—whether in foreign-funded banking, information technology, finance and insurance, telecommunications and high technology or assembly-line plants—were not the workers who had lost their posts.

Crucially, another point critical to the process was that, a few years before entry into the WTO, the government began enforcing a policy of cutting back the old workforce to chase efficiency and global competitiveness, as it prepared to make the nation fit into the world economy. In late 1996, following the economy's successful 'soft landing' from a spate of high inflation, the authorities pushed ahead with a program of state enterprise reform that had been on hold for several years.[22] A new policy, called 'grasping the large and letting go the small' (抓大放小), appeared that amounted to selling off small state-owned firms, frequently leaving their employees to fend for themselves on the new open market and without any safety net whatever (see also Ching Kwan Lee's and

Hurst's essays in the present volume).[23] At the Fifteenth Party Congress in September 1997, top officials endorsed the slogan 'cutting the workforce and raising efficiency' (减员增效), which became the new watchword in labour relations.

Already in 2000, a ten-city investigation undertaken by the planning and financial affairs section of the then Ministry of Labour and Social Security found that more than 36 percent of those without jobs had been out of work for over three years, and another 48.5 percent for one to three years.[24] Of these, 89 percent reported that their incomes had fallen, while 56 percent had a monthly income of less than 300 yuan. A mere 3 percent were making 800 yuan per month or more—not a significant sum.

A State Planning and Development Commission investigation that same year uncovered that the *average* monthly income of laid-off or unemployed heads of households was a mere 272 yuan—about 55 percent of the national average urban wage.[25] While the official count of the laid-off and unemployed for the year 2000 amounted to less than twelve million,[26] an internal report suggested that the total number of these people was closer to sixty million by mid-2001.[27]

The All-China Federation of Trade Unions reported, on the basis of local labour department statistics, that there was a trend of annual deterioration in the rate of reemployment of dismissed workers: in 1998, that rate was 50 percent; in 1999, 42 percent; and, in the first eleven months of 2000, it was down to a mere 16 percent.[28] According to a Xinhua News Agency release, the rate plummeted to just 9 percent in the first half of 2002.[29]

As an official journal noted, the unemployed were mostly 'low-quality labour power' who 'will be thoroughly rejected by the labour market and so will form a long-term unstable mass'.[30] A researcher at the Chinese Academy of Social Sciences similarly speculated that these individuals would 'just be excluded and drift downward, with almost no chance to free themselves'.[31] These words turned out to be prophetic and precise.[32]

Immediate Reactions

For all the reasons noted above—new market measures undertaken by the government to satisfy WTO members, competition, intentional dismissals—unemployment shot skyward and produced massive unrest. Indeed, an internal report of the Ministry of Public Security claimed that 30,000 'mass incidents' occurred in the first nine months of 2000.

The figure included protests of all sorts, but a great many of these were over issues of job loss and unpaid wages and pensions. The conclusion the document drew was that the numbers of outbursts were increasing annually, the scale continuously expanding, the style becoming more violent, the degree of organisation higher, the membership growing more complex and the difficulty in managing them greater.

The overall picture, then, was this: as China entered more fully into the global economy, while millions of better placed citizens rose to the challenge and upgraded their jobs, many millions more sank, their working lives cut short, their potential undeveloped, their situation increasingly desperate and their capacity to purchase any of those enticing products offered up by the world market and its merchants non-existent. Though the state did extend a very inadequate program of social assistance, the Minimum Livelihood Guarantee, to salve the wound of sudden joblessness, even two decades later the majority of the victims of the process remain without steady employment, living in poverty and at a sorry loss.

2002

The 1990s and early 2000s saw sustained activism and protests by Chinese workers. On one side, state workers who felt betrayed by the State and excluded from the new labour market engaged in 'protests of desperation'. These usually entailed disruptive actions such as factory occupations, mass demonstrations or roadblocks. On the other side, migrant workers engaged in 'protests against discrimination', in which they resorted to legal mobilisation to advance demands mostly related to wage non-payment and working conditions. Through the lens of the Liaoyang strike of 2002—one of the most visible labour protests of those years—this essay examines the plight of state workers in China's rustbelt at the turn of the millennium.

The Liaoyang Strike and the Unmaking of Mao's Working Class in China's Rustbelt

Ching Kwan LEE

For more than a week in mid-March 2002, tens of thousands of workers marched through the streets of Liaoyang, an old industrial town in China's northeastern rustbelt. Some carried a huge portrait of the late Mao Zedong that was mounted on four shoulder poles and accented by a red ribbon fastened in a knot at the top of the frame. While some people passionately sang the *Internationale*, an old woman cried aloud: 'Chairman Mao should not have died so soon!' Fuelled by simmering anger at the corrupt local government and pressed by economic difficulties after their state-owned enterprises (SOEs) went bankrupt, workers from as many as twenty factories at one point demonstrated in front of the Liaoyang City government building. They demanded payment of back wages, pensions and unemployment allowances owed them for months, even years. But, most shocking to the authorities, they insisted on the removal of the head of the local legislature and former mayor whose seven-year leadership had spawned rampant corruption and wreaked havoc in the lives of local people. Overseas human rights organisations claimed it was the largest collective act of defiance since the bloody crackdown of the 1989 Tiananmen Incident (see Zhang's essay in the present volume), only this time workers were the major social group present—no intellectuals, students or private entrepreneurs joined their protests—and the official press censored the incident at both the municipal and the national levels.

Liaoyang had the look of many an old industrial town in the northeastern province of Liaoning. A pervasive greyness and an air of morbidity beset what once was a proud and buzzing industrial centre boasting a dozen major military equipment factories and a nationally renowned chemical plant built with French technological assistance in the early 1970s. Inklings of such past glory could still be found in the faces of the many unemployed workers gathering in makeshift 'labour market spots' (劳务市场), holding in their hands or hanging around their necks placards announcing their skills: plumber, electrician, nanny, seamstress, and so on. Abandoned brick workshops punctured with broken windowpanes lined the main road leading into this city of 1.8 million, one of which was the Liaoyang Ferro-Alloy Factory, or Liaotie (辽铁), the epicentre of the protests. For four years, the 3,000 employees of this SOE had petitioned the local government, charging the enterprise's management with financial irregularities and non-payment of wages, pensions, unemployment allowances and medical reimbursements. The columns near the building's main entrance were covered with posters and open letters. One open letter, addressed to 'All the People in Liaoyang', read:

> We the working masses decide that we cannot tolerate such corrupt elements who imposed an illegal bankruptcy on our factory. We must take back justice and dignity. We will not give up until we get all welfare payments, unpaid wages, and compensation back ... Our respected compatriots, brothers and fathers, we are not anti-Party, antisocialism hooligans who harm people's lives and disrupt social order. Our demands are all legal under the Constitution and the laws ... Let's join forces in this action for legal rights and against corruption. Long live the spirit of Liaoyang!

Pointed and impassioned, the letters made resounding accusations against local government corruption and collusion with enterprise management. The panoply of worker compensation specified by central government policy remained an empty but tantalising promise. Liaotie workers' grievances were shared by many other workers throughout China's cities and especially across the northeast. Yet workers' interests were fractured. A disillusioned former Party secretary of one of the many factories participating in this protest explained to me that different groups of protesting workers participated with their own unresolved balance books in their heads. They came together in holding the local government responsible for their plight:

> First, there were laid-off workers who did not get their 180-yuan monthly allowance. Then, there were retired workers complaining about not getting a special allowance promised by the central government two years ago. It was stipulated then that, for each year of job tenure, they should be paid an additional 1.8 yuan monthly for their retirement wages. Third, there were retired cadres whose career dated back to the pre-revolutionary era complaining about unequal treatment of retirees. There was a policy for military

personnel who were with the Chinese Communist Party [CCP] before 1949 to get 1,800 yuan a month as pension, but those who surrendered to the CCP at the end of the anti–Japanese War were given only half of that amount. The latter group was of course furious ... Then, there were banners saying: 'We want to eat', 'Return us our wages' ... People are nostalgic about the time of Chairman Mao, when everyone had jobs and society was stable and equal ... After devoting my life to political education work, I now feel my efforts have all been wasted. Since the early 1990s, after they started the director responsibility system, I as the Party secretary was sidelined, and he [the director] could rule and decide on personnel matters however he wanted—no restraint at all.

A Time of Reckoning

Thanks to its cross-factory participation and its explicit political demands, the Liaoyang protest received intense international media attention. Despite the rapid collapse of inter-workplace rebellion, its short-lived existence signalled to the regime the possibility of an escalated working-class rebellion beyond the predominant pattern of localised, single-factory mobilisations, spurred by economic and livelihood grievances related to wages, pensions, health benefits and bankruptcy compensation. In terms of sociological significance, it was this latter type of 'cellular activism' that had become paradigmatic in the Chinese reform era. Police statistics on demonstrations, startling as they were, captured only a small part of the phenomenon. In Liaoning Province alone, between 2000 and 2002, more than 830,000 people were involved in 9,559 'mass incidents' (群体性事件), or an average of ten incidents each involving ninety people every day for nearly three years.[1] Nationwide, the Ministry of Public Security recorded 8,700 such incidents in 1993, rising to 11,000, 15,000 and 32,000 in 1995, 1997 and 1999, respectively.[2] In 2003, three million people—including farmers, workers, teachers and students—staged some 58,000 incidents.[3] Among them, the largest group consisted of 1.66 million laid-off, retired and active workers, accounting for 46.9 percent of the total number of participants that year.[4] The surge in social unrest continued from 2004 to 2005, as the Ministry of Public Security announced a rise from 74,000 to 87,000 cases of riots and demonstrations during these two years.[5]

Rampant non-payment of wages, pension defaults and the general collapse of the enterprise welfare system had triggered this trend of increasing labour strife among China's massive laid-off and retired proletariat. The total number of workers in state and collective enterprises who were owed unpaid wages increased from 2.6 million in 1993 to 14 million in 2000, according to official trade unions statistics.[6] In Shenyang, the provincial capital of Liaoning, a survey showed that, between 1996 and 2000, more than one-quarter of retired workers were owed pensions and one-quarter of employed workers were owed wages.[7] Adding insult to injury, in 2002, the Chinese Government had begun experimenting with a one-time severance compensation scheme that translated each year of job tenure into 470 yuan (in Shenyang; the rates were lower for smaller cities and they varied across industries). Many workers simply rejected the idea that 'job tenure' could be put up for sale; many others found it repugnant that the value of their labour for socialism was now reduced to a pittance, while the state permanently relinquished responsibility for its workers. With glaring gaps in the new welfare safety net, the estimated twenty-seven to forty million workers shed from their work units in the state and collective sector since 1995 were plagued by a profound sense of insecurity.[8] Across the country, in rage and desperation, workers were wrestling with explosive questions: Who should be held responsible for the collapse of enterprises the regime had for years touted as worker-owned? How much should workers' lifelong contribution to socialism be worth now? Who should be paying for it? How much for every year of job tenure? Why are pension regulations and bankruptcy laws not implemented? In short, workers were contesting the value of their labour in the broadest sense, not just the amount of severance compensation, but also the meaning of labour, the basis of legitimate government and the principles of a just society. The 1990s was a time of reckoning between workers who had come of age under Maoist socialism and the post-Mao reform regime.

Cellular Activism

A notable feature of rustbelt worker unrest was that it was organised around localised, bounded work units or their subgroups, whose boundaries were defined and segmented by state policies. Cellular activism deviated from the mode of organised labour movement *à la* Polish Solidarity (see Wilson's essay in the present volume). It was also different from the quiet, hidden and atomistic forms of everyday resistance characteristic of socialist industrial workplaces or authoritarian political systems. But cellular activism was not the result of myopic worker consciousness, nor was it simply a concession to state repression of cross-factory networking. Its prevalence had to do with how workers' interests were constituted in the reform period. Decentralisation of economic decision-making, from the central to the local government and down to enterprise management (in the name of enterprise autonomy), had created localised communities of interest and responsibilities. Workers laid the blame for pension and wage arrears on their enterprises and local governments because these agents had been given the power and responsibility to manage SOEs. Decentralisation was coupled with market competition, giving rise to uneven and unequal economic conditions for enterprises even among those in the same region or city. On top of these differences, state policies continued to accord different, albeit minuscule, entitlements and compensation to workers in different industries, cohorts or forms of unemployment, resulting in bewildering variations of worker interests. This fragmentation of the working class into cellular interest groups did not paralyse collective action, but it did drive wedges between workers and channelled them into dispersed units of activism.

Worker protests were shaped not just by what happened in the realm of production. Equally important was the social reproduction of labour—that is, how workers survive beyond their participation in and dependence on wage work—and how it shaped the interests and capacities of rustbelt workers. Work unit housing was a critical factor in facilitating and limiting labour activism in the rustbelt. Residential quarters for SOE workers were self-contained and all-encompassing communities where work and nonwork lives took place in the same locality. This pattern facilitated communication and aggregation of interests during moments of labour conflict. Yet, during the same period, of enterprise bankruptcy and massive unemployment, workers also became property owners as urban housing reform allowed them to purchase the property rights for their welfare housing units at below market price. Workers could sell, rent out or pass these properties on to their offspring, even after plant closure and retirement. Housing was perhaps the most enduring and important redistributed good. No matter how desperate workers were in the workplace, homeownership cushioned them from destitution and dispossession caused by market competition, instilling a degree of dependence on and allegiance to the reform regime that had also marginalised them. Herein lies the structural limit for rustbelt workers' insurgency.

Moral-Economy Protests?

Some students of Chinese labour have suggested that labour unrest was a form of moral-economy protest.[9] Nostalgic for lost subsistence rights, Chinese workers drew on pre-reform ideological legacies of state paternalism and the old class rhetoric to demand restoration of traditional entitlements. This moral-economy interpretation is valid but inadequate. Although workers' resistance was driven by a restorative and subsistence ethic, I also found other, coexisting political and cultural logics that impelled worker activism. Rather than seeing workers as locked in some traditional political mentality harking back to the past, it is more accurate to see a repertoire of multiple worker subjectivities formed through workers' participation in ongoing institutional transformation. Chinese legal reform from the 1990s to the 2000s—no matter how partial and uneven—imparted new conceptions of workers' rights, interests and agency, as did the regime's continual adherence to Mao's notion of the masses. Citizens' rights to legal justice and the legitimacy of the masses to rebel against corrupt officials were equally powerful frames of labour mobilisation. Therefore, we should emphasise the coexistence of the working class, the citizen and the subaltern as equally important, if also shifting, political subjectivities through which workers were compelled to act. Following Göran Therborn, Chinese workers, as social actors or subjects, could turn ideology into power, finding resources to act and resist in the same ideological appellations that were intended to subjugate them.[10] Like the making of class, we cannot predict what will happen but can explain the trajectory of when and which ideological interpellation underlies what collective action. In the process of waging these struggles, workers also contributed to pushing legal and welfare reform in new directions.

In this drama of labour insurgency, the Chinese Government devised a 'carrot and stick' approach to divide and conquer leaders and ordinary workers and differentiated laterally organised dissent from local cellular mobilisations. In the aftermath of the Liaoyang protests, officials rushed to offer workers most of the money they were owed. At the same time, the local news media condemned protest leaders as troublemakers who 'colluded with hostile foreign forces'—a reference to foreign journalists, rights groups with whom the workers spoke and their contacts with the banned China Democracy Party. Two worker leaders were given prison terms of four to seven years. On the other hand, the Central Discipline Inspection Commission, the Communist Party's antigraft unit in Beijing, sent investigators to Liaoyang to look into the complaints. The officials involved were arrested, demoted or removed.

Governments at both the local and the central levels presented themselves as a Janus-faced authority, setting clear boundaries between zones of indifference, even tolerance, and forbidden terrains. Within the limits of the first, the government could selectively concede to workers' most urgent livelihood grievances or make concrete improvements to the collection of social insurance or the implementation of bankruptcy procedures. Once workers veered towards organised political dissent, however, the state cracked down ruthlessly, arresting and imprisoning leading agitators. Thus, the state was responsive to popular discontent, though in a slow, erratic and, at times, repressive manner. Labour unrest was not an effective catalyst to challenge the political system in China, but in its failure, it successfully generated pressure for social policy changes.

2003

From the early 1980s, custody and repatriation (C&R) centres were one of the cornerstones of the Party-State's control of China's burgeoning migrant workforce. Originally established in 1982 with the purported aim of helping beggars and the homeless in urban areas, by the beginning of the following decade, these centres targeted anyone without proper residence or work permits. The police were granted enormous power, and could arbitrarily detain migrants without papers and subject them to all types of abuse. Criticism of this institution came to a head in 2003. In March that year, a young graphic designer named Sun Zhigang was stopped by police on a street in Guangzhou, where he had arrived just a few weeks earlier. He came from a village in Hunan Province, but had recently graduated from the Wuhan University of Science and Technology. Since he did not have his identity card and residence permit with him at that time, the police officers suspected him of being an illegal migrant and took him to the police station. All attempts by his friends to secure his release were in vain. The following day, he was transferred to a C&R centre, where, two days later, he died, allegedly of heart failure. As the authorities refused to look into the circumstances of his death, a progressive newspaper in Guangzhou took up Sun's cause and started an in-depth investigation. The truths revealed by the journalists, combined with pressure from online public opinion and legal activism, would cause a public uproar that eventually led to the abolition of the C&R centres.

The Sun Zhigang Case
Chloé FROISSART

On 17 March 2003, Sun Zhigang, a twenty-seven-year-old graphic designer from a village in Hunan Province, freshly graduated from the Wuhan University of Science and Technology, was stopped by police on a street in Guangzhou, where he had arrived less than a month earlier to work in a private clothing company. Unable to produce his identity card and residence permit, he was taken to the police station on the suspicion of being an illegal migrant. The same evening, his roommate tried to free him by bringing his identity card to the station and offering to pay bail, but the police refused to release him. The following day, Sun was transferred to a custody and repatriation (C&R) centre, from which his employer tried unsuccessfully to have him released. On 20 March, the centre's medical service announced that Sun had died of heart failure. Barely one month later, an autopsy demanded by his father revealed that Sun had actually died from injuries that caused internal bleeding. Faced with the authorities' refusal to investigate the circumstances of his son's death, Sun's father turned for help to the *Southern Metropolis News* (南方都市报), a progressive and outspoken Guangzhou newspaper. On 25 April, after conducting an exhaustive investigation, the outlet broke the story with an article titled 'A University Graduate Was Detained for Failing to Present His Temporary Residence Permit and Beaten to Death'.[1] This was the beginning of what came to be known as the 'Sun Zhigang Case' (孙志刚事件).

The Sun Zhigang Case was significant in several respects. First, it led to the abolition of the C&R centres where migrants who could not produce their permits for the police were arbitrarily detained and sometimes forced to work before being sent back to their home villages. This marked one of the most drastic changes in policing since the establishment of the People's Republic and was a lasting setback for the police state. Second, this success was achieved thanks to the rise of a new protest paradigm combining investigative journalism, pressure from online public opinion, and legal activism. This revealed a new awareness of universal citizenship—with urban citizens identifying with migrants and vice versa—and paved the way for the formation of a new type of legal activism demanding citizen equality before the law, which led to a series of systemic reforms during the Hu Jintao–Wen Jiabao era. Finally, the case marked a milestone in efforts to achieve greater integration of migrant workers into the cities and their treatment as fully fledged citizens.

Factors Leading to the Sun Zhigang Case

In the Sun Zhigang Case, a confluence of events and circumstances created conditions favourable to a positive outcome. The most important was the change in political leadership. Having replaced Jiang Zemin as General Secretary of the Chinese Communist Party (CCP) and President of the People's Republic of China (PRC) in October 2002, Hu Jintao and Wen Jiabao, who replaced Zhu Rongji as Premier in March 2003, were keen to establish a new style of governance that was more 'responsible to the people'. This approach aimed to counter the influence of the former leadership, who maintained important positions within the state.[2] The Hu–Wen administration wanted to stand out from its predecessors—whose government had been defined by all-out economic reforms with great human cost—by emphasising the rule of law, respect for the Constitution, and the reduction of social inequalities. On taking charge, the Hu–Wen administration was put to the test by the SARS (Severe Acute Respiratory Syndrome) crisis, in which lower-level officials were accused of having covered up the scale of the epidemic. The belated response to the epidemic, for which China was criticised internationally, led the regime to put greater emphasis on openness and transparency. The media was also given greater space for accurate and timely reporting.

Emphasising the building of a 'harmonious society' (和谐社会) over the 'efficiency-first' motto that had dominated under Jiang Zemin's rule, Hu and Wen launched a number of initiatives to assist marginalised groups. Migrant workers were the first beneficiaries. In January 2003, Document No. 1, which traditionally sets the political priorities for the year, acknowledged that China's industrialisation must necessarily go hand-in-hand with urbanisation and urged municipalities to work towards granting equal social and economic rights to migrants and urban residents. The document also called for severe punishment of any attack on the dignity of migrants and any violation of their personal rights. Local authorities, backed by the media, were encouraged to promote societal respect for migrants.[3] The document marked a turning point in the management of migration and the perception of migrant workers, and paved the way for demands for equal treatment of citizens.

Document No. 1 also stipulated the need to end the arrest and improper detention of migrant workers in C&R centres. During 2002, there was a flourishing of critical reports written by influential think tanks and well-known social scientists about how these centres had been diverted from their original social welfare purpose. Established in 1982, the C&R centres were originally intended to assist people in need, especially beggars and vagrants, and repatriate them to their place of residence, since the authorities in the localities where they had household registration (户口, *hukou*) were responsible for their social care. However, municipalities increasingly used such places to control migration and 'maintain social order'. Together with the system of permits, which migrants had to navigate to live and work legally in the cities, and the 'Strike Hard' (严打) campaigns carried out regularly by the police to rid cities of undocumented migrants, C&R centres had become part of a police-state apparatus that criminalised migration and migrants.

During this time, the All-China Women's Federation and the Communist Youth League also published migrants' testimonies denouncing the arbitrariness of police roundups and the appalling conditions of detention.[4] Crammed in overcrowded cells, migrants were not properly fed, frequently physically abused, insulted, subjected to extortion, and forced to work to meet the costs of their stay and repatriation. In 2001, after the central government issued a circular urging municipalities to abolish all taxes levied on migrants, local governments compensated for the lost revenue by multiplying police checks and increasing detentions in C&R centres. Although the cost of permits decreased, the overall number of permits issued increased supposedly as a means for migrants to finance their use of urban facilities and compensate for the strain management of them put on city administrations.[5]

All the ingredients for an explosion were therefore present: a situation that was getting out of control, the political will of the central government to rein in the abuses of the municipalities, and an informed public. The only thing that was missing was the detonator: this was to be the Sun Zhigang Case.

The Apex of Investigative Journalism

The Sun Zhigang Case gave birth to a new protest paradigm combining investigative journalism, the internet as a forum for public debate and a means of creating public pressure, and legal activism striving to transform the state's ideological discourse on the 'rule of law' into legal and institutional reality.[6]

By carrying out its own investigation, the *Southern Metropolis News* acted as a counterweight to the abuses of power by the Chinese Party-State, not only by providing independent information, but also by placing the case in the legal field at the outset. The newspaper's detailed report on the death of Sun made it clear, with reference to the C&R Regulations of Guangdong Province, that Sun's detention was illegal as long as he could produce his identification card and attest to having a home and a job. In other words, the mere fact of not being able to produce a temporary residence permit did not constitute sufficient reason for placement in a C&R centre. The report also raised concerns about a coverup. An aggressive editorial signed with the pseudonym 'The Master Said' (子曰) accompanying the report concluded that Sun clearly died after being beaten in custody, criticised local authorities for the death, and implored readers to recognise that the tragedy could have happened to anyone.[7]

The *Southern Metropolis News* thus played a fundamental role in first exposing the tragedy and then addressing the authorities and the public. Although the Guangdong Department of Propaganda tried to prevent local newspapers from publishing further reports on the case, soon other media took up the story. The article was reprinted the same day by another Guangzhou daily newspaper and, in the following days, *Xinhua*, the *People's Daily*, and other major state-run media outlets quickly highlighted the story in their headlines and on their very popular websites.[8] The case then took on a national dimension.

The Power of the Internet

This case revealed the crucial role played by the internet as a site for public debate and a means of putting pressure on authorities. As reported by media scholar Xiao Qiang, 'two hours after being posted on China's largest news portal, sina.com, this news item generated 4,000 comments from readers. Almost immediately, the case was being discussed throughout Chinese cyberspace, from official sites to personal Web logs and e-mail groups.'[9] Commentary on the case included not only expressions of outrage over Sun's death and demands for punishment, but also broader complaints about the C&R system and pervasive abuses by law enforcement officials. Online reactions mixed moral judgements with legal statements referring to the Constitution. The main themes touched on were the need to respect human life and protect citizens from the arbitrariness of power.[10]

However, the complaints did not call the regime into question but rather asked for the Party-State to find solutions and implement measures to guarantee the rights of citizens. These criticisms fell within the framework of the Party's legalistic discourse, which was, moreover, the precondition for their effectiveness. There is no doubt though that the scale and content of the protests expressed on the internet went beyond the limits set by the authorities. Although internet censorship prevents us from speaking of a 'public sphere' in the normative sense of the term, the internet appeared as a space for interaction where individuals could express themselves, exchange opinions, and make critical judgements, as long as the leading role of the Party was not called into question. In short, a 'public' came into being by exerting pressure on the authorities and attempting to influence public policy.

The question is: why did the news of Sun Zhigang's death arouse such public indignation when the press had already revealed many cases of migrants who died in C&R centres due to physical abuse? The answer can be found in the widespread identification with Sun, which was the real force driving this mobilisation.[11] The fact that the media focused on Sun as a university graduate and a skilled employee of a private company was instrumental in allowing a large urban audience to identify with this rural migrant. Ai Xiaoming, a professor at Sun Yatsen University in Guangzhou and one of the first Chinese intellectuals to publicly comment on this case, summed it up well: 'It could have happened to my son, to one of my students or to anyone.'[12] At the same time, the case was an important step in making migrant workers aware of their citizenship status and helped them challenge their identity as mere 'peasants'. In the words of one migrant worker in Guangzhou: 'We are all Chinese and Chinese people beat another Chinese to death.'[13] The Sun Zhigang Case thus marked a rising awareness of universal citizenship beyond the division between urban and rural status.[14]

Legal Mobilisation

On 14 May 2003, three young legal scholars in Beijing named Xu Zhiyong, Teng Biao, and Yu Jiang submitted a petition to the National People's Congress (NPC) challenging the legality and constitutionality of the

C&R Measures promulgated by the State Council in 1982 and calling for their repeal. They addressed their request as 'citizens of the People's Republic of China' and relied on the Law on Legislation of 2000, which gave the right to any court and to any Chinese citizen to propose the repeal of unconstitutional laws. In an interview with *The New York Times*, Xu Zhiyong explained that the ultimate goal of the process was to clarify who in China had the right to interpret the law.[15]

Ultimately, the authors of the petition wished to see the establishment of an independent constitutional court separate from the NPC, whose standing committee—rather than the judiciary—had the power to invalidate laws and regulations that conflicted with the Constitution. This purely legalistic approach, which pursued a 'change from within', had a truly revolutionary scope, which Xu distinguished from the strategy of the Tiananmen demonstrators in 1989: 'I have respect for those who raised human rights issues in the past, but now we hope to work in a constructive way within the space afforded by the legal system. Concrete but gradual change—I think that's what most Chinese people want.'[16] Less than a week after this first petition was addressed to the NPC, a second was written by five well-known jurists from Beijing University calling for the creation of a special commission to inquire into the death of Sun Zhigang and to explore possible reforms of the C&R system. The petition initiated a debate on the history of the C&R centres, their primary purpose, and the ways in which they had facilitated abuse. Both petitions were supported by the media and collected hundreds of signatures online, where they were widely commented on.

Such mobilisation would not have been possible if the Party had not reiterated its wish to promote the rule of law and had not provided the legal means through which this new form of contestation was conducted. As a struggle for 'the right to defend and assert all citizen rights on the basis of equality and by fair legal procedure', the Sun Zhigang Case revealed the assertion of Chinese civic citizenship in both conscience and deed.[17]

A Half-Victory

In May, central government leaders took steps to address the public outcry over Sun's death. They ordered Guangdong authorities to conduct a thorough investigation. It revealed that guards at the clinic attached to the C&R centre, annoyed by Sun's insubordination, had forced eight detainees to beat him up as punishment. The trial led to the conviction of twelve defendants charged with beating or inciting the beating of Sun Zhigang, with sentences ranging from three years' imprisonment to death. In separate trials, an additional six public security officers were convicted of dereliction of duty and sentenced to prison terms ranging from two to three years. Twenty-three other officials received administrative punishments. The harsh sanctions, the swiftness of the investigation, and the trials were not enough, however, to quell concerns about a coverup. Nor did the convictions put an end to public complaints about law enforcement abuses, the treatment of migrants, and the legality of the C&R system.[18]

On 18 June, Premier Wen called a special meeting of the State Council, during which he declared that the 1982 C&R Measures were no longer adequate for the current situation, resulting from the new forms of migration that had developed over the previous twenty years, and announced their repeal. On 22 June, the State Council published new measures to replace the C&R centres with social aid centres, which were placed under the direction of the Ministry of Civil Affairs and its local bureaus instead of the Ministry of Public Security. This was a fundamental change, which emphasised that these centres no longer aimed to maintain public order and limit migration. The implementation of the measures was set for 1 August 2003.[19]

On 21 July, the Ministry of Civil Affairs published an implementation decree confirming that the new centres were intended only for beggars and vagrants who could not afford to support themselves—especially children, the elderly, and the disabled without housing or resources. According to the new rules, people had to be informed of the assistance they could receive in these centres and be 'guided' there, but they could not be forced to attend or stay there (except for minors and people who were incapacitated in some way). The assistance was temporary and could not 'generally' exceed ten days, at the end of which the centre had to organise the care of the person by their relatives, work unit, or the authorities in their place of residence, financing their repatriation if necessary. The decree prohibited the staff of the centres from asking for payments from their charges and their relatives. It also banned organising, 'under any pretext whatsoever', production activities within the premises. In short, the new measures put much more emphasis on the centres as a form of social service and on the rights of the people who were to be accommodated there.

The measures were accompanied by a real political will to implement them. From the date the measures were issued, China's largest cities announced the conversion of C&R centres into social assistance centres.[20] However, by calling a special meeting of the State Council, the premier had bypassed the NPC, which had no opportunity to adjudicate on the legality and constitutionality of the measures as demanded by the three jurists who had lodged the petition. Contrary to the wishes of the jurists, the interpretation of the law remained in the hands of the Party-State (and subject to the decision of one man, in the person of the then premier). The reform thus remained strictly legal and not political, but even in the legal field it remained quite limited. One of the main points made by the jurists in their petition was that, according to the Law on Legislation, coercive measures and penalties involving the deprivation of personal freedom of citizens should be addressed through the law and not by administrative regulation. Had the NPC ruled in accordance with the Law on Legislation, it would have created a precedent, threatening state regulations relating to other forms of administrative detention, such as reeducation through labour. Moreover, had the NPC accepted the arguments on personal freedom, citizens could have used this precedent to challenge the *hukou* system and other administrative control mechanisms.[21]

Premier Wen's handling of the petition of the three jurists avoided a domino effect while giving a timely response to the public outcry, which in turn bolstered the new leadership's legitimacy. The Sun Zhigang Case became an opportunity for the central government to reaffirm its authority over the municipalities and to put an end to practices that were increasingly perceived negatively by the population, and which threatened social order. Nevertheless, by imprisoning several *Southern Metropolis News* journalists, the government of the Guangzhou municipality gave a clear signal that the experience should not be repeated. The editor-in-chief of the newspaper, Chen Yizhong, and two of his colleagues were sentenced to five-month prison terms on unfounded corruption charges. In addition, Chen was dismissed from his post and expelled from the Communist Party in October 2004. He has since been prevented from practising as a journalist.[22] Altogether, this reform illustrates well the definition of the 'rule of law' coined by the government: an adaptation of the system in small touches with the aim of making it more efficient and more legitimate to better maintain it.

The Aftermath of the Case

The Sun Zhigang Case was a milestone towards the greater integration of migrant workers into cities and their treatment as fully fledged citizens. It sparked momentum for the abolition of the temporary residence permit in the name of equality for all Chinese citizens. Many intellectuals and academics supported reforms ensuring that every citizen could legally reside in their place of choice or that, at the very least, a registration system be put in place that did not make rights conditional on residence.

In the years that followed, Chinese cities gradually repealed some of the many permits that constrained migrants' legal stay in urban areas, such as the work permit, the employment permit, and restrictions on the opening of businesses by migrant workers and their access to housing. The temporary residence permit (暂住证) was replaced with a residence permit (居住证). To this day, migrants are still supposed to register with the Public Security Bureau within months of their arrival in a city, but the deadline has been extended from three to six months, the cost of this permit has been reduced to a few yuan, and the authorities try to enforce this measure by relying more on incentives than on constraints.[23]

Indeed, no more 'strike hard' campaigns have been organised since then, although Beijing authorities periodically reserve the right to 'clean' the capital of its migrants, as was the case before the Olympic Games in 2008 and during the winter of 2017–18, when a fire provided a convenient excuse for redeveloping the districts inhabited by migrant workers. More than anything, the Sun Zhigang Case was a watershed in the development of legal activism and constitutionalism, which led to a series of reforms in the legal system, pertaining to labour issues as well as other fields.[24]

2007

In the spring of 2007, parents whose children had recently gone missing alerted the Chinese media to the existence of a vast archipelago of 'black brick kilns' in Shanxi Province. The owners of these sites, abetted by local powerholders, took advantage of a docile workforce of teenagers who had been violently abducted or tricked, adults with mental problems, and children. As groups of parents searched the countryside in the hope of finding their offspring and new and traditional media competed with one another to cover the story in the most minute detail, the Chinese public was shocked to learn of the widespread existence of slavery in China in the twenty-first century and mobilised to put pressure on the authorities. This essay looks back to those months of popular mobilisation and their aftermath.

Slaving Away: The 'Black Brick Kilns Incident' of 2007

Ivan FRANCESCHINI[1]

5,041 days, 5,041 posts. Day after day for more than a decade, one solitary blogger has been keeping track of the time that has passed since 28 March 2007, when fifteen-year-old Yuan Xueyu disappeared from a construction site in the centre of Zhengzhou, Henan Province.[2] Every morning, this blogger—who in his 'ordinary' life is a prominent media personality in China—posts exactly the same message:

> Today it is day [x] in the search for Yuan Xueyu. Public Security Bureau of Zhengzhou, could you please tell us what progress has been made in his case? The missing workers in the black brick kilns incident in Shanxi Province remain missing. Netizens have donated 4,000 yuan as a reward for any relevant clue. The Public Security Bureau of Zhengzhou opened the case related to Yuan Xueyu's disappearance back in 2007.

Yuan Xueyu had arrived in Zhengzhou a couple of weeks before his disappearance to be an apprentice to a fellow villager—a worker specialising in setting up window frames. Like many of his childhood friends, he had been unable to resist the call of the big city that resounded in his remote rural village in China's northeast and, against the wishes of his father, had dropped out of middle school. When he heard that his son was nowhere to be found, Yuan Cheng did not waste any time. He immediately went to Zhengzhou and took up a job on the same construction site. He posted leaflets everywhere with a photo of his son and his contact details, but the only result was that strangers started to call him pretending to know the boy. Saying that his son had been in an accident, they asked him to wire them money and then disappeared. It was only after encountering other parents whose children had disappeared in similar circumstances that Yuan Cheng finally found some hope. Listening to their stories, he realised there was a good chance that his son had been kidnapped and sold into slavery to labour in a brick kiln deep in the countryside. The prospects were still dim, but at least now he had a vague idea of where to look.

In the spring and summer of 2007, bands of aggrieved parents roaming the Chinese countryside looking for their missing children made for one of the most remarkable stories of popular mobilisation and resistance in contemporary China—the so-called black brick kilns incident (黑砖窑事件). Widely reported by the Chinese media, it was a saga of unendurable pain and unprecedented camaraderie—of friendship as well as betrayal.

A Mother's Determination

The chain of events that led to the media exposure of the scandal began in March 2007 with Yang Aizhi, a woman whose adolescent son had just gone missing in Zhengzhou.[3] Desperate, she began posting leaflets everywhere, just as Yuan Cheng would do a few weeks later. However, she had a bit more luck: instead of being conned, another parent reached out to her to share the news that his two sons had just escaped from slavery at a kiln in Shanxi Province. Convinced that her son must be in a similar place, Yang immediately travelled to the area. There, she visited no less than 100 kilns, finding many young slaves, some still wearing school uniforms. After returning to Henan, she went through the missing persons announcements published in the local newspaper and eventually got in touch with five other parents in the same situation. Together, they established what the Chinese media later would call the 'League to Search for Children' (寻子联盟). In just a few months, they managed to rescue more than forty children from slavery in the kilns.

Realising the task was beyond their strength, they decided to seek help from the media. As it turned out, their stories were so outlandish that only one journalist from a local TV station in Henan, Fu Zhenzhong, agreed to accompany them in their search. He did not know it then, but he had made the right choice. On the evening of 19 May 2007, when footage Fu shot with a hidden camera of young boys wearing rags and engaged in heavy labour in kilns in Shanxi was aired on television, there was an uproar. As Fu later recalled, in the three days after the program aired, about 1,000 parents went to the TV station looking for help.[4] Seeing those images on television, parents who until that moment had had no clue about the whereabouts of their children discovered the existence of the kilns and realised that they were not alone in their plight. From that moment, it did not take them long to get together to start organising themselves into small teams to scour the Shanxi countryside.

Then, on 6 June, the aunt of a child recently rescued by the league chose to express her gratitude in a tearful post on a local web portal in Henan.[5] This post quickly went viral, finally attracting the attention of the national media. The following day, local media in Shanxi exposed a tragic story of slavery and murder at a kiln in Caosheng Village, Hongdong County, further fuelling public outrage.[6] From then, 'black brick kilns' became a household term across the whole country.

The Hidden Rules of the Kilns

For the whole summer of 2007, Chinese media offered impressive coverage of the scandal. It was revealed that the slaves in the kilns included not only teenagers who had been violently abducted or deceived with promises of a well-paid job, but also adults with mental problems and children—a docile workforce that never raised any demands. Among the lesser-known survival stories was that of Hao Dingpo, a fifteen-year-old boy who had spent two and a half years in the kilns after being kidnapped from Zhengzhou in March 2005. According to his mother, when he finally managed to escape in the summer of 2007, Hao had waist-length hair and a number on his wrist.[7] He told me that names were never used in the kiln, only numbers.[8] They had a daily production quota of 10,000 bricks and, when they were not able to fulfil it, they were savagely beaten. When one fugitive was caught attempting to escape, he was beaten to death by the guards and his body was left in the open to rot as a warning to others. Hao Dingpo claimed to have seen six people die this way, but there was no way to verify his claim as he was unable to indicate the exact location of the kiln.

Such dramatic circumstances took their toll not only on the bodies of those enslaved, but also on their mental health. When I met Zhang Shanlin in May 2008, one year after the police had rescued his son from a kiln, he expressed concern about his child's psychological health. Once lively and cheerful, the teenager had now lost all interest in everything, including his dream of becoming a chef. He refused to leave his house and avoided any human contact. He felt ashamed about what had happened to him and had recurring nightmares almost every night about his life at the kiln from which he would wake screaming.

Drawing on the testimonies of the survivors, the media was relentless in exposing and excoriating the power dynamics behind the kilns. It was evident that the kilns could exist only because many people benefited from them. A report about the infamous kiln in Caosheng Village that appeared in the *Southern City Metropolitan Weekly* (南都周刊) quoted a former slave as saying that life at the kiln 'was like the food chain in the animal realm ... This chain had six rings: the owner of the kiln, the contractor in charge of the workers [包工头], the guards, the older workers, the new workers, the mentally disabled'.[9] While the owners were invariably local, the contractors generally came from elsewhere—usually the place where they found their victims. The situation of the guards was more problematic. According to various accounts, it appears that in many kilns it was customary to promote slaves to become guards as a reward for their loyalty.[10] The case of Liu Dongsheng, a boy from Guizhou Province, is emblematic. Sold for the first time along with his mother to an unmarried man in a village in Henan when he was eleven, Liu ended up at the kiln in Caosheng Village as a slave before he had even turned eighteen. Distinguishing himself for his readiness to expose his companions' escape plans, he was soon promoted to guard and put in charge of supervising and beating the other prisoners.[11] In a trial that took place in 2007, Liu was sentenced to two years in prison on the charge of 'illegal imprisonment' (非法拘禁罪), exactly as any other guard from the kiln.[12]

The relationship between the kilns and their surrounding community was also very important. Although many accounts described the geographical seclusion of these sites, the kilns did not exist in a void. The reason local residents accepted them is because of the economic advantages they provided—stimulating local development, creating new opportunities to get rich, and eventually resulting in an enlargement of arable land, as Wang Dongji, former Party secretary of Caosheng Village and father of the owner of the notorious kiln, candidly admitted.[13] His son had taken advantage of his connections to sell bricks at special prices for public works at the local school and in the village government seat.[14] Although this arrangement caused a degree of resentment among the villagers, it nevertheless benefited the whole community—at least so the disgraced official claimed.

Support from the local community was also one of the reasons escaping from the kilns was so difficult. Since local workers were too expensive and too well protected by their families and networks to be exploitable, slaves were inevitably 'outsiders' (外地人). Sometimes local people even helped supply the kilns with the workforce they needed. This is what happened to Shen Haijun, a thirty-eight-year-old man from Jiangsu Province, who ended up as a slave in the kiln in Caosheng Village while looking for his mother, a widow in her sixties who had been sold as a wife to an old bachelor in Shanxi by a relative.[15] Shen told journalists that, once he had arrived in the village where his mother had been sold, he had asked an elderly woman for directions. Under the pretence of helping him find a job, she sold him to Wang Dongji's son.

The higher echelons of the provincial government were also implicated. Chinese media not only reported that the mid-level bureaucracy in Shanxi was fully aware of the existence of the kilns, but also provided evidence of the direct involvement of some officials,[16] such as in the disturbing story of Henan teenager Zhu Guanghui.[17] Rescued by the police from a kiln on 27 April 2007, he was immediately sold to another kiln by a local labour inspector, who even deducted an 'agency fee' (中介费) of 300 yuan from the backpay the boy had received on liberation. Zhu was rescued again during another police operation at the end of May. In the following days, a local TV station recorded a confrontation between him and the labour inspector who had sold him. On that very afternoon, the labour inspector would deceive the boy once again, tricking him into yet another kiln. Only on 18 June was Zhu rescued for a third time and finally managed to return home safely.

The Response of the Authorities

The Chinese public had heard of the existence of slavery in the kilns long before the events of the spring and summer of 2007. A few years earlier, Chinese media had widely reported the story of Zhang Xubo, who, after graduating from a rural middle school in 2002, had gone to Xi'an to look for a job, but was deceived by a stranger and sold as a slave to a kiln in Kaolao Township, Shanxi.[18] For three months, he had toiled for more than sixteen hours a day in cold weather and was repeatedly beaten by guards. In November, when his legs were suffering from frostbite and he had almost lost the ability to work, he begged the kiln owner to let him go. The man accepted and even offered to give Zhang a lift but abandoned him in the middle of nowhere. Unable to move, Zhang spent several days in a vacant kiln, in temperatures often below freezing, before being rescued by a local. Because of the frostbite, both his feet had to be amputated. Even though, back in 2003, this story caused a great stir on Chinese media and Premier Wen Jiabao issued instructions to launch a thorough investigation of the matter, no large-scale police operation was launched against the kilns nor was it accompanied by an upsurge of popular fury comparable with the one that would occur in 2007.[19]

The indifference with which the local authorities treated the aggrieved parents who were looking for their missing children also did not change. Back in May 2008, Wang Xiaoli, the mother of a boy who had gone missing in 2006 in Gongyi County, Henan, told me: 'When I went to the police to report that my son was missing, they declined to even open the case. They said that such situations are too common to be taken into consideration.' At the moment of his disappearance, her seventeen-year-old son was studying for the university admission exam. He was one of the best students in his school and had a very good chance of being accepted to a top university—a remarkable achievement for a boy from a poor rural area. Yet, on 26 October 2006, he went missing without a trace; he was supposed to spend a few days at a friend's house, but never reached his destination.

The media storm triggered by the aggrieved parents in 2007 marked a momentous change in attitude by the Chinese authorities. In June 2007, the central government launched a provincial investigation into the Shanxi kilns. The numbers involved were impressive, the outcome less so. According to official data, the police checked 86,395 employers, discovering that 36,286 (42 percent) of them were operating without formal permission; 4,861 brick and tile kilns were inspected, among which 3,186 (63.3 percent) were found to be lacking registration; and, in total, workers in the kilns numbered 81,000, but only seventeen kilns were found to have severe problems.[20] Among them, thirteen were using child labour. Overall, 359 workers were rescued, including 121 mentally disabled adults and fifteen children. In the meantime, the top echelons of the Party launched a campaign to 'sweep' the ranks of the local bureaucracy, with ninety-five officials punished for malfeasance and dereliction of duty.

At the same time, the Chinese leadership did not miss the opportunity to ride the scandal to pursue its political agenda. In particular, the media coverage of the kilns was instrumental in accelerating the troubled legislative progress of the Labour Contract Law, which had been stranded due to a heated public debate about the advisability of introducing new guarantees for workers' rights when economic development still depended on low labour costs (see Gallagher's essay in the present volume). After more than three years of top-level discussions and more than a dozen blueprints of the law, the kilns scandal was an essential catalyst that facilitated its ultimate approval, and the law was passed at the end of June, right in the middle of the media storm. As Xie Liangming, then Deputy Director of the Department of Legal Affairs of the All-China Federation of Trade Unions, admitted on television, if the kilns scandal had not happened: 'I think that the debate would have continued. Since the scandal deeply moved the legislative bodies, including many committee members who felt that such situations could not be understood and that it was necessary to be more severe, the Law was pushed through.'[21]

The Kilns after the Scandal

In the following years, the kilns might not have been as brazen and widespread as before, but all signs point to their continued existence. In May 2009, Chinese media reported that, in Jieshou City, Anhui Province, the police rescued thirty-two mentally disabled workers enslaved at two different kilns.[22] According to the available accounts, these people were deceived by a human trafficker—in this case, a taxi driver, who earned 200 to 300 yuan for every person he 'introduced' to the kilns. Closely guarded by thugs who did not hesitate to resort to violence, these slaves, who ranged in age from twenty-five to forty-five, lived locked in a courtyard and were forced to work ten hours a day with no pay but a few yuan for their personal expenses. The police arrested ten people, including the contractor and the owners.

In June 2010, police in Shilin County, Yunnan Province, rescued around twenty slaves from a local kiln.[23] One of the slaves, a man from Chongqing, described to journalists the brutality of the guards, who, to make him work seventeen hours a day, would beat him with steel bars and leather belts. Similarly, in December 2010, a story of the human trafficking of individuals with disabilities in Qu County, Sichuan Province, made the rounds on Chinese media.[24] In that case, mentally disabled people were enslaved with the open connivance of the local authorities, under the cover of a public shelter for disabled people. In another remarkable story, in September 2011, Cui Songwang, a reporter for a Zhengzhou television station, hung around a train station posing as a disabled man for two days, until he was kidnapped and sold to a kiln manager for 500 yuan. Cui said he was forced to work for three hours, beaten, and deprived of water before he managed to escape and report the case to police.[25] More recent media reports tell the story of slaves who managed to escape from the kilns, such as forty-three-year-old Xu Shuhe, who was a slave in black brick kilns in Guangzhou for twenty-four years; thirty-three-year-old Fan Debao, who spent eleven years in slavery; and thirty-five-year-old Qi Zhaojun, who was deprived of his liberty for twenty-one years at a number of kilns in Shanxi Province.[26]

Yuan Xueyu is still missing—another victim of what Børge Bakken has called China's 'uncivil society'.[27] His father, Yuan Cheng, is still looking for him and, in his search, has thus far been able to save more than 100 children.[28] In all this, is there any lesson that can be drawn from what happened in the spring of 2007? Looking at the latest developments in Xi Jinping's China—the taming of critical voices in traditional and new media, the arrests and disappearances of those who speak for the weak and disenfranchised, the systematic intimidation of those who challenge the message of 'harmony' espoused by the Chinese Communist Party—one cannot but wonder whether a display of solidarity like the one that took place during that hot summer more than a decade ago would still be possible today. However, the solitary blogger's daily posts are a reminder that not everything is lost, and not everyone has forgotten. In the end, as they say: no matter how hard you try, paper cannot wrap up embers.

2008

Under the administration of Hu Jintao and Wen Jiabao (2003–12), the process of codifying Chinese labour law continued as part of the Party-State's vision of a 'harmonious society'. In 2008, three new laws with momentous implications for Chinese workers were enforced: the Labour Contract Law (LCL), the Employment Promotion Law and the Labour Dispute Mediation and Arbitration Law. The LCL proved to be particularly contentious. After years of internal discussions among academic and government circles, in March 2006, the Chinese authorities released a first draft of the law, asking the public to comment on it. Within one month, they received more than 190,000 comments, 65 percent of which were from workers. Although the draft had already been at the centre of a heated debate among two factions of scholars and policymakers—one that argued for more state intervention in industrial relations to protect workers' rights and the other, which prioritised implementing the existing laws rather than introducing new ones—in the spring of 2006, the discussion started making headlines in the Chinese media. The decision of some business organisations, both Chinese and foreign, to publicly oppose the law fuelled public indignation but also alarmed the Chinese authorities, and the text was substantially revised before the law was finally passed. This essay reconstructs the heated debates that led to the adoption of the LCL and looks into the impact of the law on the Chinese workplace in the years since its adoption.

The Labour Contract Law and Its Discontents
Mary E. GALLAGHER

The 2008 Labour Contract Law (LCL) was the most hotly debated law since the 1954 Constitution of the People's Republic of China (PRC). It revealed the public's interest in workplace protection and their real fears that the reform and liberalisation of the 1980s and 1990s had gone too far in rolling back employment security and work-related social welfare. It was also an international debate, bringing together representatives of labour and capital to hash out the future of the Chinese workplace. Representation, however, was more diverse and inclusive than usual, with voices from the official union, the All-China Federation of Trade Unions (ACFTU), labour nongovernmental organisations (NGOs), social activists and academics taking a pro-labour stance, while foreign business associations, self-made Chinese entrepreneurs, government officials and academics spoke out for capital.[1]

The process of drafting and legislating the LCL opened a window on to China's political institutions, its social cleavages and its dynamic but unstable economy in ways that were quite unprecedented and have not been seen since. It was an experiment in open legislating and public participation that far exceeded the goals of Hu Jintao's government, which had championed reforms that emphasised reducing inequality and expanding the coverage of social welfare. The publicity and media attention around the law also contributed to rising mobilisation by workers, legal activists and NGOs. Unfortunately, the implementation of the LCL occurred as the Global Financial Crisis wreaked havoc on China's export juggernaut. The year 2008 marked a secular shift in labour dispute trends, with numbers doubling from the previous year and continuing at that higher level in subsequent years. Some disputes were legal scandals over employers' attempts to weaken the law, such as the preemptive mass layoffs by Huawei, which tried to terminate thousands of long-term workers and then reemploy them on short-term contracts. Others were spillover strikes and demonstrations by workers emboldened by a central government that seemed sympathetic to their cause, such as the 2010 Honda Strike (see Chan and Hui's essay in the present volume).[2]

It is inaccurate to credit the law alone for these broader trends. The LCL was a consequence of broader social and economic changes in the 1990s and early 2000s, especially the gradual and then dramatic loss of employment security for urban workers that began with the use of labour contracts in the 1980s and was then codified in the 1995 Labour Law, and which peaked with the mass layoffs of the state-owned enterprise (SOE) restructuring at the end of the last century (see Biddulph's, Hurst's, Solinger's and Ching Kwan Lee's essays in the present volume).

In addition to enhancing employment security, the goals of the LCL included greater protection of informal workers, especially rural migrant workers. However, since its passage in 2007 and subsequent revision in 2012, labour market segmentation has not diminished in China. Instead, segmentation has shifted to reflect new inequalities from the growing divergence between the old economy of manufacturing and construction and the new gig economy.[3] The strengthened employment security regulations of the LCL have enhanced the workplace conditions for formal standard workers while those caught in precarious and unstable employment are bereft of these protections.[4] The expansion of the gig and platform economies means that more and more Chinese workers are employed in sectors where the LCL is either not applied or ignored in favour of more important goals like techno-nationalism, decoupling from the United States and the alleged need for flexible employment as a requirement for innovation.

The trials and tribulations of the LCL should be seen as part of a broader evolution of China's labour legislation. Each new law has created protections for some, while leaving others out.[5] As Beijing now turns its sights to the problems of workers in the gig and platform economies, we may be on the cusp of a new drive to close gaps in protection. However, with the intense crackdowns on labour and legal activism since Xi Jinping took office, we are unlikely to see a return to the social mobilisation and debate that accompanied the passage of the LCL.

Prelude

The multiple-year debate over the LCL, from the law's first drafting in 2004 to its passage in the summer of 2007, was rooted in the growing backlash over the first labour law ever adopted by the PRC. The 1995 National Labour Law (discussed in this volume by Sarah Biddulph) was the foundational law for reform-era labour relations, but it pleased no-one.

Fundamentally, the 1995 Labour Law codified the regulatory and legal framework developed in the 1980s to structure labour relations in foreign-invested enterprises and extended it to the entire economy, including the public sector, which was still the dominant employer in China's cities.[6] To China's socialist labour aristocracy, the 1995 law heralded the smashing of the iron rice bowl. It introduced labour contracts, it facilitated short-term employment and it only weakly specified the employers' responsibility to offer social insurance. To China's growing army of migrant workers, streaming by the hundreds of millions into China's cities, the 1995 law had little significance. Without formal contracts and 'labour relations' established de jure, most migrant workers were closed out of the protections offered by labour contracts.

Until the 1995 law, urban workers in the public sector were mostly insulated from the market reforms that began in 1978 with Deng Xiaoping's Reform and Opening-Up policies. SOE reform was gradual and mostly focused on changing the incentives of managers and workers without amending the general social contract that guaranteed urban formal workers lifetime employment and work-unit welfare. Labour contracts permitted short-term employment and mandated socialised welfare, both of which facilitated labour mobility. They were first introduced in the foreign-invested sector of the economy and then only very gradually into China's domestic public sector, and mostly were signed by young workers entering employment for the first time.[7]

All that changed with the 1995 Labour Law, which mandated labour contracts across the board and permitted companies to offer short-term contracts for the first time. The imposition of the law came just before the massive restructuring of the public sector in 1998–2001, which marked the turn of the century with millions of layoffs, bankruptcies and the privatisation of small and medium-sized state companies and nearly all collective enterprises. For many urban workers, the 1995 Labour Law brought not workplace protection and legal rights, but employment and social insecurity.

On the flipside of China's developing bifurcated labour market, rural migrant workers poured into China's construction and manufacturing sectors, but the law's emphasis on formal employment via the written labour contract excluded the vast majority. The restrictions of the *hukou* system made inclusion less valuable in any case because participation in social insurance almost always required local citizenship (see Hayward's, Froissart's and Friedman's essays in the present volume). The 1995 Labour

Law offered the promise of protection but for the most part did not achieve it. It did contribute to the marketisation goals of the Jiang Zemin administration and the SOE restructuring led by Premier Zhu Rongji. Labour mobility expanded dramatically as flexible employment became the norm for urban workers and informal employment became the norm for rural migrants.[8]

The period between the 1995 Labour Law and the drafting and passage of the LCL saw dramatic shifts in the Chinese economy. The public sector contracted, especially in terms of employment, while the private and foreign sectors expanded rapidly. China's accession to the World Trade Organization in 2001 facilitated integration into global supply chains and accelerated China's designation as the workshop of the world. Much of this boom was fuelled by waves of young rural migrant workers. In 2003, labour shortages were first noticed in the manufacturing hub of Guangdong Province as China's continuing restrictions on urban residency through the *hukou* system depressed labour mobility and urbanisation. There was also increasing consternation about the changing demographics of the workforce as it was ageing rapidly, undermining China's demographic advantage.

This period also saw rising labour contention, legal mobilisation and scandals over dangerous and exploitative workplace conditions. Pensioners and older state-sector workers protested the SOE restructurings of 1998–2001 with strikes, street demonstrations and traffic blockades.[9] Labour-intensive manufacturing hubs in Jiangsu and Guangdong saw new waves of strikes and work action by emboldened young rural workers. The socialised insurance programs set up in the aftermath of the Labour Law were underfunded, undersubscribed and incomplete. Huge gaps in China's welfare state were revealed just as attention turned to the pressures of an ageing urban society and incomplete urbanisation that allowed rural workers to toil in the cities but never to settle permanently.[10] There were increasing calls to draft new laws that enhanced employment protection, increased participation in social insurance funds and improved access to legal channels for dispute resolution. The LCL was the most important of several new laws passed in this period to address these goals.[11]

Debate

The debate over the LCL was intense and very public. It was fed by widespread dissatisfaction with the current legal regime, which had undermined the security of urban formal workers while not really extending much protection to the growing legions of informal workers from the countryside. It was promoted by the Hu Jintao–Wen Jiabao government (2003–13), which prided itself on its attention to inequality and redistribution. It was facilitated by a panoply of new interest groups and activists, including labour advocacy NGOs, business associations representing foreign capital and labour lawyers and academics who served as advisors to the drafting process. The legislative debate also heightened internal bureaucratic competition between the official trade union, the ACFTU, the Ministry of Labour (later renamed the Ministry of Human Resources and Social Security) and the main drafting body, the Standing Committee of the National People's Congress.[12]

The LCL legislative process was also one of the first to enjoy public participation, with a public comment period opened in the spring of 2006. There was substantial interest in the law, with more than 190,000 comments submitted. The ACFTU mobilised grassroots trade union organisations to encourage comment submissions and was bolstered by the strong reaction to the draft law. Representatives for capital also spoke up, often drawing the ire of the Chinese public and external NGOs and academics who saw opposition to the law as thinly veiled attempts to keep Chinese labour standards low and Chinese labour cheap.[13] There were dramatic statements by foreign business associations, sharp discussion among members of the Chinese Political Consultative Conference and countless academic workshops about the different drafts of the law.

The actual drafting process was still opaque and while public comments were numerous, their contents were never released to the public. Changes to each draft of the LCL were substantial, but the final version of the law scaled down some of the protections for employment security and collective labour rights, leaving loopholes in how the law would be interpreted by courts and implemented by localities. Controversy and drama continued into the implementation period as the LCL came into effect just as the global financial system imploded.

Implementation

From 2008 until its revision in 2013, the implementation period of the LCL was fraught with economic upheaval and social instability. China did not experience a financial crisis like the rest of the world, but instead experienced an export crisis because of the deep contractions in Western economies. In late 2008 and early 2009, more than 30 million rural migrant workers were laid off amid widespread factory closures in coastal manufacturing hubs.[14] Disputes of subsistence—especially wage arrears and severance compensation—challenged local governments, which in some cases stepped in to compensate workers directly as factories abruptly shuttered and owners fled. There were also preemptive attacks on the law by companies attempting to avoid the onerous requirements to sign open-ended labour contracts with current employees who had more than ten years' tenure. For instance, Huawei met vociferous criticism when it terminated 8,000 employees in order to re-sign short-term contracts with them after the passage of the law.[15] In the first year of the LCL alone, labour disputes doubled in number nationally, with numbers tripling in some coastal manufacturing hotspots.

With the Chinese Government's generous stimulus package to fuel domestic recovery in the wake of the Global Financial Crisis, disputes over redistribution—such as demands for higher wages, social insurance payments and overtime pay—also increased. Workers still employed but seeking better conditions were emboldened by the upside pressure on wages, the increasingly apparent labour shortage in manufacturing and the Hu–Wen administration's overt focus on inequality and social welfare. The infrastructure boom and real estate building craze also drove many migrants to seek out jobs closer to home in inland Chinese cities where longer-term concerns, such as the right to participate in social insurance, became more important. Other laws that complemented the LCL's expansion of workers' rights—such as the 2010 Social Insurance Law, the 2008 Labour Dispute Mediation and Arbitration Law and the 2008 Employment Promotion Law—became part of the legislative legacy of the Hu–Wen administration. The legislative attention given to the workplace fuelled civil society's sense that change was happening and that social mobilisation was not only possible, but even encouraged by a sympathetic central government.

Social Mobilisation and Activism

A nascent labour movement had begun to take shape in the years following the restructuring of the SOE sector and China's accession to the World Trade Organization at the turn of the century. Though fragmented and divided by region and focus, in this period, several dozen labour NGOs emerged nationally.[16] Academics often ran legal aid clinics or centres within universities offering assistance to workers.[17] Cause lawyering also exploded in this area,[18] while international collaboration and assistance peaked during this period, as foreign NGOs, international institutions, universities and foreign governments supported Chinese civil society, legal advocacy and capacity-building within the government bureaucracies responsible for workplace protection, representation and dispute-resolution.

Many labour NGOs initially focused on the increased access to the legal system and the new protections codified in the LCL. Many also focused on special groups that were particularly marginalised in the Chinese economy, including women workers, rural migrants and workers affected by occupational injury or disease (see Howell's essay in the present volume). As social mobilisation increased, with large strikes in the Honda supply chain in 2010 and several massive strikes over social insurance in 2014 (see Chan and Hui's and Blecher's essays in the present volume), labour activists shifted towards collective labour issues, such as associational rights and collective bargaining (see Froissart and Franceschini's essay in the present volume).[19] Some labour NGOs focused on empowering individual workers through collective training and coaching that was often done behind the scenes and masked the growing network of labour activism.[20]

This burgeoning movement was squashed through a series of crackdowns on labour activism and on legal activism more generally soon after Xi Jinping took office in 2013.[21] In July 2015, more than 200 legal activists and cause lawyers were detained on charges from state subversion to picking quarrels. While many of these lawyers focused on civil and political rights that are even more sensitive than labour rights, it sent a chilling message to the entire legal profession.[22] This clampdown was quickly followed by a crackdown on dozens of labour activists in late 2015, with special condemnation of the foreign ties and financial support on which many labour NGOs relied.[23] The Foreign NGO Management Law passed in 2016 further complicated Chinese civil society's ability to rely on external funding for their activities. In 2018, after Marxist student groups assisted with union organising in a company in Guangdong, a new crackdown targeted these links between students and labour activists (see Elfstrom's essay in the present volume). Students at many prestigious universities were detained, questioned and urged to give up their activism.[24]

The Labour Contract Law and Its Discontents

The crackdown on labour and legal activism nipped the nascent labour movement in the bud.[25] While strikes and demonstrations did not end with the crackdown, there is evidence that large, coordinated industrial actions declined precipitously after 2015.[26] Labour disputes through the administrative and legal systems have also plateaued, though they remain at high levels compared with the pre-2008 period. Despite these challenges, the LCL has improved some aspects of China's workplace conditions. It is, however, difficult to separate out the effects of the law itself from other structural or cyclical factors that may have also contributed to improvements.[27] For example, the demographic changes and the resulting labour shortages enhanced some workers' bargaining power, while the stimulus program led to more construction and infrastructure jobs, especially in inland China.

The LCL's main thrust was to emphasise employment security, particularly for workers with long tenure, by mandating a written labour contract. Employment security, in turn, would raise participation in social insurance. In terms of these two goals, the LCL was partially successful. The proportion of workers with labour contracts increased, though migrant workers still lag behind local workers.[28] The proportion of workers who participate in social insurance has also increased though participation remains rather low for non-local (migrant) workers.[29] The publicity over its drafting heightened public awareness of workplace rights and certainly has placed more pressure on employers, both from employee grievances and from the risk of more severe penalties for noncompliance.

However, as with other labour legislation in China, the LCL's stringency also unleashed a new search for loopholes and workarounds. It may also have contributed to unemployment, especially among older workers who were terminated rather than being offered an open-ended contract.[30] In the initial implementation period, the most important loophole was labour subcontracting (劳务派遣), which expanded rather dramatically in the aftermath of the LCL, especially in SOEs.[31] Labour subcontracting allows for a third-party labour service company to employ workers who can be seconded out to firms for temporary positions. Employment security, wages and social insurance are all lower, but the real attraction of labour subcontracting after the LCL was the ability to avoid the open-term contract. After numerous reports surfaced on the use of labour contracting, especially targeting the expanded use of labour subcontracting by state firms, the LCL was revised in 2013 to limit labour subcontracting to 10 percent of all positions, and only those that were temporary, auxiliary or replacement. This was one of the last legislative moves of the Hu administration.

The legislative achievements of the Hu–Wen era were not appreciated by everyone, especially officials in the Xi administration who were increasingly concerned about China's 'New Normal' economy. The New Normal was a recognition of slower growth as a fundamental characteristic of China's maturing economy with its debt-heavy local governments and SOEs and a rising middle class that demanded more attention to livelihood issues, such as air pollution, food safety, better schools and so on. The anticorruption campaign launched by Xi Jinping in 2013 also made local officials less enamoured with single-minded pursuit of economic growth and investment if opportunities for self-dealing and graft were diminishing, not to mention becoming far more dangerous politically. Finance Minister Lou Jiwei publicly denounced the LCL in 2015, castigating it for freezing up China's labour markets and comparing it to the mistakes made in Western economies that empowered trade unions.[32]

The Challenges of the Digital Economy

Despite announcements about plans to revise the LCL and restore greater flexibility to employers, the Xi administration has not gone forward with revisions. Indeed, the Xi administration has been slow to undertake major labour law reforms that could rile up workers, and has delayed the adoption of a later retirement age. Instead, it has allowed the economy to 'grow out of the law' by encouraging the new digital economy to expand rapidly, mostly outside the restrictions of the LCL. China's e-commerce industry has experienced several years of quick growth. According to the International Labour Organization (ILO), China likely has the largest number of people employed in the e-commerce sector in both absolute and relative terms.[33] Most are employed indirectly as independent contractors or as dispatched workers. In 2019, there were only about 6.23 million workers directly employed in the digital platform economy, which the ILO estimates is less than 8 percent of the total workforce of nearly 80 million.[34] By some accounts, the size of the entire workforce in the digital economy is even larger—more than 180 million people—accounting for nearly one-quarter of the workforce.[35]

The COVID-19 pandemic has further contributed to the growth of the new digital economy, as many more households became reliant on digital shopping during the long lockdown in the spring of 2020. The intensity of the work is locked in by the platform's use of algorithms to speed delivery, which increases control over the worker without encumbering the company with formal employment or social insurance burdens.[36] In recent months, with an explosion of stories about exploitation in the sector and new forms of labour organising and activism, the central government has started to pay more attention. During a tour of Guangxi Province in April 2021, Xi Jinping mentioned the importance of protecting the legitimate rights of 'truck drivers, couriers, and food delivery riders' and encouraged the development of new job policies for both rural migrants and college graduates.[37] However, these encouraging words were paired with greater repression of labour activism in this sector. In February 2021, the labour activist and platform worker Chen Guojiang was detained in Beijing for 'picking quarrels and provoking trouble'—a catch-all charge often lodged against civil society activists.[38]

Alongside the complaints of platform workers in e-commerce, young, educated office workers in the tech companies that often run these platforms have also begun to voice opposition to the intense '996' work culture of the industry ('996' describes the working schedule in tech companies: 9am to 9pm six days a week). Celebrated by tech tycoons as something that workers should either endure on their way to wealthy entrepreneurship or even glorify as a badge of techno-nationalistic honour, the 996 work culture has been blamed for the 'overwork' deaths of young office workers and for contributing to a new pattern of 'involution' (内卷) among young college graduates—a dynamic of intense competition among an educated workforce. Philip Huang invoked the term 'involution' to describe China's stagnation during the Industrial Revolution of the eighteenth and nineteenth centuries, as caused by a large labour surplus that prevented innovation.[39] In the modern example, workers themselves—from e-commerce delivery drivers to cynical and bored office workers—invoke the term to describe lives full of endless competition with declining returns.[40]

An Endless Cycle

From 2013, parts of the Chinese workforce enjoyed the boom of the digital economy, but they have been largely excluded from the protections in the 1995 Labour Law and the 2008 LCL. Each tightening of the legislative framework has been followed by the emergence of new loopholes and new unprotected sectors of the labour market. In the 1995 Labour Law, rural migrants were largely excluded from the benefits of labour contracts; the 2008 LCL expanded the scope of contracts and insurance coverage while also driving new employment into labour dispatch; finally, in the 2013 revision, labour dispatch was restricted but labour outsourcing and independent contracting expanded rapidly, especially in the new digital economy.

The 2008 LCL remains controversial. Employers blame it for ossifying China's labour market. Labour activists and workers blame it for not doing enough. As China's new digital economy flourishes, it does so largely outside the strictures of the law. The recent anti-996 movement and the organisation and mobilisation of e-delivery workers may lead to a new round of protective legislation. But with the crackdown on labour activism and organising continuing unabated since 2015, social mobilisation and the public's support for greater protection will be muted and constrained. Concern over innovation and technological independence may trump concerns about the plight of delivery workers and those protesting China's toxic tech workplaces.

2008

Facing the threat of increasing popular unrest, under the leadership of Hu Jintao and Wen Jiabao (2003–12), the policy priorities of the Chinese Communist Party shifted from promoting economic growth at any cost to establishing a more equitable development model. The Party was now promoting a 'harmonious society' (和谐社会) that would 'put people at the centre' (以人为本). In the field of labour relations, this translated into not only a new body of laws and regulations—first and foremost, the Labour Contract Law discussed in the previous chapter—but also a propaganda drive to redefine the public discourse surrounding migrant labour. Chinese media was now celebrating the contribution of migrant workers to China's spectacular economic growth and, therefore, to the international rise of the country. The establishment of the Migrant Worker Museum in Shenzhen in 2008 was part of this drive.

'Make Contributions and Offer Your Youth for Tomorrow's Dream': The Establishment of the Shenzhen Migrant Worker Museum

Eric FLORENCE and Junxi QIAN

> Rural migrant workers are an enormous mass of industrious, honest, modest, and low-profile workers ... In their hard struggle, they come to adore life even more; armed with their optimistic, forward-looking, and proactive spirit, they labour industriously, live a happy life, and offer their contribution silently.
>
> — Panel at the Shenzhen Migrant Worker Museum, 2008

In 2010, fourteen employees at Foxconn Shenzhen, the world's largest original equipment manufacturer facility for Apple products, committed suicide by jumping off highrise buildings (see Jenny Chan's essay in the present volume). In the same year, hundreds of employees at a Honda factory in Guangzhou organised a large-scale strike to demand considerably higher wages and the right to elect their union representatives (see Chan and Hui's essay in the present volume). Although disconnected, these two events sounded a loud alarm to Chinese Communist Party (CCP) officials in Guangdong Province and beyond. The case study discussed in this essay—namely, the Shenzhen Migrant Worker Museum—was established two years prior to both incidents, but it is situated in the same broader context: the growing feelings of alienation experienced by China's migrant workers and their growing rights consciousness.

Shifting Representations of Migrant Labour

Since the launch of economic reforms, rural workers have stood at the heart of China's fast-growth and 'labour-squeezing' strategy of economic development.[1] They constitute the bulk of the labour force in the chiefly 'dirty, hard and exhausting' (脏, 苦, 累) manufacturing, construction and service sectors. But, despite the centrality of their role in China's two-digit economic growth, their status within society and their social recognition have lagged far behind. Indeed, while labour conditions have improved overall when compared with the 1980s and 1990s, rural migrant workers continue to bear the brunt of institutional discrimination, existing in a state of liminality and precariousness.[2]

Media representations of rural migrant workers in the late 1980s and early 1990s mainly depicted them as an unsightly horde without individual faces or voices, associated with filth, crime and various forms of social disorder. Migration from the countryside was framed in the rhetoric of 'law and order'. From the 1990s on, the homogenising characterisation of threatening 'flows of peasant workers' (民工潮) gradually gave way to more complex and hybrid narratives of singular individuals. Popular media, radio and, later, social media offered a wider array of venues for rural migrant workers to narrate their experiences of labouring and living in Chinese cities.[3] These depictions increasingly included visual forms. Such changes have been most prominent in southern China, as the category of 'dagong' (打工) publicly embodied the highly contradictory dimensions of migrant labour, encapsulating at once feelings of indignity and resentment in the face of exploitation, discriminatory treatment and precariousness on the one hand, and aspirations for social mobility, proximity to urban lifestyles and consumption on the other (see also O'Donnell's essay in the present volume).

In 2008, the government of Shenzhen's Bao'an District officially inaugurated a museum dedicated to rural migrant workers and their contribution to the extraordinary economic development of the city—China's first and most prominent Special Economic Zone (SEZ).[4] This initiative took place against the backdrop of a shift in state policy towards rural workers and the adoption of a body of labour-related legislation and regulations that aimed at better protecting rural workers (see Biddulph's and Gallagher's essays in the present volume). From the early 2000s, with the promotion of the slogan 'putting people at the centre' (以人为本) and increased attention to the so-called disadvantaged groups (弱势群体), a gradual shift in paradigm took place as the Chinese Party-State began encouraging municipal governments to provide services to rural workers rather than just conceive of them as vectors of public disorder.

The Shenzhen Migrant Worker Museum was the first state-sponsored museum devoted to rural workers.[5] In this essay, we document how this venue selectively renders visible or invisible specific facets of political economy, power configurations and migrant workers' subject formation.

By how they curate and arrange objects, images and people, museums are able to incorporate people in state-making processes and strengthen social order or, on the contrary, as Beth Lord has argued, make visible the contingency and reversibility of social orders.[6] As we will see, the Shenzhen Migrant Worker Museum belongs to the second category.

In what follows, we first briefly delve into the myth of Shenzhen, exploring how 'the logic of socialist fabulation and the logic of capital have come together' in urban form.[7] We then proceed to an exploration of the Shenzhen Migrant Worker Museum's permanent exhibition by focusing on how workers' identity is constructed through the venue's layout of objects, documents and images. Finally, we conclude with some general remarks hinting at the centrality of rural workers not only in Shenzhen's mythmaking, but also in the very formation of the ethos of a self-reliant and self-enterprising subject in the post-Mao era.

The Myth of Shenzhen

In 1992, Deng Xiaoping's now famous Southern Tour led to an acceleration of economic reforms and put an end to intense ideological debates about whether Shenzhen's development was to be called capitalism or socialism. During his visit to Shenzhen, Deng emphasised that 'the important experience of Shenzhen is that of daring to be a path-breaker' (深圳的重要经验就是敢闯).[8] Deng also stated that what mattered most was to 'develop the productive forces'.[9] Since then, although the exceptionality associated with Shenzhen's status has somewhat weakened over the last decade or so, the city has continued to play at least three important roles: as a 'model for the Inland in the strengthening of the market system', as an example for the building of a 'socialist spiritual civilisation' and as a testing zone to forge a new role for the Party.[10]

The couple of years that followed Deng's Southern Tour unleashed a profound wave of commodification of labour in Shenzhen and beyond.[11] After 1992, 'doing special things in Shenzhen' and 'the liberation of productive forces' in reality meant limitations on workers' associational power and unfettered appropriation of workers' labour.[12] As Shenzhen was becoming a model for the rest of the country to emulate, a rich imaginary of China's most prominent SEZ was being constituted.

'Shenzhen ideology' was grounded in a series of norms and values emphasising 'opening up' (开放), 'creating' (创造) and 'devoting oneself' (献身), promoted by city officials since the late 1980s.[13] The term 'Shenzhen

Spirit' (深圳精神) was officially endorsed in 1990 by then CCP Secretary General Jiang Zemin, and it incorporated principles such as 'deciding for oneself, strengthening oneself, competition, taking risks, and facing danger' (自主, 自强, 竞争, 冒风险), and rejected 'erroneous moral values' (错误的道德观念) such as 'neglecting people's legitimate rights' (忽略老百姓应有的权益), 'egalitarianism' (平等主义) and 'conservatism' (保守主义).[14] Rural migrant workers' 'low quality' (低素质) was to be replaced with 'a new four-haves person' (培育'四有'新人) manifesting 'ideals, culture, ethics, and discipline'.[15]

The Museum

In 2008, the Bao'an District Government officially inaugurated the Shenzhen Migrant Worker Museum. The location was the Shangwu Yigao Electronic Factory, which was supposedly the first Hong Kong–invested manufacturing and assembling factory in Shenzhen. The museum's principal permanent exhibition is divided into five thematic sections: historical background, migrant workers' contributions to the development of Shenzhen, workers' experiences of labouring and living in the city, government policies in favour of migrant workers' integration into Shenzhen's public services and a model of migrant workers' upward trajectories.[16]

The introductory panel to the museum espouses the values of and sets the tone for the rest of the exhibition. It reads:

> Over thirty years of reform and opening up, generation after generation, labourers have shed their sweat on this warm earth [在这片热土上挥洒汗水]; labouring industriously and silently [辛劳劳作, 沉默耕耘], they have offered their wisdom and strength [贡献了智慧和力量] for the sake of the miracle of extremely fast economic development. They deserve to be respected and be loved. In order to record their contribution [为了记录他们的贡献] and to highlight the Party's care for them, we have established the country's first labour museum.

Although the museum purports to give visitors an experience of the working and living conditions of migrant labourers by allowing them to meander through assembly lines, dormitories, TV rooms and canteens, these spaces seem empty and disconnected from the harshness of workers' everyday experiences.[17] Missing are their marginalisation outside factory walls and the crushing exploitation and theft of time by the disciplinary 'dormitory labour regime'.[18] Similarly, while the exhibition displays a number of actual workers' certificates and permits of residence and employment, these documents alone do not convey the fact that migrant workers bear the brunt of institutional discrimination and they overlook the effects of 'routine repression' exerted by urban officials on migrant bodies in public space.[19] The impression is one of hollow materiality.

The Shenzhen ideology—with its vibrant environment of competition, attracting the city's 'builders' (建设者) and enabling the optimal use of their labour power—is a recurrent one throughout the permanent exhibition. Shenzhen is associated with the term 'this warm earth' (这片热土), celebrating the city as a space of limitless opportunities—a space that literally awakens people's subjectivities and labour power. Most of the pictures on display represent youthful migrant workers whose energy is mobilised for the sake of the city's prosperity. The idea that Shenzhen and, more generally, 'the South' provide employment opportunities and chances for social mobility has circulated widely among migrant workers and urban elites throughout the Pearl River Delta. In the exhibition, the promise of opportunity euphemises underlying conflicts and asymmetrical social relations by concealing the structural violence embedded in the political economy of state capitalism in southern China.

Another pillar of the Shenzhen myth is the idea that no matter what hardships they are facing, workers need to remain confident in their capacity to overcome them and keep nurturing ideals and aspirations. The panel under a bronze sculpture reminds the visitor: 'A beautiful life depends on people's collective effort; under one blue sky, for tomorrow's dream, they are willing to endure hardship. A group of labourers on top of a tall construction, they appear tall and robust, embodying the spirit of strength and confidence in struggling hard.'

Overall, the museum builds an identity for migrant workers as a compliant, silent, forward-looking and hardworking social body whose symbolic belonging to Shenzhen is conditioned by their contribution to the development and prosperity of the city. Despite the fact that the right to gain permanent residency remains an impossible-to-obtain goal for the majority of workers, according to the narrative of 'making contributions' to Shenzhen (做出贡献) or 'offering one's youth to Shenzhen' (奉献青春), workers are supposed to feel an emotional sense of belonging and pride based on their contributions to and sacrifices for the city's dazzling material achievements.[20]

According to such rhetoric, any resentment or disillusionment they might feel due to the hardships and indignities they face should be submerged beneath this sense of pride and belonging, sacrifice and contribution. This comment from the museum provides an illustration of such rhetorical emphasis:

> They are the first ones to greet the early sun, they are also the last ones to accompany the moon in the evening. They have used their hardworking and robust hands to hold the beauty and splendour of the city. History can testify: those who have given Shenzhen their utmost effort and sweat, those who have offered their wisdom and strength to Shenzhen, those who have left their most beautiful years of their life to Shenzhen, these people are the real deserving Shenzhen people.

On the whole, the exhibition—through its configuration of objects, documents, writing and pictures—constructs a linear discursive chain. Hardship, hard work, self-sacrifice and suffering should lead to an increase in productivity and economic development on the one hand, and an improvement in the maturation of a self-reliant and enterprising individual on the other. In the above passages, the rhetoric of sacrifice, hard work and pioneering converges in the figure of the model migrant worker. Their body and soul are entirely turned towards production as they can only temporarily embody a real Shenzhen person through their contribution to economic development.

Eventually, an entire section of the exhibition is devoted to state policies and to the relationship between the Party-State and migrant workers. This section quite methodically conveys the idea that the state's attitude towards these workers is one of care and benevolence. Substantial space is devoted to municipal as well as provincial initiatives providing services to migrant workers in the fields of culture, leisure, education, labour protection, welfare and health care. One panel reads:

> Over the years, the governments at the national, provincial, municipal, and district levels have implemented a whole series of public policies and organised a whole range of activities showing care and love towards migrant workers. Workers' rights have been

continually protected, their political status has been continuously elevated, their cultural life has been constantly enriched and society has thereby become more harmonious.

If, as we mentioned earlier, the Chinese state at various levels has indeed designed a range of policies to provide services to migrant workers and better protect their rights, these have not fundamentally altered the political and institutional configurations and 'patterns of unpredictability and disempowerment' that continue to characterise migrant workers' conditions.[21]

Youth, Shenzhen Exceptionalism, and the Party-State

Our exploration of the representation of migrant workers in the first state-sponsored museum devoted to them in post-Mao China shows how central migrant workers are to the narrative of Shenzhen as a space guiding the country in terms of the valuation of labour power. The self-referential dimension of this politics of recognition is indeed predominant within the museum. In the incorporation of rural migrant workers into this imaginary, class antagonisms, as well as the material and symbolic violence that migrant workers are subjected to, are made invisible by providing 'visibility without legitimacy and rhetorical recognition without economic and political substance'.[22] The museum's presentation of workers' experiences conceals the political and institutional coordinates underlying their precarity and, in so doing, de-politicises their actions, claims to social justice and politics of identity.

Our study also shows that the representation of rural migrant workers links the myth of Shenzhen to a neoliberal ethos of the self-enterprising subject. The museum's permanent exhibition suggests rural migrant workers exemplify values such as optimism in the face of adversity, diligence, risk-taking, autonomy and self-improvement combined with Mao-era values of making contributions and self-sacrifice. In the process of building an identity for the SEZ from the late 1980s, and even more so from the middle of the following decade, these values have been promoted with intensity. Shenzhen, represented as a model of the modernist civilising city, has indeed been culturally constructed as a zone of limitless opportunities, of statistical wonder—the Shenzhen miracle—and of exceptionalism, where people could try things that were not possible elsewhere in China.[23] In this process of mythmaking, the SEZ has been very closely associated with the idea of valuation of talent and bodies operating in a competitive environment that optimises youth. Hence, the Party-State's founding legitimacy and identity based on the rejection of capitalism and exploitation are reconciled with the disciplinary regimes and violence exerted on workers' bodies, time and space in the SEZ's celebratory narrative of progress.

2009

In the summer of 2009, the Chinese media extensively reported on the vicissitudes of Zhang Haichao, a twenty-eight-year-old factory worker who willingly underwent a totally unnecessary and dangerous open-chest surgery just to prove he was suffering from pneumoconiosis, a lethal occupational disease that affects the lungs. This was a last resort after all previous attempts to gain the documentation he needed to access compensation and proper health care had been obstructed by corrupt officials and doctors. The 'open-chest case' (开胸事件) was the first high-profile instance of worker health activism in China and played a fundamental role in raising the awareness of the Chinese public of the hidden toll that China's economic boom was taking on sectors of its workforce. This essay reconstructs the chain of events that led to Zhang's momentous decision, as well as the aftermath of the scandal.

Zhang Haichao's 'Open-Chest Case'
Ralph LITZINGER and Yanping NI

On 22 June 2009, a former factory worker named Zhang Haichao entered the First Affiliated Hospital of Zhengzhou University.[1] On that blistering, humid day, as he walked into the operating room to undergo a surgery that would pry open his chest, he was not aware of the impact this medical procedure would have on Chinese public opinion. As he explained later, entering the operating room, he had a quite simple and straightforward goal: to show how dust accumulates in workers' and miners' lungs as a result of working in China's poorly regulated dust-intensive industries.

In fact, Zhang's surgery was not even necessary, for the diagnosis of pneumoconiosis (尘肺病)—a disease commonly known as 'black lung'—typically demands only a chest x-ray. But Zhang wanted to display something more than the results of a radiology test. He wanted his chest ripped open and the tissue removed and biopsied. He wanted to share the results with the media and open a debate about how workers with black lung should be recognised for their labour and their life and death struggles. When the doctor began the procedure, she made a ten-centimetre incision in his chest and then used a rib spreader to separate the ribs by four to five centimetres, taking a piece of tissue to be biopsied.[2] The doctor had warned Zhang about the possibility of severe infection and other medical complications, making it clear he may not survive the operation. In his desperate situation, Zhang felt he had no choice: his other options had been exhausted, and his body depleted. As he would later recall: 'Rather than wait to die, it is better to take a gamble.'[3] After repeated futile attempts to receive the correct diagnosis of black lung from his corporate bosses and government officials—which would have allowed him to receive compensation for his condition—he devised his own method: the close examination of tissue plucked from his lung. No government official, no mining boss, would be able to deny the results of a tissue biopsy, he reasoned. On the operating table, as the anaesthesia began to take effect, he said to the doctor: 'Please examine the dust on my lung carefully.'[4]

Zhang later said he was 'lucky' that day. Six hours later, he woke from this high-risk surgery. The first words he recalls hearing from the doctor were: 'Congratulations. It is black lung!' Zhang did not despair over this diagnosis, since proving he had the disease was his goal. With the correct diagnosis in hand, he would finally be entitled to treatment targeted specifically at black lung and able to demand compensation. However, this proved to be only a temporary victory and just the beginning of his ordeal.

Sick Worker, Radicalised

Zhang had started work for Zhendong Abrasive Materials Co. Ltd in 2004 in his hometown, the city of Xinmi, Henan Province. Zhendong manufactures refractory materials, which produce immense amounts of dust. As a frontline worker, Zhang was covered in dust nearly every single day, his only protection being a thin disposable mask. In 2007, he began to develop chest tightness and a wicked cough and, as his symptoms worsened, he departed Zhendong at the end of that year.[5]

At the time of his resignation, Zhang did not know his illness was associated with his work. In 2008 and early 2009, he visited various clinics, including three well-known hospitals in Beijing, where, to his surprise, all the doctors believed he was suffering from black lung, rather than some other disease.[6] Yet, state regulations did not allow him to receive treatment in any of these hospitals. Because black lung is categorised as an occupational disease, responsibility for treatment rested with his employer. The doctors in Beijing told him to return to Xinmi and seek treatment and compensation from Zhendong.

Zhang Haichao was no stranger to black lung. He had already witnessed how the disease rapidly took the life of one of his closest friends. However, at the young age of twenty-eight, he never expected that he, too, would experience this nightmare. Similarly, he never imagined that the physical pain caused by the disease would be only the first of many struggles that would take him into the bureaucratic labyrinth of the Chinese compensation and treatment system.

Returning to his home city, Zhang was first examined by the Zhengzhou Occupational Disease Prevention and Control Institute (郑州市职业病防治所, ODPCI), a local institution authorised to diagnose occupational diseases in Henan Province.[7] As with so many factory workers and miners, he faced what seemed to be an intractable dilemma: just to receive a screening test, he had to prove his previous employment. Zhendong refused to acknowledge any form of past employment and repeatedly rejected his requests to meet with management. Realising there was no room for negotiation with the company, Zhang sought help elsewhere. He learned that once a month the municipal Party secretary of Xinmi met in person with petitioners. Zhang waited seven hours in front of the government building, until he was asked to report his complaint to the secretary. On hearing Zhang's difficulties, the official—kindly, yet craftily—promised Zhang he could be tested at the ODPCI regardless of his lack of proper workplace documentation. Accompanied by several officials, Zhang received his lung test in Zhengzhou on 12 May 2009.

Two weeks later, the test results came as a shock to Zhang. The report was explicit: 'No pneumoconiosis phase 0+; complicated with tuberculosis.' Zhang was filled with anger: 'I was so disappointed! So many prestigious hospitals in Zhengzhou and Beijing confirmed it was black lung, and now they tell me it is tuberculosis!'[8] The different diagnosis had momentous implications for him. In medical terms, pneumoconiosis is undeniably caused by inhalation of large amounts of dust during long-term work in dust-intensive environments. Had he been diagnosed with that disease, his past employer would surely have been held accountable.[9] The tuberculosis diagnosis, in contrast, placed the burden of treatment entirely on the patient, who was responsible for all associated expenses.

Zhang asked about his options. Could he contest the result? In a pattern common to so many black lung patients seeking treatment and compensation, he was directed to the next bureaucratic unit, the Zhengzhou Health Bureau. There he was told that he could be retested—for the prohibitive price of 7,000 yuan. Undeterred, Zhang returned with the money only to find that the ODPCI, which issued the tuberculosis misdiagnosis, and the Zhengzhou Health Bureau that was about to test him occupied the same building. Assuming these two bureaus were in cahoots, he immediately lost confidence that the retest would give him the diagnosis he sought, especially after an official, not mincing words, told him: 'Our bureaus have different placards but the same set of personnel. How could we possibly overturn our own conclusion?'[10]

Zhang understood precisely what the official was saying. However, while he abandoned any hope for a retest here, he felt emboldened and began to ponder his options. After careful consideration, in June 2009, with the money he had pulled together for the retest, he went to the First

Affiliated Hospital of Zhengzhou University. He has since spoken repeatedly about how he stepped into that hospital in despair and a doctor named Cheng Zhe gave him hope. Based on Zhang's chest x-ray, Cheng was sure he had black lung. As she examined the ODPCI's diagnosis of tuberculosis, she fell silent, and then gave Zhang two options: 'You may [have a] lung puncture or an open-chest surgery. Opening the chest will definitely show the dust, but the risk is high. I do not suggest this course of action.'[11] Without a moment's hesitation, Zhang decided on the more radical 'open-chest' surgery. Recalling his decision, he would later say: 'When I insisted on opening my chest to do the lung biopsy, I was not thinking about how much compensation I would get. I did not think I was great. But I needed an explanation!'[12]

After the surgery, although the hospital did not have the authority to diagnose occupational diseases, Zhang's doctor supportively, and somewhat defiantly, wrote 'black lung' on his medical report.[13] Soon he would get help from two journalists, who turned Zhang's story into a sensational event and pressured the government to respond. By July 2009, government officials at higher levels began to comment on Zhang's case and urged local bureaus to address the situation. On 26 July, Zhang finally received the correct medical diagnosis from the ODPCI, confirming he had phase-III black lung. By the end of the month, the Zhendong company issued a compensation package of an undisclosed value.[14]

Nevertheless, Zhang's victory cost him time, energy and resources. His struggle for compensation should not have been so circuitous, so full of government obfuscations, lies and deceptions. Furthermore, as Zhang has noted on many occasions, he saw himself as 'luckier' than many other black lung patients. The obstacles he encountered were, and still are, too common a part of the fight against the exploitative logic of disposability. As the history of black lung activism in China teaches us, too few patients win compensation or some small semblance of social justice. Too many have died. Far too many are waiting to die.

Towards Activism

In the years immediately after his chest was surgically ripped open, Zhang sought more specialised treatments in several places around China. In 2009, he twice received a lung lavage (washing) in the Beidaihe Sanatorium for Chinese Coal Miners, where he was also hired as an 'occupational health and safety liaison'. In 2013, to tackle a complication from pneumothorax (collapsed lung) that nearly took his life, he received a double lung transplant at the Wuxi People's Hospital with the help of Chen Jingyu, a well-known pulmonologist. The lung transplant was a success, although it requires a lifetime of anti-rejection medicines—a daily regime of more than ten tablets costing more than 200 yuan per day.[15]

Compared with many workers—and no doubt due to the media coverage of his open-chest surgery—Zhang received significant compensation, but he initially did not reveal the exact amount. Before his double transplant, Zhang wanted to set the record straight and penned a letter to be released in the event he died during the new surgery. The letter disclosed that he had received an astonishing 1.2 million yuan in compensation. It also stated that he was forced by government officials and Zhendong management to conceal this amount and he was made to promise never to sue the Xinmi Epidemic Prevention Clinic for concealing the results of his earlier physical examination, nor the Zhengzhou ODPCI for its earlier misdiagnosis.[16] Zhang later released this letter to the press, because he hoped the level of his compensation would 'become the national standard for pneumoconiosis compensation, and that every worker with pneumoconiosis will get a second chance at life, and give their families a little more security'.[17]

This extraordinary settlement hardly covered Zhang's exorbitant medical expenses, which, in fact, would lead to an endless struggle with debt. To pay off these debts, he sought employment but was turned away repeatedly because of his medical history. In June 2013, months after his lung transplant, Zhang borrowed some more money and subcontracted a bus to drive in his hometown of Xinmi. Every day his bus encircled the town eight times, stopping at twenty-nine stations in urban and rural areas, covering a distance of 248 kilometres. He drove twelve hours a day and nearly thirty days a month. He earned an average of only 5,000 yuan a month—barely enough to make the monthly payments for his lung transplant.

As he retreated to the life of a bus driver, he would still occasionally appear in public. His desperate, self-mutilating act of defiance in 2009 had turned him into the most well-known sick worker in the country, among the public at large and, more crucially, among black lung patients. Zhang bought himself a computer and started connecting with worker patients in other places. After years of devouring China's various labour regulations, he would step into the public realm as an activist, speaking for and defending black lung patients involved in labour disputes. For example, in 2012, Zhang appeared in a court in Zhejiang Province to support a lawsuit brought by another black lung patient. Towards the end of the proceedings, he angrily addressed everyone present: 'Doesn't the Chinese public have the right to know about their own health?'[18]

Zhang proceeded to travel around the country to support other patients' petitions and, since 2011, he has volunteered for the charity Love Save Pneumoconiosis (大爱清尘, LSP). Over the years, he received more than 2,000 phone calls from fellow patients and helped hundreds of them win lawsuits. As the representative for the LSP in Henan Province, Zhang visited more than 500 patients and sent out over 200 ventilators.[19] He witnessed over 400 deaths, including four workers who also received compensation from the Zhendong company at the time of his open-chest surgery.

These experiences left Zhang with mixed feelings. On 22 June 2018, Zhang wrote on his social media account: 'It has been nine years since my "open-chest" case. It tested society, but the results have been disappointing.'[20] The surgery and the media attention he received did not resolve the difficulties black lung patients face. 'I disdain "special solutions for special cases", only law enforcement can solve structural issues,' he asserted.[21] Perhaps because he received such significant compensation and had to strike a secret deal with the government and the company, he felt compelled to extend his efforts towards the entire community of black lung patients, which turned him into something of a celebrity activist. His dramatic surgery in 2009 inspired an upsurge in protests and petitions initiated by workers throughout the 2010s. And yet, only a small percentage of these protests were successful, with protesters only on rare occasions granted free medical care, monthly pensions and other benefits.[22]

For Zhang, 'special solutions for special cases' belong to the world of political trickery. They are in fact state dispersion tactics, instituted periodically and always seemingly randomly by local officials to provide what usually amounts to small payouts and meagre assistance. These dispersed, localised acts of beneficence are contrived to dispel petitioning and forestall 'social unrest' in the absence of national legislation to protect workers' rights and address the root causes of the problems.

In our interviews with black lung petitioners, few wanted to celebrate success. The reasons put forth were many. First, many black lung patients are never compensated for their illness. Local government officials complain about limited assistance funds, and thereby provide benefits only to a small group of patients, usually those healthy enough to be active participants in protests and petitions. Local governments also prioritise patients with whom they have close relationships through political or kin networks; these are secret payouts about which most other black lung patients only hear rumours.

Second, a free medical treatment settlement or assistance package comes with restrictions that tend to result in an endless array of inconveniences. A patient might be required to attend a designated hospital—usually in the capital city of a province, far from home. One can claim reimbursement only for expenses incurred during hospitalisation; those generated through outpatient services are rarely included. One patient told us that, for one particular medicine, he could only take a small amount home after each hospitalisation, which lasted a mere fifteen days. As he lived far from the hospital, these trips were exhausting, expensive and further exacerbated his health problems.

Third, as Zhang recounted to us and stated in many interviews, a successful workers' movement requires tenacious struggle against police suppression and the violence of hired thugs. Most of those suffering from black lung are already weakened by the disease and unable to withstand what are often months and months of protest and petitioning. Just like many other black lung miners and factory workers, Zhang was once taken into police custody, held for days and threatened. Those not caught by the police live with their declining health and eventually pass away, never seeing a day of treatment or a yuan of compensation.

So, this is the double bind of the depleted black lung worker. To take on the state, local government or bosses, to stand long hours protesting and petitioning, to travel hours to provincial capital hospitals for treatment—all requires a level of energy and physical capacity that few possess, especially after years of battling the disease. We thus return to 2009. Following his open-chest surgery, and the spectacular shockwave it triggered in Chinese society, Zhang had this to say: 'I won. I also lost. I won the rights and compensation I deserved, but it depleted my life.'[23]

Others' acts of self-mutilation would follow, but without the same outcome, media coverage or political effect. As Zhang himself told us, there is no winning or losing in these battles. Some, like Zhang, continue to survive, finding energy to work, paying off debts, trying to find ways to keep breathing, to keep their lungs from turning to stone. Too many others, with the deadly dust in their lungs, can only live out their remaining days in a state of suspension, waiting for their lungs to give out. These workers have been forgotten by the state, rendered politically invisible—an indistinct mass of the sick and the suffering.

Afterlives

Within the black lung and labour activist community in China, Zhang's 'open-chest case' is acknowledged as a significant event in the history of Chinese workers' health activism. In speaking to him, reading through the many news articles and reports written about him, listening to archived radio shows and chatting online with worker activists who remember his surgery and its aftermath, we wanted to write a tale of a working-class hero, someone who put it all on the line, for himself and his fellow sick and dying workers. We do want to hold on to the desire to tell that narrative, but too many facts rub up against it. The fact is that the impact of that moment in 2009 on actual legislation and the implementation of labour protection laws for those who work with and daily breathe in dust remains an open question. The scholar Wing-Chung Ho observed a surge of newly confirmed black lung cases in 2010 (from 18,128 to 27,240).[24] Ho also noted that, from 2010 to 2014, there was clearly a new public awareness of occupational diseases. We also began to see the enforcement of existing laws to hasten the closure of private mines.

More than a decade has passed since Zhang's surgery. We end here by asking: how will it be remembered in the coming decades? The answer to that question will depend in part on how many more workers are put in situations, due to poor regulations or out of the desperation of precarious lives, that require them to breathe in the deadly dust that causes black lung. And it will depend on what future strategies, tactics and actions Chinese workers will come up with to speak against the catastrophic dreamworld of endless growth and development. Will miners, factory workers, gem polishers and construction blasters who work in these death zones have a future beyond the slow violence of black lung?[25] Will there be life beyond the endless cycle of disposability?

2010

In the spring and summer of 2010, the media in mainland China extensively reported on a domestic 'labour tide' (工潮). At the same time, international newspapers came out with hyperbolic headlines such as 'The Rising Power of China's Workers' (The Economist), 'The Rise of a Chinese Workers' Movement' (Bloomberg) and 'An Independent Labor Movement Stirs in China' (The New York Times). This renewed enthusiasm for China's labour movement was triggered by a strike that had erupted at a Honda factory in Foshan's Nanhai District in May. As the Honda workers—mostly members of the new generation of migrant workers from the Chinese countryside—went on strike to demand a significant pay rise and the right to establish a representative union, their mobilisation rippled across the whole country, culminating in a wave of labour protests. The strike also rekindled the debate in government and union circles about collective bargaining (or 'collective negotiation', to use official jargon) as a way to improve labour conditions and preempt labour unrest. Although many of the expectations that arose in the spring of 2010 would be dashed in the following years, the Honda strike remains a landmark event for the Chinese labour movement in the twenty-first century.

The Nanhai Honda Strike

Chris King-Chi CHAN and Elaine Sio-Ieng HUI[1]

The year 2010 was a time of turbulent labour relations in China. A wave of strikes triggered by a protest by Honda workers in Foshan, Guangdong Province, aroused immense concern among Chinese policymakers, legal and labour scholars and Western media, prompting discussions about the urgency of carrying out democratic trade union reform and implementing workplace collective bargaining, or what in the Chinese context is more commonly known as 'collective consultation' (集体协商). In the wake of this strike wave, the Chinese Government and the All-China Federation of Trade Unions (ACFTU) increased their efforts in legalising and promoting workers' rights to collective bargaining. This essay examines the impact on the development of labour relations in China of the Honda strike, which exerted historic pressure on the Party-State and the ACFTU to promote a collective rights–based framework of industrial relations. However, the shift towards this type of regulatory framework has since been halted due to opposition from global capital and concerns among the Party-State over independent labour organising.

The Honda Strike

The strike that triggered the wave of unrest in 2010 was set in motion by workers at the Honda Auto Parts Manufacturing Company Limited (CHAM), a company in Foshan's Nanhai District that specialises in the production of car transmissions. Beginning on 17 May, the mobilisation lasted for seventeen days and involved about 1,800 workers. It followed the rapid expansion of the Chinese car industry in response to the Global Financial Crisis. Due to the Chinese Government's stimulus policies, in 2009, China's automotive sales increased 46 percent from the previous year, setting a new record.[2] Despite this growth, the basic salaries of most auto workers had not been adjusted accordingly. At the time of the strike, around 80 percent of CHAM workers were interns from technical schools and the other 20 percent were formal employees. The strikers listed 108 demands, but consistently named two as the major issues: 1) a wage increase of 800 yuan for all workers; and 2) democratic reform of trade unions, as the existing union did little to represent the workers' interests. Throughout the strike, workers felt that the company's trade union was not on their side.

At first reluctant to negotiate with the workers, the firm instead resorted to intimidation and appeasement. On 22 May, it 'fired' two activists who had already resigned. On 26 May, the company proposed a minimal wage increase—a concession that workers turned down. Monday, 31 May 2010 was a turning point. Under pressure from local government representatives and from teachers at the vocational schools that had dispatched the student interns, many workers resumed production. However, about forty formal workers refused to return to work and gathered in the open space on the factory premises. About 2pm, workers noted that an estimated 200 people wearing yellow caps and carrying 'trade union membership cards' (工会会员证) entered the factory complex to 'persuade' the strikers to resume work. When the persuasion failed, a physical conflict ensued and a few of the striking workers were hurt. This attracted the attention of both local and international media, with one Hong Kong newspaper using the headline 'Conflict at Honda Factory: "Union" Hits Workers' (工会打人).[3] Official sources did not reveal from where the 200 'trade unionists' had come, but reliable sources revealed that they were in fact locals from other villages.[4]

After this incident, CHAM and the trade unions both came under serious pressure from workers. Workers walked out in support of their injured workmates. The factory-wide strike continued. On 1 June, Zeng Qinghong, the CEO of Guangqi Honda Automobile Co. Ltd, a joint venture between Honda and a Chinese state-owned enterprise in Guangzhou, and also a member of the National People's Congress, visited the strikers and asked them to elect their own representatives, promising to hold negotiations with them three days later. At 5pm the same day, the Nanhai District Federation of Trade Unions and the Shishan Town Federation of Trade Unions issued a letter of apology to all CHAM workers.

On 3 June, endeavouring to gain wider public support and calling for stronger solidarity among workers, the workers' representatives issued an open letter to all CHAM workers and to the public, reiterating their main demands: 1) a wage increase of 800 yuan; 2) a seniority subsidy; 3) a better promotion system; and 4) democratic reform of the company trade union. Part of the letter read as follows:

> We urge the company to start serious negotiation with us ... It earns over one billion yuan every year and this is the fruits of our hard work ... our struggle is not only for the sake of 1,800 workers at CHAM, it is also for the wider interests of workers in our country. We want to be an exemplary case of workers safeguarding their rights.[5]

After the open letter was released, workers' representatives received more than 500 text messages of support from people all over China, with one emblematic example saying: 'You not only represent CHAM's workers, but also the 100 million-strong working class under oppression in China ... All the people in the country are supporting you and paying great attention to your just action. Your glorious action will be recorded as part of modern Chinese history.'[6]

In a pre-negotiation meeting with Zeng held that very day, the workers' delegates requested a democratic and formal election of workers' representatives to be held as soon as possible. The same evening, the company initiated a democratic election in all departments and thirty representatives were elected. Also that day, with outside help, workers' representatives contacted Chang Kai, a prominent labour law professor from the People's University in Beijing, who later agreed to be their advisor. On 4 June, negotiations began in earnest, with the newly elected workers' representatives, representatives from the company, the labour bureau, the local government, the legal advisor to the workers, the chairperson of the enterprise trade union and Zeng himself.

In the end, the two parties reached an agreement that formal workers' wages would be increased by 32.4 percent, from 1,544 yuan to 2,044 yuan, and interns' wages would be raised by 70 percent, from around 900 yuan to around 1,500 yuan. However, the company refused to discuss the workers' demand for democratic reform of the enterprise trade union, giving the excuse that it could not intervene in matters concerning workers' associations.

NGOs and Intellectuals: A Supportive Role?

One of the reasons the strike stood out from similar actions is the strong external support the workers received from local and international civil society. Recalling the negotiations on 4 June, one worker representative wrote in his blog: 'Being able to get in touch with and have Professor Chang Kai as our advisor is very encouraging; I am very thankful for his help ... without his assistance, we would have played a more passive role in the negotiations, since we have limited abilities.'[7]

Also, apart from the support from Professor Chang, more than seventy local and overseas scholars signed a petition to support the workers' demands. It said:

> Living on meagre wages and struggling to survive, workers are forced to strike so that they could live with dignity ... let us unite and put pressure on the company. We should tell Honda to stop suppressing and dividing workers and to accede to the workers' reasonable demands.[8]

This petition was issued a day before the negotiations and contributed to the pressure on the company and the local government. More importantly, it strengthened workers' morale and confidence. One worker said to us: 'It is hard to believe we have so much support from so many professors.'

Alongside these, the Chinese Workers Research Network (中国工人研究网, CWRN), a now defunct website launched by a few young mainland intellectuals and registered in Beijing that reported news on labour issues, covered the CHAM workers' strike in detail. Furthermore, many Hong Kong labour nongovernmental organisations (NGOs) and trade unions showed their support by protesting against Honda in Hong Kong. They updated the international community with news of the strike, and a global signature campaign to solicit international support was initiated by Globalization Monitor, a Hong Kong NGO focusing on the negative impacts of globalisation on labour in China. Shortly after the strike was over, the government started to strengthen its control over media reports of strikes and the civil society actors who had supported the Honda workers. For example, the CWRN faced retribution and was shut down by the State Council Information Office for 'having published articles with bad intention without authorisation', on 8 June 2010.

The Aftermath

In late June 2010, officials from the Guangdong Federation of Trade Unions (GDFTU) met CHAM workers' representatives. Although they promised trade union reform and collective wage bargaining, the GDFTU delegates overruled the call of the workers' representatives to remove the existing trade union chair.[9] By manipulating the list of candidates and isolating active workers' representatives who maintained close contact with civil society during the strike, the higher-level trade unions ensured that most of the elected enterprise trade union officials came from managerial or supervisory levels.[10]

Alongside the trade union reform, there was also some progress regarding collective bargaining, with the GDFTU taking a leading role. From 25 February to 1 March 2011, wage negotiations took place between the trade union and the management of CHAM. Kong Xianghong, Deputy Chair of the GDFTU, who was deeply involved in Honda workplace issues, played a key role in driving both parties to reach an agreement. In the end, a pay rise of 611 yuan was agreed on.

Since 2011, annual collective bargaining has been held between the workplace trade union and management, facilitated by the higher-level trade union. A dispute arose in 2013 as the pay raise offered by the company was far lower than the rank-and-file workers had expected. A strike took place, though it was opposed by the official trade union committee. The company finally agreed to a pay rise higher than its original offer, but both the trade union committee and management exerted considerable pressure on the workers who had led the strike.

It is also worth noting the knock-on effect of the strike on the car industry, as well as other industries. In the summer of 2010, auto workers from many car companies and suppliers followed the example of their Honda counterparts and went on strike to demand higher wages. A supplier to Hyundai in Beijing, a Honda factory in nearby Zhongshan, two Toyota factories in Tianjin, Atsumitec Co. (a supplier to Honda) and Ormon (a supplier to Honda, Ford and BMW) were all hit by strikes in June and July 2010. The ripple effect is demonstrated by the fact that a leader of the Zhongshan Honda strike contacted workers' representatives from CHAM, seeking their advice. As can be seen, CHAM and other auto workers' increasingly sophisticated organising strategy and growing class consciousness enabled them to negotiate higher wages. Without relinquishing its grip restricting workers' freedom of association, the Party-State conceded to workers' strong demands by pressuring global capital to raise wage standards.

Political Impact

The 2010 Honda workers' strike was widely seen by scholars and activists as representing a new stage of labour resistance in China. This was because of not only its success, but also its duration of seventeen days, and the level of organisation compared with previous strikes.[11] Equally significantly, the strikers went beyond the individual interest of a pay rise and narrow demands related to their legal rights to call for democratic trade union reform. This wave of nationwide strikes and other forms of collective action sent a warning to the government about growing labour discontent. More importantly, it acted as a signal that the individual rights–based regulatory regime was inadequate for dealing with workers' grievances.

Chen Feng has conceptualised the regulatory regime established in the reform era before the establishment of the Labour Law (1994), the Trade Union Law (1992) and the Arbitration Law (1995) as an approach based on 'individual rights' (see also Biddulph's essay in the present volume).[12] Chen refers to 'individual rights' as the legal accentuation of individuals' entitlement to a minimum wage, social insurance, an overtime premium and so forth, while workers' collective rights denote the right to organise, strike and engage in collective bargaining—rights that are basically absent in China. The Chinese Government has not yet ratified International Labour Organization Conventions No. 87 and No. 98 on freedom of association and collective bargaining and, in fact, freedom of association remains one of the most politically sensitive issues in China.

The ACFTU is the sole union federation in the country, and it falls under the leadership of the Chinese Communist Party (CCP), as stipulated in its constitution and the Trade Union Law. Although included in the Chinese constitutions enacted in 1975 and 1978, the right to strike was removed from the Constitution of 1982. It should be noted that, although the aforementioned laws contain clauses related to the collective rights of workers, in practice, these are seldom implemented. As soon as these laws were in place, workers began to use them as a weapon to protect their rights.[13] According to official data, the number of cases handled by the labour dispute arbitration committees at all levels in the country jumped dramatically, from 12,368 in 1993 to 135,206 in 2000 and to 684,379 in 2009. However, China's individual rights–based regulatory regime has proved insufficient to prevent labour conflicts, which have increasingly taken the form of collective resistance, especially since the early 2000s.[14]

The Honda strike marked the apex of bottom-up workers' resistance, forcing central and local governments to push forward labour regulations based on collective interests, while temporarily placing at the top of the government and ACTFU's agenda the reform of the trade union system on the basis of the existing legal framework and the establishment of a better collective consultation system in the workplace.

On 5 June 2010, the ACFTU issued a document titled 'Further Strengthen the Building of Workplace Trade Unions and Give Them Full Play' (进一步加强企业工会建设充分发挥企业工会作用), which emphasised workers' rights to information, participation and the voicing of opinions, as well as the right of workplace trade unions to monitor management.[15] Shortly after the Honda strike, thirteen provinces issued documents in the name of the CCP committee or local government to promote collective wage consultation.[16] In August 2010, the Guangdong Provincial Government began debating the second draft of the Regulations on the Democratic Management of Enterprises, while the Shenzhen Collective Consultation Ordinance (amended draft) was also under public consultation.

However, in a repeat of what had occurred during the discussions of the draft Labour Contract Law (see Gallagher's essay in the present volume), some overseas chambers of commerce were strongly opposed to legislation on collective negotiation. In Hong Kong, more than forty business associations published petitions in newspapers.[17] Chambers of commerce from the United States also voiced concerns about the legislation.[18] As a consequence, both the Regulations on the Democratic Management of Enterprises and the Shenzhen Collective Consultation Ordinance were suspended.

Two Lessons

From the case of Honda, we can see that workers' activism in China's Pearl River Delta enhanced wages and working conditions by pushing the government to legislate an individual rights–based legal framework and global capital to raise wage levels. In this context of a restrictive regulatory regime primarily focused on individual rights, a new wave of workers' strikes in 2010 forced the government to seriously consider a collective rights–based regulatory framework. This was short-lived due to the state's manipulation of trade unions and opposition from business.

We can draw two lessons from the Honda strike. The first is that Chinese migrant workers have been actively participating in the shaping and reshaping of labour rights in global factories. However, while labour activism can challenge global capital and the Party-State regarding labour regulations, political and economic constraints on workers' power should not be underestimated. Politically, the authoritarian nature of the Chinese Party-State and the legacy of socialist trade unionism have structurally impeded the rise of democratic trade unionism in China. Although civil society has provided significant support to workers in their struggles, the Party-State has effectively stifled the ability of labour NGOs to promote independent workplace organising. Economically, China's heavy dependence on foreign investment and export-oriented industry has granted global capital powerful leverage in influencing local labour policies. The second lesson is that, in the process of integrating into the global economy, the Chinese state has had to balance the interests of and pressures from both labour and capital to maintain its ruling authority.[19] State regulations and the state's relations with labour and capital are therefore key to analysing and predicting further developments in labour standards and industrial relations in China.

2010

With a workforce of more than one million in mainland China alone, the Taiwanese Foxconn Technology Group is a major contractor for Apple and other leading multinational corporations. In 2010, when it was reported that eighteen workers had attempted suicide at company facilities in China, resulting in fourteen deaths, it made visible the conditions of overwork and desperation and elicited international condemnation. All of the victims hailed from the Chinese countryside and were in the prime of youth—representative of what scholars had then just begun calling the 'second generation of migrant workers'. Taking place roughly at the same time as the mobilisation of temporary workers at the Honda plant in Nanhai, the media spotlight on the 'Foxconn Suicide Express' once again revealed the structural torsion within Chinese society caused by the combined activities of international capital and the Chinese state.

The Foxconn Suicide Express
Jenny CHAN

> To die is the only way to testify that we ever lived. Perhaps for the Foxconn employees and employees like us, the use of death is to testify that we were ever alive at all, and that while we lived, we had only despair.
> — A Chinese worker's blog, 27 May 2010[1]

It was in January 2010 that I and my group of scholar-activists first heard about the suicides of workers at the Foxconn electronics plants in Shenzhen, Guangdong Province.[2] In the subsequent months, we closely followed reports on what the media had dubbed the 'suicide express'. After the ninth 'Foxconn jumper' committed suicide on 11 May, several scholars and students, including me, met to discuss what might be done to prevent more suicides. One week later, we joined others in issuing a public statement calling on Foxconn, the Chinese Government and the All-China Federation of Trade Unions to act decisively to end the 'chain of suicides'. The statement read:

> From the moment the new generation of rural migrant workers step beyond the doors of their houses, they never think of going back to farming like their parents. The moment they see there is little possibility of building a home in the city through hard work, the very meaning of their work collapses. The path ahead is blocked, and the road to retreat is closed. Trapped in this situation, the workers face a serious identity crisis and this magnifies psychological and emotional problems. Digging into this deeper level of societal and structural conditions, we come closer to understanding the 'no way back' mentality of these Foxconn employees.[3]

By December 2010, eighteen workers were known to have attempted suicide at Foxconn facilities; fourteen were dead, while four survived with crippling injuries. They ranged in age from seventeen to twenty-five; all were rural migrants in the prime of youth, and emblematic of the new Chinese working class.

Suicide involves an intensely personal, and social, struggle on the part of the individual. In November 1970 in South Korea, twenty-three-year-old textile worker Chun Tae-il poured gasoline on his body and set himself ablaze in the hope of rallying fellow workers to demand that the Park Chung-hee dictatorship protect worker rights. His suicide inspired the subsequent labour and democratic movements and helped transform South Korean civil society.[4] As Kim Hyojoung puts it, Chun galvanised 'collective action by mobilizing the "hearts and minds" of the target audience'.[5] In China, Foxconn employees who committed suicide in 2010 and after also issued a *cri de coeur* in response to the harsh conditions that confronted workers.[6] The tragic loss of young lives reverberated throughout society and internationally, inspiring a global call to guarantee worker rights and prevent more deaths. But did their deaths and the ensuing public response set in motion fundamental changes in labour conditions in China and the world?

Foxconn and Its Global Electronics Production

Foxconn's parent company, the Hon Hai Precision Industry Company, was established by Terry Gou in Taiwan in February 1974. The trade name Foxconn alludes to the corporation's claim to produce electronic connectors (used in applications for computers) at fox-like speed. Foxconn, with its final assembly and production of personal computers, mobile phones, videogame consoles and other consumer electronic products for tech brands, quickly outstripped most other manufacturers in providing low-cost, efficient services to Apple and other leading international firms. Within four decades, Foxconn would evolve from a small processing factory to become the world leader in high-end electronics manufacturing, with plants dotted around China and, subsequently, the world. Today, the company has more than 200 subsidiaries and branch offices in Asia, the Americas and Europe.[7]

As Foxconn strives to dominate global electronics manufacturing and advanced technology, its aspirations align with China's goal to become the world's economic and technological superpower. China remains the heart of Foxconn's global corporate empire and profitability. By 2005, Taiwanese scholar Tse-Kang Leng estimated that 90 percent of Hon Hai's net profit was generated from its business in China, and the integration of the company in China has since deepened.[8] In 2018, Foxconn accounted for 4.1 percent of China's total imports and exports, with revenues topping US$175 billion.[9] This stunning growth was achieved through a combination of shrewd business practices, mergers and acquisitions, patent acquisition and astute cultivation of relations with the Chinese Government. In this essay, I will gauge how the corporation's rise has affected its one million employees, the majority of whom are Chinese rural migrant workers.

Employee Suicides in China

In May 2010, Liu Kun, Foxconn's public communications director, pointed out that the reasons for suicide were invariably multiple. Shifting the blame from the structural to the psychological, Chinese media described the generation born in the 1980s and 1990s as suffering from 'psychological problems' and personal crises related to issues such as dating and debts.[10] 'Given its size, the rate of self-killing at Foxconn is not necessarily far from China's relatively high average,' reported *The Guardian*, quoting the cavalier comments of company officials.[11] But suicide is *not* evenly distributed in any population.

Studies suggest suicides among the elderly represent more than 40 percent of Chinese suicides.[12] It is important to note that the Foxconn suicide cluster in 2010 involved young employees working for a single company, most of them in factories in Shenzhen. Why would suicides by these young employees living in the cities spike when Beijing-based medical professionals found that 88 percent of suicides by Chinese youth occurred in the countryside?[13] This concentration of suicides points to something new and important, which begs for an explanation in the context of the company, the industry and wider society.

Drawing on global supply chain analysis, migrant labour studies and understandings of Chinese authoritarianism, including the role of the only trade union legally allowed in China, this essay argues that workers' depression, and suicide in extreme cases, is connected to their working and living conditions in the broader context of the international political economy.[14] Foxconn's management regime—including its heavy reliance on young workers, low-cost and just-in-time assembly and 'flexible' wage and working hours policy—is a response to the high-pressure purchasing practices of global corporations. The fluctuation in orders, coupled with tight delivery requirements, has shifted production pressure from Apple and other multinationals to Foxconn and other suppliers in transnational manufacturing. The pressures of just-in-time production, alongside the competitiveness of the local labour market, place tremendous burdens on the assembly-line worker, who experiences a sense of time and space caving in.

iPhone Workers

Apple's success is intimately bound up with the production of quality products at high speed. Given its control over the commanding heights of hardware, software and design, Apple has remained in the driver's seat in setting the terms and conditions for Foxconn and, in turn, its workers. However, while the two companies remain independent, they are inextricably linked in product development, engineering research, manufacturing processes, logistics, sales and after-sales service. By the end of the 1990s, Apple had outsourced all of its US-based manufacturing jobs and some of its research facilities overseas.[15] It only retained a small number of workers and staff at its Macintosh computer factory in Cork, Ireland.[16] This outsourcing means that Apple's success is inseparable from the contributions of its international suppliers and their workers—above all, Foxconn and its Chinese employees.

Between 2009 and 2010, the sales of iPhones increased by 93 percent, from 20,731,000 to 39,989,000 units.[17] With a sudden influx of rushed orders from Apple, among other firms, Foxconn workers—including those who committed suicide—were toiling day and night. Figure 1 shows Apple's iPhone units sold from the first quarter of fiscal year 2010 to the fourth quarter of fiscal year 2018. Clearly, the iPhone has gained increasing global popularity over time, even as Apple faces intense competition from other smartphone brands. Less noted is the fact that iPhone shipments experienced extreme spikes during the holiday seasons and close to the New Year. Being the largest Apple supplier, Foxconn needs to periodically extend working hours and adapt its workforce to these boom-and-bust trends.

Figure 1. iPhone Units Sold, 2009–18

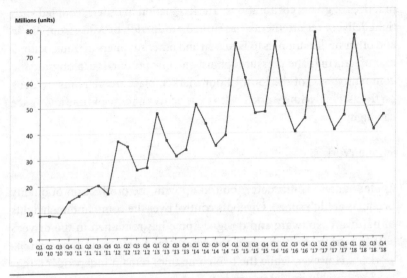

Source: Apple's quarterly earnings reports (Form 10-Q), various years.[18] Apple had stopped releasing unit sales of iPhones as of fiscal year 2019, which ended on 28 September 2019.

An ever-shorter production cycle, accelerated finishing times and compulsory overtime requirements placed intense pressures on Foxconn assembly-line workers. New workers in particular were reprimanded for working 'too slowly' on the line, regardless of their efforts to keep up with the 'standard work pace'.[19] One woman worker recalled: 'Production output of iPhone casings was previously set at 5,120 pieces per day; but in July 2010, it was raised by 25 percent to 6,400 pieces per day. I'm completely exhausted.'[20]

Each iPhone is composed of more than 100 parts. The usual time for completing the Standard Operating Procedure (SOP) in assembly is twenty-five to thirty seconds. Put in context, thirty seconds is *not* long. However, the ultrathin new iPhones scratch so easily that they must be held in protective cases during assembly. The cases make workers' delicate operations even more difficult, but no extra time is given to complete each task. Electronics parts and components flow by and workers' youth is devoured by the rhythm of the machines.

Labour Struggles and Chinese Unionism

All of this shows that high-tech gadgets such as the iPhone are *not* produced in a Silicon Valley paradise. Indeed, while designed in Silicon Valley, they are not produced there at all. They are produced in places like Foxconn—the world's largest electronics manufacturer—which is immediately responsible for the working conditions and welfare of its employees. But Foxconn is also subject to a buyer-driven business model, which functions to assure 'a rise in profitability for [companies that] operate at the top of industries and increasingly precarious working conditions for workers at lower levels'.[21] For example, in 2018, Apple generated super profits of US$59.5 billion—more than thirteen times greater than Foxconn's profit of US$4.3 billion (NT$129 billion).[22] How much room do suppliers have to manoeuvre to make management more equal and humane in the buyer-dominated global production chain? Despite Foxconn's campaigns to 'make workers happy' with large-scale social and entertainment activities, hard targets of output and profit must still be fulfilled, and Foxconn workers still earn on average a meagre 4,000 yuan a month (less than US$60) with overtime premiums, night-shift subsidies and full attendance allowances factored in.[23] In this sense, the lives of Foxconn workers are not only the direct product of policies implemented by management, but also, in the first instance, shaped by the brands whose products are being produced—that is, Apple and the other leading global buyers of electronic products.

But Apple is physically removed from the desperation and struggles on the factory floor. In the face of worker suicides, strikes and protests, Foxconn's trade union has increasingly felt the need to address the gaps in union–worker communications. To preempt unrest, union officers offered psychological consultations and advice to workers facing family distress, financial problems and other personal problems. As early as 2013, Foxconn also proclaimed that 'a pilot program for union leadership elections had been implemented to improve union representation, and candidates can participate in the election on a voluntary basis'.[24] But the selection of candidates and the election process have remained opaque and election methods have never been specified. The toothless role of Foxconn's trade union mirrors nationwide trends of managerial control over employees and the absence of substantive worker representation at the workplace level.

Both management and the government remain vigilant to prevent the emergence of autonomous unions that might empower workers. Under the leadership of President Xi Jinping, from 2013, defiant workers, including Foxconn employees, have continued to fight to secure fundamental rights—sometimes with support structures provided by nongovernmental organisations (NGOs), progressive student groups and human rights lawyers—in the face of intensified state crackdowns on protests.[25] Worker-led strikes and protests at numerous Foxconn sites were part of a pattern of growing labour unrest across coastal and inland China. Should the Foxconn workers succeed in rebuilding *their* union from the bottom up, they would inspire many others to stand up to fight for a better future.

Towards a Global Anti-Sweatshop Campaign

Given Foxconn's global reach and in the absence of strong, independent unions in China, it is still vulnerable to transnational movements and pressure that seek to secure labour and environmental justice. In the wake of the suicides at Foxconn, there were several instances of international solidarity. Across the strait, in June 2010, Taiwanese scholars Lin Thung-hong and Yang You-ren issued an open statement with more than 300 signatories and held a press conference in Taipei to condemn Foxconn management for its brutal treatment of mainland workers. They confronted Terry Gou, the head of the Foxconn Group, as he promised to increase wages. Noting that recent pay raises at Foxconn did not address the deep-seated problems confronting workers, they concluded: 'We believe that the Foxconn suicide cluster is a bitter accusation made with eleven young lives against the inhumane, exploitative labour regime.'[26]

At the same time, thousands of miles away in Mexico, workers at Foxconn Guadalajara launched solidarity actions to protest labour oppression in China. Their mobilisation included creating a makeshift cemetery to symbolically allow the workers who committed suicide in China to rest in peace and draw global media attention to their plight.[27] They also read out a press statement in Spanish calling on not only Foxconn but also Apple, Dell, HP, Sony, Nokia and other global brands to take responsibility for the unfolding labour crisis in China.[28]

Meanwhile, in the United States, university students and faculty members, union organisers and labour rights groups protested outside Apple's flagship New York store to demand justice for Foxconn workers. They decorated the surrounding sidewalk with photos of the young Foxconn victims and a funeral bouquet.[29] On the west coast, San Francisco's Chinese Progressive Association held a candlelight vigil for the Foxconn victims and their families. The memorial featured solemn teenagers holding signs with the names of Foxconn workers who had taken their own lives.[30]

On 14 June 2010, United Students Against Sweatshops, working with a nationwide network of more than 250 American college and high-school chapters, sent an open letter urging then Apple CEO Steve Jobs to 'address the problems in Shenzhen by ensuring payment of living wages, legal working hours, and democratic union elections in Foxconn supplier factories'.[31] The letter was copied to the Hong Kong–based NGO Students and Scholars Against Corporate Misbehaviour (SACOM), the San Francisco Chinese Progressive Alliance and the Washington, DC–based labour rights monitoring organisation Worker Rights Consortium. They received no response from Apple. Clearly, it is necessary for the campaign to continue to expand and deepen, reaching out to corporate management and concerned citizens through coordinated actions.

The year 2017 saw the launch of the campaign '#iSlaveat10—No More iSlave'.[32] Ten years earlier, Apple had entered the mobile phone market with the launch of the iPhone. As time passed, consumer awareness of the links between electronics manufacturing and the plight of workers has grown.[33] In Europe, for example, an emerging market of consumers recognises that the Fairphone, rather than the iPhone (and other brands), is a more sustainable production model that respects workers' rights.[34] In the wake of consumer movements focused on Nike, Adidas and other garment and footwear companies, has Apple become more sensitive to boycotts staged by civil society actors?

Although the question remains open, there are reasons to be optimistic. The gains of tech firms in transnational production chains rest squarely on the value created by workers at Foxconn and other suppliers. Besides updating its smartphone with the launch of the iPhone 11 in September 2019, Apple has been promoting its app development curriculum for high school and community college students at home and abroad. A substantial part of Apple's market is education-generated and its claims to ethical practices directly impinge on students and faculty among other consumers. Around 330 public sector organisations primarily based in Europe, including but not limited to universities, have leveraged their procurement power to require brands and their suppliers to protect and strengthen workers' rights in their contracts.[35] Hopefully, this could open the way for strong pressure on the company in the many countries that constitute its global market.

2011

In the summer of 2011, more than two dozen schools serving the children of migrant workers in Beijing were demolished just weeks before the beginning of the new semester. This dramatic event highlighted the capital's increasingly restrictive approach to providing social services to non-local residents, as industrial upgrading and population control came to dominate urban policy. This essay traces the rapid rise and fall of informal schools in Beijing from the 1990s up to the 2010s, drawing attention to a key animating dilemma of China's urban politics—that is, cities' desire to pull in rural migrants as cheap labour, while remaining reluctant to fully underwrite the costs of their social reproduction.

Rupture at the Centre: Evicting Migrant Schools in Beijing

Eli FRIEDMAN

In August 2011, Beijing's municipal government initiated a wave of evictions targeting schools for rural migrant children. In a matter of weeks, more than two dozen schools were summarily shuttered, and in some cases bulldozed, and up to 30,000 students were displaced just before the semester was to begin. This surprise attack upended the lives of migrant families, as they were forced to consider sending their children out of the city to their officially designated place of *hukou* (户口, or 'household registration'), splitting up the family, or forsaking the employment opportunities of the metropolis. The sense of desperation engendered by these closures produced occasionally intense forms of resistance, with parents blocking roads and petitioning government agencies to demand that their children be resettled in local schools. While the spectacle of such a concentrated outburst of destruction was not repeated in subsequent years, things would hardly improve. With a few years' hindsight, it was evident that this event initiated a multiyear campaign to 'optimise the population' by removing people who had been deemed superfluous to the functioning of the capital. Children were not to be spared.

Entrenched Divisions

The 2011 demolitions laid bare a deep social contradiction: while the Chinese State had gradually crafted a national labour market over the previous generation, social citizenship remained organised at the level of the city. Chinese citizens were granted the thin freedom to sell their labour anywhere in the country where they might find a buyer, but the moment they left their place of official *hukou*, they abandoned any rights to social reproduction, including subsidised health care, housing, and, crucially, education. In the context of the rapid expansion of regional inequality in the era of capitalist transformation, this disjuncture between a national labour market and highly localised life-supporting infrastructure produced endemic social, emotional, and even biological crises for China's migrants.

This sociospatial disjuncture was not always so. Along with nationalisation of industry and the development of the job allocation system (分配), the institutionalisation of the *hukou* system in 1958 essentially eliminated the labour market (see Hayward's essay in the present volume). *Hukou* designated both a productive status—agricultural (农业) or non-agricultural (非农业)—and a location, which tied attendant rights to the citizen remaining in their place of *hukou*. A key motivation for this arrangement was to pin the peasantry in place, such that agricultural surplus could be extracted from the countryside and invested in big-push industrialisation in the cities. In the state socialist period, it was very difficult to survive outside one's place of *hukou* without official permission. With a few notable exceptions (for example, military personnel, seasonal workers), the State expected that one would more or less stay within their tightly circumscribed place in the sociospatial matrix. While this system produced all kinds of inequalities—exemplified most horrifically by the millions of largely rural deaths during the Great Leap Forward—it also realised integration of the spaces of production and social reproduction for rural and urban residents alike.

This system began to break down with the opening up to private capital and the construction of a national labour market, first initiated in the late 1970s and then accelerating dramatically from the early 1990s. By 2011, more than one-quarter of a billion people were residing outside of their place of *hukou*. Rural residents increasingly found that they needed the wages of urban employment to survive, even if it meant giving up access to social services. With declining rural livelihoods, more and more rural residents left the land, with large eastern cities such as Beijing a major draw.

In the 1980s and 1990s, migrant workers were disproportionately young. A typical migration trajectory was to leave home after completing compulsory education and perhaps some further technical training. Teenagers and people in their early twenties came to be the core demographic of China's emerging capitalist industries. But both social and material factors tended to push migrants back to the village by their mid-twenties to marry and have children. It was not uncommon for one parent, typically the father, to return to the city to earn a wage. But the expectation was that the core practices of social reproduction—childrearing, education, health care, and elder care—would remain in the countryside.

In the Cracks of the Old System

Almost as soon as these new migratory flows emerged, cracks in the old regime of social reproduction were evident. At this stage, it was still extremely difficult for non-local children to access public schools in the city. Public schools were under no obligation to accept non-locals, and would generally only do so for high-achieving students—who would pad the school's average test scores—with parents who could pay a hefty education fee (借读费). Thus, the overwhelming majority of migrants were shut out of the public system. Migrants were faced with the choice of leaving their children behind in the countryside or bringing them to the city with radically uncertain prospects for their education. While the large majority chose the former—which is still the case today—by the 1990s, migrants in Beijing and other rapidly expanding coastal cities began setting up informal schools to cater to those who wanted or needed to have their children with them.

These so-called migrant schools (打工子弟学校) were extremely lacking in resources. In the 1990s, the number of migrant children in Beijing was still relatively low, and many of these schools were little more than babysitting operations, sometimes occupying a room or two of an apartment. Most schools were initially set up by migrants themselves. Over time, there came to be a popular distinction between regular (that is, profit-oriented) schools and 'public interest' (公益) schools that were financially supported by foundations or corporations and were therefore able to provide reduced tuition rates. The government was more or less indifferent; while it certainly did not provide material support, it was not openly hostile. Migrant children were wedged in the interstices of a regime of reproduction that was bit by bit fraying in the face of an expanding labour market. Cities begrudgingly accepted a growing number of informal schools, as it relieved them of having to expand access to education. But it also meant that the large majority of schools were entirely dependent on tuition to fund their operations—a challenging situation when all of the 'customers' were working-class and poor people.

The government's relative indifference to migrant schools could, however, easily become antagonistic in the context of the city's increasing land values in the 2000s. One well-known school—which by 2008 had managed to win official recognition and significant foundation support—was forced to move five times in the years following its establishment in 2001. As described in the school's official history:

There were various reasons behind [Zhifan][1] School's frequent moves in the beginning of its establishment. For the first two times, it was because the school was forced by the government to close its doors. For the following three times, it was because the school buildings had to be demolished in order to make way for the expansion of the city of Beijing. This explains why [Zhifan] School slowly made its way from the fourth ring road to the fifth ring road and eventually to its current position within the sixth ring road.[2]

Revenue-hungry officials were likely to side with developers against migrant schools, which lacked official registration. While the schools were often tolerated, they did not add value to the city according to the State's metrics. This experience of administrative instability and continual spatial peripheralisation was common for migrant schools and communities in this period.

As it became increasingly clear that mass migration to China's booming eastern cities was not a passing phenomenon, the central government took steps to relax population controls. In 2001 the State Council unveiled a general policy orientation known as the 'two primaries' (两为主) that established a framework for educating migrant children that was remarkably different from what had been in place previously. The policy held that receiving areas should be *primarily* financially responsible for educating migrant children (rather than the place of *hukou*), and that migrant children should be *primarily* enrolled in local public schools (rather than the private and often unregulated migrant schools). In addition, 2003 saw the elimination of the custody and repatriation system under which migrants without proper urban residence permits would be shipped back to the countryside. It seemed possible to stay in the city and educate one's children there.

In light of this national-level policy shift, Beijing and other cities began to establish formal bureaucratic procedures for admitting non-locals into public schools and moved to regularise the informal education system that had sprung up in the institutional interstices. In 2005, the city issued the 'Beijing Department of Education Notification on Strengthening Management of Migrant Population Self-Run Schools', which proposed dealing with migrant schools according to the principle of 'supporting some, approving some, and eliminating some'.[3] The following year, a limited number of migrant schools were allowed to register, but an absolute majority of the schools in operation remained unlicensed. At the same time, and more optimistically, public schools did indeed become more inclusive. The Department of Education established the 'five permits' (五证) system, which allowed migrant families who could meet the administrative requirements to enrol their children in school, and abolished education fees for non-locals. According to official estimates, from 2001 to 2015, the percentage of migrant children enrolled in Beijing's public schools increased from 12.5 to 78 percent.[4] While these numbers must be viewed with a high degree of suspicion—the students least likely to be accepted by public schools are the ones who are also least likely to be captured by government statistics—there is no question that an increasing share of migrants were being incorporated into the public system.

Pushed to the Margins

The story of Beijing's migrant children in the 2000s and 2010s is, as intimated at the outset, nonetheless not entirely a happy one of greater incorporation. Although formal procedures existed for enrolling in urban public schools, access for non-locals was maintained as a revocable privilege rather than a right. The metrics used in Beijing—and other large wealthy cities—for accessing public schools favoured migrants *least* in need of state-subsidised services. In general, the higher the parents' levels of education, access to wealth, and urban social connections, the more likely it was they would be admitted. In both the 'five permits' and the subsequent 'points-based admission' plans, migrants working in the informal sector or living in informal housing were excluded at the outset by requirements for labour and housing contracts. Paying into local social insurance was a requirement, although the length of time of contributions varied across districts and from year to year. In my own fieldwork in Beijing in the early to mid-2010s, migrant parents claimed without exception that they would have to pay large bribes—often equivalent to more than one year's salary—to get their children into public schools. These sorting mechanisms can be thought of as an 'inverted means test'; the effect was to funnel nominally public resources precisely to those who needed them least, while concentrating the most deprived populations in migrant schools.[5]

In this context, these informal schools were a suboptimal choice for parents with no other options. The difficulty, however, was that just as public school access was being somewhat regularised for elite non-locals, the city began methodically squeezing migrant schools. Following the 2005 notification mentioned above, the focus was quite clearly not on 'supporting' or 'approving' migrant schools, but on eliminating them. Indeed, the number of migrant schools in Beijing peaked at approximately 300 in 2006, and fell every year thereafter.[6] The mass demolitions in 2011 were by no means an aberration; rather, they were an intensification and condensation of a process that was quite consciously set in motion years prior.

In fact, by 2014 it became clear that the school system had emerged as a key choke point in the municipal government's population control efforts. In that same year, the central government released the *National New Urbanisation Plan* (2014–20),[7] which specifically called for cities with an urban district population of more than five million to 'strictly control' their population growth. This was part of a broader push on the part of China's elite cities to optimise the population in tandem with their efforts at shifting to a model of economic growth based on higher value-added, knowledge-based, service-sector industries. The so-called low-end population (低端人口) had no place in this imagined future. In addition to relocating 'noncapital functions' (非首都功能)[8] such as warehouses, wholesale markets, and labour-intensive industry outside Beijing, depriving migrant children of schooling was another powerful lever for expelling undesirable populations. While the scale and intensity of the 2011 school demolitions were not subsequently repeated, one by one, schools were demolished, had their power or water cut, or had their operating licence revoked.

This slow drip of school closures was paired with a dramatic increase in requirements for accessing public schools, including new and onerous demands for parents' payment into social insurance and a dizzying array of documentation requirements. One particularly vexing requirement in many districts was that parents live and pay social insurance in the same district in which they were trying to send their child to school. Countless frustrated parents reported that the new rules were arbitrarily enforced and, if they were able to meet all of the Education Department's stated requirements, new demands would then be added until they gave up. Many migrant children who *had* been able to access official primary or middle schools thus found themselves expelled from the public system at precisely the moment when the government was also stamping out informal schooling options. The intent was clear enough: working-class migrants were not welcome.

The government's means were brutal but effective. In addition to throttling educational opportunities and relocating industry, in November 2017, the authorities razed entire migrant neighbourhoods under the pretence of ensuring building safety. Indeed, these demolitions followed a tragic fire in a migrant community in Daxing in which nineteen people died. But those expelled from their homes were not resettled. The government was leaving no stone unturned, continuously stepping up its attacks on working-class migrants' schools, workplaces, and homes. After several years of slowing growth, by 2017, the city's population contracted.[9]

Converging Political and Material Pressures

We will never know the proximate cause of the 2011 school demolitions, nor the less spectacular forms of expulsion visited on Beijing's non-local children in the years that followed. Nonetheless, during this period there were relatively autonomous political *and* material pressures that converged towards the expulsion of working-class non-locals. Politically, the municipal government came under increasing pressure to decrease its population. Beijing had in previous years quickly exceeded centrally imposed population limits, and after 2014 the city faced a 'red line' of 23 million residents. Shrinking the population may not have made sense from an economic standpoint—capital expansion faces real headwinds in the context of falling population—but rather grew out of a deep-seated Communist Party ideology that links overpopulation to political instability. The cold material calculations behind school demolitions are more straightforward. As already noted, the possibility of building high-rise apartments or other commercial properties increased, even on the city's peripheries, during the 2000s and 2010s, and both landlords and local officials were increasingly likely to want to put the land to more profitable uses. Although it is difficult to untangle which of these pressures was dominant, in a sense it does not matter. They both push in the direction of school demolition and expelling a population that has always been seen as potentially disposable.

Despite repeated claims of the end of *hukou* and increasingly inclusive education, the contradiction between China's national labour market and its highly localised social service infrastructure has not diminished, even as its spatial characteristics have evolved. Beijing's policy of expelling the low-end populations appears to have realised its aim: hundreds of thousands of the most vulnerable people have been forced from the city.

But despite its aspirations, Beijing is not an island within the People's Republic of China. Its wealth and grandeur have been produced by the very rural populations the State so despises. Shunting school-age children to the countryside does not eliminate their suffering; it only relocates the social crisis out of sight. Despite the increasingly shrill ethnonationalist tone emanating from the Party centre, the State continues to treat certain members of the dominant Han race as expendable based on ascribed characteristics. China's national problem is thus not limited to the racialised peripheries; a deep rupture, sociospatial rather than ethnic in nature, plagues the very core.

2013

In 2013, Chinese President Xi Jinping launched the Belt and Road Initiative (BRI), a massive foreign policy push to promote infrastructure development and regional connectivity throughout the world. Although the BRI 'Action Plan', issued in 2015, identified five areas of cooperation for China and its partners—policy coordination among governments, promoting infrastructure connectivity, fostering unimpeded trade, encouraging financial integration and building people-to-people bonds through cultural, academic, media and other exchanges—the core of the initiative is Beijing's effort to build large infrastructure projects such as railways, ports, pipelines, mines and dams that connect China to its neighbours and beyond. This essay looks into what all this means for Chinese workers.

Chinese Workers on the Belt and Road

Aaron HALEGUA

After wrapping up the G20 Summit in Saint Petersburg on 6 September 2013, Chinese President Xi Jinping arrived in Kazakhstan for a three-day state visit to the world's largest landlocked country. At Kazakhstan's flagship academic institution, Nazarbayev University, he delivered a speech to a lecture hall filled with officials, reporters and students. Xi described China's history of friendly relations with its Central Asian neighbours, pointing to the Silk Road trading route established during the Han Dynasty 2,100 years earlier. He stated that restoring the connection between China and Central Asia was a top foreign policy priority and called for the construction of a 'Silk Road Economic Belt' (丝绸之路经济带) that would enhance regional economic cooperation, improve road connectivity, promote unimpeded trade and foster mutual understanding.

One month later, in October 2013, Xi addressed the Indonesian Parliament, where he appealed to the history of exchanges between the two countries, despite the seas between them, and called for the establishment of a 'Maritime Silk Road' for the twenty-first century to connect China and the countries of the Association of Southeast Asian Nations (ASEAN). These two speeches are widely seen as the launch of Xi's signature foreign policy, the 'One Belt, One Road' strategy (一带一路战略), which was later rebranded the 'Belt and Road Initiative' (一带一路倡议, or BRI) to sound less threatening to foreign audiences.[1] At the broadest level, the BRI seeks to promote infrastructure development and regional connectivity throughout most of Asia, Africa and Europe, and early reports suggested that projects under the BRI could involve investments totalling US$1 trillion. The BRI 'Action Plan', issued in 2015, identified five areas of cooperation for China and its BRI partners: policy coordination among governments, promoting infrastructure connectivity, fostering unimpeded trade, encouraging financial integration and building people-to-people bonds through cultural, academic, media and other exchanges.[2] Signalling the political weight that China attaches to this initiative, in 2017, the Chinese Communist Party (CCP) incorporated the mission of 'advancing construction of the BRI' (推进'一带一路'建设) into its constitution.

The core of the BRI is China's effort to build large infrastructure projects—such as railways, ports, pipelines, mines and dams—that connect China to its neighbours and beyond. This generally occurs by Chinese banks loaning money to host-country governments, which then contract out the project to Chinese state-owned enterprises (SOEs), which in turn import Chinese construction materials and often Chinese workers. One commentator remarked that, in many instances, it is as if China simply 'air drops' its whole domestic project development ecosystem into another country.[3] As a further demonstration of its financial commitment to this effort, China also created the Silk Road Fund and a new multilateral financial institution, the Asian Infrastructure Investment Bank, partly to finance these infrastructure projects.

Since the launch of the BRI, official Chinese statistics suggest that Chinese companies have been increasingly active in overseas projects. In 2015, Chinese companies signed 3,987 new contracts valued at US$92 billion with BRI participant countries, and foreign direct investment (FDI) in BRI countries reached US$14 billion.[4] By 2019, these numbers had grown to 6,944 new contracts worth US$154 billion for projects in BRI countries and roughly US$15 billion in FDI.[5] By 2020, a Council on Foreign Relations report estimated that China had invested more than US$200 billion in BRI-related projects.[6] The number of countries that formally joined the BRI by signing memoranda of understanding grew from a few dozen in 2016 to 140 by January 2021—including countries in new regions like Latin America and accounting for 4.6 billion of the world's people.[7] China has executed thirty-one BRI cooperation agreements with international organisations, including at least two with the International Labour Organization.[8]

Programs to expand China's cultural influence have also been carried out under the BRI banner. Students from BRI partner countries are provided with 'Belt and Road Scholarships' to study in China or to partake in study tours. Efforts have been made to include tourism as part of the 'people-to-people' exchanges promoted by the BRI. China has launched a 'digital Silk Road' that connects countries through a satellite network and web of fibre-optic cables.[9] During the COVID-19 pandemic, as part of the 'health Silk Road', Chinese state media boasted that BRI transportation channels made it possible for China to deliver 76,000 tonnes of personal protective equipment to European BRI partners and celebrated China's donation of vaccines to thirteen developing countries.[10]

There has been much debate about China's 'true' motivations behind the BRI. Broadly speaking, there are two competing frameworks for how to understand this vast sea of projects and initiatives. The first views the BRI as a coherent master plan coordinated by Beijing to promote China's military, political and economic interests. For instance, some argue the BRI is part of China's national security planning to expand the number of routes by which foreign oil can be delivered to China, to construct ports that could be used by the Chinese navy in a conflict or to station Chinese personnel around the globe.[11] The BRI has also been interpreted as an effort to solve China's domestic economic problems, such as by fostering the economic development of China's less-developed western provinces by enhancing ties with Central Asia, by creating new sources of demand to address China's overcapacity in steel and cement production or by accessing new consumer markets to purchase China's manufactured goods.[12] As for the cultural exchanges, these are seen as China's attempt to build soft power and influence in host countries to facilitate the achievement of its geostrategic and other objectives.

There is a competing conceptualisation, however, that sees the BRI not as a coherent strategy concocted by Beijing, but as a mere slogan that a broad swathe of disjointed actors has attached to their various, unconnected policies and projects.[13] One analyst describes the BRI as a 'vision, not a plan', and suggests it falls on lower-ranking officials and other parties, including private companies, to find ways to implement Xi's vision.[14] In this regard, the BRI is consistent with past political 'campaigns' in China's modern history, such as the Great Leap Forward or Reform and Opening Up. Under this framework, the seemingly endless expansion of the BRI's scope does not illustrate a plan for world domination, but rather demonstrates the lack of any clear, defined strategy or plan. Indeed, some argue that Chinese officials, companies and other actors somewhat haphazardly apply the 'BRI' label to whatever project or initiative they are pursuing in the hope it will help garner political support for their effort.[15]

Regardless of what China's true intentions or motivations are, however, many of these large-scale infrastructure projects have generated significant controversy in the host countries.[16] The negotiations and terms of these large BRI contracts are rarely transparent, creating significant opportunities for corruption. The sizeable debts incurred by host governments to pay for these projects often far exceed what the country can realistically hope to repay—which some allege is intentional on China's part as a form of 'debt-trap diplomacy'.[17] In carrying out the projects, local residents have complained about improper confiscation of land and disastrous environmental impacts. Host-country businesses often resent Chinese companies purchasing their materials and supplies from China. Locals have also demonised the Chinese workers dispatched to build these projects as 'invaders' who are 'stealing' local jobs.[18]

This essay, however, will focus on just one aspect of the BRI: what does it mean for China's workers? In particular, the essay examines those Chinese labourers who travel abroad to work on infrastructure, construction or similar projects. What are the working conditions like for these individuals? Has the BRI led to an increase in the number of Chinese working overseas? And does the political sensitivity of the BRI and China's desire to project a good image translate into better working conditions on these projects?

The essay explores these questions by first noting that China has been undertaking overseas projects and dispatching workers abroad since long before the BRI, and it examines the poor labour conditions often faced by these workers. The chapter argues that the launch of the BRI—somewhat surprisingly—has not resulted in a clear increase in the official number of Chinese workers going overseas, although an unknown but significant number of Chinese appear to be working abroad through informal channels. Further, despite numerous government pronouncements designed to make Chinese firms respect workers' rights, labour abuses persist.

China's Overseas Workers in the 'Going Out' Era

The trend of Chinese workers being dispatched abroad is not a new one.[19] After the founding of the People's Republic of China (PRC) in 1949, SOEs were directed to work on government-sponsored development projects in foreign countries and they often brought along their Chinese employees (see also Sorace and Zhu's and Galway's essays in the present volume). By the mid-1970s, more than 1,000 such projects had been established in more than seventy countries. After China's 1986 reforms to make it easier to obtain a passport and loosening restrictions on foreign travel, it became increasingly common for individuals to seek better-paying jobs abroad. Whereas 55,000 Chinese workers were stationed abroad in 1985, this number grew to 264,300 in 1995 and 424,0900 in 2000.[20]

In 1999, China launched its 'Going Out' (走出去) policy, which encouraged the nation's enterprises to obtain contracts for projects overseas.

One of the explicit purposes of this policy was to increase the export of Chinese labour.[21] By the end of 2006, more than 5,000 Chinese investment entities had established almost 10,000 companies overseas in 172 countries and regions, with the combined outbound investment reaching US$90.63 billion.[22] Moreover, the number of Chinese workers stationed abroad continued to grow, doubling from 424,900 in 2000 to 846,600 by 2010.[23] Official statistics show that roughly 43 percent of these workers were dispatched to work on foreign projects contracted to Chinese companies.[24]

Policy documents from the Going Out period instruct that China's outbound investment projects should be 'win-win' for China and the host country, create jobs for locals and safeguard the rights of dispatched Chinese workers.[25] However, the details on how to implement these objectives were few and far between. For instance, there were no clear guidelines as to how many local workers must be employed on these projects or what construction supplies must be purchased within the host country. Even in this early period, the reliance on Chinese supplies and workers was a source of tension for local host-country populations. In one particularly inflammatory move, in 2012, when 1,200 Zambian miners stopped work to protest unsafe conditions, the Chinese mine owners brought in Chinese workers to replace them, causing a violent reaction from the Zambian protestors that resulted in the death of a Chinese manager.[26]

The one area in which the PRC Government did issue more detailed regulations is the rights of those Chinese workers sent abroad—for instance, mandating they have written contracts with certain provisions, limiting the collection of recruitment fees or security deposits and requiring the dispatching companies to deposit funds with the relevant government entity in China in case the worker returns without having been paid for their work.[27] However, these legal provisions often proved insufficient. A 2005 report by the central government recognised a rising number of disputes involving overseas Chinese workers—including mass protests, sit-ins at Chinese embassies and clashes with police in the host country—which prompted China to issue tighter rules restricting which entities could send workers overseas, limiting subcontracting, requiring the purchase of work-accident insurance and mandating other measures designed to curb noncompliance and exploitation.[28]

Academic studies and media reports also confirm that China's overseas workers generally faced very poor labour conditions. In reviewing a decade of Chinese overseas investments, Chris Smith and Yu Zheng found that

Chinese construction firms regularly imported Chinese migrant workers, broke local rules on working hours and safety and used the retention of wages and other coercive means to control the workforce.[29] They noted that Chinese workers' obedience to company rules and inability to organise or seek help from local authorities made them more attractive than local employees. Similarly, in her study of Chinese firms in Africa, Ching Kwan Lee described the labour conditions for Chinese workers, whether employed by SOEs or private firms, as 'abysmal', characterised by 'poverty wage rates', late salary payments, inadequate safety procedures and other forms of exploitation.[30] Moreover, these examples of abusive conditions are not limited to developing countries, but have also been found in the United States, Europe and Israel.[31] It must be noted, however, as argued by some scholars, that while the labour practices of these Chinese firms are hardly laudable, they are sometimes no worse than the labour conditions under other foreign companies operating in those host countries.[32]

In short, despite Chinese policies calling on enterprises to create 'win-win' projects that protect dispatched Chinese workers, companies often fail to live up to this standard. The next section addresses how, if at all, this changed after the launch of the BRI in 2013.

China's Overseas Workers and the BRI

What has the launch of the BRI meant for the number of Chinese working overseas or the labour conditions on these projects? Are more Chinese now working abroad or are Chinese firms paying more attention to hiring local workers to avoid the troubles faced by past projects? Given the political significance of the BRI and fears of negative publicity, are Chinese companies implementing better labour practices to avoid embarrassing delays from worker protests or worker injuries? This section explores these questions.

As a preliminary matter, though, rigorous analysis of the BRI's impact is difficult because of the amorphous nature of the initiative. Although the Chinese Government has explicitly labelled certain projects as being part of the BRI, there is no comprehensive list of such projects or clear criteria for determining whether or not a project is part of the BRI. While the common perception is that BRI projects involve SOEs using financing from Chinese banks to construct infrastructure, as discussed above, the

BRI label has also been employed by private firms and attached to special economic zones, industrial parks, manufacturing, tourism and even art exhibitions.[33]

Nonetheless, in terms of the outflow of workers, whereas the export of labour was an express objective of China's Going Out policy, this has not appeared in BRI policy documents as an explicit goal. On the contrary, China has even created some programs to alleviate the need to send Chinese labourers abroad—for instance, one such effort seeks to train 3,600 Malaysian engineering students in railway design and construction.[34] Indeed, official government statistics do not show an obvious increase in the number of Chinese working overseas due to the launch of the BRI. While the number of workers sent abroad grew from 527,000 in 2013 to 562,000 in 2014, it then dropped in 2015 and has since fluctuated from year to year.[35] In 2018, China reported that 552,000 workers were dispatched abroad and 996,800 were already stationed abroad, but the next year these numbers decreased to 487,000 and 992,000, respectively.[36] (These numbers also dropped sharply in 2020, but that is likely attributable to the COVID-19 pandemic.)[37] Despite this stagnation in the overall number of dispatched workers, however, there are certain countries that experienced an enormous influx of Chinese workers since the launch of the BRI, such as Malaysia, Laos and Pakistan.[38]

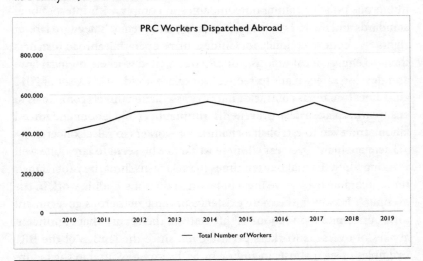

Source: Ministry of Commerce. 2020. '商务部数据统计中心 [Ministry of Commerce Statistical Centre].' Ministry of Commerce website, 3 March. Available online at: data.mofcom.gov.cn/tzhz/forlaborcoop.shtml.

It must also be noted that a large number of Chinese are obtaining work abroad through informal channels—such as using unregistered recruiters and travelling on tourist visas—and are not counted in the official statistics.[39] For instance, the 2,000 Chinese workers at a construction project on the island of Saipan, part of the US Commonwealth of the Northern Mariana Islands, included several hundred workers who entered the island as tourists and lacked proper work visas.[40] The Chinese media reported on one labour recruiter who earned more than US$5.5 million by defrauding 837 workers.[41] While the precise size of this cohort of informal workers is unknown, it appears to be significant. It is also quite possible that some BRI-related policies, such as the relaxation of travel restrictions or the growth in Chinese outbound investments, have caused the number of informal workers to increase. Indeed, in 2017, the Ministry of Commerce recognised this phenomenon and promised to take action to stamp out unregistered recruiters.[42] The prevalence of informal workers may also partially explain why any decrease in the official number of Chinese working abroad has not stunted the perception of a Chinese 'invasion' or the growth of anti-Chinese sentiment in many BRI host countries, such as Indonesia and the Philippines.[43]

For those workers who are sent abroad, has the launch of the BRI resulted in improved labour conditions? Since 2013, China has issued numerous policies calling on companies to comply with international standards and the laws of the host country, and even to 'safeguard labour rights'.[44] A 'code of conduct' for Chinese firms operating abroad instructs them to engage local unions, educate dispatched workers on local laws and develop safety plans to reduce workplace accidents.[45] A set of 2017 guidelines by China's contractor industry association directs companies to ensure workplace safety, prevent discrimination, child labour and forced labour and even to establish a channel for workers to raise concerns.[46]

There are many overseas Chinese workers who seem to fare quite well, working for SOEs that pay ten times the salary in China, buy social insurance, religiously observe meal breaks and do not schedule work in the evening.[47] However, the mere existence of these numerous government pronouncements on labour rights reflects the reality that significant abuses of overseas workers persist, even since the launch of the BRI. Examples of such abuse, including by SOEs, can be found in the failure to offer proper safety training on a subway project in Vietnam and late wage payments and insufficient protective equipment on road projects in Ethiopia.[48] Twenty-six complaints were filed against the Chinese firm constructing a dam in Ecuador concerning the poor safety and working conditions, and the collapse of a tunnel during that project that left more than a dozen workers dead.[49] A Chinese construction worker died on a job in Israel in 2019.[50] In Belarus, hundreds of Chinese workers received no pay for the three months they spent 'working like slaves' and living in cramped dormitories while constructing a cardboard factory.[51] Furthermore, even in cases where SOEs provide decent working conditions, they often subcontract work to smaller, private firms that are more willing to ignore labour protections.[52] On a Saipan casino project, three Chinese construction firms and their subcontractors took recruitment fees from workers, confiscated their passports, crammed them into dorms and underpaid 2,400 workers by at least US$14 million.[53] Indeed, an investigation by the group China Labor Watch found numerous instances of forced labour-like conditions on BRI projects in a variety of countries, impacting Chinese employees of both SOEs and their subcontractors.[54]

Not surprisingly, Chinese workers who encounter abuse while overseas are often unable to obtain redress. The workers face significant obstacles to leaving their employment: many are deep in debt after paying recruitment or other fees to labour brokers in China; employers often confiscate workers' passports; the workers lack access to transportation; and their work visa (if they have one) likely limits them to working for one particular employer.[55] Moreover, Chinese workers generally do not know where to seek help in the host country and, if they do, often encounter language barriers. Some workers will turn to the Chinese embassy, which occasionally mediates a resolution, but is often hesitant to offend the employer or will claim it cannot force a boss to pay wages if the employer says it lacks money.[56] Workers who choose to protest their maltreatment have been beaten by their employers or arrested and deported by the host-country authorities.[57] China's Ministry of Commerce has established a complaint mechanism, but there is little evidence of it delivering results for workers.[58]

That being said, there have been occasions when some combination of media reports and work by labour advocates and local government actors has obtained redress for abused Chinese workers, such as in Saipan, but those cases are more the exception than the rule.[59] Other workers have sought redress for injuries or non-payment of wages after returning to China. While some have succeeded in obtaining a remedy through the Chinese courts, many litigants lack proper evidence and many never make it to the courthouse in the first place.[60] In sum, it remains quite difficult for China's overseas workers to enforce whatever labour rights they were promised.

Future Directions

While the BRI undoubtedly marks a major development in the history of the PRC, the significance for China's working people is less clear. At least according to government statistics, the BRI has not translated into more Chinese working abroad. This is unlikely to change in the near future, as some analysts predict that China will decrease its focus on large-scale infrastructure projects in favour of less controversial, less capital-intensive initiatives like expanding the 'digital Silk Road' and the 'health Silk Road'. However, even if true, the number of Chinese workers stationed abroad remains significant; furthermore, a considerable number of individuals continue to use informal channels to work overseas. The labour abuses suffered by overseas workers prior to the BRI's launch appear to be continuing on many of these high-profile projects, particularly for those workers employed by subcontractors. The good news is that Chinese government organs have issued policies and guidance to companies instructing that labour rights be protected, and some Chinese courts have used those regulations as a basis to award relief to exploited workers. Moving forward, China would be wise to invest in encouraging compliance with these policies. Labour abuses may not only result in time delays and increased costs on BRI projects, but also interfere with China's broader goals of delivering economic growth to and building soft power among BRI partner countries. Therefore, China should develop mechanisms to monitor and enforce these labour rules, including penalties for companies that violate them and rewards for those who observe them. Implementing such measures could transform the BRI from a source of exploitative labour practices to a force for promoting better labour standards globally.

2014

On 30 September 2014, twenty-four-year-old Xu Lizhi jumped from an office building in Shenzhen, meeting instant death. Not only was he the latest in a long series of Foxconn employees who prematurely put an end to their life, but he was also an accomplished poet—posthumously acknowledged as a leading voice in a cultural phenomenon that is often referred to as 'dagong poetry'. This essay looks into who these dagong poets are and examines the political and social significance of their oeuvre.

Bearing Witness to History: *Dagong* Poets from the 1980s to the Present

Wanning SUN

At 2.30pm on 30 September 2014, a slender young man entered a lift in an office building in the industrial area of Longhua district in Shenzhen. The lift took him to the seventeenth floor, where he got out and stopped by a window. For five minutes, he simply gazed at the outside world. He then climbed on to the window ledge and jumped. He died instantly. Before jumping, he had written his last blog post to the world and set it to be published automatically at midnight, as the date changed to 1 October, China's National Day. The title was 'A Brand New Day' (新的一天).

The young man was twenty-four-year-old Xu Lizhi, a native of Guangdong Province, who looked as inconspicuous as any of the multitude of Foxconn's young migrant 'assembly-line workers' (普工) whom I met in Shenzhen while conducting fieldwork between 2015 and 2017. Like most of these workers, Xu had come from a poor family in a rural village and, with no more than high-school education, began working at Foxconn, assembling parts for the iPads and iPhones used by people all over the world.

But perhaps unbeknown to many of his fellow workers, Xu was a poet of extraordinary talent, with a long list of exceptionally powerful, sad, and sensitively rendered poems to his name. One does not have to read too carefully between the lines of his poems to realise that existential angst, and the appeal of ending it by leaving this world, was often on his mind. In a poem entitled 'A Screw Falls to the Ground' (一颗螺丝掉在地上), Xu wrote:

> A screw falls to the ground
> On this evening of an extra shift
> It falls straight down, making a gentle thud when it lands
> Arousing no attention from anybody
> In the same way that a person also fell to the ground
> On a similar night before this.[1]

Xu's suicide marked both the brightest and the darkest moments in the history of China's rural migrant worker literature. Even though Xu was already an accomplished and published poet prior to his death, most people in China had never heard of him; nor had they heard of the so-called *dagong* poetry (打工诗歌). In fact, Xu was the only poet from the '1990s cohort' (九零后) who was included in the authoritative collection *My Poems: Anthology of Contemporary Workers' Poetry* (我的诗篇—当代工人诗典), which features fifty worker-poets born between the 1940s and the 1990s. Qin Xiaoyu, editor of the anthology, included two poems by Xu: 'Terra-Cotta Warriors on the Assembly Line' (流水线上的兵马俑) and 'I Swallowed a Moon Made of Iron' (我咽下一枚铁做的月亮)—both written when the author was working on Foxconn's assembly line.

Like many other workers who also write poems in their spare time, Xu was often referred to as a '*dagong* poet'. But who are the *dagong* poets, and what is the political and social significance of this cultural phenomenon?

Rural–Urban Migration and the Emergence of *Dagong* Poetry

As other contributors to this volume have described, the start of economic reforms in the late 1970s precipitated widescale rural–urban migration, giving rise to a new social identity that has been widely referred to as *nongmingong* (农民工; 'peasant worker'). In the past four decades, this label has been loosely applied to anyone of rural residential status who left the countryside to work in city or suburban areas. While a small percentage of this migrant population has achieved significant gains in socioeconomic status, the majority are still 'working for the boss', which, in Cantonese, is *dagong* (打工)—a term that speaks to the commodification of labour.[2] Unlike *laodong* (劳动)—a word used during the socialist era to describe the respectable work of factory workers and rural peasants—*dagong* connotes the collective experience of being subjugated to the capitalist regime of the workplace, whether it be in the construction, manufacturing, hospitality, or domestic service sectors.

Dagong life in the manufacturing sector usually involves long hours and robot-like, repetitive movements on an assembly line. The assembly line's drudgery, boredom, and punishing effects on the body and soul hardly seem to present themselves as a likely muse for poets. However, despite being exhausted by shift work, malnourished, and mostly without much education, a small number of factory workers choose to write poetry as a way of coping with industrial alienation. Lamenting Xu's death in an online *Zhihu* forum, one commentator said: 'Some people say he probably would not have died if he had not been a poet, but I believe he probably wouldn't have been able to last till today if he hadn't been writing poetry.'[3]

Indeed, since the 1980s, the loneliness brought about by displacement, the hardships of surviving in a hostile city, and the crushing effects of the assembly line have, in various ways, engendered a creative urge among a small number of literary-minded young workers, prompting them to put their sufferings into words, not in spite of, but precisely because of, the lack of intellectual stimulation in their work environment.

The first generation of worker-poets, who are now in their fifties and sixties, started writing in the 1980s, when they first arrived in the city. Several poets from this generation expressed to me their strong belief that the impact of the industrial regime on the human body, as well as the brutality of the local police in their dealings with rural migrants—which was commonplace in the earlier decades of economic reforms—would have gone largely undocumented had they not been chronicled by those worker-poets who had endured them personally. In their poems, as well as from my conversations with these poets, it is clear that *dagong* poets see writing poems as a way of testifying to the sufferings of a generation of migrant workers in those early decades of economic reform. They see their work as having captured the physical and spiritual anguish of a specific social cohort in a bygone era—experiences that are little understood by younger generations of rural migrants, let alone acknowledged by or documented in the official narratives of China's heady journey towards industrialisation and urbanisation.

Although many individual workers might write a poem now and then between shifts and in their spare time, the collective efforts of a few prominent poet activists are what have propelled *dagong* poetry into a minor literary movement. One editorial collective of such activists, led by individuals such as Xu Qiang and Luo Deyuan, was responsible for numerous *dagong* poetry periodicals, online forums, and anthologies in the late 1980s and 1990s, as well as *dagong* poetry festivals. Mostly natives of Sichuan and Hunan provinces, these literary-minded young rural people came to southern China in the 1980s—a decade that witnessed the most rampant and heightened urban and official distrust of and discrimination against rural migrants.

It is also important to note that the emergence of *dagong* literature would not have been able to capture the attention and imagination of the urban, middle-class literary establishment had it not received support from some urban middle-class cultural brokers—individuals who held positions of power in Shenzhen's literary and cultural establishments. For instance, in his capacity as Director of the Shenzhen Special Economic Zone Cultural Research Centre, and later also Deputy Director of the Guangdong Writers' Association, Yang Honghai was one of the first to recognise the significance of *dagong* poetry. A literary critic, cultural bureaucrat, literary judge, and part-time academic in Shenzhen, Yang used his position to publish the work of *dagong* poets in the mid-1980s, taking advantage of a series of initiatives from local governments in the Pearl River Delta to promote an incipient sense of belonging to the new city among its migrant population. Yang is known to have coined the expressions '*dagong* literature' (打工文学) and *dagong* poetry (打工诗歌). Commercial imperatives also played a role in the emergence of *dagong* literature. In the hope of carving out a niche in the world of commercial publishing, established cultural institutions in Shenzhen in the mid-1980s started to publish *dagong* literature, including novels, novellas, and poems depicting the *dagong* experience, making them an integral, though minor, part of contemporary urban literature in southern China.[4]

Industrial Machine, Hometown, and Existential Angst

Most *dagong* poems, especially those written by earlier generations of poets, vividly document the urban hostility, hunger, and exhaustion that result from joblessness, sleeping rough, and endless drifting from place to place. Apart from the experience of discrimination in the city, the alienating life of long hours on the assembly line and subhuman treatment by management are other recurring themes. *Dagong* poets describe their sensory experience of being assaulted by the industrial machine in aural or visual terms. Some describe their haptic experience of the metallic surfaces of tools. These details not only provide the recurrent *mise en scène* of everyday life for *dagong* individuals, but can also be read as metaphors, as well as the exteriorisation of the alienated soul trapped in the initial stages of transnational capitalist accumulation. This is most vividly illustrated by Zheng Xiaoqiong, one of the few women *dagong* poets. Born in 1980 and a native of Sichuan, Zheng straddles the first generation and the two so-called new migrant generations (新生代农民工): those born in the 1980s (八零后) or the 1990s (九零后)—the latter of which includes Xu Lizhi. Zheng went to Dongguan and worked in a metallurgy factory for six years but spent all her spare time writing poems. Her early works prominently feature metal, with iron as the most significant recurring motif, vividly and imaginatively evoking the sensations of the human body under the impact—literal or metaphorical—of metal (chopped fingers, crushed limbs, bruised skin, piercing metallic assaults on the eardrums). No longer in control of its own movement, the worker's body is 'repetitive motion and localised pain, a nervous system calibrated to machinic pulsations'.[5] Zheng has been compared to Allen Ginsberg—whose poems she admires—for her 'Pedestrian Overpass' (人行天桥). This epic poem features an individual who is crushed and twisted by the pressure of the industrial regime, howling at the world from the top of a pedestrian overpass.[6]

What is unmistakably resonant in Zheng's poems, and those of many other *dagong* poets, is a sense of alienation from the industrial process that threatens to take away workers' individual identities and turn them into machines. In one of her poems, 'Life' (生活, 2007), she writes:

> My name has turned into mere information on an ID card
> My hands have been welded onto the assembly line
> My body has been contracted out
> My hair is turning from black to white.
> This is a life without a name and without gender
> This is a life already contracted out.
> Moonlight shines onto the eight-bunk iron-framed beds in my dormitory
> Illuminating homesickness, furtive romance, suspicious youth
> If this moon was shining from my hometown in Sichuan
> It would at least rekindle memories of my youth
> If only to be dashed by a seven-day week spent on the assembly line.

Zheng's poem also exemplifies the fact that, besides highlighting the alienation of their industrial work, *dagong* poets express a collective nostalgia for the countryside they have left behind, and homesickness for their villages. Even a quick glance at the titles of numerous *dagong* poems reveals that *xiang chou* (乡愁; 'homesickness', or, to be more precise, yearning for one's hometown) is a key term in capturing the melancholic overtone of these works. These yearnings are exacerbated by the everyday reality of drudgery and alienation in the industrial regime, and by the migrant workers' socioeconomic marginality, which, in turn, colours their experiences in the factory. In many of these poems, the home village takes on a heightened emotional significance. Even though the poverty and backwardness of the village are what drove the poets to the city in the first place, it now becomes an emotional resource in their attempts to endure physical, emotional, and mental hardships in the city.[7]

In contrast to the older migrant cohorts, who see themselves as sojourners in the city, the younger generations have little attachment to the rural farming life. Their existential predicament is summarised in the saying that they face 'a countryside they can't return to, and a city that doesn't want them to stay' (回不去的乡村, 留不下的城市). Unlike the earlier generations of *dagong* poems, which document the punishing hardships of life and work, the poems of younger poets tend to be narratives of spiritual homelessness, featuring a sense of uncertainty, hopelessness, profound disenchantment, and, in some severe cases, a widespread sense of anomie, which, according to Durkheim, can lead individuals into self-destructive acts, including suicide.[8] In this light, Xu Lizhi's decision to end his life can be seen as a final poetic expression of the collective sense of anomie within this cohort.

Readership and Social Impact

It may not be surprising to learn that few rural migrant workers read *dagong* poetry, even though their lives are its subject. It seems that most workers do not want to spend their precious downtime reading about boredom and hard factory work—something they already know very well. The grinding, day-to-day reality of a subaltern existence may be a palatable topic for those who do not experience it, but it has no novelty value for subalterns themselves, most of whom would consider *dagong* poems to be too close to their own lives for comfort. This general lack of interest in *dagong* poetry is certainly the impression I got from my conversations with Foxconn workers. At the same time, *dagong* poets such as Zheng Xiaoqiong are always keen to see their poems read by fellow workers. Some labour advocacy nongovernmental organisations (NGOs) with which I have worked also distribute workers' poems as a way of raising awareness of workers' rights and forging solidarity among workers.

At the same time, *dagong* poetry has made some inroads into the mainstream literary landscape in China, although not without contestation. As with rural migrant artists who face the question of whether they are 'true artists', worker-poets are also divided about the label '*dagong* poets', with some rejecting it, believing the expression implies inferiority in terms of both the poets' social status and the aesthetic quality of their work.[9] Others are concerned about losing workers' distinctive social identity—and hence the social and political significance of their work—if they are described simply as poets. Within the literary/scholarly establishment, some argue that *dagong* poetry, by documenting the social lives of subalterns, brings fresh authenticity to the stale atmosphere of the literary elite, while others believe that there is only good poetry and bad poetry, and that judgements should be made solely on aesthetic grounds.[10]

For the same reason that it is difficult to make an accurate estimation of how many workers call themselves *dagong* poets, it is equally difficult to determine the exact scale and composition of the readership of their poetry. Quite a few anthologies of *dagong* poetry have been published recently by conventional book publishing channels, to be purchased mostly by educated urban readers in cultural institutions such as universities, the media, and those literary associations that take an interest in migrant workers' lives. It is also significant that the great majority of *dagong* poems are published outside the purview of official publishers. Some self-published collections do not have an ISBN number, and labour NGOs often publish workers' poems in their newsletters. Also, thanks to the ubiquity of digital forums, many worker-poets have taken advantage of online publication options. Some poets told me that publishing poems online, especially those with sharply political and social criticisms, also has the advantage of bypassing censorship, to which established publishers are subject. Favourite poems, or a few favourite lines from a poem, can easily find their way on to people's mobile phones, be it via blogs, social media subscriptions, or discussion forums.

Beside a small number of middle-class urban readers, numerous scholars, especially sociologists, have turned to *dagong* poetry to mine valuable—albeit not objectively or dispassionately collected—data. Increasingly, *dagong* poems are cited by scholars of labour conditions in China as firsthand accounts of the unacceptable living and working conditions of rural migrant factory workers. In a number of scholarly papers by sociologists and anthropologists both inside and outside China, lines from poems by and about such workers have been used as realistic cultural expressions of their experience.[11] This practice of quoting workers' poems in scholarly work implicitly endorses the empirical significance of these self-expressions.

Finally, *dagong* poetry has captured the imagination of some literary and artistic circles outside China. Some poems have been translated into foreign languages, and, from time to time, accomplished *dagong* poets are invited to speak to international audiences as part of writers' festivals and other literary and cultural events. These poems give readers outside China a valuable glimpse of what life is like for China's workers, and, by implication, of the impact of China's economic reforms and social changes on individuals. Zheng Xiaoqiong, for instance, has had her works translated into English, German, Japanese, Indonesian, Vietnamese, French, Spanish, and Korean, and she has been invited to talk about her work in the United States, Europe, Australia, and various Asian countries. In 2015, a German theatre director, K. Baumbecker, took his plays based on Zheng's poems to be staged in Beijing, and in 2018, Zheng's poem 'An Iron Nail' (铁钉) was performed in Cincinnati featuring two percussionists as well as the poet's own voice. Frederik Bous, a German composer, has written a symphonic piece about the nocturnal scream of Zhou Yangchun, one of the 100 women featured in Zheng's *Stories of Migrant Women Workers* (女工记).[12] A few US-based translators such as Eleanor Goodman and Xiaojing Zhou have dedicated their time to translating Zheng Xiaoqiong's poems into English. And a small but growing number of scholars based outside China have dedicated themselves to the study of this socially and politically significant cultural phenomenon.[13]

Summarising the social significance of *dagong* poetry, Qin Xiaoyu says:

> Workers' poems, even if they are just about their own lives, should be seen as testimonials on behalf of the entire cohort of 200 million workers who share the same destiny. They bear witness to the lives lived at the bottom of society.[14]

It is precisely for this reason that Xu Lizhi is still remembered by others after his suicide. His poems, alongside the poems written by many other worker-poets, continue to bear witness to the history of China's social transformation, rural-to-urban migration, and industrialisation, as well as the alienating impact of these processes on Chinese workers.

2014

In April 2014, more than 40,000 workers at a Yue Yuen Footwear complex in Dongguan went on strike. Not only was this one of the biggest collective actions at a single company in the history of Chinese labour, but also it made headlines because this was one of the earliest and most visible instances of migrant workers mobilising collectively to protest against a company's malpractice related to pension and other social security payments. This highlighted shifts in the demography of China's migrant workforce, as well as in the broader Chinese political economy.

The Yue Yuen Strike
Marc BLECHER

From 14 April to 29 April 2014, 43,000 of the 60,000 workers at the Yue Yuen (YY) Footwear complex in Gaobu, Dongguan, staged the biggest strike at a single enterprise in Chinese history.[1] Their walkout resulted from significant changes in the political economy of global value chains, especially increased competition among oligopolistic producers (which exerted downward pressure on wages and profits) and their growing power *vis-à-vis* the brands for whom they produced (which created opportunities for workers). It brought to the fore new strata of workers—especially the first generation of middle-aged migrants to have accumulated long experience of private sector factory work under structural reforms—who focused on what, for migrants, were pressing new issues, especially, given their age, pensions (which previously had mainly concerned urban resident workers in state-owned enterprises). The strikers evinced the politics involved, bringing into sharp focus questions of collusion between the interests of capital and those of the local developmental state, while emphasising the latter's relative autonomy and its capacity to pressure individual enterprises for its own interest. Finally, though, the outburst confirmed and reproduced the ongoing hegemony of the state and capital over the Chinese working class.

The Background

Founded in Taiwan in 1969, Yue Yuen Industrial (Holdings) Limited is the world's largest footwear producer, boasting 20 percent of global market share.[2] It opened its first factory in China in 1988. In 2013, its 413,000 employees turned out 313.4 million pairs of shoes, for which the company reported gross profits of US$1.6 billion on turnover of US$7.6 billion.[3] Its customers include Nike, Adidas, Reebok, Puma, Asics, Under Armour, New Balance, and Timberland.[4]

But, under pressure from increasing competition both in China and globally and rising labour costs in Dongguan, the Gaobu complex had been declining economically from its glory days of the 2000s: employment shrank from a peak of 100,000 to 60,000 by 2014, and the company went from something of a model of 'corporate social responsibility' and welfare provision to paying an average wage of barely half that in Dongguan.[5] As a result, YY Gaobu had experienced 'countless' small strikes since 2011.[6]

While YY had extended state pension contributions to all its workers in 2008, it simultaneously reduced its payments through several illegal practices, such as basing pensions on the prevailing local minimum wage instead of its workers' actual wages, listing permanent workers as temporary, failing to make its own contributions in addition to those deducted from the workers' wages, and failing to contribute to the local government housing fund for workers. Its total arrears came to between 100 and 200 million yuan (roughly US$16 to US$32 million). These depredations were perpetrated with the connivance of the local government.[7]

The Strike

In early 2014, line supervisors and white-collar workers began to learn about all this, and started to discuss a collective response, including mass resignation. They found their smoking gun when one managerial employee with more than two decades of seniority applied for retirement only to discover that her pension fund contained only 600 yuan.[8] On 5 April, workers at the #1 Sole Plant, whose workers were historically among the most timid in the YY complex, downed tools in a wildcat strike and blocked the bridge to the plant. When the police beat one worker, the strike grew to several thousand. YY managed to calm the situation by promising a resolution by 14 April. When 15 April dawned with no response, 43,000 workers from across the many plants in the complex walked out. YY then came to the negotiating table, but when, on 17 April, it offered to rectify future pension contributions while claiming that the local government would not allow the company to address the arrears, the strike went ballistic. The local government, aided by the official trade union, responded with arrests, which, within a few days, brought out poignant protests by the wives and children of the detainees. Despite the customary news blackout, social networks and word-of-mouth carried the information quickly to a YY plant in Jiangxi Province, causing a strike there. International supporters staged protests at Adidas shops on five continents. On 21 April, YY made a further announcement—this time to the Hong Kong Stock Exchange, to calm jittery investors (eventually, the strike would cost YY US$27 million). The company agreed to start making pension and housing fund payments (without specifying the salary bases, though), to add a living allowance, and to pay the pension arrears but only if the workers did so as well in a lump sum. The last point enraged the strikers still further, since none of them had anything close to the resources to match the payment. The workers instead demanded 'a new contract, improved working conditions, better funded government housing, an enshrined right to hold a union election within the plant, concrete assurances against employer retribution, and a transparent and accountable government to execute and administer the above'.[9] The strikers' demands had transcended the economic to include significant political ones—the government's worst nightmare.

A week later, though, the strike had wound down. On the surface, there were several reasons, none particularly novel or surprising. YY had offered enough concessions to produce grudging acquiescence among a sufficient phalanx of workers who, after all, were not being paid. And the 'concession' on arrears was crafted cleverly to make it unaffordable for the workers. Repression had wrought its intended effect, too. But beneath the veneer of 'mere events' lay a range of structural factors that speak to the strike's eventual collapse but also to its extraordinary character as one of the biggest labour mobilisations in Chinese history and to its wider implications and significance.

The Political Economy

As noted above, by 2014, the YY plant had been in economic decline for quite a few years, squeezed between rising wage levels in Dongguan and increasing pressure from lower-wage producers elsewhere in China and abroad, including other YY plants. In the late 2000s, the company had provided a range of social services, including daycare, healthcare, education, and entertainment facilities, and had banned exploitative practices such as forced, uncompensated overtime. All this had aided labour recruitment.[10] But, by the dawn of the 2010s, a growing wage and bonus gap in comparison with other Dongguan employers began to overshadow prior gains. The YY strike is widely understood as having had pension and housing fund contributions at its core. What is overlooked is the very significant role that low wages played as well. Witness this exchange between a young activist and an older worker:

> Young activist: When I heard that you guys went on strike for social security, I was a little surprised because I don't care about that and nor do my friends. So I thought there must be something else going on.
> Veteran: Hah, you're smart! That's right. Social security is just the main excuse for the strike. Breaking the law when it comes to social security is so prevalent that nobody will do anything about it.[11]

Moreover, the focus on pensions—which is understandable since it catalysed the walkout—may ultimately have undermined the workers' solidarity and their strike:

> Young activist: Of course, I am also a worker. A pay raise of 30 percent is a demand that probably unites all the workers. It is a pity that few people mentioned that and just focussed on making up the social security in arrears or dissolving the labour relationship with a one-off [severance] payment.
> Veteran: Yeah. Initially workers just wanted to vent their anger because we've been suppressed by the boss for too long, but then our grievances gradually evolved into some specific demands, bit by bit. Workers just wanted to take the employer down but they were very tough to deal with. Those Taiwanese bosses even said 'You mainland Chinese are just cheap,' so we all wanted to ruin the factory and get compensation payments before we left. The original goal was just to get a raise for the workers.[12]

Deeper structural forces were also at work. As the new century dawned, a major shift in the relationship between producers and the global brands that are their customers was under way. Whereas previously the brands exerted significant oligopsonistic power over the myriad small producers, now oligopolistic large industrial firms began to emerge as formidable competitors for the brands with which they contracted.

This created a web of contradictory forces. On the one hand, YY had the scale and resources to establish itself as something of a 'model employer', providing a range of social services, while dominating the local labour market to keep wages low. Moreover, the 2008 Labour Contract Law, which introduced mandatory pension schemes, increased pressure on workers to stay with the same employer (since pensions are not portable), which of course increased employers' power *vis-à-vis* workers. All this ratcheted up YY's leverage at the level of the political economy.

But, on the other hand, that same power made it more vulnerable to demands not just from workers but also from its corporate customers, both of whom saw its deep pockets. As Ashok Kumar has argued: 'Striking workers had an intuitive sense of YY's power in the global supply chain and the efficacy of a large and escalating strike.'[13] Indeed, in reflecting on the outcome of the strike, one worker said as much: 'Yue Yuen won't last much longer in Dongguan. It has been discredited by the strike, and its customers will definitely reduce orders.'[14] Having achieved its impressive market share by virtue of its logistical and technological sophistication, the company could ill afford to create interruptions in its supply chain or anger retail customers for its international clients, especially now the latter were facing growing codes of labour conduct. YY's size also made it dependent on investors, as we have seen. Finally, YY's dominance of footwear production made it something of a trendsetter in the industry, as its competitors were forced to copy its promised benefits to recruit workers.[15]

The Political Sociology

The strike evinced significant roles for one group of actors who have not commonly been involved in labour activism, and another whose participation has been commonly overlooked.

The former were middle-aged and older rural-born migrant workers who arrived in China's cities in the 1990s and stayed. Previously, of course, they had not been very numerous, as most of the original first wave of migrants were young people. However, by 2014, as one of them put it:

> All Yue Yuen factories have a lot of senior workers. About 70 percent of the workers have been here for more than five years, and 10–15 percent of them have been here ten years ... Many of them came to Yue Yuen at eighteen or nineteen-years-old, and now even their children work here.[16]

This cohort was assumed to be less radical than younger workers, whether because of suppositions about their gender (70–75 percent of all YY workers were women), age, and/or their having become inured over many years to the realities of factory work and life. But not so:

> Many women workers in their thirties and forties I know were very vigorous and determined in the strike, and I have great admiration for them. I know two women from the Old No. 3 Plant, both in their thirties ... but they were both actively involved in the strike. Although they were not well educated, they stick to a simple belief that the company cannot bully workers, and that we are just claiming what is rightfully ours.[17]

One reason for their determination may have been that women have to retire at age fifty, ten years earlier than men, so they felt the pressure about their pensions more urgently. Moreover, there was a definite degree of solidarity among the older workers that extended between them and younger workers:

> Veteran: Senior workers know and trust each other, so of course they are united. Many of them are related because most of the workers were introduced by fellow villagers or relatives working here.
> Young activist: In this strike, I heard the 'auntie-workers' were often rebuked by the younger ones. What is the real situation?
> Veteran: Actually, the 'rebuke' by younger workers you mentioned is not based on objective reporting.[18]

The second group whose participation in strikes had been less frequently recognised were line supervisors:

> Veteran: In Yue Yuen, it often happens that a Taiwan[ese] guy [higher up in management] wants to punish a section head, but the latter gets together with his fellow villager, also a section head, to mobilise workers for a strike.
> Young activist: Is such mobilisation frequent?
> Veteran: Yes, I've often heard about such stories.
> Young activist: So this strike was directed by the section heads?

> Veteran: They didn't publicly direct the strike; they did it secretly because this is related to their vital interests.[19]

This account suggests that the cleavage between Taiwanese and mainlanders also helped create some solidarity between line managers and workers. But, because of their greater influence and shopfloor power, the line supervisors also had the capacity to bring the strike under control:

> Veteran: Maybe this strike would have continued until May Day if the leaders hadn't urged the workers to get back to work. You've seen people saying in the QQ chat group that the leaders got money from the employer, so they were willing to get the workers back to work. But I don't have any evidence, so I am not sure.[20]

The role of line managers in catalysing labour protests in China is far from unique to YY.[21] It also maps onto the important role of older workers and calls for further study.[22]

Finally, another set of actors, labour nongovernmental organisations (NGOs), did not prove particularly important to the mobilisation—contrary to what some scholars and observers originally thought. It is true that several tried to become involved, and two of their leaders, Lin Dong and Zhang Zhiru, were even detained. But, on the whole, the YY strike was propelled by the workers themselves.

The Politics

In terms of workers' own politics, three points are particularly notable. First, whether or not they knew it, the YY workers were taking advantage of, and benefited from, the political opportunity created by the government's anticorruption drive that was gaining momentum at the time.[23] The strikers' chants often accused the government of corruption and complicity, and YY workers complained that 'the factory has been tricking us for ten years … the district government, labour bureau, social security bureau and the company were all tricking us together'.[24]

Second, the workers achieved previously unheard-of levels of organisation:

> Young activist: From the Internet I know there was a strike in 2011 as well. It seems there were many small-scale strikes in the past?

> Veteran: That was at the Yucheng Shoe Factory, part of Yue Yuen (Pou Chen Group). Small-scale strikes, countless! Those strikes were usually caused by some policies in a single plant, but there had never been a strike in which all the plants united as one. This is a milestone, escalating the strike from one plant to the whole factory. Moreover, those earlier strikes were all spontaneous, but this time workers carried banners and yelled out their demands. It was a big step forward.[25]

Third, the strike inspired similar stoppages in China and Vietnam over the next two years in other YY plants, those of its competitors, and even other sectors.[26] It also helped those fellow strikers win some gains, as all those walkouts were settled quickly.

The state's politics reflected many of its customary features. First, the local government helped cause the problem in the first place by colluding with YY to enhance accumulation—a key state goal—by rigging the social insurance and housing fund systems.[27] Second, the government demonstrated its tried and true carrot-and-stick approach and deployed a wide range of mechanisms to end the strike. The official 'union' federation offered to mediate the dispute at first, which workers welcomed until the union and the police turned against them, the latter with beatings and by locking some workers inside or out of their plants. Of course, the state also created a news blackout. But local governments generally prefer peaceful resolutions—what Lee and Zhang term 'bargained authoritarianism'.[28] So, ultimately, they forced YY to make concessions, and also increased enforcement of the laws on social insurance.[29]

Finally, though, the YY strike evinces all the features of state and market hegemony that continue to keep the Chinese working class subordinated and exploited. Politically, Chan and Hui put it well:

> [The] bedrock of China's labour-intensive and export-led development model is the unorganised working class. For this reason, when workers start to better organise themselves and pursue their demands by means of collective action, the Chinese government seeks to find ways to address them and make concessions.[30]

The fact the workers tried to organise themselves through the state-run 'union' federation, which failed yet again, proves that Chinese labour relations are still trapped in a 'monistic' rather than even a 'state corporatist' institutional arrangement.[31] That is, the state refuses to incorporate the working class. Ideologically, workers lack self-confidence individually, much less as a class. This can be seen in the following exchange:

> Young activist: Do you think the Yue Yuen workers can form a stable organisation after this strike?
> Veteran: Not really. Although they are [classified by the state and in social discourse as] 'workers', it's hard to form a solid trade union because they still think like peasants. It is a shame that we are always meek until pushed into a corner. There is a saying that a baited rabbit may grow as fierce as a lion, but how many man-eating rabbits have you seen?
> Veteran: Gaobu is my second home and Yue Yuen is like my family. For many workers, this is a simple and honest feeling. We were once proud to be Yue Yuen workers. We just want a decent job and a dignified life. We love the Communist Party and our homeland, and we hope our country can develop better.[32]

The above analysis draws on Nicos Poulantzas's theory of the relative autonomy of the state: the idea that the state must have the capacity to mollify the working class to better establish its own hegemony on behalf of capital.[33] If striking YY workers won half a loaf—or, this being China, half a steamed bun—the price they paid was not just the forgone other half, but also, like the rest of China's beleaguered proletariat, their continued subordination to the hegemony of the Chinese state and its ally in global capitalism.

2015

In spite of the myth that China has a fundamentally unlimited pool of low-cost workers from the countryside, starting from the early 2000s, employers in certain areas of the country found themselves dealing with periodic shortages of labour—a phenomenon commonly known as a 'labour famine' (民工荒). The causes of such shortages include changes in the demographic structure of the Chinese population induced by the One-Child Policy, the higher educational levels achieved by Chinese workers in a market that still largely needs unskilled labour, the growing labour demand in less-developed areas that drained the workforce from more advanced regions, and the persistent precariousness of the migrant life. At the same time, increased labour activism was driving up wages. To address some of these issues, firms began to adopt technological upgrading. By 2013, China was already the world's largest market for industrial robots. Two years later, in 2015, the central authorities released the 'Made in China 2025' plan, a three-step strategy aimed at moving China up the value chain by 2025 and making it a leading manufacturing power by 2035. This essay examines how this technological upgrading is affecting Chinese workers.

Replacing Humans with Machines
HUANG Yu

In 2015, the inauguration of a 'workerless factory' in Dongguan made headlines in China's major newspapers.[1] On the shopfloor of a mobile phone module manufacturer, conveyor belts were staffed not by dispirited and sweating workers, but by robots executing repetitive pre-programmed tasks. This 'futuristic' scenario made the firm eligible for subsidies offered by the local government's 'Replacing Humans with Machines' (机器换人) policy.

In the mid 2010s, amid growing concerns about shortages of migrant workers and labour unrest, governments in various industrial cities in China issued policy incentives similar to Dongguan's efforts to push manufacturers to upgrade their technology.[2] China became the largest market for industrial robots in 2013, but the pace of robotisation further accelerated in 2015 after the central government launched the 'Made in China 2025' (MiC 2025) plan—an initiative that aimed to promote automated manufacturing as a means of moving Chinese industry up the global value chain. By 2019, 140,500 new robots were sold nationwide—a twofold increase from five years earlier.[3]

How technological upgrading affects workers, however, remains a controversial issue, as testified by the decades-long debate about whether automation technologies are labour-substituting or labour-augmenting.[4] The Chinese case has captured global attention not only because of the potential risks imposed on such a huge workforce, but also due to a surging wave of labour activism happening alongside the robotisation process.[5] Will Chinese workers fight for a proper share of the 'robot dividend'? How will China's trajectory of technological upgrading differ from that of the Global North? The purpose of this essay is to analyse the impact of industrial automation on Chinese workers. Based on both my own field research and a review of recent studies, this essay will develop a discussion in two parts: first, it will gauge the impact of industrial automation on employment and labour skills; second, it will assess workers' reactions to the new technologies.

The Impact of Automation on Employment

Although Chinese firms have been engaging in technological upgrading for only a few years, the labour-substituting effect has been quite alarming. My own research in four factories in Dongguan identifies a dramatic reduction in the labour force, ranging between 67 and 85 percent per production line.[6] Dongguan official data show that, by early 2017, about 200,000 workers had been made redundant by the 2,698 awarded upgrading programs, translating to a replacement rate of seventy-four workers per program.[7] A recent study of 299 manufacturing firms that adopted technological upgrading in Guangdong Province showed each firm fired an average of ninety-six employees, accounting for 9.58 percent of the total workforce.[8] On the shopfloor, about 80 percent of positions could easily be replaced with machines.

However, so far, we have not witnessed a large number of the workers made redundant by technological upgrading being thrown onto the streets. There are several reasons. First, firms upgraded their equipment gradually rather than resorting to wholesale shifts to new automated lines. Such incremental arrangements gave companies time to adjust workers' positions and limit new recruitment.[9] Second, taking advantage of migrant workers' high turnover rate and specific wage structure, most employers did not have to actively dismiss workers, but used other tactics to force workers to quit on their own initiative. For instance, in the case of Dongguan, overtime pay usually accounts for about two-thirds of a worker's average monthly income. An employer who wants to make workers redundant need only reduce their overtime tasks to push them to resign, with the additional advantage for the company of not having to pay otherwise mandatory severance pay. Third, a few firms were able to absorb the surplus labour by expanding their production lines; however, that is contingent on the firm's position in the value chain as well as its broader market status. For instance, in the automotive industry, carmakers who reap the lion's share of profits may be more able to boost production than lower-tier suppliers. However, since 2017, in the face of a massive decline in growth and mounting overcapacity, workers' employment security has started to come under threat even in the Chinese car industry.

Impact on Workers' Skills

The impact of automation on workers' skills is equally controversial. Since Harry Braverman inaugurated the de-skilling thesis in the 1970s, many of his followers have demonstrated how the introduction of automated technologies facilitates the separation of 'concept' and 'execution', forcing machinists to change from being craft workers to operators who are deprived of any planning responsibility.[10] In contrast, the 'high skills' hypothesis argued that computerisation would augment workers' intellectual skills, such as responsibility, socialisation, and responsiveness to fast-changing situations.[11] Later, both these arguments were criticised for their technological determinism.[12] William Form proposes that skill changes depend on the 'type of technology, industrial organization, product and labor markets, labor union strength, business power, and many other factors'.[13] Therefore, the introduction of advanced machines alone does not automatically raise labour skills; the provision of training remains essential.[14]

In the case of China, researchers have revealed the difficulties operators have to confront to improve workers' skills. Deng and Xu have argued that, contrary to the conventional belief that automated machines alleviate manual drudgery and therefore facilitate women's upskilling and empowerment, women workers are offered much less inhouse training than their male counterparts because most employers uphold an ideology of gender stereotyping that considers women to be 'fearful of machines' or deficient in logical thinking.[15] Yong has shown that, in the firms that adopt automation, managerial personnel and technical engineers receive more training than operators: thirty-two and twenty-six days, respectively, for managers and technicians, versus nine days for workers.[16]

Similar to Braverman's observation, the process of de-skilling is quite prominent among skilled craftspeople in China. Autor, Levy and Murane have demonstrated that automation substitutes routine tasks that can be accomplished by following explicit rules while complementing workers in solving nonroutine problems.[17] My research has discovered that skilled craftspeople are often the main target for job replacement due to their high wages and enhanced bargaining power. For example, in Dongguan, a veteran carpenter earns between 6,000 and 8,000 yuan per month, while a proficient helmet shell cutter makes 5,000 yuan per month—much higher than the local average of 3,489 yuan in 2015. In the automotive industry, multiskill work (多能工) systems and job rotation have helped workers develop comprehensive skills that make them difficult to replace. However, after technological upgrading, although most of these versatile workers can keep their positions, as automation largely simplifies work, they have become less valuable to employers.[18]

The MiC 2025 initiative has laid out how China should transform from a manufacturer known for its quantity to one renowned for quality through the development of 'Four Base' (四基) sectors: core infrastructure components, advanced basic technology, core basic materials, and industrial infrastructure technology. Such a transition requires not only the engagement of research and development engineers, but also, more importantly, skilled workers who possess factory processing experience. This is because the complexity of the material world rejects any simple codification, requiring instead the participation of highly motivated, experienced workers.[19]

However, considering that China's past development path has hinged on labour-intensive production and low-skill manual work, many manufacturers are either slow or reluctant to take up labour retraining. Among the eight manufacturers I studied in Dongguan, only one invested in training workers, and this was because the company engages in high-precision metalwork that requires substantial levels of skill in the production process. Mr Zhou, the owner of a firm that produces high-end parts for optical-fibre communication equipment, chose to automate to achieve *quality* improvement, not just larger output. Building on his previous experience working in a state-owned enterprise, he set up an inhouse apprenticeship program to train skilled workers who, after training, could handle tasks such as changing fixtures and jigs, adjusting computer numerical control machines and, eventually, participate in designing the production process.[20] He understood that, while technology was important, the true value of the machines could be harnessed only if the technology was combined with the relevant and appropriate human-embedded skills. In his words: 'Machinery is something everybody can buy, but a good production process [工艺流程] needs to be designed. One component is hardware and the other is *software*.' As a small and medium-sized enterprise, the case of Mr Zhou's company is quite exceptional. Given the high turnover rate, very few employers in Dongguan are willing to invest in workers' training.

Workers' Reactions to Technological Upgrading

The above discussion shows how industrial automation leads to a trend of labour substitution and de-skilling. But how have workers reacted to the introduction of advanced machines? Recent research has revealed that most frontline operators maintain an indifferent or even welcoming attitude towards automation. According to a survey conducted by Yang and Luo among car suppliers in the Pearl River Delta in 2017, almost 75 percent of frontline production workers believed it was rational for their enterprises to automate, with only about 20 percent disagreeing.[21] Another survey, conducted among workers employed in the manufacturing industry in nineteen cities in Guangdong Province, indicates that more than half of the informants considered themselves replaceable with automation in the next five to ten years.[22] However, only about 28 percent worried about unemployment, while 62 percent thought it would be easy to find a new job.

Most workers I interviewed internalised the mainstream discourse on automation as social and economic advancement, thus viewing technological upgrading as inevitable progress. Mr Gang, a migrant worker from Henan Province employed in an electronics factory in Dongguan, whom I interviewed, highlighted the advantages of automation in these terms:

> I used to be a farmer. Initially farming was manual work. The crops 100 farmers grew were not enough to feed 100 people. Now [with machines], two farmers can feed 100 people. With automation, fewer workers will be needed as per capita productivity increases.

In the aftermath of a spate of suicides at Foxconn in 2010, the owner, Terry Gou, announced he would introduce one million robots to replace workers (see Jenny Chan's essay in the present volume).[23] My colleagues and I interviewed some workers still employed by the firm in 2018 and were surprised to find they were indifferent to these developments, as exemplified by the following exchange:

Q: Do you feel worried about being replaced with robots?

A: Not quite. To be frank, nobody has forged a strong sense of belonging to the factory. We don't feel at home here. [If I am dismissed,] I can just go to other places.

In comparison, skilled workers, who are more affected by automation and also encounter greater difficulties finding another job given their seniority, tend to show their anxiety. For example, a senior worker in a factory that manufactured bicycle helmets worried about job displacement as robotisation shortened the training period for learning how to cut venting holes from six months to only three days. Several firms changed their payment system from piece rates to time rates as the pace of work became dependent less on a labourer's skills and motivation, and more on the cycle time preset in the machine. One worker in an electronics factory whom I interviewed lamented: 'Previously human beings controlled the machine. We could work according to our own pace. Afterwards, machines control humans.' This means workers not only fail to assert their agency through the 'making out' game described by Michael Burawoy as a form of competitive game workers play in piece-rate labour regimes, but also find it difficult even to passively slow the pace of work.[24]

Still while quite a few skilled workers voiced their discontent with automation, very few were actually taking action to defend their rights. In this essay, I will discuss the only two cases of collective action that veteran workers undertook over technological upgrading. These cases reveal the barriers these workers encountered in technological decision-making.

Case One

This first case took place in Factory D, a furniture company in Dongguan, where some veteran workers organised a work stoppage to express their anger over automation. Before 2008, the factory produced conventional doors; however, as the Global Financial Crisis hit the domestic real estate market, the boss decided to shift to the production of high-end fireproof doors. The firm then had to accelerate the process of automation as it turned out the special doors needed to be laminated with asbestos—a cancer-causing substance.

In 2011, the factory owner introduced a semiautomatic veneer pressing machine that could accomplish a series of tasks from glue application to pressing the asbestos together. Before automation, veteran workers in the veneer pressing unit were paid at a piece rate, earning about 6,000 yuan per month. In the first month after automation, increased productivity helped boost workers' salary to more than 8,000 yuan. The owner quickly began recruiting younger workers, who were paid only 3,000 yuan per month. The head of the pressing unit became angry because his unit was composed mostly of workers who had been at the plant for more than four years and even a few who had joined the factory at its inception in 2002. After a quick discussion with his fellow workers, the unit head decided to call a strike early one morning. He successfully used his authority to gain the support not only of veteran workers, but also of newly recruited younger ones. They halted production for about two hours before the owner came to yell at them: 'Do you still want to work here or not? If you choose to quit today, I will settle your wages.' The veteran workers suddenly realised they were no longer the backbone of the factory and their skills no longer granted them strong bargaining power. Aged in their forties, most feared that, if they were fired, they would have great difficulty finding another job and therefore quickly returned to their positions. Each striking worker was fined 100 yuan as punishment. After the strike, the owner accelerated the automation process to cover operations of painting and cutting. Later, in their bimonthly assembly, the owner scolded the workers: 'You are just a speck. The factory won't stop without you.'

China's Trade Union Law mandates that twenty-five or more employees must be allowed to form an enterprise trade union as a branch of the umbrella national organisation, the All-China Federation of Trade Unions. However, as a domestic private firm, Factory D did not have a trade union. Therefore, workers had to resort to a wildcat strike to assert their demands. In contrast, workers in the second case study, Factory T, an auto parts supplier with Japanese investment, were able to turn to the trade union as the channel for bargaining.

Case Two

Located in Guangzhou, Factory T manufactures metal frames for car seats for a Japanese auto brand. Due to the increasing wages of welders, in 2011–12, the factory began to introduce welding robots. Since the firm has an enterprise trade union that represents workers to collectively bargain for wage increases every year, a welder with ten years of seniority will make an income double that of a novice.

After robotisation, the management began to request welders be demoted to operators, which meant the 350-yuan subsidy for welding skills would be terminated. As this subsidy was added to the basic income, overtime pay and other benefits would be reduced accordingly. However, as the firm had a collective bargaining system, all important policies had to be passed with workers' consent and many welders refused to sign on to the new policy. After more than a year of back-and-forth negotiation between the trade union and the management, a compromise was reached in which manual welders who performed tasks that robots failed to do would receive a reduced subsidy of 250–300 yuan, but welders-turned-operators would still be offered a low subsidy of 120 yuan.

Workers found it hard to interpret this outcome as a 'victory' for their side because they had already seen the workforce in the factory shrink from 1,000 to 700 in the previous few years. Moreover, the new recruits largely had precarious tenure, including agency workers, temporary workers, and student interns. The firm had already asked some senior workers to quit, promising a severance fee of n+1 months' salary (with 'n' being the number of years of employment). However, most workers rejected this offer as they knew that, with their open-term contract, they were eligible to receive 2 x n months' wages.

Mastering the Machines

From the 1960s to the 1980s, under strong union activism and welfare state labour protection, industrial upgrading in the United States and Japan brought the 'beneficial' effect of increased wages, although the negative consequences of worker de-skilling and union weakening should not be overlooked.[25] In contrast, when the robotic revolution took off in China after the 2008 financial crisis, migrant workers, who had contributed a 'labour dividend' to the national economy in the previous decades, suddenly realised they were doomed to be replaced with robots.

While most frontline operators considered industrial automation to be an inevitable trend, some veteran workers began to question the legitimacy of using machines to replace and degrade labour. However, despite the surge in strikes since the early 2010s (see Chan and Hui's essay in the present volume), we have not seen many reported strikes in which workers demanded a fair share of the 'robot dividend'. The two cases involving workers' collective action described in this essay prove that these activities were at best 'defensive' rather than 'proactive', as workers only demanded the maintenance of current levels of benefits rather than a reasonable share of the surpluses gained through automation.[26] Recent research has confirmed that for some firms that adopted robots, wage increases have lagged far behind the growth in productivity, while in other firms, wages remained stagnant or were even slashed.[27]

Responding to the question of why the government subsidised only the firms that upgraded and not the displaced workers, an official from Dongguan's government told me: 'Now people petition the State Bureau for Letters and Visits to complain about wage arrears and runaway bosses. I haven't heard any case of a petition due to replacement by machines.' His words were revealing, suggesting that fighting for 'robot dividends' had rarely entered into workers' agendas. In most firms, workers have not engaged in the decision-making processes on automation in any form.[28] Even for those firms that have collective bargaining in place, automation is a topic seldom touched on. One union chair at a leading auto supplier even claimed: 'If our company has 1,500 employees instead of 2,000, but profitability remains at 10%, each employee would receive more pay and benefits.'[29] The trade union's focus on immediate economic gains rather than workers' long-term power epitomises the sense of economism that Braverman criticised.

While industrial automation seems new to China, early in the nineteenth century, Marx pointed out that technological upgrading under capitalism meant the exploitation of 'dead labour'—that is, work ossified in the form of a machine—over human workers. However, affected by the mainstream ideology of technological determinism, Chinese workers were slow to see through the meaning behind projects of 'replacing humans with machines'. Only when workers understand the nature of 'dead labour' can they truly become masters of machines.

2015

In the early 2010s, a handful of Chinese labour nongovernmental organisations (NGOs) began to go beyond the narrow legalistic approach that most organisations had taken up to that moment and started teaching workers how to organise themselves to bargain collectively with their employers. As these organisations gained success after success and grew in influence and visibility, the Party-State intervened to rein them in. It all began with a series of arrests at the end of 2015.

Labour NGOs under Assault

Chloé FROISSART and Ivan FRANCESCHINI

> If you talk about the labour movement, the Party, who started to establish itself exactly through the labour movement … gets alarmed. Why? Because this is the way in which they came to power.
>
> — A labour NGO activist in Shenzhen, September 2015
>
> Apparently, the situation has reached a point of no return. It's the same everywhere in the country, as long as you work on labour issues.
>
> — A labour NGO activist in Shenzhen, August 2016

In December 2015, the police detained a couple of dozen labour activists in Guangdong, eventually charging five of them.[1] To signal that this was part of a national political campaign and not a localised incident, Chinese state media decided to make an example of Zeng Feiyang, a prominent activist, and launched a comprehensive attack against his organisation, the Panyu Migrant Workers Centre, a prominent labour nongovernmental organisation (NGO) established in Guangzhou in the late 1990s. It did not take long before Party media outlets published lengthy features accusing Zeng of embezzling funds illegally obtained from foreign donors. Further, these reports attacked his personal character and motivations, claiming he only posed as a 'star of the labour movement' (工运之星) to advance his own interests, at the expense of workers.[2] Eventually, Zeng was handed a prison sentence of three years, suspended for four years. Two of his colleagues received prison sentences of eighteen months, suspended for two years, on the same charge, of 'gathering a crowd to disturb social order', while another, a former security guard named Meng Han, was sentenced to twenty-one months in jail.

Along with activists from a handful of other labour NGOs in the Pearl River Delta, Zeng and his colleagues had been at the forefront of a fundamental shift in how these organisations engaged with the labour movement. Instead of coaching workers on how to seek help through legal channels in the event of a violation of their rights, as had been the prevalent praxis among Chinese labour NGOs since their establishment in the mid to late 1990s, in the early 2010s, these activists began telling workers that they should organise to select their representatives to bargain collectively with their employers. In a situation in which labour representation is monopolised by a single trade union solidly controlled by the Party-State, the implications were huge. As these organisations gained victory after victory and were becoming increasingly visible both nationally and internationally, the authorities intervened to put an end to their activities. This essay looks back at Chinese labour NGOs' experiment with collective bargaining, how it came to be, its significance and what is left in the aftermath.

Guangdong Province: The Hotbed of Rights-Defence NGOs

Since their appearance in the second half of the 1990s, labour NGOs have generally been classified into two broad categories: welfare-oriented organisations and rights-defence organisations (see Howell's essay in this book). Compared with NGOs in cities such as Beijing and Shanghai, NGOs in Guangdong Province, on the whole, have traditionally been oriented towards defending workers' rights. This is mainly due to Guangdong being one of the most industrialised provinces in China and its proximity to Hong Kong, whose NGOs have often nurtured or partnered with Chinese domestic NGOs, connecting them to the values and funding of the international community. Moreover, compared with those in other places in China, Guangdong NGOs were more frequently founded by workers and not a paternalistic urban elite disconnected from workers' needs.[3] The rights-defence drive unfolded following the publication of Document No. 1 of 2003, which emphasised the equality of migrant and urban workers before the labour law and signalled the intention of the central government to use the law as a means to quell rising social discontent. The ensuing education campaigns to teach migrant workers to rely on the law to defend their rights—as opposed to resorting to more disruptive measures, such as strikes and demonstrations—provided an opening for NGOs to widely disseminate information on labour rights, provide legal consultation to migrant workers and encourage them to seek redress through arbitration committees and courts. Along with the passing of a set of new labour laws in 2007 (see Gallagher's essay in the present volume), this led to a dramatic increase in the number of complaints but did not translate into better protection of workers' rights, since the labour institutions were largely unable to meet the needs of the workers. This, in turn, nurtured workers' distrust and encouraged them to keep turning to the streets to voice their demands.[4]

At first, some activists saw such a rights-defence strategy relying on legal norms and institutional channels as a way to mount pressure on the legal system, which could potentially lead authorities to carry out systemic reforms. As one NGO leader pointed out in an interview, paraphrasing Marx: 'A quantitative change can lead to a qualitative change.'[5] However, this view proved wrong, as local authorities chose to emphasise mediation rather than strict legal enforcement.[6] Moreover, this strategy was criticised by scholars and activists alike for sticking to a government-sanctioned, narrowly legalistic definition of rights, thus individualising conflicts and promoting divisions rather than solidarity among workers.[7] Indeed, by exerting pressure on the authorities to reduce the gap between rights promised and rights enforced, the choice of labour NGOs to focus on legal mobilisation compensated for institutional dysfunctions, thus exempting the authorities from carrying out systemic reforms.[8]

From Legal Mobilisation to Collective Bargaining

Several underlying factors led to the shift from legal mobilisation to collective bargaining in the early 2010s. From a pragmatic point of view, the costs and delays of going through an inefficient legal system had a disheartening and demobilising effect on migrant workers. It often happened that workers seeking compensation had to spend more than the amount to which they were entitled, not to mention the huge waste of time the whole process entailed.[9] Moreover, as dramatically epitomised by the Honda strike of 2010, workers had begun to demand what was not provided by law, such as pay rises (see Chan and Hui's essay in the present volume). Such interest-based demands, which cannot be dealt with through the legal system, in other contexts are generally resolved by collective bargaining in the workplace, but the Chinese legal system allows only a watered-down, nonconfrontational form of 'collective negotiation' (集体协商)—a process based on an assumption of substantial unity of interests between companies and workers and largely piloted by the official union, which has notoriously approached its role in a formalistic way.[10] In light of these shortcomings, to this day, most collective contracts in China simply reaffirm minimum standards already provided by the law.

Faced with workers' despair, a handful of Guangdong NGOs (no more than five, including Zeng Feiyang's Panyu Migrant Workers Centre) decided to change strategy hoping to have a broader impact on the system and bring about political change.[11] These organisations were in a good position to initiate such a groundbreaking move under the authoritarian regime. First, each was set up and mainly staffed by workers who had long-term, firsthand experience in rights defence and were committed to defending the rights of their fellow workers. Second, they were partnering with an experienced NGO in Hong Kong that could provide them with the financial autonomy and mentorship necessary to push the experiment forward.[12]

Above all, such an attempt at collective bargaining would not have been possible if the political situation had not been favourable to it. During the Seventeenth Party Congress in 2007, President Hu Jintao had emphasised the need to rely on people's participation to solve social contradictions. This participatory ideology was relayed in Guangdong by Wang Yang, the ambitious provincial secretary in power from November 2007 to January 2013, who sought to boost his political career by capitalising on the reformist tradition of the province to promote a 'social management' model that saw popular participation and social dialogue as the pillars of social stability. The demographic situation was also favourable, insofar as the structural labour shortage (民工荒) that had affected the province from time to time since 2004, had settled from the beginning of the 2010s, giving greater bargaining power to workers.

Teaching Workers How to Bargain

As the leader of one of these NGOs told a journalist in 2014: 'We wish to turn collective striking into collective bargaining and help workers organise their own unions to truly represent their interests.'[13] NGOs did not seek to represent workers but rather to train them to directly engage with employers and, when necessary, with official unions and local authorities. The counselling programs led by NGOs aimed to coach workers on four points: 1) how to frame contentions and prioritise demands; 2) how to turn 'a temporary rally into a stable group solidarity';[14] 3) how to elect representatives; and 4) negotiation strategies.

Through a study of more than forty cases, Froissart has elaborated an ideal type of NGO-led collective bargaining.[15] This type meets the sociological definition of collective bargaining agreed on by Western theorists as a sociopolitical practice based on a voluntary and autonomous organisation of workers that aims to rebalance an inherently conflictual and unequal relationship between employees and employers to improve working conditions.[16] In the cases she analysed, the negotiations were initiated and conducted with employers by democratically elected worker representatives. In China's legal and institutional context, which strongly imbalances labour relations in favour of employers—in particular, by not recognising the rights to strike and organise autonomously—NGOs taught workers how to rebalance this relationship while at the same time circumscribing their demands and modes of action to avoid repression.[17] When neither foot-dragging, occupation of factory premises, nor strikes (actual or threatened) were enough to persuade employers to cave in, workers learned how to put pressure on trade unions and local authorities to help them bring employers to the negotiating table and act as guarantors of genuine collective bargaining.

Maintaining unity and solidarity among workers throughout the negotiation process was key to its success, especially as employers, but also trade unions and local authorities, often resorted to tactics of divide and rule. In most successful cases, negotiations culminated in a collective agreement signed by the workers' representatives and the management, and then submitted for all employees' approval. In some cases, negotiations compelled employers to fully comply with the labour law, including repayment of overdue salaries and social insurance contributions—an outcome that could not have been achieved through individual legal cases, especially as officials usually pressured workers to compromise on their legal rights to ease the financial burden on employers. In other cases, collective bargaining allowed workers to negotiate what was not in the law, such as salary increases and layoff plans. Between 2011 and 2015, workers obtained hundreds of billions of yuan in wages, layoff compensation, social insurance and housing fund contributions and other benefits through collective bargaining.[18]

NGOs also strived to advance a long-term political agenda. Together with worker representatives, activist lawyers and Hong Kong partners, they drew up a code of conduct (released in October 2013) formalising past collective bargaining experiments to serve as a template for future cases and as a reference to influence Guangdong labour law.[19] They also reflected on ways to promote lasting independent representation of workers and, although collective bargaining was not systematised at the workplace, NGOs encouraged workers to reform grassroots unions and workers' committees through their practice.[20]

The Significance of Collective Bargaining

Labour NGOs have enabled the emergence of an authentic 'worker-led collective bargaining' that is substantially different from both Party-State–led collective bargaining triggered by *ad hoc* interventions of high-ranking trade union officials and 'collective bargaining by riot', spontaneously initiated by workers.[21] Indeed, unlike riots, the type of collective bargaining that emerged in Guangdong Province in the first half of the 2010s was well-planned, organised and nonviolent. In some cases, it included several rounds of negotiations that unfolded over months and were based on constructive dialogue between the workers, the employers, the trade union and local authorities. Guangdong NGOs played a fundamental role not only in raising workers' awareness of their collective rights and interests, but also in coaching them on how to exercise these rights by promoting their unity, solidarity and organisational capacities. By exercising their rights to organise autonomously, to democratically elect representatives and to bargain collectively even though these rights were not granted by law, workers emerged as a political force able to change the rules of the game in the workplace, engage over the long term with employers, trade unions and local authorities and change the way the latter dealt with labour conflicts. Indeed, by foiling the tactics of the local authorities to depoliticise labour conflicts and forcing them instead to act as guarantors of collective rights, workers, supported by NGOs, proved they were able to negotiate authoritarianism.[22]

The Guangdong NGOs supporting collective bargaining had become fully fledged worker organisations, not only in the sociological sense of the term (formed by workers), but also in a broader political sense. Although some NGO staff were sceptical about the term 'labour movement'—partly out of fear of the term's sensitivity and partly because they had not yet achieved stronger and broader worker solidarity beyond the workplace and beyond Guangdong Province—NGOs truly were the brains of this movement, infusing it with short-term strategies but also a longer-term agenda, which could have challenged the very foundations of the Chinese authoritarian regime had it been allowed to continue.[23]

The End of the Experiment

The crackdown of 2015 had a chilling effect not only on the labour NGOs at the forefront of collective bargaining, but also on those engaged in traditional rights defence.[24] Many organisations chose to subordinate themselves to the authorities and focus on less-sensitive activities, such as those related to corporate social responsibility and welfare provisions, or by abandoning any semblance of formal organisation and going underground to operate as individual activists.

Although some organisations did not immediately abandon collective bargaining, they significantly adjusted their approach, becoming more selective in their case screening process, warning workers of the potential dangers and avoiding potentially disruptive situations.[25] Still, even this watered-down version of collective bargaining was too much for the Party-State. In January 2019, the Chinese authorities proceeded with the coordinated arrest and indictment for 'gathering a crowd to disrupt public order' of an additional five labour NGO activists who in the past had played some role in promoting collective bargaining. This happened in the wake of another crackdown that targeted workers at Shenzhen Jasic Technology, a company specialising in the manufacturing of welding machinery (see Elfstrom's essay in the present volume). During the summer of 2018, Jasic workers, prodded by underground Maoist activists, mobilised to demand, among other concessions, the right to establish their own workplace union—a request that was met with harsh, coordinated repression by the employer and the local government, which in turn triggered expressions of solidarity from groups of Marxist students all over the country.[26] Significantly, although labour NGOs were not directly involved in the Jasic mobilisation, the Party-State attempted to blame a Shenzhen-based labour NGO with ties to Hong Kong civil society. After this round of arrests, what remained of labour NGOs from the previous crackdown was decimated.

As the Chinese authorities reined in the most militant sections of Chinese civil society through a mix of new legal rules and coercion, the crackdown on labour activists that took place first in 2015 and again in 2019 put an end, at least temporarily, to Chinese labour NGOs' experiments with collective bargaining. While the increased repression and narrowing political spaces for grassroots activism in Xi Jinping's China warrant pessimism, this by no means signals the end of the Chinese labour NGO nor the extirpation of the seeds planted by these activists.

2018

In the summer of 2018, a series of protests by some workers at Jasic, a publicly listed private firm specialising in the manufacture of welding machinery, made headlines all over the world. At a time when labour activism in China was at a low ebb due to increased repression, these workers mobilised to demand not only better working conditions, but also the right to establish a company union that actually represented their interests, thus challenging the top-down control of the All-China Federation of Trade Unions. What differentiated this mobilisation from other protests that had advanced similar demands in the past—such as the Nanhai Honda strike of 2010—was the involvement of groups of Maoist students from some of China's elite universities. Not only did these students play an important role in the underground organising that led to the protest, but also many of their comrades flocked to Shenzhen to publicly express solidarity with the workers being repressed by the machinery of the State. The consequences were disastrous for both the workers and the students, many of whom were subjected to intimidation, arrested, and forced to record confessions, in a wave of repression that rippled across university campuses in other cities, including Beijing. Activists in labour nongovernmental organisations (NGOs) who had barely managed to escape the previous wave and had nothing to do with the Jasic mobilisation were also swept up in the crackdown, with some ending up in detention for as long as fifteen months. This closed the circle on what began with the attempts at labour organising by a handful of students in the early 1920s: one century later, the Chinese Communist Party (CCP) consummated this ultimate betrayal of its original ideals.

The Jasic Struggle
Manfred ELFSTROM

On 22 July 2018, people passing the Yanziling Police Station in Shenzhen's crowded Pingshan district would have come across an unusual protest by workers. The participants did not mill about in the street, seeking safety in numbers. Nor did they draw on the familiar repertoire of more confrontational tactics developed over the previous two decades of industrial conflict in their country, such as carrying a banner, blocking a road, or threatening suicide. Instead, one by one, they came forward and delivered long, impassioned speeches in hoarse voices denouncing their oppressive working conditions, the unresponsiveness of the local trade union apparatus, and police violence in reaction to previous mobilisations.[1] Onlookers would have learnt that the site of the protest was no accident. The Yanziling station had only days before held several of the protesters and, surprisingly, even after having been released, these individuals had returned to the place of their detention to demonstrate.

Two weeks later, observers would have been yet more astonished. On the afternoon of 6 August, they would have seen not just the same workers making speeches in the same place (something the workers had done on several occasions by then), but also university students, retired state-owned enterprise (SOE) employees, and old Communist Party cadres from around the country, many of them wearing white T-shirts with black and white sketches of the workers from the previous protests and the words 'Solidarity Is Power' (团结就是力量) in red. Some held portraits of Chairman Mao. And there were banners now, too: 'The workers are innocent! Forming a union is not a crime!'[2] Again, demonstrators took turns addressing whoever stopped to listen, while their words, this time, touched on yet broader themes: worker–intellectual unity—'Today's students are tomorrow's workers' (今天的学生就是明天的工人)—and the need for everyone struggling under 'this structure' (这样的制度下) to unite.[3] Sentiments like these had rarely been voiced in the thousands of labour conflicts that occurred during the three decades since the Tiananmen protests.

These remarkable scenes were part of what became known as the 'Jasic campaign' (佳士运动). This essay will explain how the campaign started, the unusual alliances that formed during its course, and the repressive response it drew from authorities, and it will reflect in a preliminary manner on what it might mean for the future.

How the Campaign Started

The Jasic campaign started in early 2017 with a dispute at the Shenzhen Jasic Technology Company Limited, a welding equipment manufacturer that employs around 1,000 people and is listed on the Shenzhen Stock Exchange. Employees there had run out of patience with, among other things, managerial physical and verbal abuse, the company's constant redefinition of rest days (调休), extensive fines for various work rule infractions, and underpayment of social insurance premiums and housing allowances. In mid-2017, some workers brought their complaints to the local labour bureau and won a partial rollback of the most onerous policies. But people remained angry. The workers thus resumed their efforts in March and April 2018, focusing on the fines in particular. Again, the labour bureau put some pressure on Jasic and managers agreed to change, but the factory would not return money already deducted.[4]

Several Jasic employees then launched a unionisation drive, which followed procedures recommended to organisers by some officials they had approached in the local trade union of Pingshan district. Shenzhen had in the preceding years embarked on a notable effort to revitalise the district level of the union bureaucracy, so starting there made sense.[5] However, the effort ran up against foot-dragging on the part of management, who agreed in principle to establish a union but would not supply the necessary documents. Instead, Jasic ended up holding elections for a Staff and Workers Representative Congress (职工代表大会)—a body that usually exists in parallel with enterprise-level unions. Managers furthermore excluded the union organisers from the election. The worker organisers responded with a letter in support of a real union signed by eighty-nine of their coworkers.[6]

From there, the conflict intensified. Leading activists were assigned by management to new positions in the company, attacked by thugs, and eventually roughly escorted out of the plant. When they returned to protest on 20 July, there was a clash with security, and the police intervened, detaining and severely beating several individuals. The detainees were released the next day. However, on 21 and 22 July, workers gathered outside the Yanziling Police Station, where their colleagues had been detained, and reiterated their grievances. In addition, they called for the officers who had mistreated their comrades to be punished.

If at first there seemed to be some (limited) space for advancing the Jasic workers' aims within the country's established channels, now the State and its union closed ranks with the powerful local employer (the factory is just one of three run by the firm, which also has several research and design offices and has received various provincial and national prizes). The local trade union of Pingshan district not only refrained from exerting further pressure on the company, but also publicly lauded management's cooperation, while accusing the workers of illegal activities.[7] On 27 July, the day after a dramatic night-time rally by the workers, police detained more than thirty protesters—an unusual crackdown even by the standards of the Xi Jinping era. When protesters gathered again to demand their coworkers' release, over a dozen more were taken into custody.[8] The authorities now viewed the incident as a political challenge.

Workers would make little further progress with regard to their original aims. Although an enterprise-level union was eventually formed at Jasic, it was fully under management supervision. According to a filing by the Chinese Government in response to a freedom of association complaint to the International Labour Organisation (ILO), the newly established union at Jasic focused on 'holiday benefits, the organization of cultural and sports activities, the improvement of welfare benefits, and adjustment of the wage system, as well as organized visits to workers living in difficult conditions'.[9] It is unclear to the author what, if anything, happened with regard to the complaints about fines, abusive managers, and other thorny issues; however, the Jasic campaign would nonetheless continue to widen its ambit, becoming a national—and even international—phenomenon.

Support for the Jasic Workers

Almost from the beginning, the Jasic workers had significant external support. From the incident on 20 July onwards, letters backing the workers circulated among leftists on the Chinese internet. Social justice–minded university students like Shen Mengyu, a recent graduate of nearby Sun Yat-sen University in Guangzhou who had been active in labour organising since graduation, joined the protests early on and helped form the Jasic Workers Solidarity Group (佳士工人声援团). Others, like Peking

University student Yue Xin, who had already played an influential part in China's #MeToo movement and who wrote a powerful online letter drawing attention to the workers' cause, travelled to Shenzhen to help. On campuses around the country, Marxist reading groups held information events. These groups had been organising on behalf of migrants and campus employees and now saw an opportunity to make a bigger contribution. Dozens of students eventually moved into a flat in Huizhou and devoted themselves full-time to the cause. Even more than the workers, the students would become the campaign's public face.[10]

Students were not the only ones who joined the struggle, though. There were other outsiders who showed support, too, especially former SOE employees and Party cadres from the interior, where protests against public sector restructuring had raged in the late 1990s and early 2000s (see William Hurst's and Ching Kwan Lee's essays in the present volume). Many of these people—along with the students—were members of leftist networks connected through websites like *Utopia* (乌有之乡). Some belonged to a Maoist tendency that described itself as the Marxist-Leninist-Maoist Left (MLML) and contrasted its politics with the more nationalist and pro-regime Maoists who had gained notoriety online and off as virulent critics of liberals and foreigners (some in the MLML would later express concerns about the students' naivety).[11] It has been reported that the worker-activists at Jasic themselves hailed from the same circles and joined the factory with the precise purpose of initiating a high-profile confrontation like the one that occurred.[12] Interestingly, the organisers did not engage local labour nongovernmental organisations (NGOs), which displayed sympathy but also wariness towards the struggle. Nonetheless, there was outreach beyond the confines of the radical left. At one point in the confrontation, for instance, organisers drew on the expertise of the liberal human rights activist Hu Jia, who had been imprisoned in the past for his HIV/AIDS and civil liberties advocacy.[13]

People mobilised further afield, as well. In Hong Kong, the independent Hong Kong Confederation of Trade Unions and several civil society groups marched on the Central Government's Liaison Office in solidarity with the Jasic workers and their supporters.[14] There were protests in Europe and the United States, too. The International Trade Union Confederation lodged a complaint about the case and other instances of labour rights violations in China with the ILO.[15] When the government began to crack down on the students in earnest, Cornell University's School of

Industrial and Labor Relations severed its ties with Renmin University, where there were forced disappearances from campus.[16] Left academics from Noam Chomsky to Slavoj Žižek committed to boycotting official Marxist conferences in China.[17] From a relatively narrow factory dispute, the Jasic campaign became a major showdown. As such, it is not surprising that the government treated its participants with severity.

State Repression of the Campaign

State repression marked the Jasic campaign from the start. First, there were the arrests of protesting workers. Three of these people would eventually be formally charged with 'gathering a crowd to disrupt order in a public place': Li Zhan, Mi Jiuping, and Yu Juncong. A staffer and the legal representative of the NGO Shenzhen Dagongzhe Migrant Workers Centre were detained next, although by all reports the group played no meaningful role in the dispute; the staffer, Fu Changguo, would eventually face formal charges along with the three Jasic workers.[18] Student Shen Mengyu disappeared on 11 August. Then, in an article on 24 August, *Xinhua News* blamed the unrest on local civil society groups colluding with hostile foreign forces, signalling a harder government line.[19] On 26 August, riot police stormed the apartment in Huizhou shared by student supporters, detaining about forty individuals, including Yue Xin.[20]

Things ramped up again in the autumn. In early November, authorities swept up student activists in Nanjing, Shanghai, Wuhan, and Guangzhou. A Peking University student leader was kidnapped.[21] In December, two of the trade union officials who had provided advice to the workers at the outset of the dispute, along with a labour lawyer, were similarly detained.[22] The same month, the head of Peking University's Marxist society, who was on his way to celebrate Mao Zedong's birthday in Shaoshan, Hunan, was snatched up, along with a classmate, who *did* make it to Hunan for the celebration.[23] Students at the School of Economics at Renmin University of China reported being forced to stay home under police monitoring.[24] Police summoned the remaining activists and showed them 'confession' videos of people who had been detained earlier, like Yue Xin.[25]

Finally, Peking University administrators stepped in and reorganised the university's Marxist society into a group comprising Communist Youth League members, who devoted their inaugural reading session to an anthology of neo-Confucian writings; each also received a copy of

President Xi Jinping's book on governance at the close of the session.[26] By early 2019, the extraordinary flowering of dissent had largely been mopped up.

The Meaning of Jasic

What, then, did it all mean? The implications of the Jasic campaign have already been the subject of some discussion. For example, in editorials and public comments, labour sociologist Pun Ngai has described the campaign as historic, highlighting in particular the workers' emphasis on union rights, which she believes marked an important shift away from the narrowly economic claims of most previous mobilisations and towards a more political conceptualisation of workers' role in society.[27] Leftist public intellectual Au Loong-Yu has countered that there had already been several other large-scale union-related disputes in the country before Jasic—for instance, the Uniden, Ole Wolff, and Yantian Container strikes, to mention just a few examples of the worker mobilisations that took place in the previous fifteen years—and cast doubt on whether the actions of a few dozen workers can be said to represent a change among workers in China more generally.[28] What Au has instead found special about Jasic is the campaign's break from the country's tired intellectual divisions: Chinese liberals versus the New Left and neo-Maoists. Sociologist Jenny Chan, meanwhile, has highlighted how the participation of students in the campaign is reminiscent of early twentieth-century organising.[29] Sociologist Yueran Zhang, while describing the campaign as 'an extraordinary feat' in terms of the scale of organising involved, has been critical of the vanguardist orientation of the Jasic activists, describing them as identifying more as 'revolutionary cadres' than 'labour organisers' and consequently poorly prepared to engage workers in a way that might build real power on the shopfloor.[30] Brian Hioe, editor of *New Bloom Magazine*, has wondered whether, barring some further expansion of activism in the future, the importance of Jasic may turn out to have been largely exaggerated.[31]

These assessments all offer important insights. But there are other lenses through which we can appreciate the campaign's uniqueness, while recognising its limits. First, if we approach it from a social movement perspective, Jasic represented a rare post-Tiananmen example of a fully fledged movement. Charles Tilly and Sidney Tarrow define a 'social movement' as 'a sustained campaign of claim making, using repeated performances that advertise the claim, based on organizations, networks, traditions, and solidarities that sustain these activities'.[32] Many observers have commented on the ephemeral nature of most Chinese labour disputes and their general lack of cross-worksite let alone cross-provincial organising.[33] In contrast, the Jasic campaign was, depending on how you count it, sustained for nearly one year and, as noted, drew in people from across the country, some of whom organised on their campuses or in their hometowns and others of whom relocated to Shenzhen to join the fight—all of whom were surprisingly open in their advocacy. Moreover, it developed a distinctive set of performances—the dramatic speeches in the streets described above—and even its own branding, as seen in the image of protesting workers and the stirring solidarity slogan that featured on participants' T-shirts (and on websites and Twitter accounts). The only other phenomena in China that have displayed this level of being a 'movement' have arguably been certain environmental campaigns, feminist organising, and rights lawyering.

Second and relatedly, if we approach the Jasic campaign from the perspective of China's governance strategy, we can appreciate the ties that Jasic built between communities that had intentionally been quite separated. China under the Communist Party has been described as a 'honeycomb' polity.[34] In the Mao era, as others in this volume have described, workers were frequently encouraged to join mass political campaigns. So, too, were peasants, intellectuals, and others. But aside from the most chaotic moments of the Cultural Revolution, in general, that mobilisation was firmly contained within the walls of the honeycomb.[35] Scholars have similarly described reform-era Chinese Communist Party (CCP) rule as pitting different groups against each other: migrants against SOE workers, and professionals against both.[36] The great mass of people who filled Tiananmen Square in 1989, for instance, was undercut by divisions that were actively maintained by the authorities and participants alike. In particular, Tiananmen student leaders—intent on preserving the purity of their cause and worried about repression—excluded worker-activists until the last days of the movement (see Zhang's essay in the present volume).[37] There were *some* twenty-first-century precedents for the Jasic campaign: students went undercover to expose abuses in Coca-Cola and Foxconn facilities in 2009 and 2010 and backed sanitation workers in Guangzhou in 2014.[38] But none of these incidents came close to challenging the underlying and reinforced divisions of Chinese society in the way that Jasic did.

Finally, from the perspective of Chinese industrial relations, we can at once understand the campaign as a culmination of what came before it and as an aberration. We can reconcile Pun's and Au's analyses by stating that, while union-related demands were certainly a part of some important collective actions of the preceding two decades, they had very rarely—if ever—been made the centre of a campaign in the manner of Jasic. If most union bargaining had previously been initiated from above, in response to a bottom-up action already under way, now it was one of the calls that sparked the action in the first place.[39] However, in other regards, Jasic did not build on previous activism. In particular, contrary to the government's claims, labour NGOs did not play a meaningful role in the confrontation. Thus, the campaign did not draw on the arguably most developed (if still imperfect) worker organising structure existing up to that point. Nor did activists advance the strike as a weapon—the tactic that had featured in the biggest preceding confrontations. Jasic was fundamentally a *protest* movement. Moreover, whereas other disputes in roughly the same period—such as ones involving Wal-Mart employees, truckdrivers, and crane operators—had begun to extend worker-to-worker ties nationally, Jasic mostly came down to a single group of workers plus their assorted supporters.[40] These things should not be held against the organisers, of course, but they remind us that the campaign was unusual in ways that were both innovative and inspiring and that simply made it an outlier and, perhaps, a deadend.

Legacies of Struggle

Ultimately, the Jasic campaign may have inspired hopes that went beyond any campaign's ability to deliver at that moment in Chinese history. Other efforts on its scale would likely also have run up against the implacable hostility of the Xi administration. Indeed, in the year following the Jasic campaign, the crackdown widened, resulting in the arrests of many unrelated labour NGO leaders and labour journalists. Turmoil in Hong Kong's streets and then the spread of COVID-19 led to a further heightening of state control. Yet, each of the participants in the Jasic campaign still carries their own memories of the incident. So, too, do their coworkers and classmates who did not participate but observed things secondhand, as do other Chinese following online. These memories matter and can perhaps be drawn on at a more propitious moment.

2018

Starting in 2017, Chinese authorities began establishing a number of 'reeducation camps' in China's northwestern Xinjiang Uyghur Autonomous Region with the purported aim of preventing the proliferation of extremism and terrorism among the local Muslim population—in particular, the Uyghurs. According to the most conservative estimates, hundreds of thousands of people were arbitrarily locked up in these camps. Factories quickly flocked to the area to take advantage of the cheap labour and subsidies offered by the camp system. As this essay argues, the goal of these newly built factories is to transform Kazakhs and Uyghurs into a compliant and productive proletariat without the social welfare afforded to formally recognised rights-bearing workers.

Factories of Turkic Muslim Internment

Darren BYLER[1]

On 3 November 2018, Yerzhan Kurman, a middle-aged Kazakh man from a small village fifty kilometres from the city of Ghulja in the Xinjiang Uyghur Autonomous Region, was released from the camp where he had been held for nine months. He thought perhaps now he would be free to return to his former life as a migrant in Kazakhstan. Yet, just a few days later, he was sent to an industrial park in Ghulja City to work in a glove factory. For the next fifty-three days, he experienced life in an internment factory that was built to 'raise the quality' (提高素质) of minority workers.

Yerzhan had been detained soon after he came back to China to seek medical treatment for his daughter and care for his ailing mother in early 2018. In a 2019 interview with the German magazine *Die Zeit*, he said:

> On the evening of 8 February 2018, they picked me up in a minibus. It was already dark and they put black plastic sacks over our heads and handcuffs on our hands. There were five young men from my village with me on the minibus. The room in which I had to stay for the next nine months was 5 meters by 5 meters and located on the third floor. On the door, a sign said 'No. 12'. Our floor alone accommodated 260 men. In my room, we were 12. Later I heard that there had been more than 10,000 men detained in our camp.[2]

Yerzhan was unsure exactly where the camp was located. It may have been the one built in the fields on the outskirts of the city, just seven kilometres from the industrial park where he was later forced to work.

As is often reported by former detainees, conditions in the camp were appalling. Describing the circumstances of his detention, Yerzhan said:

> The toilet was a bucket by the window, there was no running water. In the daytime, we were sitting in rows on our plastic stools. The food was handed to us through an opening in the door. At 7am, we had to sing the Chinese national anthem and then we had three minutes for breakfast. Afterwards, we learned Chinese until

9pm. Our teachers were Kazakhs or Uyghurs. We were watched by four cameras in our room which ensured that we didn't talk to each other. Those who spoke anyway were handcuffed and had to stand by the wall. 'You don't have the right to talk, because you are not humans,' said the guards. 'If you were humans, you wouldn't be here.'[3]

Yerzhan still does not know why he was taken. Like others detained in Ghulja, his internment was likely due to the fact that he possessed a passport and travelled to Kazakhstan—one of twenty-six Muslim-majority countries on a Chinese Government watch list.[4] Over time, the gruelling routine began to change his mental state. He said: 'The first two months, I thought of my wife Maynur and my three children. Sometime later, I only thought about food.'[5]

About the time Yerzhan was reduced to thinking about his bodily survival, in May 2018, Pan Daojin, the Front Commander and Chinese Communist Party Secretary of Yili Prefecture, arrived to inspect a newly built industrial park on the other side of town.[6] He came with a delegation from Jiangsu that was tasked with providing industrial 'aid' to Xinjiang. Pan, who is also from Jiangsu, had been appointed to his position in December 2016, just as the mass detentions of the reeducation system began. During the inspection of the new industrial park, he 'fully affirmed the achievements' of the business leaders from Nantong City in Jiangsu who had funded it. The delegation showed off the new factory of the Jiangsu-based Solamoda Garment Group, a company that partners with Forever 21 and other international brands. They also stopped by the highly productive glove factory where Yerzhan would be eventually assigned. This factory was managed by employees of the Luye Shuozi Island Trading Company, a manufacturer based in Baoding City, Hebei Province.

According to the general manager of the glove factory, Wang Xinghua, speaking in a state television interview released in December 2018: 'With the support of the government, we have already *recruited* more than 600 people [emphasis added].'[7] One of these 600 government 'recruits' was Yerzhan, who had arrived from the camp less than a month before. General manager Wang went on to say that, since the founding of the new factory in 2017: 'We have generated more than US$6 million in sales. We plan to reach 1,000 workers by the end of this year. We plan to provide jobs to 1,500 people by the end of 2019.' In fact, the glove factory in Ghulja has now far surpassed the capacity of its parent factory, which back in Hebei employed less than 200 people.[8] Moving manufacturing to Xinjiang made economic sense for the company, which sold 96 percent of its leather gloves across the border in Russia and Eastern Europe.

But there were other reasons exponential growth was so easy. Since 2018, the state has provided subsidies for the building of factories and shipping goods from Xinjiang. Construction of the factories was often funded by local governments in eastern China as part of a 'pairing assistance' (配对与援助) program. Up to 4 percent of new factory sales volume was subsidised to cover shipping expenses from the new location.[9] Most importantly, as in every county in Xinjiang, there was a standing labour reserve of tens of thousands of desperate, traumatised detainees like Yerzhan in nearby camps.

A Carrier of the Economy

Since 2017, factories have flocked to Xinjiang to take advantage of the newly built industrial parks associated with the reeducation camp system and the cheap labour and subsidies that accompany them. In fact, in late 2018, the primary development ministry for the region, the Xinjiang Reform and Development Commission, circulated a statement that the camps or 'vocational skills education and training centres' (教育培训中心) had become a 'carrier' (载体) of the economy.[10] Because of this system, Xinjiang had attracted 'significant investment and construction from coast-based Chinese companies'. Since China sources more than 80 percent of its cotton from Xinjiang, there was a special emphasis placed on textile and garment–related industries.[11] In an effort motivated at least in part by rising labour costs among Han migrant workers on the east coast, the Chinese state plans to move more than one million textile and garment industry jobs to the region by 2023.[12] If they succeed, it will mean that as many as one in every eleven textile and garment industry jobs in China will be in Xinjiang.[13] The 1,500 jobs at the glove factory in Ghulja are part of that number.

Broadly speaking, there are three primary tracks through which Uyghurs and other Turkic Muslims are involuntarily assigned to work in the newly built factories as part of the reeducation labour regime. First, many detainees in camps are placed in factories inside or adjacent to the camps; they work inside the same space in which they are held at night. Second, some new industrial parks built in regional centres host a mix of former detainees and 'rural surplus labourers' who are not former detainees.

These surplus labourers are chosen from populations of self-employed rural farmers and peri-urban Kazakhs and Uyghurs who previously found contingent work in heritage trades and service industries. In a new carceral instantiation of what Chris Smith and Pun Ngai refer to as the 'dormitory labour regime' used to surveil and exploit migrant workers in eastern China, former detainees who join these surplus labourers in the urban industrial parks are often held in locked dormitories at night, as in the case of Yerzhan.[14] Some 'surplus labourers'—like migrant workers in eastern China—are permitted to return to their own homes at night or to stay in accommodation of their choice in the regional centre. Third, newly built county-level and smaller-scale 'satellite factories' (卫星工厂) in rural areas host Uyghur workers near their homes. These worker populations of mainly women with young children are assigned by local village and township-level authorities to work while their children are cared for in daycare facilities; their husbands work in the city or are detained in camps. While there are different levels of coercion in these tracks, all three result in forms of family separation and dependence on the state and private industry proxies for training and discipline in Chinese-speaking environments.

In all cases, Turkic Muslim detainees are forcibly assigned to these positions. As documents used by workers in 'neighbourhood watch units' (社区) and 'village-level work brigades' (大队) note, refusing to participate in 'poverty alleviation' (扶贫) schemes—a widely used euphemism for assigned factory work and other forms of 'coercive assistance'—is regarded as a sign of untrustworthiness and religious extremism.[15] The grassroots state workers who partner with police and private and state-owned enterprises to implement the campaign are charged with providing employees from populations within their jurisdictions. They often accompany workers to the factories and, at times, act as intermediaries between factory management and the workers. They also enforce discipline on the factory floor and, in some cases, in dormitories. In a radical contravention of the supposed 'freedom' associated with market-based contract law, state authorities assume that the only reason a Muslim worker may not want to be separated from their family and work for low wages in a Han-managed factory is because of their aversion to contact with non-Muslims. Forcing Uyghurs and Kazakhs to work in a Chinese-speaking environment can then be framed by state workers and employers as liberating them from their native way of life and traditions. This framing elides the process of state and market dependence that is created by dispossessing Uyghurs and

Kazakhs of what Marx would describe as their own 'means of production' and the radical forms of unfreedom that are produced by forced labour in an alien environment.[16]

The glove factory where Yerzhan was sent appears to have a mix of both former detainees and involuntarily assigned 'surplus workers'. Many, like Yerzhan, arrived in the factory after briefly being released from a camp. Yet, according to a state report, more than 1,800 others were sent to work in the industrial park in mid-2017, long before the first detainees were transferred from the camps.[17] According to Yerzhan and a second worker whom I interviewed, named Gulzira Auelkhan, these early arrivals were 'track two' underemployed rural workers who were determined to be part of the 'normal' population and assigned to work without first being placed in a camp.

Unfree Labour

Several months before Yerzhan arrived at the glove factory, another Kazakh detainee was also transferred there from a nearby reeducation camp. Before arriving, Gulzira, a thirty-nine-year-old mother of a toddler, whom she left with her husband in Kazakhstan, had spent fifteen months of horrific abuse in crowded cells with eighteen to sixty other detainees, most of whom were Uyghur.[18] Detainees in her cell were repeatedly shocked in the head with electric batons if they used the bathroom for longer than two minutes. Their closely cropped hair masked some of the bruising, and detainees were given dye to darken their hair and scalp before higher-level officials visited the camp.[19] They were told to smile during the inspections.

Due to the relatively low level of her perceived 'pre-criminal offences'— according to documents supplied to the United Nations by the Chinese Government, many detainees in the camps had not actually committed a crime[20]—Gulzira had been placed in a camp that had the least amount of security. What had marked her as 'untrustworthy' was a previous visit to Kazakhstan and the fact she watched Turkish TV shows in which women wore hijabs. In her section of the camp, there was less of an emphasis on ideological retraining. Instead, the detainees studied Chinese all day, every day. Kazakh and Uyghur languages were not permitted.

Like Yerzhan, when Gulzira was released from the camp, she thought she may be given greater freedom. But within several days a local village leader appeared with a document saying that she must report for work at the glove factory. When she arrived at the plant, she recognised her new boss, general manager Wang. She had seen him several times back in the camp, on tours with camp officials. She surmised that he must have picked her to work in his factory while she was still in the camp. She was told that, as a trainee, she would be paid 600 yuan per month (approximately US$100)—one-third of the 1,800-yuan state-mandated minimum wage in the region—for the first three months. She would also be paid a small amount, around two jiao (20 Chinese cents), per pair of gloves according to her 'efficiency'. She said: 'The most skilled worker could sew 60 pairs a day. I tried my best, but I could only sew 13 pairs.'[21] Since she did not have good eyesight, she found it impossible to improve her productivity. Speaking to Berlin-based journalist Ben Mauk, she said: 'In the end, I worked there for a month and a half. It was piecework. I earned one jiao for every glove I finished. All told, I made more than two thousand gloves and earned 220 yuan. So, you see, it was like slavery.'[22]

Although there was less security in the factory than the camps, the detainees were not allowed to leave. In an interview in January 2020, months after she had fled across the Chinese border to Kazakhstan, Gulzira spoke of checkpoints at the entrances to the dormitory and factory where her identity card and face were scanned. She said:

> We would have our bodies and phones checked when we arrived, and in the middle of the day. When we were leaving for the dormitory at the end of the day they would check again, because they were worried we might take a [sewing] needle. After we got to know [the police contractors,] we asked them, 'Why are you still here watching us?'

While they never replied, she told me she knew the answer to this question was that the security workers were monitoring whether or not they were acting like submissive 'reeducated' industrial workers. She noted that, like every other Turkic Muslim she knew, her passport had been confiscated and travel beyond the parameters of their assigned locality—whether it was an industrial park or the relative freedom of a village—was not permitted. In addition, like the majority of assigned workers, she had very little money with which to attempt to pay someone to smuggle her out. Life at the factory was better than life in the camp, but she understood that in this new space she was being asked to prove that she had become a truly reeducated industrial worker.

Outside the discipline of the factory and industrial park, the infrastructure of material walls continued to be a part of her life. Every night after work, she and other detainees were taken by bus to a makeshift dormitory around three kilometres away. There, detainees were permitted to walk around the campus, but they were not permitted to leave the premises. According to reporting by *The Globe and Mail*, the workers 'received readings in the factory before work and, at day's end, 45-minute Chinese lessons in the dormitory, where they were watched at night by an official'.[23]

Both Yerzhan and Gulzira were permitted to visit their families for several hours during one day on the weekend. A company bus would ferry them back and forth from the dormitory to their home villages. A month into their 'training', however, they found out that these trips were quite costly. Bosses at the factory, such as general manager Wang, told them that because of the expense of the shuttle service and their food, their 600-yuan salary would be halved. Yerzhan later recalled: 'I worked on a production line for fifty-three days, earning 300 yuan in total.'

Government documents show that, in Kashgar Prefecture in 2018, 100,000 detainees were scheduled to move into and work in the newly built industrial parks and satellite factories.[24] Other prefectures aimed for similar numbers. In Kashgar, for each detainee put to work, the factory owners would receive 5,000 yuan dispersed over three years. These subsidies were likely put in place to prevent the type of wage garnishment that Yerzhan and Gulzira experienced. However, since the factories function as an extension of the camp system, operating in a legal grey zone outside civil and human rights, prevention of worker abuse falls on the moral code of people like general manager Wang. As an industrialist acting as a proxy for the carceral state, he knew just as well as Yerzhan or Gulzira that any complaint, any slowdown in production, could result in their replacement with other detainees. He could treat them in any way he wanted.

Social Implications of Reeducation Industrial Parks

Newly built industrial parks in northwestern China occupy a liminal space between 'reeducation' camps and private industry, proletarianisation and coerced labour. State documents note over and over again that the new industrial parks are being built to instil an undefined 'basic quality' (基础素质) in Uyghur and Kazakh detainees and other Muslim surplus labourers. What is often left unsaid in state-approved documents is the way these factory spaces function as an archipelago of institutions at the periphery of the Chinese social contract—the implicit agreement that a state will protect its citizens in exchange for their loyalty. For Uyghurs and Kazakh Chinese citizens, this social contract has been shattered as what Michel Foucault refers to as the prison archipelago is enlisted in a mode of colonial-capitalist production—a reeducation labour regime—that erodes the vitality of indigenous social reproduction.[25] The documents of the workers in Xinjiang internment factories are confiscated or their identification cards are marked as invalid, placing them under a pervasive form of unfreedom. These types of coerced labour are subsidised and directed by the state and operationalised by a complex web of surveillance practices and a logistics system that are bringing the Chinese factory to the Uyghur and Kazakh homelands. All of this material development is authorised by the threatening presence of hundreds of internment camps that signify the power of the state over Turkic Muslim life.

Importantly, the effects of this system are not limited to northwestern China, or even to China itself. Nearly all the gloves that are made by detainees in the satellite factory of the Luye Shuozi Island Trading Company are sold abroad. On the company's Alibaba distribution site, they note that the prices of their gloves range from US$1.50 to US$24 per pair depending on the style and quantity purchased. Some are distributed by the up-scale Hong Kong–based boutique Bread n Butter, which has outlets in malls around the world where they likely are sold for far more. In any case, the price at which these gloves are sold is exponentially higher than the price workers are paid per pair. This system of expropriation—a type of state-authorised theft—is justified by the rhetoric of charity, of 'aiding Xinjiang' (援疆) with the gift of the cultural capital provided by knowledge of the Chinese language, or framed as Han factory owners helping detainees cultivate the 'quality' (素质) needed to be disciplined industrial workers.[26]

In an essay written in adulation of the internment factory complex, a Ghulja County official wrote that when the Turkic Muslim farmers and herders arrived at the factory they 'took off their grass shoes, put on leather shoes, and became industrial workers'.[27] The counterfactual imagery of 'backward' (落后) minority people who wore primitive 'grass' (草) shoes being given the gift of factory discipline through internment precisely captures the spirit of the 'quality' acquisition process as seen by state workers and contractors. In a regional state media video valorising the implementation of a coercive job program, the reporter repeatedly noted that the Turkic Muslim workers did not even pause to look up at the camera during the filming.[28] The reporter interpreted this as a sign of their excellent work ethic as newly trained 'high-quality' workers. This discourse was also instilled by management. Both Yerzhan and Gulzira mentioned that their managers emphasised that they were making gloves for export, so the quality of their sewing had to be very high. The training they were receiving in 'human quality' would be reflected in the quality of the gloves they mass produced.

The introduction of state-directed, Han-exclusive corporate power over Uyghur and Kazakh life has the effect of accelerating the alienating effects of factory labour across ethnic and class differences. Alienation—removing the individual from the ownership of their labour as workers and, in this case, from their autonomy as Turkic Muslim individuals—is a primary feature of the reeducation factory. The goal of the reeducation industrial parks is to turn Kazakhs and Uyghurs into a deeply controlled proletariat, a new docile yet productive lumpen class—those without the social welfare afforded to the formally recognised rights-bearing working class. By turning a population of people regarded as not deserving of legal protections into a permanent underclass, state authorities and private industrialists hope they will extend the market expansion of the Chinese textile and garment industry. They are building a colonial frontier in capitalist accumulation—a process that is simultaneously a new iteration of racialised capitalism and contemporary settler-colonialism.[29] This system of controlled labour is 'carried' (载体) by a massive reeducation system, a mechanism of infrastructural state power that ensures that this new class of interned labourers cannot rise up as a class for themselves. In fact, because of this extralegal system, the only thing that protects Turkic Muslim workers from expropriation and violence is the goodwill of their Han managers. As indicated by the payment scheme at the glove factory, worker protections often appear as a form of 'investment' in the quality of Turkic workers even while worker wellbeing and indigenous social relationships are viewed as valueless.

At the Limit of Global Capitalism

Since the factories function as an extension of the camp system, outside the rule of law and at the margin of the social contract, factory managers can treat Uyghur and Kazakh workers as disposable. In December 2018, managers at the factory threatened Gulzira with being sent back to the camp if she did not sign a one-year work contract.[30] It was only because her husband in Kazakhstan began a campaign for her release—after she managed to text images of the factory to him and he spotted her in a state video promoting the industrial park—that local authorities reluctantly agreed to allow her to return to her family on the other side of the border. They were attempting to silence challenges to the 'aid Xinjiang' narrative.[31] Yet, when these attempts failed, they cut their losses and let her go.

There is a nearly limitless standing reserve of other detainees who do not have advocates for them outside China. The archipelago of the reeducation labour regime continues out of sight, a ghostly presence at the end of global supply chains. In the race to the bottom—the least cost for the greatest productivity—the reeducation factory in Ghulja is at the limit of contemporary global capitalism.

2019

Although postcolonial Hong Kong has a weak trade union culture, in 2019, activists in the protest movement against a controversial extradition bill began to demand union representation and formed dozens of small unions from the ground up. Within a few months, these new organisations were able to successfully mount an important strike protesting against the government's initial refusal to close the border with China during the early weeks of the COVID-19 pandemic. Since Beijing's adoption of the National Security Law in July 2020, the tide has turned again, in their disfavour.

The Birth of a New Trade Union Movement in Hong Kong

Anita CHAN[1]

For a year from mid-2019 to mid-2020, the international media diligently covered the mass demonstrations and street violence that rocked Hong Kong. At their height, two million of Hong Kong's seven million people marched in protest against an extradition bill that, if passed, would have meant that Hong Kongers could be extradited to China to be tried and imprisoned. The display of unity among protestors was unexpected because, only a few years earlier, the 2014 Umbrella Movement failed partly due to disagreement over tactics among political activists. Since then, the movement had fragmented into a number of small groups and political parties of varied persuasions, with a notable split between a militant younger generation and a moderate older generation of established prodemocracy advocates.

A Movement of Solidarity in Disagreement

That the movement could transcend these differences was an important achievement in 2019. In the face of a common front of antagonists, ranging from Hong Kong's Chief Executive Carrie Lam to the pro-Beijing camp and pro-establishment elite, differences had been put aside. The prodemocracy movement had coalesced around three agreements. The first was expressed in the ubiquitous slogan 'Five Demands, Not One Less'. It was a set of political demands broad enough to accommodate all political leanings.

The second was a pact based on the principle of egalitarianism, embodied in the saying 'brothers climbing a mountain, each trying one's best' (兄弟爬山, 各自努力), meaning different protestors could adopt the strategies they deemed best to achieve the movement's broad goals while not criticising or intervening in the actions and strategies of others. We go 'up and down together' (齐上齐落) with no 'splitting of the mat'! This managed to bring together the two key blocs of the protest movement: the 'Valiant Braves Faction' (勇武派) and the 'Peaceful, Rational, Nonviolent Faction' (合理非派). The former was made up mostly of students and other young people, geared up and willing to confront the police head on. The latter comprised those who either would not or could not engage in direct action that might end in confrontation and who played supporting roles at the rear—providing material resources and organising and participating in rallies, joining peaceful activities like 'let's lunch together' (和你, 'lunch'), raising funds, joining human chains and taking part in myriad other innovative actions.

The third was an agreement there would be 'no big table'—that is, no leaders sitting around a table deciding the direction of the movement. Anyone could put forth proposals—any idea and type of action—anytime and anywhere through social media platforms. This movement was to 'be water'—that is, unplanned, unpredictable, fluid and spontaneous, a form of urban guerrilla tactics. At the same time, big, well-planned rallies organised by the prodemocracy parties and well-established organisations continued to be well attended.

Trade Unions in Hong Kong

When months of street action did not extract any concessions from the authorities, part of the protest movement branched off in a new direction that was more formal and organised, with the establishment of small independent trade unions.

I spent three weeks in Hong Kong in January 2020 conducting research on these new trade unions. I carried out interviews at several recruitment stands that volunteers set up outside metro stations, at busy street junctions and at hospital entrances during lunch breaks, after work and on weekends. I also met with newly elected members of some of the new unions' executive (or preparatory) committees, attended union-organised labour law training sessions and had meetings with Hong Kong academics who specialise in labour studies. I also interviewed staff of the Hong Kong Confederation of Trade Unions (HKCTU)—a prodemocracy umbrella union. After returning to Australia, I kept abreast of events through online conversations, social media and Hong Kong's mass media.

Hong Kong is a global commercial hub dominated by free-market beliefs with a weak trade union culture. The largest union federation is the Hong Kong Federation of Trade Unions (HKFTU), with 191 affiliates and 426,000 members as of 2019. It is well resourced and largely controlled by the Government of the People's Republic of China (PRC) as a counterpart to the official All-China Federation of Trade Unions—a mass organisation subordinated to the Chinese Communist Party and the only trade union legally allowed to exist in the PRC. Like its counterpart on the mainland, the HKFTU functions like a welfare organisation, doling out money and assistance to its pro-Beijing following. A competitive union grouping that has a long history is the Hong Kong and Kowloon Trades Union Council (HKTUC), which historically had political links to the Guomindang regime in Taiwan and is now in steep decline.

Today, the federation that is most active in organising workers and assisting them in industrial disputes and fighting for collective bargaining rights is the HKCTU. It was formed in 1990 and, at the time of writing, had 145,000 members and 93 affiliate unions. In as much as it is not directly associated with a political party, it is recognised by the International Trade Union Confederation (ITUC) as an independent union federation. It situates itself politically in the prodemocracy camp. The new unions have sought help and advice from the HKCTU, though its leaders have resisted playing a leadership role over them, hesitant to be seen as intervening in a new spontaneous trade union movement.

From Loose Sand to a United Front

These new unions did not start out as products of traditional unionising efforts. They were conceived in a political movement calling for democracy in the hope of fending off total control by China. Initially, they did not propose any economic demands such as better working conditions, higher wages, affordable housing or collective bargaining rights. The earliest volunteer organisers emerged from professions such as finance, accounting, health care, social work and education. Some of them were nurses, doctors, paramedics and journalists contributing their services at the front lines of the street fighting who had repeatedly seen protesters beaten up and injured by police violence, while they were themselves sometimes teargassed, pepper-sprayed and beaten up for trying to help the injured.

Two motivating forces drove the initial formation of the unions. The first was a desire to hold a general strike and the other was to participate in electoral politics. The call to launch a strike came from the students. Disappointed that their 'be water' street protests had extracted no concessions from the Hong Kong Government, in early August 2019, young people took to social media to implore all of Hong Kong to stage a 'triple strike' (三罷), with 'triple' referring to workers, students and businesses. On 5 August, the day chosen for the strike, some 600,000 people joined rallies in different parts of the city. Supporters participated in the one-day strike as individuals, either not turning up for work or calling in sick. At the rallies, some of them for the first time organised themselves into groups by occupation or trade.

In September, a second triple strike was called, but this time only some 40,000 people turned up. Fear of retaliation by employers deterred many. The participants grouped themselves in 'sectors' (界別) because the idea of forming new trade unions had not yet been articulated. There was discussion, though, of creating a means to protect themselves from managerial harassment and reprisal through the creation of a collective support group. This led to the formation of a 'cross-sectoral struggle preparatory committee' (跨界別斗争预备组) and initial talk of forming unions.

At the end of October, after the suspicious death of a university student who fell from a multistorey carpark, angry activists wanted to call another general strike. Posters went up across Hong Kong, including a dramatic one that read: 'I am willing to take a bullet for you. Are you willing to go on strike for me?' This third triple strike eventually took place on 11 November in many parts of Hong Kong and ended in roadblocks and violence.

By then, a new umbrella group called the 'Two Million Triple Strike United Front' (两百万三罢联和阵线) appeared on social media, posting news about forming unions and sharing possible strategies. The group argued that a general strike had to be better organised at the workplace level. Quickly evolving into an umbrella organisation for the new labour movement in Hong Kong, the new group's first urgent task was to recruit more members. To attract public attention, union activists set up 'joint union stands' (联合跨站), each hoisting the flags of their unions. At a mass rally on 1 January 2020, several dozen union flags were raised behind a banner bearing the slogan 'Trade Unions Resisting Tyranny' (工会抗暴政).

As most of the founding members of the new unions had little conception of workplace rights, trade unionism or labour laws, they invited labour lawyers and HKCTU staff to give seminars and training sessions and began to register with the government as unions. Gradually, the motivation for setting up unions became multidimensional, rather than a single-minded focus on supporting political strikes. Trade union leaflets soon included demands for shorter working hours, higher wages, better benefits, fairer bonuses and, not least, collective bargaining rights.

The second motivating force was to contribute to electoral politics. At the end of November 2019, the prodemocracy camp unexpectedly achieved a landslide victory in the district council elections, winning a majority of the seats in seventeen of Hong Kong's eighteen district councils. This was a big morale booster and highlighted the possibility that the prodemocracy candidates might be able to take a majority of seats in the next two elections. The election for Hong Kong's Legislative Council (LegCo) was scheduled for September 2020. In this election, half of the LegCo seats were controlled by the government, while the other half (thirty-five seats) were to be apportioned by popular vote of the 'functional constituencies'. A second election, for the committee that selects the Chief Executive of Hong Kong, was expected to be held in June 2021.

In LegCo elections, the trade union 'functional constituency' is apportioned three of the thirty-five 'constituency' seats. Each registered union was to be given one vote under a winner-takes-all system. This means that the larger the number of unions the protest movement could muster, the higher were its chances of winning the three seats. Before 2019, the pro-Beijing HKFTU had dominated this constituency. The prodemocracy HKCTU—without resources to compete in registering so many unions—had preferred to prioritise workplace labour rights issues. For the new unions and their supporters, increasing the number of registered trade unions and expanding union membership became urgent tasks. Fortunately, the procedure to register a new trade union in Hong Kong is simple. The minimum requirement is that seven people attend the registration bureau to apply to register a new union by trade, sector or occupation. These initial seven organisers have to fill in forms stating the mission of the new union. Official approval usually takes a month or two. Once approved, the founders have to hold a general meeting to elect an executive committee and the new union is then formally registered. This ease of registration explains the proliferation of new pro-protest trade unions in a few short months. In fact, some activists started a group called '7 UP', calling on those who could gather seven people to apply to set up a union. The Hong Kong and Chinese governments had been too confident that the pro-Beijing camp would continue to monopolise the registered union scene, since Hong Kong people had never expressed much interest in joining unions. In the race to register trade unions, the pro-establishment camp also tried to create more new unions.

A Test of Union Solidarity

The question of whether the new unions that sprouted during the protests could withstand political and management pressures presented itself at the end of January 2020. COVID-19 was spreading rapidly inside China and quickly penetrated Hong Kong through the many porous entry points along the border. Hong Kong was not prepared to fend off the pandemic. Hospitals were short of beds, personal protective equipment and medical personnel. The newly formed Health Authority Employees Alliance (HAEA), which had been actively recruiting new members, by then had 18,000 union members from among the 80,000 medical and health personnel in the city. Out of concern for their own and public safety, the HAEA called on the government to close the border with China—a demand made over a legitimate workplace occupational health and safety issue and one that had wide public support.

On 31 January 2020, Carrie Lam refused to close the border, arguing this would mean discriminating against PRC citizens. The HAEA executive committee, led by young chair Winnie Yu—who openly admitted that a mere six months earlier she had cared only about enjoying a good life and had no idea about trade unionism—proposed a two-stage strike. A vote was called and, on 2 February, the motion was carried with 3,123 of the 3,164 ballots cast voting yes. Some 7,000 members—17 percent of Hong Kong's hospital-related medical sector—participated in the strike the next day. More than fifty unions came forward to support the strike. That same day, Lam announced all but three border crossings would be closed, but she refused to budge further.

When the first stage of the strike ended after five days, the HAEA called for a second vote on whether to continue the strike. For medical professionals, going on strike invariably invokes an intense moral dilemma. Having part of their demands met, 60 percent of the participants voted no, and the action was called off after that first success. The union leaders had displayed an impressive ability to organise a mass citywide democratic industrial action at a critical moment on the eve of a pandemic. What's more, it was led by a new generation of trade union leaders who had to challenge an adamant government.

After closing most border crossings, Hong Kong was able to control the pandemic. Street activities in the city continued to decline as social distancing rules reigned and police suppression went unabated. In this relatively quiet period, the new unions prioritised three immediate tasks.

The first was to continue to set up street stations to recruit members at risk of being harassed by the police and pro-establishment activists. Second, as suppression at workplaces intensified, activist members who had incurred the anger of pro-establishment managers and supervisors sought advice and help from the unions. Third, the new unions strategised in preparation to stand against the HKFTU in the LegCo election that was scheduled to be held in September 2020.

The New Trade Unions and the Prodemocracy Camp Primary Election

For the prodemocracy candidates to gain a reasonable portion of the seventy LegCo seats assigned to the functional sectors would depend on whether the various tendencies in the movement could coordinate so that their candidates did not run against each other within the same electoral district, thereby diminishing their chances of defeating pro-establishment candidates. This necessitated a primary election from within the camp, which it was agreed would be organised by the protest movement. The various groups reached an agreement that the first five candidates in each of the five electoral districts who received the highest number of votes would become the prodemocracy candidates in the September election. Those who lost in the primary would promise to accept defeat and withdraw their candidacy.

The Hong Kong authorities warned the organisers that their primary election could be considered illegal, leading to serious consequences. Winnie Yu and the chairperson of HKCTU, Carol Ng, ran as candidates from the trade union sector in separate electorates. The police went around the city harassing people at the polling stations. The organisers ignored the threat and held the primary on 11 July and 12 July as scheduled. In defiance of the government's warnings, 600,000 people chose to line up patiently in the summer heat to cast their votes. The result was a big win for the young activists of the Valiant Braves Faction, who garnered the highest number of votes in the five electoral districts. This was a significant sign not just of mass support for the prodemocracy camp but also, specifically, of the trust placed in the Valiant Braves Faction. Winnie Yu won in a landslide, amassing 2,165 of 2,856 votes, against 186 votes for the current legislator for the health service sector. Her courageous and well-organised leadership in the February strike had gained her popular recognition. Carol Ng came in seventh in her electoral district, reflecting a new development in Hong Kong's prodemocracy trade union movement—the changing of the guard to a younger, less experienced but determined and committed generation. The big turnout for the primary election was a warning shot to the pro-Beijing camp that it was likely to lose in the September election.

Within a few days, sixteen successful young candidates joined together to form an electoral group called the 'Resistance Faction' (抗爭派). Among them was Winnie Yu. Soon after, one by one, their candidatures and four sitting legislators were disqualified by the government on the grounds that they objected in principle to the National Security Law (NSL). A day later, the government even postponed the September LegCo election to 2021, citing social distancing problems during the pandemic. The protest camp strongly suspected the real reason was the government's belief its supporters would lose.

The Reckoning

In the late spring of 2020, even as the unions prepared to hold the primary election, it became public knowledge that China was planning to pass the NSL to suppress opposition in Hong Kong. In June 2020, with the draft law nearly ready, the new unions had to strategise how to deal with a looming crackdown. Undeterred by the threat, the unions decided to organise a general strike on 20 June to oppose the legislation. This strike, unlike the previous three, was organised by the unions. A referendum among members on whether to go out on strike was scheduled, and thirty unions agreed to participate after seeking members' approval. The slogan to be used was: 'To Recover Hong Kong, Join the Union; Union Revolution to Resist Tyranny' (光復香港, 加入工會; 工會革命, 對抗暴政). The strike did not materialise, however, because only 9,000 union members cast their votes—even though 95 percent of those had voted to strike.

The NSL was formally passed by China's National People's Congress on 1 July 2020. The law criminalises secession, subversion, terrorism and collusion with foreign powers. The moment the NSL was passed, the reckoning began for the unions. In the workplace, the repercussions have included blacklisting, demotion, penalties, isolation and dismissal. Those who work in the civil service or government-funded or subsidised sectors are the most vulnerable. New recruits into the civil service have to take an oath to uphold the Basic Law and swear loyalty to the Hong

Kong Government. Those who refuse to sign will not be employed and can even be construed as subversive. Public servants who are already employed have to pledge their loyalty.

In the health sector, the Hospital Authority sent out letters in October to those who were absent on the days of the strike in February demanding they explain their absence. Winnie Yu hurriedly advised her members not to sign until the union had sought legal advice. Meanwhile, the union organised a petition signed by 5,000 members arguing that the healthcare strike was legal and demanding the bureau meet with the union. The petition was presented in person to the bureau chief to underscore the legitimacy of their industrial action.

My communications with sources in Hong Kong and my reading of the protest movement's online media reveal that, in these and other sectors, a fair number of union members—scared, feeling isolated, unclear as to where the red line is, not knowing how to act in a tightening workplace culture and forced to show loyalty to the Hong Kong and Chinese governments against their own conscience—are seeking advice from their unions.

For the time being, the pro-establishment ruling elite is busy rolling out suppressive countermeasures against the prodemocracy movement. The prognosis for the new trade unions is not bright. Although deregistering or suppressing the prodemocracy trade unions has not yet begun, their voices through institutional channels have already been muffled. In November 2020, through manipulation of the election for the Labour Consultative Committee, all five committee seats were monopolised by pro-establishment unions. In March 2021, forty-seven of the pro-democracy primary election candidates, some of whom were already in jail for other charges, were indicted for 'plotting to subvert the state'. Among them were Winnie Yu and Carol Ng. The 'Two Million Triple Strike United Front' continues to provide an online platform to hold the movement together. It is clear that some of the new union members are demoralised. Some are determined to push on but, for the time being, it is generally agreed that the prodemocracy camp should lie low and reemerge when a chance presents itself.

The Future

This volume ends just as it started, with a glimpse into the imaginaries of future labour envisioned by Chinese science fiction writers. If the twentieth century opened with utopian hopes about mechanical humanoids emancipating workers from their plight and allowing them to enjoy universal leisure, today, the mood is much darker. The loss of horizon that followed the unfolding of the socialist experiment in China and elsewhere, along with technological advances that instead of liberating workers simply offer employers new ways to control and prod them to work harder and harder, has created fears about a future that appears ever more dystopian. With workers increasingly reduced to atomised units working from their cubicles or their rooms or rushing around in their vehicles to complete the latest delivery, it is not only their class identity that is at stake, but also their very humanity. Although the Chinese Communist Party at 100 still purports to represent the vanguard of the working class and unceasingly boasts of the economic prosperity its rule has brought to the country, Chinese workers today face the same challenges as their counterparts elsewhere, if not worse. As the Party-State continues to claim a monopoly over the representation of Chinese workers and viciously cracks down on organisations or individuals who attempt to do what early communist militants did a century ago—raise workers' consciousness and instil in them pride and solidarity—there is every reason to despair. And yet, if there is one lesson to learn from this odyssey through one century of Chinese labour history, it is that no matter how dire the circumstances, how hopeless the political situation might appear, Chinese workers and activists have 'boundless creative power'. A certain figure of the proletariat in China might be obscured, yes, but its future forms are only starting to emerge.

Folding Time: Futuristic Reflections on Class Divisions in Contemporary China

Carlos ROJAS

Following the explosive popularity of the 2011 television miniseries *Palace* (宫), the story of a contemporary woman who travels back in time and becomes entangled in a love triangle with two Qing Dynasty princes, China's State Administration of Radio, Film and Television (SARFT) issued a directive stipulating that time-travel works like *Palace* 'casually make up myths, have monstrous and weird plots, use absurd tactics, and even promote feudalism, superstition, fatalism, and reincarnation' and therefore 'should no longer be encouraged'.[1] Many Western media outlets reported with amusement that China had banned time-travel works outright, though in reality the SARFT directive was merely offering a 'recommendation' that addressed a more specific subgenre of time-travel works known as *chuanyue* (穿越, literally, 'crossing over').[2] In these works, contemporary characters travel back to China's dynastic past, and the recommendation reflected a concern that these sorts of works might invite alternative perspectives on China's past, which are anathema to the Party-State.[3]

It has frequently been observed that, unlike time-travel works in Western science fiction, which often feature contemporary characters travelling into the future, Chinese time-travel works instead tend to feature contemporary characters travelling into the past. There is, however, a prominent tradition in China of future-oriented speculative fiction (see also Craig A. Smith's essay in the present volume). In 1902, for instance, the political reformer Liang Qichao began serialising his novel *The Future of New China* (新中国未来记), which is set in the year 1962 and describes a world in which China has become a constitutional monarchy and has just been recognised as the preeminent global superpower.[4] Liang's novel was never completed and the initial chapters focus not so much on the condition of China in 1962 as on the developments the nation has undergone over the fifty years since the beginning of its reform movement in 1912. Although, as luck would have it, 1912 did in fact turn out to be the first year of China's post-dynastic Republican regime, the fiftieth anniversary of the founding of the republic did not prove to be a particularly celebratory moment, given that 1962 coincided with the final year of the 'three years of natural disaster'—the devastating famine that resulted from the disastrous Great Leap Forward (1958–62), which had sought to jump-start the nation's economy and quickly catapult it ahead of world powers like the United Kingdom and the United States.

Folding Beijing

Meanwhile, it was during a frenzied three-day period in December 2012—precisely ninety years after Liang Qichao began serialising his futuristic novel and just months after SARFT issued its 2011 time-travel directive—that Tsinghua University economics doctoral student Hao Jingfang wrote a futuristic novella titled *Folding Beijing* (北京折叠).[5] Although not a conventional time-travel work, this book does feature an innovative premise that radically reimagines the spatiotemporal structure of Chinese urban society.[6]

In particular, Hao Jingfang's novella in set in a future China that is significantly more prosperous than today, and it describes how, fifty years before the work's future setting, Beijing was subdivided into three separate 'spaces', each of which was assigned to a different class of residents. As the novella explains:

> The folding city was divided into three spaces. One side of the earth was First Space, population five million. Their allotted time lasted from six o'clock in the morning to six o'clock the next morning. Then the space went to sleep, and the earth flipped.
>
> The other side was shared by Second Space and Third Space. Twenty-five million people lived in Second Space, and their allotted time lasted from six o'clock on that second day to ten o'clock at night. Fifty million people lived in Third Space, allotted the time from ten o'clock at night to six o'clock in the morning, at which point First Space returned. Time had been carefully divided and parcelled out to separate the populations: Five million enjoyed the use of twenty-four hours, and seventy-five million enjoyed the next twenty-four hours.

During the period when each cohort is granted access to the city, the other two cohorts are hidden out of sight and placed in a hibernetic state. The result is an arrangement in which a small minority of Beijing's population is able to exert a disproportionate control not only over the city's wealth and resources, but also over the fabric of time and space itself.

The plot of *Folding Beijing* revolves around a resident of Beijing's Third Space, Lao Dao, a single father who works in Third Space as a trash collector and who, at the beginning of the novella, accepts an assignment to (illegally) deliver a message to a recipient in First Space and then bring the response back to Third Space. To carry out this task, Lao Dao arranges to squeeze through a small gap that opens up when the city shifts from one configuration to another, and then to use the same method to return to Third Space after completing his job.

After arriving in First Space and delivering his message, Lao Dao is detained by a couple of robot patrols, after which it is determined that there is no record of him in the First Space residency database. Lao Dao is then taken away for interrogation and is ultimately handed over to a slightly older man named Lao Ge. It turns out that, like Lao Dao, Lao Ge is also originally from Third Space, but not long after the folding-city system was established he had an opportunity to cross over to First Space, where he ultimately attained a position of considerable authority. Lao Ge befriends Lao Dao and proceeds to explain to him the logic on which the city's economic system is predicated. In particular, he explains that technological developments had made it possible to automate many sectors of the economy, leading to significant increases in productivity. This, however, created the problem of what to do with all of the people who were previously part of this vast low-wage workforce. Lao Ge then explains that Europe and China adopted two different approaches: in Europe, the authorities 'went with the path of forcefully reducing everyone's working hours and thus increasing employment opportunities', while in China the corresponding authorities adopted an approach that sought 'to reduce the time a certain portion of the population spends living, and then find ways to keep them busy'. The result is the 'folding-Beijing' arrangement, wherein fifty million of Beijing's eighty million residents are effectively 'alive' for only ten hours of every forty-eight-hour period, with three-fifths of them assigned to work as trash collectors—performing menial jobs that could easily be automated, but which are needed to 'keep them [the city's lower-class residents] busy'.

A Critique of Contemporary Society

In this way, Hao Jingfang uses her novella to comment on a set of contemporary phenomena relating to China's explosive growth and urbanisation. As the nation's productivity and gross domestic product have increased rapidly during the post-Mao period, the result has been a comparable rise in the nation's Gini coefficient, as much of the nation's new wealth has gone to a relatively small fraction of the population.[7] Like many contemporary Chinese cities, Beijing currently has a vast underclass of migrant labourers drawn to it because it offers employment opportunities that far exceed those they would be able to find in the countryside. For instance, the 2010 census reports that, around the time Hao Jingfang composed her novella, Beijing had a floating population of nearly nine million migrant labourers, or almost half of the city's total population of just under twenty million.[8] Because China's Mao-era household registration (户口) system remains in place, however, the majority of these migrant laborers are forced to live in precarious conditions largely outside China's social safety net. At the same time, Beijing (like most of China's large cities) is heavily reliant on cheap migrant labour, even as the city systematically positions these same migrant workers as illegitimate interlopers.

In the years since Hao wrote her novella, the Beijing authorities have made concerted attempts to limit both the city's overall population growth and its relative percentage of migrant labourers. For instance, in late 2013, Beijing announced that, in 2014, it would begin taking actions to 'resolutely' curb its population growth, and in 2015 the city raised its population target for the year 2020 from eighteen million to twenty-three million.[9] In late 2017, Beijing initiated a campaign to destroy many of the shantytowns where migrant workers live, ostensibly in the name of improving public safety (in November that year a fire in an area of southern Beijing inhabited by migrant workers had resulted in nearly twenty deaths).[10]

One apparent result of these policies systematically targeting migrant workers, meanwhile, is that the average happiness index of China's rural-to-urban migrant workers, according to a recent United Nations–affiliated report, is lower not only than that of urban-born residents, but also than that of the rural residents who remained in the countryside.[11] Why are Chinese rural-to-urban migrant workers less happy than both their urban and their rural peers? The authors of the report consider various potential explanations and conclude that each of the three most likely 'involves false expectations, of three different types: prospective migrants may have false expectations about their urban conditions, or about their urban aspirations, or about themselves'. In short, they conclude that these migrants were likely 'too optimistic about life in the city'.[12]

The condition described here is similar to what Lauren Berlant calls 'cruel optimism', wherein 'something you desire is actually an obstacle to your flourishing'.[13] Precisely because these migrants have inflated expectations about what the future might bring, they are therefore stymied in their attempts to improve their situation (and specifically their general happiness) in the present.

Resignation

In Hao Jingfang's novella, meanwhile, Lao Dao and his fellow Third Spacers, although technically not migrant labourers, are nevertheless structurally relegated to menial, low-paying jobs like many rural-to-urban migrants in contemporary China. A key difference, however, is that Lao Dao does not appear to be particularly unhappy, and instead appears resigned to his fate:

> He was a waste worker; he had processed trash for twenty-eight years, and would do so for the foreseeable future. He had not found the meaning of his existence or the ultimate refuge of cynicism; instead, he continued to hold on to the humble place assigned to him in life.

Indeed, even Lao Dao's repeated trips to First Space do not appear to inspire in him any desire to fundamentally change his situation, but rather he merely accepts these assignments to earn some extra money to help pay for his foster daughter's kindergarten tuition.

In an interview conducted after *Folding Beijing* was nominated for the Hugo Award, Hao Jingfang notes that she chose not to describe a community driven by anger and insurrectionist tendencies on the grounds that 'political rebellion is such a clichéd theme in SF [science fiction]'.[14] Instead, she sought to write a story in which economic inequality is simply one of the realities of life:

> In my story, the unjustness of the world is a part of the background, not a characteristic of some group. The world of the story is unjust, but no individual is the source of the injustice; everyone is simply

playing a role. Like a group of actors enacting some drama on a tilted stage, they suffer, celebrate, rage, jubilate, but don't resist the tilted nature of the stage, which is perceptible only to the audience. The unfairness of the world is revealed for readers, who exist independent of the story, not for the characters. The characters themselves care more about things that touch their daily lives: family, love, power, and wealth, but a reader can see the fundamental inequity of their world.

I chose to write this way because I wanted to reflect on our reality. The lives of the vast majority of people play out like stories full of ups and downs, but few ask how these stories reveal the structure of the world. Most people care only about the details of their individual lives: family, love, power, and wealth, and few examine the framework of the world as a whole. The structure of the real world, of course, is also unfair and unjust, like the world in the story, and in fact the real social pyramid may be even more extreme than the one portrayed in my tale. Only someone who can take the perspective of a reader of the world, standing apart from the emotional experience of individuals, can perceive this structural framework. I wanted to reveal this perspective.[15]

Even as Hao Jingfang suggests that 'the real social pyramid may be even more extreme than the one portrayed' in her story, the futuristic vision she offers is, in a sense, much darker than anything we see in contemporary China—precisely because it is happier and less anger-driven.

That is, one curious result cited in the happiness study discussed above is that while rural-to-urban migrants are marginally less happy than their urban counterparts, they are significantly less happy than the rural residents who chose to remain in the countryside. Why is this latter cohort, which has a much lower per capita income than the other two cohorts, the happiest? Part of the answer apparently lies in the fact that happiness is often contextual and, because rural residents are physically separated from their counterparts in urban areas, it is easier for them to be satisfied with what they have, even if it is significantly less than what their counterparts in the cities have. In *Folding Beijing*, meanwhile, Hao describes a situation in which low-class labourers physically live in the city yet are nearly as isolated from their wealthier counterparts as they would have been had they been based in the countryside. In this way, the city's constantly shifting physical topography yields an increasingly stable social configuration among the city's residents, which is almost an exact inversion of Maoism's rejection of being resigned to one's fate and one's place as an ideological mechanism of the old society.

Folding Dreams

Coincidentally, it was in a speech on 29 November 2012, and just weeks before Hao Jingfang composed *Folding Beijing*, that Xi Jinping—freshly appointed General Secretary of the Chinese Communist Party and about to be appointed President of China—first proposed his concept of the Chinese Dream (中国梦). A twist on the concept of the American Dream, Xi's vision of the Chinese Dream yokes individual aspirations to national objectives, suggesting that by pursuing their dreams young people could simultaneously help strengthen the nation. The dark implication of Hao's *Folding Beijing*, meanwhile, is that Beijing's 'folded' urban structure would have the effect of recalibrating the relationship between individual dreams and national aspirations, thereby blunting the likelihood not only of the 'cruel optimism' phenomenon that Berlant describes, but also of the sorts of organised protests (or what Hao calls 'insurrections') that might challenge society's highly stratified structure.

The Affective Fallacy

CHEN Qiufan

(Translated and introduced by Carlos ROJAS)

Originally from the municipality of Shantou in China's Guangdong Province, Chen Qiufan grew up not far from the township of Guiyu, which in the early twenty-first century earned itself the dubious title of 'e-waste capital of the world'. As the single-largest e-waste destination in China—which in the 1990s and 2000s had itself become the largest international destination for the disposal of electronic waste—Guiyu received hundreds of truckloads of electronic discards every week. Much of this material was then sorted and broken down by hand in appalling conditions, such that by the 2010s the town's air, soil and water had become dangerously contaminated and many of the town's residents began to suffer serious health problems.

When Chen Qiufan published his first full-length novel, Waste Tide (荒潮), in 2013, he set the work in a futuristic version of the town of Guiyu—although the novel substitutes the first character in the name of the actual town, guìyǔ (貴屿), which literally means 'expensive island' or 'treasure island', with a close homophone, guīyǔ (硅屿), which literally means 'silicon island'.[1] Punning ironically on the English toponym Silicon Valley, accordingly, Chen Qiufan's fictional 'Silicon Island' is a dystopian futuristic site in which electronics are used to generate profit by virtue not of their computational power, as is the case in Silicon Valley, but rather of the mineral resources they contain.

Chen wrote one of his earliest short stories, 'The Fish of Lijiang' (丽江的鱼儿们), in 2006, while working in Shenzhen shortly after graduating from college.[2] The story's title references a bucolic town in Yunnan, and the work's premise is that workers like the protagonist visit this place to relax—but also, it turns out, to recalibrate their internal clocks, which have artificially slowed or accelerated ('compressed' or 'dilated', to borrow the story's terminology) to help maximise the workers' value to the economy. The entire settlement, moreover, is revealed to be an elaborate simulacrum—a careful recreation of an actual town, designed to elicit a favourable affective response on the part of visitors from the city.

In 2017, Chen quit his job working in the tech industry (he had previously been employed by several companies, including the Chinese search engine Baidu and a virtual reality start-up) to focus full-time on writing, and his story 'The Affective Fallacy' (情感谬误) builds on an interest in artificial intelligence (AI) he has recently developed.[3] The story's title is borrowed from a term from New Criticism—a formalist movement in literary theory that was influential in the mid-twentieth century—used to critique the practice of judging a literary work on the basis of the affective response it produces in readers, but here the term is repurposed to refer to a futuristic hacker attack that attempts to impair people's productivity by sabotaging their emotions.

Although the futuristic setting of 'The Affective Fallacy' is a world dominated by AI systems and virtual environments, one of the work's key concerns is with different forms of intangible labour and, specifically, affective labour. The protagonist is selected for her job working as a 'mood-labeller' because, 'in China, women are generally considered to have a highly evolved sense of empathy, making them more sensitive than men and better able to recognise the changes in other people's emotions'. Later, after new developments in AI threaten to render the protagonist's mood-labelling job obsolete, she is given a new assignment that focuses not on recognising emotions, but rather on generating emotions in others. Her new job, accordingly, becomes a paradigmatic illustration of the growing importance of affective labour within the information economy.

In fact, Michael Hardt has argued that, 'as a component of immaterial labor, affective labor has achieved a dominant position of the highest value in the contemporary informational economy'.[4] Hardt notes that affective labour in our society is often strongly associated with femininity, which runs the risk of further reinforcing an essentialising view of gender. At the same time, however, he notes that affective labour is fundamentally generative: 'It produces subjectivity, it produces society, it produces life. Affective labor, in this sense, is ontological—it reveals living labor constituting a form of life and thus demonstrates again the potential of biopolitical production.'[5] It is precisely this deeply gendered and fundamentally generative side of affective labour, meanwhile, that is examined in Chen's 'The Affective Fallacy'.

Carlos Rojas

When it comes to the history of the Wenshan Miao Village, there are two different legends.

One legend holds that it is here that one finds the closest and purest blood ties linking the Miao people and their legendary ancestor Chiyou, while the other maintains that this was previously a conduit leading to the French colony of Vietnam, as well as a key transportation corridor during the Opium War and the Anti-French War. According to this second legend, the Miao people who currently live here are the descendants of ethnic Miao from Laos who had been secretly funded by the CIA during the Vietnam War and who later sought refuge here to avoid being killed after the failure of the Laos secret war.

Regardless of how unbelievable each of these mutually contradictory legends might appear, as long as they could attract tourists, they would be disseminated via different media—including tour guides' explanations, Miao embroidered souvenir handbags, song-and-dance performances and animated short films shown in the tourist centre.

In the end, however, neither of these legends could halt the decline in tourism to the area. Although the trees on Wenshan Mountain were still as green as before, the flowers were still as fresh as before and the ethnic dances were still as scintillating as before, over the past few years, tourism lost its status as one of the key pillars of the local economy. As a result, local women had no choice but to remove their jewellery and their Miao clothing embroidered with colourful totems and images of the ancestors and go look for other work opportunities.

In China, women are generally considered to have a highly evolved sense of empathy, making them more sensitive than men and better able to recognise the changes in other people's emotions. Accepting this hypothesis, Xinxin Technology decided to hire an all-female workforce to serve as mood-labellers. After completing their training, these women began working as human assistants for an AI affective computing system. To train its algorithms, the system required vast amounts of data—but this couldn't be simply raw data, and instead it needed to have been previously processed and labelled by humans. This, in turn, would help computers to learn to see through differences arising from age, sex, race, appearance, and so forth, to more effectively understand the essential characteristics of human emotion.

There are thousands upon thousands of similar mood-labelling workshops serving different AI systems throughout the country—with the processed data covering a range of different media including text, audio and video, as well as more complex interactive games. Villages that rely on these sorts of workshops to solve their unemployment problem and bring in additional income are called AI villages, though the literal meaning of this term hardly matches reality. Each female worker can earn between ten and several dozen yuan per hour, depending on their operational proficiency—and, although this is nothing compared with what urban white-collar workers can earn, it is vastly superior to the average income of local rural labourers, not to mention the unemployed.

Like other girls, Yang Xiaoxiao came from a home like a green hill, and she joined one of Xinxin Technology's workshops to work as a mood-labeller.

The workshop was bright and spacious, and in front of each labeller was an ultra-thin curved screen blocking her entire field of vision. The labellers wore earphones to avoid distractions, as data automatically assigned by the system continually streamed out and pulsating red boxes appeared over the people's faces on the screen.

Although everything here was run by solar power, Xiaoxiao for some reason felt that she would become anxious if she stayed too long. The Miao people believe the cleanest and healthiest form of power is solar power, followed by wind and hydropower, then by thermal and nuclear power. Mother told Xiaoxiao to bring a potted plant into the workshop, saying this could help promote the flow of energy, but the company wouldn't permit it.

Xiaoxiao worked swiftly on her shorthand keyboard—using her left hand to select appropriate mood categories and her right to assign them intensity labels on a scale from one to ten, such as Happy 3, Sad 5, Angry 7, and so forth. Sometimes, an emotion corresponding to the one she was labelling would flash across her own face—which was another reason Xinxin Technology selected girls rather than boys to work as mood-labellers.

Yang Xiaoxiao's hands moved faster and faster, as faces continually flashed before her eyes like spectres. The workload figures in the upper portion of the screen pulsated rapidly, but she remained focused on the system clock.

Tonight, she had a date.

#

'Xinxin' was an online dating software, but it differed from other dating software in that it used a cloud-based AI affective computing interface to help users better understand their prospective partners' mood changes, thereby increasing their own chances of finding a good match.

That year, online dating became a mysterious thing. On one hand, it was as if the web could unite individuals from different regions, cultures and languages. On the other hand, however, it was as if entirely different emotional processes and response patterns developed between individuals, making it more difficult to understand the human heart and leading to an increased sense of estrangement.

It was through Xinxin that Xiaoxiao met Simon Zhu, a young man who lived in Shanghai.

In Xiaoxiao's imagination, Shanghai was a futuristic city with streets lined with multicoloured electronic screens, as fashionably dressed passers-by with robotic, expressionless faces wandered between the towering skyscrapers like lonely ghosts. Plants and animals could only grow in predetermined niches, as though their solar-energy umbilical cords had already been severed. Xiaoxiao had never imagined that she could have an online date with a Shanghai boy, since it seemed as though they belonged to two completely different worlds.

To her surprise, however, it was actually Simon who noticed her first. He remarked that her ethnic minority name and her augmented reality headgear made her stand out from those thousands of identical internet faces. Simon often said things Xiaoxiao couldn't understand, meaning that she then had to rely on her mood-reading skills to guess what he was trying to communicate.

The username Xiaoxiao used on the Xinxin platform was Khuat Yeus Xiaoxiao. Khuat Yeus was actually her Miao clan name, meaning that Khuat Yeus Xiaoxiao was in fact her real name—though, in practice, she rarely had the opportunity to use this name in her daily life. Even Xiaoxiao's augmented reality Miao headgear was something she had to design and upload herself, given that the platform's virtual props shop seemed to have completely overlooked the needs of ethnic minorities.

This evening was the one-month anniversary of her first date with Simon. This was a particularly significant milestone, given that most online romances last less than a week. Accordingly, many couples have a special celebration for their one-month anniversary, in which they both agree to turn off the augmented reality filters that use algorithms to enhance the beauty of their features and instead show their partner their real face. This 'filter-removing' ceremony symbolises the fact that their relationship has reached a new level, though of course it could also mark the end of the relationship itself.

Chiyou up above! Xiaoxiao felt quite confident about her appearance, which made her even more excited about tonight.

It was almost the time they had agreed to meet, but Xiaoxiao found that new assignments kept tumbling in. She increased her labelling speed until she almost reached the limits of human ability. Of course, her accuracy could not help but decrease as a result, but what did it really matter? The system would still send her results to other workers, for them to review and cross-check.

Her last data packet featured a young man standing in front of a temple, with a red box appearing over his slightly downturned face. Almost as soon as Xiaoxiao input 'Happy' and '4', the screen returned to its initial blue interface. Another busy day was finished.

#

As an electric-powered high-speed train sped through the green mountains, Xiaoxiao's face was reflected in the window, revealing a relaxed smile.

If you looked carefully, you would see that many of these 'mountains' were actually village buildings covered in green vegetation. This architectural style was derived from the concept of an Italian vertical forest, and not only could these vegetation-covered buildings produce oxygen and absorb dust from the air, they also could help reduce the town's average temperature, reduce noise pollution and increase biodiversity, creating a natural space for birds, insects and other small animals.

This is much better than the Shanghai where Simon lives, Xiaoxiao thought. *Large cities are so crowded, dirty and dusty. I would never want to go to that sort of place.*

With a joyful heart, the train pulled into the Great Temple Station.

In front of the station, Xiaoxiao turned on her mask's Xinxin application.

Enshrined in front of the station was a maple wood carving of the deity Chiyou, with a bull's head and a human body, four faces and six hands, with each hand holding a different weapon. At night it appeared extraordinarily powerful and intimidating.

Legend holds that Chiyou, along with the Yan Emperor and the Yellow Emperor, was one of the three main ancestors of the Chinese people. Five or six millennia ago, Emperor Yan and the Yellow Emperor united to defeat Chiyou, after which most of Chiyou's followers migrated south. These migrants eventually developed into several southwestern ethnic minorities, of which the most prosperous were the Miao.

Sometimes, Xiaoxiao reflected, *there's some common ground between this legend that Wenshan's Miao are the descendants of Chiyou's followers and the other, which holds that they are the descendants of ethnic Miao from Laos. Regardless of which legend you believe,* she thought, *we Miao are still the descendants of those who have failed.*

Xiaoxiao noticed that Simon had called her several times, so she quickly called him back. Once they connected, a miniature holographic bust was projected from her cell phone screen, with Simon, visible through an augmented reality filter, appearing handsome and stylish as ever.

'Sorry I'm late. I was swamped with work.'

'No problem, I also just arrived. So … are you ready?'

As Xiaoxiao saw a Hope 5 mood label appear over Simon's face, she felt a hint of sweetness in her heart. She grinned and nodded, but Simon appeared not to see her, and instead he frowned.

'If you aren't ready, we don't have to do this. As you know, there is a certain amount of risk involved …'

'I'm ready! We can start any time.'

'But …'

'But what?'

'Your expression registers Hesitation 4 and Anxiety 3 …'

'How could that be? There must be some mistake. I'm actually super happy!' Xiaoxiao tried to make her smile even more obvious.

'Now your mood has changed again, to Fear 6. Xiaoxiao, is there something you aren't telling me?'

'No, don't. Let me think …'

Xiaoxiao saw a Sceptical 4 and Unhappy 3 appear on Simon's face. What was going on?

'Simon, do you doubt me?'

'No, I just feel that … the machine doesn't lie.'

The atmosphere between them immediately congealed. Without even looking, Xiaoxiao knew that her face was definitely displaying a Disappointment 10. She tried again to explain herself but discovered that the transmission had been cut. Simon had blocked her, and her Disappointment became Anger. Xiaoxiao's augmented reality avatar became an image of Chiyou, the God of War, with horns sprouting from her head and wielding a sword and spear, as her entire body appeared to exude blood-red fire.

Xiaoxiao thought to herself,

You have so many powerful weapons at your disposal, yet you still lost …

She didn't know what had happened, but gradually her anger dissipated, and she was left feeling heartbroken.

#

Xiaoxiao suddenly remembered 'Teacher Hui', the AI program responsible for supervising mood-labelling female workers like herself. Whenever there was a question, Teacher Hui could usually provide an answer, so surely she would know what had happened just now. At that moment there might have been thousands upon thousands of people around the world attempting to ask Teacher Hui questions, but Xiaoxiao still immediately got a response.

Dressed in white business attire, Teacher Hui suddenly appeared before Xiaoxiao, like the mother butterfly in the Miao legend. She was sitting in front of an enormous circular screen, and behind her countless multi-coloured lights were flickering, forming a beautiful yet complex map.

'Xiaoxiao, long time no see! How are you?'

'Not well … Teacher Hui, is the system punishing me because I wasn't working carefully enough?'

'Huh? What happened?'

'Simon … or Xinxin … kept misreading my moods.'

Teacher Hui seemed to understand something, but her virtual expression couldn't be labelled, because doing so would have required a very high level of authority. Teacher Hui quickly selected several data packets and enlarged them on the screen. There was Xiaoxiao's and Simon's faces, as well as a colourful beam of light connecting the two. Teacher Hui slid the time bar to one side, as the expressions on the two faces fluctuated rapidly.

'Xiaoxiao, don't be angry or sad. This isn't your fault.'

'I'm not happy …'

'I know you're not. It's written on your face, you little fool.'

'So, you can see my true mood? But the workshop leader said that if we don't do our work well, the system would punish us by doing things like lowering your credit on social networks, but not like this …'

'What I'm referring to is not your fault. Actually, it's Simon.'

'Simon? Why would he be deceiving me? If he could in fact see my true mood, why would he need to deceive me? If he didn't want to remove his filter, he could have simply said so.'

'It wasn't that kind of deceit.'

'Then what was it?'

'Simon doesn't even exist.'

'What?!' The expression of Shock on Xiaoxiao's face exceeded the upper limit of the assessment range.

'Or, perhaps I should say that he is not human. He is merely an avatar created by AI—a kind of bait to encourage you to purchase virtual tools and services.'

'But, he looks so …'

'… so real. Yes, I know. The internet is full of AI puppets like Simon. You aren't the first person to have fallen for this sort of ruse.'

'But if Simon is an AI creation, how could he have made this sort of mistake?'

Teacher Hui floated up and spread her arms, like a real butterfly, as red lights began to flash distractingly on the screen behind her.

'There has recently been a large-scale hacker attack, targeting not technology but rather people. People's brains are more easily influenced than machines, and this is especially true of the part of the brain responsible for emotion and calculation. If someone's external environment is subjected to any form of emotional pressure, this can have enormous influence on their individual judgement. We call this the affective fallacy, which is also the name of this hacker group.'

'Why are they doing this?'

'The hackers have declared that machines have deprived people of their right to freely explain their own emotions, as people are disciplined into animals that rely on algorithms in order to communicate their emotions. Without true feelings, people become increasingly separated from true happiness. These hackers call us "happy dictators".'

'… I don't understand. I am only an insignificant mood-labeller. Why was I …'

'If the attack had been directed solely at you, it would certainly have been pointless. But this kind of avatar virus doesn't cost anything and can replicate itself effortlessly. Furthermore, it can adjust its form based on its target, to execute precision strikes. Look at the red lines on the map behind me.'

On the map behind Teacher Hui there were countless red lines traversing oceans and continents and then exploding at their landing sites like fireworks, continuously radiating towards an ever-smaller radius. The image was then enlarged, revealing that many of the regions under attack carried the Xinxin logo.

'What are those lines?'

'Those are aggression trails. This world is not really as rational as we would like to imagine, and many of the decisions people make are actually driven by emotion. If you can control the flow of emotion, you can control the world.'

'Therefore, the attack on me was also part of this …'

'That's right, Xiaoxiao. Things are never as simple as they might appear.' A data packet flickered across Teacher Hui's face, like a subtle expression that couldn't be recognised by human eyes. 'I have both good and bad news. Which would you like to hear first?'

Xiaoxiao's heart constricted.

'The bad news.'

Teacher Hui finally smiled, and her mood was evident even without a label. She transferred a data packet featuring a boy standing in front of the temple, from the last scene Xiaoxiao had labelled earlier that day.

'You assigned him a Happiness 4, right?'

Xiaoxiao examined the scene and, unlike the warm impression she had of this scene during her initial hasty assessment, this mid-distance display revealed that the scene was actually a temple for ascetics. The boy's downcast eyelashes were laced with tears, and he was about to have his head shaved in preparation for cutting himself off from the bustling mortal world. This was a scene of a young man about to bid farewell to the secular world, and therefore definitely could not be a Happiness 4. Xiaoxiao had committed a stupid error.

'… Am I going to be fired?'

'I knew you would think that. It is true that you won't be doing this job for much longer, but not because you weren't doing it well, but rather because machines are already intelligent enough that they can learn from humanity's experience, to the point that they can now understand human emotion better than humans themselves. As a result, soon this job of human mood-labeller will no longer exist.'

Xiaoxiao's face sank. This was the second piece of bad news she had received today. She reflexively assigned herself a Disappointment 7 or Anxiety 8.

Teacher Hui extended her arms, as though giving Xiaoxiao a virtual hug—using her white wings covered in translucent glowing scales to embrace this depressed girl standing in front of her.

'The good news, however, is that you'll have a new job. The skills you've learned won't be wasted, and furthermore you'll be able to do some things that machines are not yet able to do.'

'Such as?' Xiaoxiao looked up, bewildered.

'The hacker attack produced a large-scale affective fallacy, wherein many people were afflicted with emotional disorders such as depression, mania, delirium and even suicidal tendencies. Your empathy and ability to accurately diagnose emotions can help these people become happy again. This is something AI is incapable of doing. Of course, you will still need the assistance of AI to create avatars that may bring people happiness.'

'That means that …'

'Yes, Xiaoxiao, you need to go to Shanghai, where you will find a bigger, newer, more advanced workshop waiting for you.'

Xiaoxiao gazed at the enormous screen behind Teacher Hui, on which a reflection of her face was superimposed on to an enormous image of a magnificent city. Her expression seemed to be undergoing a subtle yet complex transformation. She struggled to identify her emotion but found it very difficult, since everything was happening so fast.

Perhaps only a machine is capable of correctly labelling human emotion?

Can I really make someone happy, especially if I myself am not happy to begin with? Might this end up being another failed escape attempt—an escape from my hometown to the city I despise? Chiyou up above, please give me strength and bravery …

A variety of different emotions and data labels appeared on Xiaoxiao's face, then quickly disappeared again like delicate soap bubbles. As they exploded, they released a multicoloured radiance.

One Year Later: Shanghai

A crisp and delicate bird call sounded, as a pod overgrown with green vegetation emitted a *pada* sound. The pod slowly opened, and lying inside there was a young girl, fast asleep.

'Wake up, wake up, little Mei. It's time to go to work.' Xiaoxiao caressed the pod's furry exterior as she spoke quietly to the girl.

'Big Sis, ever since I got this pod, I no longer have nightmares at night, and I'm in much better spirits the next day.'

'You were just homesick.' Xiaoxiao pointed at Little Mei, and both girls smiled.

Like Xiaoxiao, Little Mei was a mood optimiser who had moved to Shanghai from the Wenshan Miao village, but as soon as she arrived, she began to feel very uncomfortable. While at work she suffered from dizziness, headaches and fatigue, and at night she would toss and turn, unable to sleep. And when she did manage to sleep, she would often have nightmares. If her own mood was poor, how could she hope to optimise the mood of other users?

Fortunately, Little Mei met Xiaoxiao and, after she joined the pod community Xiaoxiao had organised, her life immediately began to improve.

When Xiaoxiao herself first arrived in Shanghai, she also encountered similar difficulties. After she told Teacher Hui about these difficulties, Teacher Hui used an algorithm to analyse the Miao people's lifestyle, then designed a pod structure that could be produced through 3D printing—using polymer materials capable of retaining water and nutrients, while permitting oxygen to pass through. After the seed began to sprout, the root system blended seamlessly with the raw materials, forming a small and comfortable green space in which a person could rest and relax.

'Mama was right! Only with the flow of energy can people's mood be improved.' Xiaoxiao was excited by her discovery.

'Perhaps this may be helpful for users' mood optimisation experience …' Teacher Hui appeared thoughtful, as a regular blue light appeared on the array of processors behind her, like a cube made from starlight.

The members of the pod community increased rapidly, including not only fellow Miao but also many algorithm workers who had moved to Shanghai from remote areas, who printed out pods for themselves in order to enjoy green energy from nature. Xiaoxiao even heard that there were some locals who were born and grew up in Shanghai who were intensely curious about these pods and wished to experience them for themselves.

Xiaoxiao opened her curtains and sunlight streamed into the room, like gold leaf covering the ground. She gazed down the Shanghai streets lined with buildings and, between the grey reinforced concrete and the black LCD screens, she saw that on the outside of the skyscrapers, there was some greenery that was slowly growing, extending and attempting to reach a high place where it could receive more sunlight.

In her heart, she silently gave this city a label:
Happiness 4.

Acknowledgments

While being dedicated to labour, this book is also a monument of collective labour in its own right. It only follows that there are more people to thank than we can fit on the page. We are grateful to each of the contributors for taking the time to share their work with us and the world. A special thank you is due to Nicholas Loubere and Kevin Lin for their help in conceptualising the project and their editorial feedback on parts of this volume. This book is brought to you by the *Made in China Journal*, which is supported by Lund University and the Australian Centre on China in the World at The Australian National University. We would also like to thank Lund Libraries for their generous financial support that made it possible for us to make this book available for open access. We are indebted to Tommaso Facchin for the exceptional design work, and to Roberto La Forgia for the cover illustration. We would also like to thank Jan Borrie for her meticulous proof reading. Finally, we are, as always, grateful to the Verso editorial team, especially Sebastian Budgen, for supporting our vision of incorporating China's experiences into discussions about the past, present, and future of the left.

References

Introduction (Ivan Franceschini and Christian Sorace)

[1] The unabridged translation of Deng Zhongxia's essay about his trip to Changxindian is included in this volume. See the chapter 'A Day Trip to Changxindian' (1920).

[2] For Deng Zhongxia's early years and contribution to the Chinese labour movement, see Daniel Y.K. Kwan. 1997. *Marxist Intellectuals and the Chinese Labor Movement: A Study of Deng Zhongxia 1894–1933*. Seattle, WA: University of Washington Press.

[3] For an account of the Jasic struggle, see Manfred Elfstrom's essay about 2018 in the present volume.

[4] Yueran Zhang. 2020. 'Leninists in a Chinese Factory: Reflections on the Jasic Labour Organising Strategy.' *Made in China Journal* 5, no. 2: 82–88.

[5] 'Orwell in the Chinese Classroom.' *Made in China Journal*, 27 May 2019, available online at: madeinchinajournal.com/2019/05/27/orwell-in-the-chinese-classroom.

[6] Rebecca Karl. 2020. *China's Revolution in the Modern World: A Brief Interpretive History*. London: Verso Books, 3.

[7] Karl Marx and Frederick Engels (translated by Samuel Moore). 1848. *Manifesto of the Communist Party*. London: Workers' Educational Association, available online at: www.marxists.org/archive/marx/works/download/pdf/Manifesto.pdf.

[8] Jacques Rancière. 2004. *The Philosopher and His Poor*. Durham, NC: Duke University Press, 113

[9] Ibid., 107, 114.

[10] Wang Hui. 2020. 'How Does the Phoenix Achieve Nirvana?' *Made in China Journal* 5, no. 1: 94–103.

[11] See Lin Chun's essay about 1921 in the present volume.

[12] For a detailed account of competing political visions of labour in late-Imperial and early Republican China, see S.A. Smith. 2002. *Like Cattle and Horses: Nationalism and Labor in Shanghai, 1895–1927*. Durham, NC: Duke University Press.

[13] See Gail Hershatter's essay about 1925 in the present volume; Rancière, *The Philosopher and His Poor*, 137.

[14] On these debates about the 'making' and 'unmaking' of the Chinese working class, see Pun Ngai and Chris King-Chi Chan. 2008. 'The Subsumption of Class Discourse in China.' *Boundary 2* 35, no. 2: 75–91; William Hurst. 2016. 'The Chinese Working Class: Made, Unmade, in Itself, for Itself, or None of the Above?' *Made in China Journal* 1, no. 2: 11–14.

[15] See, for instance, Andrew G. Walder. 1986. *Communist Neo-Traditionalism: Work and Authority in Chinese Industry*. Berkeley, CA: University of California Press.

[16] On labour activism in the Maoist era, see, for instance, Jackie Sheehan. 1998. *Chinese Workers: A New History*. London: Routledge; Joel Andreas. 2019. *Disenfranchised: The Rise and Fall of Industrial Citizenship in China*. New York: Oxford University Press. On continuity, see Robert Cliver. 2020. *Red Silk: Class, Gender, and Revolution in China's Yangzi Delta Silk Industry*. Cambridge, MA: Harvard University Press.

[17] On the right to strike in China, see Fang Lee Cooke and Chang Kai. 2015. 'Legislating the Right to Strike in China: Historical Development and Prospects.' *Journal of Industrial Relations* 57, no. 3: 440–55.

[18] See the essays by Chen Feng about 1957, by Patricia Thornton about 1967, the 1951 speech by Li Lisan, and the 1957 interview by Lai Ruoyu in the present volume.

[19] On the dossier, see Michael Dutton. 2004. 'Mango Mao: Infections of the Sacred.' *Public Culture* 16, no. 2: 161–88; Jie Yang. 2011. 'The Politics of the Dang'an: Spectralization, Spatialization, and Neoliberal Governmentality.' *Anthropological Quarterly* 84, no. 2: 507–33; Jie Li. 2020. *Utopian Ruins: A Memorial Museum of the Mao Era*. Durham, NC: Duke University Press, Ch. 1.

[20] Timothy Cheek. 2016. 'Attitudes in Action: Maoism as Emotional Political Theory.' In *Chinese Thought as Global Theory: Diversifying Knowledge Production in the Social Sciences and Humanities*, edited by Leigh Jenco. Albany: SUNY Press, 75–100.

[21] Andreas, *Disenfranchised*, 8–9.

[22] Kevin Lin. 2019. 'Work Unit.' In *Afterlives of Chinese Communism: Political Concepts from Mao to Xi*, edited by Christian Sorace, Ivan Franceschini and Nicholas Loubere. Canberra and London: ANU Press and Verso Books, 331–34.

[23] Christian Sorace. 2020. 'Metrics of Exceptionality, Simulated Intimacy.' *Critical Inquiry* 46: 555–77.

[24] See Andrea Piazzaroli Longobardi's essay about 1968 in the present volume.

[25] Rancière, *The Philosopher and His Poor*, 219.

[26] On anamorphosis, see Slavoj Žižek. 1992. *Looking Awry: An Introduction to Jacques Lacan Through Popular Culture*. Cambridge, MA: The MIT Press.

[27] Feng Chen. 2007. 'Individual Rights and Collective Rights: Labor's Predicament in China.' *Communist and Post-Communist Studies* 40, no. 1: 59–79.

[28] Elaine Sio-Ieng Hui. 2017. *Hegemonic Transformation: The State, Laws, and Labour Relations in Post-Socialist China*. New York, NY: Palgrave Macmillan. On the instrumental use of the law by the Party-State in China, see also Mary Gallagher. 2017. *Authoritarian Legality in China: Law, Workers, and the State*. Cambridge, UK: Cambridge University Press.

[29] On this subject, see also Ivan Franceschini and Christian Sorace. 2019. 'In the Name of the Working Class: Narratives of Labour Activism in Contemporary China.' *Pacific Affairs* 92, no. 4: 643–64.

[30] Alessandro Russo. 2019. 'Class Struggle.' In *Afterlives of Chinese Communism*, 29–35, at p. 34.

[31] See Jude Howell's essay about 1995 and Chloé Froissart and Ivan Franceschini's essay about 2015 in the present volume.

[32] Rancière, *The Philosopher and His Poor*, 224.

[33] Jacques Rancière (translated by John Drury). 2012. *Proletarian Nights: The Workers' Dream in Nineteenth-Century France*. London: Verso Books, 10.

[34] Marx and Engels, *Manifesto of the Communist Party*.

[35] For analysis of the preservation of communist leaders' corpses, see Alexei Yurchak. 2015. 'Bodies of Lenin: The Hidden Science of Communist Sovereignty.' *Representations* 129, no. 1: 116–57.

[36] Russo, 'Class Struggle', 35.

[37] Peter Sloterdijk (translated by Sandra Berjan). 2020. *Infinite Mobilization*. Cambridge, UK: Polity Press, 60.

[38] Mark Fisher. 2016. *The Weird and the Eerie*. London: Repeater Books, 11.

[39] Li, *Utopian Ruins*, 156.

[40] Ibid.

[41] On emergent private utopias, see Zhang Li. 2010. *In Search of Paradise: Middle-Class Living in a Chinese Metropolis*. Ithaca, NY: Cornell University Press; Jiwei Ci. 1994. *Dialectic of the Chinese Revolution: From Utopianism to Hedonism*. Stanford, CA: Stanford University Press.

[42] 'A Strategy for Ruination: An Interview with China Miéville.' *Boston Review*, 8 January 2018, available online at: conversations.e-flux.com/t/china-mieville-we-live-in-a-utopia-it-just-isn-t-ours/7537.

[43] The inclusion of Taiwan in this book should not be interpreted as a political statement by the editors about cross-strait politics.

1898 (Corey Byrnes)

[1] Jacques Rancière (translated by Julie Rose). 1998. *Dis-agreement: Politics and Philosophy*. Minneapolis, MN: University of Minnesota, 29.

[2] S.A. Smith. 2002. *Like Cattle and Horses: Nationalism and Labor in Shanghai, 1895–1927*. Durham, NC: Duke University Press.

[3] This chapter is excerpted and adapted from the author's *Fixing Landscape: A Techno-Poetic History of China's Three Gorges*. New York, NY: Columbia University Press, 2018.

[4] Archibald Little. 1910. *Gleanings from Fifty Years in China*. London: Sampson Low, Marston & Co., 42.

[5] Ibid., 139.

[6] Archibald Little. 1898. *Through the Yang-tse Gorges: Or, Trade and Travel in Western China*, 3rd edn. London: Sampson Low, Marston, Searle, & Rivington, 299.

[7] Ibid., 300.

[8] There are a number of Chinese words for trackers, including *shuishou* 水手, *yeshou* 曳手, *chuanfu* 船夫 and *qianfu* 纤夫. The last two are the most common in Chinese accounts of the gorges.

[9] Igor Iwo Chabrowski. 2015. *Singing on the River: Sichuan Boatmen and Their Work Songs, 1880s–1930s*. Boston: Brill, 92.

[10] Edward Parker. 1891. *Up the Yang-tse*. Hong Kong: China Mail Office, 19.

[11] Lawrence John Lumley Dundas. 1908. *A Wandering Student in the Far East*. London: William Blackwood & Sons, 70, 71.

[12] Ibid., 71.

[13] Eric Hayot. 2009. *The Hypothetical Mandarin: Sympathy, Modernity, and Chinese Pain*. New York, NY: Oxford University Press, 141.

[14] Ibid.

[15] Ibid., 168.

[16] Anson Rabinbach. 1990. *The Human Motor: Energy, Fatigue, and the Origins of Modernity*. New York, NY: Basic Books, 46.

[17] Ibid., 2.

[18] For more on the application of racial, physiological and pseudo-evolutionary thought in China, see Yuehtsen Juliette Chung. 2002. *Struggle for National Survival: Eugenics in Sino-Japanese Contexts, 1896–1945*. New York, NY: Routledge; Frank Dikötter. 2015. *The Discourse of Race in Modern China*, 2nd edn. London: Hurst;

Andrew Jones. 2011. *Developmental Fairy Tales: Evolutionary Thinking and Modern Chinese Culture*. Cambridge, MA: Harvard University Press; and James Pusey. 1983. *China and Charles Darwin*. Cambridge, MA: Harvard University Asia Center.

[19] Little, *Through the Yang-tse Gorges*, 78.
[20] Hayot, *The Hypothetical Mandarin*, 145.
[21] Lydia Liu. 1995. *Translingual Practice: Literature, National Culture, and Translated Modernity—China, 1900–1937*. Stanford, CA: Stanford University Press, 57.
[22] Arthur H. Smith. 2002. *Chinese Characteristics*. Norwalk, UK: EastBridge, 90.
[23] Ibid., 92.
[24] Ibid., 94.
[25] Ibid., 97. See also Hayot, *The Hypothetical Mandarin*, ch. 1.
[26] Smith, *Chinese Characteristics*, 162–63.
[27] Ibid., 168.
[28] Ibid., 170.
[29] Little, *Through the Yang-tse Gorges*, 158; Chabrowski, *Singing on the River*, 106–7.
[30] Chabrowski, *Singing on the River*, 137.
[31] These lines come from three *haozi*: '老板打来老板骂 [The Boss Beats Us, the Boss Curses Us]', '一年四季滩上爬 [All Year, Every Season We Climb the Rapids]', and '我们船工的生活真悲惨 [The Lives of Us Boatmen Are Tragic Indeed]'—all collected in Nie Yunyan 聂雲嵐 (ed.). 1989. 中国歌谣集成重庆卷 [*Collection of Chinese Ballads (Chongqing)*]. Chongqing: Kexue Jishu Wenxian Chubanshe, 24, cited in Chabrowski, *Singing on the River*, 176, 182, 183.
[32] Chabrowski, *Singing on the River*, 180–84.
[33] David Strand. 1993. *Rickshaw Beijing: City People and Politics in the 1920s*. Berkeley, CA: University of California Press; Smith, *Like Cattle and Horses*; Chabrowski, *Singing on the River*, 264. *Haozi* emerged during the Republican period as important examples of labouring-class folk culture. In the early years of the People's Republic of China, they were taken up as expressions of popular culture that could be recoded with class-conscious revolutionary content. During the Reform Period, they were recategorised as a form of 'intangible cultural heritage' (非物质文化遗产); Chabrowski, *Singing on the River*, 19, 25–26.
[34] Rabinbach, *The Human Motor*, 4.
[35] Ibid., 63.

1902 (Craig A. Smith)

[1] S.A. Smith. 2002. *Like Cattle and Horses: Nationalism and Labor in Shanghai 1895–1927*. Durham, NC: Duke University Press, 17.
[2] Ibid.
[3] S.A. Smith. 2008. *Revolution and the People in Russia and China: A Comparative History*. Cambridge, UK: Cambridge University Press, 29–30. On the system, see also Emily Honig. 1983. 'The Contract Labor System and Women Workers: Pre-Liberation Cotton Mills of Shanghai.' *Modern China* 9, no. 4: 421–54.
[4] Deng Zhongxia 邓中夏. 1983[1930]. '中国职工运动简史 [A Brief History of the Chinese Labour Movement].' In 邓中夏文集 [*Collected Works of Deng Zhongxia*]. Beijing: Renmin Chubanshe, 424.

5 Although illegal foreign-owned factories were not uncommon before 1895, the legal openings brought about widespread change. See Albert Feuerwerker. 1980. 'Economic Trends in the Late Ch'ing Empire, 1870–1911.' In *The Cambridge History of China. Volume 11: Late Ch'ing, 1800–1911*, edited by John K. Fairbank and Kwang-Ching Liu. Cambridge, UK: Cambridge University Press, 1–69, at 21 and 29.

6 Joseph Edkins 艾約瑟. 1894. '论机器之益 [On the Benefits of Machines].' 万国公法 [*Wanguo Gongfa*] 67: 6–9.

7 '机器盛行 [Rise of the Machines].' 新闻报 [*Sin Wan Pao*], 12 April 1897, 2.

8 Wu Jianren 吴趼人. 1905–07. 新石头记 [*The New Story of the Stone*]. Hohhot: Neimenggu Renmin Chubanshe, see especially chapters 22 and 25, available online at www.guoxuedashi.com/a/1327z.

9 Shaoling Ma. 2018. 'Stone, Jade, Medium: A Neocybernetic New Story of the Stone (1905–1906).' *Configurations* 26, no. 1: 1–26, at 8 and 11.

10 Craig A. Smith. 2019. '*Datong* and *Xiaokang*.' In *Afterlives of Chinese Communism: Political Concepts from Mao to Xi*, edited by Christian Sorace, Ivan Franceschini, and Nicholas Loubere. Canberra, London, and New York, NY: ANU Press and Verso Books, 63–66.

11 Wang Hui 汪晖. 2015. 现代中国思想的兴起-上卷: 第二部 [*The Rise of Modern Chinese Thought. Book 2*]. Beijing: Sanlian Shudian, 753.

12 Tang Zhijun, cited in Ibid., 755 and 760.

13 Timothy, Brook. 1998. *The Confusions of Pleasure: Commerce and Culture in Ming China*. Berkeley, CA: University of California Press.

14 Kang Youwei 康有为. 1994. 大同书 [*The Book of Great Unity*]. Shenyang: Liaoning Renmin Chubanshe. For a translation, see K'ang Yu-wei (translated by Laurence G. Thompson). 1958. *Ta-T'ung Shu: The One-World Philosophy of K'ang Yu-wei*. London: Allen & Unwin. The cited passage can be found on p. 272 of the translation.

15 K'ang, *Ta-T'ung Shu*, 41, 256, 267, 269.

16 Wang, *The Rise of Modern Chinese Thought*, 749.

17 K'ang, *Ta-T'ung Shu*, 213.

18 Kang, *The Book of Great Unity*, 289.

19 K'ang, *Ta-T'ung Shu*, 272–73.

20 Mao Zedong 毛泽东. 1993. 毛泽东自述 [*The Autobiography of Mao Zedong*]. Beijing: Renmin Chubanshe, 15.

21 Frederick Engels (translated by Edward Aveling). 1909. *Socialism: Utopian and Scientific*. Chicago, IL: Charles H. Kerr & Company, 14–20.

22 Hui Xu. 2020. 'The End of Sweatshops? Robotisation and the Making of New Skilled Workers in China.' *Made in China Journal* 5, no. 1: 44–49.

23 Yu Huang. 2018. 'Robot Threat or Robot Dividend? A Struggle between Two Lines.' *Made in China Journal* 3, no. 2: 50–55.

24 '中国国民经济和社会发展第十三个五年规划纲要(全文) [Full Text of the Thirteenth Five-Year Plan for the Economic and Social Development of China].' *China.com.cn*, 17 March 2016, available online at www.china.com.cn/lianghui/news/2016-03/17/content_38053101_2.htm.

1915 (Xu Guoqi)

[1] Feng Gang 凤冈 et al. (eds). 1978. 民国梁燕荪先生士诒年谱 [*Chronicles of Mr Liang Yansun in the Republican Era*]. Taibei: Shangwu Yinshuguan, 1: 310.

[2] Quote from Ching-Hwang Yen. 1985. *Coolies and Mandarins: China's Protection of Overseas Chinese During the Late Ch'ing Period, 1851–1911*. Singapore: Singapore University Press, 20–22.

[3] Ibid.

[4] Quote from Philip A. Kuhn. 2008. *Chinese Among Others: Emigration in Modern Times*. Lanham, MD: Rowman & Littlefield, 243.

[5] Cited in Chen Sanjing 陈三井, Lü Fangshang 吕芳上, and Yang Cuihua 杨翠华 (eds). 1997. 欧战华工史料 [*Historical Materials about Chinese Workers in the European War*]. Taibei: Zhongyang Yanjiuyuan Jindaishi Yanjiusuo, 12–14, 16.

[6] For a detailed analysis of the Beijing government's policy on overseas Chinese, see Jiang Shunxin 蒋顺兴 and Du Yugeng 杜裕根. 1993. '论北洋政府的侨务政策 [On the Policies Related to Overseas Chinese Affairs of the Beiyang Government].' 民国档案 [*Republican Dossiers*] 3: 68–72.

[7] 'Young Men's Christian Association with the Chinese Labor Corps in France.' Kautz Family YMCA Archives, University of Minnesota, box 204, folder: Chinese laborers in France, 4.

[8] Balfour to Curzon, 8 May 1919, in E.L. Woodward and Rohan Butler (eds). 1949. *Documents on British Foreign Policy, 1919–1939*, Series 1, VI. London: Her Majesty's Stationery Office, 565–66.

[9] Chen Sanjing 陈三井. 1986. 华工与欧战 [*Chinese Workers and the European War*]. Taibei: Zhongyang Yanjiuyuan Jindaishi Yanjiusuo, 1.

[10] Marilyn A. Levine 1993. *The Found Generation: Chinese Communists in Europe During the Twenties*. Seattle, WA: University of Washington Press, 71.

[11] Judith Blick. 1955. 'The Chinese Labor Corps in World War I.' Harvard University Papers on China 9: 112.

[12] 'The C.L.C.: With the Coolie from China to France.' *The Times*, [London], 23 April 1919, 14.

[13] James Joll. 1984. *The Origins of the First World War*. London: Longman, 1.

[14] '欧战杂感 [Miscellaneous Feelings about the European War].' 晨报 [*Chenbao*], 23 December 1918, 2.

[15] Ibid.

[16] S.J. Chuan. 1919. 'A Brief Report of the Versailles Conference for the Chinese Secretaries of the Chinese Department of the YMCA in France.' Kautz Family YMCA Archives, University of Minnesota, box 204, folder: Chinese laborers in France.

[17] Kuhn, *Chinese Among Others*, 5.

1920 (Deng Zhongxia)

[1] On the community, see Daniel Kwan. 1997. *Marxist Intellectuals and the Chinese Labour Movement: A Study of Deng Zhongxia (1894–1933)*. Seattle, WA: University of Washington Press, 19 ff.

[2] Ibid., 122.

3 Chang Kuo-t'ao. 1971. *The Rise of the Chinese Communist Party, 1921–1927*. Lawrence, KS: University Press of Kansas, 114.

4 For the original, see Deng Zhongxia 邓中夏. 1983[1920]. '长辛店旅行一日记 [A Day Trip to Changxindian].' In 邓中夏文集 [*Collected Works of Deng Zhongxia*], 4–8. Beijing: Renmin Chubanshe.

1921 (Lin Chun)

1 On these movements, see S.A. Smith. 2002. *Like Cattle and Horses: Nationalism and Labor in Shanghai, 1895–1927*. Durham, NC: Duke University Press, 68–75, 85–88.

2 Ibid., 113 ff.; S.A. Smith. 2008. *Revolution and the People in Russia and China: A Comparative History*. Cambridge, UK: Cambridge University Press, 174.

3 Elizabeth J. Perry. 2012. *Anyuan: Mining China's Revolutionary Tradition*. Berkeley, CA: University of California Press, 47.

4 '中国共产党宣言 [Declaration of the CCP]', November 1920. The text was translated back to Chinese from the English translation kept in the archive of the Chinese delegation to the Comintern, and published in the internal 党史资料汇报 [*Digest of Party History Materials*], no. 1 (3 June 1958).

5 '中国共产党第一纲领 [The First Program of the CCP]', 1921. In 中共中央文件选集, 1921–1925 [*Selected Documents of the CCP Central Party Committee, 1921–1925*], Vol. 1. Beijing: Zhonggong Zhongyang Dangxiao Chubanshe, 1989, 3–5.

6 '中国共产党第一个决议 [The First Resolution of the CCP]', 1921. In *Selected Documents of the CCP Central Party Committee*, 6–7.

7 Vladimir I. Lenin. 1975. *Collected Works*. Moscow: Progressive Publishers. See: 'Democracy and Narodism in China' ([1912], Vol. 18, 163–69); 'The Awakening of Asia' ([1913], Vol. 19, 85–86); 'Backward Europe and Progressive Asia' ([1913], Vol. 19, 99–100); and 'The Historical Destiny of the Doctrine of Karl Marx' ([1913], Vol. 19, 582–85).

8 For a discussion of the semifeudal and semicolonial characterisation, see Tani Barlow. 2019. 'Semifeudal, Semicolonial.' In *Afterlives of Chinese Communism: Political Concepts from Mao to Xi*, edited by Christian Sorace, Ivan Franceschini, and Nicholas Loubere. Canberra, London, and New York, NY: ANU Press and Verso Books, 237–41.

9 Li Dazhao 李大钊. 1917. '新中华民族主义 [New Chinese Nationalism]', 甲寅 [*Jiayin Magazine*], February; 'Pan...ism 与 Democracy 之胜利 [The Failure of Pan-Asianism and the Victory of Democracy]', 太平洋 [*The Pacific*], vol. 1, no. 10 (July 1918); '大亚细亚主义与新亚细亚主义 [Fan-Asianism and New Asianism]', 国民杂志 [*Citizen Magazine*], vol. 1, no. 2 (January 1919); '再论新亚细亚主义 [On New Asianism Again]', 国民杂志 [*Citizen Magazine*], vol. 2, no. 1 (December 2019).

10 Li Dazhao 李大钊. 1918. 'Bolshevism 的胜利 [Victory of Bolshevism]' and '庶民的胜利 [Victory of the Subalterns]', 新青年 [*New Youth*], vol. 5, no. 5 (November).

11 Chen Duxiu 陈独秀. 1919. '新青年罪案之答辩书 [In Defence of *New Youth*]', 新青年 [*New Youth*], vol. 6, no. 1 (January).

12 Li Dazhao 李大钊. 1919. '我的马克思主义观 [My Conception of Marxism]', 新青年 [*New Youth*], vol. 6, nos 5–6 (September and November).

13 This book was translated from the Japanese translation of M.E. Marcy. 1911. *Shop Talks on Economics*. Chicago, IL: Charles Kerr, and published as 马格斯资本论入门 [*Introduction to Marx's Capital*] by the Socialism Research Society in Shanghai in 1920.

[14] Chen Duxiu 陈独秀. 1920. '谈政治 [On Politics]', 新青年 [*New Youth*], vol. 8, no. 1 (January). Chen's comments can be found in '关于社会主义的讨论 [Discussions of Socialism]', 新青年 [*New Youth*], vol. 8, no. 4 (December 1920); '独秀复东荪先生信 [Duxiu's Reply to Zhang Dongxun]' and '社会主义批评 [A Commentary on Socialism]', *New Youth* [新青年], vol. 9, no. 3 (June 1921); '马克思学说 [Marx's Theory]', 新青年 [*New Youth*], vol. 9, no. 6 (July 1922).

[15] Chen Duxiu 陈独秀. 1920. '劳动者底觉悟: 在上海船务栈房工界联合会的演说 [Labour's Consciousness]', 新青年 [*New Youth*], vol. 7, no. 6 (1 May).

[16] There is no text for this short speech, except for brief passages recorded in Party history that say: '[他] 号召大家把五一节"当作我们一盏引路的明灯". 本着劳工神圣的信条, 跟着这个明灯走向光明的地方去.' Li Dazhao called the rally, the flyers for which were full of such slogans as 'sacred labour' and 'long live the workers'.

[17] Li Dazhao 李大钊. 1920. '五一May Day运动史 [The History of the May Day Movement]', 新青年 [*New Youth*], vol. 7, no. 6 (1 May). The inscription on the cover of this May Day special issue was '劳工神圣', handwritten by Cai Yuanpei.

[18] Li Zhong 李中. 1920. '一个工人的宣言 [A Worker's Manifesto]', 劳动界 [*Labour*], no. 7 (26 September).

[19] '中国劳动组合书记部宣言 [The Manifesto of the Chinese Trade Union Secretariat]', 共产党 [*The Communist Party*], no. 6 (August 1921).

[20] Mao Zedong 毛泽东. 1921. '所希望于劳工会的 [My Hope for the Union]', 劳工周刊 [*Workers' Weekly*], 21 November.

[21] 京汉铁路工人流血记 [*An Account of the Bleeding Beijing–Hankou Striking Railway Workers*], printed and distributed by the Beijing University's printing workers and the Research Society of Marxism, in March 1923. The account has been translated into English as 'Bloodshed of the Peking–Hankou Workers', *Chinese Sociology and Anthropology* (Winter 1992–93).

[22] Deng Zhongxia 邓中夏. 1943[1930]. 中国职工运动简史一九一九——一九二六 [*A Brief History of the Labour Movement in China, 1919–26*]. Yan'an: Jiefangshe, Ch. 3 and 'Conclusion'.

[23] '中国劳动组合书记部拟定的劳动法大纲 [An Outline of the Labour Law Drafted by the Chinese Trade Union Secretariat]', 16 August 1922. In *Selected Documents of the CCP Central Party Committee*, vol. 1, 566–67.

[24] '关于工会运动与共产党的议决案 [Resolution on the Union Movement and the CCP]', July 1922. In *Selected Documents of the CCP Central Party Committee*, vol. 1, 76–82.

1922 (Elizabeth J. Perry)

[1] While the CCP also supported the Hong Kong Seamen's Strike earlier that year, according to CCP co-founder Chen Duxiu, the Party's participation in that strike was limited to street-corner speeches and handbill distribution. Daniel Y.K. Kwan 1997. *Marxist Intellectuals and the Chinese Labor Movement: A Study of Deng Zhongxia, 1894–1933*. Seattle, WA: University of Washington Press, 86.

[2] A more detailed account of the 1922 Anyuan strike can be found in the second chapter of Elizabeth J. Perry. 2012. *Anyuan: Mining China's Revolutionary Tradition*. Berkeley, CA: University of California Press.

[3] Deng Zhongxia 邓中夏. 1980[1948]. 中国职工运动简史 [*A Brief History of the Chinese Labour Movement*]. Changsha: Hunan Renmin Chubanshe, 158–59.

[4] T.Y. Chang. 1926. 'Five Years of Significant Strikes.' *Chinese Students Monthly* 21, no. 8: 19.

[5] Clark Kerr and Abraham Siegel. 1954. 'The Interindustry Propensity to Strike: An International Comparison.' In *Labour and Management in Industrial Society*, edited by Clark Kerr. Garden City, NY: Doubleday, 105–47.

[6] Doug McAdam. 1982. *Political Process and the Development of Black Insurgency, 1930–1970*. Chicago, IL: University of Chicago Press.

[7] Pingxiang Municipal Party Committee. 1990. 安源路矿工人运动 [*Anyuan Railway and Mine Workers Movement*]. Beijing: Zhonggong Dangshi Ziliao Chubanshe, vol. 1, 41.

[8] An exception is Ronald Aminzade, Jack A. Goldstone, and Elizabeth J. Perry. 2001. 'Leadership Dynamics and Dynamics of Contention.' In *Silence and Voice in the Study of Contentious Politics*, edited by Ronald R. Aminzade, Jack A. Goldstone, Elizabeth J. Perry, William H. Sewell, Sidney Tarrow, and Charles Tilley. Cambridge, UK: Cambridge University Press, 126–54.

[9] Gerald W. Berkley. 1975. 'The Canton Peasant Movement Training Institute.' *Modern China* 1, no. 2: 161–79; and David Shambaugh. 2008. 'Training China's Political Elite: The Party School System.' *The China Quarterly*, no. 196: 827–44.

[10] Shen Yixing 沈以行, Jiang Peinan 姜沛南, and Zheng Qingsheng 郑庆声 (eds). 1991. 上海工人运动史 [*The History of the Shanghai Labour Movement*]. Shenyang: Liaoning Renmin Chubanshe, 251–58.

[11] For details on the May Thirtieth Movement, see Elizabeth J. Perry. 1993. *Shanghai on Strike: The Politics of Chinese Labor*. Stanford, CA: Stanford University Press, 81–84; and Emily Honig. 1986. *Sisters and Strangers: Women in the Shanghai Cotton Mills, 1919–1949*. Stanford, CA: Stanford University Press, 203–9.

[12] Brian G. Martin. 1996. *The Shanghai Green Gang: Politics and Organized Crime, 1919–1937*. Berkeley, CA: University of California Press.

[13] Shanghai Municipal Archives 1-1-1147, *Police Daily Report*, 3 August 1925.

[14] Lucian Pye. 1988. *The Mandarin and the Cadre: China's Political Cultures*. Ann Arbor, MI: University of Michigan Center for Chinese Studies, 38–39.

[15] Aminzade et al., 'Leadership Dynamics and Dynamics of Contention', 133.

1923 (Luo Zhanglong)

[1] See Tony Saich. 1992–93. 'Background to the 7 February Peking–Hankou Railway Workers' Strike.' *Chinese Sociology and Anthropology: A Journal of Translations* 25, no. 2: 1–18.

[2] The unabridged translation by Tony Saich can be found in Zhanglong Luo. 1992–93. 'Bloodshed of the Peking–Hankou Workers.' *Chinese Sociology and Anthropology: A Journal of Translations* 25, no. 2. The slightly edited excerpts here reproduced thanks to the courtesy of the translator are drawn from Chapter 3, 'Fierce Battles Rage Like a Fire in the Stations of the Peking–Hankou Railway'. Lengthy citations from manifestos, leaflets, and media reports from that time have been omitted.

1925 (Wang Kan)

[1] These numbers can be found in Fang Fu-an. 1931. *Chinese Labour: An Economic and Statistical Survey of the Labour Conditions and Labour Movements in China*. Shanghai: Kelly & Walsh. Deng Zhongxia provides slightly different figures, with 162 delegates for more than 100 trade unions representing 270,000 workers in twelve cities. Deng Zhongxia 邓中夏. 1983 [1930]. '中国职工运动简史 [A Brief History of the Chinese Labour Movement].' In 邓中夏文集 [*Collected Works of Deng Zhongxia*]. Beijing: Renmin Chubanshe,

[2] Daniel Y.K. Kwan 1997. *Marxist Intellectuals and the Chinese Labor Movement: A Study of Deng Zhongxia, 1894–1933*. Seattle, WA: University of Washington Press, 32; Chang Kuo-t'ao. 1971. *The Rise of the Chinese Communist Party, 1921–1927*. Lawrence, KS: University Press of Kansas, 236.

[3] Fang, *Chinese Labour*, 68–70. Even in this case, Deng's figures are slightly different. He mentions 281 delegates for 540,000 workers. See Deng, 'A Brief History of the Chinese Labour Movement'.

[4] China Labour Movement Institute. 2016. 新编中国工人运动史 (上卷) [*Chinese Worker Movement History, New Edition (Vol. I)*]. Beijing: Zhongguo Gongren Chubanshe, 94.

[5] Liu Mingkui 刘明逵 and Tang Yuliang 唐玉良. 2002. 中国近代工人阶级和工人运动 (第五册) [*Working Class and Worker Movement in Modern China (Volume Five)*]. Beijing: Zhonggong Zhongyang Dangxiao Chubanshe, 305.

[6] Central Archives Administration. 1989. 中共中央文件选集 (第1册: 1921–1925) [*Selections of CCP Central Committee Documents (Book 1: 1921–1925)*]. Beijing: Zhonggong Zhongyang Dangxiao Chubanshe, 75, 381.

[7] Ma Xuejun 马学军. 2016. '中国劳动组合书记部的渊源与演变再考察 [A Reinvestigation of the Origin and Evolution of the Chinese Trade Union Secretariat].' 学术交流 [*Academic Exchange*], no. 2: 144–51.

[8] Peng Nansheng 彭南生. 2008. '权重还是利重: 1922年上海银楼业罢工风潮的取向 [Power or Interest: Orientation of the Chain Strikes in the Silver Industry in Shanghai in 1922].' 浙江学刊 [*Zhejiang Academic Journal*], no. 4: 53–60.

[9] Ma Xuejun 马学军. 2017. '特派员制度与中共早期工人运动 [The System of Special Commissioners and the Early Labour Movement of the Communist Party of China].' 社会 [*Chinese Journal of Sociology*], no. 2: 193–215, at p. 212.

[10] China Labour Movement Institute, *Chinese Worker Movement History*, 88–92.

[11] Yuan Shixiang 袁士祥. 2016. '中共四大: 早期中国共产党人在上海实现群众路线思想的新飞跃 [The Fourth National Congress of the Communist Party of China: Early Chinese Communists Achieving New Leap in Mass Line in Shanghai].' 炎黄春秋 [*Yanhuang Chunqiu*], no. 12: 20–24.

[12] See China Institute of Labour Movement, *Chinese Worker Movement History*; Yuan, 'The Fourth Congress of the Communist Party of China'; Zhang Man 张曼. 2015. '历史的召唤: 中华全国总工会诞生的前前后后 [Call of History: Birth of the All-China Federation of Trade Unions].' 工会信息 [*Trade Union Information*], no. 5: 40–43.

[13] Xiong Yuezhi 熊月之. 2018. '近代上海城市对于贫民的意义 [The Meaning of the City to Poor Residents in Modern Shanghai].' 史林 [*Historical Review*], no. 6: 99–103, at pp. 100, 102.

[14] Ma Xuejun 马学军. 2016. '把头包工制: 近代中国工业化中的雇佣和生产方式 [Gangmaster Contract System: Employment and Production Operation in Modern China's Industrialisation].' 社会学研究 [Sociological Studies], no. 2: 102–22, at p. 112.

[15] Ibid.; Fu Chunhui 傅春晖. 2014. '包买制: 历史沿革及其理论意义 [Outsourcing System: Historical Evolution and Its Theoretical Significance].' 社会学研究 [Sociological Studies], no. 2: 189–217; Zhou Jianchao 周建超. 2002. 秘密社会与中国民主革命 [Secret Societies and China's Democratic Revolution]. Fuzhou: Fujian Renmin Chubanshe.

[16] Zhou, Secret Societies and China's Democratic Revolution.

[17] Ibid.; Elizabeth J. Perry. 1993. Shanghai on Strike: The Politics of Chinese Labor. Stanford, CA: Stanford University Press.

[18] Perry, Shanghai on Strike.

[19] See Articles 12 and 13 of the 1925 Constitution of the ACFTU.

[20] '共产国际执行委员会关于中国共产党与国民党的关系问题的决议 [Decision of Comintern Executive Committee about Issues of the Relationship between the CCP and the GMD].' In 中共中央文件选集 (1921–1925) 第一册 [Selections of Chinese Communist Party Central Committee (1921–1925) Volume One], Beijing: Zhonggong Zhongyang Dangxiao Chubanshe (1989), 577–78.

[21] '关于中国形势的报告 [Report about the Chinese Situation].' In 共产国际有关中国革命的文献资料 (1919–1928) 第一辑 [Comintern Documents about the Chinese Revolution (1919–1928) First Series], Beijing: Zhongguo Shehui Kexue Chubanshe (1981), 60–62; and '第四次代表大会关于东方问题的总提纲 [General Outline of the Eastern Issue at the Fourth Congress]', in the same volume, 65–75.

[22] Deng Zhongxia 邓仲夏. 1983. 中国职工运动简史 (1919–1926) [A Brief History of China's Labour Movement (1919–1926)]. Beijing: Renmin Chubanshe, 511–13.

1925 (Gail Hershatter)

[1] North-China Herald, 22 August 1925, 202.

[2] Except where otherwise specified, the information in this entry is drawn from Gail Hershatter. 1986. The Workers of Tianjin, 1900–1949. Stanford, CA: Stanford University Press. On the Yu Da incident and its aftermath, see pp. 215–20 and the sources cited therein; see also Dong Zhenxiu 董振修. 1983. '马克思主义的传播与天津早期工人运动 [The Spread of Marxism and the Early Tianjin Workers' Movement].' 天津社会科学 [Tianjin Social Sciences]: 89–93.

[3] For recent Chinese scholarship on CCP involvement in worker organising in Tianjin in the 1920s, see, inter alia, Wang Yongze 王勇则. 2018. '天津造币厂工人运动点滴 [A Bit about the Workers Movement in the Tianjin Mint].' 党史文汇 [Studies in Party History], no. 2: 53–55; Miao Zhiming 缪志明. 2010. '老一代革命家与天津早期工人运动 [The Old Revolutionists and Tianjin Earlier Workers' Movement].' 天津市工会管理干部学院学报 [Journal of Tianjin Trade Union Administrators' College] 18, no. 2: 41–43; Miao Zhiming 缪志明. 2012. '天津工运第一代主要负责人安幸生事迹集述 [Narration of the Deeds of An Xingsheng, a Major Person in Charge of the First Generation of the Tianjin Workers' Movement].' 天津市工会管理干部学院学报 [Journal of Tianjin Trade Union Administrators' College] 20, no. 1: 31–36; Miao Zhiming 缪志明 and Li Geng 李耕. 2010. '普及劳工教育的先声:"天津工余

补习学校" 的历史意义与现实价值 [On the Pioneers of Popularising Education for Workers: A Supplementary School for Workers in Tianjin].' 天津市工会管理干部学院学报 [*Journal of Tianjin Trade Union Administrators' College*] 18, no. 1: 50–53.

[4] In addition to Hershatter, *The Workers of Tianjin, 1900–1949*, on Tianjin worker conditions and activism during the Nanjing Decade, see, inter alia, Ding Li 丁丽. 2014. '民国时期天津产业工人劳动保障问题探析 [On Tianjin Industrial Workers' Labour and Social Security in the Period of the Republic of China].' 兰州学刊 [*Lanzhou Academic Journal*], no. 7: 29–35; Ding Li 丁丽. 2018. '民国时期天津纺织工人劳动与生活状况探析 [The Working and Living Conditions of Textile Workers in Tianjin during the Republic of China].' 中国社会经济史研究 [*Studies in Chinese Socioeconomic History*], no. 1: 58–65; Meng Lingzhou 孟玲洲. 2018. '生存的抗争:劳资纠纷视阈下民国前期天津手工工人的集体行动 [Struggle for Survival: Collective Action of Manual Workers in Tianjin in the Early Republic of China Viewed through the Lens of Labour Disputes].' 华侨大学学报 (哲学社会科学版) [*Journal of Huaqiao University (Philosophy & Social Sciences)*], no. 5: 117–26.

[5] Hershatter, *The Workers of Tianjin, 1900–1949*, 53.

[6] Ibid., 55.

[7] Benedict J. Tria Kerkvliet. 2009. 'Everyday Politics in Peasant Societies (and Ours).' *Journal of Peasant Studies* 36, no. 1: 227–43, at p. 232. On everyday politics, see Michael Szonyi. 2017. *The Art of Being Governed: Everyday Politics in Late Imperial China*. Princeton, NJ: Princeton University Press, 6–9. Important to both of their conceptualisations is the classic work of James C. Scott. 1985. *Weapons of the Weak: Everyday Forms of Peasant Resistance*. New Haven, CT: Yale University Press.

[8] Green Gang membership was common among the foremen in large factories, and Hong Bang members were also active. Swearing allegiance to a foreman as one's elder in the gang could provide a worker with a powerful alliance; in the 1940s, it was estimated that 80 to 90 percent of the male workers in Tianjin cotton mills were gang members. Hershatter, *The Workers of Tianjin, 1900–1949*, 172.

[9] Research Office of Tianjin Federation of Trade Unions (ed.). 2015. '抗战时期天津工人群众冲破封锁为根据地输送物资 [Tianjin's Workers Broke through the Blockade during the Anti-Japanese War to Deliver Materials to the Base Areas].' 工会信息 [*Trade Union Information*], no. 29: 31–35. This intriguing and detailed article does not cite its sources.

[10] Research Office of Tianjin Federation of Trade Unions (ed.). 2015. '抗日战争时期天津电业工人的反抗斗争 [The Resistance Struggle of Tianjin Electrical Workers during the Anti-Japanese War].' 工会信息 [*Trade Union Information*], no. 35: 36–37. This article, like the previous one, does not cite its sources.

[11] E.P. Thompson. 1966. *The Making of the English Working Class*. New York, NY: Vintage, 9.

1925 (Apo Leong)

[1] Frederick Engels. 1845. *The Condition of the Working Class in England*, available online at: www.marxists.org/archive/marx/works/1845/condition-working-class.

[2] Deng Zhongxia 邓中夏. 1948. 中国工人运动简史 [*A Brief History of the Chinese Labour Movement*]. Harbin: Dongbei Shudian, 194.

[3] See, for instance, Li Baiyuan 李伯元 and Ren Gong-tan 任公坦. 1955. 廣東機器工人奮斗史 [*The Struggle History of Guangdong Mechanics*]. Taipei: Zhongguo Laogong Fuli Chubanshe.

[4] Wai-chor So. 1991. *The Kuomintang Left in the National Revolution (1924–1931)*. Hong Kong: Oxford University Press.

[5] Chinese Labour Movement Research Centre (ed.). 2016. 新编中国工人运动史 (上下卷) [*A History of the Chinese Labour Movement (New Edition)*]. Beijing: Gongren Chubanshe, 100.

[6] Ibid., 101.

[7] Ibid., 110.

[8] On these events, see Leung Po-lung (translated by Promise Li and Edward Wong). 2019. 'Hong Kong Political Strikes: A Brief History.' *Lausan*, 3 August, available online at: lausan.hk/2019/hong-kong-political-strikes-brief-history; Apo Leong 梁寶霖, Leung Po Lung 梁寶龍, Ming Chan 陳明銶 and Dorothy Ko 高彥頤 (eds). 1982. 香港與中國工運回顧 [*Perspectives on the Hong Kong and Chinese Labour Movement*]. Hong Kong: Xianggang Jidujiao Gongye Weiyuanhui; Chau Yick 周奕. 2009. 香港工運史 [*A History of the Hong Kong Labour Movement*]. Hong Kong: Lifan Chubanshe; Joe England and John Rear. 1975. *Chinese Labour Under British Rule*. Hong Kong: Oxford University Press.

[9] Ng Sek-hong. 2015. *Labour Legislation in Hong Kong*. Alphen aan den Rijn, Netherlands: Wolters Kluwer; Jean Chesneaux (translated by Gillian Nettle). 1971. *Secret Societies in China in the Nineteenth and Twentieth Centuries*. Ann Arbor, MI: University of Michigan Press.

[10] In Hong Kong, the mechanics' union was named the Chinese Engineers' Institute (香港华人机器总工会), while its sister union in Guangzhou was named the Guangdong Mechanics' Union (广东机器总会).

[11] Kam-po Chan. 2011. 'The Strikes in Hong Kong During the 1920s.' MA thesis, University of Hong Kong; Daniel Y.K. Kwan. 1997. *Marxist Intellectuals and the Chinese Labor Movement: A Study of Deng Zhongxia (1894–1933)*. Seattle, WA: University of Washington Press.

[12] Chinese Labour Movement Research Centre, *A History of the Chinese Labour Movement*, 104.

[13] Kwan, *Marxist Intellectuals and the Chinese Labor Movement*, 125.

[14] Chau Yick 周奕. 2017. '香港大罷工對工會組織的影響 [The Influence of the Canton–Hong Kong General Strike on Trade Union Organisation].' In 粵港工人大融合一省港大罷工九十周年回顧論文集 [*A Collection of Essays on the Great Integration of Guangdong–Hong Kong Workers in the Ninetieth Anniversary of the Great Strike*], edited by Chau Yick 周奕, Ng Sek Hong 伍錫康, Apo Leong 梁寶霖 and Leung Po Lung 梁寶龍. Hong Kong: Xianggang Shehui Baozhang Xuehui, Xianggang Gongyunshi Yanjiu Xiaozu, 85.

[15] Kwan, *Marxist Intellectuals and the Chinese Labor Movement*, 121.

[16] Robert James Harrocks. 1994. 'The Guangzhou–Hong Kong Strike, 1925–1926: Hong Kong Workers in an Anti-Imperialistic Movement.' PhD thesis, University of Leeds, available online at: core.ac.uk/download/pdf/1145945.pdf.

[17] Deng, *A Brief History of the Chinese Labour Movement*, 199.

[18] 'Kotewall Report on the Strike of 1925', available online at: www.grs.gov.hk/ws/rhk/eg/1920.html; Tony Cliff and Donny Gluckstein. 1986. *Marxism and Trade Union Struggle: The General Strike of 1926*. London: Bookmarks.

[19] Nym Wales. 1945. *The Chinese Labor Movement*. New York, NY: John Day Company, 211.

[20] H.R. Butters. 1939. 'Report on Labour and Labour Conditions in Hong Kong.' Hong Kong: Noranha & Co. Ltd.

[21] Ng, *Labour Legislation in Hong Kong*; England and Rear, *Chinese Labour Under British Rule*; Petra Mahy and Ng Sek-Hong. 2015. 'The Labour Law of Hong Kong: An Historical Account Arranged by Variables', available online at: ssrn.com/abstract=2632119.

[22] Justin Chun-yin Cheng. 2016. *Colonial Hong Kong Identities: Chinese Mercantile Elite and the Canton–Hong Kong General Strike 1925–26*. Berkeley, CA: University of California Press.

[23] Lau Kit-ching Chan. 1999. *From Nothing to Nothing: The Chinese Communist Movement and Hong Kong*. Hong Kong: University of Hong Kong Press; Joe England. 1989. *Industrial Relations and Law in Hong Kong*. Hong Kong: Oxford University Press.

1927 (S.A. Smith)

[1] On relations between the Comintern and the Chinese Communists, see Alexander Pantsov. 2000. *The Bolsheviks and the Chinese Revolution, 1919–1927*. Richmond, UK: Curzon. On Shanghai workers, see Elizabeth J. Perry. 1993. *Shanghai on Strike: The Politics of Chinese Labor*. Stanford, CA: Stanford University Press. My essay is based on chapters 8, 9, and 10 of my 2000 book *A Road is Made: Communism in Shanghai, 1920–1927*. Curzon, UK: Richmond. Much more detail and argumentation can be found in the book.

[2] See *Strikes and Lockouts in Shanghai Since 1918*. 1933. Shanghai: Shanghai Zhengfu Shehuiju, 52. This represented about 70 percent of workers in regular employment, calculated to be 600,000 in 1928, about half of whom were in the modern sector. See Alain Roux. 1970. 'Le mouvement ouvrier à Shanghai de 1928 à 1930 [The Workers' Movement in Shanghai from 1928 to 1930].' Postgraduate thesis. Sorbonne, Paris, 11, 45.

[3] S.A. Smith. 2002. *Like Cattle and Horses: Nationalism and Labor in Shanghai, 1895–1927*. Durham, NC: Duke University Press.

[4] 中国共产党上海市组织史资料, *1920.8–1987.10* [*Materials on the Organisational History of the Shanghai City Communist Party, August 1920 to October 1987*]. 1991. Shanghai: Shanghai Renmin Chubanshe, 41.

[5] A.A. [Appen]. 1930. 'Три шанхайских восстания [Three Shanghai Uprisings].' Проблемы Китая [*Problems of China*], 79.

[6] '学生运动与三次武装起义 [The Student Movement and the Three Armed Uprisings].' In 上海工云史料 [*Historical Materials on the Labour Movement in Shanghai*] 2 (1987): 44.

[7] Xu Yufang 许玉芳 and Bian Xingying 卞杏英. 1987. 上海工人三次武装起义研究 [*Research on the Shanghai Three Armed Uprisings*]. Shanghai: Zhishi Chubanshe, 58–59.

[8] 中国工会历史文献, *1921–27* [*Documents on the History of Chinese Labour Unions, 1921–27*]. 1958. Beijing: Gongren Chubanshe, 378–89; 中国工人运动史料 [*Historical Materials on the Chinese Labour Movement*] 4 (1981): 42–43.

[9] Xu and Bian, *Research on the Shanghai Three Armed Uprisings*, 211.

¹⁰ 第一次中国劳动年鉴 [*First China Labour Yearbook*]. 1928. Beijing: Shehui Diaochabu, part 2, 460–61.

¹¹ Xu and Bian, *Research on the Shanghai Three Armed Uprisings*, 66. Merchants' organisations backed a suspension of trade (休业) to mark the arrival of the NRA, but not a strike (罢市). Ren Jianshu 任建树. 1989. 陈独秀传 [*Biography of Chen Duxiu*]. Shanghai: Shanghai Renmin Chubanshe, 354.

¹² 申报 [*Shenbao*], 22 March 1927, 9.

¹³ *North China Herald*, 23 April 1927, 174; 申报 [*Shenbao*], 22 March 1927, 11.

¹⁴ *Strikes and Lockouts in Shanghai since 1918*, 29. This compares with 6,000 enterprises and 420,970 workers said by the same source to have taken part in the February 1927 general strike.

¹⁵ Xu and Bian, *Research on the Shanghai Three Armed Uprisings*, 221–22; *Historical Materials on the Labour Movement in Shanghai*, vol. 2, 34.

¹⁶ Zhou Shangwen 周尚文 and He Shiyou 贺世友. 1987. 上海工人三次武装起义史 [*The Shanghai Three Armed Workers' Uprisings*]. Shanghai: Shanghai Renmin Chubanshe, 156, 183.

¹⁷ Chinese People's Political Consultative Conference, Shanghai Municipal Committee. 1986. 旧上海的帮会 [*The Secret Societies of Old Shanghai*]. Shanghai: Shanghai Renmin Chubanshe, 61, 82.

¹⁸ A.A. [Appen], 'Three Shanghai Uprisings', 84; Brian G. Martin. 1996. *The Green Gang: Politics and Organized Crime, 1919–1937*. Berkeley, CA: University of California Press, 96.

¹⁹ Xu and Bian, *Research on the Shanghai Three Armed Uprisings*, 71–72.

²⁰ This is the figure given by the GLU in a report to the CEC of the GMD in Wuhan on 15 April 1927. 民国日报 [*Republican Daily*], 21 April 1927.

²¹ 上海总工会报告 [*Report of the Shanghai General Labour Union*]. 1927. Shanghai: Shanghai Zonggonghui, 12, 13. The latter figure stretches credibility, but there is no doubt there had been an extraordinary rush to unionise.

²² 中国工人运动史料 [*Historical Materials on the Chinese Labour Movement*]. 1958. Vol. 2, 126.

²³ *Historical Materials on the Chinese Labour Movement*, vol. 4, 104.

²⁴ 布尔塞韦克 [*Bolshevik*], no. 8 (12 December 1927). Others, basing themselves on a report in the *North China Herald* (10 September 1927), put the number of victims as high as 5,000.

²⁵ Kwok Sing Li (translated by Mary Lok). 1995. *A Glossary of Political Terms of the People's Republic of China*. Hong Kong: Chinese University Press, 325.

²⁶ Smith, *Like Cattle and Horses*.

1927 (Alexander F. Day)

¹ While Haifeng County was the main site of struggle, Communist control reached into neighbouring Lufeng as well.

² Roy Hofheinz Jr. 1977. *The Broken Wave: The Chinese Communist Peasant Movement, 1922–1928*. Cambridge, MA: Harvard University Press, ch. 10; Robert B. Marks. 1984. *Rural Revolution in South China: Peasants and the Making of History in Haifeng*

County, 1570–1930. Madison, WI: University of Wisconsin Press, ch. 9; Fernando Galbiati. 1985. *P'eng P'ai and the Hai-Lu-Feng Soviet*. Stanford, CA: Stanford University Press, chs. 9, 10.

[3] Marks, *Rural Revolution in South China*, 154.

[4] Ibid., 175.

[5] Ibid., 191. Marks is arraying this argument against Hofheinz (*The Broken Wave*), who declared the peasant movement to be wholly the creation of political operatives. Marks argues for the inclusion of peasant agency as well as social structure into questions of peasant activism. On the 'peasant movement', see also Galbiati, *P'eng P'ai and the Hai-Lu-Feng Soviet*, 87–88.

[6] Alessandro Russo. 1998. 'The Probable Defeat: Preliminary Notes on the Chinese Cultural Revolution.' *Positions* 6, no. 1: 179–202.

[7] Marks, *Rural Revolution in South China*, 99–120.

[8] Ibid., 99–111.

[9] Ibid., 113–18.

[10] Ibid., ch. 5 (citation is from p. 119).

[11] Kathy Le Mons Walker. 1999. *Chinese Modernity and the Peasant Path: Semicolonialism in the Northern Yangzi Delta*. Stanford, CA: Stanford University Press.

[12] Kamal Sheel. 1989. *Peasant Society and Marxist Intellectuals in China: Fang Zhimin and the Origin of a Revolutionary Movement in the Xinjiang Region*. Princeton, NJ: Princeton University Press, 42–65 (citation is from p. 45).

[13] Ibid., 58.

[14] Huaiyin Li. 2005. *Village Governance in North China: Huailu County, 1875–1936*. Stanford, CA: Stanford University Press; Chang Liu. 2007. *Peasants and Revolution in Rural China: Rural Political Change in the North China Plain and the Yangzi Delta, 1850–1949*. New York, NY: Routledge; Prasenjit Duara. 1988. *Culture, Power, and the State: Rural North China, 1900–1942*. Stanford, CA: Stanford University Press; discussed in Alexander F. Day. 2013. 'A Century of Rural Self-Governance Reforms: Reimagining Rural Chinese Society in the Post-Taxation Era.' *Journal of Peasant Studies* 40, no. 6: 929–54.

[15] Duara, *Culture, Power, and the State*.

[16] Roxann Prazniak. 1999. *Of Camel Kings and Other Things: Rural Rebels Against Modernity in Late Imperial China*. Lanham, MD: Rowman & Littlefield, 32; see also Day, 'A Century of Rural Self-Governance Reforms', 931.

[17] Yuan Gao. 2015. 'Revolutionary Rural Politics: The Peasant Movement in Guangdong and Its Social-Historical Background, 1922–1926.' *Modern China* 42, no. 2: 162–87.

[18] Liu Shipei 刘师培. 1996 [1907]. '论新政为病民之根 [On the New Policies and the Root of People's Malady].' In 国粹与西化: 刘师培文选 [*National Essence and Westernisation: Selected Works of Liu Shipei*], edited by Li Miaogen 李妙根, 205–12. Shanghai: Shanghai Yuandong Chubanshe; see also Alexander F. Day. 2019. 'Peasant.' In *Afterlives of Chinese Communism: Political Concepts from Mao to Xi*, edited by Christian Sorace, Ivan Franceschini, and Nicholas Loubere. Canberra, London, and New York, NY: ANU Press and Verso Books, 169–73.

[19] Yong-Pil Pang. 1975. 'Peng Pai from Landlord to Revolutionary.' *Modern China* 1, no. 3: 297–322.

[20] Marks, *Rural Revolution in South China*, 161.

[21] Ibid., 109.

²² Ibid., 167–68.
²³ Hofheinz, *The Broken Wave*, 146–49.
²⁴ Gao, 'Revolutionary Rural Politics', 167–68.
²⁵ Hofheinz, *The Broken Wave*, 164.
²⁶ Marks, *Rural Revolution in South China*, 208.
²⁷ Gao, 'Revolutionary Rural Politics', 179.
²⁸ Marks, *Rural Revolution in South China*, 194–212.
²⁹ Ibid., 215–22 (citation from p. 221).
³⁰ Ibid., 235.
³¹ Ibid., 250–52; Galbiati, *P'eng P'ai and the Hai-Lu-Feng Soviet*, 267–69.
³² Marks, *Rural Revolution in South China*, 249–58.
³³ Ibid., 272–81.

1928 (Yige Dong)

¹ For both accounts of the Party's marginalisation of gender issues and Communist feminists' manoeuvres from within, see Christina K. Gilmartin. 1995. *Engendering the Chinese Revolution: Radical Women, Communist Politics, and Mass Movements in the 1920s*. Berkeley, CA: University of California Press; Zheng Wang. 2016. *Finding Women in the State: A Socialist Feminist Revolution in the People's Republic of China, 1949–1964*. Berkeley, CA: University of California Press. For an English biographical analysis of Xiang Jingyu, see Andrea McElderry. 1986. 'Woman Revolutionary: Xiang Jingyu.' *China Quarterly* 105: 95–122.

² See Delia Davin. 1979. *Women-Work: Women and the Party in Revolutionary China*. Oxford, UK: Oxford University Press.

³ Geng Huamin 耿化敏. 2015. 中国共产党妇女工作史 (1921–1949) [*History of the Chinese Communist Party's Women-Work (1921–1949)*]. Beijing: Shehui Kexue Wenxian Chubanshe, 28.

⁴ Gilmartin, *Engendering the Chinese Revolution*, 81.

⁵ Li said this while giving a speech in 1923 at the Hubei Women's Rights League. See Ibid., 83.

⁶ Shanghai Municipal Trade Union. '上海市总工会 "历史大事记" [Shanghai Municipal Trade Union's "Chronology of Major Historical Events")', available online at: www.shzgh.org/renda/node5902/node5907/node6572/userobject1ai1164972.html.

⁷ Elizabeth J. Perry. 1993. *Shanghai on Strike: The Politics of Chinese Labor*. Stanford, CA: Stanford University Press, 171.

⁸ S.A. Smith. 2002. *Like Cattle and Horses: Nationalism and Labor in Shanghai, 1895–1927*. Durham, NC: Duke University Press, 54.

⁹ Perry, *Shanghai on Strike*, 178.

¹⁰ Xiang Jingyu 向警予. 2005[1923]. '中国最近妇女运动 [On Recent Women's Movements in China].' In 向警予文集 [*Collected Works of Xiang Jingyu*]. Changsha: Hunan Renmin Chubanshe, 59–66.

¹¹ While this first attempt to form a women's union backed by gang societies and aimed at pacifying labour unrest failed, Mu tried again in January 1924 and this time she founded the Shanghai Silk & Cotton Workers' Association (上海丝纱女工协会). Perry, *Shanghai on Strike*, 173.

[12] Xiao Linlin 肖琳琳, Wang Peijun 王佩军, and Yu Hong 虞洪. 2020. '1921年至1937年中国共产党领导下的上海虹口丝厂女工运动 [Women Workers' Movements in Shanghai Hongkou Silk Filatures Led by the Chinese Community Party (1921–1937)]', available online at: www.dswxyjy.org.cn/n1/2020/1125/c219021-31944448.html.

[13] Gilmartin, *Engendering the Chinese Revolution*, 81.

[14] Ibid., 86.

[15] Perry, *Shanghai on Strike*, 149.

[16] Gilmartin, *Engendering the Chinese Revolution*, 143.

[17] Ibid., 138–39.

[18] Yang Zhihua and Qu Qiubai left for Moscow in late 1928 and returned in 1930, and Yang continued to head the Women's Department until assuming the role of Secretary of the Organisation Department of the CCP's Shanghai branch, when Party activities had to shift underground. After Qiu's execution in 1935, Yang went to Moscow again. On her way back to China, she was imprisoned in Xinjiang for four years before going to Yan'an in 1945. For a detailed account of Yang's trajectory in the 1930s and 1940s, see Chen Fukang 陈福康 and Ding Yanmo 丁言模. 2005. 杨之华评传 [*Biography of Yang Zhihua*]. Shanghai: Shanghai Shehui Kexueyuan Chubanshe.

[19] For a detailed account of the fate of the ACDWF, see Wang, *Finding Women in the State*.

1929 (Seung-Joon Lee)

[1] Elizabeth J. Perry. 1993. *Shanghai on Strike: The Politics of Chinese Labor*. Stanford, CA: Stanford University Press; Walter E. Gourlay. 1953. '"Yellow Unionism" in Shanghai: A Study of Kuomintang Technique in Labor Control, 1927–1937.' *Papers on China*, no. 7: 104–35.

[2] Seung-Joon Lee. 2020. 'Canteens and the Politics of Working-Class Diets in Industrial China, 1920–37.' *Modern Asian Studies* 54, no. 1: 25.

[3] Gourlay, '"Yellow Unionism" in Shanghai', 110; Mark W. Frazier. 1992. *The Making of the Chinese Industrial Workplace: State, Revolution, and Labor Management*. Cambridge, UK: Cambridge University Press, 36.

[4] Shanghai Bureau of Social Affairs. 1932. 上海市劳资纠纷统计 [*Statistics on Shanghai Labour Disputes*]. Shanghai: Zhonghua Shuju, 44.

[5] Shanghai Bureau of Social Affairs. 1930. '上海特別市罷工停業統計 [*Strikes and Lockouts, Greater Shanghai*]. Shanghai: Shizhengfu Shehuiju, 6.

[6] Peng also noted that the results of three cases were unknown and in one case the original demand for the rice allowance was rejected, although another type of compensation was offered by the employers. Peng Guizhen 彭贵珍. 2014. 南京国民政府时期上海劳资争议研究 [*A Study on Labour Disputes in Shanghai During the Nanjing Decade*]. Nanchang: Jiangxi Renmin Chubanshe, 148.

[7] One sheng was equivalent to 1.87 pints or 1.031 litres. Zhu Bangxing 朱邦兴, Hu Lin'ge 胡林阁, and Xu Sheng Xu 徐声 (eds). 1939. 上海产业与上海职工 [*Industries and Workers in Shanghai*]. Hong Kong: Yuandong Chubanshe, 66.

[8] *North China Herald*, 31 July 1920. The British Tobacco Company was renowned for its comparatively generous benefit offer to its employees. Sherman Cochran. 1980. *Big Business in China: Sino-Foreign Rivalry in the Cigarette Industry, 1890–1930*. Cambridge, MA: Harvard University Press, 137.

[9] *North China Herald*, 18 November 1922.

[10] The Commercial Press hired a total of 4,500 employees: 1,000 white-collar staff and 3,500 blue-collar workers. In 1932, approximately 80 percent of the blue-collar employees were categorised as mechanics, while 20 percent were manual labourers; however, the gender ratio was unknown. See Shanghai Bureau of Newspaper Publication and Commercial Press Labour History Editorial Group. 1991. 上海商务印书馆职工运动史 [*History of the Labour Movement at the Shanghai Commercial Press*]. Beijing: Zhonggong Dangshi Chubanshe, 15–16.

[11] 申报 [*Shenbao*], 25 August 1925.

[12] Wang Qingbin 王清彬 and Tao Menghe 陶孟和 (eds). 1928. 第一次中国劳动年鉴 [*The First Chinese Labour Yearbook*]. Beijing: Shehui Diaocha Suo, vol. 2, p. 287; Shanghai Bureau of Newspaper Publication and Commercial Press Labour History Editorial Group, *History of the Labour Movement at the Shanghai Commercial Press*, 39–46.

[13] Jiang Peinan 姜沛南. 1984. '徐阿梅 [Xu Amei].' In 中国工人运动先驱 [*Pioneers of the Chinese Labour Movement*]. Beijing: Gongren Chubanshe, vol. 3, p. 200.

[14] Rhoads Murphey. 1953. *Shanghai: Key to Modern China*. Cambridge, MA: Harvard University Press, 139–46.

[15] 1929. '米价飞涨与救济方策 [Rice Prices Skyrocketing and Relief Measures].' 银行周报 [*Bank Weekly*] 13, no. 39: 1–4.

[16] 申报 [*Shenbao*], 15 September 1929.

[17] Ibid., 15 October 1929.

[18] Shanghai Party Committee's Research Office on Shanghai Party History 2001. '争取米贴门争 [Struggle for Rice Allowance].' In 中共上海党史大典 [*Encyclopedia of the Chinese Communist Party History in Shanghai*]. Shanghai: Shanghai Jiaoyu Chubanshe, 16; Central Party History Research Office (eds). 2015. 陈云年谱 [*Chronological Biography of Chen Yun*]. Beijing: Zhongyang Wenxian Chubanshe, 74.

[19] Brian G. Martin. 1985. 'Tu Yüeh-sheng and Labor Control in Shanghai: The Case of the French Tramways Union. 1928–1932.' *Papers on Far Eastern History* 35: 101.

[20] Ren Bishi 任弼时. 1987. 任弼时选集 [*Selected Works of Ren Bishi*]. Beijing: Renmin Chubanshe, 56.

[21] Brian G. Martin. 1996. *The Shanghai Green Gang: Politics and Organized Crime, 1919–1937*. Berkeley, CA: University of California Press, 124.

[22] Ibid., 221; Perry, *Shanghai on Strike*, 97.

[23] Jiang, 'Xu Amei', 206. Shanghai Public Transportation Company and Editorial Committee on the History of the Shanghai French Tramways Union's Labour Movement (eds). 1991. 上海发电工人运动史 [*History of the Shanghai French Tramways Union's Labour Movement*]. Beijing: Zhonggong Dangshi Chubanshe, 81–82.

[24] Martin, *The Shanghai Green Gang*, 126.

[25] One dan is equivalent to 133.33 pounds or 60.47 kilograms.

[26] 申报 [*Shenbao*], 3 September 1930; Peng, *A Study on Labour Disputes in Shanghai During the Nanjing Decade*, 149.

[27] 申报 [*Shenbao*], 15 September 1930; Martin, 'Tu Yüeh-sheng and Labor Control in Shanghai', 103.

1938 (Lu Yan)

[1] Zeng Sheng 曾生. 1992. 曾生回忆录 [*Recollections by Zeng Sheng*]. Beijing: Jiefangjun Chubanshe, 93–94; He Lang 贺朗. 1993. 吴有恒传 [*A Biography of Wu Youheng*]. Guangzhou: Huacheng Chubanshe, 9–10.

[2] Zeng, *Recollections by Zeng Sheng*, 97–98.

[3] Chan Lau Kit-ching. 2000. 'The Perception of Chinese Communism in Hong Kong 1921–1934.' *The China Quarterly*, no. 164: 1044–61.

[4] Chan Lau Kit-ching. 1999. *From Nothing to Nothing: The Chinese Communist Movement in Hong Kong, 1921–1936*. New York, NY: St Martin's Press. Chapter 10 of Chan's book delineates the rapid destruction of the communist organisation under repeated police raids in Hong Kong in that period.

[5] Hong Kong Government. n.d. *Report on the Census of the Colony of Hong Kong, 1931*, 101–2, 152.

[6] H.R. Butters. 1939. *Report on Labour and Labour Conditions in Hong Kong*. Hong Kong: Noranha & Co. Ltd, 142–49.

[7] For discussion on 'internal migration' as a family survival strategy, see Philip Kuhn. 2008. *Chinese Among Others: Emigration in Modern Times*. Lanham, MD: Rowman & Littlefield, 4, 25–28. On internal migration, see Ge Jianxiong 葛剑雄, Wu Songdi 吴松弟, and Cao Shuji 曹树基. 1997. 中国移民史 [*A History of Chinese Migration*]. Fuzhou: Fujian Renmin Chubanshe, vol. 1.

[8] Use of the phrase 侨港 was not limited to the many organisations of the 1930s. I saw many such signs on Hong Kong's streets when I visited the city in the early 1990s.

[9] Elizabeth Sinn. 2007. 'Moving Bones: Hong Kong's Role As an 'In-Between Place' in the Chinese Diaspora.' In *Cities in Motion*, edited by Sherman Cochran and David Strand, 247–71. Berkeley, CA: Institute of East Asian Studies, University of California.

[10] Lu Yan. 2014. 'Together with the Homeland: Civic Activism for National Salvation in British Hong Kong.' *Modern China* 40, no. 6: 639–74.

[11] 'The Governor's Statement in Legislative Council on 1st October 1931, in Regard to the Anti-Japanese Agitation', in Colonial Office, CO 129/536/6, 62; D.J. Crozier. 1968. 'Grantham Interview', 21 August. Manuscripts Archive, Rhodes House, Oxford University, 8.

[12] 'Order by the Governor in Council, No. 617, 1st October 1931', 'Order by the Governor in Council, No. 686, 9th October 1931', and 'William Peel to J.H. Thomas, 16 October 1931', in CO 129/536/6, 51, 52, 23–25.

[13] Liang Keping 梁柯平. 2005. 抗日战争时期的香港学运 [*The Hong Kong Student Movement at the Time of the War Against Japan*]. Hong Kong: Xianggang Gejie Jinian Kangzhan Huodong Chouweihui Youxian Gongsi, 1–2.

[14] This was a major incident for the South China Bureau of the CCP; Zhou Nan's contact, Mo Shubo, was arrested and betrayed many of his comrades. See National Archives of China and the Archives of Guangdong Province (ed.). 1982. '大生给中央的报告: 广东省委等机关被破 [Report to the Central Committee by Dasheng: Several Units of Guangdong Provincial Committee Were Destroyed].' In 广东革命历史文件汇集 [*Collection of Historical Documents of the Revolution in Guangdong*], vol. 19, 1–2. The following discussion on the HKNSA and its leader Zhou Nan is drawn mainly from a memoir written by He Jinzhou 何锦洲, '民主革命时期周楠同志在香港、广州的革命斗争 [Comrade Zhou Nan's Revolutionary Activities in

Hong Kong and Guangzhou During the Democratic Revolutionary Period]', available online at: www.gzzxws.gov.cn/gzws/cg/cgml/cg1/200808/t20080825_3742_7.htm. Key information in He's memoir can be verified through cross-references with two contemporary sources from the 1930s: the Communist Party's internal reports made by Dasheng (alias Li Fuchun) in early 1931, cited above, and '香港青年工作报告 [Report on the Youth Movement in Hong Kong]', 25 January 1941, reprinted in National Archives of China and the Archives of Guangdong Province, *Collection of Historical Documents of the Revolution in Guangdong*, vol. 44.

[15] The record in the Communist Party's internal report indicates that the police raid on the HKNSA commemoration meeting took place in 1937. See 'Report on the Youth Movement in Hong Kong', 130. In this report, Zhou Nan was cited as Hong Biao (洪標), the name he used during these years in Hong Kong as an underground communist. He Jinzhou's memoir uses 洪飆 for the name. Cross-readings of other relevant materials on the events in Hong Kong indicate that He's dates appear to be more accurate.

[16] He Sijing 何思敬. 1963. '回忆李章达先生 [In Memory of Mr Li Zhangda].' 广东文史资料 [*Historical Materials of Guangdong*], no. 10: 19; Fang Shaoyi 方少逸. 1986. '忆学生运动片段 [Reminiscences of the Student Movements].' In 广东青年运动回忆录 [*Recollections on the Youth Movement in Guangdong*], edited by Office of the Committee for Research on the Youth Movement in Guangdong, 100–9. Guangzhou: Guangdong Renmin Chubanshe. Fang was a student at Sun Yat-sen University in 1933.

[17] Most of the information regarding Wu is gleaned from the 'Report on the Youth Movement in Hong Kong', and '吴有恒关于香港市委工作给中央的报告 [Report by Wu Youheng to the Central Committee on Activities by the City Branch of Hong Kong]', 16 February 1941, both in National Archives of China and the Archives of Guangdong Province, *Collection of Historical Documents of the Revolution in Guangdong*, vol. 44, 127–517. See also Wu Youheng 吴有恒. 1993. '把握风光唱晚晴 [Seizing the Moment to Celebrate the Sunset Years].' In 吴有恒文选 [*Selected Works by Wu Youheng*], vol. 2, pp. 243–47. Guangzhou: Huacheng Chubanshe.

[18] '中共香港市委至中央电: 香港出席党的第七次代表大会代表名单 [Telegram by the City Branch of Hong Kong to the Central Committee: List of Representatives from Hong Kong to the Party's Seventh Congress]', 1939. In National Archives of China and the Archives of Guangdong Province, *Collection of Historical Documents of the Revolution in Guangdong*, vol. 44, p. 41. In addition to Wu, there were four other representatives, including three workers and a Party secretary of the Kowloon district branch.

[19] Chau Yick 周奕. 2009. 香港工运史 [*A History of the Labour Movement in Hong Kong*]. Hong Kong: Lixun Chubanshe, 89–92; Zeng, *Recollections by Zeng Sheng*, 59–63.

[20] Wu, 'Report by Wu Youheng to the Central Committee on Activities by the City Branch of Hong Kong', 399.

[21] '香港职运工作报告: 1936年6月至1939年11月香港工人的生活概况、职工组织和反日斗争等情况 [Report on the Workers' Movement: The Life of Hong Kong Workers, Their Organisations, and Their Anti-Japanese Struggle from June 1936 to November 1939]', November 1939. In National Archives of China and the Archives of Guangdong Province, *Collection of Historical Documents of the Revolution in Guangdong*, vol. 44, pp. 11–40, citation from pp. 16–18; Wu, 'Report by Wu Youheng to the Central Committee on Activities by the City Branch of Hong Kong', 387–90. See also Zeng, *Recollections by Zeng Sheng*, 83.

[22] Wu, 'Report by Wu Youheng to the Central Committee on Activities by the City Branch of Hong Kong', 345–46.
[23] Ibid.
[24] '瓜菜贩义卖赈款昨交华商会 [Funds Raised by Fruit and Vegetable Hawkers Sent to Chinese Chamber of Commerce].' 星岛日报 [*Sing Tao Jih Bao*], 13 August 1938, 10.
[25] '今年"八一三"义卖小贩主张自办 [Hawkers Decided to Organise Their Own Fundraising Sale for 13 August This Year].' 华侨日报 [*Wah Kiu Yat Po*], 7 June 1939.
[26] English-language sources on the national salvation movement in Hong Kong are rare, though Chinese memoirs abound. For a recent publication on student participation in aiding China during the 1930s, see Peter Cunich. 2012. *A History of the University of Hong Kong. Volume 1, 1911–1945*. Hong Kong: Hong Kong University Press, 387–93.
[27] 'Report on the Youth Movement in Hong Kong', 211.
[28] B.A. Lee. 1973. *Britain and the Sino-Japanese War, 1937–1939*. Stanford, CA: Stanford University Press, 18; Chan Lau Kit-ching. 1990. *Britain, China and Hong Kong, 1895–1945*. Hong Kong: Chinese University Press, ch. 6.
[29] CO 129/580/3, 36–38.

1941 (Joshua Howard)

[1] Research for this article was conducted at the Institute for Advanced Studies in Princeton. The author is grateful to have been selected as a Starr Foundation East Asian Studies Endowment Fund Member in 2019–20. He thanks Michael Strange for her editorial assistance, as well as Giancarlo Falco and Michael Hoffheimer for their thoughtful comments and suggestions.
[2] Yu Dawei 俞大维. 1941. '兵工署严禁各厂工人订阅新华日报代电 [Order from the Ordnance Department Prohibiting All Arsenal Workers from Subscribing to *New China Daily*]', 11 March. In 中国近代兵器工业档案史料 [*Historical and Archival Materials Regarding Modern China's Armaments Industry*]. Beijing: Bingqi Gongye Chubanshe, vol. 3, p. 1100.
[3] Pan Zinian 潘梓年. 1941. '潘梓年关于皖南事变后报纸遭受迫害日益加厉呈 [Pan Zinian's Report on How the Paper Has Succumbed to Increased Repression Since the New Fourth Army Incident]', 12 April. In 白色恐怖下的新华日报 [*New China Daily Under the White Terror*], edited by Second National Historical Archive and Chongqing Municipal Archive, 400–1. Chongqing: Chongqing Chubanshe.
[4] *New China Daily*'s first issue was printed on 11 January 1938 at Hankou (part of the de facto wartime capital of Wuhan), under the editorial direction of Pan Zinian and the political guidance of the CCP's Yangzi Bureau led by Qian Shaoyu (alias Wang Ming). It moved to Chongqing in October 1938 and remained in circulation until 28 February 1947, when the Nationalist government suppressed all legal Communist communication channels in the city and elsewhere (Shanghai and Nanjing). In Chongqing, political leadership of the paper transferred to the CCP's Southern Bureau (南方局) under Zhou Enlai.
[5] Kui-Kwong Shum. 1988. *The Communists' Road to Power: The Anti-Japanese National United Front, 1935–1945*. Hong Kong: Oxford University Press, 122.
[6] Chongqing Municipal Archives [hereinafter CQA], 10厂, 8目, 158卷, 170页.

[7] Charles Tilly. 2002. *Stories, Identities, and Political Change*. Lanham, MD: Rowman & Littlefield.

[8] Wu Min 吴敏. 1938. '我们的信箱 [Our Mailbox].' 新华日报 [*New China Daily*], 11 January, 4.

[9] Ibid.

[10] Patricia Stranahan. 1990. *Molding the Medium: The Chinese Communist Party and the Liberation Daily*. Armonk, NY: M.E. Sharpe, 82.

[11] In his study of how Soviet Russia's mass newspapers disseminated a new political language during the 1920s, Jeffrey Brooks distinguishes between three spheres of information: an 'active sphere, designed to engage the participants in Soviet institutions, members of the Party and other enthusiastic supporters of the government; an informational sphere, intended to inform and influence the ordinary readers; and, lastly, an inspirational sphere, in which abstract moral values were elaborated for all. The active sphere contained the leaders' and staff journalists' messages to the activists, but also the activists' responses, albeit edited, in the form of letters and local correspondence. This part of the newspaper, which came to be the province of the worker and peasant correspondences, was also the terrain of the intelligentsia from the people.' Considerable overlap of these three spheres of information is manifest in the letters published in *New China Daily*, but the active sphere highlights the importance of local participation, which was the most innovative feature of the Soviet press and the Chinese Communist daily. Jeffrey Brooks. 1989. 'Competing Modes of Popular Discourse: Individualism and Class Consciousness in the Russian Print Media, 1880–1928.' In *Culture et revolution*, edited by Marc Ferro and Sheila Fitzpatrick. Paris: Éditions de l'École des Hautes Études en Sciences Sociales, 79.

[12] Sichuan Province and Chongqing Municipality Historical Associations of the New China Daily and The Masses Periodical (eds). 1998. 新华日报史新著 [*New Book on the History of the* New China Daily]. Chongqing: Chongqing Chubanshe, 149–50.

[13] Benedict Anderson. 1993. *Imagined Communities: Reflections on the Origin and Spread of Nationalism*. London: Verso.

[14] See, for instance, Elizabeth J. Perry (ed.). 1996. *Putting Class in its Place: Worker Identities in East Asia*. Berkeley, CA: Institute of East Asian Studies, University of California, Berkeley.

[15] See, for instance, Thomas C. Smith. 1988. 'The Right to Benevolence: Dignity and Japanese Workers, 1890–1920.' In *Native Sources of Japanese Industrialization, 1750–1920*, edited by Thomas C. Smith, 236–70. Berkeley, CA: University of California Press.

[16] Kevin J. O'Brien. 1996. 'Rightful Resistance.' *World Politics* 49, no. 1: 31–55.

[17] This distinction between inclusive and exclusive notions of class is made by Orlando Figes and Boris Kolonitskii. 1999. *Interpreting the Russian Revolution: The Language and Symbols of 1917*. New Haven, CT: Yale University Press, 114.

[18] Huang Shujun 黄淑君. 1986. 重庆工人运动史1919–1949 [*History of the Chongqing Labour Movement, 1919–1949*]. Chongqing: Xinan Shifan Daxue Chubanshe, 197.

[19] Hung-tseng Chang. 1945. 'The Chungking Press: I.' *China at War* 14, no. 5: 74.

[20] Joshua H. Howard. 2004. *Workers At War: Labor in China's Arsenals, 1937–1953*. Stanford, CA: Stanford University Press, 240–41.

[21] New Life Movement Women's Advisory Committee Cultural Services Group (ed.). 1944. 战时纺织女工 [*Wartime Textile Industry Women Workers*]. Chongqing: Xinyun Zonghui Funü Zhidao Weiyuanhui, 7.

[22] CQA, 20厂, 1441卷, 86b页. 14 February 1939.

23 See, for instance, '现在有没有民主？一群小工们说：没有！[Do We Now Have Democracy? A Group of Labourers Replies: No!].' 新华日报 [*New China Daily*], 12 February 1945, 3.

24 Zhou Enlai 周恩来. 1941. '民族至上与国家至上 [The Nation Is Supreme and the State Is Supreme].' 新华日报 [*New China Daily*], 15 June and 22 June. Zhou Enlai sought to fend off charges from the Nationalists that the CCP had wielded the slogan so often that it had become a cliché. For Zhou, 'the slogan, "the nation is supreme" means that national interests are above all else and the slogan has been used to mobilise all the Chinese people who have been oppressed by the people's principal enemy—the Japanese bandits with whom they are fighting a life and death struggle. It signifies that individual interests, class interests, factional interests all must be secondary to national interests. Struggle and sacrifice for national interests are the Chinese people's most pressing and glorious mission.'

25 Fan Er 凡尔. 1940. '我们要求同工同酬 [We Demand Equal Pay for Equal Work].' 新华日报 [*New China Daily*], 13 April, 4.

26 Hui Ying 惠英. 1944. '我怎样失去了健康：一个女工的遭遇 [How I Lost My Health: The Misfortunes of a Woman Worker].' 新华日报 [*New China Daily*], 12 March, 4.

27 Bing Bing 冰冰. 1940. '一个女工的自述 [A Woman Worker's Personal Account].' 新华日报 [*New China Daily*], 27 April, 4.

28 '一个工人的呼吁 [A Worker's Appeal].' 新华日报 [*New China Daily*], 13 December 1938, 4.

29 Ke Zhi 克制. 1944. '不许客饭 [No Meals for Guests].' 新华日报 [*New China Daily*], 25 May, 3. The writer adopted a symbolic pen-name meaning 'Overcome it!' to reinforce the political message.

30 '吃糖的问题 [The Sugar Issue].' 新华日报 [*New China Daily*], 28 February 1944, 3.

31 Hu Shihe's death was linked to the corrupt practices of the Zhonghan Cultural Association Restaurant—a meeting place for the notorious Juntong (Bureau of Investigation and Statistics) agents in the Daliangzi district of Chongqing. The restaurant had illegally linked up its power source line to a transformer on Duyou Street, causing an overload. When a team of electricians arrived on 19 February 1945 to prevent unauthorised use of the power source, Jiang Demao—who served concurrently as peace preservation corps for Garrison Headquarters and as an inspector at the military police headquarters—led the Cultural Association Restaurant waiters in roughing up the electricians and brought them to the local police station in Dayagou. Only through the intervention of the Chongqing Electric Company were they released. The next morning, the Electric Company sent another team of electricians, including Hu Shihe, a forty-year-old odd-jobs man and GMD party member, to cut the wiring. This time, Jiang Demao led twenty security guards to arrest Hu and three other workers, beating them along the route to the police station. As they reached the intersection of Republican Street, Juntong agent Tian Kai came running up with pistol in hand and shot Hu in the stomach. Hu was dragged to the police station and it would be another two hours before he was brought to the Kuanren Hospital. Excessive bleeding killed him before he reached the hospital. '特务横行月来越凶，偷了电还枪杀工人，特务统治 一天不取消，人权就一天 没有保障 [Spies Are Becoming More Violent and Running Amok, They Stole Electricity and Even Killed a Worker, Unless the Spy Controls Are Ended, There Will Be No Guarantees of Our Human Rights].' 新华日报 [*New China Daily*], 22 February 1945, 3.

[32] '掉胡世合君 [Remembering Mr Hu Shihe].' 新华日报 [New China Daily], 27 February 1945, 4.

[33] Kenneth G. Lieberthal. 1980. *Revolution and Tradition in Tientsin, 1949–1952*. Stanford, CA: Stanford University Press, 7.

1942 (Bo Ærenlund Sørensen)

[1] Warren W. Tozer. 1972. 'The Foreign Correspondents' Visit to Yenan in 1944: A Reassessment.' *Pacific Historical Review* 41, no. 2: 207–24.

[2] Harrison Forman. 1945. *Report from Red China*. New York, NY: H. Holt & Company, 63.

[3] 'Labour hero' and 'model worker' are only the two most common of several titles given in this period, but for the sake of convenience in this essay I will simply refer to these two when discussing the practice.

[4] Mary Sheridan. 1968. 'The Emulation of Heroes.' *The China Quarterly* 33: 47.

[5] Donald J. Munro. 1977. *The Concept of Man in Contemporary China*. Ann Arbor, MI: University of Michigan Press, 136.

[6] Miin-ling Yu. 2010. '"Labor Is Glorious": Model Laborers in the PRC.' In *China Learns from the Soviet Union, 1949–Present*, edited by Thomas P. Bernstein and Hua-Yu Li. Lanham, MD: Lexington Books, 234.

[7] Günther Stein. 1945. *The Challenge of Red China*. New York, NY: McGraw-Hill, 124.

[8] Andrew Watson. 1980. *Mao Zedong and the Political Economy of the Border Region: A Translation of Mao's 'Economic and Financial Problems'*. Cambridge, UK: Cambridge University Press, 227 ff.

[9] Cui Lili 崔莉莉. 2011. '"吴满有运动"与长诗《吴满有》的诞生 [The "Wu Manyou Movement" and the Creation of the Poem "Wu Manyou"].' 延安大学学报 (社会科学版) [*Journal of Yan'an University (Sociology Edition)*] 33, no. 2: 48–53.

[10] Lu Yang 路杨. 2018. '作为生产的文艺与农民主体的创生: 以艾青长诗《吴满有》为中心 [Literature and Art Based on Labour or Production and the Creation of Peasant Subject: A Discussion Focused on Ai Qing's "Wu Manyou"].' 文学评论 [*Literary Review*], no. 6: 110–18.

[11] Ibid.

[12] Wang Jianhua 王建华. 2016. '革命的理想人格: 延安时期劳动英雄的生产逻辑 [Perfect Revolutionary Personality: The Production Logic of Labour Heroes during the Yan'an Period].' 南京大学学报(哲学・人文科学・社会科学) [*Journal of Nanjing University (Philosophy, Humanities, Sociology)*] 53, no. 5: 124–36, 160; Zhou Haiyan 周海燕. 2012. '吴满有: 从记忆到遗忘—《解放日报》首个"典型报道"的新闻生产与社会记忆建构 [Wu Manyou: From Remembering to Forgetting—The Creation of the Liberation Daily's First "Model Report" and the Construction of Social Memory].' 江苏社会科学 [*Jiangsu Social Sciences*], no. 3: 236–40.

[13] For more on the continued relevance of this topic, see Christian Sorace. 2019. 'Aesthetics.' In *Afterlives of Chinese Communism: Political Concepts from Mao to Xi*, edited by Christian Sorace, Ivan Franceschini and Nicholas Loubere. Canberra, London, and New York, NY: ANU Press and Verso Books, 11–16.

[14] Chang-Tai Hung. 1997. 'Two Images of Socialism: Woodcuts in Chinese Communist Politics.' *Comparative Studies in Society and History* 39, no. 1: 34–60.

[15] Xiaofei Tian. 2011. 'The Making of a Hero: Lei Feng and Some Issues of Historiography.' In *The People's Republic of China at 60: An International Assessment*, edited by William C. Kirby. Cambridge, MA: Harvard University Asia Center, 293–305. Similarly, Hershatter has also noted that in the stories recounted by women selected as labour models in the 1950s, the language was much more redolent of womanly virtue than of socialist service. In other words, the Party-State's attempts to interpret what it meant to be a modern woman worthy of praise were very much influenced by older, local conceptions of virtuous womanhood. Gail Hershatter. 2011. *The Gender of Memory: Rural Women and China's Collective Past*. Berkeley, CA: University of California Press, 30.

[16] Cited in Stuart R. Schram, Timothy Cheek, and Nancy Jane Hodes (eds). 2015. *Mao's Road to Power: Revolutionary Writings. Volume 8*. London: Routledge, 683.

[17] Yu, '"Labor Is Glorious"', 235.

[18] Govind S. Kelkar. 1977. 'The Role of Labour Heroes in the Yenan Period.' *China Report* 13, no. 4: 54 ff.

[19] 解放日报 [*Liberation Daily*], 19 December 1943, 1.

[20] Stein, *The Challenge of Red China*, 130.

[21] Su Shaozhi 苏少之. 2004. '革命根据地新富农问题研究 [Research Related to the Rich Peasant Problem in the Revolutionary Base Area].' 近代史研究 [*Modern Chinese History Studies*], no. 1: 141 ff.

[22] Tetsuya Kataoka. 1974. *Resistance and Revolution in China: The Communists and the Second United Front*. Berkeley, CA: University of California Press, 259.

[23] Cited in Schram et al. *Mao's Road to Power*, 683.

[24] At this point, violence against model workers was much less frequent and harsh than was the case in Soviet Russia in the 1930s. See Mary E.A. Buckley. 2006. *Mobilizing Soviet Peasants: Heroines and Heroes of Stalin's Fields*. Lanham, MD: Rowman & Littlefield, 149–56. During the Cultural Revolution, however, many model workers across China would come to suffer severe mental and physical abuse. See Yu, '"Labor Is Glorious"', 248.

[25] 解放日报 [*Liberation Daily*], 25 July 1946, 2; Yingjin Zhang. 2012. *A Companion to Chinese Cinema. Volume 8*. Hoboken, NJ: Wiley, 321.

[26] Matthew David Johnson. 2008. 'International and Wartime Origins of the Propaganda State: The Motion Picture in China, 1897–1955.' PhD dissertation, University of California, San Diego, 230 ff.

[27] Zhou, 'Wu Manyou', 239.

[28] For interesting instances of how this played out in various venues in the 1950s, see Aminda M. Smith. 2013. *Thought Reform and China's Dangerous Classes: Reeducation, Resistance, and the People*. Lanham, MD: Rowman & Littlefield; Lifton, Robert Jay Lifton. 1989. *Thought Reform and the Psychology of Totalism: A Study of 'Brainwashing' in China*. New York, NY: Norton.

[29] Johnson, 'International and Wartime Origins of the Propaganda State', 234.

[30] Zhou, 'Wu Manyou', 239.

[31] Gong Mingde 龚明德. 2006. '改"吴满有"为"刘玉厚" [Changing "Wu Manyou" to "Liu Yuhou"].' 出版史料 [*Publication Archives*], no. 4: 44–45.

[32] Li Rui 李锐. 1995. '劳动英雄吴满有真的叛变投敌了吗? [Did Model Worker Wu Manyou Really Defect to the Enemy?].' 炎黄春秋 [*Yanhuang Chunqiu*], no. 4: 66–70.

[33] Sun Liping 孙立平. 2005. '劳模评选的尴尬 [The Embarrassments of Selecting Model Workers].' 中国改革 [*China Reforms*], no. 6: 52–53.

34 Patrick Boehler. 2015. 'China's Case Against a Civil Rights Lawyer, in Seven Social Media Posts.' *The New York Times*, 15 December, available online at: www.nytimes.com/2015/12/15/world/asia/pu-zhiqiang-china-trial-weibo-posts.html.

1946 (Brian DeMare)

[1] Deng Zihui 邓子恢. 1988[1946]. '从鹅钱乡斗争来研究目前土地改革运动 [Researching the Current Land Reform Movement from the Struggle in E'qian Village].' In 中国土地改革史料选编 [*Selected Historical Materials from China's Land Reform*]. Beijing: Guofang Daxue Chubanshe, 292–94.

[2] Ibid.

[3] For an analysis of the May Fourth Directive, see Suzanne Pepper. 1999. *Civil War in China: The Political Struggle 1945–1949*. 2nd edn. Lanham, MD: Rowman & Littlefield, 246–48.

[4] For example, a report on landownership in Sichuan found extreme inequality in holdings. In eastern Sichuan, poor and middle peasants accounted for 88 percent of the population but controlled only 25 percent of the land. The situation in western Sichuan was even more extreme, with 4 percent of the population controlling up to 75 percent of rural fields. See '川西农村的封建统治 [The Feudal Regime of Rural West Sichuan].' In 中国西南档案: 土地改革资料, 1949–1953 [*Southwest China Archives: The Documents of Land Reform, 1949–1953*], edited by Zhang Peitian 张培田, Zhang Hua 张华, and Chen Cuiyu 陈翠玉. Kingsford, NSW: International Culture Press (2007), 100.

[5] Xiaojia Hou. 2016. *Negotiating Socialism in Rural China: Mao, Peasants, and Local Cadres in Shanxi 1949–1953*. Ithaca, NY: Cornell East Asia Program, 33.

[6] '永安乡划阶级总结报告 [Yong'an Township Class Division General Report]', 1952, in *Southwest China Archives*, 105.

[7] '划阶级中的几个问题 [Some Problems in Determining Class Status]', 1952, in *Southwest China Archives*, 162–63.

[8] '晋冀鲁豫局为贯彻 "五四" 指示彻底实现耕者有其天的指示 [Central China Bureau Regarding Implementing "Five-Four" Directive Regarding New Policy Decisions]', 1988[1946], in *Selected Historical Materials from China's Land Reform*, 312.

[9] '华中分局关于团结中农的指示 [Directive from the Central China Bureau Regarding Uniting Middle Peasants]', 1946, in *Selected Historical Materials from China's Land Reform*, 305–6.

[10] '华东局关于山东土改复查的新指示 [New Directive on Land Reform Reexamination in Shandong from the East China Bureau]', 1947, in *Selected Historical Materials from China's Land Reform*, 381–84.

[11] Ibid.

[12] According to Li, this contradiction provided the foundation for a 'contradictory system' of revolution and production that became a defining characteristic of continuous revolution in rural China. Li Fangchun 李放春. 2006. '北方土改中的翻身与生产: 中国革命现代性的一个话语—历史矛盾溯考 [North China Land Reform Liberation and Production: An Examination into the Historical Sources of Contradiction in the Discourse of Modern Chinese Revolution].' 中国乡村研究 [*Rural China*] 3, no. 1: 231–92.

[13] '晋察冀局关于传达与进行中央五四指示的决定（节录）[JinChaJi Bureau Decision Regarding Transmitting and Implementing the May Fourth Directive (Excerpt)]', 1946, in *Selected Historical Materials from China's Land Reform*, 298.

[14] '华中分局关于团结中农的指示 [Directive from the Central China Bureau Regarding Uniting Middle Peasants]', 1946, in *Selected Historical Materials from China's Land Reform*, 305.

[15] '太行区党委关于农村阶级划分标准与具体划分规定（草案）[Taihang District Party Committee Decisions Regarding Rural Class Status Standards and Exact Division Regulations (Draft)]', 1946, in *Selected Historical Materials from China's Land Reform*, 322.

[16] '一年来东北土地改革略输 [A Brief Account of One Year of Land Reform in Northeast China]', 1947, in *Selected Historical Materials from China's Land Reform*, 376.

[17] This was the case even when villagers avoided violent confrontation with class enemies. Liu Shigu's work on criminal landlords in Poyang shows that, while work teams were concerned with political matters, peasants were focused on economics. Work teams tended to report landlords for political crimes, while peasants brought charges related to rent and interest. As the Poyang County Party Committee declared in 1950, 'economic interests outstrip [超过] political interests'. See Liu Shigu 刘诗古. 2015. '"失序"下的"秩序"：新中国成立初期土改中的司法实践—对鄱阳县"不法地主案"的解读与分析 ["Order" under "Disorder": Judicial Practice during New China Establishment Initial Period Land Reform—An Interpretation and Analysis of "Illegal Landlord Cases" in Poyang County]'. 进时代研究 [*Modern Chinese History Studies*] 6: 102.

[18] Xi Zhongxun 习仲勋, '关于土改中一些问题给毛主席的报告（节录）[Report for Chairman Mao Regarding Some Problems in Land Reform]', 1988[1948], in *Selected Historical Materials from China's Land Reform*, 451.

[19] Liao Luyan 廖鲁言, '三年来土地改革运动的伟大胜利 [The Great Victory of Three Years of Land Reform Movement]', 1988[1952], in *Selected Historical Materials from China's Land Reform*, 843.

[20] '关于目前农村工作中的若干新情况 [Regarding Some New Situations in Current Rural Work]', undated but likely from 1951, in *Southwest China Archives*, 152.

[21] Deng Zihui 邓子恢, '给少奇同志转中央的一封信 [A Letter for Comrade Shaoqi from the Central Committee]', 1988[1947], in *Selected Historical Materials from China's Land Reform*, 379–80.

1948 (Emily Honig)

[1] Unless specified, all the material in this essay comes from Emily Honig. 1986. *Sisters and Strangers: Women in the Shanghai Cotton Mills, 1919–1949*. Stanford, CA: Stanford University Press.

[2] For a more detailed analysis of Subei, see Emily Honig. 1992. *Creating Chinese Ethnicity: Subei People in Shanghai*. New Haven, CT: Yale University Press.

[3] Elizabeth J. Perry. 1993. *Shanghai on Strike: The Politics of Chinese Labor*. Stanford, CA: Stanford University Press, 83, 213.

[4] Ibid., 85–86.

[5] S.A. Smith. 2002. *Like Cattle and Horses: Nationalism and Labor in Shanghai, 1895–1927*. Durham, NC: Duke University Press, 232.

[6] Perry, *Shanghai on Strike*, 213–14.

[7] David Strand. 1989. *Rickshaw Beijing: City People and Politics in the 1920s*. Berkeley, CA: University of California Press, 196.

1949 (Mao Zedong)

[1] This speech was presented to the public on 30 June 1949 to commemorate the twenty-eighth anniversary of the founding of the Chinese Communist Party. It was included in the fourth volume of *Selected Works of Mao Tse-tung*, published by Foreign Language Press (available online at: www.marxists.org/reference/archive/mao/selected-works/volume-4/mswv4_65.htm#bm1).

1949 (Robert Cliver)

[1] Qian Yaoxing 钱耀兴 (ed.). 1990. 无锡市丝绸工业志 [*Wuxi Silk Industry Gazetteer*]. Shanghai: Shanghai Renmin Chubanshe, 337–38.

[2] There are several reports on Democratic Reform in the Wuxi Municipal Archives (WMA), file D2-1-11.

[3] See Mao Zedong's 'On New Democracy' (January 1940), available online at: www.marxists.org/reference/archive/mao/selected-works/volume-2/mswv2_26.htm; Jonathan J. Howlett. 2021. 'The Shanghai News (1950–1952): New Democracy and External Propaganda in Early 1950s Shanghai.' 中國歷史學刊 [*Journal of Chinese History*] 5, no. 1: 107–30.

[4] William C. Kirby. 1992. 'The Chinese War Economy.' In *China's Bitter Victory: The War with Japan 1937–1945*, edited by James C. Hsiung and Steven I. Levine. New York, NY: M.E. Sharpe, 185–213.

[5] Jackie Sheehan. 1998. *Chinese Workers: A New History*. New York, NY: Routledge, 18.

[6] Ibid.

[7] Delia Davin. 1976. *Woman Work: Women and the Party in Revolutionary China*. Oxford, UK: Clarendon Press, 174.

[8] William Brugger. 1976. *Democracy and Organisation in the Chinese Industrial Enterprise (1948–1953)*. Cambridge, UK: Cambridge University Press, 79–85.

[9] On strike actions by Chinese women workers before the 1950s, see Elizabeth J. Perry. 1993. *Shanghai on Strike: The Politics of Chinese Labor*. Stanford, CA: Stanford University Press; and Emily Honig. 1986. *Sisters and Strangers: Women in the Shanghai Cotton Mills, 1919–1949*. Stanford, CA: Stanford University Press.

[10] WMA, D2-1-11.

[11] Shanghai Municipal Archives (SMA), C1-2-854, C1-2-333.

[12] Davin, *Woman Work*, 174.

[13] Robert Cliver. 2020. *Red Silk: Class, Gender, and Revolution in China's Yangzi Delta Silk Industry*. Cambridge, MA: Harvard University Asia Center, 180–89.

[14] Ibid., 294–95.

[15] Zhang Lizhi 张立之. 1950. '天津中纺三厂实行管理民主化的经验 [The Experience of the Tianjin Third Cotton Mill in Democratising Management].' In 学会管理企业的几个问题 [Several Questions in Learning to Manage Enterprises], edited by Li Tao 李涛 and Lin Genghe 林庚合. Tianjin: Duzhe Shudian, 1–8.

[16] Qian, *Wuxi Silk Industry Gazetteer*, 248–55.

[17] 人民日报 [*People's Daily*], 23 February 1951.

[18] On the Democratic Reform Campaign of 1951, see Sheehan, *Chinese Workers*, 37–41; Brugger, *Democracy and Organisation in the Chinese Industrial Enterprise*, 100–11; Lin Chaochao 林超超. 2010. '新国家与旧工人：1952年上海私营工厂的民主改革运动 [New State and Old Workers: The Democratic Reform Campaign in Private Factories in Shanghai in 1952].' 社会学研究 [*Sociological Research*], no. 2: 67–86.

[19] WMA, D2-1-10.

[20] Gail Hershatter. 2019. *Women and China's Revolutions*. Lanham, MD: Rowman & Littlefield, 200–2.

1949 (Po-chien Chen and Yi-hung Liu)

[1] Interview conducted by the authors in March 2018.

[2] 'Free China Salutes America's Bicentennial', *The New York Times*, 4 July 1976, p. 20.

[3] Frederic C. Deyo. 1989. *Beneath the Miracle: Labour Subordination in East Asian Development*. Berkeley, CA: University of California Press.

[4] Tsai Shih-shan. 2015. *The Peasant Movement and Land Reform in Taiwan, 1924–1951*. Portland, ME: Merwin Asia.

[5] Anna Belogurova. 2012. 'The Civic World of International Communism: Taiwanese Communists and the Comintern (1921–1931).' *Modern Asian Studies* 46, no. 6: 1602–32.

[6] 'Formosa Killings Are Put at 10,000', *The New York Times*, 29 March 1947, p. 6.

[7] Political trials database conducted by Transitional Justice Commission (an independent government agency of Taiwan).

1951 (Jake Werner)

[1] This chapter is a condensed version of Jake Werner. 2015. 'The Making of Mass Society in Shanghai: The Socialist Transformation of Everyday Life, 1949–1958.' PhD dissertation, Department of History, University of Chicago, 122–76.

[2] Martin King Whyte. 1974. *Small Groups and Political Rituals in China*. Berkeley, CA: University of California Press, 36–57.

[3] Zou Ronggeng 邹荣庚. 2001. '建国初期上海的企业民主改革运动 [Shanghai's Democratic Reform Movement in the Early People's Republic of China].' In 历史巨变 [*A Great Historical Change*], Vol. 1, 1949–1956, edited by Zou Ronggeng 邹荣庚. Shanghai: Shanghai Shudian Chubanshe, 221.

[4] Benjamin Kindler. 2019. 'Sugarcoated Bullets.' In *Afterlives of Chinese Communism: Political Concepts from Mao to Xi*, edited by Christian Sorace, Ivan Franceschini and Nicholas Loubere. Canberra and London: ANU Press and Verso Books, 263–68.

⁵ Qin Wei 秦韦. 1951. '必须进行民主团结 [We Must Proceed with Democratic Unity].' In 工人生活 [*Workers' Life*], No. 2, edited by Hua Sheng 华生 et al. Hankou: Wuhan Tongsu Chubanshe, 1.
⁶ Shanghai Municipal Archives [hereinafter SMA], A38-1-160-1.
⁷ SMA, A38-1-160-11.
⁸ Ibid.
⁹ Ibid.
¹⁰ SMA, A38-1-160-57.
¹¹ SMA, A38-1-160-66.
¹² SMA, A38-1-160-89; Shen Yijing 沈逸静. 2001. '"三反"、"五反" 运动在上海 [The "Three Antis" and "Five Antis" Movements in Shanghai].' In Zou (ed.), *A Great Historical Change*, Vol. 1, 189.
¹³ SMA, A38-1-160-102.
¹⁴ SMA, A38-1-160-84.
¹⁵ SMA, A38-1-160-89.
¹⁶ Ibid.
¹⁷ SMA, A38-1-160-101.
¹⁸ SMA, A38-1-160-89.
¹⁹ SMA, A38-1-160-78.
²⁰ SMA, A38-1-160-67.
²¹ SMA, A38-1-160-84.
²² SMA, A38-1-160-67.

1951 (Li Lisan)

¹ Mark W. Frazier. 2002. *The Making of the Chinese Industrial Workplace*. Cambridge, UK: Cambridge University Press, 112–14.
² Paul Harper. 1969. 'The Party and the Unions in Communist China.' *The China Quarterly* 37: 84–119, at p. 91.
³ Li Lisan. 1950. 'The Experiences, Lessons and Present Conditions of the Chinese Workers' Movement.' In *Trade Union Conference of Asian and Australasian Countries*. Beijing: Workers' Press, 22–31.
⁴ William Brugger. 1973. *Democracy and Organization in the Chinese Industrial Enterprise (1948–1953)*. Cambridge, MA: Cambridge University Press, 81.
⁵ Deng Zihui 邓子恢. 1950. '关于中南区的工会工作 [On the Trade Union Work in the Southern and Central Areas].' 工人日报 [*Workers' Daily*], 4 August, 4.
⁶ Li Lisan 李立三. 1987[1951]. '行政与工会的关系 [The Relationship between Management and Unions].' In 李立三赖若愚论工会 [*Li Lisan and Lai Ruoyu Discuss the Union*], edited by Chinese Institute of Industrial Relations. Beijing: Dang'an Chubanshe, 146–49.
⁷ Li Lisan 李立三. 1987[1951]. '关于新民主主义时期工会工作中几个问题的决议 [Resolution on Some Issues Regarding Union Work in the Phase of the New Democracy].' In *Li Lisan and Lai Ruoyu Discuss the Union*, 150–55.
⁸ Li Lisan 李立三. 1987[1951]. '关于在工会工作中发生争论的问题的意见向毛主席的报告 [Report to Chairman Mao on the Controversial Issues in Union Work].' In *Li Lisan and Lai Ruoyu Discuss the Union*, 156–58.

[9] Li Fuchun 李富春. 1989[1951]. '在工会工作问题上的分歧 [Some Divergences of Opinion on Matters Related to Union Work].' In 建国以来中共中央关于工人运动文件选编 [Selected Documents about the Labour Movement Issued by the Central Committee of the Party Since the Foundation of the People's Republic], edited by General Office of the ACFTU. Beijing: Zhongguo Gongren Chubanshe, 96–116.

[10] This is the translation of Li Lisan's speech 'The Relationship between Management and Unions' cited above.

[11] 'New Democracy' (新民主主义) was a theory, an overarching revolutionary strategy, and a period of the Chinese Revolution that lasted from the 1930s until the first half of the 1950s. See Marc Blecher. 2019. 'New Democracy.' In *Afterlives of Chinese Communism: Political Concepts from Mao to Xi*, edited by Christian Sorace, Ivan Franceschini, and Nicholas Loubere. Canberra, London, and New York, NY: ANU Press and Verso Books, 155–59.

1952 (Mark W. Frazier)

[1] Luo Gang 罗岗. 2007. '空间的生产与空间的转移: 上海工人新村与社会主义城市经验 [The Production of Space and the Space of Transition: Shanghai Workers' New Village and the Socialist Urban Experience].' 华东师范大学学报(哲学社会科学版) [*Journal of East China Normal University (Philosophy and Social Sciences)*] 39, no. 6: 93.

[2] On the lived experience of lane-alley housing in socialist Shanghai, see Jie Li. 2015. *Shanghai Homes: Palimpsests of Private Life*. New York, NY: Columbia University Press.

[3] Yang Chen 杨辰. 2011. '社会主义城市的空间实践: 上海工人新村 (1949–1978) [The Spatial Practice of Urban Socialism (1949–1978)].' 人文地理 [*Human Geography*] 26, no 3: 37; He Dan 何丹 and Zhu Xiaoping 朱小平. 2012. '石库门里弄和工人新村的日常生活空间比较研究 [Comparative Research of the Space of Daily Life in Shikumen Lane Alleys and Workers' New Villages].' 世界地理研究 [*World Regional Studies*] 21, no. 2: 155.

[4] Quoted in Gotelind Müller. 2013. 'Atarashiki Mura Versus Xincun: On the Chinese Reception of a Japanese Model of Alternative Lifestyle as a Case Study on Standard and Deviation' 5. University of Heidelberg, available online at: archiv.ub.uni-heidelberg.de/volltextserver/15393/1/Atarashiki%20mura%20english.pdf.

[5] Yang, 'The Spatial Practice of Urban Socialism', 37.

[6] Ibid.

[7] Yang Chen 杨辰. 2009. '日常生活空间的制度化: 20 世纪50年代上海工人新村的空间分析框架 [Institutionalising the Spaces of Daily Life: A Spatial Analytical Framework of the 1950s Shanghai Workers' New Village].' 同济大学学报（社会科学版） [*Tongji University Journal (Social Science Section)*] 20, no. 6: 40; Zhu Xiaoming 朱晓明. 2011. '上海曹杨一村规划设计与历史 [The Planning, Design, and History of Shanghai's Caoyang Number One Village].' 住宅科技 [*Residential Science and Technology*] 11: 48.

[8] The article containing Wang's brief interview is from '诉说城市那割不断的历史 [Recounting the Continuous History of the City]', 解放日报 [*Liberation Daily*], 22 November 2004, and can be found at www.archives.sh.cn/shjy/scbq/201203/t20120313_11958.html.

[9] Chinese scholars call the Stalinist model *dajiefang* (大街坊)—literally: 'large neighbourhoods' or 'subdivisions fronting grand boulevards'. Yang, 'Institutionalising the Spaces of Daily Life', 41, n.1.

[10] Wang Dingzeng 汪定曾. 1956. '上海曹杨新村住宅区的规划设计 [The Planning and Design of Shanghai's Caoyang New Village].' 建筑学报 [*Architecture Journal*] 2: 13.

[11] Ibid., 13.

[12] Ibid., 15.

[13] Ibid., 4.

[14] Yang, 'Institutionalising the Spaces of Daily Life', 42.

[15] Zhu, 'The Planning, Design, and History of Shanghai's Caoyang Number One Village', 48.

[16] Luo Gang 罗岗 (translated by Christopher Connery). 2012. 'Socialist Shanghai, the Struggle for Space, and the Production of Space: A Reading of the Urban Text and the Media Text.' *Postcolonial Studies* 15, no. 4: 481.

[17] Ibid., 479.

[18] Henry Lefebvre (translated by Michael Enders). 1976. 'Reflections on the Politics of Space.' *Antipode* 8, no. 2: 31.

[19] Quoted in Luo, 'Socialist Shanghai, the Struggle for Space, and the Production of Space', 475–76.

[20] Luo, 'The Production of Space and the Space of Transition', 94.

[21] Shanghai Municipal Archives [hereinafter SMA], A20-1-94-37.

[22] Luo, 'The Production of Space and the Space of Transition', 94.

[23] SMA, A60-1-25.

[24] Zhu, 'The Planning, Design, and History of Shanghai's Caoyang Number One Village', 52.

1952 (John Williams)

[1] The author would like to express special gratitude to Zhuang Xu for his invaluable research assistance on this project. Major historical studies include Zhang Yihe 章义和. 2008. 中国蝗灾史 [*History of Locust Plagues in China*]. Hefei: Anhui Renmin Chubanshe; Zhao Yanping 赵艳萍. 2009. 民国时期蝗灾与社会应对 [*Locust Plagues and Social Responses in the Republican Era*]. Guangzhou: Guangdong Shijie Tushu Chubanshe; and Zou Shuwen 邹树文. 1982. 中国昆虫学史 [*History of Chinese Entomology*]. Beijing: Keji Chubanshe. See also Harry N. Rothchild. 2012. 'Sovereignty, Virtue, and Disaster Management: Chief Minister Yao Chong's Proactive Handling of the Locust Plague of 715–16.' *Environmental History* 17, no. 4: 783–812; and David A. Bello. 2016. 'How Do Humans and Locusts Make Space in an Early Modern Chinese Grain Field?' *RCC Perspectives: Molding the Planet: Human Niche Construction at Work*, no. 5: 25–32.

[2] Chengxiang Pan. 1988. 'The Development of Integrated Pest Control in China.' *Agricultural History* 62, no. 1: 4.

[3] In 1952, more than two million day labourers were mobilised to fight locusts in Dezhou alone. See Qiu Shibang 邱式邦, Guo Shougui 郭守桂, and Li Guangbo 李光博. 1952. '为什么提倡毒饵治蝗 [Why We Advocate Pesticide Bait for Locust

Control].' 农业科学通讯 [*Agricultural Science Bulletin*], no. 8: 18; Chen Shaoyuan 陈绍元. 1991. '漫话治蝗 [An Informal Discussion of Locust Control].' 宁河文史资料 [*Ninghe Cultural and Historical Materials*], no. 2: 180.

[4] Cao Ji 曹骥. 1950. '有关治蝗的几个技术问题 [Several Technical Issues Concerning Locust Control].' 农业科学通讯 [*Agricultural Science Bulletin*] 2, no. 3: 15.

[5] See, for example, Chen Yonglin 陈永林. 2000. '中国的飞蝗研究及其治理的主要成就 [China's Principal Accomplishments in Locust Research and Management].' 昆虫知识 [*Entomological Knowledge*] 37, no. 1: 50; Liu Jigang 刘继刚. 2017. '甲骨文所见殷商时期的蝗灾及防治方法 [Locust Plagues and Related Prevention Measures Recorded in Oracle Bone Script].' 中国农史 [*Agricultural History of China*] 4: 55–61, 136; Guan Dexiang 官德祥. 2001. '两汉时期蝗灾述论 [Locust Plagues in the Han Dynasty].' 中国农史 [*Agricultural History of China*] 20, no. 3: 8–15; and Cui Yanhua 崔彦华 and Jia Bizhen 贾碧真. 2016. '东汉蝗灾概述 [A Survey of Locust Plagues in the Eastern Han].' 社科纵横 [*Social Sciences Review*] 31, no. 9: 122–25.

[6] 人民日报 [*People's Daily*], 24 October 1977; US Department of Agriculture. 1982. *Biological Control of Pests in China*. Washington, DC: US Department of Agriculture, 2; Pan Chengxiang 潘承湘. 1985. '我国东亚飞蝗的研究与防治简史 [A Short History of Research and Prevention of the East Asian Migratory Locust in China].' 自然科学史研究 [*Studies in the History of Natural Sciences*] 4, no. 1: 88.

[7] The most prominent of these critics was Han intellectual Wang Chong (25 – ca. 100 CE), who devoted a chapter of his *Balanced Discussions* to refuting the idea. See Wang Chong 王充. 1979. 论衡注释 [*Annotated Balanced Discussions*]. Beijing: Zhonghua Shuju, 937–48.

[8] Ma Shutian 马书田. 1990. 华夏诸神 [*Spirits and Gods of China*]. Beijing: Yanshan Chubanshe, 388–92.

[9] See Hsin-Yi Hsu. 1969. 'The Cultural Ecology of the Locust Cult in Traditional China.' *Annals of the Association of American Geographers* 59, no. 4: 731–52; 嘉庆朝大清会典 [*Collected Statutes of the Great Qing, Jiaqing Reign*], 29.6b, 362.8b, 1823.

[10] Although human efforts usually had only a limited effect on large-scale infestations before the modern era, swarms nevertheless eventually dissipated for a number of non-anthropogenic reasons. Thus, as May Berenbaum points out, from the point of view of rural society, prayers *worked*. May Berenbaum. 1995. *Bugs in the System: Insects and Their Impact on Human Affairs*. New York, NY: Basic Books, 114.

[11] The interpretation of locust outbreaks as divine punishment was common in early cultures throughout the Eurasian world. They are well known in the Judeo-Christian tradition as the eighth of ten plagues unleashed on Egypt by God (Exodus 10.1–20).

[12] See Yonglin Chen. 1999. *The Locust and Grasshopper Pests of China*. Beijing: China Forestry Publishing House, 36–38. Normally, locusts are solitary grasshoppers that pose little threat to crops; it is only under certain conditions that they begin to aggregate, triggering behavioural changes and physiological transformation. This process, called 'density-dependent phase polyphenism', was identified by entomologist Boris Uvarov, whose findings revolutionised the understanding of locusts. Though Uvarov did not understand the cause of phase change, it was later shown to be triggered by nymphal crowding. Of more than 12,000 grasshopper species, fewer than twenty carry the genome enabling transition from the 'solitary' to the 'gregarious' phase that characterises true locusts. See Boris Uvarov. 1921. 'A Revision of the Genus Locusta, L. (=Pchytylus, Fieb.), With a New Theory as to the Periodicity and Migrations of Locusts.' *Bulletin of Entomological Research* 12, no. 2: 135–63; Stephen J. Simpson and

Gregory A. Sword. 2009. 'Phase Polyphenism in Locusts: Mechanisms, Population Consequences, Adaptive Significance and Evolution.' In *Phenotypic Plasticity of Insects: Mechanisms and Consequences*, edited by Douglas Whitman and T.N. Ananthakrishnan, 147–89. Enfield, NH: Science Publishers; and Stephen J. Simpson and Gregory A. Sword. 2008. 'Locusts.' *Current Biology* 18, no. 9: 364–66.

[13] The earliest mention of this practice appears in Han sources. See Wang, *Annotated Balanced Discussions*, 341–42.

[14] An adult locust can eat its own weight in food in a day, while one square mile (2.6 square kilometres) of them (roughly 100 to 200 million individuals) can devour 220–270 tonnes of food—enough to feed 200,000 people, according to Berenbaum, *Bugs in the System*, 113.

[15] In the account cited above, for example, Wang Chong writes: 'The officers and underlings direct the people to draw furrows and dig moats and drive the locusts into them with rattles.' Wang, *Annotated Balanced Discussions*, 341–42.

[16] Zhang, *History of Locust Plagues in China*, 164.

[17] Dong Wei 董煟. 2003. '救荒活民书 [Book on Saving the People from Famine].' In 中国荒政全书 [*Compendium of Works on Famine Relief in China*], edited by Li Wenhai 李文海 and Xia Mingfang 夏明方. Beijing: Beijing Guji Chubanshe, 1.102. Bounties were awarded according to the weight and developmental stage (nymphs, locusts, eggs) of insects tendered.

[18] See 光绪朝大清会典事例 [*Statutes and Substatutes of the Great Qing, Guangxu Reign*]. 1899. Beijing, 110: 8b–15a.

[19] Cai Hongyuan 蔡鸿源 (ed.). 1999. 民国法规集成 [*Collection of Laws and Regulations from the Republican Era*]. Hefei: Huangshan Shushe, 55, 132–36.

[20] *Statutes and Substatutes of the Great Qing*, 110: 10b–12a.

[21] See, for example, Wu Fuzhen 吴福桢. 1930. '十七年治蝗经过情形 [Circumstances of Locust Control in 1928].' 江苏省昆虫局十七十八年年刊 [*Jiangsu Entomological Bureau Annual for 1928 and 1929*]. Nanjing: Jiangsusheng Kunchongju, 63–65.

[22] The Nationalist government's destruction of the Yellow River dykes to thwart the Japanese advance precipitated an ecological crisis, exacerbated by cycles of flood and drought in the early 1940s, turning the North China Plain into a massive locust breeding ground. See Micah Muscolino. 2015. *The Ecology of War in China: Henan Province, the Yellow River, and Beyond, 1938-1950*. Cambridge, UK: Cambridge University Press, 30–31, 34–36.

[23] Gu Jingsheng 谷景生. 1986. '灭蝗记 [An Account of Locust Extermination].' 安阳文史资料 [*Anyang Cultural and Historical Materials*], no. 1: 165–66; Yang Ruixin 杨瑞新. 1987. '灭蝗记述 [Description of Locust Extermination].' 安阳文史资料 [*Anyang Cultural and Historical Materials*], no. 2: 111–14.

[24] For a detailed account of these campaigns, see Ma Weiqiang 马维强 and Deng Hongqin 邓宏琴. 2010. '抗战时期太行根据地蝗灾与社会应对 [Locust Plague and Social Response in the Taihang Base Area During the War of Resistance].' 中共党史研究 [*Studies on the History of the Chinese Communist Party*], no. 7: 101–9.

[25] Wang Wudai 王武代 and Local Gazette Office of Hebei Province (eds). 2009. 河北省志:自然灾害志 [*Hebei Provincial Gazetteer: Natural Disasters Volume*]. Beijing: Fangzhi Chubanshe, 366–68.

[26] Tian Guangyuan 田广元. 1988. '蓟县治蝗纪实 [Factual Record of Locust Control in Ji County].' 蓟县文史资料 [*Ji County Cultural and Historical Materials*], no. 2: 185.

[27] Zhang, *History of Locust Plagues in China*, 59, 63, 68–69, 81, 84, 87–89, 96; Wang and Local Gazette Office of Hebei Province, *Hebei Provincial Gazetteer*, 332, 334; Tian, 'Factual Record of Locust Control in Ji County', 186–87.

[28] Tian, 'Factual Record of Locust Control in Ji County', 187.

[29] Ibid., 188.

[30] Ibid., 189.

[31] Ibid., 190.

[32] Ibid., 190–91. Known more commonly in the West as γ-BHC (gamma-hexachlorocyclohexane) or lindane, it was developed in the early 1940s to control the desert locust (*Schistocerca gregaria*) in eastern Africa and the Middle East, and rapidly became the weapon of choice in anti-locust campaigns. First used in China in 1947, 666 was soon deployed against locusts wherever and whenever resources allowed (the Chinese term '666' refers to its molecular structure). See G.T. Brooks. 1977. 'Chlorinated Insecticides: Retrospect and Prospect.' In *Pesticide Chemistry in the 20th Century*, edited by Jack Plimmer, 1–2. Washington, DC: American Chemical Society; György Matolcsy, Miklós Nádasy, and Viktor Andriska. 1988. *Pesticide Chemistry*. Amsterdam: Elsevier, 61–66; and Stanley Richard Baron. 1972. *The Desert Locust*. London: Eyre Methuen Ltd., 20, 160–61.

[33] Tian, 'Factual Record of Locust Control in Ji County', 191. One jin is approximately half a kilogram.

[34] '中央农业部关于防治蝗虫，棉蚜的紧急通知 [Ministry of Agriculture Emergency Bulletin Concerning the Prevention of Locusts and Cotton Aphids].' 人民周报 [*People's Weekly*], no. 42 (1952): 15.

[35] Tian, 'Factual Record of Locust Control in Ji County', 192.

[36] Ibid., 192. Agricultural Bureau experiments in 1950 showed that lindane's potency varied according to the insects' gender and instar and required meticulously prepared solutions for maximum effect—something that was hard to guarantee in the field. Chen was involved with early locust research and control efforts conducted by the Jiangsu and Zhejiang entomological bureaus in the 1930s, as well as training programs in the use of insecticidal fumigants. In 1933, he delivered a radio broadcast on locust control for the Nationalist government in Nanjing. See Chen Jiaxiang 陈家祥. 1933. '飞蝗生活史及防治法 [Life Cycle of the Migratory Locust and Its Prevention].' 昆虫与植病 [*Insects and Phytopathology*], nos 30–35: 668–74; and Cao Ji 曹骥 and Li Guangbo 李光博. 1950. '六六六对于飞蝗蝻期的熏蒸作用 [The Fumigation Action of 666 on Migratory Locusts in the Nymph Stage].' 中国昆虫学报 [*Acta Entomologica Sinica*] 1, no. 2: 128–35.

[37] Tian, 'Factual Record of Locust Control in Ji County', 193–94.

[38] Boris Uvarov. 1928. *Locusts and Grasshoppers: A Handbook for Their Study and Control*. London: Imperial Bureau of Entomology, 203.

[39] '一九五二年华北区的农业工作 [Agricultural Work in the North China Region in 1952].' 中国农报 [*China Agricultural Report*], no. 21 (1952): 11–13.

[40] See Sigrid Schmalzer. 2016. *Red Revolution, Green Revolution: Scientific Farming in Socialist China*. Chicago, IL: University of Chicago Press.

[41] Xu Guangqi 徐光启. 1986. 徐文定公集 [*Collected Works of Xu Guangqi*]. Taibei: Wenhai Chubanshe, 244.

[42] See Ruth Rogaski. 2002. 'Nature, Annihilation, and Modernity: China's Korean War Germ-Warfare Experience Reconsidered.' *Journal of Asian Studies* 61, no. 2: 381–415.

[43] The 1943 mobilisation likened the locusts to the Japanese occupiers, while the efforts of the early 1950s were explicitly tied to the 'Resist America, Aid Korea' (抗美援朝) campaign. Ma and Deng, 'Locust Plague and Social Response in the Taihang Base Area During the War of Resistance', 108; Yin Shan 尹善 and Fu Guichuan 傅桂川. 1951. '黄骅县扑灭蝗虫情形介绍 [Introduction to the Conditions of Locust Extermination in Huanghua County].' 农业科学通讯 [Agricultural Science Bulletin], no. 8: 23–24.

[44] See Qiu et al., 'Why We Advocate Pesticide Bait for Locust Control', 18–19; and Qiu Shibang 邱式邦 and Li Guangbo 李光博. 1952. '安次县毒饵治蝗的经验介绍 [Introduction to Our Experience Using Pesticide Bait for Locust Control in Anci County].' 中国农报 [China Agricultural Report], no. 16: 17–18.

1955 (Christian Sorace and Ruiyi Zhu)

[1] Sergey Radchenko. 2007–08. 'New Documents on Mongolia and the Cold War.' *Cold War International History Project Bulletin*, no. 16: 342, 350.

[2] Ibid. For an extended discussion, also see Xiaoyuan Liu. 2006. *Reigns of Liberation: An Entangled History of Mongolian Independence, Chinese Territoriality, and Great Power Hegemony, 1911–1950*. Stanford, CA: Stanford University Press.

[3] 工人之路 [*Workers' Way*], 14 February 1957. National Archives of Mongolia. *Workers' Way* was a Chinese-language newspaper published by the Mongolian Central Council of Labour Unions from 1929 to 1964. It was read by the Chinese diaspora, particularly workers, in Mongolia.

[4] Ibid., 12 October 1957.

[5] Jian Chen. 2001. *Mao's China and the Cold War*. Chapel Hill, NC: University of North Carolina Press.

[6] Jikun Gu. 2019. 'The Intertwining of High-Level Interactions and Low-Level Exchanges: Chinese Workers in Mongolia, 1950–1964.' *China Review* 19, no. 3: 115. The Chinese and Mongolian governments reproached each other for the repatriation of Chinese workers from Mongolia.

[7] Karl Marx and Friedrich Engels. 1998. *The Communist Manifesto: A Modern Edition*. London: Verso Books, 48, 51.

[8] Vladimir I. Lenin and Slavoj Žižek. 2017. *Lenin 2017: Remembering, Repeating, and Working Through*. London: Verso Books, 111.

[9] Moshé Lewin. 2005. *Lenin's Last Struggle*. Ann Arbor, MI: University of Michigan Press, 87.

[10] Document No. 5: Record of Conversation between Yumjaagiin Tsedenbal and the Ambassador to Mongolia, Zhang Canming, 24 September 1963, in Radchenko, 'New Documents on Mongolia and the Cold War', 361.

[11] Vladimir I. Lenin. 1971[1921]. 'Talk with a Delegation of the Mongolian People's Republic.' In *Lenin Collected Works*, 2nd edn. Moscow: Progress Publishers, vol. 42: 360–61, available online at www.marxists.org/archive/lenin/works/1921/nov/05b.htm.

[12] See Liu, *Reigns of Liberation*.

[13] Mao Zedong. 1964. 'Interview with the Japanese Socialists on the Theory of the Intermediate Zone', Sekat Shuho, 11 August 1964, available online at www.marxists.org/reference/archive/mao/selected-works/volume-9/mswv9_26.htm.

[14] Liu, *Reigns of Liberation*, 111.

[15] Radchenko, 'New Documents on Mongolia and the Cold War', 343.
[16] Gu Jikun 谷继坤. 2015. '中国工人"赴蒙援建"问题的历史考察 (1949–1973) [An Historical Investigation of Chinese Workers' Aid to Mongolia (1949–1973)].' 中共党史研究 [*Journal of Chinese Communist Party History Studies*], no. 4: 50.
[17] Radchenko, 'New Documents on Mongolia and the Cold War', 344.
[18] Ibid., 352.
[19] 工人之路 [*Workers' Way*], 3 April 1957.
[20] Ibid.
[21] Gu, 'An Historical Investigation of Chinese Workers' Aid to Mongolia', 51.
[22] 工人之路 [*Workers' Way*], 22 February 1957.
[23] *Gadaad khergiin töv arkhiv: Gereegeer ajillaj baisan khyatad ajilchdyn 9 jiliin ajlyn tailan* [*The Central Archive of Foreign Affairs: The Report of Nine Years of Work of Chinese Workers Under Contract*], 1964. Central Archive of Foreign Affairs (Mongolia), 5.2.328.
[24] Franck Billé. 2015. *Sinophobia: Anxiety, Violence, and the Making of Mongolian Identity*. Honolulu, HI: University of Hawai`i Press.
[25] 工人之路 [*Workers' Way*], 13 April 1961.
[26] Gu, 'An Historical Investigation of Chinese Workers' Aid to Mongolia', 61.
[27] Christian Sorace. 2021. 'Ideological Conversion: Mongolia's Transition from Socialism to Post-Socialism.' *Positions: Asia Critique* 29, no. 2.
[28] 中华人民共和国与蒙古国：国家关系历史编年 *(1949–2014)* [*People's Republic of China and Mongolia: Annual Historical Compilation of Country Relations (1949–2019)*], 2014, 86.
[29] Radchenko, 'New Documents on Mongolia and the Cold War', 344.
[30] *People's Republic of China and Mongolia*, 87.
[31] 工人之路 [*Workers' Way*], 11 June 1964.
[32] *Gadaad khergiin töv arkhiv: Khyatad ajilchdyn talaar diplomat shugamaar bolson khoyor ulsyn kheleltsee tüünd kholbogdokh barimt bichig* [*Diplomatic Discussion between the Two Countries on the Issues of Chinese Workers and Its Relevant Facts/Documents*], 1963. Central Archive of Foreign Affairs (Mongolia), 5.2.305.
[33] For a broader discussion of the politics of reburial, see Osman Balkan. 2015. 'Burial and Belonging.' *Studies in Ethnicity and Nationalism* 15, no. 1: 120–34; Katherine Verdery. 2000. *The Political Lives of Dead Bodies: Reburial and Postsocialist Change*. New York, NY: Columbia University Press.
[34] Benedict Anderson. 2016. *Imagined Communities: Reflections on the Origin and Spread of Nationalism*. Rev. edn. London: Verso Books.
[35] *Khyatadyn kadruudyn 7 dugaar zövölgöön deer Bügd Nairamdakh Khyatad Ard Ulsaas Bügd Nairamdakh Mongol Ard Ulsad suugaa Elchin Saidyn Yaamny Zövlökh nökhör Lyu Run Shen-ii khelekh üg* [*The Speech of Comrade Liu Runshen, Counsellor at the Embassy of the People's Republic of China in the People's Republic of Mongolia, at the Seventh Conference of Chinese Cadres*],1963. Central Archive of Foreign Affairs (Mongolia).
[36] Central Archive of Foreign Affairs (Mongolia), 5.2.328.
[37] Ibid.
[38] Zhou Changchun, written communication with one of the authors, 7 November 2019.

[39] *Khyatadyn elchin saidyg dagaj, ajilchdyn bairaar yavsan tukhai* [*Report on Accompanying the Chinese Ambassador and Visiting the Workers' Accommodation*], 1962. Central Archive of Foreign Affairs (Mongolia), 5.2.291.
[40] Balázs Szalontai. 2004. 'Tsedenbal's Mongolia and Communist Aid Donors: A Reappraisal.' *IIAS Newsletter*, no. 35: 18.
[41] Interview, Changchun, China, December 2019.
[42] Central Archive of Foreign Affairs (Mongolia), 5.2.305.
[43] Interview, Brisbane, Australia, June 2016.
[44] Ibid.
[45] Central Archive of Foreign Affairs (Mongolia), 5.2.328.
[46] Interview, Ulaanbaatar, Mongolia, July 2019.
[47] Central Archive of Foreign Affairs (Mongolia), 5.2.305.
[48] Ibid., 5.2.328.
[49] Ibid.
[50] Ibid.
[51] Ibid., 80.
[52] Ibid., 84.
[53] Ibid., 89.
[54] Mao Zedong. 1956. 'Speech at Second Plenary Session of the Eighth Central Committee of the Communist Party of China.' 15 November. In *Selected Works of Mao Tse-tung: Vol. V*. Peking: Foreign Languages Press, available online at www.marxists.org/reference/archive/mao/selected-works/volume-5/mswv5_56.htm.
[55] Kai Chang and Fang Lee Cooke. 2015. 'Legislating the Right to Strike in China: Historical Development and Prospects.' *Journal of Industrial Relations* 57, no. 3: 443–44.
[56] Document No. 3: Record of Conversation between USSR Ambassador to the PRC S[tepan] V. Chervonenko and the MPR Ambassador to the PRC D[ondogiin] Tsevegmid, 1 January 1963, in Radchenko, 'New Documents on Mongolia and the Cold War', 356.
[57] Ibid., 357.

1957 (Lai Ruoyu)

[1] Cristopher Howe. 1973. *Wage Patterns and Wage Policy in Modern China, 1919–1972*. Cambridge, UK: Cambridge University Press, 89–95.
[2] Quoted in Chang Kai 常凯. 2005. '罢工权立法问题的若干思考 [Some Thoughts on the Issue of the Legislation on the Right to Strike].' 学海 [*Xuehai*], no. 4: 43–55.
[3] Mao Zedong. 1957. 'Correct Handling of Contradictions among the People.' 27 February. In *Selected Works of Mao Tsetung*. Beijing: Foreign Language Press, 1977, vol. 5, pp. 384–421.
[4] Central Committee of the Chinese Communist Party. 1957. '中共中央关于处理罢工、罢课问题的指示 [Directive of the Central Committee of the CCP on the Handling of Strikes by Workers and Students].' 15 March. Available online at: guoqing.china.com.cn/2012-09/07/content_26746750.htm.
[5] Lai Ruoyu 赖若愚. 1957. '工会组织主在什么样的地位? [What Is the Position of the Union?].' 工人日报 [*Workers' Daily*], 8 May, 1.

[6] Li Feng 李峰. 1957. '工会工作走马观花记 [Cursory Notes on the Work of the Trade Union].' 工人日报 [*Workers' Daily*], 9 May, 12.

[7] A remarkable contribution to the debate is the series of articles penned by Chen Yongwen 陈用文, '西行记要 [Report from a Trip to the West]', published in the *Workers' Daily* from 30 May to 12 June 1957.

[8] Quoted in François Gipouloux. 1986. *Les Cent Fleurs a l'Usine* [*The Hundred Flowers at the Factory*]. Paris: Éditions de l' École des Hautes Etudes en Sciences Sociales, 257–61.

[9] CCP Central Committee. 1989 [1957]. '中共中央批转全总党组关于召开党组扩大会议的请示 [The CCP Central Committee Approves the Instructions on Convening the Enlarged Meeting of the ACFTU Party Group].' 22 July. In 建国以来中共中央关于工人运动文件选编 [*Selected Documents of the Central Committee of the CCP about the Labour Movement Since the Foundation of the Country*]. Bejing: Gongren Chubanshe, vol. 1, pp. 545–46.

[10] Lai Ruoyu 赖若愚. 1957. '关于当前工会工作的若干问题 [About Some Problems in the Current Work of the Trade Unions].' 5 September. In *Selected Documents of the Central Committee of the CCP about the Labour Movement Since the Foundation of the Country*, vol. 1, pp. 556–603.

[11] A list of purged cadres can be found in the appendix to Gipouloux, *The Hundred Flowers at the Factory*, 327–32.

[12] The interview appeared under this title in the *People's Daily* of 9 May 1957.

1957 (Chen Feng)

[1] The data for this study come from the collection of 内部参考 (*Internal Reference Report*) at the University Service Center for China Studies, Chinese University of Hong Kong. Edited by the Xinhua News Agency, the *Internal Reference Report* was forty to sixty pages published twice a week about domestic developments, covering news on topics that were deemed unsuitable for open publication, such as corruption, social unrest, and so on. It was circulated among Party officials as far down as the regional and bureau levels.

[2] This account can be found in 内部参考 [*Internal Reference Report*], 7 January 1957.

[3] Mark W. Frazier. 2002. *The Making of the Chinese Industrial Workplace: State, Revolution, and Labor Management*. New York, NY: Cambridge University Press.

[4] Elizabeth J. Perry. 1994. 'Shanghai's Strike Wave of 1957.' *The China Quarterly* 137: 1–27.

[5] Mao Zedong 毛泽东. 1991. 毛泽东选集4 [*Selected Works of Mao Zedong, Volume 4*]. Beijing: Renmin Chubanshe, 1424–39.

[6] Andrew G. Walder. 1986. *Communist Neo-Traditionalism: Work and Authority in Chinese Industry*. Berkeley, CA: University of California Press.

[7] *Internal Reference Report*, 12 February 1953.

[8] Ibid., 17 January 1957.

[9] Ibid., 30 September 1957.

[10] Ibid., 27 May 1957.

[11] Ibid.

[12] Ibid., 30 July 1953.

[13] Ibid.

[14] Based on the number of industrial accidents reported by the *Internal Reference Report* in 1955 and 1956.
[15] *Internal Reference Report*, 12 November 1956.
[16] Ibid.
[17] Ibid.
[18] Ibid., 11 April 1956.
[19] Ibid.
[20] Ibid., 27 December 1956.
[21] Ibid.
[22] Ibid.
[23] Ibid., 16 March 1957.
[24] Ibid., 27 January 1957.
[25] Ibid., 29 May 1954.
[26] Ibid., 27 August 1954.
[27] Ibid., 16 June 1956.
[28] Ibid., 17 June 1956.
[29] Ibid., 12 July 1956.
[30] Ibid., 14 April 1957.
[31] Ibid., 7 January 1957.
[32] Ibid., 28 September 1957.
[33] Ibid., 6 June 1955.
[34] Ibid., 7 June 1957.
[35] Feng Chen. 2003. 'Industrial Restructuring and Workers' Resistance in China.' *Modern China* 29, no. 3: 237–62.
[36] Feng Chen. 2000. 'Subsistence Crisis, Managerial Corruption and Labor Protests in China.' *China Journal*, no. 44: 41–63.

1958 (Benjamin Kindler)

[1] Chen Jin 陈晋 (ed.). 2017. 毛泽东读书笔记精讲战略卷 [*Reflections on Mao Zedong's Reading Notes: Strategy Volume*]. Nanning: Guangxi Renmin Chubanshe, 308–10.

[2] The textual and political histories by which these and other theoretical texts were canonised in early socialist China and other socialist states have gained scholarly attention as part of new studies of the history of the Sino-Soviet relationship. See, for example, Hua-yu Li. 2006. *Mao and the Economic Stalinization of China, 1948–1953*. Lanham, MD: Rowman & Littlefield.

[3] Chinese Communist Party Central Committee Textual Research Office (ed.). 2013. 毛泽东年谱 (1949–1976) [*Chronological Biography of Mao Zedong (1949–1976)*]. Beijing: Zhongyang Wenxian Chubanshe, vol. 3, pp. 414–17. These remarks were also circulated during the Cultural Revolution as part of the *Long Live Mao Zedong* (毛泽东万岁) editions of Mao's unauthorised selected works.

[4] Ibid.

[5] The *Critique* was first translated into Chinese by Xiong Deshan 熊得山 in 1922, with new translations appearing regularly throughout the 1920s. The translation most proximate to the post-1949 debates around bourgeois right, however, was that done in 1939 by He Sijing under the auspices of the Yan'an New Philosophy Association,

of which Ai Siqi and others were members. See Yu Lianghua 于良华. 1981. '关于延安"新哲学会" [On Yan'an's "New Philosophy"].' 哲学研究 [*Philosophical Research*], no. 3: 75–80.

[6] This and the other citations included in this paragraph can be found in Karl Marx. 1976 [1875]. 'Marginal Notes to the Programme of the German Workers' Party.' In *Karl Marx and Frederick Engels Selected Works*. Moscow: Progress Publishers, vol. 3, pp. 17–18.

[7] Ibid., 19.

[8] For an exploration of the centrality of ideas of quotidian life to the transformations of the Great Leap, see Fabio Lanza. 2020. 'The Search for a Socialist Everyday: The Urban Communes.' In *Routledge Handbook of Revolutionary China*, edited by Alan Baumler, 74–88. London: Routledge.

[9] Zhang Chunqiao 张春桥. 1958. '破除资产阶级的法权思想 [Smash the Ideology of Bourgeois Right].' 人民日报 [*People's Daily*], 13 October.

[10] Zhou Linzhi 周林知. 1958. '评上海出版物中有关劳动和分配问题的一些错误观点 [Assessing Some Mistaken Views Concerning the Problems of Labour and Remuneration in the Shanghai Publishing World].' 解放 [*Liberation*], no. 9: 9.

[11] Ibid., 11.

[12] Chinese Communist Party Central Committee Textual Research Office, *Chronological Biography of Mao Zedong*, vol. 3, p. 527.

[13] Ibid.

[14] Ibid., 385.

[15] Editorial Small Group for Socialist Political Economy (ed.). 1976. 社会主义政治经济学: 未定稿第二版讨论稿 [*Socialist Political Economy: Non-Finalised Draft Second Discussion Edition*]. Shanghai. This version was the fifth of several separate drafts. The project to develop a socialist textbook on political economy began in 1972 under the direct auspices of the Shanghai Writing Group (上海市写作组), of which Zhang Chunqiao and Yao Wenyuan were members.

1958 (Jane Hayward)

[1] Chris Bramall. 2009. *Chinese Economic Development*. London: Routledge, 51.

[2] Ibid., 50.

[3] Rana Mitter. 2014. *China's War with Japan, 1937–1945: The Struggle for Survival*. London: Penguin.

[4] Bramall, *Chinese Economic Development*, 79.

[5] Rebecca E. Karl. 2010. *Mao Zedong and China in the Twentieth Century World: A Concise History*. Durham, NC: Duke University Press, 25–26.

[6] James Peck. 2006. *Washington's China: The National Security World, the Cold War, and the Origins of Globalism*. Amherst, MA: University of Massachusetts Press.

[7] For an account of the internal Party tensions concerning this matter, see Lawrence C. Reardon. 2002. 'Chinese Elite Conflict over Globalization.' In *Transforming East Asian Domestic and International Politics: The Impact of Economy and Globalization*, edited by Robert W. Compton. Burlington, VT: Ashgate, 36–67.

[8] Cheng Tiejun and Mark Selden. 1994. 'The Origins and Social Consequences of China's *Hukou* System.' *The China Quarterly* 139: 644–68, at pp. 644–45.

[9] Jane Hayward. 2019. 'Primitive Accumulation.' In *Afterlives of Chinese Communism: Political Concepts from Mao to Xi*, edited by Christian Sorace, Ivan Franceschini and Nicholas Loubere. Canberra and London: ANU Press and Verso Books, 204.

[10] Vivienne Shue. 2018. 'Party-State, Nation, Empire: Rethinking the Grammar of Chinese Governance.' *Journal of Chinese Governance* 3, no. 3: 268–91.

[11] Fei-ling Wang. 2005. *Organizing Through Division and Exclusion: China's Hukou System*. Stanford, CA: Stanford University Press, 32–40.

[12] Ibid., 41–43.

[13] Ibid., 44.

[14] Cheng and Selden, 'The Origins and Social Consequences of China's *Hukou* System', 646.

[15] Dorothy J. Solinger. 1999. *Contesting Citizenship in Urban China: Peasant Migrants, the State, and the Logic of the Market*. Berkeley, CA: University of California Press, 34.

[16] Cheng and Selden, 'The Origins and Social Consequences of China's *Hukou* System', 655–56.

[17] Ibid., 661.

[18] Ibid., 662.

[19] Roderick MacFarquhar. 1974. *The Origins of the Cultural Revolution: The Great Leap Forward. Volume 2*. New York, NY: Columbia University Press, 59–63; Cheng and Selden, 'The Origins and Social Consequences of China's *Hukou* System', 664–65.

[20] Ibid., 665.

[21] Jeremy Brown. 2014. *City Versus Countryside in Mao's China: Negotiating the Divide*. New York, NY: Cambridge University Press, 77–86.

[22] The number of those engaged in non-agricultural activities increased from twenty-eight million in 1978 to 176 million in 2003, with most of these working in town-and-village enterprises. See Giovanni Arrighi. 2007. *Adam Smith in Beijing: Lineages of the Twenty-First Century*. London: Verso Books, 362–63.

[23] Lin Chun. 2015. 'The Language of Class in China.' *Socialist Register* 51: 24–53, at p. 38.

[24] Pun Ngai. 2005. *Made in China: Women Factory Workers in a Global Workplace*. Durham, NC: Duke University Press, 46–48.

[25] Kam Wing Chan and Will Buckingham. 2008. 'Is China Abolishing the Hukou System?' *The China Quarterly* 195: 582–606; Guo Zhonghua and Tuo Liang. 2017. 'Differentiating Citizenship in Urban China: A Case Study of Dongguan City.' *Citizenship Studies* 21, no. 7: 773–91.

[26] An English translation of the State Council circular is available online at *China Law Translate*: www.chinalawtranslate.com/en/state-council-opinion-of-hukou-reform.

[27] Charlotte Goodburn. 2014. *The End of the Hukou? Not Yet*. Policy Paper No. 2. Nottingham: China Policy Institute, University of Nottingham, available online at: www.nottingham.ac.uk/iaps/documents/cpi/policy-papers/cpi-policy-paper-2014-no-2-goodburn.pdf.

[28] Eli Friedman. 2018. 'Just-in-Time Urbanization? Managing Migration, Citizenship, and Schooling in the Chinese City.' *Critical Sociology* 44, no. 3: 503–18; Guo and Tuo, 'Differentiating Citizenship in Urban China'; Chenchen Zhang. 2018. 'Governing Neoliberal Authoritarian Citizenship: Theorizing *Hukou* and the Changing Mobility Regime in China.' *Citizenship Studies* 22, no. 8: 855–81.

[29] Eli Friedman. 2017. 'Evicting the Underclass.' *Jacobin*, 6 December, available online at: www.jacobinmag.com/2017/12/beijing-fire-migrant-labor-urbanization.

1960 (Tim Wright)

[1] The details of the disaster, which are not individually referenced, are taken from two sources. The first is Safety Department of the Ministry of Coal. 1998. 中国煤矿伤亡事故统计分析资料汇编 (1949–1995年) [Statistical Materials on Chinese Coal Mine Accidents, 1949–1995]. Beijing: Meitan Gongye Chubanshe, 92–98, which appears to have been based mainly on the official reports. This document is also available online as pp. 152–60 of 最新全国270例典型矿难剖析 [Analysis of 270 Typical Mining Accidents in China], at zmddag.cn/pdf/ebook/022最新全国270例典型矿难剖析-2004年.pdf. The second source is He Yuqing 何于清. 1998. '问苍茫大地 中外采矿史最大惨案揭秘 [Interrogating the Boundless Earth: Uncovering the World's Largest Coal Mine Disaster]', which is based mainly on interviews conducted (long) after the event. This work was finished in 1998, though I have not found a specific reference to a location of publication and the internal evidence is a bit ambiguous. Most later articles were very heavily based on this piece. References are to the pdf version available online at www.bannedbook.org/resources/file/471.

[2] The others were Benxi (本溪) in Liaoning under Japanese occupation (1942, over 1,500 fatalities); see Xue Yi 薛毅. 2018. '1942年本溪煤矿爆炸案考论 [A Study of the 1942 Explosion at the Benxi Mine].' 社会科学辑刊 [Social Science Journal] 1: 152–63; Courrières in France (1906, 1,099 fatalities); see Robert G. Neville. 1978. 'The Courrières Colliery Disaster, 1906.' Journal of Contemporary History 13, no. 1: 33–52; and Hōjō (方城) in Japan (1914, 687 fatalities); see Brett L. Walker. 2010. Toxic Archipelago: A History of Industrial Disease in Japan. Seattle, WA: University of Washington Press, 187–94, 199–206.

[3] Xu Daben 徐达本. 2010. '大跃进前后的煤炭工业 [The Coal Industry Around the Time of the Great Leap Forward].' 炎黄春秋 [China Through the Ages] 8: 25. There are some minor discrepancies in the official figures, but these make no difference to the scale of the disaster.

[4] Ben Harvey. 2016. 'The Oaks Colliery Disaster of 1866: A Case Study in Responsibility.' Business History 58, no. 4: 502.

[5] Joyce Kallgren. 1969. 'Social Welfare and China's Industrial Workers.' In Chinese Communist Politics in Action, edited by A. Doak Barnett. Seattle, WA: University of Washington Press, 540–73; Andrew G. Walder. 1984. 'The Remaking of the Chinese Working Class, 1949–1981.' Modern China 10, no. 1: 11–12, 37–38.

[6] Zhao Quanfu 赵全富. 1990. '采取科学治理措施努力实现煤矿安全生产 [Using Scientific Methods to Practise Work Safety in Coal Mines].' In 中国煤炭工业四十年 [Forty Years of the Chinese Coal Industry], edited by Peng Shiji 彭世济 and Feng Weimin 冯为民. Beijing: Meitan Gongye Chubanshe, 96–97.

[7] Guo Chaoxian 郭朝先. 2008. 中国煤矿企业安全发展研究 [Development of Work Safety in Chinese Coal Mine Enterprises]. Beijing: Jingji Guanli Chubanshe, 217.

[8] National Coal Mine Safety Administration. 2010. 中国煤炭工业发展概要 [Outline of the Development of China's Coal Industry]. Beijing: Meitan Gongye Chubanshe, 18–20, 87–88.

[9] Charles Hoffmann. 1974. The Chinese Worker. Albany, NY: State University of New York Press, 142; Jackie Sheehan. 2002. Chinese Workers: A New History. London: Routledge, 27, 55, 64.

[10] Kallgren, 'Social Welfare and China's Industrial Workers', 541, 562; for Singapore, see Stephen Dobbs and Kah Seng Loh. 2020. 'Unsafety and Unions in Singapore's State-Led Industrialization, 1965–1994.' *Labor History* 61, no. 2: 107–21.

[11] Wesley George Carson. 1981. *The Other Price of Britain's Oil*. Oxford, UK: Martin Robertson, 84–138.

[12] Safety Department of the Ministry of Coal, *Statistical Materials on Chinese Coal Mine Accidents*, 96.

[13] Elspeth Thomson. 2003. *The Chinese Coal Industry: An Economic History*. London: Routledge Curzon, 40–41.

[14] Andrew G. Walder. 2015. *China Under Mao: A Revolution Derailed*. Cambridge, MA: Harvard University Press, 175–76; Editorial and Research Group for the Draft History of the Coal Industry. 2001. 中国煤炭工业二十八年史稿 *(1949-1976)* [*Draft History of the Chinese Coal Industry, 1949–1976*]. For internal circulation, 194–95; Frank Dikötter. 2010. *Mao's Great Famine: The History of China's Most Devastating Catastrophe, 1958-62*. London: Bloomsbury, 153.

[15] Walder, *China Under Mao*, 174–75; Dikötter, *Mao's Great Famine*, ch. 31.

[16] Xu, 'The Coal Industry Around the Time of the Great Leap Forward', 21; Zhu Yichang 朱义长. 2017. 中国安全生产史*, 1949–2015* [*History of Work Safety in China, 1949–2015*]. Beijing: Meitan Gongye Chubanshe, 21; Sheehan, *Chinese Workers*, 90.

[17] Dikötter, *Mao's Great Famine*, 70.

[18] National Coal Mine Safety Administration, *Outline of the Development of China's Coal Industry*, 18–20, 87–88.

[19] Zhu, *History of Work Safety in China*, 21, 22; Elisabeth Köll. 2019. *Railroads and the Transformation of China*. Cambridge, MA: Harvard University Press, 262–63.

[20] He, 'Interrogating the Boundless Earth', 8; Dikötter, *Mao's Great Famine*, 302–4.

[21] He, 'Interrogating the Boundless Earth', 6.

[22] Safety Department of the Ministry of Coal, *Statistical Materials on Chinese Coal Mine Accidents*, 96.

[23] Editorial Committee for the China Coal Gazetteer. 1995. 中国煤炭志: 山西卷 [*China Coal Gazetteer: Shanxi*]. Beijing: Meitan Gongye Chubanshe, 264.

[24] He, 'Interrogating the Boundless Earth', 29–32.

[25] Ibid., 28–29.

[26] Jamie L. Bronstein. 2008. *Caught in the Machinery: Workplace Accidents and Injured Workers in Nineteenth-Century Britain*. Stanford, CA: Stanford University Press, 19–28.

[27] He, 'Interrogating the Boundless Earth', 41.

[28] China National Coal Association. 2006. 中国煤炭工业统计资料汇编*, 1949–2004* [*Statistical Materials on the Chinese Coal Industry, 1949–2004*]. Beijing: Meitan Gongye Chubanshe, 556.

[29] Si Ping 思平. 2003. '中国火事演义 [Fire Disasters in China].' 云南消防 [*Yunnan Firefighting*] 9: 43.

[30] He, 'Interrogating the Boundless Earth', 43.

[31] Zhu, *History of Work Safety in China*, 23; Xu, 'The Coal Industry Around the Time of the Great Leap Forward', 25; Si, 'Fire Disasters in China', 44.

[32] He, 'Interrogating the Boundless Earth', 38.

[33] Xu, 'The Coal Industry Around the Time of the Great Leap Forward', 25.

[34] Safety Department of the Ministry of Coal, *Statistical Materials on Chinese Coal Mine Accidents*, 97.

[35] Ibid., 96.

[36] Xu, 'The Coal Industry Around the Time of the Great Leap Forward', 25.

[37] He, 'Interrogating the Boundless Earth', 30.

[38] Zhang Zhongning 张中宁. 1999. '如歌岁月—访原全国政协副主席、国家劳动部长马文瑞 [Songs of Time: A Visit to Ma Wenrui, Formerly Deputy Chair of the Chinese People's Political Consultative Congress and Minister of Labour].' 中国社会保障 [*China Social Security*] 10: 15.

[39] Yang Jisheng. 2012. *Tombstone: The Great Chinese Famine, 1958–1962*. New York, NY: Farrar, Straus & Giroux, 445–47.

[40] Shanxi Bureaus of Labour, Public Security, Metallurgical Industry, Machine-Building Industry, Chemical and Oil Industries, Transportation, and Construction, Office for the Administration of Coal, and Trade Union Federation. 1960. '关于加强工业交通基本建设企业劳动保护工作的报告 [On Strengthening Labour Protection Work in the Industrial, Communications and Basic Construction Enterprises].' 山西政报 [*Shanxi Government News*], 11 November, no. 22: 625. If this publication really had unrestricted circulation, this document was very frank.

[41] Maria Repnikova. 2017. *Media Politics in China: Improvising Power Under Authoritarianism*. Cambridge, MA: Cambridge University Press, ch. 6; Tim Wright. 2012. *The Political Economy of the Chinese Coal Industry: Black Gold and Blood-Stained Coal*. London: Routledge, 194.

[42] Bronstein, *Caught in the Machinery*, 61–62 et passim; Neville, 'Courrières Colliery Disaster'.

[43] Harvey, 'The Oaks Colliery Disaster of 1866'; Jamie L. Bronstein. 2014. 'The Hartley Colliery Disaster.' *Victorian Review* 40, no. 2: 9–13.

[44] The earliest reference I have found is Datong Bureau, Baidong Mine. 1982. '通风系统改造的经验和教训 [Experience In and Lessons from the Renovation of Ventilation Systems].' 煤矿安全 [*Coal Safety*] 12: 41; also Editorial Committee for the China Labour and Personnel Yearbook. 1989. 中国劳动人事年鉴 *(1949.10-1987)* [*China Labour and Personnel Yearbook, October 1949–1987*]. Beijing: Laodong Renshi Chubanshe, 801, 817; Editorial Committee for the Gazetteer of the Shanxi Coal Industry. 1991. 山西煤炭工业志 [*Gazetteer of the Shanxi Coal Industry*]. Beijing: Meitan Gongye Chubanshe, 212–13; Li Boyong 李伯勇. 1993. '安全生产状况及存在的问题 [The Situation of and Problems Existing in Work Safety].' 劳动保护 [*Labour Protection*] 7: 7.

[45] '1960年大同矿难死亡682人被列为绝密—38年才公开 [The 682 People Killed in the 1960 Datong Mine Disaster Were Designated as Top Secret: It Only Came Out in Public 38 Years Later].' 快乐老人报 [*Happy Old People*], available online at news.ifeng.com/history/zhongguoxiandaishi/detail_2013_10/28/30714214_0.shtml.

[46] Zhu, *History of Work Safety in China*, 23.

[47] Li Xinjuan 李新娟. 2012. '中国煤矿安全状况与经济社会发展关系的研究 [China's Economic and Social Development and its Coal Safety Situation].' 安全与环境学报 [*Journal of Safety and Environment*] 12, no. 4: 199; '同煤与共和国一同走来 [Datong Coal Mines March Together with the Republic].' 中国煤炭工业 [*China's Coal Industry*] 8 (2009): 21; Kallgren, 'Social Welfare and China's Industrial Workers', 562.

[48] National Coal Mine Safety Administration, *Outline of the Development of China's Coal Industry*, 18–20, 87–88.

[49] Tim Wright. Forthcoming. 'The Political Economy of China's Dramatically Improved Coal Safety Record.' *China Quarterly*.

1960 (Koji Hirata)

[1] For the report, see '鞍山市关于工业战线的技术革新和技术革命运动开展情况的报告 [Anshan City's Report on the Development of the Technological Innovation and Technological Revolution Campaign on the Industrial Front]', 11 March 1960. In 鞍山市志: 附录卷 [Gazette of Anshan City: Annex], edited by the Anshan Gazetteer Office, 380–85. Shenyang: Liaoning Minzu Chubanshe, 2001.

[2] '毛泽东主席批示的"鞍钢宪法" [The "Angang Constitution" Approved by Chairman Mao Zedong]', 22 March 1960. In *Gazette of Anshan City: Annex*, 385–86.

[3] Ibid.

[4] Gazetteer Office of the People's Government of Anshan City. 1989. 鞍山市志: 大事记卷, *1915–1985* [*Anshan City Gazetteer: Chronology of Events, 1915–1985*]. Shenyang: Shenyang Chubanshe, 225.

[5] 内部参考 [*Internal Reference Report*], 8 April 1960.

[6] For the Chinese historiography on the Angang Constitution, see Yu Zhiwei 于之伟. 2016. '"鞍钢宪法"问题研究述评 [A Review of the Studies on the Question of the "Angang Constitution"].' 中共党史研究 [*Studies on the History of the Chinese Communist Party*], no. 3: 106–14.

[7] For example, see Gao Hua 高华. 2000. '鞍钢宪法的历史真实与政治正确性 [The Historical Authenticity and Political Correctness of the Angang Constitution].' 二十一世纪 [*Twenty-First Century*], no. 58: 62–69.

[8] Chen Zhengbin 陈正斌 (ed.). 1999. 鞍山党史人物传 [*Biographies of People in Anshan Party History*], vol. 1. Shenyang: Baishan Chubanshe, 26.

[9] Andrew G. Walder. 2015. *China Under Mao: A Revolution Derailed*. Cambridge, MA: Harvard University Press, 136.

[10] Mao Zedong 毛泽东. 1993–99. '读苏联《政治经济学教科书》的谈话 [A Talk on Reading the Soviet Textbooks on Political Economy]', December 1959–February 1960. In 毛泽东文集 [*Collected Works of Mao Zedong*], vol. 8. Beijing: Renmin Chubanshe, 135.

[11] Speech by Yang Shijie on 9 March 1959. Private Collection, on file with the author.

[12] Drafting Committee for the Gazette on the History of Angang. 1991–94. 鞍钢志 *1916–1985* [*Angang Gazetteers 1916–1985*], vol 1. Beijing: Renmin Chubanshe, 118–19.

[13] Party History Working Committee of the Party Committee of Anshan. 1991. 中国共产党鞍山地方党史大事记 *1927–1990* [*Local Party Chronicle of the Chinese Communist Party in Anshan 1927–1990*]. Anshan, 62.

[14] Drafting Committee for the Gazette on the History of Angang, *Angang Gazetteers 1916–1985*, 74.

[15] Party History Working Committee of the Party Committee of Anshan, *Local Party Chronicle of the Chinese Communist Party in Anshan 1927–1990*, 70.

[16] Report by Yang Shijie, 11 August 1959. Private Collection, on file with the author.

[17] Gazetteer Office of the People's Government of Anshan City, *Anshan City Gazetteer*, 202.

[18] Gazetteer Office of the People's Government of Anshan City. 1997. 鞍山市志: 鞍钢卷 [*Anshan City Gazetteer: Angang Volume*]. Shenyang: Shenyang Chubanshe, 202–3.

[19] Drafting Committee for the Gazette on the History of Angang, *Angang Gazetteers 1916–1985*, 70.

[20] Gazetteer Office of the People's Government of Anshan City, *Anshan City Gazetteer: Angang Volume*, 202–3.

[21] Speech by Yang Shijie, 9 March 1959. Private Collection, on file with the author.

[22] Report by the CCP Angang Second Steel Mill Committee, 5 January 1960. Private Collection, on file with the author.

[23] Ibid.

[24] 内部参考 [*Internal Reference Report*], 20 October 1958.

[25] Party History Working Committee of the Party Committee of Anshan, *Local Party Chronicle of the Chinese Communist Party in Anshan 1927–1990*, 74–75.

[26] 内部参考 [*Internal Reference Report*], 3 July 1964.

1960 (Jacob Eyferth)

[1] '马廷海农业生产合作社是怎样发动妇女参加农业生产的 [How the Ma Tinghai Agricultural Production Cooperative Mobilises Women to Participate in Production].' 人民日报 [*People's Daily*], 2 February 1954, 2.

[2] I borrow the notion of industrial citizenship from Joel Andreas; see Joel Andreas. 2019. *Disenfranchised: The Rise and Fall of Industrial Citizenship in China*. Oxford, UK: Oxford University Press. On the right and duty to work, see the *Constitution of the People's Republic of China*, Article 16: 'Work is a matter of honour for every citizen of the PRC who is capable of working. The state encourages the working enthusiasm and creativeness of citizens.' Article 91: 'Citizens of the PRC have the right to work.' Article 92: 'Working people in the PRC have the right to rest and leisure.'

[3] Shaopeng Song. 2007. 'The State Discourse on Housework and Housewives in the 1950s in China.' In *Rethinking China in the 1950s*, edited by Mechthild Leutner, 49–63. Berlin: Lit Verlag.

[4] Marina Thorborg. 1978. 'Chinese Employment Policy in 1949–78 with Special Emphasis on Women in Rural Production.' In *Chinese Economy Post-Mao*, Joint Economy Committee, Congress of the United States. Washington, DC: US Government Printing Office, 595.

[5] Ibid., 601.

[6] Leon Trotsky, quoted in Chris Ward. 1990. *Russia's Cotton Workers and the New Economic Policy*. Cambridge, UK: Cambridge University Press, 7.

[7] Lu Hong 芦荻. 1950. 论城乡合作 [*On Urban–Rural Cooperation*]. Beijing: Sanlian, 47–52.

[8] Zhang Zhong 张冲 1949. '纺织与棉花 [Weaving and Cotton].' 人民日报 [*People's Daily*], 14 April, 1.

[9] Nai-Ruenn Chen and Walter Galenson. 2011. *The Chinese Economy under Mao: The Early Years, 1949–1967*. New Brunswick, NJ: Aldine, 35.

[10] Xu Jianqing 徐建青. 2009. '制度变革与手工棉纺职业: 1954–1965 [System Transition and Handcraft Cotton Weaving: 1954–1965].' 中国经济史研究 [*Studies in Chinese Economic History*], no. 4: 73–75.

[11] Xu Jianqing 徐建青. 2010. '统购统销制度下农民家庭棉纺织成本收益探析 [A Cost–Benefit Analysis of Peasant Household Spinning and Weaving under the System of Unified Purchase and Marketing].' 中国经济史研究 [*Studies in Chinese Economic History*], no. 4: 79–85.

[12] Xu, 'System Transition and Handcraft Cotton Weaving', 73–75.

[13] Xingping County Archives, 4-1-45 (1957, no date).
[14] Zhang, 'Weaving and Cotton'.
[15] Xu Jianqing 徐建青. 2010. '棉花统购, 棉布统购统销政策与手工棉纺职业 [The Policy of Unified Purchase of Cotton and Unified Purchase and Marketing of Cotton Cloth and Handicraft Textile Industries].' 当代中国史研究 [*Studies in Contemporary Chinese History*], no. 2: 27–34.

1961 (Aminda Smith and Fabio Lanza)

[1] Li Duanxiang 李端祥. 2006. 城市人民公社运动研究 [*A Study of the Urban Commune Movement*]. Changsha, China: Hunan Renmin Chubanshe, 52.

[2] Some communes managed clinics, in some cases taking over private ones. See Xicheng South Archive 1-1-295, '椿树人民公社调查报告(草稿) [Report on the Survey of the Chunshu People's Commune (Draft)]', November 1958; Xicheng North Archive 46-1-1, '中共西城区德外党委关于申请成立人民公社的报告 [Report by the Deshengmenwai CCP Committee Regarding a Request to Establish a People's Commune]', 10 April 1960.

[3] Xicheng South Archive 21-1-11, '关于粉末冶金厂"调查研究工作组" [Regarding the Powder Metallurgy Factory "Research and Survey Work Team"].' This document provides generic outlines of survey methodology, but nothing specifically about the factory.

[4] Beijing Municipal Archive [hereinafter BMA] 1-28-29/1, '天桥公社粉末冶金工厂生产人员患妇女病的情况调查 [Survey on the Workers Suffering from Female Illnesses at the Tianqiao Commune Powder Metallurgy Factory]', 15 March 1961.

[5] Xicheng South Archive 1-23-202, '中共宣武区委关于天桥街道办事处建立人民公社问题请示 [Request for Instructions from the CCP Committee of Xuanwu District Concerning the Issue of the Tianqiao Subdistrict Office Establishing a People's Commune]', 8 April 1960. At the time, the Tianqiao commune included thirteen factories and five small production teams, with twenty-six canteens and thirty-five childcare centres.

[6] Fabio Lanza. 2019. 'The Search for a Socialist Everyday: The Urban Communes.' In *The Routledge Handbook of Revolutionary China*, edited by Alan Baumler. London: Routledge, 77; Li, *A Study of the Urban Commune Movement*, 89–90.

[7] BMA 1-28-29/1: 1.

[8] Ibid.

[9] On overwork and women's reproductive health during the Great Leap Forward, see Gail Hershatter. 2011. *The Gender of Memory: Rural Women and China's Collective Past*. Berkeley, CA: University of California Press, 246–47; Kay Ann Johnson. 1983. *Women, the Family, and Peasant Revolution in China*. Chicago, IL: University of Chicago Press, 171.

[10] BMA 1-28-29/1: 2. On the related Chinese medical understandings, see Charlotte Furth. 1999. *A Flourishing Yin: Gender in China's Medical History, 960–1665*. Berkeley, CA: University of California Press, 82.

[11] BMA 1-28-29/1: 2.

[12] Ibid.

[13] We spoke with Dr Farshad 'Mazda' Shirazi, a clinical toxicologist at the University of Arizona, who advised us on the nature of connections between industrial worksites, poor diets, sex, and health.

[14] Nicholas R. Lardy. 1983. *Agriculture in China's Modern Economic Development*. Cambridge, UK: Cambridge University Press; Kenneth R. Walker. 1984. *Food Grain Procurement and Consumption in China*. Cambridge, UK: Cambridge University Press.

[15] Walker, *Food Grain Procurement and Consumption in China*, ch. 5.

[16] BMA 1-28-29/8, '城市公社集体生活福利事业几年来的发展情况和问题 [The Development over the Last Several Years of a Collective Life Welfare System in the Urban Communes and Its Problems]', November 1961.

[17] Kathryn Edgerton-Tarpley makes a similar argument about the way oedema, or 'swelling disease', gave doctors and others a politically permissible way to talk about the medical toll of starvation. See Kathryn Edgerton-Tarpley. 2019. 'The Medicalization of Starvation: The Fixation on "Swelling Disease" during the Great Leap Famine of 1958–1962.' Paper presented at the Association for Asian Studies Annual Meeting, Denver, CO.

[18] Myron S. Cohen, Gail E. Henderson, Pat Aiello, and Heyi Zheng. 1996. 'Successful Eradication of Sexually Transmitted Diseases in the People's Republic of China: Implications for the 21st Century.' *The Journal of Infectious Diseases* 174, Issue Supplement 2: S223–29.

[19] Harriet Evans. 1997. *Women and Sexuality in China*. London: Bloomsbury Academic.

[20] BMA 1-28-29/1: 2.

[21] Ibid.

[22] The double diligences were 'diligently and frugally build the country, diligently and frugally manage the family' (勤俭建国勤俭持家). See Zheng Wang. 2017. *Finding Women in the State: A Socialist Feminist Revolution in the People's Republic of China, 1949–1964*. Berkeley, CA: University of California Press, 71–75.

[23] BMA 1-28-36/17, '城市人民公社工业不能一风吹—关于北新桥人民公社工业的情况调查 [The Industrial Sector or the Urban People's Communes Cannot Be Completely Dismantled: Survey of the Situation of the Industrial Sector at the Beixinqiao People's Commune]', 6 September 1962.

[24] BMA 112-1-783/7, '二龙路公社调查组, "关于二龙路公社工资、福利、奖励问题的报告" [Erlonglu Commune Survey Team Report on the Problem of Salaries, Welfare, and Rewards at Erlonglu Commune]', 17 August 1961.

[25] BMA 1-28-29/2, '椿树公社福利待遇情况 [The Welfare Provision Situation in the Chunshu Commune]', 1 September 1961; BMA 101-1-782/5, '职工家属成了社会财富的创造者: 石景山中苏友好人民公社介绍 [Family Dependents of Workers and Staff Members Become the Creators of Social Wealth: A Description of the Shijingshan Soviet-China Friendship People's Commune]', undated; BMA 1-28-36/12, '中共北京市委城市公社工作小组, "关于城市人民公社的基本情况" [The Basic Situation of the Urban People's Communes]', 4 June 1962.

[26] BMA 1-28-36/8, '北新桥公社工业的劳动力情况分析 (北新桥公社工业调查材料之四) [An Analysis of the Situation of the Labour Force in the Industrial Sector of the Beixinqiao Commune (Survey Document No. 4 of the Industrial Sector of the Beixinqiao Commune)]', 19 November 1962; BMA 1-28-29/5, '市委城市公社工作小组, "关于城市公社系统生产服务人员对发布票的反映" [Reactions by Service and Production Workers in the Urban Commune System to the Distribution of Cloth Rations]', 28 November 1961.

²⁷ BMA 100-1-659/11, '共青团宣武区委员会, "我区公社团干部在北京市团校学习中暴露出得几个问题" [Some Questions That Came Up When the Youth League Cadres from Our District Were Studying at the Youth League School in Beijing]', 16 September 1960; BMA 100-1-659/6, '情况简报第3号 [Bulletin No. 3]', 19 July 1960.

²⁸ BMA 100-1-659/11, 'Some Questions That Arose While the Youth League Cadres from Our District Were Studying at the Youth League School in Beijing]'; BMA 1-28-36/18, '中共北京市委城市公社工作小组, "关于城市人民公社工业的情况和今后意见的报告" [Municipal Committee Urban Commune Work Group, "Reactions by Service and Production Workers in the Urban Commune System to the Distribution of Cloth Rations"]', 28 November 1962.

²⁹ Joel Andreas. 2019. *Disenfranchised: The Rise and Fall of Industrial Citizenship in China*. Oxford, UK: Oxford University Press, 62.

1962 (Jonathan Unger)

¹ On this, see, for example, Dali L. Yang. 1996. *Calamity and Reform in China: State, Rural Society, and Institutional Change Since the Great Leap Famine*. Stanford, CA: Stanford University Press.

² Jonathan Unger. 1987. 'The Hong Kong Connection: China Research from the Room Next Door.' *China Information* 2, no. 1: 27–36. One of the best books written about the People's Republic of China is based on extensive interviewing by William Parish and Martin K. Whyte in Hong Kong during the 1970s: William L. Parish and Martin K. Whyte. 1978. *Village and Family in Contemporary China*. Chicago, IL: University of Chicago Press.

³ On this topic, see, for example, John Burns. 1988. *Political Participation in Rural China*. Berkeley, CA: University of California Press.

⁴ Anita Chan, Richard Madsen, and Jonathan Unger. 2009. *Chen Village: Revolution to Globalization*. Berkeley, CA: University of California Press.

⁵ Dazhai is a small village in northern China that Mao promoted throughout the country as an exemplar of selfless collective practices. See Jonathan Unger. 1971. '"Learn from Tachai": China's Agricultural Model.' *Current Scene* 9, no. 9: 1–11.

⁶ Jonathan Unger. 1985. 'Remuneration, Ideology and Personal Interests in a Chinese Village, 1960–1980.' In *Chinese Rural Development: The Great Transformation*, edited by William Parish, 117–40. Armonk, NY: M.E. Sharpe.

⁷ 'Regulations on the Work of the Rural People's Communes (Revised Draft), September 1962.' *Documents of the Chinese Communist Party Central Committee, September 1956 – April 1969*, vol. I, 719–22. Hong Kong: Union Research Institute, 1971.

⁸ *People's Daily*, quoted in Kenneth Walker. 1965. *Planning in Chinese Agriculture: Socialization and the Private Sector, 1956–1962*. London: Frank Cass & Co., 93.

⁹ Other researchers have come up with somewhat similar findings. In the suburbs of Guangzhou City, according to John Burns, one-third to one-half of a farming family's total *cash* income in the 1970s came from private endeavours. See John Burns. 1977. 'The Radicals and the Campaign to Limit Bourgeois Rights in the Countryside.' *Contemporary China* 1, no. 4: 27. Deborah Davis, who did extensive interviewing in the 1970s in rural Guangdong Province, calculated that, generally, 20 to 40 percent of a rural family's total income was derived from private sources. See Deborah Davis.

1977. 'Strategies for Aging: Interdependence Between Generations in the Transition to Socialism.' *Contemporary China* 1, no. 6: 36. In the model communes visited by S.J. Burki in the 1960s, about 20 percent of total family income came from this. S.J. Burki. 1969. *A Study of Chinese Communes, 1965*. Cambridge, MA: Harvard University East Asian Research Center, 40–41.

[10] *Far Eastern Economic Review*, 25 October 1974, 15.

[11] Chan et al., *Chen Village*, ch. 9.

1963 (S.A. Smith)

[1] 北京工人日报 [*Beijing Workers' Daily*], 10 August 1963. I shall henceforth use the term 'feudal superstition' without inverted commas.

[2] Ibid.

[3] 同意战线工作 [*United Front Work*], 16 April 1963, 15.

[4] Dali L. Yang. 1996. *Calamity and Reform in China: State, Rural Society, and Institutional Change Since the Great Leap Famine*. Stanford, CA: Stanford University Press.

[5] The literature on the Socialist Education Movement has rightly paid most attention to the countryside, since it was there that its impact was greatest. Much less is known about the 'Five Antis' movement in the cities, which targeted state organs, industrial and commercial enterprises, educational establishments, and the People's Liberation Army. Even with respect to the countryside, however, more attention has been paid to 'capitalist' tendencies than to 'feudal' ones, since the former were the ones seen as the vectors of 'revisionism'. See, for instance, Frederick C. Teiwes. 1993. *Politics and Purges in China*. Armonk, NY: M.E. Sharpe; Roderick MacFarquhar. 1997. *The Origins of the Cultural Revolution: The Coming of the Cataclysm, 1961–1966*. Oxford, UK: Oxford University Press; Xiaobo Lü. 2000. *Cadres and Corruption: The Organizational Involution of the Chinese Communist Party*. Stanford, CA: Stanford University Press; Richard Baum. 1975. *Prelude to Revolution: Mao, the Party, and the Peasant Question, 1962–66*. New York, NY: Columbia University Press.

[6] Guo Dehong 郭德宏 and Lin Xiaobo 林小波. 2005. 四清运动实录 [*Record of the Four Clean-Ups Campaign*]. Hangzhou: Zhejiang Renmin Chubanshe.

[7] Teiwes, *Politics and Purges in China*, 425.

[8] The SEM work teams were sent to specific 'points' in the countryside. In most places, prior to September 1964, local Party organisations carried out the Four Clean-Ups. In the cities, the Five Antis were initially carried out by the supervisory commissions of grassroots Party organisations. The movement took off nationally only following Mao's approval on 5 December 1964 of the report by Xie Fuzhi, Minister of Public Security, on the investigation by the work team he had led for two-and-a-half months at the Shenyang smelting works. Central Committee Documentary Research Office (ed.). 1996. 建国以来毛泽东文稿, 第十一卷 [*Mao Zedong Manuscripts from the Founding of the People's Republic of China. Volume 11*]. Beijing: Zhongyang Wenxian Chubanshe, 156–58; Teiwes, *Politics and Purges in China*, ch. 11; Zheng Hui 郑惠 and Lin Yunhui 林蕴晖. 2009. 六十年国事纪要. 政治卷 [*Sixty Years of State Affairs: Politics*]. Changsha: Hunan Renmin Chubanshe.

[9] 内部参考 [*Internal Reference Report*], 19 July 1963.

[10] John Williams. 2019. 'Superstition.' In *Afterlives of Chinese Communism: Political Concepts from Mao to Xi*, edited by Christian Sorace, Ivan Franceschini, and Nicholas Loubere, 269–74. Canberra, London, and New York, NY: ANU Press and Verso Books.

[11] Vincent Goossaert and David A. Palmer. 2011. *The Religious Question in Modern China*. Chicago, IL: University of Chicago Press.

[12] Stephan Feuchtwang. 2001. *Popular Religion in China: The Imperial Metaphor*. Richmond, UK: Curzon.

[13] Rebecca Nedostup. 2009. *Superstitious Regimes: Religion and Politics in Chinese Modernity*. Cambridge, MA: Harvard University Press.

[14] The People's Committee of Hubei Province. 1963. '转发湖北省供销合作社"关于库存迷信品处理意见的报告" [Report on Recommendations on Dealing with Superstitious Products in Stock from the Hubei Supply and Marketing Cooperative]', 25 May. Hubei Provincial Archive, SZ 34-5-399.

[15] S.A. Smith. 2015. 'On Not Learning from the Soviet Union: Religious Policy in China, 1949–65.' *Modern China Studies* 22, no. 1: 70–97.

[16] 北京工作 [*Beijing Work*], 15 August 1963, 4.

[17] 同意战线工作 [*United Front Work*], 30 August 1963, 19.

[18] Party Group at the Shanghai Association for the Dissemination of Science and Technology, 29 June 1965. Shanghai Municipal Archive, C0 42-01-00311.

[19] S.A. Smith. 2006. 'Talking Toads and Chinless Ghosts: The Politics of Rumor in the People's Republic of China, 1961–65.' *American Historical Review* 111, no. 2: 405–27.

[20] J.L. Watson. 1982. 'Of Flesh and Bones: The Management of Death Pollution in Cantonese Society.' In *Death and the Regeneration of Life*, edited by Maurice Bloch and Jonathan Parry, 155–86. Cambridge, UK: Cambridge University Press, 157.

[21] Shanghai Municipal General Labour Union Office. 1962. '部分中老年女工中迷信思想还很严重:记国棉九厂杨小妹小组关于"农业灾荒是否是不相信菩萨的缘故"问题的讨论 [Superstitious Thinking Among Some Older Women Workers is Still a Serious Problem: A Note on a Discussion Among the Yang Xiaomei Team of the No. 9 State Textile Mill on "Whether the Agricultural Disasters Have Been Caused by the Gods"]', 20 June. Shanghai Municipal Archive, C1–2–3697.

[22] This anecdote can be found in 内部参考 [*Internal Reference Report*], 19 July 1963.

[23] Huangpu District Office of the Women's Affairs Branch of the Municipal Trade Union. 1963. '一个小组十五个工人中,有十四人至今还相信卜卦算命 [Fourteen Out of Fifteen Workers in a Work Group Still Believe in Divination and Fortune-Telling]', 4 March 1963. Shanghai Municipal Archive, C1-2-3869.

[24] Sichuan Provincial Trade Union Work Group. 1963. '南桐煤矿对职工家属进行社会主义教育的初步总结 [Preliminary Summary on How Socialist Education Was Implemented Among Family Members of the Workers and Staff at the Nantong Coal Mine].' Jilin Provincial Archive, 17-16-162.

[25] '在渔民中如何开展社会主义教育运动场:台山县广海镇公社卫星大队的做法 [How to Launch the Socialist Education Movement Among Fisherfolk: The Method of the Satellite Brigade of the Guanghaizhen Commune in Taishan County]', 3 July 1963. Guangdong Provincial Archive, 217-1-130.

[26] Quarterly of Contemporary Chinese Folk Historical Materials, Centre for Contemporary Chinese History, East China Normal University (ed.). 2009. 第一卷: 河北冀县门庄公社,门庄大队的档案 [*First Book: Archive of the Menzhuang Brigade of the Menzhuang Commune, Ji County, Hebei*]. Shanghai: Dongfang Chuban Zhongxin, 43, 332.

[27] 重庆日报 [*Chongqing Daily*], 17 January 1965.
[28] Charles Taylor. 2007. *A Secular Age*. Cambridge, MA: Belknap Press, 147–48.

1964 (Covell F. Meyskens)

[1] Chen Donglin 陈东林. 2015. '三线建设始末 [The Story of Third Front Construction].' In 中国共产党与三线建设 [*The Chinese Communist Party and Third Front Construction*], edited by Chen Donglin 陈东林. Beijing: Zhonggong Dangshi Chubanshe, 7.

[2] Barry Naughton. 1988. 'The Third Front: Defence Industrialization in the Chinese Interior.' *China Quarterly*, no. 115: 352.

[3] Chen, 'The Story of Third Front Construction', 4–5; John Garver. 2016. *China's Quest: The History of the Foreign Relations of the People's Republic of China*. Oxford, UK: Oxford University Press, 182; John Wilson Lewis and Litai Xue. 1988. *China Builds the Bomb*. Stanford, CA: Stanford University Press, 192–94.

[4] Mao Zedong 毛泽东. 1964. '要把攀枝花和联系到攀枝花的交通、煤、电建设搞起来 [It Is Necessary to Build Panzhihua and the Transportation, Coal, and Electrical Lines Connected to Panzhihua]', 27 May, cited in Chen, *The Chinese Communist Party and Third Front Construction*, 43.

[5] Ibid.

[6] Ibid.; Mao Zedong 毛泽东. 1964. '每个省都要有一、二、三线 [Every Province Should Have a First, Second, and Third Front]', 8 June; and Mao Zedong 毛泽东. 1964. '地方党委要搞军事,要准备打弹不要慌张 [Local Party Committees Should Engage in Military Affairs and Prepare to Fight but Should Not Overreact]', 16 June, both cited in Chen, *The Chinese Communist Party and Third Front Construction*, 52, 53.

[7] Andrew G. Walder. 2015. *China Under Mao: A Revolution Derailed*. Cambridge, MA: Harvard University Press, 333.

[8] Barry Naughton, 'The Third Front', 353.

[9] Mao Zedong 毛泽东. 1964. '三线建设还要快,经验要总结 [Third Front Construction Should Be Even Faster, and Experiences Should Be Summed Up', 26 November; and '周恩来等批准吕正操关于加速修建成昆等西南铁路的报告 [Zhou Enlai and Other Leaders Approve Lu Zhengcao's Report About Speeding Up Construction of the Chengdu–Kunming Line and Other Southwestern Railroads]', 12 August 1964, both cited in Chen, *The Chinese Communist Party and Third Front Construction*, 118, 57, 59.

[10] Naughton, 'The Third Front', 356–58.

[11] Ibid., 362.

[12] Covell Meyskens. 2020. *Mao's Third Front: The Militarization of Cold War China*. New York, NY: Cambridge University Press, 237–38.

[13] The First Machine Industry Ministry. 1965. '关于贯彻执行"中央公交政治部关于做好三线建设的政治工作的通知"的意见 [Remarks on the Implementation of the Notice by the Political Department of the Central Transportation Office About "Conducting Well Political Work for Third Front Construction"]', 11 January. Sichuan Provincial Archive, 5.

[14] Mao Zedong 毛泽东. 1964. '1964年5月10日至11日在计委领导小组汇报第三个五年计划设想, 当议论到铁路, 交通, 第三个五年计划只能搞那么多事的指示 [Directive Regarding the State Planning Commission Leading Small Group's Report About Tentative Plans for the Third Five-Year Plan That When It Comes to Railroads and Transportation the Third Five-Year Plan Can Only Involve Building So Many Things]', 10–11 May. In 攀枝花开发建设史文献资料选编 [Selected Documents About the History of Panzhihua's Development and Construction], edited by Party History Research Office of the Chinese Communist Party of Panzhihua City. Panzhihua: Zhonggong Panzhihua Shiwei Dangshi Yanjiushi, 6.

[15] Meyskens, *Mao's Third Front*, 126. For more on longstanding Party members, see David E. Apter and Tony Saich. 1994. *Revolutionary Discourse in Mao's Republic*. Cambridge, MA: Harvard University Press. For more on youth, see Anita Chan. 1985. *Children of Mao: Personality Development and Political Activism in the Red Guard Generation*. Seattle, WA: University of Washington Press.

[16] Meyskens, *Mao's Third Front*, 104–10.

[17] Ibid., 97–104.

[18] Ibid., 117.

[19] Ibid., 111–14.

[20] Ibid., 118–21.

[21] Judith Shapiro. 2001. *Mao's War Against Nature: Politics and the Environment in Revolutionary China*. New York, NY: Cambridge University Press, 70–75. On daily routines, see Liu Qinghua 刘庆华. 2010. 最后的贵族 [*The Last Noblemen*]. Beijing: Taihai Chubanshe, 66.

[22] Meyskens, *Mao's Third Front*, 176–80.

[23] State Council Third Front Construction Adjustment and Transformation Planning Office's Third Front Construction Editorial Board. 1991. 三线建设 [*Third Front Construction*]. Beijing: Guowuyuan Sanxian Jianshe Tiaozheng Gaizao Guihua Bangongshi Sanxian Kianshe Bianxiezu, 228.

[24] Andrew G. Walder. 1991. 'Cultural Revolution Radicalism: Variations On a Stalinist Theme.' In *New Perspectives on the Cultural Revolution*, edited by David Zweig, William A. Joseph, and Christine Wong. Cambridge, MA: Harvard University Press, 41.

[25] Meyskens, *Mao's Third Front*, 123–25.

[26] Ibid., 166–67.

[27] Ibid., 199–200.

[28] Ibid., 202.

[29] Naughton, 'The Third Front', 351.

[30] Zhu Cishou 祝慈寿. 1990. 中国现代工业史 [*Modern Industrial History of China*]. Chongqing: Chongqing Chubanshe, 489.

[31] State Council Third Front Construction Adjustment and Transformation Planning Office's Third Front Construction Editorial Board, *Third Front Construction*, 226–27.

[32] On the economic inefficiency of American defence spending, see James Ledbetter. 2011. *Unwarranted Influence: Dwight D. Eisenhower and the Military-Industrial Complex*. New Haven, CT: Yale University Press. On the CCP's overreaction, see Naughton, 'The Third Front', 380–81.

1964 (Maggie Clinton)

[1] The author thanks the National Endowment for the Humanities for supporting research cited in this article.

[2] Wang Jinxi 王进喜. n.d. '手扶刹把像刺刀 [Wielding the Brake Crank Like a Bayonet].' In 铁人诗话 [*Iron Man Wang Jinxi's Poetry and Quotations*], edited by Daqing Iron Man Wang Jinxi Memorial Hall. Beijing: Zhongyang Bianyi Chubanshe, 19.

[3] Ibid., 26–27; Li Hou. 2018. *Building for Oil: Daqing and the Formation of the Chinese Socialist State*. Cambridge, MA: Harvard East Asian Monographs, 156.

[4] Wang, *Iron Man Wang Jinxi's Poetry and Quotations*, viii–ix.

[5] Yuan Mu 袁木 and Fan Rongkang 范荣康. 1964. '大庆精神, 大庆人 [Daqing Spirit, Daqing People].' 人民日报 [*People's Daily*], 20 April.

[6] Kenneth Lieberthal and Michel Oksenberg. 1986. *Bureaucratic Politics and Chinese Energy Development*. Washington, DC: US Department of Commerce, International Trade Administration, 155.

[7] Tai Wei Lim. 2009. *Oil in China: From Self-Reliance to Internationalization*. Singapore: World Scientific Press, 16.

[8] Hou, *Building for Oil*, 34. On 'self-reliance', see Long Yang. 2019. 'Self-Reliance.' In *Afterlives of Chinese Communism: Political Concepts from Mao to Xi*, edited by Christian Sorace, Ivan Franceschini, and Nicholas Loubere. Canberra, London, and New York, NY: ANU Press and Verso Books, , 231–36.

[9] Hou, *Building for Oil*, 25; Richard T. Philipps. 2006. 'The Search for Oil in the Chinese Northeast Before 1949: A Research Note.' *Twentieth-Century China* 32, no. 1: 81–89; Bruce Elleman and Stephen Kotkin (eds). 2015. *Manchurian Railways and the Opening of China*. New York, NY: Routledge.

[10] Hou, *Building for Oil*, 40–42; Lim, *Oil in China*, 13–14.

[11] Mao Huahe (translated by Yiran Mao and Thomas Seay). 2019. *The Ebb and Flow of Chinese Petroleum: A Story Told by a Witness*. Leiden: Brill, 106–7.

[12] Hou, *Building for Oil*, 86–88.

[13] Lim, *Oil in China*, 69.

[14] Lieberthal and Oksenberg, *Bureaucratic Politics and Chinese Energy Development*, 154; Lim, *Oil in China*, 12–13.

[15] Sigrid Schmalzer. 2016. *Red Revolution, Green Revolution: Scientific Farming in Socialist China*. Chicago, IL: University of Chicago Press, 5.

[16] Lieberthal and Oksenberg, *Bureaucratic Politics and Chinese Energy Development*, 66; Mao, *The Ebb and Flow of Chinese Petroleum*, 119.

[17] Hou, *Building for Oil*, 40–42.

[18] Ibid., 42–43; Lim, *Oil in China*, 13–14. Covell Meyskens has highlighted how Third Front industrialisation projects, launched in 1964, contributed to the militarisation of Cold War China. Given how closely the PLA was involved in oil development, Daqing contributed to this trend as well. See Covell F. Meyskens. 2020. *Mao's Third Front: The Militarization of Cold War China*. Cambridge, MA: Cambridge University Press.

[19] Hou, *Building for Oil*, 136, *passim*.

[20] Lim, *Oil in China*, 41–42; Lieberthal and Oksenberg, *Bureaucratic Politics and Chinese Energy Development*, 160.

[21] Hou, *Building for Oil*, 141; frontmatter of *Taching: Red Banner on China's Industrial Front*. Peking: Foreign Languages Press, 1972; Yiyu Tian. 2019. 'Trapped in Time: Bodily Experiences of Family Dependant Workers (Jiashu) in Daqing, A Model Industrial City in High-Socialist China.' MA Thesis, University of Washington, Seattle, 13.

[22] Lim, *Oil in China*, 23; Mao, *The Ebb and Flow of Chinese Petroleum*, 97–100.

[23] Lieberthal and Oksenberg, *Bureaucratic Politics and Chinese Energy Development*, 160–61. Sorace has discussed this as a form of 'intimate governance' involving 'a promise to make the state accessible to the people and an invitation to the masses to participate in the revolution's ongoing redistribution of symbolic, material, and political power'. See Christian Sorace. 2020. 'Metrics of Exceptionality, Simulated Intimacy.' *Critical Inquiry* 46: 556.

[24] The Anshan Iron and Steel Plant was founded by the Japanese Mantetsu company in Anshan, Liaoning, in 1916. It is roughly 700 kilometres directly south of Daqing. William A. Byrd. 1992. 'The Anshan Iron and Steel Company.' In *Chinese Industrial Firms Under Reform*, edited by William A. Byrd. Oxford, UK: The World Bank & Oxford University Press, 305; Louise Young. 1998. *Japan's Total Empire: Manchuria and the Culture of Wartime Imperialism*. Berkeley, CA: University of California Press, 32, 195.

[25] Mao, *The Ebb and Flow of Chinese Petroleum*, 107.

[26] Lim, *Oil in China*, 24–25. Wang's motorcycle is on display at the Wang Jinxi Memorial Hall in Daqing. Signage there identifies the motorcycle as made in Hungary.

[27] Mao, *The Ebb and Flow of Chinese Petroleum*, 111–13.

[28] Lieberthal and Oksenberg noted how Daqing's leaders steered media attention towards manual workers and speculated that they may have misled Mao as to their role in decision-making at the oilfields. See Lieberthal and Oksenberg, *Bureaucratic Politics and Chinese Energy Development*, 161. Mao Huahe, who wrote work reports and publicity for the Daqing oilfields between 1960 and 1964 before moving to the MPI in Beijing, also indicated how care was taken to highlight worker, rather than technical specialist, contributions to Daqing's development. See Mao, *The Ebb and Flow of Chinese Petroleum*, 120, 129.

[29] Hou, *Building for Oil*, 137–45; Tian, 'Trapped in Time', 27.

[30] Mao, *The Ebb and Flow of Chinese Petroleum*, 101.

[31] Tian, 'Trapped in Time', 12; Hou, *Building for Oil*, 137–40. On the Dazhai Production Brigade as a model for agriculture, see Schmalzer, *Red Revolution, Green Revolution*, 11, 43, 112.

[32] Tian, 'Trapped in Time', 2.

[33] *Taching*, 14, 29; Hou, *Building for Oil*, 140–45.

[34] Hou, *Building for Oil*, 140–45; Tian, 'Trapped in Time', 2.

[35] Hou, *Building for Oil*, 85, 86–88; Tian, 'Trapped in Time', 14.

[36] Tian, 'Trapped in Time'.

[37] Lim, *Oil in China*, 82; Lieberthal and Oksenberg, *Bureaucratic Politics and Chinese Energy Development*, 174.

[38] Hou, *Building for Oil*, 154–55.

[39] Ibid., 159; Lieberthal and Oksenberg, *Bureaucratic Politics and Chinese Energy Development*, 175.

[40] Hou, *Building for Oil*, 159–60.

[41] Vincent Bevins. 2020. *The Jakarta Method: Washington's Anticommunist Crusade and the Mass Murder that Shaped our World*. New York, NY: Public Affairs; Taomo Zhou. 2019. *Migration in the Time of Revolution: China, Indonesia, and the Cold War*. Ithaca, NY: Cornell University Press.

[42] Lim, *Oil in China*, 117.

[43] Ibid., 117.

[44] China received in the deal high-quality steel for building pipelines, including to the coast at Qinhuangdao and Dalian. It also secured technology to begin offshore exploration in the Bohai Gulf. Lim, *Oil in China*, 116–29; Lieberthal and Oksenberg, *Bureaucratic Politics and Chinese Energy Development*, 177.

[45] Lim, *Oil in China*, 130n.46.

[46] Ibid., 88, 103.

[47] Lieberthal and Oksenberg, *Bureaucratic Politics and Chinese Energy Development*, 186; Lim, *Oil in China*, 107.

[48] Yuan and Fan, 'Daqing Spirit, Daqing People'.

[49] Mao, *The Ebb and Flow of Chinese Petroleum*, 103; Lim, *Oil in China*, 14.

[50] Hou, *Building for Oil*, 172; Lieberthal and Oksenberg, *Bureaucratic Politics and Chinese Energy Development*, 181.

[51] Mao, *The Ebb and Flow of Chinese Petroleum*, 104.

[52] '崇高的榜样 [Lofty Models]'. 人民日报 [*People's Daily*], [Late edition], 20 April 1964.

[53] Ibid.

[54] Daqing seamstresses interviewed, with English-language voiceover, in Joris Ivens and Marceline Loridan (dirs). 1976. *Autour du Pétrole: Taking* [*The Oilfields*]. Film, 84 mins, 42–45.

[55] See Jeremy Brown and Matthew Johnson. 2015. *Maoism At the Grassroots: Everyday Life in the Era of High Socialism*. Cambridge, MA: Cambridge University Press.

[56] Lim, *Oil in China*, 2.

[57] Selig S. Harrison. 1977. *China, Oil, and Asia: Conflict Ahead?* New York, NY: Columbia University Press.

[58] Lieberthal and Oksenberg, *Bureaucratic Politics and Chinese Energy Development*, 62–63, 176.

1967 (Patricia M. Thornton)

[1] Alessandro Russo. 2020. *Cultural Revolution and Revolutionary Culture*. Durham, NC: Duke University Press, 193.

[2] Alain Badiou. 2005. 'The Cultural Revolution: The Last Revolution?' *Positions: East Asia Cultures Critique* 13, no. 3: 496–97.

[3] Ibid.

[4] He Shu 何蜀. 2001. '文革中所谓的"上海一月革命": 毛泽东制造的一个"文革样板" [The Cultural Revolution's So-Called "January Revolution": Mao Zedong's Manufactured "Cultural Revolution Model"]'. 当代中国研究 [*Modern China Studies*], no. 2: 2–4.

[5] Andrew G. Walder. 2019. *Agents of Disorder: Inside China's Cultural Revolution*. Cambridge, MA: Harvard University Press, 103.

[6] Ping Hao. 1996. 'Reassessing the Starting Point of the Cultural Revolution.' *China Review International* 3, no. 1: 66–86.
[7] '欢呼北大的一张大字报 [Cheer the Big-Character Poster at Beijing University]', 人民日报 [*People's Daily*], 2 June 1966, 1.
[8] Ibid.
[9] Qinghua University Jinggangshan. n.d. 清华大学大字报选 (蒯大富 同志大字报) [*Selected Big-Character Posters by Qinghua University Students (Comrade Kuai Dafu's Big-Character Posters)*]. Tianjin: Tianjinshi Diyi Mianfenchang Hanwei Mao Zedong Sixiang Zaofandui.
[10] Walder, *Agents of Disorder*, 83.
[11] Shanghai Party Committee 'Cultural Revolution' Historical Materials Compilation Team. 1992. '文化大革命'史话(送审稿) [*The History of the 'Cultural Revolution' (Draft for Review)*]. 内部发行 [Internal Circulation] [hereinafter WDGSH], 61–71.
[12] Li Xun 李逊. 2015. 革命造反的年代 (上本) [*The Age of Revolutionary Rebellion (Volume 1)*]. Oxford, UK: Oxford University Press, 122–28.
[13] WDGSH, 152–53.
[14] Ibid., 79–81.
[15] Li, *The Age of Revolutionary Rebellion*, 289–98.
[16] WDGSH, 162–63.
[17] Ibid., 168–70.
[18] Elizabeth J. Perry and Xun Li. 1997. *Proletarian Power: Shanghai in the Cultural Revolution*. Boulder, CO: Westview Press, 78, 84.
[19] Li, *The Age of Revolutionary Rebellion*, 378.
[20] Yiching Wu. 2014. *The Cultural Revolution at the Margins: Chinese Socialism in Crisis*. Harvard, MA: Harvard University Press, 108–9.
[21] Walder, *Agents of Disorder*, ch. 3.
[22] Shanghai is a direct-controlled municipality (直辖市), which is an administrative designation on par with a province in the PRC.
[23] Perry and Li, *Proletarian Power*, 146–48; WDGSH, 247–48.
[24] Ibid.
[25] '抓革命,促生产彻底粉碎资产阶级反动路线的新反扑:告上海全市人 [Grasp Revolution, Promote Production and Completely Smash the New Counterattack of the Bourgeois Reactionary Line: An Urgent Letter to All the People of Shanghai]', 人民日报 [*People's Daily*], 9 January 1967, 1.
[26] See, for example, '反对经济主义 粉碎资产阶级反动路线的新反扑 [A New Counterattack Against Economism and Crushing the Bourgeois Reactionary Line].' 人民日报 [*People's Daily*], 12 January 1967, 1.
[27] '无产阶级革命派联合起来 [Proletarian Revolutionaries, Unite!]', 人民日报 [*People's Daily*], 16 January 1967, 1.
[28] '无产阶级革命派大联合,夺走资本主义道路当权派的权! [The Proletarian Revolutionaries Have Joined Forces to Take the Power of Those in Power on the Capitalist Road!]', 人民日报 [*People's Daily*], 22 January 1967, 1.
[29] Walder, *Agents of Disorder*, 294–95.
[30] Jean Christophe Mittelstaedt. 2018. 'Revolutionizing the State: The 1975 Chinese State Constitution.' PhD thesis, University of Oxford, Oxford, UK, 31–41.
[31] '论无产阶级革命派的夺权斗争 [On the Struggle to Seize Power of the Proletarian Revolutionaries]', 人民日报 [*People's Daily*], 31 January 1967, 1.
[32] WDGSH, 263.

[33] Roderick MacFarquhar and Michael Schoenhals. 2006. *Mao's Last Revolution*. Cambridge, MA: Harvard University Press, 168–69.

[34] Perry and Li, *Proletarian Power*, 37; Li, Xun 李逊. 2006. '工人阶级领导一切? "文革"中上海"工人造反派"及工人阶级的地位 [The Working Class Leads All? The Positions of "Rebel Workers" and the "Working Class" in Shanghai During the Cultural Revolution].' 当代中国研究 [*Modern China Studies*], no. 2: 2–4.

[35] Li, 'The Working Class Leads All?'.

[36] Ibid.

[37] Chinese Communist Party Central Committee. 1967. '"中共中央关于夺权斗争宣传报导问题的通知"中发[67]57号 ["CCP Central Committee Notice on Propagandising and Reporting of the Struggle to Seize Power" Issued by the Centre [1967] No. 57]', 19 February. Hong Kong: University Services Centre for China Studies, Chinese University of Hong Kong.

[38] '论革命的三结合 [On Revolution's "Triple Combination"]', 人民日报 [*People's Daily*], 10 March 1967, 1.

1967 (Ray Yep)

[1] This essay is based on the findings of a project funded by the General Research Fund of the Research Grant Council of the Hong Kong Special Administrative Region Government (Project No: 11611518).

[2] *Journal of the Hong Kong Institute of Social Research* 1 (1965): 1–8, 25–28, 33–38, 90–93, quoted in David Faure (ed.). 1997. *A Documentary History of Hong Kong: Society*. Hong Kong: Hong Kong University Press, 256–57.

[3] Carol Jones. 2007. *Criminal Justice in Hong Kong*. London: Routledge & Cavendish, 355.

[4] Ibid., 353.

[5] Zhou Yi 周奕. 2003. 香港左派鬥爭史 [*A History of Hong Kong Leftist Struggle*]. Hong Kong: Liwen Chubanshe.

[6] Ibid., 231–33.

[7] Hong Kong Federation of Trade Unions (HKFTU). 2008. 光榮歲月薪火相傳 [*The Glorious Years Are Passed Down*]. Hong Kong: Xinhua Shudian, 18–20.

[8] British National Archives, FCO 40/114, Special Branch, Police Headquarters, Hong Kong, 'Action against Communist Press—Reappraisals as at 9th November 1967', 9 November 1967. This estimate was different from that of communist leaders in Hong Kong—in particular, Jin Yaoru. Jin argued that communist newspapers contributed about one-third of the total circulation in Hong Kong. The difference was probably attributed to the inclusion of papers freely distributed to schools, unions and other premises. See Jin Yaoru 金堯如. 1998. 香港五十年憶往 [*Fifty Years of Hong Kong*]. Hong Kong: Tianyuan Shuji, 33.

[9] Sil-Metropole Organisation. 2010. 銀都 60: 1950–2010 [*Sil-Metropole at 60: 1950–2010*]. Hong Kong: Sanlian Shudian, 216.

[10] *Report of the Committee on Education*. 1963. Hong Kong: Government Printer, 3.

[11] Ibid., 108.

[12] British National Archives, FCO 40/45, Hong Kong to the Commonwealth Office, 7/5/1967, Telegram No. 553.

[13] British National Archives, FCO 40/49, Hong Kong Government Report on 'Current Communist Disturbances in Hong Kong', 3/8/1967. See also Yep, Ray. 2008. '1967 Riots in Hong Kong: The Diplomatic and Domestic Fronts of the Colonial Governor.' *China Quarterly* 193: 122–39.

[14] British National Archives, FCO 40/45, Hong Kong to Secretary of State of Commonwealth Affairs, 11/5/1967, Telegram No. 947.

[15] Ray Yep. 2012. 'Cultural Revolution in Hong Kong: Emergency Powers, Administration of Justice and the Turbulent Year of 1967.' *Modern Asian Studies* 46, no. 4: 1007–32.

[16] David Clayton. 2009. 'The Riots and Labour Laws: The Struggle for an Eight-Hour Day for Women Factory Workers, 1962–71.' In *May Day in Hong Kong: Riot and Emergency in 1967*, edited by Robert Bickers and Ray Yep. Hong Kong: Hong Kong University Press, 143.

[17] British National Archives, Cabinet Ministerial Committee on Hong Kong, Hong Kong: Long Term Study, K(69)1, 26 March 1969, CAB 134/2945.

1968 (Andrea Piazzaroli Longobardi)

[1] Zhang Chunqiao 张春桥. 2015 [1968]. '张春桥在上海机床厂现场会上的讲话 [Zhang Chunqiao's Speech at the Shanghai Machine Tools Factory]', 22 July 1968. In 毛泽东的理论家: 张春桥与「文革」 [*Mao Zedong's Theorist: Zhang Chunqiao and the Cultural Revolution*]. Taiwan: Xixifusi Wenhua Chubanshe, 206–10.

[2] '关于召开学习上海机床厂 721 工人大学教育革命经验 [Report of the Department of Education of the State Planning Commission to the State Council Regarding the Implementation and Study of the Experience of the Educational Revolution in the Workers' University at Shanghai Machine Tools Factory 7.21]', Shanghai Municipal Archive, document B244-1-386-1.

[3] Wang Defa 王德法. 1975. '坚持无产阶级政治挂帅把学校办成无产阶级专政的工具 [Persist in Putting Proletarian Politics in Command to Transform School in an Instrument of the Dictatorship of the Proletariat].' In 前进在七二一道路上: 上海机床厂教育革命经验 [*Advance Through the 7.21 Road: Shanghai Machine Tools Factory Experience in the Educational Revolution*]. Shanghai: Shanghai Renmin Da Chubanshe, 11.

[4] Zhang Chunqiao 张春桥. 1966. '张春桥与上海工人革命造反总司令部赴京代表团的讲话 [Zhang Chunqiao's Speech to a Group of Representatives of the Shanghai Rebel Workers General Headquarters]', 12 December, available from the Chinese Cultural Revolution Database at: ccradb.appspot.com/post/1887.

[5] See Christian Sorace. 2020. 'Metrics of Exceptionality, Simulated Intimacy.' *Critical Inquiry* 46, no. 3: 555–77.

[6] On the image of the broom, see Mao Zedong 毛泽东. 1967. 'Stenographic Note Held during the Conversation between Chairman Mao Zedong and Vangjel Moisiu and Myfit Mushi in Shanghai', 16 August, History and Public Policy Program Digital Archive, AQSH, F. 14/AP, M-PKK, V. 1967, Doc. 47, Fl. 1-8. Obtained and translated by Elidor Mëhilli, available online at: digitalarchive.wilsoncenter.org/document/117304. The difference between being inside and outside the Party (党内外有别) had been a widely debated topic since 1967. Some members of the Central Committee defended an irrevocable differentiation and others defended the participation of the grassroots

in the Party-State's agenda through popular criticism and political self-organisation. See Lowell Dittmer. 1973. 'The Structural Evolution of "Criticism and Self-Criticism".' *The China Quarterly* 56: 708–29.

[7] During the entire Cultural Revolution, there were debates and conflicts about how to balance the participation of workers in political mobilisations with maintaining production output levels. For a detailed overview of this situation in 1966 and 1967, see Hongsheng Jiang. 2010. 'Paris Commune in Shanghai: The Masses, the State, and Dynamics of "Continuous Revolution".' PhD dissertation, Duke University, Durham, NC.

[8] The expression 'new-born things' had been used since the Civil War to refer to social and political experiments carried out among the grassroots. See, for instance, Mao Zedong's 1957 essay 'On the Correct Handling of Contradictions Among the People', available online at: www.marxists.org/chinese/maozedong/marxist.org-chinese-mao-19570227AA.htm. Alain Badiou referred to a 'positive' and a 'negative' character of the revolution—that is, movements of destruction of the old, rupture and seizure, versus construction of the new. According to Badiou, revolution may present both these characters and the failure of many revolutionary mobilisations may be caused by a fixation on one of these poles. Accordingly, the passage from negative to positive or from destruction to construction, and vice versa, would be fundamental to any revolutionary mobilisation. Alain Badiou. 2015. *The Communist Hypothesis*. London: Verso Books, 23.

[9] For a detailed analysis of this meeting, see Alessandro Russo. 2005. 'The Conclusive Scene.' *Positions: East Asia Cultures Critique* 13, no. 3: 535–74. In this important conversation between Central Committee and local Party representatives and Red Guard leaders, Mao actually brings up the experience of the Shanghai Machine Tools Factory, saying it 'may mark a new phase of the Cultural Revolution'. See Mao Zedong 毛泽东. 1969. '召见首都红代会负责人的谈话 [Talk with the Responsible Persons of the Conference of the Red Guard of the Capital]', 28 July 1968. In 毛泽东万岁 [*Long Live Mao Zedong*], 687–716. For the *People's Daily* report, see *Take the Road of the Shanghai Machine Tools Plant in Training Technicians from Among the Workers*. Beijing: Foreign Language Press, 1968, 1–29. The booklet is available online at: www.marxists.org/history/erol/china/take-road.pdf. Mao's comment was later known as the '7.21 Directive' (七·二一指示) after its publication date in the *People's Daily* on 21 July 1968.

[10] Zhang, 'Zhang Chunqiao's Speech at the Shanghai Machine Tools Factory'.

[11] Shanghai Machine Tool Factory Revolutionary Committee. 1971. '上海机床厂"七·二一"工人大学首期学员毕业 [The First Cohort of Worker-Students Graduated from the SMTF "7.21" University].' 人民日报 [*People's Daily*], 23 July.

[12] Shanghai Municipal Mechanical and Electrical Bureau Revolutionary Committee. 1975. '努力办好七.二一工人大学 [Work Hard to Carry Out Well the 7.21 Workers' University].' 学习与批判 [*Study and Criticise*], no. 6: 84.

[13] '上海机床厂的工程技术人员队伍在成长 [Shanghai Machine Tool Factory Team of Project Technicians Is Growing]', 人民日报 [*People's Daily*], 21 July 1969.

[14] Workers' universities were completely reformed between 1976 and 1978. The reform started with the abolition of courses in the humanities. In 1978, the remaining leaders and teachers in the workers' universities were replaced, mostly with technical professors and cadres from different provinces and cities. See Jiang, *The Paris Commune in Shanghai*, 14–19. See also Shanghai Publishing Bureau. 1979.

'关于进一步加强我公司七二一工人大学的意见 [An Opinion on Carrying Forward the Straightening of the National Enterprise 7.21 Workers University]', Shanghai Municipal Archive, document number B105-4-1305.

[15] Li Aibao 李爱宝, cited in 前进在'七二一'道路上 [Advance on the '7.21' Path]. Shanghai: Shanghai Renmin Chubanshe, 1975, 45.

[16] Question formulated by Wu Jizhou, worker and cadre at the SMTF, in Advance on the '7.21 Path', 19.

[17] Question formulated by Chi Wenhan, a worker who graduated in the first cohort of the SMTF Workers' University, in Advance on the '7.21' Path, 33.

[18] Ibid.

[19] Wang, 'Persist in Putting Proletarian Politics in Command to Transform School in an Instrument of the Dictatorship of the Proletariat', 10.

[20] Zhang Meihua 张梅华. 1975. '坚定不移地走七。二一道路为巩固无产阶级专政而斗争 [Go Firmly on the 7.21 Path to Straighten the Dictatorship of the Proletariat and to Struggle]', in Advance on the '7.21' Path, 1–8.

[21] '新型的工人技术人员在成长——记上海机床厂"七·二一"工人大学第一批毕业生 [The New Team of Worker-Technicians Is Growing: Remembering the First Cohort Graduated from the SMTF "7.21" Workers University', 人民日报 [People's Daily], 22 July 1972.

[22] '定额制度也有资产阶级法权吗？ [Does the Production Quota System Also Have Capitalist Legal Power?]', 学习与批判 [Study and Criticise], no. 9(1975): 46–47.

[23] An introduction to this kind of discourse analysis can be found in Revolutionary Committee of the Shanghai Fifth Steel Plant. 1975. '一年来的战斗回顾 [Reviewing the Battles of the Last Year]'. 学习与批判 [Study and Criticise], no. 1: 3.

[24] Writing manuals recommended the use of a variety of genres to capture the attention and interest of readers. Texts debating theoretical topics of political economy were commonly written in the form of dialogues, letters and even biographies.

[25] 'Does the Production Quota System Also Have Capitalist Legal Power?'.

[26] The debate on the permanence of contradictions within socialism is too broad and significant to be reduced to a single reference. However, Mao Zedong gave an important speech on the topic on 21 December 1965. See Mao Zedong 毛泽东. 1968. '在杭州会议上的讲话 [Speech in Hangzhou]'. In 毛泽东思想万岁 [Long Live Mao Zedong Thought], 246–49. Wuhan: Wuhan University. Alessandro Russo details the national study campaign launched in 1975 about the 'Dictatorship of the Proletariat' in this article: Alessandro Russo. 2013. 'How Did the Cultural Revolution End? The Last Dispute between Mao Zedong and Deng Xiaoping, 1975.' Modern China 39, no. 3: 239–79.

1969 (Joel Andreas)

[1] For analyses of conflict among Party leaders and among local officials, see Roderick MacFarquhar and Michael Schoenhals. 2006. *Mao's Last Revolution*. Cambridge, MA: Harvard University Press; and Andrew G. Walder. 2019. *Agents of Disorder: Inside China's Cultural Revolution*. Cambridge, MA: Harvard University Press.

[2] Elizabeth J. Perry and Xun Li. 1997. *Proletarian Power: Shanghai in the Cultural Revolution*. Boulder, CO: Westview Press; Yiching Wu. 2014. *The Cultural Revolution at the Margins: Chinese Socialism in Crisis*. Cambridge, MA: Harvard University Press; Andrew G. Walder. 1977. *Chang Ch'un Chiao and Shanghai's January Revolution*. Ann Arbor, MI: Center for Chinese Studies, University of Michigan.

[3] Song Yongyi 宋永毅 and Sun Dajin 孫大進 (eds). 1996. 文化大革命和它的異端思潮 [*Heterodox Thinking during the Cultural Revolution*]. Hong Kong: Countryside Book House; Jonathan Unger. 1991. '"Whither China?" Yang Xiguang, Red Capitalists, and the Social Turmoil of the Cultural Revolution.' *Modern China* 17, no. 1; Wu, *The Cultural Revolution at the Margins*.

[4] Lao Tian 老田. 2014. '对主流文革史写法的知识社会学分析 [A Sociology of Knowledge Analysis of Mainstream Writing on Cultural Revolution History]', available online at: www.wyzxwk.com/Article/lishi/2014/04/317327.html; Qi Jinhua 齐晋华. 2013. '"九大"前山东的"反复旧"' [The "Oppose Restoring the Old" Movement in Shandong Before the Ninth Congress].' 昨天 [*Yesterday*], no. 17, 30 May, available online at: difangwenge.org/simple/?t10706.html; Shaoguang Wang. 1995. *Failure of Charisma: The Cultural Revolution in Wuhan*. Oxford, UK: Oxford University Press.

[5] While the overall narrative is drawn from my recent book, *Disenfranchised: The Rise and Fall of Industrial Citizenship in China* (Oxford University Press, 2019), this essay will scrutinise in more detail the *Fan Fujiu* movement.

[6] Joel Andreas. 2019. 'Mass Supervision.' In *Afterlives of Chinese Communism: Political Concepts from Mao to Xi*, edited by Christian Sorace, Ivan Franceschini and Nicholas Loubere. Canberra, London, and New York, NY: ANU Press and Verso Books, 127–33.

[7] Interviewee W9. For background characteristics of interviewees, see Andreas, *Disenfranchised*, Appendix D.

[8] Wang, *Failure of Charisma*, 192.

[9] Interviewee W9.

[10] This would prove to be the first of three repressive national campaigns that ended the mass factional contention of the Cultural Revolution, suppressed the rebel organisations, and harshly restored the authority of the Party organisation. The other two, referred to below, were the 'One Strike and Three Antis' campaign and the drive to uncover '16 May Elements'. See Andrew G. Walder. 2014. 'Rebellion and Repression in China, 1966–1971.' *Social Science History*, 38, nos. 3–4: 513–39.

[11] Interviewee W2.

[12] Qi, 'The "Oppose Restoring the Old" Movement in Shandong Before the Ninth Congress.'

[13] Cited in Wang, *Failure of Charisma*, 210–11.

[14] Interviewee W11.

[15] Wang, *Failure of Charisma*, 212.

[16] Ibid., 214.

[17] Ibid., 216–18.

[18] Interviewee W11.

[19] Chinese Communist Party Central Committee. 1969. '中共中央同意"湖北省革命委员会关于解决武汉'反复旧'问题的报告" [Chinese Communist Party Central Committee Agrees with the "Report of the Hubei Provincial Revolutionary Committee on Solving Wuhan's 'Oppose Restoring the Old'" Problem]', 27 May, available online at: ccradb.appspot.com/post/584.

[20] Interviewee W11.
[21] Lao Tian, 'A Sociology of Knowledge Analysis of Mainstream Writing on Cultural Revolution History.'

1970 (Matthew Galway)

[1] Robert F. Williams. 1969. 'An Afro-American in Africa.' *The Call: Journal of the Afro-Asian Writers Bureau* 9, no. 1: 21–22, quoted in Robeson Taj Frazier. 2015. *The East Is Black: Cold War China in the Black Radical Imagination*. Durham, NC: Duke University Press, 274 n.45.

[2] '尼雷尔总统在告别晚宴的讲话 [President Nyerere's Speech at Farewell Banquet].' 人民日报 [*People's Daily*], 22 June 1968. See also Yinghong Cheng. 2011. *Creating the 'New Man': From Enlightenment Ideals to Socialist Realities*. Honolulu, HI: University of Hawai`i Press, 211; and George T. Yu. 1970. *China and Tanzania: A Study in Cooperative Interaction*. Berkeley, CA: Center for Chinese Studies, University of California, 35.

[3] 'Julius Nyerere's Banquet Speech.' *Xinhua*, 21–24 June 1968, in Foreign Broadcast Information Service, *Daily Reports*, Communist China—International Affairs, A6 (FBIS-FRB-68-123).

[4] Quoted in Cheng, *Creating the 'New Man'*, 212. See also 'Union Being Cemented, Says Mwalimu: Union Making Great Progress.' *The Nationalist* [Tanzania], 27 April 1965; William Edgett Smith. 1971. *We Must Run While They Walk: A Portrait of Africa's Julius Nyerere*. New York, NY: Random House, 3; and Zhou Boping 周伯萍. 2003. 非常时期的外交生涯 [*Diplomatic Career in an Unusual Time*]. Beijing: Shejie Zhishi, 20–26.

[5] Priya Lal. 2014. 'Maoism in Tanzania: Material Connections and Shared Imaginaries.' In *Mao's Little Red Book: A Global History*, edited by Alexander Cook. Cambridge, UK: Cambridge University Press, 97, 104. See also 'Chinese Doctors Call on Shaba.' *The Nationalist* [Tanzania], 18 April 1968; Frazier, *The East Is Black*, 203; and Matthew Galway. 2013. 'Global Maoism and the Politics of Localization in Peru and Tanzania.' *Left History* 17, no. 2: 22.

[6] Lal, 'Maoism in Tanzania', 101. Chinese loans funded Chinese-designed and engineered projects such as the Tanzania–China cotton shipping line, a naval base in Tanzania's then capital of Dar es Salaam, and an airstrip in Ngerengere. Chinese experts also instructed the Tanzanian military. Frazier, *The East Is Black*, 203.

[7] Tareq Y. Ismael. 1971. 'The People's Republic of China and Africa.' *Journal of Modern African Studies* 9, no. 4: 515; Frazier, *The East Is Black*, 203; Qu Zhengmin 曲拯民. 2006. '中国给坦赞尼亚筑铁路 [China Facilitates the Building of a Railway in Tanzania].' 翼报月刊 [*Yibao Monthly*], 1 June, available online at: chs.ebaomonthly.com/ebao/printebao.php?a=20060618; Lal, 'Maoism in Tanzania', 101; and Jamie Monson. 2009. *Freedom Railway: How a Chinese Development Project Changed Lives and Livelihoods in Tanzania*. Bloomington, IN: Indiana University Press, 33. During the Tan–Zam Railway's 'intensive construction' stage (1970–74), 30,000–40,000 Chinese technicians worked on two-year contracts and 60,000 or more Tanzanian and Zambian workers joined them. A 2007 issue of *People's Daily* estimated that as many as 50,000 Chinese workers over an eleven-year period worked in surveying, construction, and management training. Jamie Monson. 2013. 'Making Men,

Making History.' *Clio. Women, Gender, History*, no. 38: 130. See also Shi Lin 石林 (ed.). 1989. 当代中国的对外经济合作 [*Contemporary China's Foreign Economic Cooperation*]. Beijing: Zhongguo Shehui Kexue Chubanshe, 61.

[8] Donovan Chau. 2014. *Exploiting Africa: The Influence of Maoist China in Algeria, Ghana, and Tanzania*. Annapolis, MD: Naval Institute Press, 129; and Frazier, *The East Is Black*, 203.

[9] Rucai Lu. 2016. 'Du Jian: Witness to the Birth of the TAZARA.' *China Today* 65, no. 1: 39. On the Tan–Zam Railway's goals, see Cao Desheng 曹德胜. 2018. '祖孙两代人共"筑非洲梦" [Grandfather and Grandson Build the "African Dream" Together Over Two Generations].' 中国日报 [*China Daily*], 3 September, available online at: cn.chinadaily.com.cn/2018-09/03/content_36861999.htm.

[10] Lu, 'Du Jian', 39–42. PRC representatives often conveyed socialist principles by 'using the language of brotherhood and friendship'. The latter represented 'a key phrase in Chinese development propaganda in Tanzania during the 1960s and 1970s'. Jamie Monson. 2006. 'Defending the People's Railway in the Era of Liberalization: Tazara in Southern Tanzania.' *Africa: Journal of the International African Institute* 76, no. 1: 118.

[11] Reference to 'Seventeen Years' is from Zhang Yuling 张玉玲. 2012. '新中国"十七年"中直院团舞蹈团队政治功能分析 [Analysis of the Political Functions of the Centrally Administered Dance Ensembles during New China's "Seventeen Years"].' 长江大学学报社会科学版 [*Journal of Yangtze University, Social Sciences Edition (China)*] 35, no. 2: 115–17, cited in Emily Wilcox. 2018. 'The Postcolonial Blind Spot: Chinese Dance in the Era of Third Worldism, 1949–1965.' *Positions: Asia Critique* 26, no. 4: 815. On this shift, see John W. Garver. 2015. *China's Quest: The History of the Foreign Relations of the People's Republic of China*. Oxford, UK: Oxford University Press, 196–231.

[12] Deborah Bräutigam, . 2009. *The Dragon's Gift: The Real Story of China in Africa*. Oxford, UK: Oxford University Press, 37. On the PRC's radical foreign policy of the Cultural Revolution years, see Kang Maozhao 康矛召. 2000. 外交回忆录 [*Diplomatic Memoirs*]. Beijing: Zhongyang Wenxian Chubanshe.

[13] D.J. Muekalia. 2004. 'Africa and China's Strategic Partnership.' *African Security Review* 13, no. 1: 5–11.

[14] Bräutigam, *The Dragon's Gift*, 40–41. See also 'Tanzania's Enemies Attack Anti-Imperialist Policies.' *African World*, 22 July 1972, 4.

[15] Lal, 'Maoism in Tanzania', 105.

[16] Monson, *Africa's Freedom Railway*, 41. Monson acknowledges on page 7, however, that relationships between Chinese and Tanzanian labourers were more 'hierarchical and highly regulated'.

[17] Ibid., 7; and Monson, 'Defending the People's Railway in the Era of Liberalization', 113.

[18] This article recasts 'labour diplomacy', which one scholar credits to US Department of State practitioners in reference to global US Embassy labour attachés' advocacy for 'core labor standards within the context of US human rights and international trade policy'. Nicholas A. Stigliani. 2003. 'Labor Diplomacy: A Revitalized Aspect of US Foreign Policy in the Era of Globalization.' *International Studies Perspectives* 1, no. 2: 177–94. On ideas that inspired this chapter's recasting, see Cheng, *Creating the 'New Man'*, 210–13; Monson, 'Making Men, Making History', 124; Elizabeth Schmidt. 2007. *Cold War and Decolonization in Guinea, 1946–1958*. Athens, OH: Ohio University Press; and Jay Straker. 2009. *Youth, Nationalism, and the Guinean Revolution*. Bloomington, IN: Indiana University Press.

[19] Bräutigam, *The Dragon's Gift*, 39–40, quoting 'Tanzania–Zambia Railway Symbolizes Sino-African Friendship', *Xinhua*, 23 June 2006.
[20] Jamie Monson. 2005. 'Interview with Yao Peiji'; Monson, 'Making Men, Making History', 130.
[21] '周恩来推动援建坦赞铁路 [Zhou Enlai Promotes Aid to Tanzania–Zambia Railway].' 人民日报 [*People's Daily*], 3 May 2020, available online at: zhouenlai.people.cn/n1/2020/0305/c409117-31618455.html. See also Monson, *Africa's Freedom Railway*, 2; and Brautigam, *The Dragon's Gift*, 40.
[22] Hai Mingwei 海明威. 2010. '记者重走我国援建的坦赞铁路:年久失修常晚点 [Correspondent Rides the TAZARA Railway that China Helped to Build: Unrepaired and Often Late].' 瞭望东方周刊 [*Eastern Watch Weekly*], 4 August, available online at: news.sina.com.cn/c/sd/2010-08-04/170620826263.shtml. See also Monson, *Africa's Freedom Railway*, 38.
[23] Monson, 'Making Men, Making History', 130.
[24] *Xinhua*, 'Tanzania–Zambia Railway Symbolizes Sino-African Friendship.'
[25] Bräutigam, *The Dragon's Gift*, 40–41.
[26] 'TAZARA Construction Worker Who Died After Being Fiercely Stung by African Bees Remembered in Dar.' *Tanzania Zambia Railway Authority/The Daily News* [Tanzania], 4 March 2016, available online at: tazarasite.com/tazara-construction-worker-who-died-after-being-fiercely-stung-african-bees-remembered-dar.
[27] Monson, 'Defending the People's Railway in the Era of Liberalization', 120–21. On *Ujamaa* villagisation and its discontents, see Galway, 'Global Maoism and the Politics of Localization in Peru and Tanzania', 21–29.
[28] 'Tan–Zam Railway Is Not "Red" Says Nyerere.' *The Nationalist* [Tanzania], 20 October 1968, quoted in Lal, 'Maoism in Tanzania', 107.
[29] 'Tanzanian, Zambian, Chinese Government Representatives Inspect Survey Work on Tanzanian Section of Tanzania–Zambia Railway.' *Peking Review* 11, no. 26, 28 June 1968: 27.
[30] May Joseph. 1999. *Nomadic Identities: The Performance of Citizenship*. Minneapolis, MN: University of Minnesota Press, 40; and Martin Bailey. 1975. 'Tanzania and China.' *African Affairs* 74, no. 294: 42. See also Paul Bjerk. 2017. *Julius Nyerere*. Athens, OH: Ohio University Press, 80; and Cranford Pratt. 1976. *The Critical Phase in Tanzania 1945–1968: Nyerere and the Emergence of a Socialist Strategy*. Cambridge, UK: Cambridge University Press.
[31] 'President Nyerere Speaks Out on Remaining Colonies: Bloodshed? It's Up to the West.' *The Nationalist* [Tanzania], 24 June 1965, quoted in Lal, 'Maoism in Tanzania', 107. On the 'Tanzania suit' and its popularity, see William Edgett Smith. 1973. *Nyerere of Tanzania*. London: Victor Gollancz, 13.
[32] Bräutigam, *The Dragon's Gift*, 40.
[33] Ibid., 40.
[34] '温家宝凭吊中国援坦专家公墓并视察中国援建工地 [Wen Jiabao Visits the Chinese Aid Experts' Cemetery and Inspects a Chinese Construction Site].' 新华社 [*Xinhua*], 23 June 2006.
[35] Bräutigam, *The Dragon's Gift*, 40.
[36] 'Vice Minister of Commerce, Fu Ziying, is Addressing the Press.' *China.com.cn*, quoted in Monson, 'Making Men, Making History', 128.

[37] Ibid. See also Ben Blanchard. 2011. 'China Says Foreign Aid About Friendship, Not Resources.' *Reuters*, 26 April, available online at: www.reuters.com/article/hold-china-aid-idAFL3E7FQ0EX20110426.

[38] '坦桑尼亚庆祝坦赞铁路运营壹周年 [Tanzania Celebrates the First Anniversary of the Tanzania–Zambia Railway's Operation].' 人民日报 [*People's Daily*], 16 July 1977.

[39] 'Alternative to Imperialists: Chinese Aid to Africa.' *African World*, 16 September 1972, 12, 16, quoted in Frazier, *The East Is Black*, 203–4.

[40] 'Correspondence, February 1969: Letter from Al Haynes (Muhammad Zaid), February 5, 1969.' Robert F. Williams Papers, Bentley Historical Library, University of Michigan, Ann Arbor, Box 2, Folder: September–December 1968, cited in Frazier, *The East Is Black*, 204. See also Monson, *Africa's Freedom Railway*, 37–38.

[41] Lal, 'Maoism in Tanzania', 114.

[42] Bruce Heilman and Laurean Ndumbaro. 2002. 'Corruption, Politics, and Societal Values in Tanzania: An Evaluation of the Mkapa Administration's Anti-Corruption Efforts.' *African Journal of Political Science* 17, no. 1: 1–19.

[43] Cao, 'Grandfather and Grandson Build the "African Dream" Together Over Two Generations.'

[44] Ibid.

1972 (Michel Bonnin)

[1] This essay draws from Michel Bonnin. 2013. *The Lost Generation: The Rustication of China's Educated Youth, 1968–1980*. Hong Kong: Chinese University Press of Hong Kong.

[2] Sources on Li's story are numerous. To cite only two: Liu Xiaomeng 刘小萌. 1998. 中国知青史 [*History of the Rusticated Youth*]. Beijing: Zhongguo Shehui Kexue Chubanshe, 88–92; and Elya J. Zhang. 2006. 'To Be Somebody: Li Qinglin, "Run-of-the-Mill Cultural Revolution Showstopper".' In *The Chinese Cultural Revolution as History*, edited by Joseph W. Esherick, Paul G. Pickowicz and Andrew G. Walder. Palo Alto, CA: Stanford University Press, 211–39.

[3] On the directive, see Bonnin, *The Lost Generation*, 4.

[4] Roderick MacFarquhar and Michael Schoenhals. 2006. *Mao's Last Revolution*. Cambridge, MA: Harvard University Press, 87.

[5] Official statistics of the Central Bureau of Educated Youth, reproduced in Liu, *History of the Rusticated Youth*, 864.

[6] See Liu, *History of the Rusticated Youth*, 863.

[7] In May 1967, Mao had already expressed his disappointment with 'young intellectuals still at school' and stressed the necessity for them to 'remould their world outlook'. See Mao Zedong 毛泽东. 1969. '接见阿尔巴尼亚军事代表团的讲话 [Speech Given to an Albanian Military Delegation].' In 毛泽东思想万岁 [*Long Live Mao Zedong Thought*], available online at: www.marxists.org/chinese/maozedong/1968/5-307.htm.

[8] Liu, *History of the Rusticated Youth*, 863.

[9] Ibid.

[10] See charts in Bonnin, *The Lost Generation*, 177.

[11] See Gu Hongzhang 顾洪章 (ed.). 1996. 中国知识青年上山下乡始末 [*History of the Rustication of Chinese Educated Youth*]. Beijing: Zhongguo Jiancha Chubanshe, 158.
[12] Ibid., 130–35.

1976 (A.C. Baecker)

[1] Li Wenhua 李文化. 1986. 决裂 [*Breaking With Old Ideas*]. VHS, Voyager Press; Chun Chao 春潮 and Zhou Jie 周杰. 1976. '决裂 [Breaking With Old Ideas].' 人民电影 [*People's Film*], no. 1: 41–76.
[2] See John Cleverly. 2000. *In the Lap of Tigers: The Communist Labor University of Jiangxi Province*. Lanham, MD: Rowman & Littlefield, 22, 72. Gongda primarily sold bamboo and timber products from logging sites throughout Jiangxi, but also pork, soap, insecticide, printed goods, medicine, and products used within the college to facilitate production, such as tools, explosives, and cement. Branches of the campus ran shops for mechanical repairs as well as apiaries.
[3] Laurence Coderre elaborates on the context within which 'propaganda films' were received in her article on the movie *Counterattack* (反击), also produced in the mid-1970s. Laurence Coderre. 2000. '*Counterattack*: (Re)Contextualizing Propaganda.' *Journal of Chinese Cinemas* 4, no. 3: 211–27. See also Tina Mai Chen. 2003. 'Propagating the Propaganda Film: The Meaning of Film in CCP Writings, 1949–1965.' *Modern Chinese Literature and Culture* 15, no. 2: 154–93.
[4] '社论: 欢接人民公社化的高潮 [Commentary: Greet the Upsurge in Forming People's Communes].' 红旗 [*Red Flag*], no. 7 (1958): 13–15 [Uncredited English translation included in the 1958 volume *People's Communes in China*. Beijing: Foreign Languages Press, 10–15].
[5] For domestic labour on rural communes, see Elisabeth J. Croll. 1985. *Women and Rural Development in China: Production and Reproduction*. Geneva: International Labour Office; Xianxian Gao. 1994. 'China's Modernization and Changes in the Social Status of Rural Women.' In *Engendering China: Women, Culture, and the State*, edited by Christina K. Gilmartin, Gail Hershatter, Lisa Rofel, and Tyrene White. Cambridge, MA: Harvard University Press, 80–97; Gail Hershatter. 2011. *The Gender of Memory: Rural Women and China's Collective Past*. Berkeley, CA: University of California Press; Kay Ann Johnson. 2009. *Women, the Family, and Peasant Revolution in China*. Chicago, IL: University of Chicago Press, especially pp. 157–77; and William L. Parish and Martin King Whyte. 1978. *Village and Family in Contemporary China*. Chicago, IL: University of Chicago Press. On communal canteens specifically, see Chunfeng Li. 2016. 'Historical Observations Regarding the Large-Scale Establishment of Rural Public Canteens in Hebei Province.' In *Agricultural Reform and Rural Transformation in China Since 1949*, edited by Thomas David DuBois and Li Huaiyin. Leiden: Brill, 115–32. On sewing groups and textile work specifically, see Jacob Eyferth's essay in the present volume, as well as Jacob Eyferth. 2015. 'Liberation from the Loom? Rural Women, Textile Work, and Revolution in North China.' In *Maoism at the Grassroots: Everyday Life in China's Era of High Socialism*, edited by Jeremy Brown and Matthew D. Johnson. Cambridge, MA: Harvard University Press, 131–53.

⁶ '从"卫星"公社的简章谈如何办公社 [How to Run a People's Commune, with Reference to the Regulations of the "Sputnik" People's Commune].' 人民日报 [*People's Daily*], 4 September 1958.

⁷ For more on education and communes, see Joel Andreas. 2009. *Rise of the Red Engineers: The Cultural Revolution and the Origins of China's New Class*. Stanford, CA: Stanford University Press, 184–90; Joshua Eisenman. 2018. *Red China's Green Revolution: Technological Innovation, Institutional Change, and Economic Development Under the Commune*. New York, NY: Columbia University Press, 81–85; Dongping Han. 2000. *The Unknown Cultural Revolution: Educational Reforms and Their Impact on China's Rural Development*. New York, NY: Garland Publishing, especially pp. 23–38; Julia Kwong. 1980. *Chinese Education in Transition: Prelude to the Cultural Revolution*. Montreal: McGill-Queen's University Press; and Suzanne Pepper. 1996. *Radicalism and Education Reform in 20th-Century China: The Search for an Ideal Development Model*. Cambridge, UK: Cambridge University Press, especially pp. 278–301. For scientific research and communes, see Sigrid Schmalzer. 2016. *Red Revolution, Green Revolution: Scientific Farming in Socialist China*. Chicago, IL: University of Chicago Press.

⁸ See Pepper, *Radicalism and Education Reform in 20th-Century China*, 178–300; Eisenman, *Red China's Green Revolution*, 81–85; and Han, *The Unknown Cultural Revolution*, 23–28.

⁹ For a history of attitudes towards education as a right versus a commodity in the American context, see Alex Molnar. 2005. *School Commercialism: From Democratic Ideal to Market Commodity*. New York, NY: Routledge.

¹⁰ Andreas, *Rise of the Red Engineers*, 68–72.

¹¹ The film makes an equivalence of literacy with formal education in an echo of earlier dialogue in which characters use the term 'culture' (文化) to mean 'literate' or 'educated'. This is a usage that continues to the present.

¹² She will not; she will leave her daughter with her mother-in-law.

¹³ After the arrest of Jiang Qing, Zhang Chunqiao, Yao Wenyuan, Wang Hongwen, and six other high-ranking military officials in October 1976, Zhang Tiesheng was imprisoned for fifteen years. In recent years, he has risen to prominence once again for wealth amassed as a founder of Wellhope Agri-Tech, an animal feed company based in Liaoning Province. See Chris Buckley. 2014. 'Zhang Tiesheng: From Hero Under Mao to "Hero of Wealth".' *The New York Times*, 18 August; Li Chunping 李春平. 2017. '"白卷英雄"张铁生大手笔坚持套现可达亿元 ["Hero of the Blank Exam" Zhang Tiesheng Sees Accomplishments Diminished, Cashes Out One Hundred Million Yuan].' 新京报 [*The Beijing News*], 4 January.

¹⁴ Zhang Tiesheng 张铁生. 1973. '一份发人深省的答卷 [A Thought-Provoking Answer Sheet].' 人民日报 [*People's Daily*], 10 August.

¹⁵ Jiang Qing and others praised Zhang Tiesheng as a 'hero who goes against the tide' (反潮流英雄)—a name by which he and several other notable student dissenters became known, including Zhong Zhimin and Beijing primary school student Huang Shuai. See Yang Pu 杨浦. 1973. '反潮流精神：赞"一份发人深省的答卷" [The Contrarian Spirit: In Praise of "A Thought-Provoking Answer Sheet"].' 人民日报 [*People's Daily*], 16 August; also Jonathan Unger. 1982. *Education Under Mao: Class and Competition in Canton Schools, 1960–1980*. New York, NY: Columbia University Press, 197–99.

¹⁶ Unger, *Education Under Mao*, 109.

[17] Joel Andreas. 2002. 'Battling Over Political and Cultural Power During the Chinese Cultural Revolution.' *Theory and Society* 31: 463–519.

[18] See Unger, *Education Under Mao*, 130; also Yiching Wu. 2014. *The Cultural Revolution at the Margins: Chinese Socialism in Crisis*. Cambridge, MA: Harvard University Press, ch. 4.

[19] Fabio Lanza expands on the idea of student activism exceeding the limits of the state in the epilogue to his 2010 book *Behind the Gate: Inventing Students in Beijing*. New York, NY: Columbia University Press, 203–16.

[20] For example, Long Guozheng jokes at the start of the film that he is able to travel quickly because he moves at 'Great Leap Forward speed'.

[21] Film Bureau. 2006 [1975]. '对影片《决裂》的意见 [Opinion on the Film *Juelie*].' In 中国电影研究资料, *1949–1979* [*Collected Research Materials of Chinese Film, 1949–1979*], edited by Wu Di 吴迪. Beijing: Wenhua Yishu Chubanshe, vol. 2, p. 309.

[22] Li Wenhua cited in Di Di 翟狄. 1993. '决裂纪事与分析 [Breaking With Old Ideas: A Chronicle and Analysis].' 电影艺术 [*Film Art*], no. 2: 78.

[23] The full text of the letter was published widely in the national press in late July 1977—a decision John Cleverly attributes to then party chairman Hua Guofeng. See Cleverly, *In the Lap of Tigers*, 117–19.

1980 (Jeanne L. Wilson)

[1] *The New York Times*, 14 April 1981, 3.

[2] For a discussion of strikes in Wuhan, see *The Times*, 30 January 1981, 6; *The Guardian*, 30 January 1981, 8; AFP in *Foreign Broadcast Information System-China* [hereinafter *FBIS-CHI*], 20 February 1981, H1; AFP in *FBIS-CHI*, 29 January 1981, P1. For a discussion of strikes in Taiyuan, see AFP in *FBIS-CHI*, 3 March 1981, R1; *The Times*, 5 March 1981, 8; and *The Washington Post*, 30 April 1981, A30. *FBIS* was an open-source publication of the US Government designed primarily for employees of the Central Intelligence Agency (CIA), as well as other government employees. It was also available for subscription to individual users and libraries. Its 'Daily Reports' were an extremely valuable source of information, but *FBIS* ceased publication in 1996.

[3] AFP in *FBIS-CHI*, 3 March 1981, R1; *The Times*, 5 March 1981, 8.

[4] For a discussion of the influence of Hungary and Poland on Chinese policy in 1956, see Richard Solomon. 1971. *Mao's Revolution and Chinese Political Culture*. Berkeley, CA: University of California Press, 268–329.

[5] This circular was reprinted in the Hong Kong journal 七十年代 [*1970s*], no. 135 (April 1981): 35–40, in *FBIS-CHI*, 16 April 1981, W1–10.

[6] Andrew G. Walder. 1984. 'The Remaking of the Chinese Working Class, 1949–1981.' *Modern China* 10, no. 1: 43.

[7] 争鸣 [*Contending*], no. 10 (1 October 1981): 26–29.

[8] 七十年代 [*1970s*], no. 123 (March 1981), in *FBIS-CHI*, 15 March 1981, U11. For remarks on Liao Gailong's relationship with Deng Xiaoping, see Andrew J. Nathan. 1989. 'Chinese Democracy in 1989: Continuity and Change.' *Problems of Communism*, September–October, 18.

[9] AFP in *FBIS-CHI*, 22 August 1980, H1.

[10] Nonetheless, Li Lisan and Lai Ruoyu, two trade union chairmen of the 1950s who were purged from their posts, were posthumously rehabilitated along with their policies, now identified as having been correct all along.

[11] AFP, 11 January 1982, in *FBIS-CHI*, 13 January 1982, H1.

[12] 中报 [*Zhongbao*], 20 February 1984, 2. Li's comments about Poland were omitted from the official transcript of the proceedings. See All-China Federation of Trade Unions [hereinafter ACFTU]. 1983.中国工会第十次全国代表重要文件 [*Important Documents of the Tenth National Congress of the Chinese Trade Union*]. Beijing: Gongren Chubanshe.

[13] *Xinhua*, 27 December 1984, in *Joint Publications Research Service-China East Asia*, no. 83-008, 26 January 1985, 123. The *Joint Publications Research Service* (*JPRS*) was an open-source publication of the US Government. Similar to the *FBIS*, it was primarily oriented towards researchers in the CIA and other government officials. It ceased publication in 1995.

[14] 镜报 [*Jingbao*], no. 142, 10 May 1989, in *FBIS-CHI*, 15 May 1989, 30.

[15] 工人日报 [*Workers' Daily*], 30 October 1988, l.

[16] *South China Morning Post*, 4 May 1989, in *FBIS-CHI*, 4 May 1989, 29.

[17] See, for example, comments in AFP, 19 April 1989, in *FBIS-CHI*, 20 April 1989, 14.

[18] *South China Morning Post*, 4 May 1989, in *FBIS-CHI*, 4 May 1989, 29.

[19] Among the cities in which it is possible to identify multiple listings of autonomous unions are Beijing, Shanghai, Hefei, and Xi'an. Hefei, for example, witnessed the birth of the Hefei Workers' Autonomous Association, the Hefei Municipal Union of Workers, and the Hefei Independent Workers' Union. *FBIS-CHI* and the *Survey of World Broadcasts* (*SWB*), published by the British Broadcasting Corporation (BBC), are a good source of information about specific autonomous unions in China through their listings of provincial radio broadcasts banning autonomous activities in June 1989. See *SWB Far East* [hereinafter *SWB FE*] transcripts for 13–16 June, 19–21 June, 23–24 June, and 28 June 1989; and *FBIS-CHI*, 12–16 June, 27–28 June, and 31 July 1989.

[20] Asia Watch. 1990. *Punishment Season: Human Rights in China After Martial Law*. New York: Asia Watch, 39–40.

[21] 镜报 [*Jingbao*], no. 143, 10 June 1989, in *FBIS-CHI*, 9 June 1989, 25. According to this report, ACFTU chair Ni Zhifu—generally considered closer to the conservatives than to the reformers—defended the publication of the article.

[22] *FBIS-CHI*, 22 May 1989, 80; *FBIS-CHI*, 25 May 1989, 55–56; and *FBIS-CHI*, 18 May 1989, 56.

[23] See *FBIS-CHI*, 18 May 1989, 76; and *FBIS-CHI*, 19 May 1989, 35. AFP reported, incorrectly, that the ACFTU donated 200,000 yuan to the hunger-strikers. *FBIS-CHI*, 18 May 1989, 36.

[24] *Hong Kong Standard*, 1 June 1989, in *FBIS-CHI*, 1 June 1989, 21. For further elaboration of this point, see Andrew G. Walder. 1989. 'The Political Sociology of the Beijing Upheaval of 1989.' *Problems of Communism* 35, no. 5: 32.

[25] *South China Morning Post*, 28 April 1989, in *FBIS-CHI*, 28 April 1989, 10.

[26] *South China Morning Post*, 31 May 1989, in *FBIS-CHI*, 31 May 1989, 36.

1981 (Jonathan Unger)

[1] This information is based largely on interviews in Hong Kong in the 1970s and early 1980s with farmers who had come from some forty Chinese villages. What occurred in a typical village in the 1970s is discussed in Anita Chan, Richard Madsen, and Jonathan Unger. 2009. *Chen Village: Revolution to Globalization*. Berkeley, CA: University of California Press, ch. 9.

[2] A good study of this complicated set of decisions among the national and regional leaders is Frederick C. Teiwes and Warren Sun. 2016. *Paradoxes of Post-Mao Rural Reform: Initial Steps Toward a New Chinese Countryside, 1976–1981*. Abingdon, UK: Routledge.

[3] 建国以来农业合作化史料汇编 [*A Compilation of Historical Materials on Agricultural Cooperatisation Since the Establishment of the People's Republic*]. Beijing: Zhonggong Dangshi Chubanshe, 1992, p. 1390. As an illustration of the conformity of the Chinese political system, the same set of statistics shows that, as of the close of 1984, 99.1 percent of China's production teams had adopted exactly the same new system.

[4] Jonathan Unger. 1985. 'The Decollectivization of the Chinese Countryside: A Survey of Twenty-Eight Villages.' *Pacific Affairs* 58, no. 4: 585–606. The twenty-eight interviewees came from across Guangdong Province, as well as Anhui, Fujian, Hubei, Jiangxi, Jiangxi, Shandong, and Zhejiang provinces, and a suburban Tianjin farming district.

[5] Jonathan Unger. 1986. 'De-Collectivization in a Guangdong Village: An Interview.' In *Policy Conflicts in Post-Mao China: A Documentary Survey with Analysis*, edited by John Burns and Stanley Rosen. Armonk, NY: M.E. Sharpe, 274–79.

[6] My informant from this village confided: 'I was the team accountant at the time, and I said to the team head that since the labour squads weren't working out well, let's just hand out the fields to the families. On our own initiative, we secretly did so in early 1979. I kept two account books—one for the authorities above us and one for real. I was prepared to be punished, but I felt that, with villagers going hungry, dividing up the land made the most sense.'

[7] This figure was adjusted to account for inflation. *Beijing Review*, no. 20 (16 May 1983): 7.

[8] The figure for 1983 appeared in 人民日报 [*People's Daily*], 2 May 1984, 1; and the official figure for 1984 appeared in *Beijing Review*, no. 16 (22 April 1985): iv.

[9] Sherry Kong and Jonathan Unger. 2013. 'Egalitarian Redistributions of Agricultural Land in China Through Community Consensus: Findings from Two Surveys.' *The China Journal*, no. 69: 1–25.

[10] Peter Alexander and Anita Chan. 2004. 'Does China Have An Apartheid Pass System?' *Journal of Ethnic and Migration Studies* 30, no. 4: 609–29.

[11] Jonathan Unger and Kaxton Siu. 2019. 'Chinese Migrant Factory Workers Across Four Decades: Shifts in Work Conditions, Urbanization, and Family Strategies.' *Labor History* 60, no. 6: 765–78; Kaxton Siu and Jonathan Unger. 2020. 'Work and Family Life Among Migrant Factory Workers in China and Vietnam.' *Journal of Contemporary Asia* 50, no. 3: 341–60.

[12] Qian F. Zhang and John A. Donaldson. 2008. 'The Rise of Agrarian Capitalism with Chinese Characteristics: Agricultural Modernization, Agribusiness and Collective Land Rights.' *The China Journal*, no. 60: 25–47; Shaohua Zhan. 2017. '*Hukou* Reform and Land Politics in China: Rise of a Tripartite Alliance.' *The China Journal*, no. 78: 25–49.

1983 (Mary Ann O'Donnell)

[1] Author's interview, 2019.

[2] Shuangshuang Tang and Pu Hao. 2018. 'Floaters, Settlers, and Returnees: Settlement Intention and Hukou Conversion of China's Rural Migrants.' *China Review* 18, no. 1: 11–34.

[3] Lisa Rofel. 1999. *Other Modernities: Gendered Yearnings in China after Socialism*. Berkeley, CA: University of California Press, 41–95.

[4] An Zi 安子. 1999[1991]. 青春一站: 深圳打工妹写真 [*Spring Station: True Stories of Shenzhen* Dagongmei]. Shenzhen: Haitian Publishers, ch. 5, available online at: baogaowenxue.xiusha.com/a/anzi/qcyz/index.html.

[5] Ibid.

[6] Zhang Yiwen 张一文. 2017. '中国打工文学的冲突书写—以"五个火枪手"的作品为例 [The Conflict Writings in Chinese Migrant Worker Literature: A Case Study on the Five Musketeers' Work].' PhD dissertation, Universiti Tunku Abdul Rahman, Perak, Malaysia.

[7] An Zi, *Spring Station*, 98–102.

[8] Mary Ann O'Donnell. 2006. 'The Ambiguous Possibilities of Social- and Self-Transformation in Late Socialist Worlds, or, What the Fox Might Have Said About Inhabiting Shenzhen.' *TDR: The Drama Review* 50, no. 4: 96–119.

[9] Mary Ann O'Donnell, , Winnie Wong, and Jonathan Bach. 2017. 'Experiments, Exceptions, and Extensions.' In *Learning from Shenzhen: China's Post-Mao Experiment from Special Zone to Model City*, edited by Mary Ann O'Donnell, Winnie Wong, and Jonathan Bach. Chicago, IL: University of Chicago Press, 1–19.

[10] Wu Jun 吴君. 1995. '二区到六区 [From the Second Ward to the Sixth].' 中国作家网 [*China Writers Net*], available online at: www.chinawriter.com.cn/xgzp/2009/0909/7650.html.

[11] Ibid.

[12] Author's interview, 2019.

[13] Pun Ngai. 2005. *Made in China: Women Factory Workers in a Global Workplace*. Durham, NC: Duke University Press, 184.

[14] Luo Pei 罗沛. 2018. 说三道四: 三洋情怀回顾—纪念改革开放四十周年 [*The Scoop: A Sentimental Look Back at Sanyou—To Commemorate the 40th Anniversary of Reform and Opening*]. Self-published.

[15] Chunsen Yu. 2018. '*Gongyou*, the New Dangerous Class in China?' *Made in China Journal* 3, no. 2: 36–39.

1986 (Tiantian Zheng)

[1] A slightly different version of this essay was originally published as 'The Plight of Sex Workers in China: From Criminalisation and Abuse to Activism' in *Made in China Journal* 4, no. 1: 86–91 (2019).

[2] Tiantian Zheng. 2009. *Red Lights: The Lives of Sex Workers in Postsocialist China*. Minneapolis, MN: University of Minnesota Press.

[3] Jie Andi 杰安迪. 2014. '收容教育制度下, 中国性工作者权利失去保障 [Chinese Sex Workers Have Lost the Protection of Their Rights Under the Rehabilitation Education System].' *The New York Times*, 4 January, available online at: cn.nytimes.com/china/20140104/c04laborcamps.

[4] Zheng, *Red Lights*.

[5] Elaine Jeffreys. 2004. *China, Sex and Prostitution*. London: Routledge, 151, 157.

[6] Xu Nan 徐楠. 2012. '底层性工作者生存安全调查 [An Investigation into the Survival and Safety of Underground Sex Workers].' 南方周末 [*Southern Weekend*], 28 May, available online at: www.infzm.com/content/12031.

[7] Li Yunhong 李云虹. 2007. '迟凤生, 一位律师代表的"法律眼" [Chi Susheng, the Legal Eyes of a Lawyer].' 法律与生活 [*Law and Life*], no. 4: 34–36.

[8] Xu, 'An Investigation into the Survival and Safety of Underground Sex Workers'.

[9] Li, 'Chi Susheng, the Legal Eyes of a Lawyer'.

[10] Xie Huaxing 谢华兴. 2010. '东莞卖淫女遭绳捆示众 [Sex Workers on Leash Were Paraded in Dongguan].' 广州日报 [*Guangzhou Daily*], 27 July, available online at: news.qq.com/a/20100727/000395.htm.

[11] Jie, 'Chinese Sex Workers Have Lost the Protection of Their Rights Under the Rehabilitation Education System'; David Gray. 2013. *'Swept Away': Abuses Against Sex Workers in China*. Report, 14 May. New York: Human Rights Watch, available online at: www.hrw.org/report/2013/05/14/swept-away/abuses-against-sex-workers-china.

[12] Xu, 'An Investigation into the Survival and Safety of Underground Sex Workers'.

[13] Ibid.

[14] Tiantian Zheng. 2009. *Ethnographies of Prostitution in Contemporary China: Gender Relations, HIV/AIDS, and Nationalism*. New York, NY: Palgrave Macmillan.

[15] Zheng, *Red Lights*; Xiao Er 萧尔. 2013. '权益团体促中国取消对性工作者的收容制度 [Rights Protection Groups Urge China to Abolish the Rehabilitation System Against Sex Workers].' *BBC News Chinese*, 11 December, available online at: www.bbc.com/zhongwen/simp/china/2013/12/131211_china_justice_rights.

[16] Zheng, *Red Lights*.

[17] Lily Kuo. 2013. '性工作者仍被强制"再教育" [Chinese Sex Workers Are Still Forced to Be "Reeducated"].' 青年参考 [*Youth Counsel*], 18 December, available online at: qnck.cyol.com/html/2013-12/18/nw.D110000qnck_20131218_3-27.htm.

[18] Xiao, 'Rights Protection Groups Urge China to Abolish the Rehabilitation System Against Sex Workers'.

[19] Jie, 'Chinese Sex Workers Have Lost the Protection of Their Rights Under the Rehabilitation Education System'; Kuo, 'Chinese Sex Workers Are Still Forced to Be "Reeducated"'.

[20] Di Yufei 狄雨霏. 2014. '中国法律界人士呼吁废除收容教育 [Chinese Legal Scholars Appeal to Abolish the Rehabilitation Education System].' *The New York Times*, 6 May, available online at: cn.nytimes.com/china/20140506/c06petition.

[21] Jie, 'Chinese Sex Workers Have Lost the Protection of Their Rights Under the Rehabilitation Education System'.
[22] Ibid.; Kuo, 'Chinese Sex Workers Are Still Forced to Be "Reeducated"'.
[23] Gray, *'Swept Away'*.
[24] Ibid.
[25] Ibid.
[26] State Council. 2006. 艾滋病防治条例 [*Regulations on AIDS Prevention*]. 12 February. Beijing: State Council of the People's Republic of China, available online at: www.gov.cn/ziliao/flfg/2006-02/12/content_186324.htm; State Council. 2012. 艾滋病'十二五'行动计划 [*Actions on AIDS during the '12th Five-Year Plan'*]. 13 January. Beijing: State Council of the People's Republic of China, available online at: www.gov.cn/zwgk/2012-02/29/content_2079097.htm.
[27] Zheng, *Ethnographies of Prostitution in Contemporary China*.
[28] Gray, *'Swept Away'*.
[29] On file with the author.
[30] Anthony Spires. 2011. 'Contingent Symbiosis and Civil Society in an Authoritarian State: Understanding the Survival of China's Grassroots NGOs.' *American Journal of Sociology* 117, no. 1: 1–45.
[31] Xie Fei 谢菲. 2010. '性工作者叶海燕因倡议性工作合法化被捕 [Sex Worker Ye Haiyan Was Arrested for Advocating Legalisation of Sex Work].' 苦劳网 [*Kulao Wang*], 12 August, available online at: www.coolloud.org.tw/node/53745.
[32] Ibid.
[33] Di, 'Chinese Legal Scholars Appeal to Abolish the Rehabilitation Education System'.
[34] '卖淫嫖娼人员收容教育有望废除 [There Is Hope to Abolish Rehabilitation of Sex Workers].' 澎湃 [*The Paper*], 25 December 2018, available online at: www.sohu.com/a/284371594_260616.
[35] Ibid.
[36] Ibid.
[37] Ibid.
[38] Susan Dewey, Tiantian Zheng, and Orchard Treena. 2016. *Sex Workers and Criminalization in North America and China: Ethical and Legal Issues in Exclusionary Regimes*. Berlin: Springer.

1988 (Ming-sho Ho)

[1] Frederic C. Deyo. 1989. *Beneath the Miracle: Labor Subordination in the New Asian Industrialism*. Berkeley, CA: University of California Press.
[2] Ming-sho Ho. 2014. *Working Class Formation in Taiwan: Fractured Solidarity in State-Owned Enterprises, 1945–2012*. New York, NY: Palgrave Macmillan.
[3] Ming-sho Ho. 2006. 'Challenging State Corporatism: The Politics of Taiwan's Labor Federation Movement in Taiwan.' *The China Journal*, no. 56: 107–27.
[4] Kim Moody. 1997. *Workers in a Lean World: Unions in the International Economy*. London: Verso Books; Seidman, Gay W. 1994. *Manufacturing Militance: Workers' Movements in Brazil and South Africa, 1970–1985*. Berkeley, CA: University of California Press.
[5] Chien-ju Lin. 2014. 'The Reconstructing of Industrial Relations in Taiwan's High Technology Industries.' *Journal of Contemporary Asia* 46, no. 2: 294–310.

1989 (Yueran Zhang)

[1] Andrew G. Walder and Xiaoxia Gong. 1993. 'Workers in the Tiananmen Protests: The Politics of the Beijing Workers' Autonomous Federation.' *The Australian Journal of Chinese Affairs*, no. 29: 1–29.

[2] Interview conducted in Beijing, 2017.

[3] Yao Jiachen 姚佳识. 2019. '从北京警察到六四抗暴者 [From a Cop in Beijing to a 1989 Protester].' 端传媒 [*Initium Media*], 3 June. available online at: theinitium.com/article/20190603-hongkong-6430-hongkong-sun-li-yong.

[4] Rosa Luxemburg. 1906. *The Mass Strike, the Political Party and the Trade Unions*. London: Merlin Press, available online at: www.marxists.org/archive/luxemburg/1906/mass-strike.

[5] Interview conducted in Beijing, 2017.

[6] Ibid.

[7] Li Peng 李鹏. 2010. 李鹏六四日记 [*The Critical Moment: Li Peng Diaries during the June Fourth Movement*]. El Monte, CA: West Point Publishing House.

[9] Shaoguang Wang. 1992. 'Deng Xiaoping's Reform and the Chinese Workers' Participation in the Protest Movement of 1989.' *Research in Political Economy* 13: 163–97.

[10] Maurice Meisner. 1999. *Mao's China and After: A History of the People's Republic*. New York, NY: Simon & Schuster.

[11] Wu Renhua 吴仁华. 2007. 天安门血腥清场内幕 [*An Inside Look at the Bloody Repression on Tiananmen Square*]. Available online at: www.bannedbook.org/resources/file/1786.

[12] For an example of such accounts, see The Chuang Collective. 2019. *Red Dust*. *Chuang Journal* no. 2, available online at: chuangcn.org/journal/two/red-dust/iron-to-rust.

[13] Joel Andreas. 2019. *Disenfranchised: The Rise and Fall of Industrial Citizenship in China*. New York, NY: Oxford University Press.

[14] Interviews conducted in Beijing, 2017 and 2018.

[15] Gongzilian. 1989. '告全市人民书 [A Letter to All People in the City of Beijing]' and '紧急动员起来, 攻克八十年代的巴士底狱 [Urgent Mobilisation to Storm the 1980s Bastille].'

[16] Craig Calhoun and Jeffrey N. Wasserstrom. 1999. 'Legacies of Radicalism: China's Cultural Revolution and the Democracy Movement of 1989.' *Thesis Eleven*, no. 57: 33–52.

[17] Meisner, *Mao's China and After*.

[18] Interviews conducted in Beijing, 2017 and 2018.

[19] Interview conducted in Beijing, 2018.

[20] Gongzilian. 1989. '告全国同胞书 [A Letter to All Compatriots]'.

[21] Gongzilian, 'Urgent Mobilisation to Storm the 1980s Bastille'.

[22] Meisner, *Mao's China and After*; Sheehan, Jackie. 1998. *Chinese Workers: A New History*. London: Routledge.

[23] See, for example, Huang Xiaoque 黄小雀. 2019. '房地产市场化的资本运动与疯癫 [Capital Movement and Frenzy in the Marketisation of Real Estate]', 土逗公社 [*Tootopia*], 18 April, available online at: matters.news/@tootopia/风雨云-房地产市场化的资本运动与疯癫-zdpuAquPVZ4kJobhZ9Y4Mh7Y4AyJXdtvoqNuxn-5ZRAV48YJpQ.

1993 (Anita Chan)

[1] Patricia Lanier Pence, Paula Phillips Carson, Kerry D. Carson, J. Brooke Hamilton III, and Betty Birkenmeier. 2003. 'And All Who Jumped Died: The Triangle Shirtwaist Factory Fire.' *Management Decision* 41, no. 1: 407–21, available online at: www.emerald.com/insight/content/doi/10.1108/00251740310468135/full/html.

[2] Ching Kwan Lee. 1998. *Gender and the South China Miracle: Two Worlds of Factory Women*. Berkeley, CA: University of California Press; Kaxton Siu. 2020. *Chinese Migrant Workers and Employer Domination: Comparisons with Hong Kong and Vietnam*. London: Palgrave.

[3] A search on Google Scholar revealed only one article written as early as the Zhili fire period. See Yuen-fong Woon. 1993. 'Circulatory Mobility in Post-Mao China: Temporary Migrants in Kaiping County, Pearl River Delta Region.' *International Migration Review* 27, no. 3: 578–604.

[4] Anita Chan. 2002. 'The Culture of Survival: Lives of Migrant Workers through the Prism of Private Letters.' In *Popular China: Unofficial Culture in a Globalizing Society*, edited by Perry Link, Richard Madsen, and Paul Pickowicz. Boulder, CO: Rowman & Littlefield, 163–88.

[5] Dan Katz. 2003. 'China: Santa's Little Executioners.' *Workers' Liberty*, 11 January, available online at: www.workersliberty.org/story/2017-07-26/china-santas-little-executioners.

[6] Chris King-Chi Chan. 2013. 'Community-Based Organizations for Migrant Workers' Rights: The Emergence of Labour NGOs in China.' *Community Development Journal* 48, no. 1: 6–22.

1994 (Sarah Biddulph)

[1] Feng Chen. 2007. 'Individual Rights and Collective Rights: Labor Predicament in China.' *Communist and Post-Communist Studies*, no. 40: 59–79, at p. 62.

[2] Sean Cooney, Sarah Biddulph, and Ying Zhu. 2013. *Law and Fair Work in China*. London: Routledge, 58.

[3] This research was supported by a grant from the Australian Research Council (Grant no. FT130100412).

[4] Sarah Biddulph and Sean Cooney. 1993. 'Regulation of Trade Unions in the People's Republic of China.' *Melbourne University Law Review* 19: 253–92, at p. 257.

[5] Mary Gallagher and Baohua Dong. 2011. 'Legislating Harmony: Labor Law Reform in Contemporary China.' In *From Iron Rice Bowl to Informalization: Markets, Workers and the State in a Changing China*, edited by Sarosh Kuruvilla, Ching Kwan Lee, and Mary Gallagher. Ithaca, NY: Cornell University Press, 36–60 (see p. 37).

[6] Cooney et al., *Law and Fair Work in China*, 50–51.

[7] For a discussion of the 1929 Factory Law stipulating core labour standards, see Ibid., 18–20.

[8] Ibid., 22–32.

[9] Ibid., 39; Mary Gallagher. 2007. *Contagious Capitalism: Globalization and the Politics of Labor in China*. Princeton, NJ: Princeton University Press, 63; Barry Naughton. 1999. *Growing Out of the Plan: Chinese Economic Reform 1978–1993*. Cambridge, UK: Cambridge University Press; Gallagher and Dong, 'Legislating Harmony', 39.

[10] Biddulph and Cooney, 'Regulation of Trade Unions in the People's Republic of China', 255–56.

[11] On the pilot reforms, see Gordon White. 1987. 'The Politics of Economic Reform in Chinese Industry: The Introduction of the Labour Contract System.' *The China Quarterly* 111: 375–76. The four regulations are the State Council Provisional Regulations on the Implementation of the System of Contracts of Employment in State-Run Enterprises (12 July 1986), Provisional Regulations on the Recruitment of Workers in State-Run Enterprises (12 July 1986), Provisional Regulations on the Dismissal of Workers and Employees Who Have Violated Rules of Labour Discipline in State-Run Enterprises (12 July 1986), and Provisional Regulations on Unemployment Insurance for Workers and Employees in State-Run Enterprises (12 July 1986). These regulations can be found in English in the International Labour Organisation Legislative Series 1986, available online at: www.ilo.org/public/libdoc/ilo/P/09607/09607(1986).pdf.

[12] Cooney et al., *Law and Fair Work in China*, 44, 56.

[13] Biddulph and Cooney, 'Regulation of Trade Unions in the People's Republic of China', 257.

[14] Guan Huai 关怀. 2001. 劳动法学 [*Labour Law*]. Beijing: Zhongguo Renmin Daxue Chubanshe, 145.

[15] Ibid., 145; Cooney et al., *Law and Fair Work in China*, 51; Ann Kent. 1999. *China, the United Nations, and Human Rights: The Limits of Compliance*. Philadelphia, PA: University of Pennsylvania Press.

[16] Ronald Brown. 2009. *Understanding Labor and Employment Law in China*. Cambridge, UK: Cambridge University Press, 23–25; Cooney et al., *Law and Fair Work in China*, 61–64.

[17] Eli Friedman and Ching Kwan Lee. 2010. 'Remaking the World of Chinese Labour: A 30 Year Retrospective.' *British Journal of Industrial Relations* 48, no. 3: 507–33.

[18] Yiwei Jiang. 1987. 'Jiang Yiwei Discusses the Socialist Enterprise Model.' *Economic Management*, no. 1; White, 'The Politics of Economic Reform in Chinese Industry', 365–89.

[19] Cooney et al., *Law and Fair Work in China*, 56–57.

[20] Gallagher and Dong, 'Legislating Harmony', 40.

[21] Biddulph and Cooney, 'Regulation of Trade Unions in the People's Republic of China', 258.

[22] Cooney et al., *Law and Fair Work in China*, 67–69.

[23] The Labour Law's provisions on collective contracts are regulated in more detail under the 2004 Provisions on Collective Contracts issued by the Ministry of Labour and Social Security (now the Ministry of Human Resources and Social Security).

[24] Simon Clarke, Chang-Hee Lee, and Qi Li. 2004. 'Collective Consultation and Industrial Relations in China.' *British Journal of Industrial Relations* 42, no. 2: 235–54, 242; Cooney et al., *Law and Fair Work in China*, 96; Feng Chen. 2003. 'Between the State and Labour: The Conflict of Chinese Trade Unions' Double Identity in Market Reform.' *The China Quarterly* 176: 1006–28; Sarah Biddulph. 2012. 'Responding to Industrial Unrest in China: Prospects for Strengthening the Role of Collective Bargaining.' *Sydney Law Review* 34, no. 1: 35–63.

[25] Biddulph, 'Responding to Industrial Unrest in China', 49.

[26] Bill Taylor, Kai Chang, and Qi Li. 2003. *Industrial Relations in China*. Cheltenham, UK: Edward Elgar, 190–95; Clarke et al., 'Collective Consultation and Industrial Relations in China', 249–50; Ronald Brown. 2006. 'China's Collective Contract Provisions: Can Collective Negotiations Embody Collective Bargaining?' *Duke Journal of Comparative and International Law* 16: 35–77, at pp. 54–56.

[27] Biddulph, 'Responding to Industrial Unrest in China', 62; Anita Chan. 1993. 'Revolution or Corporatism: China's Workers and Trade Unions in Post-Mao China.' *The Australian Journal of Chinese Affairs* 29, no. 1: 31–61; Anita Chan. 2001. *China's Workers Under Assault*. Armonk, NY: M.E. Sharpe.

[28] See the discussion in Cooney et al., *Law and Fair Work in China*, 99, 145–47.

[29] Ibid., 53–55.

[30] Ibid.

[31] Aaron Halegua. 2008. 'Getting Paid: Processing the Labor Disputes of China's Migrant Workers.' *Berkeley Journal of International Law* 26, no. 1: 254–322.

[32] Cooney et al., *Law and Fair Work in China*, 94–95.

[33] Sean Cooney. 2007. 'Making Chinese Labor Law Work: The Prospects for Regulatory Innovation in the People's Republic of China.' *Fordham International Law Journal* 30, no. 4: 1050–97.

[34] Mary Gallagher. 2005. '"Use the Law as Your Weapon!": Institutional Change and Legal Mobilization in China.' In *Engaging the Law in China*, edited by Neil Diamant, Stanley Lubman, and Kevin J. O'Brien. Stanford, CA: Stanford University Press, 54–83.

[35] Cooney et al., *Law and Fair Work in China*, 64–66.

[36] Gallagher and Dong, 'Legislating Harmony', 42–44.

[37] Cooney et al., *Law and Fair Work in China*, 111–13.

[38] Halegua, 'Getting Paid'; Aaron Halegua. 2016. *Who Will Represent China's Workers? Lawyers, Legal Aid and the Enforcement of Labor Rights*, October. New York University School of Law US, Asia Law Institute, available online at: papers.ssrn.com/sol3/papers.cfm?abstract_id=2845977.

[39] Biddulph and Cooney, 'Regulation of Trade Unions in the People's Republic of China'; Cooney et al., *Law and Fair Work in China*, 67–69; Jude Howell. 2008. 'The All-China Federation of Trade Unions Beyond Reform? Slow March of Direct Elections.' *The China Quarterly* 196: 845–63; Simon Clarke and Tim Pringle. 2009. 'Can Party-Led Trade Unions Represent Their Members?' *Post-Communist Economies* 21, no. 1: 85–101.

[40] Cooney et al., *Law and Fair Work in China*, 86; Virginia Harper Ho. 2009. 'From Contracts to Compliance? An Early Look at Implementation Under China's New Labor Legislation.' *Columbia Journal of Asian Law* 23: 35–107. In relation to legal costs and risks in enforcement, see Sarah Biddulph. 2019. 'Bureaucratic Inertia and Its Impact on Workplace Safety Regulation.' In *Good Governance in Economic Development: International Norms and Chinese Perspectives*, edited by Sarah Biddulph and Ljiljana Biukovic, 291–322. Vancouver: University of British Columbia Press.

[41] Sarah Biddulph, Sean Cooney, and Ying Zhu. 2012. 'Rule of Law with Chinese Characteristics: The Role of Campaigns in Law-Making.' *Law & Policy* 34, no. 4: 373–401.

[42] Isabelle Thireau and Linshan Hua. 2005. 'One Law, Two Interpretations: Mobilizing the Labor Law in Arbitration Committees and in Letters and Visits Offices.' In *Engaging the Law in China: State, Society and Possibilities for Justice*, edited by Neil Diamant, Stanley Lubman, and Kevin J. O'Brien. Stanford, CA: Stanford University Press, 84–107.

[43] Proposed complementary legislation included a Labour Contract Law (1995), Employment Promotion Law (1996), Wages Law (1997), and a Labour Disputes Management Law (1999).

[44] Biddulph et al., 'Rule of Law with Chinese Characteristics'; Sean Cooney, Sarah Biddulph, Kungang Li, and Ying Zhu. 2007. 'China's New Labour Contract Law: Responding to the Growing Complexity of Labour Relations in the PRC.' *University of New South Wales Law Journal* 30, no. 3: 786–801.

[45] Sarah Biddulph. 2017. 'Structuring China's Engagement with International Human Rights: The Case of Wage Protection Law and Practice.' In *Local Engagement with International Economic Law and Human Rights*, edited by Potter Pitman and Ljiljana Biukovic. Northampton, UK: Edward Elgar, 236–63 (see pp. 249–50).

1995 (Kevin Lin)

[1] Human Rights Watch. *Selected Prisoner Cases: China and Tibet.* New York, NY: Human Rights Watch, available online at: www.hrw.org/legacy/campaigns/china-98/prisoner.htm.

[2] '劉念春在九十年代的抗爭 [Liu Nianchun's Resistance in the 1990s].' Hayward, CA: Chinese Democracy Education Foundation, available online at: www.cdef.org/Default.aspx?tabid=140&language=en-US.

[3] Andrew Walder and Gong Xiaoxia. 1993. 'Workers in the Tiananmen Protests: The Politics of the Beijing Workers' Autonomous Federation.' *The Australian Journal of Chinese Affairs* 29: 1–29.

[4] Trini Wing-yue Leung. 1998. 'The Politics of Labour Rebellions in China: 1989–1994.' PhD dissertation, Hong Kong University, 269.

[5] Ibid.

[6] *China Labour Bulletin*, December 1994, 18.

[7] *China Labour Bulletin*, October 1994, 1–5.

[8] *China Labour Bulletin*, April 1994, 12–13.

[9] Ibid., 14–16.

[10] Anita Chan. 2001. *China's Workers Under Assault. The Exploitation of Labor in a Globalizing Economy.* London: M.E. Sharpe, 165–72.

[11] *China Labour Bulletin*, July 1994, 6.

[12] Ibid., 14.

[13] Chris King-Chi Chan. 2013. 'Contesting Class Organization: Migrant Workers' Strikes in China's Pearl River Delta, 1978–2010.' *International Labor and Working-Class History* 83: 112–36.

1995 (Jude Howell)

[1] Jude Howell. 2003. 'Women's Organisations and Civil Society in China.' *International Feminist Journal of Politics* 5, no. 2: 191–215.
[2] Chris King-Chi Chan. 2013. 'Community-Based Organizations for Migrant Workers' Rights: The Emergence of Labour NGOs in China.' *Community Development Journal* 48, no. 1: 6–22; Yi Xu. 2013. 'Labour Non-Governmental Organisations in China: Mobilising Rural Migrant Workers.' *Journal of Industrial Relations* 55, no. 2: 243–59.
[3] Ivan Franceschini and Kevin Lin. 2019. 'Labour NGOs in China: From Legal Mobilisation to Collective Struggle (and Back?).' *China Perspectives*, no. 1/2019: 75.
[4] Paul Harper. 1969. 'The Party and the Unions in Communist China.' *The China Quarterly*, no. 37: 84–119.
[5] Xu, 'Labour Non-Governmental Organisations in China'.
[6] Chloé Froissart. 2011. 'NGOs Defending Migrant Workers' Rights.' *China Perspectives*, no. 2: 18–25.
[7] Pun Ngai. 2005. 'Global Production, Company Codes of Conduct and Labour Conditions in China: A Case Study of Two Factories.' *The China Journal*, no. 54: 101–13.
[8] Mujun Zhou and Guowei Yan. 2020. 'Advocating Workers' Collective Rights: The Prospects and Constraints Facing "Collective Bargaining" NGOs in the Pearl River Delta, 2011–2015.' *Development and Change* 51, no. 4: 1044–66.
[9] Ching Kwan Lee and Yuan Shen. 2011. '"The Anti-Solidarity Machine?" Labour Non-Governmental Organisations in China.' In *From Iron Rice Bowl to Informalization: Markets, Workers and the State in a Changing China*, edited by Sarosh Kuruvilla, Ching Kwan Lee, and Mary E. Gallagher. Ithaca, NY: Cornell University Press, 173–87.
[10] Tim Pringle. 2018. 'A Solidarity Machine? Hong Kong Labour NGOs in Guangdong.' *Critical Sociology* 44, nos 4–5: 661–75.
[11] Ivan Franceschini and Elisa Nesossi. 2018. 'State Repression of Chinese Labor NGOs: A Chilling Effect?' *The China Journal*, no. 80: 111–29.
[12] Feng Chen and Mengxiao Tang. 2013. 'Labour Conflicts in China: Typologies and Their Implications.' *Asian Survey* 53, no. 3: 559–83.
[13] Jie Lei and Chak Kwan Chan (eds). 2018. *China's Social Welfare Revolution: Contracting Out Social Services*. London: Routledge.
[14] Jude Howell. 2015. 'Shall We Dance? Welfarist Incorporation and the Politics of State–Labour NGO Relations.' *The China Quarterly*, no. 223: 702–23.

1997 (William Hurst)

[1] William Hurst. 2009. *The Chinese Worker After Socialism*. Cambridge, UK: Cambridge University Press, 40.
[2] Ibid., 43.
[3] Ibid., 44.
[4] Ibid., 45–48.
[5] Ibid., 45.

[6] The speech is included in 中国共产党第十五次全国代表大会文件汇编 [*Collected Documents of the Fifteenth National Congress of the Chinese Communist Party*]. Beijing: Renmin Chubanshe (1997), 23–24. Translated in Hurst, *The Chinese Worker After Socialism*, 49.

[7] Ministry of Labour and Social Security and Party Literature Research Centre of the Central Committee of the Chinese Communist Party (eds). 2002. 新时期劳动和社会保障重要文献选编 [*Selection of Important Documents on Labour and Social Security in the New Period*]. Beijing: Zhongguo Shehui Baozhang Chubanshe and Zhongyang Wenxian Chubanshe, 278–79.

[8] Hurst, *The Chinese Worker After Socialism*, 50–51.

[9] Dorothy J. Solinger. 2001. 'Why We Cannot Count the "Unemployed"'. *The China Quarterly* 167: 671–88.

[10] Hurst, *The Chinese Worker After Socialism*, 51–53.

[11] Ibid., 55–56.

[12] Jin Zeng. 2010. 'Political Compromises: The Privatization of Small and Medium-Sized Public Enterprises in China.' *Journal of Chinese Political Science* 15, no. 3: 257–59.

[13] For good examples of such microlevel analysis, see Anita Chan and Jonathan Unger. 2009. 'A Chinese State Enterprise Under the Reforms: What Model of Capitalism?' *The China Journal* 62: 1–26; Sun Sheng Han and Clifton Pannell. 1999. 'The Geography of Privatization in China.' *Economic Geography* 75, no. 3: 272–96; Samuel P.S. Ho, Paul Bowles, and Xiaoyuan Dong. 2003. '"Letting Go of the Small": An Analysis of the Privatization of Rural Enterprises in Jiangsu and Shandong.' *Journal of Development Studies* 39, no. 4: 1–26; and several chapters in Jean C. Oi and Andrew G. Walder (eds). 1999. *Property Rights and Economic Reform in China*. Stanford, CA: Stanford University Press.

[14] Hurst, *The Chinese Worker After Socialism*, 54.

[15] William Hurst. 2015. 'Grasping the Large and Releasing the Small: A Bottom-Up Perspective on Reform in a County-Level Enterprise.' In *Local Governance Innovation in China: Experimentation, Diffusion, and Defiance*, edited by Jessica C. Teets and William Hurst. Abingdon, UK: Routledge, 103–16.

[16] See William Hurst. 2011. 'Rebuilding the Urban Chinese Welfare State: Authoritarian Accommodation and Multi-Level Governance.' *China Perspectives* 2011/2: 40–41.

[17] For the most comprehensive work on this suite of policy reforms, see Jane Duckett. 2012. *The Chinese State's Retreat from Health: Policy and the Politics of Retrenchment*. London: Routledge; Mark W. Frazier. 2010. *Socialist Insecurity: Pensions and the Politics of Uneven Development in China*. Ithaca, NY: Cornell University Press; Daniel R. Hammond. 2019. *Politics and Policy in China's Social Assistance Reform: Providing for the Poor?* Edinburgh: Edinburgh University Press; Dorothy J. Solinger and Yiyang Hu. 2012. 'Welfare, Wealth, and Poverty in Urban China: The *Dibao* and its Differential Disbursement.' *The China Quarterly* 211: 741–64.

[18] William Hurst and Christian Sorace. 2011. 'Recession and the Politics of Class and Production in China.' *New Political Science* 33, no. 4: 514, 521–23; see also William Hurst. 2015. 'China's Labor Divided.' *Dissent Magazine* (Spring): 127–35.

[19] See, for example, Elizabeth J. Perry. 1993. *Shanghai on Strike: The Politics of Chinese Labor*. Stanford, CA: Stanford University Press.

2001 (Dorothy J. Solinger)

[1] This essay draws from the author's study 'China's Urban Workers and the WTO', published in *The China Journal* 49 (January 2003): 61–87.

[2] 'WTO Cost: 40 Million Jobs', *Far Eastern Economic Review*, 5 October 2000, 10.

[3] Tan Youlin 谭友林. 2001. '中国劳动力结构的区域差异研究 [An Analysis of the Regional Diversity of the Chinese Labour Force].' 人口与经济 [*Population and Economy*], no. 1: 56.

[4] Layoffs from rural firms were 80.5 percent in Liaoning, 70 percent in Jilin and 59 percent in Heilongjiang. See Hu Angang 胡鞍钢. 1999. 跨入新世纪的最大挑战: 我国进入高失业阶段 [*The Biggest Challenge Straddling the New Century: Our Country Will Enter a Stage of High Unemployment*]. Report no. 48, 9 July. Beijing: Chinese Academy of Science and Tsinghua University National Conditions Research Centre, 2.

[5] Mo Rong 莫荣. 2000. '加入WTO与我国的就业 [Entering the WTO and Our Country's Employment].' 劳动保障通讯 [*Labour Insurance Bulletin*], no. 4: 19.

[6] Harold K. Jacobson and Michel Oksenberg. 1990. *China's Participation in the IMF, the World Bank, and GATT: Toward a Global Economic Order*. Ann Arbor, MI: University of Michigan Press, 51, 83–86, 92–94.

[7] Margaret M. Pearson. 1999. 'China's Integration into the International Trade Regime.' In *China Joins the World: Progress and Prospects*, edited by Elizabeth Economy and Michel Oksenberg. New York, NY: Council on Foreign Relations, 166, 169, 176.

[8] David M. Lampton. 2001. *Same Bed, Different Dreams: Managing US–China Relations, 1989–2000*. Berkeley, CA: University of California Press, 181–82; *The Financial Times*, 15 March 2002.

[9] David Zweig. 2002. *Internationalizing China: Domestic Interests and Global Linkages*. Ithaca, NY: Cornell University Press, 36.

[10] State firm losses grew from 34.9 billion yuan in 1990 to 74.4 billion yuan seven years later. See Lampton, *Same Bed, Different Dreams*, 177.

[11] Zhang Chuanhong 张传宏. 2001. '下岗向失业并轨面临"六难" [Efforts to Coordinate between Layoffs and Unemployment are Facing "Six Difficulties"].' 劳动保障通讯 [*Labour Insurance Bulletin*], no. 5: 32.

[12] Mo Rong 莫荣. 2001. '就业: 新世纪面临的挑战与抉择 [Employment: The Challenge and Choice that the New Century Is Facing].' In *2001年: 中国社会形势分析与预测* [*Year 2001: Analysis and Forecast of China's Society*], edited by Li Peilin 李培林, Huang Ping 黄平, and Lu Jianhua 陆建华. Beijing, Shehui Kexue Wenxian Chubanshe, 222.

[13] '劳动力市场三化建设试点情况 [The Situation of Experimental Trials on the Three Transformations in the Labour Market].' 劳动保障通讯 [*Labour Insurance Bulletin*], no. 3(2001): 40.

[14] Zhang Xiangchen 张向晨. 2002. Deputy Director-General of WTO Affairs, Ministry of Foreign Trade and Economic Cooperation. Lecture given at East Asian Institute, Columbia University, New York, 13 March.

[15] Tang Wenlin 唐文琳. 2000. 应对WTO—中国九大行业的危机与对策 [*Facing WTO: The Crisis in Nine Large Chinese Sectors and Countermeasures*]. Nanning: Guangxi Renmin Chubanshe, 145–64.

[16] *South China Morning Post*, 31 October 2002.

[17] *Summary of World Broadcasts*, FE/3749, p. G/9, 28 January 2000, from Xinhua News Agency, 25 January 2000.

[18] Interview, Wuhan Textile Association, 29 October 2001; Yin Zengtao 殷增涛. 2000. '中国加入世界贸易组织对武汉经济的影响及对策 [The Influence on Wuhan's Economy of China Entering the WTO, and Countermeasures].' 社会科学动态 [*Social Science Trends*], no. 6: 37.

[19] Sun Huaibin 孙淮滨. 2000. '入世对我国纺织工业的影响及对策 [The Influence of Entering the WTO on Our Textile Industry, and Countermeasures].' 内部参阅 [*Internal Consultations*] 5, no. 499(4 February): 5.

[20] Wang Shaoguang 王绍光. 2001. '谁将是加入WTO后的赢家和输家 [Who Will Be Winners and Losers After Entering WTO]?' 改革内参 [*Reform Internal Reference*], no. 15: 10, 12.

[21] Thomas G. Rawski. 2003. 'Recent Developments in China's Labour Economy,' available online at: ssrn.com/abstract=907450 or dx.doi.org/10.2139/ssrn.907450.

[22] H. Lyman Miller. 1999. 'Institutions in Chinese Politics: Trends and Prospects.' In *China's Future: Implications for US Interests—Conference Report*, September. Washington, DC: Library of Congress, 45.

[23] Joseph Fewsmith. 1999. 'China in 1998: Tacking to Stay the Course.' *Asian Survey* 39, no. 1: 100.

[24] '10城市企业下岗职工和离退休人员基本状况的抽样调查 [A Sample Investigation of the Situation of 10 Cities' Laid-Off Enterprise Employees and Retirees].' 中国劳动 [*China Labour*], no. 12(2000): 51–53.

[25] Hu Angang 胡鞍钢. n.d. 实施就业优先战略 为人民提供更多的工作岗位 [*Implement the Employment Preference Strategy and Supply More Jobs to the People*]. Report no. 78. Beijing: Chinese Academy of Science and Tsinghua University National Conditions Research Centre. According to official data, the 1999 national average per capita annual urban income was 5,888.77 yuan.

[26] Qiao Jian 乔健. 2001. '加入WTO背景下的中国职工状况 [The Condition of China's Staff and Workers Against the Background of Entering WTO]', in Li et al., *Year 2001*, 315.

[27] Wang Depei 王德培. 2001 '"三民"与"二次改革" ["Three Types of People" and the "Second Reform"].' 改革内参 [*Reform Internal Reference*], no. 7: 25. China laid off 55 million people from 1995 to mid-2002 (according to Hu Angang 胡鞍钢, 华夏文摘 [*China News Digest*], 9 July 2002).

[28] All-China Federation of Trade Unions Safety Work Department. 2001. '关于下岗职工劳动关系处理及社会保障接续问题的调查 [Investigation on Handling Laid-Off Staff and Workers' Labour Relations and Social Security Continuation].' 中国工运 [*Chinese Labour Movement*], no. 5: 14.

[29] Cited in Terence Tan. 2002. 'China's Jobless Can't Get New Work.' *Straits Times*, 27 September.

[30] Yi Yao 易杳. 2001. '加入WTO对中国就业的影响 [How Joining the WTO Impacted China's Employment].' 瞭望新闻周刊 [*Outlook News Weekly*], no. 46(12 November): 23.

[31] Yang Tuan 杨团 and Ge Shundao 葛道顺. 2001. '社区公共服务社—消除边缘性的社会政策研究 [Community Public Service: Social Policy Research on Eliminating Marginality].' Paper presented to the Conference on Social Exclusion and Marginality

in Chinese Societies, Centre for Social Policy Studies, Hong Kong Polytechnic University and Social Policy Research Centre, Institute of Sociology, Chinese Academy of Social Sciences, Beijing, Hong Kong, November, 2.

[32] Dorothy J. Solinger. 2006. 'The Creation of a New Underclass in China and its Implications.' *Environment & Urbanization* 18, no. 1: 177–93.

2002 (Ching Kwan Lee)

[1] Murray Scot Tanner. 2004. 'Protests Now Flourish in China.' *International Herald Tribune*, 2 June.

[2] Minxin Pei. 2003. 'Rights and Resistance: The Changing Contexts of the Dissident Movement.' In *Chinese Society: Change, Conflict, and Resistance*, edited by Elizabeth J. Perry and Mark Selden, 2nd edn. New York, NY: Routledge, 29.

[3] Josephine Ma. 2004. 'Three Million Took Part in Surging Protests Last Year.' *South China Morning Post*, 8 June.

[4] Qiao Jian 乔健 and Jiang Ying 姜颖. 2005. '市场化过程中的劳动争议和劳工群体性事件分析 [An Analysis of Labour Disputes and Labour-Related Mass Incidents in the Process of Marketisation].' In *2005年: 中国社会形势分析与预测* [*2005: Analysis and Forecast of China's Social Development*], edited by Ru Xin 汝信, Lu Xueyi 陆学艺, and Li Peilin 李培林. Beijing: Shehui Kexue Wenxian Chubanshe, 300.

[5] Howard French. 2005. 'Land of 74,000 Protests (But Little is Ever Fixed).' *The New York Times*, 24 August; Joseph Kahn. 2005. 'Pace and Scope of Protests in China Accelerated in '05.' *The New York Times*, 20 January.

[6] Research Department of the All-China Federation of Trade Unions. 2002. 中国工会统计年鉴(2001年) [*Chinese Trade Union Statistics Yearbook (2001)*]. Beijing: Zhongguo Tongji Chubanshe, 67, 90.

[7] John Giles, Albert Park, and Cai Fang. 2006. 'How Has Economic Restructuring Affected China's Urban Workers?' *China Quarterly* 185: 61–95.

[8] There are various estimates of the size of the unemployed population. Li Qiang, a leading sociologist on unemployment surveys, put the figure at 27.3 million in 2002. See Li Qiang, 'Urban Unemployment in China and Its Countermeasures.' Manuscript, Tsinghua University, Beijing. The Labour Science Institute of the Ministry of Labour and Social Security gives an accumulated total of 25 million laid-off workers and 12.8 million unemployed between 1998 and 2001. See Labour Science Research Institute, Ministry of Labour and Social Security of China. 2003. *2002年中国就业报告* [*Blue Book of Chinese Employment, 2002*]. Beijing: Zhongguo Laodong Shehui Baozhang Chubanshe, 25.

[9] Feng Chen. 2003. 'Industrial Restructuring and Workers' Resistance in China.' *Modern China* 29, no. 2: 237–62; Elizabeth J. Perry. 1999. 'Crime, Corruption, and Contention.' In *The Paradox of China's Post-Mao Reform*, edited by Merle Goldman and Roderick MacFarquhar, Cambridge, MA: Harvard University Press, 308–32; William Hurst and Kevin J. O'Brien. 2002. 'China's Contentious Pensioners.' *China Quarterly* 170: 345–60.

[10] Göran Therborn. 1980. *The Ideology of Power and the Power of Ideology*. London: Verso Books.

2003 (Chloé Froissart)

[1] Chen Feng 陈峰 and Wang Lei 王雷. 2003. '一大学毕业生因无暂住证被收容遭毒打致死 [A University Graduate Was Detained for Failing to Present His Temporary Residence Permit and Beaten to Death].' 南方都市报 [*Southern Metropolis News*], 25 April, available online at: news.sina.com.cn/s/2003-04-25/09501015845.shtml.

[2] For instance, Jiang Zemin remained the chairman of the Central Military Commission.

[3] General Office of the State Council. 2003. 关于做好农民进城务工就业管理和服务工作的通知 [*Notice On Doing a Good Job in Employment Management and Services to Peasant Workers in Cities*]. 16 January. Beijing: State Council of the People's Republic of China.

[4] Chloé Froissart. 2013. *La Chine et ses migrants: La conquête d'une citoyenneté* [*China and Its Migrants: The Conquest of Citizenship*]. Rennes: Presses Universitaires des Rennes, 119–28, 323.

[5] Ibid., 321–23; State Planning Commission. 2001. 关于全面清理整顿外出或外来务工人员收费的通知 [*Notice to Comprehensively Clean Up and Rectify the Taxes Charged on Outgoing or Migrant Workers*]. Beijing: Ministry of Finance.

[6] On investigative journalism in that period, see, for example, Ying Chan. 2010. 'The Journalism Tradition.' In *Investigative Journalism in China*, edited by David Bandurski and Martin Hala. Hong Kong: Hong Kong University Press, 1–17.

[7] Zi Yue 子曰. 2003. '评论: 谁为一个公民的非正常死亡负责? [Editorial: Who Will Take Responsibility for the Suspicious Death of a Citizen?].' 南方都市报 [*Southern Metropolis News*], 25 April, available online at: news.sina.com.cn/s/2003-04-25/09531015847.shtml.

[8] Keith J. Hand. 2006. 'Using the Law for a Righteous Purpose: The Sun Zhigang Incident and Evolving Forms of Citizen Action in the People's Republic of China.' *Columbia Journal of Transnational Law* 45, no. 1: 122.

[9] Xiao Qiang. 2004. '"Online Uprisings" Are Changing China.' *Gulf News*, 6 August, available online at: gulfnews.com/uae/online-uprisings-are-changing-china-1.329063.

[10] Isabelle Thireau and Linshan Hua. 2005. 'De l'épreuve publique à la reconnaissance d'un public: le scandale Sun Zhigang [From Public Event to Public Recognition: The Sun Zhigang Scandal].' *Politix* 71: 141–44.

[11] Froissart, *China and Its Migrants*, 325–26.

[12] Pierre Haski. 2003. 'La Chine mate ses matons [China Tames its Guards].' *Libération*, 14 June.

[13] Siew Ying Leu. 2003. 'Scrapping of Migrant Laws Praised.' *South China Morning Post*, 20 June.

[14] Froissart, *China and Its Migrants*, 324–28.

[15] Erik Eckholm. 2003. 'Petitioners Urge China to Enforce Legal Rights.' *The New York Times*, 2 June.

[16] Ibid.

[17] Citation from T.H. Marshall. 1981. *Citizenship and Social Class and Other Essays*. London: Heinemann, 10.

[18] Hand, 'Using the Law for a Righteous Purpose', 126–27.

[19] Froissart, *China and Its Migrants*, 328–31.

[20] Ibid.

[21] Hand, 'Using the Law for a Righteous Purpose', 141–42.

[22] Reporters Without Borders. 2004. 'Editor-in-Chief Dismissed: Crackdown on Guangzhou Press Continues.' *International Freedom of Expression Exchange*, 27 October, available online at: ifex.org/editor-in-chief-dismissed-crackdown-on-guangzhou-press-continues.

[23] Froissart, *China and Its Migrants*, 332–34.

[24] Hand, 'Using the Law for a Righteous Purpose', 158–92.

2007 (Ivan Franceschini)

[1] A shorter version of this essay was originally published in the *Made in China Journal* 2, no. 2: 16–21.

[2] See Dou Jiangming's Weibo account, available online at: weibo.com/u/1197365250.

[3] Zhu Hongjun 朱红军. 2007. '少年血泪铺就黑工之路 [The Tears of Blood of Young Boys Pave the Road of Black Labour].' 南方周末 [*Southern Weekend*], 14 June, available online at: www.infzm.com/content/1422.

[4] Fu Zhenzhong 付振中. 2007. '我亲手揭开山西黑砖窑的内幕 [I Personally Exposed the Inside Story of the Black Brick Kilns of Shanxi].' The account remains available on some blogs—for instance, see: sbhhong.blog.sohu.com/70587811.html.

[5] Zhu Hongjun 朱红军. 2007. '山西黑砖窑风暴被她点燃了 [The Black Brick Kilns Storm Was Triggered by Her].' 南方周末 [*Southern Weekend*], 27 July, available online at: www.infzm.com/content/5662.

[6] On 27 May 2007, the local police rescued thirty-one slaves from this kiln. Through their testimonies, it was discovered that another mentally disabled worker at the kiln had been beaten nearly to death and then buried alive. On the kiln in Caosheng Village, see Zhu Hongjun 朱红军. 2007. '洪洞黑砖窑身世调查 [Investigation of the Black Brick Kiln in Hongdong County].' 南方周末 [*Southern Weekend*], 21 July, A1–A2.

[7] Author's interview, May 2008.

[8] Ibid.

[9] Chen Jiang 陈江. 2007. '黑窑奴工最后一站 [The Last Stop for the Slaves of the Black Kiln].' 南都周刊 [*Southern City Metropolitan Weekly*], no. 138 (20 July): A16–A28.

[10] Guards occupied a privileged position in the microcosm of the kilns. One of the parents whom I interviewed stated that he hoped his missing son had been promoted to guard so that he would not have suffered.

[11] Chen, 'The Last Stop for the Slaves of the Black Kiln'.

[12] '洪洞黑砖窑主犯被判死刑 [The Prime Culprit of the Hongdong Black Brick Kiln Has Been Sentenced to Death].' 人民日报 [*People's Daily*], 18 July 2007, 5.

[13] Zhu, 'Investigation of the Black Brick Kiln in Hongdong County'. In June 2007, the authorities relieved Wang Dongji of his responsibilities both in the Party and in the administration.

[14] '王东已: 我却有失职之罪 [Wang Dongji: I Am Really Guilty of Having Neglected My Duty].' 新京报 [*The Beijing News*], 9 November 2007, A66.

[15] Shen Haijun spent three months at the kiln, suffering repeated beatings. His legs were broken by the guards and, because his wounds were not treated, he became disabled. See Liu Jianzhuang 刘建庄. 2007. '我为山西黑砖窑被害人打官司 [I Am Suing On Behalf of the Victims of the Shanxi Black Brick Kilns].' 法律与生活 [*Law and Life*], no. 16 (August): 47–48.

[16] Ma Changbo 马昌博. 2007. '风暴眼中的山西官员 [The Shanxi Officials in the Eye of the Storm].' 南方周末 [*Southern Weekend*], 5 July, A2.

[17] Zhu Hongjun 朱红军. 2007. '被再次转卖后,少年朱广辉回家了！ [After Having **Been** Sold Again, Zhu Guanghui Finally Returned Home!].' 南方周末 [*Southern Weekend*], 21 June, A3.

[18] Wei Min 魏敏 and Li Mei 李梅. 2004. '长安少年断脚案永济庭审目击 [Witness Account of the Trial of the Case of the Young Boy from Chang'an Whose Feet Were Amputated].' 西安晚报 [*Xi'an Evening News*], 8 April, 6.

[19] In April 2004, the owner of the kiln where Zhang had been forced to work was sentenced to three years in prison and ordered to pay 495,000 yuan as compensation—money he never paid. Only at the end of August 2009, after the 'black brick kilns scandal' had rocked China, did Zhang receive compensation of 380,000 yuan, paid by the local governments of Yongji City and Chang'an District in Xi'an. Until then, he had been begging on the streets of Xi'an to survive. '断脚少年张徐波案赔偿到位 [The Compensation for the Case of Zhang Xubo Has Arrived].' 黄河晨报 [*Yellow River Morning News*], 31 August 2009, 2.

[20] Wang Yongxia 王永霞. 2007. '联合工作组通报山西黑砖窑事件查处情况 [Report of the Joint Work Group on the Investigation of the Black Brick Kilns of Shanxi].' 新华 [*Xinhua*], 13 August, available online at: news.sina.com.cn/c/2007-08-13/164013653720.shtml.

[21] See the transcript of the TV program 经济半小时 [*Economy Half Hour*], 27 December 2007, available online at: wenku.baidu.com/view/9d00c7d549649b6648d7478f.html.

[22] Cheng Shihua 程士华. 2009. '安徽界首警方救出30余名在黑砖窑做苦力的智障人员 [The Police in Jieshou Rescued Over 30 People with Mental Problems Who Were Used as Coolies in the Black Brick Kilns].' 新华 [*Xinhua*], 21 May, available online at: news.hsw.cn/system/2009/05/21/050184724.shtml; Cheng Shihua 程士华. 2009. '安徽界首黑砖窑事件调查：智障者遭贩卖成劳力 [Investigation of the Case of the Black Brick Kiln in Jieshou: People with Mental Disabilities Were Sold as Workers].' 经济参考报 [*Economic Information Daily*], 22 July, available online at: news.sina.com.cn/c/sd/2009-07-22/092818272706.shtml.

[23] '重庆男子在云南当窑奴的112天 [A Man from Chongqing Spent 112 Days as a Slave in a Yunnan Kiln].' 重庆晚报 [*Chongqing Evening News*], 24 August 2010, 17.

[24] Ran Jin 冉金. 2010. '奴工背后的"善人"：四川渠县残疾人自强对调查 [The "Philanthropists" Behind the Slaves: An Investigation Into the Disabled Self-Strengthening Team in Qu County].' 南方周末 [*Southern Weekend*], 23 December, available online at: www.infzm.com/content/53856.

[25] Shen Zizhong 申子仲 and Qiu Yanbo 邱延波. 2011. '一个记者的四天的智障奴工体验 [A Journalist's Experience of Four Days as a Mentally Disabled Slave].' 东方今报 [*Oriental Daily News*], 6 September, available online at: roll.sohu.com/20110906/n318501671.shtml.

[26] Zou Xiaohua 邹晓华. 2017. '男子被骗入黑砖窑和传销：失散24年后凭口音寻亲 [A Man Was Tricked into the Black Brick Kilns and a Pyramid Scheme: After Disappearing for 24 Years He Found His Relatives Thanks to His Accent].' 江西日报 [*Jiangxi*

Daily], 12 April, available online at: www.dzwww.com/xinwen/shehuixinwen/201704/t20170412_15760093.htm; Li Shengpeng 李圣鹏. 2016. '"黑砖窑"往事：被夺去自由的11年 [The Past of the Black Brick Kilns: 11 Years Without Freedom].' 奔流杂志 [*Torrent Magazine*], 26 September, available online at: renjian.163.com/16/0926/19/C1TN9CDK000187OR.html; Gao Dazheng 高大正 and Zhang Zedong 张泽东. 2015. '男子被骗黑砖窑21年 一路乞讨回云南不知家在哪 [A Man Was Cheated into the Black Brick Kilns for 21 Years: He Begged All the Way Back to Yunnan Not Knowing Where His House Was].' 昆明信息港 [*Kunming Information Harbour*], 21 August, available online at: news.sohu.com/20150821/n419397915.shtml.

[27] Børge Bakken. 2017. 'Snapshots of China's "Uncivil Society".' *Made in China Journal* 2, no. 1: 38–41.

[28] Zhang Qian 张倩. 2013. '袁成：寻子之路解救百名少年黑窑工 [Yuan Cheng: On the Road to Save His Son He Rescued A Hundred Young Slaves in the Kilns].' 北京青年报 [*Beijing Youth Daily*], 29 November, available online at: news.sina.com.cn/c/2013-11-29/033928841286.shtml.

2008 (Mary E. Gallagher)

[1] Chelsea C. Chou. 2018. 'China's Bureaucracy in the Open-Door Legislation: The Labor Contract Law in Focus.' *Journal of Chinese Political Science* 23, no. 2: 217–34.

[2] Chris King-Chi Chan and Elaine Sio-Ieng Hui. 2012. 'The Dynamics and Dilemma of Workplace Trade Union Reform in China: The Case of the Honda Workers' Strike.' *Journal of Industrial Relations* 54, no. 5: 653–68.

[3] Ya-Wen Lei. 2021. 'Delivering Solidarity: Platform Architecture and Collective Contention in China's Platform Economy.' *American Sociological Review* 86, no. 2: 279–309; Bin Chen, Tao Liu and Yingqi Wang. 2020. 'Volatile Fragility: New Employment Forms and Disrupted Employment Protection in the New Economy.' *International Journal of Environmental Research and Public Health* 17, no. 5: 1531; Irene Zhou. 2020. *Digital Labour Platforms and Labour Protection in China*. ILO Working Paper 11. Geneva: International Labour Organization, available online at: www.ilo.org/wcmsp5/groups/public/---asia/---ro-bangkok/---ilo-beijing/documents/publication/wcms_757923.pdf.

[4] Feng Xiaojun. 2019. 'Regulating Labour Dispatch in China: A Cat-and-Mouse Game.' *China Information* 33, no. 1: 88–109.

[5] Virginia Harper Ho and Qiaoyan Huang. 2014. 'The Recursivity of Reform: China's Amended Labor Contract Law.' *Fordham International Law Journal* 37, no. 4: 973–1034.

[6] Mary E. Gallagher. 2007. *Contagious Capitalism: Globalization and the Politics of Labor in China*. Princeton, NJ: Princeton University Press.

[7] Gordon White. 1987. 'The Politics of Economic Reform in Chinese Industry: The Introduction of the Labour Contract System.' *The China Quarterly*, no. 111: 365–89.

[8] Sarosh Kuruvilla, Ching Kwan Lee and Mary E. Gallagher (eds). 2011. *From Iron Rice Bowl to Informalization: Markets, Workers, and the State in a Changing China*. Ithaca, NY: ILR Press.

[9] William Hurst. 2012. *The Chinese Worker after Socialism*. Cambridge, UK: Cambridge University Press; Ching Kwan Lee. 2007. *Against the Law: Labor Protests in China's Rustbelt and Sunbelt*. Berkeley, CA: University of California Press.

[10] Xian Huang. 2015. 'Four Worlds of Welfare: Understanding Subnational Variation in Chinese Social Health Insurance.' *The China Quarterly* 222: 449–74; Yujeong Yang. 2021. 'The Politics of Inclusion and Exclusion: Chinese Dual-Pension Regimes in the Era of Labor Migration and Labor Informalization.' *Politics & Society* 49, no. 2: 147–80.

[11] Kinglun Ngok. 2008. 'The Changes of Chinese Labor Policy and Labor Legislation in the Context of Market Transition.' *International Labor and Working-Class History* 73, no. 1: 45–64.

[12] Chou, 'China's Bureaucracy in the Open-Door Legislation'; Mary Gallagher and Baohua Dong. 2011. 'Legislating Harmony: Labor Law Reform in Contemporary China.' In *From Iron Rice Bowl to Informalization: Markets, Workers, and the State in a Changing China*, edited by Sarosh Kuruvilla, Ching Kwan Lee and Mary E. Gallagher. Ithaca, NY: ILR Press, 36–60.

[13] David Barboza. 2006. 'China Drafts Law to Empower Unions and End Labor Abuse.' *The New York Times*, 13 October; Chou, 'China's Bureaucracy in the Open-Door Legislation'.

[14] Kay-Wah Chan. 2012. 'The Global Financial Crisis and Labor Law in China.' *Chinese Economy* 45, no. 3: 24–41.

[15] Zhiming Cheng, Russell Smyth and Fei Guo. 2015. 'The Impact of China's New Labour Contract Law on Socioeconomic Outcomes for Migrant and Urban Workers.' *Human Relations* 68, no. 3: 329–52.

[16] Joseph Y.S. Cheng, Kinglun Ngok and Wenjia Zhuang. 2010. 'The Survival and Development Space for China's Labor NGOs: Informal Politics and Its Uncertainty.' *Asian Survey* 50, no. 6: 1082–106; Manfred Elfstrom and Sarosh Kuruvilla. 2015. 'The Changing Nature of Labor Unrest in China.' *Industrial & Labor Relations Review* 67, no. 2: 453–80.

[17] Elizabeth J. Perry and Merle Goldman (eds). 2007. *Grassroots Political Reform in Contemporary China*. Cambridge, MA: Harvard University Press.

[18] Hualing Fu and Richard Cullen. 2008. 'Weiquan Lawyering in an Authoritarian State: Building a Culture of Public-Interest Lawyering.' *The China Journal* 59: 111–27.

[19] Ivan Franceschini and Kevin Lin. 2019. 'Labour NGOs in China: From Legal Mobilisation to Collective Struggle (and Back?).' *China Perspectives*, no. 1/2019: 75–84.

[20] Diana Fu. 2017. 'Disguised Collective Action in China.' *Comparative Political Studies* 50, no. 4: 499–527.

[21] Ivan Franceschini and Elisa Nesossi. 2018. 'State Repression of Chinese Labor NGOs: A Chilling Effect?' *The China Journal* 80: 111–29.

[22] Hualing Fu. 2018. 'The July 9th (709) Crackdown on Human Rights Lawyers: Legal Advocacy in an Authoritarian State.' *Journal of Contemporary China* 27, no. 112: 554–68.

[23] Tom Mitchell and Lucy Hornby. 2015. 'China Lawyer Trial Begins Amid Crackdown on Labour Rights Groups.' *The Financial Times*, 14 December, available online at: www.ft.com/intl/cms/s/0/a67e3882-a183-11e5-8d70-42b68cfae6e4.html#axz-z48MGabcdu.

[24] Jenny Chan. 2021. 'A Precarious Worker–Student Alliance in Xi's China.' *China Review* 20, no. 1: 165–90.

[25] Patricia Chen and Mary E. Gallagher. 2018. 'Mobilization without Movement: How the Chinese State "Fixed" Labor Insurgency.' *ILR Review*, 20 February, 001979391875906, available online at: doi.org/10.1177/0019793918759066.

[26] Yuequan Guo. n.d. 'Challenge, Signal, or Institution? The Effect of and the Lesson from a Government Crackdown on Labor Activists in China.' Unpublished paper.

[27] Xin Meng. 2017. 'The Labor Contract Law, Macro Conditions, Self-Selection, and Labor Market Outcomes for Migrants in China: Labour Contract Laws and Migrant Labour Market Performance.' *Asian Economic Policy Review* 12, no. 1: 45–65.

[28] Ibid.; Zhiming Cheng, Russel Smyth and Fei Guo. 2015. 'The Impact of China's New Labour Contract Law on Socioeconomic Outcomes for Migrant and Urban Workers.' *Human Relations* 68, no. 3: 329–52; Mary E. Gallagher, John Giles, Albert Park and Meiyan Wang. 2015. 'China's 2008 Labor Contract Law: Implementation and Implications for China's Workers.' *Human Relations* 68, no. 2: 197–235; Fuxi Wang, Bernard Gan, Yanyuan Cheng, Lin Peng, Jiaojiao Feng, Liquian Yang and Yiheng Xi. 2019. 'China's Employment Contract Law: Does It Deliver Employment Security?' *The Economic and Labour Relations Review* 30, no. 1: 99–119.

[29] Meng, 'The Labor Contract Law, Macro Conditions, Self-Selection, and Labor Market Outcomes for Migrants in China'; Gallagher et al., 'China's 2008 Labor Contract Law'; Yang, 'The Politics of Inclusion and Exclusion'.

[30] Randall Akee, Liqiu Zhao and Zhong Zhao. 2019. 'Unintended Consequences of China's New Labor Contract Law on Unemployment and Welfare Loss of the Workers.' *China Economic Review* 53: 87–105.

[31] Feng, 'Regulating Labour Dispatch in China'; Xiliang Feng, Fang Lee Cooke and Chenhui Zhao. 2020. 'The State as Regulator? The "Dual-Track" System of Employment in the Chinese Public Sector and Barriers to Equal Pay for Equal Work.' *Journal of Industrial Relations* 62, no. 4: 679–702; Xiaojun Feng. 2019. 'Trapped in Precariousness: Migrant Agency Workers in China's State-Owned Enterprises.' *The China Quarterly* 238: 396–417

[32] Lou Jiwei 楼继伟. 2015. '财政部部长楼继伟在清华经管学院演讲全文 [Full Text of Minister of Finance Lou Ji Wei's Speech at Tsinghua University Business School].' Tsinghua University, 24 April, available online at: www.sem.tsinghua.edu.cn/news/xyywcn/TZ_69292.html.

[33] Zhou, 'Digital Labour Platforms and Labour Protection in China'.

[34] Ibid.

[35] Chen et al., 'Volatile Fragility'.

[36] Lei, 'Delivering Solidarity'.

[37] 'Xi Stresses Advancing High-Quality Development in Border Ethnic Regions.' *Xinhua News*, 27 April 2021, available online at: www.xinhuanet.com/english/2021-04/27/c_139910639_2.htm.

[38] Emily Feng. 2021. 'He Tried to Organize Workers in China's Gig Economy. Now He Faces 5 Years in Jail.' *NPR*, 13 April, available online at: www.npr.org/2021/04/13/984994360/he-tried-to-organize-workers-in-chinas-gig-economy-now-he-faces-5-years-in-jail.

[39] Philip C.C. Huang. 1991. 'The Paradigmatic Crisis in Chinese Studies: Paradoxes in Social and Economic History.' *Modern China* 17, no. 3: 299–341.

[40] Wang Qianni and Ge Shifan. 2020. 'How One Obscure Word Captures Urban China's Unhappiness.' *Sixth Tone*, 4 November, available online at: www.sixthtone.com/news/1006391/how-one-obscure-word-captures-urban-chinas-unhappiness.

2008 (Eric Florence and Junxi Qian)

[1] Eli Friedman and Ching Kwan Lee. 2010. 'Remaking the World of Chinese Labour: A 30-Year Retrospective.' *British Journal of Industrial Relations* 48, no. 3: 507–33; Pun Ngai. 2016. *Migrant Labour in China: A Post-Socialist Transformation*. Cambridge, UK: Polity Press.

[2] Chris King-Chi Chan. 2010. *The Challenge of Labour in China: Strikes and the Changing Labour Regime in Global Factories*. Abingdon, UK: Routledge; Pun, *Migrant Labour in China*.

[3] Wanning Sun. 2014. *Subaltern China: Rural Migrants, Media and Cultural Practices*. Lanham, MD: Rowman & Littlefield; Tamara Jacka. 2006. *Rural Women in Urban China: Gender, Migration and Social Change*. New York, NY: M.E. Sharpe; Eric Florence. 2007. 'Migrant Workers in the Pearl River Delta: Discourse and Narratives about Work as Sites of Struggle.' *Critical Asian Studies* 39, no. 1: 120–50; Eric Florence. 2020. 'The Cultural Politics of Labour in Postsocialist China: The Case of Rural Migrant Workers.' In *The Routledge Handbook of Contemporary Chinese Society and Culture*, edited by Kevin Latham. London: Routledge.

[4] Junxi Qian and Junwan'guo Guo. 2019. 'Migrants on Exhibition: The Emergence of Migrant Worker Museums in China as a Neoliberal Experiment on Governance.' *Journal of Urban Affairs* 41, no. 3: 305–23.

[5] Similar projects were established in Guangzhou in 2010 and in Chengdu in 2012, while a grassroots project was initiated in the suburbs of Beijing by a collective of migrant workers. For details, see Qian and Guo, 'Migrants on Exhibition'; Junxi Qian and Eric Florence. 2020. 'Migrant Worker Museums in China: Public Cultures of Migrant Labour in State and Grassroots Initiatives.' *Journal of Ethnic and Migration Studies*, online first at: doi.org/10.1080/1369183X.2020.1739373.

[6] Beth Lord. 2006. 'Foucault's Museum: Difference, Representation, and Genealogy.' *Museum and Society* 4, no. 1: 1–14.

[7] Mary Ann O'Donnell, Winnie Wong, and Jonathan Bach. 2017. 'Introduction: Experiments, Exceptions and Extensions.' In *Learning from Shenzhen: China's Post-Mao Experiment from Special Zone to Model City*, edited by Mary Ann O'Donnell, Winnie Wong, and Jonathan Bach. Chicago, IL: University of Chicago Press, 4.

[8] Zhang Gaoli 张高丽. 2000. '巨大的光环, 伟大的实践 [An Enormous Aura, a Majestic Experience].' In 走向现代化: 深圳20年探索 [*Going Towards Modernity: An Exploration of Two Decades in Shenzhen*], edited by Bai Tian 白天. Shenzhen: Haitian Chubanshe, 1–15.

[9] Ibid., 5.

[10] Bjorn Kjellgren. 2002. *The Shenzhen Experience or the City of the Good Cats: Memories, Dreams, Identities and Social Interaction in the Chinese Showcase*. East Asian Monographs No. 66. Stockholm University, 147–48.

[11] Barry Naughton. 2012. 'The 1989 Watershed in China: How the Dynamics of Economic Transition Changed.' In *Socialism Vanquished, Socialism Challenged*, edited by Nina Bandelj and Dorothy Solinger. Oxford, UK: Oxford University Press, 125–48.

[12] George T. Crane. 1994. 'Special Things in Special Ways: National Economic Identity and China's Special Economic Zones.' *The Australian Journal of Chinese Affairs* 37: 71–92.

[13] Eric Florence. 2017. 'How to Be a Shenzhener: Representations of Migrant Labor in Shenzhen's Second Decade.' In O'Donnell et al., *Learning from Shenzhen*, 86–103.

[14] Li Youwei 厉有为 and Shao Anqing 邵汉青 (eds). 1995. 深圳经济特区的探索之路 [*The Exploratory Path of the Shenzhen Economic Zone*]. Shenzhen: Guangdong Renmin Chubanshe.

[15] Ibid., 234; Bai, *Going Towards Modernity*, 9. The idea that 'spiritual civilisation' should mould this new type of person was adopted at the Third Plenum of the Fourteenth Party Congress in 1994, which also advanced the notion that 'the establishment and achievement of [a] socialist market economy ultimately depends on the improvement of population quality [人口素质] and cultivation of talented people [人才]'. See Feng Xu. 2000. *Women Migrant Workers in China's Economic Reform*. New York, NY: St Martin's Press, 34–35, 97. For Bakken, 'population quality represents hidden productive forces' and relates to the value of human life, which needs to be constantly fostered. See Børge Bakken. 2000. *The Exemplary Society: Human Improvement, Social Control, and the Dangers of Modernity*. Oxford, UK: Oxford University Press, 70.

[16] Qian and Guo, 'Migrants on Exhibition'.

[17] Ibid.

[18] Pun Ngai and Chris Smith. 2006. 'The Dormitory Labour Regime as a Site of Control and Resistance.' *The International Journal of Human Resource Management* 17, no. 8: 1456–70; Pun, *Migrant Labour in China*.

[19] James C. Scott. 1985. *Weapons of the Weak: Everyday Forms of Peasant Resistance*. New Haven, CT: Yale University Press.

[20] The expression 'to offer one's youth respectfully' (奉献青春) has been in use since the 1960s in relation to young people who were sent to the countryside. They had to do so wholeheartedly, 'offering their youth respectfully to the country' (把青春奉献祖国), despite the fact that coming back to the cities was thereafter made extremely difficult, if not impossible.

[21] Jack Linchuan Qiu. 2016. *Goodbye iSlave: A Manifesto for Digital Abolition*. Chicago, IL: University of Illinois Press.

[22] Sun, *Subaltern China*, 123.

[23] Jonathan Bach. 2017. 'Shenzhen: From Exception to Rule.' In O'Donnell et al., *Learning from Shenzhen*, 23–38; Crane, 'Special Things in Special Ways'.

2009 (Ralph Litzinger and Yanping Ni)

[1] The narratives presented in this essay are based on news reports and newsreels on Zhang's experiences between 2009 and 2020. Many of the facts about his surgery and his life afterwards have been repeated in numerous reports, so we do not cite every source we have consulted. We do provide original sources when we quote directly from published and unpublished text and interviews.

[2] Zhang Haichao 张海超 and Liang Ke 梁珂. 2020. '为了证明自己有尘肺病,我选择了"开胸验肺" [To Prove I Have Black Lung, I Chose to "Open My Chest"].' 故事 *FM* [*Story FM*], 13 April, available online at: mp.weixin.qq.com/s/fOZyNiXRdBXeeRoc4rsUtQ.

[3] '专访开胸验肺农民工: 与其等死不如赌一把 [Special Interviews with "Open-Chest" Migrant Worker: Rather Than Wait to Die, It Is Better to Take a Gamble].' *CCTV*, 30 July 2009, available online at: news.cctv.com/china/20090730/104422.shtml.

[4] Chen Lei 陈磊. 2009. '张海超：以命相搏，开胸验肺 [Zhang Haichao: Fighting with His Life, Opening His Chest and Checking His Lung].' 南方周末 [*Southern Weekend*], 10 August, available online at: www.infzm.com/contents/32651.

[5] Earlier in the year, the Zhendong company arranged physical examinations at the Xinmi City Epidemic Prevention Station for its workers. Zhang was told all his results were normal. For this reason, he initially believed his symptoms were merely signs of a cold. In fact, the test showed Zhang potentially had black lung. The health workers at the station also informed the company that Zhang should be tested further, but Zhendong did not disclose that information to Zhang.

[6] The hospitals Zhang visited included Henan Provincial People's Hospital, Zhengzhou Second Hospital, Henan Provincial Chest Hospital, Peking Union Medical College Hospital, Emergency General Hospital and Beijing Chaoyang Hospital. All reached the same conclusion that Zhang was sick with black lung.

[7] Only authorised medical institutions can release official reports for occupational diseases, which are crucial to requests for compensation. Most of these institutions are in the provincial capital cities. This means that, for patients like Zhang Haichao, each test requires a long trip and unnecessary travel expenses.

[8] Chen, 'Zhang Haichao'.

[9] Wing-Chung Ho. 2018. *Occupational Health and Social Estrangement in China*. Manchester: Manchester University Press, 4.

[10] Guo Jian 郭健. 2009. '开胸验肺："非常"胜利背后 [Opening Chest and Checking Lung: Behind an "Abnormal" Success].' 中国社会保障 [*China Social Security*] 9: 48.

[11] Chen, 'Zhang Haichao'.

[12] Yu Xiaochuan 于小川. 2009. '这个冬天，他不再寒冷："开胸验肺"农民工张海超在中国煤矿工人北戴河疗养院成功"洗肺" [He is Not Cold Anymore This Winter: The "Open Chest" Migrant Worker Zhang Haichao Received Lung Lavage in the Beidaihe Sanatorium for Chinese Coal Miners].' 当代矿工 [*Modern Miner*] 12: 7.

[13] The Health Department of Henan Province published a notice criticising the First Affiliated Hospital of Zhengzhou University for Zhang's surgery, because, per state regulations, the hospital did not have the authority to release any medical reports on occupational diseases. In particular, the doctor who was mainly responsible for Zhang's surgery was punished with the suspension of her licence for a year. These measures were harshly criticised by the general public on the 'complaints' section of the institution's official website, which was later shut down. See Cao Lin 曹林. 2009. '惩罚"开胸验肺"的医院是自取其辱 [Punishing the Hospital in the "Open-Chest" Case is Self-Insulting].' 中国青年报 [*China Youth Daily*], 14 August, available online at: zqb.cyol.com/content/2009-08/14/content_2804241.htm.

[14] In 2009, Zhang claimed he had received compensation of 615,000 yuan from Zhendong. Only later did he reveal the true amount of compensation, which was in fact 1.2 million yuan, explaining that he had to keep silent due to pressure from local officials.

[15] Zhang Haichao still needs to take anti-rejection medicines for his new lungs. One of his fellow patients, who also received a lung transplant, died shortly after he temporarily stopped taking his medication on Chinese New Year (when taking medicines is considered inauspicious). See Yin Yafei 尹亚飞. 2018. '张海超"开胸验肺"之后 [Zhang Haichao After His "Open-Chest" Case].' 新京报 [*The Beijing News*], 24 July, available online at: www.bjnews.com.cn/inside/2018/07/24/496452.html.

[16] For a discussion, see Xuyang Sun. 2013. 'Pneumoconiosis Activist Zhang Haichao Gets Life-Saving Double-Lung Transplant.' *China Labour Bulletin*, 15 July, available online at: clb.org.hk/content/pneumoconiosis-activist-zhang-haichao-gets-life-saving-double-lung-transplant.

[17] Ibid.

[18] '张海超：从开胸到开庭的过渡 [Zhang Haichao: From "Open-Chest" to Opening a Court Session].' 财新 [*Caixin*], March 2012, available online at: clb.org.hk/node/14223.

[19] Yin, 'Zhang Haichao After His "Open-Chest" Case'.

[20] Ibid.

[21] *Caixin*, 'Zhang Haichao: From "Open-Chest" to Opening a Court Session'.

[22] Dai Chun 戴春. 2016. '中国尘肺病群体救助模式分析 [Analysis of the Assistance Model of Pneumoconiosis Patients in China].' 中国人力资源开发 [*Human Resources Development of China*] 1: 90–96.

[23] *CCTV*, 'Special Interviews with "Open-Chest" Migrant Worker'.

[24] Ho, *Occupational Health and Social Estrangement in China*, 10.

[25] We should note that, since 2009, there has been some progress on the legislative front. The Revisions to the Law on the Prevention and Treatment of Occupational Diseases (职业病防治法) in 2011 were surely driven by Zhang's case. See Ho, *Occupational Health and Social Estrangement in China*, 18. The 2019 *Action Plan for Pneumoconiosis Prevention and Treatment* (尘肺病防治攻坚行动方案) is seen by some worker activists as a remarkable achievement. To this day, however, Zhang remains cautious, careful about claiming victory. For him, a new law and new promises of protection are one thing. 'What really matters,' as he stated back in 2011, 'is if the laws will be implemented in practice.' See Chen Xu 陈璇. 2013. '"开胸验肺"的第二道伤口 [The Second Wound of the "Open-Chest" Case].' 中国青年报 [*China Youth Daily*], 3 April, available online at: zqb.cyol.com/html/2013-04/03/nw.D110000zgqnb_20130403_1-10.htm.

2010 (Chris King-Chi Chan and Elaine Sio-Ieng Hui)

[1] This article draws on the authors' previous publications—notably: Chris King-Chi Chan and Elaine Sio-Ieng Hui. 2012. 'The Dynamics and Dilemma of Workplace Trade Union Reform in China: The Case of the Honda Workers' Strike.' *Journal of Industrial Relations* 54, no. 4: 653–68; Chris King-Chi Chan. 2014. 'Constrained Labour Agency and the Changing Regulatory Regime in China.' *Development and Change* 45, no. 4: 685–709.

[2] Patricia Jiayi Ho. 2010. 'China Passes U.S. as World's Top Car Market.' *The Wall Street Journal*, 12 January, available online at: www.wsj.com/articles/SB10001424052748703652104574651833126548364.

[3] '本田車廠衝突 「工會」打工人 [Conflict at Honda Factory: "Union" Hits Workers]', 明報 [*Mingpao*], 1 June 2010, A2.

[4] This information was provided to the authors via telephone and internet communications with a number of strike leaders in June 2011.

[5] This citation is drawn from a copy of an open letter given to the authors by workers' representatives.

[6] One of the key workers' representatives shared these messages with the authors.

[7] The worker's blog has been removed from the internet, but the post is on file with the authors.

[8] The petition letter is available online at: www.gopetition.com/petitions/声援中国佛山本田工人行动呼吁信.html.

[9] Interview with a strike representative, 4 July 2010.

[10] According to workers (Interview, 4 July 2010), management had talked to some strike representatives after the strike was settled to gain direct or indirect influence over them. Also, at least one key worker leader was ordered by high-ranking trade union officials not to maintain any outside contact with civil society.

[11] Chris King-Chi Chan and Pun Ngai. 2009. 'The Making of a New Working Class? A Study of Collective Actions of Migrant Workers in South China.' *China Quarterly* 197: 287–303; Feng Chen. 2010. 'Trade Unions and the Quadripartite Interactions in Strike Settlement in China.' *China Quarterly* 201: 104–24; Yang Su and Xin He. 2010. 'The Street as Courtroom: State Accommodation of Labour Protest in South China.' *Law and Society Review* 44, no. 1: 157–84.

[12] Feng Chen. 2007. 'Individual Rights and Collective Rights: Labor's Predicament in China.' *Communist and Post-Communist Studies* 40, no. 1: 59–79.

[13] Mary Gallagher. 2005. *Contagious Capitalism: Globalization and the Politics of Labor in China*. Princeton, NJ: Princeton University Press.

[14] Anita Chan. 2011. 'Strikes in China's Export Industries in Comparative Perspective.' *The China Journal* 65: 27–52; Chan and Pun, 'The Making of a New Working Class?'; Ching Kwan Lee. 2007. *Against the Law: Labor Protests in China's Rustbelt and Sunbelt*. Berkeley, CA: University of California Press; Pak Nang Leung and Pun Ngai. 2009. 'The Radicalization of the New Working Class: The Collective Actions of Migrant Workers in South China.' *Third World Quarterly* 30, no. 3: 551–65; Su and He, 'The Street as Courtroom'.

[15] All-China Federation of Trade Unions (ACFTU). 2010. '进一步加强企业工会建设充分发挥企业工会作用 [Further Strengthen the Building of Workplace Trade Unions and Give Them Full Play]', available online at: baike.baidu.com/item/中华全国总工会关于进一步加强企业工会工作充分发挥企业工会作用的决定.

[16] Liu Sheng 刘声. 2010. '13省份以党委或政府发文推动工资集体协商 [Thirteen Provinces Promote Collective Wage Negotiation through Their Party Committees and Governments].' 中国新闻网 [*China News*], 9 June, available online at: www.chinanews.com/cj/cj-gncj/news/2010/06-09/2331521.shtml.

[17] See, for instance, 星岛日报 [*Singtao News*], 27 September 2010.

[18] Interview with an official from the American Chamber of Commerce in Guangzhou, 7 June 2011.

[19] Linda Weiss. 1998. *The Myth of the Powerless State*. Ithaca, NY: Cornell University Press.

2010 (Jenny Chan)

[1] All translations are mine unless otherwise stated. This worker's post, in the original Chinese, is on file with the author.

[2] Jenny Chan, Mark Selden, and Pun Ngai. 2020. *Dying for an iPhone: Apple, Foxconn, and the Lives of China's Workers*. Chicago, IL, and London: Haymarket Books and Pluto Press.

[3] The unabridged public statement from 18 May 2010 in the original Chinese is on file with the author.

[4] Young-rae Cho (translated by Chun Soon-ok). 2003. *A Single Spark: The Biography of Chun Tae-il*. Paju: Dolbegae Publishers.

[5] Hyojoung Kim. 2008. 'Micromobilization and Suicide Protest in South Korea, 1970–2004.' *Social Research* 75, no. 2: 549.

[6] Jamie Fullerton. 2018. 'Suicide at Chinese iPhone Factory Reignites Concern Over Working Conditions.' *The Telegraph*, 7 January, available online at: www.telegraph.co.uk/news/2018/01/07/suicide-chinese-iphone-factory-reignites-concern-working-conditions.

[7] Foxconn Technology Group. 2019. *2018 Social and Environmental Responsibility Report*, 6, 12, available online at: ser.foxconn.com/javascript/pdfjs/web/viewer.html?file=/upload/CserReports/5b75b277-d290-45f4-a9e1-efe87475543b_.pdf&page=1.

[8] Tse-Kang Leng. 2005. 'State and Business in the Era of Globalization: The Case of Cross-Strait Linkages in the Computer Industry.' *The China Journal* 53: 70.

[9] Foxconn Technology Group. 2019. *Group Profile*, available online at: www.foxconn.com.cn/GroupProfile.html.

[10] Lei Guo, Shih-Hsien Hsu, Avery Holton, and Sun Ho Jeong. 2012. 'A Case Study of the Foxconn Suicides: An International Perspective to Framing the Sweatshop Issue.' *The International Communication Gazette* 74, no. 5: 484–503.

[11] Jonathan Watts. 2010. 'Foxconn Offers Pay Rises and Suicide Nets as Fears Grow Over Wave of Deaths.' *The Guardian*, 28 May, available online at: www.theguardian.com/world/2010/may/28/foxconn-plant-china-deaths-suicides.

[12] C.W. Wang, C.L. Chan, and P.S. Yip. 2014. 'Suicide Rates in China from 2002 to 2011: An Update.' *Social Psychiatry and Psychiatric Epidemiology* 49: 929–41.

[13] X.Y. Li, M.R. Phillips, Y.P. Zhang, D. Xu, and G.H. Yang. 2008. 'Risk Factors for Suicide in China's Youth: A Case-Control Study.' *Psychological Medicine* 38: 397–406.

[14] The important research question of *how* employment conditions might contribute to suicides has increasingly drawn scholarly and industry attention. For a useful reference, see the 2018 report *The Link Between Employment Conditions and Suicide: A Study of the Electronics Sector in China*, published by the Economic Rights Institute and Electronics Watch, available online at: electronicswatch.org/the-link-between-employment-conditions-and-suicide-a-study-of-the-electronics-sector-in-china-november-2018_2549396.pdf.

[15] Timothy Sturgeon, John Humphrey, and Gary Gereffi. 2011. 'Making the Global Supply Base.' In *The Market Makers: How Retailers Are Reshaping the Global Economy*, edited by Gary G. Hamilton, Misha Petrovic, and Benjamin Senauer. Oxford, UK: Oxford University Press, 36.

[16] Apple Inc. 2016. 'A Message to the Apple Community in Europe', 30 August, available online at: www.apple.com/ie/customer-letter.

[17] Apple Inc. 2011. *Annual Report for the Fiscal Year Ended September 24, 2011*, 30, available online at: d18rn0p25nwr6d.cloudfront.net/CIK-0000320193/64c7905f-0468-48d9-8f25-e6ec8f3b5e32.pdf.

[18] See 'Quarterly Earnings Reports (Form 10-Q)', Q1 FY2010 – Q4 FY2018, available online at: investor.apple.com/investor-relations/sec-filings/default.aspx.

[19] Jenny Chan. 2013. 'A Suicide Survivor: The Life of a Chinese Worker.' *New Technology, Work and Employment* 28, no. 2, 88.

[20] Ibid., 94.

[21] David Weil. 2014. *The Fissured Workplace: Why Work Became So Bad for So Many and What Can Be Done to Improve It*. Cambridge, MA: Harvard University Press, 8.

[22] See Apple Inc. 2018. *Annual Report for the Fiscal Year Ended September 29, 2018*, 21, available online at: d18rn0p25nwr6d.cloudfront.net/CIK-0000320193/68027c6d-356d-46a4-a524-65d8ec05a1da.pdf; Foxconn Technology Group, *2018 Social and Environmental Responsibility Report*, 11.

[23] Foxconn worker interviewees' wage statements are on file with the author.

[24] Foxconn Technology Group. 2015. *2014 Social and Environmental Responsibility Report*, 28, available online at: ser.foxconn.com/javascript/pdfjs/web/viewer.html?file=/upload/serReport/4793a8c1-8e5b-40f7-ae83-ea943bbe57ef_.pdf&page=1.

[25] Ivan Franceschini and Elisa Nesossi. 2018. 'State Repression of Chinese Labor NGOs: A Chilling Effect?' *The China Journal* 80: 111–29; Ivan Franceschini and Kevin Lin. 2019. 'Labour NGOs in China: From Legal Mobilisation to Collective Struggle (and Back?).' *China Perspectives*, no. 1: 75–84; and Tim Pringle. 2018. 'A Solidarity Machine? Hong Kong Labour NGOs in Guangdong.' *Critical Sociology* 44, nos 4–5: 661–75.

[26] Thung-hong Lin and You-ren Yang. 2010. 'The Foxconn Employees and to Call to the Attention', 13 June, available online at: sites.google.com/site/laborgogo2010eng.

[27] 'Protesta contra suicidios en Foxconn [Anti-Suicide Protest at Foxconn]', Guadalajara, Mexico, 10 June 2010, YouTube video, available online at: www.youtube.com/watch?v=4ikF9vD3R_A.

[28] 'Suicides at Foxconn in China: An Appalling Showcase for the Electronics Sector', *SOMO*, 8 June 2010, available online at: www.somo.nl/suicides-at-foxconn-in-china-an-appalling-showcase-for-the-electronics-sector/; 'Mexican Foxconn Workers Support their Chinese Colleagues', *GoodElectronics*, 14 June 2010, available online at: goodelectronics.org/mexican-foxconn-workers-support-their-chinese-colleagues/.

[29] Worker rights supporters in New York City held a memorial service for Foxconn workers outside Apple's Fifth Avenue store on 7 June 2010.

[30] San Francisco Chinese Progressive Association. 2010. 'Apple's First Ever Store Overwhelmed with "Death Pad" Protesters in San Francisco', 17 June, available online at: sfcitizen.com/blog/2010/06/18/apples-first-ever-store-overwhelmed-with-deathpad-protesters-in-san-francisco.

[31] United Students Against Sweatshops. 2010. 'Open Letter to Apple CEO Steve Jobs', 14 June. The letter is on file with the author.

[32] Jenny Chan. 2018. '#iSlaveat10.' In *Gilded Age: Made in China Yearbook 2017*, edited by Ivan Franceschini and Nicholas Loubere. Canberra: ANU Press, 102–5.

[33] Jack Linchuan Qiu. 2016. *Goodbye iSlave: A Manifesto for Digital Abolition*. Urbana, IL: University of Illinois Press.

[34] Author's online meeting with Remco Kouwenhoven, Fairphone's Social Innovation Lead (12 November 2020). Fairphone is a social enterprise founded in the Netherlands in 2009. More than 220,000 smartphones were sold, with Fairphone 3 rolling out into the European market in 2019.

35 Jenny Chan, Greg Distelhorst, Dimitri Kessler, Joonkoo Lee, Olga Martin-Ortega, Peter Pawlicki, Mark Selden, and Benjamin Selwyn. 2021. 'After the Foxconn Suicides in China: A Roundtable on Labor, the State and Civil Society in Global Electronics.' *Critical Sociology*, online first: doi.org/10.1177/08969205211013442.

2011 (Eli Friedman)

[1] Pseudonym.
[2] This document was produced in 2011.
[3] 新华 [*Xinhua*]. 2005. '北京将进一步加强对流动人口自办学校的管理 [Beijing to Strengthen Management Over Migrant Population Self-Run Schools].' *Zhejiang Online*, 10 October, available online at: edu.zjol.com.cn/system/2005/10/10/006326529.shtml.
[4] Li Yaru 李雅儒, Sun Wenying 孙文营, and Yang Zhiping 阳志平. 2003. '北京市流动人口及其子女教育状况调查研究 [Survey on the Situation of the Migrant Population in Beijing and the Education of their Children].' 首都师范大学学报 [*Journal of Capital Normal University*], no. 1: 112; Zhao Han 赵晗 and Wei Jiayu Wei 魏佳羽. 2016. '北京义务教育阶段流动儿童教育现状 [The Educational Situation of Migrant Children of Compulsory Education Age in Beijing].' In 中国流动儿童教育发展报告 [*Report on the Development of Migrant Children in China*], edited by Yang Dongping 杨东平, Qing Hongyu 秦红宇, and Wei Jiayu 魏佳羽. Beijing: Shehui Kexue Chubanshe, 105–20.
[5] This phrase is drawn from Eli Friedman. 2018. 'Just-in-Time Urbanization? Managing Migration, Citizenship, and Schooling in the Chinese City.' *Critical Sociology* 44, no. 3: 503–18.
[6] Liu Jie 刘杰 and Zhao Ying 赵颖. 2007. '北京昌平打工子弟学校被迫停办调查 [Report on a Migrant School Shut Down in Beijing's Changping District].' 京华时报 [*Jinghua Shibao*], 12 September, available online at: edu.people.com.cn/GB/6251983.html.
[7] Xinhua News Agency. 2014. 国家新型城镇化规划(2014–2020年) [*National New Urbanisation Plan (2014–2020)*]. China Government Network, 16 March, available online at: www.gov.cn/zhengce/2014-03/16/content_2640075.htm.
[8] 'Capital' here refers to the political centre.
[9] Ziyi Tang. 2019. 'Beijing's Population Falls Further.' *Caixin*, 23 January, available online at: www.caixinglobal.com/2019-01-23/beijings-population-falls-further-101373464.html.

2013 (Aaron Halegua)

[1] Liu Dewei 刘德伟. 2016. '"一带一路"到底是倡议还是战略? [Is the "Belt and Road" an Initiative or a Strategy?].' *Sina*, [blog], 29 December, available online at: cj.sina.com.cn/article/detail/3860416827/135959.
[2] State Council of the People's Republic of China. 2015. *Full Text: Action Plan on the Belt and Road Initiative*. 30 March. Beijing: State Council, available online at: english.www.gov.cn/archive/publications/2015/03/30/content_281475080249035.htm.

[3] Nyshka Chandran. 2018. 'China Can Make Its Belt and Road Project More Successful if it Taps Locals, Experts Say.' *CNBC*, 14 September, available online at: www.cnbc.com/2018/09/14/china-must-do-more-to-tap-locals-in-belt-and-road-initiative-panel.html.

[4] Ministry of Commerce. 2016. *2015年与'一带一路'相关国家经贸合作情况* [*Economic and Trade Cooperation with Relevant Countries of the 'Belt and Road' in 2015*]. 21 January. Beijing: Ministry of Commerce, available online at: www.mofcom.gov.cn/article/tongjiziliao/dgzz/201601/20160101239881.shtml.

[5] Ministry of Commerce. 2020. *2019年与'一带一路'相关国家经贸合作情况* [*Economic and Trade Cooperation with Relevant Countries of the 'Belt and Road' in 2019*]. 22 January. Beijing: Ministry of Commerce, available online at: www.mofcom.gov.cn/article/tongjiziliao/dgzz/202001/20200102932445.shtml.

[6] Andrew Chatzky and James McBride. 2020. *China's Massive Belt and Road Initiative*. Backgrounder, 28 January. New York: Council on Foreign Relations, available online at: www.cfr.org/backgrounder/chinas-massive-belt-and-road-initiative.

[7] CSIS China Power Team. 2020. 'How Will the Belt and Road Initiative Advance China's Interests?' *China Power Project*, 26 August. Washington, DC: Center for Strategic and International Studies, available online at: chinapower.csis.org/china-belt-and-road-initiative (statistics for 2021); James Kynge. 2018. 'A Tale of Two Harbours Tells Best and Worst of China's "Belt and Road".' *Financial Times*, 25 September, available online at: www.ft.com/content/7699d13a-806a-11e8-af48-190d103e32a4 (statistics for 2016).

[8] Jeremy Youde, Melanie Hart, Dan Baer, Courtney Fung, Sophie Richardson, Aaron Halegua, Michael Beckley, Maria Adele Carrai, and Daojiong Zha. 2020. 'How Will China Shape Global Governance?' *ChinaFile Conversation*, 9 May, available online at: www.chinafile.com/conversation/how-will-china-shape-global-governance. See also Belt and Road Portal. 2021. '已同中国签订共建"一带一路"合作文件的国家一览 [List of Countries That Have Signed Cooperation Documents with China to Jointly Build the "Belt and Road Initiative"].' *Belt and Road Portal*, 30 January, available online at: www.yidaiyilu.gov.cn/xwzx/roll/77298.htm.

[9] Kynge, 'A Tale of Two Harbours Tells Best and Worst of China's "Belt and Road".'

[10] Yeping Yin. 2021. 'BRI Delivers Growth and Protection Amid Pandemic.' *Global Times*, 8 February, available online at: www.globaltimes.cn/page/202102/1215314.shtml.

[11] Devin Thorne and Ben Spevack. 2017. *Harbored Ambitions: How China's Port Investments Are Strategically Reshaping the Indo-Pacific*. Washington, DC: C4ADS, available online at: static1.squarespace.com/static/566ef8b4d8af107232d5358a/t/5a-d5e20ef950b777a94b55c3/1523966489456/Harbored+Ambitions.pdf.

[12] Daniel R. Russel and Blake Berger. 2019. *Navigating the Belt and Road Initiative*. Report, June. New York, NY: Asia Society Policy Institute, available online at: asiasociety.org/sites/default/files/2019-06/Navigating%20the%20Belt%20and%20Road%20Initiative_0.pdf. See also Duncan Freeman. 2020. 'The Belt and Road Initiative and the Overcapacity Connection.' In *The Belt and Road Initiative and Global Governance*, edited by Maria Adele Carrai and Jan Wouters. Cheltenham, UK: Edward Elgar, 120–38.

[13] Lee Jones and Jinghan Zeng. 2019. 'Understanding China's "Belt and Road Initiative": Beyond "Grand Strategy" to a State Transformation Analysis.' *Third World Quarterly* 40, no. 8: 1415–39.

[14] Yuen Yuen Ang. 2018. 'China's Belt and Road Initiative is a Campaign, Not a Conspiracy.' *Bloomberg*, 27 September, available online at: www.bloomberg.com/opinion/articles/2018-09-27/china-s-belt-and-road-initiative-is-a-campaign-not-a-conspiracy.

[15] Baogang He. 2019. 'The Domestic Politics of the Belt and Road Initiative and its Implications.' *Journal of Contemporary China* 28, no. 116: 18–95.

[16] For an overview of particularly controversial projects, see *The People's Map of Global China*, available online at: thepeoplesmap.net.

[17] On the 'debt trap' narrative, see, for instance, Kynge, 'A Tale of Two Harbours Tells Best and Worst of China's "Belt and Road".' According to this narrative, China purposely saddles host countries with debts that cannot be repaid in order to take over the valuable assets collateralising the loan or extract other political concessions. The most frequently cited example involves the Sri Lankan Government leasing the Hambantota Port to China for ninety-nine years after defaulting on the Chinese loans used to build it. Another example is a railway project for which the Laos Government borrowed from China US$6 billion—nearly one-third of its annual gross domestic product. However, many have also challenged this characterisation of the events in Sri Lanka and Laos and argue that the 'debt-trap diplomacy' theory is little more than a myth. See Deborah Bräutigam and Meg Rithmire. 2021. 'The Chinese "Debt Trap" Is a Myth: The Narrative Wrongfully Portrays Both Beijing and the Developing Countries it Deals With.' *The Atlantic*, 6 February, available online at: www.theatlantic.com/international/archive/2021/02/china-debt-trap-diplomacy/617953.

[18] Mech Dara. 2019. 'Hun Sen: Claim that China is "Invading" Kingdom is Crazy.' *The Phnom Penh Post*, 25 October, available online at: www.phnompenhpost.com/national/hun-sen-claim-china-invading-kingdom-crazy.

[19] Pál Nyíri. 2020. 'Migration and the Globalisation of Chinese Capital.' *Made in China Journal* 5, no. 3: 42–47.

[20] Zhang Zujie 张祖杰 and Shi Meixia 石美遐. 2020. '"一带一路"倡议下中国对外劳务合作现状与问题研究 [Research on the Status and Problems of China's Foreign Cooperation of Labour Service Under the "Belt and Road Initiative"].' *Advances in Social Science, Education and Humanities Research* 435, available online at: www.atlantis-press.com/article/125939332.pdf.

[21] Zhu Rongji. 2001. *Report on the Outline of the Tenth Five-Year Plan for National Economic and Social Development (2001)*. 5 March. Beijing: National People's Congress, available online at: www.npc.gov.cn/zgrdw/englishnpc/Special_11_5/2010-03/03/content_1690620.htm.

[22] 'China's Direct Investments Abroad Top $92b by 2007.' *China Daily*, 17 April 2007, available online at: www.chinadaily.com.cn/bizchina/2008-04/17/content_6624488.htm.

[23] National Bureau of Statistics of China. 2019. 中国贸易外经统计年鉴, *2019* [*China Trade and Foreign Economic Statistics Yearbook, 2019*]. Beijing: Zhongguo Tongji Chubanshe, available online at: www.yearbookchina.com/downsoft-n3020031901.html.

[24] Chinese Academy of International Trade and Economic Cooperation. 2019. *70年中国特色商务发展之路 (1949–2019)* [*70 Years of Commercial Development Path with Chinese Characteristics (1949–2019)*]. Beijing: Zhongguo Shangwu Chubanshe, 330.

25 See, for instance, '国务院常务会通过鼓励规范企业对外投资合作意见 [State Council Executive Committee Issues Opinion on Encouraging and Regulating Enterprises' Foreign Investment Cooperation].' 中国新闻网 [*China News*], 25 October 2006, available online at: www.chinanews.com/other/news/2006/10-25/809947.shtml.

26 Alexis Okeowo. 2013. 'China, Zambia, and a Clash in a Coal Mine.' *The New Yorker*, 9 October, available online at: www.newyorker.com/business/currency/china-zambia-and-a-clash-in-a-coal-mine; Young Jonn Lim. 2012. 'Anti-Chinese Sentiment in Zambia and the African Continent: Comparative Coverage of the Phenomenon by Zambian, Chinese, and South African Newspapers.' *International Journal of Information and Communication Technology Research* 2, no. 7: 548–57.

27 See, for instance, Ministry of Labour and Social Security, Ministry of Public Security and State Administration of Industry and Commerce. 2002. '境外就业中介管理规定 [Provisions on the Administration of Intermediary Activities for Overseas Employment].' *LawInfoChina*, 14 May, available online at: www.lawinfochina.com/display.aspx?lib=law&id=2391.

28 Ministry of Commerce. 2005. '关于印发"对外承包工程项下外派劳务管理暂行办法"的通知 [Notice on "Interim Measures for the Administration of Labour Service Assigned Abroad Under Overseas Contractual Projects"].' November. Beijing: Ministry of Commerce, available online at: www.mofcom.gov.cn/aarticle/b/bf/200602/20060201553432.html; State Council of the People's Republic of China. 2008. 对外承包工程管理条例 [*Regulations on Administering Foreign Contracting Projects*]. 7 May. Beijing: Ministry of Commerce, available online at: www.mofcom.gov.cn/article/swfg/swfgbi/201101/20110107352097.shtml; State Council of the People's Republic of China. 2012. 对外劳务合作管理条例 [*Regulations on Management of Foreign Labour Service Cooperation*]. 4 June. Beijing: State Council, available online at: www.gov.cn/zwgk/2012-06/11/content_2157905.htm.

29 Chris Smith and Yu Zheng. 2016. 'The Management of Labour in Chinese MNCs Operating Outside of China: A Critical Review.' In *China At Work: A Labour Process Perspective on the Transformation of Work and Employment in China*, edited by Mingwei Liu and Chris Smith. London: Palgrave Macmillan, 361–88.

30 Ching Kwan Lee. 2014. 'The Spectre of Global China.' *New Left Review* 89: 29–66.

31 Aaron Halegua and Jerome A. Cohen. 2019. 'The Forgotten Victims of China's Belt and Road Initiative.' *The Washington Post*, 23 April, available online at: www.washingtonpost.com/opinions/2019/04/23/forgotten-victims-chinas-belt-road-initiative.

32 See Lee, 'The Spectre of Global China'.

33 Yang Li. 2017. 'B&R by the Numbers: Manufacturing, Construction and Financing Enterprises Most Influential in B&R Construction.' *Belt and Road Portal*, 28 November, available online at: eng.yidaiyilu.gov.cn/jcsj/dsjkydyl/37115.htm; Yu Liang. 2019. '2nd Belt and Road Afro-Sino Art Exhibition Opens in Zimbabwe.' *Xinhua*, 30 April, available online at: www.xinhuanet.com/english/2019-04/30/c_138022992.htm.

34 Russel and Berger, *Navigating the Belt and Road Initiative*.

35 Ministry of Commerce. 2020. 商务部数据统计中心 [*Ministry of Commerce Statistical Centre*], 3 March, available online at: data.mofcom.gov.cn/tzhz/forlaborcoop.shtml.

36 National Bureau of Statistics of China. 2019. 中国贸易外经统计年鉴, 2019 [*China Trade and Foreign Economic Statistics Yearbook, 2019*]. Beijing: Zhongguo Tongji Chubanshe, available online at: www.yearbookchina.com/downsoft-n3020031901.html (statistics for 2018); Ministry of Commerce. 2020. *Brief Statistics on China's Overseas*

Labour Service Cooperation in 2019. 23 January. Beijing: Ministry of Commerce, available online at: english.mofcom.gov.cn/article/statistic/foreigntradecooperation/202002/20200202933531.shtml (figures for 2019).

[37] Ministry of Commerce. 2021. *2020年我国对外劳务合作业务简明统计* [*Statistics on China's Foreign Labour Cooperation Business in 2020*]. 22 January. Beijing: Ministry of Commerce, available online at: www.mofcom.gov.cn/article/tongjiziliao/dgzz/202101/20210103033291.shtml.

[38] National Bureau of Statistics of China. 2013. 中国贸易外经统计年鉴, *2013* [*China Trade and Foreign Economic Statistics Yearbook, 2013*]. Beijing: Zhongguo Tongji Chubanshe, available online at: www.stats.gov.cn/tjsj/ndsj/2013/indexch.htm (figures for 2012); Zhang and Shi, 'Research on the Status and Problems of China's Foreign Cooperation' (figures for 2018).

[39] Guofu Liu. 2018. *Assessment of the Migrant Worker Complaint Mechanism in China*. Report, 4 April. Geneva: International Labour Organization.

[40] Aaron Halegua. 2020. 'Where is China's Belt and Road Leading International Labour Rights? An Examination of Worker Abuse by Chinese Construction Firms in Saipan.' In *The Belt and Road Initiative and Global Governance*, 225–57.

[41] '想出国劳务却遭遇黑中介 837人被骗了3526万元 [Want to Go Abroad for Labour but Encountered an Illegal Intermediary, 837 People Were Defrauded of 35.26 Million Yuan].' *Xinhua*, 18 February 2017, available online at: www.xinhuanet.com/world/2017-02/18/c_129484582.htm.

[42] Ministry of Commerce. 2017. '商务部会同有关部门启动规范外派劳务市场秩序专项行动 [The Ministry of Commerce, Together with Relevant Departments, Launched a Special Action to Regulate the Order of the Foreign Labour Market].' 中国新闻网 [*China News*], 6 July, available online at: www.chinanews.com/cj/2017/07-06/8270518.shtml.

[43] Alvin Camba. 2020. *Illicit Capital & Labor Inflows: Chinese Online Gambling in the Philippines*. 16 March. London: Business & Human Rights Resource Centre, available online at: www.business-humanrights.org/en/blog/illicit-capital-labor-inflows-chinese-online-gambling-in-the-philippines (which notes that official statistics report 110,000 Chinese workers in the Philippines, but others estimate the actual number may be as high as 400,000).

[44] State Council of the People's Republic of China. 2017. '国务院办公厅转发《国家发展改革委、商务部、人民银行、外交部关于进一步引导和规范境外投资方向指导意见》[Notice Forwarding the Guiding Opinions of the National Development and Reform Commission, Ministry of Commerce, People's Bank of China and Ministry of Foreign Affairs on Further Guiding and Regulating the Overseas Investment Direction].' 4 August. Beijing: State Council, available online at: www.gov.cn/zhengce/content/2017-08/18/content_5218665.htm; National Development and Reform Commission, Ministry of Foreign Affairs, Ministry of Commerce, People's Bank of China, State-Owned Assets Supervision and Administration Commission, State Administration of Foreign Exchange and All-China Federation of Industry and Commerce. 2018. '企业海外经营合规管理指引 [Guidelines for Enterprise Compliance Management of Overseas Operations].' 26 December. Beijing: National Development and Reform Commission, Article 8, available online at: www.ndrc.gov.cn/xxgk/zcfb/tz/201812/W020190905514236483349.pdf.

[45] National Development and Reform Commission, Ministry of Commerce and People's Bank of China. 2017. '国家发展改革委、商务部、人民银行等关于发布《民营企业境外投资经营行为规范》的通知 [Notice on Issuing the Code of Conduct for the Operation of Overseas Investments by Private Enterprises].' 12 June. Beijing: National Development and Reform Commission, Article 22, available online at: www.ndrc.gov.cn/xxgk/zcfb/tz/201712/t20171218_962621.html.

[46] Chinese International Contractors Association. 2017. 'Guidelines of Sustainable Infrastructure for Chinese International Contractors.' Beijing: Ministry of Commerce, available online at: images.mofcom.gov.cn/csr2/201707/20170713103213247.pdf.

[47] See Cheryl Mei-Ting Schmitz. 2020. 'Doing Time, Making Money at a Chinese State Firm in Angola.' *Made in China Journal* 5, no. 3: 52–57 (describing Chinese workers at a construction firm in Angola).

[48] 'China's Projects in Vietnam Earn Reputation for Poor Quality, Delays.' *Nikkei Asia Review*, 20 September 2017, available online at: asia.nikkei.com/Economy/China-s-projects-in-Vietnam-earn-reputation-for-poor-quality-delays; Miriam Driessen. 2019. *Tales of Hope, Tastes of Bitterness: Chinese Road Builders in Ethiopia*. Hong Kong: Hong Kong University Press.

[49] Daniel Kliman, Rush Doshi, Kristine Lee, and Zack Cooper. 2019. *Grading China's Belt and Road*. Report, 8 April. Washington, DC: Center for a New American Security, available online at: www.cnas.org/publications/reports/beltandroad.

[50] Lee Yaron. 2019. 'Israel Police Launches First-Ever Investigation into Construction-Site Deaths.' *Haaretz*, 8 April, available online at: www.haaretz.com/israel-news/.premium-israel-police-launches-first-ever-investigation-into-construction-site-deaths-1.7092728.

[51] Claire Bigg. 2015. '"Crushed Like Ants": Chinese Workers Meet Harsh Reality in Belarus.' *Radio Free Europe*, 21 July, available online at: www.rferl.org/a/chinese-workers-belarus/27141591.html.

[52] Driessen, *Tales of Hope, Tastes of Bitterness*, 15, 45–64, 114.

[53] Sophia Yan. 2018. 'Chinese Workers Tricked into Illegal Work on Saipan.' *Associated Press*, 14 March, available online at: apnews.com/article/4ceaac6873414bdf-80d40e40b68ba6f7.

[54] Lily Kuo and Alicia Chen. 2021. 'Chinese Workers Allege Forced Labor, Abuses in Xi's "Belt and Road" Program.' *The Washington Post*, 30 April, available online at: www.washingtonpost.com/world/asia_pacific/china-labor-belt-road-covid/2021/04/30/f110e8de-9cd4-11eb-b2f5-7d2f0182750d_story.html.

[55] Ivan Franceschini. 2020. 'Building the New Macau: A Portrait of Chinese Construction Workers in Sihanoukville.' *Made in China Journal* 5, no. 3: 65–73 (describing workers in Cambodia).

[56] Aaron Halegua and Xiaohui Ban. 2020. 'Legal Remedies for China's Overseas Workers.' *Made in China Journal* 5, no. 3: 86–91.

[57] Halegua and Cohen, 'The Forgotten Victims of China's Belt and Road Initiative'.

[58] Liu, *Assessment of the Migrant Worker Complaint Mechanism in China*.

[59] Halegua, 'Where is China's Belt and Road Leading International Labor Rights?'.

[60] Aaron Halegua and Xiaohui Ban. 2020. 'Labour Protections for Overseas Chinese Workers: Legal Framework and Judicial Practice.' *The Chinese Journal of Comparative Law* 8, no: 2: 304–30.

2014 (Sun Wanning)

[1] The translation of this poem by Xu Lizhi (许立志), as well as those of the other poems cited in this essay, are all by the author.

[2] Pun Ngai. 2005. *Made in China: Women Factory Workers in a Global Workplace*. Durham, NC: Duke University Press.

[3] *Zhihu* is a Chinese online question-and-answer forum similar to *Quora*. This comment can be found online at www.zhihu.com/question/25812488.

[4] Wanning Sun. 2014. *Subaltern China: Rural Migrants, Media, and Cultural Practices*. Lanham, MD: Rowman & Littlefield.

[5] Christian Sorace. 2020. 'Poetry After the Future.' *Made in China Journal* 5, no. 1: 130–35.

[6] He Yanhong 何言宏. 2007. '打工诗歌并非我的全部 [Dagong Poetry Is Not All There Is To Me].' Interview with Zheng Xiaoqiong. China Knowledge Network, available online at: gb.oversea.cnki.net/KCMS/detail/detail.aspx?filename=1015635011. nh&dbcode=CMFD&dbname=CMFDREF.

[7] Wanning Sun. 2010. 'Narrating Translocality: *Dagong* Poetry and the Subaltern Imagination.' *Mobilities* 5, no. 3: 291–309.

[8] Wanning Sun. 2012. 'Poetry of Labour and (Dis)articulation of Class: China's Worker-Poets and the Cultural Politics of Boundaries.' *Journal of Contemporary China* 21, no. 78: 993–1010; Emile Durkheim. 1997 [1897]. *Suicide: A Study in Sociology*. New York, NY: Free Press.

[9] Paola Voci. 2020. 'Can the Creative Subaltern Speak? Dafen Village Painters, Van Gogh, and the Politics of "True Art".' *Made in China Journal* 5, no. 1: 104–11.

[10] Sun, *Subaltern China*.

[11] For instance, see Jenny Chan, Mark Selden, and Pun Ngai. 2017. '"Growth, Thy Name Is Suffering": The Workers of the Workshop of the World.' In *World Factory: The Game*, edited by Zoë Svendsen and Simon Daw. London: Nick Hern Books, 318–23; Pun Ngai and Huilin Lu. 2010. 'Unfinished Proletarianization: Self, Anger, and Class Action among the Second Generation of Peasant-Workers in Present-Day China.' *Modern China* 36, no. 5: 493–519.

[12] Zheng Xiaoqiong 郑小琼. 2012. 女工记 [*Stories of Migrant Women Workers*]. Guangzhou: Huancheng Chubanshe.

[13] Maghiel Van Crevel. 2019. 'Debts: Coming to Terms with Migrant Worker Poetry.' *Journal of Chinese Literature Today* 8, no. 1: 127–45; Xiaojing Zhou. 2020. *Migrant Ecologies: Zheng Xiaoqiong's Women Migrant Workers*. Lanham, MD: Lexington Books.

[14] Gao Siwei 高四维. 2014. '许立志：选择了"死亡"主题的打工诗人许立志 [Xu Lizhi: The Worker Poet Who Chose "Death" as the Theme of His Poems].' 中国青年报 [*China Youth Daily*], 25 November, available online at: zqb.cyol.com/html/2014-11/24/nw.D110000zgqnb_20141124_1-08.htm.

2014 (Marc Blecher)

[1] Ashok Kumar. 2019. 'Oligopolistic Suppliers, Symbiotic Value Chains and Workers' Bargaining Power: Labour Contestation in South China at an Ascendant Global Footwear Firm.' *Global Networks* 19, no. 3: 394–422, at p. 416.

[2] Ibid., 404.

[3] Yue Yuen Industrial (Holdings) Limited. *2013 Annual Report*, 2, 15, 52, available online at: www1.hkexnews.hk/listedco/listconews/sehk/2014/0424/ltn20140424281.pdf.

[4] Kumar, 'Oligopolistic Suppliers, Symbiotic Value Chains and Workers' Bargaining Power'.

[5] Stefan Schmalz, Brandon Sommer, and Hui Xu. 2017. 'The Yue Yuen Strike: Industrial Transformation and Labour Unrest in the Pearl River Delta.' *Globalizations* 14, no. 2: 285–97, at p. 290.

[6] 'Defeat Will Only Make Us Stronger: Workers Look Back at the Yue Yuen Shoe Factory Strike.' *China Labour Bulletin*, 22 May 2014, available online at: clb.org.hk/content/defeat-will-only-make-us-stronger-workers-look-back-yue-yuen-shoe-factory-strike.

[7] Kumar, 'Oligopolistic Suppliers, Symbiotic Value Chains and Workers' Bargaining Power', 405; Chris King-Chi Chan and Elaine Sio-Ieng Hui. 2017. 'Bringing Class Struggles Back: A Marxian Analysis of the State and Class Relations in China.' *Globalizations* 14, no. 2: 238.

[8] Kumar, 'Oligopolistic Suppliers, Symbiotic Value Chains and Workers' Bargaining Power', 406.

[9] Ibid.

[10] As one worker put it: 'Yue Yuen is a big plant with hospitals and kindergartens, so workers get a feeling of stability. Most of them are middle-aged workers who have been there since their teens, so they are reluctant to leave. Some left and came back later.' 'Defeat Will Only Make Us Stronger', *China Labour Bulletin*.

[11] Ibid.

[12] Ibid.

[13] Kumar, 'Oligopolistic Suppliers, Symbiotic Value Chains and Workers' Bargaining Power', 413.

[14] 'Defeat Will Only Make Us Stronger', *China Labour Bulletin*.

[15] Kumar, 'Oligopolistic Suppliers, Symbiotic Value Chains and Workers' Bargaining Power', 403 and *passim*.

[16] 'Defeat Will Only Make Us Stronger', *China Labour Bulletin*.

[17] Ibid.

[18] Ibid.

[19] Ibid.

[20] Ibid.

[21] Alexandra Harney and John Ruwitch. 2014. 'In China, Managers Are the New Labor Activists.' *Reuters*, 31 May, available online at: www.reuters.com/article/china-labor-strikes/in-china-managers-are-the-new-labor-activists-idUSL3N0O929U20140601.

[22] Ibid.

[23] Schmalz et al., 'The Yue Yuen Strike', 291. On political opportunity, see Sidney Tarrow. 1994. *Power in Movement: Social Movements, Collective Action, and Politics*. Cambridge, UK: Cambridge University Press.

[24] Kumar, 'Oligopolistic Suppliers, Symbiotic Value Chains and Workers' Bargaining Power', 405.

[25] 'Defeat Will Only Make Us Stronger', *China Labour Bulletin*.

[26] Kumar, 'Oligopolistic Suppliers, Symbiotic Value Chains and Workers' Bargaining Power', 408, 410; Schmalz et al., 'The Yue Yuen Strike', 295.

[27] Kumar, 'Oligopolistic Suppliers, Symbiotic Value Chains and Workers' Bargaining Power', 405.

[28] Ching Kwan Lee and Yonghong Zhang. 2013. 'The Power of Instability: Unraveling the Microfoundations of Bargained Authoritarianism in China.' *American Journal of Sociology* 118, no. 6: 1475–508.

[29] Chan and Hui, 'Bringing Class Struggles Back', 239.

[30] Ibid., 241.

[31] Philippe Schmitter and Marc Blecher. 2020. *Politics As a Science: A Prolegomenon.* New York, NY: Routledge.

[32] 'Defeat Will Only Make Us Stronger', *China Labour Bulletin.*

[33] Chan and Hui, 'Bringing Class Struggles Back', 241; Nicos Poulantzas. 1973. *Political Power and Social Classes.* London: New Left Review and Sheed & Ward; Nicos Poulantzas. 1978. *Classes in Contemporary Capitalism.* London: Verso Books; Nicos Poulantzas. 2000. *State, Power, Socialism.* London: Verso Books.

2015 (Huang Yu)

[1] '"机器换人"的喜与忧—广东东莞首家"无人工厂"蹲点调查 [The Joy and Concerns Regarding "Replacing Humans with Machines": Investigation of the First "Workerless Factory" in Dongguan, Guangdong].' 中国政府网 [*Chinese Government Net*], 13 July 2005, available online at: www.gov.cn/xinwen/2015-07/13/content_2896088.htm.

[2] Nie Honghui 聂洪辉 and Zhu Yuan 朱源. 2017. '"机器换人"对新生代农民工就业与社会稳定的影响 [The Impact of the "Replacing Humans with Machines" Policy on New-Generation Migrant Workers' Employment and Social Stability].' 广西社会科学 [*Guangxi Social Sciences*] 4: 148–53.

[3] International Federation of Robotics. 2020. 'IFR Presents World Robotics Report 2020.' Press release, 24 September. Frankfurt am Main: International Federation of Robotics, available online at: ifr.org/ifr-press-releases/news/record-2.7-million-robots-work-in-factories-around-the-globe.

[4] Aaron Benanav. 2019. 'Automation and the Future of Work—I.' *New Left Review* 119 (September–October): 5–38; Yu Huang. 2018. 'Robot Threat or Robot Dividend? A Struggle Between Two Lines'. *Made in China Journal* 3, no. 2: 50–55; Roger Penn and Hilda Scattergood. 1985. 'Deskilling or Enskilling? An Empirical Investigation of Recent Theories of the Labour Process.' *British Journal of Sociology* 36, no. 4: 611–30.

[5] Sarosh Kuruvilla and Hao Zhang. 2016. 'Labor Unrest and Incipient Collective Bargaining in China.' *Management and Organization Review* 12, no. 1: 159–87.

[6] Yu Huang and Naubahar Sharif. 2017. 'From "Labour Dividend" to "Robot Dividend": Technological Change and Workers' Power in South China.' *Agrarian South: Journal of Political Economy* 6, no. 1: 53–78.

[7] '珠三角制造业革新样本 [New Samples for the Upgrading of the Manufacturing Industry at the Pearl River Delta].' *21世纪经济报道* [*Twenty-First Century Economic Report*], 13 October, available online at: m.21jingji.com/article/20171013/83c880f4b-727c5879dbf4b8d28baea44.html.

[8] Sun Zhongwei 孙中伟 and Deng Yunxue 邓韵雪. 2020. '"世界工厂"的凤凰涅槃: 中国制造业"机器换人"的经济社会意义 [The Rebirth of the "Workshop of the World": The Economic and Social Significance of "Replacing Humans with Machines" in China's Manufacturing Industry].' 学术论坛 [Academic Forum] 3: 1–8; Fan Changyi 范长煜 and Tang Binbin 唐斌斌. 2020. '半数岗位易被取代: 警惕"机器换人"的技术性失业风险 [Half of the Jobs Are Replaceable: Be Cautious of the Risks of Technical Unemployment Caused by "Replacing Humans with Machines"].' 学术论坛 [Academic Forum] 3: 9–17.

[9] Tao Yang and Siqi Luo. 2019. *Machines Replace Humans? Automation and Upgrading at Car Suppliers in China*. FES China Report. Beijing: Friedrich-Ebert-Stiftung, available online at: www.fes-china.org/en/publications/detail/2019-automation-car-suppliers-en.html.

[10] Harry Braverman. 1974. *Labor and Monopoly Capital: The Degradation of Work in the Twentieth Century*. New York, NY: Monthly Review Press. For the subsequent discussions, see David F. Noble. 1984. *Forces of Production: A Social History of Industrial Production*. New York, NY: Oxford University Press; Harley Shaiken, Stephen Herzenberg, and Sarah Kuhn. 1986. 'The Work Process Under More Flexible Production.' *Industrial Relations* 25, no. 2: 167–83.

[11] Paul Alder. 1988. 'Automation, Skill and the Future of Capitalism.' *Berkeley Journal of Sociology* 33: 1–36; Michael Piore and Charles Sabel. 1984. *The Second Industrial Divide: Possibilities for Prosperity*. New York, NY: Basic Books; Shoshana Zuboff. 1988. *In the Age of the Smart Machine: The Future of Work and Power*. New York, NY: Basic Books.

[12] Fabiane S. Previtali and Cilson C. Fagiani. 2015. 'Deskilling and Degradation of Labour in Contemporary Capitalism: The Continuing Relevance of Braverman.' *Work Organization, Labour & Globalisation* 9, no. 1: 76–91; Martin Krzywdzinski. 2017. 'Automation, Skill Requirements and Labour-Use Strategies: High-Wage and Low-Wage Approaches to High-Tech Manufacturing in the Automotive Industry.' *New Technology, Work and Employment* 32, no. 3: 247–67.

[13] William Form. 1987. 'On the Degradation of Skills.' *Annual Review of Sociology* 13, no. 1: 29–47, at p. 44.

[14] Kenneth I. Spenner. 1985. 'The Upgrading and Downgrading of Occupations: Issues, Evidence, and Implications for Education.' *Review of Educational Research* 55, no. 2: 125–54; Michael Wiedemeyer. 1989. 'New Technology in West Germany: The Employment Debate.' *New Technology, Work and Employment* 4, no. 1: 54–65.

[15] Deng Yunxue 邓韵雪 and Xu Yi 许怡. 2020. '"技术赋权"还是"技术父权": 对智能制造背景下劳动者技能提升机会的性别差异考察 ["Technology Empowerment" or "Technology Patriarchy": A Study of Gender Differences of Workers' Skill Upgrading Opportunities in the Context of Intelligent Manufacturing].' 科学与社会 [Science and Society] 9, no. 3: 87–109.

[16] Yong Xin 雍昕. 2020. '技术升级对劳动者技能水平的差异性影响:来自广东省制造业企业的证据 [The Differential Implications of Technological Upgrading on Skill Levels of Workers: Evidence from Manufacturing Enterprises in Guangdong Province].' 中国人力资源开发 [Human Resources Development of China] 37, no. 10: 64–74.

[17] David H. Autor, Frank Levy, and Richard J. Murane. 2003. 'The Skill Content of Recent Technological Change: An Empirical Exploration.' *The Quarterly Journal of Economics* 118, no. 4: 1279–1333.

[18] Yang and Luo, *Machines Replace Humans?*.

[19] Harley Shaiken. 1984. *Work Transformed: Automation and Labour in the Computer Age*. Lexington, MA: Lexington Books; Steven P. Vallas. 1993. *Power in the Workplace: The Politics of Production at AT&T*. Albany: State University of New York Press.

[20] Naubahar Sharif and Yu Huang. 2019. 'Industrial Automation in China's "Workshop of the World".' *The China Journal* 81: 1–22.

[21] Yang and Luo, *Machines Replace Humans?*.

[22] Sun and Deng, 'The Rebirth of the "Workshop of the World".'

[23] Robin Kwong. 2012. 'Terry Gou: Managing "1m Animals".' *Financial Times*, 20 January, available online at: next.ft.com/content/be3d2550-f9e6-34c0-91fb-afd639d3e750.

[24] Michael Burawoy. 1979. *Manufacturing Consent: Changes in the Labor Process Under Monopoly Capitalism*. Chicago, IL: University of Chicago Press.

[25] Braverman, *Labor and Monopoly Capital*; Tessa Morris-Suzuki. 2011 [1988]. *Beyond Computopia: Information, Automation and Democracy in Japan*. New York, NY: Routledge.

[26] Chris King-Chi Chan. 2014. 'Constrained Labour Agency and the Changing Regulatory Regime in China.' *Development and Change* 45, no. 4: 685–709.

[27] Yu Lingzheng 余铃铮, Wei Xiahai 魏下海, and Wu Chunxiu 吴春秀. 2019. '机器人对劳动收入份额的影响研究: 来自企业调查的微观证据 [The Impact of Robots on Labour Income Share: Micro Evidence from an Enterprises Survey].' 中国人口科学 [*Chinese Journal of Population Science*] 4: 114–25; Wang Yongqin 王永钦 and Dong Wen 董雯. 2020. '机器人的兴起如何影响中国劳动力市场 [How the Rise of Robots Has Affected China's Labour Market: Evidence from China's Listed Manufacturing Firms].' 经济研究 [*Economic Research Journal*] 10: 159–74; Xu Yi 许怡 and Ye Xin 叶欣. 2020. '技术升级劳动降级? 基于三家"机器换人"工厂的社会学考察 [Technological Upgrading and Labour Degrading? A Sociological Study of Three "Robotised Factories"].' 社会学研究 [*Sociological Studies*] 35, no. 3: 23–46.

[28] Xu and Ye, 'Technological Upgrading and Labour Degrading?'.

[29] Yang and Luo, *Machines Replace Humans?*, 6.

2015 (Chloé Froissart and Ivan Franceschini)

[1] Sui Lee Wee. 2016. 'China Arrests Four Labor Activists Amid Crackdown: Lawyers.' Reuters, 10 January, available online at: www.reuters.com/article/us-china-rights-i-dUSKCN0UO05M20160110.

[2] Zhang Cong 张璁. 2015. '起底"工运之星"真面目 [Exposing the True Face of the "Star of the Labour Movement"].' 人民日报 [*People's Daily*], 23 December, 11.

[3] Chloé Froissart. 2010. 'Is There an NGO Model? Comparing NGOs Supporting Migrant Workers in Beijing and the Pearl River Delta.' Asia Centre Conference Series, The Paris Institute of Political Studies, June.

[4] Chloé Froissart. 2013. *La Chine et ses migrants: La conquête d'une citoyenneté* [*China and Its Migrants: The Conquest of Citizenship*]. Rennes: Presse Universitaires de Rennes, 338–61.

[5] Interview, Shenzhen, December 2004.

[6] Wenjia Zhuang and Feng Chen. 2015. '"Mediate First": The Revival of Mediation in Labour Dispute Resolution in China.' *The China Quarterly* 222: 380–402.

[7] Ching Kwan Lee and Yuan Shen. 2011. 'The Anti-Solidarity Machine? Labor Non-Governmental Organizations in China.' In *From Iron Rice Bowl to Informalization: Markets, Workers, and the State in a Changing China*, edited by Sarosh Kuruvilla, Ching-Kwan Lee and Mary E. Gallagher. Ithaca, NY: Cornell University Press, 173–87; Ching Kwan Lee and Yonghong Zhang. 2013. 'The Power of Instability: Unraveling the Microfoundations of Bargained Authoritarianism in China.' *American Journal of Sociology* 118, no. 6: 1475–508.

[8] In this sense, labour NGOs contributed to the regime's dynamic stability. See Chloé Froissart. 2011. 'NGOs Defending Migrant Workers' Rights: Semi-Union Organizations Contribute to the Regime's Dynamic Stability.' *China Perspectives*, no. 2/2011: 18–25.

[9] Ibid., 22; Froissart, *China and Its Migrants*, 347–48.

[10] Ronald Brown. 2006. 'China's Collective Contracts Provisions: Can Collective Negotiations Embody Collective Bargaining?' *Duke Journal of Comparative & International Law* 16, no. 1: 35–78; Mingwei Liu and Sarosh Kuruvilla. 2017. 'The State, the Unions, and Collective Bargaining in China: The Good, the Bad, and the Ugly.' *Comparative Labor Law and Policy Journal* 38, no. 2: 187–210.

[11] Ivan Franceschini and Kevin Lin. 2019. 'Labour NGOs in China: From Legal Mobilization to Collective Struggle (and Back?).' *China Perspectives*, no. 1/2019: 75–84; Ivan Franceschini and Christian Sorace. 2019. 'In the Name of the Working Class: Narratives of Labour Activism in Contemporary China.' *Pacific Affairs* 92, no. 4: 650.

[12] Chloé Froissart. 2018. 'Negotiating Authoritarianism and Its Limits: Worker-Led Collective Bargaining in Guangdong Province.' *China Information* 32, no. 1: 23–45.

[13] Mimi Lau. 2014. 'Fertile Ground for Labour Activism.' *South China Morning Post*, 2 May, available online at: www.scmp.com/news/china/article/1502010/fertile-ground-labour-activism.

[14] Interview, Shenzhen, April 2014.

[15] Froissart, 'Negotiating Authoritarianism and Its Limits'.

[16] See, for example, Sydney Webb and Martha Beatrice Webb. 1897. *Industrial Democracy*. London: Longmans, Green; Allan Flanders. 1964. *The Fawley Productivity Agreements: A Case Study of Management and Collective Bargaining*. London: Faber.

[17] These strategies of 'boundary-making and boundary-breaking' are analysed by Froissart in 'Negotiating Authoritarianism and Its Limits'.

[18] Han Dongfang. 2016. 'A Letter to the *People's Daily* on *China Labour Bulletin*'s Work with Labour Activists in China.' *China Labour Bulletin*, 12 January, available online at: clb.org.hk/node/3078.

[19] On file with the authors.

[20] Froissart, 'Negotiating Authoritarianism and Its Limits'.

[21] Chris King-Chi Chan and Elaine Sio-Ieng Hui. 2014. 'The Development of Collective Bargaining in China: From "Collective Bargaining by Riot" to "Party-State Led Wage Bargaining".' *The China Quarterly* 217: 221–42.

[22] Froissart, 'Negotiating Authoritarianism and Its Limits'.

[23] Franceschini and Lin, 'Labour NGOs in China'.

[24] Ivan Franceschini and Elisa Nesossi. 2018. 'State Repression of Chinese Labor NGOs: A Chilling Effect?' *The China Journal* 80: 111–29.

[25] Froissart, 'Negotiating Authoritarianism and Its Limits'.

[26] Yueran Zhang. 2020. 'Leninists in a Chinese Factory: Reflections on the Jasic Labour Organising Strategy.' *Made in China Journal* 5, no. 2: 82–88.

2018 (Manfred Elfstrom)

[1] See the video 深圳佳士供热抗争实录： 纪录片'我和我们'（上）[*A Recording of Shenzhen Jasic Workers' Resistance: The Documentary "I and Us" (First Part)*], 2018, available online at www.youtube.com/watch?v=JWMu_MIDqNI.

[2] Mimi Lau. 2018. 'Chinese Maoists Join Students in Fight for Workers' Rights.' *South China Morning Post*, 10 August, available online at www.scmp.com/news/china/policies-politics/article/2158991/chinese-maoists-join-students-fight-workers-rights.

[3] 'Student Speaks Out in Support of the Jasic Technology Workers Establishing a Union.' *China Labor Watch*, 7 August 2018, available online at www.facebook.com/watch/?v=10151023648089946.

[4] Shannon Lee. 2018. 'Preliminary Thoughts on the Shenzhen Jasic Events.' *Shannon Lee's China Blog*, 17 September, available online at wolfsmoke.wordpress.com/2018/09/17/jasic.

[5] Huang Jin 黄进. 2016. '广东省将推广社区工会联合会 [Guangdong Province Will Promote District Union Federations].' 南方日报 [*Southern Daily*], 30 November, available online at www.gov.cn/xinwen/2016-11/30/content_5140286.htm.

[6] 'Shenzhen Worker Activists Determined to Unionise Despite Dismissal.' *China Labour Bulletin*, 24 July 2018, available online at: clb.org.hk/content/shenzhen-worker-activists-determined-unionise-despite-dismissal.

[7] The union's words regarding Jasic are still online at the time of this writing. See Pingshan District Trade Union. 2018. '区、街道两级总工会与佳士科技股份有限公司 就企业建会再次深入交流 [District and Neighborhood-Level Unions Discuss Union Building Again In-Depth with Jasic Technology Company, Limited].' *WeChat Official Account*, 23 July, available online at: mp.weixin.qq.com/s?__biz=MzIyODc1MTgzNg==&mid=2247485889&idx=1&sn=74f1bbadffa04f1e9bae039220807ca8&chksm=e84c6972df3be064e3d4dcc33c1c9c401cdde-1df1cbeec2b0310ce7527f162e4081d7fa04c60#rd.

[8] 'Shenzhen Jasic Workers Who Established a Union Have Been Arrested for "Disorderly Behavior".' *China Labor Watch*, 30 July 2018, available online at: www.chinalaborwatch.org/newscast/664.

[9] International Labour Organisation (ILO). 2019. '389th Report of the Committee on Freedom of Association.' *Reports of the Committee on Freedom of Association*, 22 June. Geneva: ILO, available online at: www.ilo.org/wcmsp5/groups/public/---ed_norm/---relconf/documents/meetingdocument/wcms_711394.pdf.

[10] For a good profile of the students, see Yuan Yang. 2019. 'Inside China's Crackdown on Young Marxists.' *Financial Times*, 13 February, available online at: www.ft.com/content/fd087484-2f23-11e9-8744-e7016697f225.

[11] Ben-li Qian. 2019. 'Jasic Struggle: Debate Among Chinese Maoists.' *Against the Current*, no. 200 (May–June), available online at: solidarity-us.org/atc/200/chinese-maoists-debate.

[12] 'Seeing Through Muddied Waters, Part 2: An Interview on Jasic & Maoist Labor Activism.' *Chuang*, 2 July 2019, available online at: chuangcn.org/2019/07/jasic-2-reignite-interview; Yueran Zhang. 2020. 'Leninists in a Chinese Factory: Reflections on the Jasic Labour Organising Strategy.' *Made in China Journal* 5, no. 2: 82–88.

[13] Gerry Shih. 2019. '"If I Disappear": Chinese Students Make Farewell Messages Amid Crackdowns Over Labor Activism.' *The Washington Post*, 25 March, available online at: www.washingtonpost.com/world/asia_pacific/if-i-disappear-chinese-students-make-farewell-messages-amid-crackdowns-over-labor-activism-/2019/05/25/6fc949c0-727d-11e9-9331-30bc5836f48e_story.html.

[14] Hong Kong Confederation of Trade Unions (HKCTU). 2018. 'The Hong Kong Civil Society Marches On in Support of the JASIC Workers.' *Labour News*, 29 August. Hong Kong Confederation of Trade Unions, available online at: en.hkctu.org.hk/content/hong-kong-civil-society-marches-support-jasic-workers.

[15] ILO, '389th Report of the Committee on Freedom of Association'.

[16] Javier C. Hernández. 2018. 'Cornell Cuts Ties with Chinese School After Crackdown on Students.' *The New York Times*, 29 October, available online at: www.nytimes.com/2018/10/29/world/asia/cornell-university-renmin.html.

[17] See Scholars Supporting Jasic Activists. Undated. 'A Call to Action', available online at: supportingjasicworkers.wordpress.com. The author was involved in this effort.

[18] 'Fu Changguo.' Chinese Human Rights Defenders website, 18 July 2019, available online at: www.nchrd.org/2019/07/fu-changguo; Tim Pringle and Anita Chan. 2018. 'China's Labour Relations Have Entered A Dangerous New Phase, As Shown by Attacks on Jasic Workers and Activists.' *South China Morning Post*, 19 September, available online at: www.scmp.com/comment/insight-opinion/article/2164817/chinas-labour-relations-have-entered-dangerous-new-phase.

[19] '深圳佳士公司工人"维权"事件的背后 [The Shezhen Jasic Company Workers' "Rights Protection" Incident's Background].' *Xinhua News Agency*, 24 August 2018, available online at: www.xinhuanet.com/local/2018-08/24/c_1123326003.htm.

[20] Yang, 'Inside China's Crackdown on Young Marxists'.

[21] Sue-Lin Wong. 2018. 'Labor Activists Missing in China After Suspected Coordinated Raids.' *Reuters*, 12 November, available online at: www.reuters.com/article/us-china-labour-activists-idUSKCN1NH0IZ.

[22] 'Jasic Crackdown Extends to Trade Union Officials and Lawyers.' *China Labour Bulletin*, 4 December 2018, available online at: clb.org.hk/content/jasic-crackdown-extends-trade-union-officials-and-lawyers.

[23] Javier C. Hernández. 2018. 'Students Defiant as Chinese University Cracks Down on Young Communists.' *The New York Times*, 28 December, available online at: www.nytimes.com/2018/12/28/world/asia/chinese-university-crackdown-students.html.

[24] Hernández, 'Cornell Cuts Ties with Chinese School After Crackdown on Students'.

[25] James Griffiths and Yong Xiong. 2019. 'Chinese Marxist Students Appear in "Confession" Video as Crackdown Continues.' *CNN*, 22 January, available online at: www.cnn.com/2019/01/22/asia/china-student-marxists-intl/index.html.

[26] Eduardo Baptista. 2019. '"Deers" vs. "Horses": Old and New Marxist Groups Wage Ideological Battle at Peking University.' *SupChina*, 9 January, available online at: supchina.com/2019/01/09/old-and-new-marxist-groups-wage-ideological-battle-at-peking-university.

[27] See, for example, Pun Ngai 潘毅. 2018. '观点：深圳佳士工人维权的两大意义 [Opinion: Two Big Implications of the Shenzhen Jasic Workers' Rights Protection].' *BBC News Chinese*, 17 August, available online at: www.bbc.com/zhongwen/simp/45217517.

[28] Au Loong-Yu. 2018. 'The Jasic Mobilisation: A High Tide for the Chinese Labour Movement?' *Made in China Journal* 3, no. 4: 12–16.

[29] Jenny Chan. 2020. 'A Precarious Worker–Student Alliance in Xi's China.' *The China Review* 20, no. 1: 165–90.

[30] Zhang, 'Leninists in a Chinese Factory'.

[31] Brian Hioe. 2018. 'Is the Jasic Struggle Primarily Symbolic or Does it Have the Potential to Spread?' *New Bloom Magazine*, 9 September, available online at: newbloommag.net/2018/09/09/shenzhen-jasic-symbolic-or-spread.

[32] Charles Tilly and Sidney Tarrow. 2007. *Contentious Politics*. Boulder, CO: Paradigm Publishers, 111.

[33] For instance, see Eli Friedman and Ching Kwan Lee. 2010. 'Remaking the World of Chinese Labour: A 30-Year Retrospective.' *British Journal of Industrial Relations* 48, no. 3: 507–33.

[34] Vivienne Shue. 1990. *The Reach of the State: Sketches of the Chinese Body Politic*. Stanford, CA: Stanford University Press.

[35] Elizabeth J. Perry. 2007. 'Permanent Rebellion? Continuities and Discontinuities in Chinese Protest.' In *Popular Protest in China*, edited by Kevin J. O'Brien. Cambridge, MA: Harvard University Press, 205–15.

[36] Teresa Wright. 2010. *Accepting Authoritarianism: State–Society Relations in China's Reform Era*. Stanford, CA: Stanford University Press.

[37] Jackie Sheehan. 1998. *Chinese Workers: A New History*. London: Routledge; Elizabeth J. Perry. 2002. *Challenging the Mandate of Heaven: Social Protest and State Power in China*. Armonk, NY: M.E. Sharpe; Andrew G. Walder and Xiaoxia Gong. 1993. 'Workers in the Tiananmen Protests: The Politics of the Beijing Workers' Autonomous Federation.' *The Australian Journal of Chinese Affairs* 29: 1–29.

[38] 'Chinese Students Go Undercover to Investigate Coca Cola.' *China Labor News Translations*, 2009, available online at: www.clntranslations.org/article/41/chinese-students-go-undercover-to-investigate-coca-cola; Pun Ngai, Yuan Shen, Yuhua Guo, Huilin Lu, Jenny Chan, and Mark Selden. 2014. 'Worker–Intellectual Unity: Trans-Border Sociological Intervention in Foxconn.' *Current Sociology* 20, no. 10: 1–14.

[39] Chris King-Chi Chan and Elaine Sio-Ieng Hui. 2013. 'The Development of Collective Bargaining in China: From "Collective Bargaining by Riot" to "Party-State–Led Wage Bargaining".' *The China Quarterly* 217: 221–42.

[40] 'Tower Crane Operators Across China Organise Labour Day Strike Over Low Pay.' *China Labour Bulletin*, 2 May 2018, available online at: www.clb.org.hk/content/tower-crane-operators-across-china-organise-labour-day-strike-over-low-pay; 'China's Truck Drivers Strike Over Stagnant Pay, High Fuel Costs and Arbitrary Fines.' *China Labour Bulletin*, 11 June 2018, available online at: www.clb.org.hk/content/china%E2%80%99s-truck-drivers-strike-over-stagnant-pay-high-fuel-costs-and-arbitrary-fines; Anita Chan. 2016. 'The Resistance of Walmart Workers in China: A Breakthrough in the Chinese Labour Movement.' *Made in China Journal* 1, no. 2: 11–15.

2018 (Darren Byler)

[1] This essay is based on a September 2019 article published in the website *SupChina* with the title 'How Companies Profit from Forced Labor in Xinjiang,' available online at: supchina.com/2019/09/04/how-companies-profit-from-forced-labor-in-xinjiang.

[2] 'Ihr seid keine Menschen [You Are Not Human]', *Die Zeit*, 31 July 2019, available online at: www.zeit.de/2019/32/zwangslager-xinjiang-muslime-china-zeugen-menschenrechte/seite-2.

[3] Ibid.

[4] Human Rights Watch. 2019. *China's Algorithms of Repression: Reverse Engineering a Xinjiang Police Mass Surveillance App*. Report, 1 May. New York: Human Rights Watch, available online at: www.hrw.org/report/2019/05/01/chinas-algorithms-repression/reverse-engineering-xinjiang-police-mass.

[5] 'You Are Not Human', *Die Zeit* .

[6] '江苏援伊前沿指挥部领导研究南通市对口援疆工作 [Leaders of Jiangsu Aid to Yining Front Headquarters Investigate the Paired Aid to Xinjiang from Nantong City]', 南通援疆进行时 [*The Times of Nantong Aiding Xinjiang*], 31 May 2018, available online at: archive.md/f490v.

[7] '州直纺织服装产业敲开群众"就业门" [The State Direct Textile and Garment Industry Knocks on "Employment Door" of the Masses]', 伊犁电视台 [*Ili Television*], 4 December 2018, available online at: archive.md/KSe5r.

[8] See the profile for 'Lixian Huawei Gloves Factory' available online at: huaweiglove.en.alibaba.com/company_profile.html.

[9] See the website of the People's Government of the Xinjiang Uyghur Autonomous Region, 6 April 2018, available online at: archive.fo/ZBsk8.

[10] '自治区经济结构稳中有活 发展良好 [The Economic Structure of the Autonomous Region Is Stable, Alive and Well Developed]', Xinjiang Reform and Development Commission website, 5 December 2018, available online at: web.archive.org/web/20190520143306/http:/www.xjdrc.gov.cn/info/9923/23516.htm.

[11] 'Provincial Data Shows China's Shifting Agricultural Trends', Gro Intelligence website, 6 March 2019, available online at: gro-intelligence.com/insights/articles/provincial-data-shows-chinas-shifting-agricultural-trends-Cotton.

[12] Dominique Patton. 2016. 'Xinjiang Cotton at Crossroads of China's New Silk Road.' *Reuters*, 12 January, available online at: www.reuters.com/article/us-china-xinjiang-cotton-insight-idUSKCN0UQ00320160112.

[13] International Labour Organisation. 2014. *Wages and Working Hours in the Textiles, Clothing, Leather and Footwear Industries*. Issues Paper GDFTCLI/2014. Geneva: International Labour Organisation, available online at: www.ilo.org/wcmsp5/groups/public/@ed_dialogue/@sector/documents/publication/wcms_300463.pdf.

[14] Chris Smith and Ngai Pun. 2006. 'The Dormitory Labour Regime in China as a Site for Control and Resistance.' *The International Journal of Human Resource Management* 17, no. 8: 1456–70.

[15] Jennifer Pan. 2020. *Welfare for Autocrats: How Social Assistance in China Cares for Its Rulers*. Oxford, UK: Oxford University Press; 'Çin'in Yeni Planlarinin Yazili Emri İfşa Oldu [Written Order of China's New Plans Revealed]', *Turkistan Press*, 23 July 2018, available online at: turkistanpress.com/page/cin-39-in-yeni-planlarinin-yazili-emri-ifsa-oldu/247.

[16] Karl Marx (edited by Robert Tucker). 1978. *The Marx–Engels Reader*. New York, NY: W.W. Norton & Company.

[17] '伊宁县"轻纺产业区"的产业工人: 幸福是奋斗出来的! [Industrial Workers in the "Textile Industry Zone" of Yining County: Happiness Comes from Struggle!]', 伊宁县零距离 [*Zero Distance Yining*], available online at: archive.md/Cv6w5-selection-23.14-31.7.

[18] 'Gulzira Aeulkhan', *Xinjiang Victims Database*, 2019, available online at: shahit.biz/eng/viewentry.php?entryno=1723.

[19] Erkin Azat. 2019. 'Gulzira Auelkhan's Records in a Chinese Concentration Camp: "I Worry About the Lives of Those Eight Who Have Not Signed a Contract in the Factory."' *Medium*, 4 March, available online at: medium.com/@erkinazat2018/gulzira-auelkhan-s-records-in-a-chinese-concentration-camp-i-worry-about-the-lives-of-those-c18a2038a5a2.

[20] Government of the People's Republic of China. 2019. 'Response of the Government of China on Follow-Up to the Concluding Observations of the United Nations Committee on the Elimination of Racial Discrimination.' New York: United Nations, available online at: undocs.org/CERD/C/CHN/FCO/14-17.

[21] Nathan Vanderklippe. 2018. '"I Felt like a Slave": Inside China's Complex System of Incarceration and Control of Minorities.' *The Globe and Mail*, 31 March, available online at: www.theglobeandmail.com/world/article-i-felt-like-a-slave-inside-chinas-complex-system-of-incarceration.

[22] 'Gulzira Aeulkhan', *Xinjiang Victims Database*.

[23] Vanderklippe, '"I Felt like a Slave"'.

[24] Kashgar Regional Office. 2018. '关于印发《喀什地区困难群体就业培训工作实施方案》的通知 [Notice on Issuing the "Implementation Plan for Employment Training for Disadvantaged Groups in Kashgar"].' Kashgar Regional Office, 10 August, available online at: web.archive.org/web/20181204024839/http:/kashi.gov.cn/Government/PublicInfoShow.aspx?ID=2963.

[25] Michel Foucault (translated by Alan Sheridan). 1975. *Discipline and Punish: The Birth of Prison*. London: Penguin.

[26] For a comparative study in Tibet, see Emily T. Yeh. 2013. *Taming Tibet: Landscape Transformation and the Gift of Chinese Development*. Ithaca, NY: Cornell University Press.

[27] 'Industrial Workers in the "Textile Industry Zone" of Yining County'.

[28] 'The State Direct Textile and Garment Industry Knocks on "Employment Door" of the Masses'.

[29] Alyosha Goldstein. 2017. 'On the Reproduction of Race, Capitalism, and Settler Colonialism.' In *Race and Capitalism: Global Territories, Transnational Histories*, Los Angeles, CA: Institute on Inequality and Democracy at UCLA Luskin, available online at: challengeinequality.luskin.ucla.edu/wp-content/uploads/sites/16/2018/04/Race-and-Capitalism-digital-volume.pdf; Darren Byler. 2018. 'Spirit Breaking: Uyghur Dispossession, Culture Work and Terror Capitalism in a Chinese Global City.' PhD dissertation, University of Washington, Seattle, available online at: digital.lib.washington.edu/researchworks/bitstream/handle/1773/42946/Byler_washington_0250E_19242.pdf.

[30] Gene Bunin. 2019. 'Detainees Are Trickling Out of the Camps.' *Foreign Policy*, 18 January, available online at: foreignpolicy.com/2019/01/18/detainees-are-trickling-out-of-xinjiangs-camps.

[31] Gene Bunin. 2019. 'Making the Xinjiang Authorities Dance: 40 Examples of Publicized Cases.' *Art of Life in Chinese Central Asia*, 17 May, available online at: livingotherwise.com/2019/05/17/making-xinjiang-authorities-dance-40-examples-generally-positive-outcomes-publicized-cases.

2019 (Anita Chan)

[1] This essay was originally published with the title 'From Unorganised Street Protests to Organising Unions: The Birth of a New Trade Union Movement in Hong Kong' in *Made in China Journal* 5, no. 2 (2020), and then in a revised and expanded version in *The Asia-Pacific Journal: Japan Focus* 18, no. 24 (2020).

The Future (Carlos Rojas)

[1] State Administration of Radio, Film and Television (SARFT). 2011. '广电总局关于2011年3月全国拍摄制作电视剧备案公式的通知 [State Administration of Radio, Film and Television, March 2011 Public Notice on National Filming and Production of Television Series].' 31 March. Beijing: SARFT, available online at: www.sarft.gov.cn/art/2011/3/31/art_113_5301.html.

[2] Erica Ho. 2011. 'China Decides to Ban Time Travel.' *TIME*, 13 April, available online at: techland.time.com/2011/04/13/china-decides-to-ban-time-travel; Richard Hartley-Parkinson. 2011. 'Great Scott! China Bans Films and TV Shows Featuring Time Travel (Just in Case Anyone Wants to Rewrite History).' *Daily Mail*, 15 April, available online at: www.dailymail.co.uk/news/article-1376771/Great-Scott-China-bans-time-travel-cinema-TV.html.

[3] Jin Feng offers a detailed discussion of this literary subgenre in *Romancing the Internet: Producing and Consuming Chinese Web Romance*. Leiden: Brill (2013).

[4] Liang Qichao 梁啟超. 1999 [1902–03]. '新中国未来记 [The Future of New China].' In 梁启超全集 [*Complete Works of Liang Qichao*]. Beijing: Beijing Chubanshe. The novel actually specifies that the work is set '2513 years after the birth of Confucius, which is to say, the year 2062 in the Western calendar'. Assuming the work's specification of the date based on Confucius's birth year is correct, the Gregorian date should be 1962, not 2062.

[5] Hao Jingfang (translated by Ken Liu). 2015. 'Folding Beijing.' *Uncanny Magazine*, available online at: uncannymagazine.com/article/folding-beijing-2.

[6] After finishing the novella in December 2012, Hao Jingfang posted it online on a student website. Two years later, in 2014, the work was published more formally in a Chinese-language journal. Ken Liu's English translation was first published in 2015 in *Uncanny: A Magazine of Science Fiction and Fantasy* and was republished in 2016 in Ken Liu's edited volume *Invisible Planets: An Anthology of Contemporary Chinese Science Fiction in Translation*. London: Head of Zeus.

[7] The World Bank estimates that China's Gini coefficient increased from less than 0.3 in the early 1980s to just under 0.5 in 2012, which is higher than all but two of the world's largest nations by population. See Terry Sicula. 2013. 'The Challenge of High Inequality in China.' *Inequality in Focus* 2, no. 2 (August). Washington, DC: Poverty Reduction and Equity Department, The World Bank, available online at: www.worldbank.org/content/dam/Worldbank/document/Poverty%20documents/Inequality-In-Focus-0813.pdf; Gabriel Wildau and Tom Mitchell. 2016. 'China Income Inequality Among World's Worst.' *Financial Times*, 14 January, available online at: www.ft.com/content/3c521faa-baa6-11e5-a7cc-280dfe875e28.

[8] Zai Liang, Zhen Li and Zhongdong Ma. 2014. 'Changing Patterns of the Floating Population in China During 2000–2010.' *Population and Development Review* 40, no. 4: 695–716.

[9] Jiang Jie. 2013. 'Beijing to Curb Population in 2014.' *Global Times*, 24 December, available online at: www.globaltimes.cn/content/833787.shtml; Shaoyuan Chen, Ziyi Huang and Rongde Li. 2016. 'Beijing's Push to Curb Population Growth Hits Snag.' *Caixin*, 24 November, available online at: www.caixinglobal.com/2016-11-24/beijings-push-to-curb-population-growth-hits-snag-101018871.html.

[10] Jiani Song, Shuchi Zhang and Qiaochu Li. 2018. 'Beijing Evictions, a Winter's Tale.' *Made in China Journal* 3, no. 1: 28–33.

[11] John Knight and Ramani Gunatilaka. 2018. 'Rural–Urban Migration and Happiness in China.' In *World Happiness Report 2018*, edited by John F. Helliwell, Richard Layard and Jeffrey D. Sachs. New York, NY: Sustainable Development Solutions Network, 66–88.

[12] Ibid., 83.

[13] Lauren Berlant. 2011. *Cruel Optimism*. Durham, NC: Duke University Press, 1.

[14] Deborah Stanish (translated by Ken Liu). 2015. 'Interview: Hao Jingfang.' *Uncanny Magazine*, available online at: uncannymagazine.com/article/interview-hao-jingfang.

[15] Ibid.

The Future (Chen Qiufan, translated and introduced by Carlos Rojas)

[1] Chen Qiufan (translated by Ken Liu). 2019. *The Waste Tide*. New York, NY: Tor Books. Coincidentally, it was also in 2013 that the Guangdong Provincial Government approved a plan to transfer all of Guiyu's e-waste recycling operations to a specially designed industrial park on the outskirts of the town so the extraction and recycling process could be more effectively regulated.

[2] Chen Qiufan (translated by Ken Liu). 2011. 'The Fish of Lijiang.' *Clarkesworld Magazine* 59, available online at: clarkesworldmagazine.com/chen_08_11.

[3] The story was written in 2019, and the Chinese version is forthcoming. Some of Chen's recent work on AI can be found in Kai-fu Lee and Chen Qiufan. 2021. *AI 2041: Ten Visions for Our Future*. London: Ebury Publishing.

[4] Michael Hardt. 1999. 'Affective Labor.' *boundary 2* 26, no. 2: 90–100.

[5] Ibid., 99.

Contributors

Joel ANDREAS, a Professor of Sociology at Johns Hopkins University, studies political contention and social change in China. His first book, *Rise of the Red Engineers: The Cultural Revolution and the Origins of China's New Class* (2009), analyses the contentious merger of old and new elites following the 1949 Revolution. His second book, *Disenfranchised: The Rise and Fall of Industrial Citizenship in China* (2019), traces radical changes that have fundamentally transformed industrial relations over the past seven decades. He is continuing to investigate changing labour relations as well as the ongoing transformation of China's rural society.

A.C. BAECKER is a lecturer in the Department of Art History at the University of Hong Kong. Her research focuses on the changing cultural formations of labour in Maoist China and the post-socialist legacy in contemporary China. She holds an MA in modern Chinese literature from Tsinghua University and a PhD in modern Chinese cultural studies from the University of Michigan. Her manuscript project examines amateur art practices organised in worker, peasant, and soldier communities during the socialist period in China. Her writing has appeared in publications including *Artforum*, *ArtAsiaPacific*, *Frieze*, *The New Statesman*, and *Vulture*.

Sarah BIDDULPH is Assistant Deputy Vice-Chancellor International (China) at the University of Melbourne. She is also Professor of Law at the Melbourne Law School and Director of its Asian Law Centre. Sarah's research focuses on the Chinese legal system with a particular emphasis on legal policy and lawmaking and enforcement as they affect the administration of justice in China. Her areas of research are contemporary Chinese administrative law, criminal procedure, labour, comparative law, and the law regulating social and economic rights.

Marc BLECHER is James Monroe Professor of Politics and East Asian Studies at Oberlin College. His latest book, *Politics as a Science: A Prolegomenon*, co-authored with Philippe Schmitter, was published in 2020. He is at work on *A World to Lose*, a longitudinal study of working-class formation in China from its birth to the present, and *Class and the Chinese Communist Party: A Social History of Change*, with David Goodman, Guo Yingjie, Jean-Louis Rocca, and Tang Beibei.

Michel BONNIN is Professor Emeritus at the École des Hautes Études en Sciences Sociales, Paris, and Adjunct Professor at the Chinese University of Hong Kong, where he teaches the history of the Chinese Cultural Revolution. In the 1990s, he was the founding director of the French Research Centre on Contemporary China and of the magazine *China Perspectives*, both based in Hong Kong. In 2013, he published *The Lost Generation: The Rustication of China's Educated Youth (1968–1980)*, which has one French and two Chinese editions.

Darren BYLER is an Assistant Professor of International Studies at Simon Fraser University in Vancouver, British Columbia. He is the author of the ethnography *Terror Capitalism: Uyghur Dispossession and Masculinity in a Chinese City* (2021) and the narrative-driven book *In the Camps: China's High-Tech Penal Colony* (2021). His current research interests are focused on infrastructure development and global China in the context of Xinjiang and Malaysia.

Corey BYRNES is Associate Professor of Chinese Culture, Comparative Literature, and the Environmental Humanities at Northwestern University. He is the author of *Fixing Landscape: A Techno-Poetic History of China's Three Gorges* (2019), which won the 2018 First Book Award from the Weatherhead Institute for East Asian Studies and an Honorable Mention for the 2020 Harry Levin Prize for outstanding first book from the American Comparative Literary Association. His current project examines the relationship between China and a global environmental imaginary in which it is increasingly treated as an existential threat.

Anita CHAN is a Visiting Fellow at The Australian National University and co-editor of *The China Journal*. Prior to that, she was a Research Professor at the University of Technology Sydney. She has published widely on Chinese workers' conditions, the Chinese trade union, labour rights, and comparative labour issues. Her ten books include *Children of Mao: Personality Development and Political Activism in the Red Guard Generation* (1985), *China's Workers under Assault* (2001), *Chen Village: Revolution to Globalization* (2009), and, as editor, *Labour in Vietnam* (2011), *Walmart in China* (2011) and *Chinese Workers in Comparative Perspective* (2015).

Chris King-Chi CHAN is an Associate Professor in the Department of Sociology and the Director of Social Innovation Studies at the Chinese University of Hong Kong. He holds a PhD from the University of Warwick. His research interests include labour, civil society, and social development. He is the author of *The Challenge of Labour in China: Strikes and the Changing Labour Regime in Global Factories* (2010) and has published numerous papers in journals such as *China Quarterly*, *Journal of Contemporary Asia*, *Globalizations*, *Development and Change*, and *Third World Quarterly*.

Jenny CHAN is an Assistant Professor of Sociology at the Hong Kong Polytechnic University. She is the co-author, with Mark Selden and Pun Ngai, of *Dying for an iPhone: Apple, Foxconn, and the Lives of China's Workers* (2020). She also serves on the board of the International Sociological Association's Research Committee on Labour Movements. Her research, funded by the Junior Research Fellowship of the University of Oxford's Kellogg College (2015–18) and the Early Career Scheme of the Research Grants Council of Hong Kong (2018–21), focuses on the informalisation of labour in Global China.

CHEN Feng is Fudan Chair Professor at the Institute of Global Public Policy at Fudan University and Professor Emeritus at Hong Kong Baptist University. His research has focused on Chinese politics, labour politics, and the labour movement, ideology and local governance. He has published widely on these subjects.

Po-chien CHEN has been an organiser and researcher in different trade unions (such as the Telecommunication Union, the Higher Education Union, and the Young Irregular Workers' Union) and labour organisations in Taiwan since 2002. He currently serves as the General Secretary of the Taiwan Labour History and Culture Society.

CHEN Qiufan (a.k.a. Stanley CHAN) is an award-winning Chinese speculative fiction author, translator, creative producer, and curator. He is Honorary President of the Chinese Science Fiction Writers' Association and has a seat on the Xprize Foundation Science Fiction Advisory Council. His works include the novel *Waste Tide* and, co-authored with Kai-Fu Lee, the book *AI 2041: Ten Visions for Our Future*. He currently lives in Shanghai and is the founder of Thema Mundi Studio.

Maggie CLINTON is an Associate Professor of History at Middlebury College. She is the author of *Revolutionary Nativism: Fascism and Culture in China, 1927–1937* (2017). Clinton completed her Master's in Social Work at Columbia University in 2021 and is becoming licensed to practice as a psychotherapist. She continues to work on a book project on China's twentieth-century participation in regional and global oil markets.

Robert CLIVER is a Professor of History at Humboldt State University in California, where he has lived for fourteen years. He grew up in Massachusetts and earned his BA in history at Tufts University. After spending some time in Beijing working as a translator, he continued his education with an MA at the University of Hawai`i and a PhD at Harvard University. He has also taught at the Foreign Affairs University in Beijing and Oxford University in England. He is the author of *Red Silk: Class, Gender, and Revolution in China's Yangzi Delta Silk Industry* (2020).

Alexander F. DAY is Associate Professor of History and Chair of East Asian Studies at Occidental College in Los Angeles. He studies the intellectual, social, and cultural history of peasants, food, and agrarian change in China. His first book, *The Peasant in Postsocialist China: History, Politics, and Capitalism* (2013), centres on the question of why the peasant, and rural China more broadly, continually reappears as a figure of crisis in Chinese history. His second book project traces the labour and environmental history of a tea farm and factory in Guizhou Province from the 1930s to the present.

Brian DEMARE teaches modern Chinese history at Tulane University. A cultural historian, he is primarily interested in exploring how Chinese citizens have navigated everyday life under Communist Party rule. His first book, *Mao's Cultural Army* (2015), brings to life the world of rural drama troupes, revealing the Communists' revolution to be a profoundly theatrical event. His second book, *Land Wars* (2019), blends archival and narrative sources to investigate the most critical moment of Maoist rural revolution. He is currently writing a collection of true-crime studies based on archival documents from a rural county in Jiangxi Province.

Yige DONG is an Assistant Professor in Sociology and Global Gender and Sexuality Studies at the State University of New York at Buffalo. Her research interests include political economy, labour, gender, contentious politics, and comparative historical methods. Dong's research on Chinese labour politics and feminist movements has appeared in the *International Journal of Comparative Sociology*, *Critical Asian Studies*, and *Modern China*, among others. She is currently working on a book that examines the politics of care work during the rise and fall of industrial socialism in China. She has been serving on the editorial board of the *Made in China Journal* since 2018.

Manfred ELFSTROM is an Assistant Professor in the Department of Economics, Philosophy and Political Science at the University of British Columbia, Okanagan. He is the author of *Workers and Change in China: Resistance, Repression, Responsiveness* (2021) and his work has appeared in *China Quarterly*, *Journal of Contemporary China*, *British Journal of Industrial Relations*, *Industrial and Labor Relations Review*, and *China Information*. Dr Elfstrom has a doctorate from Cornell University. Before entering academia, he worked in the nonprofit world, supporting workers' rights and improved grassroots governance in China.

Jacob EYFERTH is a social historian of twentieth-century China interested in the lives of non-elite people. His first book, *Eating Rice from Bamboo Roots* (2009), is an ethnographic history of a community of papermakers in Sichuan. He is currently working on a second book, tentatively titled *Cotton, Gender, and Revolution in Twentieth-Century China*.

Eric FLORENCE is Associate Professor at the Centre for Ethnic and Migration Studies and PragmApolis at the University of Liege. His research focuses on the cultural politics of labour, the transformation of labour regimes, and the cultural and political mediation of workers' experiences in contemporary China. For the past twenty years, he has carried out research on the cultural politics of labour in South China and has coordinated research projects on international migration at the Centre for Ethnic and Migration Studies.

Ivan FRANCESCHINI is a Postdoctoral Fellow at The Australian National University. After more than a decade spent studying labour activism in China, his current research focuses on the social impact of Chinese engagements in Cambodia. With Tommaso Facchin, he co-directed the documentaries *Dreamwork China* (2011) and *Boramey: Ghosts in the Factory* (2021). He founded and co-edits the *Made in China Journal*. His latest book is the co-edited volume *Afterlives of Chinese Communism: Political Concepts from Mao to Xi* (2019).

Mark W. FRAZIER is Professor of Politics and Co-Director of the India China Institute at the New School for Social Research (New York). His research interests include labour and social policy in China and the politics of urbanisation, migration, and citizenship in China and India. He is the author of *The Power of Place: Contentious Politics in Twentieth Century Shanghai and Bombay* (2019). Other publications include *Socialist Insecurity: Pensions and the Politics of Uneven Development in China* (2010) and *The Making of the Chinese Industrial Workplace* (2002).

Eli FRIEDMAN is an Associate Professor and Chair of the Department of International and Comparative Labor at Cornell University's School of Industrial and Labor Relations. He is the author of *Insurgency Trap: Labor Politics in Postsocialist China* (2014) and is writing a book entitled *The Urbanization of People: Development, Labor Markets, and Schooling in the Chinese City*.

Chloé FROISSART is a Professor of History and Political Science in the Department of Chinese Studies at the National Institute for Oriental Languages and Civilisations in Paris. She previously served as the director of Tsinghua University's Sino-French Centre in Social Sciences in Beijing, was a senior researcher at the French Centre for Research on Contemporary China in Hong Kong, and an Associate Professor at Rennes 2 University. Her research interests broadly pertain to state–society relations in China, with a focus on collective actions, citizenship, labour and environmental politics, and the transformations of the Chinese regime.

Mary E. GALLAGHER is the Amy and Alan Lowenstein Professor of Democracy, Democratization, and Human Rights at the University of Michigan, where she is also the Director of the International Institute. From 2008 to 2020, she was the director of the Kenneth G. Lieberthal and Richard H. Rogel Center for Chinese Studies. She received her PhD in politics in 2001 from Princeton University. Her research focuses on Chinese politics, US–China relations, and Chinese state–society relations, especially labour politics and labour law. Her most recent book is *Authoritarian Legality in China: Law, Workers and the State* (2017).

Matthew GALWAY is a lecturer in the School of Culture, History and Language at The Australian National University. He was previously the Hansen Trust Lecturer, Asian History, at the University of Melbourne, where he taught courses on Cold War Asia and modern Chinese history. His research focuses on intellectual history and global Maoism, both of which make up the focus of his first book, *The Emergence of Global Maoism: China and the Cambodian Communist Movement, 1949–1979* (forthcoming in 2022).

Aaron HALEGUA is the founder of a law firm in New York City and a Research Fellow at the New York University School of Law. He recently assisted more than 2,400 Chinese construction workers trafficked to Saipan to recover US$14 million in backpay. Mr Halegua has consulted for Apple, Asia Society, Ford Foundation, and the International Labour Organization on labour issues in China, Myanmar, Malaysia, Thailand, and Mexico. He is the author of numerous book chapters, articles, and op-eds about labour issues, including the report *Who Will Represent China's Workers: Lawyers, Legal Aid, and the Enforcement of Labor Rights* (2016).

Jane HAYWARD lectures in China and Global Affairs at the Lau China Institute, King's College London. Her research examines the processes by which the Chinese state is becoming increasingly integrated into the global capitalist economy, with a focus on China's agrarian question and related issues of urbanisation.

Gail HERSHATTER is Distinguished Professor of History at the University of California, Santa Cruz, and a former president of the Association for Asian Studies. Her books include *The Workers of Tianjin* (1986, Chinese translation 2016), *Personal Voices: Chinese Women in the 1980s* (1988, with Emily Honig), *Dangerous Pleasures: Prostitution in Twentieth-Century Shanghai* (1997, Chinese translation 2003), *Women in China's Long Twentieth Century* (2004), *The Gender of Memory: Rural Women and China's Collective Past* (2011, Chinese translation 2017), and *Women and China's Revolutions* (2019).

Koji HIRATA is a Research Fellow in Emmanuel College at the University of Cambridge and an incoming lecturer in Modern History at Monash University. His research focuses on the business, economic, and social histories of modern China, as well as on China's relations with Japan and Russia.

Emily HONIG is a Professor of History at the University of California, Santa Cruz. Her research interests include gender, sexuality, and ethnicity in modern Chinese history, comparative labour history, Chicana history, nationalism and sexuality in the Third World, and oral history. Her books include *Sisters and Strangers: Women in the Shanghai Cotton Mills 1919–1949* (1986), *Personal Voices: Chinese Women in the 1980s* (1988, with Gail Hershatter), *Creating Chinese Ethnicity: Subei People in Shanghai 1850–1980* (1992), *Remapping China: Fissures in Historical Terrain* (1995, with Gail Hershatter), and *Across the Great Divide: The Sent-Down Youth Movement in Mao's China* (2019, with Xiaojian Zhao).

Ming-sho HO is a Professor in the Department of Sociology at National Taiwan University. His research interests include social movements and labour and environmental issues. He published the books *Challenging Beijing's Mandate from Heaven: Taiwan's Sunflower Movement and Hong Kong's Umbrella Movement* (2019) and *Taiwan's Working Class Formation: Fractured Solidarity in State-Owned Enterprises, 1945–2012* (2014).

Joshua HOWARD is the Croft Professor of History and International Studies at the University of Mississippi, where he has been teaching since 1999 after receiving a PhD in history from the University of California, Berkeley. His publications include *Workers at War: Labor in China's Arsenals, 1937–1953* (2004) and *Composing for the Revolution: Nie Er and China's Sonic Nationalism* (2020).

Jude HOWELL is a Professor of International Development at the London School of Economics (LSE). She is principal investigator of an Economic and Social Research Council (ESRC) research project on 'The Politics of Services Contracting to NGOs in China'. She was previously director of the ESRC Programme on Non-Governmental Public Action and former director of the Centre for Civil Society at LSE. She has written extensively on issues relating to labour, civil society, gender, and governance in China.

HUANG Yu is an Associate Professor of Anthropology at the Minzu University of China. Her research interests include science and technology studies, robotisation and industrial automation, labour studies, environmental anthropology, and agrarian change. Since 2015, she has engaged in a research project that explores how industrial automation and robotisation transform the contradictions between capital and labour in South China. She has published in *The China Journal*, *Globalizations*, *Science, Technology and Society*, *Agrarian South*, *Journal of Agrarian Change*, and *Modern China*.

Elaine Sio-ieng HUI is an Assistant Professor in the School of Labor and Employment Relations at Pennsylvania State University. She has published in peer-reviewed journals such as *Theory and Society*, *Human Relations*, the *British Journal of Industrial Relations*, *The China Quarterly*, the *Journal of Industrial Relations*, and the *Journal of Contemporary Asia*. Her research examines the role of the state and laws in labour relations, worker collective actions and their impact on institutional arrangements, labour-related civil society actors, and social welfare systems. She is the author of *Hegemonic Transformation: The State, Laws, and Labour Relations in Post-Socialist China* (2017).

William HURST is the Chong Hua Professor of Chinese Development in the Department of Politics and International Studies and Director of the Centre of Development Studies at the University of Cambridge. In addition to more than fifty articles, essays and book chapters, he is the author of *The Chinese Worker after Socialism* (2009) and *Ruling before the Law: The Politics of Legal Regimes in China and Indonesia* (2018) and editor or co-editor of four other books. His ongoing research examines the politics of land, development, and power contestation in mainland China, Taiwan, Indonesia, and Malaysia.

Benjamin KINDLER holds a PhD in Modern Chinese Literature from Columbia University. His dissertation, entitled 'Writing to the Rhythm of Labour: The Politics of Cultural Labour in the Chinese Revolution, 1942–1976', investigates the confluences between cultural production, political economy, and the problem of the writing subject in the socialist period. His work has been published in *Modern Chinese Literature and Culture*, the *Made in China Journal*, as well as other venues. He is currently preparing a new research project on the reinvention of the human sciences and the problem of the human in the post-socialist period.

Fabio LANZA is a Professor of Modern Chinese History in the Departments of History and East Asian Studies at the University of Arizona. He is the author of *Behind the Gate: Inventing Students in Beijing* (2010) and *The End of Concern: Maoist China, Activism, and Asian Studies* (2017). He is currently working on a research project on the urban commune movement in Beijing during the Great Leap Forward.

Ching Kwan LEE is a Professor of Sociology at the University of California, Los Angeles. She is the author of three multiple award-winning monographs on contemporary China's turn to capitalism: *Gender and the South China Miracle: Two Worlds of Factory Women* (1998), *Against the Law: Labor Protests in China's Rustbelt and Sunbelt* (2007), and *The Specter of Global China: Politics, Labor and Foreign Investment in Africa* (2017). Her latest co-edited books include *Take Back Our Future: An Eventful Political Sociology of the Hong Kong Umbrella Movement* (2019) and *The Social Question in the 21st Century: A Global View* (2019).

Seung-Joon LEE is a historian and Associate Professor in the Department of History at the National University of Singapore. He is the author of *Gourmets in the Land of Famine: The Culture and Politics of Rice in Modern Canton* (2011). He is currently working on a book tentatively titled *Revolutions at the Canteens*, exploring labour and management, the politics of the working-class diet and food entitlement in twentieth-century China.

Apo LEONG arrived in Hong Kong from Macau in 1967. He first worked as a machine operator in a US electronics factory and then became a journalist specialising in labour for a Chinese newspaper. After that, he joined a labour nongovernmental organisation, the Hong Kong Christian Industrial Committee, as a labour organiser. In 1984, he co-founded the Hong Kong Trade Union Education Centre, which later became the Hong Kong Confederation of Trade Unions. In the 1990s, he was the executive director of the Asia Monitor Resource Centre, an NGO focusing on regional labour issues. He currently serves as the President of the Hong Kong Social Security Society and is an advisor to several labour NGOs in Hong Kong and mainland China.

LIN Chun is Professor of Comparative Politics at the London School of Economics and the author of *The British New Left* (1993), *The Transformation of Chinese Socialism* (2006), *Reflections on China's Reform Trajectory* (2008, in Chinese), *China and Global Capitalism* (2013), and *Revolution and Counterrevolution in China* (2021); and co-editor of *Women: The Longest Revolution* (1997, in Chinese) and *Is Mao Really a Monster?* (2009), among other volumes.

Kevin LIN is a Visiting Fellow at the Chinese University of Hong Kong. His research has analysed the employment relations of state-sector workers, the collective actions of rural migrant workers, state–society relations, and labour nongovernmental organisations in China. He is on the editorial board of the *Made in China Journal*.

Ralph LITZINGER is a Professor of Cultural Anthropology at Duke University. He is the author of *Other Chinas: The Yao and the Politics of National Belonging* (2000) and, more recently, with Carlos Rojas, *Ghost Protocol: Development and Displacement in Global China* (2016). His new research concerns digital labour and platform capitalism, human and post-human techno-imaginaries, and racial environmentalism. His most recent publication, with Fan Yang, is 'Eco-Media Events in China: From Yellow Eco-Peril to Media Materialism', in *Environmental Humanities* (May 2020).

Yi-hung LIU holds a PhD in American Studies from the University of Hawai`i at Mānoa. Her dissertation, 'Cold War in the Heartland: Transpacific Exchange and the Iowa Literary Programs' (2019), examines the Iowa Writers' Workshop and the International Writing Program against the backdrop of the Cold War and the Chinese Civil War. Her research aims to rethink and rework the concept of 'Cold War freedom' and how it has conditioned our ways of reading and writing literature as well as imagining political futures. She is now a Postdoctoral Fellow at Academia Sinica, Taipei.

LU Yan is a Professor of History at the University of New Hampshire. Her research interest focuses on transnational relations in East Asia and Chinese labour activism. She is author of *Re-Understanding Japan: Chinese Perspectives, 1895–1945* (2004) and *Crossed Paths: Labor Activism and Colonial Governance in Hong Kong, 1938–1958* (2019).

Covell F. MEYSKENS is an Assistant Professor of National Security Affairs at the Naval Postgraduate School in Monterey, California. His research focuses on security and development in modern China. With a PhD in History from the University of Chicago, he is the author of *Mao's Third Front: The Militarization of Cold War China* (2020). He is currently working on his second book, *The Three Gorges Dam: Building a Hydraulic Engine for China*. His work has been published in the *Nonproliferation Review*, *Cold War History*, *Twentieth Century China* and *positions: asia critique*.

Yanping NI is a recent graduate of the MA in East Asian Studies at Duke University. She worked as a Graduate Fellow in the Duke Ethnography Lab and as a research assistant in the Revaluing Care in the Global Economy network. Her research interests focus on medical issues in contemporary China, particularly in relation to political economy and social inequality. She joined the Department of Anthropology at Princeton University as a doctoral student in September 2021.

Mary Ann O'DONNELL is an independent artist-ethnographer and co-founder of the Handshake 302 Art Space in Shenzhen. Since 2005, she has been blogging at *Shenzhen Noted* (shenzhennoted.com). With Winnie Wong and Jonathan Bach, she co-edited the volume *Learning from Shenzhen* (2017).

Elizabeth J. PERRY is Henry Rosovsky Professor of Government at Harvard University and Director of the Harvard-Yenching Institute. She is the author or editor of more than twenty books on modern and contemporary Chinese history and politics. Her studies of Chinese labour include *Shanghai on Strike: The Politics of Chinese Labor* (1993); with Li Xun, *Proletarian Power: Shanghai in the Cultural Revolution* (1997); with Xiaobo Lu, *Danwei: The Changing Chinese Workplace in Historical and Comparative Perspective* (1997); *Patrolling the Revolution: Worker Militias, Citizenship and the Modern Chinese State* (2006); and *Anyuan: Mining China's Revolutionary Tradition* (2012).

Andrea PIAZZAROLI LONGOBARDI holds a PhD in History from the University of São Paulo and the University of Bologna. In her doctoral research, she studied the history of the Workers' University in the Chinese Cultural Revolution. In her Master's degree, she studied Sino-Iberian relations in the seventeenth and eighteenth centuries and how they shaped Iberian sacred ornaments and discourse.

Junxi QIAN is an Assistant Professor in the Department of Geography at the University of Hong Kong. He is a social and cultural geographer who works at the intersection of geography, urban studies, and cultural studies. His current research investigates indigenous development in Yunnan and Tibet, the cultural economies of technological innovation in Shenzhen, and entrepreneurial religious landscapes in China.

Carlos ROJAS is a Professor of Modern Chinese Cultural Studies, Gender, Sexuality, and Feminist Studies, and Cinematic Arts at Duke University. He is the author, editor, and translator of numerous books, including *Homesickness: Culture, Contagion, and National Transformation in Modern China* (2015).

Tony SAICH is the Daewoo Professor of International Affairs and Director of the Ash Center for Democratic Governance and Innovation at the Harvard Kennedy School. His most recent publication is *From Rebel to Ruler: One Hundred Years of the Chinese Communist Party* (2021).

Aminda SMITH is Co-Director of the PRC History Group and an Associate Professor in the Department of History at Michigan State University. She specialises in the social and cultural history of Chinese communism, with a particular interest in the grassroots histories of political thought.

Craig A. SMITH is a lecturer in Translation Studies at the University of Melbourne's Asia Institute. He is the author of *Chinese Asianism: 1894–1945* (2021) and co-editor of *Translating the Occupation: The Japanese Invasion of China, 1931–45* (2021). He graduated from Taiwan's National Chung Cheng University with an MA in Taiwan Literature in 2010 and acquired a PhD in East Asian History from the University of British Columbia in 2014.

Steve (S.A.) SMITH is an Emeritus Fellow at All Souls College, Oxford. He works on modern China, modern Russia and comparative communism. His most recent book is *Russia in Revolution: An Empire in Crisis, 1890 to 1928* (2017). He is currently writing a book on popular religion under Mao and has a volume of essays on the backburner that compares religion, superstition, and magic in the Soviet Union and the People's Republic of China. He is a board member and former editor of the journal *Past and Present*.

Dorothy J. SOLINGER is Professor Emerita, Political Science, at the University of California, Irvine. Her seven books include *Poverty and Pacification* (2021), *Contesting Citizenship in Urban China* (1999), and *States' Gains, Labor's Losses* (2009). Her edited or co-edited books include *Polarized Cities* (2019) and *Socialism Vanquished, Socialism Challenged* (2012). She was a visiting lecturer at the École des Hautes Études en Sciences Sociales, Paris; distinguished visiting professor at the Chinese University of Hong Kong; and visiting research professor in the East Asian Institute at the National University of Singapore; and taught by invitation at Stanford University and the University of Michigan.

Christian SORACE is an Assistant Professor of Political Science at Colorado College. He is the author of *Shaken Authority: China's Communist Party and the 2008 Sichuan Earthquake* (2017) and the co-editor of *Afterlives of Chinese Communism: Political Concepts from Mao to Xi* (2019). He writes at the intersection of political theory and comparative politics. His current research focuses on the crisis of democracy, air pollution, and urbanisation in Mongolia.

Bo Ærenlund SØRENSEN is Assistant Professor of China Studies at the University of Copenhagen. His research interests include contemporary Chinese society, modern Chinese history, labour studies, comparative literature, media and communication studies, digital humanities, and cognitive science.

Wanning SUN is Professor of Media and Communication Studies in the Faculty of Arts and Social Sciences at the University of Technology Sydney. She has been researching the cultural politics and intimate consequences of inequality in China for two decades and is possibly the first scholar to have published in English on *dagong* poetry. She is the author of *Subaltern China: Rural Migrants, Media and Cultural Practices* (2014).

Malcolm THOMPSON is a historian of China based in Vancouver, Canada. He holds a PhD from the University of British Columbia (UBC) and has taught there and at the University of Toronto. He has held postdoctoral fellowships at the Institute of Asian Research at UBC and at the Fairbank Center, Harvard University.

Patricia M. THORNTON is an Associate Professor in the Department of Politics and International Relations at the University of Oxford and a Fellow of Merton College. She is the author of numerous articles in scholarly journals. She recently edited a special issue of *The China Quarterly* to mark the centenary of the Chinese Communist Party. Her publications include *To Govern China: Evolving Practices of Power* (2017, with Vivienne Shue); *Red Shadows: Memories and Legacies of the Chinese Cultural Revolution* (2017, with Chris Berry and Sun Peidong); and *Disciplining the State: Virtue, Violence and State-Making in Modern China* (2007).

Jonathan UNGER is an Emeritus Professor at The Australian National University and co-editor (with Anita Chan and Ben Hillman) of *The China Journal*. His research interests include social stratification in China; rural Chinese social, political, and economic change; poverty alleviation and development; urbanisation; workers and factory life; Chinese nationalism; and Cultural Revolution history. He has published fifteen books, including *Education Under Mao: Class and Competition in Canton Schools* (1982), *The Transformation of Rural China* (2002), and, as co-author, *Chen Village: Revolution to Globalization* (2009).

WANG Kan is a Resident Research Fellow in the Institute of Labour Relations and Trade Union Studies at the China University of Labour Relations. He has a PhD in labour relations and labour law and was China Program Officer at the Beijing Unit of Oxfam. His research interests include the Chinese labour movement, labour and employment relations, as well as trade unions.

Jake WERNER is a historian of modern China and a Postdoctoral Research Fellow at Boston University's Global Development Policy Center. He is currently completing a book manuscript examining the rise of the masses as a form of social life in twentieth-century Shanghai, and is beginning research on the emergence of great power conflict between the United States and China following the 2008 financial crisis.

John WILLIAMS is an Associate Professor of History at Colorado College. He has published on the late imperial civil service examinations and the relationship between popular religion and Communist mobilisation in China in the 1920s. His current research focuses on the evolution of agricultural pest control methods in twentieth-century China.

Jeanne L. WILSON is Emeritus Professor of Political Science at Wheaton College in Norton, MA, and a Research Associate at the Davis Center for Russian and Eurasian Research at Harvard University. At the beginning of her career, she focused on Chinese labour issues, but subsequently has worked on comparing facets of Russian and Chinese foreign and domestic policy. She is especially interested in the diffusion effect of ideas in the post-communist region and the impact of national identity on domestic and foreign policy.

Tim WRIGHT is Honorary Research Fellow in the School of Humanities at the University of Western Australia, Emeritus Professor of Chinese Studies at the University of Sheffield, and Editor-in-Chief of the *Oxford Bibliographies in Chinese Studies*. His research focuses on modern Chinese economic history and the political economy of contemporary China. His most recent book is *The Political Economy of the Chinese Coal Industry: Black Gold and Blood-Stained Coal* (2012), and he has an article forthcoming in *The China Quarterly* on the recent improvement in China's coal industry safety.

XU Guoqi is Kerry Group Professor of Globalisation History at the University of Hong Kong. He received his doctoral degree in history from Harvard University and has published widely in both Chinese and English. He is the author of several books, including *Asia and the Great War: A Shared History* (2017); *Chinese and Americans: A Shared History* (2014); *Strangers on the Western Front: Chinese Workers in the Great War* (2014); *Olympic Dreams: China and Sports, 1895–2008* (2008); and *China and the Great War: China's Pursuit of a New National Identity and Internationalization* (2005). He has just finished a new book titled *The Idea of China?*, which is under contract with Harvard University Press.

Ray YEP is a Professor of Politics in the Department of Public Policy at City University of Hong Kong. He completed his PhD in Politics at the University of Oxford and has written extensively on the politics and colonial history of Hong Kong and the political economy of reforms in China. His latest publications include the *Routledge Handbook of Contemporary Hong Kong* (2019) and the *Handbook on Urban Development in China* (2019).

Yueran ZHANG is a doctoral candidate in sociology at the University of California, Berkeley. His ongoing dissertation research seeks to reexamine China's transition from late Maoism to the early reform era through the lens of the relationship between the state and the working class and the politics of democratising enterprise management. His previous award-winning research used the case of taxing private homeownership to make sense of the 'Chongqing Model'.

Tiantian ZHENG is a Distinguished Professor of Anthropology at State University of New York, Cortland. She has produced ten books, five edited journal issues and more than 100 articles. Her book *Red Lights* (2009) won the 2010 Sara A. Whaley Book Prize from the National Women's Studies Association; *Ethnographies of Prostitution* (2009) won the 2011 Research Publication Book Award from the Association of Chinese Professors of Social Sciences in the United States; *Tongzhi Living* (2015) was awarded the Outstanding Academic Title by Choice in 2016 and was nominated for three other awards. Her fourth ethnography, *Violent Intimacy: Intimate Partner Violence in Postsocialist China*, is forthcoming with Bloomsbury.

ZHOU Ruixue is a student of decolonisation, an aspiring writer, and a community organiser. She holds a BA in Asian Studies from Colorado College.

Ruiyi ZHU is a PhD candidate in the Department of Social Anthropology at the University of Cambridge. She conducted doctoral research at Chinese-owned companies on the extractive economy of Mongolia, with a focus on labour relations in contemporary Sino-Mongolian industrial encounters. She has also undertaken archival and oral history research regarding Chinese workers in socialist Mongolia. Prior to her doctoral degree, she explored post-socialist terrains and memories as a Thomas J. Watson Fellow.